P9-CCF-534

# THE SCOUTING NOTEBOOK: 1996

Produced by STATS, Inc.
(Sports Team Analysis and Tracking Systems, Inc.)

John Dewan, Editor

Don Zminda, Associate Editor

Statistics by STATS, Inc.

## STATS
PUBLISHING

This book is dedicated to the families and friends of STATS employees
for the love and encouragement they give us.
I am forever grateful to my wonderful wife Gella
and to our beautiful children Jonah and Aaron.
—Bob Meyerhoff

Most of the player photographs which appear in THE SCOUTING NOTE-
BOOK: 1996 were furnished individually by 27 of the teams which comprise
Major League Baseball. Their cooperation is gratefully acknowledged: Balti-
more Orioles, Boston Red Sox, California Angels, Chicago White Sox, Cleve-
land Indians, Detroit Tigers, Kansas City Royals, Milwaukee Brewers,
Minnesota Twins, New York Yankees, Oakland Athletics, Texas Rangers,
Toronto Blue Jays, Atlanta Braves, Chicago Cubs, Cincinnati Reds, Colorado
Rockies, Florida Marlins, Houston Astros, Los Angeles Dodgers, Montreal
Expos, New York Mets, Philadelphia Phillies, Pittsburgh Pirates, St. Louis
Cardinals, San Diego Padres and San Francisco Giants.

Cover by Excel Marketing Group

Cover photos Ponzini Photography

THE SCOUTING NOTEBOOK: 1996. Copyright © 1995 by STATS, Inc.
All rights reserved. Printed in the United States of America. No part of this
book may be used or reproduced in any manner whatsoever without written
permission except in the case of brief quotations embodied in critical articles
and reviews. For information, address STATS, Inc., 8131 Monticello, Skokie,
IL 60076.

STATS is a trademark of Sports Team Analysis and Tracking Systems, Inc.

First Edition: December, 1995

ISBN 1-884064-22-1

# Acknowledgments

Just by flipping through a few pages of *The Scouting Notebook*, you could guess that putting it together requires a monumental effort—and you'd be right. Everyone at STATS has a part in making this book a reality, and we'd like to thank them here for their efforts.

Dr. Richard Cramer is the founder and Chairman of the Board of STATS, Inc., and is also responsible for developing the computer and data collection systems used by our network of reporters. STATS would not even exist today without his vision.

STATS President and CEO John Dewan is heavily involved in the production of this book and many others, and all of us continue to be amazed at how he finds the time. John's efforts over the years have laid the groundwork for STATS' continued growth and success.

Don Zminda remains the heart of *The Scouting Notebook* as our Director of Publications. It's a colossal effort to coordinate the work of all the reporters, writers, and editors for this book, and Don's got it down to a science.

Rob Neyer and Jim Henzler support Don in our Publications Department, and both were heavily involved in this book's production. Rob has too many tasks to list here, but took time out to write the scouting sections for two teams. Jim wrote most of the minor league prospect reports.

Dave Mundo performed several tasks in helping put together the book—programming, editing, and developing page layouts, to name just a few. All of the statistics and charts you see are the result of Dave and the rest of our Systems Department. Sue Dewan and Mike Canter head that busy group, which consists of Art Ashley, Jim Guthrie, Stefan Kretschmann, David Pinto and Jeff Schinski.

Chuck Miller is in a league by himself, laying out most of the book's pages and keeping track of several hundred player pictures. In his "spare" time, Chuck also helped check the stats.

But he wouldn't even *have* stats to check without the work of our Operations Department. Steve Moyer heads that group, which consists of Ethan Cooperson, Mike Hammer, Kenn Ruby, Allan Spear, and Peter Woelflein. These guys, along with our network of reporters, are responsible for collecting ream after ream of baseball data each season. Steve and his staff were our main stat checkers, along with Drew Faust and Chuck Miller.

Special thanks to Bud Podrazik for assisting Chuck with the massive "cut and paste" operation. Thom Henninger also deserves a thank you for his help editing essays.

Our appreciation also goes to the rest of the STATS staff: Kristen Beauregard, Jim Capuano, Buffy Cramer-Hammann, Brian Ernsberger, Ron Freer, Virginia Hamill, Tim Harbert, Bob Meyerhoff, Marge Morra, Betty Moy, Jim Musso, Brynne Orlando, Jim Osborne, Pat Quinn, Ross Schaufelberger, Stephanie Seburn and Leena Sheth. STATS does much more than just write books, and these people help make the rest of those things happen.

Our "Stars, Bums and Sleepers" section is greatly inspired by the pioneering work of Bill James. It's safe to say that without Bill, this *industry* wouldn't even exist, let alone a growing company like STATS. Thanks, Bill.

A big thanks to Fred Claire of the Los Angeles Dodgers for his foreword. It's truly flattering to know that one of baseball's most respected and successful executives enjoys our work. If STATS can sustain the level of long-term success that the Dodgers have, we'll all be smiling.

Thanks to Fred Barnes of *The Sporting News* and Bob Wirz and his staff at Wirz and Associates for their help in obtaining photos.

And our biggest thanks of all go to you, the fan. Without your continued enthusiasm for both STATS and the national pastime, our efforts mean nothing.

—Scott McDevitt

# The Scouting Staff

Baseball scouts are the first building blocks of any team's success—if they can't tell the stars from the bums, the team is going to have some problems. That goes for our scouts as well. *The Scouting Notebook* writing staff consists of both beat reporters and STATS reporters who cover major league baseball on a regular basis, and they know their stuff. We are proud of their work, and we'd like to recognize them for their outstanding efforts.

The scouting reports in this book were written by the following people, in conjunction with our editors:

| | |
|---|---|
| Baltimore Orioles | Mike Mittleman<br>*STATS, Inc.* |
| Boston Red Sox | Peter Gammons<br>*ESPN/The Boston Globe* |
| California Angels | Phil Rogers<br>*Dallas Morning News* |
| Chicago White Sox | Don Zminda<br>*STATS, Inc.* |
| Cleveland Indians | Paul Hoynes<br>*Cleveland Plain Dealer* |
| Detroit Tigers | Peter Pascarelli<br>*ESPN/ Baseball Weekly* |
| Kansas City Royals | Marc Bowman<br>*STATS, Inc.* |
| Milwaukee Brewers | Mat Olkin<br>*STATS, Inc.* |
| Minnesota Twins | Don Zminda<br>*STATS, Inc.* |
| New York Yankees | John Benson<br>*Diamond Analytics* |
| Oakland Athletics | Peter Pascarelli<br>*ESPN/Baseball Weekly* |
| Seattle Mariners | Rob McQuown<br>*STATS, Inc..* |
| Texas Rangers | Phil Rogers<br>*Dallas Morning News* |
| Toronto Blue Jays | Mike Mittleman<br>*STATS, Inc..* |
| Atlanta Braves | Ellen Halleran<br>*STATS, Inc.* |
| Chicago Cubs | Rob Neyer<br>*STATS, Inc.* |

| | |
|---|---|
| Cincinnati Reds | Ted Thompson<br>*STATS, Inc.* |
| Colorado Rockies | Carmen Corica<br>*STATS, Inc.* |
| Florida Marlins | Rob Neyer<br>*STATS, Inc.* |
| Houston Astros | Ivy McLemore<br>*STATS, Inc.* |
| Los Angeles Dodgers | Don Hartack<br>*STATS, Inc.* |
| Montreal Expos | Peter Pascarelli<br>*ESPN/Baseball Weekly* |
| New York Mets | John Benson<br>*Diamond Analytics* |
| Philadelphia Phillies | Peter Pascarelli<br>*ESPN/Baseball Weekly* |
| Pittsburgh Pirates | John Perrotto<br>*Beaver County Times* |
| St. Louis Cardinals | Peter Pascarelli<br>*ESPN/Baseball Weekly* |
| San Diego Padres | Rob Neyer<br>*STATS, Inc.* |
| San Francisco Giants | Barry Mednick<br>*STATS, Inc.* |

Most of the minor league prospect reports were written by Jim Henzler. Rob Neyer wrote prospect reports for the Cubs and Padres. The mini-notes on major leaguers were written by Scott McDevitt, Rob Neyer and Don Zminda.

This is the second edition of *The Scouting Notebook*. Prior to this book, STATS produced five editions of *The Scouting Report* with another publisher. Although the name of the book has changed, we're fortunate that many of our writers haven't. In fact, four have been around for *all seven* seasons of the book: John Benson, Marc Bowman, Paul Hoynes, and John Perrotto. Are any of you guys interested in a lifetime contract?

And special thanks to John Benson, Peter Gammons and Peter Pascarelli, three of the most respected baseball minds in America, for their efforts again this year.

—Scott McDevitt

# Table of Contents

# Foreword

## The Importance of Scouting

by Fred Claire

Executive Vice President and General Manager, Los Angeles Dodgers

The key to every successful baseball operation is scouting.

There is no group of individuals more important to a baseball organization than its scouts, and no person knows this more than the General Manager. The evaluation and projection of a player is absolutely critical. It begins at the amateur level and continues throughout a professional career. If a club is to make good trades and intelligent free-agent signings, it *must* have the benefit of good scouting reports.

Good scouting requires an organized approach—the act of working through many factors to come up with a clear evaluation of a player.

Good scouting is far from the obvious. It requires tremendous research into every phase of a player's game, including the player's mental approach to his job.

Good scouting is a product of knowledge, experience, information and evaluation. *The Scouting Notebook*, combining each of those qualities, has earned its place as an important source of reference for the baseball professional.

One nice thing about scouting is that, despite what some might tell you, it is *not* just a matter of opinion without a final chance for analysis. Every scout—and for that matter every book—leaves a paper trail of evaluations, and any team—or reader—which doesn't "scout its scouts," so to speak, is playing with fire.

*The Scouting Notebook* has a lengthy record in place, there to be evaluated. I think you'll find both that record and this year's edition of *The Scouting Notebook* to be worthy of your attention.

# Introduction

Welcome to the second edition of *The Scouting Notebook*. We used to do a book with a different title, and you can still find that different title in the bookstores. But the editors and the writers of that book are now working on this one. And most important, the ruling principle of this book is the same: get a bunch of intelligent baseball analysts, people who collectively cover *thousands* of games every season, and have them give us their detailed scouting reports on every major league player who saw significant action last season.

The result is a veritable encyclopedia of contemporary major league baseball. Every year, we tell you about the strengths and weaknesses of many hundreds of players—not just major league players, either, but also each club's top minor league prospects. We study the stats, we talk to the scouts, we watch the games with a keen eye, recording even the smallest details. We look for the truth, and we ignore the hype.

Things are going to happen this season—Billy Wagner will be the National League's Rookie of the Year, Javy Lopez will make the All-Star team, Andy Ashby will win 18-odd games—and you'll say to your friends, "I knew it all along."

Our scouting staff is stronger than ever and includes some of the top baseball analysts around, people like Peter Gammons and Peter Pascarelli and John Benson. This second edition offers some key improvements over last year's book. First of all, we've doubled our coverage of minor league prospects (more on that below). And second, this year you'll find what we call "mini-notes" on peripheral major leaguers. This allows us, for the first time, to cover *every* 1995 major leaguer—all 1,133 of them—in some fashion.

Along with all those lively, well-written reports, we give you our bountiful supply of useful, easy-to-understand data. This includes hitting and pitching charts based on the 1995 season. The hitting charts show you graphically where each player hit the ball, while the pitching charts measure the effectiveness of every pitcher (in four different situations) in performing his most basic task—throwing a strike.

Then there's "Stars, Bums and Sleepers." In this section, a fantasy/rotisserie smorgasbord, you'll get a feel for what to expect from each player in 1996: whether they will improve, decline, remain consistent, even come out of nowhere to surprise.

We'll get to the meat of the book—the full- and half-page player reports—later, but first let's go over the other sections in which we evaluate players.

## The "Other" Pages

Some players didn't play enough last year to earn a full- or half-page result, and aren't young enough or good enough to deserve a prospect report (see below). But they did play in the majors last year, so we can't ignore them. Following the half-page reports for each team, you'll find a page devoted to these part-timers, with each getting a three- or four-line summary. At the conclusion of each "mini-note" (as we call them), you'll find a letter grade from A to D, with the grades as follows:

**A** — should be an important contributor
**B** — should spend at least part of the season on the roster and contribute
**C** — unlikely to spend much time on a major league roster
**D** — unlikely to play in the majors at all

The grades aren't gospel, of course, and you need to watch spring-training reports to get the best reading on where all these guys will end up.

## The Prospect Pages

If major leaguers aren't enough for you, *The Scouting Notebook* presents two "prospects pages" for each team, up from one prospect page in past editions. For each club, we've chosen between six and eight outstanding minor league players—many of them ready to make a major league impact in 1994 and almost all expected to make an impact within two or three years.

As a useful guide, we include "major league equivalencies" for the position players who played Double- or Triple-A in 1995. The MLE is a tool, adjusted for league and ballpark, devised by Bill James to indicate how a minor league hitter would do at the major league level based on his minor league stats. Is this system necessary? Of course it's necessary; some minor leaguers compile their stats in a hitters' paradise like Tucson, where the average hitter batted a whopping .304 last year, while others struggled in a pitchers' yard like Trenton, where the overall batting average was .245.

Along with the top prospects for each team, we include an organization overview. Some clubs are simply better at developing talent than others; just ask fans of the Atlanta Braves (extremely good) or the Philadelphia Phillies (extremely bad).

In addition, in order to get a few more prospects in the book this year, there is a paragraph titled "Others to Watch." These are other notable prospects, with their skills outlined in a sentence or two.

## The Players

For each major league team, we have extensive reports on 23 to 27 major league players. Most include a full page of scouting information, but six or eight players from each club receive half-page reports. Because we like to get this book in your hands as soon as possible, players are listed with their 1995 clubs, but we keep abreast of post-season moves, and all player moves which took place before December 1, 1995 are noted and discussed in the texts. In addition, most of the major deals between December 1 and December 10 are also noted. If you don't know with which team a player is listed, just check the index.

## The Scouting Notebook Page

*The Scouting Notebook* page for primary players has two columns. The left column provides an in-depth report by an expert scout/analyst who follows the team on a daily basis. The right column contains statistical information. Starting at the top of the column it lists:

*Position*: The first position shown is the player's most common position in 1995. If a position player played any other positions in 10 or more games, those positions are shown also. For pitchers, SP stands for starting pitcher and RP for relief pitcher. A second pitching position is shown if a starting pitcher relieved at least four times or a relief pitcher started at least twice.

*Bats and Throws:* L=left-handed, R=right-handed, B=both (switch-hitter).

*Opening Day Age:* This is the player's age on March 31, the Sunday night on which the 1996 season will begin.

*Born:* Birth date and place.

*ML Seasons:* This number indicates the number of different major league seasons in which this player has actually appeared. For example, if a player was called up to play in September in each of the last three seasons, the number shown would be three (3). Note that this is different from the term "Major League Service," which counts only the actual number of days a player appears on a major league roster.

*Overall Statistics:* These are traditional statistics for the player's 1995 season and his career through 1995.

### Pitcher Strike Charts

The pitcher strike charts answer the question "How Often Does He Throw Strikes?" The charts are constructed based on the most extreme pitchers at throwing strikes in baseball. Our data shows that, depending on the pitcher and the situation, pitchers will toss a strike between 40 and 80 percent of the time. Therefore we've constructed the chart to represent the 40-80 percent range of throwing strikes.

Here are some ground rules: When you read your daily paper's box score or hear an announcer state that a pitcher has thrown 97 pitches, 62 of them for strikes, the strike count includes swinging strikes, taken strikes, foul balls and balls hit in play. Even though not all balls hit into play are strikes, the theory is that most of them are, and the ones that aren't would be difficult to judge. Our charts reflect this. The charts are then broken into four categories. **All Pitches** is straightforward, as is **First Pitch**. We define **Ahead** as being any time there are more strikes than balls in the count (0-1, 0-2, 1-2). **Behind** includes counts with more balls than strikes.

League averages are shown in each chart. Here are the 1995 league averages:

| Strike Percentage by League — 1995 | | |
|---|---|---|
| | American | National |
| All Pitches | 60.1% | 62.4% |
| First Pitch | 55.2% | 58.0% |
| Ahead in the Count | 58.4% | 60.3% |
| Behind in the Count | 66.2% | 67.4% |

You'll notice the National League throws a slightly higher percentage of strikes, as they have in all seven years we've kept track of this.

## Hitting Diagrams

The hitting diagrams shown in these reports are the most advanced of their kind. For every game and every ball hit into play last year (both hits and outs), STATS-trained reporters entered data into the STATS computers. They kept track of the type of batted ball—ground ball, fly ball, pop-up, line drive and bunt—as well as the distance each ball traveled. Direction is tracked by dividing the field into 26 "wedges" projecting out from home plate. Distance is measured in 10-foot increments from home plate.

Below are switch-hitting Mickey Tettleton's hitting diagrams. The chart on the left shows where Tettleton hit the ball against lefthanders, while the chart on the right shows what he did against righthanders.

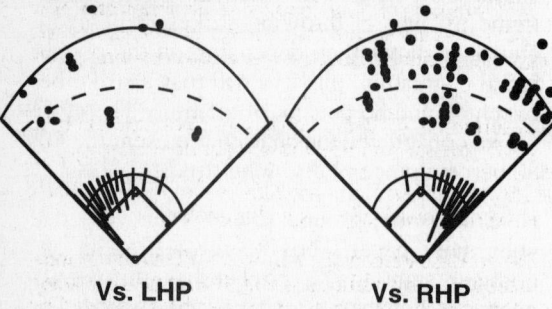

**Vs. LHP**          **Vs. RHP**

In the diagrams, ground balls and short line drives are shown by the various length lines in the infield; the longer the line, the more ground balls and liners were hit in that direction. In the outfield, batted balls are shown by dots. The dotted line in the outfield is 300 feet away from home plate, indicating a rough approximation of typical outfield defensive positions. As you can see, Tettleton is an extreme pull hitter whether he's hitting from the left or right side of the plate, and whether he hits the ball on the ground or in the air.

## Technical Information on the Diagrams

A lot of experimentation went into producing these charts. When we first started, we tried to show every single batted ball that was hit into play by each player. We found that the charts became very cluttered for everyday players. We began experimenting with trying to show only the most meaningful information. When all was said and done, here's what we ended up with:

a. Pop-ups and bunts are excluded. We excluded pop-ups because 95% of these are caught regardless of how fielders are positioned. We excluded bunts because defensing a bunt is a whole different strategy that is primarily used on a select number of players and situations.

b. Ground balls under 50 feet are excluded. These are swinging bunts and are somewhat rare. We exclude them because they don't provide a true indication of the direction of a batted ball reaching an infielder or going through the infield.

c. For everyday players, we excluded what we call isolated points in the outfield. If a player hit only one ball in a given area of the field with no other batted balls in the vicinity all season, we exclude it from the chart. We felt that one ball does not give a true indication of a tendency. This rule did not apply to balls hit farther than 380 feet; all batted balls over 380 feet are shown. See Albert Belle for many examples.

d. Similarly, for players who play infrequently, we expanded the data sample to create a larger pattern of dots in the outfield when he tended to hit in a given area more frequently.

e. For ground balls over 50 feet, we excluded only the rare isolated ground ball. For most players, almost all their ground balls are shown.

Other notes of interest:

The field itself is drawn to precise scale, with the outfield fence reaching 400 feet in center field and 330 feet down the lines. Keep in mind that parks are configured differently so that a dot that is shown inside of the diagram might actually have been a home run. Similarly, a dot outside the fence in the diagram might actually have been in play.

Liners under 170 feet are part of the infield. We

give responsibility for short line drives to the infielders.

No distinction is made between hits and outs.

## 1995 Situational Stats

There are eight situational breakdowns for every primary player. **Home** and **Road** show performance while playing in his home park and on the road. **First Half** and **Scnd Half** show performance before and after last year's All-Star break. For hitters, **LHP** and **RHP** show the player's performance versus left-handed pitchers and right-handed pitchers, respectively. For pitchers, **LHB** and **RHB** show how the opposition batters hit against that pitcher based on the side of the plate from which they hit. **Sc Pos** stands for Scoring Position. It shows batting performance when hitting with runners in scoring position.

The definition we use for **Clutch** here can be simply defined as the late innings of a close game. For those of you interested in the exact definition, clutch is when it is the seventh inning or later and the batting team is up by one run, tied, or has the tying run on base, at bat, or on deck. Our definition of Clutch is consistent with a very well-known statistic, the save.

## 1995 Rankings

This section shows how the player ranked against the league, against his teammates, and by position in significant categories. Thanks to the power of the STATS computer, we not only include traditional categories, but also the less traditional categories as shown in the Major League Leaders section of this book. The Definitions and Qualifications section below provides some details on these lesser known categories. Due to space considerations, when a player ranked high in numerous categories, we omitted some of the less interesting rankings.

## Major League Leaders

The chapter immediately following this introduction is a complete listing of Major League Leaders. The top three players in each category are shown for each league separately. You'll notice a STATS flavor to these leaders. Not only do we show the leaders for the common categories like batting average, home runs and ERA, but you'll also find less traditional categories like steals of third and pitches thrown.

## Definitions and Qualifications

The following are definitions and qualifications for the Major League Leaders and Rankings.

*Definitions:*

Times on Base — Hits plus walks plus hit by pitch.

Ground/Fly Ratio — The ratio of all ground balls hit to fly balls and pop-ups hit. Bunts and line drives are excluded completely.

Runs/Times on Base — This is calculated by dividing Runs Scored by Times on Base.

Clutch — This category shows a player's batting average in the late innings of close games: the seventh inning or later with the batting team ahead by one, tied, or has the tying run on base, at bat, or on deck.

Bases Loaded — This category shows a player's batting average in bases loaded situations.

GDP per GDP situation — A GDP situation exists any time there is a man on first with less than two outs. This statistic measures how often a player grounds into a double play in that situation.

Percentage of Pitches Taken — This tells you how often a player lets a pitch go by without swinging.

Percentage Swings Put In Play — This tells you how often a player hits the ball into fair territory, or is retired on a foul-ball out, when he swings.

Run Support per Nine Innings — This indicates how many runs are scored for a pitcher by his team while he was pitching translated into a per-nine-inning figure.

Baserunners per Nine Innings — These are the hits, walks and hit batsmen allowed per nine innings.

Strikeout/Walk Ratio — This is simply a pitcher's strikeouts divided by his walks allowed.

Stolen Base Percentage Allowed — This figure indicates how successful opposing baserunners are when attempting a stolen base. It's stolen bases divided by stolen-base attempts.

Save Percentage — This is saves divided by save opportunities. Save opportunities include saves plus blown saves.

Blown Saves — A blown save is charged any time a pitcher comes into a game where a save situation is in place and he loses the lead.

Holds — A hold is given to a pitcher when he comes into the game in a save situation, but is removed before the end of the game while maintaining his team's lead. The pitcher must retire at least one batter to get a hold.

Percentage of Inherited Runners Scored — When a pitcher comes into a game with men already on base, these runners are called inherited runners. This statistic measures the percentage of these inherited runners that the relief pitcher allows to score.

First Batter Efficiency — This statistic tells you the batting average allowed by a relief pitcher to the first batter he faces.

## Qualifications:

In order to be ranked, a player had to qualify with a minimum number of opportunities. Due to the strike, the qualifications aren't necessarily the same for players on different teams, because they ended up being "scheduled," for our purposes, for different numbers of games. The qualifications are as follows:

### Batters

Batting average, slugging percentage, on-base average, home run frequency, ground/fly ratio, runs scored per time reached base and pitches seen per plate appearance — (3.1 plate appearances) times (team games)

Percentage of pitches taken, lowest percentage of swings that missed and percentage of swings put into play — (9.26 pitches seen) times (team games)

Percentage of extra bases taken as a runner — (.09 opportunities to advance) times (team games)

Stolen base percentage — (.12 stolen-base attempts) times (team games)

Runners in scoring position — (.62 plate appearances with runners in scoring position) times (team games)

Clutch — (.31 plate appearances in the clutch) times (team games)

Bases loaded — (.06 plate appearances with the bases loaded) times (team games)

GDP per GDP situation — (.31 plate appearances with a man on first and less than two outs) times (team games)

Vs LHP — (.77 plate appearances against left-handed pitchers) times (team games)

Vs RHP — (2.33 plate appearances against right-handed pitchers) times (team games)

BA at home — (1.55 plate appearances at home) times (team games)

BA on the road — (1.55 plate appearances on the road) times (team games)

Leadoff on-base average — (.93 plate appearances in the number-one spot in the batting order) times (team games)

Cleanup slugging percentage — (.93 plate appearances in the number-four spot in the batting order) times (team games)

BA on 3-1 count — (.06 plate appearances putting the ball into play or walking on a 3-1 count) times (team games)

BA with 2 strikes — (.62 plate appearances with two strikes) times (team games)

BA on 0-2 count — (.12 plate appearances putting the ball into play or striking out on a 0-2 count) times (team games)

BA on 3-2 count — (.12 plate appearances with a 3-2 count) times (team games)

### Pitchers

Earned run average, run support per nine innings, baserunners per nine innings, batting average allowed, on-base average allowed, slugging percentage allowed, home runs per nine innings, strikeouts per nine innings, strikeout/walk ratio, stolen base percentage allowed, GDPs per nine innings, pitches thrown per batter and groundball/flyball ratio off — 1 inning pitched per team game

Winning percentage — .09 decisions per team game

GDPs induced per GDP situation — pitchers facing .19 batters in GDP situations per team game

Save Percentage — .12 save opportunities per team game

Percentage of inherited runners scoring — .19 inherited runners per team game

First batter efficiency — .25 games in relief per team game

BA allowed, runners in scoring position — pitchers facing .93 batters with men in scoring position per team game

ERA at home — .5 innings pitched at home per team game

ERA on the road — .5 innings pitched on the road per team game

Vs LHB — .77 left-handed batters faced per team game

Vs RHB — 2.33 right-handed batters faced per team game

### Relief Pitchers

ERA, batting average allowed, baserunners per nine innings, strikeouts per 9 innings — .33 relief innings per team game

### Fielders

Percentage caught stealing by catchers — catchers with .46 stolen-base attempts against them per team game

Fielding percentage — .62 games at a position per team game; .19 chances per team game for pitchers

# Major League Leaders

# 1995 American League Leaders

## Batters

### Batting Average
| | |
|---|---|
| Edgar Martinez | .356 |
| Chuck Knoblauch | .333 |
| Tim Salmon | .330 |

### Home Runs
| | |
|---|---|
| Albert Belle | 50 |
| Jay Buhner | 40 |
| Frank Thomas | 40 |

### Runs Batted In
| | |
|---|---|
| Albert Belle | 126 |
| Mo Vaughn | 126 |
| Jay Buhner | 121 |

### Games Played
| | |
|---|---|
| Frank Thomas | 145 |
| Edgar Martinez | 145 |
| 5 players tied with | 144 |

### At Bats
| | |
|---|---|
| Lance Johnson | 607 |
| Otis Nixon | 589 |
| Chad Curtis | 586 |

### Runs Scored
| | |
|---|---|
| Edgar Martinez | 121 |
| Albert Belle | 121 |
| Jim Edmonds | 120 |

### Hits
| | |
|---|---|
| Lance Johnson | 186 |
| Edgar Martinez | 182 |
| Chuck Knoblauch | 179 |

### Singles
| | |
|---|---|
| Otis Nixon | 151 |
| Lance Johnson | 146 |
| Carlos Baerga | 130 |

### Doubles
| | |
|---|---|
| Edgar Martinez | 52 |
| Albert Belle | 52 |
| Kirby Puckett | 39 |

### Triples
| | |
|---|---|
| Kenny Lofton | 13 |
| Lance Johnson | 12 |
| Brady Anderson | 10 |

### Stolen Bases
| | |
|---|---|
| Kenny Lofton | 54 |
| Tom Goodwin | 50 |
| Otis Nixon | 50 |

### Caught Stealing
| | |
|---|---|
| Otis Nixon | 21 |
| Chuck Knoblauch | 18 |
| Tom Goodwin | 18 |

### Walks
| | |
|---|---|
| Frank Thomas | 136 |
| Edgar Martinez | 116 |
| Tony Phillips | 113 |

### Intentional Walks
| | |
|---|---|
| Frank Thomas | 29 |
| Edgar Martinez | 19 |
| Kirby Puckett | 18 |

### Hit by Pitch
| | |
|---|---|
| Ed Sprague | 15 |
| Mike Macfarlane | 14 |
| Mo Vaughn | 14 |

### Strikeouts
| | |
|---|---|
| Mo Vaughn | 150 |
| Benji Gil | 147 |
| Tony Phillips | 135 |

### Ground into DP
| | |
|---|---|
| Albert Belle | 24 |
| Paul O'Neill | 23 |
| 3 players tied with | 18 |

### Sacrifice Bunts
| | |
|---|---|
| Tom Goodwin | 14 |
| Luis Alicea | 13 |
| Joey Cora | 13 |

### Sacrifice Flies
| | |
|---|---|
| Frank Thomas | 12 |
| Brent Gates | 11 |
| Paul O'Neill | 11 |
| Will Clark | 11 |

### Plate Appearances
| | |
|---|---|
| Chad Curtis | 670 |
| Brady Anderson | 657 |
| Otis Nixon | 656 |

### Times on Base
| | |
|---|---|
| Edgar Martinez | 306 |
| Frank Thomas | 294 |
| Tim Salmon | 274 |

### Total Bases
| | |
|---|---|
| Albert Belle | 377 |
| Rafael Palmeiro | 323 |
| Edgar Martinez | 321 |

### Slugging Percentage
| | |
|---|---|
| Albert Belle | .690 |
| Edgar Martinez | .628 |
| Frank Thomas | .606 |

### Slugging off LHP
| | |
|---|---|
| Frank Thomas | .849 |
| Mark McGwire | .835 |
| Chris Hoiles | .720 |

### Slugging off RHP
| | |
|---|---|
| Albert Belle | .729 |
| Mo Vaughn | .654 |
| Rafael Palmeiro | .605 |

### Cleanup Slugging
| | |
|---|---|
| Mark McGwire | .697 |
| Albert Belle | .690 |
| Juan Gonzalez | .597 |

### On-Base Average
| | |
|---|---|
| Edgar Martinez | .479 |
| Frank Thomas | .454 |
| Jim Thome | .438 |

### OBA off LHP
| | |
|---|---|
| Edgar Martinez | .562 |
| Frank Thomas | .524 |
| Manny Ramirez | .507 |

### OBA off RHP
| | |
|---|---|
| Jim Thome | .456 |
| Edgar Martinez | .449 |
| Chuck Knoblauch | .433 |

### Leadoff OBA
| | |
|---|---|
| Chuck Knoblauch | .423 |
| Wade Boggs | .420 |
| Rickey Henderson | .408 |

### AB/HR Frequency
| | |
|---|---|
| Albert Belle | 10.9 |
| Jay Buhner | 11.8 |
| Frank Thomas | 12.3 |

### Ground/Fly Ratio
| | |
|---|---|
| Otis Nixon | 3.0 |
| Tom Goodwin | 2.2 |
| Mark McLemore | 2.0 |

### % Extra Bases Taken
| | |
|---|---|
| Tim Salmon | 72.7% |
| Ray Durham | 72.2 |
| Travis Fryman | 69.6 |

### Runs/Time On Base
| | |
|---|---|
| Jim Edmonds | 55.0% |
| Kenny Lofton | 48.9 |
| Albert Belle | 48.0 |

### SB Success %
| | |
|---|---|
| Rich Amaral | 91.3% |
| Roberto Alomar | 90.9 |
| Stan Javier | 87.8 |

### Steals of third
| | |
|---|---|
| Otis Nixon | 13 |
| Vince Coleman | 13 |
| Kenny Lofton | 13 |

### BA Scoring Position
| | |
|---|---|
| Rickey Henderson | .419 |
| Kenny Lofton | .386 |
| Edgar Martinez | .384 |

### BA Late & Close
| | |
|---|---|
| Jose Canseco | .404 |
| Edgar Martinez | .397 |
| Joey Cora | .392 |

### BA Bases Loaded
| | |
|---|---|
| Mike Stanley | .818 |
| Devon White | .667 |
| Mo Vaughn | .600 |

### GDP/GDP Situation
| | |
|---|---|
| Jose Valentin | 0.0% |
| Brady Anderson | 3.2 |
| Keith Lockhart | 4.0 |

### BA vs LH Pitchers
| | |
|---|---|
| Edgar Martinez | .433 |
| Manny Ramirez | .407 |
| Frank Thomas | .389 |

### BA vs RH Pitchers
| | |
|---|---|
| Eddie Murray | .340 |
| Kevin Seitzer | .334 |
| Edgar Martinez | .331 |

### BA at Home
| | |
|---|---|
| Wade Boggs | .379 |
| Edgar Martinez | .377 |
| Chili Davis | .358 |

### BA on the Road
| | |
|---|---|
| Tim Salmon | .366 |
| Edgar Martinez | .336 |
| Chuck Knoblauch | .336 |

### BA on 3-1 Count
| | |
|---|---|
| Jorge Fabregas | .857 |
| Jon Nunnally | .714 |
| Michael Tucker | .714 |

### BA With 2 Strikes
| | |
|---|---|
| Carlos Baerga | .332 |
| Wade Boggs | .285 |
| Edgar Martinez | .283 |

### BA on 0-2 Count
| | |
|---|---|
| Garret Anderson | .405 |
| Luis Polonia | .375 |
| John Jaha | .345 |

### BA on 3-2 Count
| | |
|---|---|
| Matt Merullo | .500 |
| Jeff Reboulet | .462 |
| Lyle Mouton | .444 |

### Pitches Seen
| | |
|---|---|
| Tony Phillips | 2754 |
| Chad Curtis | 2648 |
| Brady Anderson | 2644 |

### Pitches Seen per PA
| | |
|---|---|
| Rickey Henderson | 4.37 |
| Wade Boggs | 4.32 |
| Mickey Tettleton | 4.31 |

### % Pitches Taken
| | |
|---|---|
| Mickey Tettleton | 66.9% |
| Edgar Martinez | 66.2 |
| Wade Boggs | 65.9 |

| % of Missed Swings | |
|---|---|
| **Wade Boggs** | **5.3%** |
| Joey Cora | 6.5 |
| Luis Sojo | 7.2 |

| % Swings Put In Play | |
|---|---|
| **Lance Johnson** | **61.5%** |
| Luis Sojo | 57.5 |
| Carlos Baerga | 56.0 |

| Bunts in Play | |
|---|---|
| **Otis Nixon** | **53** |
| Tom Goodwin | 43 |
| Ray Durham | 29 |

# Pitchers

| Earned Run Average | |
|---|---|
| **Randy Johnson** | **2.48** |
| Tim Wakefield | 2.95 |
| Dennis Martinez | 3.08 |

| Wins | |
|---|---|
| **Mike Mussina** | **19** |
| David Cone | 18 |
| Randy Johnson | 18 |

| Losses | |
|---|---|
| **Jason Bere** | **15** |
| **Mike Moore** | **15** |
| **Kevin Gross** | **15** |

| Win-Loss Percentage | |
|---|---|
| **Randy Johnson** | **.900** |
| David Wells | .769 |
| Erik Hanson | .750 |

| Games Pitched | |
|---|---|
| **Jesse Orosco** | **65** |
| Roger McDowell | 64 |
| Bob Wickman | 63 |
| Bobby Ayala | 63 |
| Stan Belinda | 63 |

| Games Started | |
|---|---|
| **Mark Gubicza** | **33** |
| Mike Mussina | 32 |
| Chuck Finley | 32 |

| Complete Games | |
|---|---|
| **Jack McDowell** | **8** |
| Mike Mussina | 7 |
| Scott Erickson | 7 |

| Shutouts | |
|---|---|
| **Mike Mussina** | **4** |
| Randy Johnson | 3 |
| 6 players tied with | 2 |

| Games Finished | |
|---|---|
| **Roberto Hernandez** | **57** |
| **Jose Mesa** | **57** |
| John Wetteland | 56 |

| Innings Pitched | |
|---|---|
| **David Cone** | **229.1** |
| Mike Mussina | 221.2 |
| Jack McDowell | 217.2 |

| Hits Allowed | |
|---|---|
| **Pat Hentgen** | **236** |
| Todd Stottlemyre | 228 |
| Mark Gubicza | 222 |

| Batters Faced | |
|---|---|
| **David Cone** | **954** |
| Jack McDowell | 927 |
| Todd Stottlemyre | 920 |

| Runs Allowed | |
|---|---|
| **Pat Hentgen** | **129** |
| Kevin Gross | 124 |
| Jason Bere | 120 |

| Earned Runs Allowed | |
|---|---|
| **Pat Hentgen** | **114** |
| Kevin Gross | 113 |
| Mike Moore | 111 |

| Home Runs Allowed | |
|---|---|
| **Brad Radke** | **32** |
| Kevin Gross | 27 |
| Todd Stottlemyre | 26 |
| Ricky Bones | 26 |
| Kenny Rogers | 26 |

| Walks Allowed | |
|---|---|
| **Al Leiter** | **108** |
| Jason Bere | 106 |
| Wilson Alvarez | 93 |
| Chuck Finley | 93 |

| Hit Batters | |
|---|---|
| **Roger Clemens** | **14** |
| Dennis Martinez | 12 |
| Kevin Brown | 9 |
| Tim Wakefield | 9 |

| Strikeouts | |
|---|---|
| **Randy Johnson** | **294** |
| Todd Stottlemyre | 205 |
| Chuck Finley | 195 |

| Wild Pitches | |
|---|---|
| **Al Leiter** | **14** |
| Sean Bergman | 13 |
| Chuck Finley | 13 |

| Balks | |
|---|---|
| **Tim Fortugno** | **3** |
| **Brian Anderson** | **3** |
| 14 players tied with | 2 |

| Run Support per 9 IP | |
|---|---|
| **Charles Nagy** | **8.1** |
| Mark Langston | 7.2 |
| Scott Erickson | 6.8 |

| Baserunners per 9 IP | |
|---|---|
| **Randy Johnson** | **9.7** |
| Mike Mussina | 9.7 |
| Tim Wakefield | 11.1 |

| BA Allowed | |
|---|---|
| **Randy Johnson** | **.201** |
| Kevin Appier | .221 |
| Mike Mussina | .226 |

| Slugging Pct Allowed | |
|---|---|
| **Randy Johnson** | **.303** |
| Kevin Brown | .341 |
| Kevin Appier | .351 |

| On-Base Pct Allowed | |
|---|---|
| **Randy Johnson** | **.266** |
| Mike Mussina | .270 |
| Tim Wakefield | .300 |

| Home Runs per 9 IP | |
|---|---|
| **Randy Johnson** | **.504** |
| Kevin Brown | .522 |
| Tom Gordon | .571 |

| Strikeouts per 9 IP | |
|---|---|
| **Randy Johnson** | **12.3** |
| Todd Stottlemyre | 8.8 |
| Chuck Finley | 8.6 |

| Walks per 9 IP | |
|---|---|
| **Mike Mussina** | **2.0** |
| Dennis Martinez | 2.2 |
| Brad Radke | 2.3 |

| Strikeout/Walk Ratio | |
|---|---|
| **Randy Johnson** | **4.5** |
| Mike Mussina | 3.2 |
| Todd Stottlemyre | 2.6 |

| Stolen Bases Allowed | |
|---|---|
| **Jason Bere** | **36** |
| David Cone | 28 |
| Jack McDowell | 25 |
| Sean Bergman | 25 |

| Caught Stealing Off | |
|---|---|
| **Mark Langston** | **12** |
| **Todd Stottlemyre** | **12** |
| Tim Belcher | 11 |

| SB % Allowed | |
|---|---|
| **Mark Langston** | **25.0%** |
| Tim Belcher | 26.7 |
| Mike Mussina | 40.0 |

| GDPs induced | |
|---|---|
| **Steve Sparks** | **29** |
| Orel Hershiser | 26 |
| Scott Erickson | 26 |

| GDPs induced per 9 IP | |
|---|---|
| **Orel Hershiser** | **1.4** |
| Steve Sparks | 1.3 |
| Scott Erickson | 1.2 |

| GDPs/GDP Situation | |
|---|---|
| **Jason Grimsley** | **24.2%** |
| Orel Hershiser | 23.6 |
| Ben Blomdahl | 22.2 |

| Grd/Fly Ratio Off | |
|---|---|
| **Kevin Brown** | **2.7** |
| Scott Erickson | 2.5 |
| Orel Hershiser | 2.4 |

| BA Allowed Scor Pos | |
|---|---|
| **Randy Johnson** | **.164** |
| Dennis Martinez | .183 |
| Tim Wakefield | .185 |

| Pitches Thrown | |
|---|---|
| **David Cone** | **3719** |
| Randy Johnson | 3622 |
| Steve Finley | 3520 |

| Pitches per Batter | |
|---|---|
| **Jim Abbott** | **3.48** |
| Orel Hershiser | 3.54 |
| Chris Bosio | 3.57 |

| Pickoff Throws | |
|---|---|
| **Jack McDowell** | **241** |
| David Cone | 219 |
| Mark Langston | 210 |

| ERA at Home | |
|---|---|
| **Randy Johnson** | **2.57** |
| Andy Pettitte | 2.61 |
| Orel Hershiser | 2.67 |

| ERA on the Road | |
|---|---|
| **Randy Johnson** | **2.35** |
| Jim Abbott | 2.68 |
| Dennis Martinez | 2.70 |

| BA Off by LH Batters | |
|---|---|
| **Mike Mussina** | **.209** |
| Erik Hanson | .215 |
| Chad Ogea | .226 |

| BA Off by RH Batters | |
|---|---|
| **Kevin Appier** | **.177** |
| Orel Hershiser | .196 |
| Randy Johnson | .209 |

# Relievers

| Relief ERA | |
|---|---|
| **Jose Mesa** | **1.13** |
| Norm Charlton | 1.51 |
| Troy Percival | 1.95 |

| Relief Wins | |
|---|---|
| **Julian Tavarez** | **10** |
| Stan Belinda | 8 |
| Hipolito Pichardo | 8 |

| Relief Losses | |
|---|---|
| **Roberto Hernandez** | **7** |
| **Joe Boever** | **7** |
| **John Doherty** | **7** |

| Saves | |
|---|---|
| **Jose Mesa** | **46** |
| Lee Smith | 37 |
| Rick Aguilera | 32 |
| Roberto Hernandez | 32 |

| Blown Saves | |
|---|---|
| **Roberto Hernandez** | **10** |
| Dennis Eckersley | 9 |
| Bob Wickman | 9 |

| Save Opportunities | |
|---|---|
| **Jose Mesa** | **48** |
| Roberto Hernandez | 42 |
| Lee Smith | 41 |

| Save Percentage | | Relief Strikeouts/9 IP | | Errors by C | | Errors by SS | |
|---|---|---|---|---|---|---|---|
| **Jose Mesa** | **95.8%** | **Roberto Hernandez** | **12.7** | **John Flaherty** | **11** | **Pat Meares** | **18** |
| Lee Smith | 90.2 | Troy Percival | 11.4 | Randy Knorr | 8 | Greg Gagne | 18 |
| Mike Henneman | 90.0 | Jeff Nelson | 11.0 | Joe Oliver | 8 | John Valentin | 18 |
| | | | | Ivan Rodriguez | 8 | | |

| Holds | | % Inher Rnnrs Scored | | | | Errors by LF | |
|---|---|---|---|---|---|---|---|
| **Troy Percival** | **29** | **Mike Christopher** | **9.1%** | Errors by 1B | | **Joe Carter** | **7** |
| Bob Wickman | 21 | Paul Assenmacher | 10.7 | **Mark McGwire** | **12** | Albert Belle | 6 |
| Julian Tavarez | 19 | Jim Poole | 14.8 | Mo Vaughn | 11 | Mike Greenwell | 6 |
| | | | | Tino Martinez | 8 | | |

| Relief Innings | | First Batter Efficiency | | Errors by 2B | | Errors by CF | |
|---|---|---|---|---|---|---|---|
| **John Doherty** | **107.1** | **John Doherty** | **.049** | **Joey Cora** | **22** | **Bernie Williams** | **8** |
| Joe Boever | 98.2 | Jim Poole | .083 | Carlos Baerga | 19 | Kenny Lofton | 8 |
| Roger McDowell | 85.0 | Jose Mesa | .117 | Luis Alicea | 16 | Lee Tinsley | 5 |
| Julian Tavarez | 85.0 | | | | | | |

| Relief BA Allowed | | | | Errors by 3B | | Errors by RF | |
|---|---|---|---|---|---|---|---|
| **Troy Percival** | **.147** | # Fielding | | **Tony Phillips** | **19** | **Jon Nunnally** | **6** |
| Jesse Orosco | .169 | | | Robin Ventura | 17 | Shawn Green | 6 |
| John Wetteland | .185 | Errors by P | | Ed Sprague | 16 | Ruben Sierra | 5 |
| | | **Chuck Finley** | **4** | Jim Thome | 16 | Manny Ramirez | 5 |

| Runners/9 IP - Relief | | | | | | % CS off Catchers | |
|---|---|---|---|---|---|---|---|
| **Norm Charlton** | **7.6** | **Dennis Martinez** | **4** | Tim Naehring | 16 | **Ivan Rodriguez** | **48.1%** |
| Troy Percival | 7.8 | 7 players tied with | 3 | | | Lance Parrish | 41.5 |
| John Wetteland | 7.9 | | | | | Terry Steinbach | 39.4 |

# 1995 National League Leaders

## Batters

### Batting Average
| | |
|---|---|
| **Tony Gwynn** | **.368** |
| Mike Piazza | .346 |
| Dante Bichette | .340 |

### Home Runs
| | |
|---|---|
| **Dante Bichette** | **40** |
| Larry Walker | 36 |
| Sammy Sosa | 36 |

### Runs Batted In
| | |
|---|---|
| **Dante Bichette** | **128** |
| Sammy Sosa | 119 |
| Andres Galarraga | 106 |

### Games Played
| | |
|---|---|
| **Barry Bonds** | **144** |
| **Fred McGriff** | **144** |
| **Sammy Sosa** | **144** |

### At Bats
| | |
|---|---|
| **Brian McRae** | **580** |
| Dante Bichette | 579 |
| Sammy Sosa | 564 |

### Runs Scored
| | |
|---|---|
| **Craig Biggio** | **123** |
| Barry Bonds | 109 |
| Steve Finley | 104 |

### Hits
| | |
|---|---|
| **Tony Gwynn** | **197** |
| **Dante Bichette** | **197** |
| Mark Grace | 180 |

### Singles
| | |
|---|---|
| **Tony Gwynn** | **154** |
| Steve Finley | 126 |
| Brett Butler | 126 |

### Doubles
| | |
|---|---|
| **Mark Grace** | **51** |
| Brian McRae | 38 |
| Dante Bichette | 38 |

### Triples
| | |
|---|---|
| **Brett Butler** | **9** |
| **Eric Young** | **9** |
| Steve Finley | 8 |
| Luis Gonzalez | 8 |
| Deion Sanders | 8 |

### Stolen Bases
| | |
|---|---|
| **Quilvio Veras** | **56** |
| Barry Larkin | 51 |
| Delino DeShields | 39 |

### Caught Stealing
| | |
|---|---|
| **Quilvio Veras** | **21** |
| Darren Lewis | 18 |
| Delino DeShields | 14 |

### Walks
| | |
|---|---|
| **Barry Bonds** | **120** |
| Walt Weiss | 98 |
| Craig Biggio | 80 |
| Quilvio Veras | 80 |

### Intentional Walks
| | |
|---|---|
| **Barry Bonds** | **22** |
| Jeff Branson | 14 |
| Larry Walker | 13 |

### Hit by Pitch
| | |
|---|---|
| **Craig Biggio** | **22** |
| Larry Walker | 14 |
| Andres Galarraga | 13 |

### Strikeouts
| | |
|---|---|
| **Andres Galarraga** | **146** |
| Sammy Sosa | 134 |
| Reggie Sanders | 122 |

### Ground into DP
| | |
|---|---|
| **Charlie Hayes** | **23** |
| Fred McGriff | 20 |
| Eddie Williams | 20 |

### Sacrifice Bunts
| | |
|---|---|
| **Bobby Jones** | **18** |
| Andy Ashby | 17 |
| Ramon Martinez | 13 |
| Jose Vizcaino | 13 |

### Sacrifice Flies
| | |
|---|---|
| **Jeff Conine** | **12** |
| Jeff King | 8 |
| 5 players tied with | 7 |

### Plate Appearances
| | |
|---|---|
| **Craig Biggio** | **673** |
| Brian McRae | 638 |
| Barry Bonds | 635 |

### Times on Base
| | |
|---|---|
| **Barry Bonds** | **274** |
| Craig Biggio | 269 |
| Mark Grace | 247 |

### Total Bases
| | |
|---|---|
| **Dante Bichette** | **359** |
| Larry Walker | 300 |
| Vinny Castilla | 297 |

### Slugging Percentage
| | |
|---|---|
| **Dante Bichette** | **.620** |
| Larry Walker | .607 |
| Mike Piazza | .606 |

### Slugging off LHP
| | |
|---|---|
| **Vinny Castilla** | **.769** |
| Reggie Sanders | .692 |
| Dante Bichette | .691 |

### Slugging off RHP
| | |
|---|---|
| **Larry Walker** | **.637** |
| Barry Bonds | .614 |
| Mike Piazza | .606 |

### Cleanup Slugging
| | |
|---|---|
| **Ron Gant** | **.717** |
| Mark Grace | .664 |
| Matt Williams | .643 |

### On-Base Average
| | |
|---|---|
| **Barry Bonds** | **.431** |
| Craig Biggio | .406 |
| Tony Gwynn | .404 |

### OBA off LHP
| | |
|---|---|
| **Craig Biggio** | **.493** |
| Eric Young | .449 |
| Reggie Sanders | .447 |

### OBA off RHP
| | |
|---|---|
| Barry Bonds | .447 |
| Dave Magadan | .446 |
| Mark Grace | .425 |

### Leadoff OBA
| | |
|---|---|
| John Cangelosi | .454 |
| Steve Finley | .405 |
| Eric Young | .402 |

### AB/HR Frequency
| | |
|---|---|
| Mike Piazza | 13.6 |
| Larry Walker | 13.7 |
| Ron Gant | 14.1 |

### Ground/Fly Ratio
| | |
|---|---|
| Brett Butler | 2.6 |
| Tony Gwynn | 2.5 |
| Brian McRae | 2.2 |

### % Extra Bases Taken
| | |
|---|---|
| Marquis Grissom | 76.2% |
| Jay Bell | 70.5 |
| Brian Jordan | 69.6 |

### Runs/Times On Base
| | |
|---|---|
| Raul Mondesi | 47.9% |
| Brian Jordan | 46.6 |
| Rondell White | 46.5 |

### SB Success %
| | |
|---|---|
| Barry Larkin | 91.1% |
| Bip Roberts | 90.9 |
| Tony Tarasco | 88.9 |

### Steals of third
| | |
|---|---|
| Barry Larkin | 15 |
| Quilvio Veras | 14 |
| Eric Young | 12 |

### BA Scoring Position
| | |
|---|---|
| Tony Gwynn | .394 |
| Jason Bates | .370 |
| Dante Bichette | .367 |

### BA Late & Close
| | |
|---|---|
| Ron Gant | .418 |
| Eric Young | .404 |
| Barry Larkin | .397 |

### BA Bases Loaded
| | |
|---|---|
| Danny Sheaffer | .714 |
| Tony Gwynn | .636 |
| Carl Everett | .556 |

### GDP/GDP Situation
| | |
|---|---|
| Tony Tarasco | 2.2% |
| Chuck Carr | 3.2 |
| Darren Daulton | 3.9 |

### BA vs LH Pitchers
| | |
|---|---|
| Eric Young | .400 |
| Vinny Castilla | .388 |
| Craig Biggio | .383 |

### BA vs RH Pitchers
| | |
|---|---|
| Tony Gwynn | .389 |
| Mike Piazza | .351 |
| Mark Grace | .344 |

### BA at Home
| | |
|---|---|
| Tony Gwynn | .387 |
| Vinny Castilla | .383 |
| Dante Bichette | .377 |

### BA on the Road
| | |
|---|---|
| Mike Piazza | .384 |
| Derek Bell | .361 |
| Tony Gwynn | .349 |

### BA on 3-1 Count
| | |
|---|---|
| Terry Pendleton | .750 |
| Thomas Howard | .750 |
| Mark Parent | .750 |

### BA With 2 Strikes
| | |
|---|---|
| Dave Hansen | .329 |
| Gregg Jefferies | .315 |
| Tony Gwynn | .313 |

### BA on 0-2 Count
| | |
|---|---|
| Greg Colbrunn | .345 |
| Ron Gant | .333 |
| Jerry Browne | .333 |

### BA on 3-2 Count
| | |
|---|---|
| Nelson Liriano | .533 |
| Jesus Tavarez | .500 |
| Tony Gwynn | .444 |

### Pitches Seen
| | |
|---|---|
| Craig Biggio | 2488 |
| Eric Karros | 2485 |
| Barry Bonds | 2452 |

### Pitches Seen per PA
| | |
|---|---|
| Dave Justice | 4.21 |
| Quilvio Veras | 4.16 |
| Barry Larkin | 4.16 |

### % Pitches Taken
| | |
|---|---|
| Walt Weiss | 65.4% |
| Quilvio Veras | 64.7 |
| Dave Magadan | 64.7 |

### % of Missed Swings
| | |
|---|---|
| Gregg Jefferies | 5.1% |
| Brett Butler | 5.5 |
| Tony Gwynn | 6.0 |

### % Swings Put In Play
| | |
|---|---|
| Tony Gwynn | 62.8% |
| Gregg Jefferies | 59.1 |
| Jody Reed | 58.5 |

### Bunts in Play
| | |
|---|---|
| Brett Butler | 46 |
| Chad Fonville | 38 |
| Darren Lewis | 33 |

# Pitchers

### Earned Run Average
| | |
|---|---|
| Greg Maddux | 1.63 |
| Hideo Nomo | 2.54 |
| Andy Ashby | 2.94 |

### Wins
| | |
|---|---|
| Greg Maddux | 19 |
| Pete Schourek | 18 |
| Ramon Martinez | 17 |

### Losses
| | |
|---|---|
| Paul Wagner | 16 |
| John Burkett | 14 |
| Jeff Fassero | 14 |
| Tom Candiotti | 14 |

### Win-Loss Percentage
| | |
|---|---|
| Greg Maddux | .905 |
| Pete Schourek | .720 |
| Dave Burba | .714 |

### Games Pitched
| | |
|---|---|
| Curt Leskanic | 76 |
| Dave Veres | 72 |
| Steve Reed | 71 |

### Games Started
| | |
|---|---|
| Denny Neagle | 31 |
| Mark Portugal | 31 |
| Andy Ashby | 31 |
| Esteban Loaiza | 31 |
| Doug Drabek | 31 |

### Complete Games
| | |
|---|---|
| Greg Maddux | 10 |
| Mark Leiter | 7 |
| Ismael Valdes | 6 |

### Shutouts
| | |
|---|---|
| Greg Maddux | 3 |
| Hideo Nomo | 3 |
| 10 players tied with | 2 |

### Games Finished
| | |
|---|---|
| Heathcliff Slocumb | 54 |
| Robb Nen | 54 |
| Todd Worrell | 53 |

### Innings Pitched
| | |
|---|---|
| Denny Neagle | 209.2 |
| Greg Maddux | 209.2 |
| Ramon Martinez | 206.1 |

### Hits Allowed
| | |
|---|---|
| Denny Neagle | 221 |
| Paul Quantrill | 212 |
| Bobby Jones | 209 |

### Batters Faced
| | |
|---|---|
| Denny Neagle | 876 |
| Ramon Martinez | 859 |
| Joey Hamilton | 850 |

### Runs Allowed
| | |
|---|---|
| Esteban Loaiza | 115 |
| Terry Mulholland | 112 |
| Bobby Jones | 107 |

### Earned Runs Allowed
| | |
|---|---|
| Esteban Loaiza | 99 |
| Doug Drabek | 98 |
| Terry Mulholland | 96 |

### Home Runs Allowed
| | |
|---|---|
| Kevin Foster | 32 |
| Steve Trachsel | 25 |
| Terry Mulholland | 25 |

### Walks Allowed
| | |
|---|---|
| Ramon Martinez | 81 |
| Hideo Nomo | 78 |
| Pat Rapp | 76 |
| Steve Trachsel | 76 |

### Hit Batters
| | |
|---|---|
| Mark Leiter | 17 |
| Darryl Kile | 12 |
| Joey Hamilton | 11 |
| Andy Ashby | 11 |
| Pedro Martinez | 11 |

### Strikeouts
| | |
|---|---|
| Hideo Nomo | 236 |
| John Smoltz | 193 |
| Greg Maddux | 181 |

### Wild Pitches
| | |
|---|---|
| Hideo Nomo | 19 |
| Hector Carrasco | 15 |
| John Smoltz | 13 |

### Balks
| | |
|---|---|
| Hideo Nomo | 5 |
| Wllm VanLandingham | 4 |
| Carlos Perez | 4 |

### Run Support per 9 IP
| | |
|---|---|
| Mark Portugal | 6.2 |
| Pat Rapp | 6.2 |
| Jim Bullinger | 5.9 |

### Baserunners per 9 IP
| | |
|---|---|
| Greg Maddux | 7.5 |
| Hideo Nomo | 9.7 |
| Pete Schourek | 10.0 |

### BA Allowed
| | |
|---|---|
| Hideo Nomo | .182 |
| Greg Maddux | .197 |
| Pedro Martinez | .227 |

### Slugging Pct Allowed
| | |
|---|---|
| Greg Maddux | .258 |
| Hideo Nomo | .286 |
| Tom Glavine | .334 |

### On-Base Pct Allowed
| | |
|---|---|
| Greg Maddux | .224 |
| Hideo Nomo | .270 |
| Ismael Valdes | .277 |

### Home Runs per 9 IP
| | |
|---|---|
| Greg Maddux | .343 |
| Tom Glavine | .408 |
| Pat Rapp | .538 |

### Strikeouts per 9 IP
| | |
|---|---|
| Hideo Nomo | 11.1 |
| John Smoltz | 9.0 |
| Shane Reynolds | 8.3 |

## Walks per 9 IP

| | |
|---|---|
| Greg Maddux | 1.0 |
| Shane Reynolds | 1.8 |
| Denny Neagle | 1.9 |

## Strikeout/Walk Ratio

| | |
|---|---|
| Greg Maddux | 7.9 |
| Shane Reynolds | 4.7 |
| Pete Schourek | 3.6 |

## Stolen Bases Allowed

| | |
|---|---|
| Steve Avery | 30 |
| Hideo Nomo | 29 |
| Jim Bullinger | 27 |

## Caught Stealing Off

| | |
|---|---|
| Pat Rapp | 15 |
| Pedro Martinez | 13 |
| Tom Candiotti | 13 |

## SB% Allowed

| | |
|---|---|
| Chris Hammond | 0.0% |
| Terry Mulholland | 14.3 |
| Pat Rapp | 25.0 |

## GDPs induced

| | |
|---|---|
| Tom Glavine | 26 |
| John Burkett | 26 |
| Andy Ashby | 24 |

## GDPs induced per 9 IP

| | |
|---|---|
| John Burkett | 1.2 |
| Tom Glavine | 1.2 |
| Andy Ashby | 1.1 |

## GDPs/GDP Situation

| | |
|---|---|
| Trevor Wilson | 23.9% |
| Tom Urbani | 22.2 |
| Shawn Barton | 21.6 |

## Grd/Fly Ratio Off

| | |
|---|---|
| Greg Maddux | 3.0 |
| Shane Reynolds | 2.7 |
| Joey Hamilton | 2.3 |

## BA Allowed Scor Pos

| | |
|---|---|
| Greg Maddux | .157 |
| Chris Hammond | .184 |
| Hideo Nomo | .192 |

## Pitches Thrown

| | |
|---|---|
| Ramon Martinez | 3349 |
| Denny Neagle | 3165 |
| Joey Hamilton | 3114 |

## Pitches per Batter

| | |
|---|---|
| Esteban Loaiza | 3.28 |
| Greg Maddux | 3.34 |
| Terry Mulholland | 3.36 |

## Pickoff Throws

| | |
|---|---|
| Mark Leiter | 218 |
| Jeff Fassero | 209 |
| Steve Trachsel | 208 |

## ERA at Home

| | |
|---|---|
| Hideo Nomo | 1.73 |
| Pete Schourek | 1.86 |
| Andy Ashby | 2.21 |

## ERA on the Road

| | |
|---|---|
| Greg Maddux | 1.12 |
| Tom Glavine | 2.61 |
| Jim Bullinger | 2.69 |

## BA Off by LH Batters

| | |
|---|---|
| Greg Maddux | .194 |
| Hideo Nomo | .199 |
| Pedro Martinez | .219 |

## BA Off by RH Batters

| | |
|---|---|
| Hideo Nomo | .168 |
| Dave Burba | .198 |
| Greg Maddux | .198 |

## Relief ERA

| | |
|---|---|
| Tom Henke | 1.82 |
| Todd Worrell | 2.02 |
| Mark Wohlers | 2.09 |

## Relief Wins

| | |
|---|---|
| Jim Dougherty | 8 |
| Rich DeLucia | 8 |
| Brad Clontz | 8 |

## Relief Losses

| | |
|---|---|
| Brian Williams | 8 |
| Hector Carrasco | 7 |
| Jeff Parrett | 7 |
| Robb Nen | 7 |

## Saves

| | |
|---|---|
| Randy Myers | 38 |
| Tom Henke | 36 |
| Rod Beck | 33 |

## Blown Saves

| | |
|---|---|
| Rod Beck | 10 |
| Mel Rojas | 9 |
| Trevor Hoffman | 7 |
| John Franco | 7 |
| Rene Arocha | 7 |

## Save Opportunities

| | |
|---|---|
| Randy Myers | 44 |
| Rod Beck | 43 |
| Mel Rojas | 39 |

## Save Percentage

| | |
|---|---|
| Tom Henke | 94.7% |
| Todd Worrell | 88.9 |
| Jeff Brantley | 87.5 |

## Holds

| | |
|---|---|
| Ricky Bottalico | 20 |
| Greg McMichael | 20 |
| Tim Scott | 19 |
| Dave Veres | 19 |
| Curt Leskanic | 19 |
| Tony Fossas | 19 |

## Relief Innings

| | |
|---|---|
| Dave Veres | 103.1 |
| Todd Jones | 99.2 |
| Curt Leskanic | 98.0 |

## Relief BA Allowed

| | |
|---|---|
| Ricky Bottalico | .167 |
| Doug Henry | .198 |
| Rich DeLucia | .201 |

## Runners/9 IP - Relief

| | |
|---|---|
| Steve Reed | 8.9 |
| Jeff Brantley | 9.5 |
| Ricky Bottalico | 9.9 |

## Relief Strikeouts/9 IP

| | |
|---|---|
| Mark Wohlers | 12.5 |
| Curt Leskanic | 9.8 |
| Dave Burba | 9.7 |

## % Inher Rnnrs Scored

| | |
|---|---|
| Tim Scott | 12.5% |
| Yorkis Perez | 14.3 |
| Pedro Borbon | 17.2 |

## First Batter Efficiency

| | |
|---|---|
| Mark Wohlers | .097 |
| Yorkis Perez | .105 |
| Todd Worrell | .109 |

# Fielding

## Errors by P

| | |
|---|---|
| Bobby Jones | 6 |
| Joey Hamilton | 6 |
| Mark Leiter | 4 |
| Jeff Fassero | 4 |

## Errors by C

| | |
|---|---|
| Scott Servais | 12 |
| Joe Girardi | 10 |
| Mike Piazza | 9 |

## Errors by 1B

| | |
|---|---|
| Andres Galarraga | 13 |
| Mark Johnson | 8 |
| 6 players tied with | 7 |

## Errors by 2B

| | |
|---|---|
| Eric Young | 11 |
| Delino DeShields | 11 |
| Craig Biggio | 10 |
| Jeff Kent | 10 |

## Errors by 3B

| | |
|---|---|
| Ken Caminiti | 27 |
| Chipper Jones | 25 |
| Terry Pendleton | 18 |
| Dave Magadan | 18 |
| Scott Cooper | 18 |

## Errors by SS

| | |
|---|---|
| Jose Offerman | 35 |
| Royce Clayton | 20 |
| Kurt Abbott | 19 |

## Errors by LF

| | |
|---|---|
| Ryan Klesko | 7 |
| Luis Gonzalez | 6 |
| Barry Bonds | 6 |

## Errors by CF

| | |
|---|---|
| Brian L. Hunter | 9 |
| Jacob Brumfield | 8 |
| Steve Finley | 7 |

## Errors by RF

| | |
|---|---|
| Sammy Sosa | 13 |
| Glenallen Hill | 10 |
| Derek Bell | 8 |

## % CS off Catchers

| | |
|---|---|
| Charles Johnson | 42.7% |
| Brad Ausmus | 41.9 |
| Mark Parent | 39.3 |

# Stars, Bums and Sleepers — Who's Who in 1996

What's the definition of a superstar? How about a guy who can hit .300 with 30 homers and call it an "off year"? Here at STATS, we witnessed plenty of that in 1995—players who saw a considerable drop from their 1994 level and still ended up posting impressive offensive numbers. Frank Thomas had an off year in '95. All he did was hit .308, crank out 40 home runs, and lead the majors in walks. Those numbers will win you the MVP in a lot of seasons. Jeff Bagwell saw a huge dive in his numbers, but finished with a .290 average, 21 homers, 87 RBI, and 79 walks in just 114 games (watch that hand, Jeff). How many major leaguers would like to have *that* for an off year? But the fact that both Thomas and Bagwell dropped from their 1994 levels of production should surprise absolutely no one. Both of their '94 seasons were among the most productive in baseball history. It would simply be impossible for either player to maintain that level of production over the long-term.

Thomas and Bagwell were two "gimmes" last year among what we call our annual "Stars, Bums, and Sleepers"—our predictions of which players will do better the following season, which ones will do worse, which ones will remain consistent, and who the sleepers, the surprise stars, will be. Grouping both Thomas and Bagwell in the "Production Will Drop" category was pretty easy. But trust us—for every easy analysis, there are dozens for which we break out the STATS baseball brain trust and keep our number mill churning at a fever pitch.

Those of you familiar with the work of Bill James, particularly *The Bill James Baseball Abstract*, have a pretty good idea how we come up with the list each year. For those of you that don't, remember this—past history indicates future performance. That's probably the easiest way to put it. There are general rules to the system, of course, and there are going to be a lot of exceptions to them. But over the past few years, Bill and John Dewan have created a system that puts an objective stamp on a player's ability. Using this system, and mixing in the subjective advice of our scouts and staff experts, we come up with the list you see.

What are some of the rules? Well, some are pretty obvious. For example, younger players tend to get better, while older players tend to decline, with age 27 typically being the peak offensive season for a position player. That is also the most common year for a player to have a season "over his head," which we also take into account. It's more than likely that a player who has an unexpectedly good year will have trouble repeating it. Want more? A player that improves the previous season will tend to decline the next, and vice versa. As you probably could guess, there are other guidelines we follow, too numerous to mention here, which have proven themselves over the years.

We learn a lot, too. Last year, we had Mike Piazza atop our "Production Will Drop" list among catchers. All Piazza did was increase his batting average, on-base percentage, and slugging percentage from his '94 level—pretty much proving that neither his '93 or '94 seasons were a fluke. Piazza is indeed the real deal.

## How To Use This Section

Every position is broken into four groups: "Expect A Better Year in '96," "Look for Consistency," "Production Will Drop," and "1996 Sleepers." Here's a key point to remember when looking at the first three of these categories. **A player is put into one of these three groups based on his 1995 performance.** For example, Dante Bichette is shown in the category "Production Will Drop." That means that you probably shouldn't expect him to hit .340 with a .620 slugging percentage again, with 45 homers and 144 RBI (his numbers last season projected to a full 162 games). However, Bichette (with a ton of help from Coors Field) should still put up some pretty good numbers in 1996. Bichette's level of production might drop, but it certainly won't disappear.

We do things a little differently in the section entitled "1996 Sleepers," but we continue to do them well. Last year in the sleepers section we had players like Greg Colbrunn, Ron Gant, and Rondell White—players who didn't exactly come out of nowhere, but ones who performed better than most people thought they would. We also included Roberto Mejia as a sleeper, proving that we can't win 'em all. But you can bet (not literally, of course) that many of this year's crop of sleepers will wake up the baseball world. The numbers we show in this section are each player's combined minor and major league performance for 1995. The idea here is to show what this player is *capable* of doing. We've tried to factor projected playing time into the equation as this book went to press in late 1995, but you'll get a better idea as the season starts as to who's playing and who's not.

Finally, within each grouping (for example, shortstops listed under Expect a Better Year) we've ranked the players based on our own expectations of performance from best performance to worst.

## How We Developed This Section

We broke down all the regular major league players from this book into their most common position played in 1995. We then looked at every player in two basic ways: statistical analysis and subjective rating. For our statistical model, we looked at historical patterns of performance to help us project performance for each player. Here are some of the factors that we plugged into our computer.

*Career Trends*—A player should not be judged simply on his most recent year of performance, although the tendency for most fans (and many "experts") is to do just that. While it is possible that a player who had a good year in relation to the rest of his career has suddenly become a better ballplayer, it's much more likely that it was simply a good year. While it's possible for a career .279 hitter like Sean Berry to hit .318 again, it's much more likely he'll come back down to the range that he's established for his career. The same is true about a *bad* season for most players. If his playing time does not get

severely cut, a player with a bad season will usually rebound.

*Player Age*—The best age for a position player in baseball is 27. Based on historical studies, this is the age when hitters have their best years. So, the rule of thumb is that if a batter is younger than 27, you can expect some improvement over the level of play he's established so far in his career. If a batter is over 27, you can expect some decrease in his playing performance from **the level of play he has established in recent years and over his career.** The age when a pitcher reaches his peak is somewhat more nebulous. While it isn't possible to pinpoint a specific peak age as can be done for hitters, we are able to blend in many factors based on a pitcher's career that give us an accurate indicator of those whose potential is rising or falling.

*Minor League Performance*—Years ago, Bill James discovered that minor league performance, when properly adjusted, is just as reliable in predicting major league performance as is prior major league performance. Therefore, we've looked at minor league performance here to help us project 1996, especially for the players we call "Sleepers."

We then added our own subjective considerations:

*Playing Time*—When considering how good a player will be in a given year, you first have to determine how often he'll get a chance to play. This we've done by evaluating players compared to their teammates. Do your own research this spring to find out more about a team's plans for a player if you're not sure—and don't forget to take into account a player's possible injury-prone nature.

*Pitchers' Inconsistency*—for every five hitters you can name as being reasonably consistent from year to year, there is probably only one pitcher who can compare in consistency. Some of the most consistently tough pitchers in baseball over the past several years can suddenly have a stinker. We used many subjective considerations in devising our pitcher evaluations.

# Catcher

## Expect A Better Year in '96

| | Avg. | HR | RBI | SB |
|---|---|---|---|---|
| | **1995 Statistics** | | | |
| Chris Hoiles | .250 | 19 | 58 | 1 |
| Mike Macfarlane | .225 | 15 | 51 | 2 |
| Matt Walbeck | .257 | 1 | 44 | 3 |
| Jim Leyritz | .269 | 7 | 37 | 1 |
| Bill Haselman | .243 | 5 | 23 | 0 |
| Jorge Fabregas | .247 | 1 | 22 | 0 |
| Pat Borders | .208 | 4 | 13 | 0 |
| Tim Laker | .234 | 3 | 20 | 0 |

## Look for Consistency

| | Avg. | HR | RBI | SB |
|---|---|---|---|---|
| | **1995 Statistics** | | | |
| Mike Piazza | .346 | 32 | 93 | 1 |
| Ivan Rodriguez | .303 | 12 | 67 | 0 |
| Darren Daulton | .249 | 9 | 55 | 3 |
| Javy Lopez | .315 | 14 | 51 | 0 |
| Darrin Fletcher | .286 | 11 | 45 | 0 |
| Benito Santiago | .286 | 11 | 44 | 2 |
| Ron Karkovice | .217 | 13 | 51 | 2 |
| Sandy Alomar Jr | .307 | 10 | 36 | 3 |
| Kirt Manwaring | .251 | 4 | 36 | 1 |
| Brent Mayne | .251 | 1 | 27 | 0 |
| Brian Johnson | .251 | 3 | 29 | 0 |
| Matt Merullo | .282 | 1 | 27 | 0 |
| Kelly Stinnett | .219 | 4 | 18 | 2 |

## Production Will Drop

| | Avg. | HR | RBI | SB |
|---|---|---|---|---|
| | **1995 Statistics** | | | |
| Mike Stanley | .268 | 18 | 83 | 1 |
| Terry Steinbach | .278 | 15 | 65 | 1 |
| Dan Wilson | .278 | 9 | 51 | 2 |
| Joe Girardi | .262 | 8 | 55 | 3 |
| Tony Eusebio | .299 | 6 | 58 | 0 |
| Brad Ausmus | .293 | 5 | 34 | 16 |
| Todd Hundley | .280 | 15 | 51 | 1 |
| Scott Servais | .265 | 13 | 47 | 2 |
| Joe Oliver | .273 | 12 | 51 | 2 |
| John Flaherty | .243 | 11 | 40 | 0 |
| Greg Myers | .260 | 9 | 38 | 0 |
| Mark Parent | .234 | 18 | 38 | 0 |
| Eddie Taubensee | .284 | 9 | 44 | 2 |
| Tony Pena | .262 | 5 | 28 | 1 |
| Danny Sheaffer | .231 | 5 | 30 | 0 |

## 1996 Sleepers

| | Avg. | HR | RBI | SB |
|---|---|---|---|---|
| | **1995 Statistics (includes minor leagues)** | | | |
| Charles Johnson | .245 | 11 | 39 | 0 |
| Rick Wilkins | .200 | 7 | 23 | 0 |
| Tom Pagnozzi | .234 | 3 | 18 | 0 |
| Don Slaught | .298 | 0 | 14 | 0 |
| Randy Knorr | .231 | 4 | 22 | 0 |

# First Base

## Expect A Better Year in '96

| | Avg. | HR | RBI | SB |
|---|---|---|---|---|
| | **1995 Statistics** | | | |
| Jeff Bagwell | .290 | 21 | 87 | 12 |
| John Olerud | .291 | 8 | 54 | 0 |
| Gregg Jefferies | .306 | 11 | 56 | 9 |
| Hal Morris | .279 | 11 | 51 | 1 |
| Cliff Floyd | .130 | 1 | 8 | 3 |
| Dave Hollins | .225 | 7 | 26 | 1 |

## Look for Consistency

| | Avg. | HR | RBI | SB |
|---|---|---|---|---|
| | **1995 Statistics** | | | |
| Frank Thomas | .308 | 40 | 111 | 3 |
| Mark McGwire | .274 | 39 | 90 | 1 |
| Fred McGriff | .280 | 27 | 93 | 3 |
| Andres Galarraga | .280 | 31 | 106 | 12 |
| Will Clark | .302 | 16 | 92 | 0 |
| Cecil Fielder | .243 | 31 | 82 | 0 |
| Paul Sorrento | .235 | 25 | 79 | 1 |
| John Jaha | .313 | 20 | 65 | 2 |
| Mark Carreon | .301 | 17 | 65 | 0 |
| Don Mattingly | .288 | 7 | 49 | 0 |
| Eddie Williams | .260 | 12 | 47 | 0 |
| Mark Johnson | .208 | 13 | 28 | 5 |

## Production Will Drop

| | Avg. | HR | RBI | SB |
|---|---|---|---|---|
| | **1995 Statistics** | | | |
| Rafael Palmeiro | .310 | 39 | 104 | 3 |
| Mo Vaughn | .300 | 39 | 126 | 11 |
| Tino Martinez | .293 | 31 | 111 | 0 |
| Mark Grace | .326 | 16 | 92 | 6 |
| Eric Karros | .298 | 32 | 105 | 4 |
| J.T. Snow | .289 | 24 | 102 | 2 |
| Greg Colbrunn | .277 | 23 | 89 | 11 |
| Rico Brogna | .289 | 22 | 76 | 0 |
| Wally Joyner | .310 | 12 | 83 | 3 |
| David Segui | .309 | 12 | 68 | 2 |
| Scott Livingstone | .337 | 5 | 32 | 2 |
| Dave Martinez | .307 | 5 | 37 | 8 |
| Juan Samuel | .263 | 12 | 39 | 6 |

## 1996 Sleepers

| | Avg. | HR | RBI | SB |
|---|---|---|---|---|
| | **1995 Statistics (includes minor leagues)** | | | |
| Roberto Petagine | .228 | 4 | 22 | 1 |
| John Mabry | .300 | 5 | 41 | 0 |
| Herbert Perry | .316 | 5 | 40 | 2 |
| Ron Coomer | .307 | 21 | 95 | 5 |
| Tony Clark | .241 | 17 | 74 | 0 |
| Scott Stahoviak | .270 | 3 | 28 | 7 |
| Rich Aude | .303 | 11 | 61 | 4 |

# Second Base

## Expect A Better Year in '96

| | 1995 Statistics | | | |
| | Avg. | HR | RBI | SB |
|---|---|---|---|---|
| Delino DeShields | .256 | 8 | 37 | 39 |
| Ray Durham | .257 | 7 | 51 | 18 |
| Brent Gates | .254 | 5 | 56 | 3 |
| Carlos Garcia | .294 | 6 | 50 | 8 |
| Jeff Frye | .278 | 4 | 29 | 3 |
| Bret Barberie | .241 | 2 | 25 | 3 |
| Chad Fonville | .278 | 0 | 16 | 20 |
| Damion Easley | .216 | 4 | 35 | 5 |
| John Patterson | .205 | 1 | 14 | 4 |

## Look for Consistency

| | 1995 Statistics | | | |
| | Avg. | HR | RBI | SB |
|---|---|---|---|---|
| Carlos Baerga | .314 | 15 | 90 | 11 |
| Roberto Alomar | .300 | 13 | 66 | 30 |
| Bret Boone | .267 | 15 | 68 | 5 |
| Quilvio Veras | .261 | 5 | 32 | 56 |
| Jeff Kent | .278 | 20 | 65 | 3 |
| Luis Alicea | .270 | 6 | 44 | 13 |
| Mike Lansing | .255 | 10 | 62 | 27 |
| Jody Reed | .256 | 4 | 40 | 6 |
| Mark Lemke | .253 | 5 | 38 | 2 |
| Rey Sanchez | .278 | 3 | 27 | 6 |
| Robby Thompson | .223 | 8 | 23 | 1 |
| Scott Fletcher | .231 | 1 | 17 | 1 |

## Production Will Drop

| | 1995 Statistics | | | |
| | Avg. | HR | RBI | SB |
|---|---|---|---|---|
| Craig Biggio | .302 | 22 | 77 | 33 |
| Chuck Knoblauch | .333 | 11 | 63 | 46 |
| Lou Whitaker | .293 | 14 | 44 | 4 |
| Keith Lockhart | .321 | 6 | 33 | 8 |
| Mickey Morandini | .283 | 6 | 49 | 9 |
| Eric Young | .317 | 6 | 36 | 35 |
| Randy Velarde | .278 | 7 | 46 | 5 |
| Jason Bates | .267 | 8 | 46 | 3 |
| Joey Cora | .297 | 3 | 39 | 18 |
| Fernando Vina | .257 | 3 | 29 | 6 |
| Pat Listach | .219 | 0 | 25 | 13 |
| Mariano Duncan | .287 | 6 | 36 | 1 |
| Rex Hudler | .265 | 6 | 27 | 13 |
| Manny Alexander | .236 | 3 | 23 | 11 |

## 1996 Sleepers

| | 1995 Statistics | | | |
| | (includes minor leagues) | | | |
| | Avg. | HR | RBI | SB |
|---|---|---|---|---|
| David Bell | .265 | 11 | 62 | 5 |
| Pat Kelly | .235 | 4 | 32 | 8 |
| Geronimo Pena | .287 | 3 | 14 | 3 |
| Jerry Browne | .257 | 1 | 19 | 1 |

# Third Base

## Expect A Better Year in '96

| | 1995 Statistics | | | |
| | Avg. | HR | RBI | SB |
|---|---|---|---|---|
| Travis Fryman | .275 | 15 | 81 | 4 |
| Matt Williams | .336 | 23 | 65 | 2 |
| Dean Palmer | .336 | 9 | 24 | 1 |
| Jeff Cirillo | .277 | 9 | 39 | 7 |
| Mark Lewis | .339 | 3 | 30 | 0 |
| Edgardo Alfonzo | .278 | 4 | 41 | 1 |
| Scott Cooper | .230 | 3 | 40 | 0 |

## Look for Consistency

| | 1995 Statistics | | | |
| | Avg. | HR | RBI | SB |
|---|---|---|---|---|
| Jim Thome | .314 | 25 | 73 | 4 |
| Robin Ventura | .295 | 26 | 93 | 4 |
| Chipper Jones | .265 | 23 | 86 | 8 |
| Jeff King | .265 | 18 | 87 | 7 |
| Wade Boggs | .324 | 5 | 63 | 1 |
| Charlie Hayes | .276 | 11 | 85 | 5 |
| Sean Berry | .318 | 14 | 55 | 3 |

## Production Will Drop

| | 1995 Statistics | | | |
| | Avg. | HR | RBI | SB |
|---|---|---|---|---|
| Vinny Castilla | .309 | 32 | 90 | 2 |
| Tony Phillips | .261 | 27 | 61 | 13 |
| Bobby Bonilla | .329 | 28 | 99 | 0 |
| Tim Naehring | .307 | 10 | 57 | 0 |
| Gary Gaetti | .261 | 35 | 96 | 3 |
| Ken Caminiti | .302 | 26 | 94 | 12 |
| Ed Sprague | .244 | 18 | 74 | 0 |
| Terry Pendleton | .290 | 14 | 78 | 1 |
| Kevin Seitzer | .311 | 5 | 69 | 2 |
| Mike Blowers | .257 | 23 | 96 | 2 |
| Scott Brosius | .262 | 17 | 46 | 4 |
| Scott Leius | .247 | 4 | 45 | 2 |
| Dave Magadan | .313 | 2 | 51 | 2 |
| Jeff Branson | .260 | 12 | 45 | 2 |
| Tim Wallach | .266 | 9 | 38 | 0 |
| Jeff Manto | .256 | 17 | 38 | 0 |

## 1996 Sleepers

| | 1995 Statistics (includes minor leagues) | | | |
| | Avg. | HR | RBI | SB |
|---|---|---|---|---|
| Todd Zeile | .244 | 14 | 52 | 1 |
| Chris Snopek | .323 | 13 | 62 | 3 |
| Russ Davis | .264 | 4 | 27 | 0 |
| Jason Giambi | .301 | 9 | 66 | 2 |

# Shortstop

## Expect A Better Year in '96

| | 1995 Statistics | | | |
| | Avg. | HR | RBI | SB |
|---|---|---|---|---|
| Wil Cordero | .286 | 10 | 49 | 9 |
| Jeff Blauser | .211 | 12 | 31 | 8 |
| Alex Gonzalez | .243 | 10 | 42 | 4 |
| Jose Valentin | .219 | 11 | 49 | 16 |
| Tony Fernandez | .245 | 5 | 45 | 6 |
| Benji Gil | .219 | 9 | 46 | 2 |
| Kevin Stocker | .218 | 1 | 32 | 6 |
| Andujar Cedeno | .210 | 6 | 31 | 5 |

## Look for Consistency

| | 1995 Statistics | | | |
| | Avg. | HR | RBI | SB |
|---|---|---|---|---|
| Cal Ripken | .262 | 17 | 88 | 0 |
| Jay Bell | .262 | 13 | 55 | 2 |
| Jose Vizcaino | .287 | 3 | 56 | 8 |
| Royce Clayton | .244 | 5 | 58 | 24 |
| Mike Bordick | .264 | 8 | 44 | 11 |
| Greg Gagne | .256 | 6 | 49 | 3 |
| Orlando Miller | .262 | 5 | 36 | 3 |
| Chris Gomez | .223 | 11 | 50 | 4 |
| Domingo Cedeno | .236 | 4 | 14 | 0 |
| Ozzie Guillen | .248 | 1 | 41 | 6 |
| Tripp Cromer | .226 | 5 | 18 | 0 |

## Production Will Drop

| | 1995 Statistics | | | |
| | Avg. | HR | RBI | SB |
|---|---|---|---|---|
| John Valentin | .298 | 27 | 102 | 20 |
| Barry Larkin | .319 | 15 | 66 | 51 |
| Omar Vizquel | .266 | 6 | 56 | 29 |
| Walt Weiss | .260 | 1 | 25 | 15 |
| Shawon Dunston | .296 | 14 | 69 | 10 |
| Gary DiSarcina | .307 | 5 | 41 | 7 |
| Kurt Abbott | .255 | 17 | 60 | 4 |
| Pat Meares | .269 | 12 | 49 | 10 |
| Luis Sojo | .289 | 7 | 39 | 4 |
| Jose Hernandez | .245 | 13 | 40 | 1 |
| Jose Offerman | .287 | 4 | 33 | 2 |
| Jeff Reboulet | .292 | 4 | 23 | 1 |
| Alan Trammell | .269 | 2 | 23 | 3 |

## 1996 Sleepers

| | 1995 Statistics (includes minor leagues) | | | |
| | Avg. | HR | RBI | SB |
|---|---|---|---|---|
| Derek Jeter | .311 | 2 | 52 | 20 |
| Alex Rodriguez | .309 | 20 | 64 | 6 |
| Mark Grudzielanek | .267 | 2 | 42 | 20 |

# Left Field

## Expect A Better Year in '96

| | 1995 Statistics | | | |
| | Avg. | HR | RBI | SB |
|---|---|---|---|---|
| Moises Alou | .273 | 14 | 58 | 4 |
| Bob Higginson | .224 | 14 | 43 | 6 |
| Luis Polonia | .261 | 2 | 17 | 13 |
| Billy Ashley | .237 | 8 | 27 | 0 |
| Ozzie Timmons | .263 | 8 | 28 | 3 |
| Tony Longmire | .356 | 3 | 19 | 1 |
| Melvin Nieves | .205 | 14 | 38 | 2 |

## Look for Consistency

| | 1995 Statistics | | | |
| | Avg. | HR | RBI | SB |
|---|---|---|---|---|
| Barry Bonds | .294 | 33 | 104 | 31 |
| Marty Cordova | .277 | 24 | 84 | 20 |
| Ron Gant | .276 | 29 | 88 | 23 |
| Joe Carter | .253 | 25 | 76 | 12 |
| Luis Gonzalez | .276 | 13 | 69 | 6 |
| Rickey Henderson | .300 | 9 | 54 | 32 |
| Garret Anderson | .321 | 16 | 69 | 6 |
| Al Martin | .282 | 13 | 41 | 20 |
| Bip Roberts | .304 | 2 | 25 | 20 |
| James Mouton | .262 | 4 | 27 | 25 |
| Dave Clark | .281 | 4 | 24 | 3 |
| Gerald Williams | .247 | 6 | 28 | 4 |
| Rich Amaral | .282 | 2 | 19 | 21 |

## Production Will Drop

| | 1995 Statistics | | | |
| | Avg. | HR | RBI | SB |
|---|---|---|---|---|
| Albert Belle | .317 | 50 | 126 | 5 |
| Dante Bichette | .340 | 40 | 128 | 13 |
| Jeff Conine | .302 | 25 | 105 | 2 |
| Brady Anderson | .262 | 16 | 64 | 26 |
| Bernard Gilkey | .298 | 17 | 69 | 12 |
| Tim Raines | .285 | 12 | 67 | 13 |
| Mike Greenwell | .297 | 15 | 76 | 9 |
| Ryan Klesko | .310 | 23 | 70 | 5 |
| B.J. Surhoff | .320 | 13 | 73 | 7 |
| Mark McLemore | .261 | 5 | 41 | 21 |
| Vince Coleman | .288 | 5 | 29 | 42 |
| Derrick May | .282 | 9 | 50 | 5 |
| David Hulse | .251 | 3 | 47 | 15 |
| Joe Orsulak | .283 | 1 | 37 | 1 |

## 1996 Sleepers

| | 1995 Statistics (includes minor leagues) | | | |
| | Avg. | HR | RBI | SB |
|---|---|---|---|---|
| Carlos Delgado | .285 | 25 | 85 | 0 |
| Phil Plantier | .254 | 10 | 38 | 1 |
| Marc Newfield | .275 | 12 | 63 | 3 |
| Michael Tucker | .288 | 8 | 45 | 13 |
| Darren Bragg | .277 | 7 | 43 | 19 |

# Center Field

## Expect A Better Year in '96

| | Avg. | HR | RBI | SB |
|---|---|---|---|---|
| | 1995 Statistics | | | |
| Kenny Lofton | .310 | 7 | 53 | 54 |
| Ken Griffey Jr | .255 | 17 | 42 | 4 |
| Lenny Dykstra | .264 | 2 | 18 | 10 |
| Deion Sanders | .268 | 6 | 28 | 24 |
| Ryan Thompson | .251 | 7 | 31 | 3 |

## Look for Consistency

| | Avg. | HR | RBI | SB |
|---|---|---|---|---|
| | 1995 Statistics | | | |
| Rondell White | .295 | 13 | 57 | 25 |
| Marquis Grissom | .258 | 12 | 42 | 29 |
| Devon White | .283 | 10 | 53 | 11 |
| Roberto Kelly | .278 | 7 | 57 | 19 |
| Ellis Burks | .266 | 14 | 49 | 7 |
| Brett Butler | .300 | 1 | 38 | 32 |
| Stan Javier | .278 | 8 | 56 | 36 |
| Jacob Brumfield | .271 | 4 | 26 | 22 |
| Lee Tinsley | .284 | 7 | 41 | 18 |
| Darren Lewis | .250 | 1 | 24 | 32 |
| Curtis Goodwin | .263 | 1 | 24 | 22 |
| Andy Van Slyke | .224 | 6 | 24 | 7 |

## Production Will Drop

| | Avg. | HR | RBI | SB |
|---|---|---|---|---|
| | 1995 Statistics | | | |
| Jim Edmonds | .290 | 33 | 107 | 1 |
| Bernie Williams | .307 | 18 | 82 | 8 |
| Ray Lankford | .277 | 25 | 82 | 24 |
| Chad Curtis | .268 | 21 | 67 | 27 |
| Brian McRae | .288 | 12 | 48 | 27 |
| Lance Johnson | .306 | 10 | 57 | 40 |
| Steve Finley | .297 | 10 | 44 | 36 |
| Otis Nixon | .295 | 0 | 45 | 50 |
| Darryl Hamilton | .271 | 5 | 44 | 11 |
| Tom Goodwin | .287 | 4 | 28 | 50 |
| Mike Kingery | .269 | 8 | 37 | 13 |
| Thomas Howard | .302 | 3 | 26 | 17 |

## 1996 Sleepers

| | Avg. | HR | RBI | SB |
|---|---|---|---|---|
| | 1995 Statistics (includes minor leagues) | | | |
| Johnny Damon | .324 | 19 | 77 | 33 |
| Matt Lawton | .275 | 14 | 66 | 27 |
| Brian L. Hunter | .313 | 3 | 44 | 35 |
| Rich Becker | .254 | 8 | 61 | 14 |
| Midre Cummings | .260 | 3 | 31 | 2 |
| Jesus Tavarez | .294 | 3 | 21 | 14 |

# Right Field

## Expect A Better Year in '96

| | Avg. | HR | RBI | SB |
|---|---|---|---|---|
| | 1995 Statistics | | | |
| Dave Justice | .253 | 24 | 78 | 4 |
| Gary Sheffield | .324 | 16 | 46 | 19 |
| Rusty Greer | .271 | 13 | 61 | 3 |
| Shawn Green | .288 | 15 | 54 | 1 |

## Look for Consistency

| | Avg. | HR | RBI | SB |
|---|---|---|---|---|
| | 1995 Statistics | | | |
| Manny Ramirez | .308 | 31 | 107 | 6 |
| Larry Walker | .306 | 36 | 101 | 16 |
| Ruben Sierra | .263 | 19 | 86 | 5 |
| Orlando Merced | .300 | 15 | 83 | 7 |
| Tony Tarasco | .249 | 14 | 40 | 24 |
| Jon Nunnally | .244 | 14 | 42 | 6 |
| Matt Mieske | .251 | 12 | 48 | 2 |
| Chris Jones | .280 | 8 | 31 | 2 |

## Production Will Drop

| | Avg. | HR | RBI | SB |
|---|---|---|---|---|
| | 1995 Statistics | | | |
| Tim Salmon | .330 | 34 | 105 | 5 |
| Sammy Sosa | .268 | 36 | 119 | 34 |
| Jay Buhner | .262 | 40 | 121 | 0 |
| Reggie Sanders | .306 | 28 | 99 | 36 |
| Kirby Puckett | .314 | 23 | 99 | 3 |
| Paul O'Neill | .300 | 22 | 96 | 1 |
| Brian Jordan | .296 | 22 | 81 | 24 |
| Tony Gwynn | .368 | 9 | 90 | 17 |
| Raul Mondesi | .285 | 26 | 88 | 27 |
| Mickey Tettleton | .238 | 32 | 78 | 0 |
| Derek Bell | .334 | 8 | 86 | 27 |
| Glenallen Hill | .264 | 24 | 86 | 25 |
| Troy O'Leary | .308 | 10 | 49 | 5 |
| Jim Eisenreich | .316 | 10 | 55 | 10 |
| Mike Devereaux | .299 | 11 | 63 | 8 |

## 1996 Sleepers

| | Avg. | HR | RBI | SB |
|---|---|---|---|---|
| | 1995 Statistics (includes minor leagues) | | | |
| Lyle Mouton | .298 | 13 | 68 | 11 |
| Carl Everett | .279 | 18 | 89 | 14 |
| Mark Whiten | .251 | 16 | 60 | 12 |
| Dave Nilsson | .302 | 15 | 68 | 3 |
| Jeffrey Hammonds | .263 | 5 | 34 | 7 |
| Alex Ochoa | .284 | 10 | 61 | 25 |

# Designated Hitter

## Expect A Better Year in '96

| | 1995 Statistics | | | |
| | Avg. | HR | RBI | SB |
|---|---|---|---|---|
| Juan Gonzalez | .295 | 27 | 82 | 0 |
| Danny Tartabull | .236 | 8 | 35 | 0 |
| Reggie Jefferson | .289 | 5 | 26 | 0 |

## Look for Consistency

| | 1995 Statistics | | | |
| | Avg. | HR | RBI | SB |
|---|---|---|---|---|
| Geronimo Berroa | .278 | 22 | 88 | 7 |
| Paul Molitor | .270 | 15 | 60 | 12 |
| Greg Vaughn | .224 | 17 | 59 | 10 |

## Production Will Drop

| | 1995 Statistics | | | |
| | Avg. | HR | RBI | SB |
|---|---|---|---|---|
| Edgar Martinez | .356 | 29 | 113 | 4 |
| Chili Davis | .318 | 20 | 86 | 3 |
| Jose Canseco | .306 | 24 | 81 | 4 |
| Harold Baines | .299 | 24 | 63 | 0 |
| Eddie Murray | .323 | 21 | 82 | 5 |
| Pedro Munoz | .301 | 18 | 58 | 0 |

## 1996 Sleepers

| | 1995 Statistics (includes minor leagues) | | | |
| | Avg. | HR | RBI | SB |
|---|---|---|---|---|
| Joe Vitiello | .270 | 19 | 63 | 0 |
| Bob Hamelin | .214 | 17 | 57 | 2 |
| Darryl Strawberry | .281 | 11 | 48 | 3 |

# Starting Pitchers

## Expect A Better Year in '96

| | 1995 Statistics | | | | |
| | W | L | ERA | Sv | BR/IP |
|---|---|---|---|---|---|
| Jose Rijo | 5 | 4 | 4.17 | 0 | 1.42 |
| Bret Saberhagen | 7 | 6 | 4.18 | 0 | 1.36 |
| Jimmy Key | 1 | 2 | 5.64 | 0 | 1.52 |
| Bill Swift | 9 | 3 | 4.94 | 0 | 1.57 |
| Bob Tewksbury | 8 | 7 | 4.58 | 0 | 1.48 |
| Doug Drabek | 10 | 9 | 4.77 | 0 | 1.44 |
| Bobby Witt | 5 | 11 | 4.13 | 0 | 1.49 |
| Terry Mulholland | 5 | 13 | 5.80 | 0 | 1.56 |
| Melido Perez | 5 | 5 | 5.58 | 0 | 1.47 |
| Ken Hill | 10 | 8 | 4.62 | 0 | 1.51 |
| Andy Benes | 11 | 9 | 4.76 | 0 | 1.52 |
| Marvin Freeman | 3 | 7 | 5.89 | 0 | 1.74 |
| David West | 3 | 2 | 3.79 | 0 | 1.42 |
| Trevor Wilson | 3 | 4 | 3.92 | 0 | 1.50 |
| Pete Harnisch | 2 | 8 | 3.68 | 0 | 1.25 |
| Tom Candiotti | 7 | 14 | 3.50 | 0 | 1.33 |
| Wilson Alvarez | 8 | 11 | 4.32 | 0 | 1.52 |
| Tommy Greene | 0 | 5 | 8.29 | 0 | 2.02 |
| Steve Avery | 7 | 13 | 4.67 | 0 | 1.29 |
| Willie Banks | 2 | 6 | 5.66 | 0 | 1.83 |
| Pat Hentgen | 10 | 14 | 5.11 | 0 | 1.65 |
| Cal Eldred | 1 | 1 | 3.42 | 0 | 1.48 |
| Donovan Osborne | 4 | 6 | 3.81 | 0 | 1.31 |
| Jason Bere | 8 | 15 | 7.19 | 0 | 1.91 |
| Aaron Sele | 3 | 1 | 3.06 | 0 | 1.52 |
| Jon Lieber | 4 | 7 | 6.32 | 0 | 1.67 |
| Paul Wagner | 5 | 16 | 4.80 | 1 | 1.53 |
| Frank Rodriguez | 5 | 8 | 6.13 | 0 | 1.67 |
| Scott Karl | 6 | 7 | 4.14 | 0 | 1.56 |
| Edwin Hurtado | 5 | 2 | 5.45 | 0 | 1.62 |
| Mariano Rivera | 5 | 3 | 5.51 | 0 | 1.54 |
| John Ericks | 3 | 9 | 4.58 | 0 | 1.51 |
| Danny Darwin | 3 | 10 | 7.24 | 0 | 1.64 |

## Look for Consistency

| | 1995 Statistics | | | | |
| | W | L | ERA | Sv | BR/IP |
|---|---|---|---|---|---|
| Ismael Valdes | 13 | 11 | 3.05 | 1 | 1.11 |
| Fernando Valenzuela | 8 | 3 | 4.98 | 0 | 1.49 |
| Dennis Martinez | 12 | 5 | 3.08 | 0 | 1.24 |
| Sid Fernandez | 6 | 5 | 4.56 | 0 | 1.33 |
| Kevin Gross | 9 | 15 | 5.54 | 0 | 1.62 |
| Orel Hershiser | 16 | 6 | 3.87 | 0 | 1.24 |
| Roger Clemens | 10 | 5 | 4.18 | 0 | 1.54 |
| Mark Langston | 15 | 7 | 4.63 | 0 | 1.39 |
| Zane Smith | 8 | 8 | 5.61 | 0 | 1.52 |
| Mike Bielecki | 4 | 6 | 5.97 | 0 | 1.51 |
| Chris Bosio | 10 | 8 | 4.92 | 0 | 1.68 |
| Steve Ontiveros | 9 | 6 | 4.37 | 0 | 1.43 |
| Mark Portugal | 11 | 10 | 4.01 | 0 | 1.35 |
| Chuck Finley | 15 | 12 | 4.21 | 0 | 1.44 |
| Greg Swindell | 10 | 9 | 4.47 | 0 | 1.44 |
| David Cone | 18 | 8 | 3.57 | 0 | 1.26 |
| Jamie Moyer | 8 | 6 | 5.21 | 0 | 1.30 |
| Greg Maddux | 19 | 2 | 1.63 | 0 | 0.83 |
| Kenny Rogers | 17 | 7 | 3.38 | 0 | 1.30 |
| Kevin Brown | 10 | 9 | 3.60 | 0 | 1.23 |
| Tim Belcher | 10 | 12 | 4.52 | 0 | 1.57 |
| Jack McDowell | 15 | 10 | 3.93 | 0 | 1.35 |
| John Burkett | 14 | 14 | 4.30 | 0 | 1.44 |
| Tom Glavine | 16 | 7 | 3.08 | 0 | 1.27 |
| Al Leiter | 11 | 11 | 3.64 | 0 | 1.51 |
| Ramon Martinez | 17 | 7 | 3.66 | 0 | 1.27 |
| Todd Stottlemyre | 14 | 7 | 4.55 | 0 | 1.50 |
| John Smoltz | 12 | 7 | 3.18 | 0 | 1.26 |
| Mike Harkey | 8 | 9 | 5.44 | 0 | 1.62 |
| Curt Schilling | 7 | 5 | 3.57 | 0 | 1.08 |
| Tom Gordon | 12 | 12 | 4.43 | 0 | 1.57 |
| Randy Johnson | 18 | 2 | 2.48 | 0 | 1.07 |
| Jim Abbott | 11 | 8 | 3.70 | 0 | 1.40 |
| Kevin Appier | 15 | 10 | 3.89 | 0 | 1.25 |
| Kevin Tapani | 10 | 13 | 4.96 | 0 | 1.47 |

## Look For Consistency (continued)

| | | | | |
|---|---|---|---|---|
| Kent Mercker | 7 | 8 | 4.15 | 0 | 1.43 |
| Shawn Boskie | 7 | 7 | 5.64 | 0 | 1.42 |
| Scott Erickson | 13 | 10 | 4.81 | 0 | 1.45 |
| Charles Nagy | 16 | 6 | 4.55 | 0 | 1.47 |
| Chris Hammond | 9 | 6 | 3.80 | 0 | 1.32 |
| Alex Fernandez | 12 | 8 | 3.80 | 0 | 1.30 |
| Joe Grahe | 4 | 3 | 5.08 | 0 | 1.75 |
| Jeff Fassero | 13 | 14 | 4.33 | 0 | 1.50 |
| Mark Petkovsek | 6 | 6 | 4.00 | 0 | 1.29 |
| Scott Kamieniecki | 7 | 6 | 4.01 | 0 | 1.51 |
| Chris Haney | 3 | 4 | 3.65 | 0 | 1.39 |
| Mike Mussina | 19 | 9 | 3.29 | 0 | 1.07 |
| Dave Weathers | 4 | 5 | 5.98 | 0 | 1.78 |
| Armando Reynoso | 7 | 7 | 5.32 | 0 | 1.69 |
| Ricky Bones | 10 | 12 | 4.63 | 0 | 1.52 |
| Mark Clark | 9 | 7 | 5.27 | 0 | 1.52 |
| Roger Pavlik | 10 | 10 | 4.37 | 0 | 1.40 |
| Kevin Foster | 12 | 11 | 4.51 | 0 | 1.31 |
| Jim Bullinger | 12 | 8 | 4.14 | 0 | 1.51 |
| Pedro Martinez | 14 | 10 | 3.51 | 0 | 1.21 |
| Shane Reynolds | 10 | 11 | 3.47 | 0 | 1.24 |
| Paul Quantrill | 11 | 12 | 4.67 | 0 | 1.46 |
| Mike Trombley | 4 | 8 | 5.62 | 0 | 1.56 |
| Allen Watson | 7 | 9 | 4.96 | 0 | 1.50 |
| Kirk Rueter | 5 | 3 | 3.23 | 0 | 1.01 |
| Scott Sanders | 5 | 5 | 4.30 | 0 | 1.24 |
| Bobby Jones | 10 | 10 | 4.19 | 0 | 1.37 |
| Salomon Torres | 3 | 9 | 6.30 | 0 | 1.89 |
| Brian Anderson | 6 | 8 | 5.87 | 0 | 1.43 |
| Steve Trachsel | 7 | 13 | 5.15 | 0 | 1.56 |
| Willim VanLandingham | 6 | 3 | 3.67 | 0 | 1.35 |
| Joey Hamilton | 6 | 9 | 3.08 | 0 | 1.25 |
| Jason Jacome | 4 | 10 | 6.34 | 0 | 1.64 |
| Vaughn Eshelman | 6 | 3 | 4.85 | 0 | 1.51 |
| Felipe Lira | 9 | 13 | 4.31 | 1 | 1.47 |
| Steve Sparks | 9 | 11 | 4.63 | 0 | 1.49 |
| Andy Pettitte | 12 | 9 | 4.17 | 0 | 1.41 |
| Brad Radke | 11 | 14 | 5.32 | 0 | 1.36 |
| Juan Acevedo | 4 | 6 | 6.44 | 0 | 1.64 |
| Carlos Perez | 10 | 8 | 3.69 | 0 | 1.24 |
| Michael Mimbs | 9 | 7 | 4.15 | 1 | 1.52 |
| Esteban Loaiza | 8 | 9 | 5.16 | 0 | 1.53 |
| Hideo Nomo | 13 | 6 | 2.54 | 0 | 1.08 |
| Sid Roberson | 6 | 4 | 5.76 | 0 | 1.74 |

## Production Will Drop

| | W | L | ERA | Sv | BR/IP |
|---|---|---|---|---|---|
| | | 1995 Statistics | | | |
| Mike Morgan | 7 | 7 | 3.56 | 0 | 1.32 |
| Mark Gubicza | 12 | 14 | 3.75 | 0 | 1.36 |
| Sergio Valdez | 4 | 5 | 4.75 | 0 | 1.48 |
| John Smiley | 12 | 5 | 3.46 | 0 | 1.22 |

| | | | | | |
|---|---|---|---|---|---|
| David Wells | 16 | 8 | 3.24 | 0 | 1.23 |
| Jaime Navarro | 14 | 6 | 3.28 | 0 | 1.26 |
| Kevin Ritz | 11 | 11 | 4.21 | 2 | 1.40 |
| Mark Leiter | 10 | 12 | 3.82 | 0 | 1.31 |
| Pete Schourek | 18 | 7 | 3.22 | 0 | 1.11 |
| Andy Ashby | 12 | 10 | 2.94 | 0 | 1.31 |
| Frank Castillo | 11 | 10 | 3.21 | 0 | 1.26 |
| Denny Neagle | 13 | 8 | 3.43 | 0 | 1.28 |
| Jeff Juden | 2 | 4 | 4.02 | 0 | 1.42 |
| Butch Henry | 7 | 9 | 2.84 | 0 | 1.29 |
| Pat Rapp | 14 | 7 | 3.44 | 0 | 1.44 |
| Tim Wakefield | 16 | 8 | 2.95 | 0 | 1.23 |
| Sterling Hitchcock | 11 | 10 | 4.70 | 0 | 1.35 |
| Erik Hanson | 15 | 5 | 4.24 | 0 | 1.32 |
| Dave Mlicki | 9 | 7 | 4.26 | 0 | 1.36 |
| Tyler Green | 8 | 9 | 5.31 | 0 | 1.61 |
| Mike Hampton | 9 | 8 | 3.35 | 0 | 1.29 |
| Tom Urbani | 3 | 5 | 3.70 | 0 | 1.48 |
| Sean Bergman | 7 | 10 | 5.12 | 0 | 1.77 |
| Chan Ho Park | 0 | 0 | 4.50 | 0 | 1.00 |
| Jose Lima | 3 | 9 | 6.11 | 0 | 1.45 |
| Chad Ogea | 8 | 3 | 3.05 | 0 | 1.18 |

## 1996 Sleepers

| | 1995 Statistics (includes minor leagues) | | | | |
|---|---|---|---|---|---|
| | W | L | ERA | Sv | BR/IP |
| Danny Jackson | 3 | 12 | 5.60 | 0 | 1.72 |
| Ben McDonald | 3 | 6 | 4.09 | 0 | 1.35 |
| Darryl Kile | 6 | 13 | 5.53 | 0 | 1.61 |
| Juan Guzman | 4 | 14 | 6.09 | 0 | 1.65 |
| LaTroy Hawkins | 11 | 10 | 4.36 | 0 | 1.42 |
| Joe Rosselli | 6 | 4 | 6.01 | 0 | 1.51 |
| Ugueth Urbina | 9 | 4 | 3.50 | 0 | 1.19 |
| Jim Pittsley | 4 | 1 | 3.88 | 0 | 1.25 |
| C.J. Nitkowski | 6 | 11 | 4.99 | 0 | 1.56 |
| Bill Pulsipher | 11 | 11 | 3.63 | 0 | 1.32 |
| Steve Parris | 15 | 7 | 3.88 | 0 | 1.22 |
| Glenn Dishman | 10 | 11 | 3.72 | 0 | 1.25 |
| Brian Givens | 12 | 11 | 3.94 | 0 | 1.48 |
| Rick Krivda | 8 | 12 | 3.76 | 0 | 1.33 |
| Jason Isringhausen | 20 | 4 | 2.32 | 0 | 1.14 |
| Bryan Rekar | 14 | 11 | 3.12 | 0 | 1.17 |
| Steve Wojciechowski | 8 | 6 | 4.26 | 0 | 1.40 |
| Jamie Brewington | 14 | 7 | 3.74 | 0 | 1.49 |
| Mike Bertotti | 5 | 11 | 7.08 | 0 | 1.79 |
| Bob Wolcott | 16 | 8 | 3.34 | 0 | 1.24 |
| Marc Valdes | 9 | 13 | 5.23 | 0 | 1.62 |
| Luis Andujar | 16 | 9 | 2.91 | 0 | 1.21 |
| Jimmy Haynes | 14 | 9 | 3.16 | 0 | 1.23 |
| Alan Benes | 5 | 4 | 3.75 | 0 | 1.13 |

# Relief Pitchers

## Expect A Better Year in '96

| | W | L | ERA | Sv | BR/IP |
|---|---|---|---|---|---|
| | | | 1995 Statistics | | |
| Joe Boever | 5 | 7 | 6.39 | 3 | 1.77 |
| Randy Myers | 1 | 2 | 3.88 | 38 | 1.38 |
| Eric Plunk | 6 | 2 | 2.67 | 2 | 1.23 |
| Mike Maddux | 5 | 1 | 4.10 | 1 | 1.22 |
| Doug Jones | 0 | 4 | 5.01 | 22 | 1.56 |
| Jeff Montgomery | 2 | 3 | 3.43 | 31 | 1.32 |
| Jose Bautista | 3 | 8 | 6.44 | 0 | 1.50 |
| John Wetteland | 1 | 5 | 2.93 | 31 | 0.88 |
| Tony Castillo | 1 | 5 | 3.22 | 13 | 1.25 |
| Xavier Hernandez | 7 | 2 | 4.60 | 3 | 1.44 |
| Mike Stanton | 2 | 1 | 4.24 | 1 | 1.56 |
| Brian Bohanon | 1 | 1 | 5.54 | 1 | 1.57 |
| Jeff Shaw | 1 | 6 | 4.88 | 3 | 1.40 |
| Mel Rojas | 1 | 4 | 4.12 | 30 | 1.55 |
| Mike Perez | 2 | 6 | 3.66 | 2 | 1.44 |
| Tim Scott | 2 | 0 | 3.98 | 2 | 1.28 |
| Arthur Rhodes | 2 | 5 | 6.21 | 0 | 1.54 |
| Brian Williams | 3 | 10 | 6.00 | 0 | 1.74 |
| Shawn Barton | 4 | 1 | 4.26 | 1 | 1.31 |
| Bob Wickman | 2 | 4 | 4.05 | 1 | 1.44 |
| Ken Ryan | 0 | 4 | 4.96 | 7 | 1.81 |
| Billy Brewer | 2 | 4 | 5.56 | 0 | 1.68 |
| Jerry DiPoto | 4 | 6 | 3.78 | 2 | 1.40 |
| Woody Williams | 1 | 2 | 3.69 | 0 | 1.38 |
| Hector Carrasco | 2 | 7 | 4.12 | 5 | 1.53 |
| John Hudek | 2 | 2 | 5.40 | 7 | 1.20 |
| Scott Radinsky | 2 | 1 | 4.34 | 3 | 1.43 |
| Darren Hall | 0 | 2 | 4.41 | 3 | 1.84 |
| Mark Acre | 1 | 2 | 5.71 | 0 | 1.58 |
| Scott Sullivan | 0 | 0 | 4.91 | 0 | 1.64 |
| Brian Maxcy | 4 | 5 | 6.88 | 0 | 1.80 |
| Mike Munoz | 2 | 4 | 7.42 | 2 | 1.88 |
| Marc Kroon | 0 | 1 | 10.80 | 0 | 1.80 |
| Mark Brandenburg | 0 | 1 | 5.93 | 0 | 1.61 |

## Look for Consistency

| | W | L | ERA | Sv | BR/IP |
|---|---|---|---|---|---|
| | | | 1995 Statistics | | |
| Tom Henke | 1 | 1 | 1.82 | 36 | 1.10 |
| Jesse Orosco | 2 | 4 | 3.26 | 3 | 1.13 |
| Matt Karchner | 4 | 2 | 1.69 | 0 | 1.44 |
| Mark Wohlers | 7 | 3 | 2.09 | 25 | 1.18 |
| John Franco | 5 | 3 | 2.44 | 29 | 1.26 |
| Lee Smith | 0 | 5 | 3.47 | 37 | 1.38 |
| Trevor Hoffman | 7 | 4 | 3.88 | 31 | 1.16 |
| Greg Harris | 2 | 3 | 2.61 | 0 | 1.28 |
| Alejandro Pena | 3 | 1 | 4.72 | 0 | 1.34 |
| Dennis Eckersley | 4 | 6 | 4.83 | 29 | 1.29 |
| Jeff Russell | 1 | 0 | 3.03 | 20 | 1.38 |
| Jose DeLeon | 5 | 4 | 5.45 | 0 | 1.43 |
| Bill Wegman | 5 | 7 | 5.35 | 2 | 1.60 |
| Kirk McCaskill | 6 | 4 | 4.89 | 2 | 1.67 |
| Mike Jackson | 6 | 1 | 2.39 | 2 | 1.18 |
| Mike Timlin | 4 | 3 | 2.14 | 5 | 1.36 |
| Norm Charlton | 4 | 6 | 3.36 | 14 | 1.16 |
| Jeff Brantley | 3 | 2 | 2.82 | 28 | 1.05 |
| Mike Dyer | 4 | 5 | 4.34 | 0 | 1.55 |
| Mike Fetters | 0 | 3 | 3.38 | 22 | 1.73 |
| Chuck McElroy | 3 | 4 | 6.02 | 0 | 1.54 |
| Jim Poole | 3 | 3 | 3.75 | 0 | 1.17 |
| Gil Heredia | 5 | 6 | 4.31 | 1 | 1.37 |
| Greg McMichael | 7 | 2 | 2.79 | 2 | 1.19 |
| Rene Arocha | 3 | 5 | 3.99 | 0 | 1.53 |
| Mark Dewey | 1 | 0 | 3.13 | 0 | 1.48 |
| Dave Burba | 10 | 4 | 3.97 | 0 | 1.32 |
| Larry Casian | 1 | 0 | 1.93 | 0 | 1.63 |
| Roberto Hernandez | 3 | 7 | 3.92 | 32 | 1.58 |
| Mike Magnante | 1 | 1 | 4.23 | 0 | 1.41 |
| Rod Beck | 5 | 6 | 4.45 | 33 | 1.41 |
| Rusty Meacham | 4 | 3 | 4.98 | 2 | 1.54 |
| Doug Henry | 3 | 6 | 2.96 | 4 | 1.10 |
| Anthony Young | 3 | 4 | 3.70 | 2 | 1.55 |
| Rheal Cormier | 7 | 5 | 4.07 | 0 | 1.43 |
| Yorkis Perez | 2 | 6 | 5.21 | 1 | 1.39 |
| Todd Van Poppel | 4 | 8 | 4.88 | 0 | 1.34 |
| John Doherty | 5 | 9 | 5.10 | 6 | 1.53 |
| Pat Mahomes | 4 | 10 | 6.37 | 3 | 1.57 |
| Hipolito Pichardo | 8 | 4 | 4.36 | 1 | 1.56 |
| Pedro Astacio | 7 | 8 | 4.24 | 0 | 1.31 |
| Bill Risley | 2 | 1 | 3.13 | 1 | 1.23 |
| Steve Howe | 6 | 3 | 4.96 | 2 | 1.78 |
| Richie Lewis | 0 | 1 | 3.75 | 0 | 1.28 |
| Blas Minor | 4 | 2 | 3.66 | 1 | 1.24 |
| Tim Pugh | 6 | 5 | 3.84 | 0 | 1.35 |
| Bobby Ayala | 6 | 5 | 4.44 | 19 | 1.54 |
| Omar Daal | 4 | 0 | 7.20 | 0 | 2.25 |
| Darren Oliver | 4 | 2 | 4.22 | 0 | 1.63 |
| Carlos Reyes | 4 | 6 | 5.09 | 0 | 1.51 |
| Dave Veres | 5 | 1 | 2.26 | 1 | 1.19 |
| Toby Borland | 1 | 3 | 3.77 | 6 | 1.66 |
| Joe Ausanio | 2 | 0 | 5.73 | 1 | 1.73 |
| Mark Thompson | 2 | 3 | 6.53 | 0 | 1.88 |
| Buddy Groom | 2 | 5 | 7.44 | 1 | 2.07 |
| Mike James | 3 | 0 | 3.88 | 1 | 1.40 |
| John Cummings | 3 | 1 | 4.06 | 0 | 1.42 |
| Antonio Osuna | 2 | 4 | 4.43 | 0 | 1.34 |
| Troy Percival | 3 | 2 | 1.95 | 3 | 0.86 |
| Brad Clontz | 8 | 1 | 3.65 | 4 | 1.41 |

## Look For Consistency (continued)

| | W | L | ERA | Sv | BR/IP |
|---|---|---|---|---|---|
| Roger Bailey | 7 | 6 | 4.98 | 0 | 1.57 |
| Jim Dougherty | 8 | 4 | 4.92 | 0 | 1.54 |
| Jason Christiansen | 1 | 3 | 4.15 | 0 | 1.53 |
| Don Wengert | 1 | 1 | 3.34 | 0 | 1.45 |
| Jeff McCurry | 1 | 4 | 5.02 | 1 | 1.92 |
| Armando Benitez | 1 | 5 | 5.66 | 2 | 1.66 |
| Dustin Hermanson | 3 | 1 | 6.82 | 0 | 1.83 |
| Rob Dibble | 1 | 4 | 6.45 | 2 | 2.10 |
| Ramon Morel | 0 | 1 | 2.84 | 0 | 1.26 |
| Larry Thomas | 0 | 0 | 1.32 | 0 | 1.02 |
| Terrell Wade | 0 | 1 | 4.50 | 0 | 1.75 |
| Jay Powell | 0 | 0 | 1.08 | 0 | 1.80 |

## Production Will Drop

| | 1995 Statistics | | | | |
|---|---|---|---|---|---|
| | W | L | ERA | Sv | BR/IP |
| Rick Honeycutt | 5 | 1 | 2.96 | 2 | 1.09 |
| Dave Leiper | 1 | 3 | 3.22 | 2 | 1.32 |
| Rick Aguilera | 3 | 3 | 2.60 | 32 | 1.08 |
| Roger McDowell | 7 | 4 | 4.02 | 4 | 1.48 |
| Todd Worrell | 4 | 1 | 2.02 | 32 | 1.12 |
| Dan Plesac | 4 | 4 | 3.58 | 3 | 1.34 |
| Paul Assenmacher | 6 | 2 | 2.82 | 0 | 1.23 |
| Jeff Parrett | 4 | 7 | 3.64 | 0 | 1.30 |
| Bruce Ruffin | 0 | 1 | 2.12 | 11 | 1.32 |
| Ed Vosberg | 5 | 5 | 3.00 | 4 | 1.33 |
| Bob Patterson | 5 | 2 | 3.04 | 0 | 1.16 |
| Mike Henneman | 0 | 2 | 2.15 | 26 | 1.19 |
| Jose Mesa | 3 | 0 | 1.13 | 46 | 1.03 |
| Tony Fossas | 3 | 0 | 1.47 | 0 | 1.06 |
| Jim Corsi | 2 | 4 | 2.20 | 2 | 1.31 |
| Dennis Cook | 0 | 2 | 4.53 | 2 | 1.58 |
| Mark Gardner | 5 | 5 | 4.49 | 1 | 1.53 |
| Randy Veres | 4 | 4 | 3.88 | 1 | 1.42 |
| Mark Guthrie | 5 | 5 | 4.21 | 0 | 1.50 |
| Rudy Seanez | 1 | 3 | 6.75 | 3 | 1.67 |
| Stan Belinda | 8 | 1 | 3.10 | 10 | 1.19 |
| Willie Blair | 7 | 5 | 4.34 | 0 | 1.39 |
| Darren Holmes | 6 | 1 | 3.24 | 14 | 1.32 |
| Rich DeLucia | 8 | 7 | 3.39 | 0 | 1.24 |
| Heathcliff Slocumb | 5 | 6 | 2.89 | 32 | 1.53 |
| Terry Mathews | 4 | 4 | 3.38 | 3 | 1.19 |
| Mike Christopher | 4 | 0 | 3.82 | 1 | 1.42 |
| Jeff Nelson | 7 | 3 | 2.17 | 2 | 1.16 |

| | W | L | ERA | Sv | BR/IP |
|---|---|---|---|---|---|
| Mike Butcher | 6 | 1 | 4.73 | 0 | 1.58 |
| Matt Whiteside | 5 | 4 | 4.08 | 3 | 1.28 |
| Steve Reed | 5 | 2 | 2.14 | 3 | 0.99 |
| Doug Brocail | 6 | 4 | 4.19 | 1 | 1.46 |
| Robb Nen | 0 | 7 | 3.29 | 23 | 1.31 |
| Pedro Borbon | 2 | 2 | 3.09 | 2 | 1.47 |
| Mike Mohler | 1 | 1 | 3.04 | 1 | 1.44 |
| Graeme Lloyd | 0 | 5 | 4.50 | 4 | 1.13 |
| Rich Robertson | 2 | 0 | 3.83 | 0 | 1.53 |
| Lance Painter | 3 | 0 | 4.37 | 1 | 1.48 |
| Angel Miranda | 4 | 5 | 5.23 | 1 | 1.78 |
| Eddie Guardado | 4 | 9 | 5.12 | 2 | 1.58 |
| Turk Wendell | 3 | 1 | 4.92 | 0 | 1.61 |
| Curt Leskanic | 6 | 3 | 3.40 | 10 | 1.18 |
| Albie Lopez | 0 | 0 | 3.13 | 0 | 1.09 |
| Todd Jones | 6 | 5 | 3.07 | 15 | 1.47 |
| Julian Tavarez | 10 | 2 | 2.44 | 0 | 1.18 |
| Danny Miceli | 4 | 4 | 4.66 | 21 | 1.60 |
| Dave Stevens | 5 | 4 | 5.07 | 10 | 1.63 |
| Andrew Lorraine | 0 | 0 | 3.38 | 0 | 0.75 |
| Bryce Florie | 2 | 2 | 3.01 | 1 | 1.33 |
| Ricky Bottalico | 5 | 3 | 2.46 | 1 | 1.10 |
| Tim Crabtree | 0 | 2 | 3.09 | 0 | 1.41 |
| Joe Borowski | 0 | 0 | 1.23 | 0 | 1.23 |

## 1996 Sleepers

| | 1995 Statistics (includes minor leagues) | | | | |
|---|---|---|---|---|---|
| | W | L | ERA | Sv | BR/IP |
| Danny Cox | 1 | 3 | 6.40 | 0 | 1.88 |
| Terry Clark | 3 | 7 | 3.42 | 6 | 1.35 |
| Gregg Olson | 4 | 3 | 3.40 | 16 | 1.37 |
| Dave Fleming | 2 | 6 | 5.36 | 0 | 1.69 |
| Alan Embree | 6 | 6 | 2.48 | 6 | 1.38 |
| Jason Schmidt | 10 | 8 | 2.87 | 0 | 1.38 |
| Ron Villone | 3 | 3 | 3.74 | 14 | 1.43 |
| Doug Bochtler | 6 | 7 | 3.87 | 2 | 1.41 |
| Rafael Carmona | 6 | 8 | 4.88 | 5 | 1.63 |
| Jeff Suppan | 9 | 7 | 3.66 | 0 | 1.28 |
| Paul Byrd | 5 | 5 | 2.64 | 6 | 1.13 |
| Terry Adams | 3 | 4 | 2.76 | 25 | 1.26 |
| Brian Barber | 8 | 6 | 4.81 | 0 | 1.43 |
| Bill Simas | 8 | 5 | 3.39 | 6 | 1.62 |
| John Wasdin | 13 | 9 | 5.45 | 0 | 1.32 |
| Darrell May | 6 | 10 | 3.81 | 0 | 1.25 |
| Robert Person | 8 | 5 | 3.25 | 7 | 1.09 |

# American League Players

# Brady Anderson

## 1995 Season

Brady Anderson has been the Orioles' primary leadoff hitter and left fielder for the last four years. Though he strikes out a lot and doesn't hit for a high average, Anderson compensates by getting on base frequently via the walk, and he has excellent speed and baserunning skills once he gets there. He also provides unusual power from the leadoff spot. Anderson led the O's in runs scored with 108 in 1995, achieved or tied career highs in runs and triples, and remained a steady performer in the field.

## Hitting

Anderson hits to all fields and likes the fastball at the knees. He employs a high leg kick, and he can drive the ball a long distance when he gets hold of one. Since he excels at hitting to the opposite field, pitchers tend to come inside to him with some success. He had problems with southpaws last summer, and does not hit well when behind in the count. However, he will take a lot of pitches looking for the free pass.

## Baserunning & Defense

Anderson is among the best baserunners in the American League. He had 36 successful stolen-base attempts in a row over the '94 and '95 seasons—a league record later broken by Tim Raines—and he's an aggressive, intelligent runner. Anderson is a very good outfielder who is more comfortable in left than in center. He covers good ground and has an average arm.

## 1996 Outlook

Anderson offers the Orioles stability in left field and the capability of playing center. He fulfills his leadoff responsibilities by getting on base often enough, but Curtis Goodwin may take over that role in 1996. Anderson's attributes would also fit nicely into the number-two slot, and he is likely to be moved there if Goodwin wins the leadoff job.

**Position:** LF/CF
**Bats:** L  **Throws:** L
**Ht:** 6' 1"  **Wt:** 195

**Opening Day Age:** 32
**Born:** 1/18/64 in Silver Spring, MD
**ML Seasons:** 8

### Overall Statistics

|  | G | AB | R | H | D | T | HR | RBI | SB | BB | SO | Avg | OBP | Slg |
|---|---|---|---|---|---|---|---|---|---|---|---|---|---|---|
| 1995 | 143 | 554 | 108 | 145 | 33 | 10 | 16 | 64 | 26 | 87 | 111 | .262 | .371 | .444 |
| Career | 945 | 3271 | 512 | 817 | 164 | 44 | 72 | 346 | 187 | 459 | 593 | .250 | .349 | .393 |

### Where He Hits the Ball

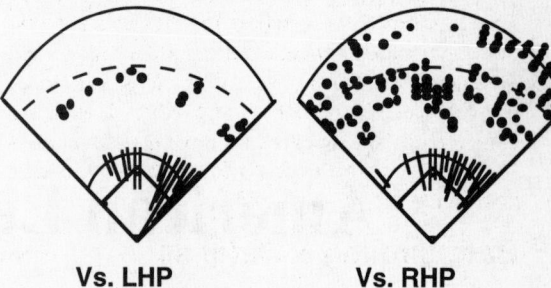

**Vs. LHP**          **Vs. RHP**

### 1995 Situational Stats

|  | AB | H | HR | RBI | Avg |  | AB | H | HR | RBI | Avg |
|---|---|---|---|---|---|---|---|---|---|---|---|
| Home | 277 | 72 | 10 | 33 | .260 | LHP | 178 | 38 | 3 | 15 | .213 |
| Road | 277 | 73 | 6 | 31 | .264 | RHP | 376 | 107 | 13 | 49 | .285 |
| First Half | 256 | 66 | 9 | 31 | .258 | Sc Pos | 123 | 35 | 4 | 48 | .285 |
| Scnd Half | 298 | 79 | 7 | 33 | .265 | Clutch | 74 | 16 | 2 | 12 | .216 |

### 1995 Rankings (American League)

→ 1st in fielding percentage in left field (.990)

→ 2nd in plate appearances (657) and least GDPs per GDP situation (3.2%)

→ 3rd in triples and pitches seen (2,644)

→ 6th in runs scored, hit by pitch (10) and highest percentage of extra bases taken as a runner (63.9%)

→ Led the Orioles in at-bats, runs scored, doubles, triples, stolen bases, walks, hit by pitch, times on base (242), strikeouts, pitches seen, plate appearances, most pitches seen per plate appearance (4.02), least GDPs per GDP situation and batting average with runners in scoring position (.285)

# Harold Baines

## 1995 Season

Just when conventional wisdom suggested that Harold Baines would demonstrate reduced productivity in 1995, the 37-year-old designated hitter came out swinging. Baines clubbed 24 round-trippers, his most since 1984, and his .540 slugging percentage nearly matched his career-high .541 mark, which led the American League in '84. Particularly remarkable was his consistency: he deftly avoided any prolonged slump.

## Hitting

Baines is a dead pull hitter who will kill the low fastball. Standing a bit off the plate, he will lay off pitches on the outside corner in an effort to force pitchers to come inside to him. This past season Baines seemed to correct a long-standing weakness against lefthanders, hitting them very well, albeit in a limited number of chances. He struck out less per at-bat than at any other time in his career. Baines, however, did have problems driving in runs and hit poorly with runners in scoring position.

## Baserunning & Defense

It's no secret that Baines has gimpy knees which prevent him from playing in the field. He hasn't stolen a base since 1992, and that was his only steal over the last nine seasons. He is a prime candidate to be removed for a pinch runner at crucial times in ballgames. He used to be a fine right fielder, but nowadays he's truly a designated hitter only.

## 1996 Outlook

Baltimore exercised its option on Baines for the 1995 season, but a new contract for a 37-year-old designated hitter is not a sure thing. One of his biggest supporters, ex-GM Roland Hemond, is no longer with the club, and the Orioles probably won't re-sign him unless terms of the contract are heavily weighted in the club's favor. If the O's don't want him back, Baines should have no trouble finding work with another American League club.

**Position:** DH
**Bats:** L **Throws:** L
**Ht:** 6' 2" **Wt:** 195

**Opening Day Age:** 37
**Born:** 3/15/59 in St. Michaels, MD
**ML Seasons:** 16

### Overall Statistics

|  | G | AB | R | H | D | T | HR | RBI | SB | BB | SO | Avg | OBP | Slg |
|---|---|---|---|---|---|---|---|---|---|---|---|---|---|---|
| 1995 | 127 | 385 | 60 | 115 | 19 | 1 | 24 | 63 | 0 | 70 | 45 | .299 | .403 | .540 |
| Career | 2183 | 7871 | 1033 | 2271 | 387 | 48 | 301 | 1261 | 30 | 804 | 1163 | .289 | .352 | .465 |

### Where He Hits the Ball

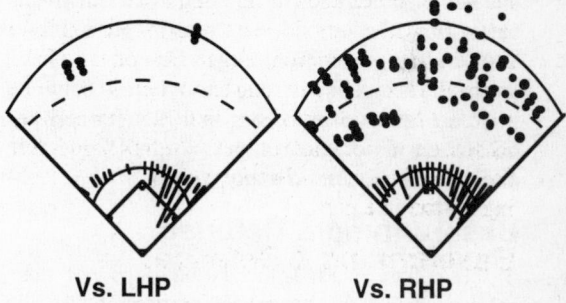

**Vs. LHP**          **Vs. RHP**

### 1995 Situational Stats

|  | AB | H | HR | RBI | Avg |  | AB | H | HR | RBI | Avg |
|---|---|---|---|---|---|---|---|---|---|---|---|
| Home | 172 | 50 | 7 | 22 | .291 | LHP | 62 | 18 | 3 | 5 | .290 |
| Road | 213 | 65 | 17 | 41 | .305 | RHP | 323 | 97 | 21 | 58 | .300 |
| First Half | 168 | 52 | 10 | 30 | .310 | Sc Pos | 92 | 22 | 5 | 39 | .239 |
| Scnd Half | 217 | 63 | 14 | 33 | .290 | Clutch | 51 | 16 | 4 | 7 | .314 |

### 1995 Rankings (American League)

- ➡ 6th in intentional walks (13) and most GDPs per GDP situation (18.2%)
- ➡ 9th in slugging percentage vs. right-handed pitchers (.557)
- ➡ 10th in on-base percentage
- ➡ Led the Orioles in intentional walks (13), GDPs (16), on-base percentage, batting average in the clutch (.314), on-base percentage vs. right-handed pitchers (.412) and batting average on the road (.305)

# Bret Barberie

## 1995 Season

Baltimore acquired Bret Barberie before the 1995 season, hoping he would stabilize the situation at second base. Barberie, however, did not rise above the rank of platoon player. Stuck in a three-man rotation at second base, he hit a paltry .219 and struck out frequently while batting in the number-two position. Once he was moved toward the end of the lineup, Barberie's hitting improved. Still, Barberie's debut in the American League fell far short of previous performances with Montreal and Florida.

## Hitting

Barberie is a switch-hitter who chokes up on the bat and slaps the ball to all fields. He hit much better from the left side last season. He exhibits very limited power from either side of the plate, though he is certainly strong enough to do better in that department than he did in 1995. Barberie is one of the more patient hitters in the league, but one who also takes too many strikes.

## Baserunning & Defense

Barberie has average speed and does not take many risks on the bases. He attempted just six steals in 1995. He has average range at second base. More noteworthy is his improvement in turning the double play since his days with the Florida Marlins. He still has a slight problem in getting to balls hit to his right when it is necessary to back-hand the ball.

## 1996 Outlook

Since the Orioles believe their second-base woes were not solved this past summer, it is reasonable to assume that Barberie will not be around when the new season starts. There are several impact second baseman who are free agents this year, including Roberto Alomar and Craig Biggio. Orioles owner Peter Angelos has shown no reluctance to spend money, so one of those big names might wind up in Baltimore. Despite his poor 1995 season, Barberie is a proven major league hitter and should have no trouble finding another job.

**Position:** 2B
**Bats:** B  **Throws:** R
**Ht:** 5'11"  **Wt:** 180

**Opening Day Age:** 28
**Born:** 8/16/67 in Long Beach, CA
**ML Seasons:** 5

### Overall Statistics

|        | G   | AB   | R   | H   | D  | T | HR | RBI | SB | BB  | SO  | Avg  | OBP  | Slg  |
|--------|-----|------|-----|-----|----|---|----|-----|----|-----|-----|------|------|------|
| 1995   | 90  | 237  | 32  | 57  | 14 | 0 | 2  | 25  | 3  | 36  | 50  | .241 | .351 | .325 |
| Career | 464 | 1405 | 159 | 387 | 73 | 6 | 15 | 131 | 16 | 159 | 257 | .275 | .360 | .368 |

### Where He Hits the Ball

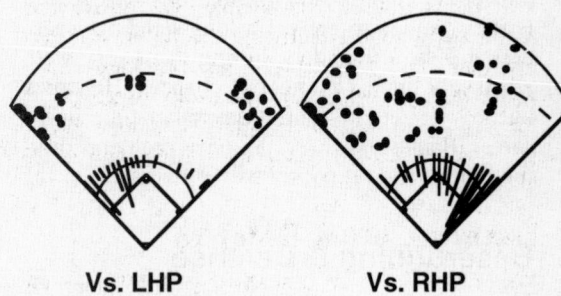

**Vs. LHP**          **Vs. RHP**

### 1995 Situational Stats

|            | AB  | H  | HR | RBI | Avg  |        | AB  | H  | HR | RBI | Avg  |
|------------|-----|----|----|-----|------|--------|-----|----|----|-----|------|
| Home       | 119 | 29 | 1  | 12  | .244 | LHP    | 79  | 12 | 0  | 8   | .152 |
| Road       | 118 | 28 | 1  | 13  | .237 | RHP    | 158 | 45 | 2  | 17  | .285 |
| First Half | 113 | 33 | 0  | 4   | .292 | Sc Pos | 55  | 16 | 1  | 23  | .291 |
| Scnd Half  | 124 | 24 | 2  | 21  | .194 | Clutch | 39  | 10 | 0  | 1   | .256 |

### 1995 Rankings (American League)

➡ 9th in errors at second base (7)

# Bobby Bonilla

## 1995 Season

Changing leagues couldn't sidetrack the supreme hitting talents of Bobby Bonilla. As a member of the New York Mets, Bonilla posted impressive numbers (.325-18-53 in 80 games). On July 28 he joined the Orioles and continued to slug away, contributing mightily as Baltimore's cleanup hitter. He split time between right field and third base, but most importantly, provided a big bat to a weak-hitting lineup.

## Hitting

Bonilla is an accomplished switch-hitter who is devastating from either side of the plate. He utilizes a high leg kick and can hit with great power to all fields. Bonilla's size enables him to cover the entire strike zone effectively, and he handles the low-and-away fastball and late-breaking slider better than almost anyone. His only weakness is the change-up. To keep Bonilla off balance, pitchers focus more on changing speeds than pitch location.

## Baserunning & Defense

While Bonilla is no basestealing threat, he's an aggressive runner and capable of taking the extra base. Whether he is better defensively as a third baseman or an outfielder remains a burning question. He has a strong arm and good range to his left at third base, but is prone to errors. In the outfield, he makes each fly ball seem like an adventure, but he gets the job done.

## 1996 Outlook

Bonilla is productive wherever he plays, but he seems a lot more comfortable in Baltimore than he did in New York. He finished the year as the Orioles' third baseman and will have the inside track on that position for 1996. He also will be the cleanup hitter and provide Rafael Palmeiro with season-long protection in the order. Bonilla will be a central figure in Baltimore's efforts to return to contention in the American League East.

**Position:** 3B/LF/RF
**Bats:** B **Throws:** R
**Ht:** 6' 3"  **Wt:** 240

**Opening Day Age:** 33
**Born:** 2/23/63 in New York, NY
**ML Seasons:** 10
**Pronunciation:** buh-NEE-yuh

### Overall Statistics

|  | G | AB | R | H | D | T | HR | RBI | SB | BB | SO | Avg | OBP | Slg |
|---|---|---|---|---|---|---|---|---|---|---|---|---|---|---|
| 1995 | 141 | 554 | 96 | 182 | 37 | 8 | 28 | 99 | 0 | 54 | 79 | .329 | .388 | .576 |
| Career | 1434 | 5191 | 809 | 1472 | 306 | 49 | 217 | 849 | 36 | 644 | 846 | .284 | .360 | .487 |

### Where He Hits the Ball

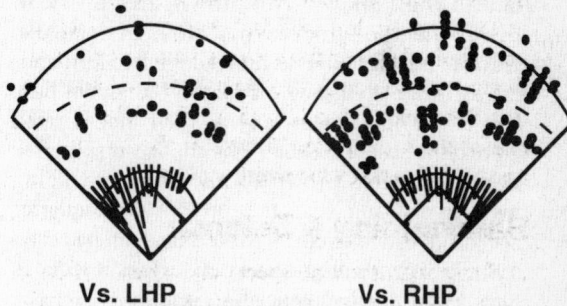

**Vs. LHP**          **Vs. RHP**

### 1995 Situational Stats

|  | AB | H | HR | RBI | Avg |  | AB | H | HR | RBI | Avg |
|---|---|---|---|---|---|---|---|---|---|---|---|
| Home | 278 | 93 | 14 | 47 | .335 | LHP | 164 | 60 | 8 | 29 | .366 |
| Road | 276 | 89 | 14 | 52 | .322 | RHP | 390 | 122 | 20 | 70 | .313 |
| First Half | 260 | 82 | 13 | 40 | .315 | Sc Pos | 145 | 45 | 4 | 63 | .310 |
| Scnd Half | 294 | 100 | 15 | 59 | .340 | Clutch | 93 | 25 | 2 | 9 | .269 |

### 1995 Rankings (American League)

→ 5th in most GDPs per GDP situation (18.3%)
→ 7th in cleanup slugging percentage (.544)
→ 8th in batting average on a 3-2 count (.400)
→ Led the Orioles in cleanup slugging percentage (.544) and batting average with two strikes (.256)

# Kevin Brown

## 1995 Season

Signed to a free-agent contract prior to the 1995 season, Kevin Brown was an early-season disappointment. Brown spent time on the disabled list with a dislocated finger on his pitching hand, and then went through a period in which he lost six straight decisions. But Brown came back and finished the season strongly, winding up among the league leaders in ERA. His mediocre 10-9 record was somewhat deceiving because he received little run support from his teammates.

## Pitching

Brown possesses some of the best stuff in the American League. His primary pitch is a sinking cut fastball that moves down and away to righthanders and produces numerous ground balls. He also uses the cutter as his lead pitch to lefthanders. Brown also throws a straight, four-seam fastball at varying speeds, and a slider that is rated among the best in baseball. His change-up is above average, as well. Brown also is fond of changing his delivery from over the top to a three-quarter arm drop. Pitching coach Mike Flanagan has tried to limit Brown's drop-down delivery, as it reduces the speed and movement of his pitches.

## Defense

Brown has one of the best moves in the game among right-handed pitchers. He is adept at keeping runners close and has a good, quick move to first. Brown is an adequate fielder who is agile coming off the mound and fields bunts well.

## 1996 Outlook

Brown is coming off a one-year deal at $4 million-plus, and is a free agent once again. Economic considerations—and the contract status of other Orioles starters—will dictate if Brown has a future in Baltimore. A pitcher who successfully induces groundballs is a perfect match for the Orioles and Camden Yards, so they'd like him back if they can afford him.

**Position:** SP
**Bats:** R  **Throws:** R
**Ht:** 6' 4"  **Wt:** 195

**Opening Day Age:** 31
**Born:** 3/14/65 in McIntyre, GA
**ML Seasons:** 9

### Overall Statistics

|        | W  | L  | Pct. | ERA  | G   | GS  | Sv | IP     | H    | BB  | SO  | HR | BR/IP |
|--------|----|----|------|------|-----|-----|----|--------|------|-----|-----|----|-------|
| 1995   | 10 | 9  | .526 | 3.60 | 26  | 26  | 0  | 172.1  | 155  | 48  | 117 | 10 | 1.18  |
| Career | 88 | 73 | .547 | 3.78 | 213 | 212 | 0  | 1451.0 | 1477 | 476 | 859 | 95 | 1.35  |

### How Often He Throws Strikes

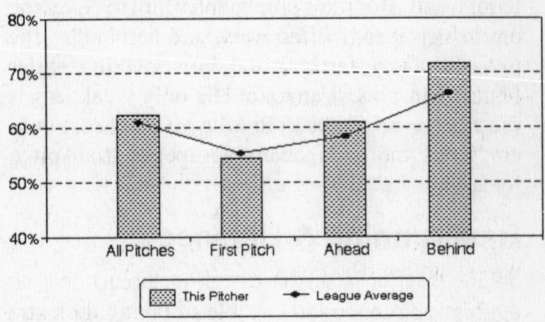

### 1995 Situational Stats

|            | W | L | ERA  | Sv | IP   |        | AB  | H  | HR | RBI | Avg  |
|------------|---|---|------|----|------|--------|-----|----|----|-----|------|
| Home       | 6 | 5 | 3.56 | 0  | 93.2 | LHB    | 364 | 90 | 5  | 34  | .247 |
| Road       | 4 | 4 | 3.66 | 0  | 78.2 | RHB    | 278 | 65 | 5  | 25  | .234 |
| First Half | 5 | 6 | 3.91 | 0  | 76.0 | Sc Pos | 131 | 31 | 2  | 47  | .237 |
| Scnd Half  | 5 | 3 | 3.36 | 0  | 96.1 | Clutch | 68  | 20 | 1  | 6   | .294 |

### 1995 Rankings (American League)

→ 1st in highest groundball/flyball ratio allowed (2.7)
→ 2nd in lowest slugging percentage allowed (.341) and least home runs allowed per 9 innings (.52)
→ 3rd in hit batsmen (9)
→ 4th in least baserunners allowed per 9 innings (11.1)
→ 5th in highest strikeout/walk ratio (2.4) , lowest on-base percentage allowed (.302) and most GDPs induced per 9 innings (1.1)
→ Led the Orioles in losses (9), hit batsmen (9), pickoff throws (174) and GDPs induced (21)

# Scott Erickson

## 1995 Season

Scott Erickson was a mainstay of the Minnesota Twins pitching staff until last July, when he was traded to the Orioles for two prospects. It was no secret that Erickson was on the block as part of the Twins' cost-cutting measures. After changing uniforms, Erickson held down the third spot in the rotation admirably. He went 9-4 with the O's, and his 3.89 ERA in a Baltimore uniform was nearly two runs lower than the mark he'd posted with the Twins.

## Pitching

Erickson relies heavily on two pitches: a 90-MPH sinking fastball that runs in on right-handed hitters, and a hard slider that he is more inclined to use when ahead in the count. His sinker is extremely effective at inducing batters to hit the ball on the ground. Erickson needs to refine an offspeed pitch—his change-up or possibly his curveball—so that hitters are less successful at timing his heat. With runners on base, Erickson sometimes encounters problems in two-out or two-strike situations. He has a tendency to overthrow and lose the hitter.

## Defense

The big righthander is an adequate fielder with good agility getting to first on grounders to the right side. He has a quick move to first from the set position and can deliver to the plate rapidly, which successfully reduces a potential basestealer's jump.

## 1996 Outlook

Although Erickson still hasn't come close to matching his 20-8 record of 1991, he made a strong impression with his solid pitching after coming over from Minnesota. However, it's uncertain whether or not the Oriole brass will re-sign the free-agent pitcher for 1996. One thing in his favor is that he makes less money than either Ben McDonald or Kevin Brown, two other O's righties who are in the same position. The club likes his arm; it'll all come down to money.

**Position:** SP
**Bats:** R  **Throws:** R
**Ht:** 6' 4"  **Wt:** 234

**Opening Day Age:** 28
**Born:** 2/2/68 in Long Beach, CA
**ML Seasons:** 6

### Overall Statistics

|        | W  | L  | Pct. | ERA  | G   | GS  | Sv | IP     | H    | BB  | SO  | HR | BR/IP |
|--------|----|----|------|------|-----|-----|----|--------|------|-----|-----|----|-------|
| 1995   | 13 | 10 | .565 | 4.81 | 32  | 31  | 0  | 196.1  | 213  | 67  | 106 | 18 | 1.43  |
| Career | 70 | 64 | .522 | 4.19 | 172 | 169 | 0  | 1088.0 | 1146 | 402 | 588 | 90 | 1.42  |

### How Often He Throws Strikes

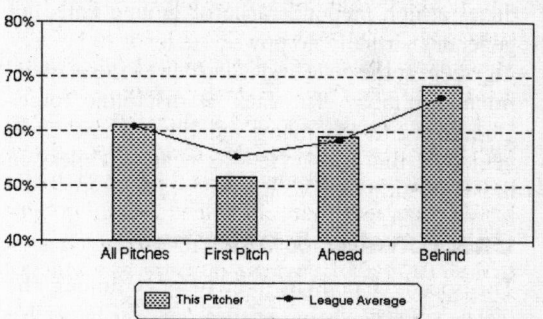

### 1995 Situational Stats

|            | W | L | ERA  | Sv | IP    |        | AB  | H   | HR | RBI | Avg  |
|------------|---|---|------|----|-------|--------|-----|-----|----|-----|------|
| Home       | 6 | 5 | 5.15 | 0  | 85.2  | LHB    | 478 | 137 | 10 | 61  | .287 |
| Road       | 7 | 5 | 4.55 | 0  | 110.2 | RHB    | 280 | 76  | 8  | 34  | .271 |
| First Half | 5 | 6 | 5.77 | 0  | 93.2  | Sc Pos | 181 | 53  | 7  | 78  | .293 |
| Scnd Half  | 8 | 4 | 3.94 | 0  | 102.2 | Clutch | 26  | 10  | 0  | 2   | .385 |

### 1995 Rankings (American League)

→ 2nd in complete games (7) , GDPs induced (26) and highest groundball/flyball ratio allowed (2.5)

→ 3rd in shutouts (2), balks (2), highest batting average allowed (.281) , most run support per 9 innings (6.8) and most GDPs induced per 9 innings (1.2)

→ 4th in games started

→ 5th in highest ERA, hits allowed and least pitches thrown per batter (3.58)

→ Led the Orioles in complete games (7), balks (2) and most GDPs induced per GDP situation (22.1%)

# Curtis Goodwin

## 1995 Season

Talk about making an entrance. In his major league debut last June 2, Curtis Goodwin singled in his first two major league at-bats. The baseball world took notice when Goodwin hit .359, scored 21 runs and stole 11 bases in the month of June. He personified what the Orioles were looking for in a leadoff hitter. However, Goodwin's impatience at the plate, a July slump, and a short stint on the disabled list took its toll. He hit a little worse with each month and finished the year not as a leadoff man, but as a number-nine hitter.

## Hitting

Goodwin is a free swinger whose flat swing produces a high preponderance of ground balls but generates virtually no power. He tends to be very impatient at the plate and will often swing at questionable pitches. The lack of discipline forces Goodwin into too many situations where he is behind in the count. He was nearly helpless in those situations last year, batting just .159.

## Baserunning & Defense

The speedy Goodwin already rates among the league's best at blazing a path around the bases. He was a 60-steal man in the minors, and looks like he could do the same at the major league level if he gets on base often enough. As a center fielder, Goodwin covers an exceptional amount of ground and is reasonably sure-handed. However, he does not possess a strong arm and is prone to making poor throwing decisions.

## 1996 Outlook

Goodwin should nail down the starting center field position for the O's next season, as they sorely need his speed in the lineup. He could develop into an Otis Nixon-type player, but needs to develop more patience at the plate and improve his outfield instincts. He intends to play winter ball this year to improve those facets of his game.

**Position:** CF
**Bats:** L **Throws:** L
**Ht:** 5'11"  **Wt:** 180

**Opening Day Age:** 23
**Born:** 9/30/72 in Oakland, CA
**ML Seasons:** 1

### Overall Statistics

|  | G | AB | R | H | D | T | HR | RBI | SB | BB | SO | Avg | OBP | Slg |
|---|---|---|---|---|---|---|---|---|---|---|---|---|---|---|
| 1995 | 87 | 289 | 40 | 76 | 11 | 3 | 1 | 24 | 22 | 15 | 53 | .263 | .301 | .332 |
| Career | 87 | 289 | 40 | 76 | 11 | 3 | 1 | 24 | 22 | 15 | 53 | .263 | .301 | .332 |

### Where He Hits the Ball

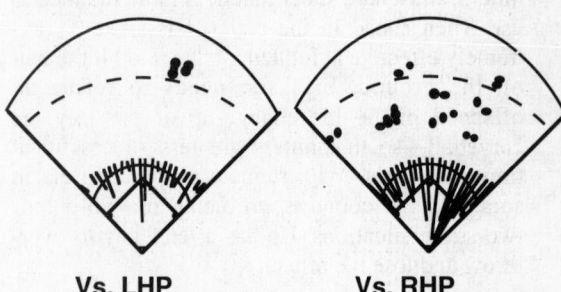

| Vs. LHP | Vs. RHP |
|---|---|

### 1995 Situational Stats

|  | AB | H | HR | RBI | Avg |  | AB | H | HR | RBI | Avg |
|---|---|---|---|---|---|---|---|---|---|---|---|
| Home | 143 | 42 | 0 | 13 | .294 | LHP | 77 | 19 | 1 | 6 | .247 |
| Road | 146 | 34 | 1 | 11 | .233 | RHP | 212 | 57 | 0 | 18 | .269 |
| First Half | 135 | 49 | 1 | 15 | .363 | Sc Pos | 67 | 16 | 0 | 20 | .239 |
| Scnd Half | 154 | 27 | 0 | 9 | .175 | Clutch | 38 | 5 | 0 | 4 | .132 |

### 1995 Rankings (American League)

- ➡ 2nd in lowest on-base percentage for a leadoff hitter (.281)
- ➡ 5th in stolen base percentage (84.6%)
- ➡ 8th in bunts in play (24)
- ➡ 9th in batting average with the bases loaded (.500)
- ➡ Led the Orioles in sacrifice bunts (7), stolen base percentage (84.6%), batting average with the bases loaded (.500) and bunts in play (24)

# Jeffrey Hammonds

## 1995 Season

Jeffrey Hammonds never had a chance to get it going in 1995. He went down with a strained right shoulder muscle in mid-July and never made it back into the lineup. It was the second straight year the promising O's outfielder had his season cut short by injuries; in 1994, it was a strained right knee that limited his playing time. Hammonds has been expected to be an everyday starter in right field since he was the fourth overall pick in the 1992 draft. Unfortunately, he has played in just 125 games in the last two years.

## Hitting

Due in good part to the injuries, Hammonds' game has not matched his potential. But they're not the only problems. With nine walks in 191 plate appearances during 1995, Hammonds obviously needs to develop more patience at the plate. He is prone to chasing outside pitches, and too intent on pulling them. He also struggles against left-handed pitching, even though he's a right-handed hitter. Despite his lack of experience, he has shown he can hit for average, as he did during his brief major league stint in 1994. He has some power as well, and looks capable of hitting 15-20 homers.

## Baserunning & Defense

When healthy, Hammonds has the speed to steal close to 50 bases and cover plenty of turf in the outfield. He committed only one error last year, but his throwing arm leaves a lot to be desired. Though he's played all three outfield positions with Baltimore, his best position is left field due to his poor throwing arm. Unfortunately, the O's already have Brady Anderson entrenched there.

## 1996 Outlook

Originally Hammonds was viewed as a leading candidate to take over center field for the Orioles. While he piled up injuries and Curtis Goodwin matured into a major league outfielder, the Oriole thinking changed. Hammonds will try to stay healthy and play a full season as Baltimore's right fielder.

**Position:** RF
**Bats:** R  **Throws:** R
**Ht:** 6' 0"  **Wt:** 195

**Opening Day Age:** 25
**Born:** 3/5/71 in Plainfield, NJ
**ML Seasons:** 3

### Overall Statistics

|        | G   | AB  | R  | H   | D  | T | HR | RBI | SB | BB | SO | Avg  | OBP  | Slg  |
|--------|-----|-----|----|-----|----|---|----|-----|----|----|----|------|------|------|
| 1995   | 57  | 178 | 18 | 43  | 9  | 1 | 4  | 23  | 4  | 9  | 30 | .242 | .279 | .371 |
| Career | 158 | 533 | 73 | 149 | 35 | 3 | 15 | 73  | 13 | 28 | 85 | .280 | .314 | .441 |

### Where He Hits the Ball

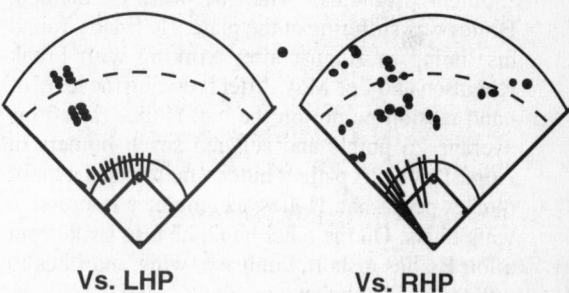

**Vs. LHP**        **Vs. RHP**

### 1995 Situational Stats

|            | AB  | H  | HR | RBI | Avg  |        | AB  | H  | HR | RBI | Avg  |
|------------|-----|----|----|-----|------|--------|-----|----|----|-----|------|
| Home       | 86  | 24 | 2  | 12  | .279 | LHP    | 53  | 11 | 0  | 7   | .208 |
| Road       | 92  | 19 | 2  | 11  | .207 | RHP    | 125 | 32 | 4  | 16  | .256 |
| First Half | 158 | 38 | 4  | 23  | .241 | Sc Pos | 43  | 14 | 2  | 20  | .326 |
| Scnd Half  | 20  | 5  | 0  | 0   | .250 | Clutch | 24  | 2  | 0  | 2   | .083 |

### 1995 Rankings (American League)

➡ Did not rank near the top or bottom in any category

# Chris Hoiles

## 1995 Season

Chris Hoiles experienced two seasons in 1995. Prior to the All-Star game, Hoiles was bothered by injuries and his numbers were abysmal. Manager Phil Regan even began to use backup Greg Zaun against certain righthanders. But Hoiles got healthy, found his stroke after some tutoring sessions and went on to have a great second half. While he failed to approach the numbers from his outstanding 1993 season (.310-29-82), Hoiles had another productive year, one remarkably similar to his solid 1994 campaign.

## Hitting

Hoiles came out of spring training with nagging shoulder problems. When he wasn't sidelined, Hoiles was suffering at the plate. He finally found his timing in August after working with Frank Robinson and Lee May. After reducing the level of hand tension he put on the bat, Hoiles raised his average 26 points and slugged seven homers in August alone. A patient hitter who looks at a lot of pitches per at-bat, Hoiles accumulates impressive walk totals. On the other hand, he also strikes out a lot. He has a short, compact swing and likes to pull the inside pitch.

## Baserunning & Defense

Hoiles is a slow runner whose extra-base hit totals are adversely affected by his lack of speed. Defensively, Hoiles is a sound catcher who makes few mistakes. He does not possess a very strong arm. Still, he is not a cinch to steal on and had some success against opposing baserunners last year.

## 1996 Outlook

Hoiles, who is signed through 1999, provides stability at the catching position with his combination of power and good defense. While his average could stand improvement, good health and a full spring training in 1996 could cure the ills that affected him early in 1995. Look for Hoiles to catch 125 games this season with continued good production.

**Position:** C
**Bats:** R  **Throws:** R
**Ht:** 6' 0"  **Wt:** 213

**Opening Day Age:** 31
**Born:** 3/20/65 in Bowling Green, OH
**ML Seasons:** 7

### Overall Statistics

|        | G   | AB   | R   | H   | D  | T | HR | RBI | SB | BB  | SO  | Avg  | OBP  | Slg  |
|--------|-----|------|-----|-----|----|---|----|-----|----|-----|-----|------|------|------|
| 1995   | 114 | 352  | 53  | 88  | 15 | 1 | 19 | 58  | 1  | 67  | 80  | .250 | .373 | .460 |
| Career | 571 | 1826 | 270 | 481 | 82 | 2 | 99 | 271 | 4  | 289 | 383 | .263 | .368 | .473 |

### Where He Hits the Ball

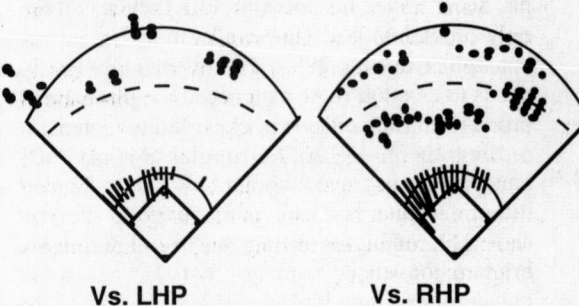

**Vs. LHP**          **Vs. RHP**

### 1995 Situational Stats

|            | AB  | H  | HR | RBI | Avg  |        | AB  | H  | HR | RBI | Avg  |
|------------|-----|----|----|-----|------|--------|-----|----|----|-----|------|
| Home       | 183 | 46 | 9  | 25  | .251 | LHP    | 100 | 30 | 12 | 27  | .300 |
| Road       | 169 | 42 | 10 | 33  | .249 | RHP    | 252 | 58 | 7  | 31  | .230 |
| First Half | 173 | 36 | 10 | 27  | .208 | Sc Pos | 91  | 25 | 4  | 35  | .275 |
| Scnd Half  | 179 | 52 | 9  | 31  | .291 | Clutch | 55  | 12 | 3  | 9   | .218 |

### 1995 Rankings (American League)

→ 1st in fielding percentage at catcher (.996)
→ 3rd in slugging percentage vs. left-handed pitchers (.720)
→ 6th in lowest batting average with two strikes (.130)
→ Led the Orioles in batting average vs. left-handed pitchers (.300), slugging percentage vs. left-handed pitchers (.720) and on-base percentage vs. left-handed pitchers (.418)

# Doug Jones

## 1995 Season

Doug Jones turned in a stellar performance as the Philadelphia Phillies' closer in 1994. His success was based upon excellent control and and keeping the ball out of the bleachers. After signing a one-year deal with Baltimore, Jones seemed to lose that pinpoint control and had tremendous difficulty pitching in Camden Yards. He did manage to record 22 saves in 25 opportunities, but he had only three saves after August 1, as the Orioles stopped using him in pressure situations.

## Pitching

Changing speeds with his fastball sets up Jones' key pitch, the change-up. His change is his out pitch and he usually keeps it low and away from right-handed hitters. Unfortunately for Jones, his location betrayed him last year. And, unlike previous years, he had more trouble with right-handed hitters than lefties. Getting less break on his once-devastating change-up, Jones went to his fastball more often and became easier to hit as the season wore on. He got hurt a lot on the first pitch, and he had problems all season long pitching with runners in scoring position.

## Defense

Simply stated, Jones is almost impossible to run on. In fact, during 1995 no one even attempted a steal against him. He wastes no motion coming to the plate and works fast, which makes it hard for runners to study him. He is a below-average fielder who is slow getting off the mound.

## 1996 Outlook

The conventional wisdom is that the Orioles will go shopping for a new closer and that Jones will not be back. He's bounced back from bad seasons before, and he'll probably get a chance to save games for someone again this year. But Jones, who turns 39 in June, is unlikely to command a salary near the $1.1 million he made in 1995.

**Position:** RP
**Bats:** R **Throws:** R
**Ht:** 6' 2" **Wt:** 195

**Opening Day Age:** 38
**Born:** 6/24/57 in Covina, CA
**ML Seasons:** 11

Baltimore Orioles

### *Overall Statistics*

|        | W  | L  | Pct. | ERA  | G   | GS | Sv  | IP    | H   | BB  | SO  | HR | BR/IP |
|--------|----|----|------|------|-----|----|-----|-------|-----|-----|-----|----|-------|
| 1995   | 0  | 4  | .000 | 5.01 | 52  | 0  | 22  | 46.2  | 55  | 16  | 42  | 6  | 1.52  |
| Career | 43 | 58 | .426 | 3.12 | 526 | 4  | 239 | 721.1 | 730 | 159 | 579 | 42 | 1.23  |

### *How Often He Throws Strikes*

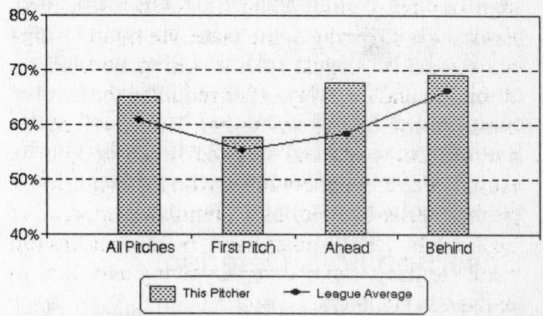

### *1995 Situational Stats*

|            | W | L | ERA  | Sv |      | IP   |        | AB  | H  | HR | RBI | Avg  |
|------------|---|---|------|-----|------|------|--------|-----|----|----|-----|------|
| Home       | 0 | 4 | 7.77 | 10 |      | 22.0 | LHB    | 105 | 24 | 1  | 17  | .229 |
| Road       | 0 | 0 | 2.55 | 12 |      | 24.2 | RHB    | 87  | 31 | 5  | 17  | .356 |
| First Half | 0 | 2 | 3.60 | 14 |      | 30.0 | Sc Pos | 54  | 19 | 1  | 28  | .352 |
| Scnd Half  | 0 | 2 | 7.56 | 8  |      | 16.2 | Clutch | 89  | 26 | 3  | 23  | .292 |

### *1995 Rankings (American League)*

- ➡ 5th in save percentage (88.0%)
- ➡ 8th in saves and games finished (47)
- ➡ 10th in save opportunities (25)
- ➡ Led the Orioles in saves, games finished (47), save opportunities, save percentage and blown saves (3)

# Jeff Manto

## 1995 Season

Chris Sabo's departure and an injury to Leo Gomez opened up the door for Jeff Manto, who has persevered through 10 minor league seasons. A slugger at the minor league level, Manto showed he could do the same when given a chance to play in the majors. He accumulated a large portion of his 17 homers during a torrid June hot streak, but then went on the disabled list with a pulled hamstring. Because of his lack of success against righthanders, Manto was platooned when he returned from the disabled list in July.

## Hitting

Manto is a straight fastball hitter who employs a slightly open batting stance. He hits with good power to both alleys. Due to his uppercut swing, he has a higher than normal flyball-to-groundball ratio. Manto's troubles with righthanders were compounded by difficulties with offspeed stuff. Batting coach Lee May worked with him, trying to get him to wait on pitches longer, and Manto hit a little better in August and September.

## Baserunning & Defense

Not blessed with great speed, Manto failed to steal a base in three attempts in '95. As expected, his glove work at the hot corner proved to be average. He has great reach with his 6'3" frame, especially going to his left, but his range overall is probably a little below average.

## 1996 Outlook

Manto is very likely in Baltimore's plans for this coming year, as the O's need powerful bats in their lineup. However, he'll have to learn to hit right-handed pitching better in order to be a full-time player. The one-time catcher is 31, so the Oriole brass view his growth potential as limited. He still figures to be useful as a bench and platoon player.

**Position:** 3B/DH
**Bats:** R  **Throws:** R
**Ht:** 6' 3"  **Wt:** 210

**Opening Day Age:** 31
**Born:** 8/23/64 in Bristol, PA
**ML Seasons:** 4

### Overall Statistics

|  | G | AB | R | H | D | T | HR | RBI | SB | BB | SO | Avg | OBP | Slg |
|---|---|---|---|---|---|---|---|---|---|---|---|---|---|---|
| 1995 | 89 | 254 | 31 | 65 | 9 | 0 | 17 | 38 | 0 | 24 | 69 | .256 | .325 | .492 |
| Career | 174 | 476 | 58 | 110 | 21 | 1 | 21 | 65 | 2 | 59 | 112 | .231 | .324 | .412 |

### Where He Hits the Ball

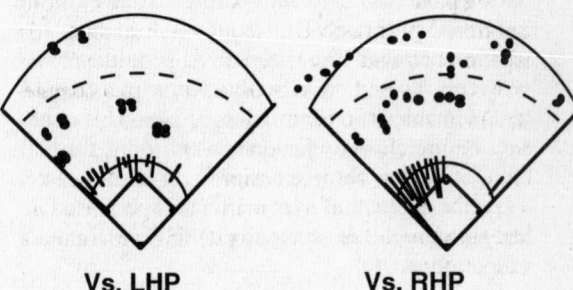

**Vs. LHP**          **Vs. RHP**

### 1995 Situational Stats

|  | AB | H | HR | RBI | Avg |  | AB | H | HR | RBI | Avg |
|---|---|---|---|---|---|---|---|---|---|---|---|
| Home | 131 | 34 | 12 | 24 | .260 | LHP | 90 | 29 | 7 | 15 | .322 |
| Road | 123 | 31 | 5 | 14 | .252 | RHP | 164 | 36 | 10 | 23 | .220 |
| First Half | 146 | 41 | 12 | 30 | .281 | Sc Pos | 58 | 12 | 3 | 19 | .207 |
| Scnd Half | 108 | 24 | 5 | 8 | .222 | Clutch | 45 | 7 | 2 | 5 | .156 |

### 1995 Rankings (American League)

→ 4th in lowest batting average in the clutch (.156)

# Ben McDonald

## 1995 Season

Ben McDonald must have felt he was trapped in a house of horrors, judging by the way the 1995 season unfolded for him. A strained right shoulder sidelined him in June. Two starts after coming off the disabled list in July, he developed tendinitis in the same shoulder, forcing him back onto the disabled list a second time. When he returned in September, McDonald was sent to the bullpen. He responded by openly criticizing management, and management responded by holding him out of the rotation.

## Pitching

McDonald and his 6'7" frame make for an intimidating presence on the mound. Just as intimidating are his 90-plus fastballs. An effective slider is part of the mix, and when the count is favorable he occasionally will try to fool hitters with a change-up. McDonald throws everything straight over the top. Once notorious for giving up lots of homers, McDonald was showing improvement until 1995, when the gopher ball was a problem again. He also struggled with his control in 1995, and his walk rate went up.

## Defense

McDonald has a long delivery, and that enables runners to get a little extra jump. He does not have a particularly sharp move to first, but he is fairly agile for such a big man. He moves well and can cover first in a hurry.

## 1996 Outlook

Ben McDonald is a big question mark for 1996—with a $4.5 million salary, a tough agent in Scott Boras, a supposed breach of trust with Oriole management, and his open contempt for being relegated to the bullpen late in the year. These factors, combined with (1) an almost certain attempt by the O's to cut his salary and (2) prospects Rick Krivda and Jimmy Haynes waiting in the wings, could spell departure time for Big Ben. If his salary demands aren't outrageous, plenty of clubs would love to have him.

**Position:** SP
**Bats:** R **Throws:** R
**Ht:** 6' 7" **Wt:** 214

**Opening Day Age:** 28
**Born:** 11/24/67 in Baton Rouge, LA
**ML Seasons:** 7

### Overall Statistics

|  | W | L | Pct. | ERA | G | GS | Sv | IP | H | BB | SO | HR | BR/IP |
|---|---|---|---|---|---|---|---|---|---|---|---|---|---|
| 1995 | 3 | 6 | .333 | 4.16 | 14 | 13 | 0 | 80.0 | 67 | 38 | 62 | 10 | 1.31 |
| Career | 58 | 53 | .523 | 3.89 | 155 | 142 | 0 | 937.0 | 838 | 334 | 638 | 100 | 1.25 |

### How Often He Throws Strikes

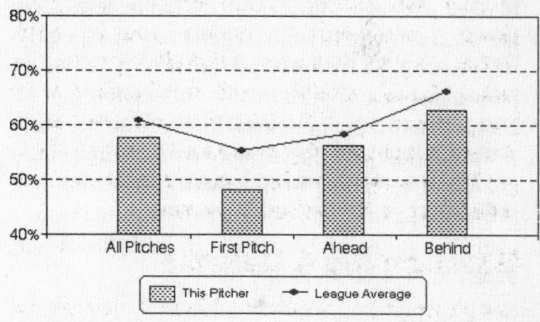

### 1995 Situational Stats

|  | W | L | ERA | Sv | IP |  | AB | H | HR | RBI | Avg |
|---|---|---|---|---|---|---|---|---|---|---|---|
| Home | 2 | 2 | 2.56 | 0 | 38.2 | LHB | 150 | 30 | 6 | 16 | .200 |
| Road | 1 | 4 | 5.66 | 0 | 41.1 | RHB | 149 | 37 | 4 | 20 | .248 |
| First Half | 2 | 4 | 4.40 | 0 | 61.1 | Sc Pos | 70 | 13 | 0 | 20 | .186 |
| Scnd Half | 1 | 2 | 3.38 | 0 | 18.2 | Clutch | 13 | 5 | 0 | 1 | .385 |

### 1995 Rankings (American League)

➡ 3rd in balks (2)
➡ Led the Orioles in wild pitches (4) and balks (2)

35

# Jamie Moyer

## 1995 Season

Despite a disappointing 1994 campaign, Jamie Moyer began the 1995 season as Baltimore's fourth starter. While he improved upon 1994's losing record, his ERA was a whopping 5.21, among the highest of his major league career. The abbreviated spring training may have contributed to Moyer's problems. He never got into a groove, alternating periods of effective pitching with long stretches where he consistently got hammered. He was hit hard in the season's final weeks, and the Orioles seemed to lose confidence in him.

## Pitching

Moyer is not an overpowering pitcher, nor is he blessed with exceptional stuff. What he does have is a great sense of rhythm. When he works quickly, he can be extremely effective. It's when baserunners cause him to slow his tempo that he becomes a different pitcher. His repertoire is basic fastball, slider and curve, and he mixes in a circle change to keep hitters off balance. Moyer has had difficulty against lefthanders, who sported a .317 average against him in 1995. He also has a tendency to give up the home run.

## Defense

Moyer's move to first is considered average, and he had problems with opposing baserunners in 1995. One problem is his pitching style: he throws more from the side than over the top, and runners seem able to read his move pretty easily. Moyer's fielding has always been solid and last year was no exception.

## 1996 Outlook

Since lefthanders are considered such a valuable commodity, Moyer's services will continue to be in demand. Baltimore's top three pitchers are right-handed, amd there's a good chance he'll be back in an O's uniform, challenging rookie southpaw Rick Krivda for a starting role. But it is unlikely, given his style and tools, that Moyer will improve much over his past performance.

**Position:** SP/RP
**Bats:** L  **Throws:** L
**Ht:** 6' 0"  **Wt:** 170

**Opening Day Age:** 33
**Born:** 11/18/62 in Sellersville, PA
**ML Seasons:** 9

### Overall Statistics

|  | W | L | Pct. | ERA | G | GS | Sv | IP | H | BB | SO | HR | BR/IP |
|---|---|---|---|---|---|---|---|---|---|---|---|---|---|
| 1995 | 8 | 6 | .571 | 5.21 | 27 | 18 | 0 | 115.2 | 117 | 30 | 65 | 18 | 1.27 |
| Career | 59 | 76 | .437 | 4.51 | 216 | 177 | 0 | 1116.2 | 1195 | 388 | 677 | 131 | 1.42 |

### How Often He Throws Strikes

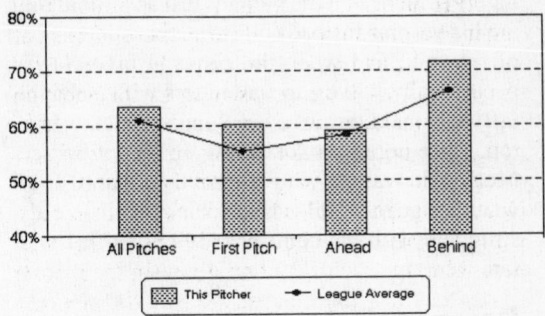

### 1995 Situational Stats

|  | W | L | ERA | Sv | IP |  | AB | H | HR | RBI | Avg |
|---|---|---|---|---|---|---|---|---|---|---|---|
| Home | 3 | 5 | 6.08 | 0 | 60.2 | LHB | 104 | 33 | 2 | 11 | .317 |
| Road | 5 | 1 | 4.25 | 0 | 55.0 | RHB | 338 | 84 | 16 | 51 | .249 |
| First Half | 4 | 3 | 3.83 | 0 | 54.0 | Sc Pos | 73 | 26 | 6 | 45 | .356 |
| Scnd Half | 4 | 3 | 6.42 | 0 | 61.2 | Clutch | 28 | 6 | 2 | 4 | .214 |

### 1995 Rankings (American League)

➡ Led the Orioles in stolen bases allowed (11)

# Mike Mussina

**Position:** SP
**Bats:** R  **Throws:** R
**Ht:** 6' 2"  **Wt:** 185

**Opening Day Age:** 27
**Born:** 12/8/68 in
Williamsport, PA
**ML Seasons:** 5

Baltimore Orioles

## 1995 Season

Battling back from a slow start that was probably due to the abbreviated spring training, Mike Mussina had another great season in 1995. Mussina was 5-5 with a 5.13 ERA after his first 11 starts, but he pitched brilliantly from then on and wound up with a career-high 19 victories. He finished the year with back-to-back shutouts and allowed only 10 hits and one run in his last 27 innings.

## Pitching

Compared to Catfish Hunter by Bill James, Mussina has an arsenal of very effective pitches. He throws two fastballs: a running fastball that hits 92 MPH and tails off to the right, and a sinking cutter that dives down and away to right-handed hitters. Add to that a hard knuckle-curve and a change-up, his most devastating pitch, and you have the makings of a dominant pitcher. He is prone to giving up the homer, usually early in games when he is trying to establish the fastballs. Once the location of his heat is locked in, the stage is set for one of the best change-ups in the business. Mussina's stuff is normally even tougher on lefties than it is on righties, and that was the case again in 1995.

## Defense

Mussina is a good fielder who is quick and agile coming off the mound. With runners on base, he has a distinctive set and delivery that is difficult to read and inhibits potential basestealers. Just four of 11 stolen-base attempts were successful all year.

## 1996 Outlook

Baltimore's ace is up for a new contract in 1996. Look for Oriole management to go the limit to sign him. Mussina is just now entering his prime and should break through the 20-win barrier that has eluded him because of two strike-shortened seasons. Unquestionably he is one of the league's stars, and a good bet for a Cy Young award within the next few seasons.

### Overall Statistics

|        | W  | L  | Pct. | ERA  | G   | GS  | Sv | IP    | H   | BB  | SO  | HR | BR/IP |
|--------|----|----|------|------|-----|-----|----|-------|-----|-----|-----|----|-------|
| 1995   | 19 | 9  | .679 | 3.29 | 32  | 32  | 0  | 221.2 | 187 | 50  | 158 | 24 | 1.07  |
| Career | 71 | 30 | .703 | 3.22 | 125 | 125 | 0  | 894.1 | 802 | 205 | 556 | 86 | 1.13  |

### How Often He Throws Strikes

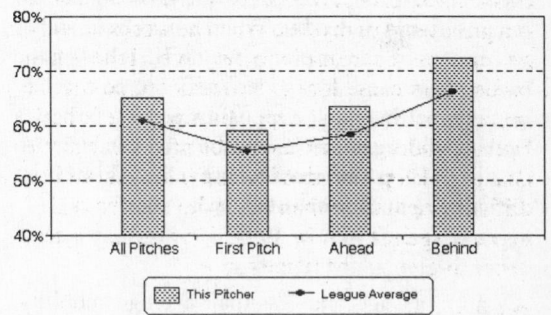

### 1995 Situational Stats

|           | W  | L | ERA  | Sv | IP    |        | AB  | H   | HR | RBI | Avg  |
|-----------|----|---|------|----|-------|--------|-----|-----|----|-----|------|
| Home      | 11 | 3 | 3.38 | 0  | 117.0 | LHB    | 483 | 101 | 9  | 32  | .209 |
| Road      | 8  | 6 | 3.18 | 0  | 104.2 | RHB    | 344 | 86  | 15 | 42  | .250 |
| First Half| 9  | 5 | 4.41 | 0  | 96.0  | Sc Pos | 146 | 31  | 4  | 47  | .212 |
| Scnd Half | 10 | 4 | 2.44 | 0  | 125.2 | Clutch | 73  | 19  | 3  | 10  | .260 |

### 1995 Rankings (American League)

➡ 1st in wins, shutouts (4) and lowest batting average allowed vs. left-handed batters (.209)

➡ 2nd in games started, complete games (7), innings pitched, highest strikeout/walk ratio (3.2), lowest on-base percentage allowed (.270), lowest groundball/flyball ratio allowed (0.8) and least baserunners allowed per 9 innings (9.7)

➡ 3rd in lowest batting average allowed (.226) and lowest stolen base percentage allowed (40.0%)

➡ Led the Orioles in ERA, wins, losses, games started, complete games (7), shutouts (4), innings pitched and hits allowed

# Jesse Orosco

## 1995 Season

Signed by the Orioles in April, veteran lefthander Jesse Orosco proved he was far from washed up. Orosco appeared in 65 games, his highest total in six years, and provided the O's with a valuable set-up man from the left side. He was tough on both righties and lefties and very reliable when he came in with runners on base. He even notched three saves in September, when the O's, who had soured on Doug Jones, were looking for someone who could come in and finish games.

## Pitching

Orosco uses three pitches: a basic fastball, a slider and a sweeping curve. The velocity on his fastball is still pretty good, and he likes to go inside with it against right-handed hitters; if he has command of the heater, he can be plenty tough. He relies on the wide curve and the slider, still his best pitch, against lefthanders. Opposing hitters batted a lowly .169 against Orosco, but his tendency to walk right-handed hitters prevented him from being the full-time set-up man.

## Defense

Despite his age and less-than-average mobility, Orosco manages to be an average fielder with a decent glove hand on grounders hit back through the box. He gives away a lot to basestealers (seven steals in 10 attempts) because his delivery has slowed and he doesn't keep runners close. The breaking pitches he predictably throws to lefties also give runners a decided edge.

## 1996 Outlook

Orosco was a bargain at $400,000, but his age will work against him as he pursues a new contract. The O's liked his work last year, and if his salary demands are reasonable he could be back. If they won't meet his price, he should have little difficulty finding another job.

**Position:** RP
**Bats:** R  **Throws:** L
**Ht:** 6' 2"  **Wt:** 205

**Opening Day Age:** 38
**Born:** 4/21/57 in Santa Barbara, CA
**ML Seasons:** 16

### Overall Statistics

| | W | L | Pct. | ERA | G | GS | Sv | IP | H | BB | SO | HR | BR/IP |
|---|---|---|---|---|---|---|---|---|---|---|---|---|---|
| 1995 | 2 | 4 | .333 | 3.26 | 65 | 0 | 3 | 49.2 | 28 | 27 | 58 | 4 | 1.11 |
| Career | 71 | 68 | .511 | 2.96 | 819 | 4 | 133 | 1021.0 | 825 | 432 | 920 | 79 | 1.23 |

### How Often He Throws Strikes

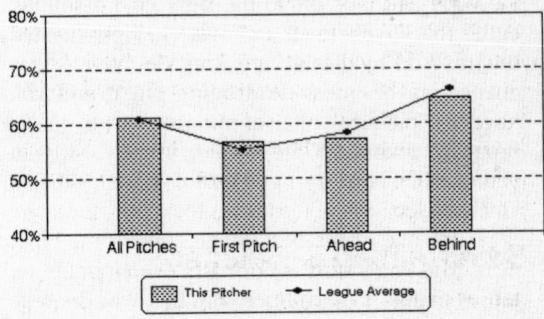

### 1995 Situational Stats

| | W | L | ERA | Sv | IP | | AB | H | HR | RBI | Avg |
|---|---|---|---|---|---|---|---|---|---|---|---|
| Home | 1 | 3 | 3.60 | 3 | 30.0 | LHB | 77 | 11 | 1 | 9 | .143 |
| Road | 1 | 1 | 2.75 | 0 | 19.2 | RHB | 89 | 17 | 3 | 16 | .191 |
| First Half | 1 | 1 | 2.75 | 0 | 19.2 | Sc Pos | 67 | 12 | 0 | 20 | .179 |
| Scnd Half | 1 | 3 | 3.60 | 3 | 30.0 | Clutch | 97 | 15 | 4 | 13 | .155 |

### 1995 Rankings (American League)

- → 1st in games pitched
- → 2nd in lowest batting average allowed in relief (.169)
- → 5th in holds (15) and lowest batting average allowed in relief with runners on base (.165)
- → 6th in most strikeouts per 9 innings in relief (10.5)
- → 7th in least baserunners allowed per 9 innings in relief (10.1)
- → Led the Orioles in games pitched, holds (15), blown saves (3) and lowest batting average allowed in relief with runners on base (.165)

# Rafael Palmeiro

## 1995 Season

Rafael Palmeiro's second season in Baltimore was just as good as his first. Relied upon to provide more power in an O's lineup short on pop, Palmeiro did just that by socking 39 homers, the third-highest total in Oriole history. The Bobby Bonilla trade in late July gave Palmeiro someone with whom to share the slugging load, and he was a terror in the second half of the season, batting .334 with 24 homers after the break.

## Hitting

Possessing the ability to mix power and average, Palmeiro has extraordinary bat speed and control. Much like a pitcher who changes speeds, he increases or decreases his bat speed depending on his read of the pitch. As a result, he strikes out far less often than most home-run hitters. He can turn on the inside heat or go to the opposite field on the back-door stuff with equal savvy. He handles left-handers nearly as well as he handles righties, and he's a patient hitter who draws a fair number of walks.

## Baserunning & Defense

Palmeiro stole 22 bases in 1993, but he's lost some speed and is no longer much of a basestealing threat. Despite his lack of speed, he'll usually make it when he takes off, and his intelligence and awareness of game situations makes him a fine baserunner. As a first baseman, Palmeiro is a reliable if not flashy fielder, and he seldom commits an error.

## 1996 Outlook

A free-agent signee who really paid off, Palmeiro has given the Orioles consistent power and average since the club signed him prior to the 1994 season. His contract still has three years to run, and with Bonilla cemented in the cleanup spot for the whole of 1996, Palmeiro figures to enjoy another banner year.

**Position:** 1B
**Bats:** L **Throws:** L
**Ht:** 6' 0"  **Wt:** 188

**Opening Day Age:** 31
**Born:** 9/24/64 in Havana, Cuba
**ML Seasons:** 10

Baltimore Orioles

### Overall Statistics

| | G | AB | R | H | D | T | HR | RBI | SB | BB | SO | Avg | OBP | Slg |
|---|---|---|---|---|---|---|---|---|---|---|---|---|---|---|
| 1995 | 143 | 554 | 89 | 172 | 30 | 2 | 39 | 104 | 3 | 62 | 65 | .310 | .380 | .583 |
| Career | 1300 | 4857 | 758 | 1455 | 296 | 27 | 194 | 706 | 60 | 494 | 541 | .300 | .365 | .491 |

### Where He Hits the Ball

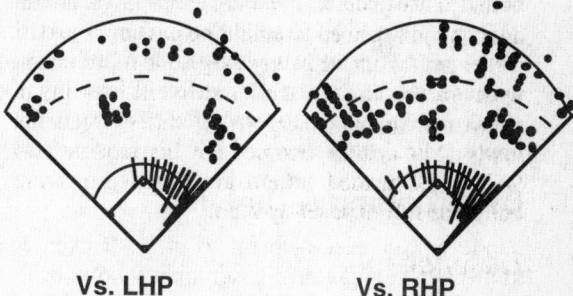

**Vs. LHP**          **Vs. RHP**

### 1995 Situational Stats

| | AB | H | HR | RBI | Avg | | AB | H | HR | RBI | Avg |
|---|---|---|---|---|---|---|---|---|---|---|---|
| Home | 265 | 89 | 21 | 58 | .336 | LHP | 202 | 59 | 14 | 37 | .292 |
| Road | 289 | 83 | 18 | 46 | .287 | RHP | 352 | 113 | 25 | 67 | .321 |
| First Half | 264 | 75 | 15 | 47 | .284 | Sc Pos | 146 | 40 | 10 | 63 | .274 |
| Scnd Half | 290 | 97 | 24 | 57 | .334 | Clutch | 74 | 19 | 5 | 16 | .257 |

### 1995 Rankings (American League)

→ 2nd in total bases (323), lowest batting average with the bases loaded (0.000) and fielding percentage at first base (.997)

→ 3rd in slugging percentage vs. right-handed pitchers (.605)

→ 4th in home runs

→ 5th in slugging percentage and lowest ground-ball/flyball ratio (0.8)

→ 6th in HR frequency (14.2 ABs per HR)

→ 8th in games played and lowest percentage of extra bases taken as a runner (33.3%)

→ Led the Orioles in batting average, home runs, at-bats, hits, singles (101), total bases, RBI and slugging percentage

# Cal Ripken

## 1995 Season

The 1995 season will be remembered as the year in which many fans boycotted baseball. But it also was the season in which Cal Ripken broke Lou Gehrig's consecutive-game streak, in the process bringing a lot of fans back to the game. Statistically speaking, Ripken did not post Gehrig-like numbers. But he continued to be one of the most productive shortstops in baseball, and his contributions go well beyond the numbers.

## Hitting

Ripken hit consistently for much of the year before slumping in August. The slump caused him to significantly close his batting stance. He rebounded shortly after breaking Gehrig's record on September 6, and had a solid September. For most of the year, Ripken was pitched down and away because pitchers seemed fearful of causing a streak-ending injury. He responded by going to the opposite field frequently.

## Baserunning & Defense

While hardly ever a threat to steal, Ripken is known as an aggressive baserunner who will hit the dirt hard to break up the double play. That makes his games-played streak even more amazing. His defense is nearly flawless. He committed just seven errors while maintaining his uncanny ability to position himself where the ball will be hit. A smooth fielder with soft hands and a good arm, he continues to rank with the best in the majors.

## 1996 Outlook

Ripken is 35 years old but remains in great shape thanks to rigorous offseason training sessions. He figures to remain productive in 1996, but he'll be watched carefully for signs of fatigue and deterioration. His power numbers have dropped off the last couple of years and this trend may force his manager to drop him lower in the batting order. Having Lou Gehrig behind him eliminates a burdensome distraction.

**Position:** SS
**Bats:** R **Throws:** R
**Ht:** 6' 4" **Wt:** 220

**Opening Day Age:** 35
**Born:** 8/24/60 in Havre de Grace, MD
**ML Seasons:** 15

### Overall Statistics

| | G | AB | R | H | D | T | HR | RBI | SB | BB | SO | Avg | OBP | Slg |
|---|---|---|---|---|---|---|---|---|---|---|---|---|---|---|
| 1995 | 144 | 550 | 71 | 144 | 33 | 2 | 17 | 88 | 0 | 52 | 59 | .262 | .324 | .422 |
| Career | 2218 | 8577 | 1272 | 2371 | 447 | 42 | 327 | 1267 | 34 | 901 | 955 | .276 | .345 | .453 |

### Where He Hits the Ball

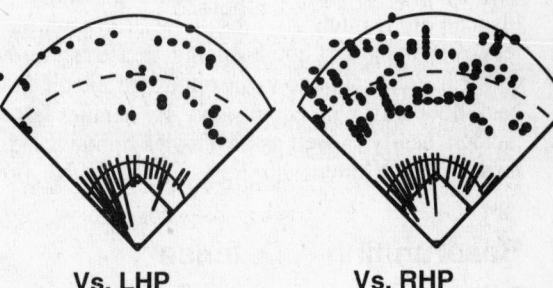

**Vs. LHP**　　　　**Vs. RHP**

### 1995 Situational Stats

| | AB | H | HR | RBI | Avg | | AB | H | HR | RBI | Avg |
|---|---|---|---|---|---|---|---|---|---|---|---|
| Home | 271 | 78 | 10 | 53 | .288 | LHP | 154 | 44 | 7 | 26 | .286 |
| Road | 279 | 66 | 7 | 35 | .237 | RHP | 396 | 100 | 10 | 62 | .253 |
| First Half | 264 | 75 | 7 | 35 | .284 | Sc Pos | 153 | 43 | 5 | 69 | .281 |
| Scnd Half | 286 | 69 | 10 | 53 | .241 | Clutch | 75 | 11 | 1 | 8 | .147 |

### 1995 Rankings (American League)

- → 1st in fielding percentage at shortstop (.989)
- → 3rd in games played and lowest batting average in the clutch (.147)
- → 5th in lowest cleanup slugging percentage (.439)
- → 6th in lowest on-base percentage vs. right-handed pitchers (.311)
- → 7th in batting average on a 3-2 count (.400)
- → 8th in doubles
- → 9th in lowest on-base percentage
- → Led the Orioles in doubles, sacrifice flies (8) and games played

# Manny Alexander

**Position**: 2B
**Bats**: R  **Throws**: R
**Ht**: 5'10"  **Wt**: 150

**Opening Day Age**: 25
**Born**: 3/20/71 in San Pedro de Macoris, DR
**ML Seasons**: 3

## Overall Statistics

|        | G   | AB  | R  | H  | D | T | HR | RBI | SB | BB | SO | Avg  | OBP  | Slg  |
|--------|-----|-----|----|----|---|---|----|-----|----|----|----|------|------|------|
| 1995   | 94  | 242 | 35 | 57 | 9 | 1 | 3  | 23  | 11 | 20 | 30 | .236 | .299 | .318 |
| Career | 101 | 247 | 37 | 58 | 9 | 1 | 3  | 23  | 11 | 20 | 33 | .235 | .297 | .316 |

## 1995 Season

Manny Alexander was supposed to get his first crack at big-league experience in 1994, but he had a tumor removed from his left thigh and spent the year rehabilitating at Triple-A Rochester. Alexander finally got his chance with the Orioles in 1995, but didn't do much with it. He rotated with Bret Barberie and Jeff Huson at second until the latter part of the season, when he was benched due to his struggles in the field.

## Hitting, Baserunning & Defense

Alexander got off to a good start with the bat last year, but he faded badly in the second half. He had particular problems with righties, who were able to overpower him. He did, however, show good speed and could be a basestealing threat if he could get on base often enough. His work at second base needs improvement since most of his minor league work has been as a shortstop. He's considered a good fielder and was rated as having the best infield arm in the International League, so the tools are obviously there.

## 1996 Outlook

The Orioles' situation at second base remains unsettled. Since Alexander is young, promising and untested, he will be given a good look this spring. But he'll have to both hit and field a lot better than he did in 1995.

# Kevin Bass

**Position**: RF/LF/DH
**Bats**: B  **Throws**: R
**Ht**: 6' 0"  **Wt**: 190

**Opening Day Age**: 36
**Born**: 5/12/59 in Redwood City, CA
**ML Seasons**: 14

## Overall Statistics

|        | G    | AB   | R   | H    | D   | T  | HR | RBI | SB  | BB  | SO  | Avg  | OBP  | Slg  |
|--------|------|------|-----|------|-----|----|----|-----|-----|-----|-----|------|------|------|
| 1995   | 111  | 295  | 32  | 72   | 12  | 0  | 5  | 32  | 8   | 24  | 47  | .244 | .303 | .336 |
| Career | 1571 | 4839 | 609 | 1308 | 248 | 40 | 118| 611 | 151 | 357 | 668 | .270 | .323 | .411 |

## 1995 Season

Kevin Bass was acquired by the Orioles to provide depth in the outfield and batting punch off the bench. Due to the injury to Jeffrey Hammonds, Bass was pressed into full-time service during the early part of the season. Bass performed well at the outset but then gave way to fatigue. He hit below .200 for July and August, and hardly played in September.

## Hitting, Baserunning & Defense

Bass is a switch-hitter once capable of hitting 15-20 homers a year in his prime, but these days his power is pretty limited. He tends to hit the ball on the ground and is most effective in the number-two position in the order, despite questionable bunting skills. Bass is somewhat slower on the basepaths these days, but he will still attempt to steal surprisingly often. He is a decent fielder with a pretty good arm.

## 1996 Outlook

Due to the lack of depth in the Oriole outfield and the anticipated move of Bobby Bonilla to third base, it is reasonable to assume that the O's will want to keep a smart veteran like Bass around for another year as a backup outfielder. But his numbers faded badly last year, and he'll have to show he can still hit.

# Armando Benitez

**Position:** RP
**Bats:** R **Throws:** R
**Ht:** 6' 4" **Wt:** 220

**Opening Day Age:** 23
**Born:** 11/3/72 in
Ramon Santana, DR
**ML Seasons:** 2

### Overall Statistics

| | W | L | Pct. | ERA | G | GS | Sv | IP | H | BB | SO | HR | BR/IP |
|---|---|---|---|---|---|---|---|---|---|---|---|---|---|
| 1995 | 1 | 5 | .167 | 5.66 | 44 | 0 | 2 | 47.2 | 37 | 37 | 56 | 8 | 1.55 |
| Career | 1 | 5 | .167 | 4.84 | 47 | 0 | 2 | 57.2 | 45 | 41 | 70 | 8 | 1.49 |

## 1995 Season

Expected to play a featured role in the Oriole bullpen, Armando Benitez suffered through a trying 1995 season. Benitez struggled with his control, pitched poorly and wound up bouncing back and forth between the big leagues and the minors. His performance was a far cry from the promise he'd shown during a brief but impressive debut with the Orioles in 1994.

## Pitching & Defense

Benitez is a power pitcher whose fastball travels nearly 95 MPH. He was extremely tough to hit when he was throwing strikes last year, and he performed pretty well in pressure situations. However, he often had trouble with his control, and he also needs to refine a pitch that will complement the heater. In 1995 he continually threw his slider too high in the strike zone, leaving him with the fastball as his only weapon. Benitez is an average fielder, but he has a long way to go in learning how to keep runners close.

## 1996 Outlook

The hard-throwing Benitez may have been rushed into a major league set-up role too soon, but he's still a bright prospect. He has the makings of a big league closer if the Orioles show patience, let him work on his control and help him develop a pitch to accompany that fantastic fastball.

# Terry Clark

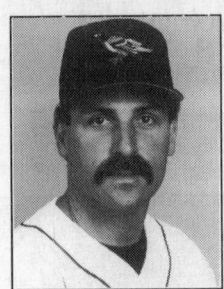

**Position:** RP
**Bats:** R **Throws:** R
**Ht:** 6' 2" **Wt:** 196

**Opening Day Age:** 35
**Born:** 10/10/60 in Los
Angeles, CA
**ML Seasons:** 4

### Overall Statistics

| | W | L | Pct. | ERA | G | GS | Sv | IP | H | BB | SO | HR | BR/IP |
|---|---|---|---|---|---|---|---|---|---|---|---|---|---|
| 1995 | 2 | 5 | .286 | 3.59 | 41 | 0 | 1 | 42.2 | 43 | 20 | 20 | 3 | 1.48 |
| Career | 8 | 13 | .381 | 4.87 | 61 | 18 | 1 | 151.2 | 185 | 57 | 68 | 11 | 1.60 |

## 1995 Season

The Orioles signed well-traveled reliever Terry Clark as a free agent last May, shortly after Clark was released by the Atlanta Braves. Not much was expected, but he proved to be a pleasant surprise, providing middle-relief help before moving into a set-up role he shared with Jesse Orosco. Clark's work prior to the All-Star break was excellent, but he ran into problems in the second half.

## Pitching & Defense

Clark tries to keep the ball down, using a combination of fastballs and sliders to keep hitters off-balance. He's not a power pitcher, however, and he lacks an effective weapon to use against left-handed hitters. He also tends to have problems when he gets behind in the count and has to come down the middle with his fastball. He is fairly adept at keeping runners close and is an average fielder.

## 1996 Outlook

After several years lingering in the minors, Clark finally got his chance to pitch regularly. He was impressive at the outset but his performance dropped off sharply, causing speculation as to whether he can remain effective in 1996. At his age (35), he's always just a few bad outings away from his release or another trip back to the minors.

# Rick Krivda

**Position:** SP
**Bats:** R **Throws:** L
**Ht:** 6' 1"  **Wt:** 180

**Opening Day Age:** 26
**Born:** 1/19/70 in
McKeesport, PA
**ML Seasons:** 1

## Overall Statistics

|        | W | L | Pct. | ERA  | G  | GS | Sv | IP   | H  | BB | SO | HR | BR/IP |
|--------|---|---|------|------|----|----|----|------|----|----|----|----|-------|
| 1995   | 2 | 7 | .222 | 4.54 | 13 | 13 | 0  | 75.1 | 76 | 25 | 53 | 9  | 1.34  |
| Career | 2 | 7 | .222 | 4.54 | 13 | 13 | 0  | 75.1 | 76 | 25 | 53 | 9  | 1.34  |

## 1995 Season

Lefthander Rick Krivda spent most of the 1995 season with Triple-A Rochester, where he was 6-5 with a 3.19 ERA. Krivda was called up on July 7 for a spot start against the Chicago White Sox, looked good, got sent down again, and then returned for good in late July. Despite his 2-7 record, Krivda showed good poise in nearly all of his 13 starts for the Orioles. Two poor outings ballooned his ERA.

## Pitching & Defense

Krivda is a southpaw with a sneaky fastball in the 85-MPH range, a three-finger change-up and a superb curveball. He works two or three innings before establishing the curve, which often leads to high pitch counts and tight jams in the early going. He needs to locate his fastball lower in the strike zone, and use it less often when behind in the count. Krivda is a good fielder. He employs two moves to first, but runners took off fairly frequently against him last year.

## 1996 Outlook

Either Jamie Moyer or Krivda figures to hold down a lefty spot in the rotation this year. Since Moyer was moved to the bullpen late last year, it might be reasonable to assume that Krivda has an edge going into spring training. He appears capable of being a decent fourth or fifth starter.

# Arthur Rhodes

**Position:** RP/SP
**Bats:** L **Throws:** L
**Ht:** 6' 2"  **Wt:** 206

**Opening Day Age:** 26
**Born:** 10/24/69 in
Waco, TX
**ML Seasons:** 5

## Overall Statistics

|        | W  | L  | Pct. | ERA  | G  | GS | Sv | IP    | H   | BB  | SO  | HR | BR/IP |
|--------|----|----|------|------|----|----|----|-------|-----|-----|-----|----|-------|
| 1995   | 2  | 5  | .286 | 6.21 | 19 | 9  | 0  | 75.1  | 68  | 48  | 77  | 13 | 1.54  |
| Career | 17 | 24 | .415 | 5.70 | 69 | 59 | 0  | 344.0 | 344 | 188 | 273 | 47 | 1.55  |

## 1995 Season

Arthur Rhodes' major league career continued according to form in 1995. Rhodes couldn't get the ball over the plate early in the year, resulting in a demotion to the minor leagues. He was recalled in late June but continued to be wild, then ended up on the disabled list with a strained left shoulder. It was yet another difficult season for Rhodes, who was expected to be a dominant pitcher by now.

## Pitching & Defense

A left-handed fireballer, Rhodes can throw a mid-90s fastball. Unfortunately, his velocity is counter-balanced by his lack of control. He will try to mix his heat with a curve, slider and change, but he has little mastery over those pitches, either. Rhodes has became easy to run on, as well, which often happens to pitchers with control problems. He is an average fielder.

## 1996 Outlook

Rhodes had a modest contract last year, but he is now facing sterner competition from a good rookie crop of starting pitchers. So his chances of rejoining the Oriole rotation look slim. At best, he will be used as a middle reliever—if he is able to lick his control problems. At 26, Rhodes' potential is no longer much of a plus. He must deliver now.

# Mark Smith

**Position:** RF/LF
**Bats:** R  **Throws:** R
**Ht:** 6' 3"  **Wt:** 205

**Opening Day Age:** 25
**Born:** 5/7/70 in
Pasadena, CA
**ML Seasons:** 2

## Overall Statistics

|  | G | AB | R | H | D | T | HR | RBI | SB | BB | SO | Avg | OBP | Slg |
|---|---|---|---|---|---|---|---|---|---|---|---|---|---|---|
| 1995 | 37 | 104 | 11 | 24 | 5 | 0 | 3 | 15 | 3 | 12 | 22 | .231 | .314 | .365 |
| Career | 40 | 111 | 11 | 25 | 5 | 0 | 3 | 17 | 3 | 12 | 24 | .225 | .304 | .351 |

## 1995 Season

Mark Smith, a first-round draft pick in 1991, has spent most of his professional career at Triple-A Rochester. Twice in 1995, however, he was recalled to get some playing time in right field. Smith was named to the International League postseason All-Star team, and showed flashes of power with the O's in a 37-game trial.

## Hitting, Baserunning & Defense

Smith has quick hands and generates excellent bat speed, which enables him to pull the outside heater and hit for power. His ability to hit the change is a different story, and he intends to work on hitting offspeed stuff while playing winter ball in Venezuela. He also needs to work on hitting righthanders, who gave him fits last year. And he must gain better baserunning savvy, particularly learning to read different pitchers' moves to first. Defensively, Smith has a decent arm and is reasonably sure-handed.

## 1996 Outlook

Smith will probably battle a veteran such as Kevin Bass for a backup role this spring, and since he's young and not making much money, his chances appear pretty good. His chances of being more than a part-time player with the O's depend upon his learning to make better contact at the plate. If he can do that, his average should rise and his playing time will increase.

# Greg Zaun

**Position:** C
**Bats:** B  **Throws:** R
**Ht:** 5'10"  **Wt:** 170

**Opening Day Age:** 24
**Born:** 4/14/71 in
Glendale, CA
**ML Seasons:** 1

## Overall Statistics

|  | G | AB | R | H | D | T | HR | RBI | SB | BB | SO | Avg | OBP | Slg |
|---|---|---|---|---|---|---|---|---|---|---|---|---|---|---|
| 1995 | 40 | 104 | 18 | 27 | 5 | 0 | 3 | 14 | 1 | 16 | 14 | .260 | .358 | .394 |
| Career | 40 | 104 | 18 | 27 | 5 | 0 | 3 | 14 | 1 | 16 | 14 | .260 | .358 | .394 |

## 1995 Season

Greg Zaun, the nephew of former Orioles catcher Rick Dempsey, was recalled from Triple-A Rochester in mid-June to back up Chris Hoiles. When Hoiles went on the disabled list in July, Zaun saw regular action behind the plate. He had a fine month, hitting .288 with three homers and 10 RBI. His playing time diminished once Hoiles returned, but Zaun made an impressive debut.

## Hitting, Baserunning & Defense

Zaun is a good fastball hitter with fair power. A switch-hitter, he has excellent discipline at the plate. He was susceptible last year to being fooled on the inside part of the plate, but experience should help cure that problem. As with most catchers, Zaun does not display much speed and poses little threat on the basepaths. His defensive abilities appear quite good. While not having a cannon arm, he did a fine job of controlling the running game.

## 1996 Outlook

The Orioles appear to have a good young catcher in Zaun. He will probably be brought along slowly behind Hoiles for the next few years, and since Hoiles is signed long-term, Zaun will have to battle for playing time. In the meantime, he should be very helpful in a backup role.

# Other Baltimore Orioles

**Jarvis Brown (Pos: CF, Age: 28, Bats: R)**

The Orioles were Brown's fourth team in four seasons, and he'll probably be looking for a fifth next year. He's just a .203 career hitter, and he'll be lucky to get another shot. 1996 Outlook: D

**Jim Dedrick (Pos: RHP, Age: 27)**

Dedrick has consistently pitched well in the Oriole system since being drafted in 1990. Despite that, he appeared in just six games in '95. He's at the age where he needs to start making things happen. 1996 Outlook: C

**John DeSilva (Pos: SP, Age: 28, Throws: R)**

DeSilva was traded from the Dodgers prior to last season after pitching very poorly in their minor league system. He continued that in 1995, spending most of the season at Triple-A Rochester with mediocre results. 1996 Outlook: D

**John Dettmer (Pos: RHP, Age: 26)**

Dettmer was acquired in May and pitched very poorly for Rochester in 1995. The organization might want to consider letting him start again. He was outstanding as a starting pitcher early on. 1996 Outlook: C

**Cesar Devarez (Pos: C, Age: 26, Bats: R)**

Devarez has very little hope for a major league career. He's a catcher, so maybe he'll turn out to be a defensive whiz. Offensively, he's been very poor in the minors, with no walks or power. 1996 Outlook: D

**Leo Gomez (Pos: 3B, Age: 29, Bats: R)**

Gomez shared time with Jeff Huson and Jeff Manto at third base before an ankle injury in late July sidelined him for the season. His batting average slipped, but he should remain a solid platoon player. 1996 Outlook: A

**Gene Harris (Pos: RHP, Age: 31)**

Harris pitched poorly for the Phillies and Orioles last season. But he's pitched poorly most of his major league career and still finds a team each spring. He'll likely find a way to do it again. 1996 Outlook: C

**Mike Hartley (Pos: RHP, Age: 34)**

Hartley didn't pitch terribly for Rochester in '95, but at his age, he's not likely to get another extended chance in the majors. 1996 Outlook: D

**Jeff Huson (Pos: 3B/2B, Age: 31, Bats: L)**

Huson appeared in 66 games for the Orioles in 1995. His role has pretty much been reduced to that of a utility infielder, but he'll likely find a spot to do the same thing next season. 1996 Outlook: C

**Mark Lee (Pos: LHP, Age: 31)**

1995 might have been Lee's final chance, as he pitched poorly for the Orioles in 39 games. Since showing some promise with Milwaukee, he's been plagued by control problems. 1996 Outlook: D

**Alan Mills (Pos: RHP, Age: 29)**

Mills bottomed out in 1995, posting a 7.43 ERA and continuing the slide from his sparkling 1992 season. His control continues to be very poor, and at his age, his opportunity might have passed. 1996 Outlook: C

**Sherman Obando (Pos: RF, Age: 26, Bats: R)**

After two fine Triple-A seasons, Obando's future looks bright, probably as a DH as opposed to the outfield, where he is not regarded with awe. Should finally get a real chance to play this year. 1996 Outlook: B

**Mike Oquist (Pos: RHP, Age: 27)**

The Orioles stuck with Oquist in 1995, despite continuing control problems that he is yet to shake. He's still young enough to develop and will probably continue to draw occasional long-relief assignments. 1996 Outlook: B

# Baltimore Orioles Minor League Prospects

## Organization Overview:

There was a time in the late 1980s to early '90s when Baltimore's farm system ranked near the bottom of the barrel in baseball. With the move into the cash cow of Camden Yards and the sale of the club to deep-pocketed Peter Angelos, the Orioles have since invested more money into player development. In 1995, Baltimore received significant contributions from rookies Curtis Goodwin, Manny Alexander, Greg Zaun and Armando Benitez. More young talent could make their presence felt in 1996, especially from among a group of live-armed right-handed pitchers, which appears to be the system's strength. The system seems thin in position players, especially middle infielders. But with Angelos offering little reluctance to fill in gaps by taking advantage of the free agent market, those deficiencies should hardly be debilitating.

## Joe Borowski

**Position:** P     **Opening Day Age:** 24
**Bats:** R **Throws:** R     **Born:** 5/4/71 in
**Ht:** 6' 2" **Wt:** 225     Bayonne, NJ

*Recent Statistics*

|                  | W | L | ERA | G | GS | Sv | IP | H | R | BB | SO | HR |
|------------------|---|---|-----|---|----|----|------|----|----|----|----|----|
| 95 AA Bowie      | 2 | 2 | 3.92 | 16 | 0 | 7 | 20.2 | 16 | 9 | 7 | 32 | 2 |
| 95 AAA Rochester | 1 | 3 | 4.04 | 28 | 0 | 6 | 35.2 | 32 | 16 | 18 | 32 | 3 |
| 95 AL Baltimore  | 0 | 0 | 1.23 | 6 | 0 | 0 | 7.1 | 5 | 1 | 4 | 3 | 0 |

During five seasons in the Baltimore system Borowski has done nothing to make the Orioles regret trading Pete Rose, Jr. in 1991 to obtain him. Despite a 1.91 ERA in 1994, Borowski was still overshadowed by the talents of Armando Benitez. In 1995, Borowski improved his already impressive strikeout rate to 11.2 per nine innings. He also continued to demonstrate an ability to close games, saving 13 between Double- and Triple-A. With a fastball that doesn't leave the mid-80s, Borowski can best be described as sneaky fast. He could at the very least be a capable set-up man in the Baltimore bullpen in the near future.

## Rocky Coppinger

**Position:** P     **Opening Day Age:** 22
**Bats:** R **Throws:** R     **Born:** 3/19/74 in El
**Ht:** 6' 5" **Wt:** 245     Paso, TX

*Recent Statistics*

|                  | W | L | ERA | G | GS | Sv | IP | H | R | BB | SO | HR |
|------------------|---|---|-----|---|----|----|------|----|----|----|----|----|
| 94 R Bluefield   | 4 | 3 | 2.45 | 14 | 13 | 0 | 73.1 | 51 | 24 | 40 | 88 | 5 |
| 95 A Frederick   | 7 | 1 | 1.57 | 11 | 11 | 0 | 68.2 | 46 | 16 | 24 | 91 | 3 |
| 95 AA Bowie      | 6 | 2 | 2.69 | 13 | 13 | 0 | 83.2 | 58 | 33 | 43 | 62 | 7 |
| 95 AAA Rochester | 3 | 0 | 1.04 | 5 | 5 | 0 | 34.2 | 23 | 5 | 17 | 19 | 2 |

Coppinger has wasted little time catching the attention of the Orioles, ascending all the way from short-season A-ball to Triple-A Rochester in a little over one season.

He has dominated at every level, limiting opponents to a .198 average in 1994 and only 127 hits in 187 innings pitched in 1995. Although he's just two seasons removed from junior college, Coppinger is already king-sized, at 6'5" and close to 250 pounds. He has the fastball to match his frame, and it's helped him maintain a strikeout pace of almost one per inning. If his slider improves, Coppinger could soon make the jump to the majors.

## Tommy Davis

**Position:** 3B     **Opening Day Age:** 22
**Bats:** R **Throws:** R     **Born:** 5/21/73 in
**Ht:** 6' 1" **Wt:** 195     Mobile, AL

*Recent Statistics*

|                | G | AB | R | H | D | T | HR | RBI | SB | BB | SO | AVG |
|----------------|----|-----|----|-----|----|---|----|-----|----|----|-----|------|
| 94 A Albany    | 61 | 216 | 35 | 59 | 10 | 1 | 5 | 35 | 2 | 18 | 52 | .273 |
| 95 A Frederick | 130 | 496 | 62 | 133 | 26 | 3 | 15 | 57 | 7 | 41 | 105 | .268 |
| 95 AA Bowie    | 9 | 32 | 5 | 10 | 3 | 0 | 3 | 10 | 0 | 1 | 9 | .313 |

Davis was the Orioles first selection in the 1994 draft, when he was considered one of the best power hitters available. He played first base in college, but began his pro career at third base. Defensive deficiencies may eventually force a move back across the diamond, but Davis should pack enough wallop for either position. He possesses impressive bat speed and demonstrated extra-base power in his first full pro season.

## Jimmy Haynes

**Position:** P     **Opening Day Age:** 23
**Bats:** R **Throws:** R     **Born:** 9/5/72 in
**Ht:** 6' 4" **Wt:** 175     Lagrange, GA

*Recent Statistics*

|                  | W | L | ERA | G | GS | Sv | IP | H | R | BB | SO | HR |
|------------------|----|---|-----|----|----|----|-------|-----|----|----|-----|----|
| 95 AAA Rochester | 12 | 8 | 3.29 | 26 | 25 | 0 | 167.0 | 162 | 77 | 49 | 140 | 16 |
| 95 AL Baltimore  | 2 | 1 | 2.25 | 4 | 3 | 0 | 24.0 | 11 | 6 | 12 | 22 | 2 |

Haynes' record suggests he has the stuff to be a staff ace. He has enjoyed nothing but success at every minor league stop, and he was far from awed in his first exposure to the majors. In his 24-inning audition with the Orioles, he struck out twice as many as he allowed hits. Haynes' fastball should only get better as he fills out, and he can already throw his curveball for strikes at two speeds. Perhaps most impressively, Haynes achieves his high strikeout totals with little cost to his excellent control. There doesn't appear to be any reason why Haynes isn't ready to contribute at the major league level in 1996.

## Calvin Maduro

**Position:** P     **Opening Day Age:** 21
**Bats:** R **Throws:** R     **Born:** 9/5/74 in
**Ht:** 6' 0" **Wt:** 175     Oranjestad, Aruba

*Recent Statistics*

| | W | L | ERA | G | GS | Sv | IP | H | R | BB | SO | HR |
|---|---|---|---|---|---|---|---|---|---|---|---|---|
| 93 R Bluefield | 9 | 4 | 3.96 | 14 | 14 | 0 | 91.0 | 90 | 46 | 17 | 83 | 4 |
| 94 A Frederick | 9 | 8 | 4.25 | 27 | 26 | 0 | 152.1 | 132 | 86 | 59 | 137 | 18 |
| 95 A Frederick | 8 | 5 | 2.94 | 20 | 20 | 0 | 122.1 | 109 | 43 | 34 | 120 | 16 |
| 95 AA Bowie | 0 | 6 | 5.09 | 7 | 7 | 0 | 35.1 | 39 | 28 | 27 | 26 | 3 |

Maduro was signed in 1991 at the age of 16 from Aruba. He was one of the youngest pitchers in the Carolina League in 1994, and continued to have success there in 1995 before his promotion to the Eastern League. Maduro struggled in his first taste of Double-A, fighting his control for the first time. He is obviously advanced for his age, possessing three quality pitches, fine mechanics and mental poise. He should get better as he matures physically.

## Billy Percibal

**Position:** P     **Opening Day Age:** 22
**Bats:** R **Throws:** R     **Born:** 2/2/74 in San
**Ht:** 6' 1" **Wt:** 160     Pedro De Macoris, DR

*Recent Statistics*

| | W | L | ERA | G | GS | Sv | IP | H | R | BB | SO | HR |
|---|---|---|---|---|---|---|---|---|---|---|---|---|
| 93 R Bluefield | 6 | 0 | 3.81 | 13 | 13 | 0 | 82.2 | 71 | 48 | 33 | 81 | 7 |
| 94 A Albany | 13 | 9 | 3.56 | 28 | 28 | 0 | 169.1 | 160 | 80 | 90 | 132 | 9 |
| 95 A High Desert | 7 | 6 | 3.23 | 21 | 20 | 0 | 128.0 | 123 | 63 | 55 | 105 | 10 |
| 95 AA Bowie | 1 | 0 | 0.00 | 2 | 2 | 0 | 14.0 | 7 | 0 | 7 | 7 | 0 |

Percibal was signed as an undrafted free agent in 1991 and began his professional career as a reliever. With command of three solid pitches, Percibal eventually became a starter, and his ERA has fallen each successive season. High Desert's Maverick Stadium is not an easy park to pitch in, as witnessed by the Mavericks' league-worst 5.78 ERA in 1995. Percibal overcame the difficult conditions to rank sixth in the California League with a 3.23 ERA. Despite being slenderly built at 160 pounds, he also ranked high in strikeouts before his promotion to Double-A.

## Brian Sackinsky

**Position:** P     **Opening Day Age:** 24
**Bats:** R **Throws:** R     **Born:** 6/22/71 in
**Ht:** 6' 4" **Wt:** 220     Pittsburgh, PA

*Recent Statistics*

| | W | L | ERA | G | GS | Sv | IP | H | R | BB | SO | HR |
|---|---|---|---|---|---|---|---|---|---|---|---|---|
| 93 A Albany | 3 | 4 | 3.20 | 9 | 8 | 0 | 50.2 | 50 | 29 | 16 | 41 | 2 |
| 93 A Frederick | 6 | 8 | 3.20 | 18 | 18 | 0 | 121.0 | 117 | 55 | 37 | 112 | 13 |
| 94 AA Bowie | 11 | 7 | 3.36 | 28 | 26 | 0 | 177.0 | 165 | 73 | 39 | 145 | 24 |
| 95 AAA Rochester | 3 | 3 | 4.60 | 14 | 11 | 0 | 62.2 | 70 | 33 | 10 | 42 | 6 |

The Orioles have had an affinity for Stanford University products in recent years, drafting Mike Mussina and Jeffrey Hammonds with first-round picks. Sackinsky, another ex-Cardinal, was taken with the Orioles' second choice in 1992. Sackinsky has always demonstrated fine control, walking fewer than two men per nine innings each of the past two seasons. Although Sackinsky possesses a good slider to complement his high-80s fastball, he's hardly overpowering, as evidenced by his 24 homers allowed in 1994. He may also not have the stamina to endure his starter's workload of 177 innings that season.

## B.J. Waszgis

**Position:** C     **Opening Day Age:** 25
**Bats:** R **Throws:** R     **Born:** 8/24/70 in
**Ht:** 6' 2" **Wt:** 210     Omaha, NE

*Recent Statistics*

| | G | AB | R | H | D | T | HR | RBI | SB | BB | SO | AVG |
|---|---|---|---|---|---|---|---|---|---|---|---|---|
| 93 A Frederick | 31 | 109 | 12 | 27 | 4 | 0 | 3 | 9 | 1 | 9 | 30 | .248 |
| 93 A Albany | 86 | 300 | 45 | 92 | 25 | 3 | 8 | 52 | 4 | 27 | 55 | .307 |
| 94 A Frederick | 122 | 426 | 76 | 120 | 16 | 3 | 21 | 100 | 6 | 65 | 94 | .282 |
| 95 AA Bowie | 130 | 438 | 53 | 111 | 22 | 0 | 10 | 50 | 2 | 70 | 91 | .253 |
| 95 MLE | 130 | 425 | 43 | 98 | 19 | 0 | 9 | 40 | 1 | 48 | 97 | .231 |

Waszgis failed to match his eye-popping numbers of 1994, when he led the Carolina League with 100 RBI. However, he continued to show two valuable offensive skillsk: plate discipline and extra-base pop. Add to that his ability to catch, and you can see why he could have value. Waszgis was the Orioles' 10th-round pick in 1991 out of McNeese State. He's made slow progress through their farm system, due in part to defensive deficiencies. He's now 25, older than Greg Zaun, and with Chris Hoiles looking to rebound, Waszgis faces a challenge to be more than a future big-league backup.

## Others to Watch

Outfielder **Harry Berrios'** exceptional 1994 season (.342, 106 RBI, 56 SB) looked like a fluke when he was hitting under .200 last June. A .316 average over the final month of 1995 helped restore his prospect status. . . First baseman **Kevin Curtis** enjoyed a breakthrough season in '95, connecting for 21 homers. He may have been helped, however, by High Desert's hitter-friendly ballpark. . . Third baseman **Scott McClain** also launched 21 homer between Double- and Triple-A. The 23-year-old was originally drafted as a pitcher back in 1990. . . First baseman **Billy Owens** slugged 27 doubles and 17 homers in 1995, but he was a Double-A repeater and will soon be 25. . . Righthander **Garrett Stephenson** was Baltimore's 18th-round selection in 1992. He's always posted strong strikeout-to-walk ratios, and will likely pitch at AAA Rochester in 1996. . . Infielder **Brad Tyler's** 17 homers and 71 walks were impressive totals in 361 at-bats. On the negative side, he hit just .258 in his second Triple-A campaign, and will turn 27 before the '96 season begins. . . Outfielder **Danny Clyburn** has been traded from the Pirates to the Reds to the Orioles since the end of '94, but he's also socked 22 and 23 homers the last two years. He'll be just 22 when the '96 season begins.

# Rick Aguilera

## 1995 Season

On the morning of July 6, the Red Sox had blown nearly half their save opportunities. That night, they completed a trade for Twins closer Rick Aguilera. Though the deal cost the Sox two prime prospects in Frankie Rodriguez and J.J. Johnson, it was worth it to Boston. Aguilera stabilized their staff and had 20 saves in 21 chances while taking them to first place before giving up a game-blowing homer to Albert Belle in the first game of the playoffs.

## Pitching

The 34-year-old Aguilera is a fairly basic pitcher. He has a decent fastball, a good slider, outstanding pitching instincts and, most of all, he has the one unhittable pitch—in his case, his forkball. When Aguilera gets ahead in counts, hitters know that he's going to throw the splitter and that chances are better than 50-50 that it will dart and zap out of the strike zone, and they still can't lay off it. He still had 52 strikeouts in 55.1 innings, and hitters know they'll get strikes; he walked only 13. Aguilera was third in the league in saves, and over the last five seasons has been a model of consistency, averaging 34 saves per season.

## Defense

A fine athlete, Aguilera is very sound defensively, but he is ridiculously easy to run on. Last year opposing basestealers were 16-for-16 against him, and they're a perfect 35-for-35 over the last five years.

## 1996 Outlook

Like most closers who are not dominant one-pitch specialists, there is the concern that as Aguilera gets into his mid-30s, he may start to lose it. Kevin Kennedy has often been impatient with his bullpen, and Aguilera was bothered by some shoulder problems that caused him to miss a week. He's a free agent and the Red Sox would love to re-sign him, but only at a reasonable price.

**Position:** RP
**Bats:** R  **Throws:** R
**Ht:** 6' 5"  **Wt:** 203

**Opening Day Age:** 34
**Born:** 12/31/61 in San Gabriel, CA
**ML Seasons:** 11
**Pronunciation:** ag-yuh-LAIR-uh

### Overall Statistics

|        | W  | L  | Pct. | ERA  | G   | GS | Sv  | IP    | H   | BB  | SO  | HR | BR/IP |
|--------|----|----|------|------|-----|----|-----|-------|-----|-----|-----|----|-------|
| 1995   | 3  | 3  | .500 | 2.60 | 52  | 0  | 32  | 55.1  | 46  | 13  | 52  | 6  | 1.07  |
| Career | 59 | 56 | .513 | 3.25 | 469 | 70 | 211 | 922.0 | 868 | 257 | 739 | 82 | 1.22  |

### How Often He Throws Strikes

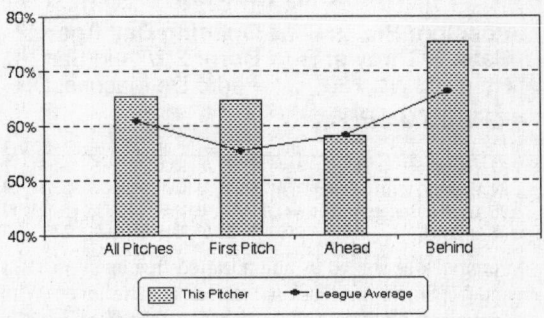

### 1995 Situational Stats

|            | W | L | ERA  | Sv |  IP  |        | AB  | H  | HR | RBI | Avg  |
|------------|---|---|------|----|------|--------|-----|----|----|-----|------|
| Home       | 2 | 2 | 1.30 | 14 | 27.2 | LHB    | 117 | 24 | 2  | 13  | .205 |
| Road       | 1 | 1 | 3.90 | 18 | 27.2 | RHB    | 87  | 22 | 4  | 8   | .253 |
| First Half | 1 | 1 | 2.42 | 13 | 26.0 | Sc Pos | 52  | 10 | 2  | 17  | .192 |
| Scnd Half  | 2 | 2 | 2.76 | 19 | 29.1 | Clutch | 127 | 25 | 2  | 17  | .197 |

### 1995 Rankings (American League)

- 3rd in saves
- 4th in games finished (51) and save percentage (88.9%)
- 5th in least baserunners allowed per 9 innings in relief (9.8)
- 6th in first batter efficiency (.163) and relief ERA (2.60)
- 7th in save opportunities (36) and lowest batting average allowed in relief with runners on base (.179)
- Led the Red Sox in saves (20), games finished (30), save opportunities (21), save percentage (95.2%) and lowest batting average allowed in relief with runners on base (.167)

# Luis Alicea

## 1995 Season

Picked up from the Cardinals during the strike for two minor leaguers, Luis Alicea became the Red Sox' everyday second baseman last year. It was Alicea's first full-time opportunity, and not only did he play a career-high 132 games at the position, but he had his best major league season.

## Hitting

Alicea is a fastball hitter who got thrown a lot of early breaking balls by American League veterans. He likes the fastball up, and can be dangerous when he can look for a pitch in his zone. California kept making those mistakes on him, and he hit a couple of huge home runs off the Angel staff. A switch-hitter, he's much better from the right side. He's a patient hitter and draws a good number of walks.

## Baserunning & Defense

Alicea set a career high with 13 steals, but since he was also caught 10 times, he is hardly a premier speed guy. What surprised many observers was how well he played defense. In St. Louis he was erratic and sometime prone to lapses of concentration, but with the Red Sox Alicea settled down after a shaky first two months. In the second half of the season, most of Alicea's errors came on meaningless plays. He doesn't have great range, but he catches what he gets to, hustles and can turn the double play. He made some tough DPs when the Red Sox were fighting for the A.L. East title in late August.

## 1996 Outlook

Even though he had worked hard at his Florida home during the spring training strike, it took Alicea awhile to get going, but from May 23 on he batted .289. The Red Sox were pleased with his performance, and while they were expected to pursue a big-name free-agent second baseman over the winter, they wouldn't feel uncomfortable having Alicea back at second again this year.

**Position:** 2B
**Bats:** B **Throws:** R
**Ht:** 5' 9"  **Wt:** 177

**Opening Day Age:** 30
**Born:** 7/29/65 in Santurce, PR
**ML Seasons:** 6
**Pronunciation:** ah-luh-SAY-uh

Boston
Red Sox

### Overall Statistics

|        | G   | AB   | R   | H   | D  | T  | HR | RBI | SB | BB  | SO  | Avg  | OBP  | Slg  |
|--------|-----|------|-----|-----|----|----|----|-----|----|-----|-----|------|------|------|
| 1995   | 132 | 419  | 64  | 113 | 20 | 3  | 6  | 44  | 13 | 63  | 61  | .270 | .367 | .375 |
| Career | 569 | 1616 | 197 | 412 | 73 | 26 | 17 | 175 | 31 | 200 | 244 | .255 | .340 | .364 |

### Where He Hits the Ball

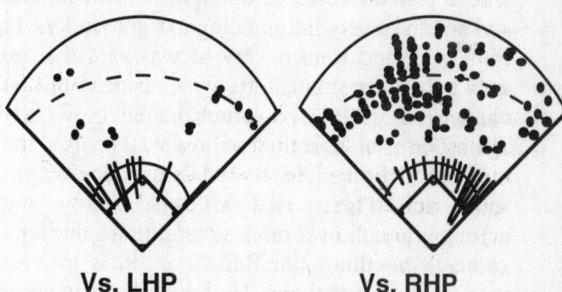

**Vs. LHP**          **Vs. RHP**

### 1995 Situational Stats

|            | AB  | H  | HR | RBI | Avg  |        | AB  | H  | HR | RBI | Avg  |
|------------|-----|----|----|-----|------|--------|-----|----|----|-----|------|
| Home       | 208 | 53 | 0  | 17  | .255 | LHP    | 99  | 29 | 2  | 12  | .293 |
| Road       | 211 | 60 | 6  | 27  | .284 | RHP    | 320 | 84 | 4  | 32  | .263 |
| First Half | 200 | 48 | 2  | 17  | .240 | Sc Pos | 110 | 27 | 1  | 37  | .245 |
| Scnd Half  | 219 | 65 | 4  | 27  | .297 | Clutch | 68  | 13 | 0  | 3   | .191 |

### 1995 Rankings (American League)

- ➡ 2nd in sacrifice bunts (13) and lowest stolen base percentage (56.5%)
- ➡ 3rd in errors at second base (16)
- ➡ 4th in lowest fielding percentage at second base (.977)
- ➡ 6th in sacrifice flies (9)
- ➡ 8th in lowest batting average at home (.255)
- ➡ 9th in caught stealing (10)
- ➡ 10th in lowest slugging percentage vs. right-handed pitchers (.372)
- ➡ Led the Red Sox in sacrifice bunts, sacrifice flies, caught stealing and bunts in play (20)

# Stan Belinda

## 1995 Season

There was a time in the early 1990s that Stan Belinda was supposed to be the Pirates' next closer. But by the time he ended up in the unsigned free agents' camp at Homestead, Florida last April, Belinda had become a journeyman whose 5.14 ERA for the '94 Royals told only part of the story of why Kansas City badly wanted to let him go. But Belinda took advantage of his opportunity to pitch in Boston and became an outstanding middle man.

## Pitching

Belinda showed he had regained his dominant stuff last year. He is essentially a sidewheeler whose fastball bores in on right-handed hitters, and he can be very intimidating to righthanders. In Pittsburgh and Kansas City, it was said that he didn't have the stomach to work inside. But that changed in 1995, and lefties batted only .209 against him, an indication of how well he used the inner half of the plate. Belinda's arm doesn't respond well to being used two days in a row, and getting him up to warm up several times during a game—something the Red Sox did a lot last year—can be a problem. He broke down in early September, and missed nearly two weeks with a sore shoulder.

## Defense

At Fenway, teams seldom try to steal runs with the game on the line, and that helped Belinda keep the running game in check. Holding runners can be a problem for him, though his delivery is deceptively quick to the plate. He is an average fielder.

## 1996 Outlook

Belinda had a stint sharing the closer role with Ken Ryan before Rick Aguilera was acquired July 6, and for the season he coverted 10 of 14 save chances. He coultake over as closer if Aguilera doesn't return this year, but it's more likely that Boston will keep him in the set-up role that suited him so well last year.

**Position:** RP
**Bats:** R  **Throws:** R
**Ht:** 6' 3"  **Wt:** 215

**Opening Day Age:** 29
**Born:** 8/6/66 in Huntingdon, PA
**ML Seasons:** 7

### Overall Statistics

|  | W | L | Pct. | ERA | G | GS | Sv | IP | H | BB | SO | HR | BR/IP |
|---|---|---|---|---|---|---|---|---|---|---|---|---|---|
| 1995 | 8 | 1 | .889 | 3.10 | 63 | 0 | 10 | 69.2 | 51 | 28 | 57 | 5 | 1.13 |
| Career | 30 | 19 | .612 | 3.70 | 345 | 0 | 72 | 406.2 | 332 | 164 | 342 | 39 | 1.22 |

### How Often He Throws Strikes

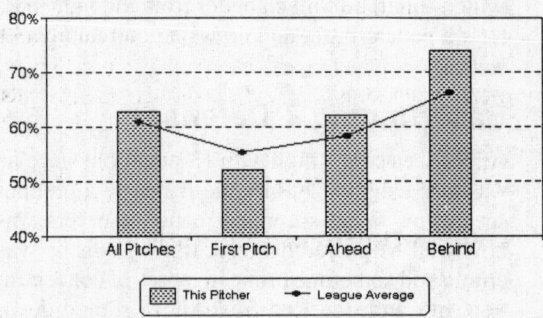

### 1995 Situational Stats

|  | W | L | ERA | Sv | IP |  | AB | H | HR | RBI | Avg |
|---|---|---|---|---|---|---|---|---|---|---|---|
| Home | 5 | 0 | 2.91 | 3 | 43.1 | LHB | 110 | 23 | 3 | 12 | .209 |
| Road | 3 | 1 | 3.42 | 7 | 26.1 | RHB | 139 | 28 | 2 | 21 | .201 |
| First Half | 7 | 1 | 3.58 | 6 | 37.2 | Sc Pos | 77 | 21 | 2 | 29 | .273 |
| Scnd Half | 1 | 0 | 2.53 | 4 | 32.0 | Clutch | 188 | 42 | 4 | 30 | .223 |

### 1995 Rankings (American League)

- → 2nd in relief wins (8)
- → 3rd in games pitched
- → 4th in holds (17)
- → 5th in lowest batting average allowed in relief (.205)
- → 10th in relief ERA (3.10)
- → Led the Red Sox in games pitched, games finished (30), holds, blown saves (4), first batter efficiency (.222), relief ERA, relief wins, relief innings (69.2), lowest batting average allowed in relief and most strikeouts per 9 innings in relief (7.4)

# Jose Canseco

## 1995 Season

When Jose Canseco was healthy last year, he was hot. In July and August, for instance, Canseco batted .344 with 17 homers, rattling 24 extra-base hits in August alone. The problem was that he wasn't healthy often enough. While Canseco appeared completely recovered from the shoulder and elbow problems that wiped him out in 1993, he still missed 42 games with rib, back, leg and elbow problems—this despite the fact that the Red Sox used him almost exclusively as a DH.

## Hitting

Canseco still is a dead fastball hitter who looks for the gas and hits it with his extraordinary bat speed. He is so strong he can get jammed and still flare singles over the infield. Pitchers try to get up and in on him—which usually leads to dramatic stares toward the mound—and then throw breaking balls out of the strike zone. But Canseco demonstrated last year that he is a good situational hitter, choking up with two strikes and going the other way.

## Baserunning & Defense

Canseco talked before the season about stealing 40 bases; he stole four, and every time he runs he looks as if he's just getting out of bed. He's now talking about playing right field in 1996, but Jose's primary interest is hitting, his defensive skills have eroded, and playing in the field may put his precarious physical condition at risk.

## 1996 Outlook

Canseco is only 31, an age at which most power hitters are still having big years. But Canseco hasn't played 120 games in a season since 1991, and the free agent's asking price might be higher than the Red Sox are willing to pay. He had a heckuva year as a hitter in 1995, but whether he'll return to Boston will probably come down to money.

**Position:** DH
**Bats:** R  **Throws:** R
**Ht:** 6' 4"  **Wt:** 235

**Opening Day Age:** 31
**Born:** 7/2/64 in Havana, Cuba
**ML Seasons:** 11
**Pronunciation:** kan-SAY-koh

### Overall Statistics

| | G | AB | R | H | D | T | HR | RBI | SB | BB | SO | Avg | OBP | Slg |
|---|---|---|---|---|---|---|---|---|---|---|---|---|---|---|
| 1995 | 102 | 396 | 64 | 121 | 25 | 1 | 24 | 81 | 4 | 42 | 93 | .306 | .378 | .556 |
| Career | 1245 | 4711 | 796 | 1275 | 229 | 12 | 300 | 951 | 153 | 560 | 1267 | .271 | .351 | .515 |

### Where He Hits the Ball

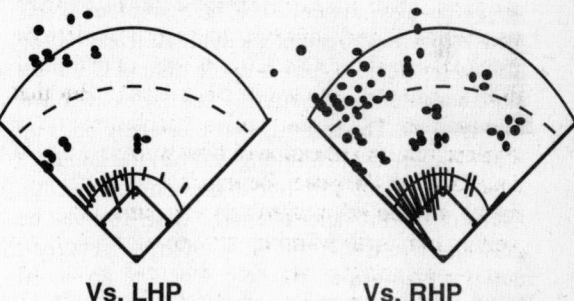

**Vs. LHP**          **Vs. RHP**

### 1995 Situational Stats

| | AB | H | HR | RBI | Avg | | AB | H | HR | RBI | Avg |
|---|---|---|---|---|---|---|---|---|---|---|---|
| Home | 199 | 67 | 10 | 44 | .337 | LHP | 93 | 26 | 12 | 21 | .280 |
| Road | 197 | 54 | 14 | 37 | .274 | RHP | 303 | 95 | 12 | 60 | .314 |
| First Half | 116 | 30 | 5 | 21 | .259 | Sc Pos | 101 | 34 | 6 | 58 | .337 |
| Scnd Half | 280 | 91 | 19 | 60 | .325 | Clutch | 47 | 19 | 3 | 13 | .404 |

### 1995 Rankings (American League)

- ➡ 1st in batting average in the clutch (.404)
- ➡ 5th in batting average on a 3-1 count (.600) and slugging percentage vs. left-handed pitchers (.699)
- ➡ 6th in cleanup slugging percentage (.564)
- ➡ 8th in batting average at home (.337)
- ➡ 10th in slugging percentage
- ➡ Led the Red Sox in batting average with runners in scoring position (.337), batting average in the clutch, batting average on a 3-1 count, cleanup slugging percentage and slugging percentage vs. left-handed pitchers

## 1995 Season

Roger Clemens started last season on the disabled list with shoulder stiffness and didn't make his first start until June 2. The Red Sox front office felt that part of Clemens' problem was that he didn't work hard enough during the eight-month layoff and came in 20-something pounds overweight. But by August 1, Clemens was back in the low 90s and starting to win, and by the end of the season Clemens was registering in the mid-90s. He went 7-2 over the last two months.

## Pitching

Some say that Clemens cannot maintain that velocity as he once did, but it appears his fastball won't be his problem. The real problem is his refusal at times to acknowledge that it isn't 1986 any more. He still charges to the mound like it's a Longhorn football Saturday and tries to blow hitters away. The result is that he usually ends up with one 25-35 pitch inning early in the game. . . which catches up with him in the sixth or seventh. Clemens has the other pitches: a nasty forkball he gets up there in the mid-80s, a terrific curveball and a sometimes-nasty slider. Pitching coach Al Nipper also taught him a circle change that gives him an extra foot on his fastball.

## Defense

Clemens will never hurt himself on any fundamental, and he meticulously works on fielding and holding runners. Of the 15 who tried to steal on him last year, only eight suceeded.

## 1996 Outlook

Clemens is 33 years old now, and his record the last three years is a combined 30-26. He has won one of his nine postseason starts. But in the Red Sox clubhouse, Clemens is still the leader of the staff. In fact, when Tim Wakefield was running off 10 straight wins and was 15-1, players reminded the media that Roger was still *the* number one.

**Position:** SP
**Bats:** R  **Throws:** R
**Ht:** 6' 4"  **Wt:** 225

**Opening Day Age:** 33
**Born:** 8/4/62 in Dayton, OH
**ML Seasons:** 12
**Nickname:** Rocket

### Overall Statistics

|  | W | L | Pct. | ERA | G | GS | Sv | IP | H | BB | SO | HR | BR/IP |
|---|---|---|---|---|---|---|---|---|---|---|---|---|---|
| 1995 | 10 | 5 | .667 | 4.18 | 23 | 23 | 0 | 140.0 | 141 | 60 | 132 | 15 | 1.44 |
| Career | 182 | 98 | .650 | 3.00 | 349 | 348 | 0 | 2533.1 | 2143 | 750 | 2333 | 175 | 1.14 |

### How Often He Throws Strikes

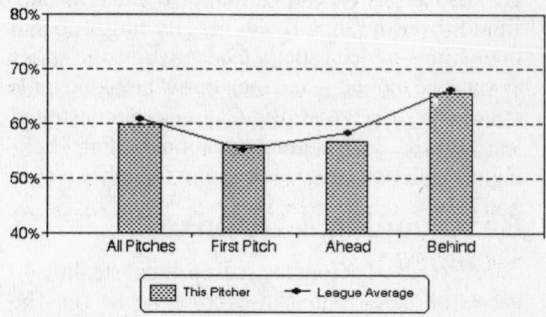

### 1995 Situational Stats

|  | W | L | ERA | Sv | IP |  | AB | H | HR | RBI | Avg |
|---|---|---|---|---|---|---|---|---|---|---|---|
| Home | 6 | 3 | 4.56 | 0 | 71.0 | LHB | 303 | 78 | 7 | 32 | .257 |
| Road | 4 | 2 | 3.78 | 0 | 69.0 | RHB | 241 | 63 | 8 | 30 | .261 |
| First Half | 2 | 1 | 4.25 | 0 | 48.2 | Sc Pos | 123 | 36 | 3 | 45 | .293 |
| Scnd Half | 8 | 4 | 4.14 | 0 | 91.1 | Clutch | 25 | 6 | 1 | 3 | .240 |

### 1995 Rankings (American League)

➡ 1st in hit batsmen (14)
➡ 10th in highest batting average allowed with runners in scoring position (.293)
➡ Led the Red Sox in hit batsmen

# Rheal Cormier

## 1995 Season

On April 8, the Red Sox traded Scott Cooper to the Cardinals for Mark Whiten. Oh yes—in the deal, Boston got Rheal Cormier and the Cardinals got Cory Bailey. By midseason, Cormier was the only significant player in the deal. Though his inconsistency was maddening at times, Cormier was a valuable member of the Boston staff because of his versatility. Most of the season, he was a long man and lefty specialist out of the bullpen, making 36 appearances. But he also made a dozen starts and went 4-3 in that role.

## Pitching

Cormier has adequate stuff, beginning with a fastball which approaches 90 miles per hour. In addition he throws a forkball which serves as his change-up, a curveball, and what at times is a nice, tight slider. But as sometimes happened in his Cardinal career, Cormier lost confidence and command last year after getting hammered by righthanders in several starts. He soon found himself back in the bullpen, where his work was better.

## Defense

Cormier's fine fielding and his ability to hold runners add to his effectiveness as a pitcher. Opponents tried to run on him only five times all season—they were successful thrice—and in five years and 554 innings, he's allowed only 19 steals.

## 1996 Outlook

While Cormier's inconsistencies frustrated the Red Sox much the way they frustrated the Cardinals, he might be one of those pitchers who takes some time to mature. Remember, this guy is an offseason lumberjack from a small town named Shediak just outside Moncton, New Brunswick—a town so small that when you get to the line, the sign reads, "You Are Now Entering Shediak, Home of Rheal Cormier." People like that sometimes don't realize how good they really are until they're in their 30s.

**Position:** RP/SP
**Bats:** L  **Throws:** L
**Ht:** 5'10"  **Wt:** 185

**Opening Day Age:** 28
**Born:** 4/23/67 in Moncton, New Britain, Canada
**ML Seasons:** 5
**Pronunciation:** RAY-al KOR-mee-ay

**Boston Red Sox**

### Overall Statistics

|  | W | L | Pct. | ERA | G | GS | Sv | IP | H | BB | SO | HR | BR/IP |
|---|---|---|---|---|---|---|---|---|---|---|---|---|---|
| 1995 | 7 | 5 | .583 | 4.07 | 48 | 12 | 0 | 115.0 | 131 | 31 | 69 | 12 | 1.41 |
| Career | 31 | 28 | .525 | 4.11 | 135 | 80 | 0 | 553.2 | 602 | 106 | 325 | 56 | 1.28 |

### How Often He Throws Strikes

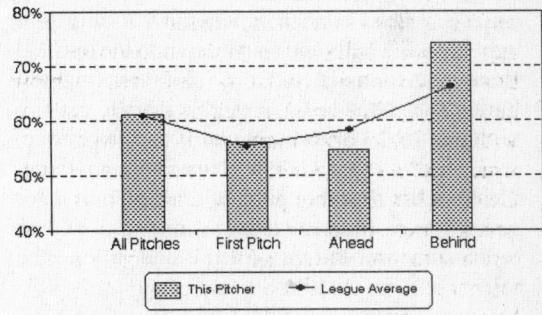

### 1995 Situational Stats

|  | W | L | ERA | Sv | IP |  | AB | H | HR | RBI | Avg |
|---|---|---|---|---|---|---|---|---|---|---|---|
| Home | 4 | 4 | 4.60 | 0 | 58.2 | LHB | 108 | 28 | 1 | 9 | .259 |
| Road | 3 | 1 | 3.51 | 0 | 56.1 | RHB | 338 | 103 | 11 | 44 | .305 |
| First Half | 3 | 1 | 3.38 | 0 | 56.0 | Sc Pos | 108 | 27 | 2 | 34 | .250 |
| Scnd Half | 4 | 4 | 4.73 | 0 | 59.0 | Clutch | 85 | 22 | 0 | 5 | .259 |

### 1995 Rankings (American League)

→ 5th in GDPs induced (23), most GDPs induced per GDP situation (21.5%) and highest batting average allowed vs. right-handed batters (.305)
→ 6th in lowest fielding percentage at pitcher (.933)
→ 8th in least strikeouts per 9 innings in relief (5.0)
→ 9th in lowest percentage of inherited runners scored (20.7%)
→ 10th in errors at pitcher (2)
→ Led the Red Sox in GDPs induced, most GDPs induced per GDP situation and lowest percentage of inherited runners scored

# Mike Greenwell

## 1995 Season

The power potential that appeared to be blossoming when Mike Greenwell hit 22 homers and knocked in 119 runs in 1988 has dissipated over the years through ankle, foot and elbow injuries. Instead, Greenwell has become a hitter who bats around .300 while providing occasional power, and he had a typical season in 1995.

## Hitting

"All you have to do is sit in Fenway for one game and you know the book on Greenwell because the fans all scream at him not to swing at the first pitch," says one American League advance scout. Indeed, Greenwell was again among the league leaders swinging at the first pitch last year. He remains a dead fastball hitter, but his ability to fight breaking balls and slap them into the outfield makes him a tough out even for breaking-ball starters. The book on Greenwell is to try to get him to chase first-pitch fastballs out of the strike zone; once he gets behind, he'll chase most anything. But hang the breaking ball, and he can pull it for power. Most of Greenwell's power is pull power, getting the bat head out in front and driving the ball.

## Baserunning & Defense

Greenwell's best position is DH, but the Red Sox have three or four of those players, so he's in left field. He is aggressive, but lacks defensive instincts and has severe problems away from Fenway, where that cozy little left-field wall has long covered up Greenwell's defensive liabilities. But give him credit for trying. He is an average baserunner who sometimes overestimates his speed, which is more a case of constant hustling.

## 1996 Outlook

Greenwell is what he is—an 11-to-15 homer, 70-to-85 RBI guy who plays as hard as he can, day after day. As long as he stays healthy—a problem throughout his career—he figures to produce at about that level again in 1996.

**Position:** LF
**Bats:** L **Throws:** R
**Ht:** 6' 0"   **Wt:** 200

**Opening Day Age:** 32
**Born:** 7/18/63 in Louisville, KY
**ML Seasons:** 11

### Overall Statistics

|  | G | AB | R | H | D | T | HR | RBI | SB | BB | SO | Avg | OBP | Slg |
|---|---|---|---|---|---|---|---|---|---|---|---|---|---|---|
| 1995 | 120 | 481 | 67 | 143 | 25 | 4 | 15 | 76 | 9 | 38 | 35 | .297 | .349 | .459 |
| Career | 1192 | 4328 | 622 | 1313 | 255 | 37 | 123 | 682 | 76 | 442 | 337 | .303 | .370 | .465 |

### Where He Hits the Ball

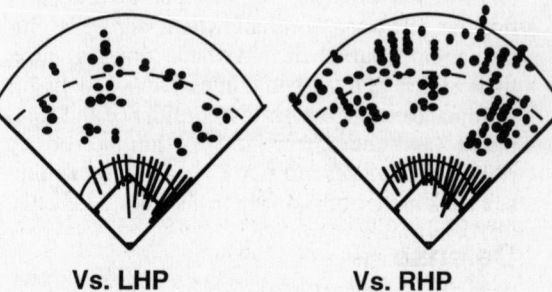

**Vs. LHP**          **Vs. RHP**

### 1995 Situational Stats

|  | AB | H | HR | RBI | Avg |  | AB | H | HR | RBI | Avg |
|---|---|---|---|---|---|---|---|---|---|---|---|
| Home | 235 | 75 | 6 | 39 | .319 | LHP | 142 | 38 | 5 | 22 | .268 |
| Road | 246 | 68 | 9 | 37 | .276 | RHP | 339 | 105 | 10 | 54 | .310 |
| First Half | 226 | 68 | 6 | 31 | .301 | Sc Pos | 137 | 43 | 3 | 60 | .314 |
| Scnd Half | 255 | 75 | 9 | 45 | .294 | Clutch | 69 | 21 | 2 | 9 | .304 |

### 1995 Rankings (American League)

➡ 2nd in errors in left field (6) and lowest fielding percentage in left field (.972)

➡ 3rd in least pitches seen per plate appearance (3.14) and highest percentage of swings on the first pitch (41.9%)

➡ 5th in highest percentage of swings put into play (53.4%) and lowest percentage of extra bases taken as a runner (31.0%)

➡ 6th in GDPs (17)

➡ Led the Red Sox in singles (99), GDPs, highest groundball/flyball ratio (1.5), lowest percentage of swings that missed (12.7%) and highest percentage of swings put into play

# Erik Hanson

## 1995 Season

One of the most successful refugees out of Camp Homestead last season was veteran righty Erik Hanson. Coming off knee surgery and a five-win 1994 season that caused serious questions about the direction of his career, Hanson was signed for $1 million by the Red Sox and became their most consistent starter.

## Pitching

Hanson proved two things in 1995. The first is that he is healthy again. One of the best-conditioned athletes in the game, he surprised doctors by working extremely hard to get his knee back in shape. He did have a strain in his forearm just below his elbow which kept him from throwing his best pitch—his curveball—in the second half, but he kept winning. The other thing Hanson proved last season was that the knocks about his heart and makeup turned out to be unfair. The guy pitched inside, he pitched hurt, he pitched tough all season. Hanson has extraordinary stuff. His fastball is just average, but he has a great change-up, that overpowering downer curveball and a cutter he developed to help make up for the loss of the curve. He's better against lefties than righties because of the curveball and change.

## Defense

A good athlete, Hanson fields his position very well. He is also more than adequate when it comes to holding runners, allowing only 11 steals in 29 starts.

## 1996 Outlook

Hanson held the Boston staff togther last year, and not just by winning 15 games. In the heat of the pennant race, he went 7-1 in August, September and October, and pitched into the eighth inning in his divisional playoff start against Cleveland only to be shut out by Orel Hershiser. He's a free agent, but the Red Sox would love to have him back.

**Position:** SP
**Bats:** R  **Throws:** R
**Ht:** 6' 6"  **Wt:** 210

**Opening Day Age:** 30
**Born:** 5/18/65 in Kinnelon, NJ
**ML Seasons:** 8

Boston Red Sox

### Overall Statistics

|        | W  | L  | Pct. | ERA  | G   | GS  | Sv | IP     | H    | BB  | SO  | HR  | BR/IP |
|--------|----|----|------|------|-----|-----|----|--------|------|-----|-----|-----|-------|
| 1995   | 15 | 5  | .750 | 4.24 | 29  | 29  | 0  | 186.2  | 187  | 59  | 139 | 17  | 1.32  |
| Career | 76 | 64 | .543 | 3.81 | 196 | 193 | 0  | 1276.2 | 1273 | 367 | 980 | 100 | 1.28  |

### How Often He Throws Strikes

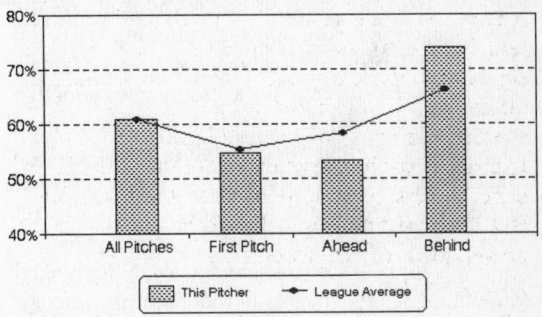

### 1995 Situational Stats

|           | W  | L | ERA  | Sv | IP   |        | AB  | H  | HR | RBI | Avg  |
|-----------|----|---|------|----|------|--------|-----|----|----|-----|------|
| Home      | 5  | 3 | 4.37 | 0  | 92.2 | LHB    | 409 | 88 | 7  | 43  | .215 |
| Road      | 10 | 2 | 4.12 | 0  | 94.0 | RHB    | 317 | 99 | 10 | 40  | .312 |
| First Half| 7  | 2 | 3.61 | 0  | 87.1 | Sc Pos | 179 | 42 | 3  | 64  | .235 |
| Scnd Half | 8  | 3 | 4.80 | 0  | 99.1 | Clutch | 51  | 8  | 1  | 1   | .157 |

### 1995 Rankings (American League)

→ 1st in highest batting average allowed vs. right-handed batters (.312)
→ 2nd in lowest batting average allowed vs. left-handed batters (.215)
→ 3rd in winning percentage
→ 5th in most run support per 9 innings (6.6)
→ 6th in highest strikeout/walk ratio (2.4)
→ 7th in most pitches thrown per batter (3.92)
→ 8th in wins, highest groundball/flyball ratio allowed (1.9) and lowest batting average allowed with runners in scoring position (.235)
→ 9th in shutouts (1) and least GDPs induced per 9 innings (0.7)
→ Led the Red Sox in games started, shutouts, hits allowed, strikeouts, and pitches thrown

# Mike Macfarlane

## 1995 Season

At the end of the 1995 season, the Red Sox declined to pick up the option on Mike Macfarlane's contract. But while Macfarlane batted only .225 and struggled behind the plate at times, the 32-year-old catcher was still an important part of the Red Sox' surprising season. He contributed both in terms of clutch late-inning hits—especially early, when the club was struggling to find its identity—and in the clubhouse, where he was an integral element on a team that was remarkably loose the entire season.

## Hitting

Macfarlane is a dead fastball hitter who likes the ball out over the plate so he can hook it. As the 1995 season wore on, opposing pitching staffs fed him a steady diet of breaking balls, and Macfarlane's power suffered as a result. He pounded lefties last year while struggling against righties, and it may be that Macfarlane's future is as a platoon catcher. His ability to rise to the occasion is demonstrated by the fact that he hit .280 with four homers in close and late situations. Macfarlane was hit by 14 pitches, and as usual he ranked among the league leaders in that painful category.

## Baserunning & Defense

Macfarlane did have his defensive problems, especially receiving the ball. But his league-leading 26 passed balls came courtesy of Tim Wakefield's knuckler. His throwing was erratic, but he tossed out 29 percent of opposing baserunners, fourth in the American League among those who caught at least 100 games. He is a strong handler of pitchers. Like most catchers, he's slow and strictly a station-to-station baserunner.

## 1996 Outlook

Macfarlane has taken some hits about his receiving, but his hard work and character transcend stats or technical skills. Wherever he plays in 1996—and whatever he hits—he figures to be a useful player.

**Position:** C
**Bats:** R **Throws:** R
**Ht:** 6' 1" **Wt:** 205

**Opening Day Age:** 31
**Born:** 4/12/64 in Stockton, CA
**ML Seasons:** 9

### Overall Statistics

|  | G | AB | R | H | D | T | HR | RBI | SB | BB | SO | Avg | OBP | Slg |
|---|---|---|---|---|---|---|---|---|---|---|---|---|---|---|
| 1995 | 115 | 364 | 45 | 82 | 18 | 1 | 15 | 51 | 2 | 38 | 78 | .225 | .319 | .404 |
| Career | 808 | 2522 | 313 | 633 | 154 | 13 | 91 | 360 | 8 | 215 | 508 | .251 | .326 | .431 |

### Where He Hits the Ball

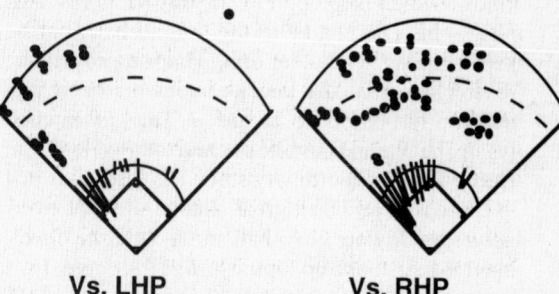

**Vs. LHP**          **Vs. RHP**

### 1995 Situational Stats

|  | AB | H | HR | RBI | Avg |  | AB | H | HR | RBI | Avg |
|---|---|---|---|---|---|---|---|---|---|---|---|
| Home | 186 | 45 | 7 | 24 | .242 | LHP | 90 | 27 | 8 | 15 | .300 |
| Road | 178 | 37 | 8 | 27 | .208 | RHP | 274 | 55 | 7 | 36 | .201 |
| First Half | 186 | 38 | 10 | 30 | .204 | Sc Pos | 105 | 17 | 4 | 38 | .162 |
| Scnd Half | 178 | 44 | 5 | 21 | .247 | Clutch | 50 | 14 | 4 | 8 | .280 |

### 1995 Rankings (American League)

→ 1st in lowest batting average with runners in scoring position (.162)
→ 2nd in hit by pitch (14)
→ 6th in fielding percentage at catcher (.993)
→ 9th in errors at catcher (5)
→ Led the Red Sox in hit by pitch

# Tim Naehring

**Position:** 3B
**Bats:** R **Throws:** R
**Ht:** 6' 2" **Wt:** 205

**Opening Day Age:** 29
**Born:** 2/1/67 in Cincinnati, OH
**ML Seasons:** 6
**Pronunciation:** NAIR-ring

## 1995 Season

If there was ever a star-crossed player, it was Tim Naehring. First, he found one leg was considerably shorter than the other, which led to back problems. When he came back, he lifted weights too vigorously and hurt his shoulder. From 1990 to 1994, he never played in as many as 81 games, and seemed destined to a career as a utility man. But last spring the Red Sox traded Scott Cooper and handed the third-base job to Naehring. He responded by hitting .307 in a career-high 126 games.

## Hitting

Naehring is similar to John Valentin in that he is very smart, a hitter who will take balls the other way to set up pitchers for key situations. Opposing pitchers feel he is a master cheater who can read and steal pitches. He can take the breaking ball to right, which gets him fastballs, and he has shown that he can look away, get jammed and still flare balls to right-center. Most clubs try to establish the breaking ball, then get him to chase balls up, out and away. He used the vast spaces of center and right-center in Fenway to hit .348 at home. Naehring's excellent plate discipline allowed him to finish with an on-base percentage over 100 points higher than his batting average, no mean feat.

## Baserunning & Defense

The back and leg injuries have taken their toll on Naehring's speed, but he has superb baserunning instincts. Defensively, he has soft, reliable hands, a strong, accurate arm and plays third base as well as anyone in the league. He is particularly adept at starting the 5-4-3 double play.

## 1996 Outlook

At the All-Star break, American League manager Buck Showalter publically apologized for not naming Naehring to the team. "Tim Naehring plays the game the way it should be played," said Showalter. Taking every play as if it were the most important of his career took its toll on Naehring, but his numbers were more than adequate, and he figures to remain the Red Sox third baseman as long as he's healthy.

### Overall Statistics

|  | G | AB | R | H | D | T | HR | RBI | SB | BB | SO | Avg | OBP | Slg |
|---|---|---|---|---|---|---|---|---|---|---|---|---|---|---|
| 1995 | 126 | 433 | 61 | 133 | 27 | 2 | 10 | 57 | 0 | 77 | 66 | .307 | .415 | .448 |
| Career | 361 | 1183 | 139 | 329 | 70 | 3 | 23 | 145 | 2 | 149 | 209 | .278 | .363 | .401 |

### Where He Hits the Ball

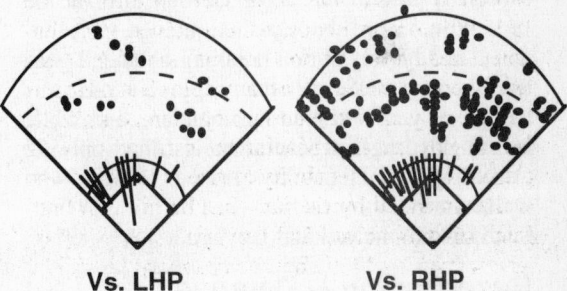

**Vs. LHP**          **Vs. RHP**

### 1995 Situational Stats

|  | AB | H | HR | RBI | Avg |  | AB | H | HR | RBI | Avg |
|---|---|---|---|---|---|---|---|---|---|---|---|
| Home | 207 | 72 | 5 | 31 | .348 | LHP | 102 | 28 | 3 | 11 | .275 |
| Road | 226 | 61 | 5 | 26 | .270 | RHP | 331 | 105 | 7 | 46 | .317 |
| First Half | 213 | 73 | 5 | 37 | .343 | Sc Pos | 118 | 36 | 3 | 48 | .305 |
| Scnd Half | 220 | 60 | 5 | 20 | .273 | Clutch | 69 | 22 | 1 | 6 | .319 |

### 1995 Rankings (American League)

- → 3rd in errors at third base (16)
- → 4th in highest percentage of pitches taken (63.7%)
- → 5th in batting average at home (.348) and fielding percentage at third base (.954)
- → 7th in on-base percentage
- → 8th in on-base percentage vs. left-handed pitchers (.439)
- → Led the Red Sox in batting average, on-base percentage, highest percentage of pitches taken and lowest percentage of swings on the first pitch (18.3%)

# Troy O'Leary

## 1995 Season

In 1987, Dan Duquette, the Brewer scouting director, was out looking at a California high-school infielder named Tom Redington. That afternoon, a kid from the opposing team hit two homers and made a spectacular catch. Duquette drafted and signed him. Then, after a 107 at-bat career in Milwaukee, Duquette spied him on the waiver wire and put in a claim. And Troy O'Leary hit .308. His season might have been even better, but in this—his first chance to play every day— O'Leary wore down late in the year.

## Hitting

O'Leary is just a good hitter. He can hit fastballs, especially low in the zone. He can turn on the fastball in on his hands, which is even more unusual, and he stays in on breaking balls and goes the other way better than many appreciate. He hits the good, hard-throwing righthanders, and while he struggled against lefties, he also had only 52 at-bats against them. He's a free swinger who walked only 29 times, but when he got that first-pitch fastball, he nailed it.

## Baserunning & Defense

O'Leary is something of a rough-hewn player. He is not a good baserunner, either in terms of stealing or simply running the bases. He also has his problems in the outfield. He has speed, but that is his best asset, as he doesn't get good angles on fly balls and doesn't have a strong arm. Worst of all, he has a scary tendency to either overthrow cutoff men or throw to the wrong base—prompting comparisons to a Boston cabbie's sense of direction.

## 1996 Outlook

Some in the Red Sox organization think that with a full season behind him, O'Leary will hit for more power and play with more consistency. Kevin Kennedy wants to get him in for a full spring training of fundamentals to see if the roughness can be sculpted.

**Position:** RF/LF/CF
**Bats:** L **Throws:** L
**Ht:** 6' 0"  **Wt:** 198

**Opening Day Age:** 26
**Born:** 8/4/69 in Compton, CA
**ML Seasons:** 3

### Overall Statistics

|  | G | AB | R | H | D | T | HR | RBI | SB | BB | SO | Avg | OBP | Slg |
|---|---|---|---|---|---|---|---|---|---|---|---|---|---|---|
| 1995 | 112 | 399 | 60 | 123 | 31 | 6 | 10 | 49 | 5 | 29 | 64 | .308 | .355 | .491 |
| Career | 158 | 506 | 72 | 153 | 35 | 7 | 12 | 59 | 6 | 39 | 85 | .302 | .353 | .470 |

### Where He Hits the Ball

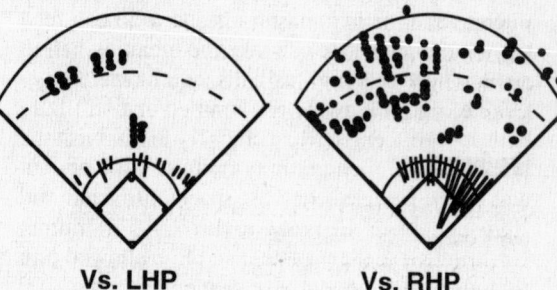

**Vs. LHP**            **Vs. RHP**

### 1995 Situational Stats

|  | AB | H | HR | RBI | Avg |  | AB | H | HR | RBI | Avg |
|---|---|---|---|---|---|---|---|---|---|---|---|
| Home | 209 | 73 | 5 | 26 | .349 | LHP | 52 | 12 | 0 | 5 | .231 |
| Road | 190 | 50 | 5 | 23 | .263 | RHP | 347 | 111 | 10 | 44 | .320 |
| First Half | 200 | 69 | 7 | 35 | .345 | Sc Pos | 95 | 27 | 3 | 39 | .284 |
| Scnd Half | 199 | 54 | 3 | 14 | .271 | Clutch | 64 | 19 | 1 | 5 | .297 |

### 1995 Rankings (American League)

→ 1st in lowest batting average on an 0-2 count (.000)
→ 3rd in lowest fielding percentage in right field (.976)
→ 4th in batting average at home (.349)
→ 5th in errors in right field (4)
→ 8th in triples
→ Led the Red Sox in triples, batting average on a 3-2 count (.323) and batting average at home

# Aaron Sele

## 1995 Season

When the shortened spring training was completed and the season opened, Aaron Sele was Boston's number-one starter. He pitched Opening Day, and beat Minnesota 9-0. By May 17, he was 3-1. Ten days later, Sele was flown back to Boston from California with a sore shoulder. He tried rest. He tried shots. He tried three or four rehabilitation stints. But by August, the 25-year-old righthander was told to shut it down for the season.

## Pitching

Sele has an over-the-top curveball that dominates hitters. His fastball is below average in terms of velocity, but because of the curveball, his willingness to pitch inside and a cutter he uses on righthanders, it looks better than average to the hitters. Because he has tended to throw so many pitches early in games, he often hits the 100-pitch level by the sixth inning.

## Defense

Sele is an average fielder. One of his biggest problems came when the club began worrying about his slow delivery to the plate. Sele struggled with the slide-step and shortening his time to the plate, and as a result often stopped throwing his best curveballs. Hey, the years Doc Gooden and Roger Clemens were a combined 48-8 in 1985-86, basestealers were 98-for-100 against them. The moral: his downer curveball is more important than his slide-step.

## 1996 Outlook

During the strike, Sele admitted he did little throwing or conditioning and wasn't in shape. When he rushed through spring training trying to make up for lost time, he hurt his shoulder. Sometimes his toughness was even questioned, which was unfair. This was the first time in Sele's brief professional career that he'd been hurt, and that is always difficult. As soon as his season was over, Dr. Framk Andrews told him to get into better shape, and by mid-November Sele was on a grueling conditioning and throwing program.

**Position:** SP
**Bats:** R  **Throws:** R
**Ht:** 6' 5"  **Wt:** 215

**Opening Day Age:** 25
**Born:** 6/25/70 in Golden Valley, MN
**ML Seasons:** 3
**Pronunciation:** SEE-lee

Boston
Red Sox

### Overall Statistics

|        | W  | L  | Pct. | ERA  | G  | GS | Sv | IP    | H   | BB  | SO  | HR | BR/IP |
|--------|----|----|------|------|----|----|----|-------|-----|-----|-----|----|-------|
| 1995   | 3  | 1  | .750 | 3.06 | 6  | 6  | 0  | 32.1  | 32  | 14  | 21  | 3  | 1.42  |
| Career | 18 | 10 | .643 | 3.32 | 46 | 46 | 0  | 287.1 | 272 | 122 | 219 | 21 | 1.37  |

### How Often He Throws Strikes

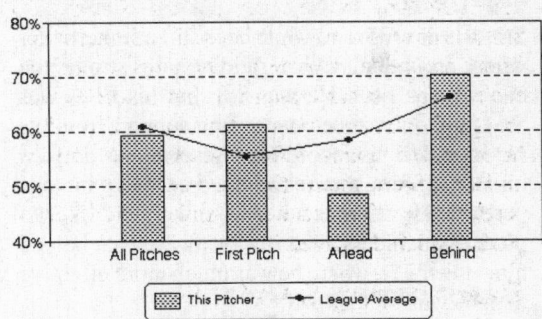

### 1995 Situational Stats

|            | W | L | ERA  | Sv | IP   |        | AB | H  | HR | RBI | Avg  |
|------------|---|---|------|----|------|--------|----|----|----|-----|------|
| Home       | 1 | 1 | 2.25 | 0  | 12.0 | LHB    | 60 | 19 | 2  | 5   | .317 |
| Road       | 2 | 0 | 3.54 | 0  | 20.1 | RHB    | 67 | 13 | 1  | 5   | .194 |
| First Half | 3 | 1 | 3.06 | 0  | 32.1 | Sc Pos | 33 | 5  | 0  | 7   | .152 |
| Scnd Half  | 0 | 0 | -    | 0  | 0.0  | Clutch | 0  | 0  | 0  | 0   | -    |

### 1995 Rankings (American League)

➡ 3rd in errors at pitcher (3)

# Zane Smith

## 1995 Season

When a New York judge effectively ended the strike and got the players back on the field, Zane Smith was one of the many who went to Homestead, Florida to work out. Like Eric Hanson and Stan Belinda, he was signed by the Red Sox at a discounted rate. But Smith never regained the consistent sinker that had once made him a reliable National League pitcher, and by the end of the year was out of the rotation and almost out of mind until he accidentally threw a 3-0 pitch over the plate to Tony Pena in the 13th inning of the first game of the divisional playoffs. Gone. In more ways than one.

## Pitching

Smith is now 35, and while he is still a sinkerballer whose groundball/flyball ratio remains strong, the end may be near. He was 8-8, but his ERA was 5.61, and only some outstanding support from his hitters made his record look respectable. Lefties hit .342 off him, and he averaged only five innings per start. He still has a decent sinker, and likes to pitch righthanders away, away, away. That helped him at Fenway, where he was much more effective than he was on the road.

## Defense

Smith is an agile fielder who moves well off the mound when he's in shape. But he was overweight last year, which caused him problems. He has a good pickoff move, but he's slow to the plate and good basestealers can take advantage of him.

## 1996 Outlook

The bite on Smith's sinker and crispness on his curveball are not what they used to be. The fact that he is left-handed may continue to land him jobs, but with a 5.69 ERA as a starter, that job likely will not be in Boston.

**Position:** SP
**Bats:** L **Throws:** L
**Ht:** 6' 1" **Wt:** 207

**Opening Day Age:** 35
**Born:** 12/28/60 in Madison, WI
**ML Seasons:** 12

### Overall Statistics

|        | W  | L   | Pct. | ERA  | G   | GS  | Sv | IP     | H    | BB  | SO  | HR  | BR/IP |
|--------|----|-----|------|------|-----|-----|----|--------|------|-----|-----|-----|-------|
| 1995   | 8  | 8   | .500 | 5.61 | 24  | 21  | 0  | 110.2  | 144  | 23  | 47  | 7   | 1.51  |
| Career | 96 | 109 | .468 | 3.68 | 344 | 275 | 3  | 1836.0 | 1876 | 562 | 964 | 115 | 1.33  |

### How Often He Throws Strikes

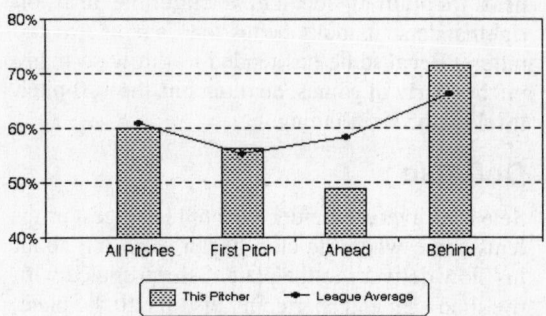

This Pitcher — League Average

### 1995 Situational Stats

|            | W | L | ERA  | Sv | IP   |        | AB  | H   | HR | RBI | Avg  |
|------------|---|---|------|----|------|--------|-----|-----|----|-----|------|
| Home       | 5 | 3 | 4.39 | 0  | 67.2 | LHB    | 73  | 25  | 0  | 17  | .342 |
| Road       | 3 | 5 | 7.53 | 0  | 43.0 | RHB    | 382 | 119 | 7  | 49  | .312 |
| First Half | 3 | 5 | 5.67 | 0  | 60.1 | Sc Pos | 120 | 42  | 1  | 57  | .350 |
| Scnd Half  | 5 | 3 | 5.54 | 0  | 50.1 | Clutch | 10  | 1   | 0  | 1   | .100 |

### 1995 Rankings (American League)

- ➡ 2nd in highest batting average allowed with runners in scoring position (.350)
- ➡ 3rd in highest batting average allowed vs. right-handed batters (.312)
- ➡ Led the Red Sox in losses and balks (1)

# Lee Tinsley

## 1995 Season

If anyone had suggested prior to the season that Lee Tinsley would hit .284, have an on-base percentage of .359—higher than Otis Nixon, the man he replaced as Red Sox center fielder—and play a reasonable center field, one would have thought Boston would have been delighted. Instead, Tinsley finished the season as a little-used benchwarmer. It was a tough finish for Tinsley, who was in his ninth professional season and playing for his fifth organization. Nagged by pulled hamstrings, a bad back and a rib-cage condition, he simply wore down late in the year.

## Hitting

Tinsley is a dead fastball hitter who likes to hit early in the count. He likes the ball from the middle down and can drive an outside pitch. A switch-hitter, he did better from the left side. Tinsley doesn't make the consistent contact most managers prefer from their leadoff man, but he does draw his fair share of walks and certainly is fast enough for the number-one slot.

## Baserunning & Defense

Thus far, Tinsley has seemed a little unsure of his ability to get good jumps on opposing pitchers. He hasn't yet begun to utilize his explosive first-step speed. Defensively, Tinsley was superb the first two months of the season, then lapsed into inconsistency, making some curious judgments. However, his speed more than made up for his mistakes until the last few weeks, when he seemed to lose confidence. His arm is below average.

## 1996 Outlook

Down the stretch and in the divisional playoffs against the Indians, Tinsley was on the bench, replaced by Dwayne Hosey, who'd been lifted from the waiver wire. But Tinsley still has the ability to become a fine major league player, and one thing Tinsley will do is work. A little more self-confidence would help, and so would some guidance. Last year the Red Sox had no hitting coach accustomed to his style, no baserunning coach, and no outfield instructor.

**Position:** CF
**Bats:** B  **Throws:** R
**Ht:** 5'10"  **Wt:** 195

**Opening Day Age:** 27
**Born:** 3/4/69 in Shelbyville, KY
**ML Seasons:** 3

Boston Red Sox

### Overall Statistics

|  | G | AB | R | H | D | T | HR | RBI | SB | BB | SO | Avg | OBP | Slg |
|---|---|---|---|---|---|---|---|---|---|---|---|---|---|---|
| 1995 | 100 | 341 | 61 | 97 | 17 | 1 | 7 | 41 | 18 | 39 | 74 | .284 | .359 | .402 |
| Career | 189 | 504 | 90 | 132 | 22 | 1 | 10 | 57 | 31 | 60 | 119 | .262 | .342 | .369 |

### Where He Hits the Ball

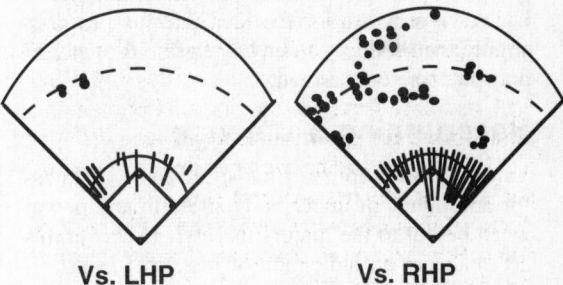

**Vs. LHP**     **Vs. RHP**

### 1995 Situational Stats

|  | AB | H | HR | RBI | Avg |  |  | AB | H | HR | RBI | Avg |
|---|---|---|---|---|---|---|---|---|---|---|---|---|
| Home | 170 | 49 | 4 | 26 | .288 | LHP |  | 88 | 22 | 3 | 9 | .250 |
| Road | 171 | 48 | 3 | 15 | .281 | RHP |  | 253 | 75 | 4 | 32 | .296 |
| First Half | 200 | 59 | 5 | 25 | .295 | Sc Pos |  | 83 | 25 | 1 | 32 | .301 |
| Scnd Half | 141 | 38 | 2 | 16 | .270 | Clutch |  | 46 | 16 | 1 | 8 | .348 |

### 1995 Rankings (American League)

- 2nd in lowest fielding percentage in center field (.979)
- 3rd in errors in center field (5)
- 7th in lowest stolen base percentage (69.2%)
- 9th in sacrifice bunts (9)
- 10th in on-base percentage for a leadoff hitter (.346)
- Led the Red Sox in on-base percentage for a leadoff hitter and steals of third (3)

# John Valentin

Overlooked

## 1995 Season

Last season was the one in which everyone found out just how good John Valentin really is. His numbers—27 homers, 102 RBI, 108 runs and 20 steals—add up to one of the most productive middle infielders on the planet.

## Hitting

Valentin is one of the smartest hitters around. He loves to get up on the plate and get a fastball; he pays a price for setting up inside, as he got hit 10 times last year. When pitchers work him away, he takes the ball the other way, but if he's at Fenway and gets a hanger, he'll hook a fly ball to left field to utilize The Wall. He has become a patient hitter, greatly improving his walk/strikeout ratio over the last few years. As for the idea that his power is simply the product of Fenway Park, 16 of his 27 homers came on the road.

## Baserunning & Defense

Valentin traded some of his speed and quickness for 25 pounds of upper-body strength and power when he got to the majors in 1992. However, his 20 steals are an indication of his street-smart instincts. He isn't fast, just intelligent. In time, those instincts could make him a premier defensive shortstop as well. His biggest problem has been occasional lapses of concentration on routine plays, especially when games are not on the line. He throws adequately, and he's worked hard to learn to read hitters.

## 1996 Outlook

Valentin's come a long way since the days when he batted ninth at Seton Hall in a lineup with Mo Vaughn and Craig Biggio. He's now one of baseball's premier middle infielders, but there is speculation that Valentin will be moved to either third base or second in 1997 to make room for minor league defensive whiz Nomar Garciaparra. Before that happens, perhaps he can become the fifth shortstop in American League history to hit 30 homers in a season.

**Position:** SS
**Bats:** R **Throws:** R
**Ht:** 6' 0" **Wt:** 185

**Opening Day Age:** 29
**Born:** 2/18/67 in Mineola, NY
**ML Seasons:** 4

### Overall Statistics

|  | G | AB | R | H | D | T | HR | RBI | SB | BB | SO | Avg | OBP | Slg |
|---|---|---|---|---|---|---|---|---|---|---|---|---|---|---|
| 1995 | 135 | 520 | 108 | 155 | 37 | 2 | 27 | 102 | 20 | 81 | 67 | .298 | .399 | .533 |
| Career | 421 | 1474 | 232 | 431 | 116 | 7 | 52 | 242 | 27 | 192 | 199 | .292 | .377 | .486 |

### Where He Hits the Ball

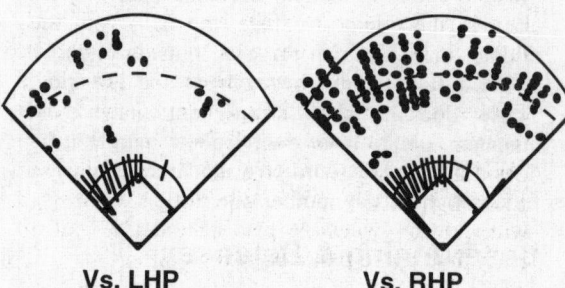

**Vs. LHP** **Vs. RHP**

### 1995 Situational Stats

|  | AB | H | HR | RBI | Avg |  | AB | H | HR | RBI | Avg |
|---|---|---|---|---|---|---|---|---|---|---|---|
| Home | 251 | 80 | 11 | 40 | .319 | LHP | 132 | 47 | 6 | 35 | .356 |
| Road | 269 | 75 | 16 | 62 | .279 | RHP | 388 | 108 | 21 | 67 | .278 |
| First Half | 257 | 73 | 14 | 42 | .284 | Sc Pos | 150 | 49 | 8 | 76 | .327 |
| Scnd Half | 263 | 82 | 13 | 60 | .312 | Clutch | 62 | 21 | 3 | 15 | .339 |

### 1995 Rankings (American League)

- → 1st in errors at shortstop (18)
- → 4th in doubles
- → 5th in pitches seen (2,554), on-base percentage vs. left-handed pitchers (.465) and lowest fielding percentage at shortstop (.973)
- → 6th in runs scored, hit by pitch (10), lowest groundball/flyball ratio (0.8) and batting average vs. left-handed pitchers (.356)
- → 7th in stolen base percentage (80.0%)
- → 8th in most pitches seen per plate appearance (4.11)
- → Led the Red Sox in runs scored, doubles, stolen bases, walks and pitches seen

# Mo Vaughn

## 1995 Season

On the field and off, Mo Vaughn led the Red Sox in 1995. What he and Jose Canseco went through in the divisional playoffs—going a combined 0-for-27 against Cleveland's underrated pitchers—didn't detract from a monster season for Vaughn. When the year ended he was rewarded with the league's Most Valuable Player award in a photo-finish over Albert Belle.

## Hitting

Granted, Vaughn strikes out too much. But because he works hard and is such a student of the game, it figures that he will improve his pitch selection and consistency. He is smart, moving around in the box and making adjustments. While the book has been to pitch him up and in with fastballs and try to get him to chase offspeed pitches down and away, late in the season he clocked a tremendous three-run homer off Indian reliever Alan Embree on a pitch that registered 96 MPH on the radar gun. That, however, is unusual; Vaughn generally goes with the pitch—though with power—when he gets an outside fastball. He's more apt to pull a breaking ball.

## Baserunning & Defense

Despite his size, Vaughn is an aggressive baserunner who can move once he gets going. His biggest deficiency is his defense. His hands are only average, and he sometimes gets his feet tangled when he's setting up for throws from his infielders, or has problems going back on pop-ups. Fortunately for him, the Red Sox don't worry much about defense.

## 1996 Outlook

Another of Vaughn's many attributes is that he shows up to play, healthy or hurting, hot or slumping. He missed only four games all season, two of those after his eye was closed when jumped by seven thugs in a local nightspot. Mo played after sitting out those two days, even though he couldn't see out of one eye. That's typical of Vaughn, and another reason why he's become one of the game's top sluggers.

**Position:** 1B
**Bats:** L **Throws:** R
**Ht:** 6' 1"  **Wt:** 245

**Opening Day Age:** 28
**Born:** 12/15/67 in Norwalk, CT
**ML Seasons:** 5
**Nickname:** The Hit Dog

### Overall Statistics

|  | G | AB | R | H | D | T | HR | RBI | SB | BB | SO | Avg | OBP | Slg |
|---|---|---|---|---|---|---|---|---|---|---|---|---|---|---|
| 1995 | 140 | 550 | 98 | 165 | 28 | 3 | 39 | 126 | 11 | 68 | 150 | .300 | .388 | .575 |
| Career | 590 | 2057 | 312 | 587 | 115 | 7 | 111 | 398 | 24 | 277 | 502 | .285 | .377 | .510 |

### Where He Hits the Ball

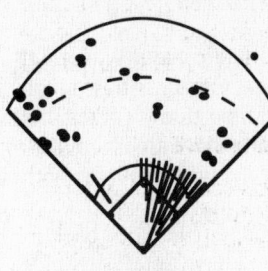
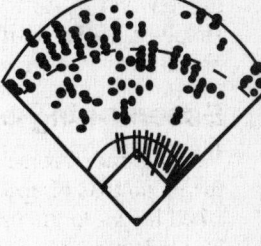

**Vs. LHP**     **Vs. RHP**

### 1995 Situational Stats

|  | AB | H | HR | RBI | Avg |  | AB | H | HR | RBI | Avg |
|---|---|---|---|---|---|---|---|---|---|---|---|
| Home | 266 | 80 | 15 | 52 | .301 | LHP | 174 | 44 | 6 | 31 | .253 |
| Road | 284 | 85 | 24 | 74 | .299 | RHP | 376 | 121 | 33 | 95 | .322 |
| First Half | 262 | 76 | 24 | 60 | .290 | Sc Pos | 149 | 50 | 8 | 84 | .336 |
| Scnd Half | 288 | 89 | 15 | 66 | .309 | Clutch | 67 | 11 | 2 | 7 | .164 |

### 1995 Rankings (American League)

→ 1st in RBI and strikeouts
→ 2nd in hit by pitch (14), slugging percentage vs. right-handed pitchers (.654), errors at first base (11) and highest percentage of swings that missed (31.6%)
→ 3rd in batting average with the bases loaded (.600) and lowest fielding percentage at first base (.992)
→ 4th in home runs and intentional walks (17)
→ 5th in total bases (316), HR frequency (14.1 ABs per HR) and lowest percentage of swings put into play (35.9%)
→ Led the Red Sox in home runs, at-bats, hits, total bases, RBI and intentional walks

# Tim Wakefield

## 1995 Season

Coming off a miserable 1994 season pitching for Buffalo in the International League, knuckleballer Tim Wakefield was released by the Pirates after one spring-training outing last year. Signed by the Red Sox and sent to their extended spring training program in Fort Myers, Wakefield hooked up with Phil Niekro. The rest of the story will be part of Boston legend for years to come. Joining the Red Sox in late May, Wakefield went 14-1 with a 1.65 ERA in his first 17 starts and carried the Sox to first place. But then Wakefield began struggling with his control. He won only two of his last nine decisions and got hammered in the division play-offs.

## Pitching

The thing that was so remarkable about Wakefield during his hot streak was that no matter how much teams tried to wait him out, he threw strikes and got ahead. But when he struggled with his control, hitters could be more patient, and he got hurt with a lot of 3-0 and 3-1 fastballs, many of which were rocketed to the bleacher seats. If he goes back to throwing strikes, the Red Sox have a staff saver for the next few years.

## Defense

A converted infielder, Wakefield does an outstanding job defensively. Though knuckleballers can be vulnerable to the stolen base because of the slow, erratic nature of the pitch, Wakefield has basically no leg kick, so runners can't do much against him.

## 1996 Outlook

Few appreciate what throwing the knuckler does to one's soul. It takes a Charlie Hough or an un-flappable Niekro to withstand the pressure of never knowing from pitch to pitch what will happen. By the end of his streak, Wakefield seemed tense and troubled, and frankly the Red Sox don't know what to expect form him this year. At worst, they hope that he is another Hough, a pitcher who throws 240 innings a year and eats up innings even if he wins only 12-14 games. . . *if* he can cope with the pressures.

**Position:** SP
**Bats:** R  **Throws:** R
**Ht:** 6' 2"  **Wt:** 204

**Opening Day Age:** 29
**Born:** 8/2/66 in Melbourne, FL
**ML Seasons:** 3

### Overall Statistics

|  | W | L | Pct. | ERA | G | GS | Sv | IP | H | BB | SO | HR | BR/IP |
|---|---|---|---|---|---|---|---|---|---|---|---|---|---|
| 1995 | 16 | 8 | .667 | 2.95 | 27 | 27 | 0 | 195.1 | 163 | 68 | 119 | 22 | 1.18 |
| Career | 30 | 20 | .600 | 3.59 | 64 | 60 | 0 | 415.2 | 384 | 178 | 229 | 39 | 1.35 |

### How Often He Throws Strikes

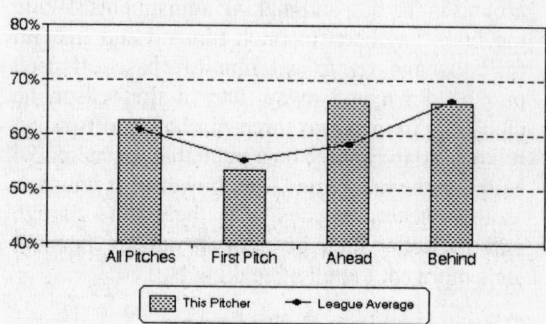

### 1995 Situational Stats

|  | W | L | ERA | Sv | IP |  | AB | H | HR | RBI | Avg |
|---|---|---|---|---|---|---|---|---|---|---|---|
| Home | 8 | 4 | 2.90 | 0 | 93.0 | LHB | 380 | 92 | 13 | 36 | .242 |
| Road | 8 | 4 | 2.99 | 0 | 102.1 | RHB | 337 | 71 | 9 | 31 | .211 |
| First Half | 7 | 1 | 1.61 | 0 | 78.1 | Sc Pos | 157 | 29 | 5 | 45 | .185 |
| Scnd Half | 9 | 7 | 3.85 | 0 | 117.0 | Clutch | 68 | 16 | 1 | 4 | .235 |

### 1995 Rankings (American League)

→ 2nd in ERA
→ 3rd in hit batsmen (9), lowest on-base percentage allowed (.300), least baserunners allowed per 9 innings (11.1) and lowest batting average allowed with runners in scoring position (.185)
→ 4th in complete games (6), wild pitches (11), lowest batting average allowed (.227), ERA at home (2.90), ERA on the road (2.99) and lowest batting average allowed vs. right-handed batters (.211)
→ Led the Red Sox in ERA, wins, losses, complete games and shutouts (1)

# Vaughn Eshelman

**Position:** SP/RP
**Bats:** L **Throws:** L
**Ht:** 6' 3" **Wt:** 210

**Opening Day Age:** 26
**Born:** 5/22/69 in
Philadelphia, PA
**ML Seasons:** 1

## Overall Statistics

| | W | L | Pct. | ERA | G | GS | Sv | IP | H | BB | SO | HR | BR/IP |
|---|---|---|---|---|---|---|---|---|---|---|---|---|---|
| 1995 | 6 | 3 | .667 | 4.85 | 23 | 14 | 0 | 81.2 | 86 | 36 | 41 | 3 | 1.49 |
| Career | 6 | 3 | .667 | 4.85 | 23 | 14 | 0 | 81.2 | 86 | 36 | 41 | 3 | 1.49 |

## 1995 Season

Red Sox general manager Dan Duquette loves bargains, and Vaughn Eshelman, plucked from right under Baltimore owner Peter Angelos' nose, was one of his better ones. The Red Sox took Eshelman for $50,000 in the December, 1994 Rule 5 draft, and Eshelman turned out to be a worthwhile investment. Thrust into the rotation at the start of the year, Eshelman began his career with 18.1 straight scoreless innings. Unfortunately, he went 3-3 with a 6.25 ERA the the rest of the way. But he'd made his contribution.

## Pitching & Defense

Eshelman has decent stuff, beginning with a tailing, running fastball he used on both sides of the plate effectively. His slider was inconsistent at times, which is why lefthanders batted .367 against him. His change-up came and went, too. Eshelman is an average fielder. He is, however, very tough to run on, with a good move to first and an exceptionally quick delivery home. Only two runners tried to steal on him; both were nailed.

## 1996 Outlook

One reason for Eshelman's fade is that he was on the disabled list three times with various shoulder problems. He also missed the entire 1992 season after surgery on his ulnar nerve. He'll need to prove he's healthy before he can make a major league roster, and a return to the minors is a strong possibility.

# Bill Haselman

**Position:** C
**Bats:** R **Throws:** R
**Ht:** 6' 3" **Wt:** 215

**Opening Day Age:** 29
**Born:** 5/25/66 in Long
Branch, NJ
**ML Seasons:** 5
Pronunciation:
HASS-el-mun

## Overall Statistics

| | G | AB | R | H | D | T | HR | RBI | SB | BB | SO | Avg | OBP | Slg |
|---|---|---|---|---|---|---|---|---|---|---|---|---|---|---|
| 1995 | 64 | 152 | 22 | 37 | 6 | 1 | 5 | 23 | 0 | 17 | 30 | .243 | .322 | .395 |
| Career | 175 | 404 | 55 | 95 | 21 | 2 | 11 | 50 | 3 | 33 | 72 | .235 | .296 | .379 |

## 1995 Season

Another of last season's "Price Club specials," catcher Bill Haselman had a nice season for the Red Sox after being signed as a minor league free agent. Haselman was a backup to Mike Macfarlane most of the season, but got an opportuunity for increased playing time after the All-Star break. While his hitting wasn't great, it was adequate, and he did a good job behind the plate. He is a mobile, athletic receiver; after all, he once was beaten out of the UCLA quarterback job by Troy Aikman.

## Hitting, Baserunning & Defense

Haselman's most memorable moment was an 11th-inning, game-winning homer on June 27 to beat the Blue Jays. Though he won't hit for much of an average, he has decent power. Haselman's main value is on defense. He caught pretty well and threw out 31 percent of opposing runners. Because he is such a good athlete, Haselman was able to fill in at both third and first bases, which enhances his value. He has decent speed for a catcher.

## 1996 Outlook

Haselman has come a long way since since 1987, when a serious shoulder operation set back his development. He played well in spots for the Red Sox last year, and could return in a backup role again this year.

# Dave Hollins

**Position**: 1B
**Bats**: B  **Throws**: R
**Ht**: 6' 1"  **Wt**: 207

**Opening Day Age**: 29
**Born**: 5/25/66 in Buffalo, NY
**ML Seasons**: 6

*Overall Statistics*

| | G | AB | R | H | D | T | HR | RBI | SB | BB | SO | Avg | OBP | Slg |
|---|---|---|---|---|---|---|---|---|---|---|---|---|---|---|
| 1995 | 70 | 218 | 48 | 49 | 12 | 2 | 7 | 26 | 1 | 57 | 45 | .225 | .391 | .394 |
| Career | 541 | 1774 | 316 | 457 | 87 | 13 | 67 | 274 | 14 | 268 | 350 | .258 | .363 | .435 |

## 1995 Season

Acquired from the Phillies in a midseason trade for Mark Whiten, Dave Hollins played only five games for the Red Sox, then fractured his wrist and missed the remainder of the season. It was the second straight season that Hollins had missed considerable time with injuries, and the second straight year he was unproductive when well enough to play.

## Hitting, Baserunning & Defense

Hollins used to be a feared switch-hitter with excellent power, but his career has been derailed by his hand and wrist injuries. Always a better hitter from the right side, he hasn't been able to catch up to the inside fastball and turn on it as he could when he was healthy. On the other hand, Hollins has become one of the more patient hitters in the majors, and his on-base average last year was excellent. Defense has been a problem; he was so weak at third that the Phils moved him off the position, but he hasn't looked comfortable at either first base or in the outfield. Hollins isn't a steal threat, but he's a good, aggressive baserunner and makes the most of his average speed.

## 1996 Outlook

Hollins' career has hit the skids. It hasn't helped that along with his other problems, he's developed a reputation for having a bad attitude. Regaining his old hitting form would solve a lot of problems, but he'll also need to find a position. He could be a productive DH if healthy.

# Reggie Jefferson

**Position**: DH
**Bats**: L  **Throws**: L
**Ht**: 6' 4"  **Wt**: 210

**Opening Day Age**: 27
**Born**: 9/25/68 in Tallahassee, FL
**ML Seasons**: 5

*Overall Statistics*

| | G | AB | R | H | D | T | HR | RBI | SB | BB | SO | Avg | OBP | Slg |
|---|---|---|---|---|---|---|---|---|---|---|---|---|---|---|
| 1995 | 46 | 121 | 21 | 35 | 8 | 0 | 5 | 26 | 0 | 9 | 24 | .289 | .333 | .479 |
| Career | 277 | 846 | 99 | 230 | 39 | 4 | 27 | 111 | 1 | 59 | 175 | .272 | .323 | .423 |

## 1995 Season

Signed as a free agent to add strength to the Red Sox bench corps, Reggie Jefferson gave Boston good production for as long as he was healthy last year. A lower back injury sidelined Jefferson for much of the second half, but he returned late in the year and made the club's postseason roster.

## Hitting, Baserunning & Defense

Formerly a switch-hitter, Jefferson had so many problems hitting righty that he became a full-time left-handed batter. He still struggles against lefties and hardly ever faces them any more. He can hit for power and likes to pull the low inside fastball. Though he's capable of going deep, he has a tendency to swing over the ball, which results in lots of grounders. Jefferson is slow on the bases and very weak defensively. He could play the outfield or first base in an emergency, but his best position is DH.

## 1996 Outlook

Since the Red Sox employed Jefferson for a relatively low salary and he provides them with additional left-handed power, there's a good chance the front office will keep him around for 1996. If the Sox don't want him back, he shouldn't have much trouble finding work. Still only 27, he's become a useful bench player and seems to be fashioning a career as a pinch hitter and platoon DH.

# Mike Maddux

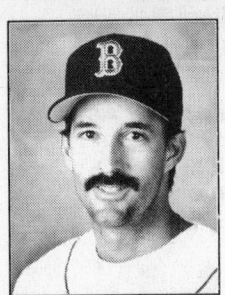

**Position**: RP/SP
**Bats**: L **Throws**: R
**Ht**: 6' 2"  **Wt**: 190

**Opening Day Age**: 34
**Born**: 8/27/61 in
Dayton, OH
**ML Seasons**: 10

*Overall Statistics*

|  | W | L | Pct. | ERA | G | GS | Sv | IP | H | BB | SO | HR | BR/IP |
|---|---|---|---|---|---|---|---|---|---|---|---|---|---|
| 1995 | 5 | 1 | .833 | 4.10 | 44 | 4 | 1 | 98.2 | 100 | 18 | 69 | 5 | 1.20 |
| Career | 29 | 28 | .509 | 3.87 | 318 | 41 | 19 | 644.0 | 633 | 200 | 430 | 39 | 1.29 |

## 1995 Season

Dropped by the lowly Pirates early last season after refusing to accept a minor league assignment, Mike Maddux signed with the Red Sox and wound up being a useful contibutor to a club which won a division championship. While he didn't exactly pitch like his younger brother Greg, Maddux served the Sox well in a middle-relief role. He also responded when given four emergency starts, going 2-0 with a 3.32 ERA.

## Pitching & Defense

Maddux has an 86-87 MPH fastball which bores in on right-handed hitters. He leans toward the third-base side when he delivers, throwing with a three-quarters motion which helps him against right-handed hitters. Maddux' fastball has a nice sink to it, and he gets a lot of groundball outs. He also throws a decent curve and slider, along with an occasional change-up. Maddux has a slow delivery and is pretty easy to steal on, but he's a good, alert fielder.

## 1996 Outlook

Signed at a bargain-basement price last year, Maddux gave the Red Sox good return on their investment. He's filed for free agency, but they'd like to have him back if his demands are reasonable. He's the kind of smart veteran teams like having in their bullpen, and his ability to start on occasion is an added bonus.

# Willie McGee

**Position**: RF/CF
**Bats**: B **Throws**: R
**Ht**: 6' 1"  **Wt**: 185

**Opening Day Age**: 37
**Born**: 11/2/58 in San
Francisco, CA
**ML Seasons**: 14

*Overall Statistics*

|  | G | AB | R | H | D | T | HR | RBI | SB | BB | SO | Avg | OBP | Slg |
|---|---|---|---|---|---|---|---|---|---|---|---|---|---|---|
| 1995 | 67 | 200 | 32 | 57 | 11 | 3 | 2 | 15 | 5 | 9 | 41 | .285 | .311 | .400 |
| Career | 1704 | 6500 | 877 | 1933 | 299 | 87 | 68 | 723 | 325 | 377 | 1010 | .297 | .335 | .402 |

## 1995 Season

What you have to know about Willie McGee is that when he arrived in Boston on July 5, the former MVP and two-time batting champion was asked about his role with the Red Sox. "I'm just here to help," replied McGee. "I'm not here to take anyone's job, I'm here to try to help if they need me." Though he was coming off an Achilles tendon operation and was bothered by foot and knee problems, McGee still managed to slash out a .285 average, including some big clutch hits.

## Hitting, Baserunning & Defnse

McGee has never been a good breaking-ball hitter. He is what scouts call an "untamed" hitter, apt to rack fastballs anywhere, over his head, on the ground. He loves to hack; he put the first pitch in play about once every five trips to the plate. Because of all the injuries, McGee doesn't run the way he once did. The injuries also affected him in the outfield. He really cannot play center field any more, but he did an adequate job in Fenway's difficult right field. His arm is strong.

## 1996 Outlook

If another's winter of rest and conditioning restores health to his legs, McGee will once again be a useful player on the field. He is always a productive teamate *off* the field.

# Ken Ryan

**Position:** RP
**Bats:** R **Throws:** R
**Ht:** 6' 3"  **Wt:** 230

**Opening Day Age:** 27
**Born:** 10/24/68 in
Pawtucket, RI
**ML Seasons:** 4

*Overall Statistics*

| | W | L | Pct. | ERA | G | GS | Sv | IP | H | BB | SO | HR | BR/IP |
|---|---|---|---|---|---|---|---|---|---|---|---|---|---|
| 1995 | 0 | 4 | .000 | 4.96 | 28 | 0 | 7 | 32.2 | 34 | 24 | 34 | 4 | 1.78 |
| Career | 9 | 9 | .500 | 3.66 | 124 | 0 | 22 | 137.2 | 127 | 75 | 120 | 9 | 1.47 |

## 1995 Season

After racking up 13 saves and a 2.44 earned-run average for the Red Sox in 1994, Ken Ryan was expected to step into the closer role last year. Instead, Ryan ended up in the minor leagues, compiling a 6.00 ERA between Double-A Trenton and Triple-A Pawtucket. Although he rejoined the club in September, he was not on the postseason roster.

## Pitching & Defense

Ryan can throw in the 90s, but because his delivery can easily get out of sync, sometimes he throws 93, sometimes 88. He cannot survive on his fastball alone because it tends to be straight when up in the zone. His best pitch may be his curveball, and when he's throwing it for strikes and using his slider to get righthanders off his fastball, he has more than enough. He has problems both defensively and holding runners.

## 1996 Outlook

Ryan fell into Kevin Kennedy's doghouse after a game-blowing gopher ball against the Indians on June 19, and he couldn't regain either his confidence or consistency. There has been speculation that coming from nearby Seekonk, with family and friends around, puts too much pressure on Ryan, particularly when he's pitching at Fenway. He is not the Mark Wohlers that locals make him out to be, and perhaps too much has been expected of him.

# Mike Stanton

**Position:** RP
**Bats:** L **Throws:** L
**Ht:** 6' 1"  **Wt:** 190

**Opening Day Age:** 28
**Born:** 6/2/67 in
Houston, TX
**ML Seasons:** 7

*Overall Statistics*

| | W | L | Pct. | ERA | G | GS | Sv | IP | H | BB | SO | HR | BR/IP |
|---|---|---|---|---|---|---|---|---|---|---|---|---|---|
| 1995 | 2 | 1 | .667 | 4.24 | 48 | 0 | 1 | 40.1 | 48 | 14 | 23 | 6 | 1.54 |
| Career | 19 | 21 | .475 | 3.94 | 326 | 0 | 55 | 310.2 | 294 | 122 | 233 | 25 | 1.34 |

## 1995 Season

As the July trading deadline approached, the Red Sox explored several possibilities. They wanted David Cone and discussed Bret Saberhagen, but took the smaller route and went for lefthander Mike Stanton, who had been lost in the Atlanta bullpen. Because of his inactivity, Stanton was "out of time," as Mick Jagger once put it, after joining the club. But he found his rhythm and posted a 1.10 ERA over his last 17 appearances.

## Pitching & Defense

Stanton has a herky-jerky delivery and tends to throw on emotion, which leaves him vulnerable to getting out of sync. His fastball only occasionally touches 90 miles per hour, but because of his spinning, short-armed delivery, it is very difficult to pick up. The fastball also runs and sinks—hard—and the more he pitched in Boston, the more his slider came back. While his fielding is poorer than average, Stanton unloads quickly to the plate, so he is very tough to run on.

## 1996 Outlook

In Atlanta, there was a time when Stanton was thought to be closer material, and some still might feel that way. He has the stuff. He also wants the ball, a quality which makes him attractive to managers. He should be getting plenty of work out of somebody's bullpen this year; it could well be Boston's.

# Other Boston Red Sox

## Brian Bark (Pos: LHP, Age: 27)

The trade from Atlanta might save Bark's career. He should at least get a chance in Boston, after pitching very well in Pawtucket in 1995. Could turn into a decent left-handed set-up man. 1996 Outlook: C

## Juan Bell (Pos: SS, Age: 28, Bats: B)

Bell's major league career appears to be finished. He spent most of 1995 in Pawtucket, and continued to hit very poorly. 1996 Outlook: D

## Chris Donnels (Pos: 3B, Age: 29, Bats: L)

Donnels came to the Red Sox from Houston in June, and continued his role as a left-handed bat. He plays a bunch of positions so he has some value. 1996 Outlook: B

## Eric Gunderson (Pos: LHP, Age: 30)

Gunderson struggled after being acquired off waivers from the Mets. Given his age, 1996 appears to be a make or break season. 1996 Outlook: C

## Scott Hatteberg (Pos: C, Age: 26, Bats: L)

Hatteberg has been buried in the minors since being drafted by the Red Sox in 1991. He's done little with the bat the last three seasons at Triple-A, but as a catcher he still might get a look in the majors. 1996 Outlook: C

## Dwayne Hosey (Pos: CF, Age: 29, Bats: B)

Hosey hit .338 in 24 games with the Red Sox after being waived by Kansas City. He hit very well at Triple-A in 1995, but the Royals let him go anyway. He should get a chance. 1996 Outlook: B

## Joe Hudson (Pos: RHP, Age: 25)

Hudson got his first shot in the majors in 1995, used almost exclusively as a set-up man with mixed results. He'll be just 25 on Opening Day, and should be a solid contributor the next few seasons. 1996 Outlook: A

## Chris James (Pos: DH, Age: 33, Bats: R)

James fought the DL most of 1995, hitting .268 in 42 games. He'll likely still play as a fourth outfielder somewhere in the majors, assuming he's healthy. 1996 Outlook: B

## Joel Johnston (Pos: RHP, Age: 29)

It's amazing he's still around, as 1995 was his fifth consecutive season in the minors with an ERA over 5.00. Still has a live arm, which is why he keeps getting opportunities. 1996 Outlook: D

## Brian Looney (Pos: LHP, Age: 26)

Despite three different call-ups from Triple-A, Looney barely got to pitch for the Red Sox in 1995. He had a decent season at Pawtucket as a starter, and has some hope at his age. 1996 Outlook: C

## Ron Mahay (Pos: CF, Age: 24, Bats: L)

Since being drafted in 1991, Mahay has consistently struggled at the plate. 1995 was no exception, as he continued to be very strikeout prone. 1996 Outlook: D

## Matt Murray (Pos: RHP, Age: 25)

Murray was an outstanding starter in the Atlanta organization before coming to Boston. His strikeout-to-walk ratios in the minors have been super, and he'll get a good look next season. 1996 Outlook: B

## Jeff Pierce (Pos: RHP, Age: 26)

Pierce pitched very poorly to start the season, issuing 14 walks in 15 innings, and was sent to Pawtucket for the rest of the year. Deserves another shot. 1996 Outlook: C

## Karl Rhodes (Pos: LF, Age: 27, Bats: L)

Rhodes was acquired off waivers from the Cubs in May, and proceeded to go 2-for-25 (.080) for the Red Sox. He's never hit well, doesn't draw walks, and is below average defensively. Outlook: C

## Carlos Rodriguez (Pos: 2B, Age: 28, Bats: B)

After a promising 1994, Rodriguez got just 30 at-bats with the Red Sox in 1995 (.333). If he's going to make it in the majors, it will probably be with another team. He's played second and shortstop. 1996 Outlook: C

## Rich Rowland (Pos: C, Age: 32, Bats: R)

Rowland's best bet is to try to catch on with a major league team carrying three catchers. He's hit very poorly (.218) in his last two stints with the Red Sox and he's not getting any younger. Outlook: D

## Keith Shepherd (Pos: RHP, Age: 28)

Shepherd was placed on the DL in May with shoulder tendinitis, and was waived soon after that. He hasn't pitched well in the minors since 1992. 1996 Outlook: D

## Terry Shumpert (Pos: 2B, Age: 29, Bats: R)

Shumpert has little to offer at this point. He hit just .234 in a short stint with Boston in 1995, slightly above his career average. He rarely walks, and strikes out much too often. 1996 Outlook: C

## Matt Stairs (Pos: LF, Age: 28, Bats: L)

Stairs hit .261 for the Red Sox in 39 games in 1995, used primarily as a pinch hitter. Still has the potential to be a decent fourth outfielder. 1996 Outlook: B

## Tim VanEgmond (Pos: RHP, Age: 26)

After leading the league in strikeouts at Double-A in 1993, nothing has gone right for VanEgmond in the majors. He's pitched very poorly in short stints the last two years. He could make it back. 1996 Outlook: C

# Boston Red Sox Minor League Prospects

## Organization Overview:

The Red Sox may have done a better job of drafting over the past three years than any team in baseball. Boston still may be a little thin in the upper levels of its farm system, but the lower levels are full of power pitchers, great athletes and exciting prospects. The rebuilding began in earnest in 1993, when the Red Sox chose Trot Nixon, Jeff Suppan, Ryan McGuire and Shawn Senior with their first four picks. In 1994, Boston followed the first-round selection of prospect Nomar Garciaparra with a host of legitimate pitching prospects, including Brian Rose, Carl Pavano and Denis McLaughlin. The Red Sox' 11th-round pick that year, shortstop Donnie Sadler, may in fact be their most exciting talent. And in 1995, Boston chose two of the finest high-school players available with its first two picks: Andy Yount, one of the draft's hardest-throwing righthanders, and Corey Jenkins, a tremendous athlete. A recurring Red Sox tactic has been to draft high school stars whom other teams may consider unsignable, pursue them aggressively, and come away with "high-ceiling" talent.

### Nomar Garciaparra

**Position:** SS **Opening Day Age:** 22
**Bats:** R **Throws:** R **Born:** 7/23/73 in
**Ht:** 6' 1" **Wt:** 175 Whittier, CA

*Recent Statistics*

|  | G | AB | R | H | D | T | HR | RBI | SB | BB | SO | AVG |
|---|---|---|---|---|---|---|---|---|---|---|---|---|
| 94 A Sarasota | 28 | 105 | 20 | 31 | 8 | 1 | 1 | 16 | 5 | 10 | 6 | .295 |
| 95 AA Trenton | 125 | 513 | 77 | 137 | 20 | 8 | 8 | 47 | 35 | 50 | 42 | .267 |
| 95 MLE | 125 | 514 | 74 | 138 | 22 | 6 | 7 | 45 | 25 | 41 | 44 | .268 |

Garciaparra is one of those players with a broad range of skills whose talents gain respect the longer he's viewed. He's a slick-fielding shortstop with a strong arm and excellent range, especially to his left. His bat makes consistent contact and shows surprising pop. Add in good strike-zone judgment and 30 stolen bases a year, and you can see why the Red Sox drafted Garciaparra with the 12th pick of the 1994 draft. Garciaparra will likely start 1996 at Triple-A.

### Jose Malave

**Position:** OF **Opening Day Age:** 24
**Bats:** R **Throws:** R **Born:** 5/31/71 in
**Ht:** 6' 2" **Wt:** 195 Cumana, Venez

*Recent Statistics*

|  | G | AB | R | H | D | T | HR | RBI | SB | BB | SO | AVG |
|---|---|---|---|---|---|---|---|---|---|---|---|---|
| 93 A Lynchburg | 82 | 312 | 42 | 94 | 27 | 1 | 8 | 54 | 2 | 36 | 54 | .301 |
| 94 AA New Britain | 122 | 465 | 87 | 139 | 37 | 7 | 24 | 92 | 4 | 52 | 81 | .299 |
| 95 AAA Pawtucket | 91 | 318 | 55 | 86 | 12 | 1 | 23 | 57 | 0 | 30 | 67 | .270 |
| 95 MLE | 91 | 314 | 48 | 82 | 12 | 0 | 19 | 50 | 0 | 26 | 70 | .261 |

Malave was the subject of trade rumors last year following a spectacular Double-A season in a tough pitcher's park. He led the Eastern League in 1994 in doubles, RBI and slugging, and although his 1995 season was stalled by injury, Malave actually improved his home-run rate after making the jump to Triple-A. Malave has quick hands, hits with power to all fields and handles breaking pitches as well as fastballs. His bat appears ready for the big leagues right now, but his glove is a concern. He doesn't look good in left field, and DH is probably his best "position."

### Glenn Murray

**Position:** OF **Opening Day Age:** 25
**Bats:** R **Throws:** R **Born:** 11/23/70 in
**Ht:** 6' 2" **Wt:** 200 Manning, SC

*Recent Statistics*

|  | G | AB | R | H | D | T | HR | RBI | SB | BB | SO | AVG |
|---|---|---|---|---|---|---|---|---|---|---|---|---|
| 93 AA Harrisburg | 127 | 475 | 82 | 120 | 21 | 4 | 26 | 96 | 16 | 56 | 111 | .253 |
| 94 AAA Pawtucket | 130 | 465 | 74 | 104 | 17 | 1 | 25 | 64 | 9 | 55 | 134 | .224 |
| 95 AAA Pawtucket | 104 | 336 | 66 | 82 | 15 | 0 | 25 | 66 | 5 | 34 | 109 | .244 |
| 95 MLE | 104 | 332 | 58 | 78 | 16 | 0 | 21 | 58 | 3 | 30 | 114 | .235 |

Murray's talents belong in the same class as Dave Kingman, Rob Deer and Cory Snyder. Like the others, Murray's home-run ability gets swallowed up by his offensive liabilities. Murray has hit at least 25 homers each of the past three seasons, but that's basically the extent of his contribution. His strikeout rate, which was never good, has actually deteriorated. His stolen bases have fallen from a high of 26 in 1992 to five last year. After seven seasons and 687 minor league games, Murray's career batting average is .234. However, his power could land him a major league job in 1996.

### Trot Nixon

**Position:** OF **Opening Day Age:** 21
**Bats:** L **Throws:** L **Born:** 4/11/74 in
**Ht:** 6' 1" **Wt:** 195 Durham, NC

*Recent Statistics*

|  | G | AB | R | H | D | T | HR | RBI | SB | BB | SO | AVG |
|---|---|---|---|---|---|---|---|---|---|---|---|---|
| 94 A Lynchburg | 71 | 264 | 33 | 65 | 12 | 0 | 12 | 43 | 10 | 44 | 53 | .246 |
| 95 A Sarasota | 73 | 264 | 43 | 80 | 11 | 4 | 5 | 39 | 7 | 45 | 46 | .303 |
| 95 AA Trenton | 25 | 94 | 9 | 15 | 3 | 1 | 2 | 8 | 2 | 7 | 20 | .160 |

Nixon's athleticism and impressive bat speed made him the seventh overall pick in the 1993 draft, but the Red Sox had to pay almost $900,000 to convince him to forego a football scholarship from North Carolina State. Nixon signed too late to compete in '93, and a back injury ended his '94 season in July. He didn't show much power in '95, possibly due to the lingering effects of the broken vertabrae. He did, however, hit .303 in the Florida State League, and continued to demonstrate a good batting eye. Nixon brings a football player's intensity to the diamond, and should his power return as he gains lower back strength, he possesses all the physical tools to become an All-Star.

## Rafael Orellano

**Position:** P **Opening Day Age:** 22
**Bats:** L **Throws:** L **Born:** 4/28/73 in
**Ht:** 6' 2" **Wt:** 160 Humacao, PR

*Recent Statistics*

|  | W | L | ERA | G | GS | Sv | IP | H | R | BB | SO | HR |
|---|---|---|---|---|---|---|---|---|---|---|---|---|
| 93 A Utica | 1 | 2 | 5.79 | 11 | 0 | 2 | 18.2 | 22 | 15 | 7 | 13 | 4 |
| 94 R Red Sox | 1 | 0 | 2.03 | 4 | 3 | 0 | 13.1 | 6 | 3 | 4 | 10 | 0 |
| 94 A Sarasota | 11 | 3 | 2.40 | 16 | 16 | 0 | 97.1 | 68 | 28 | 25 | 103 | 5 |
| 95 AA Trenton | 11 | 7 | 3.09 | 27 | 27 | 0 | 186.2 | 146 | 68 | 72 | 160 | 18 |

Orellano's career had trouble getting started after the Red Sox signed him as a free agent in 1992. Since overcoming tendinitis in his elbow and having a non-malignant tumor removed from his leg, Orellano has established himself as one of the best lefty pitching prospects around. Over the last two seasons, Orellano has allowed less than seven hits per nine innings while striking out 8.33 per nine. Many of his punchouts result from a debilitating fosh change-up taught by current Red Sox pitching coach Al Nipper. The next logical step for Orellano is Triple-A, but a lefthander with his track record could move up quickly.

## Donnie Sadler

**Position:** SS **Opening Day Age:** 20
**Bats:** R **Throws:** R **Born:** 6/17/75 in
**Ht:** 5' 6" **Wt:** 160 Clifton, TX

*Recent Statistics*

|  | G | AB | R | H | D | T | HR | RBI | SB | BB | SO | AVG |
|---|---|---|---|---|---|---|---|---|---|---|---|---|
| 94 R Red Sox | 53 | 206 | 52 | 56 | 8 | 6 | 1 | 16 | 32 | 23 | 27 | .272 |
| 95 A Michigan | 118 | 438 | 103 | 124 | 25 | 8 | 9 | 55 | 41 | 79 | 85 | .283 |

He hasn't played above slow-A, but Sadler looks like the second coming of Rickey Henderson. Sadler used his 5'6" frame to good advantage last season, drawing 79 walks to complement a .283 batting average. He may be the fastest man the Red Sox have ever had in their system, and he's a smart baserunner. Despite his size, Sadler has been known to knock over catchers, and he produced 42 extra-base hits last season. With all the walks, stolen bases and extra-base hits, Sadler seems to constantly be in scoring position, crossing the plate 103 times in only 118 games in 1995. Sadler is currently playing shortstop, but he might end up in the outfield.

## Bill Selby

**Position:** 3B **Opening Day Age:** 25
**Bats:** L **Throws:** R **Born:** 6/11/70 in
**Ht:** 5' 9" **Wt:** 190 Monroeville, AL

*Recent Statistics*

|  | G | AB | R | H | D | T | HR | RBI | SB | BB | SO | AVG |
|---|---|---|---|---|---|---|---|---|---|---|---|---|
| 93 A Lynchburg | 113 | 394 | 57 | 99 | 22 | 1 | 7 | 38 | 1 | 24 | 66 | .251 |
| 94 A Lynchburg | 97 | 352 | 58 | 109 | 20 | 2 | 19 | 69 | 3 | 28 | 62 | .310 |
| 94 AA New Britain | 35 | 107 | 15 | 28 | 5 | 0 | 1 | 18 | 0 | 15 | 16 | .262 |
| 95 AA Trenton | 117 | 451 | 64 | 129 | 29 | 2 | 13 | 68 | 4 | 46 | 52 | .286 |
| 95 MLE | 117 | 453 | 61 | 131 | 32 | 1 | 11 | 65 | 2 | 37 | 55 | .289 |

Selby was the Red Sox' 13th-round draft pick in 1992. He's hit well the past two seasons, batting a combined .292 with nice double, homer and walk totals. Selby played most of last season in Double-A at 25, so he can't be considered a great prospect. He played shortstop in college, but was moved to third base by the Red Sox. He's also been tried at second, and it will probably be as a utilityman that he eventually plays in the majors.

## Jeff Suppan

**Position:** P **Opening Day Age:** 21
**Bats:** R **Throws:** R **Born:** 1/2/75 in
**Ht:** 6' 1" **Wt:** 200 Oklahoma City, OK

*Recent Statistics*

|  | W | L | ERA | G | GS | Sv | IP | H | R | BB | SO | HR |
|---|---|---|---|---|---|---|---|---|---|---|---|---|
| 95 AA Trenton | 6 | 2 | 2.36 | 15 | 15 | 0 | 99.0 | 86 | 35 | 26 | 88 | 5 |
| 95 AAA Pawtucket | 2 | 3 | 5.32 | 7 | 7 | 0 | 45.2 | 50 | 29 | 9 | 32 | 9 |
| 95 AL Boston | 1 | 2 | 5.96 | 8 | 3 | 0 | 22.2 | 29 | 15 | 5 | 19 | 4 |

Suppan was a second-round pick out of high school in 1993, and made it to the majors two years later at the tender age of 20. While he went only 1-2, 5.96 during the crunch of the pennant race, his ERA was distorted by one bad outing, and he continued to display the high strikeout rates and excellent strikeout-to-walk ratios characteristic of his minor league career. Suppan pitches with a poise which belies his age, changing speeds effectively and mixing in three quality pitches, including the fosh change that Al Nipper is fond of. While Suppan may begin 1996 with more seasoning at Triple-A, he should soon be a fixture in the Red Sox rotation for years to come.

## Others to Watch

Righthander **Brent Hanson** was a 19th-round draft pick in 1992 who pitched well at Triple-A Pawtucket last season. His best asset has been excellent control, and last year he walked only 40 batters in roughly 170 innings. . . First baseman **Ryan McGuire** was expected to be a big home-run hitter when the Red Sox drafted him in the third round in 1993. But through three minor league seasons, he looks like Mark Grace: lots of doubles, walks and a .300 batting average. . . Besides boasting one of the best names in baseball, **Pork Chop Pough** brings legitimate power to the table. His home-run totals have risen from 11 to 13 to 20 to 26 since 1992. Pough also walks and hits doubles, but he is 26 nowRight-handed pitchers **Brian Rose** and **Carl Pavano**, New England natives both, were considered unsignable when drafted out of high school in 1994, but the Red Sox gambled and won. Rose was impressive in his 1995 pro debut, excelling in the full-season Midwest League (8-5, 3.44). Pavano, a 13th-rounder, was even harder to hit and posted a higher strikeout rate while compiling the same 3.44 ERA. . . Lefthander **Shawn Senior**, a fourth-rounder in 1993, rose to Triple-A last year. Though not overpowering, Senior does win, with a career 44-25 record in the minor leagues.

# Jim Abbott

## 1995 Season

In many ways, the California organization was scarred by Whitey Herzog's callous 1992 trade of folk hero Jim Abbott to the New York Yankees for J.T. Snow and two since-forgotten pitchers. The Angels' new regime tried to turn around that blow to their karma, making a late-July deal with the Chicago White Sox to bring Abbott back to Anaheim Stadium. He made some big starts for California—including a three-hit shutout at Texas to end a nine-game losing streak on September 24—helping keep the Angels in the hunt with the Seattle Mariners for the American League West title.

## Pitching

Abbott's good fastball was wasted in his youth. He simply does not have the stuff that helped him win 18 games during his first stint with the Angels back in 1991. He struggled to throw strikes with his curveball, forcing him too often to try and get by with just two pitches—his fastball and his cut fastball. At this point in his career, Abbott is forced to paint the corners to survive. He doesn't throw hard enough anymore to allow him to change speeds. Right-handed hitters almost never swing and miss his pitches—as his totals of 3.9 strikeouts and 2.9 walks per nine innings would indicate.

## Defense

Despite having only one hand, Abbott remains a solid fielder. He's worked hard to keep runners close, and it showed in 1995, as he held potential basestealers to a respectable 63 percent success rate. His reactions on the mound remain quick. Few pitchers have his overall presence.

## 1996 Outlook

California was expected to re-sign Abbott, who played on a one-year contract last season. He'll need some magic to repeat the 3.70 ERA he compiled with the White Sox and Angels last year. Unless his velocity returns (and there's no reason to expect it will), this could be an ugly season for Abbott. Though only 28, he's entering the post-fastball "Frank Tanana" stage of his remarkable career.

**Position:** SP
**Bats:** L **Throws:** L
**Ht:** 6' 3" **Wt:** 210

**Opening Day Age:** 28
**Born:** 9/19/67 in Flint, MI
**ML Seasons:** 7

### Overall Statistics

|  | W | L | Pct. | ERA | G | GS | Sv | IP | H | BB | SO | HR | BR/IP |
|---|---|---|---|---|---|---|---|---|---|---|---|---|---|
| 1995 | 11 | 8 | .579 | 3.70 | 30 | 30 | 0 | 197.0 | 209 | 64 | 86 | 14 | 1.39 |
| Career | 78 | 82 | .488 | 3.77 | 211 | 211 | 0 | 1418.1 | 1463 | 488 | 779 | 115 | 1.38 |

### How Often He Throws Strikes

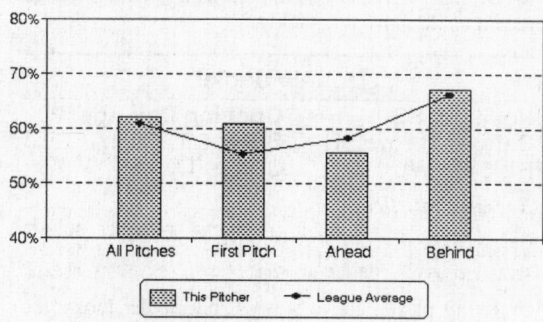

### 1995 Situational Stats

|  | W | L | ERA | Sv | IP |  | AB | H | HR | RBI | Avg |
|---|---|---|---|---|---|---|---|---|---|---|---|
| Home | 3 | 6 | 5.02 | 0 | 86.0 | LHB | 144 | 41 | 2 | 14 | .285 |
| Road | 8 | 2 | 2.68 | 0 | 111.0 | RHB | 620 | 168 | 12 | 65 | .271 |
| First Half | 4 | 4 | 3.35 | 0 | 91.1 | Sc Pos | 184 | 50 | 2 | 63 | .272 |
| Scnd Half | 7 | 4 | 4.00 | 0 | 105.2 | Clutch | 63 | 17 | 4 | 9 | .270 |

### 1995 Rankings (American League)

→ 1st in least pitches thrown per batter (3.48) and fielding percentage at pitcher (1.000)
→ 2nd in ERA on the road (2.68)
→ 4th in pickoff throws (201), GDPs induced (25), most GDPs induced per 9 innings (1.1), least strikeouts per 9 innings (3.9)
→ 5th in runners caught stealing (9) and least home runs allowed per 9 innings (.64)
→ 6th in highest groundball/flyball ratio allowed (2.0)
→ 8th in complete games (4)
→ Led the Angels in shutouts (1) and most GDPs induced per GDP situation (16.9%)

# Brian Anderson

## 1995 Season

Expectations were high for lefthander Brian Anderson in his second season in the Angel rotation. But the post-strike campaign turned out to be a nightmare instead. Anderson suffered a strained muscle in his arm during his second start and was out until late June. He never got back up to speed when he returned, and quickly lost confidence. He stopped challenging hitters and became a nibbler. Anderson got knocked out in the second inning of back-to-back starts on August 31 and September 5, then pitched in just one more game, a six-inning relief stint, the rest of the season. This was hardly the type of development the Angels hoped to see from Anderson.

## Pitching

When he's on, Anderson gets good movement on his fastball and has a sweeping curveball. He changes speeds well, and has good command of both sides of the plate. That command was often lacking last season. All too often, he worked from behind in the count—always a recipe for disaster for a finesse pitcher. Even left-handed hitters pounded Anderson last year. From both sides of the plate, it was simply "bombs away" against him. Souvenir hunters picked bleacher seats for Anderson's starts.

## Defense

Anderson is a solid fundamental fielder on come-backers and bunts. He throws to first only to hold runners on, not to pick them off. And he seemed to be constantly throwing over to first base last year.

## 1995 Outlook

Anderson's not yet 24, and there's plenty of time for him to develop. But by the end of the 1995 season, his stock had crashed. Ditto his confidence. He will get more chances to prove himself in the big leagues, but could find himself back in Triple-A this year if he can't show that his 1995 season was a fluke. The jury is out.

**Position:** SP
**Bats:** B **Throws:** L
**Ht:** 6' 1" **Wt:** 190

**Opening Day Age:** 23
**Born:** 4/26/72 in Geneva, OH
**ML Seasons:** 3

### Overall Statistics

|  | W | L | Pct. | ERA | G | GS | Sv | IP | H | BB | SO | HR | BR/IP |
|---|---|---|---|---|---|---|---|---|---|---|---|---|---|
| 1995 | 6 | 8 | .429 | 5.87 | 18 | 17 | 0 | 99.2 | 110 | 30 | 45 | 24 | 1.40 |
| Career | 13 | 13 | .500 | 5.46 | 40 | 36 | 0 | 212.2 | 241 | 59 | 96 | 38 | 1.41 |

### How Often He Throws Strikes

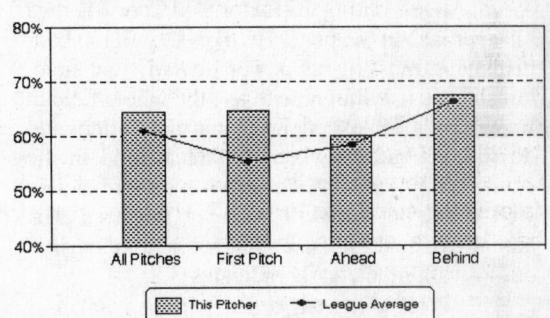

### 1995 Situational Stats

|  | W | L | ERA | Sv | IP |  | AB | H | HR | RBI | Avg |
|---|---|---|---|---|---|---|---|---|---|---|---|
| Home | 4 | 3 | 3.24 | 0 | 58.1 | LHB | 79 | 27 | 6 | 19 | .342 |
| Road | 2 | 5 | 9.58 | 0 | 41.1 | RHB | 311 | 83 | 18 | 38 | .267 |
| First Half | 2 | 2 | 4.19 | 0 | 34.1 | Sc Pos | 79 | 20 | 4 | 33 | .253 |
| Scnd Half | 4 | 6 | 6.75 | 0 | 65.1 | Clutch | 7 | 3 | 1 | 1 | .429 |

### 1995 Rankings (American League)

- ➡ 1st in balks (3)
- ➡ 8th in home runs allowed
- ➡ 10th in errors at pitcher (2)
- ➡ Led the Angels in home runs allowed and balks (3)

# Garret Anderson

## 1995 Season

A solid minor league portfolio built high expectations for Garret Anderson in 1995. But nobody thought Anderson would generate comparisons to Ken Griffey. That indeed happened, as Anderson seized the opportunity to play when California moved Tony Phillips from left field to third base in early June. Anderson wore out pitchers in July, hitting .410 and claiming American League Player of the Month honors. He slowed down late in the season, but finished second in Rookie of the Year balloting and heightened expectations for 1996.

## Hitting

Anderson has always generated tremendous bat speed. Angels hitting instructor Rod Carew helped his approach at the plate. He likes to pull the ball, displaying most of his power toward right field, but showed a willingness to use the whole field at times. He's an excellent two-strike hitter, and doesn't get ruffled when he falls behind in the count. A high-ball hitter, Anderson hit lefthanders well early, but couldn't keep up the pace. His batting eye could still use some work, as his strike-out-to-walk ratio clearly indicates.

## Baserunning & Defense

Anderson is a hitter, pure and simple—not a baserunner or defensive whiz. He doesn't run well; last year's modest total of six stolen bases was a career high for him. He's considered average in left field. He has a left fielder's arm, recording seven assists in 1995. He might be able to play center field, but doesn't throw well enough for right.

## 1996 Outlook

Anderson returns for his first full season as the Angels' regular left fielder. He could be challenged to repeat his rookie success, as pitchers built a book on him throughout the season. The most important knowledge may have come September 1, when Roger Clemens knocked him down with some high heat. Anderson, scouts say, was never the same after that.

**Position:** LF
**Bats:** L  **Throws:** L
**Ht:** 6' 3"  **Wt:** 190

**Opening Day Age:** 23
**Born:** 6/30/72 in Los Angeles, CA
**ML Seasons:** 2

### Overall Statistics

|        | G   | AB  | R  | H   | D  | T | HR | RBI | SB | BB | SO | Avg  | OBP  | Slg  |
|--------|-----|-----|----|-----|----|---|----|-----|----|----|----|------|------|------|
| 1995   | 106 | 374 | 50 | 120 | 19 | 1 | 16 | 69  | 6  | 19 | 65 | .321 | .352 | .505 |
| Career | 111 | 387 | 50 | 125 | 19 | 1 | 16 | 70  | 6  | 19 | 67 | .323 | .353 | .501 |

### Where He Hits the Ball

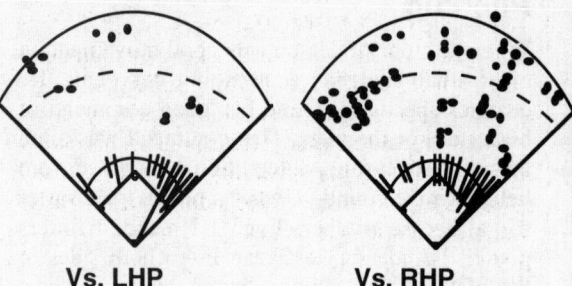

**Vs. LHP**          **Vs. RHP**

### 1995 Situational Stats

|            | AB  | H  | HR | RBI | Avg  |        | AB  | H  | HR | RBI | Avg  |
|------------|-----|----|----|-----|------|--------|-----|----|----|-----|------|
| Home       | 184 | 61 | 7  | 34  | .332 | LHP    | 115 | 29 | 5  | 23  | .252 |
| Road       | 190 | 59 | 9  | 35  | .311 | RHP    | 259 | 91 | 11 | 46  | .351 |
| First Half | 82  | 21 | 2  | 14  | .256 | Sc Pos | 111 | 32 | 3  | 52  | .288 |
| Scnd Half  | 292 | 99 | 14 | 55  | .339 | Clutch | 41  | 9  | 0  | 6   | .220 |

### 1995 Rankings (American League)

- ➡ 1st in batting average on an 0-2 count (.405)
- ➡ 3rd in lowest fielding percentage in left field (.978)
- ➡ 4th in batting average with two strikes (.282) and errors in left field (5)
- ➡ 8th in lowest on-base percentage vs. left-handed pitchers (.285)
- ➡ 10th in lowest percentage of pitches taken (48.5%)
- ➡ Led the Angels in batting average on an 0-2 count (.405) and batting average with two strikes (.282)

# Mike Bielecki

## 1995 Season

The California Angels weren't exactly counting on big things from Mike Bielecki when they signed him as a blue-light-special free agent. But the team got more than they bargained for, with Bielecki adding some valuable depth in the first half of the season. In fact, Bielecki pitched his way into the Angels' rotation before going on the disabled list with a sore right shoulder after the All-Star break. He returned in September as a reliever and was simply awful, posting an ugly 10.50 ERA during the month—allowing 10 hits and four walks in just six innings.

## Pitching

Bielecki has developed a forkball that can get left-handed hitters out. But otherwise he's your classic sinkerballer who has to keep the ball down to be effective. If he's not hitting spots, he's in big trouble. He was hit especially hard by right-handed hitters last year. At this point in his career, his value lies in his versatility to work both as a starter and long reliever. He's done both throughout his major league career.

## Defense

Age has slowed Bielecki's reactions, but until last season he hadn't committed an error since 1990. He remains tough to run on, but teams seldom have to attack him on the bases—they can beat him with their bats instead.

## 1996 Outlook

Bielecki is eligible for free agency. More than likely, he'll move on to his fourth team in four years. Wherever he goes, he'll be forced to put together a good spring and a good first half—while maintaining his health—to be in *anyone's* second-half plans. There's not much of a market for a 36-year-old righthander with weak stuff.

**Position:** SP/RP
**Bats:** R **Throws:** R
**Ht:** 6' 3"  **Wt:** 200

**Opening Day Age:** 36
**Born:** 7/31/59 in Baltimore, MD
**ML Seasons:** 12
**Pronunciation:** by-LEK-ee

*Overall Statistics*

|        | W  | L  | Pct. | ERA  | G   | GS  | Sv | IP     | H    | BB  | SO  | HR | BR/IP |
|--------|----|----|------|------|-----|-----|----|--------|------|-----|-----|----|-------|
| 1995   | 4  | 6  | .400 | 5.97 | 22  | 11  | 0  | 75.1   | 80   | 31  | 45  | 15 | 1.47  |
| Career | 63 | 63 | .500 | 4.29 | 257 | 173 | 1  | 1098.1 | 1117 | 442 | 652 | 99 | 1.42  |

*How Often He Throws Strikes*

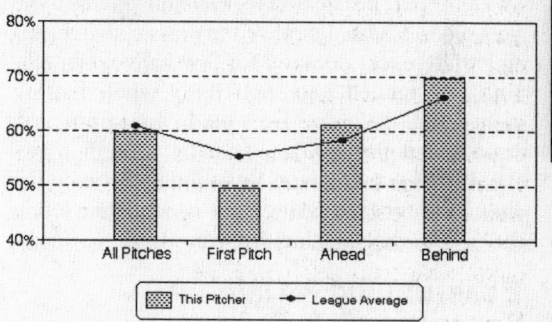

*1995 Situational Stats*

|            | W | L | ERA   | Sv | IP   |        | AB  | H  | HR | RBI | Avg  |
|------------|---|---|-------|----|------|--------|-----|----|----|-----|------|
| Home       | 1 | 3 | 6.16  | 0  | 30.2 | LHB    | 172 | 41 | 9  | 23  | .238 |
| Road       | 3 | 3 | 5.84  | 0  | 44.2 | RHB    | 121 | 39 | 6  | 27  | .322 |
| First Half | 4 | 6 | 5.10  | 0  | 65.1 | Sc Pos | 52  | 20 | 5  | 34  | .385 |
| Scnd Half  | 0 | 0 | 11.70 | 0  | 10.0 | Clutch | 1   | 0  | 0  | 1   | .000 |

*1995 Rankings (American League)*

- ➡ 8th in lowest batting average allowed vs. left-handed batters (.238)
- ➡ 10th in errors at pitcher (2)
- ➡ Led the Angels in lowest batting average allowed vs. left-handed batters (.238)

# Chili Davis

## 1995 Season

The Minnesota Twins thought Chili Davis was reaching the end of the trail when they chose not to re-sign him after the 1992 season. He continues to prove that they were wrong. Davis hit a career-high .318 at age 35, with power numbers as solid as ever. The veteran designated hitter provided a strong presence in the middle of California's lineup and played a role in the development of Garret Anderson and other rookies. Like almost every other regular, his production dropped late in the season.

## Hitting

Davis remains one of baseball's most productive switch-hitters because he makes adjustments as he gets older. He used to have the classic switch-hitting preferences, looking for low balls when batting left-handed and high balls when batting right-handed. Now he likes the ball up from *both sides* of the plate. Davis is mentally tough, a guy the Angels want at the plate with the game on the line. He was better hitting right-handed than left in 1995, but is no slouch either way.

## Baserunning & Defense

Davis, a superior athlete, still has surprising speed for the miles he has logged in the majors. He does not look to steal, however, trying just 16 times since coming to the Angels in 1993. Davis was turned into a DH because he had become a major liability in the field, and only figures to get worse at the end of his career.

## 1996 Outlook

Davis returns for his fourth season in California. He figures to remain an everyday player, but might rest more frequently than in the past. The end could come fast when his skills do erode, but that doesn't look to be on the horizon just yet. Davis has hit 20 or more homers seven of the last nine seasons. You'd be silly to turn away from that track record—even with a 36-year-old player.

**Position:** DH
**Bats:** B  **Throws:** R
**Ht:** 6' 3"  **Wt:** 217

**Opening Day Age:** 36
**Born:** 1/17/60 in Kingston, Jamaica
**ML Seasons:** 15

### Overall Statistics

| | G | AB | R | H | D | T | HR | RBI | SB | BB | SO | Avg | OBP | Slg |
|---|---|---|---|---|---|---|---|---|---|---|---|---|---|---|
| 1995 | 119 | 424 | 81 | 135 | 23 | 0 | 20 | 86 | 3 | 89 | 79 | .318 | .429 | .514 |
| Career | 1970 | 7087 | 1026 | 1934 | 348 | 29 | 270 | 1100 | 127 | 936 | 1385 | .273 | .355 | .444 |

### Where He Hits the Ball

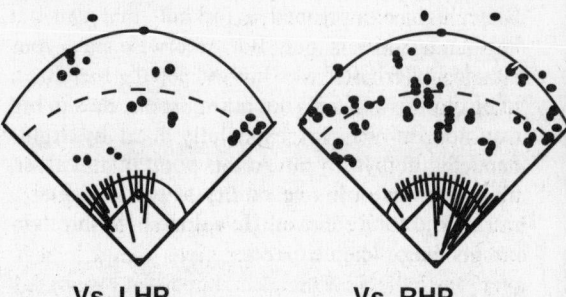

Vs. LHP          Vs. RHP

### 1995 Situational Stats

| | AB | H | HR | RBI | Avg | | AB | H | HR | RBI | Avg |
|---|---|---|---|---|---|---|---|---|---|---|---|
| Home | 212 | 76 | 11 | 50 | .358 | LHP | 129 | 45 | 6 | 30 | .349 |
| Road | 212 | 59 | 9 | 36 | .278 | RHP | 295 | 90 | 14 | 56 | .305 |
| First Half | 181 | 65 | 9 | 38 | .359 | Sc Pos | 112 | 33 | 10 | 69 | .295 |
| Scnd Half | 243 | 70 | 11 | 48 | .288 | Clutch | 47 | 13 | 1 | 3 | .277 |

### 1995 Rankings (American League)

- → 3rd in batting average at home (.358)
- → 4th in on-base percentage vs. right-handed pitchers (.430)
- → 5th in on-base percentage
- → 6th in sacrifice flies (9)
- → 7th in batting average, walks and intentional walks (12)
- → 8th in batting average vs. left-handed pitchers (.349)
- → 10th in lowest batting average with the bases loaded (.111), cleanup slugging percentage (.499) and on-base percentage vs. left-handed pitchers (.427)
- → Led the Angels in sacrifice flies (9) and intentional walks (12)

# Gary DiSarcina

**Surprise**

**Position:** SS
**Bats:** R  **Throws:** R
**Ht:** 6' 1"  **Wt:** 178

**Opening Day Age:** 28
**Born:** 11/19/67 in
Malden, MA
**ML Seasons:** 7
**Pronunciation:**
Dee-sar-SEE-nuh

## 1995 Season

One of baseball's most closely kept secrets went public in 1995. Casual fans discovered what insiders had known for two years—that Gary DiSarcina has become one of the American League's premier shortstops. DiSarcina had long been considered a good field-no hit prospect, but then he batted 65 points higher than his career average entering last season. The Angels' dramatic collapse began after he tore ligaments in his left thumb on August 3. His presence was missed defensively, offensively and in the dugout. He returned for the last 11 games, but was rusty.

## Hitting

DiSarcina accomplished one of the most difficult feats for a major-leaguer in 1995—increasing his bat speed. He had always been an opposite-field hitter, but he suddenly began to pull the ball. He also stopped hitting so many fly balls. With his increased ability to cover the entire plate, DiSarcina has become one of the league's toughest hitters to fan. He doesn't have much power, but can go deep when a pitcher gives him a "get it over" fastball. He remains an impatient hitter who doesn't walk much, but even improved in that area a little bit in 1995.

## Baserunning & Defense

DiSarcina is as reliable on routine ground balls as his idol, Larry Bird, used to be at the free-throw line. He has soft hands, quick feet, and has learned how to position himself for hitters. His absence in August and September affected both third baseman Tony Phillips and second baseman Damion Easley. DiSarcina has average speed, but is a heads-up runner. He will steal one or two bases a month, usually when he catches a pitcher napping.

## 1996 Outlook

DiSarcina's thumb should recover fully with rest. He will return as the Angels' regular shortstop and figures to have increased responsibility offensively. He hit ninth for most of 1995, but finished the season hitting second. Marcel Lachemann is likely to keep him there.

### Overall Statistics

|  | G | AB | R | H | D | T | HR | RBI | SB | BB | SO | Avg | OBP | Slg |
|---|---|---|---|---|---|---|---|---|---|---|---|---|---|---|
| 1995 | 99 | 362 | 61 | 111 | 28 | 6 | 5 | 41 | 7 | 20 | 25 | .307 | .344 | .459 |
| Career | 532 | 1799 | 219 | 459 | 84 | 10 | 14 | 164 | 25 | 79 | 155 | .255 | .292 | .336 |

### Where He Hits the Ball

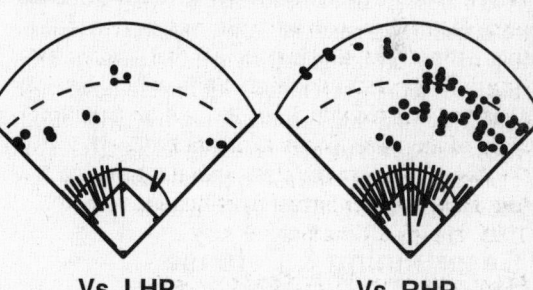

**Vs. LHP**　　　　**Vs. RHP**

### 1995 Situational Stats

|  | AB | H | HR | RBI | Avg |  | AB | H | HR | RBI | Avg |
|---|---|---|---|---|---|---|---|---|---|---|---|
| Home | 182 | 55 | 1 | 19 | .302 | LHP | 97 | 28 | 2 | 14 | .289 |
| Road | 180 | 56 | 4 | 22 | .311 | RHP | 265 | 83 | 3 | 27 | .313 |
| First Half | 250 | 81 | 4 | 33 | .324 | Sc Pos | 88 | 28 | 0 | 35 | .318 |
| Scnd Half | 112 | 30 | 1 | 8 | .268 | Clutch | 49 | 12 | 0 | 7 | .245 |

### 1995 Rankings (American League)

➡ 2nd in fielding percentage at shortstop (.986)
➡ 7th in batting average with two strikes (.263)
➡ 8th in triples
➡ Led the Angels in triples and sacrifice bunts (7)

# Damion Easley

## 1995 Season

Few American League regulars contributed as little last year as California infielder Damion Easley. He was a major disappointment at the plate, but did team with Gary DiSarcina to give the Angels strong defense up the middle. Easley showed his value by switching to shortstop for a while after DiSarcina got hurt August 3. He finished the season back at second base—but with plenty still to prove at the plate. He had just three three-hit games in 1995—all before June.

## Hitting

Pitchers have always been able to knock the bat out of Easley's hands. California hitting instructor Rod Carew wasn't able to change that. Easley has reasonable bat speed, but is so conscious of adjusting to the breaking ball that he is easy to jam. Easley is a high-ball hitter with limited power. He gets himself behind in the count by swinging at high fastballs and bad breaking balls. He especially struggles against righthanders, and has shown little ability to hit in the clutch.

## Baserunning & Defense

Easley's athleticism has always excited the Angels. Although he has good range for a second baseman and a strong arm, he does not appear to have good instincts. He's not as fast as he was as a rookie, most likely because of his flat feet and chronic shin splints. His biggest problem, though, is not being able to steal first base.

## 1996 Outlook

There is no longer any reason to expect Easley to become part of the Angels' nucleus for the future. He could be back as California's regular second baseman, but will need to get off to a good start to hold the job. He needs to stay healthy and have a productive season to regain the trust that was once placed in him by the Angels.

**Position:** 2B/SS
**Bats:** R  **Throws:** R
**Ht:** 5'11"  **Wt:** 185

**Opening Day Age:** 26
**Born:** 11/11/69 in New York, NY
**ML Seasons:** 4

### Overall Statistics

|  | G | AB | R | H | D | T | HR | RBI | SB | BB | SO | Avg | OBP | Slg |
|---|---|---|---|---|---|---|---|---|---|---|---|---|---|---|
| 1995 | 114 | 357 | 35 | 77 | 14 | 2 | 4 | 35 | 5 | 32 | 47 | .216 | .288 | .300 |
| Career | 322 | 1054 | 123 | 256 | 48 | 5 | 13 | 99 | 24 | 97 | 156 | .243 | .314 | .335 |

### Where He Hits the Ball

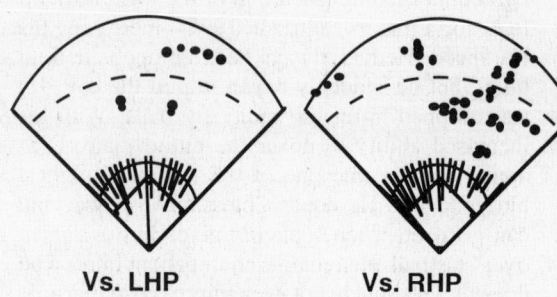

Vs. LHP          Vs. RHP

### 1995 Situational Stats

|  | AB | H | HR | RBI | Avg |  | AB | H | HR | RBI | Avg |
|---|---|---|---|---|---|---|---|---|---|---|---|
| Home | 170 | 35 | 1 | 16 | .206 | LHP | 118 | 29 | 2 | 13 | .246 |
| Road | 187 | 42 | 3 | 19 | .225 | RHP | 239 | 48 | 2 | 22 | .201 |
| First Half | 187 | 37 | 4 | 25 | .198 | Sc Pos | 109 | 20 | 2 | 32 | .183 |
| Scnd Half | 170 | 40 | 0 | 10 | .235 | Clutch | 24 | 6 | 0 | 2 | .250 |

### 1995 Rankings (American League)

- ➡ 1st in lowest batting average with the bases loaded (.000)
- ➡ 3rd in lowest batting average with runners in scoring position (.183)
- ➡ 9th in errors at second base (7)
- ➡ Led the Angels in hit by pitch (6), bunts in play (14) and highest percentage of swings put into play (52.4%)

# Jim Edmonds

## 1995 Season

There was no bigger surprise in the American League than California center fielder Jim Edmonds. The Angels surprised other teams by trading Chad Curtis to Detroit for Tony Phillips, opening up center for Edmonds. But they obviously knew what they were doing. Edmonds played a major role in California's success. He hit so well that he knocked teammate Tim Salmon off the All-Star team, while providing better-than-adequate defense.

## Hitting

Rafael Palmeiro might have a sweeter swing than Edmonds, but there are few others who can duplicate his classic stroke. He is a very fluid hitter with good bat speed who can handle the league's best pitchers when in a groove. He caught up to the righthanders who had strangely enough held him in check in 1994. In addition, he showed good power to the opposite field. Edmonds' stats would have been even more impressive last year had he done a better job hitting with men in scoring position. He also had problems hitting in pressure situations, though his 4-for-5 performance the last day of the regular season helped put California in the playoff game against Seattle.

## Baserunning & Defense

Edmonds' play in center field was a revelation. He covers ground and catches what he gets to, committing only one error all season. He shows no fear going to the wall or chasing balls. Plus he's got a strong arm. That's the total package defensively. Edmonds is a below-average baserunner who does not get a good jump. He's just 5-for-13 stealing in his major league career.

## 1996 Outlook

There are skeptics who doubt that Edmonds can come close to his 1995 level again. Those suspicions picked up momentum when he slumped down the stretch. But he was playing with an injured back, and should be fine in 1996. A .300 season is hardly out of the question, especially if Marcel Lachemann hits him in front of Tim Salmon.

**Position:** CF
**Bats:** L  **Throws:** L
**Ht:** 6' 1"  **Wt:** 190

**Opening Day Age:** 25
**Born:** 6/27/70 in Fullerton, CA
**ML Seasons:** 3

### Overall Statistics

| | G | AB | R | H | D | T | HR | RBI | SB | BB | SO | Avg | OBP | Slg |
|---|---|---|---|---|---|---|---|---|---|---|---|---|---|---|
| 1995 | 141 | 558 | 120 | 162 | 30 | 4 | 33 | 107 | 1 | 51 | 130 | .290 | .352 | .536 |
| Career | 253 | 908 | 160 | 256 | 47 | 6 | 38 | 148 | 5 | 83 | 218 | .282 | .344 | .472 |

### Where He Hits the Ball

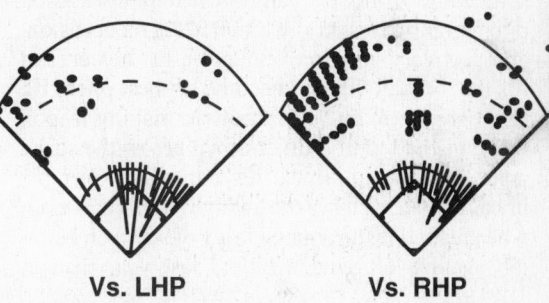

**Vs. LHP**                    **Vs. RHP**

### 1995 Situational Stats

| | AB | H | HR | RBI | Avg | | AB | H | HR | RBI | Avg |
|---|---|---|---|---|---|---|---|---|---|---|---|
| Home | 270 | 81 | 16 | 58 | .300 | LHP | 164 | 48 | 7 | 29 | .293 |
| Road | 288 | 81 | 17 | 49 | .281 | RHP | 394 | 114 | 26 | 78 | .289 |
| First Half | 261 | 76 | 13 | 52 | .291 | Sc Pos | 160 | 42 | 9 | 73 | .263 |
| Scnd Half | 297 | 86 | 20 | 55 | .290 | Clutch | 60 | 10 | 1 | 7 | .167 |

### 1995 Rankings (American League)

- ➡ 2nd in fielding percentage in center field (.998)
- ➡ 3rd in runs scored
- ➡ 4th in strikeouts
- ➡ 6th in at-bats and total bases (299)
- ➡ 7th in RBI and lowest batting average in the clutch (.167)
- ➡ 8th in pitches seen (2,513) and slugging percentage vs. right-handed pitchers (.558)
- ➡ 9th in home runs
- ➡ Led the Angels in at-bats, runs scored and RBI

**California Angels**

# Chuck Finley

## 1995 Season

Conditioning was a concern earlier in Chuck Finley's career, but he returned in good shape after the strike and produced a vintage Finley season—topping 200 innings for the fifth time in six years. He didn't get his first win until May 23, starting the season 0-4, but then went 15-8 the rest of the way. He was a workhorse, throwing more pitches than anyone in the majors not named David Cone or Randy Johnson. Despite the strike, he produced a career high in strikeouts, finishing third in the league behind Johnson and Todd Stottlemyre.

## Pitching

Finley, like teammate Mark Langston, has lost something off his fastball, but it remains a good pitch for him. He can still hit 90 MPH on occasion, and gets very good movement on his heater. But it's the forkball that has become his best pitch. He has a great arm angle to throw it, making it look like a fastball until it dives down below the strike zone. He also improved his command over his breaking ball, a slurve, throwing it for strikes even when behind in the count. Finley did a much better job against left-handed hitters last year than in 1994.

## Defense

Finley has always been awkward on the mound. He chooses to lumber toward, rather than pounce on, bunts and dribblers toward the left side of the mound. For a lefthander, he is surprisingly easy to run on. But he remains a good competitor who understands game situations. His lapses seldom come at crucial times.

## 1996 Outlook

Finley's success last season came, not surprisingly, in the last season of his four-year contract. He entered free agency for the first time, and was sure to generate attention. The Angels want to keep him, but only if he's willing to take less than the $4.875 million he earned in 1995. He is certain to receive a lucrative three- or four-year contract, whether from California or someone else.

**Position:** SP
**Bats:** L  **Throws:** L
**Ht:** 6' 6"  **Wt:** 214

**Opening Day Age:** 33
**Born:** 11/26/62 in Monroe, LA
**ML Seasons:** 10

### Overall Statistics

|        | W | L | Pct. | ERA | G | GS | Sv | IP | H | BB | SO | HR | BR/IP |
|--------|---|---|------|-----|---|----|----|----|---|----|----|----|-------|
| 1995   | 15 | 12 | .556 | 4.21 | 32 | 32 | 0 | 203.0 | 192 | 93 | 195 | 20 | 1.40 |
| Career | 114 | 98 | .538 | 3.58 | 309 | 252 | 0 | 1836.1 | 1744 | 756 | 1369 | 164 | 1.36 |

### How Often He Throws Strikes

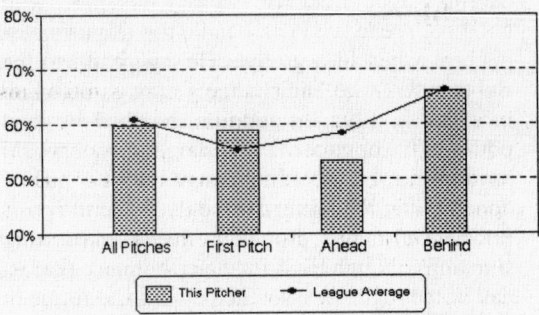

### 1995 Situational Stats

|            | W | L | ERA | Sv | IP |       | AB | H | HR | RBI | Avg |
|------------|---|---|-----|----|----|-------|----|---|----|-----|-----|
| Home       | 9 | 5 | 3.55 | 0 | 106.1 | LHB | 113 | 28 | 1 | 15 | .248 |
| Road       | 6 | 7 | 4.93 | 0 | 96.2 | RHB | 658 | 164 | 19 | 82 | .249 |
| First Half | 7 | 7 | 3.56 | 0 | 98.2 | Sc Pos | 187 | 52 | 9 | 78 | .278 |
| Scnd Half  | 8 | 5 | 4.83 | 0 | 104.1 | Clutch | 44 | 10 | 2 | 4 | .227 |

### 1995 Rankings (American League)

- 1st in errors at pitcher (4)
- 2nd in games started and wild pitches (13)
- 3rd in walks allowed, strikeouts, pitches thrown (3,520), highest stolen base percentage allowed (80.8%), most pitches thrown per batter (4.00) and most strikeouts per 9 innings (8.6)
- 4th in most run support per 9 innings (6.7)
- 7th in batters faced (880) and stolen bases allowed (21)
- 8th in wins
- Led the Angels in ERA, wins, losses, games started, complete games (2), shutouts (1), innings pitched, batters faced (880), walks allowed, hit batsmen (7) and strikeouts

# Mike Harkey

## 1995 Season

Once considered a top prospect with the Chicago Cubs, Mike Harkey's star faded after a horrible season with Colorado in 1994. Harkey took advantage of a new start in the American League, earning a spot as Oakland's fifth starter in spring training. He survived for 12 starts before Tony La Russa decided to move Todd Van Poppel from the bullpen to the rotation. California claimed Harkey on waivers, and he joined the Angels' rotation shortly after the All-Star break. He lasted through five innings in seven of eight starts with California, finishing the season with an 8-9 record, which was somewhat deceiving. He simply wasn't that good.

## Pitching

A 90-plus fastball was once Harkey's calling card, but not any more. Injuries have taken a toll on his arm and shoulder, leaving him able to throw only about 85. He improved his change-up greatly working with Oakland pitching coach Dave Duncan, and has developed a forkball that he throws to left-handed hitters. But he's effective only when throwing his curveball for strikes. Improved control was a subtle key for Harkey last season.

## Defense

Harkey has never moved well on the mound, and he's not a good defensive player. He has trouble both covering bunts and fielding comebackers. He has a below-average move to first, and opposing baserunners took advantage of him in 1995.

## 1996 Outlook

Harkey isn't expected to return to California, leaving him to again troll the free-agent waters. He is quickly approaching 30 and no longer has the arm he once did. He figures to land a job filling out someone's staff, and might add to his value by showing the ability to pitch out of the bullpen. In the end, his value may be more as a swing man than a full-time starter.

**Position:** SP/RP
**Bats:** R  **Throws:** R
**Ht:** 6' 5"  **Wt:** 235

**Opening Day Age:** 29
**Born:** 10/25/66 in San Diego, CA
**ML Seasons:** 7

California Angels

### Overall Statistics

|  | W | L | Pct. | ERA | G | GS | Sv | IP | H | BB | SO | HR | BR/IP |
|---|---|---|---|---|---|---|---|---|---|---|---|---|---|
| 1995 | 8 | 9 | .471 | 5.44 | 26 | 20 | 0 | 127.1 | 155 | 47 | 56 | 24 | 1.59 |
| Career | 35 | 36 | .493 | 4.49 | 121 | 104 | 0 | 641.1 | 708 | 220 | 310 | 72 | 1.45 |

### How Often He Throws Strikes

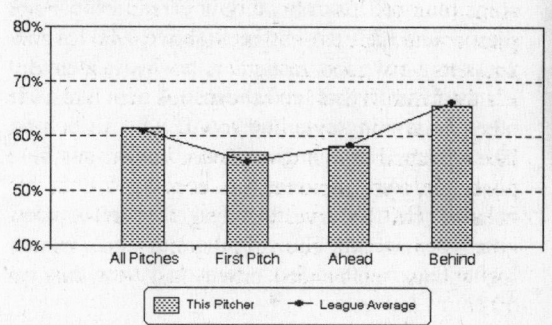

This Pitcher ▨    League Average ●

### 1995 Situational Stats

|  | W | L | ERA | Sv | IP |  | AB | H | HR | RBI | Avg |
|---|---|---|---|---|---|---|---|---|---|---|---|
| Home | 6 | 7 | 5.08 | 0 | 88.2 | LHB | 281 | 86 | 16 | 41 | .306 |
| Road | 2 | 2 | 6.28 | 0 | 38.2 | RHB | 233 | 69 | 8 | 29 | .296 |
| First Half | 4 | 6 | 6.27 | 0 | 66.0 | Sc Pos | 121 | 33 | 4 | 45 | .273 |
| Scnd Half | 4 | 3 | 4.55 | 0 | 61.1 | Clutch | 8 | 3 | 1 | 2 | .375 |

### 1995 Rankings (American League)

➡ 8th in home runs allowed
➡ 9th in highest ERA at home (5.08)
➡ 10th in stolen bases allowed (18)

# Mark Langston

## 1995 Season

Mark Langston once had the best stuff of any pitcher who couldn't win. But last season he had unquestionably the worst stuff of any 15-game winner in the major leagues. Langston has completely lost the fastball that won him three American League strikeout crowns, but he has gained a new level of toughness, which was evident when he battled Randy Johnson for seven innings in the one-game American League West playoff. Luck never hurts, either. California averaged 6.2 runs while going 21-10 in his 31 starts.

## Pitching

Langston hasn't been the same since having bone chips removed from his elbow early in the 1994 season, and his ERA has been above 4.60 for two years in a row. His fastball is now just average. Langston's curveball and slider look a lot like each other, bedeviling even the scouts who sit behind home plate. His change-up has become his best pitch, and does a good job keeping hitters off balance. He really struggled against left-handed hitters last season, allowing them to hit 22 points higher than righthanders. A season earlier, they hit 63 points *lower*.

## Defense

Okay, Langston does try to do too much sometimes. Witness the throw from Tim Salmon he unnecessarily cut off, then fired past the catcher to turn Joey Cora's playoff triple into a de facto grand slam. But he remains the best in the league at fielding his position. He is technically perfect with his fielding mechanics, and has an outstanding pickoff move that keeps runners close to the bag.

## 1996 Outlook

Heavy workloads almost always haunt pitchers late in their careers. That is the case with Langston. Although he remains a consummate professional who prepares himself for the job ahead, he requires close supervision from management after wearing down at the end of both 1994 and '95. He's quickly becoming a six- or seven-inning pitcher, but still has enough tricks for another 12-14 win season.

**Position:** SP
**Bats:** R **Throws:** L
**Ht:** 6' 2" **Wt:** 184

**Opening Day Age:** 35
**Born:** 8/20/60 in San Diego, CA
**ML Seasons:** 12

### Overall Statistics

|        | W   | L   | Pct. | ERA  | G   | GS  | Sv | IP     | H    | BB   | SO   | HR  | BR/IP |
|--------|-----|-----|------|------|-----|-----|----|--------|------|------|------|-----|-------|
| 1995   | 15  | 7   | .682 | 4.63 | 31  | 31  | 0  | 200.1  | 212  | 64   | 142  | 21  | 1.38  |
| Career | 166 | 141 | .541 | 3.81 | 383 | 380 | 0  | 2648.2 | 2370 | 1145 | 2252 | 265 | 1.33  |

### How Often He Throws Strikes

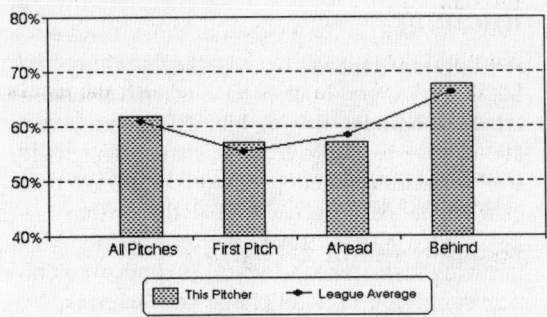

### 1995 Situational Stats

|            | W | L | ERA  | Sv | IP    |        | AB  | H   | HR | RBI | Avg  |
|------------|---|---|------|----|-------|--------|-----|-----|----|-----|------|
| Home       | 9 | 2 | 3.81 | 0  | 101.2 | LHB    | 127 | 37  | 3  | 11  | .291 |
| Road       | 6 | 5 | 5.47 | 0  | 98.2  | RHB    | 651 | 175 | 18 | 86  | .269 |
| First Half | 8 | 1 | 4.15 | 0  | 97.2  | Sc Pos | 172 | 57  | 3  | 70  | .331 |
| Scnd Half  | 7 | 6 | 5.08 | 0  | 102.2 | Clutch | 52  | 20  | 1  | 9   | .385 |

### 1995 Rankings (American League)

- ➡ 1st in runners caught stealing (12) and lowest stolen base percentage allowed (25.0%)
- ➡ 2nd in most run support per 9 innings (7.2)
- ➡ 3rd in pickoff throws (210), highest ERA on the road (5.47) and errors at pitcher (3)
- ➡ 4th in games started
- ➡ 5th in highest batting average allowed with runners in scoring position (.331)
- ➡ 6th in hits allowed
- ➡ 7th in least GDPs induced per 9 innings (0.6) and lowest fielding percentage at pitcher (.938)
- ➡ 8th in highest ERA and wins
- ➡ Led the Angels in wins, complete games (2), shutouts (1) and hits allowed

# Greg Myers

## 1995 Season

In 1995, injuries continued to take a toll on Greg Myers, a former top prospect for the Toronto Blue Jays who is getting old before his time. Myers did an adequate job for the California Angels when he was available, but fought shoulder problems all season. In all, he went on the disabled list three times in 1995. While able to play most of the second half, Myers' fragility forced Marcel Lachemann to go with Jorge Fabregas and Andy Allanson down the stretch—not an ideal situation for a team in the playoff hunt.

## Hitting

Myers struggles at the plate when pitchers keep the ball down. He likes it up, and still has the ability to spray it from power alley to power alley. His nine home runs in 1995 were a career high, but he too often seemed to be swinging for the fences rather than trying to keep innings alive, and pitchers seemed to know it. After the All-Star break, throwing strikes to Myers was all but optional. He struck out 30 times, while walking just once.

## Baserunning & Defense

Accidents have seemed to find Myers through the years, taking a toll on his body. He has lost his quickness behind the plate, which affects his ability to throw out basestealers. Myers has always relied on a quick release, not a cannon arm—and he's just not as quick anymore. Nor is he as likely to block the plate as he was earlier in his career. He remains a below-average baserunner, and struggles to go from first to third on a single to right.

## 1996 Outlook

Myers' run as a regular appears to have come to an end. He was eligible for free agency over the winter, and appeared likely to land somewhere as a number-two catcher. He could still play a long time, because there's always a market for left-handed-hitting catchers.

**Position:** C/DH
**Bats:** L  **Throws:** R
**Ht:** 6' 2"  **Wt:** 215

**Opening Day Age:** 29
**Born:** 4/14/66 in Riverside, CA
**ML Seasons:** 8

California Angels

### Overall Statistics

|  | G | AB | R | H | D | T | HR | RBI | SB | BB | SO | Avg | OBP | Slg |
|---|---|---|---|---|---|---|---|---|---|---|---|---|---|---|
| 1995 | 85 | 273 | 35 | 71 | 12 | 2 | 9 | 38 | 0 | 17 | 49 | .260 | .304 | .418 |
| Career | 486 | 1379 | 135 | 340 | 66 | 3 | 32 | 158 | 3 | 94 | 224 | .247 | .293 | .368 |

### Where He Hits the Ball

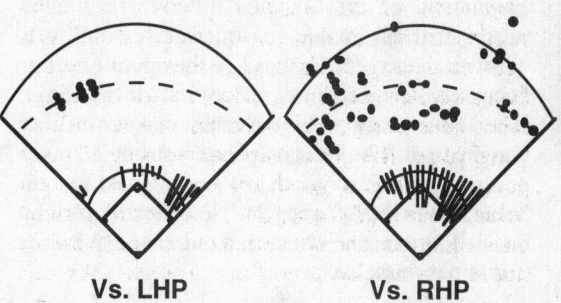

**Vs. LHP**          **Vs. RHP**

### 1995 Situational Stats

|  | AB | H | HR | RBI | Avg |  | AB | H | HR | RBI | Avg |
|---|---|---|---|---|---|---|---|---|---|---|---|
| Home | 128 | 32 | 6 | 22 | .250 | LHP | 75 | 18 | 0 | 9 | .240 |
| Road | 145 | 39 | 3 | 16 | .269 | RHP | 198 | 53 | 9 | 29 | .268 |
| First Half | 126 | 32 | 4 | 24 | .254 | Sc Pos | 72 | 19 | 0 | 25 | .264 |
| Scnd Half | 147 | 39 | 5 | 14 | .265 | Clutch | 34 | 9 | 2 | 6 | .265 |

### 1995 Rankings (American League)

➡ Did not rank near the top or bottom in any category

# Troy Percival

## 1995 Season

To quote one senior scout speaking about Troy Percival, hitters "didn't bat out of turn to get to this guy." Percival exploded onto the American League scene like one of his fastballs. California manager Marcel Lachemann brought the converted catcher along skillfully, using him as a set-up man for Lee Smith. He has better stuff than any closer in the A.L., and should benefit by his apprenticeship under Smith. Percival's rate of 11.4 strikeouts per nine innings is his calling card.

## Pitching

Percival's fastball doesn't just hit the upper 90s on the radar gun. It has some nasty natural movement, running in on right-handed hitters. The biggest surprise of his rookie season was his ability to throw strikes, getting ahead in the count to set up a curveball one scout describes as "devastating," The improvement in his curveball makes him even tougher to hit. American Leaguers struggled much more against Percival than Pacific Coast League hitters had in 1993 and '94. He is death on right-handed hitters, and not such a pleasant experience for lefties, either.

## Defense

Percival was drafted as a strong-armed catcher and did not make the transition to the mound until 1991. He remains a work in progress in regard to his ability to hold runners and field his position. He has trouble on comebackers and can be bunted on. But he is getting better in all phases of the game.

## 1996 Outlook

With Lee Smith back for the final season of his contract, Percival will get a second full season in a set-up role. But Lachemann should have the confidence to put him in more save situations. He seems a lock to get 10-plus saves if he's healthy in 1996. Depending on how Smith performs, he could get a lot more.

**Position:** RP
**Bats:** R  **Throws:** R
**Ht:** 6' 3"  **Wt:** 200

**Opening Day Age:** 26
**Born:** 8/9/69 in Fontana, CA
**ML Seasons:** 1

### Overall Statistics

|        | W | L | Pct. | ERA  | G  | GS | Sv | IP   | H  | BB | SO | HR | BR/IP |
|--------|---|---|------|------|----|----|----|------|----|----|----|----|-------|
| 1995   | 3 | 2 | .600 | 1.95 | 62 | 0  | 3  | 74.0 | 37 | 26 | 94 | 6  | 0.85  |
| Career | 3 | 2 | .600 | 1.95 | 62 | 0  | 3  | 74.0 | 37 | 26 | 94 | 6  | 0.85  |

### How Often He Throws Strikes

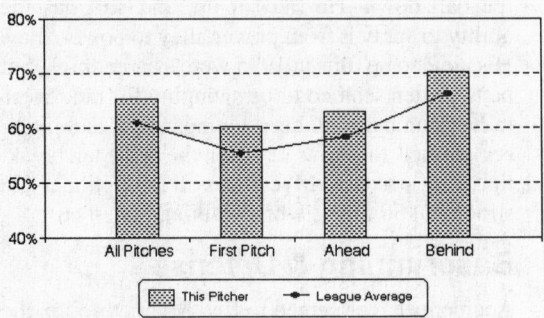

### 1995 Situational Stats

|            | W | L | ERA  | Sv | IP   |        | AB  | H  | HR | RBI | Avg  |
|------------|---|---|------|----|------|--------|-----|----|----|-----|------|
| Home       | 1 | 1 | 1.67 | 0  | 37.2 | LHB    | 116 | 20 | 2  | 7   | .172 |
| Road       | 2 | 1 | 2.23 | 3  | 36.1 | RHB    | 136 | 17 | 4  | 14  | .125 |
| First Half | 1 | 0 | 2.45 | 0  | 33.0 | Sc Pos | 60  | 12 | 0  | 13  | .200 |
| Scnd Half  | 2 | 2 | 1.54 | 3  | 41.0 | Clutch | 155 | 26 | 5  | 17  | .168 |

### 1995 Rankings (American League)

➡ 1st in holds (29) and lowest batting average allowed in relief (.147)
➡ 2nd in least baserunners allowed per 9 innings in relief (7.8) and most strikeouts per 9 innings in relief (11.4)
➡ 3rd in balks (2) and relief ERA (1.95)
➡ 4th in lowest batting average allowed in relief with runners on base (.154)
➡ 5th in lowest percentage of inherited runners scored (17.0%)
➡ 6th in games pitched and least GDPs induced per GDP situation (2.3%)
➡ Led the Angels in games pitched, holds (29) and first batter efficiency (.175)

# Tony Phillips

## 1995 Season

California's best move of the year was acquiring Tony Phillips from Detroit for Chad Curtis in a swap of leadoff hitters. Phillips improved the batting order and gave the Angels a little bit of toughness (they could still use more). There were times when he seemed to be the only one with a pulse in the California dugout. He gets carried away with his intensity level sometimes, losing it with opponents and umpires, but he's a big-game player.

## Hitting

The switch-hitting Phillips has unusual power for a leadoff hitter. He has the skill to work pitchers from both sides of the plate, seeming to spend the entire season at three-ball counts. He generates good bat speed and has admirable discipline at the plate. Phillips is better batting right-handed than left-handed. His home run and runs scored totals were both career highs despite the shortened schedule.

## Baserunning & Defense

Phillips' value is his versatility, but he was anchored at third base last year. He can play left field and second base, as well as third, although his arm is weak in the outfield. He has good hands but is erratic defensively—as was evidenced after shortstop Gary DiSarcina went on the disabled list. Phillips is an aggressive baserunner, but not as fast as he was a few years ago, going just 13-for-23 in stolen-base attempts in 1995.

## 1996 Outlook

Phillips' future with California is tenuous. He may have a few more good years in him, but the Angels need to look at youngsters George Arias and Eduardo Perez at third base. There is no room for Phillips in the Angels' outfield. It's a dubious fit. Scouts believe Phillips' skills will fade fast when they start to go, because he depends so much on his superb hand-eye coordination. This could be the year that starts to happen.

**Position:** 3B/LF
**Bats:** B **Throws:** R
**Ht:** 5'10" **Wt:** 175

**Opening Day Age:** 36
**Born:** 4/25/59 in Atlanta, GA
**ML Seasons:** 14

**California Angels**

### Overall Statistics

| | G | AB | R | H | D | T | HR | RBI | SB | BB | SO | Avg | OBP | Slg |
|---|---|---|---|---|---|---|---|---|---|---|---|---|---|---|
| 1995 | 139 | 525 | 119 | 137 | 21 | 1 | 27 | 61 | 13 | 113 | 135 | .261 | .394 | .459 |
| Career | 1696 | 5860 | 975 | 1557 | 257 | 41 | 121 | 629 | 139 | 974 | 1105 | .266 | .370 | .385 |

### Where He Hits the Ball

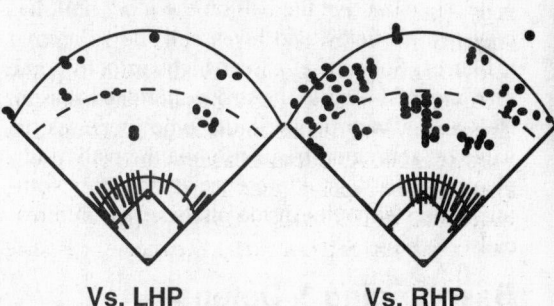

**Vs. LHP**　　　　**Vs. RHP**

### 1995 Situational Stats

| | AB | H | HR | RBI | Avg | | AB | H | HR | RBI | Avg |
|---|---|---|---|---|---|---|---|---|---|---|---|
| Home | 267 | 68 | 13 | 31 | .255 | LHP | 132 | 37 | 7 | 13 | .280 |
| Road | 258 | 69 | 14 | 30 | .267 | RHP | 393 | 100 | 20 | 48 | .254 |
| First Half | 250 | 70 | 14 | 37 | .280 | Sc Pos | 118 | 26 | 6 | 37 | .220 |
| Scnd Half | 275 | 67 | 13 | 24 | .244 | Clutch | 58 | 15 | 2 | 6 | .259 |

### 1995 Rankings (American League)

- ➡ 1st in pitches seen (2,754) and errors at third base (19)
- ➡ 2nd in lowest stolen base percentage (56.5%)
- ➡ 3rd in walks and strikeouts
- ➡ 4th in runs scored, most pitches seen per plate appearance (4.28) and on-base percentage for a leadoff hitter (.396)
- ➡ 5th in times on base (253)
- ➡ 7th in plate appearances (643), on-base percentage vs. left-handed pitchers (.441) and lowest batting average at home (.255)
- ➡ Led the Angels in stolen bases, caught stealing (10), walks, strikeouts, pitches seen (2,754), plate appearances (643) and stolen base percentage (56.5%)

# Tim Salmon

## 1995 Season

If anyone is still waiting for Tim Salmon to back-slide, they can give it a rest. The 1993 Rookie of the Year has now had three outstanding seasons in a row. He didn't get off to as fast of a start as some of his California teammates, but turned in a strong wire-to-wire effort nonetheless. Salmon was about the only hitter Marcel Lachemann could count on down the stretch. There's practically nothing he doesn't do well.

## Hitting

Salmon generates his bat speed from tremendous wrist action at the plate. He hits for power with a short stroke that allows him to cover the whole plate. He can drive the ball on the inner half, has power to all fields, and loves balls down around his knees. Salmon set career highs in both home runs and RBI despite the strike-shortened season. He's also a very patient hitter who increases his value by getting on frequently via the walk. Simply put, he has a great presence at the plate. Nothing bothers him. Not inside pitches. Not umpires' calls. Nothing.

## Baserunning & Defense

Salmon is among the league's best right fielders. He covers a lot of ground and does a good job anticipating where balls will be hit. He has a strong arm—although not in Jay Buhner's league—and is one of the most accurate throwers in the league. How accurate? He has 28 outfield assists the last three seasons. Salmon is not fast, but his great baserunning instincts more than compensate.

## 1996 Outlook

Salmon entered the prime of his career last season and should be able to repeat that performance for years to come. His challenge will be to stay as healthy as he did in 1995, when he missed only two games. If he's in the lineup, he's going to produce.

**Position:** RF
**Bats:** R **Throws:** R
**Ht:** 6' 3" **Wt:** 220

**Opening Day Age:** 27
**Born:** 8/24/68 in Long Beach, CA
**ML Seasons:** 4
**Pronunciation:** SA-men

### Overall Statistics

|  | G | AB | R | H | D | T | HR | RBI | SB | BB | SO | Avg | OBP | Slg |
|---|---|---|---|---|---|---|---|---|---|---|---|---|---|---|
| 1995 | 143 | 537 | 111 | 177 | 34 | 3 | 34 | 105 | 5 | 91 | 111 | .330 | .429 | .594 |
| Career | 408 | 1504 | 279 | 444 | 88 | 6 | 90 | 276 | 12 | 238 | 371 | .295 | .394 | .541 |

### Where He Hits the Ball

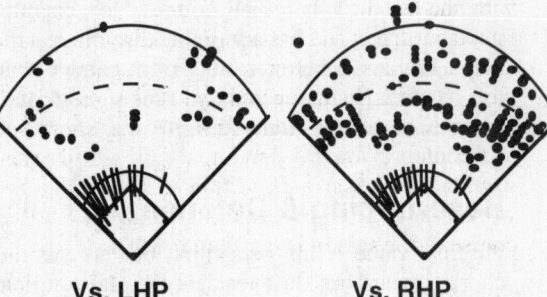

Vs. LHP          Vs. RHP

### 1995 Situational Stats

|  | AB | H | HR | RBI | Avg |  |  | AB | H | HR | RBI | Avg |
|---|---|---|---|---|---|---|---|---|---|---|---|---|
| Home | 258 | 75 | 15 | 47 | .291 | LHP | | 139 | 47 | 11 | 31 | .338 |
| Road | 279 | 102 | 19 | 58 | .366 | RHP | | 398 | 130 | 23 | 74 | .327 |
| First Half | 251 | 73 | 15 | 42 | .291 | Sc Pos | | 145 | 48 | 9 | 72 | .331 |
| Scnd Half | 286 | 104 | 19 | 63 | .364 | Clutch | | 59 | 21 | 5 | 15 | .356 |

### 1995 Rankings (American League)

→ 1st in batting average on the road (.366) and highest percentage of extra bases taken as a runner (72.7%)

→ 2nd in fielding percentage in right field (.988)

→ 3rd in batting average and times on base (274)

→ 4th in hits, total bases (319), slugging percentage and on-base percentage

→ 5th in runs scored and errors in right field (4)

→ 6th in doubles, walks, pitches seen (2,519), batting average vs. right-handed pitchers (.327) and on-base percentage vs. left-handed pitchers (.456)

→ Led the Angels in batting average, home runs, hits, doubles, total bases (319), hit by pitch (6) and times on base (274)

# Lee Smith

## 1995 Season

Like Old Man River, Lee Smith just keeps rolling on. Smith was supposed to be washed up two years ago, but instead he has extended his streak of saving 30-plus games to six years. He greatly improved the California bullpen—a major reason for their success. Smith was unhittable early in the season, converting 19 straight save opportunities before allowing a run. His age showed in the second half of the season, but he earned his fifth consecutive trip to the All-Star Game.

## Pitching

No, Smith doesn't have the fastball he used to throw in Wrigley Field. But he can get hitters out with the one he does have. His secret is simply throwing strikes. He's usually ahead in the count, challenging hitters to put the ball in play. He'll then go to his split-fingered fastball to get strikeouts. His control was not as sharp last season as it had been previously—sending up an alarm. You wouldn't call him a conditioning freak, but he worked enough to maintain his fastball over the course of the season better than in 1994.

## Defense

Smith moves slowly in everything he does, making him a target to be attacked on the mound. Teams run on him. They also bunt on him, causing his control to unravel as he hurries his delivery to get into fielding position. More teams might try to bunt on him—or make him think they are going to—this season.

## 1996 Outlook

Smith has one year left on his contract, but doesn't know if he will spend that year in California. With Troy Percival waiting to assume the closer's role, a trade is not out of the question. In any case, Smith will have to prove he still has it. Maybe this is the year baseball's all-time saves leader starts the swift fall from a likely Hall of Fame career. If nothing else, Smith could provide a nice security blanket until Percival takes over the closing chores.

**Position:** RP
**Bats:** R  **Throws:** R
**Ht:** 6' 6"  **Wt:** 269

**Opening Day Age:** 38
**Born:** 12/4/57 in Jamestown, LA
**ML Seasons:** 16

*California Angels*

### Overall Statistics

|  | W | L | Pct. | ERA | G | GS | Sv | IP | H | BB | SO | HR | BR/IP |
|---|---|---|---|---|---|---|---|---|---|---|---|---|---|
| 1995 | 0 | 5 | .000 | 3.47 | 52 | 0 | 37 | 49.1 | 42 | 25 | 43 | 3 | 1.36 |
| Career | 68 | 87 | .439 | 2.95 | 943 | 6 | 471 | 1213.0 | 1048 | 452 | 1195 | 83 | 1.24 |

### How Often He Throws Strikes

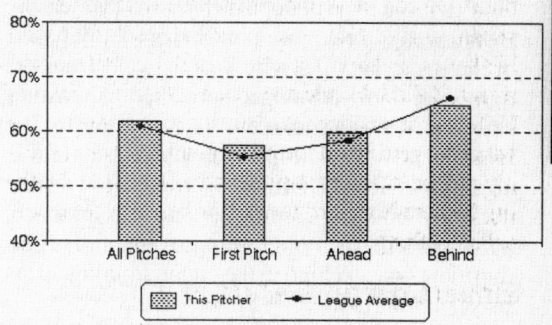

### 1995 Situational Stats

|  | W | L | ERA | Sv | IP |  | AB | H | HR | RBI | Avg |
|---|---|---|---|---|---|---|---|---|---|---|---|
| Home | 0 | 2 | 1.99 | 17 | 22.2 | LHB | 102 | 24 | 1 | 10 | .235 |
| Road | 0 | 3 | 4.73 | 20 | 26.2 | RHB | 75 | 18 | 2 | 12 | .240 |
| First Half | 0 | 2 | 3.22 | 20 | 22.1 | Sc Pos | 52 | 12 | 2 | 19 | .231 |
| Scnd Half | 0 | 3 | 3.67 | 17 | 27.0 | Clutch | 142 | 37 | 3 | 20 | .261 |

### 1995 Rankings (American League)

- ➡ 2nd in saves and save percentage (90.2%)
- ➡ 3rd in save opportunities (41)
- ➡ 4th in games finished (51)
- ➡ 7th in least GDPs induced per GDP situation (2.3%)
- ➡ 9th in lowest batting average allowed in relief with runners on base (.191)
- ➡ Led the Angels in saves, games finished (51), save opportunities (41), save percentage (90.2%) and blown saves (4)

# J.T. Snow

## 1995 Season

Which is the real J.T. Snow? The one who disappointed the California Angels badly in 1994 or the one who surpassed expectations in 1995? The answer probably lies somewhere in the middle. Snow rebounded nicely from a disastrous '94 by hitting well from both sides of the plate while playing first base as well as it can be played. Yet to visit the disabled list in his major league career, Snow missed just two games in 1995. He was a big part of the Angels' surprising success.

## Hitting

The switch-hitting Snow has always been considered weak against right-handed pitching, but he didn't show a huge platoon differential last season. He showed a little more power from the left side of the plate, but otherwise was as solid from the right side. Snow developed some bad habits after early success as a rookie in '93, swinging for the fences nearly every at-bat even when a single was all that was needed. Hitting instructor Rod Carew improved both his confidence and his approach, but Snow still has room for improvement. He gets impatient when behind in the count, running up his strikeout total.

## Baserunning & Defense

Snow, the son of former Los Angeles Rams wide receiver Jack Snow, is a natural athlete who does it all at first base. He has better-than-average range and is as skillful as anyone scooping throws in the dirt. He also makes some amazing catches going out on pop-ups. League managers and coaches were impressed enough to vote Snow his first of perhaps many Gold Gloves. He has adequate speed, but doesn't steal and isn't counted on to score from second base on a single.

## 1996 Outlook

Snow has established himself as the Angels' unquestioned first baseman, but he may have trouble maintaining the offensive standards he established in 1995. In particular, Snow isn't likely to see as many fastballs as he did in the first half of last season. The key for Snow will be developing a little more discipline and making better adjustments against breaking balls.

**Position:** 1B
**Bats:** B  **Throws:** L
**Ht:** 6' 2"  **Wt:** 202

**Opening Day Age:** 28
**Born:** 2/26/68 in Long Beach, CA
**ML Seasons:** 4

### Overall Statistics

|        | G   | AB   | R   | H   | D  | T | HR | RBI | SB | BB  | SO  | Avg  | OBP  | Slg  |
|--------|-----|------|-----|-----|----|---|----|-----|----|-----|-----|------|------|------|
| 1995   | 143 | 544  | 80  | 157 | 22 | 1 | 24 | 102 | 2  | 52  | 91  | .289 | .353 | .465 |
| Career | 340 | 1200 | 163 | 309 | 45 | 3 | 48 | 191 | 5  | 131 | 232 | .258 | .332 | .420 |

### Where He Hits the Ball

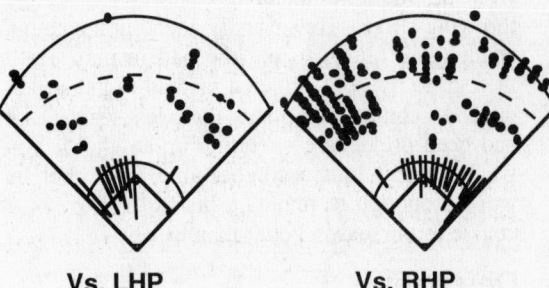

Vs. LHP          Vs. RHP

### 1995 Situational Stats

|            | AB  | H  | HR | RBI | Avg  |        | AB  | H   | HR | RBI | Avg  |
|------------|-----|----|----|-----|------|--------|-----|-----|----|-----|------|
| Home       | 270 | 82 | 14 | 60  | .304 | LHP    | 161 | 43  | 5  | 28  | .267 |
| Road       | 274 | 75 | 10 | 42  | .274 | RHP    | 383 | 114 | 19 | 74  | .298 |
| First Half | 259 | 79 | 11 | 51  | .305 | Sc Pos | 170 | 50  | 11 | 86  | .294 |
| Scnd Half  | 285 | 78 | 13 | 51  | .274 | Clutch | 67  | 15  | 5  | 14  | .224 |

### 1995 Rankings (American League)

➡ 3rd in fielding percentage at first base (.997)
➡ 7th in lowest groundball/flyball ratio (0.8)
➡ 8th in games played
➡ 10th in errors at first base (4)
➡ Led the Angels in singles (110), GDPs (16), games played, batting average with the bases loaded (.471), lowest percentage of swings that missed (14.4%) and lowest percentage of swings on the first pitch (21.7%)

# Shawn Boskie

**Position:** SP
**Bats:** R **Throws:** R
**Ht:** 6' 3" **Wt:** 200

**Opening Day Age:** 29
**Born:** 3/28/67 in
Hawthorne, NV
**ML Seasons:** 6

*Overall Statistics*

|  | W | L | Pct. | ERA | G | GS | Sv | IP | H | BB | SO | HR | BR/IP |
|---|---|---|---|---|---|---|---|---|---|---|---|---|---|
| 1995 | 7 | 7 | .500 | 5.64 | 20 | 20 | 0 | 111.2 | 127 | 25 | 51 | 16 | 1.36 |
| Career | 30 | 43 | .411 | 4.79 | 147 | 90 | 0 | 586.1 | 627 | 195 | 301 | 74 | 1.40 |

## 1995 Season

Cast adrift by the Cubs and Phillies, Shawn Boskie did an unusual thing for a pitcher—moving to the heavier-hitting American League but revitalizing his career. Boskie earned a spot in the Angels' rotation in spring training, and was terrific at the start of the season, not losing until June 19. But Boskie missed six weeks with injuries in July and August, and wasn't the same when he returned. He did hurl a five-hitter September 11, but lasted less than three innings in three of his last four starts.

## Pitching & Defense

Boskie is the classic sinkerball pitcher. He has an average fastball which he must keep down to get movement. He's developed a forkball that he can sometimes get left-handed hitters to chase. The best thing he does is throw strikes, averaging just 2.0 walks per nine innings last year. Boskie is agile on the mound, and does a good job holding runners close. Runners attempted to steal just four times against him in 1995.

## 1996 Outlook

Despite making 20 starts, Boskie was considered expendable by the Angels. He should generate some interest as a bargain free agent, however. He earned only $200,000 last year and delivered just as much as more highly paid free agents.

# Mike Butcher

**Position:** RP
**Bats:** R **Throws:** R
**Ht:** 6' 1" **Wt:** 200

**Opening Day Age:** 29
**Born:** 5/10/66 in
Davenport, IA
**ML Seasons:** 4

*Overall Statistics*

|  | W | L | Pct. | ERA | G | GS | Sv | IP | H | BB | SO | HR | BR/IP |
|---|---|---|---|---|---|---|---|---|---|---|---|---|---|
| 1995 | 6 | 1 | .857 | 4.73 | 40 | 0 | 0 | 51.1 | 49 | 31 | 29 | 7 | 1.56 |
| Career | 11 | 4 | .733 | 4.47 | 115 | 0 | 9 | 137.0 | 130 | 82 | 96 | 14 | 1.55 |

## 1995 Season

Two-and-zero. Three-and-one. Those were the counts that haunted Mike Butcher last season. The California Angels' middle reliever won six games in the first three months of the season, but was considered too erratic to get meaningful second-half innings for a contender. Rookie Troy Percival supplanted the wild Butcher as the primary set-up man for Lee Smith. It was a missed opportunity that Butcher may never know again.

## Pitching & Defense

Butcher has a sharp curveball that can be effective against both right-handed and left-handed hitters. But he struggled mechanically with the pitch last year, not throwing it consistently for strikes. He has an average fastball that can be effective if he's getting his curveball over. But he needs to throw more first-pitch strikes than he did in 1995. Butcher is an awkward fielder who seldom helps himself. Teams usually aren't afraid to run against him, but he did a much better job holding runners in 1995.

## 1996 Outlook

Butcher was dropped from the Angels' 40-man roster after the season in a move that freed up roster space. He has done little in the last two seasons to create a market for himself, and may need to spend the winter getting in peak condition before finding his way to training camp this spring.

California
Angels

# Jorge Fabregas

**Position**: C
**Bats**: L  **Throws**: R
**Ht**: 6' 3"  **Wt**: 205

**Opening Day Age**: 26
**Born**: 3/13/70 in Miami, FL
**ML Seasons**: 2
**Pronunciation**: FA-ber-gas

## Overall Statistics

|  | G | AB | R | H | D | T | HR | RBI | SB | BB | SO | Avg | OBP | Slg |
|---|---|---|---|---|---|---|---|---|---|---|---|---|---|---|
| 1995 | 73 | 227 | 24 | 56 | 10 | 0 | 1 | 22 | 0 | 17 | 28 | .247 | .298 | .304 |
| Career | 116 | 354 | 36 | 92 | 13 | 0 | 1 | 38 | 2 | 24 | 46 | .260 | .306 | .305 |

## 1995 Season

After getting a taste of the big leagues in 1994, Jorge Fabregas came to stay in 1995—but found himself struggling along the way. Playing almost as much as number-one catcher Greg Myers, Fabregas did not hit as well as he did as a rookie, and failed to make the defensive strides the Angels had hoped to see. He got valuable experience, but suffered a blow to his ego when Marcel Lachemann turned to journeyman Andy Allanson with Myers out down the stretch.

## Hitting, Baserunning & Defense

Fabregas has never regained the pop he had with an aluminum bat in college. He is a decent contact hitter, but seldom drives balls. He's developed an inside-out swing and likes to hit the ball to the opposite field. Defensively, he struggled catching the Angels' hard throwers. He smoothed out his throwing mechanics some, but it provided little consolation for what was largely a lost season. He runs like a catcher—and a slow one at that.

## 1996 Outlook

Nothing is likely to be given to Fabregas on a team that expects to be a contender. The Angels appeared likely to add a veteran catcher to platoon with the lefty-hitting Fabregas. It's time for Fabregas to step forward—or be passed by prospect Todd Greene.

# Dave Gallagher

**Position**: RF/CF
**Bats**: R  **Throws**: R
**Ht**: 6' 0"  **Wt**: 185

**Opening Day Age**: 35
**Born**: 9/20/60 in Trenton, NJ
**ML Seasons**: 9

## Overall Statistics

|  | G | AB | R | H | D | T | HR | RBI | SB | BB | SO | Avg | OBP | Slg |
|---|---|---|---|---|---|---|---|---|---|---|---|---|---|---|
| 1995 | 73 | 173 | 13 | 53 | 13 | 0 | 1 | 12 | 0 | 18 | 21 | .306 | .370 | .399 |
| Career | 794 | 2081 | 273 | 564 | 100 | 10 | 17 | 190 | 20 | 187 | 251 | .271 | .331 | .353 |

## 1995 Season

Nomadic life seems to suit Dave Gallagher. The extra outfielder continues to produce despite constantly changing addresses. He played most of the season with Philadelphia, before moving to the California Angels in a late move—his fourth team in the last three seasons. He hit .318 as the Phillies' fourth outfielder, but arrived in California with the Angels beginning their collapse. He strained a rib-cage muscle shortly after getting to California and played in only 11 games with his new team.

## Hitting, Baserunning & Defense

Gallagher remains a good contact hitter with a short stride. He knows the strike zone, and usually has about as many walks as strikeouts. Capable of playing all three outfield positions, he's still considered a good outfielder despite his declining range. He knows the hitters in both leagues, and does a great job positioning himself, helping compensate for an average arm. On the bases, Gallagher's use as a pinch runner has ended. He hasn't stolen a base since 1993.

## 1996 Outlook

Gallagher will find work somewhere, because he's still considered a valuable player off the bench. It's very possible that he'll return to the National League, where he revived his career last season.

# Rex Hudler

**Position:** 2B/LF
**Bats:** R  **Throws:** R
**Ht:** 6' 0"  **Wt:** 195

**Opening Day Age:** 35
**Born:** 9/2/60 in Tempe, AZ
**ML Seasons:** 10

## Overall Statistics

| | G | AB | R | H | D | T | HR | RBI | SB | BB | SO | Avg | OBP | Slg |
|---|---|---|---|---|---|---|---|---|---|---|---|---|---|---|
| 1995 | 84 | 223 | 30 | 59 | 16 | 0 | 6 | 27 | 13 | 10 | 48 | .265 | .310 | .417 |
| Career | 607 | 1302 | 182 | 335 | 71 | 7 | 35 | 117 | 92 | 58 | 231 | .257 | .292 | .403 |

## 1995 Season

Rex "The Wonder Dog" Hudler epitomized the can-do spirit of the surprising California Angels. He received more playing time than expected, and responded with one of the best performances of his long career. He'll play anywhere without complaint. There are hundreds of better athletes in the majors, but few with his desire. Hudler, in fact, is so happy to be in the big leagues he sometimes cries from the sheer joy of being on the field. Honest.

## Hitting, Baserunning & Defense

Hudler is a fastball hitter who likes to get pitches up in the strike zone. He doesn't look like much at the plate, but has surprising power when pitchers don't bear down on him. Breaking balls have always given him trouble. Hudler's best position is second base, but he can play third, first and the outfield. He doesn't have blazing speed, but he knows when to run. He was 13-for-13 stealing bases in 1995.

## 1996 Outlook

Hudler is a popular player who has hustled his way to a good career. He should return to the Angels' bench, but figures to see diminishing playing time. Some organization will have a coaching or minor league managing job waiting for him when he decides to hang his spikes up.

# Mike James

**Position:** RP
**Bats:** R  **Throws:** R
**Ht:** 6' 3"  **Wt:** 180

**Opening Day Age:** 28
**Born:** 8/15/67 in Fort Walton, FL
**ML Seasons:** 1

## Overall Statistics

| | W | L | Pct. | ERA | G | GS | Sv | IP | H | BB | SO | HR | BR/IP |
|---|---|---|---|---|---|---|---|---|---|---|---|---|---|
| 1995 | 3 | 0 | 1.000 | 3.88 | 46 | 0 | 1 | 55.2 | 49 | 26 | 36 | 6 | 1.35 |
| Career | 3 | 0 | 1.000 | 3.88 | 46 | 0 | 1 | 55.2 | 49 | 26 | 36 | 6 | 1.35 |

## 1995 Season

Some players simply develop late. That could be the case with reliever Mike James. He arrived in the big leagues last season with good enough stuff to make scouts wonder why he had spent so much time in the minors. He was unbeaten in middle relief, and finished the season pitching behind only Lee Smith and Troy Percival in the California bullpen. James' work out of the pen was a quiet key for the Angels in July and early August.

## Pitching & Defense

James has everything scouts look for in a reliever. He has an outstanding arm and gets very good deception from his motion. Hitters make contact against his pitches, but do little with them. His fastball runs in on right-handed hitters, breaking their bats. James is an average fielder. His slow delivery makes him a potential target for basestealers, but they didn't take advantage in 1995.

## 1996 Outlook

James returns to the California bullpen, where he is projected as the set-up man once Percival supplants Smith as the closer. James' test will be to build on the success he had last year. James is considered a major flake, leading to questions about his work ethic and mental toughness. But the tools are there for a good career.

# Spike Owen

**Position**: 3B/2B/SS
**Bats**: B  **Throws**: R
**Ht**: 5'10"  **Wt**: 170

**Opening Day Age**: 34
**Born**: 4/19/61 in
Cleburne, TX
**ML Seasons**: 13

*Overall Statistics*

| | G | AB | R | H | D | T | HR | RBI | SB | BB | SO | Avg | OBP | Slg |
|---|---|---|---|---|---|---|---|---|---|---|---|---|---|---|
| 1995 | 82 | 218 | 17 | 50 | 9 | 3 | 1 | 28 | 3 | 18 | 22 | .229 | .288 | .312 |
| Career | 1544 | 4930 | 587 | 1211 | 215 | 59 | 46 | 439 | 82 | 569 | 519 | .246 | .324 | .341 |

## 1995 Season

California attempted to unload Spike Owen's contract in spring training, but eventually was glad that no one took them up. The days are over when Owen is considered as an alternative at shortstop, but his experience and versatility are still pluses on the bench. He was not able to fill the shortstop spot when Gary DiSarcina was out in August and September, but did a good job when not overexposed.

## Hitting, Baserunning & Defense

The switch-hitting Owen hit better left-handed than right-handed last year, and contributed some big hits for the Angels in 1995. He still handles the bat well, making him a good hit-and-run guy. In addition, he usually draws as many walks as he strikes out. As he approaches 35, Owen doesn't have much range in the field, and wears down when he gets extended playing time. He hustles, but is no longer a threat to steal.

## 1996 Outlook

Owen is a free agent who may have to earn a job with some team in spring training. He's still a solid extra player, and could have value to a team with a young shortstop. His presence in California contributed to Gary DiSarcina's development into an All-Star.

# Bob Patterson

**Position**: RP
**Bats**: R  **Throws**: L
**Ht**: 6'2"  **Wt**: 192

**Opening Day Age**: 36
**Born**: 5/16/59 in
Jacksonville, FL
**ML Seasons**: 10

*Overall Statistics*

| | W | L | Pct. | ERA | G | GS | Sv | IP | H | BB | SO | HR | BR/IP |
|---|---|---|---|---|---|---|---|---|---|---|---|---|---|
| 1995 | 5 | 2 | .714 | 3.04 | 62 | 0 | 0 | 53.1 | 48 | 13 | 41 | 6 | 1.14 |
| Career | 34 | 30 | .531 | 4.14 | 371 | 21 | 19 | 483.0 | 490 | 136 | 355 | 53 | 1.30 |

## 1995 Season

Coming off a couple of so-so seasons, Bob Patterson was a pleasant surprise for the California Angels. He reverted to the same type of situational lefthander he had been with Pittsburgh's division championship teams in 1990-92, holding his own against the league's top left-handed hitters. Angels manager Marcel Lachemann used him more judiciously than Kevin Kennedy had in Texas, and Patterson responded. While he made 62 appearances, he compiled only 53.1 innings.

## Pitching & Defense

Patterson gets left-handed hitters out when he throws his slider for strikes. He did that in 1995, posting three times as many strikeouts as walks. The trouble starts when he gets narrowed down to a fastball, but his control was good enough last season that it didn't happen much. Patterson remains an outstanding fielder—he's never made an error in the major leagues—with a good pickoff move.

## 1996 Outlook

Patterson pitched well enough to keep the Angels interested in his services, but was expected to test free agency. After taking a cut in pay for 1995, he may be the rare veteran who is able to make up the difference this time around. Effective left-handed relievers are a valuable commodity.

# Other California Angels

**Mike Aldrete** (**Pos**: 1B/LF, **Age**: 35, **Bats**: L)

Aldrete was traded to the Angels from Oakland in late August, and he continued to fill his role as a left-handed bat coming off the bench. It suits him well, and he'll be able to do it again in 1996. 1996 Outlook: B

**Andy Allanson** (**Pos**: C, **Age**: 34, **Bats**: R)

Allanson's career appears to be in jeopardy. The Angels released him after the season, after he hit just .171 in 25 games. Considering last season's injury problems and his age, another chance isn't likely. 1996 Outlook: D

**Rod Correia** (**Pos**: SS, **Age**: 29, **Bats**: R)

Correia has seen stints with the Angels the last three seasons, but never enough to make a dent in the organization. It's highly unlikely that he'll ever be more than a utility man, if that. 1996 Outlook: C

**Mark Dalesandro** (**Pos**: C, **Age**: 28, **Bats**: R)

With Fabregas, Myers, and Turner ahead of him, Dalesandro will have to fight awfully hard to get the California catching duties. He saw just 11 games with the Angels in 1995, but might get a chance. 1996 Outlook: C

**Ken Edenfield** (**Pos**: RHP, **Age**: 29)

Edenfield's strikeout numbers have always been impressive in the minors, but time is running out on him. He saw just seven games with California in 1995, and needs a chance to prove himself. 1996 Outlook: C

**Tim Fortugno** (**Pos**: RHP, **Age**: 34)

After pitching poorly for the White Sox, Fortugno was traded to the Angels in July, but never saw any action. He was a decent prospect in 1990, but at this point he's about at the end of the line. 1996 Outlook: D

**Rene Gonzales** (**Pos**: 3B, **Age**: 35, **Bats**: R)

Gonzales was called up by the Angels for the season's final month, spending much of his time as a late defensive replacement for Tony Phillips at third. There's not much pop left in his bat. 1996 Outlook: C

**John Habyan** (**Pos**: RHP, **Age**: 32)

Habyan was traded to California from St. Louis in July, and pitched better than expected for both clubs. He should continue in his role as a set-up man for somebody. 1996 Outlook: A

**Mark Holzemer** (**Pos**: RHP, **Age**: 27)

Holzemer has had short stints with the Angels in 1993 and 1995, pitching poorly both times. He deteriorated in the minors as a starter, and is now pitching in relief at both levels. He'll get a chance. 1996 Outlook: C

**Jose Lind** (**Pos**: 2B, **Age**: 32, **Bats**: R)

Lind was waived by both Kansas City and California in 1995, with his fielding ability no longer justifying is poor hitting (.236 in 1995). He'll likely find a spot somewhere, because a lot of people still love his defense. 1996 Outlook: B

**Carlos Martinez** (**Pos**: 3B, **Age**: 31, **Bats**: R)

Martinez was waived by the Angels in July after hitting poorly in 1995. He has very little to offer anyone. 1996 Outlook: D

**Rich Monteleone** (**Pos**: RHP, **Age**: 33)

After being waived by the Giants last season, Monteleone was called up by the Angels for the stretch drive, but saw just nine innings of work. He should be on a major league team next season, if healthy. 1996 Outlook: C

**Orlando Palmeiro** (**Pos**: CF, **Age**: 27, **Bats**: L)

You wonder why Palmeiro doesn't get a chance. He's hit well when given the opportunity in the majors, as well as at Triple-A. He walks more than he strikes out, and has some speed. He deserves a shot. 1996 Outlook: C

**Eduardo Perez** (**Pos**: 3B, **Age**: 27, **Bats**: R)

Perez has hit very poorly during his stints the last three seasons with California. At the rate he strikes out, he'll never be a major league regular. At 27, there is time to work on it. 1996 Outlook: C

**Scott Sanderson** (**Pos**: RHP, **Age**: 39)

1995 was probably the end of the line for Sanderson, as back surgery ended his season after seven starts with the Angels. He appears to be done, with 163 major league wins. 1996 Outlook: D

**Dick Schofield** (**Pos**: SS, **Age**: 33, **Bats**: R)

After the Dodgers released Schofield, the Angels gave him a September homecoming. He got just 20 at-bats during the callup. With DiSarcina healthy, he'll have to go elsewhere. 1996 Outlook: D

**Chris Turner** (**Pos**: C, **Age**: 27, **Bats**: R)

He saw just five games with the Angels in 1995, having hit .248 in stints over the last three seasons. He'll be one of many fighting for the Angels' catching job in 1996. 1996 Outlook: C

**Mitch Williams** (**Pos**: RP, **Age**: 31, **Throws**: L)

After a horrible start with the Angels, Williams was released in mid-June and announced his retirement the next day. Simply put, he was never the same after Joe Carter's home run. 1996 Outlook: D

# California Angels Minor League Prospects

## Organization Overview:

The Angels' farm system gets little respect, but over the past three years California has promoted an American League Rookie of the Year (Tim Salmon), a power-hitting centerfielder (Jim Edmonds), one of the game's most impressive young relievers (Troy Percival), and another .300-hitting outfielder (Garret Anderson). Some of the disrespect stems from some curious draft picks, such as the selection of mission-bound McKay Christensen (now with the White Sox) with the sixth pick of 1994. However, California loosened the purse strings to sign 1995's top overall pick, Darin Erstad, for a $1.575 million signing bonus. Still, the talent in California's minor league organization looks a bit thin right now, with question marks attached to many of the following prospects.

### George Arias

**Position:** 3B | **Opening Day Age:** 24
**Bats:** R **Throws:** R | **Born:** 3/12/72 in
**Ht:** 5' 11" **Wt:** 190 | Tucson, AZ

*Recent Statistics*

|  | G | AB | R | H | D | T | HR | RBI | SB | BB | SO | AVG |
|---|---|---|---|---|---|---|---|---|---|---|---|---|
| 93 A Cedar Rapds | 74 | 253 | 31 | 55 | 13 | 3 | 9 | 41 | 6 | 31 | 65 | .217 |
| 94 A Lk Elsinore | 134 | 514 | 89 | 144 | 28 | 3 | 23 | 80 | 6 | 58 | 111 | .280 |
| 95 AA Midland | 134 | 520 | 91 | 145 | 19 | 10 | 30 | 104 | 3 | 63 | 119 | .279 |
| 95 MLE | 134 | 499 | 70 | 124 | 15 | 5 | 25 | 81 | 1 | 41 | 128 | .248 |

Only two other players at the Double- or Triple-A level hit more than the 30 homers Arias totaled last season, one of them being fellow Angel farmhand Todd Greene. Like Greene, Arias was drafted by the Angels in 1993, in round seven. Unlike Greene, third baseman Arias is a solid defender. Arias led the Texas League in both homers and RBI, and he rounded out his offense with 29 other extra-base hits and a good walk rate. He'll begin 1996 at Triple-A, and since the Angels don't appear to have a long-term solution to their third-base situation on the big club, Arias could make a major league impact soon.

### Darin Erstad

**Position:** OF | **Opening Day Age:** 21
**Bats:** L **Throws:** L | **Born:** 6/4/74 in
**Ht:** 6' 02" **Wt:** 195 | Jamestown, ND

*Recent Statistics*

|  | G | AB | R | H | D | T | HR | RBI | SB | BB | SO | AVG |
|---|---|---|---|---|---|---|---|---|---|---|---|---|
| 95 R Angels | 4 | 18 | 2 | 10 | 1 | 0 | 0 | 1 | 1 | 1 | 1 | .556 |
| 95 A Lk Elsinore | 25 | 113 | 24 | 41 | 7 | 3 | 5 | 24 | 3 | 6 | 22 | .363 |

The Angels chose Erstad with the first overall selection last June, and he didn't disappoint in his first pro action. His stay in the rookie-level Arizona League lasted just four games, where a 10-for-18 (.556) performance convinced the Angels he was ready to make the jump to the fast-A California League. Erstad wasn't slowed by the higher competition, hitting .363 with power and flashing the speed and range to play center field. While the Angel outfield appears set, a number-one pick with Erstad's talent is on the fast track to the bigs.

### Todd Greene

**Position:** C | **Opening Day Age:** 24
**Bats:** R **Throws:** R | **Born:** 5/8/71 in
**Ht:** 5' 10" **Wt:** 195 | Augusta, GA

*Recent Statistics*

|  | G | AB | R | H | D | T | HR | RBI | SB | BB | SO | AVG |
|---|---|---|---|---|---|---|---|---|---|---|---|---|
| 93 A Boise | 76 | 305 | 55 | 82 | 15 | 3 | 15 | 71 | 4 | 34 | 44 | .269 |
| 94 A Lk Elsinore | 133 | 524 | 98 | 158 | 39 | 2 | 35 | 124 | 10 | 64 | 96 | .302 |
| 95 AA Midland | 82 | 318 | 59 | 104 | 19 | 1 | 26 | 57 | 3 | 17 | 55 | .327 |
| 95 AAA Vancouver | 43 | 168 | 28 | 42 | 3 | 1 | 14 | 35 | 1 | 11 | 36 | .250 |
| 95 MLE | 125 | 467 | 69 | 127 | 17 | 0 | 33 | 74 | 2 | 20 | 97 | .272 |

Greene does nothing but hit. Despite crushing the third-most home runs in NCAA history, he wasn't drafted until round 12 in 1993. Since then, he's captured MVP honors in two leagues, led the minors in RBI in 1994 and in homers in 1995. His 40 dingers last year were the minors' most since '85. Greene's performance dipped when he reached Triple-A, as he hit .250 with a loss of doubles power in the PCL, but his hitting isn't a question. Defense is. A converted outfielder, Greene led the minors with 44 passed balls in 1994. Reportedly his defense improved last season, and if he continues to hammer the ball, the Angels will either move him to another position or learn to live with his defense.

### Aaron Guiel

**Position:** 2B | **Opening Day Age:** 23
**Bats:** L **Throws:** R | **Born:** 10/5/72 in
**Ht:** 5' 10" **Wt:** 190 | Vancouver, BC, Can.

*Recent Statistics*

|  | G | AB | R | H | D | T | HR | RBI | SB | BB | SO | AVG |
|---|---|---|---|---|---|---|---|---|---|---|---|---|
| 93 A Boise | 35 | 104 | 24 | 31 | 6 | 4 | 2 | 12 | 3 | 26 | 21 | .298 |
| 94 A Cedar Rapds | 127 | 454 | 84 | 122 | 30 | 1 | 18 | 82 | 21 | 64 | 93 | .269 |
| 95 A Lk Elsinore | 113 | 409 | 73 | 110 | 25 | 7 | 7 | 58 | 7 | 69 | 96 | .269 |

Guiel, a native of that baseball mecca, Langley, British Columbia, was taken by the Angels in the 21st round of the 1992 draft. He didn't begin his pro career until 1993, and has remained in A ball since, albeit moving up a level of competition each year. Guiel is a lefthanded-hitting second baseman with power, which has some value in itself. His 1995 production was down sharply from 1994 when he hit 18 homers with 21 stolen bases in the Midwest League. If the 23 year old can recover that performance in Double-A and maintain his high walk rate, Guiel looks like he can one day be another Dick McAuliffe.

## Pete Janicki

**Position:** P **Opening Day Age:** 25
**Bats:** R **Throws:** R **Born:** 1/26/71 in
**Ht:** 6' 4" **Wt:** 190 Parma, OH

### Recent Statistics

|  | W | L | ERA | G | GS | Sv | IP | H | R | BB | SO | HR |
|---|---|---|---|---|---|---|---|---|---|---|---|---|
| 93 A Palm Spring | 0 | 0 | 10.80 | 1 | 1 | 0 | 1.2 | 3 | 2 | 2 | 2 | 0 |
| 94 AA Midland | 2 | 6 | 6.94 | 14 | 14 | 0 | 70.0 | 86 | 68 | 33 | 54 | 4 |
| 94 A Lk Elsinore | 1 | 2 | 6.75 | 3 | 3 | 0 | 12.0 | 17 | 12 | 4 | 12 | 2 |
| 95 A Lk Elsinore | 9 | 4 | 3.06 | 20 | 20 | 0 | 123.1 | 130 | 66 | 28 | 106 | 7 |
| 95 AAA Vancouver | 1 | 4 | 7.03 | 9 | 9 | 0 | 48.2 | 64 | 38 | 23 | 34 | 8 |

Janicki was the Angels' first pick in 1992 and the eighth player taken overall. But while competing in the NCAA regionals for UCLA that spring, he hurt his elbow through overwork. The stress fracture set him back until 1994. His first full campaign was a disaster, as he went 3-8 with a 6.91 ERA before shutting down with tendinitis. He started to turn things around in 1995, although he later struggled in Triple-A. Before the injury, Janicki's fastball reached the low 90s. If he can maintain his velocity, Janicki is most likely the Angels' most-advanced pitching prospect.

## Deshawn Warren

**Position:** P **Opening Day Age:** 21
**Bats:** L **Throws:** L **Born:** 5/5/74 in
**Ht:** 6' 0" **Wt:** 172 Meridian, MS

### Recent Statistics

|  | W | L | ERA | G | GS | Sv | IP | H | R | BB | SO | HR |
|---|---|---|---|---|---|---|---|---|---|---|---|---|
| 93 R Angels | 2 | 4 | 4.10 | 9 | 9 | 0 | 41.2 | 27 | 26 | 34 | 63 | 0 |
| 94 A Cedar Rapds | 7 | 4 | 3.40 | 22 | 21 | 0 | 98.0 | 76 | 43 | 76 | 88 | 3 |
| 95 A Cedar Rapds | 2 | 3 | 3.26 | 7 | 7 | 0 | 30.1 | 20 | 12 | 13 | 26 | 2 |

Warren hails from the same high school which produced Johnny Ruffin, another pitcher with a great arm who was quite raw when first drafted. Although he's just 6'0", 172 pounds and lefthanded, Warren throws a lot more like Randy Johnson than Randy Jones, with a fastball that reaches 94 MPH. The challenge will be developing an acceptable breaking pitch that can keep hitters from sitting on the heater. In his first three professional seasons, Warren walked over seven men per nine innings. He cut that rate nearly in half last year, before a strained left elbow cut short his season. If he can harness his control and expand his repertoire, Warren could be a dominant starter. If he struggles, he may experience more success coming out of the bullpen.

## Mike Wolff

**Position:** OF **Opening Day Age:** 25
**Bats:** R **Throws:** R **Born:** 12/19/70 in
**Ht:** 6' 1" **Wt:** 195 Wilmington, NC

### Recent Statistics

|  | G | AB | R | H | D | T | HR | RBI | SB | BB | SO | AVG |
|---|---|---|---|---|---|---|---|---|---|---|---|---|
| 93 A Cedar Rapds | 120 | 407 | 63 | 100 | 18 | 5 | 17 | 72 | 8 | 74 | 104 | .246 |
| 94 AA Midland | 113 | 397 | 64 | 115 | 30 | 1 | 13 | 58 | 10 | 54 | 91 | .290 |
| 95 AA Midland | 127 | 445 | 76 | 135 | 28 | 3 | 14 | 70 | 10 | 65 | 83 | .303 |
| 95 MLE | 127 | 425 | 59 | 115 | 22 | 1 | 11 | 54 | 6 | 43 | 89 | .271 |

Wolff was the Angels 16th-round draft pick in 1992 out of Georgia Tech, and he's been an offensive plus every season since. Still, he was asked to repeat Double-A last year, where he virtually duplicated his 1994 season. Midland is a good hitters park, however, so Wolff's numbers are probably not as impressive as they might appear. Despite that, a .300 average with lots of walks, some extra-base power and a few stolen bases are a good combination. Wolff should advance to Triple-A at age 25 in 1996, and he could eventually make a push for big-league service time.

## Others to Watch

Lefthanded pitcher **Matt Beaumont**, a fourth-round pick in 1994, has looked impressive in his two pro seasons, with a strikeout-to-walk ratio of nearly three-to-one and more K's than hits allowed. He has three solid pitches, and will likely begin 1996 in Double-A. . . First baseman **John Donati** was chosen in the fourth round of 1991 out of high school. He's been slow to develop, as he finished his fifth professional season still in Class-A last year, but the power is coming along (16 HR, 24 doubles in 381 AB) and he's only 22. . . Righthanded pitcher **Ryan Hancock** was Brigham Young's quarterback before tearing the anterior-cruciate ligament in his knee. The Angels drafted him in the second round of '92, expecting his velocity to return, but judging by his stats (175.2 IP, 222 hits, 79 K's) at Double-A, Hancock still has a ways to go. . . Outfielder **Aaron Iatarola**, a 21st-round pick in 1993, showed some pop last season (16 HR, 69 RBI in 388 AB), but he was a second-year repeater in the Midwest League, and he's now 24. . . Righthander **Korey Keling** is even older, 27, but he enjoyed a fine 1995 season, going 8-5 with a 3.46 ERA at Midland, a tough park for pitchers, before getting his first taste of Triple-A. . . Catcher **Ben Molina** hit .329 with a slugging percentage close to .500 last season, but his 231 at-bats were a career high in three pro seasons. . . Third baseman **Gregory Morris** played shortstop in college before the Angles drafted him in the fifth round of 1994. He showed power and great plate discipline (14 HR, 62 BB in 355 AB) in his first full pro season at Class A. . . Righthander **Travis Thurmond** enjoyed an 11-8 campaign with great peripheral stats (140.1 IP, 111 hits, 148 K, 51 BB) between Class-A Boise and Cedar Rapids.

# Wilson Alvarez

## 1995 Season

The White Sox expected Wilson Alvarez to have a big year in 1995. Instead, they got a guy with a big belly. Alvarez reported to spring training in terrible shape, and the season was half over before he started looking like the pitcher who'd never had a losing record since joining the Sox back in 1991. A good second half got the critics off his back a little, but it came too late to salvage a disappointing season.

## Pitching

Alvarez pitched a no-hitter in his first start for the Sox, and it was no fluke: his stuff is that good. He throws a 90-plus fastball and a sharp-breaking curve, and his change and slider are also effective pitches. Along with conditioning, his biggest problem has been an inability to throw strikes consistently—especially with his curveball. After showing marked improvement in 1994, the control troubles returned last year. Alvarez had better command of the strike zone once he got himself in shape, and his strikeout-to-walk ratio was greatly improved, as was his ERA and his won-lost record. The club hopes he learned a lesson from that.

## Defense

Alvarez is a sure-handed fielder—he played errorless ball last year—but his reflexes are slow and his lack of agility hurts him when he has to move off the mound. He once had a lot of problems holding runners, but he's developed an excellent move and he now keeps most runners close to first.

## 1996 Outlook

Good lefthanders are hard to find, and the White Sox remain fond of Alvarez despite his problems last year. If he shows up for spring training in better shape, half the battle figures to be won. The other half of the battle will be to show that he can throw strikes more consistently than he did in 1995.

**Position:** SP
**Bats:** L  **Throws:** L
**Ht:** 6' 1"  **Wt:** 235

**Opening Day Age:** 26
**Born:** 3/24/70 in Maracaibo, VZ
**ML Seasons:** 6

### Overall Statistics

|        | W  | L  | Pct. | ERA  | G   | GS  | Sv | IP    | H   | BB  | SO  | HR | BR/IP |
|--------|----|----|------|------|-----|-----|----|-------|-----|-----|-----|----|-------|
| 1995   | 8  | 11 | .421 | 4.32 | 29  | 29  | 0  | 175.0 | 171 | 93  | 118 | 21 | 1.51  |
| Career | 43 | 33 | .566 | 3.81 | 129 | 103 | 1  | 701.0 | 639 | 373 | 479 | 74 | 1.44  |

### How Often He Throws Strikes

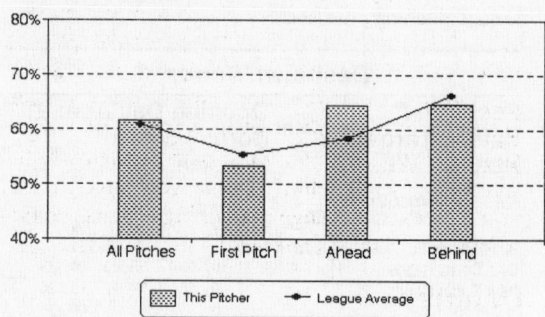

### 1995 Situational Stats

|            | W | L | ERA  | Sv | IP    |        | AB  | H   | HR | RBI | Avg  |
|------------|---|---|------|----|-------|--------|-----|-----|----|-----|------|
| Home       | 7 | 2 | 4.80 | 0  | 84.1  | LHB    | 108 | 32  | 2  | 18  | .296 |
| Road       | 1 | 9 | 3.87 | 0  | 90.2  | RHB    | 555 | 139 | 19 | 70  | .250 |
| First Half | 2 | 5 | 5.45 | 0  | 74.1  | Sc Pos | 145 | 37  | 3  | 54  | .255 |
| Scnd Half  | 6 | 6 | 3.49 | 0  | 100.2 | Clutch | 31  | 11  | 1  | 5   | .355 |

### 1995 Rankings (American League)

- ➡ 1st in fielding percentage at pitcher (1.000)
- ➡ 3rd in walks allowed and balks (2)
- ➡ 5th in runners caught stealing (9) and lowest stolen base percentage allowed (47.1%)
- ➡ 6th in lowest strikeout/walk ratio (1.3) and most pitches thrown per batter (3.93)
- ➡ Led the White Sox in home runs allowed, pickoff throws (147), runners caught stealing (9), GDPs induced (16), lowest stolen base percentage allowed (47.1%), most GDPs induced per 9 innings (0.8), ERA on the road (3.87) and lowest batting average allowed with runners in scoring position (.255)

# Jason Bere

## 1995 Season

When the 1995 season started, Jason Bere was rated as one of the best young starting pitchers in major league baseball. But Bere simply couldn't get the ball over the plate last year, and the result was a disastrous campaign. After going 24-7 in 1993-94, he posted an 8-15 mark, and the biggest mystery about the record was how he managed to win eight games. He ranked at or near the bottom of the league in losses, ERA, walks, gopher balls, stolen bases allowed. . . In a year's time, Bere went from one of the best in the league to one of the very worst.

## Pitching

Bere has terrific stuff, starting with a 90-plus fastball and a tricky "fosh" change-up. He also throws a slider and curve, and all his pitches have great movement. . . maybe more movement than he knows what to do with. Even when he was winning in 1993 and '94, Bere had problems with control, but nothing like what he went through last year. Not even a change in pitching coaches could help him turn things around.

## Defense

As messed up as Bere was last year, he didn't have time to bother with stuff like holding runners, and they ran wild on him. It's an area where he needs a lot of work. He's not a great fielder, but he handles his defensive responsibilities well enough and didn't commit an error in 1995.

## Overall

If Bere keeps pitching the way he did last year, there's no way he's going to get another 27 starts to try to straighten himself out. Especially not from the White Sox, who aren't ones to coddle their young starters. When Jack McDowell, Wilson Alvarez and Alex Fernandez ran into problems early in their careers, each got sent back to the minor leagues for a while. The same thing could happen to Bere, who'll be watched closely this spring.

**Position:** SP
**Bats:** R  **Throws:** R
**Ht:** 6' 3"  **Wt:** 185

**Opening Day Age:** 24
**Born:** 5/26/71 in Cambridge, MA
**ML Seasons:** 3
**Pronunciation:** bur-RAY

### Overall Statistics

| | W | L | Pct. | ERA | G | GS | Sv | IP | H | BB | SO | HR | BR/IP |
|---|---|---|---|---|---|---|---|---|---|---|---|---|---|
| 1995 | 8 | 15 | .348 | 7.19 | 27 | 27 | 0 | 137.2 | 151 | 106 | 110 | 21 | 1.87 |
| Career | 32 | 22 | .593 | 4.80 | 75 | 75 | 0 | 422.0 | 379 | 267 | 366 | 50 | 1.53 |

### How Often He Throws Strikes

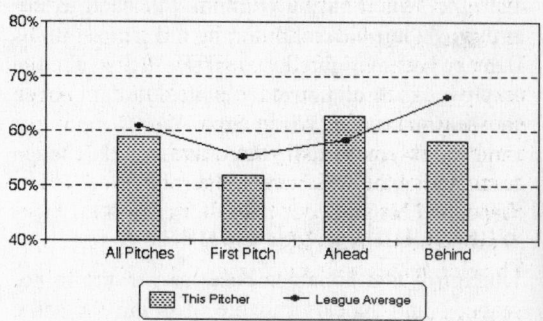

### 1995 Situational Stats

| | W | L | ERA | Sv | IP | | AB | H | HR | RBI | Avg |
|---|---|---|---|---|---|---|---|---|---|---|---|
| Home | 3 | 6 | 7.70 | 0 | 66.2 | LHB | 284 | 87 | 9 | 47 | .306 |
| Road | 5 | 9 | 6.72 | 0 | 71.0 | RHB | 261 | 64 | 12 | 53 | .245 |
| First Half | 4 | 7 | 5.31 | 0 | 84.2 | Sc Pos | 164 | 53 | 7 | 82 | .323 |
| Scnd Half | 4 | 8 | 10.19 | 0 | 53.0 | Clutch | 32 | 6 | 0 | 2 | .188 |

### 1995 Rankings (American League)

→ 1st in losses and stolen bases allowed (36)
→ 2nd in walks allowed
→ 6th in lowest winning percentage
→ 7th in highest batting average allowed with runners in scoring position (.323)
→ Led the White Sox in losses, home runs allowed, walks allowed, hit batsmen (6) and stolen bases allowed (36)

# Ray Durham

## 1995 Season

The White Sox were so high on rookie Ray Durham last year that they got rid of their regular second baseman, Joey Cora, in order to open up the position. Though he showed a few rough edges, Durham played regularly all year and flashed enough skills to indicate his potential as an above-average major league player.

## Hitting

Compared to Joe Morgan when he was coming up through the White Sox system, Durham is short but strong, with fine power for a second baseman. He had 40 extra-base hits last year and appears capable of hitting 15-20 homers. In order to do that, the switch-hitting Durham will need to improve as a left-handed hitter; he did almost all his damage batting righty last year. He'll also need to improve his discipline at the plate. Durham began the season as the White Sox leadoff man, but didn't look comfortable there and couldn't reach base often enough to handle the role.

## Baserunning & Defense

Durham was a 30-stolen-base man in the minor leagues, and appears capable of doing the same thing at the major league level. He has great speed and baserunning instincts. Durham looked a lot less polished in the field, committing 15 errors and having some problems with positioning. But he made enough spectacular plays to indicate that he can develop into a fine fielder if he keeps working on his weaknesses.

## 1996 Outlook

A lot was expected of Durham last year, and he couldn't live up to those Joe Morgan comparisons. At times he seemed to get down on himself and wound up suffering through a couple of extended slumps—including a big one at the end of the year. But the year of experience should help him in 1996, when he figures to be a much-improved player.

**Position:** 2B
**Bats:** B **Throws:** R
**Ht:** 5' 8" **Wt:** 170

**Opening Day Age:** 24
**Born:** 11/30/71 in Charlotte, NC
**ML Seasons:** 1

### Overall Statistics

|  | G | AB | R | H | D | T | HR | RBI | SB | BB | SO | Avg | OBP | Slg |
|---|---|---|---|---|---|---|---|---|---|---|---|---|---|---|
| 1995 | 125 | 471 | 68 | 121 | 27 | 6 | 7 | 51 | 18 | 31 | 83 | .257 | .309 | .384 |
| Career | 125 | 471 | 68 | 121 | 27 | 6 | 7 | 51 | 18 | 31 | 83 | .257 | .309 | .384 |

### Where He Hits the Ball

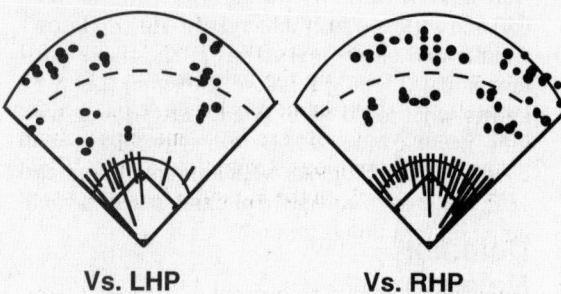

Vs. LHP          Vs. RHP

### 1995 Situational Stats

|  | AB | H | HR | RBI | Avg |  | AB | H | HR | RBI | Avg |
|---|---|---|---|---|---|---|---|---|---|---|---|
| Home | 230 | 54 | 1 | 20 | .235 | LHP | 149 | 47 | 3 | 17 | .315 |
| Road | 241 | 67 | 6 | 31 | .278 | RHP | 322 | 74 | 4 | 34 | .230 |
| First Half | 234 | 62 | 3 | 27 | .265 | Sc Pos | 137 | 35 | 2 | 44 | .255 |
| Scnd Half | 237 | 59 | 4 | 24 | .249 | Clutch | 81 | 17 | 0 | 8 | .210 |

### 1995 Rankings (American League)

- ➡ 2nd in lowest on-base percentage vs. right-handed pitchers (.277) and highest percentage of extra bases taken as a runner (72.2%)
- ➡ 3rd in lowest batting average at home (.235), lowest fielding percentage at second base (.973) and bunts in play (29)
- ➡ 4th in lowest batting average vs. right-handed pitchers (.230) and errors at second base (15)
- ➡ 5th in lowest on-base percentage
- ➡ Led the White Sox in doubles, hit by pitch (6), bunts in play (29) and highest percentage of extra bases taken as a runner (72.2%)

# Alex Fernandez

## 1995 Season

When the White Sox traded Jack McDowell to the Yankees after the 1994 season, the hope was that number-two starter Alex Fernandez would step into the role of staff ace. Instead—like many of his teammates—Fernandez got off to a terrible start, and at midseason his ERA was well over 5.00. But he finally got it together over the final two months of the season, winning his last seven decisions to finish with respectable numbers.

## Pitching

Fernandez throws the standard repertoire of fastball, curve, slider and change, and all of them are excellent pitches. He has a smooth, compact delivery, and when he's on his game any of the four are capable of tying up a hitter. Unfortunately, he's prone to stretches where his control is a little off and he'll start aiming the ball. He also still goes through periods when he lets his emotions get the best of him. Early last year, he seemed upset about losing an acrimonious arbitration to the White Sox, and his work on the mound reflected that.

## Defense

Fernandez commits an occasional error, but overall he's an excellent defensive player who moves quickly off the mound and displays good reflexes on balls hit up the middle. He's developed a nice, quick move to first, and holds runners about as well as any righthander around.

## 1996 Outlook

Fernandez has yet to become the big winner he was projected to be as an amateur, when two teams (Brewers and White Sox) made him their number-one draft choice. On the other hand, he's now had three winning seasons in a row, and he's never had a serious injury in five years in the Sox rotation. There aren't too many pitchers around like that. Whether Fernandez develops into a staff ace or not, he's already proven himself to be a quality major league starter.

**Position:** SP
**Bats:** R  **Throws:** R
**Ht:** 6' 1"  **Wt:** 215

**Opening Day Age:** 26
**Born:** 8/13/69 in Miami Beach, FL
**ML Seasons:** 6

### Overall Statistics

|        | W  | L  | Pct. | ERA  | G   | GS | Sv | IP     | H    | BB  | SO  | HR  | BR/IP |
|--------|----|----|------|------|-----|----|----|--------|------|-----|-----|-----|-------|
| 1995   | 12 | 8  | .600 | 3.80 | 30  | 30 | 0  | 203.2  | 200  | 65  | 159 | 19  | 1.30  |
| Career | 63 | 53 | .543 | 3.86 | 164 | 162| 0  | 1088.1 | 1058 | 354 | 751 | 114 | 1.30  |

### How Often He Throws Strikes

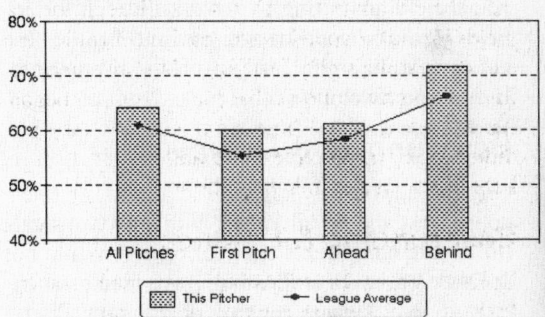

### 1995 Situational Stats

|            | W | L | ERA  | Sv | IP    |       | AB  | H   | HR | RBI | Avg  |
|------------|---|---|------|----|-------|-------|-----|-----|----|-----|------|
| Home       | 8 | 3 | 3.39 | 0  | 114.0 | LHB   | 412 | 114 | 11 | 51  | .277 |
| Road       | 4 | 5 | 4.32 | 0  | 89.2  | RHB   | 371 | 86  | 8  | 38  | .232 |
| First Half | 4 | 6 | 5.69 | 0  | 87.0  | Sc Pos| 172 | 46  | 5  | 69  | .267 |
| Scnd Half  | 8 | 2 | 2.39 | 0  | 116.2 | Clutch| 65  | 17  | 1  | 8   | .262 |

### 1995 Rankings (American League)

- → 3rd in shutouts (2), errors at pitcher (3) and lowest fielding percentage at pitcher (.925)
- → 4th in highest strikeout/walk ratio (2.4)
- → 6th in strikeouts and lowest batting average allowed vs. right-handed batters (.232)
- → 7th in complete games (5)
- → 8th in innings pitched and most strikeouts per 9 innings (7.0)
- → Led the White Sox in ERA, wins, games started, complete games (5), shutouts (2), innings pitched, hits allowed, b (858), strikeouts, pitches thrown (3,305), and GDPs induced (16)

# Craig Grebeck

## 1995 Season

For six years, Craig Grebeck has been the White Sox' primary reserve infielder, one who can fill in or perform occasional platoon duty at short, third and second. Grebeck wound up starting 44 games in 1995, most of them at shortstop, and turned in numbers pretty much in line with the rest of his career.

## Hitting

Grebeck is considered one of the best fastball hitters on the White Sox team, and though the little man won't homer very often, he can reach the gaps often enough to keep the defenses honest. Usually, though, he'll hit the ball on the ground, using the whole field and trying to drive it through the infield. He has a good batting eye and handles the bat very well, so he's useful on the hit-and-run. He's also a fine bunter. .

## Baserunning & Defense

Grebeck has only average speed at best, and he's no threat at all to steal a base, with only two steals (in 10 attempts) in his six-year career. While not spectacular, he's a competent glove man, particularly at short, displaying both decent range and a strong arm for an infielder. He's a little less skilled at second and third, but he does a fine job at both positions.

## 1996 Outlook

Grebeck was a free agent when the 1995 season ended, and he might be tempted to shop his skills in hopes of finally landing a regular position. There are worse shortstops around, but since he's 31 and has never been more than a utility player, he's more likely to continue as a part-time player. It's a role he handles extremely well, and if his salary demands are reasonable, the White Sox would love to have him back.

**Position:** SS/3B
**Bats:** R  **Throws:** R
**Ht:** 5' 7"  **Wt:** 148

**Opening Day Age:** 31
**Born:** 12/29/64 in Johnstown, PA
**ML Seasons:** 6
**Pronunciation:** GRAY-beck

### Overall Statistics

|  | G | AB | R | H | D | T | HR | RBI | SB | BB | SO | Avg | OBP | Slg |
|---|---|---|---|---|---|---|---|---|---|---|---|---|---|---|
| 1995 | 53 | 154 | 19 | 40 | 12 | 0 | 1 | 18 | 0 | 21 | 23 | .260 | .360 | .357 |
| Career | 414 | 1071 | 129 | 273 | 62 | 6 | 12 | 110 | 2 | 135 | 152 | .255 | .342 | .358 |

### Where He Hits the Ball

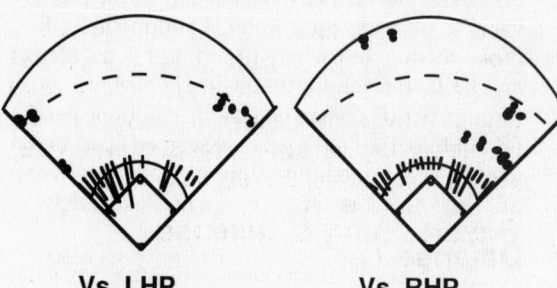

**Vs. LHP**          **Vs. RHP**

### 1995 Situational Stats

|  | AB | H | HR | RBI | Avg |  | AB | H | HR | RBI | Avg |
|---|---|---|---|---|---|---|---|---|---|---|---|
| Home | 73 | 25 | 0 | 7 | .342 | LHP | 87 | 21 | 1 | 4 | .241 |
| Road | 81 | 15 | 1 | 11 | .185 | RHP | 67 | 19 | 0 | 14 | .284 |
| First Half | 81 | 24 | 1 | 10 | .296 | Sc Pos | 39 | 11 | 0 | 17 | .282 |
| Scnd Half | 73 | 16 | 0 | 8 | .219 | Clutch | 21 | 4 | 0 | 2 | .190 |

### 1995 Rankings (American League)

➡ 1st in lowest batting average on a 3-1 count (.000)

# Ozzie Guillen

## 1995 Season

For the first three months of the 1995 season, Ozzie Guillen threatened to become the first White Sox shortstop to hit .300 in many years. But then Guillen went into a deep slump. He barely hit .200 after the All-Star break and wound up hitting just .248, the lowest full-season average of his career. He continued to play his usual steady defense, however.

## Hitting

Guillen is the quintessential slap hitter. He sprays the ball around the diamond with his thick-handled bat, going to the opposite field frequently. He has very little power and almost no discipline, consistently drawing fewer than 20 walks a year. He likes the fastball upstairs and will jump on it as soon as he sees it. He remains one of the better clutch hitters on the White Sox, and he's a fine bunter. Lefthanders bothered him a lot in 1995, and he wound up being platooned with Craig Grebeck for much of the second half.

## Baserunning & Defense

A one-time Gold Glove winner, Guillen continues to be one of the most dependable shortstops in the game. Though his range isn't as good as it was before he tore ligaments in his right knee in 1992, it's still above average, and he knows how to play the hitters. He gets rid of the ball quickly and is excellent on the double play. The knee injury robbed him of a lot of his speed, and he's no longer the baserunning threat he once was.

## 1996 Outlook

Guillen turned off a lot of the club's brass last year with his lackluster play in the second half. He figures to remain the club's primary shortstop. . . especially since he's signed through 1997. But if he wants to avoid a platoon role, he'll have to prove that last year's second-half slump was only temporary.

**Position:** SS
**Bats:** L **Throws:** R
**Ht:** 5'11" **Wt:** 164

**Opening Day Age:** 32
**Born:** 1/20/64 in Ocumare del Tuy, VZ
**ML Seasons:** 11
**Pronunciation:** GEY-un

### Overall Statistics

|  | G | AB | R | H | D | T | HR | RBI | SB | BB | SO | Avg | OBP | Slg |
|---|---|---|---|---|---|---|---|---|---|---|---|---|---|---|
| 1995 | 122 | 415 | 50 | 103 | 20 | 3 | 1 | 41 | 6 | 13 | 25 | .248 | .270 | .318 |
| Career | 1451 | 5078 | 572 | 1357 | 195 | 54 | 16 | 468 | 152 | 161 | 409 | .267 | .298 | .336 |

### Where He Hits the Ball

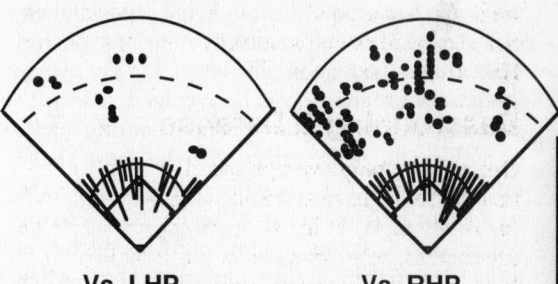

**Vs. LHP**          **Vs. RHP**

### 1995 Situational Stats

|  | AB | H | HR | RBI | Avg |  | AB | H | HR | RBI | Avg |
|---|---|---|---|---|---|---|---|---|---|---|---|
| Home | 216 | 62 | 1 | 27 | .287 | LHP | 101 | 20 | 0 | 8 | .198 |
| Road | 199 | 41 | 0 | 14 | .206 | RHP | 314 | 83 | 1 | 33 | .264 |
| First Half | 186 | 53 | 0 | 24 | .285 | Sc Pos | 111 | 29 | 0 | 37 | .261 |
| Scnd Half | 229 | 50 | 1 | 17 | .218 | Clutch | 84 | 15 | 0 | 6 | .179 |

### 1995 Rankings (American League)

- ➡ 6th in fielding percentage at shortstop (.976)
- ➡ 9th in lowest batting average in the clutch (.179)
- ➡ Led the White Sox in caught stealing (7) and batting average with the bases loaded (.444)

# Roberto Hernandez

## 1995 Season

Roberto Hernandez has done a lot of excellent pitching in his three seasons as the White Sox closer, but at the same time he's failed to show the consistency expected of a top relief ace. His 1995 season was typical: Hernandez ranked among the American League leaders with 32 saves, but he also blew 10 opportunities, the top total in the majors. While he finished the season strongly, he did nothing to indicate that he can give a team a full season of top relief work.

## Pitcher

The classic power reliever, Hernandez can blow away hitters with his 90-plus fastball. His split-fingered fastball is another excellent pitch, and he throws an occasional slider to help keep the hitters off balance. The combination of three good pitches makes him all but unhittable when he's got everything working, and in 1995 he averaged close to 13 strikeouts per nine innings pitched. Unfortunately, he has way too many games when he *doesn't* have everything working. Lack of control continues to be a major problem for him—either he's walking hitters, or he's taking too much off his pitches in order to keep them in the strike zone. That's when he gets hurt, especially by the gopher ball.

## Defense

Though he's a huge man, Hernandez has quick reflexes and surprising agility, and he helps himself with his defense. A high leg-kicker, he's not very good at holding runners but he does well enough to get by.

## 1996 Outlook

Hernandez hasn't been in the major leagues all that long, but he's no kid—he'll be 31 when the 1996 season starts. So it's unrealistic to expect him to develop much more at this point in his professional career. He has a great arm, and if he continues to close you can expect a good number of saves. . . but also a good number of *blown* saves.

**Position:** RP
**Bats:** R  **Throws:** R
**Ht:** 6' 4"  **Wt:** 235

**Opening Day Age:** 31
**Born:** 11/11/64 in Santurce, PR
**ML Seasons:** 5

### Overall Statistics

|  | W | L | Pct. | ERA | G | GS | Sv | IP | H | BB | SO | HR | BR/IP |
|---|---|---|---|---|---|---|---|---|---|---|---|---|---|
| 1995 | 3 | 7 | .300 | 3.92 | 60 | 0 | 32 | 59.2 | 63 | 28 | 84 | 9 | 1.53 |
| Career | 18 | 18 | .500 | 3.24 | 227 | 3 | 96 | 272.0 | 236 | 94 | 279 | 25 | 1.21 |

### How Often He Throws Strikes

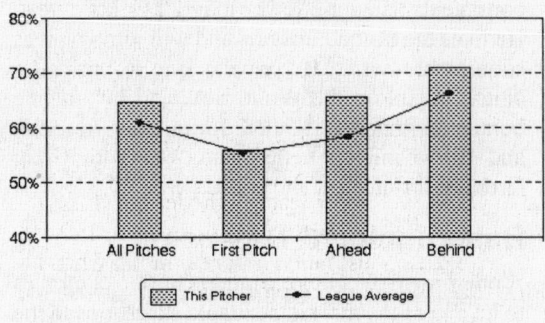

### 1995 Situational Stats

|  | W | L | ERA | Sv | IP |  | AB | H | HR | RBI | Avg |
|---|---|---|---|---|---|---|---|---|---|---|---|
| Home | 2 | 1 | 2.90 | 21 | 31.0 | LHB | 127 | 34 | 5 | 19 | .268 |
| Road | 1 | 6 | 5.02 | 11 | 28.2 | RHB | 110 | 29 | 4 | 21 | .264 |
| First Half | 2 | 3 | 4.23 | 12 | 27.2 | Sc Pos | 80 | 18 | 4 | 32 | .225 |
| Scnd Half | 1 | 4 | 3.66 | 20 | 32.0 | Clutch | 183 | 51 | 7 | 31 | .279 |

### 1995 Rankings (American League)

→ 1st in games finished (57) , blown saves (10), relief losses (7) and most strikeouts per 9 innings in relief (12.7)
→ 2nd in save opportunities (42)
→ 3rd in saves (32) and lowest save percentage (76.2%)
→ 4th in highest percentage of inherited runners scored (48.5%)
→ Led the White Sox in games pitched (60), saves (32), games finished (57), save opportunities (42), save percentage (76.2%), blown saves (10), relief ERA (3.92), relief losses (7) and most strikeouts per 9 innings in relief (12.7)

# Lance Johnson

**Position:** CF
**Bats:** L  **Throws:** L
**Ht:** 5'11"  **Wt:** 160

**Opening Day Age:** 32
**Born:** 7/6/63 in Cincinnati, OH
**ML Seasons:** 9
**Nickname:** One Dog

## 1995 Season

A consistent .280-to-.310 hitter throughout his White Sox career, Lance Johnson got off to a slow start in 1995. At the end of June, he was hitting only .250. But Johnson hit well over .300 the rest of the way and wound up becoming the first White Sox player in 35 years to lead the league in hits. The biggest shock was his unexpected home run power. After entering 1995 with a career total of seven homers in eight years, Johnson belted 10 out of the park last year—all of them in the last three months.

## Hitting

Johnson's sudden power surge coincided with his switch to a heavier bat; he was able to get better wood on the ball without suffering any noticeable loss in bat speed. He also hit better after being moved to the leadoff spot in the batting order, though his lack of discipline makes him less than ideal in that role. He loves high pitches, especially fastballs, and his great speed enables him to leg out a lot of triples. After leading the league in three-baggers a record four straight times from 1991 to 1994, Johnson just failed to repeat in '95 when he lost out to Kenny Lofton on the last day of the season.

## Baserunning & Defense

Speed and defense are Johnson's strengths. Though his throwing arm is weak, he covers as much ground as any center fielder around. He plays relatively shallow, but is able to race to the wall to track down long drives. He's also an outstanding baserunner and a consistent high-percentage basestealer.

## 1996 Outlook

The Sox did not pick up Johnson's option for 1996, but they still hope to re-sign him if the price is reasonable. A dependable hitter, a great baserunner, and one of the top defensive outfielders in the game, Johnson ranks among the best center fielders in White Sox history.

### Overall Statistics

|  | G | AB | R | H | D | T | HR | RBI | SB | BB | SO | Avg | OBP | Slg |
|---|---|---|---|---|---|---|---|---|---|---|---|---|---|---|
| 1995 | 142 | 607 | 98 | 186 | 18 | 12 | 10 | 57 | 40 | 32 | 31 | .306 | .341 | .425 |
| Career | 979 | 3618 | 487 | 1031 | 108 | 78 | 17 | 334 | 232 | 214 | 264 | .285 | .324 | .372 |

### Where He Hits the Ball

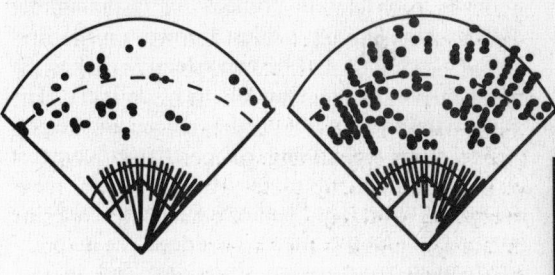

**Vs. LHP**          **Vs. RHP**

### 1995 Situational Stats

|  | AB | H | HR | RBI | Avg |  | AB | H | HR | RBI | Avg |
|---|---|---|---|---|---|---|---|---|---|---|---|
| Home | 311 | 90 | 2 | 28 | .289 | LHP | 171 | 49 | 1 | 13 | .287 |
| Road | 296 | 96 | 8 | 29 | .324 | RHP | 436 | 137 | 9 | 44 | .314 |
| First Half | 264 | 70 | 1 | 17 | .265 | Sc Pos | 128 | 41 | 2 | 45 | .320 |
| Scnd Half | 343 | 116 | 9 | 40 | .338 | Clutch | 90 | 26 | 1 | 10 | .289 |

### 1995 Rankings (American League)

→ 1st in at-bats, hits, least pitches seen per plate appearance (2.92), highest percentage of swings put into play (61.5%), and lowest batting average with the bases loaded (.000)

→ 2nd in singles (146) and triples

→ 4th in stolen base percentage (87.0%), fielding percentage in center field (.991), lowest percentage of swings that missed (8.1%) and highest percentage of swings on the first pitch (41.1%)

→ Led the White Sox in at-bats, hits, singles (146), triples, stolen bases, highest ground-ball/flyball ratio (1.9), and stolen base percentage (87.0%)

# Matt Karchner

**Position:** RP
**Bats:** R  **Throws:** R
**Ht:** 6' 4"  **Wt:** 210

**Opening Day Age:** 28
**Born:** 6/28/67 in Berwick, PA
**ML Seasons:** 1

## 1995 Season

The White Sox have had a number of top pitching prospects in their farm system over the last several years, so it's easy to see how righthander Matt Karchner got neglected. A former Royals prospect who'd been held back by arm problems, Karchner didn't make his major league debut until last July, several weeks after his 28th birthday. He made an immediate positive impression, working 11 scoreless outings before giving up his first run. By season's end he was the club's most reliable set-up man and a big part of the club's plans for 1996.

## Pitching

An imposing figure on the mound at 6-4 and 210 pounds, Karchner is primarily a fastball/slider pitcher. He's not the hardest thrower on the fireballing Sox staff, but he consistently reaches the high 80s with his smooth, easy delivery. His pitches have a nice sinking movement, and he gets a good number of ground balls. Karchner's biggest asset, however, might be his aggressive, take-charge attitude. The White Sox love the way he goes right after the hitters. He doesn't seem bothered much by pressure situations, and in fact pitched much better with runners on base than with the bases empty last year.

## Defense

Karchner helps himself with his defense. He moves quickly off the mound, reacts well on balls hit up the middle and isn't afraid to go after the lead runner when he thinks he can get him. He also does a fairly good job of holding baserunners.

## 1996 Outlook

Arm problems have slowed Karchner's development, but whenever he's been healthy and working out of the bullpen, he's turned in excellent numbers. It's a stretch to suggest he'll keep *that* up, but he figures to get a lot of work out of the Sox pen this year, and judging by past performance, he's likely to perform very well.

### Overall Statistics

|  | W | L | Pct. | ERA | G | GS | Sv | IP | H | BB | SO | HR | BR/IP |
|---|---|---|---|---|---|---|---|---|---|---|---|---|---|
| 1995 | 4 | 2 | .667 | 1.69 | 31 | 0 | 0 | 32.0 | 33 | 12 | 24 | 2 | 1.41 |
| Career | 4 | 2 | .667 | 1.69 | 31 | 0 | 0 | 32.0 | 33 | 12 | 24 | 2 | 1.41 |

### How Often He Throws Strikes

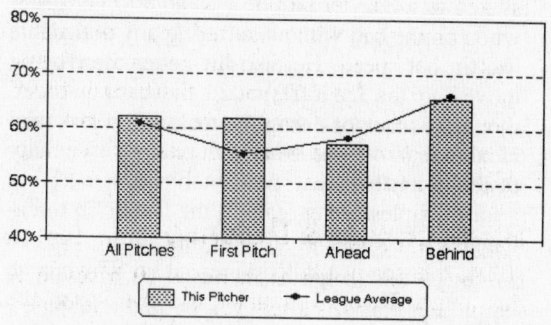

### 1995 Situational Stats

|  | W | L | ERA | Sv | IP |  | AB | H | HR | RBI | Avg |
|---|---|---|---|---|---|---|---|---|---|---|---|
| Home | 2 | 2 | 2.75 | 0 | 19.2 | LHB | 54 | 16 | 0 | 4 | .296 |
| Road | 2 | 0 | 0.00 | 0 | 12.1 | RHB | 66 | 17 | 2 | 12 | .258 |
| First Half | 0 | 0 | - | 0 | 0.0 | Sc Pos | 39 | 10 | 0 | 14 | .256 |
| Scnd Half | 4 | 2 | 1.69 | 0 | 32.0 | Clutch | 77 | 22 | 2 | 11 | .286 |

### 1995 Rankings (American League)

➡ 7th in holds (13)
➡ Led the White Sox in holds (13) and lowest batting average allowed in relief with runners on base (.197)

# Ron Karkovice

## 1995 Season

Since he succeeded Carlton Fisk as the regular White Sox catcher a few years ago, Ron Karkovice has been valued primarily for his excellent defense behind the plate. At bat, Karkovice has always been a low-average hitter, but one who's provided some home-run power. His defensive work remained very good in 1995, and Karkovice continued to show the patience at the plate that has helped increase his offensive value.

## Hitting

Karkovice is no finesse hitter. He swings hard and uses an uppercut stroke to try to hit the ball a long way. He'll never hit for much of an average, he's always going to strike out a lot, and when he's hitting pop-ups instead of homers he's not going to contribute much. But with his new-found ability to draw some walks, Karkovice has turned himself into a better-than-average offensive performer compared with most other catchers. He can also lay down a bunt.

## Baserunning & Defense

Karkovice has stolen as many as 10 bases in a season, but that was a few years—and one major knee injury—ago. He still moves those stiff legs of his as fast as they can go; they just don't go very fast. Karkovice's defensive stats weren't exceptional last year, particularly in throwing out opposing runners, but the wild throwers who make up the Sox staff are the biggest reason for that. He remains one of the top defensive catchers in the game.

## 1996 Outlook

Karkovice spent a long time backing up Fisk before getting his chance as a regular, and it's a little shocking to realize he'll turn 33 before the '96 season is over. The Sox can't count on him for more than about 120 games, but he figures to provide his usual combination of some home runs, some walks, and a lot of great defense.

**Position:** C
**Bats:** R  **Throws:** R
**Ht:** 6' 1"  **Wt:** 219

**Opening Day Age:** 32
**Born:** 8/8/63 in Union, NJ
**ML Seasons:** 10

### Overall Statistics

|  | G | AB | R | H | D | T | HR | RBI | SB | BB | SO | Avg | OBP | Slg |
|---|---|---|---|---|---|---|---|---|---|---|---|---|---|---|
| 1995 | 113 | 323 | 44 | 70 | 14 | 1 | 13 | 51 | 2 | 39 | 84 | .217 | .306 | .387 |
| Career | 777 | 2104 | 282 | 471 | 95 | 6 | 80 | 279 | 24 | 198 | 624 | .224 | .295 | .389 |

### Where He Hits the Ball

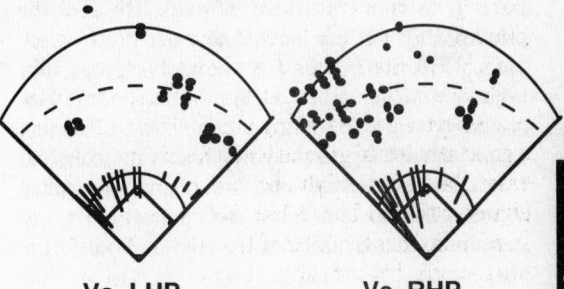

**Vs. LHP**          **Vs. RHP**

### 1995 Situational Stats

|  | AB | H | HR | RBI | Avg |  | AB | H | HR | RBI | Avg |
|---|---|---|---|---|---|---|---|---|---|---|---|
| Home | 150 | 31 | 5 | 26 | .207 | LHP | 104 | 24 | 2 | 14 | .231 |
| Road | 173 | 39 | 8 | 25 | .225 | RHP | 219 | 46 | 11 | 37 | .210 |
| First Half | 155 | 32 | 7 | 24 | .206 | Sc Pos | 99 | 23 | 5 | 42 | .232 |
| Scnd Half | 168 | 38 | 6 | 27 | .226 | Clutch | 48 | 11 | 4 | 10 | .229 |

### 1995 Rankings (American League)

- 4th in highest percentage of runners caught stealing as a catcher (30.9%)
- 6th in errors at catcher (6) and lowest percentage of swings put into play (36.5%)
- 7th in lowest batting average with two strikes (.131)
- 9th in sacrifice bunts (9)
- Led the White Sox in sacrifice bunts (9)

# Dave Martinez

## 1995 Season

When the White Sox signed journeyman outfielder Dave Martinez prior to the start of the 1995 season, expectations were modest. Martinez figured to spell Mike Devereaux in right field, pinch hit, and fill in here and there while spending most of his time on the bench. Your typical Dave Martinez season, in other words. But after a slow start, Martinez got hot in July and never cooled off. He was a terror over the second half, saw considerable playing time and wound up hitting over .300 for the first time in his 10-year career.

## Hitting

Martinez is a line-drive and groundball-type of hitter who won't hit many homers. He uses the whole field and can handle the bat pretty well. He's also a fine bunter. He's never hit lefties very well, and he remained a platoon player in 1995. Working with Sox hitting coach Walt Hriniak helped make Martinez' bat noticeably quicker, and it was easier for him to turn on a fastball. Martinez is primarily a lowball hitter and pitchers will try to get him to chase offerings upstairs and out of the strike zone.

## Baserunning & Defense

Martinez has always had good speed, and though he didn't run very often last year, he was an effective basestealer. He's always been a fine defensive player, and that remained one of his strengths last year. He started games at all three outfield positions, displaying fine range and a decent arm, and he was exceptionally good when filling in for Frank Thomas at first base late in the year.

## 1996 Outlook

Martinez was a free agent when the 1995 season ended, and his excellent performance greatly increased his market value. It would be surprising if he kept hitting like he did late last year, but he figures to remain a useful and versatile player for several more years.

**Position:** 1B/LF/RF
**Bats:** L  **Throws:** L
**Ht:** 5'10"  **Wt:** 175

**Opening Day Age:** 31
**Born:** 9/26/64 in Brooklyn, NY
**ML Seasons:** 10

### Overall Statistics

|  | G | AB | R | H | D | T | HR | RBI | SB | BB | SO | Avg | OBP | Slg |
|---|---|---|---|---|---|---|---|---|---|---|---|---|---|---|
| 1995 | 118 | 303 | 49 | 93 | 16 | 4 | 5 | 37 | 8 | 32 | 41 | .307 | .371 | .436 |
| Career | 1142 | 3334 | 429 | 897 | 136 | 45 | 53 | 319 | 124 | 294 | 527 | .269 | .329 | .385 |

### Where He Hits the Ball

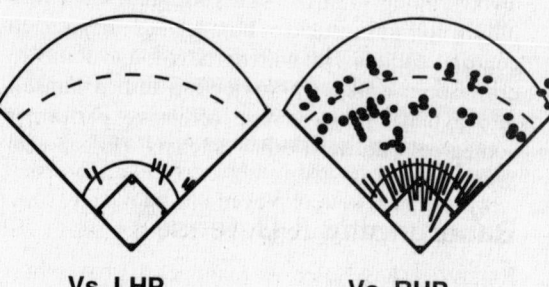

**Vs. LHP**          **Vs. RHP**

### 1995 Situational Stats

|  | AB | H | HR | RBI | Avg |  | AB | H | HR | RBI | Avg |
|---|---|---|---|---|---|---|---|---|---|---|---|
| Home | 136 | 38 | 2 | 18 | .279 | LHP | 33 | 7 | 0 | 1 | .212 |
| Road | 167 | 55 | 3 | 19 | .329 | RHP | 270 | 86 | 5 | 36 | .319 |
| First Half | 95 | 23 | 3 | 10 | .242 | Sc Pos | 71 | 24 | 2 | 30 | .338 |
| Scnd Half | 208 | 70 | 2 | 27 | .337 | Clutch | 44 | 14 | 1 | 7 | .318 |

### 1995 Rankings (American League)

→ 4th in batting average on a 3-1 count (.636)
→ 9th in sacrifice bunts (9)
→ Led the White Sox in sacrifice bunts (9), batting average with runners in scoring position (.338) and batting average on a 3-1 count (.636)

# Lyle Mouton

## 1995 Season

Lyle Mouton is a big, strong outfielder who spent most of his minor league career in the Yankee system. Mouton came to the White Sox last year as the player to be named later in the Jack McDowell trade, and his performance indicated that the Sox got some value back in the deal. Mouton hit his way into the lineup after the All-Star break and played so solidly that he'll go into spring training with a regular outfield spot pretty much wrapped up.

## Hitting

Mouton looks a little like Frank Thomas or maybe Bobby Bonilla, and at 240 pounds, he can give the ball a ride. Thus far in his career he's looked more like a 15-to-20 home-run man than a big-time slugger, but his power to the gaps is impressive. Mouton came up with a reputation as a bit of a wild swinger, and he'll probably strike out 125 times or more if he's in the lineup on a regular basis. But he also draws a reasonable number of walks, and he's not the kind of kind of player who panics and starts chasing everything once he gets behind in the count.

## Baserunning & Defense

Mouton has surprising speed for a big guy, and though he stole only one base with the White Sox, he's capable of stealing in double figures. He played both right and left field after joining the club, and handled both positions more than adequately. His arm is good but not great, and he'll probably wind up spending most of his time in left.

## 1996 Outlook

Mouton made such a strong impression last year that the Sox dealt away their regular right fielder, Mike Devereaux, with a month left in the season. He could be in right again this year—or left, if the club moves Tim Raines. One thing's pretty certain: he'll play somewhere.

**Position:** RF/LF
**Bats:** R **Throws:** R
**Ht:** 6' 4"  **Wt:** 240

**Opening Day Age:** 26
**Born:** 5/13/69 in Lafayette, LA
**ML Seasons:** 1
**Pronunciation:** moo-TAHN

### Overall Statistics

|  | G | AB | R | H | D | T | HR | RBI | SB | BB | SO | Avg | OBP | Slg |
|---|---|---|---|---|---|---|---|---|---|---|---|---|---|---|
| 1995 | 58 | 179 | 23 | 54 | 16 | 0 | 5 | 27 | 1 | 19 | 46 | .302 | .373 | .475 |
| Career | 58 | 179 | 23 | 54 | 16 | 0 | 5 | 27 | 1 | 19 | 46 | .302 | .373 | .475 |

### Where He Hits the Ball

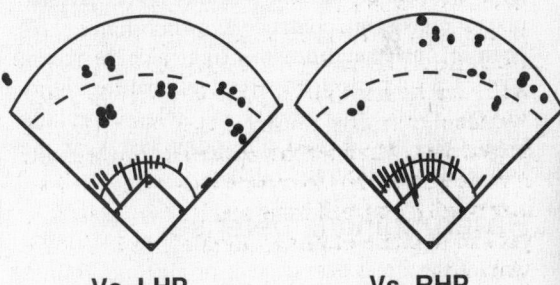

**Vs. LHP**　　　　**Vs. RHP**

### 1995 Situational Stats

|  | AB | H | HR | RBI | Avg |  | AB | H | HR | RBI | Avg |
|---|---|---|---|---|---|---|---|---|---|---|---|
| Home | 82 | 29 | 4 | 12 | .354 | LHP | 78 | 23 | 2 | 10 | .295 |
| Road | 97 | 25 | 1 | 15 | .258 | RHP | 101 | 31 | 3 | 17 | .307 |
| First Half | 16 | 3 | 1 | 2 | .188 | Sc Pos | 50 | 14 | 1 | 22 | .280 |
| Scnd Half | 163 | 51 | 4 | 25 | .313 | Clutch | 22 | 8 | 2 | 5 | .364 |

### 1995 Rankings (American League)

- ➡ 3rd in batting average on a 3-2 count (.444)
- ➡ 6th in batting average with two strikes (.263)
- ➡ Led the White Sox in batting average on a 3-2 count (.444) and batting average with two strikes (.263)

# Tim Raines

## 1995 Season

At 36, Tim Raines continues to be an excellent offensive performer. Raines contributed speed and power to the White Sox attack in 1995 and had one of the highest RBI totals of his career. But Raines also had season-long problems on defense, and his future as an everyday player—at least with the White Sox—is uncertain.

## Hitting

For many years Raines was one of the best leadoff men in baseball, but he's a little slower and heavier than he once was, and the White Sox used him mostly as their number-two hitter last year. It's a good spot for him, since he has both on-base ability and the power to drive a runner home. He also makes consistent contact. A switch-hitter, he's been inconsistent from the right side in recent years, but he performed effectively batting righty in 1995. He has fine power to all fields, especially from the left side. At one point last year, he homered in three straight games.

## Baserunning & Defense

One of the great basestealers of all time, Raines continues to be a high-percentage base thief. However, he picks his spots very carefully these days. He set an American League record by stealing 40 straight bases before getting caught last September. . . but those 40 steals were spread over three seasons. Defensively, Raines was a disaster in 1995, misplaying numerous fly balls and displaying his usual shaky arm. His speed is no longer quite good enough for him to outrun his mistakes the way he once could.

## 1996 Outlook

Raines has a year left on his contract, and his offensive contributions notwithstanding, the Sox would love for someone to take him off their hands. His best hope of remaining a regular would be to find a club that needs a DH and part-time outfielder.

**Position:** LF/DH
**Bats:** B  **Throws:** R
**Ht:** 5' 8"  **Wt:** 186

**Opening Day Age:** 36
**Born:** 9/16/59 in Sanford, FL
**ML Seasons:** 17
**Nickname:** Rock

### Overall Statistics

| | G | AB | R | H | D | T | HR | RBI | SB | BB | SO | Avg | OBP | Slg |
|---|---|---|---|---|---|---|---|---|---|---|---|---|---|---|
| 1995 | 133 | 502 | 81 | 143 | 25 | 4 | 12 | 67 | 13 | 70 | 52 | .285 | .374 | .422 |
| Career | 2053 | 7766 | 1374 | 2295 | 371 | 109 | 146 | 829 | 777 | 1134 | 809 | .296 | .385 | .428 |

### Where He Hits the Ball

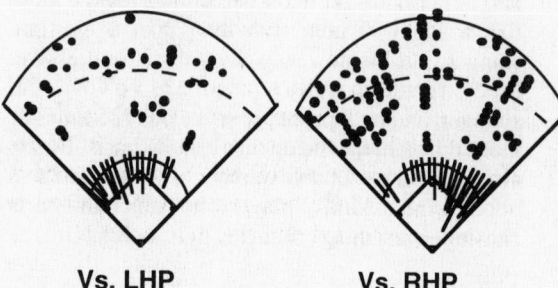

**Vs. LHP**            **Vs. RHP**

### 1995 Situational Stats

| | AB | H | HR | RBI | Avg | | AB | H | HR | RBI | Avg |
|---|---|---|---|---|---|---|---|---|---|---|---|
| Home | 239 | 71 | 6 | 31 | .297 | LHP | 140 | 39 | 3 | 16 | .279 |
| Road | 263 | 72 | 6 | 36 | .274 | RHP | 362 | 104 | 9 | 51 | .287 |
| First Half | 247 | 74 | 8 | 32 | .300 | Sc Pos | 128 | 37 | 1 | 52 | .289 |
| Scnd Half | 255 | 69 | 4 | 35 | .271 | Clutch | 89 | 19 | 3 | 12 | .213 |

### 1995 Rankings (American League)

➡ 4th in lowest fielding percentage in left field (.980)
➡ 5th in errors in left field (4)
➡ Led the White Sox in batting average at home (.297)

# Jeff Shaw

**Position:** RP
**Bats:** R  **Throws:** R
**Ht:** 6' 2"  **Wt:** 200

**Opening Day Age:** 29
**Born:** 7/7/66 in
Washington
Courthouse, OH
**ML Seasons:** 6

## 1995 Season

Righty reliever Jeff Shaw came to the White Sox from Montreal last August in a straight-up deal for another middle man, Jose DeLeon. Shaw had a couple of decent years with the Expos, but he wasn't pitching all that well at the time of the trade and he didn't turn a lot of heads with the White Sox, either. While he pitched better than his ERA would indicate, he did little to clinch a 1996 job.

## Pitching

Shaw has a decent fastball, along with a slider and a split-fingered fastball. His repertoire isn't the type that can blow hitters away, so he needs pin-point control in order to succeed. In 1995 Shaw's location wasn't as good as in the past, and he began easing up on his delivery in order to get ahead in the count. The hitters noticed and started whaling away at his first offering, with disastrous results for Shaw. Despite his difficulties, Shaw maintained his effectiveness in pressure situations. He pitched exceptionally well with men on base, and was one of the best relievers in baseball at preventing inherited runners from scoring.

## Defense

Shaw has had some problems with opposing runners in the past, but he's worked on his move and basestealers didn't bother him much in 1995. He's always been a good fielder.

## 1996 Outlook

If his contract demands are reasonable, it's not out of the realm for Shaw to return to the White Sox. The club wouldn't mind having another veteran in the bullpen, especially one who can handle pressure. In the minors Shaw maintained his poise during a streak in which he lost 17 straight decisions, and that kind of toughness is always in demand. His arm appears healthy, and he figures to be somewhere in the majors this year.

### Overall Statistics

|  | W | L | Pct. | ERA | G | GS | Sv | IP | H | BB | SO | HR | BR/IP |
|---|---|---|---|---|---|---|---|---|---|---|---|---|---|
| 1995 | 1 | 6 | .143 | 4.88 | 59 | 0 | 3 | 72.0 | 70 | 27 | 51 | 6 | 1.35 |
| Career | 11 | 25 | .306 | 4.50 | 203 | 19 | 5 | 363.2 | 380 | 125 | 207 | 45 | 1.39 |

### How Often He Throws Strikes

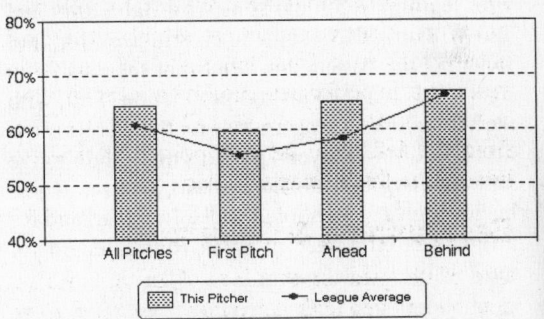

### 1995 Situational Stats

|  | W | L | ERA | Sv | IP |  | AB | H | HR | RBI | Avg |
|---|---|---|---|---|---|---|---|---|---|---|---|
| Home | 1 | 4 | 5.66 | 2 | 35.0 | LHB | 122 | 36 | 2 | 14 | .295 |
| Road | 0 | 2 | 4.14 | 1 | 37.0 | RHB | 148 | 34 | 4 | 12 | .230 |
| First Half | 1 | 4 | 4.89 | 2 | 42.1 | Sc Pos | 78 | 14 | 0 | 17 | .179 |
| Scnd Half | 0 | 2 | 4.85 | 1 | 29.2 | Clutch | 58 | 15 | 0 | 8 | .259 |

### 1995 Rankings (American League)

➡ Did not rank near the top or bottom in any category

# Frank Thomas

## 1995 Season

Although he didn't win the MVP award for the first time in three years, Frank Thomas had another outstanding season in 1995. Despite being hampered by a shoulder injury that prevented him from playing in the field for much of the second half, Thomas reached the 40-home-run level for the second time in his career. He also became the first player in major league history to bat .300, hit 20 or more homers, and log 100 runs, RBI and walks for five straight seasons.

## Hitting

The most disciplined slugger in the game, Thomas combines power and patience on a level that invites legitimate comparisons with Babe Ruth and Ted Williams. He's sometimes criticized for "not swinging the bat enough," but that seems silly in light of his tremendous run production. Still, with the White Sox lacking a consistent power threat to hit behind him last year, pitchers often didn't give him *anything* to hit. Thomas was given a major-league high 29 intentional walks last year, and for a time was on a pace to break Ruth's record for most walks in a season.

## Baserunning & Defense

Thomas is one of the biggest players in the game, and though he runs the bases intelligently, he doesn't run them very quickly. His defense, a career-long problem, was probably worse than ever in 1995. His shoulder injury forced him into a DH role, and though he strongly prefers to play in the field, he might become a full-time designated hitter before long.

## 1996 Outlook

By Frank Thomas standards, 1995 wasn't a great year. He hit a career-low .308 and his slugging average dropped by more than 100 points from 1994. But then, Thomas has the standards of a true baseball immortal. If he's fully healthy in 1996, another MVP award is a real possibility.

**Position:** 1B/DH
**Bats:** R  **Throws:** R
**Ht:** 6' 5"  **Wt:** 257

**Opening Day Age:** 27
**Born:** 5/27/68 in Columbus, GA
**ML Seasons:** 6
**Nickname:** Big Hurt

### Overall Statistics

|  | G | AB | R | H | D | T | HR | RBI | SB | BB | SO | Avg | OBP | Slg |
|---|---|---|---|---|---|---|---|---|---|---|---|---|---|---|
| 1995 | 145 | 493 | 102 | 152 | 27 | 0 | 40 | 111 | 3 | 136 | 74 | .308 | .454 | .606 |
| Career | 789 | 2764 | 565 | 893 | 185 | 8 | 182 | 595 | 16 | 661 | 443 | .323 | .450 | .593 |

### Where He Hits the Ball

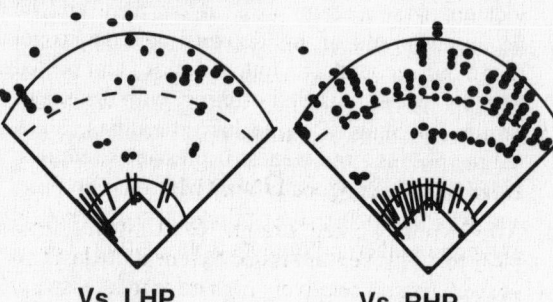

**Vs. LHP**          **Vs. RHP**

### 1995 Situational Stats

|  | AB | H | HR | RBI | Avg |  |  | AB | H | HR | RBI | Avg |
|---|---|---|---|---|---|---|---|---|---|---|---|---|
| Home | 247 | 73 | 15 | 49 | .296 |  | LHP | 126 | 49 | 16 | 35 | .389 |
| Road | 246 | 79 | 25 | 62 | .321 |  | RHP | 367 | 103 | 24 | 76 | .281 |
| First Half | 228 | 74 | 21 | 53 | .325 |  | Sc Pos | 126 | 42 | 4 | 61 | .333 |
| Scnd Half | 265 | 78 | 19 | 58 | .294 |  | Clutch | 74 | 19 | 7 | 11 | .257 |

### 1995 Rankings (American League)

→ 1st in sacrifice flies (12), walks, intentional walks (29), games played, slugging percentage vs. left-handed pitchers (.849) and lowest percentage of extra bases taken as a runner (28.3%)

→ 2nd in home runs, times on base (294), on-base percentage, on-base percentage vs. left-handed pitchers (.524) and lowest fielding percentage at first base (.991)

→ 3rd in slugging percentage, HR frequency (12.3 ABs per HR) and batting average vs. left-handed pitchers (.389)

→ Led the White Sox in batting average, home runs, runs scored, and doubles

# Robin Ventura

## 1995 Season

Though he was the subject of constant trade rumors, Robin Ventura had one of the best seasons of his career in 1995. Ventura hit a career-high 26 home runs and tied a major league record with two grand slams in one game. And though he committed a few too many careless errors, the three-time Gold Glove winner continued to show great range and instincts at third base.

## Hitting

Ventura has a long, smooth batting stroke, finishing with his hands high and his top hand slipping off the bat. He has consistent line-drive power to all fields, and can be counted for 20-plus homers and 90 or more RBI every year. He has good discipline at the plate and handles lefthanders very well, though he has much more power against righties. Pitchers tend to work him away in an effort to get him to go to the opposite field.

## Baserunning & Defense

After winning three straight Gold Gloves from 1991 to 1993, Ventura failed to repeat the last two years due to his relatively high error total. Usually the errors come when he tries to force a throw after making a good play; the problems are compounded by having an immobile first baseman in Frank Thomas. If he can cut down on the errors, there will be more Gold Gloves in his future, as he can make all the plays. Ventura is below average in speed and no threat to steal.

## 1996 Outlook

A hot rumor late last year had Ventura going to the Dodgers for the stretch run. It didn't happen, but the Sox have a promising young infielder in Chris Snopek, and it's possible Ventura will be dealt over the winter. Wherever he plays, he figures to remain one of the best third basemen in the game.

**Position:** 3B/1B
**Bats:** L  **Throws:** R
**Ht:** 6' 1"  **Wt:** 198

**Opening Day Age:** 28
**Born:** 7/14/67 in Santa Maria, CA
**ML Seasons:** 7

*Overall Statistics*

|  | G | AB | R | H | D | T | HR | RBI | SB | BB | SO | Avg | OBP | Slg |
|---|---|---|---|---|---|---|---|---|---|---|---|---|---|---|
| 1995 | 135 | 492 | 79 | 145 | 22 | 0 | 26 | 93 | 4 | 75 | 98 | .295 | .384 | .498 |
| Career | 881 | 3183 | 451 | 873 | 147 | 5 | 110 | 519 | 13 | 477 | 446 | .274 | .367 | .427 |

*Where He Hits the Ball*

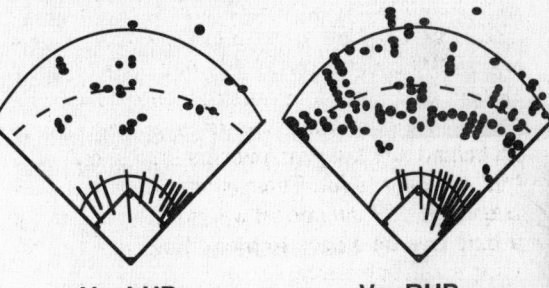

**Vs. LHP**          **Vs. RHP**

*1995 Situational Stats*

|  | AB | H | HR | RBI | Avg |  |  | AB | H | HR | RBI | Avg |
|---|---|---|---|---|---|---|---|---|---|---|---|---|
| Home | 222 | 63 | 8 | 36 | .284 | LHP | | 132 | 35 | 5 | 31 | .265 |
| Road | 270 | 82 | 18 | 57 | .304 | RHP | | 360 | 110 | 21 | 62 | .306 |
| First Half | 245 | 73 | 15 | 49 | .298 | Sc Pos | | 166 | 44 | 7 | 71 | .265 |
| Scnd Half | 247 | 72 | 11 | 44 | .291 | Clutch | | 82 | 28 | 2 | 15 | .341 |

*1995 Rankings (American League)*

- ➡ 2nd in errors at third base (17)
- ➡ 3rd in lowest cleanup slugging percentage (.423)
- ➡ 5th in lowest fielding percentage at third base (.948)
- ➡ 7th in least GDPs per GDP situation (4.8%)
- ➡ 8th in intentional walks (11)
- ➡ 10th in sacrifice flies (8)
- ➡ Led the White Sox in strikeouts, most pitches seen per plate appearance (4.00), least GDPs per GDP situation (4.8%), batting average in the clutch (.341) and slugging percentage vs. right-handed pitchers (.531)

Chicago White Sox

# Luis Andujar

**Position**: SP
**Bats**: R  **Throws**: R
**Ht**: 6' 2"  **Wt**: 175

**Opening Day Age**: 23
**Born**: 11/22/72 in Bani, DR
**ML Seasons**: 1

## Overall Statistics

|  | W | L | Pct. | ERA | G | GS | Sv | IP | H | BB | SO | HR | BR/IP |
|---|---|---|---|---|---|---|---|---|---|---|---|---|---|
| 1995 | 2 | 1 | .667 | 3.26 | 5 | 5 | 0 | 30.1 | 26 | 14 | 9 | 4 | 1.32 |
| Career | 2 | 1 | .667 | 3.26 | 5 | 5 | 0 | 30.1 | 26 | 14 | 9 | 4 | 1.32 |

## 1995 Season

Making a remarkable recovery from an ulnar nerve transplant that took place late in 1994, Puerto Rican righthander Luis Andujar reached the major leagues a year later. Andujar, who had gone 14-8 with a 2.85 ERA at Double-A Birmingham, pitched impressively in five September starts with the White Sox.

## Pitching & Defense

Only 23 years old, Andujar was moving rapidly up the White Sox system when his elbow began bothering him in 1994. He recovered quickly from the surgery, and his 88-91 MPH fastball had plenty of pop both at Birmingham—where he was voted the league's outstanding pitcher—and with the White Sox. Andujar also throws a slider and change, and while he was bothered by the home-run ball during his five White Sox starts, his stuff looked excellent. He's a decent fielder but had some problems holding runners.

## 1996 Outlook

Andujar hadn't pitched above the Double-A level prior to his September recall to the White Sox, so it's likely he'll be sent back to Triple-A to get some experience. But the Sox are very high on him, and there's a good chance he'll be a member of their rotation before the '96 season is over.

# Mike LaValliere

**Position**: C
**Bats**: L  **Throws**: R
**Ht**: 5' 9"  **Wt**: 205

**Opening Day Age**: 35
**Born**: 8/18/60 in Charlotte, NC
**ML Seasons**: 12
**Pronunciation**: luh-VAL-yur
**Nickname**: Spanky

## Overall Statistics

|  | G | AB | R | H | D | T | HR | RBI | SB | BB | SO | Avg | OBP | Slg |
|---|---|---|---|---|---|---|---|---|---|---|---|---|---|---|
| 1995 | 46 | 98 | 7 | 24 | 6 | 0 | 1 | 19 | 0 | 9 | 15 | .245 | .303 | .337 |
| Career | 879 | 2473 | 185 | 663 | 109 | 5 | 18 | 294 | 5 | 321 | 244 | .268 | .351 | .338 |

## 1995 Season

A long-time regular who's settled into a backup-catcher role the last few years, Mike LaValliere didn't have a very satisfying season in 1995. LaValliere spent a long time on the disabled list and needed a late-season surge to lift his average above the low .200s. However, his defense remained excellent.

## Hitting, Baserunning & Defense

A line-drive type of hitter, LaValliere isn't much of a power threat. But he usually makes contact, and the Sox have found him to be a dependable hitter with men on base. Since he's old and not in the best of shape, one would think lack of mobility would be a problem behind the plate. But LaValliere is still surprisingly agile, and his throwing arm remains outstanding. He runs like an old woman.

## 1996 Outlook

LaValliere is still a solid defensive catcher, and if he can stay healthy he should be good for another year of backup duty. But he couldn't stay healthy in 1995, and at 35 the clock is ticking. LaValliere could be modeling another uniform in 1996—if he's wearing any uniform at all.

# Norberto Martin

**Position:** 2B
**Bats:** R **Throws:** R
**Ht:** 5'10" **Wt:** 164

**Opening Day Age:** 29
**Born:** 12/10/66 in
Santo Domingo, DR
**ML Seasons:** 3
**Pronunciation:**
mar-TEEN

## Overall Statistics

| | G | AB | R | H | D | T | HR | RBI | SB | BB | SO | Avg | OBP | Slg |
|---|---|---|---|---|---|---|---|---|---|---|---|---|---|---|
| 1995 | 72 | 160 | 17 | 43 | 7 | 4 | 2 | 17 | 5 | 3 | 25 | .269 | .281 | .400 |
| Career | 125 | 305 | 39 | 84 | 14 | 5 | 3 | 35 | 9 | 13 | 42 | .275 | .302 | .384 |

## 1995 Season

Utility man Norberto Martin got off to a horrible start in 1995, and didn't get his average over the Mendoza line until after the All-Star break. Then he turned things around completely, soaring above the .300 mark for a brief period. A September slump dropped Martin back down to .269, which is about where he belonged all along.

## Hitting, Baserunning & Defense

A notorious hacker, Martin will swing at anything that moves. Though he usually hits the ball on the ground, he has a little bit of extra-base power. He has excellent speed and he's versatile, capable of playing both the infield and outfield. Martin's best position is second base and he does an adequate job there; his skills are strictly the fill-in variety at short, third or the outfield, but he always hustles and usually won't embarrass himself. His arm is below average.

## 1996 Outlook

With his ability to swing the bat and play a lot of positions, Martin is an ideal bench player. He adds to his value by being a fine pinch hitter. His chances of playing regularly are pretty remote, but he can give any club a decent 200 at-bats or so if a starter happened to go down.

# Kirk McCaskill

**Position:** RP
**Bats:** R **Throws:** R
**Ht:** 6' 1" **Wt:** 205

**Opening Day Age:** 34
**Born:** 4/9/61 in
Kapuskasing, Ontario,
Canada
**ML Seasons:** 11

## Overall Statistics

| | W | L | Pct. | ERA | G | GS | Sv | IP | H | BB | SO | HR | BR/IP |
|---|---|---|---|---|---|---|---|---|---|---|---|---|---|
| 1995 | 6 | 4 | .600 | 4.89 | 55 | 1 | 2 | 81.0 | 97 | 33 | 50 | 10 | 1.60 |
| Career | 101 | 103 | .495 | 4.03 | 351 | 238 | 7 | 1677.1 | 1676 | 634 | 975 | 148 | 1.38 |

## 1995 Season

After working effectively out of the White Sox bullpen in 1993 and '94, veteran righthander Kirk McCaskill suffered through a tough season in 1995. McCaskill got lit up regularly early in the year, and the club eventually lost confidence in him. After beginning the season as the club's primary set-up man, he finished it as a mop-up man who was kept well away from pressure situations.

## Pitching & Defense

McCaskill throws the standard fastball, curve, slider and change, with the best pitches being his curveball and change-up. He needs to keep the ball down in the strike zone in order to succeed, and his fastball needs to be good enough to keep hitters honest. In 1995 his location was horrendous, and he hung a number of curves that wound up in the bleachers. A great natural athlete, McCaskill fields his position very well and also does a fine job of controlling the running game.

## 1996 Outlook

McCaskill is signed through '96, and his salary is too high to make him easy to trade. Unless the club is willing to swallow his contract, he figures to be back in the Sox pen this year. He'll need to get off to a solid start in order to get his old set-up role back.

# Scott Radinsky

**Position**: RP
**Bats**: L **Throws**: L
**Ht**: 6' 3" **Wt**: 204

**Opening Day Age**: 28
**Born**: 3/3/68 in
Glendale, CA
**ML Seasons**: 5
**Nickname**: Rads

*Overall Statistics*

|  | W | L | Pct. | ERA | G | GS | Sv | IP | H | BB | SO | HR | BR/IP |
|---|---|---|---|---|---|---|---|---|---|---|---|---|---|
| 1995 | 2 | 1 | .667 | 5.45 | 46 | 0 | 1 | 38.0 | 46 | 17 | 14 | 7 | 1.66 |
| Career | 24 | 16 | .600 | 3.62 | 316 | 0 | 32 | 275.2 | 261 | 129 | 201 | 18 | 1.41 |

## 1995 Season

After missing the entire 1994 season while suffering from Hodgkin's disease, lefthander Scott Radinsky returned to the White Sox bullpen last year. He may have been rushing things, because his velocity was nowhere near as good as it had been prior to the illness. It wasn't until late in the year that Radinsky began pitching effectively, and even then he was relying more on finesse than power. Radinsky's season was notable mostly for some verbal sparring he did with Sox manager Terry Bevington, though the two eventually smoothed things over.

## Pitching & Defense

Radinsky's best pitch has always been his low-90s fastball. He also throws a curve and an occasional change-up, and with his three-quarter/sidearm delivery he can be extremely tough on left-handed hitters. But in 1995 the fastball didn't have its old heat, and he had even more problems with lefties than with righties. He has a good move to first, and his defense, a problem at times in the past, was excellent.

## 1996 Outlook

It's not easy to snap back from a serious illness, and Radinsky's 1995 problems were predictable. He should continue to get stronger, and the hope is that his old velocity will return. If it doesn't, his career is probably going to be over very quickly.

# Bill Simas

**Position**: RP
**Bats**: R **Throws**: R
**Ht**: 6' 3" **Wt**: 225

**Opening Day Age**: 24
**Born**: 11/28/71 in
Hanford, CA
**ML Seasons**: 1

*Overall Statistics*

|  | W | L | Pct. | ERA | G | GS | Sv | IP | H | BB | SO | HR | BR/IP |
|---|---|---|---|---|---|---|---|---|---|---|---|---|---|
| 1995 | 1 | 1 | .500 | 2.57 | 14 | 0 | 0 | 14.0 | 15 | 10 | 16 | 1 | 1.79 |
| Career | 1 | 1 | .500 | 2.57 | 14 | 0 | 0 | 14.0 | 15 | 10 | 16 | 1 | 1.79 |

## 1995 Season

Bill Simas is a big right-handed reliever who pitched in the Angels system until the middle of 1995, when he went to the White Sox in the Jim Abbott deal. Simas was considered one of the Angels' better prospects, and he pitched effectively out of the White Sox bullpen after making his debut on August 15.

## Pitching & Defense

Simas both started and relieved in the minors, but his career took off when he was switched exclusively to the bullpen in 1994. He's primarily a fastball/slider pitcher, and with his limited repertoire the pen is probably the best place for him. Though the White Sox didn't use him to finish games, he handled that job in the minors, and he has the sort of aggressiveness and power repertoire that are suitable for late relief. Simas didn't have a fielding chance during his limited trial, but his move to first seems okay.

## 1996 Outlook

Simas has only had four years of professional experience, and it's quite possible the Sox will send him back to Triple-A to start the year. He should be back, however, and he would be a closer candidate if Roberto Hernandez continues to struggle.

# Chris Snopek

**Position**: 3B
**Bats**: R **Throws**: R
**Ht**: 6' 1"  **Wt**: 185

**Opening Day Age**: 25
**Born**: 9/20/70 in
Cynthiana, KY
**ML Seasons**: 1

## Overall Statistics

|  | G | AB | R | H | D | T | HR | RBI | SB | BB | SO | Avg | OBP | Slg |
|---|---|---|---|---|---|---|---|---|---|---|---|---|---|---|
| 1995 | 22 | 68 | 12 | 22 | 4 | 0 | 1 | 7 | 1 | 9 | 12 | .324 | .403 | .426 |
| Career | 22 | 68 | 12 | 22 | 4 | 0 | 1 | 7 | 1 | 9 | 12 | .324 | .403 | .426 |

## 1995 Season

Infielder Chris Snopek came a long way in 1995. After posting good numbers at Triple-A Nashville, Snopek continued to impress during a September trial with the White Sox. The Sox will need to do some roster shuffling to open up a spot for him in '96, but Snopek played well enough to make them consider it.

## Hitting, Baserunning & Defense

Primarily a third baseman, Snopek doesn't have the sort of home-run power most clubs like to have at the position, but he's not a singles hitter: he has good power to the gaps, and looks capable of hitting 15 dingers or so per season. He has excellent discipline at the plate for a young player, and he also possesses good speed on the bases. Snopek is an excellent defensive third baseman but only fair at short, where he's also been given some playing time.

## 1996 Outlook

Snopek looks capable of playing regularly in the majors, but at the moment Robin Ventura and Ozzie Guillen stand in his way. The Sox have considered trading Ventura or moving him to first, and that would give Snopek his chance. If that doesn't happen, he might return to the minors this year so he can play every day.

# Larry Thomas

**Position**: RP
**Bats**: R **Throws**: L
**Ht**: 6' 1"  **Wt**: 195

**Opening Day Age**: 26
**Born**: 10/25/69 in
Miami, FL
**ML Seasons**: 1

## Overall Statistics

|  | W | L | Pct. | ERA | G | GS | Sv | IP | H | BB | SO | HR | BR/IP |
|---|---|---|---|---|---|---|---|---|---|---|---|---|---|
| 1995 | 0 | 0 | - | 1.32 | 17 | 0 | 0 | 13.2 | 8 | 6 | 12 | 1 | 1.02 |
| Career | 0 | 0 | - | 1.32 | 17 | 0 | 0 | 13.2 | 8 | 6 | 12 | 1 | 1.02 |

## 1995 Season

Lefthander Larry Thomas has been considered one of the White Sox' top pitching prospects for several years, and in 1995 he finally began showing why. Recalled from Double-A Birmingham in August, Thomas did an excellent job in middle relief and worked his way into the club's plans for 1996.

## Pitching & Defense

Thomas was primarily a starter prior to 1995, but after a poor season at Double-A Birmingham in '94, the Sox shifted him to the bullpen and he took to the role immediately. His fastball is only the mid-80s variety, but he has a nice slider and an excellent change-up, and he knows how to keep hitters off balance. He also knows how to pitch inside, and his stuff is effective against both right and left-handed hitters. Thomas has a good move to first and appears to be a decent fielder.

## 1996 Outlook

Thomas was so good in relief last year that the Sox, who could use an effective lefty in their pen, will probably keep him there. But they could also use a left-handed starter, and he might get a chance to start again eventually. In either case, he appears to have secured a spot on the club's pitching staff for this season.

# Other Chicago White Sox

**James Baldwin** (**Pos**: RHP, **Age**: 24)

Considered the White Sox' top pitching prospect, Baldwin opened the year in the rotation but got hammered. He went back to Triple-A and had more problems. He's still highly regarded. 1996 Outlook: B

**Rodney Bolton** (**Pos**: RHP, **Age**: 27)

Long one of the best pitchers in the White Sox minor league system, Bolton has been hammered regularly when promoted to the majors, and 1995 was no different. He probably needs a new team. 1996 Outlook: C

**Doug Brady** (**Pos**: 2B, **Age**: 26, **Bats**: B)

A slick-fielding second baseman, Brady didn't hit much until 1995, when he hit .295 at Triple-A Nashville. He's a switch-hitter and has good speed; he could stick as a reserve infielder. 1996 Outlook: B

**Mike Cameron** (**Pos**: RF, **Age**: 23, **Bats**: R)

Still only 23, Cameron hasn't hit for average, but he has a little power, some speed and a terrific glove. He draws some walks and might make it as a sub this year, but Triple-A seems more likely. 1996 Outlook: C

**Julio Franco** (**Pos**: DH/1B, **Age**: 34, **Bats**: R)

Franco was one of many solid major leaguers who fled the labor strife for Japan last year. We're listing him with the White Sox because that's who he last played for, but Franco could return with any club, most likely in the A.L., where he can DH. 1996 Outlook: A (but only if he comes back)

**Atlee Hammaker** (**Pos**: LHP, **Age**: 38)

After being out of baseball for two years, Hammaker came back in 1994, then amazed one and all by making the Sox Opening Day roster in 1995. But that was the end of the happy story. 1996 Outlook: D

**Brian Keyser** (**Pos**: RHP, **Age**: 29)

A righty finesse pitcher, Keyser got called up by the White Sox when their younger pitchers were having problems. Given 10 starts, he didn't show much to indicate he can win in the majors. 1996 Outlook: C

**John Kruk** (**Pos**: DH, **Age**: 35, **Bats**: L)

The White Sox signed Kruk, who was out of baseball, when they were desperate for a DH last year. He got off to a good start, but then wore down and abruptly retired. Slight chance he'll come back. 1996 Outlook: D

**Barry Lyons** (**Pos**: C, **Age**: 35, **Bats**: R)

After spending several years in the majors as a backup catcher, Lyons went back to the minors and had a big year in Triple-A in 1994. The Sox brought him back last year, and he hit pretty well. 1996 Outlook: B

**Isidro Marquez** (**Pos**: RHP, **Age**: 30)

A Mexican League veteran, Marquez came to the White Sox in a 1993 trade for Ron Coomer. A submariner, he looks like he can pitch but didn't show it in a brief trial with the Sox. 1996 Outlook: C

**Dave Righetti** (**Pos**: LHP, **Age**: 37)

Considered washed up, Righetti went back to the minors as a starter and returned to the majors with the Sox last summer. He pitched pretty well in nine starts, and could catch on with someone this year. 1996 Outlook: B

**Scott Ruffcorn** (**Pos**: RHP, **Age**: 26)

A former number-one draft choice, Ruffcorn has pitched great in the minors but can't get the side out in the majors. He's had arm problems, too, and the Sox seemed tired of him. A trade would help. 1996 Outlook: B

**Mike Sirotka** (**Pos**: LHP, **Age**: 24)

A lefty breaking-ball pitcher, Sirotka got six starts with the Sox last year and didn't do too badly. He's only pitched briefly in Triple-A, so a return to the minors is likely, but he should be back. 1996 Outlook: B

**Chris Tremie** (**Pos**: C, **Age**: 26)

A catcher with a good glove, Tremie got a little playing time when Mike LaValliere got hurt last year. He's never hit higher than .225 even in the minors, so his chances are minimal. 1996 Outlook: D

# Chicago White Sox Minor League Prospects

## Organization Overview:

The White Sox have enjoyed great success in recent years developing the commodity every team covets: starting pitching. Jack McDowell, Alex Fernandez, Jason Bere and Wilson Alvarez, the starting corps for the 1993 division champions, were all developed by the White Sox, although Alvarez was originally signed by Texas. Entering 1995, Chicago thought it had enough prospects, such as Scott Ruffcorn, James Baldwin and Steve Schrenk, to adequately replace Black Jack in the rotation. Each one disappointed, however, as Ruffcorn and Schrenk were injured and Baldwin struggled in Triple-A. Despite those setbacks, pitching still appears to be the strength of the organization, though it doesn't look like Chicago will have a rookie everyday player make an impact in 1996.

### Jeff Abbott

**Position:** OF      **Opening Day Age:** 23
**Bats:** R **Throws:** L      **Born:** 8/17/72 in
**Ht:** 6' 2" **Wt:** 190      Dunwoody, GA

*Recent Statistics*

|  | G | AB | R | H | D | T | HR | RBI | SB | BB | SO | AVG |
|---|---|---|---|---|---|---|---|---|---|---|---|---|
| 94 R White Sox | 4 | 15 | 4 | 7 | 1 | 0 | 1 | 3 | 2 | 4 | 0 | .467 |
| 94 A Hickory | 63 | 224 | 47 | 88 | 16 | 6 | 6 | 48 | 2 | 38 | 33 | .393 |
| 95 A Pr. William | 70 | 264 | 41 | 92 | 16 | 0 | 4 | 47 | 7 | 26 | 25 | .348 |
| 95 AA Birmingham | 55 | 197 | 25 | 63 | 11 | 1 | 3 | 28 | 1 | 19 | 20 | .320 |

Through two pro seasons and stints with four teams, Abbott has yet to hit below .320 at any level. He was promoted to Double-A last season one year after being drafted in the fourth round by the White Sox. He might have been drafted higher had he not missed most of his last college season due to mononucleosis. Abbott has doubles power right now, and it's hoped that he'll hit homers too after learning to pull the ball. Abbott is a good defensive outfielder with enough speed to steal a few bases. He could reach Chicago by 1997.

### Mike Bertotti

**Position:** P      **Opening Day Age:** 26
**Bats:** L **Throws:** L      **Born:** 1/18/70 in
**Ht:** 6' 1" **Wt:** 185      Jersey City, NJ

*Recent Statistics*

|  | W | L | ERA | G | GS | Sv | IP | H | R | BB | SO | HR |
|---|---|---|---|---|---|---|---|---|---|---|---|---|
| 95 AA Birmingham | 2 | 7 | 5.00 | 12 | 12 | 0 | 63.0 | 60 | 38 | 36 | 53 | 4 |
| 95 AAA Nashville | 2 | 3 | 8.72 | 7 | 6 | 0 | 32.0 | 41 | 34 | 17 | 35 | 8 |
| 95 AL Chicago | 1 | 1 | 12.56 | 4 | 4 | 0 | 14.1 | 23 | 20 | 11 | 15 | 6 |

Bertotti established himself as a solid prospect with a strong 1994 performance (11-9, 3.28) between A and Double-A. While Bertotti wasn't as impressive in 1995, the White Sox still promoted him to the majors for a couple of weeks last August. Signed as a 31st-round draft pick in 1991, Bertotti toiled most of his first two minor league seasons as a reliever. He struggled to find the plate coming out of the bullpen, but his control showed immediate improvement when he was converted to a starter in 1993. As a lefthander who throws a fastball that touches the upper 80s, Bertotti is almost certain to receive more big-league chances in the future.

### Scott Christman

**Position:** P      **Opening Day Age:** 24
**Bats:** L **Throws:** L      **Born:** 12/3/71 in
**Ht:** 6' 3" **Wt:** 190      Vancouver, WA

*Recent Statistics*

|  | W | L | ERA | G | GS | Sv | IP | H | R | BB | SO | HR |
|---|---|---|---|---|---|---|---|---|---|---|---|---|
| 93 R White Sox | 0 | 0 | 0.00 | 4 | 2 | 1 | 11.1 | 3 | 1 | 4 | 15 | 0 |
| 93 A Sarasota | 0 | 1 | 0.87 | 2 | 2 | 0 | 10.1 | 5 | 4 | 5 | 6 | 0 |
| 94 A Pr. William | 6 | 11 | 3.80 | 20 | 20 | 0 | 116.0 | 116 | 64 | 44 | 94 | 7 |
| 95 AA Birmingham | 2 | 5 | 6.39 | 12 | 12 | 0 | 62.0 | 76 | 49 | 24 | 37 | 6 |
| 95 A Pr. William | 4 | 4 | 3.59 | 13 | 13 | 0 | 85.1 | 83 | 38 | 19 | 56 | 7 |

Although Christman has not been a big winner in the minors, he is still a quality prospect. The 24-year-old's fastball reached 90 MPH at Oregon State, which helped convince the Sox to select him with their first pick of 1993. Christman wasn't throwing that hard in his first couple of pro seasons, but his fastball does have good sinking action. He also possesses a good curveball, and his change-up may be his best pitch. Christman struggled in his first action above Class A last year, and he's probably a year or two away from the White Sox staff.

### Tom Fordham

**Position:** P      **Opening Day Age:** 22
**Bats:** L **Throws:** L      **Born:** 2/20/74 in San
**Ht:** 6' 2" **Wt:** 210      Diego, CA

*Recent Statistics*

|  | W | L | ERA | G | GS | Sv | IP | H | R | BB | SO | HR |
|---|---|---|---|---|---|---|---|---|---|---|---|---|
| 93 R White Sox | 1 | 1 | 1.80 | 3 | 0 | 0 | 10.0 | 9 | 2 | 3 | 12 | 0 |
| 93 A Sarasota | 0 | 0 | 0.00 | 2 | 0 | 0 | 5.0 | 3 | 1 | 3 | 5 | 0 |
| 93 A Hickory | 4 | 3 | 3.88 | 8 | 8 | 0 | 48.2 | 36 | 21 | 21 | 27 | 3 |
| 94 A Hickory | 10 | 5 | 3.14 | 17 | 17 | 0 | 109.0 | 101 | 47 | 30 | 121 | 10 |
| 94 A South Bend | 4 | 4 | 4.34 | 11 | 11 | 0 | 74.2 | 82 | 46 | 14 | 48 | 4 |
| 95 A Pr. William | 9 | 0 | 2.04 | 13 | 13 | 0 | 84.0 | 66 | 20 | 35 | 78 | 7 |
| 95 AA Birmingham | 6 | 3 | 3.38 | 14 | 14 | 0 | 82.2 | 79 | 35 | 28 | 61 | 9 |

Fordham was selected in the 11th round of the same draft in which the White Sox chose Christman in round one. But through three minor league seasons, Fordham has actually outpitched Christman. Fordham enjoyed a great 1995 campaign, going 15-3 with a 2.70 ERA between Class-A Prince William and Double-A Birmingham. That followed a strong 1994 in which he struck out 10 batters per nine innings in the South Atlantic League. Like Christman, Fordham is a lefthander whose best pitch is probably his change-up. The White Sox have a number of intriguing pitchers in their farm system, but Fordham's performance in the minors has been as good as any of them.

## Andrew Lorraine

**Position:** P
**Bats:** L **Throws:** L
**Ht:** 6' 3" **Wt:** 195

**Opening Day Age:** 23
**Born:** 8/11/72 in Los Angeles, CA

### Recent Statistics

|  | W | L | ERA | G | GS | Sv | IP | H | R | BB | SO | HR |
|---|---|---|---|---|---|---|---|---|---|---|---|---|
| 95 AAA Vancouver | 6 | 6 | 3.96 | 18 | 18 | 0 | 97.2 | 105 | 49 | 30 | 51 | 7 |
| 95 AAA Nashville | 4 | 1 | 6.00 | 7 | 7 | 0 | 39.0 | 51 | 29 | 12 | 26 | 4 |
| 95 AL Chicago | 0 | 0 | 3.38 | 5 | 0 | 0 | 8.0 | 3 | 3 | 2 | 5 | 0 |

Lorraine has already had an eventful professional career. He was selected by California in the fourth round of the '93 draft. He finished that summer in a short-season A-league, yet made it to the big leagues in 1994. And last July he was a principal participant in the Jim Abbott trade with the White Sox. All that before he turned 23. As a pitcher, Lorraine has added 3-4 miles an hour to his fastball since he was drafted, though it's still only average velocity-wise. His best asset is his control of four pitches. It's possible Lorraine could join Wilson Alvarez as another lefty in the Sox rotation this spring.

## Olmedo Saenz

**Position:** 3B
**Bats:** R **Throws:** R
**Ht:** 6' 2" **Wt:** 185

**Opening Day Age:** 25
**Born:** 10/8/70 in Chitre Herrera, Panama

### Recent Statistics

|  | G | AB | R | H | D | T | HR | RBI | SB | BB | SO | AVG |
|---|---|---|---|---|---|---|---|---|---|---|---|---|
| 93 A South Bend | 13 | 50 | 3 | 18 | 4 | 1 | 0 | 7 | 1 | 7 | 7 | .360 |
| 93 A Sarasota | 33 | 121 | 13 | 31 | 9 | 4 | 0 | 27 | 3 | 9 | 18 | .256 |
| 93 AA Birmingham | 49 | 173 | 30 | 60 | 17 | 2 | 6 | 29 | 2 | 20 | 21 | .347 |
| 94 AAA Nashville | 107 | 383 | 48 | 100 | 27 | 2 | 12 | 59 | 3 | 30 | 57 | .261 |
| 95 AAA Nashville | 111 | 415 | 60 | 126 | 26 | 1 | 13 | 74 | 0 | 45 | 60 | .304 |
| 95 MLE | 111 | 409 | 56 | 120 | 24 | 0 | 12 | 70 | 0 | 42 | 61 | .293 |

Saenz has played in the White Sox organization since 1991. He spent parts of three seasons at Class A, never showing much home run sock, but his power has developed as he's matured. Saenz achieved his career high with 13 homers at Triple-A Nashville last season, as well as career peaks in walks (45) and RBI (74). It was Saenz' second tour of duty at Triple-A, however, and a player will often enjoy greater success after repeating a level. Saenz, who plays third base, didn't turn 25 until after the season, and his future with the White Sox depends to a great degree on Robin Ventura's status. He isn't likely to run Ventura—or for that matter, prospect Chris Snopek—off the position.

## Archie Vazquez

**Position:** P
**Bats:** R **Throws:** R
**Ht:** 6' 4" **Wt:** 233

**Opening Day Age:** 23
**Born:** 4/4/72 in Manhattan, NY

### Recent Statistics

|  | W | L | ERA | G | GS | Sv | IP | H | R | BB | SO | HR |
|---|---|---|---|---|---|---|---|---|---|---|---|---|
| 94 A Hickory | 7 | 3 | 1.21 | 50 | 0 | 28 | 67.0 | 37 | 14 | 22 | 78 | 5 |
| 95 A Pr. William | 3 | 4 | 3.59 | 47 | 0 | 20 | 57.2 | 53 | 26 | 30 | 70 | 5 |

Vazquez missed most of the 1993 season, pitching only five innings for the Sioux Falls Canaries in the Northern League. Originally drafted by San Diego in the 43rd round of 1991, Vazquez had lasted only two years in the Padre system before landing in baseball's equivalent of the scrap heap. The White Sox signed him right before the 1994 season, and over the last two seasons, Vazquez has saved 48 games and struck out 10.7 batters per nine innings, and at times he seems almost unhittable.

## Harold Williams

**Position:** 1B-DH
**Bats:** L **Throws:** L
**Ht:** 6' 4" **Wt:** 200

**Opening Day Age:** 25
**Born:** 2/14/71 in Garyville, LA

### Recent Statistics

|  | G | AB | R | H | D | T | HR | RBI | SB | BB | SO | AVG |
|---|---|---|---|---|---|---|---|---|---|---|---|---|
| 93 R White Sox | 52 | 186 | 18 | 52 | 6 | 4 | 1 | 21 | 4 | 17 | 40 | .280 |
| 94 A Hickory | 137 | 535 | 99 | 162 | 27 | 3 | 24 | 104 | 1 | 53 | 103 | .303 |
| 95 A Pr. William | 129 | 472 | 56 | 133 | 30 | 1 | 14 | 72 | 4 | 48 | 98 | .282 |

Williams is one of the better power prospects in the White Sox organization. He led the South Atlantic League in 1994 in runs scored and RBI, and while his 1995 season wasn't as impressive, Williams did improve his doubles rate and still led Prince William in RBI. But at 24, Williams, a 26th-round pick in 1993, was a bit old for a prospect in the Carolina League. He may not have a position, either. He was converted from the outfield to first base by the White Sox, and made 21 errors there in 1994.

## Others to Watch

Lorraine wasn't the only good prospect acquired by the White Sox in the Jim Abbott deal. They also picked up outfielder **McKay Christensen**. Unfortunately, Christensen has yet to play an inning as a professional. Shortly after the Angels used the fifth pick in the 1994 draft to select him, Christensen embarked on his Mormon mission. He should play in 1996, but will start in the low minors and is probably at least three years from the majors. . . One player the White Sox had high hopes for, outfielder **Jimmy Hurst**, hit just .189 at Birmingham. If Hurst can reduce his strikeouts (95 in 301 AB) he could be a 20-25 homer man. . . **Nilson Robledo** led the Midwest League with 108 RBI, but he'll be 27 in 1996 and the Sox have other first-base prospects ahead of him. . . One of those prospects is **Juan Thomas**, who smacked 26 homers in the Carolina League at age 23. But Thomas also struck out 156 times and hit just .235. . . Outfielder **Charles Poe**, a sixth-round pick in 1990, enjoyed a solid Double-A season at age 23 last year (.283, 13, 60). Poe also steals bases and draws some walks. . . **Jason Pierson** was drafted in the 25th round in 1992, and has gone 40-25 in four pro seasons. He's a crafty lefthander who doesn't beat himself with bases on balls.

# Sandy Alomar

## 1995 Season

Sandy Alomar began last season on the disabled list after hurting his left knee—which had already been operated on during the offseason—in spring training. Another surgery was performed in late April, and Alomar didn't return to the Cleveland lineup until late June. From that point forward, the Indians used him wisely, catching him three or four days a week and then resting him. Alomar rarely caught a day game after a night game, and the philosophy seemed to work as he hit .348 in his first 30 games back.

## Hitting

Alomar is an aggressive hitter, often swinging at the first pitch he sees, especially with runners in scoring position. Pitchers who throw high fastballs can get him out in that situation, and breaking balls away continue to give him problems. Alomar is generally a line-drive hitter, but his power continues to increase. He's knocked 24 homers over the last two seasons, despite missing considerable time due to the strike and injuries. After years of spraying hits to all fields, Alomar pulled the ball more to left last season. In addition, he dramatically improved his performance against the lefties who used to overwhelm him.

## Baserunning & Defense

In spite of his knee surgeries, Alomar still runs well for a big man. He'll steal a base now and then, but he's constantly warned to be cautious on the bases in order to stay off the DL. He remains among the finest defensive catchers in the game, as his big frame helps him block low pitches and his strong throwing arm deters potential basestealers.

## 1996 Outlook

Alomar's left knee needed about four more months of rehabilitation last season, but he came back early because the Indians truly needed him. If he works hard during the winter, he might finally be ready to play a full season. When healthy, he's clearly one of the best all-around catchers in the game.

**Position:** C
**Bats:** R  **Throws:** R
**Ht:** 6' 5"  **Wt:** 215

**Opening Day Age:** 29
**Born:** 6/18/66 in Salinas, PR
**ML Seasons:** 8
**Pronunciation:** AL-a-mar

*Overall Statistics*

|  | G | AB | R | H | D | T | HR | RBI | SB | BB | SO | Avg | OBP | Slg |
|---|---|---|---|---|---|---|---|---|---|---|---|---|---|---|
| 1995 | 66 | 203 | 32 | 61 | 6 | 0 | 10 | 35 | 3 | 7 | 26 | .300 | .332 | .478 |
| Career | 490 | 1658 | 193 | 451 | 80 | 4 | 42 | 215 | 21 | 92 | 191 | .272 | .317 | .401 |

*Where He Hits the Ball*

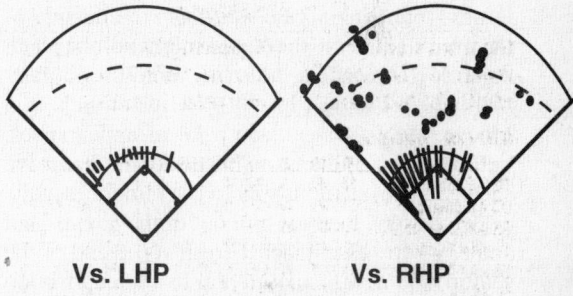

**Vs. LHP**          **Vs. RHP**

*1995 Situational Stats*

|  | AB | H | HR | RBI | Avg |  | AB | H | HR | RBI | Avg |
|---|---|---|---|---|---|---|---|---|---|---|---|
| Home | 104 | 34 | 4 | 17 | .327 | LHP | 44 | 16 | 4 | 12 | .364 |
| Road | 99 | 27 | 6 | 18 | .273 | RHP | 159 | 45 | 6 | 23 | .283 |
| First Half | 20 | 10 | 1 | 4 | .500 | Sc Pos | 55 | 16 | 3 | 25 | .291 |
| Scnd Half | 183 | 51 | 9 | 31 | .279 | Clutch | 37 | 10 | 3 | 9 | .270 |

*1995 Rankings (American League)*

➡ Did not rank near the top or bottom in any category

# Paul Assenmacher

## 1995 Season

Signed as a free agent, Paul Assenmacher became a big part of the American League's best bullpen in 1995. Used primarily by the Indians to face left-handed hitters late in the game and set the table for Jose Mesa, Assenmacher didn't allow an earned run until his 15th appearance of the season. He never hit a bad stretch, averaging more than a strikeout per inning along the way. He was a rock of stability during Cleveland's postseason run, as batters went just 1-for-15 hitting against him.

## Pitching

The 6-foot-3 Assenmacher throws a nasty curveball at a couple of different speeds. His big-breaking curve is especially tough against lefties—breaking all the way from the outside of the front shoulder to the outside corner of the plate. Against righthanders, he relies more on his fastball, which can still hit 90 MPH when he's in a groove. He's always made a lot of appearances, but last year Indians manager Mike Hargrove seemed to go out of his way to use him for just one or two batters, then get him out of the game. That strategy kept Assenmacher fresh at the end of the season, and never exposed him to a lineup for too long.

## Defense

Assenmacher remains a fine fielder, having made just two errors in his entire major league career. Like many fearsome relievers, he doesn't have a great move to first base. He hasn't caught a runner stealing since 1993, and basestealers went a perfect 5-for-5 against him last season. But he remains mobile, more than capable of getting off the mound in time to cover first.

## 1996 Outlook

The Indians liked Assenmacher so much that they signed him to a two-year deal, with a club option for a third, as soon as the World Series ended. His role in 1996 will likely be the same as last year. Despite his turning 35 during the offseason, there's no reason to think Assenmacher can't pitch another 35-50 quality relief innings again next year.

**Position:** RP
**Bats:** L  **Throws:** L
**Ht:** 6' 3"   **Wt:** 210

**Opening Day Age:** 35
**Born:** 12/10/60 in Allen Park, MI
**ML Seasons:** 10

### Overall Statistics

|  | W | L | Pct. | ERA | G | GS | Sv | IP | H | BB | SO | HR | BR/IP |
|---|---|---|---|---|---|---|---|---|---|---|---|---|---|
| 1995 | 6 | 2 | .750 | 2.82 | 47 | 0 | 0 | 38.1 | 32 | 12 | 40 | 3 | 1.15 |
| Career | 48 | 36 | .571 | 3.40 | 622 | 1 | 48 | 680.0 | 624 | 250 | 638 | 56 | 1.29 |

### How Often He Throws Strikes

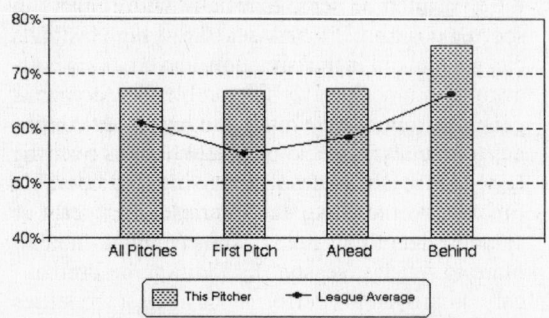

### 1995 Situational Stats

|  | W | L | ERA | Sv | IP |  | AB | H | HR | RBI | Avg |
|---|---|---|---|---|---|---|---|---|---|---|---|
| Home | 3 | 1 | 3.48 | 0 | 20.2 | LHB | 62 | 11 | 1 | 4 | .177 |
| Road | 3 | 1 | 2.04 | 0 | 17.2 | RHB | 80 | 21 | 2 | 7 | .263 |
| First Half | 2 | 2 | 1.98 | 0 | 13.2 | Sc Pos | 36 | 6 | 0 | 8 | .167 |
| Scnd Half | 4 | 0 | 3.28 | 0 | 24.2 | Clutch | 57 | 12 | 1 | 5 | .211 |

### 1995 Rankings (American League)

- ➡ 2nd in lowest percentage of inherited runners scored (10.7%)
- ➡ 6th in relief wins (6)
- ➡ 8th in lowest batting average allowed in relief with runners on base (.185)
- ➡ Led the Indians in lowest batting average allowed in relief with runners on base (.185) and lowest percentage of inherited runners scored (10.7%)

# Carlos Baerga

**Position:** 2B
**Bats:** B **Throws:** R
**Ht:** 5'11" **Wt:** 200

**Opening Day Age:** 27
**Born:** 11/4/68 in San Juan, PR
**ML Seasons:** 6
**Pronunciation:** by-AIR-ga

## 1995 Season

Carlos Baerga watched his weight during the 1994-95 offseason, and came to spring training in much better shape than in 1994. Although he made a frightening 19 errors at second base, Baerga more than made up for it with his bat, finding himself in the prime of his major league career. After a torrid tear in June he made a trip to the All-Star Game, but had some problems down the stretch. He went more than a month without a home run, and was bothered by ankle and wrist injuries late in the regular season and during the postseason.

## Hitting

One word describes the switch-hitting Baerga at the plate—dangerous. In 1995 he hit .361 with runners in scoring position and an amazing .332 with two strikes. Still a sucker for the occasional high fastball, Baerga makes contact, à la Kirby Puckett, on what seems like every pitch, spraying line drives to any part of the field. Despite his propensity to swing, Baerga remains very difficult to strike out, fanning just once in every 19.4 plate appearances last season.

## Baserunning & Defense

Baerga is an outstanding percentage basestealer, and still goes from first to third well when he keeps his playing weight in check. But when he gets heavier, he resembles a sitting penguin when he runs. Baerga's fielding continues to be a big concern for the Indians. He moves well to his left, but still has problems going behind second base to make a play. Baerga turns the double play very well, primarily because of his lower leg strength and strong throwing arm.

## 1996 Outlook

Manager Mike Hargrove calls Baerga "the heart and soul" of the Indians. Anyone who saw him struggle through the World Series on one leg knows what Hargrove means. When the Indians lost the Series, a disappointed Baerga said they'd be back. Assuming his left ankle heals during the offseason, there seems little reason to doubt that.

### Overall Statistics

|  | G | AB | R | H | D | T | HR | RBI | SB | BB | SO | Avg | OBP | Slg |
|---|---|---|---|---|---|---|---|---|---|---|---|---|---|---|
| 1995 | 135 | 557 | 87 | 175 | 28 | 2 | 15 | 90 | 11 | 35 | 31 | .314 | .355 | .452 |
| Career | 819 | 3185 | 491 | 971 | 165 | 15 | 93 | 505 | 47 | 178 | 351 | .305 | .345 | .454 |

### Where He Hits the Ball

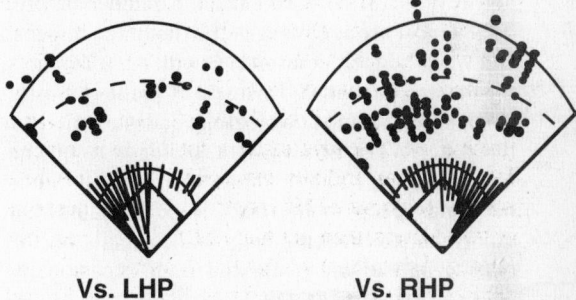

**Vs. LHP**          **Vs. RHP**

### 1995 Situational Stats

|  | AB | H | HR | RBI | Avg |  | AB | H | HR | RBI | Avg |
|---|---|---|---|---|---|---|---|---|---|---|---|
| Home | 265 | 89 | 7 | 48 | .336 | LHP | 160 | 53 | 4 | 29 | .331 |
| Road | 292 | 86 | 8 | 42 | .295 | RHP | 397 | 122 | 11 | 61 | .307 |
| First Half | 281 | 92 | 11 | 45 | .327 | Sc Pos | 144 | 52 | 4 | 70 | .361 |
| Scnd Half | 276 | 83 | 4 | 45 | .301 | Clutch | 80 | 30 | 0 | 13 | .375 |

### 1995 Rankings (American League)

- ➝ 1st in batting average with two strikes (.332)
- ➝ 2nd in errors at second base (19), lowest fielding percentage at second base (.973) and lowest percentage of swings on the first pitch (7.5%)
- ➝ 3rd in singles (130) and highest percentage of swings put into play (56.0%)
- ➝ 5th in hits, least pitches seen per plate appearance (3.41), batting average in the clutch (.375) and batting average on a 3-2 count (.405)
- ➝ 6th in batting average on an 0-2 count (.313)
- ➝ Led the Indians in at-bats, hits, singles (130) and intentional walks (6)

# Albert Belle

**Position:** LF
**Bats:** R **Throws:** R
**Ht:** 6' 2" **Wt:** 210

**Opening Day Age:** 29
**Born:** 8/25/66 in Shreveport, LA
**ML Seasons:** 7
**Nickname:** Joey

## 1995 Season

Albert Belle had a season—a second half, really—that simply defied description. He hit 36 homers after the All-Star break, becoming the first man in history to hit 50 homers and 50 doubles in one season. He beat Toronto in consecutive games with extra-inning homers in late August, and that propelled him into an unbelievable September. Belle finished 1995 with 103 extra-base hits, just the eighth player to crack 100 or more in a season. Amazingly, he finished second to Mo Vaughn in the MVP balloting.

## Hitting

Knowledge of the opposing pitcher is very important to Belle. If he hasn't faced a pitcher before, he'll almost always swing at the first pitch he sees. But when he feels comfortable with a pitcher, he's much more patient, and dangerous. Belle is mostly a pull hitter, thriving on breaking balls left out over the plate. When he struggles, he tends to hit the ball through the middle or go to right field. Since he stands deep in the box, Belle is somewhat vulnerable to breaking balls and fastballs on the outside part of the plate, and he'll occasionally chase an eye-level fastball.

## Baserunning & Defense

Belle still gets from first to third and second to home quickly, and has no qualms about breaking up a double play, but his basestealing days are behind him. Defensively, Belle is better than he showed in the postseason. He's far from a Gold Glove outfielder, but he's average at the very least. In particular, he has improved going back on the ball, but he still struggles when he has to go to his left or right. Bell possesses a decent arm but he often ignores the cutoff man.

## 1996 Outlook

If the Indians don't sign Belle to a multi-year deal, he can be a free agent after the 1996 season. Belle has already made it clear that he wants "market value," which for a slugger of his caliber means in excess of $7 million a year. The Indians say that's too high. Consequently, they feel compelled to trade one of the best power hitters in the game.

### *Overall Statistics*

| | G | AB | R | H | D | T | HR | RBI | SB | BB | SO | Avg | OBP | Slg |
|---|---|---|---|---|---|---|---|---|---|---|---|---|---|---|
| 1995 | 143 | 546 | 121 | 173 | 52 | 1 | 50 | 126 | 5 | 73 | 80 | .317 | .401 | .690 |
| Career | 755 | 2839 | 468 | 827 | 185 | 13 | 194 | 603 | 50 | 297 | 535 | .291 | .360 | .571 |

### *Where He Hits the Ball*

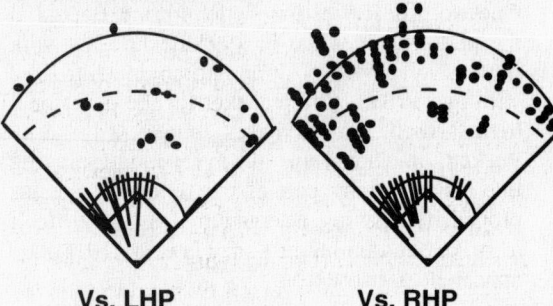

**Vs. LHP**          **Vs. RHP**

### *1995 Situational Stats*

| | AB | H | HR | RBI | Avg | | AB | H | HR | RBI | Avg |
|---|---|---|---|---|---|---|---|---|---|---|---|
| Home | 268 | 88 | 25 | 53 | .328 | LHP | 133 | 39 | 8 | 25 | .293 |
| Road | 278 | 85 | 25 | 73 | .306 | RHP | 413 | 134 | 42 | 101 | .324 |
| First Half | 260 | 81 | 14 | 51 | .312 | Sc Pos | 148 | 40 | 13 | 76 | .270 |
| Scnd Half | 286 | 92 | 36 | 75 | .322 | Clutch | 85 | 24 | 7 | 18 | .282 |

### *1995 Rankings (American League)*

→ 1st in home runs, runs scored, doubles, total bases (377), RBI, GDPs (24), slugging percentage, HR frequency (10.9 ABs per HR) and slugging percentage vs. right-handed pitchers (.729)

→ 2nd in cleanup slugging percentage (.690) and errors in left field (6)

→ 3rd in most GDPs per GDP situation (18.8%)

→ 5th in fielding percentage in left field (.981)

→ 7th in hits and times on base (252)

→ 8th in batting average and games played

→ Led the Indians in hit by pitch (6), times on base (252), plate appearances (631), games played, slugging percentage (.690), and cleanup slugging percentage (.690)

# Mark Clark

## 1995 Season

Mark Clark started the year in the Cleveland rotation, but struggled because of the strike-induced layoff. Clark's layoff was longer than most, since he suffered a broken right wrist before the strike began in 1994. A short spring training didn't help, and after six starts for the Indians he was sent to Triple-A to strengthen his arm and regain some confidence. He went 4-0 at Buffalo, and returned to Cleveland with a spot in the rotation. He was 7-5 after his return, but still failed to make the team's postseason roster, getting squeezed after the acquisition of Ken Hill.

## Pitching

Clark throws four pitches: sinking fastball, slider, split-finger and change-up. When he went 11-3 in 1994, he was throwing all four of them for strikes. But last year he had control problems. In particular, his sinking fastball simply didn't sink, and he was hit hard as a result. That was bad news, considering the sinker is his best pitch, and he usually gets a lot of ground balls with it—especially when reaching 85-88 MPH on the radar gun, of which he is capable. His split-fingered pitch is also a good one.

## Defense

Clark is still improving as a fielder. He hasn't made an error since 1993, and starts the 1-6-3 double play very well. He has a decent move to first, and has worked hard at controlling the running game. But there certainly seems to be room for improvement, as 19 of 26 runners successfully stole against him in 1995.

## 1996 Outlook

Clark hasn't peaked as a starter but he may have to do it somewhere besides Cleveland. The Indians didn't pick up his option for 1996, and were trying to renegotiate a deal for less money at press time. If a deal couldn't be worked, they were not expected to offer Clark a chance to go to arbitration, which would make him a free agent. If he does return to Cleveland, he'll compete for the third, fourth or fifth spot in the rotation.

**Position:** SP
**Bats:** R  **Throws:** R
**Ht:** 6' 5"  **Wt:** 225

**Opening Day Age:** 27
**Born:** 5/12/68 in Bath, IL
**ML Seasons:** 5

### Overall Statistics

|        | W  | L  | Pct. | ERA  | G  | GS | Sv | IP    | H   | BB  | SO  | HR | BR/IP |
|--------|----|----|------|------|----|----|----|-------|-----|-----|-----|----|-------|
| 1995   | 9  | 7  | .563 | 5.27 | 22 | 21 | 0  | 124.2 | 143 | 42  | 68  | 13 | 1.48  |
| Career | 31 | 26 | .544 | 4.44 | 95 | 78 | 0  | 497.0 | 529 | 154 | 242 | 60 | 1.37  |

### How Often He Throws Strikes

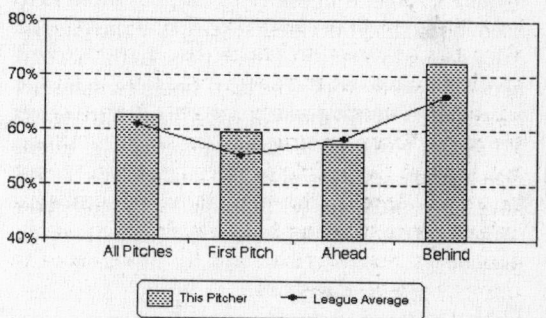

### 1995 Situational Stats

|            | W | L | ERA  | Sv | IP   |        | AB  | H  | HR | RBI | Avg  |
|------------|---|---|------|----|------|--------|-----|----|----|-----|------|
| Home       | 5 | 2 | 5.01 | 0  | 59.1 | LHB    | 283 | 90 | 10 | 47  | .318 |
| Road       | 4 | 5 | 5.51 | 0  | 65.1 | RHB    | 214 | 53 | 3  | 23  | .248 |
| First Half | 4 | 3 | 7.46 | 0  | 41.0 | Sc Pos | 137 | 37 | 5  | 55  | .270 |
| Scnd Half  | 5 | 4 | 4.20 | 0  | 83.2 | Clutch | 22  | 3  | 0  | 0   | .136 |

### 1995 Rankings (American League)

- ➡ 8th in stolen bases allowed (19) and highest batting average allowed vs. left-handed batters (.318)
- ➡ Led the Indians in losses, wild pitches (8), stolen bases allowed (19) and runners caught stealing (7)

Cleveland Indians

# Orel Hershiser

## 1995 Season

Counting the postseason, where he went 4-1, Orel Hershiser finished 20-7 overall in his first season with the Indians—a nice surprise for a team anticipating 10-12 wins at the time they signed him. His impressive campaign was a testament to both his healed right shoulder and the best offense in baseball, which gave him runs with which to work. Despite seeing a stint on the disabled list after pulling a muscle in his spinal cord in late June, Hershiser came back to go 11-2 in the season's second half.

## Pitching

Hershiser is a "hands on" pitcher—learning more about each opposing hitter as he goes along. He used the first half of his first season in the American League to check out the hitters. In the second half, he went to work. The hard sinker remains his best pitch, and he threw it even harder (over 90 MPH) last year with more movement. In addition, Hershiser mixes in a curve and change-up. He did have some problems keeping the ball in the park, allowing 21 homers, many on bad fastballs up in the zone.

## Defense

Hershiser is not a bad fundamental fielder, but he often tries to do way too much on defense. However, he can still handle balls hit through the box, a skill he displayed to the baseball world during the postseason. His move to first base remains good and keeps runners close. Potential basestealers barely broke even against him in 1995.

## 1996 Outlook

The Indians had an option on Hershiser for 1996, and they exercised it in November. He might replace Dennis Martinez as the club's number-one starter, and will be counted on for both quality innings and veteran leadership.

**Position:** SP
**Bats:** R  **Throws:** R
**Ht:** 6' 3"  **Wt:** 195

**Opening Day Age:** 37
**Born:** 9/16/58 in Buffalo, NY
**ML Seasons:** 13
**Nickname:** Bulldog

### Overall Statistics

|  | W | L | Pct. | ERA | G | GS | Sv | IP | H | BB | SO | HR | BR/IP |
|---|---|---|---|---|---|---|---|---|---|---|---|---|---|
| 1995 | 16 | 6 | .727 | 3.87 | 26 | 26 | 0 | 167.1 | 151 | 51 | 111 | 21 | 1.21 |
| Career | 150 | 108 | .581 | 3.06 | 369 | 329 | 5 | 2323.1 | 2085 | 704 | 1554 | 147 | 1.20 |

### How Often He Throws Strikes

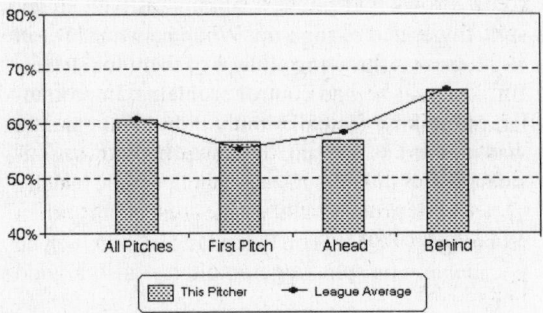

### 1995 Situational Stats

|  | W | L | ERA | Sv | IP |  | AB | H | HR | RBI | Avg |
|---|---|---|---|---|---|---|---|---|---|---|---|
| Home | 9 | 2 | 2.67 | 0 | 81.0 | LHB | 349 | 98 | 12 | 46 | .281 |
| Road | 7 | 4 | 5.00 | 0 | 86.1 | RHB | 271 | 53 | 9 | 27 | .196 |
| First Half | 5 | 4 | 4.11 | 0 | 76.2 | Sc Pos | 127 | 36 | 7 | 57 | .283 |
| Scnd Half | 11 | 2 | 3.67 | 0 | 90.2 | Clutch | 25 | 8 | 0 | 3 | .320 |

### 1995 Rankings (American League)

→ 1st in most GDPs induced per 9 innings (1.4)
→ 2nd in GDPs induced (26), least pitches thrown per batter (3.54), most GDPs induced per GDP situation (23.6%) and lowest batting average allowed vs. right-handed batters (.196)
→ 3rd in highest groundball/flyball ratio allowed (2.4) and ERA at home (2.67)
→ 4th in winning percentage
→ 5th in wins, least baserunners allowed per 9 innings (11.1) and most home runs allowed per 9 innings (1.13)
→ Led the Indians in wins, home runs allowed, GDPs induced (26) and winning percentage

# Ken Hill

## 1995 Season

The Indians acquired Ken Hill from St. Louis in late July, knowing they were heading for postseason play at the time of the deal. Cleveland's huge lead in the American League Central turned out to be a blessing, because it took pitching coach Mark Wiley most of the second half to correct the flaws in Hill's delivery. When the postseason did come, Hill went 2-1 in four appearances, and Wiley's work had made the deal pay off.

## Pitching

Hill has four pitches—a fastball, forkball, slider and change-up. His best pitches are the fastball and forkball, but because he continued to throw across his body and drop his right arm early in the year, his velocity fell. Before the Indians acquired Hill, scouts were saying that he must have a sore arm, because he wasn't throwing as hard as before. What the Indians liked is that he was *still* throwing in the low 90s. With the Indians' staff full of sinker/slider pitchers, Hill gave the team a change of pace. Despite Wiley's help, control remains a problem for Hill.

## Defense

Like Hershiser, Hill is great at fielding balls hit back up the middle. His reflexes are astounding, and he gets off the mound quickly to cover first. He doesn't have much of a move, and with his awkward delivery, Hill was very easy to run on during his years in the National League. After he came over to Cleveland, he did a little better job—probably due in part to having Sandy Alomar and Tony Pena behind the plate.

## 1996 Outlook

The Indians would love to re-sign Hill, but money is a problem. He made $4.375 million last year—a pretty big bite for a 10-game winner who required so much work on his mechanics. If the Indians could re-sign him for $2-3 million, they'd do it in a heartbeat. They liked the competitiveness he showed in the postseason, and the fact that the team went 9-2 in his 11 regular-season starts.

**Position:** SP
**Bats:** R  **Throws:** R
**Ht:** 6' 2"  **Wt:** 205

**Opening Day Age:** 30
**Born:** 12/14/65 in Lynn, MA
**ML Seasons:** 8

### Overall Statistics

|  | W | L | Pct. | ERA | G | GS | Sv | IP | H | BB | SO | HR | BR/IP |
|---|---|---|---|---|---|---|---|---|---|---|---|---|---|
| 1995 | 10 | 8 | .556 | 4.62 | 30 | 29 | 0 | 185.0 | 202 | 77 | 98 | 21 | 1.51 |
| Career | 74 | 61 | .548 | 3.67 | 198 | 191 | 0 | 1212.0 | 1125 | 475 | 720 | 84 | 1.32 |

### How Often He Throws Strikes

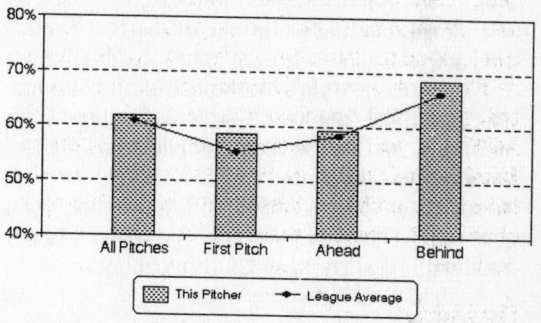

### 1995 Situational Stats

|  | W | L | ERA | Sv | IP |  | AB | H | HR | RBI | Avg |
|---|---|---|---|---|---|---|---|---|---|---|---|
| Home | 5 | 6 | 4.53 | 0 | 105.1 | LHB | 371 | 103 | 11 | 49 | .278 |
| Road | 5 | 2 | 4.74 | 0 | 79.2 | RHB | 353 | 99 | 10 | 47 | .280 |
| First Half | 5 | 6 | 4.56 | 0 | 100.2 | Sc Pos | 203 | 53 | 3 | 69 | .261 |
| Scnd Half | 5 | 2 | 4.70 | 0 | 84.1 | Clutch | 50 | 18 | 2 | 8 | .360 |

### 1995 Rankings (American League)

➡ Did not rank near the top or bottom in any category

Cleveland Indians

# Kenny Lofton

Gold Glover

## 1995 Season

Involved in strike negotiations during the offseason, Kenny Lofton didn't come to camp in game shape last spring. The lack of work showed most where he makes his living—in his legs. Hamstring problems, a bruised nerve in his lower back, and a pulled rib cage nagged Lofton all year. He also fell in love with the home run. . . only most of his hard swings ended up as fly balls instead. It wasn't until the season's final month, when he stole 22 bases, that he started playing like his old self. Lofton carried that momentum into October, and was dazzling at times during the postseason.

## Hitting

For much of the season, Lofton turned his back on the things that made him one of the best leadoff hitters in the game. He didn't walk, he didn't bunt for hits, and he didn't hit the ball on the ground. One school of thought was that his legs were hurting so bad that he didn't feel he could put any excess stress on them. He swung at a lot of high fastballs, and popped them up. But when he's in a groove, he takes sliders and outside fastballs to left field with line drives, and pulls anything inside to right field for doubles and triples.

## Baserunning & Defense

Six steals behind then-leader Tom Goodwin entering September, Lofton stole 14 bases in the last 11 games of the season to win his fourth straight stolen-base title. He has great range in all directions in center field, but especially going back on the ball. His arm is above average with good accuracy, but he hates the cutoff man. The entire package was enough to earn Lofton his third straight Gold Glove.

## 1996 Outlook

Lofton is at his best when he's doing anything he can to reach base, and then driving the defense crazy. . . not when he's trying to be a slugger. If he chooses to be that kind of player in 1996, and takes care of his legs during the winter, he can challenge for the MVP this year.

**Position:** CF
**Bats:** L  **Throws:** L
**Ht:** 6' 0"  **Wt:** 180

**Opening Day Age:** 28
**Born:** 5/31/67 in East Chicago, IN
**ML Seasons:** 5

### Overall Statistics

|  | G | AB | R | H | D | T | HR | RBI | SB | BB | SO | Avg | OBP | Slg |
|---|---|---|---|---|---|---|---|---|---|---|---|---|---|---|
| 1995 | 118 | 481 | 93 | 149 | 22 | 13 | 7 | 53 | 54 | 40 | 49 | .310 | .362 | .453 |
| Career | 546 | 2159 | 419 | 673 | 98 | 38 | 25 | 194 | 252 | 246 | 261 | .312 | .381 | .427 |

### Where He Hits the Ball

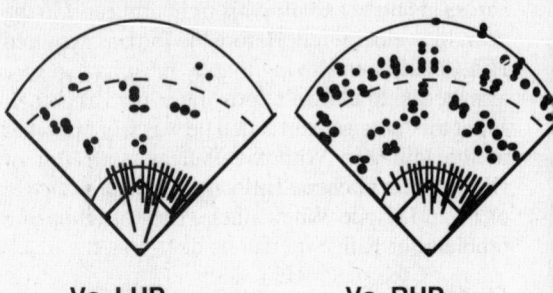

**Vs. LHP**　　　　**Vs. RHP**

### 1995 Situational Stats

|  | AB | H | HR | RBI | Avg |  | AB | H | HR | RBI | Avg |
|---|---|---|---|---|---|---|---|---|---|---|---|
| Home | 273 | 87 | 5 | 26 | .319 | LHP | 146 | 40 | 0 | 12 | .274 |
| Road | 208 | 62 | 2 | 27 | .298 | RHP | 335 | 109 | 7 | 41 | .325 |
| First Half | 249 | 78 | 5 | 27 | .313 | Sc Pos | 88 | 34 | 2 | 43 | .386 |
| Scnd Half | 232 | 71 | 2 | 26 | .306 | Clutch | 68 | 20 | 0 | 5 | .294 |

### 1995 Rankings (American League)

→ 1st in triples, stolen bases, errors in center field (8), lowest fielding percentage in center field (.970) and steals of third (13)
→ 2nd in batting average with runners in scoring position (.386)
→ 5th in caught stealing (15) and on-base percentage for a leadoff hitter (.363)
→ 6th in bunts in play (25)
→ 9th in stolen base percentage (78.3%), batting average vs. right-handed pitchers (.325) and lowest percentage of swings that missed (10.5%)
→ Led the Indians in caught stealing (15), intentional walks (6) and stolen base percentage (78.3%)

# Dennis Martinez

**Position:** SP
**Bats:** R   **Throws:** R
**Ht:** 6' 1"   **Wt:** 180

**Opening Day Age:** 40
**Born:** 5/14/55 in
Granada, Nicaragua
**ML Seasons:** 20

## 1995 Season

Dennis Martinez had two seasons in one. He started 9-0, and was the talk of baseball—a 40-year-old grandfather who just happened to be the top starter on a team headed for the playoffs. But then Martinez' old body caught up with him. He tore cartilage in his left knee and strained a muscle in his right forearm. Finally, his right shoulder stiffened because of changes he made in his mechanics to compensate for the sore knee. He went 3-5 in his last 12 starts, and reached his first-half form only once, hurling seven scoreless innings in Game 6 of the ALCS.

## Pitching

When Martinez takes the mound, it's like a matador walking into a bullfight—all eyes are on him. He'll do anything to win—throw sidearm, knock down a hitter, and according to some, doctor the ball. His best pitch is a combination curve-slider. But his forearm problems robbed much of the bite from his breaking ball. His fastball only gets up to 85-87 MPH, but he hits his spots well. Martinez also has a change-up that he hangs on the outside edge of the plate. He's durable, but needs to be monitored closely if he's pitching hurt.

## Defense

Martinez still comes off the mound well to field balls in front of the plate, but he's error prone, with 13 miscues in the last five seasons. His move to first is still adequate, as he picked off three runners last season. But his slow delivery and high leg kick make him inviting to run on.

## 1996 Outlook

Martinez will be back this year because the Tribe renegotiated his option year. He was scheduled to undergo surgery on his left knee during the offseason. If Martinez comes through the surgery all right, and his forearm and shoulder rebound, he should have at least one more good season left. But that's a lot of ifs for a body that has thrown so many innings.

### Overall Statistics

| | W | L | Pct. | ERA | G | GS | Sv | IP | H | BB | SO | HR | BR/IP |
|---|---|---|---|---|---|---|---|---|---|---|---|---|---|
| 1995 | 12 | 5 | .706 | 3.08 | 28 | 28 | 0 | 187.0 | 174 | 46 | 99 | 17 | 1.18 |
| Career | 231 | 176 | .568 | 3.60 | 610 | 528 | 6 | 3748.0 | 3601 | 1080 | 2022 | 344 | 1.25 |

### How Often He Throws Strikes

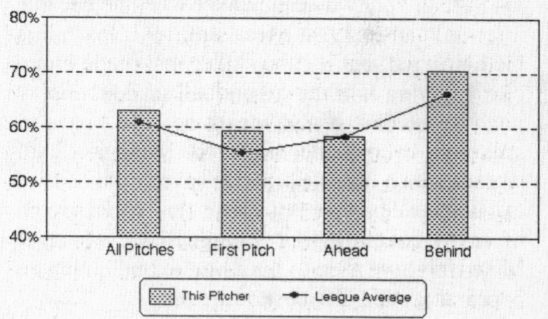

### 1995 Situational Stats

| | W | L | ERA | Sv | IP | | AB | H | HR | RBI | Avg |
|---|---|---|---|---|---|---|---|---|---|---|---|
| Home | 4 | 3 | 3.49 | 0 | 90.1 | LHB | 424 | 97 | 11 | 38 | .229 |
| Road | 8 | 2 | 2.70 | 0 | 96.2 | RHB | 281 | 77 | 6 | 23 | .274 |
| First Half | 8 | 0 | 2.37 | 0 | 95.0 | Sc Pos | 169 | 31 | 3 | 44 | .183 |
| Scnd Half | 4 | 5 | 3.82 | 0 | 92.0 | Clutch | 41 | 10 | 1 | 2 | .244 |

### 1995 Rankings (American League)

- ➡ 1st in errors at pitcher (4)
- ➡ 2nd in hit batsmen (12) and lowest batting average allowed with runners in scoring position (.183)
- ➡ 3rd in ERA, shutouts (2) and ERA on the road (2.70)
- ➡ 4th in lowest on-base percentage allowed (.302)
- ➡ 5th in lowest slugging percentage allowed (.367) and lowest batting average allowed vs. left-handed batters (.229)
- ➡ 6th in least baserunners allowed per 9 innings (11.2)
- ➡ Led the Indians in ERA, complete games (3), shutouts (2) and innings pitched

# Jose Mesa

## 1995 Season

Jose Mesa's first season as a closer turned out to be a dream year. The Indians spent all spring looking for a closer. When they couldn't find one, they gave the job to Mesa, a wild-armed starter for most of his career. All he did was save 46 games in 48 chances, including his first 38 in a row to set a major league single-season record. Mesa's favorite saying is "No doubt about it." That's exactly how the Indians felt when he came into a game in a save situation.

## Pitching

Mesa is a power pitcher. After years of starting, he put away his split-finger and curveball, going to his fastball and two-seam sinker when he became a set-up man in 1994. Mesa's mid-90s fastball is his best pitch, but it's the sinker that made him a closer, giving him the groundball or double-play pitch he needed. It also meant he didn't have to strike out every batter he faced. Mesa is a hard worker with a durable arm. He saved both ends of a doubleheader twice last season, and had a stretch of saves covering four straight days. Manager Mike Hargrove tried to limit him to one inning an appearance, and did most of the time.

## Defense

Mesa is not the greatest fielder in the world, making six errors in the last three years. Like many closers, he doesn't worry much about stolen bases, and his move is average at best. One reason he neglects runners is that very few even reach base against him.

## 1996 Outlook

Hargrove would gladly take a repeat of last season. Mesa's numbers might not be as gaudy as they were last year—his 1.13 ERA was the lowest ever by a Tribe pitcher with 60 or more innings. But if he stays healthy and gets regular use, there's no reason to think he can't save 30-40 games a year.

**Position:** RP
**Bats:** R **Throws:** R
**Ht:** 6' 3" **Wt:** 225

**Opening Day Age:** 29
**Born:** 5/22/66 in Azua, DR
**ML Seasons:** 7
**Pronunciation:** MAY-sa

### Overall Statistics

|       | W  | L  | Pct.  | ERA  | G   | GS | Sv | IP    | H   | BB  | SO  | HR | BR/IP |
|-------|----|----|-------|------|-----|----|----|-------|-----|-----|-----|----|-------|
| 1995  | 3  | 0  | 1.000 | 1.13 | 62  | 0  | 46 | 64.0  | 49  | 17  | 58  | 3  | 1.03  |
| Career| 37 | 45 | .451  | 4.55 | 211 | 95 | 48 | 708.0 | 747 | 279 | 406 | 61 | 1.45  |

### How Often He Throws Strikes

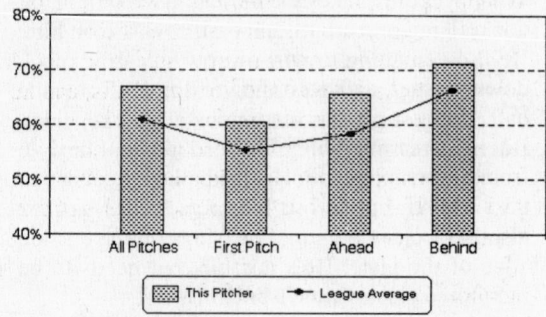

### 1995 Situational Stats

|            | W | L | ERA  | Sv |  IP  |        | AB  | H  | HR | RBI | Avg  |
|------------|---|---|------|----|------|--------|-----|----|----|-----|------|
| Home       | 1 | 0 | 0.28 | 21 | 31.2 | LHB    | 126 | 29 | 0  | 4   | .230 |
| Road       | 2 | 0 | 1.95 | 25 | 32.1 | RHB    | 101 | 20 | 3  | 8   | .198 |
| First Half | 1 | 0 | 1.84 | 21 | 29.1 | Sc Pos | 49  | 6  | 1  | 10  | .122 |
| Scnd Half  | 2 | 0 | 0.52 | 25 | 34.2 | Clutch | 172 | 39 | 3  | 10  | .227 |

### 1995 Rankings (American League)

→ 1st in saves, games finished (57), save opportunities (48), save percentage (95.8%) and relief ERA (1.13)
→ 2nd in lowest batting average allowed in relief with runners in scoring position (.122)
→ 3rd in first batter efficiency (.117)
→ 4th in least baserunners allowed per 9 innings in relief (9.3)
→ 6th in games pitched
→ 9th in lowest batting average allowed in relief (.216)
→ Led the Indians in games pitched, lowest batting average allowed in relief with runners in scoring position (.122) and relief ERA (1.13)

# Eddie Murray

## 1995 Season

Eddie Murray became the 19th man in baseball history to reach 3,000 hits on June 30, when he singled against Minnesota's Mike Trombley. In July, he went on the disabled list for just the second time in his career, with two broken ribs resulting from a collision at the plate. He had a torrid September, but in October was once again the victim of his World Series jinx, going just 2-for-19 (.105) against Atlanta.

## Hitting

Murray can take some of the worst swings in the world with that log he calls a bat. When you see him do that, it's easy to think that time has finally caught up to him. On the next pitch, he'll put everything together and hit the ball 400 feet. Murray is a guess hitter with power, who can be fooled by breaking balls away and good fastballs, and he loves to swing at the first pitch he sees. A switch-hitter, Murray is a much better hitter for both average and power left-handed than right-handed, and is still dangerous with runners in scoring position.

## Baserunning & Defense

Murray is one of the slowest men in the game going down the line, but doesn't embarrass himself going from first to third or second to home. He studies pitchers, and on occasion he'll still surprise with a steal. A former Gold Glove first baseman, Murray can still play the position well for a day or two. Any more than that, and his lack of range and mobility become apparent.

## 1996 Outlook

Murray was a free agent at the end of the 1995 season, and the Indians weren't sure if he'd be back. Wherever he goes, he will do three things—drive in big runs, become a team leader, and leave the news media without a quote. Murray needs 21 homers to become just the third man to have 3,000 hits and 500 homers. He wants it badly.

**Position:** DH/1B
**Bats:** B **Throws:** R
**Ht:** 6' 2"  **Wt:** 220

**Opening Day Age:** 40
**Born:** 2/24/56 in Los Angeles, CA
**ML Seasons:** 19

### Overall Statistics

|  | G | AB | R | H | D | T | HR | RBI | SB | BB | SO | Avg | OBP | Slg |
|---|---|---|---|---|---|---|---|---|---|---|---|---|---|---|
| 1995 | 113 | 436 | 68 | 141 | 21 | 0 | 21 | 82 | 5 | 39 | 65 | .323 | .375 | .516 |
| Career | 2819 | 10603 | 1545 | 3071 | 532 | 34 | 479 | 1820 | 105 | 1257 | 1403 | .290 | .362 | .482 |

### Where He Hits the Ball

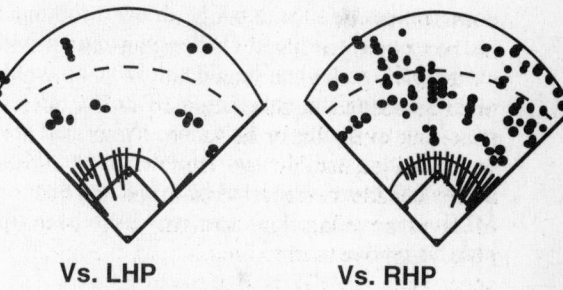

**Vs. LHP**       **Vs. RHP**

### 1995 Situational Stats

|  | AB | H | HR | RBI | Avg |  | AB | H | HR | RBI | Avg |
|---|---|---|---|---|---|---|---|---|---|---|---|
| Home | 210 | 73 | 11 | 47 | .348 | LHP | 104 | 28 | 3 | 16 | .269 |
| Road | 226 | 68 | 10 | 35 | .301 | RHP | 332 | 113 | 18 | 66 | .340 |
| First Half | 232 | 75 | 12 | 45 | .323 | Sc Pos | 114 | 40 | 6 | 60 | .351 |
| Scnd Half | 204 | 66 | 9 | 37 | .324 | Clutch | 63 | 14 | 5 | 7 | .222 |

### 1995 Rankings (American League)

- 1st in batting average vs. right-handed pitchers (.340)
- 5th in batting average and highest percentage of swings on the first pitch (40.3%)
- 6th in batting average at home (.348)
- 8th in batting average with runners in scoring position (.351)
- 10th in slugging percentage vs. right-handed pitchers (.551)
- Led the Indians in batting average, batting average vs. right-handed pitchers (.340) and batting average at home (.348)

# Charles Nagy

## 1995 Season

Charles Nagy conquered two things last year. One was a lack of confidence in his fastball. The other was fear of the unknown, as he pitched without a contract for the first time in his six-year career. The result was a second half in which Nagy went 9-2 in 15 starts, helping him reach his second-highest season win total in the big leagues. Nagy was sharp during his starts in the Divisional Play-offs and LCS, but struggled in his only World Series outing.

## Pitching

Nagy throws a sinking fastball, breaking ball, split-finger and change-up. His best pitch is his breaking ball, a hybrid slider/curve. It can be a dominant pitch for him, but he threw it too much last season. He stopped challenging hitters with his fastball, and when he did throw it, he would nibble, driving the coaching staff crazy. After a poor August outing in Baltimore, Nagy had several meetings with the staff and decided to throw the fastball more, which has been clocked up to 90 MPH. There was talk that he may have been tipping his pitches.

## Defense

Nagy fields his position well, starting four double plays last year alone. He gets off the mound quickly to cover first, and his 54 chances were the second-most among the Cleveland staff in 1995. His Achilles heel is the running game, which he hasn't controlled well since 1992. His move to first didn't scare anybody last season, as runners stole 18 bases in 21 attempts.

## 1996 Outlook

Nagy's long-term contract expired last year. That means he could have become a free agent during the winter and signed with another club. The Indians wanted to keep him, but at the right price. Nagy, drafted and raised in the Tribe's system, came of age last year. He showed the rest of the league, especially in the postseason, that he can deliver in big-game situations. He'll pitch and win wherever he goes this year.

**Position:** SP
**Bats:** L  **Throws:** R
**Ht:** 6' 3"  **Wt:** 200

**Opening Day Age:** 28
**Born:** 5/5/67 in Fairfield, CT
**ML Seasons:** 6
**Pronunciation:** NAG-ee

### Overall Statistics

|  | W | L | Pct. | ERA | G | GS | Sv | IP | H | BB | SO | HR | BR/IP |
|---|---|---|---|---|---|---|---|---|---|---|---|---|---|
| 1995 | 16 | 6 | .727 | 4.55 | 29 | 29 | 0 | 178.0 | 194 | 61 | 139 | 20 | 1.43 |
| Career | 57 | 49 | .538 | 3.97 | 136 | 135 | 0 | 905.0 | 966 | 266 | 581 | 74 | 1.36 |

### How Often He Throws Strikes

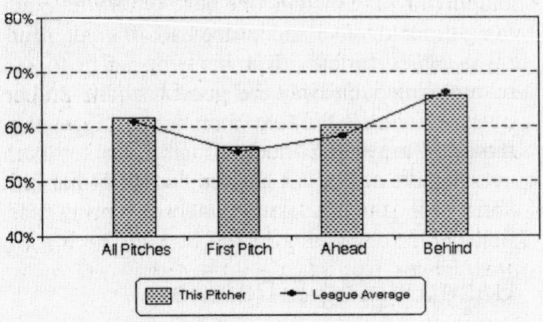

### 1995 Situational Stats

|  | W | L | ERA | Sv | IP |  | AB | H | HR | RBI | Avg |
|---|---|---|---|---|---|---|---|---|---|---|---|
| Home | 10 | 3 | 3.48 | 0 | 108.2 | LHB | 377 | 118 | 6 | 42 | .313 |
| Road | 6 | 3 | 6.23 | 0 | 69.1 | RHB | 320 | 76 | 14 | 45 | .238 |
| First Half | 7 | 4 | 3.61 | 0 | 87.1 | Sc Pos | 180 | 48 | 5 | 65 | .267 |
| Scnd Half | 9 | 2 | 5.46 | 0 | 90.2 | Clutch | 31 | 8 | 1 | 2 | .258 |

### 1995 Rankings (American League)

→ 1st in highest stolen base percentage allowed (85.7%) and most run support per 9 innings (8.1)
→ 4th in winning percentage and highest groundball/flyball ratio allowed (2.1)
→ 5th in wins
→ 7th in highest batting average allowed (.278), highest slugging percentage allowed (.433) and most strikeouts per 9 innings (7.0)
→ 8th in highest strikeout/walk ratio (2.3)
→ 9th in shutouts (1)
→ 10th in stolen bases allowed (18)
→ Led the Indians in wins, games started, hits allowed, batters faced (771), walks allowed, strikeouts and pitches thrown (2,887)

# Chad Ogea

**Position:** SP/RP
**Bats:** R **Throws:** R
**Ht:** 6' 2" **Wt:** 200

**Opening Day Age:** 25
**Born:** 11/9/70 in Lake Charles, LA
**ML Seasons:** 2
**Pronunciation:** OH-jay

## 1995 Season

Chad Ogea bounced back and forth three times between Cleveland and Triple-A Buffalo in 1995. In between, he showed the Indians he could pitch well as both a starter and long reliever. After three appearances out of the bullpen, 14 of his next 15 appearances came as a starter. He won his first four of those starts, but was eventually used as only a spot starter, allowing the Indians to juggle their starters and keep their rotation fresh for the play-offs.

## Pitching

Ogea has a good understanding of how he needs to pitch to be successful. With his stuff, rated average to below average at best, he needs every edge he can get. He relies on his change-up, as well as an 85-88 MPH fastball. But if he doesn't put his heater in the right spot, he gets hurt. The proper sequence of pitches is also a big key for Ogea. He must mix his change-up and fastball well, or the result can be disastrous. He showed the Indians he could do two things last year—throw strikes, and pitch well after sitting in the bullpen for a long time. That's why he made the postseason roster instead of Mark Clark.

## Defense

Ogea is a decent fielder, but it almost hurts to watch him walk between the dugout and the mound because of his five knee operations. In addition, he pays very little attention to the running game. Of the 16 runners who tried to steal against him in 1995, only two were thrown out.

## 1996 Outlook

Depending on what free-agent moves the Indians make during the winter, Ogea could be their fourth or fifth starter. If not that, he'll at least get a good look as the team's long man. After going 41-23 in the minors, Ogea doesn't have much more to prove there. At age 25, his career can still go in a lot of directions, but he seems well-suited for long relief.

### Overall Statistics

|  | W | L | Pct. | ERA | G | GS | Sv | IP | H | BB | SO | HR | BR/IP |
|---|---|---|---|---|---|---|---|---|---|---|---|---|---|
| 1995 | 8 | 3 | .727 | 3.05 | 20 | 14 | 0 | 106.1 | 95 | 29 | 57 | 11 | 1.17 |
| Career | 8 | 4 | .667 | 3.45 | 24 | 15 | 0 | 122.2 | 116 | 39 | 68 | 13 | 1.26 |

### How Often He Throws Strikes

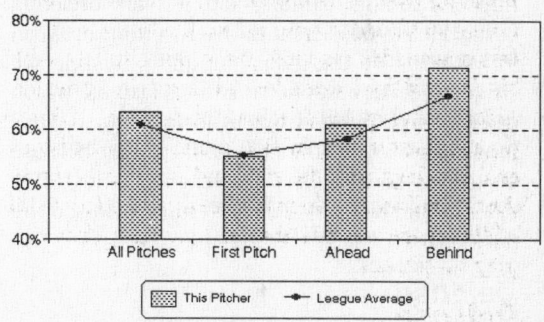

### 1995 Situational Stats

|  | W | L | ERA | Sv | IP |  | AB | H | HR | RBI | Avg |
|---|---|---|---|---|---|---|---|---|---|---|---|
| Home | 5 | 1 | 2.23 | 0 | 64.2 | LHB | 235 | 53 | 6 | 22 | .226 |
| Road | 3 | 2 | 4.32 | 0 | 41.2 | RHB | 171 | 42 | 5 | 14 | .246 |
| First Half | 5 | 1 | 2.19 | 0 | 53.1 | Sc Pos | 89 | 15 | 3 | 25 | .169 |
| Scnd Half | 3 | 2 | 3.91 | 0 | 53.0 | Clutch | 14 | 3 | 0 | 1 | .214 |

### 1995 Rankings (American League)
- ➡ 3rd in lowest batting average allowed vs. left-handed batters (.226)
- ➡ Led the Indians in lowest batting average allowed vs. left-handed batters (.226)

**Cleveland Indians**

# Eric Plunk

## 1995 Season

Until he was sidelined in early September with a sore right shoulder, Eric Plunk was in the process of giving the Indians another heavy-duty season as a right-handed set-up man. Plunk has been the Tribe's most consistent reliever over the last four years, posting a 2.92 ERA in 225 appearances over that period. Last year he teamed with Julian Tavarez as Jose Mesa's right-handed set-up combo. He also saved two games when Mesa needed a break.

## Pitching

Like Mesa, Plunk is a power pitcher. He'll get cute now and then with a slow curveball, but mostly he throws fastballs, sliders, and a sharp-breaking curve. He's a consistent thrower, hitting between 92-94 MPH on the radar gun and pounding the strike zone. His best pitch is still his fastball, which can turn right-handed hitters' bats to mush. He's prone to giving up the occasional homer because he throws so hard, but the league hit just .211 against him, and just .229 with runners in scoring position.

## Defense

The 6-foot-6 Plunk is not the smoothest fielder. He looks awkward coming off the mound, but for the second straight season didn't make an error. He'll cover first base and back up third and the plate, but needs work on controlling the running game. He was tough to run on early in his career, but basestealers have their way with him now. They're 27-for-34 (79 percent) stealing over the past three seasons.

## 1996 Outlook

The Indians were concerned about the wear-and-tear X-rays showed on Plunk's right shoulder last September. He received cortisone shots and pitched in the postseason, but not effectively. If Plunk comes back at full strength, he'll assume his duties as a key part of a very successful bullpen. If not, the Indians will have a hard time finding anyone that will give them such consistent production.

**Position:** RP
**Bats:** R **Throws:** R
**Ht:** 6' 6" **Wt:** 220

**Opening Day Age:** 32
**Born:** 9/3/63 in Wilmington, CA
**ML Seasons:** 10

### Overall Statistics

|        | W  | L  | Pct. | ERA  | G   | GS | Sv | IP    | H   | BB  | SO  | HR | BR/IP |
|--------|----|----|------|------|-----|----|----|-------|-----|-----|-----|----|-------|
| 1995   | 6  | 2  | .750 | 2.67 | 56  | 0  | 2  | 64.0  | 48  | 27  | 71  | 5  | 1.17  |
| Career | 57 | 44 | .564 | 3.73 | 472 | 41 | 32 | 859.2 | 743 | 504 | 793 | 80 | 1.45  |

### How Often He Throws Strikes

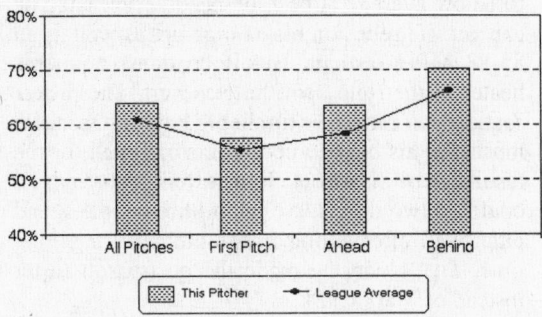

### 1995 Situational Stats

|            | W | L | ERA  | Sv | IP   |        | AB  | H  | HR | RBI | Avg  |
|------------|---|---|------|----|------|--------|-----|----|----|-----|------|
| Home       | 4 | 0 | 2.67 | 2  | 30.1 | LHB    | 108 | 24 | 0  | 13  | .222 |
| Road       | 2 | 2 | 2.67 | 0  | 33.2 | RHB    | 120 | 24 | 5  | 9   | .200 |
| First Half | 4 | 1 | 1.85 | 1  | 34.0 | Sc Pos | 48  | 11 | 1  | 18  | .229 |
| Scnd Half  | 2 | 1 | 3.60 | 1  | 30.0 | Clutch | 138 | 34 | 5  | 19  | .246 |

### 1995 Rankings (American League)

➡ 5th in first batter efficiency (.163)
➡ 6th in relief wins (6)
➡ 7th in relief ERA (2.67) and most strikeouts per 9 innings in relief (10.0)
➡ 8th in lowest batting average allowed in relief (.211)
➡ Led the Indians in lowest batting average allowed in relief (.211) and most strikeouts per 9 innings in relief (10.0)

# Manny Ramirez

## 1995 Season

Manny Ramirez had a great power year at the bottom of the Tribe lineup. Pitchers had to deal with Lofton, Baerga, Belle and Murray before they got to Ramirez, who often supplied the finisher. After a torrid first half, he made the A.L. All-Star team. By the time the season ended, Ramirez had become just the 25th player to surpass 30 homers and 100 RBI at age 23 or younger. But his inconsistency in October took a little shine off those regular-season accomplishments.

## Hitting

With a smooth, quick swing, Ramirez uses the whole field, and can hit homers to left and right. But when his swing gets long, he's vulnerable to both breaking balls away and fastballs up and in. Consequently, his strikeout total remained high, but so did his walks. In fact, there were times when Ramirez took so many pitches that he'd lose track of the count. If he walked, the umpire had to tell him to take first base. If he struck out, the ump had to tell him to go sit down. Honest. Manager Mike Hargrove called it "tunnel vision."

## Baserunning & Defense

Ramirez might be the worst baserunner in the league. When he gets on base, his mind goes blank. He rarely knows how many outs there are, runs into stupid double plays, and is always a threat to get picked off. In right field, Ramirez is "fence shy," and doesn't go back on balls well. Although he improved going into the gap in right-center, he often gives an uneven effort—hustling after one ball, loafing after the next. His arm is average, but it's allergic to cutoff men.

## 1996 Outlook

Ramirez is at home with a bat in his hand. When he's at the plate, he's a big-league veteran. Anywhere else on the field, he's the rawest of rookies. His game needs to be refined, his concentration level improved, and his maturity increased if he's going to be a franchise player. He has the talent.

**Position:** RF
**Bats:** R **Throws:** R
**Ht:** 6' 0" **Wt:** 190

**Opening Day Age:** 23
**Born:** 5/30/72 in Santo Domingo, DR
**ML Seasons:** 3

### Overall Statistics

|  | G | AB | R | H | D | T | HR | RBI | SB | BB | SO | Avg | OBP | Slg |
|---|---|---|---|---|---|---|---|---|---|---|---|---|---|---|
| 1995 | 137 | 484 | 85 | 149 | 26 | 1 | 31 | 107 | 6 | 75 | 112 | .308 | .402 | .558 |
| Career | 250 | 827 | 141 | 236 | 49 | 1 | 50 | 172 | 10 | 119 | 192 | .285 | .375 | .528 |

### Where He Hits the Ball

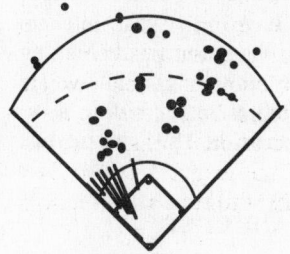
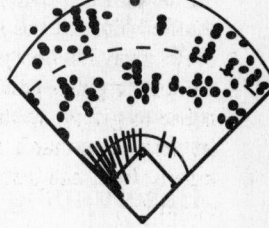

**Vs. LHP**          **Vs. RHP**

### 1995 Situational Stats

|  | AB | H | HR | RBI | Avg |  | AB | H | HR | RBI | Avg |
|---|---|---|---|---|---|---|---|---|---|---|---|
| Home | 225 | 65 | 12 | 46 | .289 | LHP | 123 | 50 | 7 | 28 | .407 |
| Road | 259 | 84 | 19 | 61 | .324 | RHP | 361 | 99 | 24 | 79 | .274 |
| First Half | 231 | 74 | 18 | 52 | .320 | Sc Pos | 129 | 44 | 7 | 74 | .341 |
| Scnd Half | 253 | 75 | 13 | 55 | .296 | Clutch | 64 | 19 | 3 | 13 | .297 |

### 1995 Rankings (American League)

- 2nd in batting average vs. left-handed pitchers (.407)
- 3rd in on-base percentage vs. left-handed pitchers (.507) and errors in right field (5)
- 5th in lowest fielding percentage in right field (.978)
- 6th in most pitches seen per plate appearance (4.18), slugging percentage vs. left-handed pitchers (.659) and batting average on the road (.324)
- 7th in RBI
- 8th in slugging percentage and HR frequency (15.6 ABs per HR)
- Led the Indians in intentional walks (6) and pitches seen (2,388)

# Paul Sorrento

## 1995 Season

To say the least, 1995 was a streaky year for Paul Sorrento. He set career highs in both homers and RBI, but his .235 batting average was his lowest in four seasons with Cleveland. The year started like a dream for him. Ten of his first 21 hits were homers, and he drove in 21 runs in his first 15 games. But at the end of the year, he went 0-for-29 after straining his right hamstring and left rib cage.

## Hitting

The left-handed Sorrento's mechanics have to be perfect to produce. When they are, and he hits the ball in front of his body instead of getting jammed by fastballs and sliders, he has good power to right field. But when his mechanics are bad, he lunges at the ball too quickly. Late in the year, pitchers baffled him with sliders, change-ups and breaking balls away, as his swing grew long and slow. He also struggled against lefties. After hitting a respectable .270 against them in 1994, he hit just .163 last year.

## Baserunning & Defense

Sorrento has below-average speed. He's not going to clog the bases, but he's not going to beat out a lot of infield hits, either. He's turned himself into a solid defensive first baseman, excellent at digging low throws out of the dirt. But his range is lacking. He tries to make up for it, making diving stops on almost any ball that requires him to take more than three steps. Those plays look good, but couldn't prevent him from making seven errors last year.

## 1996 Outlook

The Indians did not pick up the option on Sorrento's contract. It appears they're willing to trade his power for a hitter who isn't vulnerable to so many hot and cold streaks. If for some reason he does return, he'll give them what he always has—power in streaks. But the Tribe will want him to come to camp in better shape. They felt his injuries at the end of the season were due to lack of conditioning.

**Position:** 1B
**Bats:** L  **Throws:** R
**Ht:** 6' 2"  **Wt:** 220

**Opening Day Age:** 30
**Born:** 11/17/65 in Somerville, MA
**ML Seasons:** 7

### Overall Statistics

|  | G | AB | R | H | D | T | HR | RBI | SB | BB | SO | Avg | OBP | Slg |
|---|---|---|---|---|---|---|---|---|---|---|---|---|---|---|
| 1995 | 104 | 323 | 50 | 76 | 14 | 0 | 25 | 79 | 1 | 51 | 71 | .235 | .336 | .511 |
| Career | 568 | 1755 | 239 | 450 | 84 | 3 | 84 | 293 | 5 | 215 | 395 | .256 | .336 | .451 |

### Where He Hits the Ball

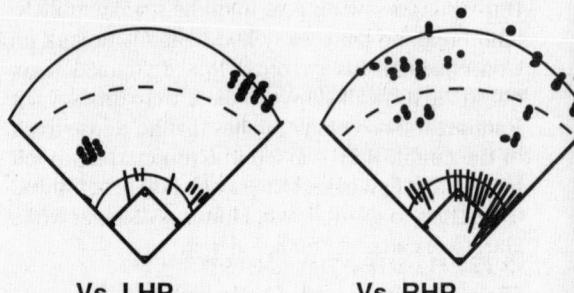

**Vs. LHP**          **Vs. RHP**

### 1995 Situational Stats

|  | AB | H | HR | RBI | Avg |  | AB | H | HR | RBI | Avg |
|---|---|---|---|---|---|---|---|---|---|---|---|
| Home | 161 | 37 | 12 | 38 | .230 | LHP | 43 | 7 | 2 | 14 | .163 |
| Road | 162 | 39 | 13 | 41 | .241 | RHP | 280 | 69 | 23 | 65 | .246 |
| First Half | 159 | 41 | 13 | 41 | .258 | Sc Pos | 100 | 26 | 6 | 51 | .260 |
| Scnd Half | 164 | 35 | 12 | 38 | .213 | Clutch | 47 | 12 | 3 | 12 | .255 |

### 1995 Rankings (American League)

➡ 4th in errors at first base (7) and lowest fielding percentage at first base (.992)
➡ 8th in batting average on a 3-1 count (.583)
➡ 10th in highest percentage of pitches taken (61.7%)
➡ Led the Indians in intentional walks (6), batting average with the bases loaded (.364), batting average on a 3-1 count (.583) and highest percentage of pitches taken (61.7%)

# Jim Thome

## 1995 Season

Jim Thome was another hitter who flourished at the bottom of the Tribe's lineup. The left-handed hitting Thome is big, strong and hit some home runs that had to be seen to be believed. He grew to be a very patient hitter, walking 47 times after August 1. In addition, he was remarkably consistent throughout the season, hitting over .300 in May, June, July and August.

## Hitting

Thome has a swift, powerful swing. He's susceptible to split-fingers and sinking fastballs (he'll swing over them), and cut fastballs and sliders in on his hands, but he'll crush mistakes. Thome has finally learned to turn on the ball and drive it to right field, but his natural power is still from left-center to right-center. Pitchers stopped challenging him in the second half, and he adjusted by walking more, but the Indians want to see him swing the bat. Given a chance to face more lefties, Thome responded, hitting .275. He was rested only against certain lefties such as Randy Johnson.

## Baserunning & Defense

Thome has good speed for a man his size. He gets down the line quickly, and has caught more than one infield napping. He's not much of a threat to steal, but is far from brain dead on the bases. Thome's range and mobility at third are good, he comes in well on bunts and choppers, and he can go down the line and into foul territory to catch a foul pop. His problems stem from spurts of erratic throwing. When he stays low and throws from the side, he's fine. But when he stands upright and throws, he's in trouble.

## 1996 Outlook

Just 25, Thome should do nothing but get better. He's clearly a potential All-Star who just might be a 100-RBI guy if he hits higher in the batting order. It remains to be seen if he'll be a consistent .300 hitter, but all the tools are there.

**Position:** 3B
**Bats:** L **Throws:** R
**Ht:** 6' 4" **Wt:** 220

**Opening Day Age:** 25
**Born:** 8/27/70 in Peoria, IL
**ML Seasons:** 5
**Pronunciation:** TOE-mee

### Overall Statistics

|  | G | AB | R | H | D | T | HR | RBI | SB | BB | SO | Avg | OBP | Slg |
|---|---|---|---|---|---|---|---|---|---|---|---|---|---|---|
| 1995 | 137 | 452 | 92 | 142 | 29 | 3 | 25 | 73 | 4 | 97 | 113 | .314 | .438 | .558 |
| Career | 349 | 1142 | 193 | 318 | 67 | 7 | 55 | 168 | 12 | 187 | 283 | .278 | .382 | .494 |

### Where He Hits the Ball

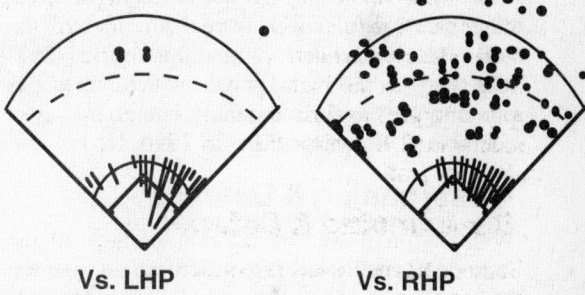

**Vs. LHP**          **Vs. RHP**

### 1995 Situational Stats

|  | AB | H | HR | RBI | Avg |  | AB | H | HR | RBI | Avg |
|---|---|---|---|---|---|---|---|---|---|---|---|
| Home | 226 | 69 | 13 | 37 | .305 | LHP | 109 | 30 | 3 | 13 | .275 |
| Road | 226 | 73 | 12 | 36 | .323 | RHP | 343 | 112 | 22 | 60 | .327 |
| First Half | 212 | 70 | 17 | 39 | .330 | Sc Pos | 124 | 30 | 8 | 51 | .242 |
| Scnd Half | 240 | 72 | 8 | 34 | .300 | Clutch | 72 | 26 | 6 | 16 | .361 |

### 1995 Rankings (American League)

- ➡ 1st in on-base percentage vs. right-handed pitchers (.456)
- ➡ 3rd in on-base percentage and errors at third base (16)
- ➡ 4th in lowest fielding percentage at third base (.948)
- ➡ 5th in walks, most pitches seen per plate appearance (4.23) and slugging percentage vs. right-handed pitchers (.601)
- ➡ 7th in batting average vs. right-handed pitchers (.327) and batting average on the road (.323)
- ➡ Led the Indians in walks, strikeouts and on-base percentage

Cleveland Indians

# Omar Vizquel

## 1995 Season

Omar Vizquel had another Gold Glove season at shortstop in 1995, playing the position differently than most. For one thing, he makes more bare-handed plays than anyone in the league. After watching him in the ALCS, Seattle manager Lou Piniella said, "The guy doesn't need to use a glove." In addition, Vizquel set career highs in homers, stolen bases and RBI, hitting in the number-two spot behind Kenny Lofton.

## Hitting

Vizquel is a switch-hitter who doesn't scare anybody with his bat, but does do enough to get by. He hit well with runners in scoring position, especially with two outs. Vizquel is mostly a spray hitter, with equal punch from both sides of the plate. He's a good breaking-ball hitter, so pitchers rely more on the high fastball, which Vizquel is prone to pop up. He's a quality bunter, and even contributed 10 sacrifice flies in 1995.

### Baserunning & Defense

With Lofton slowed by leg injuries most of the season, Vizquel took it upon himself to give the Tribe some speed at the top of the lineup. He stole bases with his head rather than his feet, since he had to be careful not to run the Tribe's big hitters out of too many innings. In the field, he has great range going to the hole or behind the bag. Vizquel is fearless when he has to turn the double play and gets rid of the ball quickly, which makes up for not having a cannon arm. Like teammate Kenny Lofton, Vizquel picked up his third Gold Glove in as many years.

## 1996 Outlook

The Indians will probably drop Vizquel down to the number-nine spot in the batting order, since defense is what he clearly does best. He's what former Tribe manager Doc Edwards calls a "100-RBI man"—he'll drive in 50, and save 50 with his glove. Cleveland picked up his option for 1996, but after that he might be too expensive for them to keep. The front office thinks he doesn't hit enough to justify $3.35 million a year, but teammates would disagree.

**Position:** SS
**Bats:** B   **Throws:** R
**Ht:** 5' 9"   **Wt:** 165

**Opening Day Age:** 28
**Born:** 4/24/67 in Caracas, VZ
**ML Seasons:** 7
**Pronunciation:** viz-KELL

### Overall Statistics

| | G | AB | R | H | D | T | HR | RBI | SB | BB | SO | Avg | OBP | Slg |
|---|---|---|---|---|---|---|---|---|---|---|---|---|---|---|
| 1995 | 136 | 542 | 87 | 144 | 28 | 0 | 6 | 56 | 29 | 59 | 59 | .266 | .333 | .351 |
| Career | 865 | 2939 | 349 | 753 | 98 | 16 | 13 | 220 | 81 | 255 | 290 | .256 | .315 | .314 |

### Where He Hits the Ball

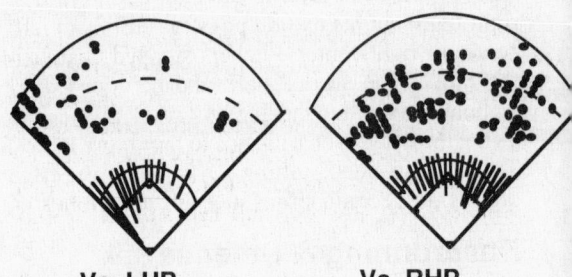

**Vs. LHP**          **Vs. RHP**

### 1995 Situational Stats

| | AB | H | HR | RBI | Avg | | AB | H | HR | RBI | Avg |
|---|---|---|---|---|---|---|---|---|---|---|---|
| Home | 258 | 69 | 3 | 28 | .267 | LHP | 168 | 44 | 2 | 19 | .262 |
| Road | 284 | 75 | 3 | 28 | .264 | RHP | 374 | 100 | 4 | 37 | .267 |
| First Half | 272 | 70 | 4 | 26 | .257 | Sc Pos | 140 | 41 | 1 | 51 | .293 |
| Scnd Half | 270 | 74 | 2 | 30 | .274 | Clutch | 74 | 19 | 1 | 6 | .257 |

### 1995 Rankings (American League)

- ➠ 3rd in fielding percentage at shortstop (.986)
- ➠ 5th in sacrifice bunts (10), sacrifice flies (10) and lowest slugging percentage
- ➠ 6th in least GDPs per GDP situation (4.7%) and lowest slugging percentage vs. right-handed pitchers (.340)
- ➠ 7th in caught stealing (11)
- ➠ 8th in highest percentage of swings put into play (53.1%)
- ➠ 9th in lowest HR frequency (90.3 ABs per HR) and bunts in play (23)
- ➠ 10th in stolen bases
- ➠ Led the Indians in sacrifice bunts (10), sacrifice flies (10) and least GDPs per GDP situation (4.7%)

# Alan Embree

**Position:** RP
**Bats:** L  **Throws:** L
**Ht:** 6' 2"  **Wt:** 190

**Opening Day Age:** 26
**Born:** 1/23/70 in
Vancouver, WA
**ML Seasons:** 2

*Overall Statistics*

| | W | L | Pct. | ERA | G | GS | Sv | IP | H | BB | SO | HR | BR/IP |
|---|---|---|------|-----|---|----|----|----|----|----|----|----|-------|
| 1995 | 3 | 2 | .600 | 5.11 | 23 | 0 | 1 | 24.2 | 23 | 16 | 23 | 2 | 1.58 |
| Career | 3 | 4 | .429 | 5.91 | 27 | 4 | 1 | 42.2 | 42 | 24 | 35 | 5 | 1.55 |

## 1995 Season

Alan Embree made three different trips between Cleveland and Triple-A last year. But while he was outstanding at Buffalo, he never made a big mark with the Indians. To be fair, he pitched better than his statistics would indicate, as September disasters against Boston and Minnesota ballooned his ERA. Prior to that, he had put together 10 straight scoreless appearances from late August to mid-September.

## Pitching & Defense

A hard-throwing lefty, Embree was used mostly in the late innings to face left-handed power hitters, relying on his fastball and slider against them. The low-90s fastball is his best pitch, and since most left-handed power hitters like the ball at the knees, Embree uses his arm strength to challenge them high in the strike zone. He missed most of the 1993 season following ligament transplant surgery, but his elbow has come back. He's a decent fielder but not very good at holding runners.

## 1996 Outlook

Except for his September slump, Embree did everything right last year. His performance should be enough to win a spot in the bullpen this year, especially considering the way he helped neutralize Atlanta's left-handed bats in the World Series. He can also back up Jose Mesa as a closer.

# Wayne Kirby

**Position:** RF/CF
**Bats:** L  **Throws:** R
**Ht:** 5'10"  **Wt:** 190

**Opening Day Age:** 32
**Born:** 1/22/64 in
Williamsburg, VA
**ML Seasons:** 5

*Overall Statistics*

| | G | AB | R | H | D | T | HR | RBI | SB | BB | SO | Avg | OBP | Slg |
|---|----|-----|-----|-----|----|---|----|-----|----|----|-----|------|------|------|
| 1995 | 101 | 188 | 29 | 39 | 10 | 2 | 1 | 14 | 10 | 13 | 32 | .207 | .260 | .298 |
| Career | 352 | 898 | 146 | 230 | 38 | 7 | 13 | 103 | 39 | 68 | 128 | .256 | .309 | .357 |

## 1995 Season

Wayne Kirby was a major disappointment to the Indians in 1995. After spending 10 seasons in the minors fighting to get to the majors, Kirby made the big leagues to stay in 1993. He followed with a good 1994 season and was rewarded with a multi-year deal last spring. The new contract seemed to make him complacent. When Kenny Lofton was injured after the All-Star break, the Tribe needed Kirby to fill the leadoff spot, but he hit just .168 in that role.

## Hitting, Baserunning & Defense

Kirby looked lost at the plate last year. His swing was long and lazy, and he was easy prey to inside breaking balls. The fastballs he used to drive into the gaps, he simply missed. But he still has good speed, and next to Lofton is the best basestealer on the club. Defensively, Kirby played all three outfield positions with center and right his strongest. His arm is strong with a quick release, but his accuracy needs to improve.

## 1996 Outlook

Kirby, who took to jogging to first base on routine grounders, may have played himself right off one of the best teams in baseball. The Tribe has two left-handed-hitting outfielders—Brian Giles and Jeromy Burnitz—waiting for a chance. Kirby may have given it to them.

# Albie Lopez

**Position**: RP
**Bats**: R  **Throws**: R
**Ht**: 6' 2"  **Wt**: 205

**Opening Day Age**: 24
**Born**: 8/18/71 in Mesa, AZ
**ML Seasons**: 3

## Overall Statistics

|  | W | L | Pct. | ERA | G | GS | Sv | IP | H | BB | SO | HR | BR/IP |
|---|---|---|---|---|---|---|---|---|---|---|---|---|---|
| 1995 | 0 | 0 | - | 3.13 | 6 | 2 | 0 | 23.0 | 17 | 7 | 22 | 4 | 1.04 |
| Career | 4 | 3 | .571 | 4.92 | 19 | 15 | 0 | 89.2 | 86 | 45 | 65 | 14 | 1.46 |

## 1995 Season

Righthander Albie Lopez spent most of the year at Triple-A Buffalo, where he sulked because he wasn't in Cleveland. The fact that he went 5-10 in Buffalo didn't seem to bother him. In all, he was called up three times—the first two were temporary, but his September call-up was to check him out for next year. After all the complaining, he strained his right biceps muscle and was unable to pitch after making just one start.

## Pitching & Defense

Lopez has a good fastball, which he can throw between 92-95 MPH, and a good curveball, with the fastball being his better pitch. The Indians have been trying to get him to throw a change-up, with mixed results. There are also questions about Lopez's heart, and fears that he may bail in tough situations on the mound. He's an ordinary fielder, and didn't get to pitch enough last season to show his fundamentals.

## 1996 Outlook

Lopez has a bad attitude, but he has one thing working in his favor—he's out of options. The Indians must keep him on their roster this year or risk losing him through waivers. He has a great young arm, but don't be surprised if the Indians trade him. The team was just two wins short of a world championship in 1995, and they don't need the headache.

# Tony Pena

**Position**: C
**Bats**: R  **Throws**: R
**Ht**: 6' 0"  **Wt**: 185

**Opening Day Age**: 38
**Born**: 6/4/57 in Monte Cristi, DR
**ML Seasons**: 16
**Nickname**: El Gato

## Overall Statistics

|  | G | AB | R | H | D | T | HR | RBI | SB | BB | SO | Avg | OBP | Slg |
|---|---|---|---|---|---|---|---|---|---|---|---|---|---|---|
| 1995 | 91 | 263 | 25 | 69 | 15 | 0 | 5 | 28 | 1 | 14 | 44 | .262 | .302 | .376 |
| Career | 1881 | 6229 | 647 | 1638 | 290 | 27 | 106 | 671 | 80 | 430 | 805 | .263 | .311 | .369 |

## 1995 Season

For the second straight year, Tony Pena bailed the Indians out by catching the staff while Sandy Alomar recovered from knee surgery. Pena's biggest moment came during Game 1 of the playoffs against Boston, when he won the game with a homer in the 13th inning. He did nothing to hurt his reputation as a tireless worker and a good influence in the clubhouse.

## Hitting, Baserunning & Defense

Pena still has the all-or-nothing swing which netted him five homers off fastballs high in the strike zone. He always hits the ball hard, but that results in a lot of double plays. Pena also runs hard, but his age and catcher's knees are big barriers. He's one of the best when it comes to handling pitchers, but his once-feared throwing arm has faded, as he threw out just 21 percent of runners attempting to steal. How well does he handle a staff? The Tribe's ERA with Pena catching was 3.38, compared to 4.40 with Alomar.

## 1996 Outlook

Pena filed for free agency after the season. The Indians would like to bring him back to keep the peace in the clubhouse and fill in for Alomar. Pena was hurt when the Indians didn't let him catch Dennis Martinez in the Boston series. But in Game 6 of the ALCS, the starting battery was Martinez and Pena.

# Herbert Perry

**Position:** 1B
**Bats:** R  **Throws:** R
**Ht:** 6' 2"  **Wt:** 215

**Opening Day Age:** 26
**Born:** 9/15/69 in Live Oak, FL
**ML Seasons:** 2

### Overall Statistics

|  | G | AB | R | H | D | T | HR | RBI | SB | BB | SO | Avg | OBP | Slg |
|---|---|---|---|---|---|---|---|---|---|---|---|---|---|---|
| 1995 | 52 | 162 | 23 | 51 | 13 | 1 | 3 | 23 | 1 | 13 | 28 | .315 | .376 | .463 |
| Career | 56 | 171 | 24 | 52 | 13 | 1 | 3 | 24 | 1 | 16 | 29 | .304 | .374 | .444 |

## 1995 Season

Herbert Perry fell into something good when future Hall of Famer Dave Winfield went on the disabled list with a strained left rotator cuff on June 11. Perry was promoted from Triple-A Buffalo and spent the rest of the year in the big leagues, playing first base against lefties. In his sixth big-league game on June 17, he went 3-for-4 with two homers off New York lefty Andy Pettitte. He was solid the rest of the way.

## Hitting, Baserunning & Defense

Perry's big body says home run, but he's more of a line-drive hitter with gap power. He's a good fastball hitter, but also showed the ability to take breaking balls into right field. He's nothing special as a baserunner, but the Indians say he's the best defensive first baseman in the organization. Perry picks balls out of the dirt with ease, and goes to the line well. His arm is good enough to start the 3-6-3 double play.

## 1996 Outlook

If the Indians don't pick up Paul Sorrento's option, they could give the full-time first base job to Perry. If they don't think he's ready, he could share it again in a platoon situation, or make the club as an extra player off the bench. Whatever direction they choose to go, it appears Perry has earned a spot on the club.

# Jim Poole

**Position:** RP
**Bats:** L  **Throws:** L
**Ht:** 6' 2"  **Wt:** 203

**Opening Day Age:** 29
**Born:** 4/28/66 in Rochester, NY
**ML Seasons:** 6

### Overall Statistics

|  | W | L | Pct. | ERA | G | GS | Sv | IP | H | BB | SO | HR | BR/IP |
|---|---|---|---|---|---|---|---|---|---|---|---|---|---|
| 1995 | 3 | 3 | .500 | 3.75 | 42 | 0 | 0 | 50.1 | 40 | 17 | 41 | 7 | 1.13 |
| Career | 9 | 6 | .600 | 3.25 | 186 | 0 | 3 | 177.0 | 141 | 70 | 135 | 17 | 1.19 |

## 1995 Season

After a horrible year with Baltimore in 1994, Jim Poole redeemed himself with the Indians. Signed during the strike to a minor league contract, Poole started the year at Triple-A but returned to spring training when the big leaguers were invited back to work by the owners. He made the club and was part of an effective one-two-three left-handed bullpen punch, as batters hit just .217 against him. Most of that dominance came at Jacobs Field, where Poole's ERA was an incredible four-and-a-half runs lower than his figure on the road.

## Pitching & Defense

The key to Poole's season was the return of his curveball. He's got a pretty good one—good enough to make lefties look helpless—but it vanished during his 1994 slide. Poole also throws a fastball, but if he leaves it up in the strike zone it gets crushed. He gave up seven homers in just over 50 innings of work last season.

## 1996 Outlook

Look for Poole to be back in the same role this year. If not, the Indians might sign him, as he was eligible for arbitration at the end of last year, and then trade him. Lefties who can get people out are a hot commodity in the majors. The only roadblock for Poole might be offseason elbow surgery.

Cleveland Indians

# Julian Tavarez

**Position:** RP
**Bats:** R **Throws:** R
**Ht:** 6' 2" **Wt:** 165

**Opening Day Age:** 22
**Born:** 5/22/73 in Santiago, DR
**ML Seasons:** 3

### Overall Statistics

| | W | L | Pct. | ERA | G | GS | Sv | IP | H | BB | SO | HR | BR/IP |
|---|---|---|---|---|---|---|---|---|---|---|---|---|---|
| 1995 | 10 | 2 | .833 | 2.44 | 57 | 0 | 0 | 85.0 | 76 | 21 | 68 | 7 | 1.14 |
| Career | 12 | 5 | .706 | 3.93 | 66 | 8 | 0 | 123.2 | 135 | 35 | 87 | 15 | 1.37 |

## 1995 Season

Julian Tavarez' 10 wins were the most ever by a rookie reliever for the Tribe. He played a key role, along with Eric Plunk, as right-handed set-up man for closer Jose Mesa. A starter throughout his minor league career, Tavarez adapted to the bullpen quickly. The Indians were 43-14 when he pitched, and righties batted just .205 against him. Cleveland's habit of making late-inning comebacks helped Tavarez win his first six decisions before losing a game.

## Pitching & Defense

Tavarez has a good repertoire of pitches—a fastball, sinker and slider. He usually throws his fastball between 89-93 MPH, and his long, lean arms allow him to get a lot of sinking action on his pitches. Tavarez struggled defensively, especially on balls hit to or near the mound. He doesn't have a great move to first, but his quick delivery to the plate helped catchers throw out three of the five runners who tried to steal against him.

## 1996 Outlook

If the Indians don't sign a big-name free agent over the winter, Tavarez will likely shift to the rotation. If not, the Indians would be happy to keep him in the role in which he thrived last year. His consideration for Rookie of the Year was very well deserved.

# Dave Winfield

**Position:** DH
**Bats:** R **Throws:** R
**Ht:** 6' 6" **Wt:** 245

**Opening Day Age:** 44
**Born:** 10/3/51 in St. Paul, MN
**ML Seasons:** 22

### Overall Statistics

| | G | AB | R | H | D | T | HR | RBI | SB | BB | SO | Avg | OBP | Slg |
|---|---|---|---|---|---|---|---|---|---|---|---|---|---|---|
| 1995 | 46 | 115 | 11 | 22 | 5 | 0 | 2 | 4 | 1 | 14 | 26 | .191 | .285 | .287 |
| Career | 2973 | 11003 | 1669 | 3110 | 540 | 88 | 465 | 1833 | 223 | 1216 | 1686 | .283 | .353 | .475 |

## 1995 Season

Stick a fork in Dave Winfield. He's done. The future Hall of Famer suffered through the worst season of his career in 1995. First, he showed he couldn't fill his role on the club—ride the bench and face one or two lefties a week. Then he tore the rotator cuff in his left shoulder while trying to steal a base. Finally, he was left off the Tribe's postseason roster.

## Hitting, Baserunning & Defense

Winfield's swing is so long that he couldn't possibly stay sharp by getting four to eight at-bats a week. He had a good spring, but once his playing time decreased it was embarrassing to watch him play. At 43, he couldn't catch up with a fastball and offspeed pitchers made him look silly. Surprisingly, he could still run well enough to beat out infield singles. The former Gold Glove winner hasn't played right field regularly for over two years.

## 1996 Outlook

Hopefully, Winfield will retire and head to Cooperstown. He ended last year knowing he needed surgery on his left shoulder and upset that the Indians didn't put him on the postseason roster. But in a show of class, Winfield, at the request of his teammates, traveled and dressed with the club to offer support on the bench and in the clubhouse.

# Other Cleveland Indians

### Ruben Amaro (**Pos**: CF, **Age**: 31, **Bats**: B)

With a .227 lifetime batting average and not much power, Amaro's not in much danger of winning a full-time job. He is a useful bench player, with decent speed and good defense. 1996 Outlook: C

### Bud Black (**Pos**: LHP, **Age**: 38)

Beset by injuries the last four seasons, Black finally drew his release last July. He remained with the Indians as a coach without portfolio, and was in uniform for the World Series. 1996 Outlook: D

### Jeromy Burnitz (**Pos**: LF, **Age**: 26, **Bats**: L)

Once a decent prospect with the Mets, Burnitz hit the cover off the ball in Triple-A Buffalo (.284-19-85), but of course there was no room for him in the Indians outfield. Should play somewhere. 1996 Outlook: B

### Alvaro Espinoza (**Pos**: 2B/3B, **Age**: 34, **Bats**: R)

He's a terrible hitter, but Espinoza can play three infield positions and the Indians seem to like him. Should fill a utility role again this season. 1996 Outlook: A

### John Farrell (**Pos**: RHP, **Age**: 33)

He was an Indian for the down years; now John Farrell is trying to make it back with Cleveland for the up years. Started 28 games last year for Buffalo, with a 4.54 ERA. 1996 Outlook: C

### Jason Grimsley (**Pos**: RHP, **Age**: 28)

Grimsley pitched very well in 10 starts with Buffalo last season (5-3, 2.91), not so well in Cleveland (6.09 ERA in 15 games). He's still got a decent arm, but time is running out. 1996 Outlook: B

### Jesse Levis (**Pos**: C, **Age**: 27, **Bats**: L)

A .297 career hitter in the minor leagues, Levis has been held back by his defense. If Tony Pena ever retires, Levis is first in line to serve as Alomar's backup. 1996 Outlook: B

### Billy Ripken (**Pos**: 2B, **Age**: 31, **Bats**: R)

Always a second baseman in the majors, Ripken played shortstop last year in Buffalo, and played it well. He's just as good a hitter as Espinoza and three years younger, and might win a utility job. 1996 Outlook: B

### Joe Roa (**Pos**: RHP, **Age**: 24)

He's pitched well at nearly every stop in the minors, but Roa doesn't have a great arm so he's not a hot prospect. He *did* go 17-3 with Buffalo last season, which should impress someone, somewhere. 1996 Outlook: B

### Paul Shuey (**Pos**: RHP, **Age**: 25)

Shuey was briefly the Indians' closer in 1994, but the emergence of Jose Mesa relegated Shuey to Buffalo most of last season. He pitched well when healthy, striking out 27 batters in as many innings. 1996 Outlook: B

### Scooter Tucker (**Pos**:C, **Age**: 29, **Bats**: R)

Tucker opened last season with Houston, was traded to the Indians, released in late June, and signed by the Braves. Sent straight to Triple-A Richmond, Tucker rarely played as Eddie Perez' backup. 1996 Outlook: C

# Cleveland Indians Minor League Prospects

## Organization Overview:

For years the poster child for mismanagement and front-office ineptitude, Cleveland is suddenly baseball's model organization. General manager John Hart anticipated and successfully dealt with the game's changing economics when he signed key players such as Carlos Baerga, Kenny Lofton and Albert Belle to long-term contracts a few years back. He and the organization made the decision to reverse decades of inconsistency with a commitment to their youthful talent base. In addition, the Indians improved their minor league system through a series of successful drafts which produced budding stars such as Manny Ramirez and Jim Thome, as well as a horde of quality arms. It is the pitching which now appears to be the organization's strength, and the Indians hope that pitching will eventually provide a nice balance to Cleveland's already potent offensive lineup. The Indians appear poised for a successful ride the next few years, quite a change after decades of floundering.

### Bartolo Colon

**Position:** P
**Bats:** R **Throws:** R
**Ht:** 6' 0" **Wt:** 185
**Opening Day Age:** 20
**Born:** 5/24/75 in Altamira, DR

*Recent Statistics*

|  | W | L | ERA | G | GS | Sv | IP | H | R | BB | SO | HR |
|---|---|---|---|---|---|---|---|---|---|---|---|---|
| 94 R Burlington | 7 | 4 | 3.14 | 12 | 12 | 0 | 66.0 | 46 | 32 | 44 | 84 | 3 |
| 95 A Kinston | 13 | 3 | 1.96 | 21 | 21 | 0 | 128.2 | 91 | 31 | 39 | 152 | 8 |

Colon was signed as a free agent in 1993. He has flat-out dominated both leagues in which he has pitched, and was named the Carolina League's Pitcher of the Year for 1995. Colon may be the hardest-throwing pitcher in the system, yet he maintains remarkable control. Although he missed the last month of the season, Colon still led the Carolina League in strikeouts and fell just one win short of leading in victories. He needs to work on his curve and change-up, but the future looks bright.

### Einar Diaz

**Position:** C
**Bats:** R **Throws:** R
**Ht:** 5' 10" **Wt:** 165
**Opening Day Age:** 23
**Born:** 12/28/72 in Chiriqui Rep., Panama

*Recent Statistics*

|  | G | AB | R | H | D | T | HR | RBI | SB | BB | SO | AVG |
|---|---|---|---|---|---|---|---|---|---|---|---|---|
| 93 R Burlington | 60 | 231 | 40 | 69 | 15 | 3 | 5 | 33 | 7 | 8 | 7 | .299 |
| 93 A Columbus | 1 | 5 | 0 | 0 | 0 | 0 | 0 | 0 | 0 | 0 | 1 | .000 |
| 94 A Columbus | 120 | 491 | 67 | 137 | 23 | 2 | 16 | 71 | 4 | 17 | 34 | .279 |
| 95 A Kinston | 104 | 373 | 46 | 98 | 21 | 0 | 6 | 43 | 3 | 12 | 29 | .263 |

Diaz was originally signed as a free-agent third baseman, but the Indians decided to make him a catcher in 1993. The results have been encouraging. Diaz was voted the South Atlantic League's best defensive catcher in 1994, and he's enjoyed success in throwing out runners. Offensively, Diaz has demonstrated extra-base power, with a high of 16 homers in '94. He rarely walks, however, and his on-base percentage dipped below .300 in '95. Still, his defensive ability alone may be enough to earn Diaz an eventual major league audition.

### Brian Giles

**Position:** OF
**Bats:** L **Throws:** L
**Ht:** 5' 11" **Wt:** 195
**Opening Day Age:** 25
**Born:** 1/20/71 in El Cajon, CA

*Recent Statistics*

|  | G | AB | R | H | D | T | HR | RBI | SB | BB | SO | AVG |
|---|---|---|---|---|---|---|---|---|---|---|---|---|
| 95 AAA Buffalo | 123 | 413 | 67 | 128 | 18 | 8 | 15 | 67 | 7 | 54 | 40 | .310 |
| 95 AL Cleveland | 6 | 9 | 6 | 5 | 0 | 0 | 1 | 3 | 0 | 0 | 1 | .556 |
| 95 MLE | 123 | 409 | 65 | 124 | 18 | 6 | 14 | 65 | 5 | 51 | 41 | .303 |

Giles hasn't received a lot of notice, but since he was drafted in the 17th round back in 1989 he has been a career .306 hitter in the minors, with lots of walks and continually improving slugging averages. Giles' last three seasons in Double- and Triple-A have been his best, and he slugged over .500 at Buffalo last year. Giles has nothing left to prove in the minors, but he faces a tough nut to crack in the talented Cleveland outfield. He may have to go to another organization to get a major league shot.

### Damian Jackson

**Position:** SS
**Bats:** R **Throws:** R
**Ht:** 5' 10" **Wt:** 160
**Opening Day Age:** 22
**Born:** 8/16/73 in Los Angeles, CA

*Recent Statistics*

|  | G | AB | R | H | D | T | HR | RBI | SB | BB | SO | AVG |
|---|---|---|---|---|---|---|---|---|---|---|---|---|
| 93 A Columbus | 108 | 350 | 70 | 94 | 19 | 3 | 6 | 45 | 26 | 41 | 61 | .269 |
| 94 AA Canton-Akrn | 138 | 531 | 85 | 143 | 29 | 5 | 5 | 46 | 37 | 60 | 121 | .269 |
| 95 AA Canton-Akrn | 131 | 484 | 67 | 120 | 20 | 2 | 3 | 34 | 40 | 65 | 103 | .248 |
| 95 MLE | 131 | 477 | 63 | 113 | 20 | 1 | 2 | 32 | 30 | 51 | 108 | .237 |

The Indians have two young, talented shortstop prospects in Jackson and Enrique Wilson. Jackson is a couple of years older and one level more advanced, but though he repeated Double-A in 1995, Jackson's offensive production actually regressed. Jackson doesn't hit with as much power as Wilson, but he walks far more often and has averaged 33 stolen bases a year in his four professional seasons. Jackson wasn't drafted until the 44th round in 1991, but he has the quick hands and strong arm necessary to be a big-league shortstop. The question will be if he can stay ahead of Wilson in the Indians' system.

## Richie Sexson

**Position:** 1B          **Opening Day Age:** 21
**Bats:** R **Throws:** R   **Born:** 12/29/74 in
**Ht:** 6' 6" **Wt:** 206    Portland, OR

*Recent Statistics*

| | G | AB | R | H | D | T | HR | RBI | SB | BB | SO | AVG |
|---|---|---|---|---|---|---|---|---|---|---|---|---|
| 93 R Burlington | 40 | 97 | 11 | 18 | 3 | 0 | 1 | 5 | 1 | 18 | 21 | .186 |
| 94 A Columbus | 130 | 488 | 88 | 133 | 25 | 2 | 14 | 77 | 7 | 37 | 87 | .273 |
| 95 A Kinston | 131 | 494 | 80 | 151 | 34 | 0 | 22 | 85 | 4 | 43 | 115 | .306 |

Sexson is yet another prospect from the dynamite Kinston club which romped to the Carolina League championship. Sexson provided much of the power, leading the team in doubles, slugging and RBI. He was the Indians' 24th-round draft choice in 1993 after playing shortstop in high school. He now plays first base and continues to fill out a rangy 6'6" frame. He has gotten better each season since being drafted, and projects as a legitimate home-run threat.

## Casey Whitten

**Position:** P          **Opening Day Age:** 23
**Bats:** L **Throws:** L   **Born:** 5/23/72 in
**Ht:** 6' 0" **Wt:** 175    Evansville, IN

*Recent Statistics*

| | W | L | ERA | G | GS | Sv | IP | H | R | BB | SO | HR |
|---|---|---|---|---|---|---|---|---|---|---|---|---|
| 93 A Watertown | 6 | 3 | 2.42 | 14 | 14 | 0 | 81.2 | 75 | 28 | 18 | 81 | 8 |
| 94 A Kinston | 9 | 10 | 4.28 | 27 | 27 | 0 | 153.1 | 127 | 78 | 64 | 148 | 21 |
| 95 AA Cantn-Akrn | 9 | 8 | 3.31 | 20 | 20 | 0 | 114.1 | 100 | 49 | 38 | 91 | 10 |

The Indians have had so many pitching prospects in their system recently that Whitten hasn't gotten as much attention as he might in another organization. Whitten was chosen in the second round of 1993, the same year Cleveland landed hard-throwing Daron Kirkreit in round one. They've risen together in the minors, but Whitten has enjoyed the greater success. Whitten has displayed fine control, a hard breaking ball, and has gotten many of his strikeouts by changing speeds effectively. The next logical step is Triple-A, but the majors may not be far away for a lefthander with his live arm.

## Enrique Wilson

**Position:** SS          **Opening Day Age:** 20
**Bats:** B **Throws:** R   **Born:** 7/27/75 in Santo
**Ht:** 5' 11" **Wt:** 160    Domingo, DR

*Recent Statistics*

| | G | AB | R | H | D | T | HR | RBI | SB | BB | SO | AVG |
|---|---|---|---|---|---|---|---|---|---|---|---|---|
| 93 R Elizabethtn | 58 | 197 | 42 | 57 | 8 | 4 | 13 | 50 | 5 | 14 | 18 | .289 |
| 94 A Columbus | 133 | 512 | 82 | 143 | 28 | 12 | 10 | 72 | 21 | 44 | 34 | .279 |
| 95 A Kinston | 117 | 464 | 55 | 124 | 24 | 7 | 6 | 52 | 18 | 25 | 38 | .267 |

The Twins are still kicking themselves for trading Wilson to the Tribe for Shawn Bryant, a lefthander who is 9-10 with a 5.91 ERA since the swap. Wilson is yet another gifted middle infielder from the Dominican Republic, and he was named the best defensive shortstop in the Carolina League for 1995. He also shows the potential to be an above-average offensive shortstop for average and power. Wilson doesn't strike out much, but he also doesn't walk often, and his offensive production should improve if his plate discipline does likewise. Since he enters the 1996 season just 20 years of age, Wilson has plenty of time to elevate all areas of his game.

## Jaret Wright

**Position:** P          **Opening Day Age:** 20
**Bats:** R **Throws:** R   **Born:** 12/29/75 in
**Ht:** 6' 2" **Wt:** 220    Anaheim, CA

*Recent Statistics*

| | W | L | ERA | G | GS | Sv | IP | H | R | BB | SO | HR |
|---|---|---|---|---|---|---|---|---|---|---|---|---|
| 94 R Burlington | 0 | 1 | 5.40 | 4 | 4 | 0 | 13.1 | 13 | 10 | 9 | 16 | 1 |
| 95 A Columbus | 5 | 6 | 3.00 | 24 | 24 | 0 | 129.0 | 93 | 55 | 79 | 113 | 9 |

Wright is the son of former big-league pitcher Clyde Wright. Unlike his father, Jaret is righthanded and throws hard, with a fastball that registers in the mid-90s. The Indians selected Wright with the 10th pick overall in 1994, and paid enough money to talk him out of a scholarship to UCLA. In his limited pro experience, Wright has demonstrated he can be overpowering when he has his good curveball to complement the hard heater. He has shown the need for better control, which he should acquire as he gets more innings. The Indians believe Wright has the talent to be their ace within the next couple of years.

## Others to Watch

Third baseman **Russ Branyan**, the Indians' seventh-round selection in 1994, hit 19 home runs in the South Atlantic League last year at the age of 19. He also struck out 120 times in 277 at-bats... **Danny Graves** may have been the most dominant reliever in the minors last season, rocketing through three levels all the way up to Triple-A. On his way to collecting 31 saves, the Indians' 1994 fourth-round draft pick allowed just 45 hits and 15 walks in 70.1 innings, while compiling a 0.64 ERA... There was a good reason Cleveland's number one pick in 1993, righthander **Daren Kirkreit**, suffered a loss in velocity from the low 90s to high 80s last year. He had a rotator-cuff injury which doesn't appear career threatening. If he's healthy, Kirkreit can be dominating... First baseman/DH **Rod McCall** spent most of last season playing on a co-op team in the California League, where he smacked 20 homers. When the Indians promoted him to Double-A, he slugged another nine taters in just 95 at-bats... The Indians have done a great job stockpiling pitching prospects throughout their system. Righthander **Wilmer Montoya** saved 31 games in the South Atlantic League while striking out 91 in 80.2 innings... The Midas touch extended to righthander **Jeff Sexton**, who became a full-time starter in '95 and responded with an 11-3 record, a 2.33 ERA and a strikeout-to-walk ratio of five-to-one in Class A. He did all that at the age of 23, however.

# Danny Bautista

## 1995 Season

Baseball seasons come and go, but one problem remains the same—the Detroit Tigers are still waiting for a lot of their younger players to put their skills together. Danny Bautista continued to tease Detroit with flashes of ability in 1995, but his batting average, slugging percentage, and on-base percentage all took a tumble—so much so that the Tigers sent him back to Triple-A for much of August.

## Hitting

Bautista still has not made the adjustments needed to cope with the velocity of major league pitchers. Though he's not a chronic overswinger, Bautista has trouble hitting hard stuff up in the strike zone. So pitchers continue to challenge him with fastballs and pound him inside. Until he can catch up to those pitches, he'll never see the change-ups or breaking pitches against which he has more success. Bautista is also a very anxious hitter when he gets behind in the count, which is often. He struck out in over a quarter of his at-bats last year, and hit an abysmal .181 with runners in scoring position.

## Baserunning & Defense

On a team sorely lacking in athletic skill, Bautista stands out with his above-average speed. Unfortunately, he is a tentative basestealer who still lacks the technique and savvy necessary to be a major threat. But he has a chance to be an outstanding defensive outfielder, combining a center fielder's range with a right fielder's arm. He needs work on judging balls, however.

## 1996 Outlook

It's a whole new ballgame in Detroit, and for a young player with talent that can mean a whole new chance. Bautista has the physical tools and, at just 23 years of age, can still develop into a quality major league outfielder. But he no longer has the luxury of being protected by the Detroit organization simply because he's a rare home-grown product with potential. He needs to show improvement to stick around.

**Position:** RF
**Bats:** R  **Throws:** R
**Ht:** 5'11"  **Wt:** 170

**Opening Day Age:** 23
**Born:** 5/24/72 in Santo Domingo, DR
**ML Seasons:** 3
**Pronunciation:** bo-TEASE-tah

### Overall Statistics

|  | G | AB | R | H | D | T | HR | RBI | SB | BB | SO | Avg | OBP | Slg |
|---|---|---|---|---|---|---|---|---|---|---|---|---|---|---|
| 1995 | 89 | 271 | 28 | 55 | 9 | 0 | 7 | 27 | 4 | 12 | 68 | .203 | .237 | .314 |
| Career | 137 | 431 | 46 | 97 | 16 | 1 | 12 | 51 | 8 | 16 | 96 | .225 | .252 | .350 |

### Where He Hits the Ball

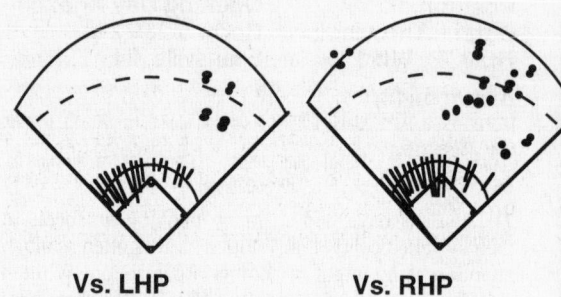

Vs. LHP          Vs. RHP

### 1995 Situational Stats

|  | AB | H | HR | RBI | Avg |  | AB | H | HR | RBI | Avg |
|---|---|---|---|---|---|---|---|---|---|---|---|
| Home | 136 | 23 | 3 | 9 | .169 | LHP | 95 | 18 | 4 | 9 | .189 |
| Road | 135 | 32 | 4 | 18 | .237 | RHP | 176 | 37 | 3 | 18 | .210 |
| First Half | 167 | 36 | 1 | 15 | .216 | Sc Pos | 83 | 15 | 1 | 18 | .181 |
| Scnd Half | 104 | 19 | 6 | 12 | .183 | Clutch | 35 | 5 | 0 | 2 | .143 |

### 1995 Rankings (American League)

➡ 2nd in lowest batting average with runners in scoring position (.181)
➡ 4th in lowest batting average with two strikes (.124)
➡ 5th in lowest batting average on an 0-2 count (.042)
➡ Led the Tigers in bunts in play (13)

# Sean Bergman

## 1995 Season

Part of a season-long youth movement on the Tiger pitching staff, Sean Bergman ended up getting more starts than any other Detroit pitcher in 1995. But his extended trial yielded very few positive results. Opposing hitters batted .307 against Bergman, who allowed a frightening 169 hits in just 135.1 innings. After struggling in limited trials with the Tigers the previous two seasons, this wasn't the way he had hoped to make his mark.

## Pitching

A sinker/slider pitcher with velocity in the high-80s, Bergman simply hasn't been consistent enough with his location to be effective. He pitches from behind in the count far too often, especially with his limited stuff, and it showed last year—Bergman led an awful Detroit staff in both walks and hits allowed. In the starts where Bergman was throwing strikes, he showed some potential, getting ground balls with the sinker and strikeouts with the slider. But all too often, he was up or out of the strike zone. Until he improves his command, he'll have difficulty being a consistent winner.

## Defense

Bergman does not have a good move to first, and his slow delivery home makes him very vulnerable to stolen bases. Runners simply did what they wanted against him in '95, stealing 25 bases in 28 attempts. He also needs work on his fielding, and needs to show more agility around the mound.

## 1996 Outlook

With Detroit's farm system still very thin, Bergman has been given every chance to develop into a rare home-grown starting pitcher. However, he's had just two seasons in his entire professional career in which his ERA was under 4.00, and last season's mediocre performance didn't help his chances. For the first time, other young Detroit pitchers have passed him in terms of potential, and Bergman will have a fight on his hands to remain part of the revamped Tiger rotation.

**Position:** SP
**Bats:** R  **Throws:** R
**Ht:** 6' 4"  **Wt:** 230

**Opening Day Age:** 25
**Born:** 4/11/70 in Joliet, IL
**ML Seasons:** 3

### Overall Statistics

|        | W  | L  | Pct. | ERA  | G  | GS | Sv | IP    | H   | BB | SO  | HR | BR/IP |
|--------|----|----|------|------|----|----|----|-------|-----|----|-----|----|-------|
| 1995   | 7  | 10 | .412 | 5.12 | 28 | 28 | 0  | 135.1 | 169 | 67 | 86  | 19 | 1.74  |
| Career | 10 | 15 | .400 | 5.28 | 40 | 37 | 0  | 192.2 | 238 | 97 | 117 | 27 | 1.74  |

### How Often He Throws Strikes

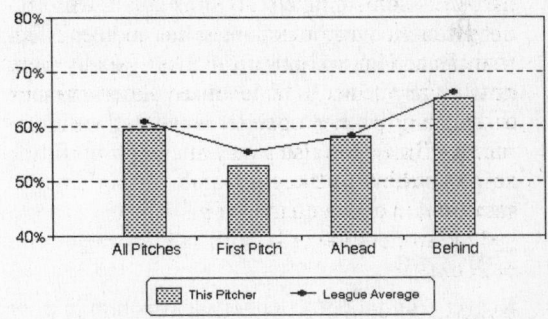

### 1995 Situational Stats

|            | W | L | ERA  | Sv | IP   |        | AB  | H   | HR | RBI | Avg  |
|------------|---|---|------|----|------|--------|-----|-----|----|-----|------|
| Home       | 3 | 4 | 4.74 | 0  | 62.2 | LHB    | 335 | 107 | 15 | 65  | .319 |
| Road       | 4 | 6 | 5.45 | 0  | 72.2 | RHB    | 216 | 62  | 4  | 21  | .287 |
| First Half | 3 | 5 | 4.88 | 0  | 62.2 | Sc Pos | 157 | 45  | 5  | 64  | .287 |
| Scnd Half  | 4 | 5 | 5.33 | 0  | 72.2 | Clutch | 13  | 3   | 0  | 0   | .231 |

### 1995 Rankings (American League)

➡ 1st in lowest fielding percentage at pitcher (.889)
➡ 2nd in wild pitches (13)
➡ 3rd in stolen bases allowed (25) and errors at pitcher (3)
➡ 4th in highest ERA on the road (5.45)
➡ 7th in highest batting average allowed vs. left-handed batters (.319)
➡ 9th in shutouts (1)
➡ Led the Tigers in games started, shutouts (1), wild pitches, pickoff throws (70), stolen bases allowed, GDPs induced (18) and ERA on the road (5.45)

Detroit Tigers

# Joe Boever

## 1995 Season

For better or worse, Joe Boever has always been the kind of reliever who will take the ball without complaint when he's asked. Last year, it was usually for the worse. Though he led Detroit in appearances and ranked among the league leaders in relief innings, Boever had the worst season of his up-and-down major-league career.

## Pitching

The palmball has always been Boever's trademark pitch. It's an offspeed pitch, and one which has a nice sinking action when it's working. But Boever needs to throw it for strikes to be effective. He also needs another, harder pitch to show hitters and give them something else to think about. Unfortunately for Boever, he no longer has another effective pitch. His mid-80s fastball is usually very hittable, and he hangs far too many sliders to make that pitch reliable. So Boever is reduced to throwing palmballs, too many of which end up in the strike zone where they become batting-practice pitches.

## Defense

Boever's unorthodox delivery leaves him in poor fielding position. That, combined with his slow reaction time and lack of agility, makes him a poor fielder. Lacking a decent pickoff move, Boever's delivery is also very easy to read, and he's fair game for potential basestealers. Runners reduced their steal attempts against Boever last season, but that's understandable, considering the way the hitters were beating him up.

## 1996 Outlook

Boever's value as a bullpen innings-eater begins to plummet when he gets lit up like he did last season. Detroit needs some veteran arms to ease their transition to a younger pitching staff, but Boever could have trouble reviving interest in his services. More than likely, he'll need to shop his 35-year-old arm around baseball in hopes of landing a job.

**Position:** RP
**Bats:** R  **Throws:** R
**Ht:** 6' 1"  **Wt:** 205

**Opening Day Age:** 35
**Born:** 10/4/60 in St. Louis, MO
**ML Seasons:** 11
**Pronunciation:** BAY-vur

### Overall Statistics

|        | W  | L  | Pct. | ERA  | G   | GS | Sv | IP    | H   | BB  | SO  | HR | BR/IP |
|--------|----|----|------|------|-----|----|----|-------|-----|-----|-----|----|-------|
| 1995   | 5  | 7  | .417 | 6.39 | 60  | 0  | 3  | 98.2  | 128 | 44  | 71  | 17 | 1.74  |
| Career | 34 | 43 | .442 | 3.90 | 503 | 0  | 47 | 739.1 | 734 | 337 | 535 | 73 | 1.45  |

### How Often He Throws Strikes

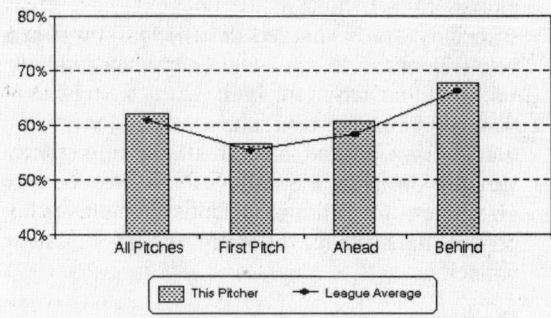

### 1995 Situational Stats

|            | W | L | ERA  | Sv | IP   |        | AB  | H  | HR | RBI | Avg  |
|------------|---|---|------|----|------|--------|-----|----|----|-----|------|
| Home       | 3 | 4 | 6.28 | 2  | 53.0 | LHB    | 221 | 66 | 10 | 52  | .299 |
| Road       | 2 | 3 | 6.50 | 1  | 45.2 | RHB    | 180 | 62 | 7  | 36  | .344 |
| First Half | 4 | 4 | 4.37 | 3  | 47.1 | Sc Pos | 130 | 46 | 9  | 78  | .354 |
| Scnd Half  | 1 | 3 | 8.24 | 0  | 51.1 | Clutch | 135 | 36 | 2  | 14  | .267 |

### 1995 Rankings (American League)

→ 1st in highest batting average allowed with runners in scoring position (.354) and relief losses (7)

→ 2nd in highest relief ERA (6.39), relief innings (98.2) and highest batting average allowed in relief (.319)

→ 3rd in most baserunners allowed per 9 innings in relief (16.0)

→ 5th in worst first batter efficiency (.377)

→ 9th in highest percentage of inherited runners scored (45.3%)

→ Led the Tigers in games pitched, games finished (27), blown saves (3), relief losses and most strikeouts per 9 innings in relief (6.5)

# Brian Bohanon

## 1995 Season

Used as a spot starter and middle reliever after coming to the Tigers last year, lefthander Brian Bohanon didn't do much to impress his new employers. Bohanon's only real success came against lefties Overall, he held them to a .250 batting average—a decent performance for someone pitching in Tiger Stadium with its short right-field porch. But apart from that he struggled, showing why the Texas Rangers gave up on him. After a career full of injuries, Bohanon at least showed he could stay healthy for a full season. His 52 appearances were a career high.

## Pitching

Bohanon's effectiveness against lefties last year offers some hope that he can fashion a career as a relief specialist who can come in to handle a left-handed hitter. Relief pitching would seem his best chance to hang around, since his repertoire as a starter is not imposing. After a series of arm injuries, his fastball is now only slightly above average in velocity. In addition, his curve remains inconsistent, his slider is not sharp enough to handle good right-handed hitters, and his change-up is not fully developed. He also needs to improve his control.

## Defense

Bohanon possesses a better-than-average move to first base, and is fairly quick delivering the ball to the plate. Both help to combat would-be basestealers, and he kept them under reasonable control last season. Bohanon is agile for a big pitcher, and shows decent instincts in the field.

## 1996 Outlook

Once a big-time prospect in the Texas organization, Bohanon's chances of success have been largely thwarted by his career-long injury problems. His one hope is that he'll regain enough velocity to make it as a middle-inning, left-handed reliever.

**Position:** RP/SP
**Bats:** L  **Throws:** L
**Ht:** 6' 3"  **Wt:** 220

**Opening Day Age:** 27
**Born:** 8/1/68 in Denton, TX
**ML Seasons:** 6

### Overall Statistics

|  | W | L | Pct. | ERA | G | GS | Sv | IP | H | BB | SO | HR | BR/IP |
|---|---|---|---|---|---|---|---|---|---|---|---|---|---|
| 1995 | 1 | 1 | .500 | 5.54 | 52 | 10 | 1 | 105.2 | 121 | 41 | 63 | 10 | 1.53 |
| Career | 12 | 14 | .462 | 5.59 | 139 | 47 | 1 | 376.2 | 442 | 161 | 212 | 42 | 1.60 |

### How Often He Throws Strikes

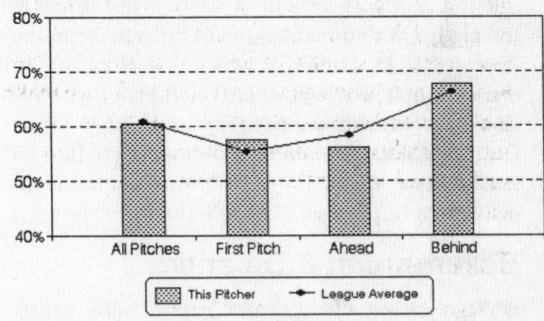

### 1995 Situational Stats

|  | W | L | ERA | Sv | IP |  | AB | H | HR | RBI | Avg |
|---|---|---|---|---|---|---|---|---|---|---|---|
| Home | 1 | 0 | 6.60 | 0 | 43.2 | LHB | 128 | 32 | 3 | 16 | .250 |
| Road | 0 | 1 | 4.79 | 1 | 62.0 | RHB | 296 | 89 | 7 | 51 | .301 |
| First Half | 0 | 1 | 6.39 | 0 | 50.2 | Sc Pos | 137 | 38 | 3 | 57 | .277 |
| Scnd Half | 1 | 0 | 4.75 | 1 | 55.0 | Clutch | 53 | 18 | 0 | 10 | .340 |

### 1995 Rankings (American League)

➡ 7th in highest batting average allowed vs. right-handed batters (.301)

➡ 9th in least strikeouts per 9 innings in relief (5.0)

➡ Led the Tigers in holds (10), lowest batting average allowed in relief (.275) and least baserunners allowed per 9 innings in relief (12.6)

Detroit Tigers

# Chad Curtis

## 1995 Season

Sent to Detroit in the trade that made Tony Phillips an Angel, Chad Curtis gave the Tigers their most consistent center-field play in recent years. Enjoying the move to Tiger Stadium, he broke through to set career highs in home runs and RBI. In addition, he led the Tigers in both stolen bases and runs scored while playing every game. He was a fresh addition to a stale team, adding speed and aggressiveness on the bases.

## Hitting

Curtis concentrated more on pulling the ball for power after coming to the Tigers last year. That translated into more strikeouts but also more production, and without a huge drop in selectivity at the plate. He's strong enough to do damage to the opposite field, which is why most clubs try to crowd him inside with hard pitches rather than going away with offspeed or breaking pitches. Curtis has good bat speed, allowing him to turn on fastballs over the plate—especially from lefthanders, whom he crushed at a .348 clip in '95.

## Baserunning & Defense

In Tiger Stadium's spacious center field, Curtis was able to make some spectacular plays. He's still guilty of misjudging some balls, and needs constant reminders about playing hitters properly. His arm is average at best, but he makes up for it by aggressively charging the ball. His quick jump makes him a basestealing threat. But his speed is not exceptional, which makes him vulnerable to overstepping himself on the bases. He's been caught 68 times in just four seasons.

## 1996 Outlook

Curtis has rubbed some teammates the wrong way with his cockiness, but he's a very underrated talent, ready to become a legitimate offensive force. Center fielders who steal over 20 bases and hit over 20 homers are difficult to find, and Detroit made a solid move for the future by acquiring Curtis. He should be part of the Tigers' evolving foundation for years to come.

**Position:** CF
**Bats:** R  **Throws:** R
**Ht:** 5'10"  **Wt:** 175

**Opening Day Age:** 27
**Born:** 11/6/68 in Marion, IN
**ML Seasons:** 4

### Overall Statistics

|  | G | AB | R | H | D | T | HR | RBI | SB | BB | SO | Avg | OBP | Slg |
|---|---|---|---|---|---|---|---|---|---|---|---|---|---|---|
| 1995 | 144 | 586 | 96 | 157 | 29 | 3 | 21 | 67 | 27 | 70 | 93 | .268 | .349 | .435 |
| Career | 549 | 2063 | 316 | 553 | 93 | 12 | 48 | 222 | 143 | 228 | 322 | .268 | .344 | .395 |

### Where He Hits the Ball

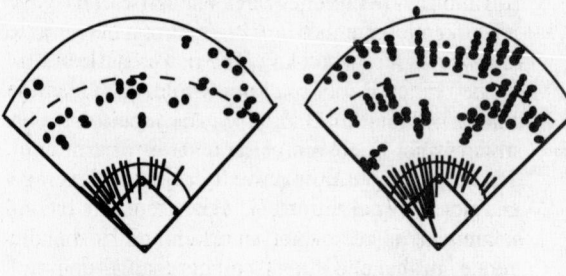

**Vs. LHP**          **Vs. RHP**

### 1995 Situational Stats

|  | AB | H | HR | RBI | Avg |  |  | AB | H | HR | RBI | Avg |
|---|---|---|---|---|---|---|---|---|---|---|---|---|
| Home | 281 | 78 | 11 | 38 | .278 |  | LHP | 135 | 47 | 5 | 16 | .348 |
| Road | 305 | 79 | 10 | 29 | .259 |  | RHP | 451 | 110 | 16 | 51 | .244 |
| First Half | 284 | 80 | 12 | 44 | .282 |  | Sc Pos | 105 | 27 | 0 | 40 | .257 |
| Scnd Half | 302 | 77 | 9 | 23 | .255 |  | Clutch | 76 | 21 | 2 | 3 | .276 |

### 1995 Rankings (American League)

- 1st in plate appearances (670)
- 2nd in pitches seen (2,648)
- 3rd in at-bats, games played and fielding percentage in center field (.992)
- 4th in lowest stolen base percentage (64.3%)
- 5th in caught stealing (15)
- 6th in errors in center field (3) and highest percentage of pitches taken (62.8%)
- 7th in lowest batting average vs. right-handed pitchers (.244)
- 9th in batting average vs. left-handed pitchers (.348) and on-base percentage for a leadoff hitter (.350)
- Led the Tigers in at-bats, runs scored, hits, doubles and total bases (255)

# John Doherty

## 1995 Season

Frustrated with his lack of development as a starting pitcher, the Tigers made John Doherty a full-time reliever for the first time in 1995. The results were mixed. Used in a variety of bullpen roles, including that of closer, Doherty showed durability and managed five wins and six saves. He pitched very well at times, particularly in June, but could never maintain a consistent level of quality.

## Pitching

Doherty throws a heavy, sinking fastball which, when it comes down in the strike zone, can produce a lot of easy ground balls. He's also come up with an improved slider that gives a different look to right-handed hitters. But Doherty doesn't have an effective offspeed pitch—one reason why he was converted to full-time relief. His best outings came when he concentrated on going after the hitters with his sinker and slider, with which he has always had fairly good command. To succeed, Doherty cannot fall into the habit of nibbling with his so-so breaking stuff. His control suffered somewhat as he adapted to relief, and he remains homer-prone, allowing 10 dingers in 113 innings.

## Defense

With a quick pickoff move and a hard-to-gauge delivery, Doherty has been one of the more effective righthanders at holding down basestealers. However, he did not do a good job in this area last year. He falls off the mound into poor fielding position, and doesn't possess either agility or good instincts when going after grounders.

## 1996 Outlook

At one point the Tigers thought Doherty could be an ace starter. But he never made it as a starting pitcher, and the bullpen might be the place where he makes or breaks his major league career. He does not have a closer's stuff, and at best it would appear he is destined to be a middle reliever who can eat up some innings.

**Position:** RP
**Bats:** R **Throws:** R
**Ht:** 6' 4" **Wt:** 215

**Opening Day Age:** 28
**Born:** 6/11/67 in Bronx, NY
**ML Seasons:** 4
**Pronunciation:** DOUGH-er-tee

### Overall Statistics

|        | W  | L  | Pct. | ERA  | G   | GS | Sv | IP    | H   | BB  | SO  | HR | BR/IP |
|--------|----|----|------|------|-----|----|----|-------|-----|-----|-----|----|-------|
| 1995   | 5  | 9  | .357 | 5.10 | 48  | 2  | 6  | 113.0 | 130 | 37  | 46  | 10 | 1.48  |
| Career | 32 | 31 | .508 | 4.86 | 145 | 61 | 9  | 515.0 | 605 | 136 | 174 | 46 | 1.44  |

### How Often He Throws Strikes

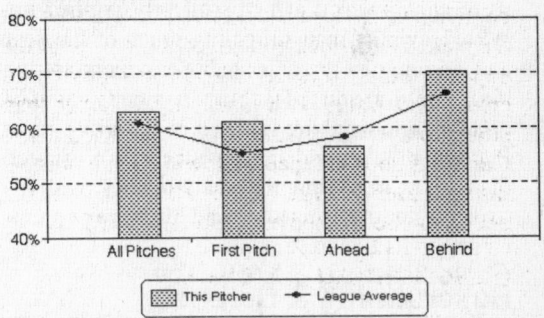

### 1995 Situational Stats

|            | W | L | ERA  | Sv | IP   |        | AB  | H  | HR | RBI | Avg  |
|------------|---|---|------|----|------|--------|-----|----|----|-----|------|
| Home       | 2 | 3 | 4.48 | 3  | 64.1 | LHB    | 234 | 76 | 7  | 30  | .325 |
| Road       | 3 | 6 | 5.92 | 3  | 48.2 | RHB    | 217 | 54 | 3  | 30  | .249 |
| First Half | 4 | 3 | 5.49 | 1  | 59.0 | Sc Pos | 117 | 38 | 1  | 48  | .325 |
| Scnd Half  | 1 | 6 | 4.67 | 5  | 54.0 | Clutch | 132 | 36 | 6  | 14  | .273 |

### 1995 Rankings (American League)

→ 1st in first batter efficiency (.049), relief losses (7), relief innings (107.1), and fielding percentage at pitcher (1.000)
→ 2nd in least strikeouts per 9 innings in relief (3.9)
→ 6th in highest batting average allowed vs. left-handed batters (.325) and highest batting average allowed with runners in scoring position (.325)
→ 8th in lowest winning percentage
→ Led the Tigers in blown saves (3), first batter efficiency (.049), relief losses and relief innings

Detroit Tigers

# Cecil Fielder

**Pure Power**

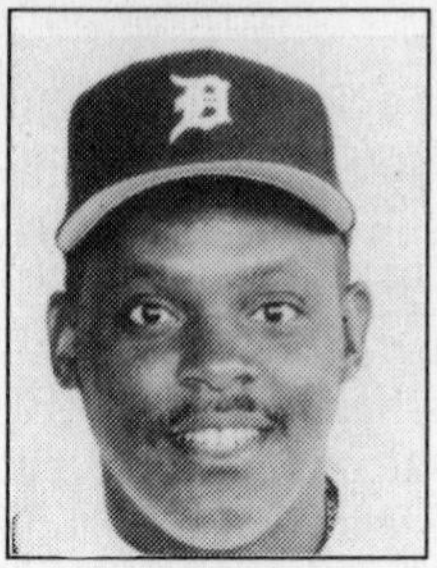

**Position:** 1B/DH
**Bats:** R **Throws:** R
**Ht:** 6' 3" **Wt:** 250

**Opening Day Age:** 32
**Born:** 9/21/63 in Los Angeles, CA
**ML Seasons:** 10
**Nickname:** Big Daddy

## 1995 Season

For a normal player, 31 home runs and 82 RBI is not a bad year's work. But for Cecil Fielder, it's a disappointing season. Fielder started the 1995 campaign in poor physical condition—even by his own loose standards—after being actively involved in the strike negotiations. As a result, he got off to a slow start. Though he got hot for a few stretches of the season, he never put together the kind of power run for which he is known.

## Hitting

Fielder was heavier than usual when the season started, and his bat speed was noticeably slowed by the extra weight. Fastballs he used to turn on were either waved at or harmlessly popped up. With Travis Fryman struggling much of the year and no one else putting up big numbers around him, Fielder started seeing a steady diet of offspeed and breaking stuff out of the strike zone. Pitchers didn't mind if he walked. A frustrated Fielder began chasing too many pitches, with his strikeouts piling up as usual and his average plummeting to its final resting place.

## Baserunning & Defense

Fielder's next stolen base will be the first of his career. With Charlie Hough retired, he is quite possibly the slowest runner in the majors. And though it might make for witty one-liners from sportswriters and pundits, Fielder's slowness means loads of double-play groundballs, and it usually takes three hits to get Fielder home from first. In the field, Fielder's bulk also works against him. He catches what he reaches, but his range is roughly the width of an easy chair.

## 1996 Outlook

With an $8 million salary this year, Fielder isn't going to be traded. For all that money, the Tigers can count on a bunch of home runs and RBI. . . along with a bunch of strikeouts and double plays. He is the ultimate one-dimensional player.

***Overall Statistics***

| | G | AB | R | H | D | T | HR | RBI | SB | BB | SO | Avg | OBP | Slg |
|---|---|---|---|---|---|---|---|---|---|---|---|---|---|---|
| 1995 | 136 | 494 | 70 | 120 | 18 | 1 | 31 | 82 | 0 | 75 | 116 | .243 | .346 | .472 |
| Career | 1095 | 3789 | 570 | 973 | 148 | 6 | 250 | 762 | 0 | 502 | 979 | .257 | .345 | .497 |

***Where He Hits the Ball***

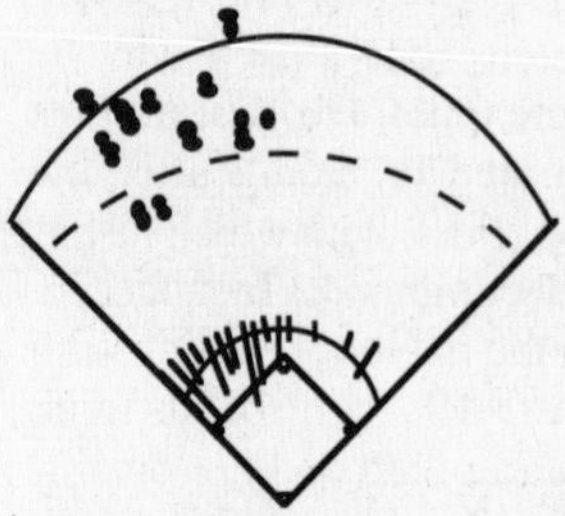

**Vs. LHP**

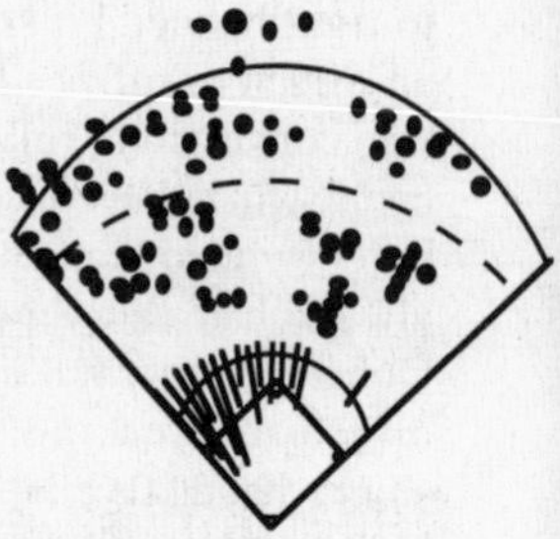

**Vs. RHP**

***1995 Situational Stats***

| | AB | H | HR | RBI | Avg | | AB | H | HR | RBI | Avg |
|---|---|---|---|---|---|---|---|---|---|---|---|
| Home | 247 | 57 | 16 | 46 | .231 | LHP | 102 | 27 | 6 | 18 | .265 |
| Road | 247 | 63 | 15 | 36 | .255 | RHP | 392 | 93 | 25 | 64 | .237 |
| First Half | 251 | 64 | 20 | 51 | .255 | Sc Pos | 122 | 27 | 6 | 43 | .221 |
| Scnd Half | 243 | 56 | 11 | 31 | .230 | Clutch | 68 | 14 | 2 | 6 | .206 |

***1995 Rankings (American League)***

- ➡ 2nd in lowest batting average at home (.231)
- ➡ 4th in lowest percentage of swings put into play (35.2%) and lowest percentage of extra bases taken as a runner (29.7%)
- ➡ 5th in lowest batting average vs. right-handed pitchers (.237)
- ➡ 6th in lowest batting average (.243), GDPs (17) and highest percentage of swings that missed (28.7%)
- ➡ 7th in strikeouts
- ➡ 8th in errors at first base (5)
- ➡ Led the Tigers in home runs, RBI, walks, intentional walks (8), strikeouts, slugging percentage and HR frequency (15.9 ABs per HR)

# John Flaherty

## 1995 Season

Despite wearing down over the last few weeks of the season, John Flaherty still had a career year, marked by a surprise All-Star berth for the long-time journeyman. Flaherty put together a solid first half. But he hit just .192 after the All-Star break, taking some shine off what was otherwise a breakthrough season.

## Hitting

Flaherty has worked hard to add strength, and as a result, he's become a hitter whom pitchers need to respect. He was pulling mistake pitches for power last season, and made contact consistently enough to be troublesome in RBI spots. Unlike many of the Tigers, Flaherty kept his strikeouts somewhat in check. He fanned only 47 times, with many of those whiffs coming late in the season when it was obvious he was slowing down from playing every day. Flaherty has trouble against good offspeed stuff, and will try to pull too many balls on the outer edge of the plate, resulting in weak ground balls.

## Baserunning & Defense

A decent runner for a catcher, Flaherty is capable of taking the extra base but no threat to steal. He is an excellent receiver and handler of pitchers, adept at blocking balls in the dirt and framing pitches behind the plate. Flaherty's arm is above average, but at times he will sail his throws to second. Consequently, runners stole at a rate above the league rate against him in '95. He will also hurry his throws at times, accounting for too many errors.

## 1996 Outlook

No one will start comparing Flaherty to Johnny Bench, but he has established himself as a bona fide big-league catcher who can catch a healthy share of games. Ideally, he should not play every day, but his occasional power, excellent attitude and catching savvy make him a valuable man on the roster.

**Position:** C
**Bats:** R  **Throws:** R
**Ht:** 6' 1"  **Wt:** 200

**Opening Day Age:** 28
**Born:** 10/21/67 in New York, NY
**ML Seasons:** 4

### Overall Statistics

|  | G | AB | R | H | D | T | HR | RBI | SB | BB | SO | Avg | OBP | Slg |
|---|---|---|---|---|---|---|---|---|---|---|---|---|---|---|
| 1995 | 112 | 354 | 39 | 86 | 22 | 1 | 11 | 40 | 0 | 18 | 47 | .243 | .284 | .404 |
| Career | 194 | 485 | 47 | 108 | 27 | 1 | 11 | 48 | 0 | 24 | 71 | .223 | .263 | .351 |

### Where He Hits the Ball

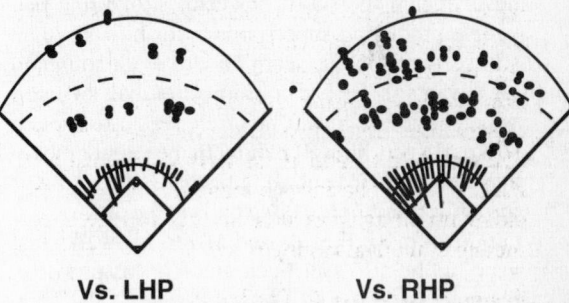

Vs. LHP          Vs. RHP

### 1995 Situational Stats

|  | AB | H | HR | RBI | Avg |  | AB | H | HR | RBI | Avg |
|---|---|---|---|---|---|---|---|---|---|---|---|
| Home | 171 | 46 | 6 | 21 | .269 | LHP | 86 | 18 | 0 | 8 | .209 |
| Road | 183 | 40 | 5 | 19 | .219 | RHP | 268 | 68 | 11 | 32 | .254 |
| First Half | 172 | 51 | 9 | 26 | .297 | Sc Pos | 74 | 18 | 0 | 25 | .243 |
| Scnd Half | 182 | 35 | 2 | 14 | .192 | Clutch | 44 | 9 | 2 | 7 | .205 |

### 1995 Rankings (American League)

→ 1st in errors at catcher (11) and lowest fielding percentage at catcher (.982)

→ 7th in batting average on a 3-1 count (.600)

→ Led the Tigers in sacrifice bunts (8) and batting average on a 3-1 count

Detroit Tigers

# Travis Fryman

## 1995 Season

A late-season revival wasn't quite enough to prevent Travis Fryman from having a disappointing 1995 season. Fryman's home-run and RBI totals were his lowest since becoming an everyday player in 1991, and his .409 slugging percentage was the lowest of his career. The only big positive Tiger fans saw was the continued improvement in his third-base defense.

## Hitting

Fryman is extremely talented, but there are far too many times when just making contact seems impossible for him. He is prone to numbing streaks of ineptitude, and at times it seems like he will never regain the short, powerful stroke that had people predicting superstardom for him. Fryman still seems unable to learn how to work counts to his advantage. He is a notorious first-ball swinger, which of course means he rarely sees a first-pitch strike. He gets himself behind in the count quickly and then is prone to chasing fastballs up and out of the strike zone, or breaking balls in the dirt. He did cut down his strikeouts and add to his walks last year, but he also sacrificed much of his power in the process.

## Baserunning & Defense

Fryman fits right into the recent Tigers mold—below-average speed and only the most occasional threat to steal. However, he has shown outstanding judgment and often takes the extra base when given the opportunity. Apparently settled at third for good, he has improved his range and overall knowledge of the position. He will occasionally boot routine grounders and has trouble on balls hit to his left. But he makes up for many of his flaws with a strong and usually accurate arm.

## 1996 Outlook

Like many good players on poor teams, Fryman has been worn down by Detroit's long stretch of losing seasons. Now there is a new regime in place and Fryman can only benefit from the improved atmosphere. He still has the ability to be a franchise player and is just entering his prime at 27.

**Position:** 3B
**Bats:** R **Throws:** R
**Ht:** 6' 1" **Wt:** 195

**Opening Day Age:** 27
**Born:** 3/25/69 in Lexington, KY
**ML Seasons:** 6

### Overall Statistics

|        | G   | AB   | R   | H   | D   | T  | HR | RBI | SB | BB  | SO  | Avg  | OBP  | Slg  |
|--------|-----|------|-----|-----|-----|----|----|-----|----|-----|-----|------|------|------|
| 1995   | 144 | 567  | 79  | 156 | 21  | 5  | 15 | 81  | 4  | 63  | 100 | .275 | .347 | .409 |
| Career | 785 | 3086 | 427 | 848 | 170 | 23 | 105| 477 | 38 | 287 | 700 | .275 | .337 | .447 |

### Where He Hits the Ball

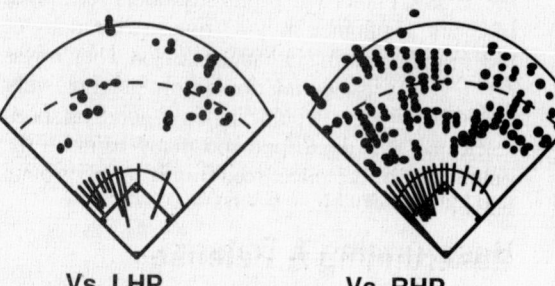

Vs. LHP          Vs. RHP

### 1995 Situational Stats

|            | AB  | H  | HR | RBI | Avg  |        | AB  | H   | HR | RBI | Avg  |
|------------|-----|----|----|-----|------|--------|-----|-----|----|-----|------|
| Home       | 267 | 78 | 9  | 41  | .292 | LHP    | 128 | 27  | 1  | 16  | .211 |
| Road       | 300 | 78 | 6  | 40  | .260 | RHP    | 439 | 129 | 14 | 65  | .294 |
| First Half | 271 | 74 | 7  | 36  | .273 | Sc Pos | 137 | 40  | 4  | 68  | .292 |
| Scnd Half  | 296 | 82 | 8  | 45  | .277 | Clutch | 71  | 19  | 3  | 14  | .268 |

### 1995 Rankings (American League)

→ 2nd in fielding percentage at third base (.969)
→ 3rd in GDPs (18), games played, lowest batting average vs. left-handed pitchers (.211) and highest percentage of extra bases taken as a runner (69.6%)
→ 4th in at-bats
→ 5th in lowest slugging percentage vs. left-handed pitchers (.281)
→ 6th in lowest on-base percentage vs. left-handed pitchers (.275)
→ 7th in singles (115) and errors at third base (14)
→ Led the Tigers in batting average, singles (115), triples, sacrifice flies (7) and GDPs (18)

# Chris Gomez

## 1995 Season

Former Detroit skipper Sparky Anderson once compared Chris Gomez to Dave Concepcion. But though Gomez' flashes of power could remind you at times of the former Reds shortstop, there were large chunks of last season when Gomez reminded you more of *Onix* Concepcion, the forgettable Kansas City infielder of the early 1980s. Gomez' bat was anemic the entire season, and a .161 September put an exclamation point on his problems.

## Hitting

Since the All-Star break of '94, Gomez has hit just .219 over roughly 500 at-bats. He still takes too big a swing and is easy pickings for major league breaking stuff. He is also easily crowded with fastballs, often getting himself out with nervous overswinging. Gomez has surprising power and can occasionally go deep with a mistake. And when he controls his swing, he's a threat to send extra-base hits to the alleys. However, Gomez remains too impatient to consistently maintain a good groove, and thus is easy to pitch to.

## Baserunning & Defense

Gomez will steal bases once in a while, but he is an average runner at best. He also has some rough spots in the field. His arm strength is questioned by many scouts, and he will occasionally bounce throws from the shortstop hole. However, he has soft hands and his range is boosted by Tiger Stadium's knee-high infield grass. Gomez can also play second adequately, though he is rather crude at turning the double play.

## 1996 Outlook

Gomez was rushed to the major leagues, and he's been paying the price with his offensive struggles. However, he has decent tools, and if he can get rid of some of the rough edges, he has time to mature into a productive big-league shortstop. A new regime in Detroit provides a good opportunity to wipe the slate clean.

**Position:** SS/2B
**Bats:** R  **Throws:** R
**Ht:** 6' 1"  **Wt:** 188

**Opening Day Age:** 24
**Born:** 6/16/71 in Los Angeles, California
**ML Seasons:** 3

### Overall Statistics

|        | G   | AB  | R  | H   | D  | T | HR | RBI | SB | BB | SO  | Avg  | OBP  | Slg  |
|--------|-----|-----|----|-----|----|---|----|-----|----|----|-----|------|------|------|
| 1995   | 123 | 431 | 49 | 96  | 20 | 2 | 11 | 50  | 4  | 41 | 96  | .223 | .292 | .355 |
| Career | 253 | 855 | 92 | 204 | 46 | 3 | 19 | 114 | 11 | 83 | 177 | .239 | .309 | .366 |

### Where He Hits the Ball

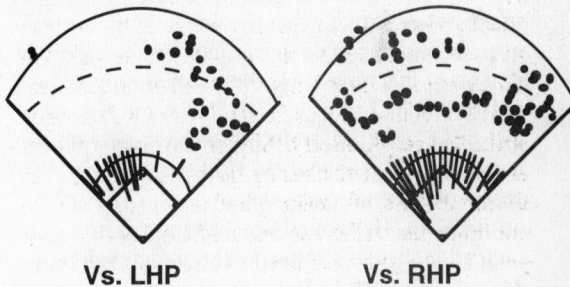

**Vs. LHP**          **Vs. RHP**

### 1995 Situational Stats

|            | AB  | H  | HR | RBI | Avg  |        | AB  | H  | HR | RBI | Avg  |
|------------|-----|----|----|-----|------|--------|-----|----|----|-----|------|
| Home       | 221 | 52 | 5  | 29  | .235 | LHP    | 113 | 32 | 3  | 21  | .283 |
| Road       | 210 | 44 | 6  | 21  | .210 | RHP    | 318 | 64 | 8  | 29  | .201 |
| First Half | 182 | 44 | 7  | 27  | .242 | Sc Pos | 110 | 26 | 0  | 33  | .236 |
| Scnd Half  | 249 | 52 | 4  | 23  | .209 | Clutch | 55  | 8  | 0  | 5   | .145 |

### 1995 Rankings (American League)

→ 1st in lowest batting average vs. right-handed pitchers (.201) and lowest on-base percentage vs. right-handed pitchers (.261)
→ 2nd in lowest batting average, lowest on-base percentage, lowest batting average in the clutch (.145) and lowest slugging percentage vs. right-handed pitchers (.321)
→ 4th in lowest batting average at home (.235) and lowest batting average on the road (.210)
→ 6th in lowest slugging percentage and lowest fielding percentage at shortstop (.973)
→ 7th in errors at shortstop (12)
→ Led the Tigers in highest groundball/flyball ratio (1.6)

**Detroit Tigers**

# Bob Higginson

## 1995 Season

Not considered one of the Tigers' better prospects until fairly recently, Bob Higginson suddenly blossomed into a home-run threat over the last two seasons. Higginson hit 23 homers at Triple-A Toledo in 1994, then broke in with Detroit last year and belted 14 more. Higginson would have hit even more if not for a September dry spell—perhaps an indication that the wear and tear of the season was getting to him.

## Hitting

Higginson perfectly fits the mold of the Tigers of the 1990s—he is prone to strikeouts but capable of home runs. Originally viewed as a high-average hitter with occasional power, he developed a legitimate power stroke while playing at Toledo. However, he has sacrificed discipline and selectivity in pursuit of that power. He too often simply swings for the fences, and as a result chases pitches out of the strike zone. In addition, he gets tied up too easily with inside pitches. However, as the 1995 season wore on he started showing more patience at the plate. He wound up walking 62 times, an indication that he has the potential to develop into a good all-around hitter.

## Baserunning & Defense

An above-average runner, Higginson should be able to steal a dozen or so bases a year. He is aggressive in looking to take the extra base. Higginson has decent outfield range, but will probably wind up as a left fielder since his arm is not really strong enough for right. At times he has problems judging fly balls, but he's young and still learning.

## 1996 Outlook

Higginson has the classic left-handed stroke that could be made to order for Tiger Stadium. With the Tigers needing more left-handed pop, Higginson will get every chance to stick with the club. He needs to put more balls in play, but the first impressions of his potential were mostly positive.

**Position:** RF/LF
**Bats:** L  **Throws:** R
**Ht:** 5'11"  **Wt:** 180

**Opening Day Age:** 25
**Born:** 8/18/70 in Philadelphia, PA
**ML Seasons:** 1

*Overall Statistics*

|  | G | AB | R | H | D | T | HR | RBI | SB | BB | SO | Avg | OBP | Slg |
|---|---|---|---|---|---|---|---|---|---|---|---|---|---|---|
| 1995 | 131 | 410 | 61 | 92 | 17 | 5 | 14 | 43 | 6 | 62 | 107 | .224 | .329 | .393 |
| Career | 131 | 410 | 61 | 92 | 17 | 5 | 14 | 43 | 6 | 62 | 107 | .224 | .329 | .393 |

*Where He Hits the Ball*

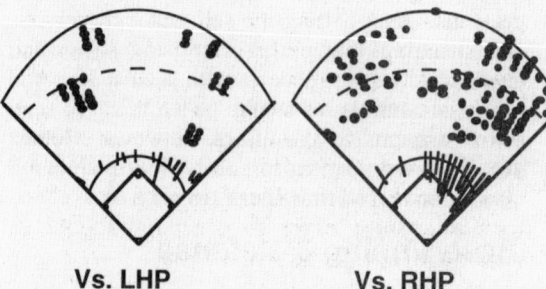

**Vs. LHP**          **Vs. RHP**

*1995 Situational Stats*

|  | AB | H | HR | RBI | Avg |  | AB | H | HR | RBI | Avg |
|---|---|---|---|---|---|---|---|---|---|---|---|
| Home | 206 | 44 | 10 | 24 | .214 | LHP | 66 | 14 | 2 | 5 | .212 |
| Road | 204 | 48 | 4 | 19 | .235 | RHP | 344 | 78 | 12 | 38 | .227 |
| First Half | 199 | 49 | 10 | 28 | .246 | Sc Pos | 88 | 18 | 2 | 28 | .205 |
| Scnd Half | 211 | 43 | 4 | 15 | .204 | Clutch | 60 | 14 | 1 | 3 | .233 |

*1995 Rankings (American League)*

➡ 1st in lowest batting average at home (.214)
➡ 3rd in lowest batting average (.224), lowest groundball/flyball ratio (0.7) and lowest batting average vs. right-handed pitchers (.227)
➡ 5th in lowest batting average with runners in scoring position (.205)
➡ 6th in lowest batting average with the bases loaded (.083)
➡ 7th in most pitches seen per plate appearance (4.12)
➡ 9th in lowest batting average on the road (.235)
➡ Led the Tigers in triples, sacrifice flies (7), most pitches seen per plate appearance and least GDPs per GDP situation (5.2%)

# Felipe Lira

**Position:** SP/RP
**Bats:** R **Throws:** R
**Ht:** 6' 0" **Wt:** 170

**Opening Day Age:** 23
**Born:** 4/26/72 in
Miranda, VZ
**ML Seasons:** 1

## 1995 Season

After first being given some innings in middle relief, rookie Felipe Lira joined the Tiger rotation last season. He gave indications that he might stay there for a while. Lira led the Tigers in strikeouts while compiling a decent 4.31 ERA, and he was especially effective in Tiger Stadium, where his ERA was nearly a run and a half better than on the road.

## Pitching

Lira's velocity is unexceptional but adequate, usually in the mid to high 80s. What makes him effective is the movement of his pitches. He throws a hard cutting fastball that runs away from left-handed hitters. He also throws a slider and a good change-up, which he can sink either in or away from righties. Lira will battle his control at times, and he also goes through period when he gets his fastball up. When the heater comes in high and straight, it often winds up in the seats. However, Lira has the stuff to strike himself out of trouble, and his knowledge of pitching is excellent for such a young hurler. He is not afraid to throw inside, and hit eight batters last year.

## Defense

Lira has not yet developed a great pickoff move, but he did an exceptional job keeping runners in check last season. Runners were just 6-for-13 stealing against him in '95. He is a good athlete who should develop into the kind of fielder who can help himself.

## 1996 Outlook

Lira got his feet wet last season, and should profit from the experience. The Tigers are likely to go with youth in their starting rotation, and Lira arrives this spring with one of those spots pretty much wrapped up. There's no reason why he won't be able to take another step and become a 10- to 12-game winner, at the very least.

### Overall Statistics

|        | W | L  | Pct. | ERA  | G  | GS | Sv | IP    | H   | BB | SO | HR | BR/IP |
|--------|---|----|------|------|----|----|----|-------|-----|----|----|----|-------|
| 1995   | 9 | 13 | .409 | 4.31 | 37 | 22 | 1  | 146.1 | 151 | 56 | 89 | 17 | 1.41  |
| Career | 9 | 13 | .409 | 4.31 | 37 | 22 | 1  | 146.1 | 151 | 56 | 89 | 17 | 1.41  |

### How Often He Throws Strikes

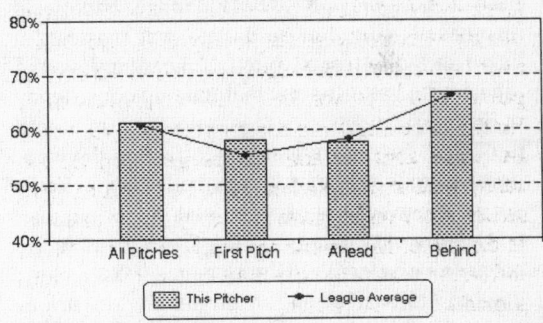

### 1995 Situational Stats

|            | W | L | ERA  | Sv | IP   |        | AB  | H  | HR | RBI | Avg  |
|------------|---|---|------|----|------|--------|-----|----|----|-----|------|
| Home       | 6 | 5 | 3.66 | 0  | 78.2 | LHB    | 332 | 87 | 8  | 35  | .262 |
| Road       | 3 | 8 | 5.05 | 1  | 67.2 | RHB    | 226 | 64 | 9  | 34  | .283 |
| First Half | 6 | 4 | 3.54 | 0  | 73.2 | Sc Pos | 123 | 27 | 4  | 48  | .220 |
| Scnd Half  | 3 | 9 | 5.08 | 1  | 72.2 | Clutch | 54  | 20 | 3  | 11  | .370 |

### 1995 Rankings (American League)

- → 2nd in least run support per 9 innings (3.9)
- → 4th in lowest stolen base percentage allowed (46.2%)
- → 5th in hit batsmen (8) and lowest batting average allowed with runners in scoring position (.220)
- → 6th in highest slugging percentage allowed (.437)
- → 8th in losses
- → 10th in lowest groundball/flyball ratio allowed (1.1) and most home runs allowed per 9 innings (1.05)
- → Led the Tigers in ERA, innings pitched, batters faced (635), hit batsmen, strikeouts and pitches thrown (2,339)

Detroit Tigers

155

# C.J. Nitkowski

## 1995 Season

Acquired from Cincinnati in the trade that sent David Wells to the Reds, rookie C.J. Nitkowski struggled in the 11 late-season starts the Tigers gave him. He won only once and averaged less than four innings per start while posting an ugly 7.09 ERA. Despite that, the Tigers remain high on Nitkowski, who's considered a top prospect.

## Pitching

A former first-round draft pick, Nitkowski has been rushed to the majors while still lacking many of the elements a major league pitcher needs in order to succeed. His velocity is not eye-popping, but he throws a heavy sinking fastball that has been clocked in the 87-89 MPH range. Nitkowski also has a slider, but he has not yet mastered a curve or an offspeed pitch. Like many young pitchers, he has difficulty maintaining consistency in his release point. Consequently, his arm comes to the plate at different angles, affecting the location and movement of his fastball. Nitkowski is not someone who is likely to overpower anyone, and he obviously needs to pitch from ahead in the count to be effective. Hitters batted .322 against him last year, and he had an alarmingly low strikeout total in his major league action.

## Defense

Nitkowski has a fairly high leg kick and a slow delivery home, making him fair game for basestealers until he develops a decent pickoff move. Runners stole against him at about the league rate last season. He is a decent athlete and capable of fielding his position, two errors last season notwithstanding.

## 1996 Outlook

Judging Nitkowski off his brief trial last year is not fair, and he will get a longer look this spring. He might need more seasoning to work on consistent mechanics and a better offspeed pitch. However, his grim numbers aside, a lefthander who throws strikes could have a bright future in Tiger Stadium.

**Position:** SP
**Bats:** L  **Throws:** L
**Ht:** 6' 3"  **Wt:** 190

**Opening Day Age:** 23
**Born:** 3/3/73 in Suffren, NY
**ML Seasons:** 1

### Overall Statistics

|        | W | L | Pct. | ERA  | G  | GS | Sv | IP   | H  | BB | SO | HR | BR/IP |
|--------|---|---|------|------|----|----|----|------|----|----|----|----|-------|
| 1995   | 2 | 7 | .222 | 6.66 | 20 | 18 | 0  | 71.2 | 94 | 35 | 31 | 11 | 1.80  |
| Career | 2 | 7 | .222 | 6.66 | 20 | 18 | 0  | 71.2 | 94 | 35 | 31 | 11 | 1.80  |

### How Often He Throws Strikes

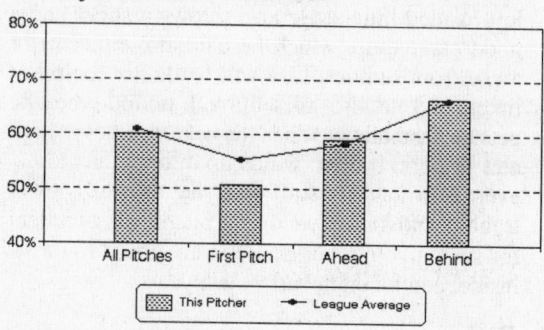

### 1995 Situational Stats

|            | W | L | ERA  | Sv | IP   |        | AB  | H  | HR | RBI | Avg  |
|------------|---|---|------|----|------|--------|-----|----|----|-----|------|
| Home       | 0 | 5 | 8.56 | 0  | 27.1 | LHB    | 55  | 15 | 0  | 9   | .273 |
| Road       | 2 | 2 | 5.48 | 0  | 44.1 | RHB    | 237 | 79 | 11 | 47  | .333 |
| First Half | 1 | 2 | 5.27 | 0  | 27.1 | Sc Pos | 83  | 30 | 3  | 46  | .361 |
| Scnd Half  | 1 | 5 | 7.51 | 0  | 44.1 | Clutch | 3   | 0  | 0  | 0   | .000 |

### 1995 Rankings (American League)

→ Did not rank near the top or bottom in any category

# Alan Trammell

## 1995 Season

In what was likely his last season with the Tigers, Alan Trammell played through assorted aches and pains. Trammell provided the Tigers with occasional production in what was mostly a utility role. Tramell managed only two homers but remained dangerous in the clutch, batting .340 with runners in scoring position.

## Hitting

With his bat speed in decline, Trammell is no longer able to turn on the balls he used to routinely send over Tiger Stadium's friendly left-field fence. However, as he's done throughout his career, Trammell gives away a minimum of at-bats. He still can do damage when he gets a count in his favor and puts the pitcher in a fastball situation. In recent years he's been prone to reach for too many balls away from him, resulting in weak fly balls to right and right-center. He also is much less effective against right-handed pitching in his declining years. He has trouble catching up with many righthanders' stuff.

## Baserunning & Defense

Trammell's days as a basestealer have long since passed, especially after a series of ankle and hamstring problems. However, there are few more intelligent baserunners around, and he still looks to take the extra base when the opportunity arises. Trammell's range at shortstop has largely disappeared, but he still has soft hands and an accurate arm. His knowledge of hitters helps him compensate somewhat for the declining range. In recent years, Trammell has made himself into a serviceable utilityman by working to learn the mechanics of playing third and left field.

## 1996 Outlook

It appeared likely at season's end that Trammell would retire. If he does come back, he would be welcomed by many clubs as a proven veteran reserve with enough left to help occasionally off the bench. If he hangs it up, then the American League will say goodbye to one of its class acts of the last 20 years.

**Position:** SS
**Bats:** R  **Throws:** R
**Ht:** 6' 0"  **Wt:** 185

**Opening Day Age:** 38
**Born:** 2/21/58 in Garden Grove, CA
**ML Seasons:** 19

### Overall Statistics

|  | G | AB | R | H | D | T | HR | RBI | SB | BB | SO | Avg | OBP | Slg |
|---|---|---|---|---|---|---|---|---|---|---|---|---|---|---|
| 1995 | 74 | 223 | 28 | 60 | 12 | 0 | 2 | 23 | 3 | 27 | 19 | .269 | .345 | .350 |
| Career | 2227 | 8095 | 1215 | 2320 | 410 | 55 | 184 | 987 | 230 | 840 | 847 | .287 | .353 | .419 |

### Where He Hits the Ball

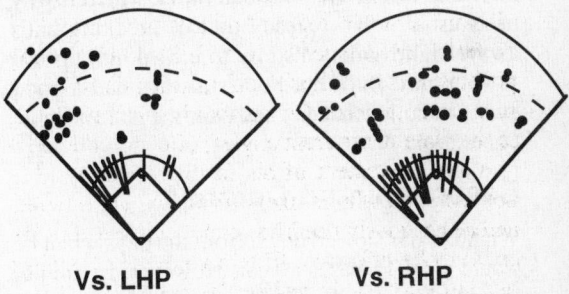

**Vs. LHP**          **Vs. RHP**

### 1995 Situational Stats

|  | AB | H | HR | RBI | Avg |  | AB | H | HR | RBI | Avg |
|---|---|---|---|---|---|---|---|---|---|---|---|
| Home | 121 | 34 | 1 | 15 | .281 | LHP | 90 | 28 | 1 | 11 | .311 |
| Road | 102 | 26 | 1 | 8 | .255 | RHP | 133 | 32 | 1 | 12 | .241 |
| First Half | 125 | 38 | 2 | 15 | .304 | Sc Pos | 50 | 17 | 1 | 22 | .340 |
| Scnd Half | 98 | 22 | 0 | 8 | .224 | Clutch | 46 | 11 | 1 | 9 | .239 |

### 1995 Rankings (American League)

➡ Did not rank near the top or bottom in any category

# Lou Whitaker

## 1995 Season

Used almost exclusively in a platoon role last season, Lou Whitaker showed that he still hasn't lost his classic Tiger Stadium stroke. His .293 average was the best on the club, and he added 14 homers, all but one coming against right-handed pitching. Still productive at 38, Whitaker proved he could still show the team's younger players a thing or two.

## Hitting

As long as he faces only righthanders, Whitaker's bat is quick enough to turn around a fastball. He also is quick to hit a mistake hung out over the plate. Even at his advanced age, Whitaker is known as an excellent fastball hitter, which is why he is usually fed a steady diet of breaking balls away. Righthanders also try to crowd him up and in with hard stuff, but he has always had a good eye... meaning that any ball over the plate is liable to be smoked.

## Baserunning & Defense

Whitaker has slowed down from the days when he would steal 15 bases a year. However, he cannot be entirely ignored, as he'll still pick his spots and swipe a base now and then. He has always been alert to taking the extra base, and rarely makes a baserunning mistake. Whitaker's fielding range has declined, but after a poor fielding year in '94 he was again a dependable, if unspectacular, second baseman. However, his best days in the field are well behind him.

## 1996 Outlook

His home-run numbers indicate that Whitaker still has something left in his tank, and the Tigers could bring him back for another season in 1996. He is reduced to platoon duty and may be more suited to designated hitter than anything. But there is still life left in that classic lefty stroke.

**Position:** 2B
**Bats:** L  **Throws:** R
**Ht:** 5'11"  **Wt:** 185

**Opening Day Age:** 38
**Born:** 5/12/57 in New York, NY
**ML Seasons:** 19
**Nickname:** Sweet Lou

### Overall Statistics

|  | G | AB | R | H | D | T | HR | RBI | SB | BB | SO | Avg | OBP | Slg |
|---|---|---|---|---|---|---|---|---|---|---|---|---|---|---|
| 1995 | 84 | 249 | 36 | 73 | 14 | 0 | 14 | 44 | 4 | 31 | 41 | .293 | .372 | .518 |
| Career | 2390 | 8570 | 1386 | 2369 | 420 | 65 | 244 | 1084 | 143 | 1197 | 1099 | .276 | .363 | .426 |

### Where He Hits the Ball

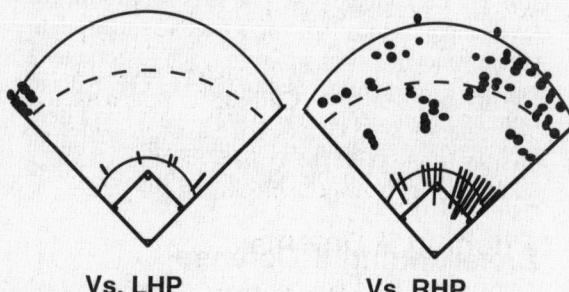

Vs. LHP                Vs. RHP

### 1995 Situational Stats

|  | AB | H | HR | RBI | Avg |  | AB | H | HR | RBI | Avg |
|---|---|---|---|---|---|---|---|---|---|---|---|
| Home | 123 | 34 | 11 | 26 | .276 | LHP | 26 | 8 | 1 | 5 | .308 |
| Road | 126 | 39 | 3 | 18 | .310 | RHP | 223 | 65 | 13 | 39 | .291 |
| First Half | 122 | 38 | 5 | 18 | .311 | Sc Pos | 61 | 18 | 5 | 33 | .295 |
| Scnd Half | 127 | 35 | 9 | 26 | .276 | Clutch | 54 | 12 | 3 | 14 | .222 |

### 1995 Rankings (American League)

➡ Did not rank near the top or bottom in any category

# Mike Christopher

**Position:** RP
**Bats:** R **Throws:** R
**Ht:** 6' 5" **Wt:** 205

**Opening Day Age:** 32
**Born:** 11/3/63 in
Petersburg, VA
**ML Seasons:** 4

## Overall Statistics

|        | W | L | Pct.  | ERA  | G  | GS | Sv | IP   | H   | BB | SO | HR | BR/IP |
|--------|---|---|-------|------|----|----|----|------|-----|----|----|----|-------|
| 1995   | 4 | 0 | 1.000 | 3.82 | 36 | 0  | 1  | 61.1 | 71  | 14 | 34 | 8  | 1.39  |
| Career | 4 | 0 | 1.000 | 3.51 | 58 | 0  | 1  | 95.0 | 104 | 29 | 57 | 13 | 1.40  |

## 1995 Season

A refugee of assorted organizations, righty reliever Mike Christopher showed for the first time last year that he might be able to pitch successfully at the major league level. Christopher earned the first four major league victories of his career, added his first save, and aside from a handful of bad outings, gave the Tigers respectable innings all year.

## Pitching & Defense

Christopher does not blow people away. His velocity is average (mid-80s), but he has developed a decent enough split-fingered pitch to have reasonable success when he has control of it. But Christopher's margin for error remains very small. If he is off just a bit with the location of his splitter, he's in trouble, because he'll likely get hit. Although he's not "walk wild," he's proven to be "extra-base wild." Over a third of the 71 hits he allowed went for extra bases, including eight homers. He does a decent job of holding runners and is a competent fielder.

## 1996 Outlook

Christopher is not likely to fill the void at closer left by Mike Henneman's departure. But he was as good as any of the nondescript arms floating through the Detroit bullpen last season, so he should be able to land a middle-relief role.

# Milt Cuyler

**Position:** LF
**Bats:** B **Throws:** R
**Ht:** 5'10" **Wt:** 185

**Opening Day Age:** 27
**Born:** 10/7/68 in
Macon, GA
**ML Seasons:** 6
**Pronunciation:** KUY-ler

## Overall Statistics

|        | G   | AB   | R   | H   | D  | T  | HR | RBI | SB | BB  | SO  | Avg  | OBP  | Slg  |
|--------|-----|------|-----|-----|----|----|----|-----|----|-----|-----|------|------|------|
| 1995   | 41  | 88   | 15  | 18  | 1  | 4  | 0  | 5   | 2  | 8   | 16  | .205 | .271 | .307 |
| Career | 433 | 1270 | 205 | 304 | 44 | 21 | 7  | 104 | 70 | 107 | 254 | .239 | .304 | .324 |

## 1995 Season

After returning to the active roster following some early-season injuries and a lengthy stint in Triple-A, Milt Cuyler found little playing time available to him last year. He had only 88 at-bats all season, and he did little with those infrequent opportunities, managing only five extra-base hits (four of them triples). His batting average, on-base percentage, and slugging percentage were all the lowest of his career.

## Hitting, Baserunning & Defense

The switch-hitting Cuyler is slightly more dangerous from the left side, though that wasn't saying much last year. He's always been an impatient hitter who is prone to chasing bad pitches, and he's vulnerable to good hard stuff. Cuyler has some bunting skill which he has never fully exploited. His four triples show he can still run, but Cuyler has never become the basestealer the Tigers thought he'd become. Playing part-time has hurt his defensive skills, which once were superb. He doesn't get the same break on fly balls that he once did, and he committed four errors in very limited play last season. His arm is below average.

## 1996 Outlook

Still a young man, Cuyler could find himself needing to revive his career with a return to the minors. He does not seem to have a future in Detroit, and there would appear to be little market for him after his recent performance.

# Scott Fletcher

**Position**: 2B
**Bats**: R **Throws**: R
**Ht**: 5'11" **Wt**: 172

**Opening Day Age**: 37
**Born**: 7/30/58 in Fort Walton Beach, FL
**ML Seasons**: 15

### Overall Statistics

| | G | AB | R | H | D | T | HR | RBI | SB | BB | SO | Avg | OBP | Slg |
|---|---|---|---|---|---|---|---|---|---|---|---|---|---|---|
| 1995 | 67 | 182 | 19 | 42 | 10 | 1 | 1 | 17 | 1 | 19 | 27 | .231 | .312 | .313 |
| Career | 1612 | 5258 | 688 | 1376 | 243 | 38 | 34 | 510 | 99 | 514 | 541 | .262 | .332 | .342 |

## 1995 Season

Veteran infielder Scott Fletcher always seems able to squeeze a little more major league time from his overachieving career. Fletcher filled in mostly at second base for the Tigers last year, but his production was very weak. He had a solid May, but then a strained left hamstring killed Fletcher's momentum and he never really got back on track.

## Hitting, Baserunning & Defense

Fletcher tries to spray the ball wherever it's pitched, and usually is able to make contact. He is no power threat, but he hangs tough in RBI situations and is a good man to use on the hitting end of a hit-and-run play. He can be overpowered with hard stuff inside. Fletcher does not have basestealing speed, but he's a smart baserunner who does not run into outs. He has sure hands wherever he plays in the infield, though at this stage of his career his range and arm basically limit him to second base. In a pinch, he can still fill in at short or third.

## 1996 Outlook

Fletcher is likely to find himself in the familiar position of having to earn a job in spring training this season. He is an intelligent, hard-working player who has gotten the maximum from his ability. He would be a steady veteran hand on any bench, but one who won't contribute much on offense.

# Jose Lima

**Position**: SP
**Bats**: R **Throws**: R
**Ht**: 6'2" **Wt**: 170

**Opening Day Age**: 23
**Born**: 9/30/72 in Santiago, DR
**ML Seasons**: 2
**Pronunciation**: LEE-mah

### Overall Statistics

| | W | L | Pct. | ERA | G | GS | Sv | IP | H | BB | SO | HR | BR/IP |
|---|---|---|---|---|---|---|---|---|---|---|---|---|---|
| 1995 | 3 | 9 | .250 | 6.11 | 15 | 15 | 0 | 73.2 | 85 | 18 | 37 | 10 | 1.40 |
| Career | 3 | 10 | .231 | 6.72 | 18 | 16 | 0 | 80.1 | 96 | 21 | 44 | 12 | 1.46 |

## 1995 Season

There was a time when Jose Lima was considered the best pitching prospect in the Tiger organization. But others have started moving past him, especially after a discouraging 1995 season in which he was ripped for a 6.11 ERA while averaging less than five innings per start.

## Pitching & Defense

Lima's best pitch is his excellent change-up, and at one time scouts compared him to a young Mario Soto. However, Lima's velocity is not in Soto's class, and he has no exceptional pitch to play off the change. As a result, he throws the pitch too often, and when it's up in the strike zone it gets crushed. He has picked up a split-fingered pitch and a slider, and his velocity has increased as he's matured physically and improved his throwing mechanics. Lima did a reasonable job keeping the running game in check last year, and didn't hurt the Tigers as a fielder.

## 1996 Outlook

Lima is much too young to be given up on yet, and the Tigers think that additional coaching and added maturity can help him turn into a useful major league starting pitcher. However, he is now just one of a group of young Detroit pitchers, and will need to earn a spot to stay.

# Brian Maxcy

**Position:** RP
**Bats:** R **Throws:** R
**Ht:** 6' 1" **Wt:** 170

**Opening Day Age:** 24
**Born:** 5/4/71 in Amory, MS
**ML Seasons:** 1

## Overall Statistics

| | W | L | Pct. | ERA | G | GS | Sv | IP | H | BB | SO | HR | BR/IP |
|---|---|---|---|---|---|---|---|---|---|---|---|---|---|
| 1995 | 4 | 5 | .444 | 6.88 | 41 | 0 | 0 | 52.1 | 61 | 31 | 20 | 6 | 1.76 |
| Career | 4 | 5 | .444 | 6.88 | 41 | 0 | 0 | 52.1 | 61 | 31 | 20 | 6 | 1.76 |

## 1995 Season

Righty reliever Brian Maxcy was probably rushed to the majors ahead of schedule last year. Maxcy started off sharp after being recalled from Triple-A Toledo last May, but he got consistently worse from month to month, capping his frustrations with a disastrous September. Used frequently in middle relief during the season's second half, Maxcy's final numbers were pretty brutal, but he pitched fairly well for much of the year.

## Pitching & Defense

Maxcy was converted to relief pitching relatively recently, and he's just starting to get comfortable in the bullpen. He has a sinking fastball that was devastating in the minors, but he needs to develop better control of it. His velocity is in the high 80s, which makes his sinker a heavy ball. His mechanics are still inconsistent, and he got too many pitches up last year to be effective. Maxcy holds runners fairly well, but struggled a bit in fielding his position during his first season.

## 1996 Outlook

In a bullpen that is wide open entering this season, Maxcy will be part of the crowd auditioning for a job. His stuff is probably a little short to be considered a closer candidate, but he could end up sticking in a middle-inning or set-up role.

# Todd Steverson

**Position:** LF
**Bats:** R **Throws:** R
**Ht:** 6' 2" **Wt:** 200

**Opening Day Age:** 24
**Born:** 11/15/71 in Los Angeles, CA
**ML Seasons:** 1

## Overall Statistics

| | G | AB | R | H | D | T | HR | RBI | SB | BB | SO | Avg | OBP | Slg |
|---|---|---|---|---|---|---|---|---|---|---|---|---|---|---|
| 1995 | 30 | 42 | 11 | 11 | 0 | 0 | 2 | 6 | 2 | 6 | 10 | .262 | .340 | .405 |
| Career | 30 | 42 | 11 | 11 | 0 | 0 | 2 | 6 | 2 | 6 | 10 | .262 | .340 | .405 |

## 1995 Season

Acquired from the Toronto organization in the Rule 5 draft, former number-one draft choice Todd Steverson showed promise in limited play with the Tigers last year. The Tigers needed to keep Steverson on their major league roster or risk losing him, and he spent most of the year either on the bench or on the injured list. A sprained right wrist kept him on the shelf from June until September.

## Hitting, Baserunning & Defense

When Steverson was first drafted, scouts saw him as a multi-tool player, one who combined power, speed and hitting for average. But his skills never developed in the Blue Jays' organization; in fact, they seemed to be deteriorating. He has a smooth stroke but tends to overswing. Steverson has worked to both cut down his swing and to stop trying to pull everything, because he can be overpowered with just average stuff. For a big man, he has good speed and could develop into a solid basestealer. He has an above-average arm, but often had trouble in the minors misjudging balls.

## 1996 Outlook

Steverson has intriguing skills and is still young enough to fashion a solid career. The Tigers are likely to give him every chance, because the organization simply does not have many pure athletes like this. He'll be one of many young Tigers trying to impress the new regime in the spring.

Detroit Tigers

# Franklin Stubbs

**Position**: 1B/LF
**Bats**: L  **Throws**: L
**Ht**: 6' 2"  **Wt**: 209

**Opening Day Age**: 35
**Born**: 10/21/60 in
Laurinburg, NC
**ML Seasons**: 10

## Overall Statistics

|      | G | AB | R | H | D | T | HR | RBI | SB | BB | SO | Avg | OBP | Slg |
|------|---|-----|-----|-----|-----|----|-----|-----|----|-----|-----|------|------|------|
| 1995 | 62 | 116 | 13 | 29 | 11 | 0 | 2 | 19 | 0 | 19 | 27 | .250 | .358 | .397 |
| Career | 945 | 2591 | 323 | 602 | 109 | 12 | 104 | 348 | 74 | 260 | 626 | .232 | .303 | .404 |

## 1995 Season

Veteran slugger Franklin Stubbs returned to the majors last season after a two-year hiatus in Japan. Stubbs had hopes of reviving what was once a promising career, but a June nosedive took some bite out of his numbers. Stubbs did provide occasional power to the Tiger offense, but his overall contributions were limited.

## Hitting, Baserunning & Defense

Stubbs has always been a notorious low-fastball hitter, and has never been able to hit change-ups or breaking balls with any consistency. He is also vulnerable to anything above the belt, and that's where pitchers try to stay with their offerings. Stubbs is strictly a platoon player, and his only real chance of doing damage comes against righties. He is a below-average runner who is no threat to steal, and he'll make mistakes on the bases. Originally a first baseman, Stubbs has also played the outfield though he has a weak arm and poor hands. He also has little range, whether in the outfield or infield.

## 1996 Outlook

Because he bats left-handed and has a track record of occasionally hitting homers, Stubbs could conceivably find a job as a bench player this year. But at 35 and with little success since 1990, he'll be fortunate if the opportunity comes.

# Ron Tingley

**Position**: C
**Bats**: R  **Throws**: R
**Ht**: 6' 2"  **Wt**: 195

**Opening Day Age**: 36
**Born**: 5/27/59 in
Presque Isle, ME
**ML Seasons**: 9

## Overall Statistics

|      | G | AB | R | H | D | T | HR | RBI | SB | BB | SO | Avg | OBP | Slg |
|------|---|-----|-----|-----|-----|----|-----|-----|----|-----|-----|------|------|------|
| 1995 | 54 | 124 | 14 | 28 | 8 | 1 | 4 | 18 | 0 | 15 | 38 | .226 | .307 | .403 |
| Career | 278 | 563 | 52 | 110 | 27 | 3 | 10 | 55 | 2 | 54 | 165 | .195 | .270 | .307 |

## 1995 Season

Career backup catcher Ron Tingley had some productive moments in his limited playing time with the Tigers last year. But there were some big gaps between those moments. Tingley still set career highs in batting average, on-base percentage, and slugging percentage while starting 40 games behind the plate.

## Hitting, Baserunning & Defense

Tingley can pull pitches on the inner half of the plate with power on occasion. He has home-run strength to left, and he can also drive a ball to the opposite field when he gets his arms extended. Tingley has trouble with offspeed stuff, and will also chase too many breaking balls—one reason why he has never been able to stay in the lineup on an everyday basis. He's no baserunning threat whatsoever. Behind the plate Tingley has a fairly quick release, and even though his throws to second tend to dip into the dirt, he caught runners at above the league rate last season. In addition, he does a solid job of blocking balls and handling pitchers.

## 1996 Outlook

Backup catchers are like left-handed relief pitchers. They always seem to eventually find work somewhere. Tingley is no exception, and his ability to hit an occasional home run makes him a player who can help any number of major league benches.

# Other Detroit Tigers

**Pat Ahearne** (**Pos**: RHP, **Age**: 26)

With the Tigers desperate (as always) for pitching, Ahearne was called up in June. He was hammered (11.70 ERA) in four games, and returned to Toledo. He'll probably spend four years in Triple-A. 1996 Outlook: C

**Ben Blomdahl** (**Pos**: RHP, **Age**: 25)

A starter his first four years in the minors, Blomdahl shifted to relief last season and pitched fairly well in Toledo. He'll be one of many weak candidates for the Detroit closer job this spring. 1996 Outlook: B

**Mike Gardiner** (**Pos**: RHP, **Age**: 30)

Hampered by severe sinus problems much of last season, Gardiner allowed 27 hits and five homers in just 12 innings. He was waived by Detroit at the end of the season, leaving his career in jeopardy. 1996 Outlook: C

**Kirk Gibson** (**Pos**: DH, **Age**: 38, **Bats**: L)

After his amazing comeback in 1994, Gibson hit .341 with eight homers last May. But he hit just .214 with no power after that, and retired on August 11. You never know, he might return once more. . . 1996 Outlook: D

**Greg Gohr** (**Pos**: RHP, **Age**: 28)

The Tigers' number-one draft pick back in 1989, Gohr missed most of last season after arm surgery, but he came back in September and pitched well in relief. Might get a tryout as closer this spring, and should fill some role. 1996 Outlook: A

**Joe Hall** (**Pos**: LF, **Age**: 30, **Bats**: R)

Hall is 30, and he's only got 43 major league at-bats to his credit. On the other hand, Hall's Triple-A batting average the last two seasons is .315, and the Tigers don't have a lot of prospects. 1996 Outlook: C

**Dwayne Henry** (**Pos**: RHP, **Age**: 34)

Henry, who still throws a plus fastball and sharp slider, pitched well at Triple-A Toledo last year, recording 52 strikeouts in 48 innings with a 3.35 ERA. The Tigers waived him in October anyway. 1996 Outlook: B

**Phil Hiatt** (**Pos**: RF, **Age**: 26, **Bats**: R)

After passing off Hiatt as a prospect for years, the Royals traded him to Detroit for Juan Samuel. If the Tigers let him play enough, he'd threaten the single-season strikeout record. They won't. 1996 Outlook: C

**Mike Moore** (**Pos**: RHP, **Age**: 36)

Over the last three seasons, Moore compiled a 5.90 ERA in 86 starts with the Tigers. That might be the longest period of utter ineffectiveness in major league history. Hasn't officially retired yet. 1996 Outlook: D

**Mike Myers** (**Pos**: LHP, **Age**: 26)

No, he wasn't in *Halloween*, and he wasn't in *Wayne's World*. This Mike Myers is a pitcher whose minor league record the last three seasons is 8-24. Decent arm, but that's about it. 1996 Outlook: C

**Phil Nevin** (**Pos**: LF/3B, **Age**: 25, **Bats**: R)

The Astros had the first pick in the draft in 1992, and they used it on Phil Nevin. Last year they got tired of waiting, and traded Nevin to the Tigers. He's a bust thus far, but still has room for growth. 1996 Outlook: B

**Shannon Penn** (**Pos**: 2B, **Age**: 26, **Bats**: B)

Penn isn't much of a hitter, but if Lou Whitaker really does retire the Tigers will need another middle infielder, at least in a utility role. Penn will take a walk and has good speed. 1996 Outlook: C

**Steve Rodriguez** (**Pos**: 2B, **Age**: 25, **Bats**: R)

Speaking of Lou Whitaker, Rodriguez is another candidate to take over at second base. He's not much of a hitter, .241 average last season in Triple-A Pawtucket, but is regarded as a solid defender. 1996 Outlook: B

**Clint Sodowsky** (**Pos**: RHP, **Age**: 23)

Despite a low strikeout rate, Sodowsky went 10-6 with a 2.65 ERA at Double- and Triple-A last season. He didn't fare so well in six starts with the Tigers, but he's very young and could develop. 1996 Outlook: B

**Derrick White** (**Pos**: 1B, **Age**: 26, **Bats**: R)

Noted for his defensive work, White had his best season last year with Toledo, blasting 14 homers in 87 games. He won't play with the Tigers unless Fielder gets hurt, and probably not even then. 1996 Outlook: C

**Sean Whiteside** (**Pos**: LHP, **Age**: 24)

One of many young Tiger hurlers thrown to the lions last year, Whiteside was called up from Double-A Jacksonville and pitched four innings. He's got a nice left arm, which is a good sign. 1996 Outlook: C

**Detroit Tigers**

# Detroit Tigers Minor League Prospects

## Organization Overview:

It's been almost 20 years since the Tigers promoted the glorious triumvirate of Alan Trammell, Lou Whitaker and Jack Morris, a trio which fueled years of success culminating in a World Championship in 1984. Since then, though, the fruits produced by Detroit's farm system have been few and far between. The only home-grown talent to make an impact recently has been Travis Fryman. For years the Tigers were notorious for neglecting their farm system, and they continue to pay the price for that. In the last few seasons, however, the Tigers have increased their number of farm teams to six, enlarged the size of their player development staff and improved the quality of their drafts. The benefits resulting from that change in philosophy have been slow to materialize, and it appears it will be at least a couple more years before legitimate prospects are playing in the Motor City. But the days when Detroit plugged holes temporarily with retreads and free agents appear to be over. The Tigers commitment to youth looks genuine.

## Frank Catalanotto

**Position:** 2B  
**Bats:** L **Throws:** R  
**Ht:** 6' 0"  **Wt:** 170  
**Opening Day Age:** 21  
**Born:** 4/27/74 in Smithtown, NY

### Recent Statistics

|              | G | AB | R | H | D | T | HR | RBI | SB | BB | SO | AVG |
|--------------|---|----|----|-----|----|----|----|-----|----|----|----|------|
| 93 R Bristol | 55 | 199 | 37 | 61 | 9 | 5 | 3 | 22 | 3 | 15 | 19 | .307 |
| 94 A Fayetteville | 119 | 458 | 72 | 149 | 24 | 8 | 3 | 56 | 4 | 37 | 54 | .325 |
| 95 AA Jacksonville | 134 | 491 | 66 | 111 | 19 | 5 | 8 | 48 | 13 | 49 | 56 | .226 |
| 95 MLE | 134 | 487 | 65 | 107 | 17 | 4 | 8 | 47 | 10 | 41 | 60 | .220 |

Catalanotto struggled in making the jump from slow-A to Double-A last season, but he was just 21, relatively young for that move upward. His 1994 season was very good, both offensively and defensively. Although he isn't a home-run threat, Catalanotto's 35 extra-base hits that year nicely complemented a .325 batting average. He also flashed exceptional range at second base. His 1995 season was a letdown by comparison, but he did improve his plate discipline and increased his stolen-base total to 13. With Lou Whitaker approaching the end of his brilliant career, Catalanotto will soon figure in Detroit's second base plans.

## Tony Clark

**Position:** 1B-DH  
**Bats:** B **Throws:** R  
**Ht:** 6' 8"  **Wt:** 240  
**Opening Day Age:** 23  
**Born:** 6/15/72 in Newton, KS

### Recent Statistics

|              | G | AB | R | H | D | T | HR | RBI | SB | BB | SO | AVG |
|--------------|---|----|----|-----|----|----|----|-----|----|----|----|------|
| 95 AAA Toledo | 110 | 405 | 50 | 98 | 17 | 2 | 14 | 63 | 0 | 52 | 129 | .242 |
| 95 AL Detroit | 27 | 101 | 10 | 24 | 5 | 1 | 3 | 11 | 0 | 8 | 30 | .238 |
| 95 MLE | 110 | 403 | 51 | 96 | 15 | 1 | 17 | 64 | 0 | 54 | 137 | .238 |

Clark's second full professional season wasn't as impressive as his first, but he continued to flash the power potential which made him the second player selected overall in 1990. Clark is listed at 6'8" and 240 pounds, and when he gets hold of the ball no park will contain it. As a former college basketball player he's quite coordinated for a player his size, although he did have trouble making contact in Triple-A, striking out almost once every three at-bats. The time Clark missed while he was chasing his basketball dream has surely slowed his development, but he still won't turn 24 until this June. He may soon ease Cecil Fielder into the DH role for the Tigers.

## Cade Gaspar

**Position:** P  
**Bats:** R **Throws:** R  
**Ht:** 6' 3"  **Wt:** 175  
**Opening Day Age:** 22  
**Born:** 8/21/73 in Mission Viejo, CA

### Recent Statistics

|              | W | L | ERA | G | GS | Sv | IP | H | R | BB | SO | HR |
|--------------|---|----|------|----|----|----|------|----|----|----|----|----|
| 94 A Lakeland | 1 | 3 | 5.58 | 8 | 8 | 0 | 30.2 | 28 | 25 | 8 | 25 | 6 |
| 95 A Lakeland | 7 | 6 | 3.90 | 23 | 23 | 0 | 99.1 | 95 | 48 | 44 | 97 | 5 |

Gaspar is yet another son of an ex-big leaguer. Cade's father, Rod Gaspar, played briefly for the Mets and Padres. Cade was the Tigers' top draft pick in 1994. His second tour of duty in the Florida State League was more successful than his first, with his biggest improvement coming in a drastically reduced home-run rate. Gaspar has three quality pitches, including a fastball, change and curveball, his best pitch. He played a lot of shortstop in junior college, so Gaspar is still relatively inexperienced as a pitcher. He'll almost surely begin 1996 in Double-A, with a chance to soon help Detroit's beleaguered big league staff.

## Rudy Pemberton

**Position:** OF      **Opening Day Age:** 26
**Bats:** R **Throws:** R    **Born:** 12/17/69 in San
**Ht:** 6' 1" **Wt:** 185     Pedro De Macoris, DR

### Recent Statistics

|  | G | AB | R | H | D | T | HR | RBI | SB | BB | SO | AVG |
|---|---|---|---|---|---|---|---|---|---|---|---|---|
| 95 AAA Toledo | 67 | 224 | 31 | 77 | 15 | 3 | 7 | 23 | 8 | 15 | 36 | .344 |
| 95 AL Detroit | 12 | 30 | 3 | 9 | 3 | 1 | 0 | 3 | 0 | 1 | 5 | .300 |
| 95 MLE | 67 | 222 | 31 | 75 | 14 | 2 | 7 | 23 | 6 | 15 | 38 | .338 |

This guy deserves a shot. Since 1991, Pemberton's batting average has risen from .229 to .265 to .276 to .303, and finally to .344 last season. His slugging percentage has also shown steady improvement, increasing from .304 in 1991 to .531 last year. This has all been accomplished while the caliber of competition increased from Class A to Triple-A. Pemberton doesn't walk much, but he'll hit an occasional home run and has stolen as many as 30 bases. He's no longer a pup, and since the Tigers gave him only 30 at-bats in his only big-league experience last year, he may not fit in their plans.

## Cam Smith

**Position:** P      **Opening Day Age:** 22
**Bats:** R **Throws:** R    **Born:** 9/20/73 in
**Ht:** 6' 3" **Wt:** 190     Brooklyn, NY

### Recent Statistics

|  | W | L | ERA | G | GS | Sv | IP | H | R | BB | SO | HR |
|---|---|---|---|---|---|---|---|---|---|---|---|---|
| 93 R Bristol | 3 | 1 | 3.58 | 9 | 7 | 0 | 37.2 | 25 | 22 | 22 | 33 | 5 |
| 93 A Niagara Fal | 0 | 0 | 18.00 | 2 | 2 | 0 | 5.0 | 12 | 11 | 6 | 0 | 0 |
| 94 A Fayettevlle | 5 | 13 | 6.06 | 26 | 26 | 0 | 133.2 | 133 | 100 | 86 | 128 | 10 |
| 95 A Fayettevlle | 13 | 8 | 3.81 | 29 | 29 | 0 | 149.0 | 110 | 75 | 87 | 166 | 6 |

Smith is one of the hardest throwers in Detroit's system, and he struck out slightly more than 10 batters per nine innings last season. It was his second year in slow-A ball, and he showed improvement across the board. He lowered his ERA from 6.06 to 3.81 while reversing his record from 5-13 to 13-8. He also reduced his walks and home runs allowed and was one of the toughest pitchers to make contact against in the Sally League, allowing only 6.6 hits per nine innings. Smith, the Tigers' third-round draft pick in 1993, needs to work on developing a consistent breaking pitch. He could skip the Florida State League and reach Double-A this season.

## Justin Thompson

**Position:** P      **Opening Day Age:** 23
**Bats:** L **Throws:** L    **Born:** 3/8/73 in San
**Ht:** 6' 3" **Wt:** 175     Antonio, TX

### Recent Statistics

|  | W | L | ERA | G | GS | Sv | IP | H | R | BB | SO | HR |
|---|---|---|---|---|---|---|---|---|---|---|---|---|
| 93 A Lakeland | 4 | 4 | 3.56 | 11 | 11 | 0 | 55.2 | 65 | 25 | 16 | 46 | 1 |
| 93 AA London | 3 | 6 | 4.09 | 14 | 14 | 0 | 83.2 | 96 | 51 | 37 | 72 | 9 |
| 95 A Lakeland | 2 | 1 | 4.88 | 6 | 6 | 0 | 24.0 | 30 | 13 | 8 | 20 | 1 |
| 95 AA Jacksonvlle | 6 | 7 | 3.73 | 18 | 18 | 0 | 123.0 | 110 | 55 | 38 | 98 | 7 |

Thompson was once the Tigers' top pitching prospect before being shelved for the entire 1994 season with an elbow injury. He came back as strong as ever in 1995, and at 23 he's again established himself as a pitcher to watch. Thompson's curveball is his best pitch, and while he throws with just average velocity he is left-handed. He was the Tigers' top pick in 1991 out of high school, but has been bothered with various ailments throughout his professional career. If he can remain healthy, Thompson should eventually acquire some big-league service time.

## Bubba Trammell

**Position:** OF      **Opening Day Age:** 24
**Bats:** R **Throws:** R    **Born:** 11/6/71 in
**Ht:** 6' 2" **Wt:** 205     Knoxville, TN

### Recent Statistics

|  | G | AB | R | H | D | T | HR | RBI | SB | BB | SO | AVG |
|---|---|---|---|---|---|---|---|---|---|---|---|---|
| 94 A Jamestown | 65 | 235 | 37 | 70 | 18 | 6 | 5 | 41 | 9 | 23 | 32 | .298 |
| 95 A Lakeland | 122 | 454 | 61 | 129 | 32 | 3 | 16 | 72 | 13 | 48 | 80 | .284 |

In what other organization would a prospect named "Trammell" sound more natural? Unlike Alan, Bubba plays the outfield, but his hitting does show as much promise. Drafted in the 11th round in 1994 out of Tennessee, Bubba smacked 16 homers in the pitcher-friendly Florida State League last season. Trammell has also banged out 50 doubles in just 689 professional at-bats. Many of those doubles might become homers as he matures and moves into more neutral ballparks. Trammell will be 24 years old when he plays in 1996, most likely at Double-A Jacksonville.

## Others to Watch

Outfielder **Jayson Bass**, the Tigers' fifth-round selection in 1993, shows potential, but he's had trouble making contact. Bass struck out 111 times in 368 at-bats at low-A last year, an unacceptable rate that contributed to a disappointing .215 average. . . **Ivan Cruz** hit more homers at the Double-A or Triple-A level, 31, than anyone other than California's Todd Greene. But Cruz did so at Double-A Jacksonville, which was a demotion from the previous season. . . Outfielder **Juan Encarnacion** hit 16 homers and 31 doubles in the Sally League at age 19 last year. One area that needs improvement is plate discipline. . . Righthander **Jason Jordan**, Detroit's 17th-round pick in 1994 out of Wichita State, has a 2.47 ERA through his two pro seasons. Jordan isn't overpowering but knows how to pitch. . . Lefthander **Greg Whiteman** posted Randy Johnson-like strikeout totals last year, with 165 Ks in 145 innings. However, the 1994 third-round draft choice managed just a 7-10 record and 4.47 ERA at the Class-A level.

# Kevin Appier

## 1995 Season

Kevin Appier avoided his usual slow start as he rushed to the pinnacle of A.L. pitchers through the first half of the 1995 season. But whether due to the strain of leading a four-man rotation or not, tendinitis landed him on the disabled list after a few poor midseason starts. It was the second straight year that minor shoulder problems hampered Appier. Returning to the (by then five-man) rotation in mid-August, Appier gradually regained his form down the stretch.

## Pitching

Appier throws three pitches very hard: fastball, slider and splitter. Falling off the mound toward the first-base line, coupled with his high, overhead delivery, often results in much side-to-side movement of both his low-90s fastball and a slider that moves in on lefties' hands. His split-finger pitch works especially well against hitters who sit on the fastball or slider, but Appier can't always control it. Early in a game, Appier will work first with inside fastballs, then add the other pitches the next time through the order. While he throws hard from start to finish, Appier occasionally overthrows late in the game, missing wild and high. Even he can't get away with grooving fastballs.

## Defense

An exaggerated delivery often leaves Appier out of position to field hot grounders back through the box. This delivery and a below-average pickoff move give baserunners an advantage; Appier allowed nine successful stolen bases in 13 attempts in 1995. His throws to the bases are inconsistent and his poor footwork makes him look clumsy when covering first base.

## 1996 Outlook

Appier has the great hard stuff expected of a staff ace, and he's in the prime of his career. Simply, he is one of the best—and most competitive—pitchers in baseball. The delivery which provides that power pitching has recently been a cause of shoulder problems, and some have long predicted that his arm wouldn't last. But as long as he's healthy, Appier has to be considered a top Cy Young candidate.

**Position:** SP
**Bats:** R  **Throws:** R
**Ht:** 6' 2"  **Wt:** 195

**Opening Day Age:** 28
**Born:** 12/6/67 in Lancaster, CA
**ML Seasons:** 7
**Pronunciation:** APE-ee-er

### Overall Statistics

|  | W | L | Pct. | ERA | G | GS | Sv | IP | H | BB | SO | HR | BR/IP |
|---|---|---|---|---|---|---|---|---|---|---|---|---|---|
| 1995 | 15 | 10 | .600 | 3.89 | 31 | 31 | 0 | 201.1 | 163 | 80 | 185 | 14 | 1.21 |
| Career | 81 | 54 | .600 | 3.22 | 190 | 178 | 0 | 1218.1 | 1068 | 419 | 961 | 72 | 1.22 |

### How Often He Throws Strikes

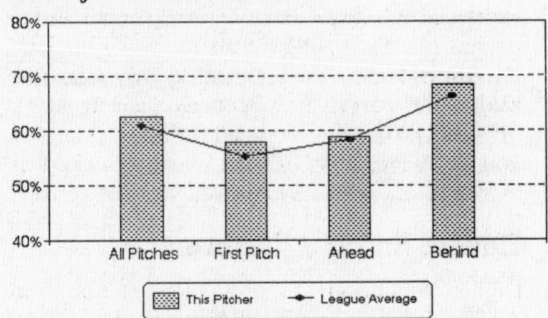

### 1995 Situational Stats

|  | W | L | ERA | Sv | IP |  | AB | H | HR | RBI | Avg |
|---|---|---|---|---|---|---|---|---|---|---|---|
| Home | 7 | 6 | 4.38 | 0 | 109.0 | LHB | 427 | 108 | 11 | 53 | .253 |
| Road | 8 | 4 | 3.31 | 0 | 92.1 | RHB | 311 | 55 | 3 | 26 | .177 |
| First Half | 11 | 5 | 3.04 | 0 | 121.1 | Sc Pos | 156 | 44 | 3 | 59 | .282 |
| Scnd Half | 4 | 5 | 5.18 | 0 | 80.0 | Clutch | 46 | 14 | 2 | 10 | .304 |

### 1995 Rankings (American League)

- ➡ 1st in lowest batting average allowed vs. right-handed batters (.177)
- ➡ 2nd in lowest batting average allowed (.221) and most pitches thrown per batter (4.03)
- ➡ 3rd in lowest slugging percentage allowed (.351)
- ➡ 4th in games started, least home runs allowed per 9 innings (.63) and most strikeouts per 9 innings (8.3)
- ➡ 5th in hit batsmen (8) and strikeouts
- ➡ 6th in lowest on-base percentage allowed (.303) and ERA on the road (3.31)
- ➡ Led the Royals in wins, complete games (4), hit batsmen (8) and strikeouts

# Johnny Damon

**Position:** CF
**Bats:** L **Throws:** L
**Ht:** 6' 0"  **Wt:** 175

**Opening Day Age:** 22
**Born:** 11/5/73 in Fort Riley, KS
**ML Seasons:** 1

## 1995 Season

The future arrived in Kansas City on August 11, when Johnny Damon and several other youngsters were called up to the majors. The centerpiece of the Royal youth movement, Damon was dropped straight into a pennant race, batting leadoff nearly every game. He produced from the outset, hitting over .300 his first month while scoring or driving in several important runs. Damon wound up collecting a total of 198 hits in 1995, leading all professional players.

## Hitting

Using a relaxed, slightly open stance, Damon is a slashing hitter who hits the ball where it's pitched. He'll take outside pitches to left field or pull inside pitches into the right-field gap or down the line. Damon had some trouble against lefthanders; he hasn't yet learned how to read their breaking pitches. Damon showed good patience in the minors, posting a .434 OBA for Wichita, but he was more aggressive in his major league stint.

## Baserunning & Defense

Damon used his great speed to steal 152 bases as a minor leaguer. He ran the bases cautiously as a rookie, and finished the year with seven steals in seven tries. He's still learning to use his speed; he'll only get more dangerous when he does. Damon's speed helps him roam the outfield with ease, and he took over in center field last summer from Tom Goodwin, a fine defender in his own right. Only a subpar arm prevents Damon from being a top all-around center fielder, but Damon has worked hard at improving his throwing skills, and he helps himself by charging the ball hard.

## 1996 Outlook

The Royals see Damon as an emerging star who embodies their commitment to youth. He'll open 1996 as the club's starting center fielder and lead-off man. As Damon matures as a hitter and his power increases, he's expected to move into the third spot in the lineup. Damon gave Royals fans a glimpse of his potential over the last seven weeks of 1995. They'll see the whole package in 1996.

### Overall Statistics

|  | G | AB | R | H | D | T | HR | RBI | SB | BB | SO | Avg | OBP | Slg |
|---|---|---|---|---|---|---|---|---|---|---|---|---|---|---|
| 1995 | 47 | 188 | 32 | 53 | 11 | 5 | 3 | 23 | 7 | 12 | 22 | .282 | .324 | .441 |
| Career | 47 | 188 | 32 | 53 | 11 | 5 | 3 | 23 | 7 | 12 | 22 | .282 | .324 | .441 |

### Where He Hits the Ball

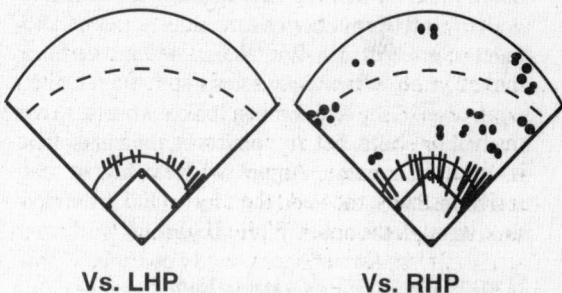

**Vs. LHP**          **Vs. RHP**

### 1995 Situational Stats

|  | AB | H | HR | RBI | Avg |  | AB | H | HR | RBI | Avg |
|---|---|---|---|---|---|---|---|---|---|---|---|
| Home | 100 | 29 | 1 | 12 | .290 | LHP | 39 | 9 | 0 | 4 | .231 |
| Road | 88 | 24 | 2 | 11 | .273 | RHP | 149 | 44 | 3 | 19 | .295 |
| First Half | 0 | 0 | 0 | 0 | - | Sc Pos | 41 | 12 | 0 | 19 | .293 |
| Scnd Half | 188 | 53 | 3 | 23 | .282 | Clutch | 26 | 6 | 1 | 2 | .231 |

### 1995 Rankings (American League)
- → 7th in lowest batting average on a 3-2 count (.067)
- → 10th in lowest on-base percentage for a lead-off hitter (.345)

# Gary Gaetti

## 1995 Season

As the Royals' sole source of power throughout the 1995 season, Gary Gaetti carried a huge burden. Batting cleanup in a weak lineup, he rarely got a good pitch to hit. Nevertheless, Gaetti ended up with one of his best seasons ever. He set a career high with 35 homers, the second-highest total in Royals history. Gaetti's importance to the Royal offense can't be overestimated; when he slumped over the final two weeks of the season, the club's scoring rate fell off by almost two runs per game.

## Hitting

An aggressive hitter with a slight uppercut swing, Gaetti looks to pull the first fastball he sees. The worst mistake a pitcher can make is to get behind Gaetti early in the count. When he can sit on a fastball, he's simply devastating. On the other hand, when Gaetti's behind in the count he'll wave at breaking balls off the plate. Opponents often placed three infielders to the left-field side of second base, but Gaetti's a flyball hitter and grounded into only seven double plays all year.

## Baserunning & Defense

No speed demon at 37, Gaetti knows his limitations and rarely takes risks on the bases. A four-time Gold Glover at third base, Gaetti still has quick reflexes around the hot corner. His range is average-plus and he throws accurately. Gaetti occasionally spelled Wally Joyner at first base, where he was out of place, reacting slowly on grounders to the right side and looking awkward on difficult chances.

## 1996 Outlook

It's easy to write off a 37 year old who has just had his career year. However, Gaetti has shown remarkable resiliency and the ability to adjust to different methods of pitching. Once again a free agent, Gaetti should command a healthy reward for his fantastic 1995 showing. He's having fun again and should be a regular power threat wherever he plays in 1996.

**Position:** 3B/1B
**Bats:** R  **Throws:** R
**Ht:** 6' 0"  **Wt:** 200

**Opening Day Age:** 37
**Born:** 8/19/58 in Centralia, IL
**ML Seasons:** 15
**Pronunciation:** guy-ETT-ee

### Overall Statistics

|  | G | AB | R | H | D | T | HR | RBI | SB | BB | SO | Avg | OBP | Slg |
|---|---|---|---|---|---|---|---|---|---|---|---|---|---|---|
| 1995 | 137 | 514 | 76 | 134 | 27 | 0 | 35 | 96 | 3 | 47 | 91 | .261 | .329 | .518 |
| Career | 1972 | 7203 | 914 | 1832 | 349 | 32 | 292 | 1075 | 86 | 499 | 1301 | .254 | .306 | .433 |

### Where He Hits the Ball

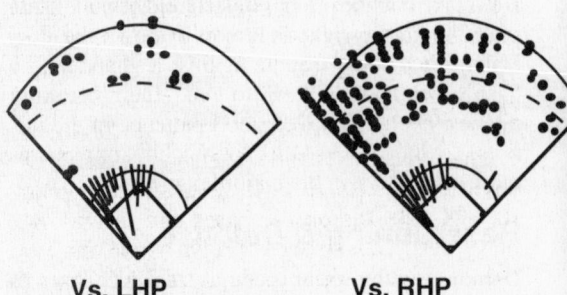

Vs. LHP          Vs. RHP

### 1995 Situational Stats

|  | AB | H | HR | RBI | Avg |  | AB | H | HR | RBI | Avg |
|---|---|---|---|---|---|---|---|---|---|---|---|
| Home | 257 | 70 | 16 | 43 | .272 | LHP | 132 | 28 | 9 | 23 | .212 |
| Road | 257 | 64 | 19 | 53 | .249 | RHP | 382 | 106 | 26 | 73 | .277 |
| First Half | 240 | 64 | 17 | 49 | .267 | Sc Pos | 154 | 37 | 11 | 62 | .240 |
| Scnd Half | 274 | 70 | 18 | 47 | .255 | Clutch | 91 | 25 | 11 | 20 | .275 |

### 1995 Rankings (American League)

→ 2nd in highest percentage of swings on the first pitch (47.9%)
→ 4th in lowest batting average vs. left-handed pitchers (.212) and fielding percentage at third base (.954)
→ 5th in lowest percentage of pitches taken (45.7%)
→ 6th in errors at third base (15)
→ 7th in home runs and HR frequency (14.7 ABs per HR)
→ Led the Royals in home runs, at-bats, runs scored, total bases (266) and RBI

# Greg Gagne

## 1995 Season

Greg Gagne's 1995 season was a carbon copy of the campaigns he authored in his first two years as a Royal: useful hitting for a middle infielder and fantastic defensive play. A midseason knee strain sidelined him for a few weeks, but Gagne returned in time for the Royals' stretch run.

## Hitting

Primarily a singles hitter, Gagne is an aggressive first-pitch hitter who's prone to overswinging at high fastballs. He's also vulnerable to inside hard stuff, then breaking balls outside and in the dirt. Gagne typically pulls ground balls but hits fly balls to the opposite field; he has decent gap power. One of the most consistent offensive players from year to year, Gagne is extremely streaky within each season.

## Baserunning & Defense

Gagne's speed is barely average but he'll take baserunning risks. In 1995, he wasn't able to outrun his mistakes on the bases and ran into too many outs. Glovework is Gagne's area of expertise. Like many top shortstops, as Gagne's physical skills have aged, he has compensated with mental adjustments. He makes difficult plays look easy and impossible plays routine. Gagne always reaches many more balls than the average shortstop, and his range factor and zone rating were again among the best in the majors. He did make an unusually large number of errors in 1995, most on relatively easy plays. Gagne turns the double play well and sports a strong, accurate arm, often under-appreciated because of his smooth, easy throwing motion.

## 1996 Outlook

The Royals simply couldn't afford to re-sign the free-agent Gagne, and on November 30 he signed a deal with the Los Angeles Dodgers. Gagne's sure hands will be a welcome change from Jose Offerman, but his hitting numbers should suffer as he moves to pitcher-friendly Dodger Stadium.

**Position:** SS
**Bats:** R  **Throws:** R
**Ht:** 5'11"  **Wt:** 180

**Opening Day Age:** 34
**Born:** 11/12/61 in Fall River, MA
**ML Seasons:** 13
**Pronunciation:** GAG-nee

### Overall Statistics

| | G | AB | R | H | D | T | HR | RBI | SB | BB | SO | Avg | OBP | Slg |
|---|---|---|---|---|---|---|---|---|---|---|---|---|---|---|
| 1995 | 120 | 430 | 58 | 110 | 25 | 4 | 6 | 49 | 3 | 38 | 60 | .256 | .316 | .374 |
| Career | 1526 | 4731 | 615 | 1202 | 263 | 45 | 92 | 492 | 102 | 286 | 908 | .254 | .299 | .387 |

### Where He Hits the Ball

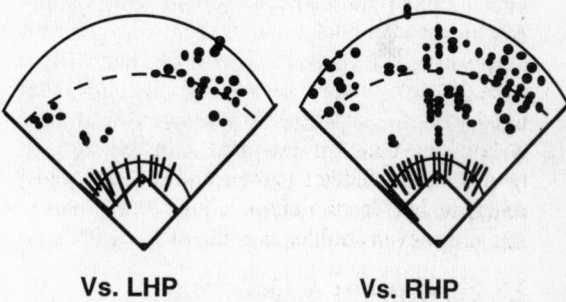

Vs. LHP          Vs. RHP

### 1995 Situational Stats

| | AB | H | HR | RBI | Avg | | AB | H | HR | RBI | Avg |
|---|---|---|---|---|---|---|---|---|---|---|---|
| Home | 202 | 55 | 2 | 25 | .272 | LHP | 117 | 29 | 1 | 10 | .248 |
| Road | 228 | 55 | 4 | 24 | .241 | RHP | 313 | 81 | 5 | 39 | .259 |
| First Half | 167 | 45 | 2 | 19 | .269 | Sc Pos | 116 | 26 | 0 | 38 | .224 |
| Scnd Half | 263 | 65 | 4 | 30 | .247 | Clutch | 62 | 18 | 1 | 3 | .290 |

### 1995 Rankings (American League)

- ➡ 1st in errors at shortstop (18)
- ➡ 3rd in lowest fielding percentage at shortstop (.969)
- ➡ 6th in lowest on-base percentage
- ➡ 7th in lowest on-base percentage vs. right-handed pitchers (.319)
- ➡ 8th in lowest batting average with the bases loaded (.091)
- ➡ 10th in lowest batting average and lowest slugging percentage
- ➡ Led the Royals in most pitches seen per plate appearance (3.63) and batting average on an 0-2 count (.267)

Kansas City Royals

# Tom Goodwin

## 1995 Season

Tom Goodwin had always been considered a speedster who couldn't hit enough to play in the majors. With the trade of Brian McRae to the Cubs before last season began, Goodwin was thrust into the role of starting center fielder and number-two hitter. By placing among team leaders in hits and runs scored, and battling Kenny Lofton down to the season's final weekend for the league's stolen-base crown, Goodwin proved that he belongs in the big leagues.

## Hitting

Goodwin hits from a wide-open, upright stance, nearly facing the pitcher head on. He then strides into the pitch and slaps at the ball with a slight downward swing, hoping to take advantage of his excellent speed. He has a short stroke and will hit the ball—albeit not very far—to all fields. Platooned late in the season by manager Bob Boone, who was trying to spread around the at-bats, Goodwin had better luck getting on base against righthanders. The only type of pitcher that particularly gave him trouble were hard throwers who busted him inside with fastballs.

## Baserunning & Defense

Stealing bases is Goodwin's forte. He had early-season problems reading pitchers' moves, and was picked off a few times. Working closely with then-teammate Vince Coleman helped improve Goodwin's success rate dramatically, and he succeeded in 48 of his last 60 attempts. Despite a mediocre arm, Goodwin's great range makes him an above-average left or center fielder. He's especially adept at running down flies deep in the gaps.

## 1996 Outlook

Goodwin's fine 1995 campaign showed he can play major league ball. He became a free agent at year's end and the Royals were lethargic about re-signing him. Still, Goodwin should be able to find major league employment for 1996, whether in Kansas City or elsewhere. He'll never be a star, but Goodwin supplies good defense and speedy baserunning, an attractive combination for many major league teams.

**Position:** CF/LF
**Bats:** L **Throws:** R
**Ht:** 6' 1" **Wt:** 170

**Opening Day Age:** 27
**Born:** 7/27/68 in Fresno, CA
**ML Seasons:** 5

### Overall Statistics

|        | G   | AB  | R  | H   | D  | T | HR | RBI | SB | BB | SO | Avg  | OBP  | Slg  |
|--------|-----|-----|----|-----|----|---|----|-----|----|----|----|------|------|------|
| 1995   | 133 | 480 | 72 | 138 | 16 | 3 | 4  | 28  | 50 | 38 | 72 | .288 | .346 | .358 |
| Career | 238 | 579 | 96 | 161 | 18 | 4 | 4  | 32  | 59 | 45 | 87 | .278 | .335 | .344 |

### Where He Hits the Ball

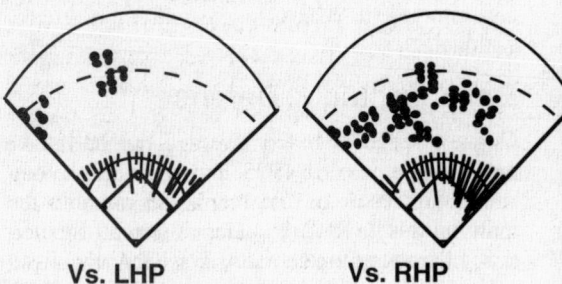

Vs. LHP          Vs. RHP

### 1995 Situational Stats

|           | AB  | H  | HR | RBI | Avg  |        | AB  | H   | HR | RBI | Avg  |
|-----------|-----|----|----|-----|------|--------|-----|-----|----|-----|------|
| Home      | 239 | 73 | 2  | 12  | .305 | LHP    | 115 | 29  | 0  | 6   | .252 |
| Road      | 241 | 65 | 2  | 16  | .270 | RHP    | 365 | 109 | 4  | 22  | .299 |
| First Half| 214 | 62 | 1  | 10  | .290 | Sc Pos | 109 | 26  | 1  | 25  | .239 |
| Scnd Half | 266 | 76 | 3  | 18  | .286 | Clutch | 64  | 18  | 1  | 4   | .281 |

### 1995 Rankings (American League)

- ➡ 1st in sacrifice bunts (14)
- ➡ 2nd in stolen bases, caught stealing (18), highest groundball/flyball ratio (2.2) and bunts in play (43)
- ➡ 3rd in lowest HR frequency (120.0 ABs per HR)
- ➡ 5th in lowest fielding percentage in center field (.986), steals of third (9) and highest percentage of extra bases taken as a runner (65.4%)
- ➡ 6th in errors in center field (3)
- ➡ Led the Royals in singles (115), sacrifice bunts (14), stolen bases, caught stealing (18), highest groundball/flyball ratio (2.2) and bunts in play (43)

# Tom Gordon

## 1995 Season

Inconsistency dogged Tom Gordon throughout the 1995 campaign, much as it has throughout his career. As the Royals' number-three starter, Gordon began the season well enough, winning five of his first seven decisions. But he posted a 5.13 ERA over his last 16 starts and finished the year on a particularly sour note, allowing six runs in the first inning of each of his last two starts.

## Pitching

Gordon works primarily with a sharp curveball and a fastball thrown in the mid-80s. He throws both with an overhand delivery which causes curves to drop straight down. When he gets behind his curve, it's nearly unhittable. Always a durable starter, Gordon usually runs high pitch counts which force him out of the game before the eighth inning. The key for Gordon is control. If he gets his curve over for strikes he can work effectively with either the fastball or the curveball. When he doesn't throw the curveball for strike one, a long count often results as the hitter lays back and waits for a hittable fastball. In games when he allowed fewer than four walks, Gordon's ERA was 3.88; when he allowed *more* than three walks, his ERA ballooned to 6.04.

## Defense

Reliance on breaking pitches has historically limited Gordon's ability to contain the running game. After leading the American League in stolen bases allowed in 1994, Gordon did improve last season, permitting only 12 steals in 17 tries. Gordon throws accurately to the bases and fields his position well enough.

## 1996 Outlook

A free agent following the 1995 season, Gordon will likely move on to another team for 1996. While Gordon has obvious talents—he was once *Baseball America's* Minor League Player of the Year—he doesn't consistently have the command necessary to be anything more than a good second or third starter. On the other hand, Gordon is durable and could be a big winner with the benefit of better run support.

**Position:** SP
**Bats:** R **Throws:** R
**Ht:** 5' 9" **Wt:** 180

**Opening Day Age:** 28
**Born:** 11/18/67 in Sebring, FL
**ML Seasons:** 8
**Nickname:** Flash

### Overall Statistics

| | W | L | Pct. | ERA | G | GS | Sv | IP | H | BB | SO | HR | BR/IP |
|---|---|---|---|---|---|---|---|---|---|---|---|---|---|
| 1995 | 12 | 12 | .500 | 4.43 | 31 | 31 | 0 | 189.0 | 204 | 89 | 119 | 12 | 1.55 |
| Career | 79 | 71 | .527 | 4.02 | 274 | 144 | 3 | 1149.2 | 1040 | 587 | 999 | 91 | 1.42 |

### How Often He Throws Strikes

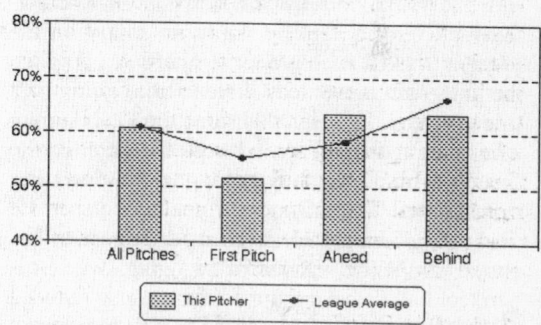

### 1995 Situational Stats

| | W | L | ERA | Sv | IP | | AB | H | HR | RBI | Avg |
|---|---|---|---|---|---|---|---|---|---|---|---|
| Home | 4 | 7 | 3.46 | 0 | 91.0 | LHB | 395 | 125 | 5 | 54 | .316 |
| Road | 8 | 5 | 5.33 | 0 | 98.0 | RHB | 336 | 79 | 7 | 32 | .235 |
| First Half | 5 | 5 | 3.96 | 0 | 86.1 | Sc Pos | 188 | 51 | 3 | 74 | .271 |
| Scnd Half | 7 | 7 | 4.82 | 0 | 102.2 | Clutch | 65 | 14 | 1 | 5 | .215 |

### 1995 Rankings (American League)

- ➡ 3rd in least home runs allowed per 9 innings (.57)
- ➡ 4th in games started, highest on-base percentage allowed (.356) and most baserunners allowed per 9 innings (14.1)
- ➡ 6th in highest batting average allowed (.279), highest stolen base percentage allowed (70.6%), least run support per 9 innings (4.8), most GDPs induced per 9 innings (1.0) and highest ERA on the road (5.33)
- ➡ 7th in walks allowed, GDPs induced (21) and highest groundball/flyball ratio allowed (1.9)
- ➡ Led the Royals in walks allowed, wild pitches (9), stolen bases allowed (12), runners caught stealing (5) and GDPs induced (21)

# Mark Gubicza

## 1995 Season

In 1995, Mark Gubicza completed his transformation from power pitcher to finesse artist. A one-hit shutout of Oakland was probably his finest game ever, and he closed the campaign with a four-hit shutout against the White Sox. Gubicza's losing record primarily resulted from poor run support; the Royals scored more than three runs in just 16 of his 33 starts. In fact, only two starters in the American League received less support than did Gubicza.

## Pitching

Gubicza works both sides of the plate with sinking fastballs thrown inside to righthanders and sweeping sliders that tail away. His fastball has below-average velocity, but his ability to spot it on the corners makes it an effective pitch. A 120-pitch ceiling often prevented Gubicza from going past the seventh inning, but that same limit kept him in the rotation all year. As a result, Gubicza led the majors with 33 starts. Keeping the ball down has transformed Gubicza into a groundball pitcher. He has to fool hitters to succeed, and most of his strikes are called instead of swinging. While his strikeout totals have dropped, he has also reduced the walks and is now one of the game's top control pitchers.

## Defense

Gubicza's maturation process has had a profound effect upon his glove work and his ability to control opposition baserunners. Once a hothead with a big leg kick, Gubicza has shortened his delivery and improved his pickoff move. He has worked hard to become one of the team's better fielders; he throws well to the bases and moves quickly to field bunts.

## 1996 Outlook

The dean of the Royal staff, Gubicza leads active major league pitchers in service time with one club (12 years), and he's the last player left from the 1985 championship club. As the Royals seek to infuse their pitching staff with more youngsters, Gubicza's leadership will become even more important, and the club would like him back in 1996.

**Position:** SP
**Bats:** R **Throws:** R
**Ht:** 6' 5" **Wt:** 230

**Opening Day Age:** 33
**Born:** 8/14/62 in Philadelphia, PA
**ML Seasons:** 12
**Pronunciation:** GOO-ba-zah

### Overall Statistics

|        | W   | L   | Pct. | ERA  | G   | GS  | Sv | IP     | H    | BB  | SO   | HR  | BR/IP |
|--------|-----|-----|------|------|-----|-----|----|--------|------|-----|------|-----|-------|
| 1995   | 12  | 14  | .462 | 3.75 | 33  | 33  | 0  | 213.1  | 222  | 62  | 81   | 21  | 1.33  |
| Career | 128 | 123 | .510 | 3.85 | 363 | 308 | 2  | 2099.1 | 2094 | 749 | 1311 | 131 | 1.35  |

### How Often He Throws Strikes

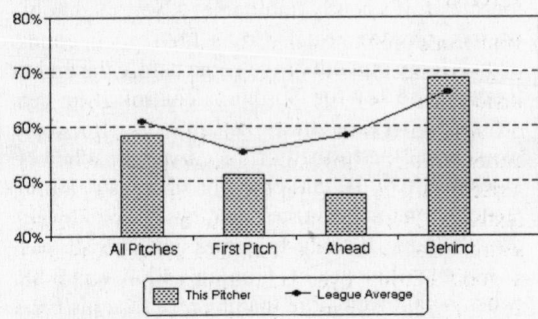

### 1995 Situational Stats

|            | W | L | ERA  | Sv | IP    |        | AB  | H   | HR | RBI | Avg  |
|------------|---|---|------|----|-------|--------|-----|-----|----|-----|------|
| Home       | 6 | 8 | 3.69 | 0  | 124.1 | LHB    | 455 | 123 | 9  | 49  | .270 |
| Road       | 6 | 6 | 3.84 | 0  | 89.0  | RHB    | 360 | 99  | 12 | 38  | .275 |
| First Half | 6 | 7 | 3.43 | 0  | 102.1 | Sc Pos | 174 | 47  | 5  | 61  | .270 |
| Scnd Half  | 6 | 7 | 4.05 | 0  | 111.0 | Clutch | 50  | 14  | 0  | 3   | .280 |

### 1995 Rankings (American League)

→ 1st in games started, least strikeouts per 9 innings (3.4) and fielding percentage at pitcher (1.000)
→ 3rd in shutouts (2), hits allowed and least run support per 9 innings (4.0)
→ 4th in losses and least pitches thrown per batter (3.58)
→ 5th in innings pitched, batters faced (898), pickoff throws (198) and highest groundball/flyball ratio allowed (2.0)
→ 7th in GDPs induced (21) and lowest strikeout/walk ratio (1.3)
→ 10th in ERA
→ Led the Royals in ERA, losses, games started, shutouts (2) and innings pitched

# Bob Hamelin

## 1995 Season

Heading into last season, the question was, would Bob Hamelin become the next Ron Kittle or the next Joe Charboneau? Early returns suggest the latter. Hamelin struggled mightily throughout the 1995 season, striking out frequently while missing the power which made him the 1994 Rookie of the Year. He was hitting .175 with just two homers when first demoted to Triple-A in mid-June. He regained his power stroke in Omaha, but lost it again after returning to Kansas City. A second demotion didn't cure his hitting ills, and Hamelin finished the year riding the bench with the lowest batting average of his professional career.

## Hitting

Hamelin's problems were primarily caused by hitting too much off his front foot. He saw a lot of inside fastballs early in the season; they got him off-stride and he tried to adjust in order to make better contact. The result was a drop in power and a rise in strikeouts. A pull hitter who feasts on low fastballs, Hamelin mostly saw breaking pitches away or fastballs up and in. Usually possessed of a good batting eye, Hamelin swung wildly in 1995, trying too hard to break out of his year-long slump.

## Baserunning & Defense

He's obviously not fast, but Hamelin is an adept baserunner. He'll never steal many bases, but he does a good job of moving up an extra base on hits to the outfield. Hamelin doesn't have much range at first base and he has yet to acquire a knack for digging low throws out of the dirt. His destiny is probably as a designated hitter, assuming he can stay in the majors.

## 1996 Outlook

Hamelin isn't well regarded by Kansas City's current managerial regime. Weight problems and a perceived reluctance to take coaching have put him in the doghouse. The Royals publicly state that Hamelin is important to the organization, but he will have to fully regain his power stroke—and lose some weight—before he'll again be counted on as a regular.

**Position:** DH
**Bats:** L  **Throws:** L
**Ht:** 6' 0"  **Wt:** 235

**Opening Day Age:** 28
**Born:** 11/29/67 in Elizabeth, NJ
**ML Seasons:** 3
**Pronunciation:** HAM-lin

### Overall Statistics

|        | G   | AB  | R  | H   | D  | T | HR | RBI | SB | BB | SO  | Avg  | OBP  | Slg  |
|--------|-----|-----|----|-----|----|---|----|-----|----|----|-----|------|------|------|
| 1995   | 72  | 208 | 20 | 35  | 7  | 1 | 7  | 25  | 0  | 26 | 56  | .168 | .278 | .313 |
| Career | 189 | 569 | 86 | 134 | 35 | 2 | 33 | 95  | 4  | 88 | 133 | .236 | .342 | .478 |

### Where He Hits the Ball

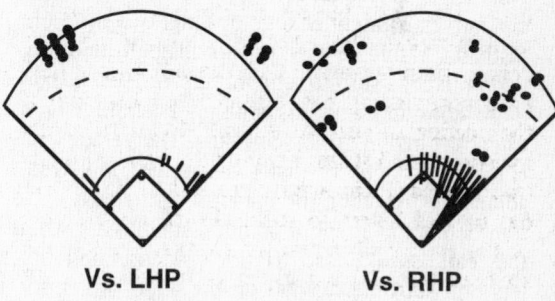

**Vs. LHP**          **Vs. RHP**

### 1995 Situational Stats

|            | AB  | H  | HR | RBI | Avg  |        | AB  | H  | HR | RBI | Avg  |
|------------|-----|----|----|-----|------|--------|-----|----|----|-----|------|
| Home       | 98  | 15 | 3  | 11  | .153 | LHP    | 30  | 7  | 4  | 10  | .233 |
| Road       | 110 | 20 | 4  | 14  | .182 | RHP    | 178 | 28 | 3  | 15  | .157 |
| First Half | 123 | 22 | 3  | 13  | .179 | Sc Pos | 68  | 10 | 2  | 19  | .147 |
| Scnd Half  | 85  | 13 | 4  | 12  | .153 | Clutch | 31  | 7  | 4  | 7   | .226 |

### 1995 Rankings (American League)

→ Did not rank near the top or bottom in any category

# Chris Haney

## 1995 Season

Chris Haney jumped from the bullpen into the Royal rotation last year and made an immediate impact. Sporting a 3-1 record and a 2.34 ERA through his first nine starts, Haney suffered a herniated disk in his back which forced him onto the disabled list. Treatment for the condition didn't help much, and Haney simply wasn't the same pitcher when he returned late in the season. He could no longer throw with the same velocity or sharpness, and hitters wracked him for a 9.72 ERA over his last four starts before he finished the year back on the DL.

## Pitching

Haney has a wide repertoire which includes sliders, curves, straight change-ups and two different fastballs. While he used to spot fastballs and rely upon offspeed stuff to retire hitters, in 1995 he had more confidence in his sinking fastball, which often resulted in groundball outs. The velocity on Haney's straight fastball was much improved, sometimes reaching the upper 80s. His easy motion belies the strength of his fastball; he's what they call "sneaky fast." Haney's sidearm delivery lets him start the fastball on the plate and run it inside to lefthanders; his breaking balls run down and away from them. It was a devastating combination as he limited lefties to a .224 slugging average on just two extra-base hits.

## Defense

Haney holds runners well enough, despite an inconsistent move to first. An above-average fielder, Haney showed good poise and often helped himself out of tight spots with good glove work.

## 1996 Outlook

Postseason back surgery was deemed successful, and Haney pitched in the Florida Instructional League during the fall. The Royals desperately need a left-handed starter, so if Haney's completely healthy he'll open the season in the rotation. Haney has been a long-term project; the Royals hope he lives up to the promise they saw in 1995.

**Position:** SP
**Bats:** L **Throws:** L
**Ht:** 6' 3" **Wt:** 195

**Opening Day Age:** 27
**Born:** 11/16/68 in Baltimore, MD
**ML Seasons:** 5

### Overall Statistics

|        | W  | L  | Pct. | ERA  | G  | GS | Sv | IP    | H   | BB  | SO  | HR | BR/IP |
|--------|----|----|------|------|----|----|----|-------|-----|-----|-----|----|-------|
| 1995   | 3  | 4  | .429 | 3.65 | 16 | 13 | 0  | 81.1  | 78  | 33  | 31  | 7  | 1.36  |
| Career | 21 | 28 | .429 | 4.93 | 77 | 71 | 0  | 398.1 | 424 | 166 | 219 | 39 | 1.48  |

### How Often He Throws Strikes

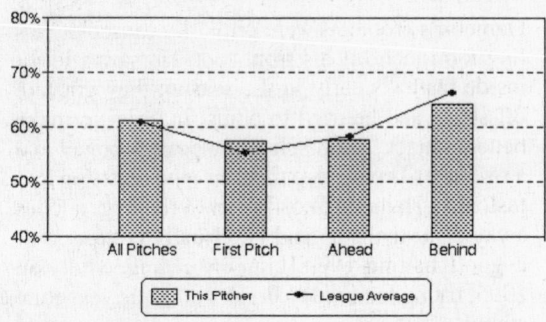

### 1995 Situational Stats

|            | W | L | ERA   | Sv |  IP  |        | AB  | H  | HR | RBI | Avg  |
|------------|---|---|-------|----|------|--------|-----|----|----|-----|------|
| Home       | 1 | 2 | 4.26  | 0  | 38.0 | LHB    | 49  | 9  | 0  | 1   | .184 |
| Road       | 2 | 2 | 3.12  | 0  | 43.1 | RHB    | 249 | 69 | 7  | 32  | .277 |
| First Half | 3 | 3 | 3.06  | 0  | 79.1 | Sc Pos | 69  | 16 | 1  | 22  | .232 |
| Scnd Half  | 0 | 1 | 27.00 | 0  | 2.0  | Clutch | 25  | 4  | 0  | 0   | .160 |

### 1995 Rankings (American League)

➡ 8th in most GDPs induced per GDP situation (19.2%)

# Jason Jacome

## 1995 Season

After five terrible starts for the Mets and eight mediocre outings in the International League, Jason Jacome joined the Royals via a minor league trade. He was immediately inserted into the rotation to replace the injured Chris Haney. After a rough A.L. start, Jacome won four straight decisions and was named Royals Pitcher of the Month for August. However, September wasn't kind as Jacome finished the year with four straight losses.

## Pitching

Jacome sports a fastball that barely reaches the mid-80s, so he relies upon pinpoint control and deception. He can hit corners with his curve or slider and throws an above-average change-up. His control is good enough to throw any pitch on any count; Jacome walked more than two batters in just one of his 14 starts for the Royals. He works batters with fastballs and sliders inside, then curveballs or change-ups away, hoping to induce ground balls. Jacome's troubles come when his low-velocity offerings catch too much of the plate. He allowed 15 homers in just 84 innings, and a team-high .501 slugging average.

## Defense

Possessed of a good move to first, Jacome limited opponents to eight steals in 11 attempts and picked off two runners himself. His defense was relatively good considering his youth, despite occasional mental lapses. Jacome fielded his position quite well and his throws to first were accurate.

## 1996 Outlook

Finesse pitchers often make a better showing their first time around the league. After a good first trip around the National League, hitters caught on to Jacome's trickery and lit him up; he carried a 10.29 ERA when the Mets demoted him in May. The Royals hope he's able to adjust as American League hitters get their second (and third) looks at his offspeed stuff. If successful, he'll battle Haney for the lefty starter spot in the Royal rotation.

**Position:** SP
**Bats:** L  **Throws:** L
**Ht:** 6' 0"  **Wt:** 180

**Opening Day Age:** 25
**Born:** 11/24/70 in Tulsa, OK
**ML Seasons:** 2
**Pronunciation:** HOCK-uh-mee

### Overall Statistics

|  | W | L | Pct. | ERA | G | GS | Sv | IP | H | BB | SO | HR | BR/IP |
|---|---|---|---|---|---|---|---|---|---|---|---|---|---|
| 1995 | 4 | 10 | .286 | 6.34 | 20 | 19 | 0 | 105.0 | 134 | 36 | 50 | 18 | 1.62 |
| Career | 8 | 13 | .381 | 5.09 | 28 | 27 | 0 | 159.0 | 188 | 53 | 80 | 21 | 1.52 |

### How Often He Throws Strikes

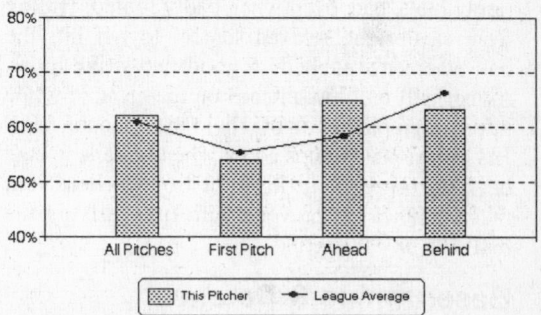

### 1995 Situational Stats

|  | W | L | ERA | Sv | IP |  | AB | H | HR | RBI | Avg |
|---|---|---|---|---|---|---|---|---|---|---|---|
| Home | 4 | 3 | 4.56 | 0 | 51.1 | LHB | 69 | 21 | 2 | 10 | .304 |
| Road | 0 | 7 | 8.05 | 0 | 53.2 | RHB | 360 | 113 | 16 | 63 | .314 |
| First Half | 0 | 4 | 10.29 | 0 | 21.0 | Sc Pos | 109 | 40 | 5 | 56 | .367 |
| Scnd Half | 4 | 6 | 5.36 | 0 | 84.0 | Clutch | 17 | 5 | 0 | 1 | .294 |

### 1995 Rankings (American League)

➡ 9th in highest batting average allowed vs. right-handed batters (.296)

➡ Led the Royals in balks (1)

Kansas City Royals

# Wally Joyner

## 1995 Season

Contact-hitting skills and a good batting eye might have made Wally Joyner an ideal second-place hitter, but the power shortage in Kansas City forced Joyner into an RBI role. He produced his usual .300-plus average and finished second on the team in RBI. Often Joyner and Gary Gaetti were the only productive hitters in a lineup that was the league's weakest. An ankle injury shortened Joyner's season, but not before he acquired the necessary 500 plate appearances which extended his large contract another year.

## Hitting

Joyner possesses a smooth, controlled swing; he rarely looks bad, even when badly fooled. Hitting from an upright, relaxed stance, Joyner hits the ball where it's pitched. A good two-strike hitter, Joyner will pull low pitches on the ground, while hitting high pitches on the fly to the opposite field. His occasional slumps come when he fails to stay back, drifting out onto his front foot; this helps him make contact but prevents him from driving the ball with any strength.

## Baserunning & Defense

Strictly a station-to-station baserunner, Joyner rarely takes chances and almost never runs into an out. By the same token, he shows little willingness to risk an extra base even when situations call for it and he's difficult to score from second base on a single. Joyner has a reputation for excellent defense. He's usually quick to snare hot grounders down the first-base line and always makes accurate throws. Unfortunately, he sometimes lacks concentration and allows easy grounders to sneak through.

## 1996 Outlook

As the only veteran everyday Royal under contract for 1996, Joyner is locked into a full-time role as the club's regular first baseman. However, he will undoubtedly move to another team after that. In the meantime, he'll fill a spot in the middle of the Royal lineup and continue his steady if unspectacular hitting.

**Position:** 1B
**Bats:** L **Throws:** L
**Ht:** 6' 2"  **Wt:** 200

**Opening Day Age:** 33
**Born:** 6/16/62 in Atlanta, GA
**ML Seasons:** 10

### Overall Statistics

| | G | AB | R | H | D | T | HR | RBI | SB | BB | SO | Avg | OBP | Slg |
|---|---|---|---|---|---|---|---|---|---|---|---|---|---|---|
| 1995 | 131 | 465 | 69 | 144 | 28 | 0 | 12 | 83 | 3 | 69 | 65 | .310 | .394 | .447 |
| Career | 1364 | 5105 | 725 | 1481 | 290 | 19 | 158 | 789 | 50 | 560 | 556 | .290 | .359 | .447 |

### Where He Hits the Ball

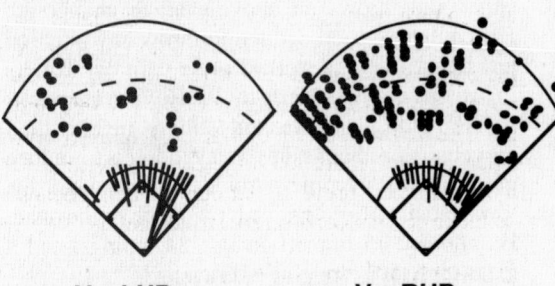

Vs. LHP          Vs. RHP

### 1995 Situational Stats

| | AB | H | HR | RBI | Avg | | AB | H | HR | RBI | Avg |
|---|---|---|---|---|---|---|---|---|---|---|---|
| Home | 220 | 74 | 6 | 41 | .336 | LHP | 146 | 40 | 0 | 9 | .274 |
| Road | 245 | 70 | 6 | 42 | .286 | RHP | 319 | 104 | 12 | 74 | .326 |
| First Half | 220 | 65 | 5 | 41 | .295 | Sc Pos | 122 | 40 | 3 | 67 | .328 |
| Scnd Half | 245 | 79 | 7 | 42 | .322 | Clutch | 67 | 21 | 2 | 12 | .313 |

### 1995 Rankings (American League)

→ 1st in fielding percentage at first base (.998)
→ 3rd in lowest batting average on an 0-2 count (0.000)
→ 6th in sacrifice flies (9) and on-base percentage vs. right-handed pitchers (.422)
→ 7th in lowest slugging percentage vs. left-handed pitchers (.295)
→ 8th in batting average vs. right-handed pitchers (.326) and batting average with two strikes (.261)
→ 9th in intentional walks (10) and batting average at home (.336)
→ 10th in batting average on a 3-2 count (.367)
→ Led the Royals in batting average, hits, doubles, sacrifice flies (9) and walks

# Keith Lockhart

## 1995 Season

Rookie Keith Lockhart turned in one of the Royals' most pleasantly surprising seasons, leading the club in hitting, batting near the top of the lineup during the pennant race and providing steady defense. When Chico Lind went AWOL halfway through the season, it was the versatile Lockhart who stepped forward to fill a large hole and post a productive season as the team's regular second baseman.

## Hitting

A line-drive hitter, Lockhart usually swings at the first hittable pitch, trying to hit the ball where it's pitched. He doesn't have much power, but was able to turn on a few balls and drive them deep to right field. Pitchers who work both sides of the plate give Lockhart the most difficulty and he has never shown that he can hit much against lefthanders. The Royals' best hitter—at least for average—against right-handed pitching, Lockhart is the type most managers prefer to bat number two, because he makes contact and rarely strikes out.

## Baserunning & Defense

Lockhart showed surprisingly good range and a consistently sure glove around second base; he hadn't been considered a good fielder before winning a regular job with the Royals. His play at third base was less stellar, though, as his reflexes aren't quick enough for him to play there regularly. Lockhart's intelligent baserunning often contributed to the Royals' running game both on the hit-and-run and with eight steals in nine attempts. He picked the right spots to take chances and made the most of those opportunities.

## 1996 Outlook

Second base is up for grabs, but Lockhart's surprising performance makes him the leading candidate for 1996. It remains to be seen if he can continue to hit .300 and play a good second base over a full season. Still, Lockhart can be useful even in a platoon or utility role. His main competition for regular play will come from gloveman David Howard and youngster Chris Stynes.

**Position:** 2B/3B
**Bats:** L **Throws:** R
**Ht:** 5'10" **Wt:** 170

**Opening Day Age:** 31
**Born:** 11/10/64 in Whittier, CA
**ML Seasons:** 2

### Overall Statistics

|  | G | AB | R | H | D | T | HR | RBI | SB | BB | SO | Avg | OBP | Slg |
|---|---|---|---|---|---|---|---|---|---|---|---|---|---|---|
| 1995 | 94 | 274 | 41 | 88 | 19 | 3 | 6 | 33 | 8 | 14 | 21 | .321 | .355 | .478 |
| Career | 121 | 317 | 45 | 97 | 19 | 3 | 8 | 39 | 9 | 18 | 31 | .306 | .345 | .461 |

### Where He Hits the Ball

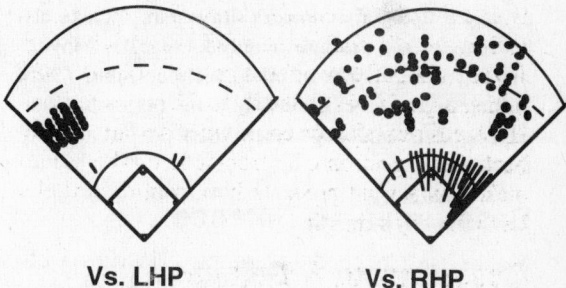

**Vs. LHP**          **Vs. RHP**

### 1995 Situational Stats

|  | AB | H | HR | RBI | Avg |  | AB | H | HR | RBI | Avg |
|---|---|---|---|---|---|---|---|---|---|---|---|
| Home | 131 | 44 | 3 | 14 | .336 | LHP | 16 | 3 | 0 | 0 | .188 |
| Road | 143 | 44 | 3 | 19 | .308 | RHP | 258 | 85 | 6 | 33 | .329 |
| First Half | 73 | 28 | 1 | 9 | .384 | Sc Pos | 66 | 17 | 2 | 27 | .258 |
| Scnd Half | 201 | 60 | 5 | 24 | .299 | Clutch | 35 | 8 | 1 | 3 | .229 |

### 1995 Rankings (American League)

➤ 3rd in least GDPs per GDP situation (4.0%)
➤ 9th in errors at second base (7)
➤ Led the Royals in least GDPs per GDP situation (4.0%)

Kansas City Royals

# Brent Mayne

## 1995 Season

The departure of Mike Macfarlane to Boston via free agency gave Brent Mayne his chance to play regularly. Mayne once said he could hit .300 if he played every day. While he briefly flirted with that mark early in the year, a two-month slump dropped his average below .220 in late August. Only a torrid September, in which Mayne hit .381, pulled his average to a more respectable level.

**Position:** C
**Bats:** L  **Throws:** R
**Ht:** 6' 1"  **Wt:** 190

**Opening Day Age:** 27
**Born:** 4/19/68 in Loma Linda, CA
**ML Seasons:** 6

## Hitting

A slashing, opposite-field hitter, Mayne has doubles power only; his season high in homers is three (1991). He prefers low pitches and is frequently overmatched by good fastballs. Mayne also lacks a good batting eye. While he doesn't strike out excessively, he also doesn't draw many walks, as his career .306 on-base average suggests. Mayne has never been able to hit lefthanders, and 1995 was no exception. Mayne hits far better against righthanders and has decent gap power against them.

## Baserunning & Defense

Mayne isn't a good baserunner. He runs well enough for a catcher, but is difficult to advance more than one base at a time and he can't steal. Despite a reputation for superior defensive skills, Mayne has never had success throwing out opponent baserunners. His career caught-stealing percentage was a poor 26 percent entering last season, and 1995 was even worse as he nailed just 15 of 70 (21 percent). Mayne's take-charge attitude helps him manage Royal pitchers well; their collective ERA was significantly better with Mayne behind the plate (4.21) than with other Royal catchers (5.01).

## 1996 Outlook

Mayne is among the league's weaker-hitting catchers. His solid work calling pitches helps offset his poor offense, but a platoon situation would clearly improve the lineup, and would still leave Mayne catching most of the time. For 1996, the Royals will likely search for a reliable right-handed-hitting complement to Mayne.

### Overall Statistics

|        | G   | AB   | R   | H   | D  | T | HR | RBI | SB | BB | SO  | Avg  | OBP  | Slg  |
|--------|-----|------|-----|-----|----|---|----|-----|----|----|-----|------|------|------|
| 1995   | 110 | 307  | 23  | 77  | 18 | 1 | 1  | 27  | 0  | 25 | 41  | .251 | .313 | .326 |
| Career | 399 | 1113 | 104 | 275 | 50 | 3 | 8  | 119 | 6  | 94 | 170 | .247 | .306 | .319 |

### Where He Hits the Ball

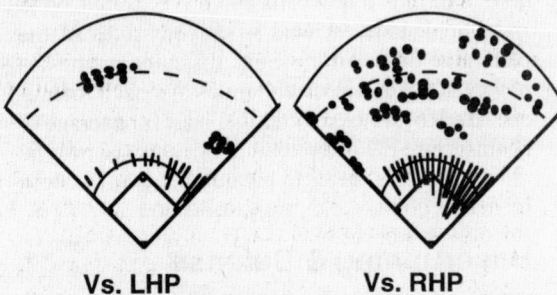

**Vs. LHP**          **Vs. RHP**

### 1995 Situational Stats

|            | AB  | H  | HR | RBI | Avg  |        | AB  | H  | HR | RBI | Avg  |
|------------|-----|----|----|-----|------|--------|-----|----|----|-----|------|
| Home       | 137 | 40 | 1  | 14  | .292 | LHP    | 45  | 8  | 0  | 2   | .178 |
| Road       | 170 | 37 | 0  | 13  | .218 | RHP    | 262 | 69 | 1  | 25  | .263 |
| First Half | 149 | 31 | 1  | 12  | .208 | Sc Pos | 76  | 20 | 0  | 25  | .263 |
| Scnd Half  | 158 | 46 | 0  | 15  | .291 | Clutch | 46  | 10 | 0  | 3   | .217 |

### 1995 Rankings (American League)

➡ 1st in most GDPs per GDP situation (28.6%)
➡ 2nd in fielding percentage at catcher (.995)
➡ 4th in sacrifice bunts (11)
➡ Led the Royals in GDPs (16) and batting average with the bases loaded (.333)

# Rusty Meacham

## 1995 Season

The 1995 season was the worst of Rusty Meacham's career, as his 4.98 ERA was his highest for any full season. As a right-handed set-up reliever, Meacham was expected to retire right-handed hitters; instead they hit .320 (up almost 80 points over 1994) and slugged .516 against him. The Royals lost confidence in Meacham: first he lost his set-up job, then he was sent to the minors in late August. Although Meacham returned in September, he continued to pitch poorly.

## Pitching

Rail-thin Meacham is ready to throw the next pitch almost as soon as the previous offering hits the catcher's mitt. He implores his catcher to return the ball quickly, and he's so impatient to pitch that he plays catch with himself if the hitter dawdles. Meacham relies on sinking fastballs down and in and sliders away. His fastball is average at best, but the sinking movement will induce grounders. Meacham normally has good movement on all his pitches, but in 1995 they came in too straight and he also had occasional control problems. His tendency to get behind in the count hurt badly, as Meacham lacks the kind of stuff to blow away major league hitters. The results were unfortunate, as Meacham allowed 25 extra-base hits and a .477 opponent slugging average.

## Defense

Because Meacham works so quickly, and because he was being hit so hard, few baserunners even attempted to steal against him; only two tried in 1995, one was caught. He has an average move to first, but a deceptive delivery. Like the rest of his game, Meacham's defense was subpar.

## 1996 Outlook

The outlook is grim for Meacham. He finished the year on a severe downward trend, just as other righty relievers were stepping forward. Meacham has likely lost his spot in the Royal bullpen. No matter where he goes in 1996, Meacham will have to battle just for a job pitching long relief.

**Position:** RP
**Bats:** R **Throws:** R
**Ht:** 6' 2" **Wt:** 175

**Opening Day Age:** 28
**Born:** 1/27/68 in Stuart, FL
**ML Seasons:** 5

### Overall Statistics

|  | W | L | Pct. | ERA | G | GS | Sv | IP | H | BB | SO | HR | BR/IP |
|---|---|---|---|---|---|---|---|---|---|---|---|---|---|
| 1995 | 4 | 3 | .571 | 4.98 | 49 | 0 | 2 | 59.2 | 72 | 19 | 30 | 6 | 1.53 |
| Career | 21 | 13 | .618 | 3.94 | 174 | 4 | 8 | 260.2 | 277 | 68 | 157 | 24 | 1.32 |

### How Often He Throws Strikes

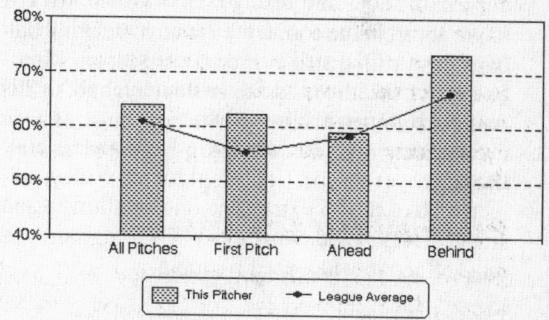

### 1995 Situational Stats

|  | W | L | ERA | Sv | IP |  | AB | H | HR | RBI | Avg |
|---|---|---|---|---|---|---|---|---|---|---|---|
| Home | 0 | 1 | 4.55 | 2 | 31.2 | LHB | 115 | 33 | 2 | 25 | .287 |
| Road | 4 | 2 | 5.46 | 0 | 28.0 | RHB | 122 | 39 | 4 | 25 | .320 |
| First Half | 2 | 2 | 4.33 | 0 | 27.0 | Sc Pos | 70 | 25 | 2 | 41 | .357 |
| Scnd Half | 2 | 1 | 5.51 | 2 | 32.2 | Clutch | 57 | 21 | 1 | 11 | .368 |

### 1995 Rankings (American League)

- 1st in highest percentage of inherited runners scored (57.5%)
- 4th in highest batting average allowed in relief (.304)
- 5th in least strikeouts per 9 innings in relief (4.5)
- 8th in worst first batter efficiency (.372) , highest batting average allowed in relief with runners on base (.347) and highest relief ERA (4.98)
- Led the Royals in holds (7)

# Jeff Montgomery

## 1995 Season

For the 1995 Royals, Jeff Montgomery was the most reliable part of a generally unreliable bullpen. He got the call when the game was on the line and responded with another fine season, collecting 31 saves to place among the league's best for the sixth straight year. Montgomery was at his best when the Royals were in the thick of the wild-card chase, saving most of their victories down the stretch.

## Pitching

Montgomery is anything *but* your typical closer. Rather than rely upon one or two great pitches, Montgomery throws four very good ones: fastball, curveball, slider and change. His favorite trick is to get ahead in the count, then snap a breaking ball over for a called strike three. Last season, Montgomery worked on adding a knuckleball to his repertoire, but with limited success (just as Dan Quisenberry did a decade ago). Lefthanders continued to get the best of Montgomery; they collected 10 of the 15 extra-base hits he allowed and slugged .419. Like many closers, Montgomery is most effective when used frequently.

## Defense

Like most closers—especially righthanders— Montgomery doesn't pay much attention to baserunners, who rarely run in close ballgames anyway. He is steady on defense, covers first base when he's supposed to and throws well to all bases. Montgomery is particularly quick to field bunts.

## 1996 Outlook

Montgomery is about as sure a bet as you'll find. He's still got good stuff, along with the durability to pitch on consecutive days. His 217 saves since 1989 are better than any closer over that span except Lee Smith and Dennis Eckersley. The kind of salary that top closers command may result in Montgomery leaving Kansas City, but he'll certainly be serving as the relief ace somewhere.

**Position:** RP
**Bats:** R  **Throws:** R
**Ht:** 5'11"  **Wt:** 180

**Opening Day Age:** 34
**Born:** 1/7/62 in Wellston, OH
**ML Seasons:** 9

### Overall Statistics

|        | W  | L  | Pct. | ERA  | G   | GS | Sv   | IP    | H   | BB  | SO  | HR | BR/IP |
|--------|----|----|------|------|-----|----|------|-------|-----|-----|-----|----|-------|
| 1995   | 2  | 3  | .400 | 3.43 | 54  | 0  | 31   | 65.2  | 60  | 25  | 49  | 7  | 1.29  |
| Career | 38 | 33 | .535 | 2.72 | 492 | 1  | 218  | 638.2 | 543 | 216 | 559 | 43 | 1.19  |

### How Often He Throws Strikes

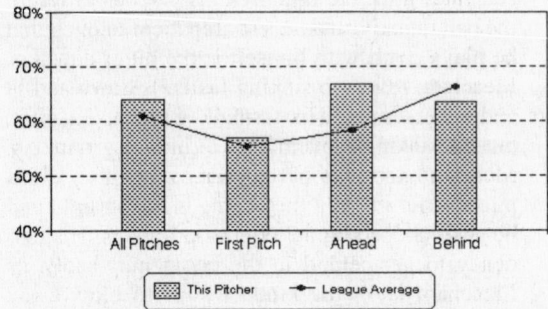

This Pitcher — League Average

### 1995 Situational Stats

|            | W | L | ERA  | Sv |  IP  |        | AB  | H  | HR | RBI | Avg  |
|------------|---|---|------|----|------|--------|-----|----|----|-----|------|
| Home       | 2 | 0 | 3.09 | 9  | 32.0 | LHB    | 136 | 38 | 4  | 20  | .279 |
| Road       | 0 | 3 | 3.74 | 22 | 33.2 | RHB    | 102 | 22 | 3  | 14  | .216 |
| First Half | 0 | 1 | 3.45 | 14 | 28.2 | Sc Pos | 60  | 18 | 1  | 25  | .300 |
| Scnd Half  | 2 | 2 | 3.41 | 17 | 37.0 | Clutch | 157 | 44 | 2  | 24  | .280 |

### 1995 Rankings (American League)

- ➥ 4th in save opportunities (38)
- ➥ 5th in saves
- ➥ 6th in lowest save percentage (81.6%) and blown saves (7)
- ➥ 7th in most GDPs induced per GDP situation (20.0%)
- ➥ 9th in games finished (46)
- ➥ Led the Royals in games pitched, saves, games finished (46), balks (1), save opportunities (38), save percentage (81.6%), blown saves (7), most GDPs induced per GDP situation (20.0%), first batter efficiency (.244), relief ERA (3.43), relief innings (65.2) and lowest batting average allowed in relief (.252)

# Jon Nunnally

## 1995 Season

Jumping straight from Class-A ball to the majors as a Rule 5 pick from the Indians, Jon Nunnally homered in his first big-league at-bat and finished the year second on the club in home runs. He showed the expected signs of inexperience, but was one of the Royals' few power threats for the first half of the season. However, Nunnally slumped to finish the year, averaging just .190 with no homers over his last 100 at-bats.

## Hitting

A pull hitter with deceptive power for his size, Nunnally is an aggressive, high-fastball hitter, and he's looking to go downtown on any pitch. He generates great bat speed, but lacks the discipline to lay off bad breaking pitches, especially when they're thrown by lefthanders. Nunnally's upper-cut swing makes him especially vulnerable to finesse pitchers. He got lots of hittable fastballs early the season, but didn't adjust to the breaking pitches he saw later in the year.

## Baserunning & Defense

Nunnally set a team record with four steals of home, but don't be fooled—three of the four were the front ends of double steals, and he's merely an average baserunner. His aggressive hitting style carried over onto the basepaths where he sometimes ran into outs. Nunnally's arm is mediocre for right field and he often didn't get a good jump on deep flies. Recently converted from second base, he hasn't yet acquired sufficient outfielder's instincts.

## 1996 Outlook

Nunnally survived the jump from Class-A to the majors, but now needs to make several adjustments in order to stay there. He has the right-field job for now, but he'll earn a quick ticket to Triple-A should he continue hitting as poorly as he did last September. Nunnally's aggressive hitting style and hustling baserunning and defense remind some of Hal McRae. The Royals will be thrilled if Nunnally becomes half the player that McRae was.

**Position:** RF/LF
**Bats:** L **Throws:** R
**Ht:** 5'10" **Wt:** 190

**Opening Day Age:** 24
**Born:** 11/9/71 in Pelham, NC
**ML Seasons:** 1

### Overall Statistics

| | G | AB | R | H | D | T | HR | RBI | SB | BB | SO | Avg | OBP | Slg |
|---|---|---|---|---|---|---|---|---|---|---|---|---|---|---|
| 1995 | 119 | 303 | 51 | 74 | 15 | 6 | 14 | 42 | 6 | 51 | 86 | .244 | .357 | .472 |
| Career | 119 | 303 | 51 | 74 | 15 | 6 | 14 | 42 | 6 | 51 | 86 | .244 | .357 | .472 |

### Where He Hits the Ball

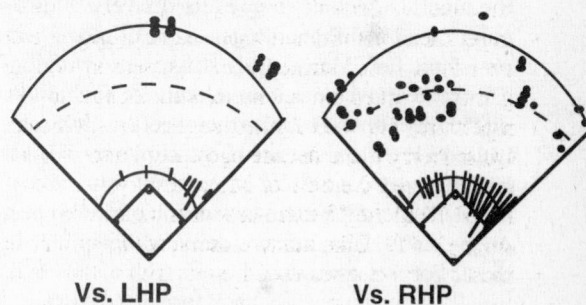

**Vs. LHP**     **Vs. RHP**

### 1995 Situational Stats

| | AB | H | HR | RBI | Avg | | AB | H | HR | RBI | Avg |
|---|---|---|---|---|---|---|---|---|---|---|---|
| Home | 141 | 32 | 6 | 16 | .227 | LHP | 37 | 6 | 1 | 4 | .162 |
| Road | 162 | 42 | 8 | 26 | .259 | RHP | 266 | 68 | 13 | 38 | .256 |
| First Half | 133 | 38 | 11 | 21 | .286 | Sc Pos | 73 | 18 | 3 | 28 | .247 |
| Scnd Half | 170 | 36 | 3 | 21 | .212 | Clutch | 48 | 9 | 3 | 6 | .188 |

### 1995 Rankings (American League)

- ➡ 1st in errors in right field (6) and lowest fielding percentage in right field (.967)
- ➡ 2nd in batting average on a 3-1 count (.714) and lowest percentage of swings put into play (32.5%)
- ➡ 3rd in highest percentage of swings that missed (30.7%)
- ➡ 8th in triples
- ➡ 9th in lowest batting average with two strikes (.136)
- ➡ 10th in lowest batting average in the clutch (.188)
- ➡ Led the Royals in triples (6) and batting average on a 3-1 count (.714)

# Hipolito Pichardo

## 1995 Season

In his second year as a full-time reliever, Hipolito Pichardo was one of the few positives in an otherwise mediocre Royal bullpen. Pichardo began the year in long relief, but his consistently good outings caused him to be used more often in set-up roles. Pichardo gave the Royals an effective right-handed set-up man; he held opponents to a .341 slugging average overall, and permitted right-handed hitters just three extra-base hits all year.

## Pitching

Pitching out of a long, whirling delivery, Pichardo throws a fastball, splitter and slider. All of his pitches are thrown hard with his fastball reaching the high 80s. His three-quarters delivery is difficult to read and Pichardo gets a lot of movement on his pitches. Many of his strikes are swinging. The good movement and velocity of Pichardo's pitches kept hitters back on their heels in 1995, and caused a lot of defensive swings. However, he also has difficulty controlling his hard stuff; his rate of 4.2 walks per nine innings was one of the highest on the staff. He sometimes delivers the splitter in the dirt or misses high and away with his fastball, usually when he reaches back for a little extra.

## Defense

Pichardo has a long delivery and his pickoff move is below average; four of five opponents attempting to steal were successful. His lanky frame makes Pichardo look awkward, but he's a good fielder and covers ground quickly to field bunts or cover first base.

## 1996 Outlook

The position of set-up reliever is often volatile, changing from one year to the next. Since Pichardo lacks the stamina to be a starter and the fastball to close games, he'll have to fill the role of right-handed set-up relief. While it's an important role for any team, Pichardo can't be considered anything more than a role player at this point in his career.

**Position:** RP
**Bats:** R  **Throws:** R
**Ht:** 6' 1"   **Wt:** 185

**Opening Day Age:** 26
**Born:** 8/22/69 in Esperanza, DR
**ML Seasons:** 4
**Pronunciation:** e-POL-uh-toe puh-CHAR-doh

### Overall Statistics

|  | W | L | Pct. | ERA | G | GS | Sv | IP | H | BB | SO | HR | BR/IP |
|---|---|---|---|---|---|---|---|---|---|---|---|---|---|
| 1995 | 8 | 4 | .667 | 4.36 | 44 | 0 | 1 | 64.0 | 66 | 30 | 43 | 4 | 1.50 |
| Career | 29 | 21 | .580 | 4.19 | 150 | 49 | 4 | 440.1 | 479 | 158 | 208 | 27 | 1.44 |

### How Often He Throws Strikes

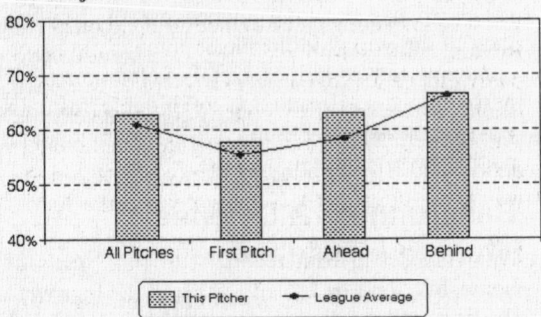

### 1995 Situational Stats

|  | W | L | ERA | Sv | IP |  | AB | H | HR | RBI | Avg |
|---|---|---|---|---|---|---|---|---|---|---|---|
| Home | 6 | 2 | 3.73 | 1 | 31.1 | LHB | 129 | 36 | 3 | 12 | .279 |
| Road | 2 | 2 | 4.96 | 0 | 32.2 | RHB | 120 | 30 | 1 | 12 | .250 |
| First Half | 5 | 3 | 3.89 | 1 | 34.2 | Sc Pos | 66 | 18 | 0 | 19 | .273 |
| Scnd Half | 3 | 1 | 4.91 | 0 | 29.1 | Clutch | 115 | 27 | 1 | 5 | .235 |

### 1995 Rankings (American League)

- ➡ 2nd in relief wins (8)
- ➡ 9th in worst first batter efficiency (.372)
- ➡ Led the Royals in balks (1), holds (7) and relief wins (8)

# Billy Brewer

**Position:** RP
**Bats:** L  **Throws:** L
**Ht:** 6' 1"  **Wt:** 175

**Opening Day Age:** 27
**Born:** 4/15/68 in Ft. Worth, TX
**ML Seasons:** 3

## Overall Statistics

| | W | L | Pct. | ERA | G | GS | Sv | IP | H | BB | SO | HR | BR/IP |
|---|---|---|---|---|---|---|---|---|---|---|---|---|---|
| 1995 | 2 | 4 | .333 | 5.56 | 48 | 0 | 0 | 45.1 | 54 | 20 | 31 | 9 | 1.63 |
| Career | 8 | 7 | .533 | 3.95 | 144 | 0 | 3 | 123.0 | 113 | 56 | 84 | 19 | 1.37 |

## 1995 Season

Billy Brewer's 1995 campaign was easily the worst of his young career. Once counted on as the Royals' lefty set-up man, Brewer stumbled so badly that he was demoted to Class-A at one point (if only for one game), with the hopes that he could find himself. Walks and homers are a bad combination, and Brewer allowed plenty of both on the way to the worst ERA of his professional career.

## Pitching & Defense

To be successful, Brewer must throw his high-80s fastball on the inside part of the plate and keep his hard slider low and away. However, all too often last year the fastball stayed out or the slider stayed up, and those pitches were hit hard, often for extra bases. Even worse, opposition lefties teed off on him. A below-average fielder who occasionally throws wildly to the bases, Brewer's pickoff move is average for a lefthander—he allowed four steals in four tries in 1995.

## 1996 Outlook

Brewer is still young enough to revive his career, but he may have to first rediscover his pitches in the minors. As young as Brewer is, it seems likely that last year was an aberration, and he should be given every chance this spring to win back his old lefty set-up job.

# Dave Fleming

**Position:** RP/SP
**Bats:** L  **Throws:** L
**Ht:** 6' 3"  **Wt:** 200

**Opening Day Age:** 26
**Born:** 11/7/69 in Queens, NY
**ML Seasons:** 5

## Overall Statistics

| | W | L | Pct. | ERA | G | GS | Sv | IP | H | BB | SO | HR | BR/IP |
|---|---|---|---|---|---|---|---|---|---|---|---|---|---|
| 1995 | 1 | 6 | .143 | 5.96 | 25 | 12 | 0 | 80.0 | 84 | 53 | 40 | 19 | 1.71 |
| Career | 38 | 32 | .543 | 4.67 | 116 | 97 | 0 | 610.1 | 669 | 248 | 303 | 67 | 1.50 |

## 1995 Season

A reclamation project from the Mariners, left-hander Dave Fleming had some limited success for the Royals in five late-season spot starts. Fleming also worked a few games in relief, but wasn't used in critical situations.

## Pitching & Defense

Finesse pitcher Fleming will mix in curveballs, sliders and change-ups to offset his mid-80s fastball. To succeed he has to keep hitters off stride by changing speeds and hitting corners; his curve is particularly effective against lefthanders. Fleming will occasionally use a sidearm delivery to give hitters a different look. When he makes his pitches too good, it's basically batting practice as hitters tee off on his soft stuff; he surrendered four homers in just 32 innings as a Royal. Overall he allowed 19 homers in 80 innings, one every four frames. Fleming's defense is average and his move to first is poor.

## 1996 Outlook

It's hard to get excited about Fleming's future. He has struggled for more than two years to regain the fine control which let him go 30-15 over his first two full seasons. Should his control return, he's still no more than a third starter at best. Fleming is most likely destined for the minors to continue the search for his control.

# David Howard

**Position**: 2B/SS/LF/CF
**Bats**: B **Throws**: R
**Ht**: 6' 0" **Wt**: 175

**Opening Day Age**: 29
**Born**: 2/26/67 in
Sarasota, FL
**ML Seasons**: 5

## Overall Statistics

|  | G | AB | R | H | D | T | HR | RBI | SB | BB | SO | Avg | OBP | Slg |
|---|---|---|---|---|---|---|---|---|---|---|---|---|---|---|
| 1995 | 95 | 255 | 23 | 62 | 13 | 4 | 0 | 19 | 6 | 24 | 41 | .243 | .310 | .325 |
| Career | 324 | 817 | 76 | 189 | 30 | 7 | 3 | 69 | 16 | 68 | 157 | .231 | .289 | .296 |

## 1995 Season

It took some doing, but manager Bob Boone found a niche for David Howard, who (all together now) was once protected from the expansion draft instead of Jeff Conine. Howard platooned some at second base with Keith Lockhart, played late-inning defense, even started in the outfield occasionally. Even better, Howard reached new career highs in virtually all offensive categories.

## Hitting, Baserunning & Defense

Howard often looks overmatched by even average pitching. In 1995 he took a more aggressive posture at the plate, often swinging early at fastballs. He also made better contact than ever before, reducing his strikeout rate substantially. Howard's excellent glove work is best displayed in the middle infield, where he shows great range and a strong, accurate arm. As an outfielder, Howard occasionally got the wrong break on balls hit shallow or deep. Howard is an average baserunner. His six stolen bases were a career best, and he often takes an extra base on hits to the outfield.

## 1996 Outlook

Howard hasn't suddenly become a good or even average hitter; his role is still that of a defense-oriented utility man. His versatility is a plus and his excellent defense will keep him employed in the majors. However, Howard simply doesn't hit enough to justify being in the lineup regularly. On the other hand, the departure of Greg Gagne might give Howard the shortstop job by default.

# Mike Magnante

**Position**: RP
**Bats**: L **Throws**: L
**Ht**: 6' 1" **Wt**: 190

**Opening Day Age**: 30
**Born**: 6/17/65 in
Glendale, CA
**ML Seasons**: 5
**Pronunciation**:
mag-NAN-tee

## Overall Statistics

|  | W | L | Pct. | ERA | G | GS | Sv | IP | H | BB | SO | HR | BR/IP |
|---|---|---|---|---|---|---|---|---|---|---|---|---|---|
| 1995 | 1 | 1 | .500 | 4.23 | 28 | 0 | 0 | 44.2 | 45 | 16 | 28 | 6 | 1.37 |
| Career | 8 | 16 | .333 | 4.15 | 153 | 19 | 0 | 271.1 | 307 | 101 | 138 | 22 | 1.50 |

## 1995 Season

Mike Magnante emerged from the shadows of long relief last year to grab an important set-up role down the stretch. In July, he pitched well enough to be named Royals Pitcher of the Month, and by season's end Magnante had established himself as the primary lefthander in the bullpen.

## Pitching & Defense

An extreme finesse pitcher, Magnante's fastball barely reaches 80 MPH. He spots that "fastball" on the corners and throws an above-average change of pace which is particularly effective against free swingers. Magnante has been trying to develop a better slider to complement his fastball. His success against lefties in 1995 is unusual; he had previously shown no platoon differential. Magnante is a decent fielder, mobile off the mound despite the knee braces he has worn for years. He also sports a good pickoff move; only two baserunners stole against Magnante and two others were caught trying.

## 1996 Outlook

He doesn't fit the classic mold of a lefty set-up man, but Magnante has been relatively successful in that role. Because he doesn't throw very hard, he's more likely to be used in long relief. Magnante is a marginal major league pitcher who will get more opportunities because of the dearth of left-handed relief pitching in the majors.

# Gregg Olson

**Position:** RP
**Bats:** R  **Throws:** R
**Ht:** 6' 4"  **Wt:** 212

**Opening Day Age:** 29
**Born:** 10/11/66 in
Scribner, NE
**ML Seasons:** 8

### Overall Statistics

| | W | L | Pct. | ERA | G | GS | Sv | IP | H | BB | SO | HR | BR/IP |
|---|---|---|---|---|---|---|---|---|---|---|---|---|---|
| 1995 | 3 | 3 | .500 | 4.09 | 23 | 0 | 3 | 33.0 | 28 | 19 | 21 | 4 | 1.42 |
| Career | 20 | 26 | .435 | 2.67 | 359 | 0 | 164 | 398.0 | 328 | 190 | 378 | 15 | 1.30 |

## 1995 Season

Serious shoulder problems appear to be behind Gregg Olson for the first time in years. After toiling briefly in the minors for the Indians, Olson was signed by the Royals and quickly exerted a steadying influence on the shaky Royal bullpen. Olson was often used in close games to set up relief ace Jeff Montgomery.

## Pitching & Defense

Olson throws a mid-80s fastball, but it's just for show; his sharp curveball remains his out pitch. The slow curve—though certainly not the feared weapon it once was—is still equally effective against both left- and right-handed hitters. Olson's control was occasionally spotty, but he limited opponents to a .235 batting average with little power. However, frequent offspeed offerings and a poor pickoff move let runners steal at will; 13 opponents tried to steal, and only one was caught. Olson is not a good fielder. His throws to the bases are erratic and he's slow to react on grounders through the middle.

## 1996 Outlook

Olson has made a remarkable comeback to once again be a valuable reliever. Given the possible departure of Jeff Montgomery, Olson might spend spring training in a competition with Rick Huisman for the closer job. Otherwise, he'll fight for the role of primary right-handed setup man.

# Juan Samuel

**Position:** 1B/LF/DH
**Bats:** R  **Throws:** R
**Ht:** 5'11"  **Wt:** 180

**Opening Day Age:** 35
**Born:** 12/9/60 in San
Pedro de Macoris, DR
**ML Seasons:** 13
**Pronunciation:**
sam-WELL

### Overall Statistics

| | G | AB | R | H | D | T | HR | RBI | SB | BB | SO | Avg | OBP | Slg |
|---|---|---|---|---|---|---|---|---|---|---|---|---|---|---|
| 1995 | 91 | 205 | 31 | 54 | 10 | 1 | 12 | 39 | 6 | 29 | 49 | .263 | .360 | .498 |
| Career | 1563 | 5748 | 812 | 1494 | 272 | 95 | 149 | 660 | 369 | 408 | 1336 | .260 | .314 | .418 |

## 1995 Season

Juan Samuel continued his nomadic ways in 1995, moving to his fourth team in as many years with a late-August trade from Detroit to Kansas City. Samuel provided the Tigers unexpected power when filling in for Lou Whitaker at second base. Desperate for right-handed power as they fought for a playoff spot, the Royals traded for Samuel in early September, but he failed to help them much.

## Hitting, Baserunning & Defense

An aggressive, first-pitch fastball hitter, Samuel does his best to pull the ball to left field. He can be overmatched by finesse pitchers who throw fastballs inside, then work breaking balls away. But don't throw him a hittable fastball or he'll bash it a long way. Samuel is no longer capable of stealing 30-40 bases per season; at best, he's an average runner at this late stage of his career. Samuel's defensive skills have also eroded; he lacks sufficient range to play second base and his arm and speed aren't good enough for the outfield.

## 1996 Outlook

Journeyman is the best way to describe Samuel at this stage. While Samuel can help a team as an experienced right-handed bat off the bench, he will never again be a regular. For 1996, he'll reprise his role, somewhere, as pinch hitter and bench jockey.

# Michael Tucker

**Position:** LF/DH
**Bats:** L  **Throws:** R
**Ht:** 6' 2"  **Wt:** 185

**Opening Day Age:** 24
**Born:** 6/25/71 in South Boston, VA
**ML Seasons:** 1

*Overall Statistics*

| | G | AB | R | H | D | T | HR | RBI | SB | BB | SO | Avg | OBP | Slg |
|---|---|---|---|---|---|---|---|---|---|---|---|---|---|---|
| 1995 | 62 | 177 | 23 | 46 | 10 | 0 | 4 | 17 | 2 | 18 | 51 | .260 | .332 | .384 |
| Career | 62 | 177 | 23 | 46 | 10 | 0 | 4 | 17 | 2 | 18 | 51 | .260 | .332 | .384 |

## 1995 Season

As the 1995 season opened, the Royals' left-field job was Michael Tucker's to lose. That's just what he did. Tentative swings had Bob Boone wondering how Tucker impressed so many scouts, and the youngster was sent back to Triple-A Omaha. Tucker regained his pretty swing in the minors, and returned to finish the campaign impressively.

## Hitting, Baserunning & Defense

Once he leveled out his uppercut swing, Tucker began to drive the ball again. He was a much more aggressive hitter when recalled to the majors, mostly pulling the ball to right field. Tucker has the speed to be a dangerous baserunner but his judgment was poor in 1995. He lost track of the number of outs on several occasions and sometimes underestimated opponent's arms when trying for an extra base. Despite his good speed, the one-time infielder is still a below-average outfielder at this point. He doesn't read the ball very well off the bat, and his arm limits him to left field.

## 1996 Outlook

Once again Tucker is the leading candidate for the left-field job, but it won't be handed to him. Still, the Royals believe he will eventually hit for both power and average, making him an idea cleanup hitter. For now—assuming he wins a spot in the lineup—Tucker will hit near the top of the order.

# Joe Vitiello

**Position:** DH
**Bats:** R  **Throws:** R
**Ht:** 6' 2"  **Wt:** 215

**Opening Day Age:** 25
**Born:** 4/11/70 in Cambridge, MA
**ML Seasons:** 1
**Pronunciation:** vit-ee-EL-oh

*Overall Statistics*

| | G | AB | R | H | D | T | HR | RBI | SB | BB | SO | Avg | OBP | Slg |
|---|---|---|---|---|---|---|---|---|---|---|---|---|---|---|
| 1995 | 53 | 130 | 13 | 33 | 4 | 0 | 7 | 21 | 0 | 8 | 25 | .254 | .317 | .446 |
| Career | 53 | 130 | 13 | 33 | 4 | 0 | 7 | 21 | 0 | 8 | 25 | .254 | .317 | .446 |

## 1995 Season

Joe Vitiello, the Royals' number-one draft pick in 1991, posted excellent Triple-A numbers in 1994 before being shelved with a knee injury. Offseason surgery limited Vitiello early last season, and he was 0-for-11 before being sent back to Omaha when the major league rosters were cut down. Vitiello regained his stroke, was recalled to Kansas City on July 27, and finished strong with five home runs in September.

## Hitting, Baserunning & Defense

Vitiello's swing is fairly compact for a big guy. He covers the plate well, doesn't try to pull everything, and consequently is able to hit the ball to all fields. Though Vitiello struggled against righthanders in the majors last season, he didn't have that problem in Triple-A and should eventually show just normal platoon splits. Vitiello was slow when the Royals drafted him, and he's certainly not getting faster as he gets older. Once talked about as an outfielder, his wheels limit him to first base or, even better, designated hitter.

## 1996 Outlook

In 359 professional at-bats last season, Vitiello hit 19 homers and knocked in 63 runs. The Royals desperately need power, so he should be in line to share the DH job with a lefty hitter, perhaps Bob Hamelin. And should Hamelin falter again, Vitiello might end up with the job all for himself.

# Other Kansas City Royals

**Scott Anderson (Pos: RHP, Age: 33)**

Anderson has generally pitched well at the Triple-A level, not so well in the majors. At his age, he's about out of chances to do either. 1996 Outlook: C

**Tom Browning (Pos: LHP, Age: 35)**

Browning's comeback attempt was aborted after two poor starts, as he hit the disabled list with an arm strain and didn't pitch again. Seems unlikely that he'll pitch well again. 1996 Outlook: D

**Mel Bunch (Pos: RHP, Age: 24)**

Bunch jumped all the way from A-ball to the majors last spring, then was sent to Triple-A Omaha three different times. He's got a live arm, and will be a prime candidate for one of the open rotation spots. 1996 Outlook: B

**Edgar Caceres (Pos: 2B, Age: 31, Bats: B)**

An 11-year minor league vet, Caceres finally got a chance to play when Jose Lind went AWOL. He didn't hit much, hurt his kneecap, and lost most of his playing time to Keith Lockhart. 1996 Outlook: C

**Wes Chamberlain (Pos: RF, Age: 29, Bats: R)**

Chamberlain still has power, but not much else. The Royals have a batch of young outfielders, and it's extremely unlikely that Chamberlain will beat any of them out of a job. Needs to find another tea, and even then he'll have to battle. 1996 Outlook: B

**Jim Converse (Pos: RHP, Age: 24)**

The Royals stockpiled young arms last season, and picked up Converse in a deal with the Mariners. He's posted good minor league numbers, but has generally been hammered in the majors. 1996 Outlook: B

**Brent Cookson (Pos: OF, Age: 26)**

After walloping the ball in the minors for three years, Cookson was called up by the Royals last summer. But when the club needed roster space Cookson was waived, and the Red Sox picked him up. 1996 Outlook: B

**Jeff Grotewold (Pos: DH, Age: 30, Bats: L)**

Once a catcher in the Phillies system, Grotewold spent part of 1994 with a Northern League team. He hit well in Omaha last year, and would be a useful player if he could still catch, but is now a DH. 1996 Outlook: C

**Billy Hatcher (Pos: RF, Age: 35, Bats: R)**

Hatcher's only real tool was his speed, and at 34 last year, that was just about gone. After a few games with the Rangers, Hatcher signed with the Royals but retired after a month in Omaha. 1996 Outlook: D

**Rick Huisman (Pos: RHP, Age: 26)**

In 1991, Huisman was one of the top starters in the minor leagues. Two teams and one arm injury later, he's a short reliever. If Montgomery leaves via free agency, Huisman is top candidate for closer. 1996 Outlook: A

**Doug Linton (Pos: RHP, Age: 30)**

The Royals were Linton's fourth organization in as many seasons. With a career major league ERA of 6.48, Linton's prospects don't look too bright. His arm has never been anything special. 1996 Outlook: C

**Russ McGinnis (Pos: 1B, Age: 32, Bats: R)**

Jeff Grotewold, Part II. McGinnis wasn't much of a hitter when he was a catcher, and now that he can hit he's not much of a catcher. Hit great in Triple-A in 1993 and '94, but done nothing since. 1996 Outlook: D

**Henry Mercedes (Pos: C, Age: 26, Bats: R)**

A .223 lifetime hitter in the minors, Mercedes got a chance to play last year when the Royals needed a backup catcher after trading Pat Borders. Mercedes has a good defensive rep. 1996 Outlook: B

**Keith Miller (Pos: LF, Age: 32, Bats: R)**

One of the most injury-prone players ever, Miller has spent most of the last three seasons on the DL. He's unlikely to get healthy all of a sudden. 1996 Outlook: D

**Jose Mota (Pos: 2B, Age: 31, Bats: B)**

After nearly 10 full seasons in the minors, Mota was finally going to get a chance to play last summer. Then he tore a groin muscle in just his second game, and others played second base. 1996 Outlook: D

**Les Norman (Pos: RF, Age: 27, Bats: R)**

Norman's not much of a prospect, but he's probably the only guy on the team with a legitimate right fielder's arm, and he has the instincts for center. Could stick with the Royals if he gets hot this spring. 1996 Outlook: B

**Joe Randa (Pos: 3B, Age: 26, Bats: R)**

Randa has been billed as prospect ever since Sean Berry was traded, and he is a good third baseman. But he's no hitter, and might end up a utility man. 1996 Outlook: B

**Dennis Rasmussen (Pos: LHP, Age: 36)**

He can still fool Triple-A hitters, but Rasmussen doesn't fare so well against the big boys. After a brief stint in K.C., the Royals released him in July. 1996 Outlook: D

**Dilson Torres (Pos: RHP, Age: 25)**

Torres has been terrific at his last three minor league stops, but struggled in brief action with the Royals last year. He'll get another shot, and could be effective in middle relief. 1996 Outlook: B

# Kansas City Royals Minor League Prospects

## Organization Overview:

The long-anticipated prospects are beginning to arrive in Kansas City. A year after Bob Hamelin was named the A.L.'s Rookie of the Year in 1994, outfielder Johnny Damon electrified the Royals with his speed, center field defense and .282 batting average. Michael Tucker's power potential made Vince Coleman expendable. And Joe Vitiello, the American Association's 1994 leading hitter, made a favorable impression in his 130 big league at-bats. Other prospects will soon be making impacts. The Royals are flush with talent, and are especially rich in two commodities all teams would envy, catching and left-handed pitching. The farm system's productivity has come at an opportune time, since the Royals have abandoned their free-spending ways under the late Ewing Kauffman in favor of the realities of small-market economics. If the prospects perform as expected, Kansas City appears to be the one team in the American League Central which could possibly challenge Cleveland's dominance over the next few years.

## Sal Fasano

**Position:** C     **Opening Day Age:** 24
**Bats:** R **Throws:** R     **Born:** 8/10/71 in
**Ht:** 6' 2"   **Wt:** 220     Chicago, IL

### Recent Statistics

|  | G | AB | R | H | D | T | HR | RBI | SB | BB | SO | AVG |
|---|---|---|---|---|---|---|---|---|---|---|---|---|
| 93 A Eugene | 49 | 176 | 25 | 47 | 11 | 1 | 10 | 36 | 4 | 19 | 49 | .267 |
| 94 A Rockford | 97 | 345 | 61 | 97 | 16 | 1 | 25 | 81 | 8 | 33 | 66 | .281 |
| 94 A Wilmington | 23 | 90 | 15 | 29 | 7 | 0 | 7 | 32 | 0 | 13 | 24 | .322 |
| 95 A Wilmington | 23 | 88 | 12 | 20 | 2 | 1 | 2 | 7 | 0 | 5 | 16 | .227 |
| 95 AA Wichita | 87 | 317 | 60 | 92 | 18 | 2 | 20 | 66 | 3 | 27 | 61 | .290 |
| 95 MLE | 87 | 302 | 46 | 77 | 16 | 1 | 12 | 51 | 2 | 17 | 62 | .255 |

Fasano's history and hitting record is reminiscent of Mike Piazza. Like Piazza, Fasano was a late-round draftee, getting selected in the 37th round of 1993. And like Piazza, Fasano is a hard-hitting catcher with the invaluable talent of knocking the ball out of the park. He slammed 32 homers in 1994 when he was named the Midwest League's MVP, and followed that with 22 dingers last season, mostly at Double-A. Fasano will begin 1996 at 24, the age at which Piazza was named the National League's Rookie of the Year. Receivers with Fasano's power are hard to come by, but with other Royal catching prospects likely to compete for playing time in the not distant future, Fasano may eventually be moved to another position.

## Felix Martinez

**Position:** SS     **Opening Day Age:** 21
**Bats:** B **Throws:** R     **Born:** 5/18/74 in
**Ht:** 6' 0"   **Wt:** 168     Nagua, DR

### Recent Statistics

|  | G | AB | R | H | D | T | HR | RBI | SB | BB | SO | AVG |
|---|---|---|---|---|---|---|---|---|---|---|---|---|
| 93 R Royals | 57 | 165 | 23 | 42 | 5 | 1 | 0 | 12 | 22 | 17 | 26 | .255 |
| 94 A Wilmington | 117 | 400 | 65 | 107 | 16 | 4 | 2 | 43 | 19 | 30 | 91 | .268 |
| 95 AA Wichita | 127 | 426 | 53 | 112 | 15 | 3 | 3 | 30 | 44 | 31 | 71 | .263 |
| 95 MLE | 127 | 412 | 41 | 98 | 13 | 3 | 1 | 23 | 31 | 20 | 69 | .238 |

The Royals have challenged Martinez the last two years, bumping him from the rookie league in 1993 to high-A ball in 1994, before pushing him to Double-A in 1995. Martinez has handled the moves well, although there are still plenty of areas he needs to work on. He hasn't demonstrated any real power yet, his walk rate is low, and he committed 50 errors last season. But he also led the Texas League with 44 stolen bases and possesses all the tools, including great range and a strong arm, to be an outstanding defensive shortstop. Martinez won't turn 22 until May, so he still has plenty of time to improve. However, the Royals have demonstrated they won't hesitate to promote him through their system quickly.

## Jim Pittsley

**Position:** P     **Opening Day Age:** 21
**Bats:** R **Throws:** R     **Born:** 4/3/74 in
**Ht:** 6' 7"   **Wt:** 215     Dubois, PA

### Recent Statistics

|  | W | L | ERA | G | GS | Sv | IP | H | R | BB | SO | HR |
|---|---|---|---|---|---|---|---|---|---|---|---|---|
| 95 AAA Omaha | 4 | 1 | 3.21 | 8 | 8 | 0 | 47.2 | 38 | 20 | 16 | 39 | 5 |
| 95 AL Kansas City | 0 | 0 | 13.50 | 1 | 1 | 0 | 3.1 | 7 | 5 | 1 | 0 | 3 |

The Royals made Pittsley the first high school pitcher selected in the 1992 draft, and he justified that status by pitching briefly in the big leagues last season at age 21. But Pittsley's problem has been that he's had difficulty staying healthy. Only once has he pitched more than 80.1 innings in a season, and his 1995 season ended after nine appearances due to a slight tear in his elbow. The injury wasn't as serious as initially feared, and it's hoped Pittsley's 90-plus fastball will return, as will his improving curveball and change-up. Everywhere he's pitched, Pittsley has compiled high strikeout rates and low walk totals, displaying great control for a pitcher who's 6'7". Since his experience above A-ball consists of just 51 innings, he will most likely begin 1996—once he's healthy enough to pitch—back in Omaha.

## Ken Ray

**Position:** P **Opening Day Age:** 21
**Bats:** R **Throws:** R **Born:** 11/27/74 in
**Ht:** 6' 2" **Wt:** 160 Atlanta, GA

*Recent Statistics*

|  | W | L | ERA | G | GS | Sv | IP | H | R | BB | SO | HR |
|---|---|---|---|---|---|---|---|---|---|---|---|---|
| 93 R Royals | 2 | 3 | 2.28 | 13 | 7 | 0 | 47.1 | 44 | 21 | 17 | 45 | 1 |
| 94 A Rockford | 10 | 4 | 1.82 | 27 | 18 | 3 | 128.2 | 94 | 34 | 56 | 128 | 5 |
| 95 A Wilmington | 6 | 4 | 2.69 | 13 | 13 | 0 | 77.0 | 74 | 32 | 22 | 63 | 3 |
| 95 AA Wichita | 4 | 5 | 5.97 | 14 | 14 | 0 | 75.1 | 83 | 55 | 46 | 53 | 7 |

Ray's fastball has gained steam since he was drafted in the 18th round of 1993. It may get even faster as he matures and gains even more strength. Last year, only two years removed from high school, Ray ascended all the way to Double-A, where he experienced his first growing pains. Prior to the move to Wichita, Ray had compiled a 2.17 ERA with a strikeout/walk ratio of 236 to 95 in 253 minor league innings. He might return to Double-A, but it isn't out of the question that Ray will reach the majors at some point during this season.

## Glendon Rusch

**Position:** P **Opening Day Age:** 21
**Bats:** L **Throws:** L **Born:** 11/7/74 in
**Ht:** 6' 2" **Wt:** 170 Seattle, WA

*Recent Statistics*

|  | W | L | ERA | G | GS | Sv | IP | H | R | BB | SO | HR |
|---|---|---|---|---|---|---|---|---|---|---|---|---|
| 93 R Royals | 4 | 2 | 1.60 | 11 | 10 | 0 | 62.0 | 43 | 14 | 11 | 48 | 0 |
| 93 A Rockford | 0 | 1 | 3.38 | 2 | 2 | 0 | 8.0 | 10 | 6 | 7 | 8 | 0 |
| 94 A Rockford | 8 | 5 | 4.66 | 28 | 17 | 1 | 114.0 | 111 | 61 | 34 | 122 | 5 |
| 95 A Wilmington | 14 | 6 | 1.74 | 26 | 26 | 0 | 165.2 | 110 | 41 | 34 | 147 | 5 |

Rusch dominated the Carolina League last year, and his stat line was one of the best in the minors. In 165.2 innings Rusch struck out 37 more batters than he allowed hits, and his hits plus walks combined was still lower than eight per nine innings. Rusch keeps hitters offstride with a great change-up, which complements an average fastball. His control within the strike zone is superb, and he rarely beats himself with walks. The Royals didn't grab Rusch until the 17th round of the 1993 draft, but his season last year, plus the fact that he's left-handed, marks him as a pitcher to keep an eye on.

## Chris Stynes

**Position:** 2B **Opening Day Age:** 23
**Bats:** R **Throws:** R **Born:** 1/19/73 in
**Ht:** 5' 9" **Wt:** 170 Queens, NY

*Recent Statistics*

|  | G | AB | R | H | D | T | HR | RBI | SB | BB | SO | AVG |
|---|---|---|---|---|---|---|---|---|---|---|---|---|
| 95 AAA Omaha | 83 | 306 | 51 | 84 | 12 | 5 | 9 | 42 | 4 | 27 | 24 | .275 |
| 95 AL Kansas City | 22 | 35 | 7 | 6 | 1 | 0 | 0 | 2 | 0 | 4 | 3 | .171 |
| 95 MLE | 83 | 295 | 40 | 73 | 10 | 4 | 5 | 32 | 2 | 20 | 23 | .247 |

Stynes was part of the package Kansas City received from Toronto when the Royals unloaded David Cone. Stynes played most of 1995 at Triple-A, but did see some major league action over three different stints with Kansas City. His walk rate, though still mediocre last

season, was actually the best of his pro career and more than double his rate from 1994. He also flashed more home run power than ever before, though his .275 batting average was his lowest ever, and his four stolen bases were a sharp drop from the 28 he pilfered the year before. Originally drafted as a shortstop in the third round of 1991, Stynes has moved from third base to second as a pro, and his defensive versatility is a plus.

## Mike Sweeney

**Position:** C **Opening Day Age:** 22
**Bats:** R **Throws:** R **Born:** 7/22/73 in
**Ht:** 6' 1" **Wt:** 195 Orange, CA

*Recent Statistics*

|  | G | AB | R | H | D | T | HR | RBI | SB | BB | SO | AVG |
|---|---|---|---|---|---|---|---|---|---|---|---|---|
| 95 A Wilmington | 99 | 332 | 61 | 103 | 23 | 1 | 18 | 53 | 6 | 60 | 39 | .310 |
| 95 AL Kansas City | 4 | 4 | 1 | 1 | 0 | 0 | 0 | 0 | 0 | 0 | 0 | .250 |

The Royals have a number of highly-regarded catching prospects bubbling through their system, but Sweeney is the best of them. His presence at Wilmington bumped Carlos Mendez from behind the plate to first base, and the Royals promoted Sweeney all the way from Class A when they needed catching depth last September. Sweeney's .310 batting average and .548 slugging percentage both led the Carolina League, while his .424 on-base average ranked second. Ever since the Royals drafted Sweeney in the 10th round of 1991, his numbers have gotten better each season. He's also a capable defensive receiver with an above-average arm, and at 22 he's two years younger than Sal Fasano.

## Others to Watch

**Mike Bovee** was the Royals sixth-round pick in 1991 and reached Double-A last year. The husky righthander's most impressive stat is a career strikeout-to-walk ratio of 3.37 to 1. . . **Nevin Brewer's** career ERA finally moved above 1.00 in his third professional season. Brewer doesn't throw hard, and he's likely to encounter less success as he faces stiffer competition. . . The left-handed pitching talent at Wilmington last year was exceptionally strong. 1994 fifth-rounder **Tim Byrdak** had a season nearly identical (11-5, 2.16 ERA, 166.1 IP, 118 hits, 45 BB, 127 K) to teammate Glendon Rusch's, but he's a year older. . . A third Blue Rock lefthander, **Jose Rosado**, pales only a little in comparison (10-7, 3.13 ERA, 138 IP, 128 hits, 30 BB, 117 K). The 21 year old was the Royals' 12th pick in 1994. . . Outfielder **Raul Gonzalez** spent most of 1995 at Wilmington, his third straight impressive season in the Carolina League. Gonzalez shows a range of offensive skills and will be only 22 in 1996. . . Talented second baseman **Sergio Nunez** struggled in making the jump from rookie ball, where he hit .397 in 1994, to fast-A last year, managing to bat just .237 while battling an injury.

# Ricky Bones

## 1995 Season

After Ricky Bones' breakthrough season in 1994, the Brewers had high hopes for their young control artist. When Cal Eldred went down early in the year, Phil Garner looked to Bones for the innings to stabilize his young staff. Bones responded admirably, pitching into the eighth inning fairly consistently in the first half of the season. Unfortunately, the increased workload caught up with him, and he faded badly in August and September. He wound up winning 10 games again, his exact average for his four full seasons with the Brewers.

## Pitching

Bones won't overpower anyone, but his pitches move just enough to stay off the sweet part of the bat. He works just off the edge of the plate and frequently falls behind in the count. But even then, batters have trouble making solid contact against him. A good Bones game features few strikeouts, but many grounders and weakly-hit pop flies. His money pitch is a sinker that runs in on right-handed hitters. He will also mix in a late-biting slider, an overhand curve and a straight change. When he tires, his pitches straighten out, and if he gets them up in the strike zone, he's easy pickings.

## Defense

Bones controls the running game by cutting down on his high leg kick, and his more compact stretch delivery yields few stolen-base attempts. In the field, Bones has sure hands and good reactions, and he fields bunts very well. His move to first is above average.

## 1996 Outlook

Bones is neither as good as he looked in '94, nor as bad as he looked at the end of '95. He was miscast as a staff ace, and the continued development of the Brewers' other young pitchers should enable him to settle into a more comfortable role. If his stamina isn't continually tested, he can be a valuable number-three starter.

**Position:** SP
**Bats:** R  **Throws:** R
**Ht:** 6' 0"  **Wt:** 193

**Opening Day Age:** 26
**Born:** 4/7/69 in Salinas, PR
**ML Seasons:** 5
**Pronunciation:** BONE-us

### Overall Statistics

|        | W  | L  | Pct. | ERA  | G   | GS  | Sv | IP    | H   | BB  | SO  | HR  | BR/IP |
|--------|----|----|------|------|-----|-----|----|-------|-----|-----|-----|-----|-------|
| 1995   | 10 | 12 | .455 | 4.63 | 32  | 31  | 0  | 200.1 | 218 | 83  | 77  | 26  | 1.50  |
| Career | 44 | 48 | .478 | 4.43 | 130 | 125 | 0  | 792.0 | 832 | 257 | 293 | 101 | 1.38  |

### How Often He Throws Strikes

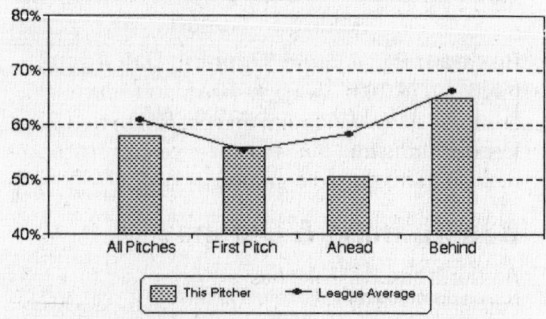

### 1995 Situational Stats

|            | W | L | ERA  | Sv | IP    |        | AB  | H   | HR | RBI | Avg  |
|------------|---|---|------|----|-------|--------|-----|-----|----|-----|------|
| Home       | 5 | 6 | 5.80 | 0  | 94.2  | LHB    | 449 | 126 | 10 | 49  | .281 |
| Road       | 5 | 6 | 3.58 | 0  | 105.2 | RHB    | 327 | 92  | 16 | 48  | .281 |
| First Half | 4 | 7 | 3.79 | 0  | 99.2  | Sc Pos | 165 | 37  | 3  | 63  | .224 |
| Scnd Half  | 6 | 5 | 5.45 | 0  | 100.2 | Clutch | 35  | 9   | 3  | 3   | .257 |

### 1995 Rankings (American League)

- 1st in lowest strikeout/walk ratio (0.9)
- 2nd in least strikeouts per 9 innings (3.5), highest ERA at home (5.80) and fielding percentage at pitcher (1.000)
- 3rd in home runs allowed and balks (2)
- 4th in games started, hits allowed, highest batting average allowed (.281), highest slugging percentage allowed (.450) and most home runs allowed per 9 innings (1.17)
- 6th in GDPs induced (22), highest on-base percentage allowed (.349) and most baserunners allowed per 9 innings (13.7)
- Led the Brewers in ERA, wins, losses, games started, complete games (3) and hits allowed

# Jeff Cirillo

## 1995 Season

The most impressive young hitter on the 1995 Brewers was rookie third baseman Jeff Cirillo. He spent the first few months of the season playing late-inning defense for Kevin Seitzer, but by early July he had simply hit his way into the lineup. Installed at third base, he kept his average over .300 for most of the year, and even saw some time at second base. Only a September slump kept Cirillo from a .300 season.

## Hitting

Crowding the plate and striding open to generate hip torque, Cirillo's swing faintly resembles Jeff Bagwell's. However, unlike Bagwell, Cirillo hasn't yet learned to pull and lift the ball. He hits the ball where it's pitched, spraying liners to all fields, and shows surprising power to right field on pitches high and away. If you pitch him inside, he'll pull in his hands and line the ball to right. The key to getting him out is to keep the ball down and make him hit it on the ground.

## Baserunning & Defense

At third base, Cirillo has all the tools to be an outstanding defender, showing good range and reactions, and a strong, accurate arm. He has had limited experience at second base, and his pivot was a bit rusty, but his play there was adequate overall. Cirillo has decent speed and runs the bases intelligently.

## 1996 Outlook

Cirillo enters the 1996 season as the club's starting third baseman. If the need arises, he could even take over at second base. At age 26, he is not likely to develop into a superstar. Still, his season was no fluke, and he should easily maintain his 1995 level of production, which would make him one of the better-hitting third basemen in the league. And if he ever learns to pull, his power could come quickly.

**Position:** 3B/2B
**Bats:** R  **Throws:** R
**Ht:** 6' 2"  **Wt:** 188

**Opening Day Age:** 26
**Born:** 9/23/69 in Pasadena, CA
**ML Seasons:** 2
**Pronunciation:** suh-RILL-oh

### Overall Statistics

|  | G | AB | R | H | D | T | HR | RBI | SB | BB | SO | Avg | OBP | Slg |
|---|---|---|---|---|---|---|---|---|---|---|---|---|---|---|
| 1995 | 125 | 328 | 57 | 91 | 19 | 4 | 9 | 39 | 7 | 47 | 42 | .277 | .371 | .442 |
| Career | 164 | 454 | 74 | 121 | 28 | 4 | 12 | 51 | 7 | 58 | 58 | .267 | .354 | .425 |

### Where He Hits the Ball

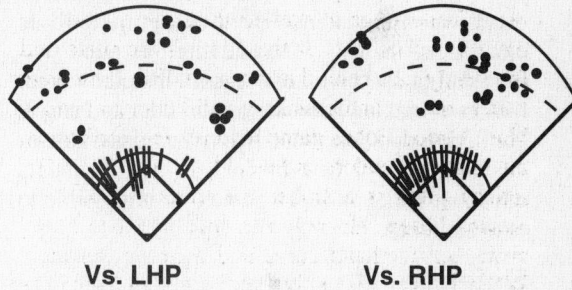

**Vs. LHP**          **Vs. RHP**

### 1995 Situational Stats

|  | AB | H | HR | RBI | Avg |  | AB | H | HR | RBI | Avg |
|---|---|---|---|---|---|---|---|---|---|---|---|
| Home | 153 | 49 | 6 | 22 | .320 | LHP | 119 | 35 | 2 | 15 | .294 |
| Road | 175 | 42 | 3 | 17 | .240 | RHP | 209 | 56 | 7 | 24 | .268 |
| First Half | 119 | 36 | 3 | 8 | .303 | Sc Pos | 80 | 18 | 2 | 32 | .225 |
| Scnd Half | 209 | 55 | 6 | 31 | .263 | Clutch | 57 | 16 | 0 | 3 | .281 |

### 1995 Rankings (American League)

➡ 1st in lowest fielding percentage at third base (.939)
➡ 10th in batting average with the bases loaded (.500) and errors at third base (13)
➡ Led the Brewers in batting average on a 3-2 count (.333) and highest percentage of pitches taken (60.0%)

# Mike Fetters

## 1995 Season

For Mike Fetters, the 1995 season offered a chance to solidify his role as the team's closer. For the first half of the season, he did just that. When he was bothered by elbow tendinitis in May and June, Brewer manager Phil Garner gave him light work, and Fetters responded by converting his first 15 save opportunities. Unfortunately, the tender elbow caught up with him. He endured a horrible stretch run, blowing five saves and losing three games in August and September. Despite the injuries and the late slump, Fetters had a fine season overall, saving a career-high 22 games.

## Pitching

Fetters throws hard and keeps the ball down, a deadly combination. His sinking fastball is clocked in the low 90s, and his out pitch is a devastating forkball. Last season, his elbow kept him from making good use of his slider and curve. He'll give up some walks when he misses downstairs, but when he's on he can get grounders almost at will, and it can be next to impossible to take him deep.

## Defense

As a fielder, Fetters is mostly a spectator since his motion leaves him in a poor position to field grounders. Still, he is generally reliable when handling the ball. He lacks a good move to first but has made great strides against the running game, and no stolen bases were even attempted against him last year.

## 1996 Outlook

On a team with no other qualified candidates, Fetters is unquestionably the closer. If his health permits, he could excel in that role. Remember, before his elbow really got cranky he had converted 32 of his last 34 save opportunities—an amazing accomplishment. If Garner continues to use him for just one inning at a time, Fetters should keep right on rolling.

**Position:** RP
**Bats:** R  **Throws:** R
**Ht:** 6' 4"  **Wt:** 224

**Opening Day Age:** 31
**Born:** 12/19/64 in Van Nuys, CA
**ML Seasons:** 7

### Overall Statistics

|        | W | L | Pct. | ERA | G | GS | Sv | IP | H | BB | SO | HR | BR/IP |
|--------|---|---|------|-----|---|----|----|-----|-----|-----|-----|----|-------|
| 1995   | 0 | 3 | .000 | 3.38 | 40 | 0 | 22 | 34.2 | 40 | 20 | 33 | 3 | 1.73 |
| Career | 12 | 17 | .414 | 3.36 | 223 | 6 | 42 | 318.1 | 313 | 142 | 193 | 24 | 1.43 |

### How Often He Throws Strikes

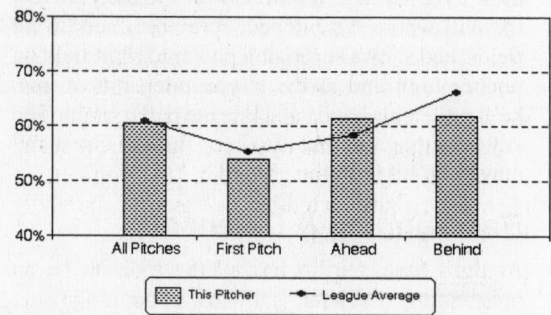

| This Pitcher | League Average |

### 1995 Situational Stats

|           | W | L | ERA | Sv | IP |       | AB | H | HR | RBI | Avg |
|-----------|---|---|------|----|------|--------|----|----|----|----|------|
| Home      | 0 | 0 | 2.87 | 6  | 15.2 | LHB    | 74 | 22 | 2 | 16 | .297 |
| Road      | 0 | 3 | 3.79 | 16 | 19.0 | RHB    | 66 | 18 | 1 | 7  | .273 |
| First Half| 0 | 0 | 1.72 | 10 | 15.2 | Sc Pos | 42 | 15 | 1 | 21 | .357 |
| Scnd Half | 0 | 3 | 4.74 | 12 | 19.0 | Clutch | 99 | 30 | 2 | 21 | .303 |

### 1995 Rankings (American League)

- ➡ 5th in lowest save percentage (81.5%)
- ➡ 8th in saves and save opportunities (27)
- ➡ 9th in blown saves (5)
- ➡ 10th in games finished (34)
- ➡ Led the Brewers in games pitched, saves, games finished (34), wild pitches (5), save opportunities (27), save percentage (81.5%), blown saves (5) and first batter efficiency (.222)

# Brian Givens

## 1995 Season

What a longshot! Signed over the winter as a minor league free agent, lefthander Brian Givens only hoped that his five-times-surgically-repaired left elbow would hold out for another season. He pitched replacement ball in the spring, then went to Triple-A when the big boys returned. But when injuries hit the Brewer rotation in June, they sent for Givens, and he responded with several respectable starts during their wild-card push in July and August. Although he faded in September, of all the replacement players who made the majors, his contribution was perhaps the most significant.

## Pitching

Givens left his overpowering fastball on one of many operating tables. His sinking fastball still has respectable velocity, but to be effective he must mix his pitches and get his big-breaking curve over the plate. He also has a hard slider and a change that he turns over, and he'll throw them anywhere in the count. Stamina is a problem, as his breaking pitches tend to lose their bite after he hits the 90-pitch mark.

## Defense

Givens' slow move to the plate gives basestealers an extra step, and they never have to wait long to get a breaking pitch to run on. He doesn't have a pickoff move, so he simply doesn't throw over. Givens is sometimes clumsy getting off the mound, but he knows what to do with the ball when he gets it.

## 1996 Outlook

If his Tommy John-rigged elbow has enough mileage left on it, Givens should start the year in the Milwaukee rotation. Still, his spot is far from secure. The return of Cal Eldred, combined with the development of some of the young pitchers, may squeeze out the 30-year-old Givens. If that happens, the Brewers may consider using this lefty out of the pen.

**Position:** SP
**Bats:** R  **Throws:** L
**Ht:** 6' 6"  **Wt:** 220

**Opening Day Age:** 30
**Born:** 11/6/65 in Lompac, CA
**ML Seasons:** 1

Milwaukee Brewers

### Overall Statistics

|        | W | L | Pct. | ERA | G | GS | Sv | IP | H | BB | SO | HR | BR/IP |
|--------|---|---|------|-----|---|----|----|-----|-----|----|----|----|-------|
| 1995   | 5 | 7 | .417 | 4.95 | 19 | 19 | 0 | 107.1 | 116 | 54 | 73 | 11 | 1.58 |
| Career | 5 | 7 | .417 | 4.95 | 19 | 19 | 0 | 107.1 | 116 | 54 | 73 | 11 | 1.58 |

### How Often He Throws Strikes

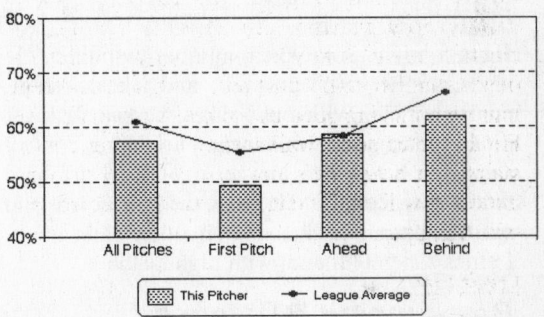

### 1995 Situational Stats

|            | W | L | ERA | Sv | IP |          | AB | H | HR | RBI | Avg |
|------------|---|---|------|----|------|----------|-----|-----|----|-----|------|
| Home       | 3 | 4 | 5.28 | 0 | 44.1 | LHB      | 66 | 14 | 0 | 4 | .212 |
| Road       | 2 | 3 | 4.71 | 0 | 63.0 | RHB      | 356 | 102 | 11 | 58 | .287 |
| First Half | 0 | 2 | 7.64 | 0 | 17.2 | Sc Pos   | 112 | 32 | 4 | 48 | .286 |
| Scnd Half  | 5 | 5 | 4.42 | 0 | 89.2 | Clutch   | 15 | 4 | 0 | 0 | .267 |

### 1995 Rankings (American League)

➞ 3rd in balks (2)
➞ 10th in errors at pitcher (2)
➞ Led the Brewers in balks (2)

# Darryl Hamilton

## 1995 Season

In possibly his last season in Milwaukee, Darryl Hamilton made a strong recovery from injuries, only to see his fortunes—and the team's—go down the drain in September. After undergoing Tommy John (ligament transplant) surgery on his right elbow in 1994, Hamilton's ability to return to center field was in question. He quickly erased those doubts, playing his usual good defense and keeping his average around .280 for most of the season. But in September, as the club went into free-fall, Hamilton stopped hitting and ended up on the bench. A dispute developed over a plate appearance-triggered option in his contract, and as a result he will almost certainly not return.

## Hitting

Hamilton is a prototypical number-two hitter. He waits on the ball very well, and takes a short, controlled cut. With two strikes, he can flick off pitches all day. His emphasis on making contact sacrifices his power, and most of his extra-base hits are leg doubles. He likes the ball down, and will drag a bunt when the situation calls for it. Lefties can get him out with high fastballs.

## Baserunning & Defense

Hamilton can still chase down balls in the gaps, but his repaired arm is a weakness and baserunners know they can challenge him. He has scaled back his running game, going only when the team truly needs it, but he remains a good percentage stealer. When he does choose to run, Hamilton lulls the pitcher with an innocent lead, then swipes second with his good acceleration.

## 1996 Outlook

Hamilton has yielded little to his age, and still possesses an attractive package of skills. The Brewers may miss his presence in center field, at the number-two spot, and in the clubhouse. Although he will be wearing new colors, he will undoubtedly be getting on base and chasing down flies for someone.

**Position:** CF
**Bats:** L **Throws:** R
**Ht:** 6' 1" **Wt:** 188

**Opening Day Age:** 31
**Born:** 12/3/64 in Baton Rouge, LA
**ML Seasons:** 7

### Overall Statistics

|  | G | AB | R | H | D | T | HR | RBI | SB | BB | SO | Avg | OBP | Slg |
|---|---|---|---|---|---|---|---|---|---|---|---|---|---|---|
| 1995 | 112 | 398 | 54 | 108 | 20 | 6 | 5 | 44 | 11 | 47 | 35 | .271 | .350 | .389 |
| Career | 666 | 2193 | 323 | 637 | 94 | 21 | 23 | 253 | 109 | 206 | 215 | .290 | .351 | .384 |

### Where He Hits the Ball

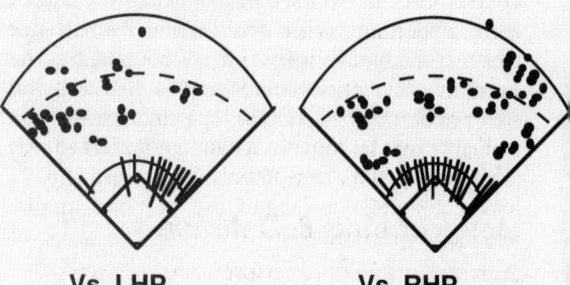

**Vs. LHP**          **Vs. RHP**

### 1995 Situational Stats

|  | AB | H | HR | RBI | Avg |  | AB | H | HR | RBI | Avg |
|---|---|---|---|---|---|---|---|---|---|---|---|
| Home | 209 | 57 | 3 | 25 | .273 | LHP | 114 | 27 | 0 | 9 | .237 |
| Road | 189 | 51 | 2 | 19 | .270 | RHP | 284 | 81 | 5 | 35 | .285 |
| First Half | 208 | 55 | 2 | 20 | .264 | Sc Pos | 81 | 23 | 1 | 35 | .284 |
| Scnd Half | 190 | 53 | 3 | 24 | .279 | Clutch | 52 | 13 | 0 | 7 | .250 |

### 1995 Rankings (American League)

- ➡ 5th in lowest percentage of swings that missed (8.7%) and lowest percentage of swings on the first pitch (13.2%)
- ➡ 6th in lowest slugging percentage vs. left-handed pitchers (.289), errors in center field (3) and fielding percentage in center field (.989)
- ➡ 7th in lowest batting average with the bases loaded (.091)
- ➡ 8th in triples
- ➡ 10th in lowest HR frequency (79.6 ABs per HR)
- ➡ Led the Brewers in sacrifice bunts (8) and lowest percentage of swings that missed (8.7%)

# John Jaha

**Position:** 1B
**Bats:** R  **Throws:** R
**Ht:** 6' 1"  **Wt:** 222

**Opening Day Age:** 29
**Born:** 5/27/66 in Portland, OR
**ML Seasons:** 4
**Pronunciation:** JAH-hah

## 1995 Season

For John Jaha, 1995 was both his breakout year and his breakdown year. Prior to the season, rumors had Dave Nilsson taking his job at first base, and his future with Milwaukee appeared uncertain—but Jaha fixed that. Although he missed most of May and July with groin injuries, for the three months when he was healthy he was one of the most dangerous hitters in the league. Most important, he finally fulfilled long-overdue expectations, growing into a middle-of-the-order hitter and solidifying his hold on the first-base job.

## Hitting

Jaha likes the ball inside, and shows good power from dead center to the left field foul pole. He gets himself in trouble when he tries to pull the outside pitch, resulting in a lot of 6-3 groundouts. He gets good lift on high pitches, and is content to turn a low pitch into a solid ground ball. Deadly with runners on base, Jaha set a club record last season with three grand slams in only 88 games.

## Baserunning & Defense

Although his fielding performance has been shaky in the past, Jaha was a solid defender in 1995. He has an accurate arm and shows decent range, especially when moving to his right. On the bases, Jaha is deceptively agile for a man his size, but he knows his limitations. His 1992 stolen-base performance—10-for-10 in only 47 games—was a fluke, and he'll probably only steal a handful of bases per season from now on.

## 1996 Outlook

With an offense sorely lacking power, the Brewers will continue to look to Jaha for production. As long as he isn't burdened with unrealistic expectations or injury, Jaha can be a solid contributor. He may have been over his head last season, and his skills don't support a .300 batting average, but he's a safe bet to stabilize around .280, with enough power to keep hitting fourth or fifth.

### Overall Statistics

|  | G | AB | R | H | D | T | HR | RBI | SB | BB | SO | Avg | OBP | Slg |
|---|---|---|---|---|---|---|---|---|---|---|---|---|---|---|
| 1995 | 88 | 316 | 59 | 99 | 20 | 2 | 20 | 65 | 2 | 36 | 66 | .313 | .389 | .579 |
| Career | 372 | 1255 | 199 | 335 | 58 | 3 | 53 | 184 | 28 | 131 | 280 | .267 | .344 | .445 |

### Where He Hits the Ball

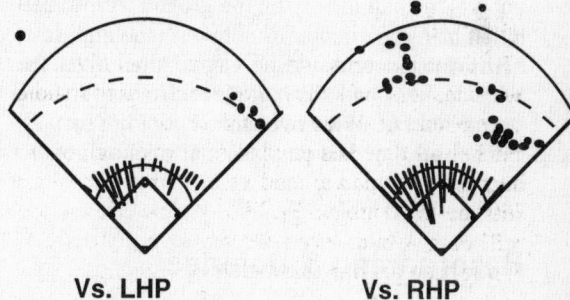

**Vs. LHP**          **Vs. RHP**

### 1995 Situational Stats

|  | AB | H | HR | RBI | Avg |  | AB | H | HR | RBI | Avg |
|---|---|---|---|---|---|---|---|---|---|---|---|
| Home | 153 | 43 | 8 | 29 | .281 | LHP | 71 | 23 | 2 | 13 | .324 |
| Road | 163 | 56 | 12 | 36 | .344 | RHP | 245 | 76 | 18 | 52 | .310 |
| First Half | 105 | 34 | 6 | 21 | .324 | Sc Pos | 81 | 25 | 9 | 47 | .309 |
| Scnd Half | 211 | 65 | 14 | 44 | .308 | Clutch | 47 | 14 | 3 | 7 | .298 |

### 1995 Rankings (American League)

- ➙ 3rd in batting average on an 0-2 count (.345)
- ➙ 9th in cleanup slugging percentage (.530) and batting average with two strikes (.261)
- ➙ Led the Brewers in home runs and batting average on an 0-2 count (.345)

# Pat Listach

**Position:** 2B/SS
**Bats:** B  **Throws:** R
**Ht:** 5' 9"  **Wt:** 180

**Opening Day Age:** 28
**Born:** 9/12/67 in Natchitoches, LA
**ML Seasons:** 4

## 1995 Season

Last year Pat Listach finally came back, but his speed didn't come with him. Coming off knee surgery, he started the year as Milwaukee's leadoff hitter and second baseman. Phil Garner, disappointed with Listach's inability to get on base and his slow pivot, benched him before the end of June. Although he continued to log time at second base and shortstop, he never saw the top of the batting order again. Continually bothered by leg injuries, Listach never showed the skills that made him A.L. Rookie of the Year in 1992.

## Hitting

Listach takes a bigger cut than you would expect, but hits the ball mostly on the ground. A low-ball hitter, he has particular trouble with the high fastball. From the right side, he's a pull hitter; from the left side, he sprays the ball more. He used to be a strong hitter from the right side, but didn't hit well from either side last year. He's always a threat to bunt, but he failed to execute too many times last season.

## Baserunning & Defense

Listach has good range and reactions at second base, his natural position. On the double play, his slow release and poor arm are handicaps. While he's still a capable shortstop, he won't reclaim his spot there. He ran tentatively at times, and didn't show his old quickness.

## 1996 Outlook

Listach's speed is his central skill, so his leg problems last year affected his entire game. If he recovers some of his old speed, he can still be a useful second baseman. He may yet win back the second-base job, and taking an optimistic view, he could even be a darkhorse candidate for the center-field position. Unfortunately, many suspect that his knee problems may have permanently rendered him a backup.

### Overall Statistics

|  | G | AB | R | H | D | T | HR | RBI | SB | BB | SO | Avg | OBP | Slg |
|---|---|---|---|---|---|---|---|---|---|---|---|---|---|---|
| 1995 | 101 | 334 | 35 | 73 | 8 | 2 | 0 | 25 | 13 | 25 | 61 | .219 | .276 | .254 |
| Career | 364 | 1323 | 186 | 344 | 45 | 9 | 4 | 104 | 87 | 120 | 263 | .260 | .323 | .317 |

### Where He Hits the Ball

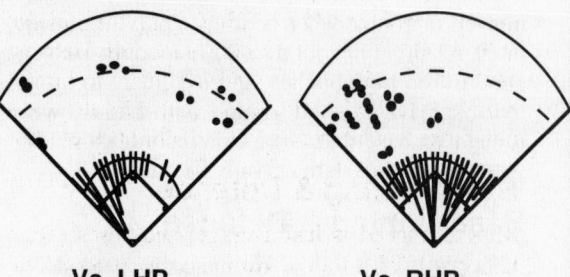

**Vs. LHP**          **Vs. RHP**

### 1995 Situational Stats

|  | AB | H | HR | RBI | Avg |  | AB | H | HR | RBI | Avg |
|---|---|---|---|---|---|---|---|---|---|---|---|
| Home | 159 | 36 | 0 | 12 | .226 | LHP | 141 | 30 | 0 | 5 | .213 |
| Road | 175 | 37 | 0 | 13 | .211 | RHP | 193 | 43 | 0 | 20 | .223 |
| First Half | 170 | 36 | 0 | 16 | .212 | Sc Pos | 83 | 23 | 0 | 24 | .277 |
| Scnd Half | 164 | 37 | 0 | 9 | .226 | Clutch | 53 | 15 | 0 | 9 | .283 |

### 1995 Rankings (American League)

- ➡ 1st in lowest on-base percentage for a leadoff hitter (.270)
- ➡ 3rd in lowest slugging percentage vs. left-handed pitchers (.269)
- ➡ 5th in lowest batting average vs. left-handed pitchers (.213) and lowest on-base percentage vs. left-handed pitchers (.273)

# Matt Mieske

## 1995 Season

After trading Gary Sheffield to get him, and releasing Troy O'Leary to play him, you can't say that the Brewers aren't committed to Matt Mieske. They keep waiting for him to show he's capable of playing right field full time, but so far, he's been unable to break out of his platoon role. While he continued to batter lefties last year, Mieske showed no signs of having solved righthanders, who have always given him trouble.

## Hitting

Mieske is a low-ball hitter who always looks to pull the ball down and in. Lefthanders' breaking pitches arc right into his wheelhouse, but when he faces a righty, it's a different story. He pulls off the breaking pitch down and away, and has problems with high fastballs in on his hands. Although he can work the count, there are some pitches he can't hit even when ahead in the count. He's mostly a pull hitter, but he can line a fastball the other way.

## Baserunning & Defense

Mieske's speed is just average, and basestealing isn't part of his game. He has good tools in the field, including the strongest outfield arm on the club, but he sometimes misreads fly balls, putting himself in poor position to throw.

## 1996 Outlook

Mieske will be in right field every time the Brewers see a southpaw, but his opportunity to earn a full-time job will depend on a variety of circumstances. The team needs to keep Dave Nilsson's bat in the lineup, so he may continue to play at Mieske's expense. While Mieske can be expected to continue to be a productive platoon player, he's 28 years old and is probably as good as he'll ever be. If he hasn't solved righthanders by now, it's not likely that he ever will.

**Position:** RF
**Bats:** R **Throws:** R
**Ht:** 6' 0" **Wt:** 192

**Opening Day Age:** 28
**Born:** 2/13/68 in Midland, MI
**ML Seasons:** 3
**Pronunciation:** MEE-skee

### Overall Statistics

|  | G | AB | R | H | D | T | HR | RBI | SB | BB | SO | Avg | OBP | Slg |
|---|---|---|---|---|---|---|---|---|---|---|---|---|---|---|
| 1995 | 117 | 267 | 42 | 67 | 13 | 1 | 12 | 48 | 2 | 27 | 45 | .251 | .323 | .442 |
| Career | 224 | 584 | 90 | 148 | 26 | 2 | 25 | 93 | 5 | 52 | 121 | .253 | .319 | .433 |

### Where He Hits the Ball

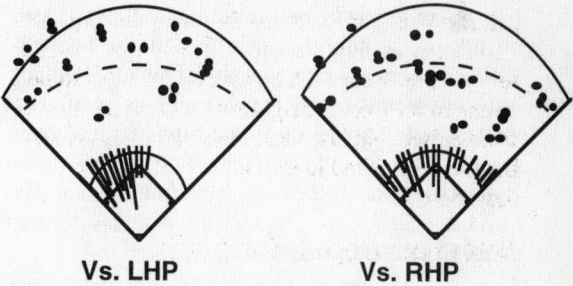

**Vs. LHP**        **Vs. RHP**

### 1995 Situational Stats

|  | AB | H | HR | RBI | Avg |  | AB | H | HR | RBI | Avg |
|---|---|---|---|---|---|---|---|---|---|---|---|
| Home | 120 | 26 | 3 | 18 | .217 | LHP | 121 | 37 | 9 | 31 | .306 |
| Road | 147 | 41 | 9 | 30 | .279 | RHP | 146 | 30 | 3 | 17 | .205 |
| First Half | 107 | 29 | 5 | 23 | .271 | Sc Pos | 84 | 21 | 7 | 41 | .250 |
| Scnd Half | 160 | 38 | 7 | 25 | .238 | Clutch | 53 | 11 | 4 | 11 | .208 |

### 1995 Rankings (American League)

➡ 5th in errors in right field (4) and fielding percentage in right field (.979)

➡ Led the Brewers in sacrifice flies (5) and slugging percentage vs. left-handed pitchers (.587)

# Angel Miranda

## 1995 Season

Angel Miranda began the season in the best Brewer tradition—recovering from an injury. After his 1994 season was ruined by surgery to reconstruct a torn ligament in his left knee, Miranda worked to rebuild his stamina during the early season. He re-aggravated the knee injury in late May, and then tore cartilage in the same knee in June, undergoing surgery and missing the month of July. When he returned in August, he was finally throwing without pain. Pitching sparingly out of the pen during the season's final months, Miranda continued to post mixed results.

## Pitching

Miranda is well known for his tantalizing screwball. He relies on its fading action, but uses it as a change-up, so he must set it up with the fastball. Unfortunately, his gimpy push-off leg affected not only his stamina, but his velocity as well. His fastball only topped out in the high 80s last year. He throws a two-seam fastball that runs in to righthanders, as well as a straight four-seamer. He also has a slow curve, and he'll use it early in the count to a good fastball hitter.

## Defense

Miranda is an erratic fielder, and the momentum of his delivery makes it difficult for him to cover first base. He seemed to regain some of his mobility after the surgery last year. While he's never been adept at holding runners, he showed some improvement last year.

## 1996 Outlook

Miranda could be the sleeper of the staff in 1996. His arm hasn't been overworked, and if his knee is finally sound he could regain his lost velocity—making his screwball much more effective. Look for him to vie for a spot in the rotation in the spring. At worst, he'll be a "long man" out of the bullpen, but if he's up to it, he'll crack the rotation sometime in 1996.

**Position:** RP/SP
**Bats:** L  **Throws:** L
**Ht:** 6' 1"  **Wt:** 195

**Opening Day Age:** 26
**Born:** 11/9/69 in Arecibo, PR
**ML Seasons:** 3

### Overall Statistics

|  | W | L | Pct. | ERA | G | GS | Sv | IP | H | BB | SO | HR | BR/IP |
|---|---|---|---|---|---|---|---|---|---|---|---|---|---|
| 1995 | 4 | 5 | .444 | 5.23 | 30 | 10 | 1 | 74.0 | 83 | 49 | 45 | 8 | 1.78 |
| Career | 10 | 15 | .400 | 4.28 | 60 | 35 | 1 | 240.0 | 222 | 128 | 157 | 28 | 1.46 |

### How Often He Throws Strikes

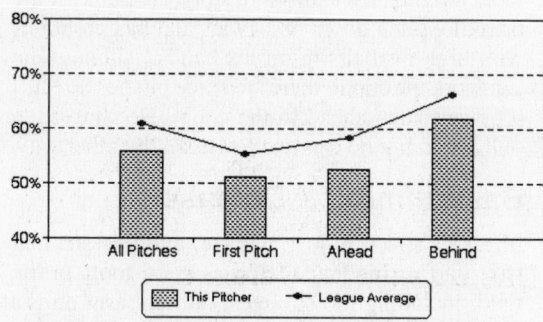

### 1995 Situational Stats

|  | W | L | ERA | Sv | IP |  | AB | H | HR | RBI | Avg |
|---|---|---|---|---|---|---|---|---|---|---|---|
| Home | 2 | 3 | 4.78 | 1 | 32.0 | LHB | 53 | 15 | 0 | 3 | .283 |
| Road | 2 | 2 | 5.57 | 0 | 42.0 | RHB | 232 | 68 | 8 | 37 | .293 |
| First Half | 4 | 3 | 5.26 | 0 | 53.0 | Sc Pos | 87 | 21 | 0 | 29 | .241 |
| Scnd Half | 0 | 2 | 5.14 | 1 | 21.0 | Clutch | 29 | 8 | 3 | 7 | .276 |

### 1995 Rankings (American League)

➡ Led the Brewers in wild pitches (5)

# Dave Nilsson

## 1995 Season

Dave Nilsson did the impossible in 1995—he came down with an affliction the Brewers hadn't already seen. Over the winter, he contracted Ross River Fever, a rare mosquito-transmitted virus from Down Under. The illness kept him out of action until late June, and continued to drain his strength all year. He had been slated to move to first base, but John Jaha's resurgence nixed that plan, so Nilsson instead went to the outfield. Playing mostly right field, he was surprisingly adequate. His power continued to develop, and he was having a good year at the plate until he wore down in September.

## Hitting

Nilsson always makes good contact, and can turn on the inside fastball—especially if it's down low. Lefties can sometimes get him to wave at the breaking ball down and away, but by the end of the year, Nilsson had earned Phil Garner's confidence that he could handle southpaws. He was on a home-run tear in early August, and appears to have truly emerged as a middle-of-the-order hitter.

## Baserunning & Defense

At full strength, Nilsson's an average runner at best, and the illness last year slowed him further. His experience as an outfielder in the Australian winter league enabled him to make a smooth transition to the garden. His range isn't great, but he takes good angles to the ball and looks comfortable in both left and right field. He throws with average strength and good accuracy.

## 1996 Outlook

Nilsson is on the brink of developing into one of the Brewers' most dangerous hitters. In a full, healthy year, he is capable of hitting for both power and average. The club will find some way to get his bat in the lineup every day, whether it's in right field, left field, at first base or DH. All he needs to do is stay healthy.

**Position:** RF/LF/DH
**Bats:** L **Throws:** R
**Ht:** 6' 3" **Wt:** 215

**Opening Day Age:** 26
**Born:** 12/14/69 in Brisbane, Queensland, Australia
**ML Seasons:** 4
**Pronunciation:** NILL-son

### Overall Statistics

|  | G | AB | R | H | D | T | HR | RBI | SB | BB | SO | Avg | OBP | Slg |
|---|---|---|---|---|---|---|---|---|---|---|---|---|---|---|
| 1995 | 81 | 263 | 41 | 73 | 12 | 1 | 12 | 53 | 2 | 24 | 41 | .278 | .337 | .468 |
| Career | 341 | 1120 | 142 | 296 | 58 | 6 | 35 | 187 | 8 | 112 | 156 | .264 | .328 | .421 |

### Where He Hits the Ball

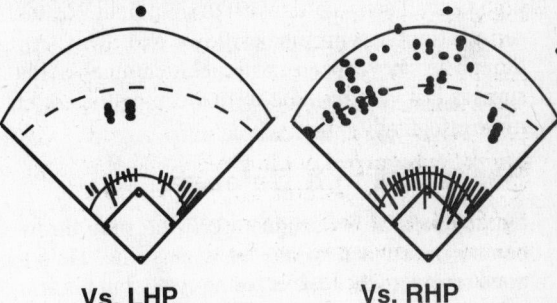

**Vs. LHP**          **Vs. RHP**

### 1995 Situational Stats

|  | AB | H | HR | RBI | Avg |  | AB | H | HR | RBI | Avg |
|---|---|---|---|---|---|---|---|---|---|---|---|
| Home | 139 | 44 | 7 | 30 | .317 | LHP | 55 | 15 | 2 | 9 | .273 |
| Road | 124 | 29 | 5 | 23 | .234 | RHP | 208 | 58 | 10 | 44 | .279 |
| First Half | 43 | 10 | 2 | 8 | .233 | Sc Pos | 80 | 20 | 4 | 41 | .250 |
| Scnd Half | 220 | 63 | 10 | 45 | .286 | Clutch | 44 | 11 | 3 | 8 | .250 |

### 1995 Rankings (American League)

- → 8th in cleanup slugging percentage (.538)
- → 10th in batting average with the bases loaded (.500)
- → Led the Brewers in sacrifice flies (5), intentional walks (4) and cleanup slugging percentage (.538)

# Joe Oliver

## 1995 Season

After missing most of 1994 with synovitis, an inflammation of the joints, Joe Oliver signed a one-year deal with the Brewers. He was a real bargain, showing surprising pop with his bat and handling the young pitching staff with a veteran's savvy. A broken wrist put him out for a month in midseason, but his bat was a stabilizing presence in the lineup for the rest of the year. He enjoyed a complete recovery in all phases of his game, and he should draw attention in the free-agent market.

## Hitting

A high-ball hitter, Oliver looks for fastballs to drive. He tries to pull most pitches, but if he sees a high fastball away he'll take it to right field. He has serious trouble with pitches down and away. Although he's never been a patient hitter, much of his success last year resulted from working the count more effectively.

## Baserunning & Defense

On defense, Oliver's signature is the snap throw behind the runner, to any base, anytime. He's a good receiver who blocks pitches well, but his arm is just average. Young pitchers enjoy working with him, as he keeps a close eye on their mechanics. On the bases, he has all the speed of an oncoming glacier, and there's no reason for him to ever attempt six stolen bases in a season again.

## 1996 Outlook

The Brewers don't have any hot young catching prospects, and they'd love to have Oliver back if they can afford him. However, after playing a year at a cut rate just to prove that he'd recovered, Oliver may prefer to test the free-agent waters. Wherever he goes, he will provide stability, although he may not duplicate last year's offensive exploits.

**Position:** C
**Bats:** R  **Throws:** R
**Ht:** 6' 3"  **Wt:** 220

**Opening Day Age:** 30
**Born:** 7/24/65 in Memphis, TN
**ML Seasons:** 7

### Overall Statistics

|        | G   | AB   | R   | H   | D   | T | HR | RBI | SB | BB  | SO  | Avg  | OBP  | Slg  |
|--------|-----|------|-----|-----|-----|---|----|-----|----|-----|-----|------|------|------|
| 1995   | 97  | 337  | 43  | 92  | 20  | 0 | 12 | 51  | 2  | 27  | 66  | .273 | .332 | .439 |
| Career | 649 | 2107 | 194 | 525 | 115 | 1 | 59 | 304 | 5  | 152 | 391 | .249 | .300 | .389 |

### Where He Hits the Ball

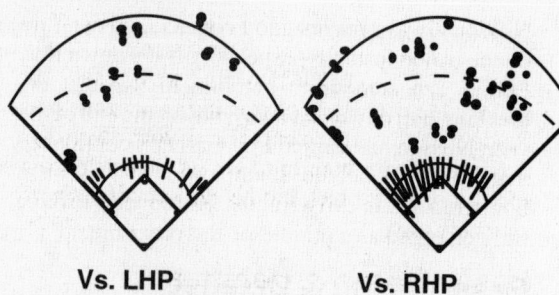

Vs. LHP          Vs. RHP

### 1995 Situational Stats

|            | AB  | H  | HR | RBI | Avg  |        | AB  | H  | HR | RBI | Avg  |
|------------|-----|----|----|-----|------|--------|-----|----|----|-----|------|
| Home       | 140 | 40 | 4  | 21  | .286 | LHP    | 77  | 20 | 1  | 8   | .260 |
| Road       | 197 | 52 | 8  | 30  | .264 | RHP    | 260 | 72 | 11 | 43  | .277 |
| First Half | 221 | 64 | 9  | 33  | .290 | Sc Pos | 88  | 30 | 3  | 38  | .341 |
| Scnd Half  | 116 | 28 | 3  | 18  | .241 | Clutch | 54  | 9  | 0  | 3   | .167 |

### 1995 Rankings (American League)

➡ 2nd in errors at catcher (8) and lowest fielding percentage at catcher (.982)

➡ 8th in lowest batting average in the clutch (.167)

# Kevin Seitzer

**Position:** 3B/1B/DH
**Bats:** R  **Throws:** R
**Ht:** 5'11"  **Wt:** 193

**Opening Day Age:** 34
**Born:** 3/26/62 in Springfield, IL
**ML Seasons:** 10
**Pronunciation:** SITE-ser

## 1995 Season

The heart and soul of the Brewers, as well as their lone All-Star last year, Kevin Seitzer enjoyed his best season in years. After getting both knees scoped over the offseason, he started off hot. Then came a frightening beaning by Scott Erickson on May 29—his second serious beaning in as many years. Remarkably, Seitzer missed only one game, returning with a black eye, a customized batting helmet. . . and a three-hit game. He stayed hot, and went on to win A.L. Player of the Month honors for June. Hitting in the number-two and three spots, he kept his average well over .300 all year.

## Hitting

Seitzer covers the entire plate and hits the ball where it's pitched. His doubles power comes on pitches up, and with a runner on first he'll happily shoot the ball through the hole on the right side. He has trouble digging out breaking balls from left-handers. With his great bat control, you can always play hit-and-run with him. He no longer has the speed to bunt for hits, but he can sacrifice whenever necessary.

## Baserunning & Defense

Never a Brooks Robinson, Seitzer has lost most of what little range he had. He has a weak arm and is forced to compensate with a quick release. He now seems more at home at first base, where he's shown a flair for digging out low throws. Once an active basestealer, Seitzer rarely runs anymore, attempting just five steals in the past two seasons combined.

## 1996 Outlook

A free agent after the season, Seitzer, sadly, may not be back with the Brewers in 1996. With his strong season last year, he may have priced himself out of their range. Wherever he winds up playing, he'll need to keep hitting like he has the last two years, as his other skills aren't enough to keep him in the lineup.

### Overall Statistics

|  | G | AB | R | H | D | T | HR | RBI | SB | BB | SO | Avg | OBP | Slg |
|---|---|---|---|---|---|---|---|---|---|---|---|---|---|---|
| 1995 | 132 | 492 | 56 | 153 | 33 | 3 | 5 | 69 | 2 | 64 | 57 | .311 | .395 | .421 |
| Career | 1221 | 4507 | 627 | 1317 | 236 | 32 | 59 | 511 | 74 | 564 | 513 | .292 | .372 | .398 |

### Where He Hits the Ball

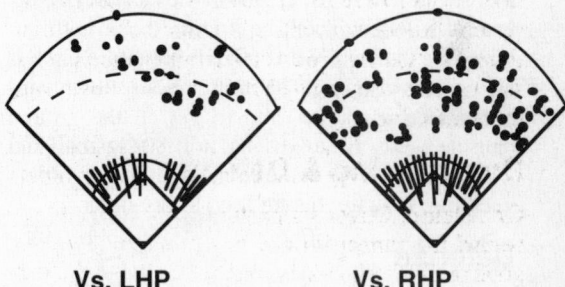

Vs. LHP          Vs. RHP

### 1995 Situational Stats

|  | AB | H | HR | RBI | Avg |  | AB | H | HR | RBI | Avg |
|---|---|---|---|---|---|---|---|---|---|---|---|
| Home | 237 | 72 | 1 | 23 | .304 | LHP | 139 | 35 | 0 | 14 | .252 |
| Road | 255 | 81 | 4 | 46 | .318 | RHP | 353 | 118 | 5 | 55 | .334 |
| First Half | 232 | 75 | 2 | 37 | .323 | Sc Pos | 125 | 47 | 1 | 60 | .376 |
| Scnd Half | 260 | 78 | 3 | 32 | .300 | Clutch | 71 | 21 | 1 | 13 | .296 |

### 1995 Rankings (American League)

- ➡ 2nd in batting average vs. right-handed pitchers (.334) and lowest percentage of extra bases taken as a runner (28.8%)
- ➡ 5th in lowest HR frequency (98.4 ABs per HR), batting average with runners in scoring position (.376) and batting average with the bases loaded (.533)
- ➡ 6th in lowest percentage of swings that missed (10.1%)
- ➡ 8th in doubles
- ➡ 9th in singles (112) and batting average on the road (.318)
- ➡ Led the Brewers in at-bats, hits, singles (112), doubles, total bases (207), walks, times on base (223) and GDPs (12)

# Steve Sparks

## 1995 Season

On a pitching staff beset with injuries, rookie knuckleballer Steve Sparks was a rock of stability in 1995. After beginning the year as a swing man, he joined the rotation for good in June and became one of the team's most dependable starters. He was a great asset to a staff that was in shambles, starting many games on short rest and relieving between starts several times. By the end of the year, he had made it clear that he will be honing his craft with the Brewers for years to come.

## Pitching

The intriguing thing about Sparks is his ability to change speeds with the knuckler. He can get it up there at around 75 MPH, one of the hardest floaters batters will see. Then, he'll come back with another one that barely hits 60. His signature pitch is also noteworthy for its tremendous downward break, which enables him to get all the ground balls he needs. He mixes in a mid-80s fastball and will use it any time in the count, just to keep hitters guessing. It's rare that he'll go to his slider.

## Defense

As he finishes his delivery upright and square to the plate, Sparks becomes a capable fifth infielder, adeptly handling anything he can reach. He has a compact stretch delivery designed to deter basestealers, but hasn't shown a good pickoff move. On balance, he's a bit worse than average at controlling the running game.

## 1996 Outlook

"Sparky" brings something that's always in short supply on the Brewer staff—durability. Ironically, this virtue served to mask his effectiveness last year; he was left in to absorb a few poundings, and he wasn't quite as sharp when brought back on short rest. If the rotation is more stable in 1996, Sparks may benefit nicely. He will continue to be an innings-eater, and as he gradually sharpens his control he should evolve into a quality starter.

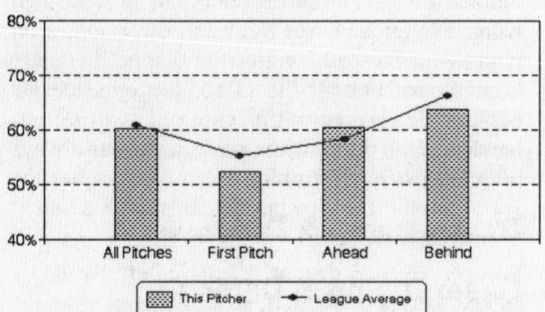

**Position:** SP/RP
**Bats:** R  **Throws:** R
**Ht:** 6' 0"  **Wt:** 180

**Opening Day Age:** 30
**Born:** 7/2/65 in Tulsa, Oklahoma
**ML Seasons:** 1

### Overall Statistics

|  | W | L | Pct. | ERA | G | GS | Sv | IP | H | BB | SO | HR | BR/9 |
|---|---|---|---|---|---|---|---|---|---|---|---|---|---|
| 1995 | 9 | 11 | .450 | 4.63 | 33 | 27 | 0 | 202.0 | 210 | 86 | 96 | 17 | 1.47 |
| Career | 9 | 11 | .450 | 4.63 | 33 | 27 | 0 | 202.0 | 210 | 86 | 96 | 17 | 1.47 |

### How Often He Throws Strikes

[Chart showing percentages for All Pitches, First Pitch, Ahead, Behind with This Pitcher (bars) and League Average (line)]

### 1995 Situational Stats

|  | W | L | ERA | Sv | IP |  | AB | H | HR | RBI | Avg |
|---|---|---|---|---|---|---|---|---|---|---|---|
| Home | 3 | 6 | 5.69 | 0 | 93.1 | LHB | 447 | 124 | 9 | 50 | .277 |
| Road | 6 | 5 | 3.73 | 0 | 108.2 | RHB | 320 | 86 | 8 | 35 | .269 |
| First Half | 5 | 3 | 3.44 | 0 | 89.0 | Sc Pos | 192 | 52 | 3 | 66 | .271 |
| Scnd Half | 4 | 8 | 5.58 | 0 | 113.0 | Clutch | 63 | 21 | 2 | 9 | .333 |

### 1995 Rankings (American League)

- → 1st in GDPs induced (29)
- → 2nd in most GDPs induced per 9 innings (1.3)
- → 3rd in lowest strikeout/walk ratio (1.1) and highest ERA at home (5.69)
- → 5th in least strikeouts per 9 innings (4.3)
- → 7th in highest ERA, pickoff throws (159) and least home runs allowed per 9 innings (.76)
- → 8th in highest on-base percentage allowed (.346) and least pitches thrown per batter (3.65)
- → 9th in hits allowed and least run support per 9 innings (4.9)
- → Led the Brewers in complete games (3), innings pitched, walks allowed and strikeouts

# B.J. Surhoff

## 1995 Season

For B.J. Surhoff, always regarded as somewhat of a disappointment, 1995 was a year of redemption. After his 1994 season was curtailed by a severe abdominal strain, Surhoff was re-signed as a utility player, taking a huge pay cut just to return. But when the bell rang he started hitting, getting off to a good start for the first time in years. His versatility proved to be a huge asset, and he remained among the batting leaders until a knee injury dragged down his average in September.

## Hitting

At the plate, Surhoff waits on the ball well and uses his strong wrists to lash the ball wherever it's pitched. With his quick, controlled swing, he remains dangerous when behind in the count, even with two strikes. He has learned to get good lift on high pitches, and he'll hit sharp grounders if you pitch him down. He stays back very well on the breaking ball, and can mash one from either a lefthander or a righthander.

## Baserunning & Defense

Surhoff showed decent range in left field but looked unsure of himself, sometimes taking poor approaches to the ball. His throwing was inconsistent, but he threw out his share of the runners who tested him. As a first baseman, he looked more comfortable. He had trouble when asked to catch, but it was later discovered that he'd been playing with torn cartilage in his right knee. Surhoff still has good speed and will run on occasion.

## 1996 Outlook

Freed from the demands of catching, Surhoff has made real strides as a hitter. He's always had what it takes to hit .300; the question now is where he'll play. As a free agent at the end of the year, he'll be expecting a nice reward for his impressive season, but with the Brewers continuing to downsize their payroll, it's not clear whether his salary will fit anymore.

**Position:** 1B/C/LF
**Bats:** L  **Throws:** R
**Ht:** 6' 1"  **Wt:** 204

**Opening Day Age:** 31
**Born:** 8/4/64 in Bronx, NY
**ML Seasons:** 9

### Overall Statistics

|  | G | AB | R | H | D | T | HR | RBI | SB | BB | SO | Avg | OBP | Slg |
|---|---|---|---|---|---|---|---|---|---|---|---|---|---|---|
| 1995 | 117 | 415 | 72 | 133 | 26 | 3 | 13 | 73 | 7 | 37 | 43 | .320 | .378 | .492 |
| Career | 1102 | 3884 | 472 | 1064 | 194 | 24 | 57 | 524 | 102 | 294 | 323 | .274 | .323 | .380 |

### Where He Hits the Ball

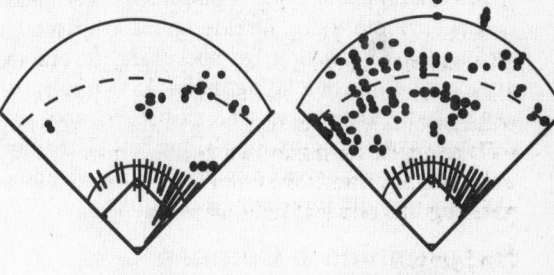

**Vs. LHP**  **Vs. RHP**

### 1995 Situational Stats

|  | AB | H | HR | RBI | Avg |  | AB | H | HR | RBI | Avg |
|---|---|---|---|---|---|---|---|---|---|---|---|
| Home | 205 | 70 | 7 | 49 | .341 | LHP | 128 | 47 | 3 | 22 | .367 |
| Road | 210 | 63 | 6 | 24 | .300 | RHP | 287 | 86 | 10 | 51 | .300 |
| First Half | 145 | 54 | 4 | 32 | .372 | Sc Pos | 107 | 41 | 6 | 63 | .383 |
| Scnd Half | 270 | 79 | 9 | 41 | .293 | Clutch | 60 | 15 | 2 | 6 | .250 |

### 1995 Rankings (American League)

- ➡ 4th in batting average with runners in scoring position (.383), batting average with the bases loaded (.556) and batting average vs. left-handed pitchers (.367)
- ➡ 5th in batting average with two strikes (.270)
- ➡ 6th in batting average
- ➡ 7th in batting average on an 0-2 count (.310) and batting average at home (.341)
- ➡ 8th in least pitches seen per plate appearance (3.48)
- ➡ 9th in highest percentage of swings put into play (53.1%)
- ➡ Led the Brewers in batting average, runs scored, RBI and intentional walks (4)

# Jose Valentin

## 1995 Season

Behind the low batting average and the errors lies a player who can help you win in a lot of ways. That's why Phil Garner stuck with Jose Valentin through a dreadful early-season slump, sending him out to shortstop every day, until his season was effectively ended by a broken finger in September. Valentin made small improvements in several areas of his game, and was one of the few constants on a team in flux.

## Hitting

A switch-hitter, Valentin shows surprising power from the left side. He looks to pull, and can turn on the inside fastball. The low pitch is his favorite, but if you pitch him away he'll pull it for a harmless grounder. From the right side he's a completely different hitter, lacking bat speed and forced to compensate by committing early. As a result, he can be badly fooled by anything offspeed, and still can be overmatched by a good fastball. The time may have come to give up switch-hitting. Valentin can bunt expertly for a hit or a sacrifice.

## Baserunning & Defense

With great range, a strong throwing arm and good hands, Valentin has quietly become one of the premier defensive shortstops in the league. He always receives the ball in a position to get off a strong throw, and as his fundamentals have improved his errors have shrunk. His quick release helps the team turn a huge number of double plays. He's learned to use his good speed on the bases, becoming the best baserunner on the team.

## 1996 Outlook

Valentin is one of the few Brewers to enter the year with a regular job virtually guaranteed. He'll never hit for a high enough average to get the recognition he deserves, but at 26 he may be coming into his own. If can learn to hit lefthanders a little better, he'll be a complete player.

**Position:** SS
**Bats:** B **Throws:** R
**Ht:** 5'10" **Wt:** 166

**Opening Day Age:** 26
**Born:** 10/12/69 in Manati, PR
**ML Seasons:** 4

### Overall Statistics

| | G | AB | R | H | D | T | HR | RBI | SB | BB | SO | Avg | OBP | Slg |
|---|---|---|---|---|---|---|---|---|---|---|---|---|---|---|
| 1995 | 112 | 338 | 62 | 74 | 23 | 3 | 11 | 49 | 16 | 37 | 83 | .219 | .293 | .402 |
| Career | 232 | 679 | 120 | 155 | 43 | 5 | 23 | 103 | 29 | 82 | 174 | .228 | .311 | .408 |

### Where He Hits the Ball

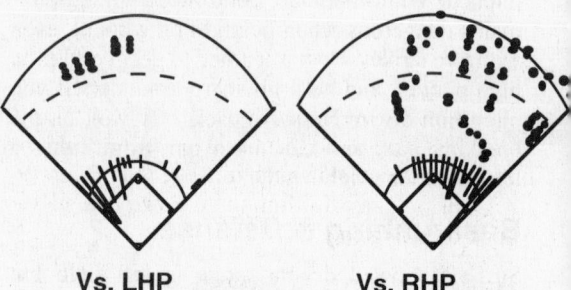

Vs. LHP          Vs. RHP

### 1995 Situational Stats

| | AB | H | HR | RBI | Avg | | AB | H | HR | RBI | Avg |
|---|---|---|---|---|---|---|---|---|---|---|---|
| Home | 172 | 31 | 3 | 23 | .180 | LHP | 83 | 11 | 0 | 4 | .133 |
| Road | 166 | 43 | 8 | 26 | .259 | RHP | 255 | 63 | 11 | 45 | .247 |
| First Half | 198 | 46 | 7 | 29 | .232 | Sc Pos | 103 | 22 | 3 | 39 | .214 |
| Scnd Half | 140 | 28 | 4 | 20 | .200 | Clutch | 48 | 13 | 1 | 6 | .271 |

### 1995 Rankings (American League)

→ 1st in least GDPs per GDP situation (0.0%)
→ 3rd in lowest batting average with two strikes (.122)
→ 4th in lowest fielding percentage at shortstop (.971)
→ 6th in lowest stolen base percentage (66.7%) and errors at shortstop (15)
→ 7th in lowest batting average with runners in scoring position (.214)
→ Led the Brewers in stolen bases, caught stealing (8) and least GDPs per GDP situation (0.0%)

# Greg Vaughn

## 1995 Season

Following offseason rotator-cuff surgery on both shoulders, Greg Vaughn never really found his groove in 1995. Still lacking bat speed in the first half, he endured a frightful slump. Since Vaughn was earning almost one-third of the team's payroll, he quickly became a lightning rod for fans' discontent. Although his bat came around in July and August, he continued to frustrate Phil Garner with his frequent strikeouts. When a hamstring injury ended his season in early September, it brought a merciful end to what he repeatedly called "the worst year of my life."

## Hitting

Vaughn's theory of hitting is simple: get a pitch you're looking for, and pull it in the air. He has an extreme uppercut swing, and he pulls the ball so much that some teams employ an infield shift. He's a guess hitter, and looks for a high fastball until he's convinced that he won't see one. He can even pull the outside pitch if it's up, but his uppercut makes it hard for him to go down and get the good breaking ball.

## Baserunning & Defense

A series of shoulder surgeries have relegated Vaughn to a DH role. There's been no speculation that he'll return to left field any time soon. He can still use his surprising speed to steal a base, and has done a much better job picking his spots to run over the past couple of seasons.

## 1996 Outlook

With a fresh start in 1996, Vaughn should be expected to rebound. Always a hard worker, he won't have to contend with the lingering effects of shoulder surgery that bothered him last year. If he can avoid the nagging injuries that have cut into his playing time in the past, he should be able to return to form. Look for him to provide good production in the middle of the Brewers' lineup.

**Position:** DH
**Bats:** R  **Throws:** R
**Ht:** 6' 0"  **Wt:** 202

**Opening Day Age:** 30
**Born:** 7/3/65 in Sacramento, CA
**ML Seasons:** 7

### Overall Statistics

|  | G | AB | R | H | D | T | HR | RBI | SB | BB | SO | Avg | OBP | Slg |
|---|---|---|---|---|---|---|---|---|---|---|---|---|---|---|
| 1995 | 108 | 392 | 67 | 88 | 19 | 1 | 17 | 59 | 10 | 55 | 89 | .224 | .317 | .408 |
| Career | 801 | 2869 | 450 | 694 | 142 | 13 | 138 | 471 | 57 | 363 | 662 | .242 | .327 | .445 |

### Where He Hits the Ball

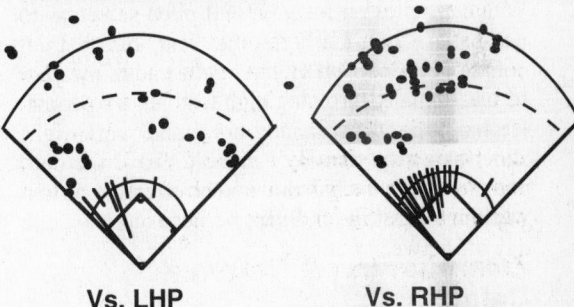

**Vs. LHP**            **Vs. RHP**

### 1995 Situational Stats

|  | AB | H | HR | RBI | Avg |  | AB | H | HR | RBI | Avg |
|---|---|---|---|---|---|---|---|---|---|---|---|
| Home | 189 | 50 | 8 | 31 | .265 | LHP | 118 | 29 | 5 | 18 | .246 |
| Road | 203 | 38 | 9 | 28 | .187 | RHP | 274 | 59 | 12 | 41 | .215 |
| First Half | 232 | 44 | 8 | 34 | .190 | Sc Pos | 112 | 26 | 5 | 42 | .232 |
| Scnd Half | 160 | 44 | 9 | 25 | .275 | Clutch | 59 | 12 | 3 | 7 | .203 |

### 1995 Rankings (American League)

→ 1st in lowest cleanup slugging percentage (.266) and lowest batting average on the road (.187)
→ 4th in lowest batting average
→ 5th in highest percentage of swings that missed (29.2%)
→ 7th in lowest on-base percentage
→ 10th in lowest percentage of swings put into play (37.0%)
→ Led the Brewers in strikeouts, HR frequency (23.1 ABs per HR) and steals of third (4)

# Bill Wegman

## 1995 Season

Bill Wegman's downward slide continued early in 1995 when a series of disastrous early-season starts had him contemplating retirement. Then Phil Garner asked him to do something he'd never done before: work out of the bullpen. Wegman tried it, and amazingly his arm came back to life. For the remainder of the year, he posted decent numbers as both a set-up man and middle relievere—peaking in July and August. In addition, he was able to avoid the disabled list after making trips there the previous two seasons.

## Pitching

Always known for his ability to throw strikes, Wegman relies on location and pitch selection to get batters out. Early in the year, his fastball couldn't crack 80 MPH, but by the end of the year he was actually throwing high fastballs by people. He has a good overhand curve, and works in a slider and a splitter. He's hittable above the belt, and must keep the ball down to be effective. When working out of the bullpen, he needs at least one day off between outings.

## Defense

Wegman still moves well for a big man, and can still get over to cover first when he needs to. Despite his poor pickoff move and slow delivery to the plate, Wegman remains capable of controlling the running game. Baserunners attempted just five steals against him last season.

## 1996 Outlook

Wegman's contract was up at the end of the year, and it's not clear whether he wants to give the game one more season. If he does, it will have to be for significantly less money. Considering the number of young starting candidates the Brewers have, Wegman will probably remain in the bullpen for good, but he could still give the team some decent middle-relief innings.

**Position:** RP/SP
**Bats:** R  **Throws:** R
**Ht:** 6' 5"  **Wt:** 220

**Opening Day Age:** 33
**Born:** 12/19/62 in Cincinnati, OH
**ML Seasons:** 11

### Overall Statistics

|  | W | L | Pct. | ERA | G | GS | Sv | IP | H | BB | SO | HR | BR/IP |
|---|---|---|---|---|---|---|---|---|---|---|---|---|---|
| 1995 | 5 | 7 | .417 | 5.35 | 37 | 4 | 2 | 70.2 | 89 | 21 | 50 | 14 | 1.56 |
| Career | 81 | 90 | .474 | 4.16 | 262 | 216 | 2 | 1482.2 | 1567 | 352 | 696 | 187 | 1.29 |

### How Often He Throws Strikes

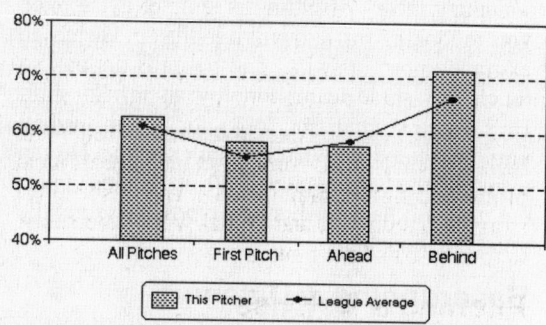

### 1995 Situational Stats

|  | W | L | ERA | Sv | IP |  |  | AB | H | HR | RBI | Avg |
|---|---|---|---|---|---|---|---|---|---|---|---|---|
| Home | 3 | 3 | 5.02 | 1 | 37.2 | LHB | | 144 | 47 | 8 | 25 | .326 |
| Road | 2 | 4 | 5.73 | 1 | 33.0 | RHB | | 141 | 42 | 6 | 19 | .298 |
| First Half | 1 | 3 | 6.57 | 1 | 37.0 | Sc Pos | | 70 | 21 | 4 | 30 | .300 |
| Scnd Half | 4 | 4 | 4.01 | 1 | 33.2 | Clutch | | 77 | 24 | 4 | 12 | .312 |

### 1995 Rankings (American League)

➡ 3rd in highest batting average allowed in relief (.306)
➡ Led the Brewers in relief innings (58.0)

# Rob Dibble

**Position**: RP
**Bats**: L  **Throws**: R
**Ht**: 6' 4"  **Wt**: 220

**Opening Day Age**: 32
**Born**: 1/24/64 in
Bridgeport, CT
**ML Seasons**: 7

# Cal Eldred

**Position**: SP
**Bats**: R  **Throws**: R
**Ht**: 6' 4"  **Wt**: 236

**Opening Day Age**: 28
**Born**: 11/24/67 in
Cedar Rapids, IA
**ML Seasons**: 5

## Overall Statistics

| | W | L | Pct. | ERA | G | GS | Sv | IP | H | BB | SO | HR | BR/IP |
|---|---|---|------|-----|---|----|----|------|-----|-----|-----|----|-------|
| 1995 | 1 | 2 | .333 | 7.18 | 31 | 0 | 1 | 26.1 | 16 | 46 | 26 | 2 | 2.35 |
| Career | 27 | 25 | .519 | 2.98 | 385 | 0 | 89 | 477.0 | 332 | 238 | 645 | 27 | 1.19 |

## Overall Statistics

| | W | L | Pct. | ERA | G | GS | Sv | IP | H | BB | SO | HR | BR/IP |
|---|---|---|------|-----|---|----|----|-------|-----|-----|-----|----|-------|
| 1995 | 1 | 1 | .500 | 3.42 | 4 | 4 | 0 | 23.2 | 24 | 10 | 18 | 4 | 1.44 |
| Career | 41 | 30 | .577 | 3.82 | 82 | 82 | 0 | 577.0 | 510 | 214 | 368 | 65 | 1.25 |

## 1995 Season

Continuing his comeback from shoulder surgery, Rob Dibble began the 1995 season in middle relief with the Chicago White Sox. With a Steve Blass-like walk rate, he earned his release by midsummer. The Brewers, desperate for middle relief and believing they could correct Dibble's mechanical problems, signed him in July. But his control struggles continued, and he saw very little action in the season's final month.

## Pitching & Defense

Milwaukee took a chance on Dibble because he can still bring the fastball in the low 90s. Unfortunately, his inability to get it over prevents him from setting up his slider. On the rare occasions that he got the ball over, he was still tough to hit, but all too often there was no need to swing the bat. His long, chaotic delivery renders him useless as a fielder, and gives basestealers enough time to relace their shoes and still get a good jump.

## 1996 Outlook

Dibble will probably pitch somewhere in 1996, as his fastball will continue to fetch him tryouts. But his Milwaukee audition is probably over, as they seemed to give up on him in September. For Rob Dibble, the path to success will always be over the plate. Don't be surprised if he gets a few more chances to rediscover the route.

## 1995 Season

After enduring two years of heavy use, Cal Eldred's elbow blew out after his fourth start of the 1995 season. On June 22 he underwent Tommy John (elbow ligament transplant) surgery and was lost for the year. For a young Milwaukee pitching staff, both Eldred's leadership and innings were sorely missed.

## Pitching & Defense

Eldred starts off hitters with high fastballs in the low 90s, later mixing in a dipping overhand curve and an occasional change-up. Despite having excellent stuff, his game is less than the sum of its parts. He surrenders his share of longballs, often on first-pitch fastballs. His walks are usually the result from missing upstairs. In addition, his high heat yields mostly fly balls, keeping him from inducing the double play. Eldred rarely commits a fielding error, and shows good athleticism for his size. His high-kicking delivery and lack of a good pickoff move frequently allow baserunners to have their way.

## 1996 Outlook

Phil Garner expects Eldred to return to action in May or June, and to be at full strength by the end of the year. But Eldred may be forced to alter his pitching style. Before the injury, he used his high heat to get strikeouts and fly balls. With even a small loss in velocity, his high fastballs may be rendered eminently hittable.

# David Hulse

**Position**: LF/CF/RF
**Bats**: L  **Throws**: L
**Ht**: 5'11"  **Wt**: 175

**Opening Day Age**: 28
**Born**: 2/25/68 in San Angelo, TX
**ML Seasons**: 4

## Overall Statistics

| | G | AB | R | H | D | T | HR | RBI | SB | BB | SO | Avg | OBP | Slg |
|---|---|---|---|---|---|---|---|---|---|---|---|---|---|---|
| 1995 | 119 | 339 | 46 | 85 | 11 | 6 | 3 | 47 | 15 | 18 | 60 | .251 | .285 | .345 |
| Career | 342 | 1148 | 189 | 310 | 32 | 20 | 5 | 97 | 65 | 68 | 188 | .270 | .311 | .346 |

## 1995 Season

Acquired from the Rangers, David Hulse had an up-and-down year in 1995. He started quickly, carrying a .300 average into July, and for a good portion of the season he was a semi-regular in the outfield. But Hulse's average plunged after the All-Star break, and his playing time diminished. By the end of the year, his role had been reduced to fourth outfielder.

## Hitting, Baserunning & Defense

Hulse will jump on the first low pitch he sees. With two strikes, he's content to try to hit everything the other way, and he frustrates pitchers by flicking off pitches at the last moment. Lefties had given him problems in the past, but he hung in well against them last year. A fearless fielder, Hulse gets a good jump on the ball and his speed gives him good range at all three outfield spots. His throwing accuracy has improved, and his arm is just strong enough for center field. On the bases, Hulse picks his spots well.

## 1996 Outlook

With the anticipated departure of Darryl Hamilton, Hulse may see significant time in center field in 1996. While he may play regularly out of necessity, Phil Garner would prefer to have him available as a pinch hitter, pinch runner, and defensive substitute. Hulse is well-suited for the role.

# Scott Karl

**Position**: SP/RP
**Bats**: L  **Throws**: L
**Ht**: 6' 2"  **Wt**: 195

**Opening Day Age**: 24
**Born**: 8/9/71 in Fontana, CA
**ML Seasons**: 1

## Overall Statistics

| | W | L | Pct. | ERA | G | GS | Sv | IP | H | BB | SO | HR | BR/IP |
|---|---|---|---|---|---|---|---|---|---|---|---|---|---|
| 1995 | 6 | 7 | .462 | 4.14 | 25 | 18 | 0 | 124.0 | 141 | 50 | 59 | 10 | 1.54 |
| Career | 6 | 7 | .462 | 4.14 | 25 | 18 | 0 | 124.0 | 141 | 50 | 59 | 10 | 1.54 |

## 1995 Season

The Brewers have high hopes for their young John Tudor wanna-be, Scott Karl. After his recall in June, the rookie stepped into the rotation and pitched like a veteran. Although his velocity won't light up the radar gun, Karl showed impressive poise, intelligence, and command. When the dust had settled, he had the lowest ERA in the Brewers' rotation.

## Pitching & Defense

Karl's bread and butter is a heavy palmball. He sets it up with a mid-80s fastball that buzzes in on the hands of righties, and an average curve. Changing speeds and working both sides of the plate, Karl may make great strides when he learns to stay ahead of the hitters a bit more. Runners beware: his outstanding pickoff move won't be a well-kept secret much longer. In the field, Karl made three errors last year, which was a complete fluke—he's a sure fielder who rarely will hurt himself with the glove.

## 1996 Outlook

It may take time, but Karl is the type of pitcher who can learn how to win big without needing to rack up a high number of strikeouts. While he may experience growing pains this year, the Brewers will give him every opportunity to develop.

# Graeme Lloyd

**Position:** RP
**Bats:** L **Throws:** L
**Ht:** 6' 7" **Wt:** 234

**Opening Day Age:** 28
**Born:** 4/9/67 in
Geelong, Victoria,
Australia
**ML Seasons:** 3

*Overall Statistics*

|  | W | L | Pct. | ERA | G | GS | Sv | IP | H | BB | SO | HR | BR/IP |
|---|---|---|---|---|---|---|---|---|---|---|---|---|---|
| 1995 | 0 | 5 | .000 | 4.50 | 33 | 0 | 4 | 32.0 | 28 | 8 | 13 | 4 | 1.13 |
| Career | 5 | 12 | .294 | 3.97 | 131 | 0 | 7 | 142.2 | 141 | 36 | 75 | 13 | 1.24 |

## 1995 Season

Working in his customary set-up role, Graeme Lloyd got off to a slow start in 1995, but he got rolling as the season progressed. Mike Fetters' tender elbow gave Lloyd a few opportunities to close out games, but the results were mixed at best. Just when he got on a roll, a finger injury ended his season in July. Overall, he was a valuable member of the bullpen, and pitched better than his ERA would indicate.

## Pitching & Defense

Unlike Randy Johnson, Lloyd's size doesn't translate into great velocity. His sinking fastball only reaches the high 80s, but it has good sink. He will mix in his big sweeping curve, occasionally dropping in a fading change. He makes his living by setting down left-handed batters. While he can look awkward at times, he's mobile enough to make all the plays in the field. Despite his large frame, Lloyd continued to do an excellent job controlling the running game. Runners attempted to steal against him only four times in 1995.

## 1996 Outlook

Lloyd is talented enough to remain in his role as lefty specialist, but he's not likely to go any further. Still, he should continue to be a useful man out the pen.

# Mike Matheny

**Position:** C
**Bats:** R **Throws:** R
**Ht:** 6' 3" **Wt:** 205

**Opening Day Age:** 25
**Born:** 9/22/70 in
Columbus, Ohio
**ML Seasons:** 2
**Pronunciation:**
muh-THEE-nee

*Overall Statistics*

|  | G | AB | R | H | D | T | HR | RBI | SB | BB | SO | Avg | OBP | Slg |
|---|---|---|---|---|---|---|---|---|---|---|---|---|---|---|
| 1995 | 80 | 166 | 13 | 41 | 9 | 1 | 0 | 21 | 2 | 12 | 28 | .247 | .306 | .313 |
| Career | 108 | 219 | 16 | 53 | 12 | 1 | 1 | 23 | 2 | 15 | 41 | .242 | .303 | .320 |

## 1995 Season

In his first full year in the big leagues, Mike Matheny proved himself to be a capable backup receiver. He started 47 games behind the plate for the Brewers, and came in to play defense in 33 more. When Joe Oliver went down for a month with an injury, Matheny handled the bulk of the catching chores adequately. Still, he never came close to breaking out of his backup role.

## Hitting, Baserunning & Defense

Matheny wasn't expected to hit well, and he didn't. He takes a defensive swing, generating no lift and no power. He can protect the plate with two strikes, but his hits are mostly grounders that find holes. A good fastball can sit him down. Matheny has good speed for a catcher, but rarely uses it on the basepaths. He came to the majors with a great defensive reputation, and his throws are indeed very strong and accurate. He blocks balls well, though he had trouble at times with Steve Sparks' knuckleball.

## 1996 Outlook

Matheny has shown enough to stay on as the backup catcher in Milwaukee. If circumstances ever force him into a regular job, he probably won't hit well enough to hold on to the spot. Still, the Brewers will be glad to have him back, especially at his low salary.

# Sid Roberson

**Position**: SP/RP
**Bats**: L  **Throws**: L
**Ht**: 5' 9"  **Wt**: 170

**Opening Day Age:** 24
**Born:** 9/7/71 in Jacksonville, Florida
**ML Seasons:** 1

### Overall Statistics

| | W | L | Pct. | ERA | G | GS | Sv | IP | H | BB | SO | HR | BR/IP |
|---|---|---|---|---|---|---|---|---|---|---|---|---|---|
| 1995 | 6 | 4 | .600 | 5.76 | 26 | 13 | 0 | 84.1 | 102 | 37 | 40 | 16 | 1.65 |
| Career | 6 | 4 | .600 | 5.76 | 26 | 13 | 0 | 84.1 | 102 | 37 | 40 | 16 | 1.65 |

## 1995 Season

After an excellent minor league season in 1994, Sid Roberson brought his breaking stuff to the Milwaukee rotation in May. Initially, Roberson had modest success, but his season unraveled as he encountered an uncharacteristic inability to throw strikes. Sent down at the end of July, he shuttled between Triple-A and the Brewer bullpen for the remainder of the year.

## Pitching & Defense

Roberson works quickly, gets grounders, and doesn't overpower anyone. His calling card is his enormous curveball, which he throws at two different speeds. He'll throw it up to 80 percent of the time, and when he can't get it over, as was often the case last year, he's out there naked. His 84-MPH cut fastball runs in on righthanders, and is a hittable pitch when he gets it up in the zone. He mixes in an occasional straight change. Roberson had a poor year in the field as well, though he's usually a sure fielder. He needs work on holding runners more effectively.

## 1996 Outlook

Roberson probably won't get another crack at the Milwaukee rotation until he shows he can get his curve over again. He had an impeccable control record in the minors, so improvement is not out of the question. Still, it may take him a while to learn how to win in the majors with his stuff.

# Fernando Vina

**Position**: 2B
**Bats**: L  **Throws**: R
**Ht**: 5' 9"  **Wt**: 170

**Opening Day Age:** 26
**Born:** 4/16/69 in Sacramento, CA
**ML Seasons:** 3
**Pronunciation:** VEE-nah

### Overall Statistics

| | G | AB | R | H | D | T | HR | RBI | SB | BB | SO | Avg | OBP | Slg |
|---|---|---|---|---|---|---|---|---|---|---|---|---|---|---|
| 1995 | 113 | 288 | 46 | 74 | 7 | 7 | 3 | 29 | 6 | 22 | 28 | .257 | .327 | .361 |
| Career | 216 | 457 | 71 | 115 | 15 | 7 | 3 | 37 | 15 | 38 | 42 | .252 | .340 | .335 |

## 1995 Season

After beginning the year as a defensive replacement, Fernando Vina got hot in June and claimed the second base/leadoff job. However, he soon went into a month-long slump, reverting to his original bench role. He played more in September, but only after a wave of injuries hit the team.

## Hitting, Baserunning & Defense

Vina is a high-ball hitter who pulls liners and grounders to the right side. Fastballs inside tie him up. He loves to try the swinging bunt, and often squares around just to draw in the third baseman. He has no power, but has a particular penchant for reaching base via the hit-by-pitch. There's no better defensive second baseman on the team than Vina. He features a lightning-quick double-play pivot, good range, and he charges balls ferociously. On the bases, he takes huge leads and gets himself picked off far too often.

## 1996 Outlook

Vina has what it takes to be useful off the bench, but his skills don't merit full-time play—a conclusion Phil Garner seemed to reach last year. Vina should continue to come off the bench and play part-time at second base in 1996.

# Other Milwaukee Brewers

**Jeff Bronkey** (**Pos**: RHP, **Age**: 30)

Bronkey missed most of last season with an injury to his right shoulder, and the Brewers released him in October. 1996 Outlook: C

**Mike Ignasiak** (**Pos**: RHP, **Age**: 30)

In four seasons as a Brewer, Ignasiak's record is 10-4 despite a 4.80 ERA. Does he know how to win? No, he's just lucky. Appears to have little left, and will have to scrape—probably successfully—for a spot this spring. 1996 Outlook: B

**Mark Kiefer** (**Pos**: RHP, **Age**: 27)

Over the last two seasons, Kiefer went 17-9 as a starter at Triple-A New Orleans. He also pitched well as a reliever with the Brewers last season, so he could fill one of many roles. 1996 Outlook: A

**Jamie McAndrew** (**Pos**: RHP, **Age**: 28)

Former replacement player McAndrew drew attention when he pitched eight strong innings against the Indians in late August. Two starts later, he was lost for the season with a strained knee. 1996 Outlook: B

**Jose Mercedes** (**Pos**: RHP, **Age**: 25)

Mercedes missed most of last season with a very sore elbow. The Brewers must like Mercedes, because they've been moving him up despite mediocre minor league numbers. 1996 Outlook: C

**Al Reyes** (**Pos**: RHP, **Age**: 24)

After Reyes posted 35 saves for Double-A Harrisburg in 1994, the Brewers grabbed him from Montreal in the Rule 5 draft. He was pitching well last season before tearing an elbow tendon. 1996 Outlook: C

**Ron Rightnowar** (**Pos**: RHP, **Age**: 31)

If nothing else, Rightnowar will always be known as the first replacement player to actually play in 1995. He got lit up in the majors, and didn't pitch as well in New Orleans as his 2.67 ERA suggests. 1996 Outlook: C

**Bob Scanlan** (**Pos**: RHP, **Age**: 29)

1995 was basically a nightmare for Scanlan, who suffered from a sore elbow most of the season. Given a strong right arm, Scanlan is a serviceable spot starter/middle reliever. 1996 Outlook: B

**Joe Slusarski** (**Pos**: RHP, **Age**: 29)

At least he's consistent. In each of Slusarski's four major league seasons, he's compiled ERAs between 5.19 and 5.45. Slusarski pitched great in New Orleans last summer, and probably deserves another shot. 1996 OIutlook: C

**Mike Thomas** (**Pos**: LHP, **Age**: 26)

Thomas saved 20 games for El Paso in 1994, but last year in New Orleans he was a situational lefty. After pitching one game for the Brewers, Thomas strained his cervix, and he was waived in August. 1996 Outlook: D

**Tim Unroe** (**Pos**: 1B, **Age**: 25, **Bats**: R)

Unroe posted some nice numbers at El Paso in 1994, but that's a great hitter's park. He didn't do much at New Orleans last season, and is very close to losing his prospect status. 1996 Outlook: D

**Turner Ward** (**Pos**: LF/RF, **Age**: 30, **Bats**: B)

Ward was posting the best numbers of his career when knocked out by a hamstring injury in late July. He's decent at each outfield position and he can run a little, so he should fit in somewhere as a spare part. 1996 Outlook: B

**Kevin Wickander** (**Pos**: LHP, **Age**: 31)

At 31, Wickander is trying to carve out a career as a situational lefty, and he may yet do it. In 23 innings last year, he posted a 1.93 ERA, and was excellent after a trade to Milwaukee in August. 1996 Outlook: B

# Milwaukee Brewers Minor League Prospects

## Organization Overview:

If an organization's minor league won-lost record translated into major league success, Milwaukee would long ago have won some kind of title. The Brewers' minor league system hasn't posted a losing record since 1981, yet its bona fide big-league prospects have been few and far between. The organization is still trying to recover from wasted first-round draft picks who didn't sign (Alex Fernandez, Kenny Henderson), the loss of premium draft picks used as compensation for questionable free-agent signings (Dave Parker, Franklin Stubbs), and just plain poor selections (Gordon Powell, Tyrone Hill). The Brewers have high hopes for their last two top draft picks, Antone Williamson and Geoffrey Jenkins, but they may not arrive until 1997. For a small-market team which won't make a splash in the free-agent market, a productive farm system that produces talent as well as victories is vital to future hopes.

### Byron Browne

**Position:** P  
**Bats:** R **Throws:** R  
**Ht:** 6' 7" **Wt:** 200  
**Opening Day Age:** 25  
**Born:** 8/8/70 in Camden, NJ

#### Recent Statistics

| | W | L | ERA | G | GS | Sv | IP | H | R | BB | SO | HR |
|---|---|---|---|---|---|---|---|---|---|---|---|---|
| 93 A Stockton | 10 | 5 | 4.07 | 27 | 27 | 0 | 143.2 | 117 | 73 | 117 | 110 | 9 |
| 94 A Stockton | 2 | 6 | 2.76 | 11 | 11 | 0 | 62.0 | 46 | 30 | 30 | 67 | 4 |
| 94 AA El Paso | 2 | 1 | 2.48 | 5 | 5 | 0 | 29.0 | 26 | 11 | 13 | 33 | 3 |
| 95 AA El Paso | 10 | 4 | 3.43 | 25 | 20 | 0 | 126.0 | 106 | 55 | 78 | 110 | 7 |

Browne really struggled to find his control after the Brewers made him their 13th-round pick in 1991. He appeared to still be growing into his body during his first three professional seasons, walking 298 batters while striking out 289 in 336.1 innings. He finally began to come around in an injury-marred 1994, reducing his walk rate to 4.25 per nine innings while compiling a 2.67 ERA. He continued to pitch well at El Paso last season, not the best place for a pitcher, although he still labored to locate the plate at times. Browne has one of the best arms in the organization, and he's one of those pitchers that hitters just don't feel comfortable facing.

### Jeffrey D'Amico

**Position:** P  
**Bats:** R **Throws:** R  
**Ht:** 6' 7" **Wt:** 250  
**Opening Day Age:** 20  
**Born:** 12/27/75 in St. Petersburg, FL

#### Recent Statistics

| | W | L | ERA | G | GS | Sv | IP | H | R | BB | SO | HR |
|---|---|---|---|---|---|---|---|---|---|---|---|---|
| 95 A Beloit | 13 | 3 | 2.39 | 21 | 20 | 0 | 132.0 | 102 | 40 | 31 | 119 | 7 |

There are two Jeff D'Amico's in pro ball, and both were chosen in the first two rounds of 1993. The other Jeff D'Amico plays shortstop in the Oakland organization. This Jeff took two years to get started after signing late

in '93 and missing all of '94 due to elbow surgery. But his pro debut in the Midwest League last year was very impressive. He threw four pitches for strikes, including a heavy forkball. Even though he just turned 20 in December, D'Amico is already a mountain of a man, and his size helps him deliver his fastball in the 90s, but he may need to watch his weight as he gets older.

### Ken Felder

**Position:** OF  
**Bats:** R **Throws:** R  
**Ht:** 6' 3" **Wt:** 220  
**Opening Day Age:** 25  
**Born:** 2/9/71 in Harrisburg, PA

#### Recent Statistics

| | G | AB | R | H | D | T | HR | RBI | SB | BB | SO | AVG |
|---|---|---|---|---|---|---|---|---|---|---|---|---|
| 93 A Beloit | 32 | 99 | 12 | 18 | 4 | 2 | 3 | 8 | 1 | 10 | 40 | .182 |
| 94 A Stockton | 121 | 435 | 56 | 119 | 21 | 2 | 10 | 60 | 4 | 32 | 112 | .274 |
| 95 AA El Paso | 114 | 367 | 51 | 100 | 24 | 4 | 12 | 55 | 2 | 48 | 94 | .272 |
| 95 MLE | 114 | 352 | 38 | 85 | 20 | 2 | 8 | 41 | 1 | 30 | 98 | .241 |

The jury's still out on whether the Brewers blew their first pick in 1992 by choosing Felder with the 12th choice overall. Felder's baseball experience was limited after playing collegiate football at Florida State, but the Brewers were intrigued by his vast power potential. However, the 15 homers he hit while playing rookie ball in 1992 is his career high, and he missed most of 1993 due to an old football shoulder injury which required surgery. Still, he improved his plate discipline while making the jump to Double-A last year, and he retains his legitimate longball power. Much depends on whether Felder can continue to reduce his strikeout rate. If he makes better contact, the home runs should come naturally.

### Mark Loretta

**Position:** SS  
**Bats:** R **Throws:** R  
**Ht:** 6' 0" **Wt:** 175  
**Opening Day Age:** 24  
**Born:** 8/14/71 in Santa Monica, CA

#### Recent Statistics

| | G | AB | R | H | D | T | HR | RBI | SB | BB | SO | AVG |
|---|---|---|---|---|---|---|---|---|---|---|---|---|
| 95 AAA Nw Orleans | 127 | 479 | 48 | 137 | 22 | 5 | 7 | 79 | 8 | 34 | 47 | .286 |
| 95 AL Milwaukee | 19 | 50 | 13 | 13 | 3 | 0 | 1 | 3 | 1 | 4 | 7 | .260 |
| 95 MLE | 127 | 473 | 44 | 131 | 21 | 3 | 6 | 73 | 6 | 31 | 48 | .277 |

Loretta has a chance to be the best shortstop the Brewers have produced since Robin Yount. He has the arm and range to play the position in the big leagues, but it's his offense which may make Loretta special. He led the American Association in RBI until late in the season and now carries a .299 batting average through 306 minor league games. He was the Brewers' seventh-round selection in 1993 out of Northwestern, after being named the Big 10 Conference's Player of the Year that spring. Loretta auditioned in Milwaukee last September and hit .407 in his last nine games. He may stick for good at some point this season.

## Duane Singleton

**Position:** OF
**Bats:** L **Throws:** R
**Ht:** 6' 1" **Wt:** 170

**Opening Day Age:** 23
**Born:** 8/6/72 in Staten Island, NY

*Recent Statistics*

| | G | AB | R | H | D | T | HR | RBI | SB | BB | SO | AVG |
|---|---|---|---|---|---|---|---|---|---|---|---|---|
| 95 AAA Nw Orleans | 106 | 355 | 48 | 95 | 10 | 4 | 4 | 29 | 31 | 39 | 63 | .268 |
| 95 AL Milwaukee | 13 | 31 | 0 | 2 | 0 | 0 | 0 | 0 | 1 | 1 | 10 | .065 |
| 95 MLE | 106 | 352 | 44 | 92 | 9 | 3 | 3 | 26 | 25 | 36 | 64 | .261 |

Singleton has seen action in the big leagues each of the past two seasons. His best asset is his speed, which allows him to outrun balls in center field and steal 30 bases a year. He also possesses a strong throwing arm and has led a couple of leagues in outfield assists. Singleton is no home-run hitter, and he probably strikes out too much for someone with his limited power. The Brewers have disciplined Singleton a number of times during his minor league career with suspensions and demotions due to off-the-field problems. But if he can keep those problems behind him, Singleton is likely the first outfielder the Brewers will promote this season.

## Derek Wachter

**Position:** OF
**Bats:** R **Throws:** R
**Ht:** 6' 2" **Wt:** 195

**Opening Day Age:** 25
**Born:** 8/28/70 in Bethpage, NY

*Recent Statistics*

| | G | AB | R | H | D | T | HR | RBI | SB | BB | SO | AVG |
|---|---|---|---|---|---|---|---|---|---|---|---|---|
| 93 A Stockton | 115 | 420 | 75 | 123 | 20 | 4 | 22 | 108 | 3 | 64 | 93 | .293 |
| 94 AA El Paso | 30 | 117 | 14 | 45 | 9 | 5 | 0 | 24 | 3 | 13 | 24 | .385 |
| 94 AAA Nw Orleans | 65 | 221 | 33 | 63 | 15 | 1 | 5 | 39 | 3 | 24 | 57 | .285 |
| 95 AAA Nw Orleans | 112 | 382 | 44 | 98 | 23 | 1 | 8 | 45 | 2 | 39 | 67 | .257 |
| 95 MLE | 112 | 377 | 40 | 93 | 22 | 0 | 6 | 41 | 1 | 36 | 68 | .247 |

Wachter's production has slowed considerably since he was promoted to Triple-A in May of 1994. Since then, he has continued to show some nice offensive skills, including adequate strike-zone judgment and extra-base power. However, his 1993 season, when he broke through with 22 homers and 108 RBI in the California League, looks like a fluke. He doesn't have much speed and his defense is nothing special, so Wachter will have to hit better than the .257 average he produced last year in order to have a major league career.

## Doug Webb

**Position:** P
**Bats:** R **Throws:** R
**Ht:** 6' 3" **Wt:** 195

**Opening Day Age:** 22
**Born:** 8/25/73 in Salt Lake City, UT

*Recent Statistics*

| | W | L | ERA | G | GS | Sv | IP | H | R | BB | SO | HR |
|---|---|---|---|---|---|---|---|---|---|---|---|---|
| 94 R Brewers | 0 | 0 | 0.00 | 1 | 0 | 0 | 1.0 | 0 | 0 | 0 | 1 | 0 |
| 94 A Stockton | 0 | 2 | 5.40 | 29 | 0 | 0 | 35.0 | 38 | 33 | 27 | 34 | 2 |
| 95 A Stockton | 0 | 0 | 1.70 | 32 | 0 | 22 | 37.0 | 17 | 7 | 8 | 34 | 3 |
| 95 AA El Paso | 2 | 1 | 4.42 | 18 | 0 | 8 | 18.1 | 11 | 9 | 13 | 11 | 3 |

Webb was nearly unhittable in the California League, allowing a total of 25 baserunners on hits plus walks in 37 innings, while also converting 22 of 23 save oppor-

tunities. He wasn't as dominating after his promotion to Double-A El Paso, although he did save an additional eight games to reach 30 for the season. Webb pitched collegiately at San Diego State before the Brewers picked him in round two of the 1994 draft. His fastball is his best pitch, and his success depends on how well he controls it. If he avoids walks as he did at Stockton last season, Webb can eventually help a major league bullpen.

## Antone Williamson

**Position:** 3B
**Bats:** L **Throws:** R
**Ht:** 6' 1" **Wt:** 195

**Opening Day Age:** 22
**Born:** 7/18/73 in Torrance, CA

*Recent Statistics*

| | G | AB | R | H | D | T | HR | RBI | SB | BB | SO | AVG |
|---|---|---|---|---|---|---|---|---|---|---|---|---|
| 94 R Helena | 6 | 26 | 5 | 11 | 2 | 1 | 0 | 4 | 0 | 2 | 4 | .423 |
| 94 A Stockton | 23 | 85 | 6 | 19 | 4 | 0 | 3 | 13 | 0 | 7 | 19 | .224 |
| 94 AA El Paso | 14 | 48 | 8 | 12 | 3 | 0 | 1 | 9 | 0 | 7 | 8 | .250 |
| 95 AA El Paso | 104 | 392 | 62 | 121 | 30 | 6 | 7 | 90 | 3 | 47 | 57 | .309 |
| 95 MLE | 104 | 376 | 46 | 105 | 26 | 3 | 5 | 67 | 2 | 30 | 59 | .279 |

Williamson probably won't hit as many home runs as you'd like from a third baseman, although his power may develop as he matures. Still, he is a line-drive hitter who could bat .300 regularly, with the gap power to produce 30 doubles annually. He did exactly that in the Texas League last season, his first full year in professional baseball. Williamson draws enough walks to bat high in the order, and he also drove in 90 runs for El Paso. The Brewers chose Williamson with the fourth pick overall in 1994, following an All-America career at Arizona State. He'll likely begin this season in Triple-A, and looks to be the Brewers' third sacker of the future.

## Others to Watch

Outfielder **Brian Banks**, the Brewers' second-round pick in 1993, enjoyed his best season at hitter-friendly El Paso, batting .308, drawing tons of walks, and banging 61 hits for extra bases. He's 25. . . Outfielder **Todd Dunn** stroked 23 homers in '94 and was hitting .293 at Stockton last season before breaking his hand. He was a supplemental first-round pick in 1993 who can run, throw, and hit for power, but at 25 he has yet to reach Double-A. . . The Brewers used the ninth overall selection in last year's draft to choose outfielder **Geoffrey Jenkins** from USC. Jenkins then played at three levels in less than three months, and Milwaukee envisions him as a middle-of-the-order bopper in the near future. . . Shortstop **Danny Klassen** missed the first part of last season recovering from a torn knee ligament. He's got good defensive skills and some offensive pop. . . Like the pitcher by the same name in Minnesota, **Frankie Rodriguez** is a hard-throwing righthander who generates strikeouts. The Brewers' Rodriguez will likely begin 1996 in Triple-A.

# Rich Becker

## 1995 Season

Considered one of the brightest prospects in baseball for several years, Rich Becker finally got his first extended major league trial in 1995. Unfortunately, Becker had a difficult rookie season. He batted only .237, looked tentative in the field and on the bases, and had so much trouble hitting lefties that he abandoned switch-hitting and started hitting lefty full-time.

## Hitting

Becker hit for both power and average during his outstanding minor league career, but he hit for neither with the Twins last year. He seemed to press after getting off to a slow start and looked awkward at the plate, with a much slower bat than expected. He started swinging wildly and didn't show the patience at the plate that was one of the hallmarks of his minor league career. The Twins stuck with him and Becker finished the year on an up note, though his problems with lefties continued. Becker went to the instructional league after the season to work on his batting stroke.

## Baserunning & Defense

Becker also had problems stealing bases, but he was still getting over a serious knee injury he suffered early in 1994. He's a smart baserunner and should be able to steal 15-plus sacks once he learns the pitchers. Even with the knee injury, he has above-average speed and can cover a lot of ground in the outfield. However, he had problems adjusting to playing in the Metrodome and didn't flash the brilliance he'd shown in the minors. His arm is strong and accurate.

## 1996 Outlook

The Twins are still high on Becker, who has the kind of work ethic and intensity that Tom Kelly likes. But he'll need to show he can handle lefties, and he'll have to battle rookie prospect Matt Lawton for playing time this year. He's only 24 and there's still plenty of time.

**Position:** CF
**Bats:** L **Throws:** L
**Ht:** 5'10"  **Wt:** 199

**Opening Day Age:** 24
**Born:** 2/1/72 in Aurora, IL
**ML Seasons:** 3

### Overall Statistics

|  | G | AB | R | H | D | T | HR | RBI | SB | BB | SO | Avg | OBP | Slg |
|---|---|---|---|---|---|---|---|---|---|---|---|---|---|---|
| 1995 | 106 | 392 | 45 | 93 | 15 | 1 | 2 | 33 | 8 | 34 | 95 | .237 | .303 | .296 |
| Career | 137 | 497 | 60 | 121 | 20 | 1 | 3 | 41 | 15 | 52 | 124 | .243 | .319 | .306 |

### Where He Hits the Ball

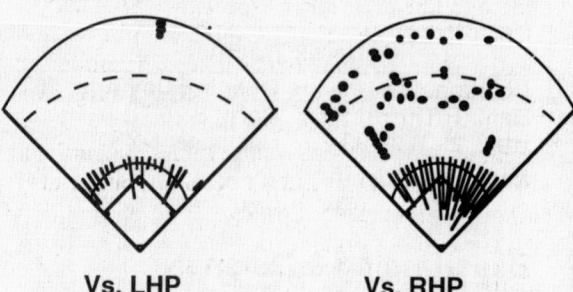

**Vs. LHP**          **Vs. RHP**

### 1995 Situational Stats

|  | AB | H | HR | RBI | Avg |  | AB | H | HR | RBI | Avg |
|---|---|---|---|---|---|---|---|---|---|---|---|
| Home | 180 | 39 | 1 | 14 | .217 | LHP | 87 | 13 | 0 | 2 | .149 |
| Road | 212 | 54 | 1 | 19 | .255 | RHP | 305 | 80 | 2 | 31 | .262 |
| First Half | 130 | 31 | 1 | 10 | .238 | Sc Pos | 94 | 20 | 1 | 32 | .213 |
| Scnd Half | 262 | 62 | 1 | 23 | .237 | Clutch | 60 | 12 | 1 | 8 | .200 |

### 1995 Rankings (American League)

- → 1st in lowest stolen base percentage (47.1%)
- → 4th in lowest slugging percentage vs. right-handed pitchers (.334), errors in center field (4) and lowest fielding percentage in center field (.986)
- → 6th in lowest batting average with runners in scoring position (.213)
- → 10th in lowest on-base percentage vs. right-handed pitchers (.322)
- → Led the Twins in sacrifice bunts (6), batting average on a 3-1 count (.533) and bunts in play (8)

# Marty Cordova

## 1995 Season

After a big season at Triple-A Salt Lake City in 1994, Marty Cordova didn't miss a beat when he moved up to the major league level last year. Cordova was one of the outstanding rookies in the American League, hitting for power and performing competently in the outfield and on the bases. He beat out Garret Anderson for American League Rookie of the Year honors, and was one of the best first-year players in Twins history.

## Hitting

Cordova is a hard-nosed hitter who dives into the ball and isn't afraid of the inside pitch. Though he's capable of hitting 30-plus homers, he's primarily a line-drive hitter, especially when facing a lefthander. Cordova uses a shorter stroke against lefties than he does with righties, resulting in fewer home runs but a much better average; he tends to swing from the heels more against righthanders. He's had some vision problems and will probably always strike out a lot, but he also draws a fair number of walks.

## Baserunning & Defense

Cordova surprised a few people by stealing 20 bases last year. He doesn't have blinding speed, but he's a smart baserunner and moves pretty well once he gets going. He's fast enough to play center field on occasion, but he's best suited for left, where his range is well above average. His arm isn't overly strong, but it's very accurate and he gets rid of the ball quickly. Cordova tied teammate Rich Becker for second in the league with 12 assists last year.

## 1996 Outlook

Cordova's impressive performance last year was no fluke. He's a hustling player with a strong work ethic, and there seems little danger that he'll get complacent. He should be able to match last year's performance with little trouble, and there's an excellent chance that he'll improve on it.

**Position:** LF/CF
**Bats:** R  **Throws:** R
**Ht:** 6' 0"  **Wt:** 193

**Opening Day Age:** 26
**Born:** 7/10/69 in Las Vegas, NV
**ML Seasons:** 1
**Pronunciation:** cor-DOH-vuh

**Minnesota Twins**

### Overall Statistics

| | G | AB | R | H | D | T | HR | RBI | SB | BB | SO | Avg | OBP | Slg |
|---|---|---|---|---|---|---|---|---|---|---|---|---|---|---|
| 1995 | 137 | 512 | 81 | 142 | 27 | 4 | 24 | 84 | 20 | 52 | 111 | .277 | .352 | .486 |
| Career | 137 | 512 | 81 | 142 | 27 | 4 | 24 | 84 | 20 | 52 | 111 | .277 | .352 | .486 |

### Where He Hits the Ball

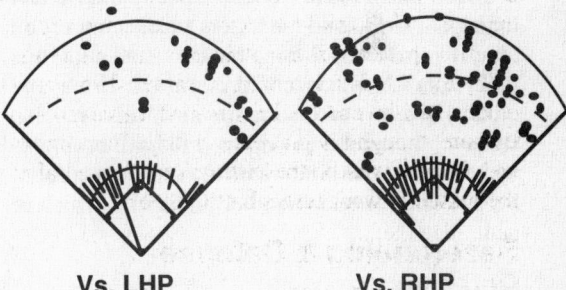

**Vs. LHP**          **Vs. RHP**

### 1995 Situational Stats

| | AB | H | HR | RBI | Avg | | AB | H | HR | RBI | Avg |
|---|---|---|---|---|---|---|---|---|---|---|---|
| Home | 241 | 68 | 16 | 48 | .282 | LHP | 124 | 40 | 3 | 20 | .323 |
| Road | 271 | 74 | 8 | 36 | .273 | RHP | 388 | 102 | 21 | 64 | .263 |
| First Half | 228 | 60 | 12 | 37 | .263 | Sc Pos | 143 | 37 | 6 | 55 | .259 |
| Scnd Half | 284 | 82 | 12 | 47 | .289 | Clutch | 73 | 15 | 4 | 11 | .205 |

### 1995 Rankings (American League)

→ 1st in highest percentage of swings on the first pitch (48.7%)
→ 2nd in fielding percentage in left field (.988)
→ 5th in errors in left field (4)
→ 6th in hit by pitch (10)
→ 9th in lowest batting average with the bases loaded (.091)
→ Led the Twins in home runs, sacrifice flies (5), strikeouts, games played, HR frequency (21.3 ABs per HR) and stolen base percentage (74.1%)

# Eddie Guardado

**Position:** RP/SP
**Bats:** R  **Throws:** L
**Ht:** 6' 0"  **Wt:** 193

**Opening Day Age:** 25
**Born:** 10/2/70 in
Stockton, California
**ML Seasons:** 3
**Pronunciation:**
gwar-DAH-doe

## 1995 Season

After continuing to struggle in a starting role, lefthander Eddie Guardado found success when the Twins shifted him to the bullpen last year. Guardado was one of Tom Kelly's most reliable pitchers down the stretch and nailed down a position on the Minnesota pitching staff for 1996.

## Pitching

With his stuff, Guardado *looks* like he should be a successful starting pitcher. Throwing with a compact motion, he features an 88-90 MPH fastball, along with a curveball and change. He works up in the strike zone a lot, and he's usually okay as long as he has good velocity. His problem as a starter has been that he tends to lose velocity after a few innings of work, and the hitters start teeing off on him. He also tends to hang his curveball a lot. In a relief role Guardado could come out firing and didn't have to worry so much about his stamina. But even in relief, he continued to have problems with righties, and if he wants to succeed he probably needs to develop another pitch with which to neutralize them.

## Defense

Guardado doesn't have the slickest pickoff move around, but he does a pretty good job holding runners. He's a good athlete and does a fine job of fielding his position.

## 1996 Outlook

Guardado is one of the better talents on the Twins' beleaguered pitching staff, and he figures to see plenty of action this year. He handled middle relief very well last year, but the club will probably be tempted to give him another shot as a starter. He'll need to improve his stamina if he's going to succeed in a starting role, and he'll also probably need to develop a pitch he can use against righties. If he fails again they can always return him to relief.

### Overall Statistics

|        | W | L | Pct. | ERA | G | GS | Sv | IP | H | BB | SO | HR | BR/IP |
|--------|---|---|------|-----|---|----|----|-----|-----|----|-----|----|-------|
| 1995   | 4 | 9 | .308 | 5.12 | 51 | 5 | 2 | 91.1 | 99 | 45 | 71 | 13 | 1.58 |
| Career | 7 | 19 | .269 | 5.90 | 74 | 25 | 2 | 203.0 | 248 | 85 | 125 | 29 | 1.64 |

### How Often He Throws Strikes

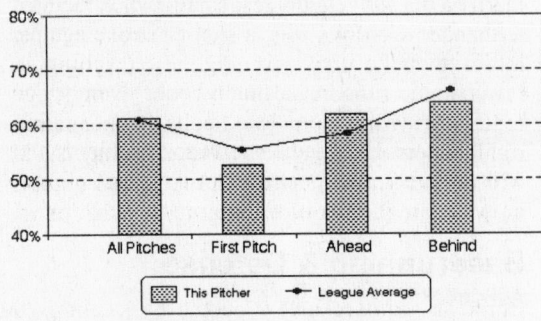

### 1995 Situational Stats

|            | W | L | ERA | Sv | IP |      | AB | H | HR | RBI | Avg |
|------------|---|---|-----|----|------|------|-----|----|----|-----|------|
| Home       | 3 | 4 | 3.60 | 2 | 40.0 | LHB | 121 | 27 | 2 | 15 | .223 |
| Road       | 1 | 5 | 6.31 | 0 | 51.1 | RHB | 233 | 72 | 11 | 42 | .309 |
| First Half | 0 | 7 | 5.92 | 0 | 48.2 | Sc Pos | 86 | 25 | 4 | 44 | .291 |
| Scnd Half  | 4 | 2 | 4.22 | 2 | 42.2 | Clutch | 71 | 15 | 1 | 5 | .211 |

### 1995 Rankings (American League)

➡ 4th in highest batting average allowed vs. right-handed batters (.309)
➡ 5th in lowest winning percentage
➡ 10th in least GDPs induced per GDP situation (2.9%)
➡ Led the Twins in balks (1), runners caught stealing (5), first batter efficiency (.250), lowest batting average allowed in relief with runners on base (.276), relief ERA (3.86), relief innings (70.0) and most strikeouts per 9 innings in relief (7.8)

# Chuck Knoblauch

## 1995 Season

The Twins seem to keep getting worse, but Chuck Knoblauch just keeps getting better. Last year Knoblauch batted a career-high .333—second in the league behind Edgar Martinez—and reached career highs in numerous other categories. He continued to sparkle in the field and on the bases, embellishing his reputation as one of the very best infielders in the major leagues.

## Hitting

Knoblauch has always batted from a crouch, but as the 1995 season wore on, the crouch became more extreme. It seemed to help his ability to turn on a fastball, as he was an absolute terror after the All-Star break. The biggest surprise was the way he hit for power—after hitting 11 home runs in his first four and a half seasons, he hit 10 dingers in less than three months. Knoblauch probably won't develop into a slugger, but he can drive the ball into the gaps and he's capable of hitting 12-15 homers per season. He also draws a good number of walks, making him even more valuable on offense.

## Baserunning & Defense

An aggressive but intelligent baserunner, Knoblauch stole a career-high 46 bases last year. His success rate was down a little, but that was probably due to an attempt to make things happen with the Twins struggling. He figures to do better this year. He's an excellent fielder with soft hands, good range, an accurate arm and the ability to turn the double play.

## 1996 Outlook

Knoblauch is about to enter his free-agent years, and the big question in Minnesota is whether the Twins can afford him. He loves the Twin Cities and would probably settle for less money in order to stay there. He's the type of player a club needs to build around, and the Twins will do their best to satisfy his demands.

**Position:** 2B
**Bats:** R **Throws:** R
**Ht:** 5' 9"  **Wt:** 181

**Opening Day Age:** 27
**Born:** 7/7/68 in Houston, TX
**ML Seasons:** 5
**Pronunciation:** NOB-lock

**Minnesota Twins**

### Overall Statistics

|        | G   | AB   | R   | H   | D   | T  | HR | RBI | SB  | BB  | SO  | Avg  | OBP  | Slg  |
|--------|-----|------|-----|-----|-----|----|----|-----|-----|-----|-----|------|------|------|
| 1995   | 136 | 538  | 107 | 179 | 34  | 8  | 11 | 63  | 46  | 78  | 95  | .333 | .424 | .487 |
| Career | 704 | 2750 | 456 | 822 | 149 | 27 | 21 | 261 | 169 | 331 | 295 | .299 | .378 | .396 |

### Where He Hits the Ball

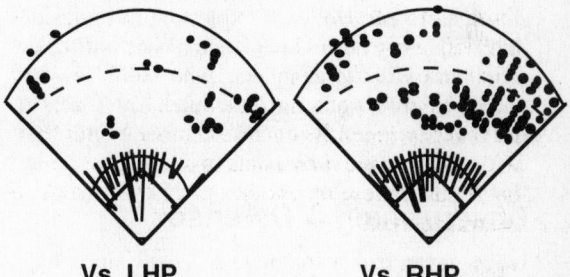

Vs. LHP          Vs. RHP

### 1995 Situational Stats

|            | AB  | H   | HR | RBI | Avg  |        | AB  | H   | HR | RBI | Avg  |
|------------|-----|-----|----|-----|------|--------|-----|-----|----|-----|------|
| Home       | 282 | 93  | 4  | 34  | .330 | LHP    | 141 | 50  | 4  | 30  | .355 |
| Road       | 256 | 86  | 7  | 29  | .336 | RHP    | 397 | 129 | 7  | 33  | .325 |
| First Half | 253 | 79  | 1  | 23  | .312 | Sc Pos | 113 | 41  | 1  | 48  | .363 |
| Scnd Half  | 285 | 100 | 10 | 40  | .351 | Clutch | 76  | 25  | 2  | 10  | .329 |

### 1995 Rankings (American League)

→ 1st in on-base percentage for a leadoff hitter (.423)

→ 2nd in batting average, caught stealing (18) and fielding percentage at second base (.985)

→ 3rd in hits, on-base percentage vs. right-handed pitchers (.433) and batting average on the road (.336)

→ 4th in singles (126), stolen bases, times on base (267) and batting average on an 0-2 count (.333)

→ 5th in triples and steals of third (9)

→ Led the Twins in batting average, at-bats, runs scored, hits, singles (126), triples, stolen bases, caught stealing (18) and walks

# Scott Leius

## 1995 Season

About all you can say for Scott Leius' 1995 season is that he kept his batting average at its usual level. Over his last three full seasons (he missed almost all of 1993 after rotator-cuff surgery), Leius has batted .249, .246 and .247. Unfortunately, he didn't maintain the home-run power he'd shown in 1994, and he needed a late surge to get his average as high as .247. His future as a regular is very much in jeopardy.

## Hitting

After hitting 14 homers in 97 games in 1994, Leius spent the winter working out with weights in order to develop even more power. He may have bulked up a little too much, because his bat seemed much slower last year. He wasn't able to turn on inside pitches the way he did in '94, and he had particular problems with righthanders, who were able to overpower him. Leius did look much better later in the year, hitting .318 after September 1. But that was a little too late to salvage his season.

## Baserunning & Defense

Leius never had a lot of speed, and since he's gotten more muscular, he's even slower than in the past. He'll usually only steal as part of a hit-and-run play. At third base he has good hands and a strong arm, but with the added bulk he missed more balls to his left last year than he used to. He can play shortstop, also, but strictly as a fill-in.

## 1996 Outlook

After the way he played last year, there's no guarantee that Leius will return to the Twins. Even if he does he'll have to hustle to win a regular job, as the club has other alternatives at third. It'll help if he shows up for spring training a little less lighter than last year.

**Position:** 3B
**Bats:** R **Throws:** R
**Ht:** 6' 3" **Wt:** 200

**Opening Day Age:** 30
**Born:** 9/24/65 in Yonkers, NY
**ML Seasons:** 6
**Pronunciation:** LAY-us

### Overall Statistics

|        | G   | AB   | R   | H   | D  | T  | HR | RBI | SB | BB  | SO  | Avg  | OBP  | Slg  |
|--------|-----|------|-----|-----|----|----|----|-----|----|-----|-----|------|------|------|
| 1995   | 117 | 372  | 51  | 92  | 16 | 5  | 4  | 45  | 2  | 49  | 54  | .247 | .335 | .349 |
| Career | 476 | 1373 | 201 | 346 | 58 | 10 | 26 | 155 | 15 | 154 | 214 | .252 | .327 | .366 |

### Where He Hits the Ball

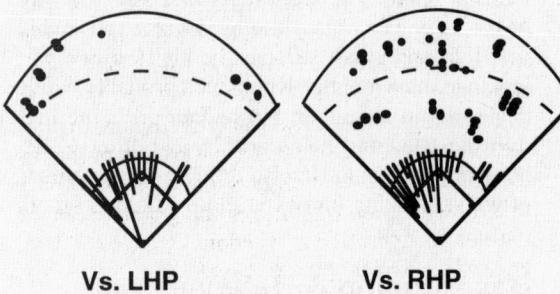

**Vs. LHP**          **Vs. RHP**

### 1995 Situational Stats

|            | AB  | H  | HR | RBI | Avg  |        | AB  | H  | HR | RBI | Avg  |
|------------|-----|----|----|-----|------|--------|-----|----|----|-----|------|
| Home       | 179 | 40 | 2  | 22  | .223 | LHP    | 117 | 32 | 1  | 13  | .274 |
| Road       | 193 | 52 | 2  | 23  | .269 | RHP    | 255 | 60 | 3  | 32  | .235 |
| First Half | 203 | 47 | 3  | 29  | .232 | Sc Pos | 103 | 24 | 2  | 41  | .233 |
| Scnd Half  | 169 | 45 | 1  | 16  | .266 | Clutch | 49  | 8  | 1  | 5   | .163 |

### 1995 Rankings (American League)

- ➡ 2nd in lowest fielding percentage at third base (.945)
- ➡ 5th in lowest batting average in the clutch (.163)
- ➡ 7th in errors at third base (14)
- ➡ 10th in lowest batting average on a 3-1 count (.083) and highest percentage of extra bases taken as a runner (60.5%)
- ➡ Led the Twins in highest percentage of pitches taken (58.9%) and highest percentage of swings put into play (50.3%)

# Pat Mahomes

## 1995 Season

Talented but enigmatic, Pat Mahomes still hasn't had the major league success that's long been predicted for him. Mahomes began the '95 season in the Twins' rotation, but after going 0-4 with a double-digit ERA he was moved to the bullpen. Mahomes pitched pretty well in relief for a period of about two months, but tailed off again later in the year.

## Pitching

Everyone agrees that Mahomes has great stuff. He was rated a Top 10 prospect by *Baseball America* four times during his minor league career, and he went 28-19 at the Double- and Triple-A level from 1991 to 1993. Perhaps the hardest thrower on the Minnesota staff, he can reach 95 MPH on a good day. Unfortunately, he has too many *bad* days, ones on which his heater doesn't get past the mid-80s. Mahomes is inconsistent with his curveball as well; it has good movement, but he has problems controlling it. He also throws an occasional slider and a change-up which has the potential to be another good pitch. The weapons clearly are there. The results, so far at least, haven't been.

## Defense

Mahomes can do a good job of holding runners when he works at it, but in 1995 he didn't and they ran wild against him. One area that didn't slip was his defense. He's a good athlete with quick reactions and excellent instincts in the field.

## 1996 Outlook

Despite all his struggles, Mahomes is only 25 years old and he's still got that great arm. And of course, he's not exactly pitching on a staff full of Cy Young candidates. So he'll probably get another chance to try to establish himself on the major league level. He figures to stay in relief, where he found most of his success last year.

**Position:** RP/SP
**Bats:** R **Throws:** R
**Ht:** 6' 4" **Wt:** 212

**Opening Day Age:** 25
**Born:** 8/9/70 in Bryan, TX
**ML Seasons:** 4
**Pronunciation:** muh-HOMES

### Overall Statistics

|        | W  | L  | Pct. | ERA  | G  | GS | Sv | IP    | H   | BB  | SO  | HR | BR/IP |
|--------|----|----|------|------|----|----|----|-------|-----|-----|-----|----|-------|
| 1995   | 4  | 10 | .286 | 6.37 | 47 | 7  | 3  | 94.2  | 100 | 47  | 67  | 22 | 1.55  |
| Career | 17 | 24 | .415 | 5.62 | 94 | 46 | 3  | 321.2 | 341 | 162 | 187 | 57 | 1.56  |

### How Often He Throws Strikes

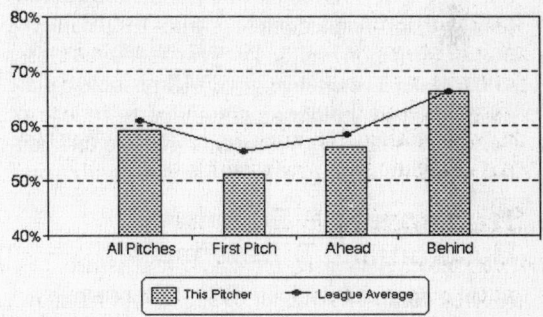

### 1995 Situational Stats

|            | W | L | ERA  | Sv |  IP  |        | AB  | H  | HR | RBI | Avg  |
|------------|---|---|------|----|------|--------|-----|----|----|-----|------|
| Home       | 1 | 5 | 9.20 | 0  | 46.0 | LHB    | 202 | 63 | 12 | 31  | .312 |
| Road       | 3 | 5 | 3.70 | 3  | 48.2 | RHB    | 167 | 37 | 10 | 40  | .222 |
| First Half | 0 | 4 | 7.63 | 0  | 46.0 | Sc Pos | 91  | 30 | 8  | 52  | .330 |
| Scnd Half  | 4 | 6 | 5.18 | 3  | 48.2 | Clutch | 107 | 26 | 5  | 16  | .243 |

### 1995 Rankings (American League)

→ 4th in lowest winning percentage and relief losses (6)

→ Led the Twins in walks allowed, wild pitches (6), blown saves (4), relief losses (6), lowest batting average allowed in relief (.239) and least baserunners allowed per 9 innings in relief (12.1)

# Pat Meares

## 1995 Season

Pat Meares has improved steadily in his three seasons with the Twins. He's raised his average each year that he's been with the club, and in 1995 he even began hitting for power, reaching double figures in home runs for the first time in his professional career. Meares has also improved on defense, though he continues to make a few too many errors.

## Hitting

Meares is an extremely aggressive hitter who tends to swing at everything. He's worked a lot on driving the ball and the difference was really evident last year, when his power surprised a lot of opposing clubs. In the past he's had a lot of problems with left-handed pitchers who could paint the outside corner on him, so last year he moved closer to the plate. The change gave Meares better plate coverage, and though he continued to be one of those rare hitters with a reverse platoon differential, he finally began to hit lefties with some power.

## Baserunning & Defense

Meares doesn't have a lot of speed, but he knows what he's doing on the bases and is capable of stealing 10 or 15 bases a year. He's a fine athlete and it shows on defense, where he displays good range and a strong arm. He's also solid on the double play. His arm tends to be erratic, however, and he still makes too many careless throwing errors.

## 1996 Outlook

Meares bears more than a few similarities to Greg Gagne, his predecessor as the Minnesota shortstop. Like Gagne, he's a good fielder and a .260-ish hitter with a little power but not much patience. If he can cut down on the throwing errors and continue his offensive development, he could have the same sort of long run at the position that Gagne did before him.

**Position:** SS
**Bats:** R **Throws:** R
**Ht:** 6' 0" **Wt:** 188

**Opening Day Age:** 27
**Born:** 9/6/68 in Salina, KS
**ML Seasons:** 3

### Overall Statistics

| | G | AB | R | H | D | T | HR | RBI | SB | BB | SO | Avg | OBP | Slg |
|---|---|---|---|---|---|---|---|---|---|---|---|---|---|---|
| 1995 | 116 | 390 | 57 | 105 | 19 | 4 | 12 | 49 | 10 | 15 | 68 | .269 | .311 | .431 |
| Career | 307 | 965 | 119 | 253 | 45 | 8 | 14 | 106 | 19 | 36 | 170 | .262 | .295 | .369 |

### Where He Hits the Ball

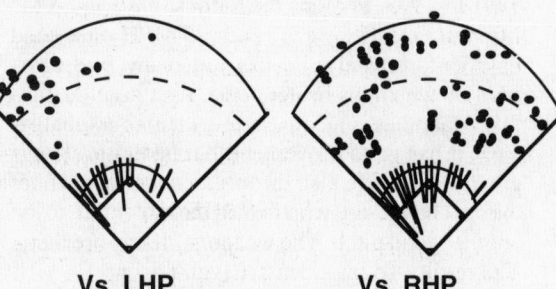

**Vs. LHP**              **Vs. RHP**

### 1995 Situational Stats

| | AB | H | HR | RBI | Avg | | AB | H | HR | RBI | Avg |
|---|---|---|---|---|---|---|---|---|---|---|---|
| Home | 194 | 52 | 3 | 20 | .268 | LHP | 121 | 28 | 5 | 11 | .231 |
| Road | 196 | 53 | 9 | 29 | .270 | RHP | 269 | 77 | 7 | 38 | .286 |
| First Half | 181 | 51 | 7 | 21 | .282 | Sc Pos | 108 | 25 | 2 | 37 | .231 |
| Scnd Half | 209 | 54 | 5 | 28 | .258 | Clutch | 49 | 13 | 2 | 7 | .265 |

### 1995 Rankings (American League)

- ➡ 1st in errors at shortstop (18)
- ➡ 2nd in lowest fielding percentage at shortstop (.965)
- ➡ 3rd in lowest on-base percentage vs. left-handed pitchers (.254) and lowest batting average on a 3-2 count (.056)
- ➡ 4th in hit by pitch (11)
- ➡ 6th in lowest percentage of pitches taken (46.0%)
- ➡ 7th in most GDPs per GDP situation (17.8%)
- ➡ Led the Twins in sacrifice flies (5), hit by pitch (11), GDPs (16) and bunts in play (8)

# Pedro Munoz

## 1995 Season

Talented but maddeningly inconsistent in past seasons, Pedro Munoz had the best year of his career in 1995. Settling into the DH role which seems made to order for him, Munoz avoided the long slumps which plagued him in previous years. The result was a career-high 18 homers and the first .300 average of his major league career.

## Hitting

Munoz is not the most scientific of hitters. He has a big swing and not much discipline, and he's had a tendency to chase high fastballs and offspeed pitches out of the strike zone. While he hasn't exactly turned into Frank Thomas, Munoz has started to lay off those bad pitches a little more over the past couple of years. His strikeout-to-walk ratio is still pretty bad, and pitchers with superior location can make him look foolish. But he's improving. He likes to use the whole field, and gets a good percentage of his hits to right field.

## Baserunning & Defense

Munoz didn't play much in the field last year, and that's just as well. He doesn't get a very good jump on the ball, knee problems have severely limited his mobility, and he doesn't have a very good arm, either. He's one of the poorest baserunners on the Twins, strictly a station-to-station guy, and with his bad knees, no threat at all to steal.

## 1996 Outlook

Munoz has tried the Twins' patience at times with his lack of discipline, but they've stuck with him for one good reason: he can hit. Though the club has other possibilities at DH, none of them can belt the ball quite like Munoz, so there's a good chance he'll be back. If not, he should have few problems finding work with an A.L. club looking for a DH.

**Position:** DH/RF
**Bats:** R  **Throws:** R
**Ht:** 5'10"  **Wt:** 208

**Opening Day Age:** 27
**Born:** 9/19/68 in Ponce, PR
**ML Seasons:** 6
Pronunciation: moon-YOHS

### Overall Statistics

|        | G   | AB   | R   | H   | D  | T | HR | RBI | SB | BB | SO  | Avg  | OBP  | Slg  |
|--------|-----|------|-----|-----|----|---|----|-----|----|----|-----|------|------|------|
| 1995   | 104 | 376  | 45  | 113 | 17 | 0 | 18 | 58  | 0  | 19 | 86  | .301 | .338 | .489 |
| Career | 483 | 1587 | 186 | 436 | 70 | 8 | 61 | 234 | 11 | 91 | 387 | .275 | .316 | .444 |

### Where He Hits the Ball

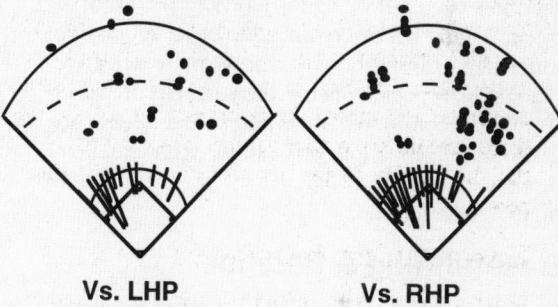

**Vs. LHP**          **Vs. RHP**

### 1995 Situational Stats

|            | AB  | H  | HR | RBI | Avg  |        | AB  | H  | HR | RBI | Avg  |
|------------|-----|----|----|-----|------|--------|-----|----|----|-----|------|
| Home       | 177 | 58 | 10 | 34  | .328 | LHP    | 126 | 39 | 7  | 23  | .310 |
| Road       | 199 | 55 | 8  | 24  | .276 | RHP    | 250 | 74 | 11 | 35  | .296 |
| First Half | 183 | 53 | 12 | 31  | .290 | Sc Pos | 126 | 34 | 4  | 39  | .270 |
| Scnd Half  | 193 | 60 | 6  | 27  | .311 | Clutch | 47  | 16 | 2  | 5   | .340 |

### 1995 Rankings (American League)

→ 3rd in lowest percentage of pitches taken (42.2%) and lowest percentage of swings put into play (35.0%)

→ 9th in lowest batting average on an 0-2 count (.050) and highest percentage of swings that missed (27.5%)

→ 10th in most GDPs per GDP situation (17.1%)

→ Led the Twins in batting average in the clutch (.340) and cleanup slugging percentage (.473)

# Kirby Puckett

**Hall of Famer**

## 1995 Season

Continuing his journey toward Cooperstown, Kirby Puckett had another great year in 1995. Puckett battled back from a slow start to hit .314, which is just below his career average, and topped 20 homers and 90 RBI for the sixth time each. However, Puckett's season ended on a frightening note on September 28, when a pitch by Cleveland's Dennis Martinez fractured his left jawbone. Puckett, who bore no malice toward Martinez, is expected to be at full strength when spring training begins.

## Hitting

Puckett loves the fastball, and throughout his career he's been notorious for jumping on the first-pitch heater. Puckett continued to be an aggressive hitter in 1995, but he was a little more selective than usual, especially late in the year. His 56 walks were the second-most of his career and double his 1994 total. He's a line-drive hitter with excellent power to all fields, and one of the best clutch hitters in the game.

## Baserunning & Defense

Puckett could steal 20-plus bases when he was a young man, but he's put on a lot of weight since then and is no longer a threat to steal. He still runs pretty well and is a very intelligent baserunner. Moved from center to right a few years ago, Puckett has lost some range but he's still a fine outfielder with a solid arm. He's the captain of the Twins outfield, taking charge and helping the other outfielders with their positioning.

## 1996 Outlook

Puckett will need to show he's recovered from the Martinez beaning, but you can pretty much count on another great year. There's talk that the budget-conscious Twins might want to unload his high salary, but Kirby is still the cornerstone of the franchise and, with two years still left on his contract, it seems unlikely they would let him go.

**Position:** RF/DH
**Bats:** R **Throws:** R
**Ht:** 5' 9" **Wt:** 223

**Opening Day Age:** 35
**Born:** 3/14/61 in Chicago, IL
**ML Seasons:** 12

### Overall Statistics

| | G | AB | R | H | D | T | HR | RBI | SB | BB | SO | Avg | OBP | Slg |
|---|---|---|---|---|---|---|---|---|---|---|---|---|---|---|
| 1995 | 137 | 538 | 83 | 169 | 39 | 0 | 23 | 99 | 3 | 56 | 89 | .314 | .379 | .515 |
| Career | 1783 | 7244 | 1071 | 2304 | 414 | 57 | 207 | 1085 | 134 | 450 | 965 | .318 | .360 | .477 |

### Where He Hits the Ball

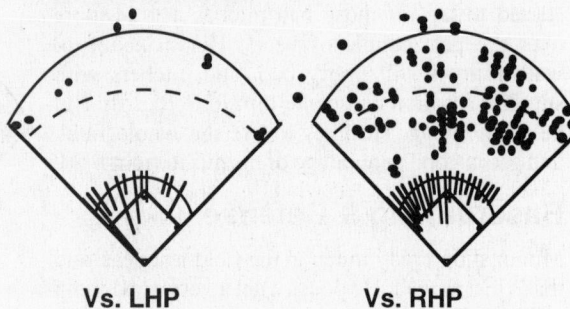

**Vs. LHP**      **Vs. RHP**

### 1995 Situational Stats

| | AB | H | HR | RBI | Avg | | AB | H | HR | RBI | Avg |
|---|---|---|---|---|---|---|---|---|---|---|---|
| Home | 277 | 84 | 13 | 52 | .303 | LHP | 128 | 41 | 6 | 23 | .320 |
| Road | 261 | 85 | 10 | 47 | .326 | RHP | 410 | 128 | 17 | 76 | .312 |
| First Half | 264 | 74 | 10 | 40 | .280 | Sc Pos | 155 | 49 | 10 | 80 | .316 |
| Scnd Half | 274 | 95 | 13 | 59 | .347 | Clutch | 85 | 25 | 4 | 15 | .294 |

### 1995 Rankings (American League)

- 3rd in doubles and intentional walks (18)
- 4th in least pitches seen per plate appearance (3.36), batting average on the road (.326) and fielding percentage in right field (.980)
- 5th in errors in right field (4)
- 9th in batting average and total bases (277)
- 10th in hits
- Led the Twins in at-bats, doubles, total bases (277), RBI, sacrifice flies, intentional walks (18), games played, slugging percentage, slugging percentage vs. right-handed pitchers (.512) and on-base percentage vs. left-handed pitchers (.404)

# Brad Radke

**Position:** SP
**Bats:** R  **Throws:** R
**Ht:** 6' 2"   **Wt:** 186

**Opening Day Age:** 23
**Born:** 10/27/72 in Eau Claire, WI
**ML Seasons:** 1

## 1995 Season

When the 1995 season began, Brad Radke was a 22-year-old youngster who'd never pitched above the Double-A level. By the time it ended, he was the number-one starter on the Minnesota Twins pitching staff. Admittedly, Radke became an "ace by default" after the Twins dealt away Scott Erickson and Kevin Tapani prior to the July 31 trading deadline. But though his record was pretty ugly, Radke impressed the Twins with his poise, stuff and willingness to take the ball. In the midst of disaster, the Twins think they may have found a pretty good pitcher.

## Pitching

Tall and fairly slender, Radke has only a mid-80s fastball. But he has a good curveball, a fine change-up and pinpoint control, and he uses his stuff intelligently. Radke isn't afraid to challenge the hitters, and he pays a price for it, yielding a major league-high 32 home runs last year. However, the vast majority of his gopher balls last year came with the bases empty. Radke's not afraid to bust the ball inside against a left-handed hitter, and he was actually more effective against lefties than righties last year.

## Defense

A fundamentally sound player, Radke does an excellent job of holding runners. Despite pitching from the stretch much of the time, he permitted only seven stolen bases last year. He's also a very fine fielder, quick off the mound and very sure-handed.

## 1996 Outlook

Radke went into the 1995 season with less than four years of professional experience, and most organizations would have had him at the Triple-A level, picking up experience. Instead Radke did his learning at the major league level, and it wasn't always a pleasant experience. But the Twins were very impressed with the way he handled things, and he should be much better with that first year under his belt.

*Overall Statistics*

|  | W | L | Pct. | ERA | G | GS | Sv | IP | H | BB | SO | HR | BR/IP |
|---|---|---|---|---|---|---|---|---|---|---|---|---|---|
| 1995 | 11 | 14 | .440 | 5.32 | 29 | 28 | 0 | 181.0 | 195 | 47 | 75 | 32 | 1.34 |
| Career | 11 | 14 | .440 | 5.32 | 29 | 28 | 0 | 181.0 | 195 | 47 | 75 | 32 | 1.34 |

*How Often He Throws Strikes*

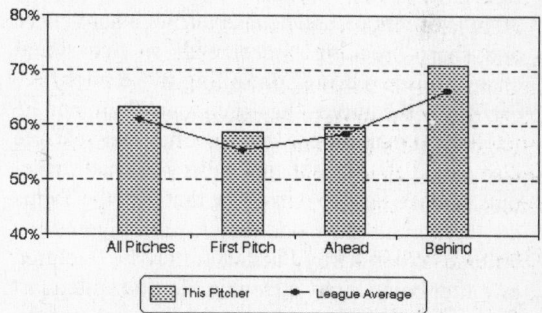

*1995 Situational Stats*

|  | W | L | ERA | Sv | IP |  | AB | H | HR | RBI | Avg |
|---|---|---|---|---|---|---|---|---|---|---|---|
| Home | 6 | 8 | 4.64 | 0 | 104.2 | LHB | 400 | 107 | 14 | 47 | .268 |
| Road | 5 | 6 | 6.25 | 0 | 76.1 | RHB | 309 | 88 | 18 | 58 | .285 |
| First Half | 5 | 7 | 6.08 | 0 | 77.0 | Sc Pos | 149 | 40 | 5 | 66 | .268 |
| Scnd Half | 6 | 7 | 4.76 | 0 | 104.0 | Clutch | 37 | 8 | 1 | 2 | .216 |

*1995 Rankings (American League)*

➡ 1st in home runs allowed, highest slugging percentage allowed (.487), lowest ground-ball/flyball ratio allowed (0.8), most home runs allowed per 9 innings (1.59), highest ERA on the road (6.25), and fielding percentage at pitcher (1.000)

➡ 2nd in highest ERA

➡ 3rd in least strikeouts per 9 innings (3.7)

➡ 4th in losses

➡ 6th in least pitches thrown per batter (3.63)

➡ 9th in shutouts (1) and highest batting average allowed (.275)

➡ Led the Twins in ERA, wins, losses, games started, shutouts (1), innings pitched, hits allowed and batters faced (772)

# Frankie Rodriguez

**Position:** SP/RP
**Bats:** R  **Throws:** R
**Ht:** 6' 0"  **Wt:** 195

**Opening Day Age:** 23
**Born:** 12/11/72 in Brooklyn, NY
**ML Seasons:** 1

## 1995 Season

When the Twins decided to deal away relief ace Rick Aguilera at the trading deadline last year, they demanded a top prospect in return. They got one in Red Sox farmhand Frankie Rodriguez. A great all-around athlete who'd been a minor league All-Star both at shortstop and on the mound, Rodriguez was one of the most celebrated players in the Boston system. Put in the Twins' rotation immediately after the trade, the young righthander struggled. However, the club was greatly impressed with his stuff and competitive fire.

## Pitching

Rodriguez throws hard. His fastball usually tops 90 miles per hour, and he also throws a hard curve and sharp-breaking slider, with an occasional change-up mixed in. Controlling those pitches—especially the curve—has been a problem, and he fell behind in the count way too often last year. He also issued almost as many walks as he had strikeouts, and it's hard to win doing that. But the Twins are high on his stuff, and they love his aggressive attitude. When Kirby Puckett suffered a fractured jaw after being hit by a Dennis Martinez pitch last September, Rodriguez immediately retaliated by plunking Albert Belle.

## Defense

It's no exaggeration to call Rodriguez a "fifth infielder," and you can see from his splendid defensive work why a lot of people think he could have made it to the majors as a shortstop. He also does an excellent job holding runners, permitting only four steals last year.

## 1996 Outlook

Just 23 and a full-time pitcher for only a few years, Rodriguez is still pretty raw. But the Twins see him as a potential star, and with the club in a rebuilding mode, they figure to be patient with him. Unless he starts getting hammered badly enough to weaken his confidence, he should be in the rotation all year.

### Overall Statistics

|  | W | L | Pct. | ERA | G | GS | Sv | IP | H | BB | SO | HR | BR/IP |
|---|---|---|---|---|---|---|---|---|---|---|---|---|---|
| 1995 | 5 | 8 | .385 | 6.13 | 25 | 18 | 0 | 105.2 | 114 | 57 | 59 | 11 | 1.62 |
| Career | 5 | 8 | .385 | 6.13 | 25 | 18 | 0 | 105.2 | 114 | 57 | 59 | 11 | 1.62 |

### How Often He Throws Strikes

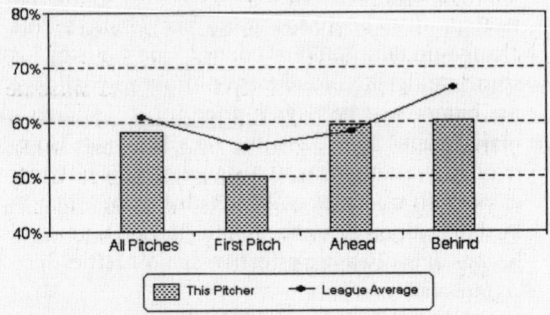

### 1995 Situational Stats

|  | W | L | ERA | Sv | IP |  | AB | H | HR | RBI | Avg |
|---|---|---|---|---|---|---|---|---|---|---|---|
| Home | 3 | 4 | 5.45 | 0 | 67.2 | LHB | 219 | 59 | 3 | 30 | .269 |
| Road | 2 | 4 | 7.34 | 0 | 38.0 | RHB | 192 | 55 | 8 | 34 | .286 |
| First Half | 0 | 3 | 10.31 | 0 | 18.1 | Sc Pos | 104 | 33 | 3 | 53 | .317 |
| Scnd Half | 5 | 5 | 5.26 | 0 | 87.1 | Clutch | 11 | 3 | 0 | 1 | .273 |

### 1995 Rankings (American League)

→ 1st in fielding percentage at pitcher (1.000)
→ 10th in lowest winning percentage
→ Led the Twins in walks allowed (47), hit batsmen (5), GDPs induced (14) and lowest batting average allowed vs. left-handed batters (.267)

# Scott Stahoviak

## 1995 Season

After a good season at Triple-A Salt Lake City in 1994, former first-round pick Scott Stahoviak joined the Twins last season. Stahoviak played both first and third, displaying a good glove at first and hitting pretty well except for one dry period in July. He was doing his best hitting of the year when he went on the shelf in early September with bone chips in his right elbow. Stahoviak underwent surgery but should be ready for spring training.

## Hitting

Stahoviak is a big man at 6-5 and 222 pounds, and he hits a lot of batting-practice home runs. But he shortens his stroke when the game begins and doesn't go deep as often as the Twins would like. He'll probably never be a Kent Hrbek, but he should be able to hit 12-15 dingers, and since he hits some doubles and draws a few walks, that would make him a decent offensive performer. The Twins used Stahoviak almost exclusively against righties last year, but he handled lefties in the minors and could probably do the same in the majors if given a chance.

## Baserunning & Defense

Stahoviak has pretty good speed for a big guy and can steal a few bases. He's an excellent defensive first baseman with good range and the ability to stretch for the ball. He is much less sure of himself at third, where he looks awkward and makes a lot of mistakes. He used to have a strong arm, but it's been weakened by chronic elbow problems.

## 1996 Outlook

The Twins are committed to their young players, and Stahoviak figures to get an opportunity to play this year, especially at first base. However, the club has other players waiting in the wings and he'll need to hit more home runs if he wants to secure a regular job.

**Position:** 1B/3B
**Bats:** L **Throws:** R
**Ht:** 6' 5"   **Wt:** 222

**Opening Day Age:** 26
**Born:** 3/6/70 in Waukegan, IL
**ML Seasons:** 2

**Minnesota Twins**

### Overall Statistics

|        | G   | AB  | R  | H  | D  | T | HR | RBI | SB | BB | SO | Avg  | OBP  | Slg  |
|--------|-----|-----|----|----|----|---|----|-----|----|----|----|------|------|------|
| 1995   | 94  | 263 | 28 | 70 | 19 | 0 | 3  | 23  | 5  | 30 | 61 | .266 | .341 | .373 |
| Career | 114 | 320 | 29 | 81 | 23 | 0 | 3  | 24  | 5  | 33 | 83 | .253 | .323 | .353 |

### Where He Hits the Ball

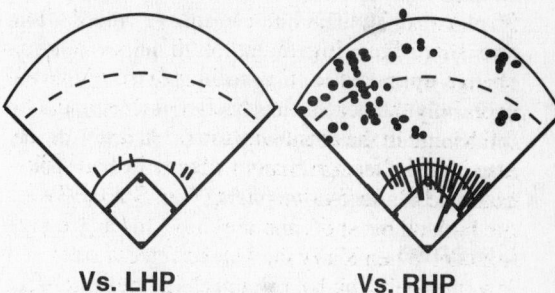

**Vs. LHP**          **Vs. RHP**

### 1995 Situational Stats

|            | AB  | H  | HR | RBI | Avg  |        | AB  | H  | HR | RBI | Avg  |
|------------|-----|----|----|-----|------|--------|-----|----|----|-----|------|
| Home       | 134 | 35 | 1  | 10  | .261 | LHP    | 13  | 1  | 0  | 0   | .077 |
| Road       | 129 | 35 | 2  | 13  | .271 | RHP    | 250 | 69 | 3  | 23  | .276 |
| First Half | 152 | 40 | 2  | 11  | .263 | Sc Pos | 70  | 18 | 1  | 21  | .257 |
| Scnd Half  | 111 | 30 | 1  | 12  | .270 | Clutch | 37  | 9  | 1  | 2   | .243 |

### 1995 Rankings (American League)

➡ 4th in least GDPs per GDP situation (4.6%)
➡ Led the Twins in least GDPs per GDP situation (4.6%)

# Dave Stevens

## 1995 Season

The Twins have been intrigued with righty reliever Dave Stevens ever since they obtained him from the Cubs after the 1993 season. When they dealt Rick Aguilera to the Red Sox last July, it gave them a chance to try Stevens in the closer role for the first time. Stevens went through a rough period in August, but he pitched very well apart from that, converting 10 saves in 12 chances. He finished the year strongly, posting a 1.72 ERA in his last 15 appearances.

## Pitching

Stevens *looks* like a closer. He's a big guy with a Goose Gossage-style manner on the mound, and he goes right after the hitters. His best pitch is a 90-plus fastball. The pitch has good velocity but often comes in a little too straight, and it's pretty obvious that he's not going to be able to survive on the fastball alone. Stevens has been working on a split-fingered fastball, but thus far it's still in the experimental stages. He also throws a slider, but it hasn't been an effective pitch.

## Defense

Stevens had some problems holding runners last year, but it wasn't a major problem because he was usually in the game at times when the opposition was reluctant to risk a steal. He's not the most mobile guy in the world, but he does a pretty fair job of fielding his position.

## 1996 Outlook

The Twins haven't anointed Stevens as *the* closer for 1996, saying they're going to go with a bull-pen-by-committee. It's pretty obvious, though, that Stevens is going to be the guy getting most of the save opportunities, at least at the start of the year. He has the arm and the demeanor, but he's probably going to need another effective pitch in order to become a top closer.

**Position:** RP
**Bats:** R  **Throws:** R
**Ht:** 6' 3"  **Wt:** 205

**Opening Day Age:** 26
**Born:** 3/4/70 in Fullerton, CA
**ML Seasons:** 2

### Overall Statistics

|  | W | L | Pct. | ERA | G | GS | Sv | IP | H | BB | SO | HR | BR/IP |
|---|---|---|---|---|---|---|---|---|---|---|---|---|---|
| 1995 | 5 | 4 | .556 | 5.07 | 56 | 0 | 10 | 65.2 | 74 | 32 | 47 | 14 | 1.61 |
| Career | 10 | 6 | .625 | 5.77 | 80 | 0 | 10 | 110.2 | 129 | 55 | 71 | 20 | 1.66 |

### How Often He Throws Strikes

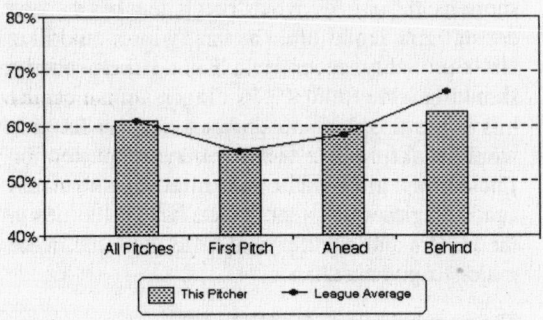

### 1995 Situational Stats

|  | W | L | ERA | Sv | IP |  | AB | H | HR | RBI | Avg |
|---|---|---|---|---|---|---|---|---|---|---|---|
| Home | 2 | 2 | 6.64 | 6 | 39.1 | LHB | 129 | 41 | 3 | 21 | .318 |
| Road | 3 | 2 | 2.73 | 4 | 26.1 | RHB | 131 | 33 | 11 | 29 | .252 |
| First Half | 3 | 0 | 5.60 | 1 | 35.1 | Sc Pos | 91 | 22 | 3 | 34 | .242 |
| Scnd Half | 2 | 4 | 4.45 | 9 | 30.1 | Clutch | 114 | 32 | 3 | 25 | .281 |

### 1995 Rankings (American League)

→ 4th in worst first batter efficiency (.386)
→ 7th in highest relief ERA (5.07)
→ 8th in most baserunners allowed per 9 innings in relief (14.7)
→ 9th in highest batting average allowed in relief (.285)
→ 10th in games finished (34)
→ Led the Twins in games pitched and games finished (34)

# Mike Trombley

## 1995 Season

After a rough season in relief for the Twins in 1994, Mike Trombley began the '95 season in the minors. He was recalled in June, and this time the Twins used him as a starter. Trombley worked in the rotation for the rest of the year, but like most of his Minnesota mound-mates, he got hit pretty hard.

## Pitching

Trombley has relied mostly on his fastball during his major league career, and that might not be enough. The heater has pretty good velocity and he's recorded some impressive strikeout totals with it, but the pitch doesn't always have good movement, and when it doesn't the hitters start teeing off. Trombley also throws an overhand curveball with a nice break, but he's had problems throwing it for strikes. His change-up isn't much of a weapon. Trombley works up in the strike zone a lot, and if he doesn't have good command of his pitches he's going to be in trouble. Unfortunately that's the case way too often, and hitters have taken him out of the yard regularly during his major league career.

## Defense

With all the pitching problems last year, Trombley didn't pay much attention to baserunners, and they took advantage by stealing nine bases in 10 attempts. A good all-around athlete, he moves well off the mound and helps himself with his defense.

## 1996 Outlook

Trombley's been with the Twins for four seasons now, and he's failed to establish himself either as a starter or in relief. The Twins have stuck with him because he throws pretty hard, and because they've been desperate for pitching. But he'll need to have a good spring to keep his slot in the rotation, and he won't remain in the majors if he keeps pitching as badly as he did in 1995.

**Position:** SP
**Bats:** R  **Throws:** R
**Ht:** 6' 2"  **Wt:** 206

**Opening Day Age:** 28
**Born:** 4/14/67 in Springfield, MA
**ML Seasons:** 4

### Overall Statistics

|  | W | L | Pct. | ERA | G | GS | Sv | IP | H | BB | SO | HR | BR/IP |
|---|---|---|---|---|---|---|---|---|---|---|---|---|---|
| 1995 | 4 | 8 | .333 | 5.62 | 20 | 18 | 0 | 97.2 | 107 | 42 | 68 | 18 | 1.53 |
| Career | 15 | 16 | .484 | 5.11 | 98 | 35 | 2 | 306.2 | 337 | 118 | 223 | 48 | 1.48 |

### How Often He Throws Strikes

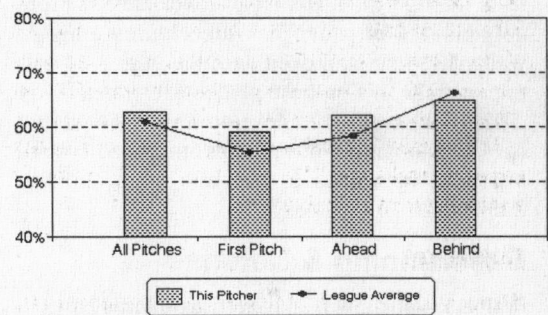

### 1995 Situational Stats

|  | W | L | ERA | Sv | IP |  | AB | H | HR | RBI | Avg |
|---|---|---|---|---|---|---|---|---|---|---|---|
| Home | 3 | 3 | 5.16 | 0 | 45.1 | LHB | 219 | 65 | 8 | 27 | .297 |
| Road | 1 | 5 | 6.02 | 0 | 52.1 | RHB | 173 | 42 | 10 | 31 | .243 |
| First Half | 1 | 3 | 4.50 | 0 | 24.0 | Sc Pos | 108 | 25 | 5 | 41 | .231 |
| Scnd Half | 3 | 5 | 5.99 | 0 | 73.2 | Clutch | 20 | 7 | 2 | 2 | .350 |

### 1995 Rankings (American League)

➡ Did not rank near the top or bottom in any category

# Matt Walbeck

## 1995 Season

Matt Walbeck entered the 1995 season as the Twins' number-one catcher, but with the knowledge that his job would be in danger if he didn't improve on the .204 average he'd posted as a rookie in '94. Walbeck came through, hitting .257 and performing well in the clutch. His defense, meanwhile, remained solid.

## Hitting

Walbeck improved as a hitter when he shortened his stroke and concentrated on making contact. He hit only one homer with the new style, but he was never much of a power threat anyway, so that was no great loss. A switch-hitter, he's much better from the right side. His biggest weakness is probably his lack of patience. Walbeck drew only 25 walks last year, and even with the improved batting average, his on-base percentage was a lowly .302. He also needs to develop a more consistent stroke. Though his hitting was improved overall last year, he tended to alternate good and bad months.

## Baserunning & Defense

Walbeck somehow managed to steal three bases in four attempts last year, but don't count on it happening again: this guy is *slow*. His defense is what keeps him in the lineup. Walbeck is very nimble behind the plate and the Twins love the way he handles a pitching staff. His arm isn't all that strong, but he makes up for it with a quick release. His throw-out rate wasn't very good last year (23 percent), but that was mostly the fault of a struggling, inexperienced pitching staff.

## 1996 Outlook

Walbeck solidified his hold on the Twins' catching job with his improved hitting last year. He'll probably never be much of an offensive threat, but he doesn't need to be. As long as he plays well on defense, he's pretty much assured of a job.

**Position:** C
**Bats:** B  **Throws:** R
**Ht:** 5'11"  **Wt:** 188

**Opening Day Age:** 26
**Born:** 10/2/69 in Sacramento, CA
**ML Seasons:** 3

### Overall Statistics

|  | G | AB | R | H | D | T | HR | RBI | SB | BB | SO | Avg | OBP | Slg |
|---|---|---|---|---|---|---|---|---|---|---|---|---|---|---|
| 1995 | 115 | 393 | 40 | 101 | 18 | 1 | 1 | 44 | 3 | 25 | 71 | .257 | .302 | .316 |
| Career | 223 | 761 | 73 | 176 | 32 | 1 | 7 | 85 | 4 | 43 | 114 | .231 | .274 | .304 |

### Where He Hits the Ball

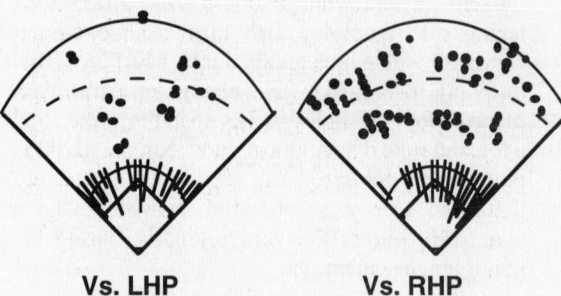

Vs. LHP          Vs. RHP

### 1995 Situational Stats

|  | AB | H | HR | RBI | Avg |  | AB | H | HR | RBI | Avg |
|---|---|---|---|---|---|---|---|---|---|---|---|
| Home | 190 | 55 | 1 | 23 | .289 | LHP | 117 | 36 | 0 | 15 | .308 |
| Road | 203 | 46 | 0 | 21 | .227 | RHP | 276 | 65 | 1 | 29 | .236 |
| First Half | 169 | 40 | 1 | 18 | .237 | Sc Pos | 101 | 31 | 0 | 42 | .307 |
| Scnd Half | 224 | 61 | 0 | 26 | .272 | Clutch | 69 | 18 | 0 | 11 | .261 |

### 1995 Rankings (American League)

➡ 5th in lowest fielding percentage at catcher (.991)
➡ 6th in errors at catcher (6)
➡ 9th in lowest percentage of pitches taken (48.2%)

# Jerald Clark

**Position:** LF/1B
**Bats:** R **Throws:** R
**Ht:** 6' 4"  **Wt:** 205

**Opening Day Age:** 32
**Born:** 8/10/63 in
Crockett, TX
**ML Seasons:** 7

### Overall Statistics

|        | G   | AB   | R   | H   | D  | T  | HR | RBI | SB | BB | SO  | Avg  | OBP  | Slg  |
|--------|-----|------|-----|-----|----|----|----|-----|----|----|-----|------|------|------|
| 1995   | 36  | 109  | 17  | 37  | 8  | 3  | 3  | 15  | 3  | 2  | 11  | .339 | .354 | .550 |
| Career | 515 | 1609 | 170 | 414 | 79 | 16 | 44 | 208 | 17 | 83 | 295 | .257 | .301 | .408 |

## 1995 Season

After spending the 1994 season with the Yakult Swallows of the Japanese League, former Padre and Rockie outfielder Jerald Clark returned to the majors with the Twins last year. Clark was terrific when he was healthy, hitting .339 with good power, but he wasn't healthy very often. He missed most of the season with a strained right knee.

## Hitting & Defense

Clark isn't a big home-run hitter, but he has good power to the gaps, and he's capable of hitting 10-15 dingers a year. He loves the fastball and he's a notorious hacker, drawing only two walks last season. He's an excellent athlete with above-average speed when the knee isn't bothering him, and he can steal a few bases. He can play all three outfield positions, as well as first base, but he's not a great fielder and doesn't have a good arm.

## 1996 Season

Clark played very well for the Twins, but he's 32 years old and they'd prefer to go with younger players. But .339 is .339, and if he's healthy he should be able to land another job if his salary demands are reasonable.

# Alex Cole

**Position:** CF
**Bats:** L **Throws:** L
**Ht:** 6' 0"  **Wt:** 184

**Opening Day Age:** 30
**Born:** 8/17/65 in
Fayetteville, NC
**ML Seasons:** 6

### Overall Statistics

|        | G   | AB   | R   | H   | D  | T  | HR | RBI | SB  | BB  | SO  | Avg  | OBP  | Slg  |
|--------|-----|------|-----|-----|----|----|----|-----|-----|-----|-----|------|------|------|
| 1995   | 28  | 79   | 10  | 27  | 3  | 2  | 1  | 14  | 1   | 8   | 15  | .342 | .409 | .468 |
| Career | 549 | 1688 | 273 | 477 | 53 | 25 | 5  | 110 | 143 | 209 | 285 | .283 | .362 | .352 |

## 1995 Season

Veteran outfielder Alex Cole was off to a sensational start when he suffered a broken right fibula and dislocated right ankle in a game at Milwaukee on May 30. Cole was placed on the 60-day disabled list and didn't return until late September, when he had four hitless at-bats.

## Hitting, Baserunning & Defense

Cole is a line-drive/groundball hitter who's always relied on his legs to beat out a lot of hits, so the broken leg has to be a cause for concern. He draws enough walks to be used as a leadoff man, though the Twins used him mostly as a number-two hitter last year. He has problems with lefties and needs to be platooned. Cole was always an effective basestealer prior to 1995, but his speed doesn't help him all that much in the outfield, where he gets a poor jump on the ball. His arm is weak.

## 1996 Outlook

Tom Kelly has always liked Cole, and there's a good chance the Twins will re-sign him. Speed is his biggest asset and he'll need to show that his leg has healed, but he's only 30 and should have several years left as a part-time outfielder.

# Ron Coomer

**Position:** 1B/3B
**Bats:** R **Throws:** R
**Ht:** 5'11" **Wt:** 205

**Opening Day Age:** 29
**Born:** 11/18/66 in Crest Hill, IL
**ML Seasons:** 1

## Overall Statistics

| | G | AB | R | H | D | T | HR | RBI | SB | BB | SO | Avg | OBP | Slg |
|---|---|---|---|---|---|---|---|---|---|---|---|---|---|---|
| 1995 | 37 | 101 | 15 | 26 | 3 | 1 | 5 | 19 | 0 | 9 | 11 | .257 | .324 | .455 |
| Career | 37 | 101 | 15 | 26 | 3 | 1 | 5 | 19 | 0 | 9 | 11 | .257 | .324 | .455 |

## 1995 Season

Veteran minor league infielder Ron Coomer finally got a chance to play at the big-league level when the Twins acquired him from the Dodgers last summer in the Kevin Tapani trade. Coomer didn't hit for a great average, but his power production was excellent and he worked his way into the Twins' plans for 1996.

## Hitting, Baserunning & Defense

Though he's new to the majors, Coomer is just a year shy of 30. He spent three years at the Double-A level, played for three different organizations and took awhile to establish his credentials. He's a line-drive hitter with good power to the gaps, and he's tough on left-handed pitchers—his first major league home run came off Randy Johnson. He had problems with righties, however, and might need to be platooned. He can play both first and third acceptably; he has pretty decent range, but his arm is erratic. Coomer's a slow runner and no threat to steal.

## 1996 Outlook

Coomer is one of many Twins fighting for playing time at the infield corners. Given his lefty/righty splits, his best chance might be in a platoon situation with someone like Scott Stahoviak. The thing most in his favor is that the Twins need help at both his primary positions.

# Chip Hale

**Position:** DH
**Bats:** L **Throws:** R
**Ht:** 5'11" **Wt:** 186

**Opening Day Age:** 31
**Born:** 12/2/64 in Santa Clara, CA
**ML Seasons:** 5

## Overall Statistics

| | G | AB | R | H | D | T | HR | RBI | SB | BB | SO | Avg | OBP | Slg |
|---|---|---|---|---|---|---|---|---|---|---|---|---|---|---|
| 1995 | 69 | 103 | 10 | 27 | 4 | 0 | 2 | 18 | 0 | 11 | 20 | .262 | .333 | .359 |
| Career | 234 | 476 | 54 | 134 | 22 | 1 | 6 | 62 | 2 | 46 | 58 | .282 | .349 | .370 |

## 1995 Season

One of baseball's best pinch hitters, Chip Hale had another good season in 1995. Hale collected 14 pinch hits and batted .298 when practicing his specialty, and he hit .400 with men in scoring position. Hale didn't perform as well when used as a designated hitter, but overall he posted another successful season.

## Hitting, Baserunning & Defense

Hale doesn't have much power, but he has a nice quick stroke and the ability to handle anybody's fastball. He likes to go after the first pitch, and a hurler who can get ahead of him in the count usually won't have much trouble. Though he seldom plays in the field, Hale isn't a bad infielder, especially at second base. He can also fill in at first and third. He doesn't have much speed and he's a below-average baserunner.

## 1996 Outlook

A specialist like Hale is always a slump away from a ticket out of town, and even when he's going well he has to be willing to work cheap. Hale keeps on hitting and his salary demands remain reasonable, so he figures to stay in Minnesota, pounding out those pinch hits.

# Dan Masteller

**Position**: 1B/RF
**Bats**: L **Throws**: L
**Ht**: 6' 0" **Wt**: 190

**Opening Day Age**: 28
**Born**: 3/17/68 in
Toledo, Ohio
**ML Seasons**: 1

## Overall Statistics

|  | G | AB | R | H | D | T | HR | RBI | SB | BB | SO | Avg | OBP | Slg |
|---|---|---|---|---|---|---|---|---|---|---|---|---|---|---|
| 1995 | 71 | 198 | 21 | 47 | 12 | 0 | 3 | 21 | 1 | 18 | 19 | .237 | .303 | .343 |
| Career | 71 | 198 | 21 | 47 | 12 | 0 | 3 | 21 | 1 | 18 | 19 | .237 | .303 | .343 |

## 1995 Season

Dan Masteller made headlines in 1995 not for his performance, but because of his status as a replacement player. Masteller may not have been the most popular player on the Twins after deciding to cross the picket line, but the club liked his work ethic and his ability to play several positions.

## Hitting, Baserunning & Defense

Masteller got off to a slow start after joining the Twins, understandable considering the controversy surrounding his replacement status. However, he finished solidly. He's a contact hitter with a short stroke but not much power. A lefty swinger, he has problems with southpaws and probably won't ever be more than a platoon player. He's a battler, and though he hit only three home runs, they came off Jack McDowell, Lee Smith and Kevin Appier. Masteller has a good glove at first base but is just average in the outfield, with a so-so arm. He has only average speed on the bases, but doesn't make mistakes.

## 1996 Outlook

Masteller doesn't figure to play regularly at the major league level, but the Twins think he could be a useful bench player. Minnesota manager Tom Kelly likes his hustle and intensity, and sees a little of himself in Masteller. He has a good chance to stick around this year.

# Matt Merullo

**Position**: C/DH
**Bats**: L **Throws**: R
**Ht**: 6' 2" **Wt**: 200

**Opening Day Age**: 30
**Born**: 8/4/65 in
Ridgefield, CT
**ML Seasons**: 6

## Overall Statistics

|  | G | AB | R | H | D | T | HR | RBI | SB | BB | SO | Avg | OBP | Slg |
|---|---|---|---|---|---|---|---|---|---|---|---|---|---|---|
| 1995 | 76 | 195 | 19 | 55 | 14 | 1 | 1 | 27 | 0 | 14 | 27 | .282 | .335 | .379 |
| Career | 223 | 496 | 37 | 116 | 17 | 2 | 7 | 59 | 0 | 32 | 69 | .234 | .281 | .319 |

## 1995 Season

Matt Merullo is a left-handed-hitting catcher with a fine minor league hitting record but no success in the majors prior to 1995. Merullo entered the year with a .203 lifetime average, but Twins gave him another chance, and he proved beyond any doubt that he could handle major league pitching. He did have problems behind the plate, but that was no major surprise.

## Hitting, Baserunning & Defense

Merullo is a line-drive hitter who won't hit many homers, but he has good power to the gaps. He has a smooth stroke and can hold his own against lefties. He doesn't walk a whole lot, but he doesn't strike out much, either. Merullo gives it his best shot behind the plate, but he's not a good catcher, and his arm is a real liability. He's a slow baserunner.

## 1996 Outlook

Merullo proved last year that his minor league success was no fluke, and that he can handle major league pitching. Unfortunately, he also proved that he's a very poor catcher. He can help a lot of clubs with his bat, but if he gets more than 200 at-bats, it'll probably be as a first baseman or designated hitter.

# Jeff Reboulet

**Position:** SS/1B/2B/3B
**Bats:** R **Throws:** R
**Ht:** 6' 0" **Wt:** 171

**Opening Day Age:** 31
**Born:** 4/30/64 in
Dayton, OH
**ML Seasons:** 4
**Pronunciation:**
REB-uh-lay

## Overall Statistics

|  | G | AB | R | H | D | T | HR | RBI | SB | BB | SO | Avg | OBP | Slg |
|---|---|---|---|---|---|---|---|---|---|---|---|---|---|---|
| 1995 | 87 | 216 | 39 | 63 | 11 | 0 | 4 | 23 | 1 | 27 | 34 | .292 | .373 | .398 |
| Career | 343 | 782 | 115 | 200 | 37 | 2 | 9 | 77 | 9 | 103 | 120 | .256 | .346 | .343 |

## 1995 Season

Jeff Reboulet has been a fine bench player for the Twins for several seasons now, and the 1995 campaign was his best yet. Reboulet batted a career-high .292 while playing all four infield positions, and he even filled in behind the plate on one occasion. He was a terror in midsummer, batting .391 in July and August.

## Hitting, Baserunning & Defense

A very disciplined hitter, Reboulet knows how to work a count and he seldom swings at a bad pitch. He's not a home-run threat, but he gets a fair number of extra-base hits for a middle infielder. In the field, Reboulet can do a good job just about anywhere, but he's best at shortstop, where he has above-average range. His throwing arm can be erratic, however. At 31, Reboulet has lost a little speed, but he's a solid baserunner. He's not much of a threat to steal, however.

## 1996 Outlook

Prior to 1995, Reboulet never hit as high as .292 even in the minors, and he can't really be expected to repeat his performance. But he's a useful role player even hitting 50 points lower than that, and he figures to help the Twins this year.

# Rich Robertson

**Position:** RP/SP
**Bats:** L **Throws:** L
**Ht:** 6' 4" **Wt:** 175

**Opening Day Age:** 27
**Born:** 9/15/68 in
Nacogdoches, TX
**ML Seasons:** 3

## Overall Statistics

|  | W | L | Pct. | ERA | G | GS | Sv | IP | H | BB | SO | HR | BR/IP |
|---|---|---|---|---|---|---|---|---|---|---|---|---|---|
| 1995 | 2 | 0 | 1.000 | 3.83 | 25 | 4 | 0 | 51.2 | 48 | 31 | 38 | 4 | 1.53 |
| Career | 2 | 1 | .667 | 4.72 | 42 | 4 | 0 | 76.1 | 83 | 45 | 51 | 6 | 1.68 |

## 1995 Season

Former Pirate Rich Robertson was one of the few bright lights on the shell-shocked Minnesota pitching staff last year. Robertson was outstanding in three late-season starts, going 2-0 with a 1.50 ERA, and overall he was one of the most effective pitchers on the staff. The Twins are desperate for a lefty starter, and Robertson's performance put him in the running for a rotation spot in 1996.

## Pitching & Defense

A slick lefthander, Robertson tries to keep the ball down and get the batter to hit the ball on the ground. His fastball is only low- to mid-80s, but the pitch has good movement, and he gets a surprising number of strikeouts both with the fastball and his sharp-breaking curve. Control has been a problem for him, but when he throws strikes he can be very effective. He has a good move to first and fields his position smartly.

## 1996 Outlook

Robertson spent five seasons in the minors, but he's only 27 and may just now be coming into his own. His performance late last year greatly impressed the Twins' brass, and barring disaster he's almost certain to be one of the club's starters when they break camp.

# Other Minnesota Twins

### Bernardo Brito (Pos: DH, Age: 32, Bats: R)

Crash Davis was a piker compared to Bernando Brito, who's hit 278 minor league homers but had only 73 major league at-bats. The Twins gave Btito his release last summer, allowing him to sign with a Japanese team. 1996 Outlook: D

### Kevin Campbell (Pos: RHP, Age: 31)

Considering how badly the Twins needed pitching, it's surprising they didn't give Campbell more of a chance. His control is not very good, but he's as good as many relievers who've had more chances. 1996 Outlook: C

### Steve Dunn (Pos: 1B, Age: 25, Bats: L)

A first baseman with impressive size, Dunn has batted .300 at several minor league stops, and hit as many as 26 homers. He probably won't hit that many in the majors, but he could hit .280 with 15 homers. 1996 Outlook: A

### Greg W. Harris (Pos: RHP, Age: 32)

This is the Greg Harris who throws with *one* hand, and the one who used to be a good pitcher with the Padres. Last five major league ERAs: 2.23, 4.12, 4.59, 6.65, 8.82. How high can it go? 1996 Outlook: C

### Denny Hocking (Pos: SS, Age: 25, Throws: B)

Hocking's had two decent years at Salt Lake, and he's about ready. Below-average hitter but not horrible, good speed, pretty good glove, hustling type that Tom Kelly usually likes, but for some reason he hasn't gotten much of a chance yet. 1996 Outlook: B

### Vince Horsman (Pos: LHP, Age: 29)

Hey, Tony La Russa: you left the bullpen gate open and a Hors(man) escaped! Your basic lefty specialist, good in the right situation with the right manager, but this doesn't look like the place for him. 1996 Outlook: C

### Riccardo Ingram (Pos: OF/DH, Age: 29, Bats: R)

Ingram's spent the last four seasons in Triple-A, hitting a little better each year, capped by a .348 season at Salt Lake last year. Bad glove, probably not enough power to be a major league DH. 1996 Outlook: C

### Scott Klingenbeck (Pos: RHP, Age: 25)

A righty swingman, Klingenbeck came to the Twins in the Scott Erickson deal with the O's. He was a good starter in the minors, but didn't pitch well in the majors last year. Still a fine prospect. 1996 Outlook: A

### Oscar Munoz (Pos: RHP, Age: 26)

Munoz is big, strong, and throws pretty hard, with some impressive records up through Double-A ball. His Triple-A and major league work hasn't been as good; he may need another pitch. 1996 Outlook: C

### Jose Parra (Pos: RHP, Age: 23)

Parra came to the Twins in the Tapani deal. He has a good fastball and slider, but struggles with his control. Only 23, he probably needs more minor league seasoning. 1996 Outlook: B

### Brian Raabe (Pos: 2B, Age: 28, Bats: R)

A 28-year-old second baseman, Raabe has had two .300 seasons in Triple-A. Runs well, not a great glove man, and obviously he's not going to beat out Knoblauch. Could stick as a utility man. 1996 Outlook: C

### Mo Sanford (Pos: RHP, Age: 29)

Sanford's curveball has made him a minor league strike-out king, but in the majors he hasn't been able to throw it for strikes. He also throws a lot of gopher balls. About out of chances. 1996 Outlook: D

### Erik Schullstrom (Pos: RHP, Age: 27)

A big righthander, Schullstrom can throw in the 90s but his velocity is inconsistent. Minor league record isn't great, and he struggled in the Twins' pen last year. 1996 Outlook: C

### Scott Watkins (Pos: LHP, Age: 26)

A tall, thin lefty reliever, Watkins had 20 saves in 45 games at Salt Lake last year, but was only fair in 27 games with the Twins. His great minor league record alone gives him a chance. 1996 Outlook: B

### Carl Willis (Pos: RHP, Age: 35)

Willis had some nice seasons for the Twins, throwing a "sinker" a lot of people thought was a spitter. He appeared to reach the end of the line last year, and barring a miracle he won't be back. 1996 Outlook: D

# Minnesota Twins Minor League Prospects

## Organization Overview:

The Twins are one of those small-market teams which depend on a thriving farm system in order to remain competitive. In recent years, the Twins have lost Shane Mack to Japan, and Kevin Tapani and Rick Aguilera in trades because the club just couldn't afford to sign them. The pitching situation is particularly troubling, given Minnesota's recent difficulty in developing competent hurlers. The Twins have provided extensive big-league trials to highly-regarded talent such as Pat Mahomes, Mike Trombley, LaTroy Hawkins and Eddie Guardado, but each has struggled. The Twins enjoyed more success last season with a an outfielder: Rookie of the Year Marty Cordova. The Twins still haven't given up on some of the pitchers who've failed to live up to expectations. But their best prospect is probably Todd Walker, at this point a second baseman (see below).

### LaTroy Hawkins

**Position:** P    **Opening Day Age:** 23
**Bats:** R **Throws:** R    **Born:** 12/21/72 in
**Ht:** 6' 5" **Wt:** 195    Gary, IN

*Recent Statistics*

|  | W | L | ERA | G | GS | Sv | IP | H | R | BB | SO | HR |
|---|---|---|---|---|---|---|---|---|---|---|---|---|
| 95 AAA Salt Lake | 9 | 7 | 3.55 | 22 | 22 | 0 | 144.1 | 150 | 63 | 40 | 74 | 7 |
| 95 AL Minnesota | 2 | 3 | 8.67 | 6 | 6 | 0 | 27.0 | 39 | 29 | 12 | 9 | 3 |

The Twins' pitching staff has been a mess the last few seasons, and Minnesota entertained hopes that Hawkins was ready to help at age 22 last year. After all, no minor league pitcher won more games than the 18 Hawkins accumulated between three levels in 1994. Unfortunately, by May he had proven he was overmatched by big-league hitters, losing all three of his starts while compiling a 13.50 ERA. Dispatched back to Triple-A, Hawkins pitched better as the season progressed, and actually won two games upon his return to the Twins in September. He still has his 90-plus fastball and a loose, live arm, so he'll get more opportunities with the Twins. And soon.

### Torii Hunter

**Position:** OF    **Opening Day Age:** 20
**Bats:** R **Throws:** R    **Born:** 7/18/75 in Pine
**Ht:** 6' 2" **Wt:** 205    Bluff, AR

*Recent Statistics*

|  | G | AB | R | H | D | T | HR | RBI | SB | BB | SO | AVG |
|---|---|---|---|---|---|---|---|---|---|---|---|---|
| 93 R Twins | 28 | 100 | 6 | 19 | 3 | 0 | 0 | 8 | 4 | 4 | 23 | .190 |
| 94 A Fort Wayne | 91 | 335 | 57 | 98 | 17 | 1 | 10 | 50 | 8 | 25 | 80 | .293 |
| 95 A Fort Myers | 113 | 391 | 64 | 96 | 15 | 2 | 7 | 36 | 7 | 38 | 77 | .246 |

Hunter's 1995 season was a disappointment, in that his numbers fell off after the short jump from slow- to fast-A. Since the Twins expended a first-round pick to select Hunter in 1993, they were expecting better re-

sults. He's a potential five-tool talent, possessing home run power and far-ranging speed in center field. One hopeful sign for future improvement was better plate discipline last year. His 38 walks were a career high, and though he fanned 77 times, he actually reduced his strikeout rate. Hunter is probably at least two seasons removed from Minnesota.

### Matt Lawton

**Position:** OF    **Opening Day Age:** 24
**Bats:** L **Throws:** R    **Born:** 11/3/71 in
**Ht:** 5' 9" **Wt:** 180    Gulfport, MS

*Recent Statistics*

|  | G | AB | R | H | D | T | HR | RBI | SB | BB | SO | AVG |
|---|---|---|---|---|---|---|---|---|---|---|---|---|
| 95 AA New Britain | 114 | 412 | 75 | 111 | 19 | 5 | 13 | 54 | 26 | 56 | 70 | .269 |
| 95 AL Minnesota | 21 | 60 | 11 | 19 | 4 | 1 | 1 | 12 | 1 | 7 | 11 | .317 |
| 95 MLE | 114 | 408 | 74 | 107 | 18 | 4 | 13 | 53 | 21 | 48 | 77 | .262 |

Lawton has now delivered three straight solid seasons in Minnesota's system, and he wasn't overwhelmed by last year's jump to Double-A New Britain. Though his average sank to .269, Lawton continued to score lots of runs because he still drew walks and stole bases. He also improved his slugging percentage by cracking a career-high 13 homers. Lawton plays an adequate center field and does the kinds of things which help a team's offense. However, he turned 24 years of age in November, has yet to reach Triple-A, and is actually three months older than Rich Becker, with whom he may compete for playing time.

### Travis Miller

**Position:** P    **Opening Day Age:** 23
**Bats:** R **Throws:** L    **Born:** 11/2/72 in
**Ht:** 6' 3" **Wt:** 205    Dayton, OH

*Recent Statistics*

|  | W | L | ERA | G | GS | Sv | IP | H | R | BB | SO | HR |
|---|---|---|---|---|---|---|---|---|---|---|---|---|
| 94 A Fort Wayne | 4 | 1 | 2.60 | 11 | 9 | 0 | 55.1 | 52 | 17 | 12 | 50 | 2 |
| 94 AA Nashville | 0 | 0 | 2.84 | 1 | 1 | 0 | 6.1 | 3 | 3 | 2 | 4 | 0 |
| 95 AA New Britain | 7 | 9 | 4.37 | 28 | 27 | 0 | 162.2 | 172 | 93 | 65 | 151 | 17 |

Miller is the player the Twins have to show for failing to sign catcher Jason Varitek. When Varitek refused to ink a contract with the Twins after they chose him in the first round of '93, Minnesota received a supplemental pick in '94 and used it to grab Miller. So far, Miller has done his best to compensate. The lefthander pitched in Double-A last season at 22 and posted a respectable strikeout-to-innings ratio, a good indicator of future success. He'll likely face a strong test this season in the stronger hitting environment of the Pacific Coast League. If he passes, he should eventually join Dustin Hermanson in the majors. The two were teammate at Kent University, and both were selected in the 1994 draft.

## Dan Serafini

**Position:** P
**Bats:** B **Throws:** L
**Ht:** 6' 1" **Wt:** 185

**Opening Day Age:** 22
**Born:** 1/25/74 in San Francisco, CA

### Recent Statistics

|  | W | L | ERA | G | GS | Sv | IP | H | R | BB | SO | HR |
|---|---|---|---|---|---|---|---|---|---|---|---|---|
| 93 A Fort Wayne | 10 | 8 | 3.65 | 27 | 27 | 0 | 140.2 | 117 | 72 | 83 | 147 | 5 |
| 94 A Fort Myers | 9 | 9 | 4.61 | 23 | 23 | 0 | 136.2 | 149 | 84 | 57 | 130 | 11 |
| 95 AA New Britain | 12 | 9 | 3.38 | 27 | 27 | 0 | 162.2 | 155 | 74 | 72 | 123 | 7 |
| 95 AAA Salt Lake | 0 | 0 | 6.75 | 1 | 0 | 1 | 4.0 | 4 | 3 | 1 | 4 | 2 |

Serafini was the Twins' first draft selection in 1992, the 26th player taken overall. He's made steady, though uneven progress throughout his career. After moving up to fast-A in '94, Serafini actually improved his record and ERA in making the jump to Double-A last year. His fastball is only average velocity-wise, but for a left-hander with his movement it's still a strikeout pitch. Serafini's curve also has a sharp break to it, though it's one of the pitches he's still working on. Serafini will likely begin 1996 in Triple-A. At 22, he's on target for a rotation spot in Minnesota in the near future.

## Hector Trinidad

**Position:** P
**Bats:** R **Throws:** R
**Ht:** 6' 2" **Wt:** 190

**Opening Day Age:** 22
**Born:** 9/8/73 in Los Angeles, CA

### Recent Statistics

|  | W | L | ERA | G | GS | Sv | IP | H | R | BB | SO | HR |
|---|---|---|---|---|---|---|---|---|---|---|---|---|
| 93 A Peoria | 7 | 6 | 2.47 | 22 | 22 | 0 | 153.0 | 142 | 56 | 29 | 118 | 6 |
| 93 AA Orlando | 1 | 3 | 6.57 | 4 | 4 | 0 | 24.2 | 34 | 19 | 7 | 13 | 5 |
| 94 A Daytona | 11 | 9 | 3.23 | 28 | 27 | 0 | 175.2 | 171 | 72 | 40 | 142 | 8 |
| 95 AA New Britain | 4 | 11 | 4.61 | 23 | 22 | 0 | 121.0 | 137 | 67 | 22 | 92 | 6 |

Trinidad's 1995 season was not quite as bad as his 4-11 record would indicate. He continued to walk very few batters, and his strikeout-to-walk ratio, always excellent, was 4.18-to-1. He allowed just six home runs in over 120 innings. Trinidad was originally a sixth-round draft pick of the Cubs. He was sent to the Twins as compensation for the Cubs' acquisition of club president Andy MacPhail. Trinidad doesn't throw hard, so he must have command of all his pitches in order to be effective.

## Jose Valentin

**Position:** C
**Bats:** B **Throws:** R
**Ht:** 5' 10" **Wt:** 185

**Opening Day Age:** 20
**Born:** 9/19/75 in Manati, PR

### Recent Statistics

|  | G | AB | R | H | D | T | HR | RBI | SB | BB | SO | AVG |
|---|---|---|---|---|---|---|---|---|---|---|---|---|
| 93 R Twins | 32 | 103 | 18 | 27 | 6 | 1 | 1 | 19 | 0 | 14 | 19 | .262 |
| 93 R Elizabethtn | 9 | 24 | 3 | 5 | 1 | 0 | 0 | 3 | 0 | 4 | 2 | .208 |
| 94 R Elizabethtn | 54 | 210 | 23 | 44 | 5 | 0 | 9 | 27 | 0 | 15 | 44 | .210 |
| 95 A Fort Wayne | 112 | 383 | 59 | 123 | 26 | 5 | 19 | 65 | 0 | 47 | 75 | .321 |

Valentin's brother, also named Jose, plays shortstop for the Brewers. This Jose is making a name for himself with both his hitting and his defensive work behind the plate. The Twins drafted Valentin in the third round of 1993 out of Puerto Rico, and he followed with two rather lackluster seasons in rookie ball. He broke out in a big way last year, hitting .321 with 19 homers at Class-A Fort Wayne. He was also voted the Midwest League's best defensive catcher. There aren't many commodities more valuable than a switch-hitting catcher with power. Valentin's throwing arm draws raves, but he does need work on calling a game.

## Todd Walker

**Position:** 2B
**Bats:** L **Throws:** R
**Ht:** 6' 0" **Wt:** 180

**Opening Day Age:** 22
**Born:** 5/25/73 in Bakersfield, CA

### Recent Statistics

|  | G | AB | R | H | D | T | HR | RBI | SB | BB | SO | AVG |
|---|---|---|---|---|---|---|---|---|---|---|---|---|
| 94 A Fort Myers | 46 | 171 | 29 | 52 | 5 | 2 | 10 | 34 | 6 | 32 | 15 | .304 |
| 95 AA New Britain | 137 | 513 | 83 | 149 | 27 | 3 | 21 | 85 | 23 | 63 | 101 | .290 |
| 95 MLE | 137 | 508 | 82 | 144 | 26 | 2 | 22 | 84 | 18 | 54 | 111 | .283 |

Walker has hit at every level. He was drafted by the Twins in the first round in 1994 after a glorious career at Louisiana State in which he helped lead the Tigers to a College World Series championship and was twice named All-American. Walker's range of offensive skills are broad and deep. He draws walks, steals bases, and hits for both average and power, as exhibited by the 21 homers he clubbed for New Britain, whose Beehive Field is notorious as a hitter's graveyard. Drafted as a second baseman, Walker's defensive deficiencies were expected to force a move to third, but he improved that area of his game as well last season. With Chuck Knoblauch in Minnesota, a position switch is still likely.

## Others to Watch

On the surface, outfielder **Rafael Alvarez'** season may not look impressive (.283, 5 HR, 36 RBI), but keep in mind he accomplished that at the age of 18 in the Midwest League. . . Righthander **Marc Barcelo**, another first-rounder from '93, looked like a world beater in '94 (11-6, 2.65 at Double-A), but crashed to earth last year (8-13, 7.05 ERA at Triple-A). If there's no long-term arm problem, he can still recover. . . **Troy Carrasco** (12-4, 3.13) turned in an awfully impressive season for a 20-year-old lefthander in only his second full pro season. . . **Jake Patterson**, a 31st-round selection in 1993, hit 14 homers at Fort Wayne last season, a year after clubbing 18 in 63 games at rookie-level Elizabethton. He may not have a defensive position, however. . . The Twins selected **Benj Sampson**, a left-hander from an Iowa high school, in the sixth round in '93. Sampson has pitched okay the last two seasons in A-ball (17-18, 3.63 ERA). . . Second baseman **Mitch Simons** has hit .317 and .325 with doubles power and at least 30 stolen bases the last last two seasons at Double- and Triple-A. He's now 27 years old, though, and faces big obstacles in Chuck Knoblauch and Todd Walker.

# Wade Boggs

## 1995 Season

Wade Boggs started and ended the last year of his Yankee contract in a big way. He batted .400 in the first nine games (New York was 7-2), and didn't make an error in the field until July 14. His .354 tear after moving into the leadoff slot August 4 helped the Yanks go 34-22 thereafter. Also during the hot streak, he collected his 2,500th major league hit. A strained left hamstring kept him out of the final three games.

## Hitting

Boggs is a wizard with the bat. His inside-out swing lines single after single to left-center field, and he knows how to turn on the ball to take advantage of Yankee Stadium's short right-field porch. He is at his best in day games. No hitter since Ted Williams has been able to influence umpires' strike zones on the basis of his batting eye more than Boggs. He's also an excellent two-strike hitter, though his strikeout total rose a bit in '95.

## Baserunning & Defense

Buck Showalter's managing style, rarely using the stolen base, allowed him to use Boggs as the lead-off batter even though he has almost no speed (one steal in two attempts). Boggs plays the game intelligently on the bases and in the field. He could always hit, but he's worked hard and successfully to overcome the defensive mediocrity that marked his early career. Shrewd positioning and good hands turned him into a Gold Glover in 1994, and he garnered the award again in '95.

## 1996 Outlook

The Yankees ended the 1995 season facing a decision as to which singles-hitting, free-agent corner infielder to re-sign—Boggs or Don Mattingly. But Mattingly made the decision moot when he announced a tentative retirement. That greatly increased the likelihood that Boggs would return to the Bronx, and he'll play regularly whether at third base, first, or even designated hitter.

**Position:** 3B
**Bats:** L  **Throws:** R
**Ht:** 6' 2"  **Wt:** 197

**Opening Day Age:** 37
**Born:** 6/15/58 in Omaha, NE
**ML Seasons:** 14

### Overall Statistics

|  | G | AB | R | H | D | T | HR | RBI | SB | BB | SO | Avg | OBP | Slg |
|---|---|---|---|---|---|---|---|---|---|---|---|---|---|---|
| 1995 | 126 | 460 | 76 | 149 | 22 | 4 | 5 | 63 | 1 | 74 | 50 | .324 | .412 | .422 |
| Career 1991 | 7599 | 1287 | 2541 | 489 | 53 | 103 | 864 | 19 | 1213 | 598 | .334 | .424 | .453 |

### Where He Hits the Ball

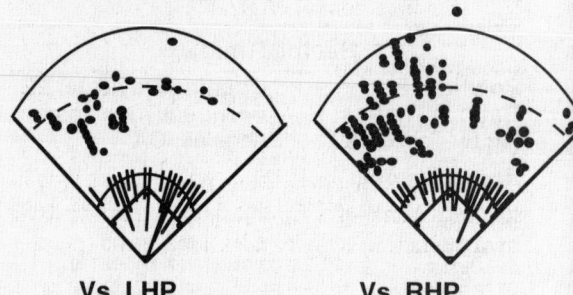

**Vs. LHP**          **Vs. RHP**

### 1995 Situational Stats

|  | AB | H | HR | RBI | Avg |  | AB | H | HR | RBI | Avg |
|---|---|---|---|---|---|---|---|---|---|---|---|
| Home | 253 | 96 | 4 | 35 | .379 | LHP | 132 | 41 | 1 | 15 | .311 |
| Road | 207 | 53 | 1 | 28 | .256 | RHP | 328 | 108 | 4 | 48 | .329 |
| First Half | 207 | 61 | 2 | 28 | .295 | Sc Pos | 112 | 34 | 1 | 56 | .304 |
| Scnd Half | 253 | 88 | 3 | 35 | .348 | Clutch | 56 | 14 | 2 | 9 | .250 |

### 1995 Rankings (American League)

→ 1st in batting average at home (.379), fielding percentage at third base (.981), lowest percentage of swings that missed (5.3%) and lowest percentage of swings on the first pitch (7.0%)

→ 2nd in most pitches seen per plate appearance (4.32), on-base percentage for a leadoff hitter (.420) and batting average with two strikes (.285)

→ 3rd in highest percentage of pitches taken (65.9%)

→ Led the Yankees in batting average, singles (118), and on-base percentage

# David Cone

## 1995 Season

When Toronto traded David Cone to the Yankees for three minor league pitchers on July 28, New York was one game under .500. Toronto won just 20 more games, but the Yanks finished 38-23 and made it to the playoffs, with Cone's 9-2 stretch run a big key. He went at least 6.1 innings in every start with his new team. So he solidified the rotation, and took pressure off the bullpen. Overall, he won 18 games, the second-highest total of his career.

## Pitching

Few pitchers have Cone's extensive repertoire. His best pitch is his split-fingered fastball, but he also throws a high-velocity fastball and a slider, both with fine control. Against right-handed batters, he can drop down to throw his "Laredo" sidearm slider. With the Jays, Cone let his defense do much of the work instead of trying for strikeouts. He put that strategy on hold with the Yankees, increasing his strikeout ratio to 8.1 per nine innings. That meant a lot of pitches—126 per start as a Yank—for Cone, who led the American League in innings, batters faced and pitches thrown.

## Defense

Cone is overcoming a tendency earlier in his career to blow up easily and make bad plays in the field. He now is a fair fielder. However, he still has trouble holding runners and getting the ball to the plate quickly. He has consistently allowed 75 percent of basestealers to advance successfully, and permitted 28 steals in 1995.

## 1996 Outlook

Cone ended the '95 season again eligible for free agency. The Yankees were hoping to re-sign him, but faced lots of competition. Last year's finish elevated the perception of Cone as a competitor who can carry a pitching staff, and a team, on his back. He won one playoff game, and led another but ran out of gas after throwing 147 pitches against Seattle. He remains one of the majors' best pitchers.

**Position:** SP
**Bats:** L **Throws:** R
**Ht:** 6' 1" **Wt:** 190

**Opening Day Age:** 33
**Born:** 1/2/63 in Kansas City, MO
**ML Seasons:** 10

### Overall Statistics

|  | W | L | Pct. | ERA | G | GS | Sv | IP | H | BB | SO | HR | BR/IP |
|---|---|---|---|---|---|---|---|---|---|---|---|---|---|
| 1995 | 18 | 8 | .692 | 3.57 | 30 | 30 | 0 | 229.1 | 195 | 88 | 191 | 24 | 1.23 |
| Career | 129 | 78 | .623 | 3.17 | 288 | 259 | 1 | 1922.0 | 1589 | 716 | 1741 | 151 | 1.20 |

### How Often He Throws Strikes

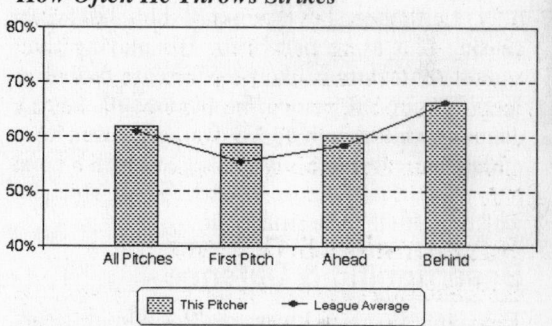

### 1995 Situational Stats

|  | W | L | ERA | Sv | IP |  | AB | H | HR | RBI | Avg |
|---|---|---|---|---|---|---|---|---|---|---|---|
| Home | 10 | 3 | 3.27 | 0 | 104.2 | LHB | 497 | 116 | 13 | 52 | .233 |
| Road | 8 | 5 | 3.83 | 0 | 124.2 | RHB | 358 | 79 | 11 | 35 | .221 |
| First Half | 7 | 5 | 3.64 | 0 | 106.1 | Sc Pos | 197 | 47 | 5 | 62 | .239 |
| Scnd Half | 11 | 3 | 3.51 | 0 | 123.0 | Clutch | 97 | 18 | 4 | 10 | .186 |

### 1995 Rankings (American League)

➡ 1st in innings pitched , batters faced (954) and pitches thrown (3,719)
➡ 2nd in wins, pickoff throws (219), stolen bases allowed (28) and least GDPs induced per 9 innings (0.4)
➡ 3rd in shutouts (2) and errors at pitcher (3)
➡ 4th in complete games (6), strikeouts, wild pitches (11), lowest groundball/flyball ratio allowed (0.9), highest stolen base percentage allowed (75.7%) and lowest fielding percentage at pitcher (.929)
➡ Led the Yankees in lowest batting average allowed vs. left-handed batters (.225)

# Tony Fernandez

## 1995 Season

The Yankees signed Tony Fernandez as a free agent in December, 1994. Though he played third base for Cincinnati in 1994, New York returned him to shortstop, where he'd played his first 11 seasons. Fernandez missed time early last year after suffering a rib-cage injury; then in September he sat out because of a knee injury. His season highlight came August 1, when his two-run single in the seventh inning beat Milwaukee. When it ended he'd batted .245, the worst average of his 13-year career.

## Hitting

Fernandez may now be a switch-hitter in name only. Lefthanders overpowered him last year, causing him to be platooned. His playing time against southpaws is likely to decrease further in 1996. Batting left-handed, Fernandez still can be a dangerous hitter with above-average power for a middle infielder. He also has good strike-zone judgment; last season was the seventh in which he walked more than he struck out.

## Baserunning & Defense

The young Fernandez was good for 20-plus steals a year. The current version managed just six, with a 50-percent success rate, in '95. He still has an exasperating tendency to lose concentration and make baserunning and fielding errors. People question Fernandez's arm because of his nonchalant manner of flipping the ball to first base, but he still can go into the hole and make a seemingly underhand toss on target and on time.

## 1996 Outlook

Fernandez signed a two-year deal worth $3 million through 1996. The thinking was that he could play shortstop one year, then help break in Derek Jeter. Fernandez will likely be hitting near the bottom of the order. If Jeter shows he can handle the position, expect Fernandez to become a backup or be sent elsewhere. His injury history and sometimes-difficult personality make him a questionable candidate for a utility role.

**Position:** SS
**Bats:** B **Throws:** R
**Ht:** 6' 2" **Wt:** 175

**Opening Day Age:** 33
**Born:** 6/30/62 in San Pedro de Macoris, DR
**ML Seasons:** 13

### Overall Statistics

| | G | AB | R | H | D | T | HR | RBI | SB | BB | SO | Avg | OBP | Slg |
|---|---|---|---|---|---|---|---|---|---|---|---|---|---|---|
| 1995 | 108 | 384 | 57 | 94 | 20 | 2 | 5 | 45 | 6 | 42 | 40 | .245 | .322 | .346 |
| Career | 1682 | 6408 | 847 | 1808 | 312 | 89 | 66 | 638 | 220 | 538 | 605 | .282 | .339 | .390 |

### Where He Hits the Ball

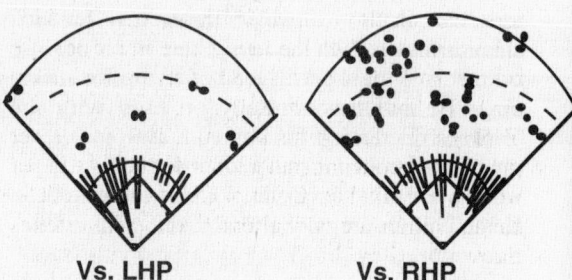

Vs. LHP          Vs. RHP

### 1995 Situational Stats

| | AB | H | HR | RBI | Avg | | AB | H | HR | RBI | Avg |
|---|---|---|---|---|---|---|---|---|---|---|---|
| Home | 189 | 47 | 3 | 23 | .249 | LHP | 128 | 25 | 2 | 13 | .195 |
| Road | 195 | 47 | 2 | 22 | .241 | RHP | 256 | 69 | 3 | 32 | .270 |
| First Half | 191 | 46 | 2 | 25 | .241 | Sc Pos | 101 | 29 | 1 | 40 | .287 |
| Scnd Half | 193 | 48 | 3 | 20 | .249 | Clutch | 56 | 14 | 0 | 7 | .250 |

### 1995 Rankings (American League)

- ➡ 2nd in lowest batting average vs. left-handed pitchers (.195), lowest slugging percentage vs. left-handed pitchers (.266) and lowest on-base percentage vs. left-handed pitchers (.241)
- ➡ 5th in fielding percentage at shortstop (.976)
- ➡ 7th in lowest percentage of swings that missed (10.3%)
- ➡ 8th in most GDPs per GDP situation (17.7%)
- ➡ 9th in errors at shortstop (10)
- ➡ Led the Yankees in caught stealing (6) and highest percentage of extra bases taken as a runner (56.5%)

# Sterling Hitchcock

## 1995 Season

Sterling Hitchcock spent much of the season dodging trade rumors and the wrath of George Steinbrenner. The lefthander was mentioned in various trade talks that might have brought Randy Johnson or Mark Langston to the Big Apple. Steinbrenner criticized Hitchcock after just two starts; Hitchcock went out the next day and held Boston to two hits in seven innings. After missing one turn following the David Cone acquisition, he came back and finished 7-4 down the stretch.

## Pitching

Hitchcock's out pitch is a no-nonsense, 90-MPH four-seam fastball. To set up the heater, he mixes in a two-seam sinker, a splitter, a straight change and two sliders with different speeds. He is a classic power/flyball pitcher, and improved his control some last year, to 3.6 walks per nine innings. He has fair stamina, evidenced by four complete games last year, but still uses too many pitches, meaning the bullpen needs to be ready for work when Hitchcock starts. Only the better left-handed hitters are now allowed to face the southpaw, but they have obviously made some adjustments.

## Defense

Hitchcock is a steady but unspectacular fielder. His pitching style doesn't generate a lot of ground balls, so he doesn't get many assists. Hitchcock works to hold baserunners and has a good pickoff move, but in 1995 the opposition got away with 23 of 27 steal attempts, partly due to the throwing problems of the Yankee catchers.

## 1996 Outlook

Last year Hitchcock appeared solid in the rotation with a 5-1 finish, but was sent to the bullpen for the playoffs in an attempt to compensate for Steve Howe's late-season struggles. Hitchcock held up well under pennant-race pressure, but the Yankees have never been ones to value a good young arm, and in December he went to Seattle in the Tino Martinez deal. Hitchcock will almost certainly join the Mariner rotation this spring.

**Position:** SP
**Bats:** L  **Throws:** L
**Ht:** 6' 1"  **Wt:** 192

**Opening Day Age:** 24
**Born:** 4/29/71 in Fayetteville, NC
**ML Seasons:** 4

New York Yankees

### Overall Statistics

|  | W | L | Pct. | ERA | G | GS | Sv | IP | H | BB | SO | HR | BR/IP |
|---|---|---|---|---|---|---|---|---|---|---|---|---|---|
| 1995 | 11 | 10 | .524 | 4.70 | 27 | 27 | 0 | 168.1 | 155 | 68 | 121 | 22 | 1.32 |
| Career | 16 | 15 | .516 | 4.78 | 59 | 41 | 2 | 261.2 | 258 | 117 | 190 | 31 | 1.43 |

### How Often He Throws Strikes

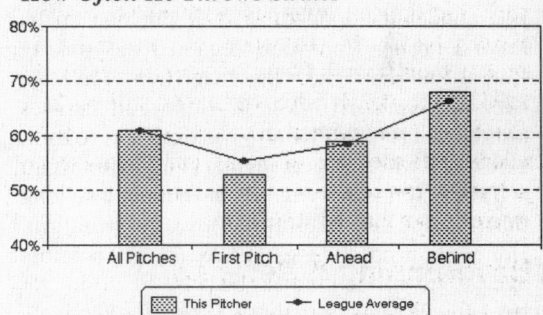

### 1995 Situational Stats

|  | W | L | ERA | Sv | IP |  | AB | H | HR | RBI | Avg |
|---|---|---|---|---|---|---|---|---|---|---|---|
| Home | 6 | 5 | 4.33 | 0 | 79.0 | LHB | 112 | 34 | 6 | 23 | .304 |
| Road | 5 | 5 | 5.04 | 0 | 89.1 | RHB | 520 | 121 | 16 | 51 | .233 |
| First Half | 3 | 5 | 5.03 | 0 | 78.2 | Sc Pos | 123 | 35 | 6 | 53 | .285 |
| Scnd Half | 8 | 5 | 4.42 | 0 | 89.2 | Clutch | 45 | 12 | 1 | 6 | .267 |

### 1995 Rankings (American League)

- 2nd in highest stolen base percentage allowed (85.2%)
- 3rd in balks (2) and most home runs allowed per 9 innings (1.18)
- 4th in most pitches thrown per batter (3.98)
- 5th in stolen bases allowed (23)
- 6th in highest ERA and lowest groundball/fly-ball ratio allowed (0.9)
- 7th in highest ERA on the road (5.04) and lowest batting average allowed vs. right-handed batters (.233)
- 8th in complete games (4) and pickoff throws (147)
- Led the Yankees in losses, hit batsmen (5) and balks (2)

# Rick Honeycutt

## 1995 Season

Part of a mini-reunion of the Glory Days Athletics, Rick Honeycutt returned to Oakland last season after a one-year stay in Texas. Amazingly, at 41 years old Honeycutt revived his long career as one of the game's best specialty left-handed relievers. He won five games and saved two more while holding left-handed hitters to a .188 average and allowing only 46 baserunners in 44.2 innings. On September 25, with the Yankees desperate for lefty bullpen as the playoffs approached, Honeycutt was sold to New York, where he pitched just one inning.

## Pitching

Back under the watchful eye of pitching coach Dave Duncan, Honeycutt regained the sinking fastball and sharp slider that made him so reliable over the years. At his best, Honeycutt induces mostly ground balls. He also has excellent control, especially when he gets regular work. Honeycutt is a great competitor who has been around so long that he doesn't get rattled in any situation. Honeycutt needs to be spotted as much as possible against left-handed hitters, because he no longer has enough velocity to throw his stuff effectively against right-handed hitters, who hit six homers off him last year. He also cannot pitch more than an inning at a time.

## Defense

Honeycutt does a good job of holding runners and will surprise baserunners with his quick move to first. He remains a good athlete whose pitching delivery leaves him in good fielding position.

## 1996 Outlook

No one knows Honeycutt better than La Russa, who extracted the maximum from him. Now, you have to wonder if another manager will have the same appreciation or interest in someone who will turn 42 this season. On the other hand, Honeycutt demonstrated last season that he still has some mileage left, and he should last as long as he can retire lefties.

**Position:** RP
**Bats:** L  **Throws:** L
**Ht:** 6' 1"  **Wt:** 195

**Opening Day Age:** 41
**Born:** 6/29/54 in Chattanooga, TN
**ML Seasons:** 19

### Overall Statistics

|        | W   | L   | Pct. | ERA  | G   | GS  | Sv | IP     | H    | BB  | SO   | HR  | BR/IP |
|--------|-----|-----|------|------|-----|-----|-----|--------|------|-----|------|-----|-------|
| 1995   | 5   | 1   | .833 | 2.96 | 52  | 0   | 2   | 45.2   | 39   | 10  | 21   | 6   | 1.07  |
| Career | 107 | 142 | .430 | 3.73 | 734 | 268 | 34  | 2110.1 | 2136 | 649 | 1006 | 182 | 1.32  |

### How Often He Throws Strikes

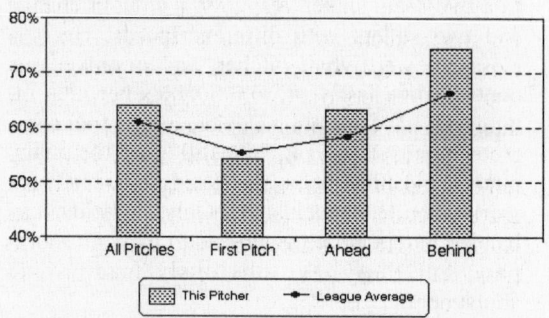

### 1995 Situational Stats

|           | W | L | ERA  | Sv | IP   |        | AB | H  | HR | RBI | Avg  |
|-----------|---|---|------|----|------|--------|----|----|----|-----|------|
| Home      | 5 | 0 | 3.32 | 1  | 19.0 | LHB    | 84 | 15 | 0  | 10  | .179 |
| Road      | 0 | 1 | 2.70 | 1  | 26.2 | RHB    | 81 | 24 | 6  | 18  | .296 |
| First Half| 4 | 1 | 3.32 | 1  | 21.2 | Sc Pos | 44 | 18 | 3  | 23  | .409 |
| Scnd Half | 1 | 0 | 2.63 | 1  | 24.0 | Clutch | 75 | 14 | 3  | 12  | .187 |

### 1995 Rankings (American League)

➡ 6th in most GDPs induced per GDP situation (20.7%)
➡ 7th in highest batting average allowed in relief with runners in scoring position (.409)
➡ 10th in holds (12)

# Steve Howe

## 1995 Season

It was not a happy year for Steve Howe. Controversy dogged him from the beginning, when he worked in the ticket office during spring training replacement games. Then there were unsubstantiated (but nonetheless publicized) rumors that he was providing amphetamines to teammates. And there was an obvious decline in Howe's performance. He started slowly, allowing 20 hits in his first 8.2 innings, then righted himself during June. But Howe was inconsistent through the summer and wasn't used much after August. By season's end, the Yankees had obtained Rick Honeycutt as a left-handed set-up man.

## Pitching

Howe's fastball can still reach the low 90s. His biggest problem last year was that he wasn't getting righthanders out by running his slider in on their hands. Righties absolutely pounded Howe in 1995. He also gave up his first home run to a left-handed batter in more than two years when Dave Nilsson connected for a two-run shot on August 2. Howe walked batters about twice as frequently as he had in 1994, and registered fewer strikeouts in critical situations.

## Defense

Howe remains a solid defensive asset, although his movement around the mound has slowed a bit with age. He has been paying somewhat more attention to baserunners recently (having more to worry about) and allowed only one steal by the opposition last year.

## 1996 Outlook

At this stage of his career, Howe is no longer a closer candidate. He lost the team's confidence, and his own job security as a set-up man, last year. Unless he regains his ability to retire right-handed batters (and that would require some team giving him the opportunity), Howe will be cast in the role of lefty-lefty match-up specialist for the remainder of his career. Nonetheless, he has come back from adversity before.

**Position:** RP
**Bats:** L **Throws:** L
**Ht:** 6' 2" **Wt:** 198

**Opening Day Age:** 38
**Born:** 3/10/58 in Pontiac, MI
**ML Seasons:** 11

### Overall Statistics

|        | W  | L  | Pct. | ERA  | G   | GS | Sv | IP    | H   | BB  | SO  | HR | BR/IP |
|--------|----|----|------|------|-----|----|----|-------|-----|-----|-----|----|-------|
| 1995   | 6  | 3  | .667 | 4.96 | 56  | 0  | 2  | 49.0  | 66  | 17  | 28  | 7  | 1.69  |
| Career | 47 | 40 | .540 | 2.93 | 472 | 0  | 90 | 589.1 | 567 | 133 | 323 | 31 | 1.19  |

### How Often He Throws Strikes

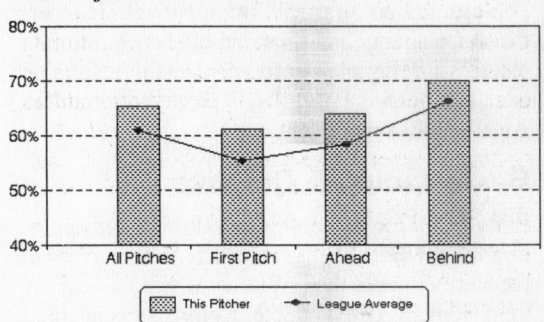

### 1995 Situational Stats

|            | W | L | ERA  | Sv | IP   |        | AB  | H  | HR | RBI | Avg  |
|------------|---|---|------|----|------|--------|-----|----|----|-----|------|
| Home       | 5 | 1 | 6.39 | 1  | 25.1 | LHB    | 79  | 19 | 1  | 10  | .241 |
| Road       | 1 | 2 | 3.42 | 1  | 23.2 | RHB    | 125 | 47 | 6  | 27  | .376 |
| First Half | 3 | 3 | 4.30 | 1  | 23.0 | Sc Pos | 73  | 26 | 2  | 31  | .356 |
| Scnd Half  | 3 | 0 | 5.54 | 1  | 26.0 | Clutch | 92  | 30 | 3  | 17  | .326 |

### 1995 Rankings (American League)

→ 1st in highest batting average allowed in relief (.324)
→ 2nd in most baserunners allowed per 9 innings in relief (16.0)
→ 6th in relief wins (6)
→ 9th in highest relief ERA (4.96)
→ Led the Yankees in relief wins (6)

New York Yankees

# Pat Kelly

## 1995 Season

Coming off a career year, Pat Kelly might have blossomed, but his 1995 season was a general collapse. He underwent arthroscopic surgery to repair a torn ligament in his left wrist June 1, and was out until July 7. When he returned, he hit so poorly—including an 0-for-21 slump—that he lost his everyday job to Randy Velarde. Kelly's best moment came September 29, when his ninth-inning homer at Toronto helped put the Yankees into the playoffs.

## Hitting

Kelly regressed at the plate partly because of his injury, but also because he hits too many flies and pop-ups and doesn't walk often enough. His performance against right-handed pitchers put him in danger of being platooned permanently. He is an excellent bunter, a useful skill at the bottom of an American League order.

## Baserunning & Defense

Kelly's defense had nothing to do with his demotion to part-time status. He made fewer errors in far more chances than Velarde at second base. A tremendously gifted athlete, Kelly also is adept at turning double plays. He has good speed and is one of the Yankees' best basestealers, but Buck Showalter sent runners less often than any other American League manager. With Showalter's departure and the arrival of new manager Joe Torre, Kelly might steal 20 bases.

## 1996 Outlook

The Yankees were unsure about offering arbitration to Kelly, because he probably would receive more than $1 million in the current market. As a free agent, he would be very attractive to a team needing defensive help at second base, bat-handling low in the order, and some speed on the bases. He's also just a year removed from a .280 season at the plate. If he can recover his offensive output, he would be an even bigger bargain. The downside is his history of injuries.

**Position:** 2B
**Bats:** R **Throws:** R
**Ht:** 6' 0" **Wt:** 182

**Opening Day Age:** 28
**Born:** 10/14/67 in Philadelphia, PA
**ML Seasons:** 5

### Overall Statistics

|        | G   | AB   | R   | H   | D  | T  | HR | RBI | SB | BB  | SO  | Avg  | OBP  | Slg  |
|--------|-----|------|-----|-----|----|----|----|-----|----|-----|-----|------|------|------|
| 1995   | 89  | 270  | 32  | 64  | 12 | 1  | 4  | 29  | 8  | 23  | 65  | .237 | .307 | .333 |
| Career | 511 | 1578 | 189 | 399 | 91 | 10 | 24 | 171 | 48 | 106 | 308 | .253 | .309 | .369 |

### Where He Hits the Ball

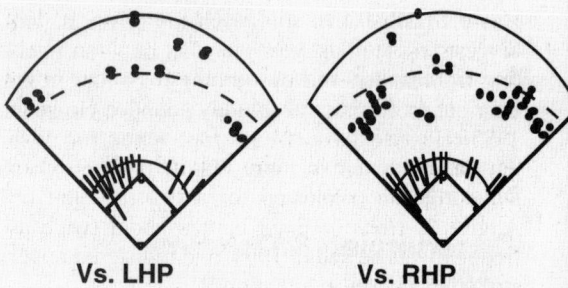

Vs. LHP          Vs. RHP

### 1995 Situational Stats

|            | AB  | H  | HR | RBI | Avg  |        | AB  | H  | HR | RBI | Avg  |
|------------|-----|----|----|-----|------|--------|-----|----|----|-----|------|
| Home       | 140 | 33 | 1  | 14  | .236 | LHP    | 92  | 25 | 3  | 13  | .272 |
| Road       | 130 | 31 | 3  | 15  | .238 | RHP    | 178 | 39 | 1  | 16  | .219 |
| First Half | 84  | 23 | 3  | 7   | .274 | Sc Pos | 69  | 12 | 0  | 22  | .174 |
| Scnd Half  | 186 | 41 | 1  | 22  | .220 | Clutch | 30  | 7  | 2  | 7   | .233 |

### 1995 Rankings (American League)

➡ 5th in sacrifice bunts (10)
➡ 9th in errors at second base (7)
➡ Led the Yankees in sacrifice bunts (10) and bunts in play (17)

# Jim Leyritz

## 1995 Season

Jim Leyritz continued to attract attention in 1995, even while his power output declined from his big '94 season. Leyritz started the season in the shadows, but soon found the spotlight. He arrived late for one May contest, then hit a home run and was cited for a controversial quote saying the homer was more important than the fine he'd receive. On May 31, after a Randy Johnson fastball broke a bone in Leyritz' face, the incident ignited ill feelings between the Yankees and Mariners that lasted into the playoffs. Leyritz's crowning blow was the 15th-inning home run that won Game 2.

## Hitting

Leyritz' home-run frequency was significantly lower in 1995 than in 1993-94, and his batting average was nothing special, either. At 32 he might be declining a little, but Leyritz can still go with a pitch to any field, and he can still turn on inside pitches with home-run power. His open, stiff-legged stance gives him some trouble hitting breaking balls outside.

## Baserunning & Defense

Leyritz has stolen just one base in the last two years. Defensively, his problem is the running game. Basestealers were successful on 80 percent of attempts against him. He made three errors last season: two behind the plate and one at first base. Despite those shortcomings, every primary Yankee starter but Jack McDowell had a lower ERA with Leyritz catching than with Mike Stanley. Andy Pettitte's 6-1 finish came with Leyritz as his regular battery-mate.

## 1996 Outlook

Leyritz has said he wouldn't mind being traded from a team plagued by "chaos." His return to New York was also uncertain because Stanley is a better hitter, rookie Jorge Posada is superior defensively, and the Yankees traded for Joe Girardi in November. Alternatively, if Leyritz regains his home-run stroke he could become the Yankees' new first baseman.

**Position:** C/1B/DH
**Bats:** R  **Throws:** R
**Ht:** 6' 0"  **Wt:** 195

**Opening Day Age:** 32
**Born:** 12/27/63 in Lakewood, OH
**ML Seasons:** 6
Pronunciation: LAY-ritz

### Overall Statistics

|  | G | AB | R | H | D | T | HR | RBI | SB | BB | SO | Avg | OBP | Slg |
|---|---|---|---|---|---|---|---|---|---|---|---|---|---|---|
| 1995 | 77 | 264 | 37 | 71 | 12 | 0 | 7 | 37 |  | 1 | 37 | 73 | .269 | .374 | .394 |
| Career | 434 | 1296 | 180 | 346 | 60 | 1 | 50 | 203 | 3 | 163 | 281 | .267 | .362 | .431 |

### Where He Hits the Ball

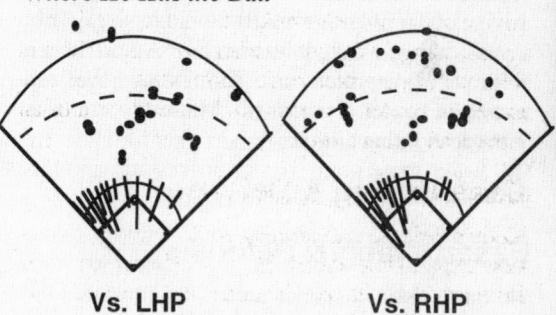

Vs. LHP          Vs. RHP

### 1995 Situational Stats

|  | AB | H | HR | RBI | Avg |  | AB | H | HR | RBI | Avg |
|---|---|---|---|---|---|---|---|---|---|---|---|
| Home | 140 | 39 | 3 | 20 | .279 | LHP | 115 | 37 | 5 | 18 | .322 |
| Road | 124 | 32 | 4 | 17 | .258 | RHP | 149 | 34 | 2 | 19 | .228 |
| First Half | 164 | 46 | 4 | 22 | .280 | Sc Pos | 78 | 22 | 1 | 30 | .282 |
| Scnd Half | 100 | 25 | 3 | 15 | .250 | Clutch | 32 | 10 | 0 | 4 | .313 |

### 1995 Rankings (American League)

→ 9th in on-base percentage vs. left-handed pitchers (.435)

→ Led the Yankees in hit by pitch (8), least GDPs per GDP situation (6.5%), batting average vs. left-handed pitchers (.322), on-base percentage vs. left-handed pitchers (.435) and batting average on a 3-2 count (.355)

# Don Mattingly

## 1995 Season

Few players had a year as eventful as Don Mattingly's. He drove in all four runs as the Yankees won their second game of the season, then six days later homered in an eighth-inning rally. He scored his 1,000th run. He suffered from hamstring and back injuries and a serious eye infection. Even with a bad eye he could read "Donnie's Done" tabloid headlines. And then came Mattingly's first postseason play after 14 years.

## Hitting

Last year it became embarrassing on Yankee radio broadcasts to report a charitable contributions drive based on Mattingly RBI output, which all but stalled during a 20-game stretch in August when he drove in just three runs. Though his home-run power is much diminished, Mattingly remains adept at shooting doubles down either foul line. He still walks more often than he strikes out, and hits lefthanders almost as well as righties.

## Baserunning & Defense

Mattingly isn't fast, but he knows how to pick spots and run when defenses aren't paying attention. Unfortunately he's even slower than he used to be, which was pretty slow, and he was thrown out in his only two steal attempts last year. He has more Gold Gloves than any first baseman but Keith Hernandez. Mattingly is a wily veteran who positions himself well. He also helps his pitchers' pickoff moves by faking off the base, then backtracking to catch unwary baserunners.

## 1996 Outlook

With the Yankees lukewarm about re-signing Mattingly after last season, he beat them to the punch and announced he would try a sort of "trial retirement." In other words, if he gets sick of fishing and watching television, he might come back. For now, Mattingly can content himself with the knowledge that at least he finally got the experience of postseason competition.

**Position:** 1B
**Bats:** L  **Throws:** L
**Ht:** 6' 0"  **Wt:** 200

**Opening Day Age:** 34
**Born:** 4/20/61 in Evansville, IN
**ML Seasons:** 14

### Overall Statistics

|  | G | AB | R | H | D | T | HR | RBI | SB | BB | SO | Avg | OBP | Slg |
|---|---|---|---|---|---|---|---|---|---|---|---|---|---|---|
| 1995 | 128 | 458 | 59 | 132 | 32 | 2 | 7 | 49 | 0 | 40 | 35 | .288 | .341 | .413 |
| Career | 1785 | 7003 | 1007 | 2153 | 442 | 20 | 222 | 1099 | 14 | 588 | 444 | .307 | .358 | .471 |

### Where He Hits the Ball

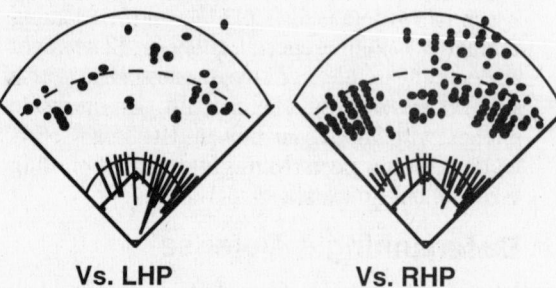

**Vs. LHP**      **Vs. RHP**

### 1995 Situational Stats

|  | AB | H | HR | RBI | Avg |  | AB | H | HR | RBI | Avg |
|---|---|---|---|---|---|---|---|---|---|---|---|
| Home | 238 | 72 | 5 | 27 | .303 | LHP | 151 | 40 | 2 | 15 | .265 |
| Road | 220 | 60 | 2 | 22 | .273 | RHP | 307 | 92 | 5 | 34 | .300 |
| First Half | 193 | 53 | 1 | 20 | .275 | Sc Pos | 126 | 29 | 0 | 35 | .230 |
| Scnd Half | 265 | 79 | 6 | 29 | .298 | Clutch | 62 | 23 | 2 | 7 | .371 |

### 1995 Rankings (American League)

- 4th in errors at first base (7) and highest percentage of swings put into play (55.3%)
- 5th in lowest batting average with the bases loaded (.083)
- 6th in GDPs (17), least pitches seen per plate appearance (3.44) and fielding percentage at first base (.994)
- 7th in batting average in the clutch (.371)
- 10th in sacrifice flies (8)
- Led the Yankees in doubles, batting average in the clutch (.371) and highest percentage of swings put into play (55.3%)

# Jack McDowell

## 1995 Season

Jack McDowell's regular season began with a controversy about his congenital hip defect, which almost caused the Yankees to void their trade with the White Sox. It ended with a bone scan to determine whether he had a stress fracture in his back. In between, the finger he waived at Yankee fans August 10 cost him $5,000. Before David Cone joined the team, McDowell was the one big workhorse holding the pitching staff together all season long, and the Yankees' second-half surge coincided with Black Jack's fine work.

## Pitching

McDowell's best pitch is a split-fingered fastball, which he can throw hard or offspeed. The splitter sets up his 90-MPH fastball as a true major league out pitch, when it would otherwise be hittable. McDowell needs control of the splitter for this method to work, and when he can't get the splitter over he is indeed quite hittable. For that reason, McDowell has been making increased use of his curve in recent years, with good effect.

## Defense

McDowell's competitive spirit is visible in his fielding. He covers his position aggressively and acts sure-handedly in all situations. He works hard at holding runners and owns a fine pickoff move, but with the Yankees in 1995 he yielded 25 stolen bases and a 71-percent success rate to the opposition. He did make eight successful pickoffs.

## 1996 Outlook

The strained back muscle that caused McDowell to miss his first start since his rookie season, and to be lost for two playoff games, left some lingering concern for 1996. The Yankees, with as much information as anyone has about McDowell, nonetheless intended to pursue him for another contract, well aware of what he did for them in 1995 and hoping for more of the same.

**Position:** SP
**Bats:** R **Throws:** R
**Ht:** 6' 5" **Wt:** 188

**Opening Day Age:** 30
**Born:** 1/16/66 in Van Nuys, CA
**ML Seasons:** 8

### Overall Statistics

|  | W | L | Pct. | ERA | G | GS | Sv | IP | H | BB | SO | HR | BR/IP |
|---|---|---|---|---|---|---|---|---|---|---|---|---|---|
| 1995 | 15 | 10 | .600 | 3.93 | 30 | 30 | 0 | 217.2 | 211 | 78 | 157 | 25 | 1.33 |
| Career | 106 | 68 | .609 | 3.56 | 221 | 221 | 0 | 1561.1 | 1469 | 497 | 1075 | 130 | 1.26 |

### How Often He Throws Strikes

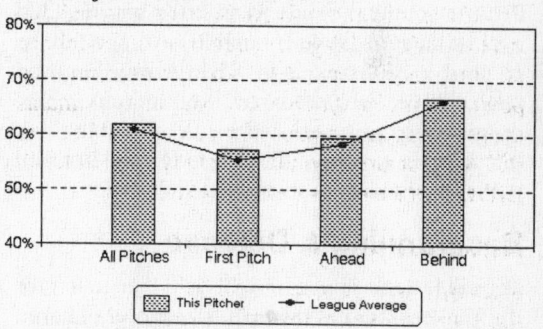

This Pitcher — League Average

### 1995 Situational Stats

|  | W | L | ERA | Sv | IP |  | AB | H | HR | RBI | Avg |
|---|---|---|---|---|---|---|---|---|---|---|---|
| Home | 7 | 6 | 4.24 | 0 | 116.2 | LHB | 475 | 121 | 15 | 59 | .255 |
| Road | 8 | 4 | 3.56 | 0 | 101.0 | RHB | 355 | 90 | 10 | 39 | .254 |
| First Half | 6 | 5 | 4.56 | 0 | 106.2 | Sc Pos | 195 | 50 | 5 | 70 | .256 |
| Scnd Half | 9 | 5 | 3.32 | 0 | 111.0 | Clutch | 107 | 18 | 2 | 9 | .168 |

### 1995 Rankings (American League)

- ➡ 1st in complete games (8) and pickoff throws (241)
- ➡ 2nd in batters faced (927)
- ➡ 3rd in shutouts (2), innings pitched, stolen bases allowed (25) and least GDPs induced per 9 innings (0.5)
- ➡ 4th in runners caught stealing (10)
- ➡ 5th in pitches thrown (3,460) and highest stolen base percentage allowed (71.4%)
- ➡ 6th in home runs allowed
- ➡ 7th in hits allowed
- ➡ 8th in wins, strikeouts and ERA on the road (3.56)
- ➡ Led the Yankees in ERA, wins, losses, games started and complete games

New York Yankees

# Paul O'Neill

## 1995 Season

The 1994 batting champion, Paul O'Neill picked up where he left off with a .412 average in the first nine games, including a big eighth-inning homer May 4. But then a wrist injury put the Yankees' number-three hitter on the disabled list in May. He recovered well enough to hit three home runs August 31, but slumped weakly down the stretch. His didn't initially object to playing left field when Darryl Strawberry arrived, but O'Neill cooled to the idea and soon returned to right.

## Hitting

O'Neill's batting average has been a function of how well he hits lefthanders, and he slumped against southpaws last year after batting .305 against them in 1994. Though his average fell, he reached a career high in RBI. Always a good fastball hitter, he has adapted well to Yankee Stadium and to the American League's breaking-ball pitchers. He can drive the ball to left field or pull it over the Stadium's short right-field fence.

## Baserunning & Defense

O'Neill is better suited to right field than to left for the Yankees. He has the team's best outfield arm, except perhaps for Gerald Williams'. O'Neill also is not fast enough to cover the stadium's vast left field pasture as speedsters like Rickey Henderson, Luis Polonia and Roberto Kelly have done. American League baserunners have given up trying to run on O'Neill. Consequently, he had only three assists in 1995. On the bases, he goes station to station and would not be a serious threat to steal even on a running team.

## 1996 Outlook

The Yankees are well served with O'Neill batting third and playing right field. They're likely to keep him in those roles, and concentrate their efforts on sorting out their crowded left field and designated hitter situations. He is under contract through 1998, so he'll almost certainly be back.

**Position:** RF/LF
**Bats:** L **Throws:** L
**Ht:** 6' 4"  **Wt:** 215

**Opening Day Age:** 33
**Born:** 2/25/63 in Columbus, OH
**ML Seasons:** 11

### Overall Statistics

|  | G | AB | R | H | D | T | HR | RBI | SB | BB | SO | Avg | OBP | Slg |
|---|---|---|---|---|---|---|---|---|---|---|---|---|---|---|
| 1995 | 127 | 460 | 82 | 138 | 30 | 4 | 22 | 96 | 1 | 71 | 76 | .300 | .387 | .526 |
| Career | 1170 | 3944 | 542 | 1104 | 236 | 13 | 159 | 665 | 69 | 493 | 657 | .280 | .359 | .467 |

### Where He Hits the Ball

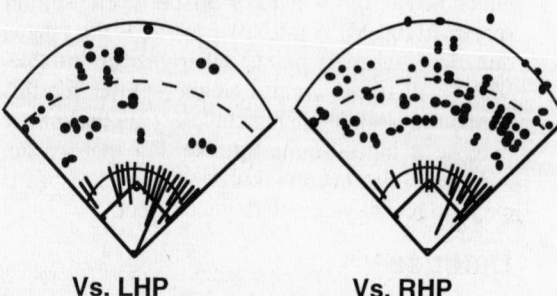

**Vs. LHP**        **Vs. RHP**

### 1995 Situational Stats

|  | AB | H | HR | RBI | Avg |  |  | AB | H | HR | RBI | Avg |
|---|---|---|---|---|---|---|---|---|---|---|---|---|
| Home | 226 | 72 | 12 | 59 | .319 | | LHP | 170 | 44 | 9 | 38 | .259 |
| Road | 234 | 66 | 10 | 37 | .282 | | RHP | 290 | 94 | 13 | 58 | .324 |
| First Half | 185 | 64 | 11 | 39 | .346 | | Sc Pos | 131 | 38 | 6 | 71 | .290 |
| Scnd Half | 275 | 74 | 11 | 57 | .269 | | Clutch | 53 | 16 | 2 | 10 | .302 |

### 1995 Rankings (American League)

→ 2nd in sacrifice flies (11) and GDPs (23)
→ 3rd in fielding percentage in right field (.985)
→ 9th in errors in right field (3)
→ 10th in on-base percentage vs. right-handed pitchers (.419)
→ Led the Yankees in home runs, RBI, sacrifice flies (11), intentional walks (8), GDPs (23), slugging percentage, HR frequency (20.9 ABs per HR), slugging percentage vs. right-handed pitchers (.545) and on-base percentage vs. right-handed pitchers (.419)

# Melido Perez

## 1995 Season

Melido Perez was the Yankees' number-three starter behind Jimmy Key and Jack McDowell when the 1995 season started. But then, like the Yankees as a whole, he slumped into the inconsistency that typifies a .500 record. The year went straight down after a June 30 bombing in Milwaukee. An inflamed right shoulder put Perez on the disabled list until September, when he came back for just one relief inning.

## Pitching

The only pitcher who can surpass Perez's animation on the mound is his brother Carlos. And few pitchers have the healthy Melido's repertoire, which includes a 92-MPH fastball and a sharp-dropping forkball. Perez uses the fastball to get ahead, then throws forkballs that batters can only wave at, or pound into the dirt. In 1995, Perez walked 4.0 batters per nine innings while his strikeout ratio dropped to 5.7. In years past, he has struggled as the season wore on.

## Defense

Perez moves off the mound quickly to field ground balls, which he handles smoothly. He is adept at holding runners, wearing them out with frequent throws to first. Only one of five basestealing attempts was successful against him last year.

## 1996 Outlook

The fact that he couldn't pitch in the second half of last year, because of recurring shoulder problems, casts a big cloud over Perez' future. His career has been checkered with other minor ailments. When healthy, he is a visibly maturing pitcher, but still has never put together two winning seasons in a row. Perez must now be regarded as a question mark—brilliant when healthy, but unreliable for full-year planning purposes. Even with a contract set for 1996, he will need to prove himself to keep his starter's role.

**Position:** SP
**Bats:** R **Throws:** R
**Ht:** 6' 4" **Wt:** 210

**Opening Day Age:** 30
**Born:** 2/15/66 in San Cristobal, DR
**ML Seasons:** 9
**Pronunciation:** purr-EZZ

### Overall Statistics

|  | W | L | Pct. | ERA | G | GS | Sv | IP | H | BB | SO | HR | BR/IP |
|---|---|---|---|---|---|---|---|---|---|---|---|---|---|
| 1995 | 5 | 5 | .500 | 5.58 | 13 | 12 | 0 | 69.1 | 70 | 31 | 44 | 10 | 1.46 |
| Career | 78 | 85 | .479 | 4.17 | 243 | 201 | 1 | 1354.2 | 1268 | 551 | 1092 | 144 | 1.34 |

### How Often He Throws Strikes

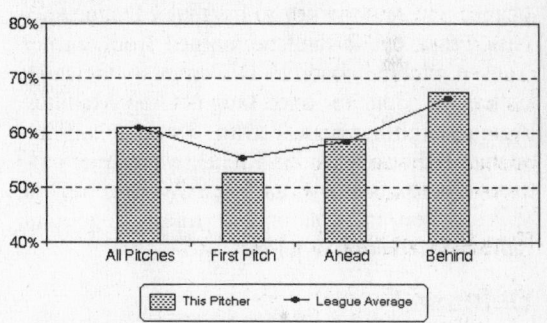

### 1995 Situational Stats

|  | W | L | ERA | Sv | IP |  | AB | H | HR | RBI | Avg |
|---|---|---|---|---|---|---|---|---|---|---|---|
| Home | 3 | 1 | 3.94 | 0 | 29.2 | LHB | 146 | 38 | 6 | 23 | .260 |
| Road | 2 | 4 | 6.81 | 0 | 39.2 | RHB | 122 | 32 | 4 | 18 | .262 |
| First Half | 5 | 5 | 5.66 | 0 | 68.1 | Sc Pos | 67 | 21 | 2 | 30 | .313 |
| Scnd Half | 0 | 0 | 0.00 | 0 | 1.0 | Clutch | 20 | 6 | 2 | 2 | .300 |

### 1995 Rankings (American League)

➡ Did not rank near the top or bottom in any category

# Andy Pettitte

## 1995 Season

The Yankees proceeded slowly with Andy Pettitte, a big winner in the minors. He pitched well enough in five relief appearances that they moved him into a starting role on May 27. Despite a 3-6 beginning, they never took him out of the rotation. After hitting bottom with his two worst starts in late August, Pettitte went at least seven innings in each of his last seven appearances, going 6-1 in New York's stretch drive when every game was critical.

## Pitching

Pettitte has pitching maturity beyond his years. He throws a 93-MPH four-seam fastball, an 87-89 MPH two-seamer, a hard curve and a straight change. He said the key to his major league success was a cut fastball he learned from former Yankee pitching coach Billy Connors—the same cutter that Connors once taught Greg Maddux. Against righthanders, Pettitte works his four-seamer and cutter inside with his two-seamer outside. He can throw as a power pitcher in strikeout/pop-up situations, or finesse a ground ball as the situation requires.

## Defense

Pettitte's maturity also shows itself in his fielding ability. He covers his position quickly and surely. One of his biggest assets is holding baserunners. He watches them closely, and has a deceptive motion that led the American League with 12 pickoffs. He also picked off two Mariners in his playoff start. Runners who did try to steal were only 9-for-17.

## 1996 Outlook

The future looks bright for Pettitte. He ended 1995 as the top lefthander on the Yankee staff. His control is on a par with David Cone and Jack McDowell, though he doesn't yet have their strikeout ability. Pettitte merely needs to find a style that works away from Yankee Stadium to become a consistent 15-to-18 game winner.

**Position:** SP/RP
**Bats:** L  **Throws:** L
**Ht:** 6' 5"  **Wt:** 235

**Opening Day Age:** 23
**Born:** 6/15/72 in Baton Rouge, LA
**ML Seasons:** 1

### Overall Statistics

|  | W | L | Pct. | ERA | G | GS | Sv | IP | H | BB | SO | HR | BR/IP |
|---|---|---|---|---|---|---|---|---|---|---|---|---|---|
| 1995 | 12 | 9 | .571 | 4.17 | 31 | 26 | 0 | 175.0 | 183 | 63 | 114 | 15 | 1.41 |
| Career | 12 | 9 | .571 | 4.17 | 31 | 26 | 0 | 175.0 | 183 | 63 | 114 | 15 | 1.41 |

### How Often He Throws Strikes

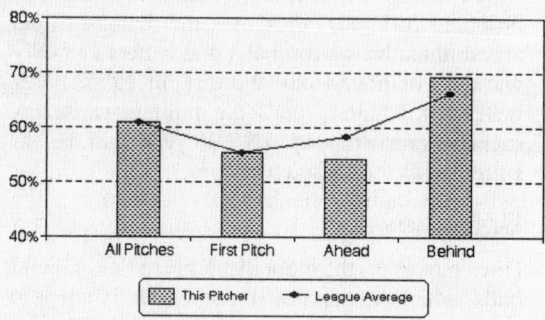

### 1995 Situational Stats

|  | W | L | ERA | Sv | IP |  | AB | H | HR | RBI | Avg |
|---|---|---|---|---|---|---|---|---|---|---|---|
| Home | 8 | 2 | 2.61 | 0 | 100.0 | LHB | 117 | 30 | 1 | 10 | .256 |
| Road | 4 | 7 | 6.24 | 0 | 75.0 | RHB | 555 | 153 | 14 | 64 | .276 |
| First Half | 3 | 6 | 4.80 | 0 | 60.0 | Sc Pos | 150 | 46 | 2 | 55 | .307 |
| Scnd Half | 9 | 3 | 3.83 | 0 | 115.0 | Clutch | 43 | 14 | 1 | 6 | .326 |

### 1995 Rankings (American League)

→ 2nd in ERA at home (2.61) and highest ERA on the road (6.24)
→ 8th in least home runs allowed per 9 innings (.77) and highest batting average allowed with runners in scoring position (.307)
→ 9th in runners caught stealing (8) and lowest stolen base percentage allowed (52.9%)
→ Led the Yankees in GDPs induced (16), highest groundball/flyball ratio allowed (1.2), lowest stolen base percentage allowed (52.9%), least home runs allowed per 9 innings (.77), most GDPs induced per 9 innings (0.8) and ERA at home (2.61)

# Ruben Sierra

## 1995 Season

In his third season with Oakland, Ruben Sierra had his second season of difficulty with manager Tony La Russa. The media sided with La Russa and labeled Sierra as lax in the field, unwilling to take a walk, and far short of the superstar he was once projected to become. In an exchange of two unhappy players, Sierra came to New York July 28 for Danny Tartabull. Sierra became a valuable asset in the Yankees' late surge, contributing 44 RBI in little more than two months, mostly as a designated hitter.

## Hitting

The Sierra Hall of Fame Express has been sidetracked ever since his last great year, 1991, when he batted .307 with 116 RBI. The switch-hitter still hits lefthanders better than righties, but does not dominate southpaws as he once did. The book on him, from either side of the plate, is to throw breaking pitches away. He can't reach them, because unlike other batters who lift their front leg before swinging, Sierra tends to land straight ahead on that foot instead of striding into pitches. He still crushes mistakes, however, and is always dangerous.

## Baserunning & Defense

The Yankees decided to find out for themselves about Sierra's defense in right field. Within two weeks, he had been replaced in the field—by Darryl Strawberry! Sierra stole a career-high 25 bases just three years ago, but was only 5-for-9 in '95. He has been susceptible to hamstring pulls which have reduced his baserunning aggressiveness.

## 1996 Outlook

George Steinbrenner seemed more committed to Strawberry than Sierra as the primary designated hitter for 1996, so another move to another city may well be in Sierra's future. At age 30, it's crucial for him to once again concentrate on making news on the field rather than off it.

**Position:** RF/DH
**Bats:** B  **Throws:** R
**Ht:** 6' 1"   **Wt:** 200

**Opening Day Age:** 30
**Born:** 10/6/65 in Rio Piedras, PR
**ML Seasons:** 10

### Overall Statistics

|        | G    | AB   | R   | H    | D   | T  | HR  | RBI | SB  | BB  | SO  | Avg  | OBP  | Slg  |
|--------|------|------|-----|------|-----|----|-----|-----|-----|-----|-----|------|------|------|
| 1995   | 126  | 479  | 73  | 126  | 32  | 0  | 19  | 86  | 5   | 46  | 76  | .263 | .323 | .449 |
| Career | 1454 | 5679 | 809 | 1547 | 306 | 50 | 220 | 952 | 126 | 419 | 834 | .272 | .318 | .460 |

### Where He Hits the Ball

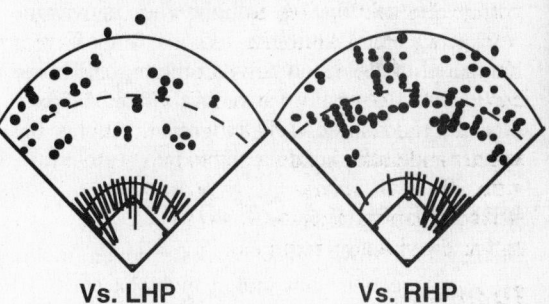

**Vs. LHP**          **Vs. RHP**

### 1995 Situational Stats

|            | AB  | H  | HR | RBI | Avg  |        | AB  | H  | HR | RBI | Avg  |
|------------|-----|----|----|-----|------|--------|-----|----|----|-----|------|
| Home       | 219 | 55 | 8  | 42  | .251 | LHP    | 161 | 44 | 5  | 28  | .273 |
| Road       | 260 | 71 | 11 | 44  | .273 | RHP    | 318 | 82 | 14 | 58  | .258 |
| First Half | 245 | 65 | 12 | 42  | .265 | Sc Pos | 132 | 41 | 6  | 67  | .311 |
| Scnd Half  | 234 | 61 | 7  | 44  | .261 | Clutch | 67  | 15 | 2  | 12  | .224 |

### 1995 Rankings (American League)

→ 3rd in errors in right field (5)
→ 6th in lowest cleanup slugging percentage (.440) and lowest batting average at home (.251)
→ 8th in lowest on-base percentage (.323) and lowest on-base percentage vs. right-handed pitchers (.321)
→ 10th in sacrifice flies (8)
→ Led the Yankees in batting average on a 3-1 count (.833) and cleanup slugging percentage (.431)

# Mike Stanley

## 1995 Season

Veteran catcher Mike Stanley missed time early in 1995 with a finger injury after being hit by a pitch. But he soon reclaimed his status as a valuable run producer. His 1995 highlights included driving in the only run in a 1-0 shutout of Kansas City July 27, and belting three home runs against Cleveland in the first game of an August 10 doubleheader.

## Hitting

Stanley is a flyball hitter with above-average power. He was so adept at hitting with the bases loaded, including two more grand slams (making a career total of eight), that his teammates began calling him "Slammo," a flashback to the nickname "Sluggo" for Don Slaught when he was the Yankee catcher. Although '95 was an off year compared to 1994, Stanley had the highest home batting average of any Yankee right-handed hitter. He has good strike-zone judgment, but his bat speed is not quite what it used to be.

## Baserunning & Defense

Stanley is a slow but savvy baserunner. In his 10-year career, he has stolen eight bases in 10 attempts. On the other side of the running game, behind the plate, he regressed, throwing out only 19 percent of basestealers after reaching 42 percent in 1994. When Stanley tires in late innings, he sometimes becomes lax in blocking outside pitches.

## 1996 Outlook

After the Rangers gave up on him, Stanley has become a star with the Yankees. However, his playing time could be curtailed this season if rookie Jorge Posada makes a huge impression in spring training. The Yankees are already loaded with designated hitters. Stanley's greatest advantage is that he's a veteran catcher who can bat in the middle of the order.

**Position:** C
**Bats:** R  **Throws:** R
**Ht:** 6' 0"  **Wt:** 190

**Opening Day Age:** 32
**Born:** 6/25/63 in Ft. Lauderdale, FL
**ML Seasons:** 10

### Overall Statistics

|  | G | AB | R | H | D | T | HR | RBI | SB | BB | SO | Avg | OBP | Slg |
|---|---|---|---|---|---|---|---|---|---|---|---|---|---|---|
| 1995 | 118 | 399 | 63 | 107 | 29 | 1 | 18 | 83 | 1 | 57 | 106 | .268 | .360 | .481 |
| Career | 850 | 2272 | 325 | 614 | 116 | 6 | 85 | 371 | 8 | 333 | 507 | .270 | .364 | .439 |

### Where He Hits the Ball

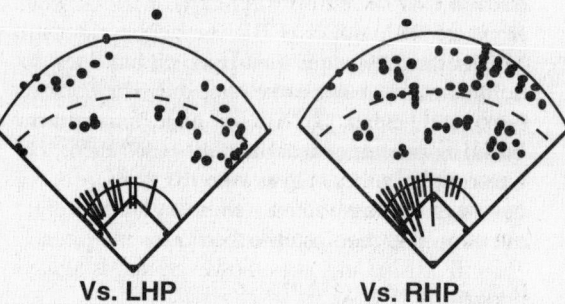

**Vs. LHP**          **Vs. RHP**

### 1995 Situational Stats

|  | AB | H | HR | RBI | Avg |  | AB | H | HR | RBI | Avg |
|---|---|---|---|---|---|---|---|---|---|---|---|
| Home | 195 | 61 | 13 | 44 | .313 | LHP | 139 | 39 | 8 | 24 | .281 |
| Road | 204 | 46 | 5 | 39 | .225 | RHP | 260 | 68 | 10 | 59 | .262 |
| First Half | 181 | 47 | 7 | 34 | .260 | Sc Pos | 97 | 31 | 4 | 64 | .320 |
| Scnd Half | 218 | 60 | 11 | 49 | .275 | Clutch | 49 | 18 | 1 | 9 | .367 |

### 1995 Rankings (American League)

→ 1st in batting average with the bases loaded (.818)
→ 2nd in lowest percentage of runners caught stealing as a catcher (18.7%)
→ 6th in sacrifice flies (9) and lowest batting average on the road (.225)
→ 8th in batting average in the clutch (.367)
→ 9th in errors at catcher (5) and lowest percentage of extra bases taken as a runner (33.3%)
→ 10th in lowest groundball/flyball ratio (0.8)
→ Led the Yankees in strikeouts, batting average with runners in scoring position (.320) and batting average with the bases loaded (.818)

# Darryl Strawberry

## 1995 Season

Darryl Strawberry began the season serving a 60-day suspension for violating provisions of his drug after-care program. The Giants then released him. Strawberry's uncertain future took shape when the Yankees signed him. He made his Yankee Stadium debut on August 7, receiving a 20-minute ovation before going 0-for-3. He went on to hit .276, his best average in five years, and he also swung with more power than he had in several years. His on-field highlight was a homer against Tim Wakefield September 8.

## Hitting

Strawberry's power stroke causes right-handed pitchers to work him very carefully. As a result, he draws enough walks to have an above-average on-base percentage even when his batting average is low. Against lefthanders, Strawberry's long swing and tendency to bail out make him an easy victim of sweeping breaking pitches. When he's in a groove, he has a swing as sweet as anybody's. At this stage of his career, it's a question whether he can play enough to get into that groove.

## Baserunning & Defense

It has been nine years since Strawberry was a 30-30 man. He hasn't stolen a base since 1993. Even in his prime, Strawberry could have been characterized as an uninspired baserunner and fielder. While his speed has faded, his arm remains strong. He had two assists in 11 games as an outfielder. He replaced Ruben Sierra in right field, but Strawberry's defensive deficiencies restored Paul O'Neill to that position, and Darryl became a designated hitter.

## 1996 Outlook

Because George Steinbrenner views Strawberry as a reclamation project and assigned Dick Williams as his personal tutor, it appeared likely that New York would bring Straw back rather than take the option of buying him out. Unless the Yanks try him as a first baseman to get some power into the lineup, Strawberry's role would be limited to platoon designated hitter.

**Position:** DH
**Bats:** L **Throws:** L
**Ht:** 6' 6" **Wt:** 215

**Opening Day Age:** 34
**Born:** 3/12/62 in Los Angeles, CA
**ML Seasons:** 13

### Overall Statistics

|  | G | AB | R | H | D | T | HR | RBI | SB | BB | SO | Avg | OBP | Slg |
|---|---|---|---|---|---|---|---|---|---|---|---|---|---|---|
| 1995 | 32 | 87 | 15 | 24 | 4 | 1 | 3 | 13 | 0 | 10 | 22 | .276 | .364 | .448 |
| Career | 1384 | 4843 | 808 | 1256 | 226 | 36 | 297 | 899 | 205 | 719 | 1182 | .259 | .356 | .505 |

### Where He Hits the Ball

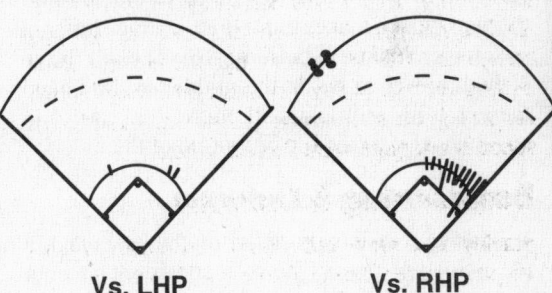

**Vs. LHP**          **Vs. RHP**

### 1995 Situational Stats

|  | AB | H | HR | RBI | Avg |  | AB | H | HR | RBI | Avg |
|---|---|---|---|---|---|---|---|---|---|---|---|
| Home | 42 | 12 | 3 | 8 | .286 | LHP | 12 | 2 | 0 | 0 | .167 |
| Road | 45 | 12 | 0 | 5 | .267 | RHP | 75 | 22 | 3 | 13 | .293 |
| First Half | 0 | 0 | 0 | 0 | - | Sc Pos | 23 | 8 | 2 | 10 | .348 |
| Scnd Half | 87 | 24 | 3 | 13 | .276 | Clutch | 6 | 0 | 0 | 0 | .000 |

### 1995 Rankings (American League)

→ Did not rank near the top or bottom in any category

# Randy Velarde

## 1995 Season

Randy Velarde was one of the success stories from the free agents' spring camp at Homestead, Florida. The Yankees re-signed him to a $350,000 contract—a reduction of $775K from his 1994 salary. That was an exceptional bargain for the Yankees. After excelling in his utility role at five positions, he played regularly down the stretch, mostly at second base, while Pat Kelly wasn't hitting.

## Hitting

Velarde has developed consistency at the plate. His giant step forward last season was learning patience; before 1995 he had almost a 2.5-to-1 strikeout-to-walk ratio. He can drive the ball into the gaps, which makes him a high-average hitter in spacious Yankee Stadium. He doesn't have enough power to bat in the middle of the lineup there, but his multiple skills make him useful in any other slot, at the top or bottom of the order.

## Baserunning & Defense

Velarde is occasionally stellar on the bases and in the field, but overall he is inconsistent at both aspects. He has become more selective as a basestealer, picking his spots last year. As a utility-man, he is a defensive asset, but at any single position, he can be a liability, as he showed in left field during the playoffs. He has a strong enough arm to play on the left side of the infield or in right field on occasion. His strength is versatility, not excellence at any position.

## 1996 Outlook

If he were a steadier defensive player, Velarde would have been a long-time regular instead of a career utility player. As it stands, his versatility makes him extremely valuable for creating options for any manager. Velarde is due for a sizable raise.

**Position:** 2B/3B/SS/LF
**Bats:** R  **Throws:** R
**Ht:** 6' 0"  **Wt:** 192

**Opening Day Age:** 33
**Born:** 11/24/62 in Midland, TX
**ML Seasons:** 9

*Overall Statistics*

|  | G | AB | R | H | D | T | HR | RBI | SB | BB | SO | Avg | OBP | Slg |
|---|---|---|---|---|---|---|---|---|---|---|---|---|---|---|
| 1995 | 111 | 367 | 60 | 102 | 19 | 1 | 7 | 46 | 5 | 55 | 64 | .278 | .375 | .392 |
| Career | 658 | 1935 | 263 | 511 | 99 | 10 | 43 | 208 | 22 | 186 | 382 | .264 | .333 | .392 |

*Where He Hits the Ball*

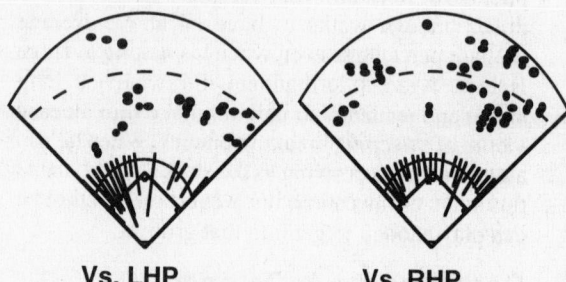

**Vs. LHP**　　　　**Vs. RHP**

*1995 Situational Stats*

|  | AB | H | HR | RBI | Avg |  | AB | H | HR | RBI | Avg |
|---|---|---|---|---|---|---|---|---|---|---|---|
| Home | 162 | 49 | 2 | 24 | .302 | LHP | 136 | 38 | 1 | 10 | .279 |
| Road | 205 | 53 | 5 | 22 | .259 | RHP | 231 | 64 | 6 | 36 | .277 |
| First Half | 174 | 46 | 3 | 19 | .264 | Sc Pos | 105 | 29 | 1 | 35 | .276 |
| Scnd Half | 193 | 56 | 4 | 27 | .290 | Clutch | 45 | 13 | 1 | 4 | .289 |

*1995 Rankings (American League)*
➡ 2nd in lowest batting average with the bases loaded (.000)

# John Wetteland

## 1995 Season

How important is a closer? One of the Yankees' first moves after the strike ended was trading two minor leaguers and $1.4 million to Montreal to make sure they had an ace reliever. When New York won early in the season, it was John Wetteland saving the games. When the team stumbled, Wetteland stumbled, too. And when they won 11 of 12 down the stretch to make the playoffs, Wetteland saved six of them, finishing with eight saves and a 0.84 ERA for the month of September.

## Pitching

Wetteland is a classic power pitcher, with a moving 95 MPH fastball. When he can get his curve and occasional change-up over, he's virtually unhittable. When he's not striking out batters (9.7 per nine innings), he gets most of his outs on fly balls. He is an equal-opportunity pitcher—tough on lefty and righty hitters alike. He explained two blown saves against Cleveland during August: "It's a simple matter of velocity. It's down." That came during one of two stretches when he pitched three days in a row.

## Defense

Wetteland is an agile fielder, but his rising fastball rarely leads to grounders near the mound; he is even tough to bunt on. His high leg kick makes him poor at holding baserunners. Seven of eight basestealers were successful against him last season, bringing to three the total thrown out over the last three years.

## 1996 Outlook

Wetteland lost one of his biggest supporters when Buck Showalter announced he would not return as Yankee manager. Despite Showalter's departure, Wetteland will likely remain in New York. At only 29 years of age, he sits among the top handful of relief aces in all of baseball. Assuming he remains healthy, there's no reason to think he won't continue his level of success.

**Position:** RP
**Bats:** R **Throws:** R
**Ht:** 6' 2"  **Wt:** 215

**Opening Day Age:** 29
**Born:** 8/21/66 in San Mateo, CA
**ML Seasons:** 7

### Overall Statistics

|  | W | L | Pct. | ERA | G | GS | Sv | IP | H | BB | SO | HR | BR/IP |
|---|---|---|---|---|---|---|---|---|---|---|---|---|---|
| 1995 | 1 | 5 | .167 | 2.93 | 60 | 0 | 31 | 61.1 | 40 | 14 | 66 | 6 | 0.88 |
| Career | 26 | 30 | .464 | 2.93 | 308 | 17 | 137 | 448.1 | 338 | 153 | 487 | 34 | 1.10 |

### How Often He Throws Strikes

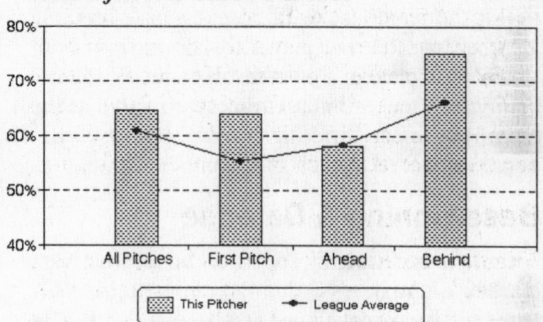

This Pitcher — League Average

### 1995 Situational Stats

|  | W | L | ERA | Sv | IP |  | AB | H | HR | RBI | Avg |
|---|---|---|---|---|---|---|---|---|---|---|---|
| Home | 0 | 4 | 4.06 | 15 | 31.0 | LHB | 113 | 21 | 3 | 18 | .186 |
| Road | 1 | 1 | 1.78 | 16 | 30.1 | RHB | 103 | 19 | 3 | 9 | .184 |
| First Half | 1 | 1 | 2.51 | 12 | 28.2 | Sc Pos | 52 | 16 | 2 | 21 | .308 |
| Scnd Half | 0 | 4 | 3.31 | 19 | 32.2 | Clutch | 131 | 25 | 5 | 21 | .191 |

### 1995 Rankings (American League)

- ➡ 3rd in games finished (56), lowest batting average allowed in relief (.185) and least baserunners allowed per 9 innings in relief (7.9)
- ➡ 5th in saves
- ➡ 6th in save opportunities (37) and save percentage (83.8%)
- ➡ 7th in blown saves (6)
- ➡ 8th in relief ERA (2.93)
- ➡ 10th in games pitched, first batter efficiency (.190) and most strikeouts per 9 innings in relief (9.7)
- ➡ Led the Yankees in saves, games finished (56), save opportunities (37) and save percentage (83.8%)

# Bernie Williams

## 1995 Season

As the Yankees marched unsteadily toward their playoff berth, one constant was Bernie Williams, who patrolled center field in all 144 Yankee contests. He started the season well enough, but saved his best for the latter part of the season. After he was installed in the number-two slot in the batting order August 4, he batted .366 over his next 164 at-bats, and tied Mike Piazza for the major league lead with 46 hits in August.

## Hitting

Williams has become a true switch-hitter, adept from both sides of the plate. He is primarily a groundball hitter, but drove the ball well enough to tie for the team lead with 56 extra-base hits. He also became the first player to homer from both sides of the plate in a postseason game. Williams' batting eye makes him extremely effective at the top of the lineup, offering contact, power, or patience as needed in each situation.

## Baserunning & Defense

Although he has the speed to cover the vast reaches of Yankee Stadium's center field, Williams still hasn't developed as a basestealer. But he has become a much more "heads-up" baserunner who can take an extra base with ease. In the field, he committed eight errors last year, but ran down 29 more fly balls than any other American League outfielder. Williams also has enough arm strength to make throws from the Stadium's deep gaps.

## 1996 Outlook

Williams is a pronounced example of a star player whose true value is not quickly visible in any of the usual statistics. He does everything well without generating any glittering numbers to highlight his excellence in any specific area. To the Yankees, he is an invaluable top-of-the-order batter with unusual power and a defensive anchor who is just coming into his prime.

**Position:** CF
**Bats:** B **Throws:** R
**Ht:** 6' 2" **Wt:** 205

**Opening Day Age:** 27
**Born:** 9/13/68 in San Juan, PR
**ML Seasons:** 5

### Overall Statistics

| | G | AB | R | H | D | T | HR | RBI | SB | BB | SO | Avg | OBP | Slg |
|---|---|---|---|---|---|---|---|---|---|---|---|---|---|---|
| 1995 | 144 | 563 | 93 | 173 | 29 | 9 | 18 | 82 | 8 | 75 | 98 | .307 | .392 | .487 |
| Career | 538 | 2119 | 322 | 592 | 122 | 20 | 50 | 267 | 50 | 266 | 351 | .279 | .362 | .427 |

### Where He Hits the Ball

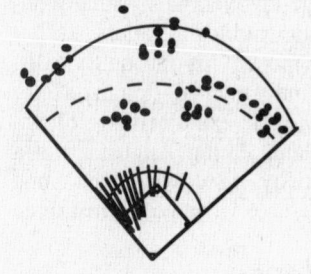

**Vs. LHP**          **Vs. RHP**

### 1995 Situational Stats

| | AB | H | HR | RBI | Avg | | AB | H | HR | RBI | Avg |
|---|---|---|---|---|---|---|---|---|---|---|---|
| Home | 280 | 92 | 7 | 39 | .329 | LHP | 195 | 59 | 13 | 35 | .303 |
| Road | 283 | 81 | 11 | 43 | .286 | RHP | 368 | 114 | 5 | 47 | .310 |
| First Half | 254 | 65 | 9 | 38 | .256 | Sc Pos | 146 | 46 | 3 | 61 | .315 |
| Scnd Half | 309 | 108 | 9 | 44 | .350 | Clutch | 75 | 24 | 1 | 16 | .320 |

### 1995 Rankings (American League)

- 1st in errors in center field (8)
- 3rd in games played and lowest fielding percentage in center field (.982)
- 4th in triples and plate appearances (648)
- 5th in at-bats and times on base (253)
- 6th in singles (117)
- 7th in hits
- 9th in slugging percentage vs. left-handed pitchers (.590)
- 10th in pitches seen (2,461)
- Led the Yankees in at-bats, runs scored, hits, triples, total bases (274), caught stealing (6), walks, times on base (253), pitches seen (2,461), plate appearances (648) and games played (144)

# Joe Ausanio

**Position**: RP
**Bats**: R  **Throws**: R
**Ht**: 6' 1"  **Wt**: 205

**Opening Day Age**: 30
**Born**: 12/9/65 in
Kingston, NY
**ML Seasons**: 2
**Pronunciation**:
aw-SAN-ee-oh

## Overall Statistics

|  | W | L | Pct. | ERA | G | GS | Sv | IP | H | BB | SO | HR | BR/IP |
|---|---|---|---|---|---|---|---|---|---|---|---|---|---|
| 1995 | 2 | 0 | 1.000 | 5.73 | 28 | 0 | 1 | 37.2 | 42 | 23 | 36 | 9 | 1.73 |
| Career | 4 | 1 | .800 | 5.57 | 41 | 0 | 1 | 53.1 | 58 | 29 | 51 | 12 | 1.63 |

## 1995 Season

In his eighth professional year and with his third organization, righthander Joe Ausanio finally got a real chance to show what he could do in the major leagues. Ausanio picked up two relief wins in the Yankees' first 14 games, but after blowing two save opportunities in May he rarely appeared when games were on the line, and didn't work at all after September 15.

## Pitching & Defense

A minor league closer at times, Ausanio doesn't have the dominant stuff for such a role in the majors. His job is mainly to soak up innings while the more important pitchers save their arms. In 1995 he pitched in 28 games; the Yankees won just eight. Walking more than five batters per nine innings, Ausanio gets behind hitters, and as a fly-ball pitcher he gives up a lot of home runs. Basestealers were 2-for-2 against Ausanio, who never achieved excellence at holding runners in the minors.

## 1996 Outlook

At age 30 it is unlikely that Ausanio can rise to a critical role in a major league bullpen, especially on a team that favors veterans with starry track records. At best, he might improve his control and get more work as a middle reliever, and possibly build from there. He'll get a chance to do just that with the cross-town Mets, with whomAusanio signed a minor league contract in November.

# Russ Davis

**Position**: 3B
**Bats**: R  **Throws**: R
**Ht**: 6' 0"  **Wt**: 195

**Opening Day Age**: 26
**Born**: 9/13/69 in
Birmingham, AL
**ML Seasons**: 2

## Overall Statistics

|  | G | AB | R | H | D | T | HR | RBI | SB | BB | SO | Avg | OBP | Slg |
|---|---|---|---|---|---|---|---|---|---|---|---|---|---|---|
| 1995 | 40 | 98 | 14 | 27 | 5 | 2 | 2 | 12 | 0 | 10 | 26 | .276 | .349 | .429 |
| Career | 44 | 112 | 14 | 29 | 5 | 2 | 2 | 13 | 0 | 10 | 30 | .259 | .325 | .393 |

## 1995 Season

Prospect Russ Davis finally arrived in the majors last year, but only as a platoon third baseman and off-the-bench role player. He showed the power that allowed him to hit 110 home runs in the minors. At third his range was comparable to Wade Boggs, but Davis is not yet as sure-handed. Overall he found his part-time role challenging.

## Hitting, Baserunning & Defense

Davis is capable of hitting liners into the gaps at Yankee Stadium. Because opponents prefer to use lefty starters in New York, Yankee fans were somewhat spared from seeing Davis struggle on the road against righties. Davis has fair patience at the plate, but hasn't yet shown the ability to make contact consistently. He hasn't yet developed defensive consistent, either. He was not much of a basestealer in the minors, and won't be with the Yankees.

## 1996 Outlook

Other major league clubs have long hungered for power-prospect Davis, and last December one of those clubs finally got their man. Along with Sterling Hitchcock, Davis was traded to Seattle for Tino Martinez, Jeff Nelson and prospect Jim Mecir. With Mike Blowers now a Dodger, Davis should fit nicely into the lineup at third base.

# Dion James

**Position**: DH/LF
**Bats**: L **Throws**: L
**Ht**: 6' 1" **Wt**: 185

**Opening Day Age**: 33
**Born**: 11/9/62 in
Philadelphia, PA
**ML Seasons**: 10

## Overall Statistics

|  | G | AB | R | H | D | T | HR | RBI | SB | BB | SO | Avg | OBP | Slg |
|---|---|---|---|---|---|---|---|---|---|---|---|---|---|---|
| 1995 | 85 | 209 | 22 | 60 | 6 | 1 | 2 | 26 | 4 | 20 | 16 | .287 | .346 | .354 |
| Career | 911 | 2696 | 361 | 779 | 142 | 21 | 32 | 266 | 42 | 317 | 305 | .289 | .364 | .393 |

## 1995 Season

Dion James didn't like playing in Japan, so he came back to the last team he'd played for in the U.S., signing a $300,000 contract with the Yankees. After Luis Polonia was traded, James assumed a more important role as a platoon outfielder against righthanders. He also played first base, and saw considerable time as the team's designated hitter.

## Hitting, Baserunning & Defense

James hits right-handed pitching well, spraying line drives and coming up with timely hits. Though he doesn't have much power, he has batted third and fifth. Because he's patient, he has also been tried as a leadoff batter. James doesn't dive into the ball like he used to, so he's less susceptible to being pitched inside. He has some speed which he uses wisely. James picked his spots to steal four bases in five attempts. He doesn't have much range in the field, and has a below-average outfield throwing arm.

## 1996 Outlook

James can no longer be considered for a regular job, but he fits nicely into the Yankees' roster as a utility player. They can use him in the outfield, at first base, as a pinch hitter and as a pinch runner. He is a less expensive, more versatile alternative to some higher-profile players.

# Scott Kamieniecki

**Position**: SP
**Bats**: R **Throws**: R
**Ht**: 6' 0" **Wt**: 195

**Opening Day Age**: 31
**Born**: 4/19/64 in Mt.
Clemens, MI
**ML Seasons**: 5
**Pronunciation**:
kam-uh-NICK-ee

## Overall Statistics

|  | W | L | Pct. | ERA | G | GS | Sv | IP | H | BB | SO | HR | BR/IP |
|---|---|---|---|---|---|---|---|---|---|---|---|---|---|
| 1995 | 7 | 6 | .538 | 4.01 | 17 | 16 | 0 | 89.2 | 83 | 49 | 43 | 8 | 1.47 |
| Career | 35 | 37 | .486 | 4.08 | 106 | 89 | 1 | 604.2 | 608 | 263 | 308 | 59 | 1.44 |

## 1995 Season

Scott Kamieniecki finally earned a spot in the Yankee rotation last year, but then was knocked out May 5th by a sprained elbow ligament that sidelined him for 10 weeks. He finished strong for the second year in a row, going 3-1 down the stretch. That was after Mariano Rivera had replaced him for one start.

## Pitching & Defense

Kamieniecki throws a 90-MPH fastball, overhand curve, slider and change-up—but none is a true major league out pitch. To get by, he has to change speeds and move the ball in and out. He also helps himself with good defense and above-average ability at holding runners. At times he has trouble throwing strikes, a problem not helped by signs of temper that umpires sometimes consider attempts to show them up.

## 1996 Outlook

The Yankees ended 1995 with a $1 million option on Kamieniecki's services for 1996. Depending on who else the team signs, he could be the first pitcher dumped from the rotation. Kamieniecki has had stamina problems over the years and might fit better as a long reliever.

# Jimmy Key

**Position:** SP
**Bats:** R **Throws:** L
**Ht:** 6' 1" **Wt:** 185

**Opening Day Age:** 34
**Born:** 4/22/61 in
Huntsville, AL
**ML Seasons:** 12

## Overall Statistics

| | W | L | Pct. | ERA | G | GS | Sv | IP | H | BB | SO | HR | BR/IP |
|---|---|---|---|---|---|---|---|---|---|---|---|---|---|
| 1995 | 1 | 2 | .333 | 5.64 | 5 | 5 | 0 | 30.1 | 40 | 6 | 14 | 3 | 1.52 |
| Career | 152 | 93 | .620 | 3.40 | 381 | 314 | 10 | 2130.2 | 2060 | 505 | 1228 | 204 | 1.20 |

## 1995 Season

Something wasn't right when staff ace Jimmy Key gave up 19 hits in 11.1 innings during two starts in May. Here's what was wrong: recurring tendinitis and inflammation in his rotator cuff. The pain became so great after 10 pitches in a simulated game in Tampa that in July, Key underwent surgery for the second time in nine months.

## Pitching & Defense

Even when healthy, Key throws only a mid-80s fastball, but few pitchers can spot their curve, change and slider as precisely. He walks very few batters and can come up with double-play grounders like magic when he needs them—valuable qualities for a pitcher who gives up lots of hits. Key's smooth delivery leaves him in excellent fielding position. Key does a great job holding runners, and he didn't give up a stolen base in his five games last season.

## 1996 Outlook

If Key pitches at all in 1996, it won't be until the latter part of the season. Of last year's injury, he said, "This time I feel pain." The most discouraging aspect of his injury is that it was essentially the same problem that surgery in 1994 was supposed to fix.

# Mariano Rivera

**Position:** SP/RP
**Bats:** R **Throws:** R
**Ht:** 6' 2" **Wt:** 168

**Opening Day Age:** 26
**Born:** 11/29/69 in
Panama City, Panama
**ML Seasons:** 1

## Overall Statistics

| | W | L | Pct. | ERA | G | GS | Sv | IP | H | BB | SO | HR | BR/IP |
|---|---|---|---|---|---|---|---|---|---|---|---|---|---|
| 1995 | 5 | 3 | .625 | 5.51 | 19 | 10 | 0 | 67.0 | 71 | 30 | 51 | 11 | 1.51 |
| Career | 5 | 3 | .625 | 5.51 | 19 | 10 | 0 | 67.0 | 71 | 30 | 51 | 11 | 1.51 |

## 1995 Season

Mariano Rivera was dominant in seven starts at Triple-A Columbus (2.10 ERA, 30 strikeouts in 30 innings), earning three in-season promotions to the Yankees. He was hit hard the first time up, then put it together for eight innings of two-hit ball in Chicago on July 4, a game regarded as Rivera's major league breakthrough. He was 4-1 with a 4.15 ERA in his final 15 appearances, then did some excellent work in the postseason.

## Pitching & Defense

Shoulder and elbow injuries limited Rivera to 400 innings in his first five minor league seasons. The arm trouble didn't take away from his mid-90s fastball, however. He also throws a change-up, but needs work on his hard slider. In late '95 he was developing a split-fingered pitch that he hasn't yet used in games. He said the key to success is keeping the ball down in the strike zone. For a hard thrower, he's not bad at holding runners.

## 1996 Outlook

Rivera has not pitched enough innings, nor has he thrown enough strikes, to be projected into the Yankee rotation. However, his repertoire and his success in the playoffs (5.1 scoreless innings, eight strikeouts) point toward a career as a potentially outstanding reliever if doesn't catch on as a starter.

# Bob Wickman

**Position:** RP
**Bats:** R **Throws:** R
**Ht:** 6' 1" **Wt:** 212

**Opening Day Age:** 27
**Born:** 2/6/69 in Green Bay, WI
**ML Seasons:** 4

### Overall Statistics

|  | W | L | Pct. | ERA | G | GS | Sv | IP | H | BB | SO | HR | BR/IP |
|---|---|---|------|-----|---|----|----|-----|-----|-----|-----|----|-------|
| 1995 | 2 | 4 | .333 | 4.05 | 63 | 1 | 1 | 80.0 | 77 | 33 | 51 | 6 | 1.38 |
| Career | 27 | 13 | .675 | 4.10 | 165 | 28 | 11 | 340.1 | 338 | 149 | 198 | 24 | 1.43 |

## 1995 Season

Early in the year, Wickman was part of Yankee radio announcer John Sterling's bullpen "terrific troika" with John Wetteland and Steve Howe. When the Yankees struggled, so did Wickman, who blew nine saves and received his only save by default when a game got rained out. Team and pitcher both righted themselves by season's end, and Wickman wound up recording 21 holds, second most in the league behind Troy Percival.

## Pitching & Defense

Wickman throws a 90 MPH fastball which he likes to cut, a mid-80s slider and a sinker. Because he throws a heavy ball, he gets a lot of groundball outs. When called in with runners on base, Wickman stranded 78 percent of them. He is not good at holding runners. All nine basestealing attempts against him last season were successful. Wickman is also not a nimble fielder.

## 1996 Outlook

With Wetteland as the bullpen horse, Wickman's role as a set-up man was better defined last season. He made one "see what happens" start while Scott Kamieniecki was injured, but then went back to the bullpen. Wickman remained a Yankee despite trade rumors, and his strong finish suggests he will return in the same role in '96.

# Gerald Williams

**Position:** LF/RF
**Bats:** R **Throws:** R
**Ht:** 6' 2" **Wt:** 190

**Opening Day Age:** 29
**Born:** 8/10/66 in New Orleans, LA
**ML Seasons:** 4

### Overall Statistics

|  | G | AB | R | H | D | T | HR | RBI | SB | BB | SO | Avg | OBP | Slg |
|---|---|----|---|---|---|---|----|-----|----|----|----|-----|-----|-----|
| 1995 | 100 | 182 | 33 | 45 | 18 | 2 | 6 | 28 | 4 | 22 | 34 | .247 | .327 | .467 |
| Career | 214 | 362 | 70 | 88 | 30 | 5 | 13 | 53 | 9 | 27 | 68 | .243 | .297 | .461 |

## 1995 Season

Gerald Williams earned more at-bats last season than in his first three major league visits combined. He appeared in a right-handed platoon, played late-inning outfield defense and pinch ran. His versatility endeared him to manager Buck Showalter, who found ways to use Williams 100 times.

## Hitting, Baserunning & Defense

If Williams ever got a chance to play every day, he could be a 20-homer, 20-steal man, although he probably wouldn't hit for much of an average. Though he's nearly 30, Williams is still improving his game, most noticeably in his patience at the plate. His walk frequency last season was four times greater than in his other years. He is as quick on the bases as any Yankee and is an intelligent baserunner. Williams' speed is most noticeable in the field, where he chased down long drives from all three outfield positions. His strong arm enabled him to lead the team with six outfield assists.

## 1996 Outlook

Williams has accepted his status as a role player about as quickly as any recent major leaguer, while at the same time working to improve his game. If Williams could hit righthanders, he would be the complete package.

# Other New York Yankees

**Scott Bankhead** (**Pos**: RHP, **Age**: 32)

Bankhead's career appears to be in jeopardy. He pitched terribly in 20 games for the Yankees, and even worse later on for Triple-A Edmonton (Oakland). He'll be lucky to find a team next season. 1996 Outlook: C

**Todd Benzinger** (**Pos**: 1B, **Age**: 33, **Bats**: B)

Benzinger was released by the Giants after a poor start, signed by the Yankees, and played sparingly at Triple-A Columbus after that. He has no hope of being a regular, barring a batch of injuries. 1996 Outlook: C

**Brian Boehringer** (**Pos**: RHP, **Age**: 26)

Boehringer was shelled in his three starts for the Yankees, but continues to be a very effective starting pitcher in the minor leagues. He still has time to improve. 1996 Outlook: C

**Matt Dunbar** (**Pos**: LHP, **Age**: 27)

Dunbar was taken by the Marlins in the Rule 5 draft a year ago, but went back to the Yankees in May after a poor start. Up until last season, he had been superb in the minor leagues. He needs to improve his control dramatically to rebound. 1996 Outlook: C

**Robert Eenhoorn** (**Pos**: SS, **Age**: 28, **Bats**: R)

A second-round pick by the Yankees in 1990, Eenhoorn played sparingly for the team in 1995. He's hit very poorly at Triple-A the last two seasons, has little power, and rarely walks. He is regarded as a top-flight defensive shortstop. 1996 Outlook: D

**Dave Eiland** (**Pos**: RHP, **Age**: 29)

Eiland continues to get chances in the majors, but has never pitched well during any stint. He pitched well at Triple-A in 1995, but at 29 his opportunities are quickly running out. 1996 Outlook: C

**Dwight Gooden** (**Pos**: RHP, **Age**: 31)

Can he still pitch? Unless something goes wrong between now and April, we'll find out this spring. Gooden is unlikely to throw mid-90s fastballs, but he could be a decent third starter. 1996 Outlook: A

**Kevin Maas** (**Pos**: DH/1B, **Age**: 31, **Bats**: L)

Maas was reacquired by the Yankees after a poor start with the Twins. It's been downhill for him since he exploded onto the scene in 1990. He remains a huge liability in the field. 1996 Outlook: D

**Bob MacDonald** (**Pos**: RHP, **Age**: 30)

The Yankees gave him a lot of work, but MacDonald pitched poorly in his relief role. He hasn't pitched well since 1991, and at 30 he needs to prove himself again. 1996 Outlook: B

**Josias Manzanillo** (**Pos**: RHP, **Age**: 28)

Manzanillo was acquired by the Yankees after a poor start with the Mets. He pitched pretty well from that point forward, at least until an inflamed elbow ended his season. He'll find a team, if healthy. 1996 Outlook: B

**Jeff Patterson** (**Pos**: RHP, **Age**: 27)

Patterson got a cup of coffee with the Yankees, pitching pretty well at Triple-A the remainder of the season. He's only 27, but his control has gotten progressively worse since 1989. 1996 Outlook: C

**Dave Pavlas** (**Pos**: RHP, **Age**: 33)

Pavlas pitched extremely well as a closer at Triple-A Columbus in 1995, but his hopes of jumping back to the majors are all but gone. He's pitched well when given a chance, but his time is up. 1996 Outlook: D

# New York Yankees Minor League Prospects

## Organization Overview:

The Yankees have always had a productive farm system, but the prospects often end up getting traded for veterans. Though that tendency had waned in recent years, the behavior may be re-emerging. The Yankees traded three prospects, including prized arm Marty Janzen, in order to acquire David Cone last July. Last year, the Yankees promoted Andy Pettitte, the top American League rookie pitcher, and received a contribution from power-hitting Russ Davis, who could see extensive action in 1996. Also on the near horizon are two of the most eagerly anticipated prospects in baseball: Derek Jeter and Ruben Rivera. But beyond those two, the Yankees are not especially deep in minor league talent.

### Nick Delvecchio

**Position:** 1B  
**Bats:** L **Throws:** R  
**Ht:** 6' 5" **Wt:** 203  
**Opening Day Age:** 26  
**Born:** 1/23/70 in Natick, MA

*Recent Statistics*

| | G | AB | R | H | D | T | HR | RBI | SB | BB | SO | AVG |
|---|---|---|---|---|---|---|---|---|---|---|---|---|
| 93 A Greensboro | 137 | 485 | 90 | 131 | 30 | 3 | 21 | 80 | 4 | 80 | 156 | .270 |
| 94 R Yankees | 4 | 13 | 1 | 5 | 0 | 0 | 0 | 0 | 0 | 2 | 3 | .385 |
| 94 A Tampa | 27 | 95 | 17 | 27 | 3 | 0 | 7 | 18 | 0 | 11 | 20 | .284 |
| 95 AA Norwich | 125 | 430 | 66 | 112 | 23 | 4 | 19 | 74 | 2 | 72 | 133 | .260 |
| 95 MLE | 125 | 421 | 57 | 103 | 21 | 2 | 17 | 64 | 1 | 51 | 141 | .245 |

Delvecchio is an intriguing power prospect with numerous holes in his game. First the good news: Delvecchio has averaged 23 homers and 79 walks for every 500 minor league at-bats. Unfortunately, he's also averaged 153 strikeouts, and his best position may be DH. Now 25, Delvecchio hasn't played in Triple-A yet, so he'll likely never be a star. But he could eventually grab a major league job as a left-handed bat off the bench.

### Matt Drews

**Position:** P  
**Bats:** R **Throws:** R  
**Ht:** 6' 8" **Wt:** 205  
**Opening Day Age:** 21  
**Born:** 8/29/74 in Sarasota, FL

*Recent Statistics*

| | W | L | ERA | G | GS | Sv | IP | H | R | BB | SO | HR |
|---|---|---|---|---|---|---|---|---|---|---|---|---|
| 94 A Oneonta | 7 | 6 | 2.10 | 14 | 14 | 0 | 90.0 | 76 | 31 | 19 | 69 | 1 |
| 95 A Tampa | 15 | 7 | 2.27 | 28 | 28 | 0 | 182.0 | 142 | 73 | 58 | 140 | 5 |

Drews is the grandson of Karl Drews, who pitched for four teams, including the Yanks, in the late '40s-early '50s. Matt was the Yankees' top pick in 1993 and has pitched sensationally since. In 272 pro innings, he's allowed just 218 hits and 77 walks while striking out 209 and compiling a 2.22 ERA. His 15 victories last year led the Florida State League. Drews breaks bats with a low-90s sinking fastball. He also has an improving curveball and a competent change-up. At 225 pounds, Drews looks like a workhorse.

### Mike Figga

**Position:** C  
**Bats:** R **Throws:** R  
**Ht:** 6' 0" **Wt:** 200  
**Opening Day Age:** 25  
**Born:** 7/31/70 in Tampa, FL

*Recent Statistics*

| | G | AB | R | H | D | T | HR | RBI | SB | BB | SO | AVG |
|---|---|---|---|---|---|---|---|---|---|---|---|---|
| 93 A San Bernrdo | 83 | 308 | 48 | 82 | 17 | 1 | 25 | 71 | 2 | 17 | 84 | .266 |
| 93 AA Albany-Colo | 6 | 22 | 3 | 5 | 0 | 0 | 0 | 2 | 1 | 2 | 9 | .227 |
| 94 AA Albany-Colo | 1 | 2 | 1 | 1 | 0 | 0 | 0 | 0 | 0 | 0 | 1 | .500 |
| 94 A Tampa | 111 | 420 | 48 | 116 | 17 | 5 | 15 | 75 | 3 | 22 | 94 | .276 |
| 95 AA Norwich | 109 | 399 | 59 | 108 | 22 | 4 | 13 | 61 | 1 | 43 | 90 | .271 |
| 95 AAA Columbus | 8 | 25 | 2 | 7 | 1 | 0 | 1 | 3 | 0 | 3 | 5 | .280 |
| 95 MLE | 117 | 411 | 52 | 102 | 20 | 2 | 11 | 54 | 0 | 32 | 100 | .248 |

Figga had been an afterthought for much of his early career. He played at a junior college in Florida, was drafted in the 44th round of 1989, didn't sign until the following year, and then proceeded to hit less than .200 at two different stops in 1991 and 1992. That led to a co-op assignment in the California League in 1993, in which Figga suddenly found the power to jack 25 homers, more than four times his previous career total over three seasons. The Yankees snatched him back and he's been an all-star three times running. Last year he was voted the top defensive catcher in the Eastern League. One hurdle he faces in the future is fellow Yankee farmhand Jorge Posada, who at 24 is one year younger and one level more advanced.

### Andy Fox

**Position:** 3B-SS  
**Bats:** L **Throws:** R  
**Ht:** 6' 4" **Wt:** 185  
**Opening Day Age:** 25  
**Born:** 1/12/71 in Sacramento, CA

*Recent Statistics*

| | G | AB | R | H | D | T | HR | RBI | SB | BB | SO | AVG |
|---|---|---|---|---|---|---|---|---|---|---|---|---|
| 93 AA Albany-Colo | 65 | 236 | 44 | 65 | 16 | 1 | 3 | 24 | 12 | 32 | 54 | .275 |
| 94 AA Albany-Colo | 121 | 472 | 75 | 105 | 20 | 3 | 11 | 43 | 22 | 62 | 102 | .222 |
| 95 AA Norwich | 44 | 175 | 23 | 36 | 3 | 5 | 5 | 17 | 8 | 19 | 36 | .206 |
| 95 AAA Columbus | 82 | 302 | 61 | 105 | 16 | 6 | 9 | 37 | 22 | 43 | 41 | .348 |
| 95 MLE | 126 | 465 | 73 | 129 | 16 | 7 | 12 | 47 | 21 | 50 | 80 | .277 |

A year ago, Fox had hit above .248 in only one of six previous professional seasons. Now he's pushed his way into the picture as a possible successor to Wade Boggs. 1995 didn't start off well for Fox, as he was again languishing with a .206 batting average at Norwich, his third season in Double-A. Upon his promotion to Triple-A Columbus, however, he suddenly caught fire. Fox proceeded to bat .348 in 82 games, with his usual high walk and stolen base totals. They were the kind of numbers the Yankees had envisioned when they drafted Fox in the second round of 1989 out of high school, their top selection that year. Although 1996 will be Fox' eighth professional season, he'll still be just 25. And if he can pick up where he left off last season, he's very much in the Yankees' future plans.

## Derek Jeter

**Position:** SS      **Opening Day Age:** 21
**Bats:** R **Throws:** R    **Born:** 6/26/74 in
**Ht:** 6' 3" **Wt:** 175     Pequannock, NJ

### Recent Statistics

|                | G | AB | R | H | D | T | HR | RBI | SB | BB | SO | AVG |
|----------------|---|----|---|---|---|---|----|-----|----|----|----|-----|
| 95 AAA Columbus | 123 | 486 | 96 | 154 | 27 | 9 | 2 | 45 | 20 | 61 | 56 | .317 |
| 95 AL New York | 15 | 48 | 5 | 12 | 4 | 1 | 0 | 7 | 0 | 3 | 11 | .250 |
| 95 MLE | 123 | 471 | 85 | 139 | 25 | 6 | 1 | 40 | 15 | 52 | 58 | .295 |

You have to look hard to find holes in Jeter's game. He doesn't hit many home runs, at least not yet, but he still had enough gap power to total 27 doubles and nine triples at Triple-A last year. Some observers feel he may always have difficulty making the play from the short-stop hole, but that's nitpicking. Jeter has the range and quick feet necessary to play the position. If he can stay there he'll be a tremendous offensive asset, since he should be a .300 hitter with good strike-zone judgment. At 21, Jeter is ready to stick. He and the two Alexes, Rodriguez and Gonzalez, could be the American League's top shortstops for the next decade.

## Jim Musselwhite

**Position:** P      **Opening Day Age:** 24
**Bats:** R **Throws:** R    **Born:** 10/25/71 in
**Ht:** 6' 1" **Wt:** 190     Pompano Beach, FL

### Recent Statistics

|                   | W | L | ERA | G | GS | Sv | IP | H | R | BB | SO | HR |
|-------------------|---|---|-----|---|----|----|----|---|---|----|----|----|
| 93 A Oneonta | 1 | 1 | 2.25 | 5 | 4 | 0 | 20.0 | 15 | 7 | 8 | 18 | 0 |
| 93 A Greensboro | 5 | 3 | 2.79 | 11 | 10 | 0 | 67.2 | 60 | 29 | 24 | 60 | 4 |
| 94 A Tampa | 9 | 6 | 3.43 | 17 | 17 | 0 | 107.2 | 87 | 50 | 23 | 106 | 8 |
| 94 AA Albany-Colo | 2 | 1 | 1.21 | 5 | 5 | 0 | 29.2 | 28 | 4 | 5 | 31 | 0 |
| 95 AA Norwich | 5 | 9 | 4.58 | 24 | 24 | 0 | 131.2 | 136 | 75 | 34 | 96 | 11 |

Musselwhite is one of those pitchers who may have difficulty succeeding against higher levels of competition. Last year, in his first full season above Class A, he compiled a 5-9 record with a 4.58 ERA at Double-A Norwich. It was the first time he had struggled. Drafted in the fifth round of 1993, Musselwhite has great control of four pitches: fastball, slider, change-up and split-finger. The problem is, his mid-80s fastball may be a bit short. He'll probably pitch at Triple-A this season.

## Jorge Posada

**Position:** C      **Opening Day Age:** 24
**Bats:** B **Throws:** R    **Born:** 8/17/71 in
**Ht:** 6' 0" **Wt:** 167     Santurce, PR

### Recent Statistics

|                | G | AB | R | H | D | T | HR | RBI | SB | BB | SO | AVG |
|----------------|---|----|---|---|---|---|----|-----|----|----|----|-----|
| 95 AAA Columbus | 108 | 368 | 60 | 94 | 32 | 5 | 8 | 51 | 4 | 54 | 101 | .255 |
| 95 AL New York | 1 | 0 | 0 | 0 | 0 | 0 | 0 | 0 | 0 | 0 | 0 | - |
| 95 MLE | 108 | 359 | 53 | 85 | 29 | 3 | 7 | 45 | 2 | 45 | 104 | .237 |

Posada is sort of the reverse of Craig Biggio, in that Posada was drafted as a second baseman but shifted to catcher. His defensive skills behind the plate, particularly his footwork, rate above average. Posada repeated Triple-A last season, a year after suffering a broken leg.

His numbers generally improved across the board, especially his doubles total, which zoomed to 32 in just 368 at-bats. Posada is a switch-hitting catcher, which of course has value in itself. When his plate discipline and defensive skills are factored in, you can see why other organizations are interested in his services. The Yankees will likely promote him this season.

## Ruben Rivera

**Position:** OF      **Opening Day Age:** 22
**Bats:** R **Throws:** R    **Born:** 11/14/73 in
**Ht:** 6' 3" **Wt:** 190     Chorrera, Panama

### Recent Statistics

|                | G | AB | R | H | D | T | HR | RBI | SB | BB | SO | AVG |
|----------------|---|----|---|---|---|---|----|-----|----|----|----|-----|
| 95 AA Norwich | 71 | 256 | 49 | 75 | 16 | 8 | 9 | 39 | 16 | 37 | 77 | .293 |
| 95 AAA Columbus | 48 | 174 | 37 | 47 | 8 | 2 | 15 | 35 | 8 | 26 | 62 | .270 |
| 95 AL New York | 5 | 1 | 0 | 0 | 0 | 0 | 0 | 0 | 0 | 0 | 1 | .000 |
| 95 MLE | 119 | 416 | 75 | 108 | 21 | 6 | 20 | 64 | 17 | 48 | 145 | .260 |

Rivera is a scout's dream, as he possesses all the tools they look for in a prospect. Rivera emerged as one of the most coveted properties in baseball when he belted 33 homers, drove in 101 runs and stole 48 bases in 1994. While the raw numbers were not as impressive in 1995, Rivera actually improved his on-base percentage from .357 to .390, and his slugging average from .541 to .553. He did that while making the jump to Double- and Triple-A. Also encouraging was that his home run rate actually increased at Triple-A. Another positive sign was more walks, though he continued to strike out an awful lot. The Yankees envision Rivera as their next superstar.

## Others to Watch

The Yankees have a few catching prospects in their system and **Chris Ashby** is one of their greenest. But a 20-year-old catcher who draws 61 walks in 288 at-bats with power (23 doubles, 9 HR at Class-A Greensboro) catches your attention. . . Outfielder **Brian Buchanan** nearly lost his leg after a terrible break in a game last season. The Yankees hope their 1994 first-round draft choice makes a full recovery. . . Righthander **Ramiro Mendoza** reached Triple-A last season at 23. He's compiled ERA's in the low three's the last two years with good strikeout-to-walk ratios. . . Right-handed reliever **Dan Rios** compiled a 0.70 ERA while saving 19 games in 1994. He saved 24 games last year while striking out 72 in 67.1 innings. . . Lefthander **Brien Taylor**, the former wunderkind who was the top overall draft selection in 1991, just hasn't been the same since an offseason arm injury he suffered in a fight in December of 1993. Last year, Taylor was starting over in rookie ball, and failing miserably, going 2-5 with a 6.08 ERA and 54 walks in 40 innings.

# Mark Acre

## 1995 Season

Many people in the Oakland organization have hoped that righthander Mark Acre could develop into a closer-caliber reliever, and become the heir apparent to Dennis Eckersley. After all, Acre once saved 30 games in a minor league season, and at 6'8" he certainly *looks* like a closer. However, Acre didn't do much to assume such a role in 1995. Used mostly in set-up and mop-up roles, Acre had a rough sophomore campaign, permitting 82 baserunners in only 52 innings. After two seasons, he's still looking for that first major league save.

## Pitching

Seen for the first time, Acre presents an imposing image on the mound. However, American League hitters have become accustomed to his size and delivery, and they've also discovered that his stuff doesn't match his brawn. One glaring example was that right-handed batters hit Acre 105 points better than they hit him a year ago. Acre's fastball rarely tops 90 miles per hour, and while he has worked on both a slider and split-fingered pitch, he has yet to throw either with much consistency. Acre has difficulty maintaining solid mechanics, which results in shaky control.

## Defense

For a big man, Acre does a pretty fair job of holding runners. His slow delivery would appear to leave him vulnerable to basestealers, but he keeps close check on them. A former college basketball player, Acre is a decent athlete who fields his position fairly well.

## 1996 Outlook

If he can find a consistent release point, Acre is still capable of picking up a couple of miles on his fastball and becoming a dominant reliever. However, he remains a question mark, and at this point he probably wouldn't be the A's first choice to finish games should Eckersley falter. He's likely to remain in middle relief for the foreseeable future.

**Position:** RP
**Bats:** R **Throws:** R
**Ht:** 6' 8" **Wt:** 240

**Opening Day Age:** 27
**Born:** 9/16/68 in Concord, CA
**ML Seasons:** 2

### Overall Statistics

|  | W | L | Pct. | ERA | G | GS | Sv | IP | H | BB | SO | HR | BR/IP |
|---|---|---|---|---|---|---|---|---|---|---|---|---|---|
| 1995 | 1 | 2 | .333 | 5.71 | 43 | 0 | 0 | 52.0 | 52 | 28 | 47 | 7 | 1.54 |
| Career | 6 | 3 | .667 | 4.80 | 77 | 0 | 0 | 86.1 | 76 | 51 | 68 | 11 | 1.47 |

### How Often He Throws Strikes

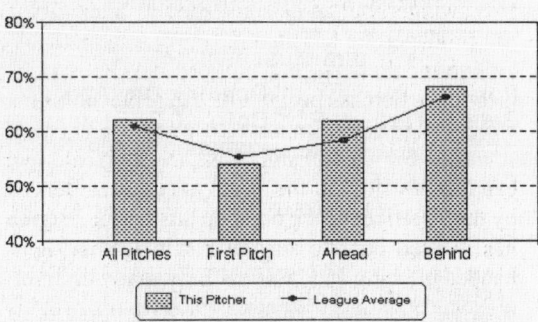

### 1995 Situational Stats

|  | W | L | ERA | Sv | IP |  | AB | H | HR | RBI | Avg |
|---|---|---|---|---|---|---|---|---|---|---|---|
| Home | 0 | 0 | 6.00 | 0 | 18.0 | LHB | 93 | 23 | 2 | 15 | .247 |
| Road | 1 | 2 | 5.56 | 0 | 34.0 | RHB | 110 | 29 | 5 | 26 | .264 |
| First Half | 1 | 2 | 5.91 | 0 | 32.0 | Sc Pos | 71 | 17 | 3 | 34 | .239 |
| Scnd Half | 0 | 0 | 5.40 | 0 | 20.0 | Clutch | 52 | 20 | 4 | 17 | .385 |

### 1995 Rankings (American League)

→ 3rd in highest relief ERA (5.71)
→ 10th in most baserunners allowed per 9 innings in relief (14.2)
→ Led the Athletics in balks (1)

# Geronimo Berroa

Oakland Athletics

## 1995 Season

Without any fanfare, longtime minor league veteran Geronimo Berroa has produced two straight productive seasons and established himself as a major leaguer. Berrora led the Athletics with 88 RBI and 87 runs last season, and ranked second with 22 homers and 88 RBI. And on a team riddled by injuries, Berroa played in more games than any other Oaklander. He looked like an All-Star in May, batting .340 with eight homers, but settled down after that and wound up with decent numbers for a DH/left fielder.

## Hitting

Berroa came to the majors with a reputation as a free swinger, but as he's emerged as a legitimate run producer, he has also improved his plate discipline and drawn a good number of walks. Berroa is tough to defense because he can drive the ball to either left or right. Improved batting eye notwithstanding, Berroa will still chase breaking balls and can lose touch with the strike zone, as evidenced by the 98 strikeouts he piled up last season. Berroa has worked hard to stay in better against right-handed pitching and last year he actually hit righties some 50 points better than lefties, with 19 of his homers coming against right-handed pitching.

## Baserunning & Defense

Berroa is an aggressive baserunner who managed three triples last year and will steal an occasional base. His speed is not exceptional, however. Used often as a DH, Berroa has improved his outfield defense, but he misjudges more than a few fly balls and his arm is neither strong nor accurate.

## 1996 Outlook

His solid '95 season proved Berroa's emergence was no fluke. Depending on the makeup of their club, Berroa might have to play more outfield than the Athletics would prefer. But he should once again post solid offensive numbers in the middle of the Oakland lineup.

**Position:** DH/LF/RF
**Bats:** R  **Throws:** R
**Ht:** 6' 0"  **Wt:** 195

**Opening Day Age:** 31
**Born:** 3/18/65 in Santo Domingo, DR
**ML Seasons:** 6
**Pronunciation:** ber-ROH-uh

### Overall Statistics

|  | G | AB | R | H | D | T | HR | RBI | SB | BB | SO | Avg | OBP | Slg |
|---|---|---|---|---|---|---|---|---|---|---|---|---|---|---|
| 1995 | 141 | 546 | 87 | 152 | 22 | 3 | 22 | 88 | 7 | 63 | 98 | .278 | .351 | .451 |
| Career | 352 | 1075 | 154 | 300 | 46 | 5 | 37 | 162 | 14 | 116 | 201 | .279 | .348 | .434 |

### Where He Hits the Ball

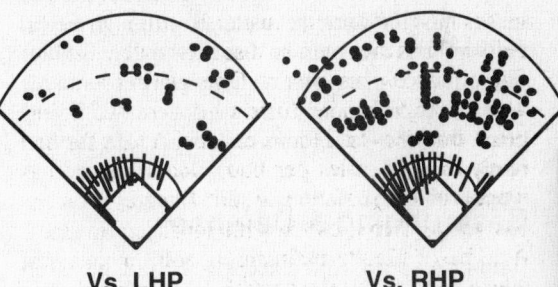

**Vs. LHP**          **Vs. RHP**

### 1995 Situational Stats

|  | AB | H | HR | RBI | Avg |  | AB | H | HR | RBI | Avg |
|---|---|---|---|---|---|---|---|---|---|---|---|
| Home | 264 | 76 | 10 | 36 | .288 | LHP | 152 | 36 | 3 | 17 | .237 |
| Road | 282 | 76 | 12 | 52 | .270 | RHP | 394 | 116 | 19 | 71 | .294 |
| First Half | 259 | 70 | 12 | 42 | .270 | Sc Pos | 139 | 36 | 3 | 53 | .259 |
| Scnd Half | 287 | 82 | 10 | 46 | .286 | Clutch | 86 | 22 | 2 | 13 | .256 |

### 1995 Rankings (American League)

→ 9th in errors in right field (3)
→ 10th in lowest batting average on an 0-2 count (.053)
→ Led the Athletics in at-bats, runs scored, hits, singles (105), total bases (246), times on base (216), strikeouts, pitches seen (2,398), plate appearances (616), games played, slugging percentage and HR frequency (24.8 ABs per HR)

# Mike Bordick

## 1995 Season

Now established as one of baseball's most dependable shortstops, Mike Bordick had a typically solid season in 1995. He hit .264, virtually his career average. He chipped in with some key RBI, fielded steadily—and at times spectacularly—at shortstop, and was the Athletics' leader on the field during a difficult season.

## Hitting

Bordick has closed his stance and shortened his swing in order to better fight off hard inside stuff. He's improved so much in that area that he hit righthanders better than lefties last season. A good breaking-ball hitter, Bordick hits the ball where it's pitched and can occasionally go deep when he gets a mistake over the plate. But though he hit eight homers last year, he's mostly a singles hitter with one of the lower slugging percentages around. An impatient hitter, he doesn't walk very often, but he also seldom strikes out. He's a fine bunter.

## Baserunning & Defense

Bordick's speed isn't exceptional, but he is an aggressive, smart baserunner and has become a high-percentage basestealer. His greatest value is in the field, where he is among the best half-dozen shortstops in baseball. Bordick has the whole defensive package: good range, excellent knowledge of hitters, an accurate and strong arm, and soft hands. He made only 10 errors last year, despite his willingness to attempt plays few other shortstops could even hope to make.

## 1996 Outlook

On a club likely headed for a major transition, Bordick's hustle, reliability and leadership—especially at a key position like shortstop—is a major asset. His offensive production is ordinary at best, but his defense more than makes up for that. With luck, his value won't be lost on the new regime which is taking over the Oakland franchise and might not want to spend the money to keep its veteran players.

**Position:** SS
**Bats:** R **Throws:** R
**Ht:** 5'11" **Wt:** 175

**Opening Day Age:** 30
**Born:** 7/21/65 in Marquette, MI
**ML Seasons:** 6

### Overall Statistics

|        | G   | AB   | R   | H   | D  | T  | HR | RBI | SB | BB  | SO  | Avg  | OBP  | Slg  |
|--------|-----|------|-----|-----|----|----|----|-----|----|-----|-----|------|------|------|
| 1995   | 126 | 428  | 46  | 113 | 13 | 0  | 8  | 44  | 11 | 35  | 48  | .264 | .325 | .350 |
| Career | 668 | 2118 | 227 | 556 | 76 | 11 | 16 | 198 | 43 | 188 | 250 | .263 | .329 | .331 |

### Where He Hits the Ball

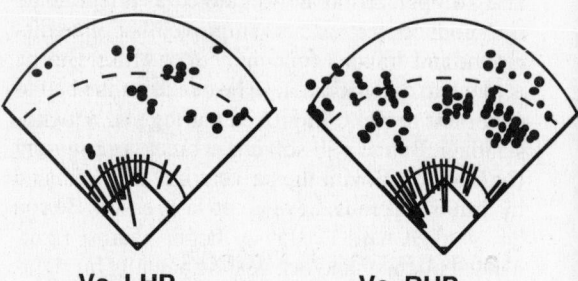

**Vs. LHP**          **Vs. RHP**

### 1995 Situational Stats

|            | AB  | H  | HR | RBI | Avg  |        | AB  | H  | HR | RBI | Avg  |
|------------|-----|----|----|-----|------|--------|-----|----|----|-----|------|
| Home       | 204 | 55 | 2  | 17  | .270 | LHP    | 109 | 26 | 2  | 9   | .239 |
| Road       | 224 | 58 | 6  | 27  | .259 | RHP    | 319 | 87 | 6  | 35  | .273 |
| First Half | 181 | 49 | 2  | 14  | .271 | Sc Pos | 97  | 24 | 1  | 34  | .247 |
| Scnd Half  | 247 | 64 | 6  | 30  | .259 | Clutch | 71  | 20 | 1  | 5   | .282 |

### 1995 Rankings (American League)

➡ 4th in lowest slugging percentage and highest fielding percentage at shortstop (.983)
➡ 7th in highest percentage of swings put into play (53.2%)
➡ 9th in lowest slugging percentage vs. left-handed pitchers (.303), lowest slugging percentage vs. right-handed pitchers (.367) and errors at shortstop (10)
➡ 10th in lowest on-base percentage and lowest percentage of swings that missed (10.5%)
➡ Led the Athletics in sacrifice bunts (7), lowest percentage of swings that missed and highest percentage of swings put into play

# Scott Brosius

## 1995 Season

Playing much of the season as Oakland's regular third baseman, Scott Brosius continued his development into a power-hitting threat. He ranked third on the Athletics with a career-high 17 homers, and was fourth on the club with 69 runs scored. However, Brosius continued to struggle in RBI situations, a problem that has kept him from producing acceptable RBI totals. And his defense remained adequate at best.

## Hitting

Brosius is strong enough to hit the ball out of the park to any field, and he has worked to cut down his swing, thus leaving himself less vulnerable to change-ups and breaking balls. He has kept his strikeouts under control and though he does not walk all that much, he has improved his selectivity at the plate. Brosius' biggest problem is that he continues to press in RBI situations. He hit only .219 with runners in scoring position last season, the worst mark among the Oakland regulars, and his career figure is .239.

## Baserunning & Defense

Brosius has passable speed, is aggressive on the bases and will swipe the occasional sack. He has made some strides as a third baseman, improving his range and his hands, but he remains error-prone. Most of his fielding problems come on throws; Brosius has a strong arm but will often overthrow balls into the dirt or sail them wide of first. Brosius supplies some versatility, as he's got experience at all the infield positions and the outfield.

## 1996 Outlook

Brosius has the kind of power that is not easily dismissed, and though he still lacks consistency and hasn't really settled down on defense, he remains a valuable player. If Brosius gets 400 at-bats, he is likely to hit 20 or more home runs, and right-handed power like that is tough to find.

**Position:** 3B/1B/CF/RF
**Bats:** R  **Throws:** R
**Ht:** 6' 1"  **Wt:** 185

**Opening Day Age:** 29
**Born:** 8/15/66 in Hillsboro, OR
**ML Seasons:** 5
**Pronunciation:** BRO-shus

### Overall Statistics

|        | G   | AB   | R   | H   | D  | T | HR | RBI | SB | BB | SO  | Avg  | OBP  | Slg  |
|--------|-----|------|-----|-----|----|---|----|-----|----|----|-----|------|------|------|
| 1995   | 123 | 389  | 69  | 102 | 19 | 2 | 17 | 46  | 4  | 41 | 67  | .262 | .342 | .452 |
| Career | 363 | 1081 | 148 | 267 | 50 | 4 | 43 | 137 | 18 | 85 | 185 | .247 | .306 | .420 |

### Where He Hits the Ball

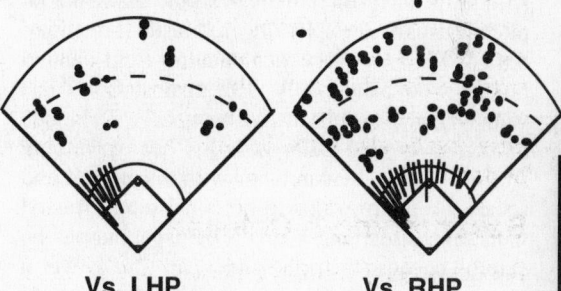

**Vs. LHP**          **Vs. RHP**

### 1995 Situational Stats

|            | AB  | H  | HR | RBI | Avg  |        | AB  | H  | HR | RBI | Avg  |
|------------|-----|----|----|-----|------|--------|-----|----|----|-----|------|
| Home       | 177 | 48 | 12 | 25  | .271 | LHP    | 124 | 29 | 3  | 8   | .234 |
| Road       | 212 | 54 | 5  | 21  | .255 | RHP    | 265 | 73 | 14 | 38  | .275 |
| First Half | 195 | 45 | 5  | 14  | .231 | Sc Pos | 96  | 21 | 3  | 29  | .219 |
| Scnd Half  | 194 | 57 | 12 | 32  | .294 | Clutch | 55  | 12 | 0  | 2   | .218 |

### 1995 Rankings (American League)

➡ 8th in lowest batting average with runners in scoring position (.219)
➡ 9th in highest percentage of swings on the first pitch (36.8%)

# Jim Corsi

## 1995 Season

Jim Corsi's destiny apparently lies in Oakland. He began his career there in 1988, pitched a season in Houston, returned to the Athletics in 1992, was selected by Florida in the expansion draft, and was an Athletic again last season. Bouncing back from shoulder troubles, Corsi's third stint in Oakland was largely successful, though he did spend about six weeks on the disabled list with a recurrence of shoulder problems. Used mostly as a set-up man, he led all Oakland pitchers with a 2.20 ERA while allowing only 31 hits in 45 innings.

## Pitching

Despite his many physical problems, Corsi can still throw his fastball in the low 90s. His strikeout pitch is usually the split-fingered fastball or slider, both of which are very tough against right-handed hitters, who batted only .192 against Corsi last year. When Corsi is at his best, he will induce numerous ground balls with his heavy, sinking stuff. However, he can labor with his control and issues too many walks to be consistently trusted with save situations. Corsi's manager has to be careful, because the righthander can't really warm up several times during a game. When he heats up, he needs to pitch or he has trouble getting loose again for the next few days.

## Defense

Corsi has difficulty holding runners and is fairly slow to the plate, but last year only three runners tried to steal, and two of them were gunned down. He is an average fielder at best.

## 1996 Outlook

Trusting Corsi from year to year has been risky because of his long history of injuries. He gave the Athletics a solid season, and when healthy he's an effective reliever. Corsi got a third chance in Oakland only because of his past relationship with Tony La Russa and pitching coach Dave Duncan. If the new Athletic brain trust doesn't want him, he'll probably get a look in St. Louis.

**Position:** RP
**Bats:** R  **Throws:** R
**Ht:** 6' 1"  **Wt:** 220

**Opening Day Age:** 34
**Born:** 9/9/61 in Newton, MA
**ML Seasons:** 6

### Overall Statistics

|        | W | L  | Pct. | ERA  | G   | GS | Sv | IP    | H   | BB | SO  | HR | BR/IP |
|--------|---|----|------|------|-----|----|----|-------|-----|----|-----|----|-------|
| 1995   | 2 | 4  | .333 | 2.20 | 38  | 0  | 2  | 45.0  | 31  | 26 | 26  | 2  | 1.27  |
| Career | 7 | 16 | .304 | 2.99 | 165 | 1  | 2  | 246.2 | 225 | 93 | 136 | 14 | 1.29  |

### How Often He Throws Strikes

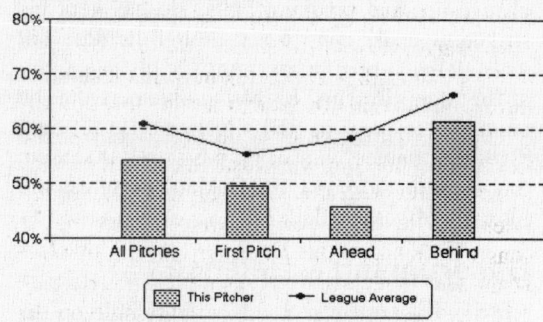

### 1995 Situational Stats

|            | W | L | ERA  | Sv | IP   |        | AB | H  | HR | RBI | Avg  |
|------------|---|---|------|----|------|--------|----|----|----|-----|------|
| Home       | 1 | 3 | 1.86 | 1  | 19.1 | LHB    | 80 | 17 | 0  | 7   | .213 |
| Road       | 1 | 1 | 2.45 | 1  | 25.2 | RHB    | 73 | 14 | 2  | 6   | .192 |
| First Half | 2 | 3 | 1.67 | 2  | 27.0 | Sc Pos | 46 | 6  | 0  | 11  | .130 |
| Scnd Half  | 0 | 1 | 3.00 | 0  | 18.0 | Clutch | 88 | 21 | 1  | 7   | .239 |

### 1995 Rankings (American League)

➡ 3rd in lowest batting average allowed in relief with runners on base (.137) and lowest batting average allowed in relief with runners in scoring position (.130)
➡ 4th in most GDPs induced per GDP situation (22.0%)
➡ 7th in holds (13)
➡ Led the Athletics in holds, lowest batting average allowed in relief with runners on base and lowest batting average allowed in relief with runners in scoring position

# Dennis Eckersley

## 1995 Season

It is a measure of the greatness of Dennis Eckersley that a 29-save season was widely viewed as perhaps the end of the line for one of the all-time great relievers. However, behind the save numbers were some distressing developments. Eckersley blew nine saves, suffered six losses, posted a 4.83 ERA—his highest ever as a reliever—and for a second straight season allowed more hits than innings pitched.

## Pitching

Eckersley still can have stretches when he has perfect control of his slider and running fastball, and that makes the job of closing games seem easy. However, Eckersley's margin for error has all but disappeared. He used to establish every at-bat with a first-pitch fastball strike, but now that fastball is thrown in the mid 80s rather than the low 90s. So hitters are aggressive early in the count against Eckersley if he's throwing fastballs. And if he tries to get ahead with the slider or forkball, hitters often will lay off what once were pitches they'd chase. Lefthanders hit Eckersley hard (.347 last year), and though he remains deadly vs. righties (.145), Eckersley did allow two homers to righthanders, including a monster, game-losing shot to Manny Ramirez. Eckersley works much deeper counts than he did a few years ago.

## Defense

Though he works hard to hold runners, Eckersley does not have a good pickoff move and is easy to run on because of his distinctive delivery. He is an excellent fielder.

## 1996 Outlook

Eckersley toyed with retirement, especially with Tony La Russa now in St. Louis, but decided to return to Oakland for another season. At 41, he'll be watched carefully for further signs of deterioration. The end is near.

**Position:** RP
**Bats:** R  **Throws:** R
**Ht:** 6' 2"  **Wt:** 195

**Opening Day Age:** 41
**Born:** 10/3/54 in Oakland, CA
**ML Seasons:** 21

### Overall Statistics

| | W | L | Pct. | ERA | G | GS | Sv | IP | H | BB | SO | HR | BR/IP |
|---|---|---|---|---|---|---|---|---|---|---|---|---|---|
| 1995 | 4 | 6 | .400 | 4.83 | 52 | 0 | 29 | 50.1 | 53 | 11 | 40 | 5 | 1.27 |
| Career | 192 | 159 | .547 | 3.48 | 901 | 361 | 323 | 3133.0 | 2916 | 716 | 2285 | 324 | 1.16 |

### How Often He Throws Strikes

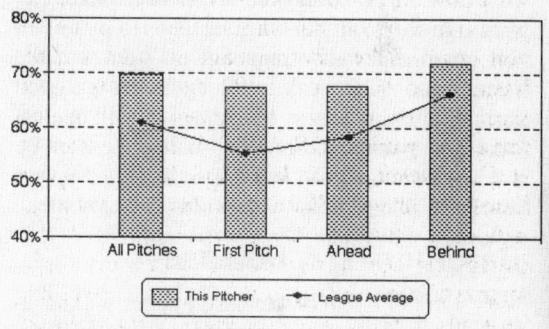

### 1995 Situational Stats

| | W | L | ERA | Sv | IP | | AB | H | HR | RBI | Avg |
|---|---|---|---|---|---|---|---|---|---|---|---|
| Home | 3 | 3 | 5.68 | 19 | 25.1 | LHB | 121 | 42 | 3 | 21 | .347 |
| Road | 1 | 3 | 3.96 | 10 | 25.0 | RHB | 76 | 11 | 2 | 7 | .145 |
| First Half | 2 | 2 | 3.10 | 18 | 29.0 | Sc Pos | 52 | 15 | 2 | 23 | .288 |
| Scnd Half | 2 | 4 | 7.17 | 11 | 21.1 | Clutch | 121 | 36 | 5 | 24 | .298 |

### 1995 Rankings (American League)

- → 2nd in blown saves (9)
- → 4th in save opportunities (38), lowest save percentage (76.3%) and relief losses (6)
- → 6th in first batter efficiency (.163)
- → 7th in saves and games finished (48)
- → Led the Athletics in games pitched, saves, games finished, save opportunities, save percentage, blown saves, first batter efficiency and relief losses

Oakland Athletics

# Brent Gates

**Position:** 2B
**Bats:** B  **Throws:** R
**Ht:** 6' 1"  **Wt:** 180

**Opening Day Age:** 26
**Born:** 3/14/70 in Grand Rapids, MI
**ML Seasons:** 3

## 1995 Season

Finally injury free, Brent Gates recovered from a slow start to have a solid, if unspectacular, season as Oakland's regular second baseman. Gates knocked in 56 runs, thanks to a .286 batting average with men in scoring position. Gates' biggest problem was consistency. He was hitting just .183 at the end of May, then tended to alternate good and bad months.

## Hitting

The switch-hitting Gates hit 20 points higher from the right side than the left, though that difference is so small as to be meaningless. The Athletics think he will get stronger and develop more extra-base power than he showed last season. Gates can spray the ball to all fields but he tends to try to pull too often, especially from the left side, and the result is too many weak ground balls. He is a good fastball hitter, however, and hangs in well against offspeed stuff and breaking balls. He can be pitched inside, but if his bat speed keeps improving, he should eventually be a .285 to .300 hitter.

## Baserunning & Defense

Only a minor threat on the bases, Gates will occasionally attempt to steal a base. He has good judgment and is aggressive in taking the extra base. At second base, Gates looks shaky at times when turning the double play, and he'll occasionally have concentration lapses on routine grounders. However, he also has excellent range and good overall skills.

## 1996 Outlook

Gates needed part of last year to get himself sharp after missing much of 1994 with thumb and knee injuries. He has the talent to be one of the top second basemen in the American League, and the offensive ability to put up strong numbers. On a club with loads of future questions, Gates at least is a major source of potential.

### Overall Statistics

|  | G | AB | R | H | D | T | HR | RBI | SB | BB | SO | Avg | OBP | Slg |
|---|---|---|---|---|---|---|---|---|---|---|---|---|---|---|
| 1995 | 136 | 524 | 60 | 133 | 24 | 4 | 5 | 56 | 3 | 46 | 84 | .254 | .308 | .344 |
| Career | 339 | 1292 | 153 | 354 | 64 | 7 | 14 | 149 | 13 | 123 | 191 | .274 | .334 | .367 |

### Where He Hits the Ball

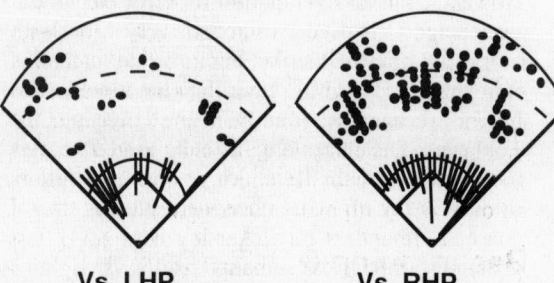

Vs. LHP          Vs. RHP

### 1995 Situational Stats

| | AB | H | HR | RBI | Avg | | AB | H | HR | RBI | Avg |
|---|---|---|---|---|---|---|---|---|---|---|---|
| Home | 259 | 72 | 3 | 20 | .278 | LHP | 134 | 36 | 2 | 13 | .269 |
| Road | 265 | 61 | 2 | 36 | .230 | RHP | 390 | 97 | 3 | 43 | .249 |
| First Half | 234 | 54 | 2 | 23 | .231 | Sc Pos | 119 | 34 | 1 | 50 | .286 |
| Scnd Half | 290 | 79 | 3 | 33 | .272 | Clutch | 84 | 18 | 2 | 15 | .214 |

### 1995 Rankings (American League)

→ 2nd in sacrifice flies (11) and lowest slugging percentage
→ 3rd in lowest slugging percentage vs. right-handed pitchers (.326)
→ 4th in lowest on-base percentage, lowest HR frequency (104.8 ABs per HR), highest groundball/flyball ratio (1.9), lowest on-base percentage vs. right-handed pitchers (.303) and fielding percentage at second base (.982)
→ 5th in errors at second base (12)
→ 8th in lowest batting average on the road (.230)
→ Led the Athletics in triples, sacrifice flies, GDPs (15) and highest groundball/flyball ratio (1.9)

# Rickey Henderson

## 1995 Season

The mercurial Rickey Henderson can still play the game at a very high level. The trouble is, it's so difficult to know when he is interested in playing. He took himself out of the lineup on numerous occasions last year, to the point where Tony La Russa finally lost patience and ripped Henderson's attitude. Lost amid the personalities was Henderson's production, as he hit .300 with 31 doubles, 54 RBI and 32 steals.

## Hitting

Henderson remains one of the game's most selective hitters. He goes deep into counts with a regularity unmatched in baseball. As a result, he walks a ton and continues to top the .400 mark in on-base percentage. However, in recent years pitchers have been able to throw fastballs by Henderson more frequently, so his strikeouts have increased and his power has gone backward. Though he often infuriates his team with his attitude, Henderson remains a great clutch hitter who last season hit over .400 with men in scoring position.

## Baserunning & Defense

Henderson's frequent muscle pulls, real or imagined, have made him a far less disruptive basestealer. Though he was back among the league leaders last year, his basestealing percentage was not good, and at times he appeared reluctant to run, perhaps understandable given his leg woes. When his mind is in the game, he is one of the game's premier left fielders with still-fine range and an accurate, if not particularly strong, arm. Henderson will allow a handful of balls to go over his head when he gets late jumps.

## 1996 Outlook

What's so frustrating about Henderson is that even at his advanced age, he still has those Hall of Fame skills. However, he's now a day-to-day question mark for a manager filling out a lineup card, and many clubs will undoubtedly be reluctant to sign such a player. Not that Henderson will have any problems finding work this season; just don't count on him for more than 120 or so games.

**Position:** LF/DH
**Bats:** R **Throws:** L
**Ht:** 5'10" **Wt:** 190

**Opening Day Age:** 37
**Born:** 12/25/58 in Chicago, IL
**ML Seasons:** 17

### Overall Statistics

|  | G | AB | R | H | D | T | HR | RBI | SB | BB | SO | Avg | OBP | Slg |
|---|---|---|---|---|---|---|---|---|---|---|---|---|---|---|
| 1995 | 112 | 407 | 67 | 122 | 31 | 1 | 9 | 54 | 32 | 72 | 66 | .300 | .407 | .447 |
| Career | 2192 | 8063 | 1719 | 2338 | 395 | 57 | 235 | 858 | 1149 | 1550 | 1101 | .290 | .406 | .441 |

### Where He Hits the Ball

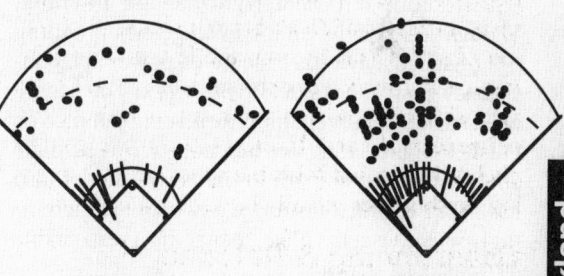

Vs. LHP          Vs. RHP

### 1995 Situational Stats

|  | AB | H | HR | RBI | Avg |  | AB | H | HR | RBI | Avg |
|---|---|---|---|---|---|---|---|---|---|---|---|
| Home | 208 | 62 | 3 | 25 | .298 | LHP | 120 | 28 | 2 | 10 | .233 |
| Road | 199 | 60 | 6 | 29 | .302 | RHP | 287 | 94 | 7 | 44 | .328 |
| First Half | 210 | 58 | 5 | 28 | .276 | Sc Pos | 74 | 31 | 1 | 43 | .419 |
| Scnd Half | 197 | 64 | 4 | 26 | .325 | Clutch | 56 | 20 | 2 | 9 | .357 |

### 1995 Rankings (American League)

→ 1st in most pitches seen per plate appearance (4.37) and batting average with runners in scoring position (.419)
→ 3rd in on-base percentage for a leadoff hitter (.408) and fielding percentage in left field (.988)
→ 4th in steals of third (11)
→ 5th in batting average vs. right-handed pitchers (.328) and highest percentage of pitches taken (63.5%)
→ 6th in lowest percentage of swings on the first pitch (13.3%)
→ Led the Athletics in batting average, doubles, caught stealing (10) and on-base percentage

# Stan Javier

## 1995 Season

Stan Javier's second stint as an Athletic has proven to be a beneficial one, both for himself and the club. Labeled a part-time player for most of his career, Javier has finally established himself as someone who can put together front-line numbers. He gave Oakland a second straight solid season, getting most of his playing time as an everyday center fielder, along with occasional time in left subbing for the oft-injured Rickey Henderson. Javier set career highs with 56 RBI, 81 runs and 36 steals.

## Hitting

Javier over the last few years has held his own against both left- and right-handed pitching. Though a better hitter for average when batting right-handed, Javier is capable of power and consistency from either side. He has worked on a more open stance to prevent him from being jammed so much by hard stuff, yet has not sacrificed plate coverage or his strength to the alleys. Javier also has kept his strikeouts down and become increasingly selective at the plate, managing a respectable 49 walks last season.

## Baserunning & Defense

Javier has excellent speed and gets a very quick start away from first, making him an outstanding basestealer. With his increased playing time of late, his knowledge of pitchers' moves has made him one of the league's best percentage runners. Javier is solid at each of the three outfield positions, displaying solid range. His arm is just decent, but Javier compensates by charging the ball and throwing quickly.

## 1996 Outlook

It's unlikely that Javier will ever be an All-Star, but he's a solid player with a range of offensive and defensive skills. In December, Javier moved across the Bay after signing a two-year deal with the San Francisco Giants. Pending the disposition of Deion Sanders, Javier should be in line for a regular job with the Giants.

**Position:** CF/LF
**Bats:** B  **Throws:** R
**Ht:** 6' 0"  **Wt:** 185

**Opening Day Age:** 32
**Born:** 1/9/64 in San Francisco de Macoris, DR
**ML Seasons:** 11
**Pronunciation:** HAV-ee-air

### Overall Statistics

|  | G | AB | R | H | D | T | HR | RBI | SB | BB | SO | Avg | OBP | Slg |
|---|---|---|---|---|---|---|---|---|---|---|---|---|---|---|
| 1995 | 130 | 442 | 81 | 123 | 20 | 2 | 8 | 56 | 36 | 49 | 63 | .278 | .353 | .387 |
| Career | 1089 | 2896 | 439 | 748 | 120 | 23 | 31 | 275 | 155 | 316 | 481 | .258 | .332 | .348 |

### Where He Hits the Ball

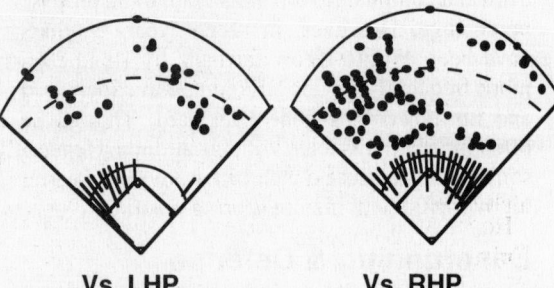

**Vs. LHP**          **Vs. RHP**

### 1995 Situational Stats

|  | AB | H | HR | RBI | Avg |  | AB | H | HR | RBI | Avg |
|---|---|---|---|---|---|---|---|---|---|---|---|
| Home | 202 | 52 | 3 | 25 | .257 | LHP | 119 | 36 | 3 | 18 | .303 |
| Road | 240 | 71 | 5 | 31 | .296 | RHP | 323 | 87 | 5 | 38 | .269 |
| First Half | 216 | 56 | 4 | 18 | .259 | Sc Pos | 132 | 37 | 2 | 47 | .280 |
| Scnd Half | 226 | 67 | 4 | 38 | .296 | Clutch | 77 | 19 | 2 | 11 | .247 |

### 1995 Rankings (American League)

- ➡ 1st in fielding percentage in center field (1.000)
- ➡ 3rd in stolen base percentage (87.8%)
- ➡ 5th in bunts in play (26) and steals of third (9)
- ➡ 7th in stolen bases, lowest batting average on an 0-2 count (.045) and lowest slugging percentage vs. right-handed pitchers (.356)
- ➡ 8th in highest groundball/flyball ratio (1.7)
- ➡ 9th in lowest batting average at home (.257)
- ➡ Led the Athletics in stolen bases, stolen base percentage, batting average vs. left-handed pitchers (.303) and bunts in play

# Mark McGwire

## 1995 Season

Between lengthy absences due to back and hamstring problems, Mark McGwire had a monster year that might have reached historic proportions if he'd been able to play a full season. In only 317 at-bats, McGwire blasted 39 home runs for a ratio unsurpassed in major league history. He added 90 RBI on only 87 hits, another rare feat.

## Hitting

McGwire's many injuries have not eroded one of the great power swings in baseball. His bat speed remains awesome, and with his plate coverage and great strength, it is very difficult to sneak a fastball by him. McGwire can be handled at times with offspeed stuff, but he chases few bad pitches because of his outstanding plate discipline. McGwire is a dead pull hitter. He has the strength to hit a ball out anywhere, but rarely tries to take pitches to the opposite field, preferring to wait for deliveries he can turn on. Pitchers will try to crowd McGwire in order to prevent him from extending his arms. However, if a pitcher misses just a little over the plate, he'll get burned.

## Baserunning & Defense

Known—as well he should be—for his power, McGwire doesn't get the recognition he deserves for his excellent fielding. Though he had some error problems last season, his hands are usually as soft as any first baseman in the American League, and he excels at scooping throws in the dirt. He also has an accurate arm and good range for a man so big. He's a plodder on the basepaths.

## 1996 Outlook

When Oakland's new owners took over the club, one of the partners suggested McGwire was unreliable because of his injuries. However, his injuries last year were unrelated to his chronic heel problem and McGwire is a fanatic about conditioning. All baseball fans should hope that McGwire can stay healthy for a full season, because if that ever happens we might see some truly historic numbers.

**Position:** 1B
**Bats:** R  **Throws:** R
**Ht:** 6' 5"  **Wt:** 250

**Opening Day Age:** 32
**Born:** 10/1/63 in Pomona, CA
**ML Seasons:** 10

### Overall Statistics

|        | G    | AB   | R   | H   | D   | T | HR  | RBI | SB | BB  | SO  | Avg  | OBP  | Slg  |
|--------|------|------|-----|-----|-----|---|-----|-----|----|-----|-----|------|------|------|
| 1995   | 104  | 317  | 75  | 87  | 13  | 0 | 39  | 90  | 1  | 88  | 77  | .274 | .441 | .685 |
| Career | 1094 | 3659 | 621 | 921 | 150 | 5 | 277 | 747 | 7  | 673 | 833 | .252 | .369 | .523 |

### Where He Hits the Ball

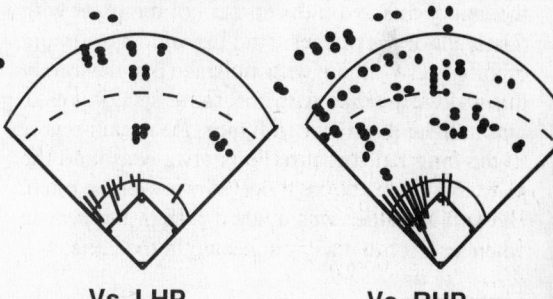

**Vs. LHP**          **Vs. RHP**

### 1995 Situational Stats

|            | AB  | H  | HR | RBI | Avg  |        | AB  | H  | HR | RBI | Avg  |
|------------|-----|----|----|-----|------|--------|-----|----|----|-----|------|
| Home       | 145 | 36 | 15 | 38  | .248 | LHP    | 79  | 22 | 14 | 28  | .278 |
| Road       | 172 | 51 | 24 | 52  | .297 | RHP    | 238 | 65 | 25 | 62  | .273 |
| First Half | 212 | 58 | 24 | 59  | .274 | Sc Pos | 69  | 21 | 9  | 45  | .304 |
| Scnd Half  | 105 | 29 | 15 | 31  | .276 | Clutch | 47  | 12 | 5  | 14  | .255 |

### 1995 Rankings (American League)

→ 1st in cleanup slugging percentage (.697), errors at first base (12) and lowest fielding percentage at first base (.986)

→ 2nd in slugging percentage vs. left-handed pitchers (.835)

→ 4th in home runs, hit by pitch (11) and on-base percentage vs. left-handed pitchers (.478)

→ 8th in walks, lowest batting average with two strikes (.135) and highest percentage of pitches taken (62.0%)

→ 10th in highest percentage of swings that missed (27.5%)

→ Led the Athletics in home runs, RBI, walks, intentional walks (5) and hit by pitch

# Steve Ontiveros

## 1995 Season

After winning the American League ERA title in 1994, Steve Ontiveros got off to a great start last year and made the All-Star team. But the oft-injured Ontiveros had his second half spoiled by neck and shoulder problems. He won only once after the break, with his ERA rising from 3.09 to 4.37.

## Pitching

Health permitting, Ontiveros is a craftsman on the mound. He throws both a cut fastball and a sinker, both of them in the mid 80s. He can change speeds with both and also mixes in an excellent overhand curve, an occasional slider and a forkball. He has the ability to stay on the corners of the plate with nearly all of his pitches. And his wide assortment of offerings—along with the fact that he rarely throws two pitches with the same speed—make him a difficult pitcher to figure. He is vulnerable to the long ball because he is always around the plate and does not have one overpowering pitch. His stiff shoulder was evident late in the season when he left too many pitches up in the zone.

## Defense

A martial-arts devotee, Ontiveros is a very good athlete who does the little things to help himself out on the mound. He can be exasperatingly diligent about keeping runners close. He's got a decent pickoff move to first plus a quick delivery home, both of which limit the stolen base. He is one of the better fielding pitchers around.

## 1996 Outlook

It all comes down to whether he stays healthy. Ontiveros works hard to stay in shape and he is a great competitor, always looking for a new edge. But he has not been able to keep himself in the rotation because of the physical woes. If he *can* stay in one piece, Ontiveros is certainly capable of winning 15 games for the A's—or some other team—over a full season.

**Position:** SP
**Bats:** R  **Throws:** R
**Ht:** 6' 0"  **Wt:** 190

**Opening Day Age:** 35
**Born:** 3/5/61 in Tularosa, NM
**ML Seasons:** 9
**Pronunciation:** on-tuh-VAIR-ohs

### Overall Statistics

|  | W | L | Pct. | ERA | G | GS | Sv | IP | H | BB | SO | HR | BR/IP |
|---|---|---|------|-----|---|----|----|-----|---|----|----|----|-------|
| 1995 | 9 | 6 | .600 | 4.37 | 22 | 22 | 0 | 129.2 | 144 | 38 | 77 | 12 | 1.40 |
| Career | 33 | 30 | .524 | 3.62 | 204 | 72 | 19 | 656.1 | 613 | 203 | 381 | 59 | 1.24 |

### How Often He Throws Strikes

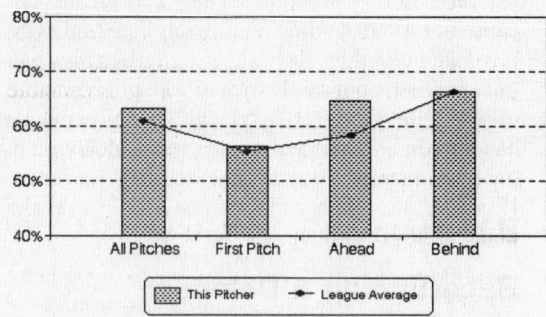

### 1995 Situational Stats

|  | W | L | ERA | Sv | IP |  | AB | H | HR | RBI | Avg |
|---|---|---|-----|----|-----|---|-----|----|----|-----|------|
| Home | 5 | 3 | 3.88 | 0 | 67.1 | LHB | 328 | 86 | 8 | 33 | .262 |
| Road | 4 | 3 | 4.91 | 0 | 62.1 | RHB | 180 | 58 | 4 | 29 | .322 |
| First Half | 8 | 3 | 3.09 | 0 | 84.1 | Sc Pos | 112 | 31 | 4 | 49 | .277 |
| Scnd Half | 1 | 3 | 6.75 | 0 | 45.1 | Clutch | 21 | 6 | 1 | 2 | .286 |

### 1995 Rankings (American League)

→ 1st in fielding percentage at pitcher (1.000)
→ 9th in shutouts (1)
→ Led the Athletics in complete games (2) and shutouts

# Craig Paquette

## 1995 Season

When Mark McGwire was on the disabled list last year, the A's moved Scott Brosius to first and gave Craig Paquette an extended stretch of playing time at third. Paquette responded with encouraging power, producing 13 homers and 49 RBI in only 283 at-bats. However, Paquette had difficulty making contact and struck out once every three at-bats.

## Hitting

Paquette is strong enough to hit a mistake over the fence. However, his problem is that he makes contact on virtually nothing except those occasional mistakes. He is a wild swinger with little patience. His big swing has holes, and he's easily exploited by hard stuff inside and offspeed stuff low and away. Paquette walked only 12 times last year while fanning 88 times, a totally unacceptable ratio. He is not appreciably better against left-handed pitching, which negates the option of trying him in a platoon situation.

## Baserunning & Defense

An aggressive runner, Paquette has surprising speed and can steal an occasional base though he is hardly a big-time threat on the bases. At third, he has decent range but needs to work on his footwork, which is awkward and sometimes prevents him from getting to balls he should reach. Paquette has fairly good hands and a strong but erratic arm, with most of his miscues being throwing errors.

## 1996 Outlook

Paquette has been a "prospect" for some time and his power alone will probably keep him around in some kind of role this year. However, he's a .217 lifetime hitter who never walks, and an occasional home run isn't going to make up for that kind of weak production. The A's have other third-base prospects on the way and Paquette won't get too many more chances to win a regular job unless he starts making more consistent contact.

**Position:** 3B/LF
**Bats:** R **Throws:** R
**Ht:** 6' 0" **Wt:** 190

**Opening Day Age:** 27
**Born:** 3/28/69 in Long Beach, CA
**ML Seasons:** 3
**Pronunciation:** pah-KET

### Overall Statistics

|  | G | AB | R | H | D | T | HR | RBI | SB | BB | SO | Avg | OBP | Slg |
|---|---|---|---|---|---|---|---|---|---|---|---|---|---|---|
| 1995 | 105 | 283 | 42 | 64 | 13 | 1 | 13 | 49 | 5 | 12 | 88 | .226 | .256 | .417 |
| Career | 224 | 725 | 77 | 157 | 35 | 5 | 25 | 95 | 10 | 26 | 210 | .217 | .243 | .382 |

### Where He Hits the Ball

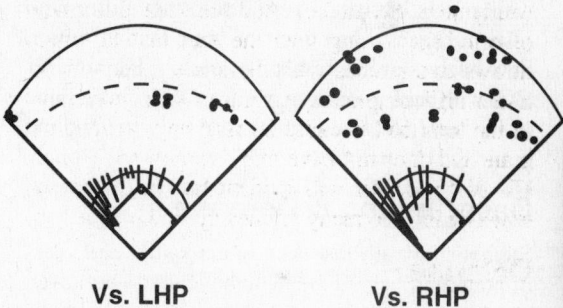

**Vs. LHP**          **Vs. RHP**

### 1995 Situational Stats

|  | AB | H | HR | RBI | Avg |  | AB | H | HR | RBI | Avg |
|---|---|---|---|---|---|---|---|---|---|---|---|
| Home | 154 | 37 | 8 | 22 | .240 | LHP | 108 | 23 | 6 | 16 | .213 |
| Road | 129 | 27 | 5 | 27 | .209 | RHP | 175 | 41 | 7 | 33 | .234 |
| First Half | 118 | 28 | 8 | 23 | .237 | Sc Pos | 78 | 21 | 4 | 38 | .269 |
| Scnd Half | 165 | 36 | 5 | 26 | .218 | Clutch | 34 | 8 | 1 | 5 | .235 |

### 1995 Rankings (American League)

- ➡ 4th in lowest on-base percentage vs. left-handed pitchers (.254)
- ➡ 6th in lowest batting average vs. left-handed pitchers (.213)
- ➡ 10th in lowest batting average with two strikes (.136)

# Terry Steinbach

## 1995 Season

On an Oakland team riddled by injuries and changes, Terry Steinbach remains a rock of stability. Steinback had another excellent season in 1995, driving in 65 runs and hitting 15 homers, the second-highest total of his career. He also remains, in the estimation of many A.L. managers and scouts, the best defensive catcher in the league, one who is unsurpassed at handling pitchers.

## Hitting

Steinbach is a solid all-around hitter who hangs in against all kinds of pitching. He used to be susceptible to being crowded by righthanders, but he moved off the plate a little and last year had nine home runs off righty pitching. Steinbach doesn't walk much, but he's a very disciplined hitter who seldom chases a bad pitch. A good fastball hitter, Steinbach is at his best in the clutch. He hit over .300 with men in scoring position and remains one of the better pressure hitters, not only in Oakland but in the entire league.

## Baserunning & Defense

Steinbach wasn't fast even in his youth, and years of pounding behind the plate have made him even slower. However, he will not make mistakes on the bases and his intelligence can sometimes translate into an extra base. Defensively he has few peers. Steinbach has a strong and accurate arm, plus perhaps the quickest release in baseball. He blocks balls as well as anyone, and serves as another coach on the field with his knowledge of hitters and ability to keep his own pitchers focused.

## 1996 Outlook

The Athletics' new owners are likely to engage in wholesale cost-cutting, but they would be wise to leave Steinbach in place. Catchers of his quality are too valuable to simply discard with no replacement in sight, and if Oakland made him available there would be several teams immediately interested in one of the game's top catchers.

**Position:** C
**Bats:** R **Throws:** R
**Ht:** 6' 1" **Wt:** 195

**Opening Day Age:** 34
**Born:** 3/2/62 in New Ulm, MN
**ML Seasons:** 10
**Pronunciation:** STINE-bok

### Overall Statistics

|        | G    | AB   | R   | H    | D   | T  | HR | RBI | SB | BB  | SO  | Avg  | OBP  | Slg  |
|--------|------|------|-----|------|-----|----|----|-----|----|-----|-----|------|------|------|
| 1995   | 114  | 406  | 43  | 113  | 26  | 1  | 15 | 65  | 1  | 25  | 74  | .278 | .322 | .458 |
| Career | 1054 | 3648 | 419 | 1004 | 180 | 13 | 97 | 495 | 15 | 258 | 574 | .275 | .326 | .411 |

### Where He Hits the Ball

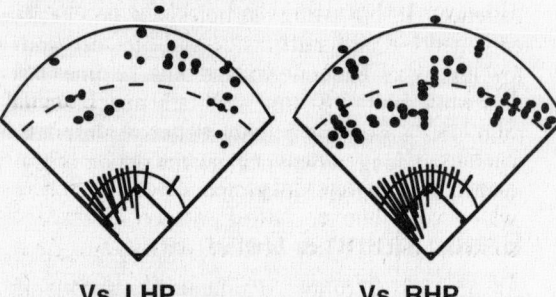

**Vs. LHP**          **Vs. RHP**

### 1995 Situational Stats

|            | AB  | H  | HR | RBI | Avg  |        | AB  | H  | HR | RBI | Avg  |
|------------|-----|----|----|-----|------|--------|-----|----|----|-----|------|
| Home       | 189 | 51 | 9  | 36  | .270 | LHP    | 123 | 37 | 6  | 25  | .301 |
| Road       | 217 | 62 | 6  | 29  | .286 | RHP    | 283 | 76 | 9  | 40  | .269 |
| First Half | 226 | 59 | 10 | 44  | .261 | Sc Pos | 94  | 31 | 9  | 57  | .330 |
| Scnd Half  | 180 | 54 | 5  | 21  | .300 | Clutch | 76  | 25 | 5  | 23  | .329 |

### 1995 Rankings (American League)

- → 3rd in highest percentage of runners caught stealing as a catcher (35.5%)
- → 4th in lowest percentage of pitches taken (45.5%)
- → 9th in errors at catcher (5)
- → Led the Athletics in GDPs (15)

# Todd Stottlemyre

## 1995 Season

Long viewed as an underachiever, Todd Stottlemyre left Toronto last year and proceeded to post a breakthrough season in Oakland. In that world of mortals not inhabited by Randy Johnson, Stottlemyre recorded the most strikeouts in the league while gaining credit for 14 of the Athletics' 67 victories.

## Pitching

There has never been anything wrong with Stottlemyre's physical ability. He throws a nasty sinking fastball in the low 90s, along with a change-up thrown with excellent mechanics, a good curve and a slider which can be devastating. However, he has always had problems keeping his good stuff beyond six or seven innings and maintaining consistency from one start to the next. Working with pitching coach Dave Duncan, Stottlemyre found better consistency with his mechanics. He also came up with a mean splitter (some A.L. hitters suspected illegal doctoring) which gave him an added weapon and a new strikeout pitch. When Stottlemyre did struggle, it all started with lack of control. He walked 80 batters, but more important, he was sometimes wild in the strike zone on the way to allowing a staff-high 26 homers.

## Defense

Stottlemyre's rather high leg kick makes him fairly easy for basestealers to measure. He also lacks a consistent pickoff move and as a result is vulnerable to the stolen base. On the other hand, Stottlemyre is a good athlete who usually leaves himself in good fielding position and can range off the mound to make tough plays on slow rollers.

## 1996 Outlook

The good news for Stottlemyre is that he came close to realizing his big potential for the first time, and seems to have gotten past his career-long inconsistency. However, unless he ends up in St. Louis, Stottlemyre won't have Duncan around to tutor him, and he will have to maintain his new-found power pitching under new leadership.

**Position:** SP
**Bats:** L **Throws:** R
**Ht:** 6' 3" **Wt:** 200

**Opening Day Age:** 30
**Born:** 5/20/65 in Yakima, WA
**ML Seasons:** 8
**Pronunciation:** STAH-tull-my-er

### Overall Statistics

|  | W | L | Pct. | ERA | G | GS | Sv | IP | H | BB | SO | HR | BR/IP |
|---|---|---|---|---|---|---|---|---|---|---|---|---|---|
| 1995 | 14 | 7 | .667 | 4.55 | 31 | 31 | 0 | 209.2 | 228 | 80 | 205 | 26 | 1.47 |
| Career | 83 | 77 | .519 | 4.41 | 237 | 206 | 1 | 1348.2 | 1410 | 494 | 867 | 141 | 1.41 |

### How Often He Throws Strikes

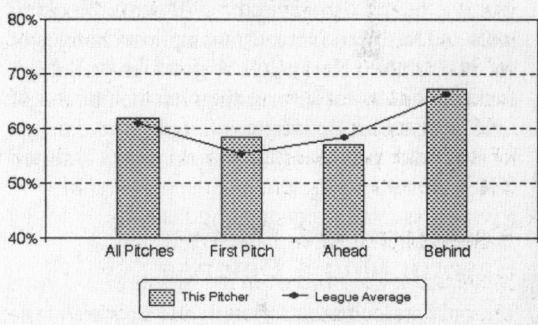

### 1995 Situational Stats

|  | W | L | ERA | Sv | IP |  | AB | H | HR | RBI | Avg |
|---|---|---|---|---|---|---|---|---|---|---|---|
| Home | 6 | 5 | 3.89 | 0 | 118.0 | LHB | 483 | 125 | 11 | 49 | .259 |
| Road | 8 | 2 | 5.40 | 0 | 91.2 | RHB | 343 | 103 | 15 | 56 | .300 |
| First Half | 7 | 2 | 3.84 | 0 | 96.0 | Sc Pos | 201 | 58 | 5 | 78 | .289 |
| Scnd Half | 7 | 5 | 5.15 | 0 | 113.2 | Clutch | 54 | 11 | 1 | 4 | .204 |

### 1995 Rankings (American League)

- → 1st in runners caught stealing (12)
- → 2nd in hits allowed, strikeouts and most strikeouts per 9 innings (8.8)
- → 3rd in batters faced (920), home runs allowed and highest strikeout/walk ratio (2.6)
- → 4th in games started, wild pitches (11) and pitches thrown (3,485)
- → 5th in highest ERA on the road (5.40)
- → 6th in innings pitched
- → 7th in most run support per 9 innings (6.5) and most home runs allowed per 9 innings (1.12)
- → Led the Athletics in ERA, wins, games started, complete games (2), innings pitched, hits allowed, batters faced, home runs allowed, walks allowed and hit batsmen (6)

# Danny Tartabull

## 1995 Season

After wearing out his welcome in New York with his often indifferent play, Danny Tartabull was swapped to Oakland last summer for another problem child, Ruben Sierra. However, Tartabull was damaged goods when he joined the Athletics, and the injury-prone slugger managed only a handful of at-bats for his new club. He was in and out of the lineup with physical problems over the season's final two months.

## Hitting

Tartabull has always been known as a dead fastball hitter who will try to work long counts, with the hope of eventually forcing the pitcher to come in with the heater. However, he will chase breaking balls and has been inconsistent against changes of speed. Tartabull has always been a high walk/high strikeout hitter, not surprising given the number of pitches he takes. He has the strength to do damage to any field, but many scouts think his assorted injuries have cost Tartabull bat speed, resulting in a weakness against outstanding fastballs.

## Baserunning & Defense

The only stolen bases Tartabull attempts are at the front end of hit-and-run plays. He has little speed, though when the spirit moves him he can be an aggressive runner. Defensively, his best position is DH. He is an indifferent outfielder with awful range and poor judgment on balls over his head. He ends up playing very deep to keep those balls to a minimum, which of course means too many balls drop untouched in shallow right. His arm is strong if not particularly accurate.

## 1996 Outlook

Oakland is stuck with Tartabull's contract for another year, so all they can do is hope he stays relatively healthy, settles into the DH slot, and returns to the 30-homer, 100-RBI level. Getting out of pressure-packed New York should help, but Tartabull's best days are far behind.

**Position:** DH/RF
**Bats:** R **Throws:** R
**Ht:** 6' 1" **Wt:** 204

**Opening Day Age:** 33
**Born:** 10/30/62 in Miami, FL
**ML Seasons:** 12

### Overall Statistics

| | G | AB | R | H | D | T | HR | RBI | SB | BB | SO | Avg | OBP | Slg |
|---|---|---|---|---|---|---|---|---|---|---|---|---|---|---|
| 1995 | 83 | 280 | 34 | 66 | 16 | 0 | 8 | 35 | 0 | 43 | 82 | .236 | .335 | .379 |
| Career | 1271 | 4532 | 696 | 1246 | 266 | 19 | 235 | 824 | 36 | 700 | 1230 | .275 | .371 | .498 |

### Where He Hits the Ball

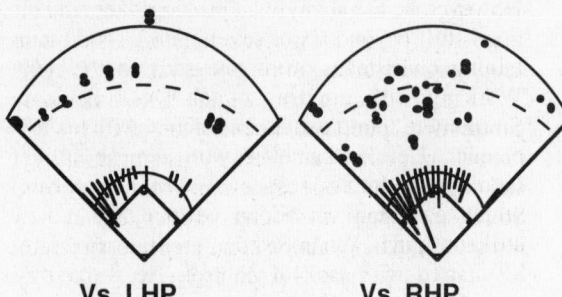

Vs. LHP          Vs. RHP

### 1995 Situational Stats

| | AB | H | HR | RBI | Avg | | AB | H | HR | RBI | Avg |
|---|---|---|---|---|---|---|---|---|---|---|---|
| Home | 113 | 31 | 3 | 18 | .274 | LHP | 99 | 25 | 6 | 17 | .253 |
| Road | 167 | 35 | 5 | 17 | .210 | RHP | 181 | 41 | 2 | 18 | .227 |
| First Half | 187 | 43 | 6 | 28 | .230 | Sc Pos | 73 | 16 | 1 | 26 | .219 |
| Scnd Half | 93 | 23 | 2 | 7 | .247 | Clutch | 46 | 13 | 2 | 8 | .283 |

### 1995 Rankings (American League)

➡ 1st in lowest batting average with two strikes (.096)
➡ 2nd in lowest cleanup slugging percentage (.369)
➡ 7th in lowest batting average on an 0-2 count (.045)

# Todd Van Poppel

## 1995 Season

Everyone knows the story of Todd Van Poppel, one of the most highly regarded pitching prospects of the last 20 years. After signing for a huge bonus out of high school in 1990, Van Poppel made it to the majors for good four years later, but finished with a 6.09 ERA and topped the American League in walks. He opened last season in the bullpen for the first time in his career, and he performed very well in that role. Not content to leave well enough alone, the A's shifted Van Poppel back to the rotation, and he went 3-6 with a 5.60 ERA as a starter.

## Pitching

Maintaining consistency remains the biggest challenge for Van Poppel. His high-80s fastball moves sharply and is tough to hit. He's also developed a good change-up and a big-time curve. When he's throwing them all for strikes, Van Poppel can dominate. But like many tall pitchers, Van Poppel struggles to maintain his good mechanics, and when he gets out of sync his control wavers. Still, Van Poppel made great strides in that area last season. After walking more men than he struck out in both 1993 and '94, Van Poppel reversed that trend in a big way, registering more than twice as many strikeouts as walks.

## Defense

Van Poppel lacks a decent pickoff move and has a slow delivery to the plate. He's become so concerned with holding runners that he tends to lose his rhythm with men on base. He is a good fielder for such a big man.

## 1996 Outlook

Van Poppel has struggled in his big-league career, but it's easy to forget that he's still only 24 and more than young enough to emerge as a dominant pitcher. Though the A's would still like him to make it as a starter, last season's performance indicates that Van Poppel's future might be in the bullpen, perhaps as a dominant closer.

**Position:** RP/SP
**Bats:** R  **Throws:** R
**Ht:** 6' 5"   **Wt:** 210

**Opening Day Age:** 24
**Born:** 12/9/71 in Hinsdale, IL
**ML Seasons:** 4

### Overall Statistics

|  | W | L | Pct. | ERA | G | GS | Sv | IP | H | BB | SO | HR | BR/IP |
|---|---|---|---|---|---|---|---|---|---|---|---|---|---|
| 1995 | 4 | 8 | .333 | 4.88 | 36 | 14 | 0 | 138.1 | 125 | 56 | 122 | 16 | 1.31 |
| Career | 17 | 24 | .415 | 5.39 | 76 | 54 | 0 | 343.2 | 316 | 209 | 258 | 47 | 1.53 |

### How Often He Throws Strikes

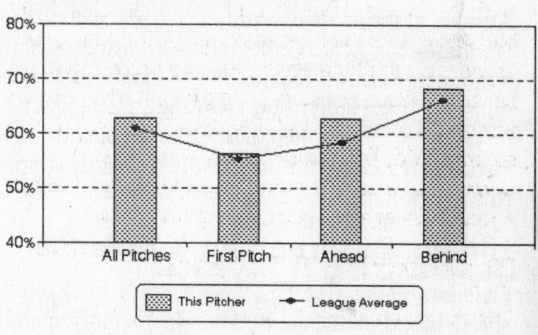

### 1995 Situational Stats

|  | W | L | ERA | Sv | IP |  | AB | H | HR | RBI | Avg |
|---|---|---|---|---|---|---|---|---|---|---|---|
| Home | 2 | 5 | 4.00 | 0 | 81.0 | LHB | 290 | 72 | 10 | 39 | .248 |
| Road | 2 | 3 | 6.12 | 0 | 57.1 | RHB | 223 | 53 | 6 | 34 | .238 |
| First Half | 1 | 2 | 3.46 | 0 | 41.2 | Sc Pos | 105 | 39 | 6 | 58 | .371 |
| Scnd Half | 3 | 6 | 5.49 | 0 | 96.2 | Clutch | 63 | 14 | 3 | 6 | .222 |

### 1995 Rankings (American League)

➡ 6th in least baserunners allowed per 9 innings in relief (9.9)

➡ 7th in lowest batting average allowed in relief (.209)

➡ Led the Athletics in losses, lowest batting average allowed vs. left-handed batters (.248), relief ERA (3.54), lowest batting average allowed in relief, least baserunners allowed per 9 innings in relief and most strikeouts per 9 innings in relief (8.6)

# Mike Gallego

**Position**: 2B/3B/SS
**Bats:** R  **Throws:** R
**Ht:** 5' 8"  **Wt:** 175

**Opening Day Age:** 35
**Born:** 10/31/60 in
Whittier, CA
**ML Seasons:** 11
**Pronunciation:**
guy-YAY-go

## Overall Statistics

| | G | AB | R | H | D | T | HR | RBI | SB | BB | SO | Avg | OBP | Slg |
|---|---|---|---|---|---|---|---|---|---|---|---|---|---|---|
| 1995 | 43 | 120 | 11 | 28 | 0 | 0 | 0 | 8 | 0 | 9 | 24 | .233 | .292 | .233 |
| Career | 1033 | 2745 | 356 | 663 | 107 | 12 | 42 | 277 | 24 | 313 | 428 | .242 | .324 | .335 |

## 1995 Season

Another of the many ex-Athletics to return to Oakland last year, Mike Gallego had a wasted season as he spent nearly three months on the disabled list with a strained arch in his right foot. He appeared in only 43 games, had just eight RBI and was virtually a non-factor in the Tony Phillips-type role the Athletics had envisioned for him.

## Hitting, Baserunning & Defense

Gallego still handles the bat pretty well, but his bat speed has diminished of late. In his infrequent appearances last year he had problems catching up with decent hard stuff and often chased breaking pitches out of the strike zone. He has occasional power, but remarkably he had no extra-base hits in 120 at-bats last year. He is at his best when he concentrates on spraying the ball to all fields. He rarely tries to steal because of his below-average speed, the result of frequent leg problems. Gallego's best defensive position is second base, since his arm and range aren't good enough for him to play shortstop every day. He can also fill in at third or even in left field if necessary.

## 1996 Outlook

His lost '95 season could make it tough for Gallego to re-establish himself as a solid utility player. At his age, he will likely find it difficult to get more than just an un-guaranteed invitation to spring training.

# Jason Giambi

**Position**: 3B/1B
**Bats:** L  **Throws:** R
**Ht:** 6' 2"  **Wt:** 200

**Opening Day Age:** 25
**Born:** 1/8/71 in West
Covina, CA
**ML Seasons:** 1
**Pronunciation:**
jee-AHM-bee

## Overall Statistics

| | G | AB | R | H | D | T | HR | RBI | SB | BB | SO | Avg | OBP | Slg |
|---|---|---|---|---|---|---|---|---|---|---|---|---|---|---|
| 1995 | 54 | 176 | 27 | 45 | 7 | 0 | 6 | 25 | 2 | 28 | 31 | .256 | .364 | .398 |
| Career | 54 | 176 | 27 | 45 | 7 | 0 | 6 | 25 | 2 | 28 | 31 | .256 | .364 | .398 |

## 1995 Season

Infield prospect Jason Giambi reached the majors last year in just his fourth professional season. Called up early in the season, he spent a week with the Athletics, was sent back to Edmonton, and was then recalled for good on July 7. Giambi didn't make any big headlines, but he held his own in an extended trial at both third base and first.

## Hitting, Baserunning & Defense

The A's think Giambi might be a late bloomer in terms of developing power. He hit six home runs last year and demonstrated the ability to pull fastballs with some pop. He battled big-league breaking balls pretty well and also displayed patience and a decent knowledge of the strike zone. Giambi is a very aggressive player who needs to show a little more control on the bases. He has the lumbering gait of a power hitter and is no threat to steal. Giambi was a third baseman in the minors and has decent range, a strong arm and fairly good hands. He's adequate at first base.

## 1996 Outlook

Oakland will likely give Giambi a long look this spring. They like his emerging power and work ethic and will give him a chance to win at least a platoon role at third. However, Giambi's moderate defensive skills and the presence of prospect Scott Spiezio might mean a position switch in the near future.

# Jose Herrera

**Position:** CF
**Bats:** L **Throws:** L
**Ht:** 6' 0" **Wt:** 165

**Opening Day Age:** 23
**Born:** 8/30/72 in Santo Domingo, DR
**ML Seasons:** 1

## Overall Statistics

|      | G  | AB | R | H  | D | T | HR | RBI | SB | BB | SO | Avg | OBP | Slg |
|------|----|----|---|----|---|---|----|-----|----|----|----|------|------|------|
| 1995 | 33 | 70 | 9 | 17 | 1 | 2 | 0 | 2 | 1 | 6 | 11 | .243 | .299 | .314 |
| Career | 33 | 70 | 9 | 17 | 1 | 2 | 0 | 2 | 1 | 6 | 11 | .243 | .299 | .314 |

## 1995 Season

Back in 1993, the Athletics traded Rickey Henderson to Toronto in exchange for pitcher Steve Karsay and outfielder Jose Herrera. Karsay was viewed as the key man in the deal from Oakland's point of view, but his career has been derailed by arm problems. Herrera, meanwhile, continues to rise in Oakland's estimation. Herrera was given a late-season look last year and didn't look overmatched in 70 fairly uneventful at-bats.

## Hitting, Baserunning & Defense

Herrera has power potential, but he is still something of a wild swinger who chases too many balls out of the strike zone. But unlike similar young, raw players, Herrera will also draw his share of walks. He has gap power to both left- and right-center fields, and an encouraging ability to hang tough against breaking balls. Herrera has excellent speed and should improve as a basestealer as he learns the game better. He has all the tools to be an excellent outfielder, including range and a big-time throwing arm.

## 1996 Outlook

Herrera could probably use more seasoning—he skipped Triple-A last season—but a big spring could allow him to challenge for a job. He has major league tools, and the Athletics think that he might eventually hit 20-odd homers and steal 20 bases per season.

# Mike Mohler

**Position:** RP
**Bats:** R **Throws:** L
**Ht:** 6' 2" **Wt:** 195

**Opening Day Age:** 27
**Born:** 7/26/68 in Dayton, OH
**ML Seasons:** 3

## Overall Statistics

|      | W | L | Pct. | ERA | G | GS | Sv | IP | H | BB | SO | HR | BR/IP |
|------|---|---|------|------|----|----|----|------|----|----|----|----|-------|
| 1995 | 1 | 1 | .500 | 3.04 | 28 | 0 | 1 | 23.2 | 16 | 18 | 15 | 0 | 1.44 |
| Career | 2 | 8 | .200 | 4.98 | 71 | 10 | 1 | 90.1 | 75 | 64 | 61 | 11 | 1.54 |

## 1995 Season

After working in 42 games for Oakland in 1993, lefthander Mike Mohler missed almost all of 1994 with a serious shoulder injury. Mohler returned last season to pitch decently at both Triple-A Edmonton (2.60 ERA) and in the majors. While he wasn't Oakland's top lefty reliever—that job was held by Rick Honeycutt until the season's final week—Mohler did pitch well enough to make a good impression.

## Pitching & Defense

Mohler throws a steady diet of sinkers, forkballs and offspeed pitches in an effort to get ground balls. He can get an occasional strikeout with the forkball, but Mohler has small margin for error and will nibble around the strike zone, as shown by the 18 walks he issued in only 23.2 innings. He will just as soon walk a hitter as give in and throw a two-strike fastball, and as a result Mohler did not allow a home run last season. Mohler has a decent move to first and fields his position adequately.

## 1996 Outlook

With the departure of Honeycutt, there is an opening for a lefty specialist in the Athletic bullpen. Mohler showed enough last season to be considered a top candidate, but he'll need to demonstrate a little more confidence in his fastball. Relievers who walk nearly a batter per inning don't last long. . . even if they are left-handed.

# Carlos Reyes

**Position**: RP
**Bats**: B **Throws**: R
**Ht**: 6' 1"  **Wt**: 190

**Opening Day Age**: 26
**Born**: 4/4/69 in Miami, FL
**ML Seasons**: 2
**Pronunciation**: RAY-ess

## Overall Statistics

|  | W | L | Pct. | ERA | G | GS | Sv | IP | H | BB | SO | HR | BR/IP |
|---|---|---|---|---|---|---|---|---|---|---|---|---|---|
| 1995 | 4 | 6 | .400 | 5.09 | 40 | 1 | 0 | 69.0 | 71 | 28 | 48 | 10 | 1.43 |
| Career | 4 | 9 | .308 | 4.59 | 67 | 10 | 1 | 147.0 | 142 | 72 | 105 | 20 | 1.46 |

## 1995 Season

After being selected in the Rule 5 draft from Atlanta, righthander Carlos Reyes started nine games in 1994, which was unusual because he'd started only three times in three pro seasons. Reyes didn't show enough endurance for that role, and last season Reyes pitched in middle and long relief. However, he continued to struggle.

## Pitching & Defense

Reyes largely lives and dies with his change-up, which can be an effective strikeout pitch when he's throwing it down in the strike zone. Reyes also features a good slider, especially against right-handed hitters, who hit just .242 against him last season. However, when Reyes falls behind in the count he does not have the stuff to recover. He hangs more than a few of those sliders and also leaves his change-up high in the strike zone on occasion, which accounts for Reyes allowing 10 home runs in 69 innings. He varies his delivery home to help combat basestealers, but doesn't have much of a move to first. Reyes makes all the routine plays as a fielder.

## 1996 Outlook

Reyes has a good minor league record, and the A's still think he can be an effective middle reliever. If he can avoid the gopher ball this spring, he has a chance to win a spot in the club's bullpen.

# Andy Tomberlin

**Position**: RF/CF
**Bats**: L **Throws**: L
**Ht**: 5'11"  **Wt**: 180

**Opening Day Age**: 29
**Born**: 11/7/66 in Monroe, NC
**ML Seasons**: 3

## Overall Statistics

|  | G | AB | R | H | D | T | HR | RBI | SB | BB | SO | Avg | OBP | Slg |
|---|---|---|---|---|---|---|---|---|---|---|---|---|---|---|
| 1995 | 46 | 85 | 15 | 18 | 0 | 0 | 4 | 10 | 4 | 5 | 22 | .212 | .256 | .353 |
| Career | 90 | 163 | 20 | 37 | 0 | 2 | 6 | 16 | 5 | 13 | 48 | .227 | .288 | .362 |

## 1995 Season

Originally a pitcher in the Atlanta system, Andy Tomberlin was switched to the outfield in 1988. After cups of coffee with the Pirates and Red Sox, Tomberlin signed with the Athletics for the 1995 season. Tomberlin was given an early-season look by the A's, who were looking for some left-handed pop off the bench. Tomberlin did produce four homers in 85 at-bats, but he managed just a .212 average and was demoted to Triple-A Edmonton.

## Hitting, Baserunning & Defense

Tomberlin can be easily pitched to with breaking balls. He will chase pitches out of the strike zone and tries to pull almost every pitch, which leads to a lot of weak grounders to the second baseman. Tomberlin is quick enough to turn on even good fastballs, but he does not adjust his swing for offspeed stuff and is too anxious a hitter. He is an average baserunner who occasionally will attempt a steal. Tomberlin is a below-average outfielder with a decent arm. He often has trouble judging balls hit over his head and his range is poor.

## 1996 Outlook

One of those fringe players who turns up somewhere every spring, Tomberlin could fill in on someone's bench simply because of his ability to hit an occasional home run. However, those home runs are virtually the only asset he brings to the table.

# Don Wengert

**Position**: RP
**Bats**: R  **Throws**: R
**Ht**: 6' 2"  **Wt**: 205

**Opening Day Age**: 26
**Born**: 11/6/69 in Sioux City, IA
**ML Seasons**: 1

## Overall Statistics

|        | W | L | Pct. | ERA  | G  | GS | Sv | IP   | H  | BB | SO | HR | BR/IP |
|--------|---|---|------|------|----|----|----|------|----|----|----|----|-------|
| 1995   | 1 | 1 | .500 | 3.34 | 19 | 0  | 0  | 29.2 | 30 | 12 | 16 | 3  | 1.42  |
| Career | 1 | 1 | .500 | 3.34 | 19 | 0  | 0  | 29.2 | 30 | 12 | 16 | 3  | 1.42  |

## 1995 Season

A starting pitcher for nearly all of his minor league career, Don Wengert was converted to relief last year at Triple-A Edmonton, and enjoyed some success in a set-up role after being summoned to Oakland. He earned his first major league victory and compiled a solid 3.34 ERA in 19 appearances.

## Pitching & Defense

Wengert has a good split-fingered fastball with some nice downward movement. His fastball hits the mid 80s, and he also throws a change-up and slider on occasion. Wengert has some potential as a strikeout pitcher and his control is generally solid. Wengert has to keep the ball down, because his offerings are very hittable when up in the strike zone. The slider gives him an effective weapon against right-handed hitters. Wengert has no pick-off move to speak of but didn't have a steal attempted against him last year. He fields his position adequately.

## 1996 Outlook

With their bullpen in flux, the Athletics are likely to give Wengert a chance to make the club in spring training. He might not have closer-caliber stuff, but he has a real chance to become a solid set-up man as he gains more experience as a reliever.

# George Williams

**Position**: C
**Bats**: B  **Throws**: R
**Ht**: 5'10"  **Wt**: 190

**Opening Day Age**: 26
**Born**: 4/22/69 in Lacrosse, WI
**ML Seasons**: 1

## Overall Statistics

|        | G  | AB | R  | H  | D | T | HR | RBI | SB | BB | SO | Avg  | OBP  | Slg  |
|--------|----|----|----|----|---|---|----|-----|----|----|----|------|------|------|
| 1995   | 29 | 79 | 13 | 23 | 5 | 1 | 3  | 14  | 0  | 11 | 21 | .291 | .383 | .494 |
| Career | 29 | 79 | 13 | 23 | 5 | 1 | 3  | 14  | 0  | 11 | 21 | .291 | .383 | .494 |

## 1995 Season

Considered a decent catching prospect a few years ago, George Williams had his career delayed by a shoulder injury he suffered in 1994. Williams got a late start in 1995, but after crushing the ball at Triple-A he was summoned to Oakland on three different occasions. He continued to post impressive numbers as an Athletic, and has to be considered part of the club's future.

## Hitting, Baserunning & Defense

Switch-hitting catchers are tough to find, which is what makes the late-blooming Williams an intriguing player. He appears to have more power from the right side of the plate but holds his own batting left-handed, too. Not surprisingly, Williams needs work against big-league offspeed stuff, and he'll chase breaking balls out of the zone. However, he is already a solid fastball hitter. He has no speed and has problems behind the plate, particularly with an erratic throwing arm.

## 1996 Outlook

Terry Steinbach is established as the A's catcher, but with cost-cutting imminent it's conceivable that his Oakland days are numbered. It's an open question as to whether Williams is strong enough defensively to catch every day. But managers like guys who can hit, and if he continues to swing the bat as well as he did last year, they'll find a place for him.

**Oakland Athletics**

# Other Oakland Athletics

**Scott Baker (Pos:** LHP, **Age:** 25)

Baker pitched great at Double-A in 1994 (10-4, 1.78) but got roughed up last year at Triple-A Edmonton. He's got a fine arm, but has yet to harness his control for an extended stretch. 1996 Outlook: C

**John Briscoe (Pos:** RHP, **Age:** 28)

Briscoe's 8.35 ERA last season can be partially blamed on the shoulder injury that cost him half the season. But in parts of five major league seasons he's walked more than he's struck out. 1996 Outlook: C

**Ron Darling (Pos:** RHP, **Age:** 35)

Sporting a 6.23 ERA last August 20, Darling drew his release. He hasn't officially retired, and might draw a spring-training invite from someone. Hasn't pitched well since 1992. 1996 Outlook: D

**Chris Eddy (Pos:** LHP, **Age:** 26)

Eddy has decent stuff and knows how to pitch, but got hit hard when the Royals promoted him to Triple-A last summer. He ended up in Oakland, and pitched in six games. 1996 Outlook: C

**Ramon Fermin (Pos:** RHP, **Age:** 23)

Fermin blossomed in 1994, his fourth season in the California League. Moved up to Double-A last year, he pitched well enough to earn a late call to Oakland, where he appeared in one game. 1996 Outlook: C

**Brian Harper (Pos:** C, **Age:** 36, **Bats:** R)

When it happened, it happened fast. Harper, a .300 machine for so many years, went 0-for-7 with the A's, spurned a demotion and retired. 1996 Outlook: D

**Eric Helfand (Pos:** C, **Age:** 27, **Bats:** L)

The Athletics went through all sorts of contortions to avoid losing Helfand back in the expansion draft a few years ago. It probably wasn't worth the trouble, as Helfand hasn't hit his weight in the majors. 1996 Outlook: C

**Doug Johns (Pos:** LHP, **Age:** 28)

Johns doesn't have great stuff, but he's been successful in the minors, going 21-13 over the last two seasons. Johns went 5-3, 4.61 with Oakland last year, and is a candidate for the rotation. 1996 Outlook: B

**Steve Karsay (Pos:** RHP, **Age:** 24)

Karsay looked like one of the top young pitchers in baseball after the Athletics got him in the Rickey Henderson trade back in 1993. But he hurt his elbow in '94, and has yet to pitch again. Obviously a major question mark at this point. 1996 Outlook: C

**Troy Neel (Pos:** DH/1B, **Age:** 30)

After two very similar, solid seasons in 1993 and '94, Neel left for Japan. Assuming a solid labor agreement, he's likely to return to the States this spring. He'll hit 20-25 home runs if he plays regularly. 1996 Outlook: A (if playing)

**Steve Phoenix (Pos:** RHP, **Age:** 28)

Phoenix has a great split-fingered pitch, but his fastball tops out around 85 miles an hour. He generally pitched well in the minors until 1995, when he was hit hard in Triple-A. Has a chance to stick as a middle man. 1996 Outlook: C

**Ariel Prieto (Pos:** RHP, **Age:** 26)

There was a big competition to sign Prieto, a Cuban defector. Oakland won, and everyone's been impressed with Prieto's stuff and his acumen. However, he suffered biceps tendinitis and made only nine starts. 1996 Outlook: A

**Dave Stewart (Pos:** RHP, **Age:** 39)

It was sort of like one big retirement party in Oakland last year. Brian Harper retired, Ron Darling retired, Dave Stewart retired, and Bob Welch should have. Stewart ended his career with a 6.89 ERA last season. 1996 Outlook: D

**Billy Taylor (Pos:** RHP, **Age:** 34)

Remember this guy? As a 32-year-old rookie in 1994, he finished with a 3.50 ERA and looked like yet another brilliant acquisition by the Athletics brain trust. Unfortunately, he missed all of last season after April knee surgery, and he's not getting any younger. 1996 Outlook: C

**Todd Williams (Pos:** RHP, **Age:** 25)

Williams was a closer earlier in his career, but his side-arm motion leaves him vulnerable to lefties and now he's a middle reliever. He got roughed up in the majors last season, but it was only 16 games. 1996 Outlook: C

**Steve Wojciechowski (Pos:** LHP, **Age:** 25)

The lefthander with the uniform-defying name pitched decently as a starter in Double- and Triple-A the last two seasons, but he was hammered with the Athletics last season (5.18 ERA). 1996 Outlook: B

**Ernie Young (Pos:** RF/CF, **Age:** 26)

Young hit .277 with good power for Edmonton last season, but that was in a great hitter's park. In 80 major league at-bats, his average is just .150, and he needs an extended chance to play. 1996 Outlook: B

# Oakland Athletics Minor League Prospects

## Organization Overview:

The Oakland farm system has stalled since the late '80s, a period when the A's promoted three straight Rookies of the Year in Jose Canseco, Mark McGwire and Walt Weiss. Part of the problem has been a reduced commitment to player development due to economic constraints, but the A's have also endured their share of bad luck. A watershed year was 1990, when Oakland drafted what was described as their four future aces in the first round. Unfortunately, Don Peters, David Zancanaro and Kirk Dressendorfer were derailed by arm problems, and Todd Van Poppel has yet to live up to expectations. Despite those setbacks, pitching still appears to be the strength of the organization, as several talented hurlers are getting close to making major league contributions. Position-wise, the A's don't look to be as deep, and many of the prospects come with questions attached.

### Willie Adams

**Position:** P  **Opening Day Age:** 23
**Bats:** R **Throws:** R  **Born:** 10/8/72 in
**Ht:** 6' 7"  **Wt:** 215  Gallup, NM

*Recent Statistics*

|  | W | L | ERA | G | GS | Sv | IP | H | R | BB | SO | HR |
|---|---|---|---|---|---|---|---|---|---|---|---|---|
| 94 A Modesto | 7 | 1 | 3.38 | 11 | 5 | 2 | 45.1 | 41 | 17 | 10 | 42 | 7 |
| 94 AA Huntsville | 4 | 3 | 4.30 | 10 | 10 | 0 | 60.2 | 58 | 32 | 23 | 33 | 3 |
| 95 AA Huntsville | 6 | 5 | 3.01 | 13 | 13 | 0 | 80.2 | 75 | 33 | 17 | 72 | 8 |
| 95 AAA Edmonton | 2 | 5 | 4.37 | 11 | 10 | 0 | 68.0 | 73 | 35 | 15 | 40 | 2 |

Adams doesn't throw as hard as you might expect for someone with a classic pitcher's build. Still, he's coordinated for his size and has great control of his pitches. Last year Adams walked fewer than two batters per nine innings while striking out 2.5 times as many. Should his fastball pick up a few extra miles per hour and reach the upper 80s, Adams could be even more effective. He was a supplemental first-round draft pick in 1993 out of Stanford, a school which has developed a lot of pitching prospects recently. He'll be 23 in 1996, and could reach the big leagues at some point this summer.

### Tony Batista

**Position:** SS  **Opening Day Age:** 22
**Bats:** R **Throws:** R  **Born:** 12/9/73 in
**Ht:** 6' 0"  **Wt:** 180  Luperon, Puerto Plata, Dr

*Recent Statistics*

|  | G | AB | R | H | D | T | HR | RBI | SB | BB | SO | AVG |
|---|---|---|---|---|---|---|---|---|---|---|---|---|
| 94 A Modesto | 119 | 466 | 91 | 131 | 26 | 3 | 17 | 68 | 7 | 54 | 108 | .281 |
| 95 AA Huntsville | 120 | 419 | 55 | 107 | 23 | 1 | 16 | 61 | 7 | 29 | 98 | .255 |
| 95 MLE | 120 | 410 | 52 | 98 | 20 | 0 | 14 | 58 | 5 | 23 | 108 | .239 |

Batista was signed as a free agent from the Dominican Republic in 1991, and he has now hit 17 and 16 home runs the past two seasons. For a shortstop with a good defensive reputation, his slugging totals are mighty impressive. He competed at Double-A Hunstville at the age of 21 last year. Even though his walk rate was down in 1995, Batista has demonstrated a good eye in the past. In addition to the home runs, he's also shown doubles power and should be an offensive plus. In the field, Batista has range, good hands and a strong arm. He'll probably play at Triple-A this season and be ready to challenge for a big league job in 1997, if not sooner.

### Steven Cox

**Position:** 1B  **Opening Day Age:** 21
**Bats:** L **Throws:** L  **Born:** 10/31/74 in
**Ht:** 6' 4"  **Wt:** 200  Delano, CA

*Recent Statistics*

|  | G | AB | R | H | D | T | HR | RBI | SB | BB | SO | AVG |
|---|---|---|---|---|---|---|---|---|---|---|---|---|
| 93 A Sou. Oregon | 15 | 57 | 10 | 18 | 4 | 1 | 2 | 16 | 0 | 5 | 15 | .316 |
| 94 A W. Michigan | 99 | 311 | 37 | 75 | 19 | 2 | 6 | 32 | 2 | 41 | 95 | .241 |
| 95 A Modesto | 132 | 483 | 95 | 144 | 29 | 3 | 30 | 110 | 5 | 84 | 88 | .298 |

Cox had trouble staying healthy after the A's chose him in the fifth round of 1992. He never played in as many as 100 games in any of his first three seasons, and was knocked out of action during 1994 by a batting-practice line drive which broke some bones in his face and led to the discovery that he needed corrective lenses. With contact lenses in place, Cox led the California League last season in both home runs and RBI. It was a remarkable breakthrough for Cox, who had never before hit more than six homers in any season. The power appears to be legitimate, as Cox is a big, strapping lad of 6'4", 200 pounds, with the outstanding plate discipline that forces hurlers to throw pitches he can handle.

### Fausto Cruz

**Position:** SS  **Opening Day Age:** 24
**Bats:** R **Throws:** R  **Born:** 1/5/72 in Monte
**Ht:** 5' 11"  **Wt:** 165  Christi, DR

*Recent Statistics*

|  | G | AB | R | H | D | T | HR | RBI | SB | BB | SO | AVG |
|---|---|---|---|---|---|---|---|---|---|---|---|---|
| 95 AAA Edmonton | 114 | 448 | 72 | 126 | 23 | 2 | 11 | 67 | 7 | 34 | 67 | .281 |
| 95 AL Oakland | 8 | 23 | 0 | 5 | 0 | 0 | 0 | 5 | 1 | 3 | 5 | .217 |
| 95 MLE | 114 | 426 | 55 | 104 | 18 | 1 | 8 | 51 | 5 | 26 | 72 | .244 |

Cruz is a fine defensive shortstop who has delivered four straight solid offensive seasons. He's a career .294 hitter through 503 minor league games, with enough walks to possibly bat near the top of the order. Last year, at the age of 23, Cruz delivered a career-high 11 homers. Cruz has played parts of the last three seasons in Triple-A and has experience at second and third base. His versatility could earn him a spot on the A's roster in '96, with the possibility of an expanded role.

## Brian Lesher

**Position:** OF     **Opening Day Age:** 25
**Bats:** R **Throws:** L     **Born:** 3/5/71 in
**Ht:** 6' 5" **Wt:** 205     Belgium

*Recent Statistics*

| | G | AB | R | H | D | T | HR | RBI | SB | BB | SO | AVG |
|---|---|---|---|---|---|---|---|---|---|---|---|---|
| 93 A Madison | 119 | 394 | 63 | 108 | 13 | 5 | 5 | 47 | 20 | 46 | 102 | .274 |
| 94 A Modesto | 117 | 393 | 76 | 114 | 21 | 0 | 14 | 68 | 11 | 81 | 84 | .290 |
| 95 AA Huntsville | 127 | 471 | 78 | 123 | 23 | 2 | 19 | 71 | 7 | 64 | 110 | .261 |
| 95 MLE | 127 | 461 | 74 | 113 | 20 | 1 | 17 | 68 | 5 | 52 | 121 | .245 |

Many of the A's prospects in recent years have drawn walks, and Lesher is a case in point. He coaxed 81 free passes in under 400 at-bats in 1994, and followed with 64 last year. Along with, or perhaps because of the plate discipline, Lesher is developing his power potential. He smacked a career-high 19 homers last year in his first season above Class A, and at 6'5" and better than 200 pounds, Lesher has the build of a slugger. He was drafted in the 25th round of 1992 as a first baseman, but is now a fine defensive outfielder. He'll be 25 when his 1996 season begins, most likely at Triple-A.

## Jason McDonald

**Position:** SS     **Opening Day Age:** 24
**Bats:** B **Throws:** R     **Born:** 3/20/72 in
**Ht:** 5' 8" **Wt:** 175     Modesto, CA

*Recent Statistics*

| | G | AB | R | H | D | T | HR | RBI | SB | BB | SO | AVG |
|---|---|---|---|---|---|---|---|---|---|---|---|---|
| 93 A Sou. Oregon | 35 | 112 | 26 | 33 | 5 | 2 | 0 | 8 | 22 | 31 | 17 | .295 |
| 94 A W. Michigan | 116 | 404 | 67 | 96 | 11 | 9 | 2 | 31 | 52 | 81 | 87 | .238 |
| 95 A Modesto | 133 | 493 | 109 | 129 | 25 | 7 | 6 | 50 | 70 | 110 | 84 | .262 |

McDonald looks like he could be the eventual heir to Rickey Henderson as the A's leadoff man. Although McDonald led the minor leagues with 70 stolen bases in 1995, it's his ability to get on base which makes him so valuable offensively. In addition to the stolen bases, he also led the minors with 110 walks, which helped produce a .409 on-base percentage and 109 runs scored. McDonald, who is Henderson-sized, is also developing extra-base power, which would get him into scoring position even more often. Drafted in the fourth round of 1992, McDonald has played shortstop and the outfield in the past, but may be moved to second base next season.

## Brad Rigby

**Position:** P     **Opening Day Age:** 22
**Bats:** R **Throws:** R     **Born:** 5/14/73 in
**Ht:** 6' 6" **Wt:** 194     Milwaukee, WI

*Recent Statistics*

| | W | L | ERA | G | GS | Sv | IP | H | R | BB | SO | HR |
|---|---|---|---|---|---|---|---|---|---|---|---|---|
| 94 A Modesto | 2 | 1 | 3.80 | 11 | 1 | 2 | 23.2 | 20 | 10 | 10 | 28 | 0 |
| 95 A Modesto | 11 | 4 | 3.84 | 31 | 23 | 2 | 154.2 | 135 | 79 | 48 | 145 | 5 |

Rigby was part of the powerhouse Georgia Tech team of 1994 which also sent first-round picks Nomar Garciaparra to the Red Sox, Jay Payton to the Mets, and Jason Varitek to the Mariners. Rigby went in the second round, and has spent his first two professional seasons at Modesto in the California League. His stats indicate that he could have been challenged at a higher level last season, as his minor league ledger is now 13-5 with a three-to-one strikeout/walk ratio. Rigby appears to be all arms and legs on the mound, but his mechanics are sound and he has command of four pitches.

## John Wasdin

**Position:** P     **Opening Day Age:** 23
**Bats:** R **Throws:** R     **Born:** 8/5/72 in Fort
**Ht:** 6' 2" **Wt:** 195     Belvoir, VA

*Recent Statistics*

| | W | L | ERA | G | GS | Sv | IP | H | R | BB | SO | HR |
|---|---|---|---|---|---|---|---|---|---|---|---|---|
| 95 AAA Edmonton | 12 | 8 | 5.52 | 29 | 28 | 0 | 174.1 | 193 | 117 | 38 | 111 | 26 |
| 95 AL Oakland | 1 | 1 | 4.67 | 5 | 2 | 0 | 17.1 | 14 | 9 | 3 | 6 | 4 |

Wasdin was the A's top draft pick in 1993 and has pitched like a polished product throughout his pro career. His stats were not overwhelming last year, with a 5.52 ERA and 193 hits allowed in 174.1 innings, but Edmonton is not the place to pitch if you desire eye-catching numbers. The bottom line is that Wasdin went 12-8 in the Pacific Coast League and continued to be issue walks at a very low rate, fewer than two per nine innings. One possible reason to temper one's enthusiasm for him is that Wasdin doesn't record strikeouts at high rates. But he does throw three pitches for strikes, and wasn't overmatched in his brief major league trial last season. He'll likely pitch again in Oakland at some point in 1996.

## Others to Watch

Right-handed pitcher **Bobby Chouinard** was originally drafted by Baltimore in 1990. He pitched at Double-A last season and is now 26-13 with a 3.14 ERA since 1994. . . Outfielder **Ben Grieve** is the son of former Texas GM Tom Grieve and was the second player drafted in 1994. He competed in the Midwest and California Leagues at 19 last season, and posted decent numbers (.262, 6 HR, 76 RBI). . . Outfielder **Demond Smith** could one day make the Angels regret their pennant-chase trade which sent Smith to the A's in exchange for Mike Aldrete. Smith was originally drafted in the sixth round in 1990, and did almost nothing until last year, when he enjoyed one of the best seasons of any minor leaguer (.342, 16 HR, 70 RBI, 54 SB). . . Third baseman **Scott Spiezio** is the son of Ed, the ex-big leaguer. Scott has been very consistent the past two seasons, with double-digit homers, 30-plus doubles, .280-range batting averages and high walk rates.

# Bobby Ayala

## 1995 Season

Something went wrong with Bobby Ayala last season. Ayala only allowed about one hit per inning, didn't walk too many batters, and he struck out more than a batter a frame. But he also gave up nine homers, dried up down the stretch, and all but pitched himself off the Mariners' postseason roster. He looked like he might have been fighting a nagging injury—or perhaps a severe loss of confidence. Whatever the reason, the Mariners were fortunate that Norm Charlton was around, since Ayala was struggling as the season wound down.

## Pitching

Ayala's repertoire is simple: splitter and fastball. In 1994 Ayala confounded American League hitters by successfully disguising the two pitches. Not so in 1995; Ayala had trouble finding the strike zone with the splitter. If he countered by throwing it a little higher in the strike zone, then it wouldn't bite. Righthanders in particular found Ayala to their liking, teeing off for a .529 slugging average against the former closer. When Ayala has command of his split-fingered pitch, neither lefties or righties can distinguish the pitch from his fastball until it's too late, making him almost unhittable.

## Defense

Ayala doesn't show much concern for the finer points of the game, such as fielding and holding runners. He's worrying about the "out" at the plate when he's pitching, and runners can take advantage of this. His delivery leaves him off balance and in poor fielding position.

## 1996 Outlook

Look for Ayala to find a happy medium somewhere between his 1994 success and 1995 struggles. He still can be dominant when he finds his mechanics and control. It remains to be seen whether that will happen often enough to once again place him among the elite closers in the league. But even if he can't assume his old closer role, he's still capable of helping the M's in middle relief.

**Position:** RP
**Bats:** R  **Throws:** R
**Ht:** 6' 3"  **Wt:** 200

**Opening Day Age:** 26
**Born:** 7/8/69 in Ventura, CA
**ML Seasons:** 4
**Pronunciation:** eye-YAH-luh

### Overall Statistics

|        | W  | L  | Pct. | ERA  | G   | GS | Sv | IP    | H   | BB  | SO  | HR | BR/IP |
|--------|----|----|------|------|-----|----|----|-------|-----|-----|-----|----|-------|
| 1995   | 6  | 5  | .545 | 4.44 | 63  | 0  | 19 | 71.0  | 73  | 30  | 77  | 9  | 1.45  |
| Career | 19 | 19 | .500 | 4.52 | 157 | 14 | 40 | 254.2 | 254 | 114 | 241 | 28 | 1.45  |

### How Often He Throws Strikes

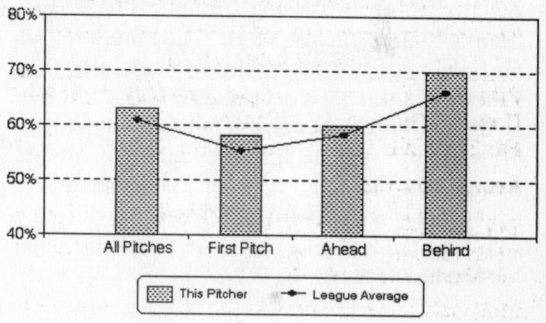

### 1995 Situational Stats

|            | W | L | ERA  | Sv | IP   |        | AB  | H  | HR | RBI | Avg  |
|------------|---|---|------|----|------|--------|-----|----|----|-----|------|
| Home       | 5 | 0 | 3.41 | 11 | 37.0 | LHB    | 175 | 40 | 5  | 31  | .229 |
| Road       | 1 | 5 | 5.56 | 8  | 34.0 | RHB    | 104 | 33 | 4  | 19  | .317 |
| First Half | 2 | 2 | 3.18 | 13 | 34.0 | Sc Pos | 98  | 30 | 3  | 42  | .306 |
| Scnd Half  | 4 | 3 | 5.59 | 6  | 37.0 | Clutch | 153 | 35 | 5  | 26  | .229 |

### 1995 Rankings (American League)

→ 2nd in lowest save percentage (70.4%)
→ 3rd in games pitched
→ 4th in blown saves (8) and lowest batting average allowed vs. left-handed batters (.229)
→ 6th in games finished, highest percentage of inherited runners scored (47.1%) and relief wins (6)
→ 8th in save opportunities (27) and most strikeouts per 9 innings in relief (9.8)
→ 10th in relief innings (71.0)
→ Led the Mariners in games pitched, saves, games finished (50), hit batsmen (6), save opportunities, save percentage (70.4%) and blown saves

# Tim Belcher

## 1995 Season

Not many thought the Mariners' acquisition of veteran righty Tim Belcher last May would work out. After all, he was a flyball pitcher coming to the homer-happy Kingdome, and he'd lost a few inches off his fastball in recent years. But while the numbers weren't pretty, Belcher didn't embarrass himself. He came back strongly from his terrible 1994 season with the Tigers, and his veteran leadership and workhorse approach were notable assets on a young Seattle club. After winning 10 games in the regular season, Belcher was one of the most-used Mariners in the postseason.

## Pitching

Belcher's fastball is losing steam, and he's never been a control pitcher, so he relies more on his breaking stuff and his ability to keep hitters off balance. He still has a decent curveball, and when he throws it for strikes he can be very tough to hit. With a loss in velocity, his slider doesn't confound righties as it once did. And when a slider hangs, it's a pretty easy pitch to drive. Belcher also throws a split-fingered fastball, but it wasn't a reliable pitch for him last year.

## Defense

Belcher may not have the great stuff he used to have, but he has the right stuff on the field. He's attentive to the running game (recovering from a lapse in 1994), and fields his position quite well. His head is always in the game.

## 1996 Outlook

Lou Piniella likes tough players, and Belcher fits the mold. He has the demeanor, work ethic and fundamentals to again be a very good pitcher, but he hasn't yet developed the control to compensate for his reduced velocity. His future will depend upon his ability to make these adjustments. He'll get more opportunities.

**Position:** SP
**Bats:** R  **Throws:** R
**Ht:** 6' 3"  **Wt:** 220

**Opening Day Age:** 34
**Born:** 10/19/61 in Sparta, OH
**ML Seasons:** 9

### Overall Statistics

|        | W  | L  | Pct. | ERA  | G   | GS  | Sv | IP     | H    | BB  | SO   | HR  | BR/IP |
|--------|----|----|------|------|-----|-----|----|--------|------|-----|------|-----|-------|
| 1995   | 10 | 12 | .455 | 4.52 | 28  | 28  | 0  | 179.1  | 188  | 88  | 96   | 19  | 1.54  |
| Career | 94 | 90 | .511 | 3.78 | 260 | 239 | 5  | 1583.2 | 1459 | 581 | 1089 | 133 | 1.29  |

### How Often He Throws Strikes

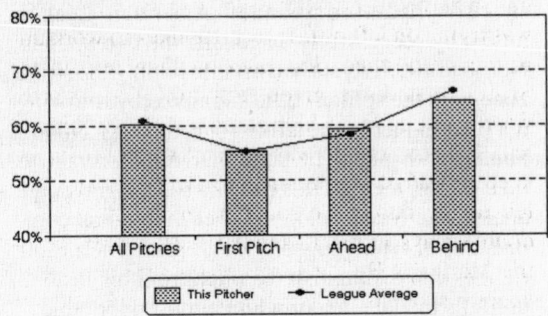

### 1995 Situational Stats

|            | W | L | ERA  | Sv | IP    |        | AB  | H   | HR | RBI | Avg  |
|------------|---|---|------|----|-------|--------|-----|-----|----|-----|------|
| Home       | 5 | 7 | 4.36 | 0  | 99.0  | LHB    | 425 | 114 | 9  | 45  | .268 |
| Road       | 5 | 5 | 4.71 | 0  | 80.1  | RHB    | 275 | 74  | 10 | 39  | .269 |
| First Half | 4 | 4 | 4.78 | 0  | 69.2  | Sc Pos | 170 | 41  | 6  | 66  | .241 |
| Scnd Half  | 6 | 8 | 4.35 | 0  | 109.2 | Clutch | 50  | 10  | 0  | 2   | .200 |

### 1995 Rankings (American League)

- → 2nd in lowest strikeout/walk ratio (1.1) and lowest stolen base percentage allowed (26.7%)
- → 3rd in runners caught stealing (11)
- → 4th in least run support per 9 innings (4.4)
- → 5th in highest on-base percentage allowed (.352) and most baserunners allowed per 9 innings (14.1)
- → 6th in least GDPs induced per 9 innings (0.6)
- → 7th in lowest groundball/flyball ratio allowed (1.0)
- → 8th in highest slugging percentage allowed (.430) and least strikeouts per 9 innings (4.8)
- → Led the Mariners in losses, home runs allowed and walks allowed

# Andy Benes

## 1995 Season

With the Mariners hovering around .500 in July, Seattle management made one of the boldest moves in team history, dealing two top prospects for San Diego starter Andy Benes. The Mariners needed a workhorse like Benes, who has averaged about seven innings every fifth day since 1990. As a Mariner, his 7-2 record belies the fact that he was anything but effective. Benes averaged little more than five innings per start, and posted a woeful 5.86 ERA.

## Pitching

Benes has an excellent fastball which consistently tops 90 miles an hour. He also throws a cut fastball, a hard slider, a slurve, and a circle change he was trying on lefties last year. He likes to work up in the strike zone. The high pitching mound in Seattle may have given him trouble. He also wasn't getting many high strike calls in the American League, and he was hit hard when he didn't keep the ball down. Pitching high in the strike zone led to the dubious distinction of inducing zero double plays in his 12 regular-season starts with the Mariners. He's a fast worker, though, which keeps his defense in the game.

## Defense

Benes is a good athlete and is very alert on the mound, pouncing on bunts and snagging liners. He quieted the running game last season with a quick pickoff move and good stretch delivery. In all, runners succeeded less than half the time against Benes—tremendous results for a power pitcher.

## 1996 Outlook

Benes didn't pitch well for the M's, but he's posted good numbers throughout his career—especially considering that he's pitched in front of defensively challenged teams in unfriendly home parks. Those numbers should be much better in 1996, given that a higher strike zone is supposed to be in place this year. The '96 season could also mean a new team for Benes. One of the most attractive free agents of the past offseason, he figured to command plenty of interest.

**Position:** SP
**Bats:** R  **Throws:** R
**Ht:** 6' 6"  **Wt:** 240

**Opening Day Age:** 28
**Born:** 8/20/67 in Evansville, IN
**ML Seasons:** 7
**Nickname:** Big Train
**Pronunciation:** BEN-es

### Overall Statistics

|      | W  | L  | Pct. | ERA  | G   | GS  | Sv | IP     | H    | BB  | SO   | HR  | BR/IP |
|------|----|----|------|------|-----|-----|----|--------|------|-----|------|-----|-------|
| 1995 | 11 | 9  | .550 | 4.76 | 31  | 31  | 0  | 181.2  | 193  | 78  | 171  | 18  | 1.49  |
| Career | 76 | 77 | .497 | 3.68 | 199 | 198 | 0  | 1298.0 | 1200 | 435 | 1081 | 123 | 1.26  |

### How Often He Throws Strikes

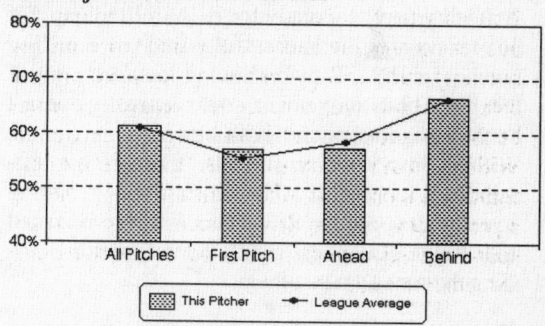

### 1995 Situational Stats

|            | W | L | ERA  | Sv |   | IP   |        | AB  | H   | HR | RBI | Avg  |
|------------|---|---|------|----|---|------|--------|-----|-----|----|-----|------|
| Home       | 4 | 6 | 4.35 | 0  |   | 99.1 | LHB    | 381 | 108 | 7  | 50  | .283 |
| Road       | 7 | 3 | 5.25 | 0  |   | 82.1 | RHB    | 332 | 85  | 11 | 45  | .256 |
| First Half | 3 | 5 | 3.73 | 0  |   | 94.0 | Sc Pos | 168 | 46  | 3  | 71  | .274 |
| Scnd Half  | 8 | 4 | 5.85 | 0  |   | 87.2 | Clutch | 40  | 5   | 0  | 0   | .125 |

### 1995 Rankings (American League)

➡ 1st in least GDPs induced per GDP situation (0.0%)
➡ 5th in highest batting average allowed vs. left-handed batters (.329)

# Mike Blowers

## 1995 Season

With Edgar Martinez becoming a full-time designated hitter, Mike Blowers took over the Mariners' third-base job in 1995. He responded well to becoming an everyday player, hitting with good power and driving in 96 runs, a career high by plenty. Blowers reached career bests in numerous other categories, and continued his career-long trend of crushing the ball with the bases loaded. Only a postseason swoon put a damper on his first season as a full-time player.

## Hitting

Blowers has a pretty slow bat for a power hitter. Like most major league hitters, he can crush a fastball when he's ready for it. And like many of his teammates, he successfully laid off breaking pitches in 1995. Blowers' swing includes a lot of head and body movement, so he generally doesn't fare well against pitches with a lot of break. For the second time in three seasons, Blowers hit left-handed pitchers like a Hall of Famer. His batting average dropped in '95, largely because he faced the league's toughest righthanders instead of riding the pines against them.

## Baserunning & Defense

Blowers remains one of the easiest double-play marks in the league. He takes big swings, ends up off balance, and has limited acceleration out of the box. His acceleration on the basepaths isn't much better, but he doesn't make many mental mistakes. Defensively, Blowers' range is about average. He handles most of the plays that come his way, and makes strong, accurate throws to other bases.

## 1996 Outlook

With Edgar Martinez going to winter ball to brush up on his third-base skills, Blowers was deemed expendable by the M's, and on November 29 he was traded to the Dodgers for a pair of minor leaguers. With Los Angeles, Blowers will take over as the everyday third baseman. However, the move the Dodger Stadium is likely to hurt his hitting stats; he hit just .213 on the road last year.

**Position:** 3B
**Bats:** R  **Throws:** R
**Ht:** 6' 2"   **Wt:** 210

**Opening Day Age:** 30
**Born:** 4/24/65 in Wurzburg, Germany
**ML Seasons:** 7
Pronunciation: BLAU-erz

### Overall Statistics

|        | G   | AB   | R   | H   | D  | T | HR | RBI | SB | BB  | SO  | Avg  | OBP  | Slg  |
|--------|-----|------|-----|-----|----|---|----|-----|----|-----|-----|------|------|------|
| 1995   | 134 | 439  | 59  | 113 | 24 | 1 | 23 | 96  | 2  | 53  | 128 | .257 | .335 | .474 |
| Career | 453 | 1378 | 179 | 355 | 67 | 4 | 54 | 229 | 6  | 147 | 372 | .258 | .329 | .430 |

### Where He Hits the Ball

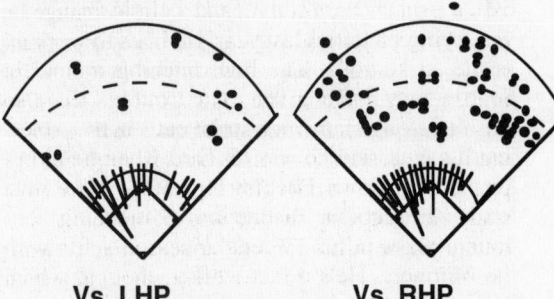

Vs. LHP          Vs. RHP

### 1995 Situational Stats

|            | AB  | H  | HR | RBI | Avg  |        | AB  | H  | HR | RBI | Avg  |
|------------|-----|----|----|-----|------|--------|-----|----|----|-----|------|
| Home       | 232 | 69 | 17 | 59  | .297 | LHP    | 129 | 44 | 7  | 34  | .341 |
| Road       | 207 | 44 | 6  | 37  | .213 | RHP    | 310 | 69 | 16 | 62  | .223 |
| First Half | 190 | 43 | 6  | 32  | .226 | Sc Pos | 135 | 43 | 8  | 74  | .319 |
| Scnd Half  | 249 | 70 | 17 | 64  | .281 | Clutch | 73  | 16 | 3  | 11  | .219 |

### 1995 Rankings (American League)

- 2nd in lowest batting average vs. right-handed pitchers (.223)
- 3rd in GDPs (18) and lowest fielding percentage at third base (.947)
- 4th in most GDPs per GDP situation (18.8%)
- 5th in strikeouts, lowest on-base percentage vs. right-handed pitchers (.306) and lowest batting average on the road (.213)
- 6th in batting average with the bases loaded (.500) and lowest batting average on an 0-2 count (.043)
- 7th in errors at third base (14)
- Led the Mariners in strikeouts, GDPs and highest groundball/flyball ratio (1.4)

# Chris Bosio

## 1995 Season

Pitching through most of the 1995 season with a sore shoulder, Chris Bosio showed what a pitcher can do on sheer determination. Pain didn't prevent him from making a reputable showing both during the regular season and the playoffs. His postseason starts against the Yankees were a study in "knowing how to pitch" versus "having good stuff." Unlike David Cone, his Game 1 opponent, Bosio looked hittable on nearly every pitch. Still, guile and deception kept Bosio and the M's in the game against one of the premier power pitchers of the era. That's Chris Bosio in a nutshell.

## Pitching

Bosio usually throws the ball just hard enough to make his change-up, curve, slider, and other junk baffling. While he knows what he's doing on the mound, he's not the same pitcher he was when his arm was healthy. But when he's sharp and exhibiting his trademark pinpoint control, there are few pitchers as frustrating to hit against as Bosio. He'll study the scouting reports and consistently feed hitters pitches they don't like, most often down in the strike zone. He doesn't need much velocity to be effective, but he needs a little more than he showed in 1995.

## Defense

Bosio may not be the best fielding pitcher in the league, but he's very good. The big guy devours grounders like an all-you-can-eat buffet. His efficient delivery and fine pickoff move keeps runners at bay.

## 1996 Outlook

While Bosio is not Orel Hershiser, his injury was similar and he has a similar pitching style. Hershiser has said that last season was the first in which he felt healthy since undergoing surgery in 1989. Bosio seems to be taking good care of his right arm, and he's a fierce competitor, so his effectiveness may return when he gains another three or four miles per hour on the radar gun. That could be as soon as this season.

**Position:** SP
**Bats:** R  **Throws:** R
**Ht:** 6' 3"  **Wt:** 225

**Opening Day Age:** 32
**Born:** 4/3/63 in Carmichael, CA
**ML Seasons:** 10
**Pronunciation:** BOZ-e-oh

### Overall Statistics

|  | W | L | Pct. | ERA | G | GS | Sv | IP | H | BB | SO | HR | BR/IP |
|---|---|---|---|---|---|---|---|---|---|---|---|---|---|
| 1995 | 10 | 8 | .556 | 4.92 | 31 | 31 | 0 | 170.0 | 211 | 69 | 85 | 18 | 1.65 |
| Career | 90 | 89 | .503 | 3.89 | 291 | 237 | 9 | 1649.1 | 1670 | 457 | 1020 | 154 | 1.29 |

### How Often He Throws Strikes

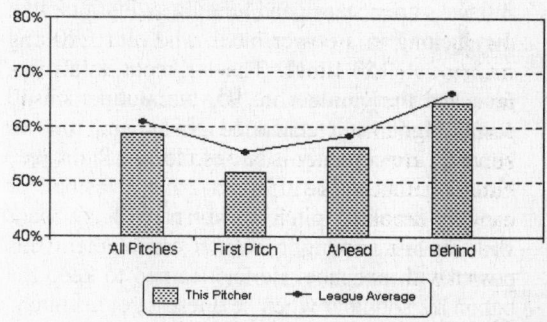

### 1995 Situational Stats

|  | W | L | ERA | Sv | IP |  | AB | H | HR | RBI | Avg |
|---|---|---|---|---|---|---|---|---|---|---|---|
| Home | 8 | 4 | 5.52 | 0 | 88.0 | LHB | 377 | 118 | 5 | 46 | .313 |
| Road | 2 | 4 | 4.28 | 0 | 82.0 | RHB | 298 | 93 | 13 | 41 | .312 |
| First Half | 6 | 3 | 4.85 | 0 | 78.0 | Sc Pos | 182 | 44 | 6 | 73 | .242 |
| Scnd Half | 4 | 5 | 4.99 | 0 | 92.0 | Clutch | 15 | 6 | 1 | 2 | .400 |

### 1995 Rankings (American League)

➡ 1st in highest batting average allowed (.313), highest on-base percentage allowed (.375) and most baserunners allowed per 9 innings (15.1)

➡ 2nd in highest slugging percentage allowed (.476) and highest batting average allowed vs. right-handed batters (.312)

➡ 3rd in least pitches thrown per batter (3.57)

➡ 4th in highest ERA and games started

➡ 5th in lowest strikeout/walk ratio (1.2) and highest ERA at home (5.52)

➡ 6th in least strikeouts per 9 innings (4.5)

➡ 7th in hits allowed

➡ Led the Mariners in games started, hits allowed and wild pitches (10)

# Jay Buhner

## 1995 Season

Much to the chagrin of Seattle's American League foes, Jay Buhner opted to stay with the Mariners at the end of the 1994 season. Most observers expected the Bald One to depart as a free agent, but Buhner stuck around to have his career year in Seattle. His run production helped the M's survive the loss of Ken Griffey, and his heroics in the League Championship Series kept the Mariners' hopes alive. But his season was notable for more than a couple of postseason homers. His presence in the lineup, in right field, and in the clubhouse were instrumental to Seattle's success.

## Hitting

Buhner's open stance and lunging swing look like they belong to a power hitter who hits .220 and strikes out 150 times. The strikeout totals approached that number in '95, but Buhner hit 40 points higher and generated power and runs in bunches. He certainly is one of the best "mistake" hitters in the league. He can drive a fastball or hanging breaking pitch to any part of any park with his brute strength. Buhner complements his power with patience. He has learned to keep the bat on his shoulder when he doesn't get his pitch.

## Baserunning & Defense

Buhner runs hard, but desire can propel you around the bases only so fast. After what was perhaps the worst fielding gaffe of his career—a misplayed fly in Game 3 of the LCS—he said he thought of himself as a "Gold Glove-type fielder." He's not. His range is about average, but the strength and accuracy of his throwing arm exceeds all but a handful of major league outfielders.

## 1996 Outlook

Buhner looks like he's fully maximized his skills as a ballplayer. Through hard work and good coaching, he covers for his weaknesses and accentuates his great strengths. His plate discipline, power, and throwing arm should remain at or near their current levels for quite some time, much to the delight of the fans in Seattle.

**Position:** RF
**Bats:** R  **Throws:** R
**Ht:** 6' 3"  **Wt:** 210

**Opening Day Age:** 31
**Born:** 8/13/64 in Louisville, KY
**ML Seasons:** 9
**Pronunciation:** BYOO-ner

### Overall Statistics

|  | G | AB | R | H | D | T | HR | RBI | SB | BB | SO | Avg | OBP | Slg |
|---|---|---|---|---|---|---|---|---|---|---|---|---|---|---|
| 1995 | 126 | 470 | 86 | 123 | 23 | 0 | 40 | 121 | 0 | 60 | 120 | .262 | .343 | .566 |
| Career | 875 | 2990 | 463 | 769 | 146 | 16 | 169 | 548 | 6 | 415 | 794 | .257 | .350 | .486 |

### Where He Hits the Ball

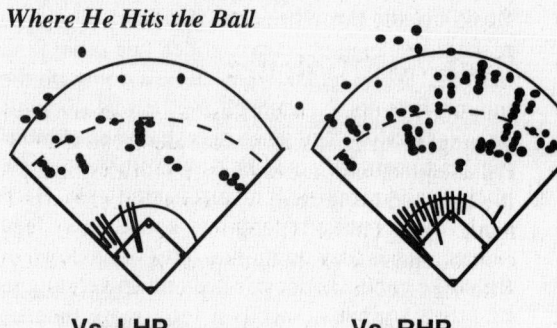

Vs. LHP          Vs. RHP

### 1995 Situational Stats

|  | AB | H | HR | RBI | Avg |  | AB | H | HR | RBI | Avg |
|---|---|---|---|---|---|---|---|---|---|---|---|
| Home | 236 | 67 | 21 | 62 | .284 | LHP | 118 | 30 | 8 | 30 | .254 |
| Road | 234 | 56 | 19 | 59 | .239 | RHP | 352 | 93 | 32 | 91 | .264 |
| First Half | 197 | 54 | 11 | 46 | .274 | Sc Pos | 157 | 45 | 15 | 90 | .287 |
| Scnd Half | 273 | 69 | 29 | 75 | .253 | Clutch | 72 | 21 | 5 | 17 | .292 |

### 1995 Rankings (American League)

- → 1st in fielding percentage in right field (.989)
- → 2nd in home runs and HR frequency (11.8 ABs per HR)
- → 3rd in RBI
- → 4th in highest percentage of swings that missed (29.6%)
- → 6th in strikeouts, batting average with the bases loaded (.500) and slugging percentage vs. right-handed pitchers (.588)
- → 7th in slugging percentage
- → 10th in lowest cleanup slugging percentage (.459)
- → Led the Mariners in home runs, RBI, sacrifice flies (6) and HR frequency

# Norm Charlton

## 1995 Season

Slow to recover from the major elbow surgery which cost him the entire 1994 season, veteran lefty Norm Charlton got off to a terrible start with his new club, the Philadelphia Phillies, last year. By July, the Phils had seen enough and they gave Charlton his release. Charlton had a friend in Seattle, however: Lou Piniella, his former skipper with both the Reds and Mariners. Given a tryout, Charlton threw about eight pitches on the sidelines before Piniella told him to get fitted for a Mariner uniform. The rest, as they say, is history. Charlton's microscopic 1.51 ERA as a Mariner pushed incumbent closer Bobby Ayala into a set-up role, and Charlton's work in the playoffs will be the talk of the town for years to come.

## Pitching & Defense

Charlton has three pitches: fastball, slider and devastating splitter. His arm, considered suspect in Philadelphia, returned to full strength after joining the M's, and his fastball was topping the 90-MPH mark. As a Phillie, Charlton struggled with his control and release point. After he was reunited with Piniella, however, he found both, and once again the hard-throwing lefty was nearly unhittable. He was almost equally effective against both righties and lefties, which allowed Piniella to use him in any situation.

## Defense

Charlton has a good pickoff move, but he often ignores baserunners and he gave up eight steals in nine attempts last year. He falls off the mound as part of his delivery, and that impairs his fielding ability.

## 1996 Outlook

While recuperating from his injury, Charlton helped the construction workers who were building his new home. He claims that hammering nails left his arm stronger than before. His success in the postseason is a testament to his novel "rehab program." Charlton is the Mariner closer until someone takes the job from him.

**Position:** RP
**Bats:** B **Throws:** L
**Ht:** 6' 3" **Wt:** 205

**Opening Day Age:** 33
**Born:** 1/6/63 in Fort Polk, LA
**ML Seasons:** 7

### Overall Statistics

|  | W | L | Pct. | ERA | G | GS | Sv | IP | H | BB | SO | HR | BR/IP |
|---|---|---|---|---|---|---|---|---|---|---|---|---|---|
| 1995 | 4 | 6 | .400 | 3.36 | 55 | 0 | 14 | 69.2 | 46 | 31 | 70 | 4 | 1.11 |
| Career | 36 | 33 | .522 | 3.00 | 327 | 37 | 61 | 605.0 | 497 | 238 | 539 | 42 | 1.21 |

### How Often He Throws Strikes

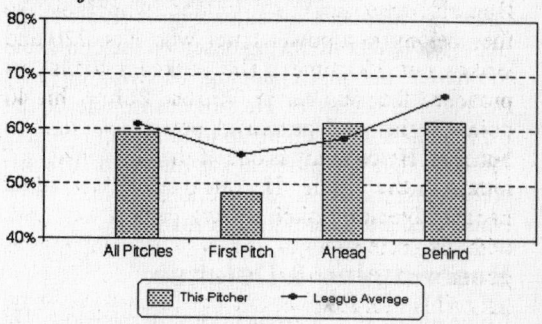

This Pitcher — League Average

### 1995 Situational Stats

|  | W | L | ERA | Sv | IP |  | AB | H | HR | RBI | Avg |
|---|---|---|---|---|---|---|---|---|---|---|---|
| Home | 4 | 1 | 3.19 | 5 | 36.2 | LHB | 77 | 15 | 1 | 7 | .195 |
| Road | 0 | 5 | 3.55 | 9 | 33.0 | RHB | 166 | 31 | 3 | 18 | .187 |
| First Half | 2 | 5 | 7.36 | 0 | 22.0 | Sc Pos | 68 | 15 | 0 | 19 | .221 |
| Scnd Half | 2 | 1 | 1.51 | 14 | 47.2 | Clutch | 139 | 24 | 2 | 14 | .173 |

### 1995 Rankings (American League)

→ 1st in least baserunners allowed per 9 innings in relief (7.6)
→ 2nd in relief ERA (1.51)
→ 4th in most strikeouts per 9 innings in relief (11.0)
→ 5th in lowest batting average allowed in relief with runners in scoring position (.143)
→ 6th in lowest batting average allowed in relief with runners on base (.167)
→ Led the Mariners in lowest batting average allowed in relief with runners on base (.167), lowest batting average allowed in relief with runners in scoring position (.143), relief ERA (1.51) and least baserunners allowed per 9 innings in relief (7.6)

# Vince Coleman

## 1995 Season

Cast aside by the Kansas City Royals in the heat of the wild-card race, Vince Coleman landed on his feet in Seattle. . . and eventually the playoffs. Coleman supplied a much-needed spark to the Mariners' September drive toward their first-ever postseason play. While Coleman struggled in the field and remained his usual impatient self at the plate, he gave the M's all they could have expected.

## Hitting

A smart hitter who knows where his strength lies, Coleman does a great job of bouncing the ball off the turf for singles. And while he never has had a "pure" swing, he is a battler who is smart at the plate. He'll alter his swing based on the count and the hurler: bunting, chopping, or swinging from the heels as necessary. He still has trouble laying off high heat, or catching up to it. Making contact often enough is a problem for him, and so is his career-long failure to draw enough walks to be considered a top-level leadoff man.

## Baserunning & Defense

Coleman is still a tremendous basestealer. He reads pitchers' moves successfully and reaches top speed with one step. Because his reflexes and raw speed have deteriorated a little with age, he's getting thrown out a bit more often than in the past. Still, he's a terror to opposing batteries. Coleman often seems fooled by the direction of balls hit to the outfield. Once he figures out where the ball's going, he gets to it in a hurry. His weak arm leads to "opportunity assists."

## 1996 Outlook

It's difficult to be a liability hitting .290, and Coleman filled a void for the Mariners last season. However, Coleman's future with Seattle is probably a short-term proposition. Because of his success on the basepaths, look for him to hang on with an Astroturf team for a few more years.

**Position:** LF/RF
**Bats:** B **Throws:** R
**Ht:** 6' 1"  **Wt:** 185

**Opening Day Age:** 34
**Born:** 9/22/61 in Jacksonville, FL
**ML Seasons:** 11

### Overall Statistics

|  | G | AB | R | H | D | T | HR | RBI | SB | BB | SO | Avg | OBP | Slg |
|---|---|---|---|---|---|---|---|---|---|---|---|---|---|---|
| 1995 | 115 | 455 | 66 | 131 | 23 | 6 | 5 | 29 | 42 | 37 | 80 | .288 | .343 | .398 |
| Career | 1332 | 5308 | 839 | 1411 | 175 | 88 | 27 | 342 | 740 | 467 | 926 | .266 | .326 | .347 |

### Where He Hits the Ball

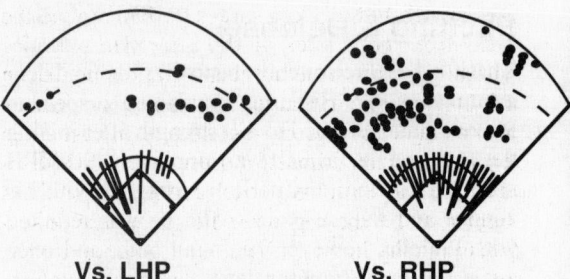

Vs. LHP          Vs. RHP

### 1995 Situational Stats

|  | AB | H | HR | RBI | Avg |  | AB | H | HR | RBI | Avg |
|---|---|---|---|---|---|---|---|---|---|---|---|
| Home | 240 | 70 | 3 | 16 | .292 | LHP | 138 | 35 | 3 | 10 | .254 |
| Road | 215 | 61 | 2 | 13 | .284 | RHP | 317 | 96 | 2 | 19 | .303 |
| First Half | 199 | 59 | 2 | 13 | .296 | Sc Pos | 73 | 20 | 2 | 25 | .274 |
| Scnd Half | 256 | 72 | 3 | 16 | .281 | Clutch | 70 | 19 | 1 | 5 | .271 |

### 1995 Rankings (American League)

- → 1st in steals of third (13)
- → 4th in caught stealing (16), fielding percentage in left field (.984) and bunts in play (27)
- → 5th in stolen bases and lowest batting average on a 3-2 count (.063)
- → 7th in errors in left field (3)
- → 8th in triples and lowest HR frequency (91.0 ABs per HR)
- → 9th in highest groundball/flyball ratio (1.7) and lowest on-base percentage for a leadoff hitter (.343)
- → 10th in least pitches seen per plate appearance (3.55)
- → Led the Mariners in on-base percentage for a leadoff hitter (.337)

# Joey Cora

## 1995 Season

A little-noted move by Mariner general manager Woody Woodward during the 1994-95 offseason was his acquisition of second baseman Joey Cora. Cora wasn't handed the second-base job; he seized it after others failed. He batted 30 points higher in 1995 than his career average, and his .359 on-base percentage was one of the highest in recent memory for a Mariner leadoff or number-two hitter. Cora also showed that he knows a thing or two about winning in the postseason. Though he had a few rough moments in the field, he played a big part in making the 1995 postseason more than just a footnote for the Mariners.

## Hitting

The switch-hitting Cora sprays the ball around the field from both sides of the plate. He provides virtually no power to a lineup—his big home run off David Cone in Game 5 of the Division Series was a major aberration—but he gets on base often enough to make himself a useful player. He handles the bat extremely well and is an excellent bunter, as he showed when he started the series-winning rally in the 11th inning of that same playoff game with a beautiful bunt down the first-base line.

## Baserunning & Defense

Cora has consistently stolen about 25 bases per 600 at-bats in his career, and he will take advantage of pitchers who ignore him. As a second baseman, Cora has average range but is error prone, leading all major league second sackers with 22 miscues last year. His weak, erratic arm contributes to his error total and reduces his ability to throw off balance and complete double plays.

## 1996 Outlook

Cora's not the best second baseman in the game, but he understands his limitations and plays within himself. He also has shown that he's willing to do whatever it takes to help the team. Look for him to get a lot of playing time again next season, even if he isn't slated to start.

**Position:** 2B
**Bats:** B **Throws:** R
**Ht:** 5' 8" **Wt:** 155

**Opening Day Age:** 30
**Born:** 5/14/65 in Caguas, PR
**ML Seasons:** 8

### Overall Statistics

|  | G | AB | R | H | D | T | HR | RBI | SB | BB | SO | Avg | OBP | Slg |
|---|---|---|---|---|---|---|---|---|---|---|---|---|---|---|
| 1995 | 120 | 427 | 64 | 127 | 19 | 2 | 3 | 39 | 18 | 37 | 31 | .297 | .359 | .372 |
| Career | 671 | 2028 | 318 | 543 | 67 | 25 | 7 | 163 | 91 | 219 | 195 | .268 | .344 | .336 |

### Where He Hits the Ball

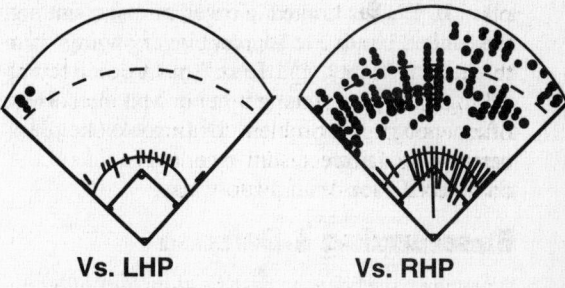

**Vs. LHP**          **Vs. RHP**

### 1995 Situational Stats

|  | AB | H | HR | RBI | Avg |  | AB | H | HR | RBI | Avg |
|---|---|---|---|---|---|---|---|---|---|---|---|
| Home | 198 | 58 | 1 | 17 | .293 | LHP | 40 | 13 | 0 | 5 | .325 |
| Road | 229 | 69 | 2 | 22 | .301 | RHP | 387 | 114 | 3 | 34 | .295 |
| First Half | 204 | 58 | 1 | 17 | .284 | Sc Pos | 105 | 35 | 1 | 37 | .333 |
| Scnd Half | 223 | 69 | 2 | 22 | .309 | Clutch | 74 | 29 | 0 | 9 | .392 |

### 1995 Rankings (American League)

→ 1st in errors at second base (22) and lowest fielding percentage at second base (.955)
→ 2nd in sacrifice bunts (13), lowest HR frequency (142.3 ABs per HR) and lowest percentage of swings that missed (6.5%)
→ 3rd in batting average in the clutch (.392)
→ 6th in batting average on a 3-2 count (.404)
→ 7th in lowest on-base percentage for a leadoff hitter (.332) and highest percentage of extra bases taken as a runner (63.8%)
→ 9th in lowest slugging percentage
→ Led the Mariners in singles (103), sacrifice bunts, batting average on a 3-2 count and bunts in play (17)

# Alex Diaz

## 1995 Season

Picked up on waivers from the Brewers after the 1994 season, reserve outfielder Alex Diaz wound up playing a lot more for the Mariners than anyone anticipated. Diaz manned center field while Ken Griffey was on the shelf, taking over after fellow reserve Rich Amaral played himself out of a job. Although he wasn't much of a factor with a bat in his hands, Diaz played hard and his steady glove work gave Seattle pitchers more confidence. When Diaz reached base—which admittedly wasn't very often—his basestealing helped spark the Mariner offense.

## Hitting

The switch-hitting Diaz chops at the ball from the left side. He has limited success as a slap-hitting left-handed batter. He takes a bigger swing when he's batting righty, and Diaz is a more effective offensive player against left-handed pitchers. He's also a petty good bunter. Diaz looks helpless against good offspeed stuff from either side of the plate, and he seldom draws a walk.

## Baserunning & Defense

Diaz may have been the best-fielding outfielder on the Mariners roster last season. His glove kept him in the lineup while Griffey was out, even though he wasn't contributing much on offense. And he was around to fill in for defensive liability Vince Coleman down the stretch and in the postseason. His only real weakness is that he doesn't have a strong arm. Diaz is a fleet baserunner who will pressure the defensive team on those rare occasions when he's on base.

## 1996 Outlook

Diaz' mug could appear in Webster's Dictionary under "fourth outfielder." He brings a number of skills to the park and plays hard. Only his inability to get on base keeps him from being an everyday player in the major leagues. Given his defensive contibutions, he could conceivably be a number-nine hitter on a team deep in offensive punch.

**Position:** CF/LF
**Bats:** B  **Throws:** R
**Ht:** 5'11"  **Wt:** 180

**Opening Day Age:** 27
**Born:** 10/5/68 in Brooklyn, NY
**ML Seasons:** 4

### *Overall Statistics*

|        | G | AB | R | H | D | T | HR | RBI | SB | BB | SO | Avg | OBP | Slg |
|--------|---|----|---|---|---|---|----|-----|----|----|----|-----|-----|-----|
| 1995   | 103 | 270 | 44 | 67 | 14 | 0 | 3 | 27 | 18 | 13 | 27 | .248 | .286 | .333 |
| Career | 236 | 535 | 75 | 137 | 21 | 7 | 4 | 46 | 31 | 23 | 58 | .256 | .287 | .344 |

### *Where He Hits the Ball*

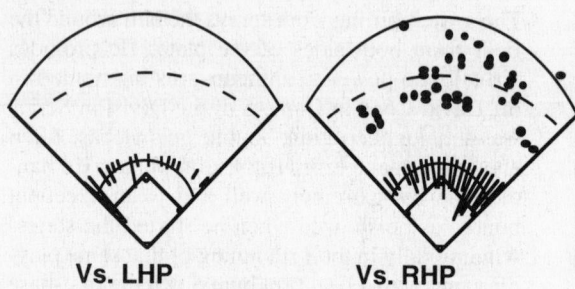

Vs. LHP          Vs. RHP

### *1995 Situational Stats*

|            | AB | H | HR | RBI | Avg |   |        | AB | H | HR | RBI | Avg |
|------------|----|---|----|-----|-----|---|--------|----|---|----|-----|-----|
| Home       | 147 | 38 | 3 | 14 | .259 |   | LHP    | 46 | 14 | 1 | 8 | .304 |
| Road       | 123 | 29 | 0 | 13 | .236 |   | RHP    | 224 | 53 | 2 | 19 | .237 |
| First Half | 167 | 44 | 2 | 17 | .263 |   | Sc Pos | 67 | 16 | 2 | 26 | .239 |
| Scnd Half  | 103 | 23 | 1 | 10 | .223 |   | Clutch | 50 | 11 | 1 | 4 | .220 |

### *1995 Rankings (American League)*
➡ 7th in lowest stolen base percentage (69.2%)
➡ Led the Mariners in caught stealing (8)

# Ken Griffey

**Position:** CF
**Bats:** L **Throws:** L
**Ht:** 6' 3" **Wt:** 205

**Opening Day Age:** 26
**Born:** 11/21/69 in Donora, PA
**ML Seasons:** 7
**Nickname:** Junior

## 1995 Season

"Get well soon, Junior." That was the message of Kingdome banners after Ken Griffey's frightful collision with the center field wall on May 26. Seattle's superstar would come back to put up a couple weeks' worth of Griffian stats in late September, then go on to tie the postseason record for most homers. Undoubtedly the new Century Park in Seattle will come to be known as "The House that Griffey Built"—and rightfully so, since it's unlikely the funding would have come without his late-season heroics.

## Hitting

Griffey wasn't on top of his game when he went down last year. And after he came back, his injured wrist affected his swing. Even with a slightly slower bat, Griffey was able to cover more of the strike zone than almost anyone in the league. The book on him is to bust him up-and-in or up-and-away. Yet, he is quick enough to get on top of high heat and smash outside offerings to left. He is a pure hitter who might bat .350 if he focused on being a singles hitter.

## Baserunning & Defense

Sometimes overlooked in the Griffey package are his excellent baserunning skills. He gets around the bases quickly, and gets a good jump off the bag. The Mariners seldom need a stolen base from him, but he will pick his spots when it's good for the team. His defensive abilities remain top-notch, including an outstanding arm. Griffey surprised many by winning his sixth straight Gold Glove despite missing half the season.

## 1996 Outlook

Griffey's injury forced him to recognize that he's mortal, which actually seemed to revitalize the young star. He enjoyed Seattle's winning ways, and he's the type of player fans love to see win. If the Mariners stay competitive, he will continue to build on his almost-legendary status in the Northwest.

### Overall Statistics

|  | G | AB | R | H | D | T | HR | RBI | SB | BB | SO | Avg | OBP | Slg |
|---|---|---|---|---|---|---|---|---|---|---|---|---|---|---|
| 1995 | 72 | 260 | 52 | 67 | 7 | 0 | 17 | 42 | 4 | 52 | 53 | .258 | .379 | .481 |
| Career | 917 | 3440 | 570 | 1039 | 201 | 19 | 189 | 585 | 92 | 426 | 530 | .302 | .379 | .536 |

### Where He Hits the Ball

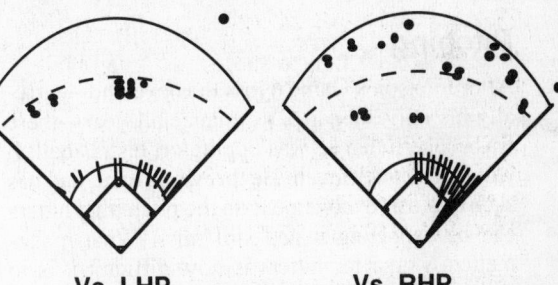

Vs. LHP          Vs. RHP

### 1995 Situational Stats

|  | AB | H | HR | RBI | Avg |  | AB | H | HR | RBI | Avg |
|---|---|---|---|---|---|---|---|---|---|---|---|
| Home | 133 | 41 | 13 | 29 | .308 | LHP | 86 | 24 | 3 | 10 | .279 |
| Road | 127 | 26 | 4 | 13 | .205 | RHP | 174 | 43 | 14 | 32 | .247 |
| First Half | 99 | 26 | 7 | 15 | .263 | Sc Pos | 77 | 19 | 4 | 26 | .247 |
| Scnd Half | 161 | 41 | 10 | 27 | .255 | Clutch | 33 | 8 | 2 | 8 | .242 |

### 1995 Rankings (American League)

➡ Led the Mariners in batting average on a 3-1 count (.545)

# Randy Johnson

## 1995 Season

Randy "Cy" Johnson isn't perfect. He isn't a one-man team. And he isn't the best pitcher in history. But last October, Mariner fans may have thought otherwise. Following a career year including a brilliant performance in the one-game playoff that won Seattle the A.L. West title, Johnson earned his first Cy Young Award. He also defeated the Yankees twice in the divisional playoffs, including the series finale in a rare relief appearance. He started and pitched brilliantly in Game 3 of the League Championship Series against Cleveland, though he didn't get credit for the win. Losing the last game of the team's first postseason had to be Johnson's only disappointment in a remarkable year.

## Pitching

After Johnson's Game 6 loss to Cleveland—virtually his only subpar performance all year—there was concern that he was tipping off his fastball. It wouldn't matter much. He throws so hard, and has such explosive movement on the pitch, that hitters can be expecting it and still miss. What makes matters worse for hitters is how difficult it is to distinguish the fastball from his hard slider. The slider leaves righties flailing and lefties talking to themselves. And when Johnson drops down for a slow curve, hitters are lucky to foul it off.

## Defense

Johnson is so focused when he pitches that he's able to overcome his lanky, off-balance delivery to field his position quite well. Mentally, he almost never makes a mistake. His pickoff move atones for some of his problems at holding runners, but he's still vulnerable to basestealers.

## 1996 Outlook

The common phrase about Greg Maddux is that he "knows how to pitch." The American League Cy Young winner is showing that Maddux doesn't have a monopoly on that trait. With the unbelievable stuff that Johnson throws, and his knowledge of the game, there seem few limits on how many wins Randy Johnson can amass over the next few seasons.

**Position:** SP
**Bats:** R  **Throws:** L
**Ht:** 6'10"  **Wt:** 225

**Opening Day Age:** 32
**Born:** 9/10/63 in
Walnut Creek, CA
**ML Seasons:** 8
**Nickname:** The Big Unit

### Overall Statistics

|        | W  | L  | Pct. | ERA  | G   | GS  | Sv | IP     | H    | BB  | SO   | HR  | BR/IP |
|--------|----|----|------|------|-----|-----|----|--------|------|-----|------|-----|-------|
| 1995   | 18 | 2  | .900 | 2.48 | 30  | 30  | 0  | 214.1  | 159  | 65  | 294  | 12  | 1.05  |
| Career | 99 | 64 | .607 | 3.52 | 218 | 216 | 1  | 1459.2 | 1125 | 755 | 1624 | 118 | 1.29  |

### How Often He Throws Strikes

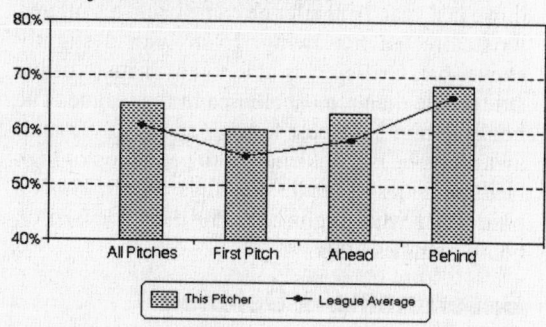

### 1995 Situational Stats

|            | W  | L | ERA  | Sv | IP    |        | AB  | H   | HR | RBI | Avg  |
|------------|----|---|------|----|-------|--------|-----|-----|----|-----|------|
| Home       | 11 | 1 | 2.57 | 0  | 122.1 | LHB    | 85  | 11  | 0  | 5   | .129 |
| Road       | 7  | 1 | 2.35 | 0  | 92.0  | RHB    | 707 | 148 | 12 | 54  | .209 |
| First Half | 9  | 1 | 2.88 | 0  | 109.1 | Sc Pos | 183 | 30  | 5  | 48  | .164 |
| Scnd Half  | 9  | 1 | 2.06 | 0  | 105.0 | Clutch | 77  | 16  | 1  | 7   | .208 |

### 1995 Rankings (American League)

➡ 1st in ERA, strikeouts, winning percentage, highest strikeout/walk ratio (4.5), lowest batting average allowed (.201), lowest slugging percentage allowed (.303), lowest on-base percentage allowed (.266), most pitches thrown per batter (4.18), least baserunners allowed per 9 innings (9.7), least home runs allowed per 9 innings (.50), least GDPs induced per 9 innings (0.3) and most strikeouts per 9 innings (12.3)

➡ 2nd in wins, shutouts (3) and pitches thrown (3,622)

➡ Led the Mariners in wins, complete games (6), shutouts (3) and innings pitched

# Edgar Martinez

## 1995 Season

Healthy again and thriving in his new role as a full-time designated hitter, Edgar Martinez helped the Mariners survive the loss of Ken Griffey with one of the best seasons turned in by a right-handed hitter in many years. Martinez led the American League in hitting, on-base average, runs and doubles while reaching career highs in numerous categories. He followed with a sensational Division Series against the Yankees, driving in seven runs in Game 4 and then plating the series-winning runs with an 11th-inning double the next night. Martinez ended the year on a down note as he batted only .087 against the Indians in the LCS. But everyone in Seattle knew that without Martinez, the M's never would have made it as far as they did.

## Hitting

Martinez is a line-drive hitter who can handle pitches almost anywhere around the plate. He'll often perch on a first-pitch fastball up in the zone and try to pull it. He's at his best, though, waiting for breaking pitches, since he excels at keeping his head still and hands back. He's also adept at using the whole field. With the best batting eye west of Chicago, Martinez always is willing to take a free pass and let his teammates have a shot. Often that's a good compromise for opposing hurlers.

## Baserunning & Defense

Although he filled in at the corners at times, Martinez basically became a full-time designated hitter in 1995. Reportedly he is polishing his third-base skills in winter ball this year, in case the Mariners need him to take the field again. He still is a smart baserunner with some speed, but he seldom tries to steal a base.

## 1996 Outlook

Like Paul Molitor, Martinez was able to shake his long-time injury problems by becoming a designated hitter. However, with the trade of Mike Blowers, Martinez will likely return to third base this season. If he can stay healthy, his sweet swing and superb batting eye should generate impressive numbers for a few more years.

**Position:** DH
**Bats:** R **Throws:** R
**Ht:** 5'11" **Wt:** 190

**Opening Day Age:** 33
**Born:** 1/2/63 in New York, NY
**ML Seasons:** 9

### Overall Statistics

|  | G | AB | R | H | D | T | HR | RBI | SB | BB | SO | Avg | OBP | Slg |
|---|---|---|---|---|---|---|---|---|---|---|---|---|---|---|
| 1995 | 145 | 511 | 121 | 182 | 52 | 0 | 29 | 113 | 4 | 116 | 87 | .356 | .479 | .628 |
| Career | 797 | 2777 | 483 | 868 | 204 | 9 | 91 | 381 | 27 | 432 | 381 | .313 | .408 | .491 |

### Where He Hits the Ball

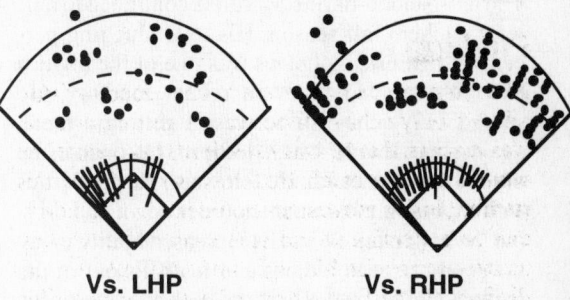

**Vs. LHP**      **Vs. RHP**

### 1995 Situational Stats

|  | AB | H | HR | RBI | Avg |  |  | AB | H | HR | RBI | Avg |
|---|---|---|---|---|---|---|---|---|---|---|---|---|
| Home | 252 | 95 | 16 | 59 | .377 | | LHP | 127 | 55 | 8 | 32 | .433 |
| Road | 259 | 87 | 13 | 54 | .336 | | RHP | 384 | 127 | 21 | 81 | .331 |
| First Half | 240 | 87 | 14 | 56 | .363 | | Sc Pos | 138 | 53 | 9 | 85 | .384 |
| Scnd Half | 271 | 95 | 15 | 57 | .351 | | Clutch | 73 | 29 | 4 | 27 | .397 |

### 1995 Rankings (American League)

- ➡ 1st in batting average (.356), runs scored, doubles, times on base (306), games played, on-base percentage, batting average vs. left-handed pitchers (.433) and on-base percentage vs. left-handed pitchers (.562)
- ➡ 2nd in hits, walks, intentional walks (19), slugging percentage, batting average in the clutch (.397), on-base percentage vs. right-handed pitchers (.449), batting average at home (.377), batting average on the road (.336) and highest percentage of pitches taken (66.2%)
- ➡ Led the Mariners in hits, total bases (321), walks and intentional walks (19)

# Tino Martinez

## 1995 Season

Most years, a guy who hits almost .300, slugs above .551 with 31 homers and 111 RBI, plays good defense and gets his team into the playoffs, is talked about as an MVP candidate. Tino Martinez, Seattle's "other" Martinez, did all of the above last year, but received surprisingly little recognition. Martinez' lefty bat was critical to the Mariners' playoff push with Ken Griffey out for much of the season. Throw in the stability he lent to the club's oft-shifting infield, and maybe this ex-Olympian should have received more notoriety for his career year.

## Hitting

The left-handed-hitting Martinez continued to hurt lefty pitchers last season. His .605 slugging percentage against southpaws was one of the highest by a left-handed hitter in recent memory. He started 137 games, so he wasn't getting a break against the league's best lefties. (Of course, he didn't have to face Randy Johnson.) He hits lefties well by keeping his front shoulder down and driving the ball to left field. His increased ability to lay off good offspeed pitches and fastballs out of the strike zone led to the best on-base average of his career.

## Baserunning & Defense

All baserunners are in scoring position when Jay Buhner's at the plate. Martinez and manager Lou Piniella respected that fact last year, as Martinez attempted no steals. He remains one of the slower non-catchers in the league. His first step is quick enough in the field, and he has soft hands and throws well for a first baseman.

## 1996 Outlook

Martinez has improved his home-run total every year he's been in the major leagues, and last year he finally arrived as an impact player. Only 28, he seems a good bet to have another outstanding season. If he does, there will be plenty of people around to notice. In December, Martinez was traded to the New York Yankees, where his left-handed power swing should be a perfect fit.

**Position:** 1B
**Bats:** L  **Throws:** R
**Ht:** 6' 2"  **Wt:** 210

**Opening Day Age:** 28
**Born:** 12/7/67 in Tampa, FL
**ML Seasons:** 6

### Overall Statistics

|  | G | AB | R | H | D | T | HR | RBI | SB | BB | SO | Avg | OBP | Slg |
|---|---|---|---|---|---|---|---|---|---|---|---|---|---|---|
| 1995 | 141 | 519 | 92 | 152 | 35 | 3 | 31 | 111 | 0 | 62 | 91 | .293 | .369 | .551 |
| Career | 543 | 1896 | 250 | 502 | 106 | 6 | 88 | 312 | 3 | 198 | 309 | .265 | .334 | .466 |

### Where He Hits the Ball

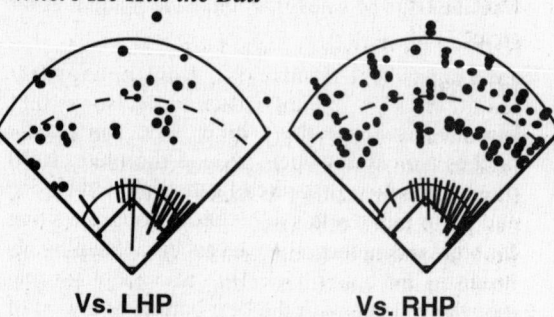

Vs. LHP          Vs. RHP

### 1995 Situational Stats

|  | AB | H | HR | RBI | Avg |  | AB | H | HR | RBI | Avg |
|---|---|---|---|---|---|---|---|---|---|---|---|
| Home | 256 | 70 | 14 | 56 | .273 | LHP | 152 | 49 | 10 | 46 | .322 |
| Road | 263 | 82 | 17 | 55 | .312 | RHP | 367 | 103 | 21 | 65 | .281 |
| First Half | 241 | 72 | 18 | 58 | .299 | Sc Pos | 150 | 46 | 11 | 86 | .307 |
| Scnd Half | 278 | 80 | 13 | 53 | .288 | Clutch | 93 | 27 | 5 | 22 | .290 |

### 1995 Rankings (American League)

→ 3rd in errors at first base (8)
→ 4th in cleanup slugging percentage (.571)
→ 5th in doubles, RBI, intentional walks (15) and lowest fielding percentage at first base (.993)
→ 8th in total bases (286) and slugging percentage vs. left-handed pitchers (.605)
→ 9th in lowest percentage of extra bases taken as a runner (33.3%)
→ Led the Mariners in at-bats, triples, sacrifice flies (6), least GDPs per GDP situation (6.1%) and cleanup slugging percentage

# Jeff Nelson

## 1995 Season

What a difference a little control and a little self-confidence can make. Jeff Nelson, always one of the toughest pitchers in the league for righties to hit, found a way to retire lefties last season. The results were nothing short of amazing. He struck out nearly 11 batters per nine innings, and his ERA was under 2.20. His 3.1 walks per nine innings was, by far, a career low. During postseason play analysts more often raved about the bullpens of Seattle's opponents, but Nelson made a strong case for Mariner relievers. He often bailed out Seattle's starters, recording two saves and a team-high 14 holds.

## Pitching

Nelson still throws the fastball/slider combo that once again kept righthanders from hitting .200 against him. The big difference for Nelson is that he can now consistently drop his slider on the outside corner against left-handed hitters, which leaves them stretching to make contact. To make this pitch more effective, Nelson isn't afraid to work up-and-in to lefties, which keeps them from sitting on the backdoor slider. His slider, by tthe way, just might have the best late movement of any in the league. Although he pitches aggressively, Nelson's smart enough to let a hitter walk instead of grooving a pitch when he's behind in the count.

## Defense

His move to first is fine, but Nelson has a huge leg kick which he needs in order to throw his pitches effectively. That makes him vulnerable to the running game. Nelson is unremarkable as a fielder, though probably a little above average for a power pitcher.

## 1996 Outlook

With his new-found control and success against lefthanders, Nelson is maturing into a potential big-league closer. For now, though, he'll serve as John Wetteland's chief set-up man, after being traded to the Yankees last December along with Tino Martinez. Nelson should be a welcome addition to the Yankees' beleaguered middle-relief corps.

**Position:** RP
**Bats:** R **Throws:** R
**Ht:** 6' 8"  **Wt:** 235

**Opening Day Age:** 29
**Born:** 11/17/66 in Baltimore, MD
**ML Seasons:** 4

### Overall Statistics

|        | W  | L  | Pct. | ERA  | G   | GS | Sv | IP    | H   | BB  | SO  | HR | BR/IP |
|--------|----|----|------|------|-----|----|----|-------|-----|-----|-----|----|-------|
| 1995   | 7  | 3  | .700 | 2.17 | 62  | 0  | 2  | 78.2  | 58  | 27  | 96  | 4  | 1.08  |
| Career | 13 | 13 | .500 | 3.16 | 227 | 0  | 9  | 262.0 | 221 | 125 | 247 | 19 | 1.32  |

### How Often He Throws Strikes

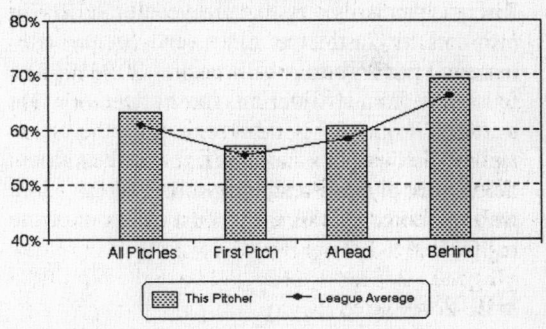

### 1995 Situational Stats

|            | W | L | ERA  | Sv | IP   |        | AB  | H  | HR | RBI | Avg  |
|------------|---|---|------|----|------|--------|-----|----|----|-----|------|
| Home       | 5 | 2 | 1.24 | 1  | 43.2 | LHB    | 120 | 28 | 2  | 11  | .233 |
| Road       | 2 | 1 | 3.34 | 1  | 35.0 | RHB    | 157 | 30 | 2  | 15  | .191 |
| First Half | 3 | 1 | 1.50 | 1  | 36.0 | Sc Pos | 99  | 18 | 0  | 21  | .182 |
| Scnd Half  | 4 | 2 | 2.74 | 1  | 42.2 | Clutch | 94  | 23 | 2  | 10  | .245 |

### 1995 Rankings (American League)

- → 3rd in most strikeouts per 9 innings in relief (11.0)
- → 4th in relief ERA (2.17) and relief wins (7)
- → 5th in relief innings (78.2)
- → 6th in games pitched, holds (14) and lowest batting average allowed in relief (.209)
- → 8th in least baserunners allowed per 9 innings in relief (10.4)
- → Led the Mariners in hit batsmen (6), holds, relief wins, relief innings, lowest batting average allowed in relief and most strikeouts per 9 innings in relief

# Bill Risley

## 1995 Season

Seattle fans didn't call them the "Nasty Boys," or give them some other catchy nickname, but the Mariners had four hard-throwing relievers who each averaged more than a strikeout per inning last year... just like the legendary relief corps that M's skipper Lou Piniella used to manage in Cincinnati. One of Seattle's bullpen stars was Montreal castoff Bill Risley. The big righthander picked up where he left off in 1994, logging quality innings as a long reliever and set-up man. That role proved extremely valuable, given the difficulties experienced by Seattle starters throughout the summer.

## Pitching

Risley is primarily a fastball/curveball pitcher. He also cuts his fastball at times, and occasionally tosses a slider. The fastball reaches 90 MPH and tails away from lefties. He is most effective when he keeps it out of the strike zone or on the black. He'll try to bust it up-and-in to right-handed hitters before dropping curves in for strikes. If the curve isn't working, righties will take it right out of the ballpark.

## Defense

Previously known for ignoring men on base, Risley surprised people by paying attention to baserunners last season. In the past he'd been reluctant to pitch from the stretch, but with an improved pickoff move and pitch selection, he was able to cut down the running game quite well for a power pitcher. His defense is adequate.

## 1996 Outlook

After two seasons in the Seattle organization, Risley now has to be considered among the league's better set-up men. He played a big role in Seattle's postseason and responded admirably to the pressure. He might even develop into a closer someday, though for now he'll remain in middle relief. Lou Piniella has a knack for uncovering hard-throwing relievers and getting good work out of them, and Risley is yet another example.

**Position:** RP
**Bats:** R  **Throws:** R
**Ht:** 6' 2"  **Wt:** 215

**Opening Day Age:** 28
**Born:** 5/29/67 in Chicago, IL
**ML Seasons:** 4

### Overall Statistics

|        | W  | L | Pct. | ERA  | G  | GS | Sv | IP    | H  | BB | SO  | HR | BR/IP |
|--------|----|---|------|------|----|----|----|-------|----|----|-----|----|-------|
| 1995   | 2  | 1 | .667 | 3.13 | 45 | 0  | 1  | 60.1  | 55 | 18 | 65  | 7  | 1.21  |
| Career | 12 | 7 | .632 | 3.28 | 85 | 1  | 1  | 120.2 | 92 | 40 | 130 | 15 | 1.09  |

### How Often He Throws Strikes

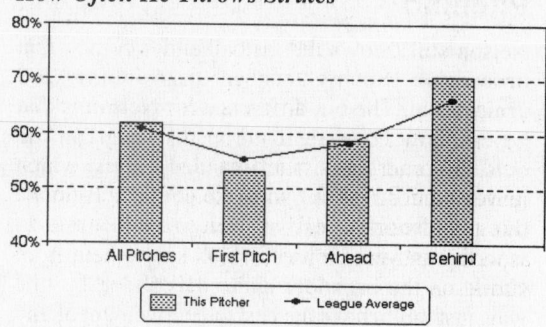

### 1995 Situational Stats

|            | W | L | ERA  | Sv | IP   |        | AB  | H  | HR | RBI | Avg  |
|------------|---|---|------|----|------|--------|-----|----|----|-----|------|
| Home       | 1 | 0 | 2.73 | 1  | 33.0 | LHB    | 128 | 30 | 3  | 18  | .234 |
| Road       | 1 | 1 | 3.62 | 0  | 27.1 | RHB    | 97  | 25 | 4  | 17  | .258 |
| First Half | 1 | 1 | 1.42 | 1  | 31.2 | Sc Pos | 66  | 20 | 3  | 29  | .303 |
| Scnd Half  | 1 | 0 | 5.02 | 0  | 28.2 | Clutch | 105 | 28 | 3  | 20  | .267 |

### 1995 Rankings (American League)

➡ 6th in highest percentage of inherited runners scored (47.1%)
➡ 7th in holds (13) and blown saves (6)
➡ 9th in most strikeouts per 9 innings in relief (9.7)

# Luis Sojo

## 1995 Season

"Been there. Done that. Swung at those." That could be Luis Sojo's motto. The free-swinging Venezuelan veteran was the survivor of the short-stop shootout in Seattle last season, and Emerald City denizens are thankful. His base-clearing double in the one-game playoff against California locked up a West Division crown and a postseason berth for the Mariners. All season long Sojo was doing whatever the team needed. His power was fine for a shortstop, and he provided some extra pop behind the big guns. He also filled in at second base and in left field when needed.

## Hitting

Sojo will swing at most any pitch, and he makes good contact with many deliveries well out of the strike zone. Pitchers are advised to avoid the straight stuff. Sojo is about as good at hitting the high fastball as anyone in the league. Only the low inside fastball gives him occasional trouble. Despite a career-high 23 walks in 1995, he seldom takes the free pass. His strikeouts are infrequent, as well. Last year, for the first time in his career, he struck out fewer times than he walked.

## Baserunning & Defense

He looks fast. He runs the bases well. Still, Sojo isn't a good basestealer. As a shortstop, he is reliable. His range isn't quite what you'd like, but he has a good arm that allows him to play a little deeper. His ability to fill in and provide solid defense at any infield spot makes him a defensive asset.

## 1996 Outlook

Nobody's job is safe in the Mariner infield, but Sojo is versatile and valuable to a contending team. He's played on several contenders in his career, and knows what it takes to win. Sojo does whatever management asks and gives an honest effort. Look for Sojo's name in most of Seattle's box scores next summer, too.

**Position:** SS/2B
**Bats:** R  **Throws:** R
**Ht:** 5'11"  **Wt:** 175

**Opening Day Age:** 30
**Born:** 1/3/66 in Barquisimeto, VZ
**ML Seasons:** 6
**Pronunciation:** SO-ho

### Overall Statistics

| | G | AB | R | H | D | T | HR | RBI | SB | BB | SO | Avg | OBP | Slg |
|---|---|---|---|---|---|---|---|---|---|---|---|---|---|---|
| 1995 | 102 | 339 | 50 | 98 | 18 | 2 | 7 | 39 | 4 | 23 | 19 | .289 | .335 | .416 |
| Career | 436 | 1411 | 176 | 377 | 58 | 8 | 24 | 139 | 18 | 68 | 101 | .267 | .304 | .371 |

### Where He Hits the Ball

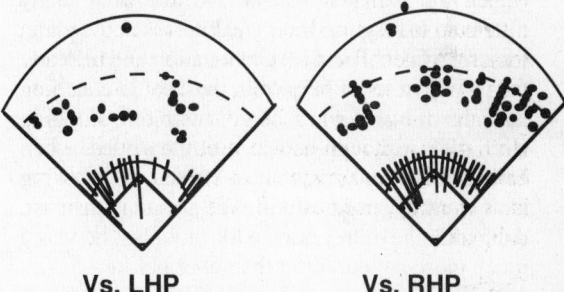

**Vs. LHP**          **Vs. RHP**

### 1995 Situational Stats

| | AB | H | HR | RBI | Avg | | AB | H | HR | RBI | Avg |
|---|---|---|---|---|---|---|---|---|---|---|---|
| Home | 189 | 49 | 4 | 28 | .259 | LHP | 111 | 40 | 5 | 19 | .360 |
| Road | 150 | 49 | 3 | 11 | .327 | RHP | 228 | 58 | 2 | 20 | .254 |
| First Half | 138 | 37 | 2 | 12 | .268 | Sc Pos | 71 | 20 | 1 | 28 | .282 |
| Scnd Half | 201 | 61 | 5 | 27 | .303 | Clutch | 42 | 8 | 1 | 9 | .190 |

### 1995 Rankings (American League)

→ 2nd in highest percentage of swings put into play (57.5%)
→ 3rd in lowest percentage of swings that missed (7.2%)
→ 5th in batting average vs. left-handed pitchers (.360)
→ Led the Mariners in highest percentage of swings put into play

Seattle Mariners

# Dan Wilson

## 1995 Season

One of the major surprises of the 1995 season, Dan Wilson had his finest year at the plate since his days at Barrington (Illinois) High School. It might be time to remove the "light-hitting" moniker from his name, as Wilson seemed to make a believer of himself last year. Once a tentative hitter, he performed like a confident veteran, as if he finally believed that he belonged in the major leagues. That confidence carried over to his catching, where he did a fine job of handling the Seattle staff.

## Hitting

We're not talking Johnny Bench here, but Wilson ripped the ball last season. He did what many hitters do to disguise their weaknesses at the plate: look for a fastball in a certain location and be ready for it. With a lot of help from the Seattle coaching staff, he did well when he got his pitch, slugging over .400. Although he was pretty harmless when forced to hit breaking pitches, Wilson didn't swing at as many offspeed offerings as he had in the past. And while he didn't draw a lot of walks, he was a much more patient hitter than ever before.

## Baserunning & Defense

Wilson isn't the slowest Mariner. In fact, he went two-for-three on steal attempts last season. His athletic ability serves him well in the field: he is mobile behind the plate, and smoothly handles pop-ups and grounders. His throwing arm is strong and his release quick.

## 1996 Outlook

While he's undoubtedly a better hitter than he was a couple of years ago, Wilson never hit anywhere near this well prior to 1995, and his numbers figure to drop a little. But Wilson should keep his job even if he falls off a little at bat, since most of his value derives from his ability to play defense and to call a game. Many teams would be happy to have someone so qualified behind the plate.

**Position:** C
**Bats:** R **Throws:** R
**Ht:** 6' 3" **Wt:** 190

**Opening Day Age:** 27
**Born:** 3/25/69 in Arlington Heights, IL
**ML Seasons:** 4

### Overall Statistics

| | G | AB | R | H | D | T | HR | RBI | SB | BB | SO | Avg | OBP | Slg |
|---|---|---|---|---|---|---|---|---|---|---|---|---|---|---|
| 1995 | 119 | 399 | 40 | 111 | 22 | 3 | 9 | 51 | 2 | 33 | 63 | .278 | .336 | .416 |
| Career | 258 | 782 | 72 | 198 | 40 | 5 | 12 | 89 | 3 | 55 | 144 | .253 | .303 | .363 |

### Where He Hits the Ball

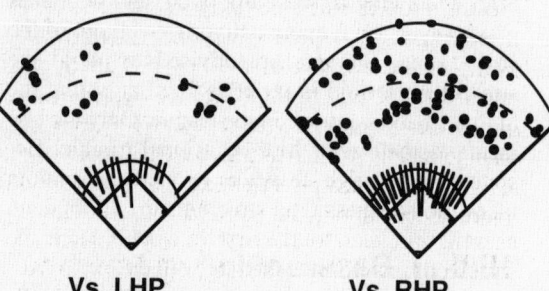

Vs. LHP          Vs. RHP

### 1995 Situational Stats

| | AB | H | HR | RBI | Avg | | AB | H | HR | RBI | Avg |
|---|---|---|---|---|---|---|---|---|---|---|---|
| Home | 193 | 55 | 5 | 29 | .285 | LHP | 102 | 24 | 3 | 16 | .235 |
| Road | 206 | 56 | 4 | 22 | .272 | RHP | 297 | 87 | 6 | 35 | .293 |
| First Half | 168 | 44 | 2 | 15 | .262 | Sc Pos | 97 | 31 | 1 | 41 | .320 |
| Scnd Half | 231 | 67 | 7 | 36 | .290 | Clutch | 50 | 18 | 2 | 5 | .360 |

### 1995 Rankings (American League)

- → 3rd in fielding percentage at catcher (.995)
- → 9th in errors at catcher (5)
- → 10th in batting average with the bases loaded (.500)
- → Led the Mariners in triples

# Rich Amaral

**Position:** LF/CF
**Bats:** R **Throws:** R
**Ht:** 6' 0"  **Wt:** 175

**Opening Day Age:** 33
**Born:** 4/1/62 in Visalia, CA
**ML Seasons:** 5
**Pronunciation:** AM-r-all

## Overall Statistics

|  | G | AB | R | H | D | T | HR | RBI | SB | BB | SO | Avg | OBP | Slg |
|---|---|---|---|---|---|---|---|---|---|---|---|---|---|---|
| 1995 | 90 | 238 | 45 | 67 | 14 | 2 | 2 | 19 | 21 | 21 | 33 | .282 | .342 | .382 |
| Career | 326 | 955 | 146 | 260 | 51 | 5 | 8 | 88 | 49 | 84 | 136 | .272 | .333 | .361 |

## 1995 Season

Seattle's fourth outfielder for much of the season, Rich Amaral provided some offensive spark while Ken Griffey was out of the lineup. Amaral was pushed to the end of the bench down the stretch, however, when Griffey returned and Vince Coleman joined the team. His playing time dropped off even further when reserve Alex Diaz proved to be more dependable in the outfield.

## Hitting, Baserunning, & Defense

Amaral stays within himself. He hits fastballs, and he's patient enough to draw some walks and slap breaking pitches around. He knows how to bunt —although he struggled with his bunting in '95— and he makes good contact on the hit-and-run. Though he doesn't have blinding speed, Amaral is an outstanding baserunner. His stolen-base record last season was a remarkable 21-for-23, and he always takes the extra base when it's there. As a center fielder, the converted infielder didn't make anyone forget the Gold Glover whom he was replacing in. But he's improving, and he can fill in just about anywhere in the infield or outfield.

## 1996 Outlook

Amaral's offensive levels are a bit low for a starting outfielder. As his instincts in the outfield improve, he could become a very good defensive player. Coupled with his ability to get on base and run, and his willingness to play anywhere, Amaral should see plenty of action this year.

# Darren Bragg

**Position:** LF/RF
**Bats:** L **Throws:** R
**Ht:** 5' 9"  **Wt:** 180

**Opening Day Age:** 26
**Born:** 9/7/69 in Waterbury, CT
**ML Seasons:** 2

## Overall Statistics

|  | G | AB | R | H | D | T | HR | RBI | SB | BB | SO | Avg | OBP | Slg |
|---|---|---|---|---|---|---|---|---|---|---|---|---|---|---|
| 1995 | 52 | 145 | 20 | 34 | 5 | 1 | 3 | 12 | 9 | 18 | 37 | .234 | .331 | .345 |
| Career | 60 | 164 | 24 | 37 | 6 | 1 | 3 | 14 | 9 | 20 | 42 | .226 | .321 | .329 |

## 1995 Season

Given a chance at the left-field post vacated by Eric Anthony last year, rookie Darren Bragg couldn't snap an early-season slump and had to go back to Triple-A Tacoma. A scrappy type whom Lou Piniella took a liking to, Bragg worked hard, played well in the outfield, drew some walks and ran the bases effectively. He just didn't hit. However, he was back with the team in September and likely would have made the postseason roster if not for the acquisition of Vince Coleman.

## Hitting, Baserunning, & Defense

The lefty-swinging Bragg has a quick, compact swing from his open stance. His on-base average against lefthanders was nearly .500, and his success against lefties bodes well for his chances as an everyday player if he can push his game to major league standards. A perfect nine-for-nine on stolen-base attempts, Bragg looks like he could steal 30 bases a year in the majors. He is a good fielder whose defensive skills would be an asset to any team.

## 1996 Outlook

It's not unheard of for players to emerge at the age of 26. Bragg has two things going for him: he's always done very well in the minors, and Piniella likes his rookies to demonstrate a great deal of maturity before giving them a shot. Bragg will have a chance in left field again this year.

# Felix Fermin

**Position:** SS/2B
**Bats:** R **Throws:** R
**Ht:** 5'11" **Wt:** 170

**Opening Day Age:** 32
**Born:** 10/9/63 in Mao,
Valverde, DR
**ML Seasons:** 9
**Pronunciation:**
fair-MEAN
**Nickname:** Gato

*Overall Statistics*

| | G | AB | R | H | D | T | HR | RBI | SB | BB | SO | Avg | OBP | Slg |
|---|---|---|---|---|---|---|---|---|---|---|---|---|---|---|
| 1995 | 73 | 200 | 21 | 39 | 6 | 0 | 0 | 15 | 2 | 6 | 6 | .195 | .232 | .225 |
| Career | 892 | 2751 | 290 | 716 | 85 | 11 | 4 | 206 | 27 | 164 | 147 | .260 | .306 | .304 |

## 1995 Season

It was a difficult summer for veteran infielder Felix Fermin, who played himself out of a job and a postseason roster spot. While Fermin was sitting, more than a few people in Seattle were noting that the man he'd been acquired for back in 1993, Omar Vizquel, was helping lead Cleveland past the Mariners in the playoffs. It was a difficult season, but Fermin never uttered a disparaging word or stopped hustling.

## Hitting, Baserunning, & Defense

Fermin's game has always been slapping at the ball, then sprinting toward first base. Last year he wasn't chopping the ball successfully, and his hustle didn't make up for his deteriorating physical skills. Fermin remains one of the best bunters and toughest strikeouts in the league. He has matured as a baserunner, and doesn't make outs on the bases on those rare occasions that he's aboard. As a fielder, he's a rangy second baseman and a reliable shortstop, not spectacular but solid.

## 1996 Outlook

While Fermin's 1994 batting average (.317) was an aberration on the high side, last year was likely a downside fluke. Fermin doesn't really help a team offensively, but he has the skills to be a .260 hitter. His ability to play on both sides of second base should keep him in the game for a few more years.

# Warren Newson

**Position:** LF/RF
**Bats:** L **Throws:** L
**Ht:** 5' 7" **Wt:** 202

**Opening Day Age:** 31
**Born:** 7/3/64 in
Newnan, GA
**ML Seasons:** 5
**Nickname:** The Deacon

*Overall Statistics*

| | G | AB | R | H | D | T | HR | RBI | SB | BB | SO | Avg | OBP | Slg |
|---|---|---|---|---|---|---|---|---|---|---|---|---|---|---|
| 1995 | 84 | 157 | 34 | 41 | 2 | 2 | 5 | 15 | 2 | 39 | 45 | .261 | .411 | .395 |
| Career | 307 | 567 | 98 | 148 | 15 | 2 | 14 | 64 | 8 | 127 | 152 | .261 | .397 | .369 |

## 1995 Season

The Mariners, who were looking for a left fielder and for hitters to plug into the top two spots in the lineup, picked up two outfielders during the 1995 season. Warren Newson was one of them. Newson's career on-base average is nearly .400 and he's scored 98 runs in 567 career at-bats. His lack of speed and finesse in the field, however, took him out of contention for regular duty with the Mariners, and he didn't see anywhere near the amount of action the M's other outfield import— Vince Coleman—did.

## Hitting, Baserunning & Defense

As a pinch hitter, Newson is always ready to hit fastballs in the heart of the strike zone. His small strike zone and great batting eye induce a great number of walks. He also has pretty good power and can hit the ball out on occasion. Once Newson's on the bases he hustles and runs smartly, but he's not fast. As a fielder, he isn't very mobile and has an arm barely adequate for left field.

## 1996 Outlook

At the end of the season the Mariners released Newson, whose only opportunity to play in Seattle was in the designated hitter slot because he's not a solid fielder and not considered fast enough to lead off. He should continue to be a useful bit player for someone, and his winning personality makes him a good person to have around the clubhouse.

# Alex Rodriguez (Top Prospect)

**Position:** SS
**Bats:** R **Throws:** R
**Ht:** 6' 3" **Wt:** 190

**Opening Day Age:** 20
**Born:** 7/27/75 in New York, NY
**ML Seasons:** 2

*Overall Statistics*

| | G | AB | R | H | D | T | HR | RBI | SB | BB | SO | Avg | OBP | Slg |
|---|---|---|---|---|---|---|---|---|---|---|---|---|---|---|
| 1995 | 48 | 142 | 15 | 33 | 6 | 2 | 5 | 19 | 4 | 6 | 42 | .232 | .264 | .408 |
| Career | 65 | 196 | 19 | 44 | 6 | 2 | 5 | 21 | 7 | 9 | 62 | .224 | .257 | .352 |

## 1995 Season

Alex Rodriguez, the boy wonder of the Seattle Mariners, has impressed everyone en route to the major leagues. Everyone, that is, except manager Lou Piniella, the one man he needs to win over before he can remain in the major leagues. Rodriguez spent the 1995 season on the shuttle between Seattle and Triple-A Tacoma, fine-tuning his game for his eventual—and almost certainly long-term—stay.

## Hitting, Baserunning, & Defense

Rodriguez has an explosive swing, capable of destroying minor league pitching (.360-15-45 last year in just 214 Triple-A at-bats). Although fans often liken the current state of pitching to that of Triple-A, Rodriguez barely slugged .400 in the bigs. That number should improve markedly as Rodriguez gains experience and physically matures. Defensively he covers ground like a tarp in the infield. However, he doesn't have a polished pick-and-throw motion and still makes a lot of errors. Despite his large frame, he should routinely reach double-digit steals each season.

## 1996 Outlook

Don't look for Rodriguez to step in as Seattle's shortstop until Piniella says he is ready. The good thing about Piniella's demanding nature is, when the kid joins the starting lineup, he *will* be ready. There won't be any glaring holes in his game that Mariner fans will be forced to overlook. It shouldn't be too much longer.

# Doug Strange

**Position:** 3B
**Bats:** B **Throws:** R
**Ht:** 6' 1" **Wt:** 185

**Opening Day Age:** 31
**Born:** 4/13/64 in Greenville, SC
**ML Seasons:** 6

*Overall Statistics*

| | G | AB | R | H | D | T | HR | RBI | SB | BB | SO | Avg | OBP | Slg |
|---|---|---|---|---|---|---|---|---|---|---|---|---|---|---|
| 1995 | 74 | 155 | 19 | 42 | 9 | 2 | 2 | 21 | 0 | 10 | 25 | .271 | .323 | .394 |
| Career | 411 | 1164 | 126 | 275 | 56 | 4 | 16 | 127 | 12 | 95 | 184 | .236 | .298 | .332 |

## 1995 Season

Given another chance after batting a weak .212 in 1994, Doug Strange proved to be a useful bit player for the 1995 Mariners. Working on his hitting with manager Lou Piniella helped him put up better numbers. Strange's .274 batting average against righties made him a key role player on a team overloaded with right-handed hitters. He usually was the first player off the bench, and he spelled Mike Blowers at third base against tough righthanders.

## Hitting, Baserunning & Defense

Strange is a good first-pitch fastball hitter, so he fills the role of pinch hitter quite well. He is far less successful, though, at hitting breaking pitches. Pitchers often find it more productive to work this free swinger out of the strike zone. He's an average baserunner who's a step slow in the field. He is best suited to third base, though he can also play second base and the outfield. His arm is below average.

## 1996 Outlook

There are a lot of guys bouncing around the majors who can hit fastballs. And there are quite a few more who can fill in at a couple of infield positions and play the outfield. Strange can do all of the above. He's a useful player for a manager such as Lou Piniella, who likes to make a host of moves in the course of a game.

**Seattle Mariners**

# Salomon Torres

**Position:** SP/RP
**Bats:** R  **Throws:** R
**Ht:** 5'11"  **Wt:** 165

**Opening Day Age:** 24
**Born:** 3/11/72 in San Pedro de Macoris, DR
**ML Seasons:** 3

## Overall Statistics

|        | W | L  | Pct. | ERA  | G  | GS | Sv | IP    | H   | BB  | SO  | HR | BR/IP |
|--------|---|----|------|------|----|----|----|-------|-----|-----|-----|----|-------|
| 1995   | 3 | 9  | .250 | 6.30 | 20 | 14 | 0  | 80.0  | 100 | 49  | 47  | 16 | 1.86  |
| Career | 8 | 22 | .267 | 5.47 | 44 | 36 | 0  | 209.0 | 232 | 110 | 112 | 31 | 1.64  |

## 1995 Season

Salomon Torres posted a 3.21 ERA and allowed eight fewer hits than innings pitched last season. Okay, so it was at Triple-A Tacoma, but that's about all of Torres' 1995 performance that's fit for family viewing. Even the Giants, who finally gave up on Torres, were hoping that a trade to Seattle would help the talented but troubled righthander. But Torres, who struggled in 13 starts with Seattle, still wasn't the cocksure flame-thrower who ripped through the Giants' minor league system.

## Pitching & Defense

Torres has a complete repertoire. He throws a fastball with great movement. He mixes in a good curve and a hard slider. Unfortunately, he can't get any of those pitchers over the plate consistently. He had particular problems with left-handed hitters last year, although both righties and lefties took him out of the yard with regularity. Torres' high leg kick hurts him when he attempts to prevent the running game, and also leaves him in poor fielding position.

## 1996 Outlook

Overlooked in the ledger of Torres flaws is the fact that he is still only 24 years old. His pitches work on high-level minor leaguers, and his confidence should return with some additional fine-tuning at Tacoma. After floundering for two years following his loss in San Francisco s pennant-deciding finale in 1993, Torres gets a fresh start, and he could begin to revive his once-promising career.

# Bob Wolcott

**Position:** SP
**Bats:** R  **Throws:** R
**Ht:** 6'0"  **Wt:** 190

**Opening Day Age:** 22
**Born:** 9/8/73 in Huntington Beach, CA
**ML Seasons:** 1

## Overall Statistics

|        | W | L | Pct. | ERA  | G | GS | Sv | IP   | H  | BB | SO | HR | BR/IP |
|--------|---|---|------|------|---|----|----|------|----|----|----|----|-------|
| 1995   | 3 | 2 | .600 | 4.42 | 7 | 6  | 0  | 36.2 | 43 | 14 | 19 | 6  | 1.55  |
| Career | 3 | 2 | .600 | 4.42 | 7 | 6  | 0  | 36.2 | 43 | 14 | 19 | 6  | 1.55  |

## 1995 Season

One month after his 22nd birthday, "Bullet Bob" Wolcott returned to the Mariners in time for the first League Championship Series game against the hard-hitting Cleveland Indians. Initially left off the first-round playoff roster, Wolcott was activated due to an injury. He turned in one of the most memorable performances in LCS history—one in which he walked the bases loaded in the first inning, escaped without a run being scored, and went on to go seven innings and pick up the win.

## Pitching & Defense

Wolcott is a power pitcher who throws a fastball and a curve. He can run a high fastball by most hitters, and on nights when he has good command of his curveball, he can be very tough. He struggled in a number of regular-season starts, but his poise in a big postseason game is noteworthy. Controlling his curve will be his ticket to major league success, and developing a reliable third pitch also would help. The jury is still out on his defense. He's not very good at holding runners.

## 1996 Outlook

Some say that the best swimmers are those who get thrown into the water and are forced to survive. Wolcott certainly did that—and then some—against the Indians last year. Seattle fans will pull for him as he fights to retain a spot in the rotation this spring.

# Other Seattle Mariners

### Rafael Carmona (Pos: RHP, Age: 23)

This guy could be a real keeper. Carmona shot through the minors in less than three seasons, pitching in relief until last summer at Triple-A Tacoma. He was hit hard in the majors, but he's got a good arm and youth on his side. 1996 Outlook: B

### Tim Davis (Pos: LHP, Age: 25)

Davis pitched pretty well in the M's pen in 1994, but was converted to a starting role last year. He came down with shoulder problems and missed most of the season. Could be back if healthy. 1996 Outlook: C

### Scott Davison (Pos: RHP, Age: 25)

Originally drafted by the Expos as a shortstop, Davison couldn't hit, got hurt and dropped out of baseball for two years. He came back with the M's as a reliever and has looked impressive at times. 1996 Outlook: B

### Lee Guetterman (Pos: LHP, Age: 37)

Yes, Lee Guetterman is still around, sucking up the innings that used to belong to Paul Mirabella. He pitched badly in 1995, but that's never stopped teams from giving him another chance. Ah, lefties. . . 1996 Outlook: C

### Tim Harikkala (Pos: RHP, Age: 24)

A former 34th-round draft choice, Harikkala had terrific success in the low minors, but has been less impressive in Double- and Triple-A. Probably needs more seasoning, and maybe another pitch. 1996 Outlook: C

### Kevin King (Pos: LHP, Age: 27)

"King of the Kingdome" seems like a natural, but the lefty reliever hasn't done much to impress in three stints with Seattle. He'll need a good spring to make a major league roster. 1996 Outlook: C

### Chad Kreuter (Pos: C, Age: 31, Bats: B)

Kreuter had a good year with the bat for the Tigers in 1993, but since then has returned to his old .220-ish level. His defensive skills are good but not great; he needs to hit better to stick around. 1996 Outlook: C

### Bill Krueger (Pos: LHP, Age: 37)

Krueger's now nearly 38, and he's had two straight years with ERAs over 6.00. He's a good guy and always seems to find a job, but the end may be here. 1996 Outlook: D

### Jim Mecir (Pos: RHP, Age: 25)

A former third-round pick, Mecir had a good year in Double-A in 1994, and another good year at Triple-A Tacoma in '95. The M's have a lot of righty relievers, but he could stick this year. 1996 Outlook: B

### Greg Pirkl (Pos: 1B, Age: 25, Bats: R)

Lou Piniella doesn't seem to like Pirkl, a big, hulking first baseman/designated hitter with great power. His best hope would be a trade, but better strike-zone judgment would help as well. 1996 Outlook: B

### Gary Thurman (Pos: LF, Age: 31, Bats: R)

Once considered a pretty good prospect with the Royals, Thurman is now 31 and has yet to establish himself as a major league player. He can run and play the outfield; he just can't hit. 1996 Outlook: C

### Bob Wells (Pos: RHP, Age: 29)

Wells came up with the Phillies, but didn't get a real major league chance until he was dealt to the M's in 1994. He had a poor '95 season, but his minor league record suggests he can pitch. 1996 Outlook: B

# Seattle Mariners Minor League Prospects

## Organization Overview:

Baseball's future in Seattle appears quite bright. The Mariners electrified their fans with a dramatic second-half run last year which didn't end until the American League Championship Series. The wave of enthusiasm which swept their fans has evidently inspired the community to pay for a new ballpark, which would not only keep the team in Seattle but make the Mariners a much more competitive club economically. And from a baseball perspective, the Mariners boast one of the most exciting and talented teams in the game. Start with Ken Griffey, arguably the best player of this generation. Surrounding him is one of baseball's strongest offensive lineups. Randy Johnson is the top pitcher in the American League. And the top-line talent in their minor league chain has other clubs envious. Alex Rodriguez was the first player drafted in 1993 and should combine with Griffey to form a dynamic offensive duo at two of the more important defensive positions. The Mariners' last two top picks, catcher Jason Varitek and outfielder Jose Cruz, Jr., could also be special. If a couple of their young pitchers come through, the Mariners could be the class of the A.L. West for the foreseeable future.

## James Bonnici

**Position:** 1B
**Bats:** R **Throws:** R
**Ht:** 6' 4" **Wt:** 230
**Opening Day Age:** 24
**Born:** 1/21/72 in Omaha, NE

### Recent Statistics

|  | G | AB | R | H | D | T | HR | RBI | SB | BB | SO | AVG |
|---|---|---|---|---|---|---|---|---|---|---|---|---|
| 93 A Riverside | 104 | 375 | 69 | 115 | 21 | 1 | 9 | 58 | 0 | 58 | 72 | .307 |
| 94 A Riverside | 113 | 397 | 71 | 111 | 23 | 3 | 10 | 71 | 1 | 58 | 81 | .280 |
| 95 AA Port City | 138 | 508 | 75 | 144 | 36 | 3 | 20 | 91 | 2 | 76 | 97 | .283 |
| 95 MLE | 138 | 507 | 73 | 143 | 39 | 2 | 19 | 89 | 1 | 65 | 108 | .282 |

Bonnici lasted until the 58th round in 1990, which is almost as incredible as the fact that he was actually drafted as a shortstop. Unless you're Cal Ripken, if you're 6'4" and 230 pounds then your career as a shortstop is usually brief. It was for Bonnici, who became a catcher first, then played most of last year at first base. He certainly hits like a first baseman, as he improved virtually all his offensive numbers last season due to increased playing time. Two stats which jump out are his 76 walks and 36 doubles in 508 at-bats. The walks are no fluke, as Bonnici has always shown great strike-zone judgment, and the doubles suggest that his 20 homers were also legitimate. Bonnici will be 24 in 1996, and will likely play at Triple-A.

## Raul Ibanez

**Position:** C
**Bats:** L **Throws:** R
**Ht:** 6' 2" **Wt:** 200
**Opening Day Age:** 23
**Born:** 6/2/72 in Manhattan, NY

### Recent Statistics

|  | G | AB | R | H | D | T | HR | RBI | SB | BB | SO | AVG |
|---|---|---|---|---|---|---|---|---|---|---|---|---|
| 93 A Appleton | 52 | 157 | 26 | 43 | 9 | 0 | 5 | 21 | 0 | 24 | 31 | .274 |
| 93 A Bellingham | 43 | 134 | 16 | 38 | 5 | 2 | 0 | 15 | 0 | 21 | 23 | .284 |
| 94 A Appleton | 91 | 327 | 55 | 102 | 30 | 3 | 7 | 59 | 10 | 32 | 37 | .312 |
| 95 A Riverside | 95 | 361 | 59 | 120 | 23 | 9 | 20 | 108 | 4 | 41 | 49 | .332 |

The Mariners probably rank with the Royals as boasting the most good catching prospects in baseball. Ibanez is the rawest of the other top Mariner backstoppers (Varitek, Widger), but his offense takes a backseat to neither right now. Ibanez led the California League with a .612 slugging percentage last year while driving in 108 runs in just 95 games. He's yet another late-round draft pick (36th round, 1992) who began his pro career at another position (outfield) only to find greater success after putting on the shinguards. Ibanez was 23 years of age last year, mature by Class-A standards, so it'll be interesting to see how he adjusts to higher classifications.

## Trey Moore

**Position:** P
**Bats:** L **Throws:** L
**Ht:** 6' 1" **Wt:** 200
**Opening Day Age:** 23
**Born:** 10/2/72 in Houston, TX

### Recent Statistics

|  | W | L | ERA | G | GS | Sv | IP | H | R | BB | SO | HR |
|---|---|---|---|---|---|---|---|---|---|---|---|---|
| 94 A Bellingham | 5 | 2 | 2.63 | 11 | 10 | 0 | 61.2 | 48 | 18 | 24 | 73 | 4 |
| 95 A Riverside | 14 | 6 | 3.09 | 24 | 24 | 0 | 148.1 | 122 | 65 | 58 | 134 | 6 |

Texas A&M has produced a number of quality lefthanders in recent years, including first-rounders Jeff Granger to the Royals in '93 and Kelly Wunsch to the Brewers the following spring. Moore dropped to the second round in 1994, where the Mariners happily snatched him, and he's been more impressive than any of the others. In 210 professional innings, Moore has allowed 170 hits while fanning 207. It's translated into a 19-8 record and an ERA under three. His slider is his best pitch, and while his fastball is only major league average, it may be fast enough for a lefthander with decent movement. Moore is ready to be challenged at Double-A in 1996.

## Arquimedez Pozo

**Position:** 2B  **Opening Day Age:** 22
**Bats:** R **Throws:** R  **Born:** 8/24/73 in Santo
**Ht:** 5' 10"  **Wt:** 180  Domingo, DR

*Recent Statistics*

| | G | AB | R | H | D | T | HR | RBI | SB | BB | SO | AVG |
|---|---|---|---|---|---|---|---|---|---|---|---|---|
| 95 AAA Tacoma | 122 | 450 | 57 | 135 | 19 | 6 | 10 | 62 | 3 | 26 | 31 | .300 |
| 95 AL Seattle | 1 | 1 | 0 | 0 | 0 | 0 | 0 | 0 | 0 | 0 | 0 | .000 |
| 95 MLE | 122 | 439 | 49 | 124 | 19 | 3 | 8 | 53 | 2 | 23 | 33 | .282 |

Pozo has made steady progress through the Mariners' farm system since 1992. However, his production has dropped somewhat as he's ascended the ladder, at least since his sensational performance in A-ball in 1993 (.342, 13 HR, 83 RBI). He was still a .300 hitter at Triple-A Tacoma last year, but his walk rate and slugging percentage have fallen sharply, and his stolen-base total dipped to single digits for the first time ever. Pozo's range is reportedly limited, yet he's posted decent defensive stats throughout his career. He hits enough now to be an offensive plus at second, but if his production returns to previous levels, Pozo might move to third.

## Desmond Relaford

**Position:** SS  **Opening Day Age:** 22
**Bats:** B **Throws:** R  **Born:** 9/16/73 in
**Ht:** 5' 8"  **Wt:** 155  Valdosta, GA

*Recent Statistics*

| | G | AB | R | H | D | T | HR | RBI | SB | BB | SO | AVG |
|---|---|---|---|---|---|---|---|---|---|---|---|---|
| 94 AA Jacksonville | 37 | 143 | 24 | 29 | 7 | 3 | 3 | 11 | 10 | 22 | 28 | .203 |
| 94 A Riverside | 99 | 374 | 95 | 116 | 27 | 5 | 5 | 59 | 27 | 78 | 78 | .310 |
| 95 AA Port City | 90 | 352 | 51 | 101 | 11 | 2 | 7 | 27 | 25 | 41 | 58 | .287 |
| 95 AAA Tacoma | 30 | 113 | 20 | 27 | 5 | 1 | 2 | 7 | 6 | 13 | 24 | .239 |
| 95 MLE | 120 | 461 | 67 | 124 | 17 | 1 | 8 | 32 | 24 | 47 | 92 | .269 |

Relaford has played at shortstop for most of his professional career, but with the Alex Rodriguez era about to begin in Seattle, Relaford is likely destined for second base. Relaford has twice been the youngest player in his league, and has shown a tendency to need a lengthy adjustment period. His range and footwork are good enough to play either middle-infield position. Offensively, he shows occasional power, great plate discipline and the speed to steal 30 bases a year. He may need a full season in Triple-A, but should arrive in Seattle by 1997.

## Matt Wagner

**Position:** P  **Opening Day Age:** 23
**Bats:** R **Throws:** R  **Born:** 4/4/72 in Cedar
**Ht:** 6' 5"  **Wt:** 215  Falls, IA

*Recent Statistics*

| | W | L | ERA | G | GS | Sv | IP | H | R | BB | SO | HR |
|---|---|---|---|---|---|---|---|---|---|---|---|---|
| 94 A Appleton | 4 | 2 | 0.83 | 15 | 1 | 1 | 32.2 | 23 | 8 | 8 | 48 | 2 |
| 95 AA Port City | 5 | 8 | 2.82 | 23 | 23 | 0 | 137.0 | 121 | 57 | 33 | 111 | 9 |
| 95 AAA Tacoma | 1 | 5 | 6.27 | 6 | 6 | 0 | 33.0 | 43 | 29 | 17 | 33 | 3 |

Wagner was feared to be a medical risk by some teams coming out of college. The Mariners' selection of him in the third round in 1994 may turn out to be one of the bigger steals of the draft. One year later, Wagner had already reached Triple-A. His won-lost record last season (6-13) doesn't convey how well he pitched. He allowed fewer hits than innings pitched, and his strikeouts nearly tripled his walks. He may be the hardest thrower in the system, with a fastball that reaches the mid-90s. He throws a hard slider as well. Even though Wagner is a big kid, the Mariners may need to be cautious with his workload. It will be interesting to see how he rebounds from last season's 170 innings pitched.

## Chris Widger

**Position:** C  **Opening Day Age:** 24
**Bats:** R **Throws:** R  **Born:** 5/21/71 in
**Ht:** 6' 3"  **Wt:** 195  Wilmington, DE

*Recent Statistics*

| | G | AB | R | H | D | T | HR | RBI | SB | BB | SO | AVG |
|---|---|---|---|---|---|---|---|---|---|---|---|---|
| 95 AAA Tacoma | 50 | 174 | 29 | 48 | 11 | 1 | 9 | 21 | 0 | 9 | 29 | .276 |
| 95 AL Seattle | 23 | 45 | 2 | 9 | 0 | 0 | 1 | 2 | 0 | 3 | 11 | .200 |

Widger saw action down the stretch and in the playoffs with the Mariners. Despite his relative big-league inexperience, the Mariners were impressed enough with his defense and handling of pitchers to play him in crucial games. While Widger's defense is almost universally acclaimed, his offense isn't shabby, either. He raised his batting average to .276 at Triple-A last season, and his slugging percentage topped .500. The Mariners don't need him to produce those kinds of numbers with their lineup already loaded. But he could be an upgrade over Dan Wilson should Wilson regress.

## Others to Watch

Second baseman **Miguel Cairo** came to the M's in the Mike Blowers deal last November, and he stole 33 bases in Double-A last year at age 21. . . Righthander **Ken Cloude** was chosen in the sixth round in 1993. His strikeout totals have exceeded his hits allowed in both his pro seasons, and he's recorded a combined ERA of 2.95, albeit in the low minors. . . Last year's top pick, **Jose Cruz, Jr.**, is almost certain to become the fourth member of his family to play in the big leagues, joining his father and two uncles, Hector and Tommy. Cruz wasn't overmatched after jumping almost immediately to the fast-A California League. . . Lefthander **Osvaldo Fernandez** will be 26 in April and is close to a finished product. He's gone 20-9 with a 3.32 ERA during his two seasons in the organization. . . Righthander **Marino Santana** is a product of the Dominican Republic. He's been an all-star the past two seasons and fanned 10.4 batters per nine innings in 1995. . . It seemed as though the **Jason Varitek** signing saga would take forever, but the two-time first-rounder finally inked with Seattle and played at Double-A last season. The former all-American catcher hit just .224 and struck out at an alarming rate (126 times in 352 AB), but hit with power and drew walks.

# Will Clark

## 1995 Season

Will Clark demonstrated his toughness in 1995, persevering through a series of ailments to put together a quietly productive season that was just below his All-Star level of 1994. Clark missed 21 games with injuries, the worst of which was a broken bone in his elbow, sustained after crashing into a sign board in pursuit of a foul ball in the season's third game. He also missed games with a strained groin and back spasms, but rebounded with a solid September, a good sign for 1996.

## Hitting

Elbow pain forced Clark to make constant adjustments in his hitting approach, and he wound up as more of a pull hitter than he was in 1994. Although he likes to hit the ball toward left-center, he lacked the strength to drive it past outfielders when going that way. Consequently, many of his well-hit balls hung up and were caught. Clark's ratio of home runs to at-bats fell near the 1992-93 levels that hastened his departure from the San Francisco Giants. But he still remains a strong situational hitter, and finished with 18 more walks than strikeouts in 1995.

## Baserunning & Defense

Clark made the second-fewest errors of his career (seven) and was solid, if not spectacular, at first base. He did a good job picking up low throws but showed a lack of range, especially on pops into the outfield. His own throws were weaker than ever following the elbow injury. He has adequate speed for a first baseman, but takes few chances on the bases.

## 1996 Outlook

Give Clark 162 games and keep him healthy, and he should have his first 100-RBI season since 1991. Health is a major question, however, as he enters the third season of a five-year contract—he hasn't played more than 148 games since 1990. But Clark hungers to lead his team into the postseason, and he should come out breathing fire in 1996.

**Position:** 1B
**Bats:** L **Throws:** L
**Ht:** 6' 1" **Wt:** 196

**Opening Day Age:** 32
**Born:** 3/13/64 in New Orleans, LA
**ML Seasons:** 10

### Overall Statistics

|  | G | AB | R | H | D | T | HR | RBI | SB | BB | SO | Avg | OBP | Slg |
|---|---|---|---|---|---|---|---|---|---|---|---|---|---|---|
| 1995 | 123 | 454 | 85 | 137 | 27 | 3 | 16 | 92 | 0 | 68 | 50 | .302 | .389 | .480 |
| Career | 1393 | 5112 | 845 | 1543 | 300 | 42 | 205 | 881 | 57 | 645 | 853 | .302 | .379 | .497 |

### Where He Hits the Ball

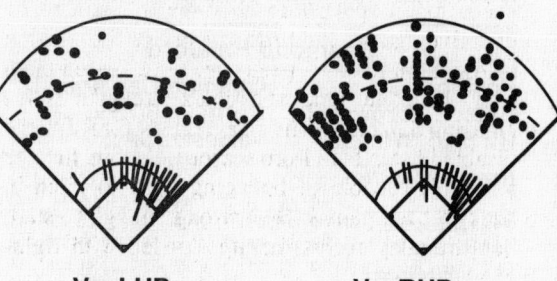

Vs. LHP          Vs. RHP

### 1995 Situational Stats

|  | AB | H | HR | RBI | Avg |  | AB | H | HR | RBI | Avg |
|---|---|---|---|---|---|---|---|---|---|---|---|
| Home | 218 | 66 | 10 | 42 | .303 | LHP | 148 | 43 | 4 | 32 | .291 |
| Road | 236 | 71 | 6 | 50 | .301 | RHP | 306 | 94 | 12 | 60 | .307 |
| First Half | 192 | 54 | 8 | 36 | .281 | Sc Pos | 129 | 44 | 3 | 72 | .341 |
| Scnd Half | 262 | 83 | 8 | 56 | .317 | Clutch | 56 | 19 | 1 | 12 | .339 |

### 1995 Rankings (American League)

- → 2nd in sacrifice flies (11)
- → 4th in lowest groundball/flyball ratio (0.7) and errors at first base (7)
- → 5th in fielding percentage at first base (.994)
- → 9th in batting average on an 0-2 count (.296)
- → 10th in batting average with runners in scoring position (.341)
- → Led the Rangers in RBI, sacrifice flies, intentional walks (6), least GDPs per GDP situation (5.8%), batting average with runners in scoring position (.341), batting average vs. right-handed pitchers (.307), batting average on a 3-1 count (.438), batting average on an 0-2 count (.296) and slugging percentage vs. left-handed pitchers (.453)

# Dennis Cook

## 1995 Season

A native Texan with an accent Dennis Weaver would love, Cook was happy to be traded to the Texas Rangers from Cleveland in midseason. He had fallen between the cracks in the Indians' deep pitching staff, but was appreciated in Texas, where he filled a need as a left-handed long reliever. He pitched better with regular use in Texas than with sporadic use in Cleveland but still didn't distinguish himself, performing poorly down the stretch with a 6.14 ERA in September. There's indeed a reason he's been with six teams in seven years.

## Pitching

Cook throws a fastball, forkball and slider. He needs to hit spots with all three of them to be effective against right-handed hitters, but he can be tough on lefties if he gets either offspeed pitch over the plate. One of Cook's strengths is his amazing durability—he's never been forced to the disabled list in his 11 pro seasons. Despite that, he still isn't capable of bouncing back to pitch in back-to-back games. He's strong enough to start, but struggles against lineups loaded with right-handed hitters.

## Defense

Nobody runs on Cook. He has a good move to first and is quick to the plate. That combination of skills held baserunners to just two stolen bases in six attempts in 1995. He moves quicker on the mound than he talks, which allows him to be a good fielder.

## 1996 Outlook

Baseball loves lefties. There will be a job for Cook somewhere, provided he doesn't get greedy. He is eligible for free agency, but wants to return to a contending Texas club. At age 33 and with the clock ticking on his career, he might be better off moving to the National League after spending the last four seasons facing American League hitters.

**Position:** RP
**Bats:** L **Throws:** L
**Ht:** 6' 3" **Wt:** 190

**Opening Day Age:** 33
**Born:** 10/4/62 in Lamarque, TX
**ML Seasons:** 8

### Overall Statistics

|  | W | L | Pct. | ERA | G | GS | Sv | IP | H | BB | SO | HR | BR/IP |
|---|---|---|---|---|---|---|---|---|---|---|---|---|---|
| 1995 | 0 | 2 | .000 | 4.53 | 46 | 1 | 2 | 57.2 | 63 | 26 | 53 | 9 | 1.54 |
| Career | 32 | 28 | .533 | 3.91 | 235 | 71 | 3 | 619.1 | 596 | 218 | 361 | 90 | 1.31 |

### How Often He Throws Strikes

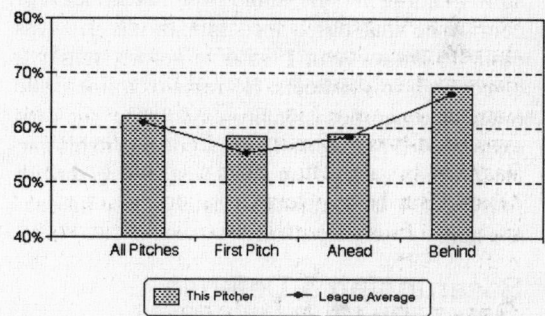

### 1995 Situational Stats

|  | W | L | ERA | Sv | IP |  | AB | H | HR | RBI | Avg |
|---|---|---|---|---|---|---|---|---|---|---|---|
| Home | 0 | 1 | 4.73 | 1 | 26.2 | LHB | 88 | 25 | 3 | 21 | .284 |
| Road | 0 | 1 | 4.35 | 1 | 31.0 | RHB | 130 | 38 | 6 | 23 | .292 |
| First Half | 0 | 0 | 4.50 | 1 | 26.0 | Sc Pos | 73 | 18 | 2 | 33 | .247 |
| Scnd Half | 0 | 2 | 4.55 | 1 | 31.2 | Clutch | 33 | 8 | 2 | 9 | .242 |

### 1995 Rankings (American League)

→ 8th in highest batting average allowed in relief (.287)

# Jeff Frye

## 1995 Season

For the third season in a row, Jeff Frye's production was down because of injuries. He saw two stints on the disabled list with hamstring problems, and has now been on the DL four times in the last three seasons. Frye got off to a strong start, but simply wasn't the same after going on the DL June 3. He shared second base with Mark McLemore in the second half of the season, often failing to produce when given the chance.

## Hitting

Frye's quick bat and disciplined approach make him the kind of pesky hitter that pitchers hate to face. But a steady diet of breaking pitches is slowly cutting into the "mind over matter" level of confidence that has helped him thrive. He was easier to put away in 1995 than before, setting a career high in strikeouts. He remains a line drive hitter who can occasionally exploit the gaps for extra bases. Frye even still has some pop in his bat, leading the Rangers over one 13-game stretch with four homers. Unfortunately, that was also his season total.

## Baserunning & Defense

Frye turns the double play well despite an average arm. That lack of arm strength prevents him from playing on the left side of the infield. He has limited range, and made too many errors last season, including some on routine plays. He was a basestealer in the minor leagues but hasn't regained the step he lost when he tore the anterior cruciate ligament in his right knee before the 1993 season.

## 1996 Outlook

Frye felt threatened by the presence of Mark McLemore last season, and could be deemed expendable—especially since he lacks the versatility that manager Johnny Oates and GM Doug Melvin value so highly. He is also eligible for salary arbitration for the first time. The Rangers are unlikely to go through the process to keep him unless they consider him an everyday player. Those days may be gone.

**Position:** 2B
**Bats:** R  **Throws:** R
**Ht:** 5' 9"  **Wt:** 165

**Opening Day Age:** 29
**Born:** 8/31/66 in Oakland, CA
**ML Seasons:** 3

### Overall Statistics

|        | G   | AB  | R  | H   | D  | T | HR | RBI | SB | BB | SO | Avg  | OBP  | Slg  |
|--------|-----|-----|----|-----|----|---|----|-----|----|----|----|------|------|------|
| 1995   | 90  | 313 | 38 | 87  | 15 | 2 | 4  | 29  | 3  | 24 | 45 | .278 | .335 | .377 |
| Career | 214 | 717 | 99 | 205 | 44 | 6 | 5  | 59  | 10 | 69 | 95 | .286 | .352 | .385 |

### Where He Hits the Ball

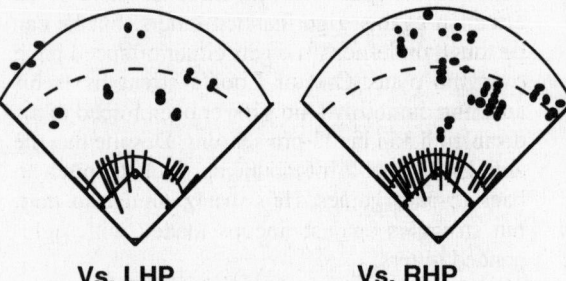

Vs. LHP          Vs. RHP

### 1995 Situational Stats

|           | AB  | H  | HR | RBI | Avg  |        | AB  | H  | HR | RBI | Avg  |
|-----------|-----|----|----|-----|------|--------|-----|----|----|-----|------|
| Home      | 154 | 46 | 2  | 16  | .299 | LHP    | 92  | 25 | 3  | 12  | .272 |
| Road      | 159 | 41 | 2  | 13  | .258 | RHP    | 221 | 62 | 1  | 17  | .281 |
| First Half| 165 | 49 | 0  | 12  | .297 | Sc Pos | 74  | 22 | 2  | 27  | .297 |
| Scnd Half | 148 | 38 | 4  | 17  | .257 | Clutch | 49  | 11 | 1  | 2   | .224 |

### 1995 Rankings (American League)

→ 4th in highest percentage of extra bases taken as a runner (66.7%)
→ 6th in errors at second base (11)
→ Led the Rangers in highest percentage of extra bases taken as a runner (66.7%)

# Benji Gil

**Position:** SS
**Bats:** R **Throws:** R
**Ht:** 6' 2" **Wt:** 182

**Opening Day Age:** 23
**Born:** 10/6/72 in
Tijuana, MX
**ML Seasons:** 2

## 1995 Season

When the Rangers committed to Benji Gil as their number-one shortstop, they said they would be happy if he just made all the routine plays. He did that, and more, in 1995. Gil, who committed 37 errors at Triple-A in 1994, emerged as one of the league's best defensive shortstops. He flashed power and showed a quick enough bat to handle the league's best pitchers on occasion. But he raised a caution flag by collapsing offensively after the All-Star break.

## Hitting

There are lots of holes in Gil's swing, as American League pitchers eventually pointed out. Despite that, Gil finished with the most home runs by a Texas shortstop since Toby Harrah's 15 in 1976. He hit only .161 when he started behind in the count, and finished second in the majors in strikeouts. A right-handed hitter, he was simply abysmal against lefties. He did not show the skills needed for a number-nine hitter, lacking the bat control to consistently get down bunts or work the hit-and-run.

## Baserunning & Defense

Gil profited greatly from regular work with infield instructor Bucky Dent. He has good range and a strong, accurate throwing arm. Dent helped Gil iron out fundamental flaws that had plagued him in the minors, and boosted his confidence. Among A.L. shortstops, he ranked behind only John Valentin in total chances, and behind only Valentin and Cal Ripken in double plays. He has good speed but lacks polish as a baserunner. He could eventually steal 10-20 bases a year, but needs work.

## 1996 Outlook

Gil returns as the Rangers' regular shortstop, and should be better offensively in his second full season. Johnny Oates, however, would be satisfied with a defensive shortstop who makes all the routine plays. Gil has the tools to be an All-Star, but it won't come easily. He must continue to make the kinds of strides offensively that he already has defensively.

### Overall Statistics

|  | G | AB | R | H | D | T | HR | RBI | SB | BB | SO | Avg | OBP | Slg |
|---|---|---|---|---|---|---|---|---|---|---|---|---|---|---|
| 1995 | 130 | 415 | 36 | 91 | 20 | 3 | 9 | 46 | 2 | 26 | 147 | .219 | .266 | .347 |
| Career | 152 | 472 | 39 | 98 | 20 | 3 | 9 | 48 | 3 | 31 | 169 | .208 | .257 | .320 |

### Where He Hits the Ball

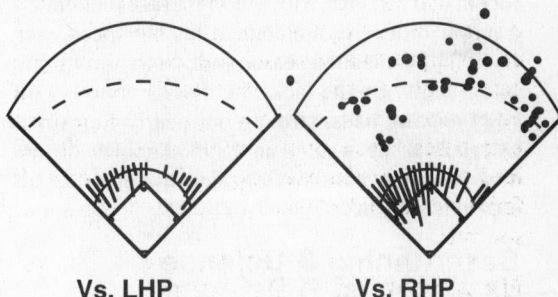

Vs. LHP          Vs. RHP

### 1995 Situational Stats

|  | AB | H | HR | RBI | Avg |  | AB | H | HR | RBI | Avg |
|---|---|---|---|---|---|---|---|---|---|---|---|
| Home | 203 | 51 | 5 | 22 | .251 | LHP | 102 | 11 | 0 | 8 | .108 |
| Road | 212 | 40 | 4 | 24 | .189 | RHP | 313 | 80 | 9 | 38 | .256 |
| First Half | 223 | 54 | 7 | 29 | .242 | Sc Pos | 108 | 30 | 2 | 37 | .278 |
| Scnd Half | 192 | 37 | 2 | 17 | .193 | Clutch | 49 | 5 | 1 | 4 | .102 |

### 1995 Rankings (American League)

- ➡ 1st in lowest batting average, lowest on-base percentage, lowest batting average in the clutch (.102), lowest batting average vs. left-handed pitchers (.108), lowest slugging percentage vs. left-handed pitchers (.157), lowest on-base percentage vs. left-handed pitchers (.225), highest percentage of swings that missed (36.7%) and lowest percentage of swings put into play (30.9%)
- ➡ 2nd in strikeouts and lowest batting average on the road (.189)
- ➡ 3rd in lowest slugging percentage
- ➡ 4th in errors at shortstop (17)
- ➡ Led the Rangers in sacrifice bunts (10) and strikeouts

Texas
Rangers

# Juan Gonzalez

## 1995 Season

For a guy who was hurt for about half the season, Juan Gonzalez put up numbers any rotisserie player would love. He missed the first 33 games with a herniated disc in his back, and returned to the disabled list in July with a pinched nerve in his neck. After about a week of playing with his assorted ailments, Gonzalez happily moved from left field to designated hitter.

## Hitting

Gonzalez has continued the curve his career began after a 1993 season in which he showed promise of being a complete hitter. After seeing his average drop from .310 in 1993 to .275 in 1994, Gonzalez rebounded last year with a .295 mark, excellent for a power hitter. He maintained his bat speed even in an injury-plagued season, allowing him to turn on fastballs. But he lacks the discipline to lay off bad breaking balls, striking out nearly four times as much as he walked in 1995. Pitchers do not have to pitch around Gonzalez as much as his statistics suggest.

## Baserunning & Defense

Gonzalez has regressed significantly in the field. His arm, which was better than average when he played right field in the minor leagues, is simply average for a left fielder in the majors. He has decent speed but runs the bases gingerly, trying to protect his fragile body.

## 1996 Outlook

Look for Gonzalez to report to camp in 1993 condition—215 pounds and lacking the bulging biceps that defined him last spring. Gonzalez and the Rangers both believe he can regain the flexibility necessary to play left field again. If he can remain healthy, he should put up monster numbers. But back problems have a way of recurring—a thought that haunts the club that still owes him $20.7 million guaranteed over the next three years.

**Position:** DH
**Bats:** R  **Throws:** R
**Ht:** 6' 3"  **Wt:** 235

**Opening Day Age:** 26
**Born:** 10/16/69 in Vega Baja, PR
**ML Seasons:** 7

### Overall Statistics

|  | G | AB | R | H | D | T | HR | RBI | SB | BB | SO | Avg | OBP | Slg |
|---|---|---|---|---|---|---|---|---|---|---|---|---|---|---|
| 1995 | 90 | 352 | 57 | 104 | 20 | 2 | 27 | 82 | 0 | 17 | 66 | .295 | .324 | .594 |
| Career | 683 | 2589 | 391 | 717 | 139 | 11 | 167 | 515 | 14 | 169 | 527 | .277 | .326 | .533 |

### Where He Hits the Ball

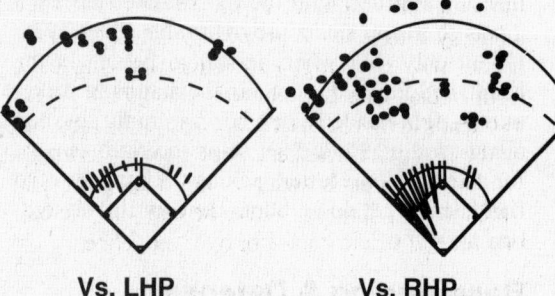

**Vs. LHP**            **Vs. RHP**

### 1995 Situational Stats

|  | AB | H | HR | RBI | Avg |  | AB | H | HR | RBI | Avg |
|---|---|---|---|---|---|---|---|---|---|---|---|
| Home | 161 | 51 | 15 | 44 | .317 | LHP | 101 | 33 | 9 | 26 | .327 |
| Road | 191 | 53 | 12 | 38 | .277 | RHP | 251 | 71 | 18 | 56 | .283 |
| First Half | 137 | 38 | 12 | 33 | .277 | Sc Pos | 94 | 27 | 8 | 53 | .287 |
| Scnd Half | 215 | 66 | 15 | 49 | .307 | Clutch | 49 | 11 | 2 | 9 | .224 |

### 1995 Rankings (American League)

→ 3rd in cleanup slugging percentage (.597)
→ Led the Rangers in GDPs (14) and cleanup slugging percentage

# Rusty Greer

## 1995 Season

There was no sophomore jinx for Rusty Greer in 1995. Greer wasn't as consistent as in his rookie season, when he batted .314, but he remained a productive player. Though he suffered through some prolonged slumps, Greer compensated with a flare for the dramatic. Of his 13 home runs, five of his first six were game-winners—including two as a pinch hitter. A left-handed batter, Greer was platooned at times but emerged as an everyday player late in the season.

## Hitting

Greer takes his hitting cues from teammate Will Clark, getting a lot of line drives out of a compact, fundamentally sound stroke. In addition, he's mentally tough and is not easily intimidated by inside heat. He struggles against breaking balls from lefthanders, but otherwise hangs tough. He also tends to be a little overanxious, often jumping on the first pitch whether or not it's an offering he can handle. Greer's swing is well suited for The Ballpark in Arlington, where he can pull the ball into the right-field corner or over the fence.

## Baserunning & Defense

Greer, who was an everyday first baseman in the Texas League as recently as 1993, is skillful at all three outfield positions, although Johnny Oates is not as quick to use him in center field as was predecessor Kevin Kennedy. He appeared. . . well, rusty. . . when used occasionally at first base. Greer is an accurate thrower with slightly above-average arm strength. He is a smart baserunner but no threat to steal, with just four attempts in 211 career games.

## 1996 Outlook

With Juan Gonzalez expected to return to left field, Greer should be pretty well anchored in right. Accordingly, his plate appearance total should increase for the second consecutive year, and he should hit closer to .300 than his .271 performance of last season.

**Position:** RF/LF
**Bats:** L **Throws:** L
**Ht:** 6' 0" **Wt:** 190

**Opening Day Age:** 27
**Born:** 1/21/69 in Fort Rucker, Alabama
**ML Seasons:** 2

### Overall Statistics

|  | G | AB | R | H | D | T | HR | RBI | SB | BB | SO | Avg | OBP | Slg |
|---|---|---|---|---|---|---|---|---|---|---|---|---|---|---|
| 1995 | 131 | 417 | 58 | 113 | 21 | 2 | 13 | 61 | 3 | 55 | 66 | .271 | .355 | .424 |
| Career | 211 | 694 | 94 | 200 | 37 | 3 | 23 | 107 | 3 | 101 | 112 | .288 | .378 | .450 |

### Where He Hits the Ball

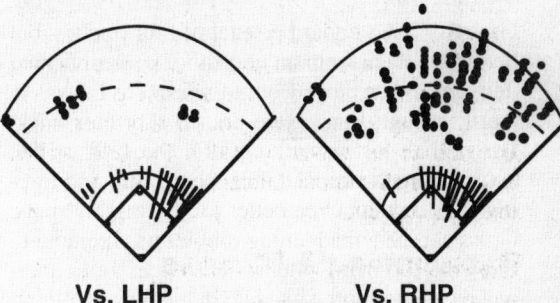

Vs. LHP          Vs. RHP

### 1995 Situational Stats

|  | AB | H | HR | RBI | Avg |  | AB | H | HR | RBI | Avg |
|---|---|---|---|---|---|---|---|---|---|---|---|
| Home | 190 | 44 | 7 | 30 | .232 | LHP | 78 | 19 | 2 | 9 | .244 |
| Road | 227 | 69 | 6 | 31 | .304 | RHP | 339 | 94 | 11 | 52 | .277 |
| First Half | 197 | 51 | 6 | 33 | .259 | Sc Pos | 121 | 33 | 6 | 52 | .273 |
| Scnd Half | 220 | 62 | 7 | 28 | .282 | Clutch | 65 | 15 | 4 | 12 | .231 |

### 1995 Rankings (American League)

→ 4th in lowest fielding percentage in right field (.977)
→ 9th in errors in right field (3)

# Kevin Gross

## 1995 Season

Given unlimited authority in his first season as the Texas Rangers' general manager, Doug Melvin made a rookie mistake by committing $6 million to sign Kevin Gross before the signing freeze that followed the 1994 season. Many better pitchers were available for less. Melvin loved Gross' durability, and he indeed got what he paid for in that respect, but Gross had an ugly transition from the National League that had him contemplating retirement after 10 starts. He got pounded by hitters and struggled with the A.L. strike zone. He pitched decently after the All-Star break, but it was already a lost season for him statistically.

## Pitching

Gross has the standard arsenal of four pitches, but he throws them from an unorthodox, complicated delivery. When he gets out of whack, as he was in April through June, there are no shortcuts back. His fastball lost something after the 1994 strike, neutralizing the impact of his change-up and forcing him to do an even better job hitting his spots. Gross can be a maddening nibbler on the mound, throwing too many pitches. His slider and curveball developed some bite late in the season, giving some hope for 1996.

## Defense

Gross' big leg kick and slow delivery make him a basestealer's delight, and things would be even worse if he didn't have Ivan Rodriguez around to catch him. His reactions are slowing down as he hits his mid-30s, as he almost never handles liners or one-hoppers up the middle.

## 1996 Outlook

Gross is a competitor who wants to repay Melvin for his contract. He showed reason for hope in August and September, but it is yet to be seen if he can produce a sub-5.00 ERA in the A.L. This is the final year of his contract, so he needs a strong showing to extend his shelf life.

**Position:** SP
**Bats:** R  **Throws:** R
**Ht:** 6' 5"  **Wt:** 227

**Opening Day Age:** 34
**Born:** 6/8/61 in Downey, CA
**ML Seasons:** 13

### Overall Statistics

|  | W | L | Pct. | ERA | G | GS | Sv | IP | H | BB | SO | HR | BR/IP |
|---|---|---|---|---|---|---|---|---|---|---|---|---|---|
| 1995 | 9 | 15 | .375 | 5.54 | 31 | 30 | 0 | 183.2 | 200 | 89 | 106 | 27 | 1.57 |
| Career | 129 | 149 | .464 | 4.02 | 434 | 346 | 5 | 2333.0 | 2338 | 916 | 1629 | 207 | 1.39 |

### How Often He Throws Strikes

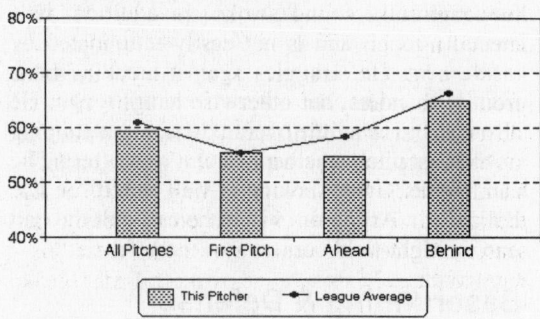

### 1995 Situational Stats

|  | W | L | ERA | Sv | IP |  | AB | H | HR | RBI | Avg |
|---|---|---|---|---|---|---|---|---|---|---|---|
| Home | 4 | 7 | 6.35 | 0 | 79.1 | LHB | 378 | 106 | 11 | 52 | .280 |
| Road | 5 | 8 | 4.92 | 0 | 104.1 | RHB | 338 | 94 | 16 | 49 | .278 |
| First Half | 3 | 8 | 7.49 | 0 | 73.1 | Sc Pos | 155 | 44 | 4 | 72 | .284 |
| Scnd Half | 6 | 7 | 4.24 | 0 | 110.1 | Clutch | 26 | 5 | 0 | 1 | .192 |

### 1995 Rankings (American League)

➡ 1st in highest ERA, losses and highest ERA at home (6.35)
➡ 2nd in home runs allowed and most home runs allowed per 9 innings (1.32)
➡ 3rd in highest slugging percentage allowed (.454), highest on-base percentage allowed (.362) and most baserunners allowed per 9 innings (14.6)
➡ 4th in lowest strikeout/walk ratio (1.2)
➡ 5th in hit batsmen (8) and highest batting average allowed (.279)
➡ 7th in walks allowed
➡ Led the Rangers in losses, complete games (4), hits allowed, home runs allowed, hit batsmen (8) and stolen bases allowed (13)

# Roger McDowell

## 1995 Season

Roger McDowell was unusually candid after the Texas Rangers signed him during spring training, saying "they ain't getting Christy Mathewson." No, they weren't. But the Rangers had no complaints about what McDowell gave them. He returned to form with more regular use than Tommy Lasorda had given him in a subpar 1994 season, and was invaluable to the Texas bullpen. No right-handed reliever got more work in the American League than McDowell.

## Pitching

McDowell is the prototypical sinkerball pitcher. He still has good velocity, which helps make his knee-high sinkers tough for hitters to handle. McDowell uses his slider only enough to let hitters know he has one. His versatility allows him to be used in a variety of roles—from long man to closer. He remains remarkably durable, and has no problem pitching four times a week or in back-to-back games, which he did 11 times in 1995. Although he struggled with his control early last season, McDowell was able to make the adjustment to the A.L. strike zone by the All-Star break.

## Defense

Unlike many relief pitchers, McDowell does a good job holding runners, and he permitted only two steals last year. He's a natural athlete who fields his position well, and moves well off of the mound, making it tough for opposing teams to bunt against him.

## 1996 Outlook

McDowell is a free agent whose salary has been reduced by the recent market. He should be welcome somewhere in the majors as long as he does not demand a return to his financial gravy days. He is effective enough to pitch for any team. Texas will miss him if he doesn't return, just as the Los Angeles Dodgers missed him in 1995.

**Position:** RP
**Bats:** R  **Throws:** R
**Ht:** 6' 1"  **Wt:** 195

**Opening Day Age:** 35
**Born:** 12/21/60 in Cincinnati, OH
**ML Seasons:** 11

### Overall Statistics

|  | W | L | Pct. | ERA | G | GS | Sv | IP | H | BB | SO | HR | BR/IP |
|---|---|---|---|---|---|---|---|---|---|---|---|---|---|
| 1995 | 7 | 4 | .636 | 4.02 | 64 | 0 | 4 | 85.0 | 86 | 34 | 49 | 5 | 1.41 |
| Career | 69 | 69 | .500 | 3.24 | 682 | 2 | 155 | 990.2 | 976 | 387 | 504 | 43 | 1.38 |

### How Often He Throws Strikes

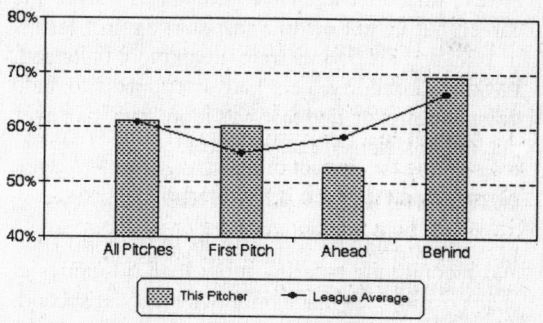

### 1995 Situational Stats

|  | W | L | ERA | Sv | IP |  | AB | H | HR | RBI | Avg |
|---|---|---|---|---|---|---|---|---|---|---|---|
| Home | 4 | 1 | 3.43 | 1 | 42.0 | LHB | 134 | 36 | 2 | 15 | .269 |
| Road | 3 | 3 | 4.60 | 3 | 43.0 | RHB | 177 | 50 | 3 | 26 | .282 |
| First Half | 4 | 1 | 4.07 | 1 | 42.0 | Sc Pos | 90 | 21 | 1 | 32 | .233 |
| Scnd Half | 3 | 3 | 3.98 | 3 | 43.0 | Clutch | 141 | 30 | 1 | 13 | .213 |

### 1995 Rankings (American League)

- ➡ 2nd in games pitched
- ➡ 3rd in relief innings (85.0)
- ➡ 4th in relief wins (7)
- ➡ 7th in worst first batter efficiency (.373)
- ➡ 10th in highest batting average allowed in relief (.277)
- ➡ Led the Rangers in games pitched, holds (9), blown saves (4), most GDPs induced per GDP situation (17.4%), relief ERA (4.02), relief wins (7) and relief innings (85.0)

Texas Rangers

# Mark McLemore

## 1995 Season

Kevin Gross got the headlines when he and Mark McLemore signed two-year contracts with the Rangers in December, 1994. But it was McLemore who carried Texas to a 39-30 start in 1995. Filling in for the injured Juan Gonzalez in left field, he was the team's early-season MVP. The Rangers' second-half decline followed his performance, as he played his way back to the statistical level he established with Baltimore in 1993-94.

## Hitting

The switch-hitting McLemore is a groundball hitter and a patient swinger who draws a good number of walks. He's also a fine bunter. He had always hit better against righthanders during his career, but he got off to a fast start against lefties in 1995 and his figures were much more balanced. Lacking durability, he's had a tendency to fade down the stretch, and that was more true than ever playing in steamy Texas last year.

## Baserunning & Defense

McLemore enjoyed fine seasons in both left field and second base, starting more than 50 games at each position. He made only two errors at second, and used his outfielder's skill to run down pop-ups that were falling between right fielder Mickey Tettleton and first baseman Will Clark. After stealing 17 bases in the first half of the season, McLemore wasn't the same in the second half. He suffered a partially torn rotator cuff the last weekend of the season, which could affect his ability to play the outfield.

## 1996 Outlook

McLemore is a favorite of Johnny Oates and GM Doug Melvin, and will remain a regular. Where he should play is still the big question. He might see more time at second base, especially if Juan Gonzalez is fit enough to play the outfield. Or he might be rested more in the first half, in hope that he'll avoid second-half burnout again. He's hit .225 after the All-Star break the last two seasons, dropping his career second-half average to .241.

**Position:** LF/2B
**Bats:** B  **Throws:** R
**Ht:** 5'11"  **Wt:** 207

**Opening Day Age:** 31
**Born:** 10/4/64 in San Diego, CA
**ML Seasons:** 10

### Overall Statistics

|        | G   | AB   | R   | H   | D  | T  | HR | RBI | SB  | BB  | SO  | Avg  | OBP  | Slg  |
|--------|-----|------|-----|-----|----|----|----|-----|-----|-----|-----|------|------|------|
| 1995   | 129 | 467  | 73  | 122 | 20 | 5  | 5  | 41  | 21  | 59  | 71  | .261 | .346 | .358 |
| Career | 783 | 2513 | 361 | 632 | 95 | 19 | 17 | 244 | 118 | 286 | 388 | .251 | .327 | .325 |

### Where He Hits the Ball

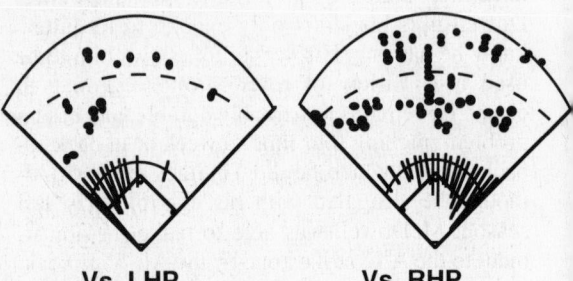

Vs. LHP        Vs. RHP

### 1995 Situational Stats

|            | AB  | H  | HR | RBI | Avg  |        | AB  | H  | HR | RBI | Avg  |
|------------|-----|----|----|-----|------|--------|-----|----|----|-----|------|
| Home       | 240 | 70 | 3  | 25  | .292 | LHP    | 131 | 35 | 1  | 6   | .267 |
| Road       | 227 | 52 | 2  | 16  | .229 | RHP    | 336 | 87 | 4  | 35  | .259 |
| First Half | 238 | 70 | 3  | 31  | .294 | Sc Pos | 105 | 30 | 4  | 39  | .286 |
| Scnd Half  | 229 | 52 | 2  | 10  | .227 | Clutch | 62  | 17 | 1  | 9   | .274 |

### 1995 Rankings (American League)

- ➡ 3rd in highest groundball/flyball ratio (2.0)
- ➡ 5th in sacrifice bunts (10) and lowest stolen base percentage (65.6%)
- ➡ 6th in lowest HR frequency (93.4 ABs per HR)
- ➡ 7th in caught stealing (11), lowest slugging percentage and lowest batting average on the road (.229)
- ➡ 8th in lowest slugging percentage vs. right-handed pitchers (.357)
- ➡ Led the Rangers in triples, sacrifice bunts (10), intentional walks (6) and highest percentage of swings put into play (51.5%)

# Otis Nixon

**Position:** CF
**Bats:** B  **Throws:** R
**Ht:** 6' 2"  **Wt:** 180

**Opening Day Age:** 37
**Born:** 1/9/59 in
Evergreen, NC
**ML Seasons:** 13

## 1995 Season

General manager Doug Melvin took a PR blood-bath by trading Jose Canseco to Boston for Otis Nixon and Luis Ortiz after the 1994 season, but Texas fans were sold on Nixon after watching him for a year. Nixon is 37, looks like he's 47, and plays like he's 27. He had a fine year with the Rangers, setting career highs in both RBI and runs scored, while stealing 50 bases for the first time since 1991. He was the centerpiece of the Rangers' transition from a team built around power hitters to one that emphasizes speed and defense.

## Hitting

Nobody slaps the ball around like Nixon. The switch-hitter takes quick, short swings to put the ball in play. He works the count, fouling off pitch after pitch when he's in a groove. He hits fastballs well enough to bedevil even Randy Johnson, and makes breaking balls fall into the strike zone before going after them. He led the league with 151 singles, including 23 on bunts, and an amazing 49 infield hits. He might never hit another home run, but Nixon still finished 1995 with a career high in extra-base hits as well. He is marginally better batting right-handed than left-handed.

## Baserunning & Defense

Nixon is a pest once he's on base, forcing frequent throws to first. Pitchers who guess right can pick him off—a tendency that contributed to him setting a Texas club record with 21 times caught stealing. He is a threat to steal third as well as second. He still covers a ton of ground in center field, which is a prerequisite in the left-center pasture at The Ballpark in Arlington. His arm is a liability, and everyone runs on him.

## 1996 Outlook

Nixon must slow down sometime, but there are no signs that will happen this season. He keeps himself in good shape and has a greyhound's body. The Rangers didn't excercise their 1996 contract option, and Nixon signed a two-year deal with Toronto, where he'll replace the departed Devon White in center field.

### Overall Statistics

|  | G | AB | R | H | D | T | HR | RBI | SB | BB | SO | Avg | OBP | Slg |
|---|---|---|---|---|---|---|---|---|---|---|---|---|---|---|
| 1995 | 139 | 589 | 87 | 174 | 21 | 2 | 0 | 45 | 50 | 58 | 85 | .295 | .357 | .338 |
| Career | 1245 | 3444 | 605 | 920 | 101 | 16 | 7 | 217 | 444 | 382 | 477 | .267 | .339 | .312 |

### Where He Hits the Ball

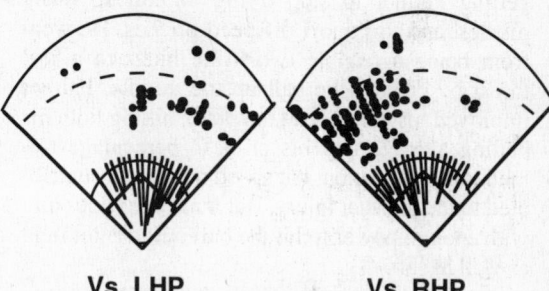

**Vs. LHP**          **Vs. RHP**

### 1995 Situational Stats

|  | AB | H | HR | RBI | Avg |  | AB | H | HR | RBI | Avg |
|---|---|---|---|---|---|---|---|---|---|---|---|
| Home | 299 | 82 | 0 | 29 | .274 | LHP | 177 | 59 | 0 | 13 | .333 |
| Road | 290 | 92 | 0 | 16 | .317 | RHP | 412 | 115 | 0 | 32 | .279 |
| First Half | 288 | 83 | 0 | 23 | .288 | Sc Pos | 138 | 40 | 0 | 43 | .290 |
| Scnd Half | 301 | 91 | 0 | 22 | .302 | Clutch | 79 | 22 | 0 | 11 | .278 |

### 1995 Rankings (American League)

➡ 1st in singles (151), caught stealing (21), lowest slugging percentage, lowest HR frequency (589 ABs without a HR), highest ground-ball/flyball ratio (3.0), lowest slugging percentage vs. right-handed pitchers (.320), bunts in play (53) and steals of third (13)

➡ 2nd in at-bats and stolen bases

➡ 3rd in plate appearances (656)

➡ 4th in errors in center field (4)

➡ 5th in fielding percentage in center field (.989)

➡ Led the Rangers in at-bats, runs scored, hits, singles (151), stolen bases, caught stealing, times on base (232) and pitches seen (2,429)

# Dean Palmer

## 1995 Season

Dean Palmer, always a popular player in Texas, was on his way to a possible All-Star appearance when he ruptured the biceps tendon in his left arm June 3. It was a grotesque injury that required surgery and kept him out until the final days of the season. Palmer's absence illustrated his importance to the organization that drafted him in the third round 10 years ago. The Rangers missed his bat in the middle of the lineup and his quiet, steady presence on the field and in the clubhouse.

## Hitting

Rudy Jaramillo, the Rangers' first-year hitting instructor, got through to Palmer like no other has—getting Palmer to stop trying to pull so many pitches, and to lay off offspeed pitches. He went from being a terrible two-strike hitter to a real threat by driving the ball up the middle. Palmer improved his patience at the plate, hiking both his batting average and his on-base percentage tremendously. His great bat speed may have contributed to the unusual injury. But it also provides him with enough power to hit the ball out to right field as well as left.

## Baserunning & Defense

Palmer improved his throwing technique, which was blamed for his horrific .912 fielding percentage in 1994, but was still headed toward another 20-error season when he went out with the injury. He doesn't figure to win a Gold Glove, but with improvement he can be average defensively. He has below-average speed but good instincts on the bases.

## 1996 Outlook

Palmer will be closely watched in spring training, but the Rangers believe he has made a complete recovery from the torn bicep. Doctors say he could be stronger than he was before the injury, and the Rangers need him to hit for power. But they would accept a little loss in that power if Palmer can pick up where he left off last year—hitting for average and working the count.

**Position:** 3B
**Bats:** R **Throws:** R
**Ht:** 6' 2" **Wt:** 195

**Opening Day Age:** 27
**Born:** 12/27/68 in Tallahassee, FL
**ML Seasons:** 6

### Overall Statistics

|        | G   | AB   | R   | H   | D  | T | HR  | RBI | SB | BB  | SO  | Avg  | OBP  | Slg  |
|--------|-----|------|-----|-----|----|---|-----|-----|----|-----|-----|------|------|------|
| 1995   | 36  | 119  | 30  | 40  | 6  | 0 | 9   | 24  | 1  | 21  | 21  | .336 | .448 | .613 |
| Career | 526 | 1808 | 280 | 427 | 87 | 6 | 102 | 289 | 25 | 194 | 528 | .236 | .315 | .460 |

### Where He Hits the Ball

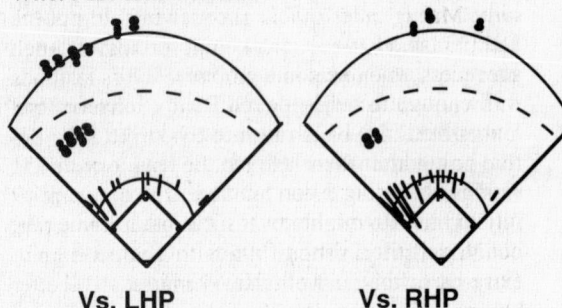

Vs. LHP          Vs. RHP

### 1995 Situational Stats

|            | AB  | H  | HR | RBI | Avg  |        | AB | H  | HR | RBI | Avg  |
|------------|-----|----|----|-----|------|--------|----|----|----|-----|------|
| Home       | 71  | 24 | 5  | 17  | .338 | LHP    | 37 | 16 | 3  | 10  | .432 |
| Road       | 48  | 16 | 4  | 7   | .333 | RHP    | 82 | 24 | 6  | 14  | .293 |
| First Half | 115 | 38 | 9  | 24  | .330 | Sc Pos | 27 | 7  | 1  | 13  | .259 |
| Scnd Half  | 4   | 2  | 0  | 0   | .500 | Clutch | 13 | 4  | 3  | 4   | .308 |

### 1995 Rankings (American League)

➡ Led the Rangers in batting average on a 3-2 count (.273)

# Roger Pavlik

## 1995 Season

Talk about a puzzling pitcher. Roger Pavlik was alternately horrible and brilliant last season, which follows the trend of his career. After a great 1993, he was woeful in 1994 when he tried to pitch through a partially-torn rotator cuff. Having completely recovered from that injury, Pavlik barely stayed in the starting rotation during the first half of last season, then kept Texas in the wild-card hunt down the stretch. He finished second on the staff in innings and wins.

## Pitching

Pavlik's across-the-body delivery defies everything pitching coaches try to teach, but it works for him. Manager Johnny Oates and pitching coach Dick Bosman tried—following the lead of their predecessors—to smooth out his delivery, but then threw up their hands, deeming him uncoachable. Undaunted, Pavlik thrived, showing his bosses that he could do it on his own. He has a curve and change, but succeeded as a de facto two-pitch pitcher—throwing his fastball to get ahead in the count, and then getting hitters to chase his split-fingered fastball out of the strike zone.

## Defense

Pavlik's crossfire delivery gets to the plate quickly. Like all Texas pitchers, he benefits from Ivan Rodriguez' strong arm, which lessens the temptation of opponents to run. Pavlik looks somewhat gangly when coming off the mound, but he remains a decent fielder.

## 1996 Outlook

Conventional thinkers, the Rangers included, swear that Pavlik is headed toward a major breakdown because of his delivery. His partial rotator cuff tear in 1994 supports that prediction. But Pavlik is young and strong, and could be the exception to the rule. If that's true, Texas would be silly to trade him away, which they were considering during the winter. It's a gamble. . . he could win big, or he could break down completely.

**Position:** SP
**Bats:** R **Throws:** R
**Ht:** 6' 2" **Wt:** 220

**Opening Day Age:** 28
**Born:** 10/4/67 in Houston, TX
**ML Seasons:** 4

### Overall Statistics

|  | W | L | Pct. | ERA | G | GS | Sv | IP | H | BB | SO | HR | BR/IP |
|---|---|---|---|---|---|---|---|---|---|---|---|---|---|
| 1995 | 10 | 10 | .500 | 4.37 | 31 | 31 | 0 | 191.2 | 174 | 90 | 149 | 19 | 1.38 |
| Career | 28 | 25 | .528 | 4.36 | 81 | 80 | 0 | 470.1 | 452 | 234 | 356 | 48 | 1.46 |

### How Often He Throws Strikes

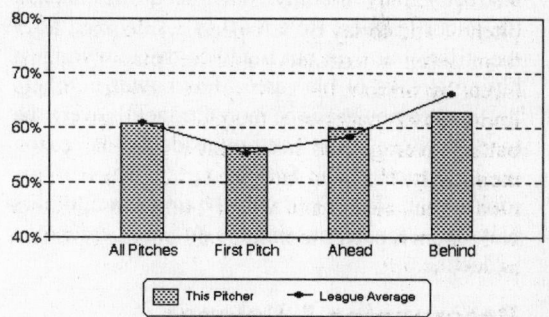

This Pitcher / League Average

### 1995 Situational Stats

|  | W | L | ERA | Sv | IP |  | AB | H | HR | RBI | Avg |
|---|---|---|---|---|---|---|---|---|---|---|---|
| Home | 6 | 6 | 5.29 | 0 | 100.1 | LHB | 410 | 96 | 10 | 43 | .234 |
| Road | 4 | 4 | 3.35 | 0 | 91.1 | RHB | 306 | 78 | 9 | 37 | .255 |
| First Half | 5 | 4 | 5.60 | 0 | 82.0 | Sc Pos | 169 | 44 | 5 | 61 | .260 |
| Scnd Half | 5 | 6 | 3.45 | 0 | 109.2 | Clutch | 79 | 22 | 2 | 8 | .278 |

### 1995 Rankings (American League)

- 4th in games started
- 5th in walks allowed and least run support per 9 innings (4.4)
- 7th in highest ERA at home (5.29), lowest ERA on the road (3.35) and lowest batting average allowed vs. left-handed batters (.234)
- 8th in wild pitches (10) and lowest stolen base percentage allowed (52.9%)
- 9th in shutouts (1), runners caught stealing (8), lowest batting average allowed (.243) and most strikeouts per 9 innings (7.0)
- 10th in strikeouts
- Led the Rangers in games started, shutouts (1), walks allowed, strikeouts, wild pitches (10) and runners caught stealing (8)

# Ivan Rodriguez

## 1994 Season

Ivan Rodriguez is a wonder. He enters this season at age 24, the same as Mike Piazza when he came from nowhere to be the National League Rookie of the Year in 1993. But Rodriguez went to his *fourth* All-Star Game last year, his third as a starter, and he just keeps getting better. He has improved his batting average three consecutive years. His tools behind the plate are unparalleled in the major leagues, and he has been on the disabled list only once in five seasons.

## Hitting

Few players hit the ball as consistently hard as Rodriguez. He thrived when reunited with hitting instructor Rudy Jaramillo, his first batting coach in the minor leagues. He got off to a slow start after the strike, but then put together the four longest hitting streaks of his career. His power numbers declined somewhat as he more frequently went the other way for a hit. The downside to his season was a return to the free-swinging ways of his rookie year. He walked only 16 times in 500-plus plate appearances, causing his on-base percentage to decline.

## Baserunning & Defense

Rodriguez returned after the strike throwing harder and more accurately than he did in 1994. He improved his percentage throwing out runners from 33.9 to a major league-best 43.7. New manager Johnny Oates, a former catcher, let Rodriguez call his own game behind the plate, which helped him develop confidence. His inconsistency blocking pitches in the dirt was reflected by the Rangers having the third-most wild pitches in the A.L. He shies away from contact with runners. Still, the total defensive package is impressive, and Rodriguez garnered his fourth Gold Glove in as many seasons. He has decent speed for a catcher, but doesn't use it.

## 1996 Outlook

Rodriguez surpassed Juan Gonzalez to become the Rangers' hottest property last season, and he still has room to improve. He has the ability to put together a 20-homer, 40-double season if he maintains the focus he carried to the plate in 1995.

**Position:** C
**Bats:** R **Throws:** R
**Ht:** 5' 9" **Wt:** 205

**Opening Day Age:** 24
**Born:** 11/30/71 in Vega Baja, PR
**ML Seasons:** 5
**Nickname:** Pudge

### Overall Statistics

|        | G   | AB   | R   | H   | D   | T | HR | RBI | SB | BB  | SO  | Avg  | OBP  | Slg  |
|--------|-----|------|-----|-----|-----|---|----|-----|----|-----|-----|------|------|------|
| 1995   | 130 | 492  | 56  | 149 | 32  | 2 | 12 | 67  | 0  | 16  | 48  | .303 | .327 | .449 |
| Career | 577 | 2028 | 231 | 569 | 111 | 8 | 49 | 254 | 14 | 105 | 275 | .281 | .318 | .416 |

### Where He Hits the Ball

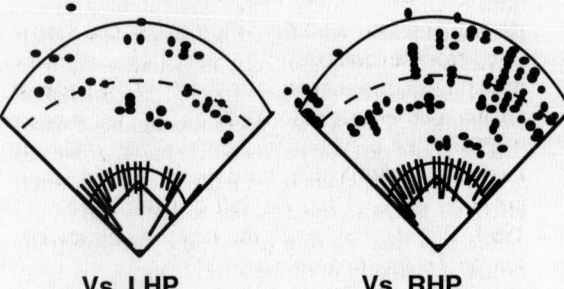

**Vs. LHP**          **Vs. RHP**

### 1995 Situational Stats

|            | AB  | H  | HR | RBI | Avg  |        | AB  | H   | HR | RBI | Avg  |
|------------|-----|----|----|-----|------|--------|-----|-----|----|-----|------|
| Home       | 232 | 69 | 5  | 31  | .297 | LHP    | 146 | 44  | 4  | 16  | .301 |
| Road       | 260 | 80 | 7  | 36  | .308 | RHP    | 346 | 105 | 8  | 51  | .303 |
| First Half | 211 | 70 | 6  | 31  | .332 | Sc Pos | 140 | 38  | 1  | 50  | .271 |
| Scnd Half  | 281 | 79 | 6  | 36  | .281 | Clutch | 69  | 22  | 1  | 13  | .319 |

### 1995 Rankings (American League)

→ 1st in lowest percentage of pitches taken (37.3%) and highest percentage of runners caught stealing as a catcher (43.7%)

→ 2nd in least pitches seen per plate appearance (3.08) and errors at catcher (8)

→ 7th in highest percentage of swings on the first pitch (38.8%)

→ 9th in lowest on-base percentage vs. right-handed pitchers (.321)

→ Led the Rangers in batting average, doubles, total bases (221) and batting average with two strikes (.236)

# Kenny Rogers

**Tough On Lefties**

## 1995 Season

Randy Johnson, Tom Glavine, and Pete Schourek—those are the only lefthanders in all of baseball better than a former 39th-round draft choice of the Rangers. Kenny Rogers blossomed into a legitimate ace in 1995, despite the departure of close friend and role model Kevin Brown. Rogers started strong, earning his first trip to the All-Star game by throwing a club-record 39 consecutive scoreless innings in May. And he finished strong, winning his last five starts including an October 1 victory on three days' rest over Seattle, forcing the Mariners into the one-game playoff with California.

## Pitching

Rogers is a late bloomer who has learned something from several pitching coaches. He can throw four pitches for strikes, including one of the best change-ups in baseball. And he's learned how to win with his curveball and cut fastball when his fastball doesn't have its normal pop. After a disappointing season against left-handed hitters in 1994, Rogers was again the death of lefties last season. His mistakes have a tendency to end up in the bleacher seats, and last year he allowed a career-high 26 home runs. Of course, Rogers rarely makes those mistakes with runners on base.

## Defense

Rogers' pickoff move is one of the most feared in baseball. Teams almost never run on him. He's a good athlete and a solid fielder. He sometimes tries to make the impossible play, beating himself in the process.

## 1996 Outlook

After 14 one-year contracts in the Texas organization, Rogers finally made it to free agency after last season. The Rangers identified him as their number-one offseason priority, but agent Scott Boras was determined that Rogers explore all his options. Wherever he goes, he faces a new challenge—coping with the pressures that come with a big contract.

**Position:** SP
**Bats:** L **Throws:** L
**Ht:** 6' 1" **Wt:** 205

**Opening Day Age:** 31
**Born:** 11/10/64 in Savannah, GA
**ML Seasons:** 7

### Overall Statistics

|  | W | L | Pct. | ERA | G | GS | Sv | IP | H | BB | SO | HR | BR/IP |
|---|---|---|---|---|---|---|---|---|---|---|---|---|---|
| 1995 | 17 | 7 | .708 | 3.38 | 31 | 31 | 0 | 208.0 | 192 | 76 | 140 | 26 | 1.29 |
| Career | 70 | 51 | .579 | 3.88 | 376 | 100 | 28 | 943.1 | 925 | 370 | 680 | 97 | 1.37 |

### How Often He Throws Strikes

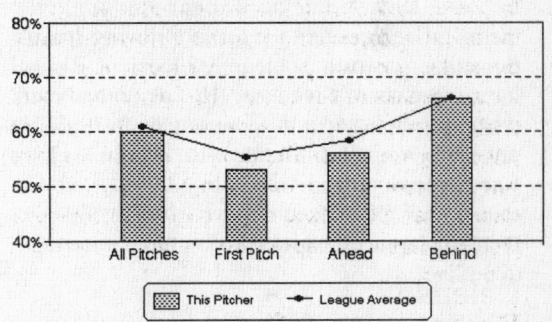

This Pitcher — League Average

### 1995 Situational Stats

|  | W | L | ERA | Sv | IP |  | AB | H | HR | RBI | Avg |
|---|---|---|---|---|---|---|---|---|---|---|---|
| Home | 9 | 1 | 2.96 | 0 | 109.1 | LHB | 115 | 18 | 2 | 9 | .157 |
| Road | 8 | 6 | 3.83 | 0 | 98.2 | RHB | 676 | 174 | 24 | 68 | .257 |
| First Half | 8 | 4 | 3.05 | 0 | 94.1 | Sc Pos | 135 | 33 | 3 | 47 | .244 |
| Scnd Half | 9 | 3 | 3.64 | 0 | 113.2 | Clutch | 74 | 24 | 2 | 5 | .324 |

### 1995 Rankings (American League)

→ 3rd in home runs allowed
→ 4th in wins and games started
→ 5th in ERA
→ 6th in winning percentage, lowest stolen base percentage allowed (50.0%), most home runs allowed per 9 innings (1.13) and ERA at home (2.96)
→ 7th in innings pitched
→ 8th in batters faced (877) and lowest batting average allowed (.243)
→ 9th in shutouts (1), pitches thrown (3,350), lowest on-base percentage allowed (.309) and least baserunners allowed per 9 innings (11.7)
→ Led the Rangers in ERA, wins, games started, shutouts and innings pitched

**Texas Rangers**

# Jeff Russell

## 1995 Season

Baseball has a way of keeping its hold on people. Jeff Russell believed he had retired after the 1994 season. He was on his way to film a fishing show when an offer came to pitch for the Rangers. He said yes, and wound up contributing 20 of the 34 saves the Texas staff recorded. It was a struggle all the way, however, as he reported to spring training late and out of shape, then battled a herniated disc in the second half of the season. He paid the price with cortisone shots.

## Pitching

There's nothing fancy about Russell's approach—fastballs around 90 miles per hour, complemented by hard sliders and occasional split-fingered fastballs. He comes in the game throwing strikes. Sometimes it works, sometimes it doesn't. Russell has always had a tendency to fail dramatically when he failed, and it happened again in 1995. He gave up a pinch-hit homer to Seattle's Doug Strange September 19 that was a turning point in the season for both teams. Russell has always been mentally tough enough to deal with such blows.

## Defense

Few teams run on Russell, primarily because of his ability to get the ball quickly to the plate. In fact, there have been only eight stolen-base attempts against him (five successful) the last three seasons. Russell has always been a good fielder, but his back problems limited his movement around the mound last season.

## 1996 Outlook

Russell took a major cut in salary to play for the Rangers last season. He was able to drive to work from his home in Colleyville, Texas. He again is considering retirement, but doesn't want to hang it up without a championship ring. If the Rangers ask him to come back, he'll probably play. After being an All-Star as both a starter and stopper, it's time for him to become an above-average set-up man.

**Position:** RP
**Bats:** R  **Throws:** R
**Ht:** 6' 3"  **Wt:** 205

**Opening Day Age:** 34
**Born:** 9/2/61 in Cincinnati, OH
**ML Seasons:** 13

### Overall Statistics

|        | W  | L  | Pct.  | ERA  | G   | GS | Sv  | IP     | H    | BB  | SO  | HR | BR/IP |
|--------|----|----|-------|------|-----|----|-----|--------|------|-----|-----|----|-------|
| 1995   | 1  | 0  | 1.000 | 3.03 | 37  | 0  | 20  | 32.2   | 36   | 9   | 21  | 3  | 1.38  |
| Career | 53 | 70 | .431  | 3.77 | 534 | 79 | 183 | 1043.2 | 1007 | 393 | 670 | 95 | 1.34  |

### How Often He Throws Strikes

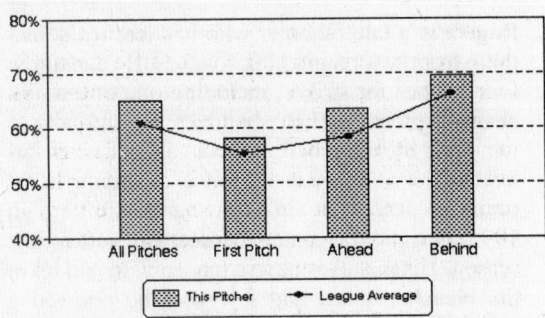

### 1995 Situational Stats

|            | W | L | ERA  | Sv | IP   |        | AB | H  | HR | RBI | Avg  |
|------------|---|---|------|----|------|--------|----|----|----|-----|------|
| Home       | 0 | 0 | 4.40 | 8  | 14.1 | LHB    | 73 | 20 | 2  | 6   | .274 |
| Road       | 1 | 0 | 1.96 | 12 | 18.1 | RHB    | 57 | 16 | 1  | 11  | .281 |
| First Half | 1 | 0 | 3.06 | 12 | 17.2 | Sc Pos | 42 | 15 | 2  | 16  | .357 |
| Scnd Half  | 0 | 0 | 3.00 | 8  | 15.0 | Clutch | 85 | 25 | 2  | 12  | .294 |

### 1995 Rankings (American League)

➡ 7th in save percentage (83.3%)
➡ 10th in saves
➡ Led the Rangers in saves, games finished (32), save opportunities (24), save percentage (83.3%) and blown saves (4)

# Mickey Tettleton

## 1995 Season

Few of the players who began the season at the free-agent camp in Homestead, Florida, panned out as well as Mickey Tettleton. The Rangers signed him late in spring training—after the Chicago White Sox had inexplicably rejected him to sign Chris Sabo—and he became a life preserver for an offense that missed Juan Gonzalez and Dean Palmer for much of the season. Tettleton also accommodated the move of Gonzalez to designated hitter by playing the outfield on a bad knee. Everybody should have this guy's attitude.

## Hitting

Tettleton must have been born with a 3-2 count. He seems to be there every trip to the plate, as he refuses to swing at any borderline pitch until he has two strikes against him. For the fifth time in his career, he topped 100 in both strikeouts and walks. A switch-hitter, Tettleton is more dangerous from the left side. His power perfectly suits The Ballpark in Arlington, where he hit 22 of his 32 home runs. That total matched a career high. He's a good all-around hitter, who contributes far beyond the scope of his .242 career average.

## Baserunning & Defense

Tettleton clogs the basepaths, and was often lifted late in the game for a pinch runner/defensive replacement. He played the outfield—mostly in right—more last season than ever before. He has limited range, but catches what he can reach. He still owns shin guards, but almost never catches on a team with Ivan Rodriguez and David Valle. His arm from the outfield is average.

## 1996 Outlook

Tettleton is eligible for free agency and deserves more than the $1.1 million in salary and incentive bonuses he earned from the Rangers, who would love to have him back. There's no guarantee he will receive a better offer on the shrunken market. Wherever he goes, he will probably return to more of a DH role. Texas will have room for him if Juan Gonzalez is able to return to left field.

**Position:** RF/DH
**Bats:** B  **Throws:** R
**Ht:** 6' 2"  **Wt:** 212

**Opening Day Age:** 35
**Born:** 9/16/60 in
Oklahoma City, OK
**ML Seasons:** 12

### Overall Statistics

|  | G | AB | R | H | D | T | HR | RBI | SB | BB | SO | Avg | OBP | Slg |
|---|---|---|---|---|---|---|---|---|---|---|---|---|---|---|
| 1995 | 134 | 429 | 76 | 102 | 19 | 1 | 32 | 78 | 0 | 107 | 110 | .238 | .396 | .510 |
| Career | 1325 | 4163 | 628 | 1007 | 183 | 15 | 218 | 645 | 21 | 851 | 1158 | .242 | .371 | .450 |

### Where He Hits the Ball

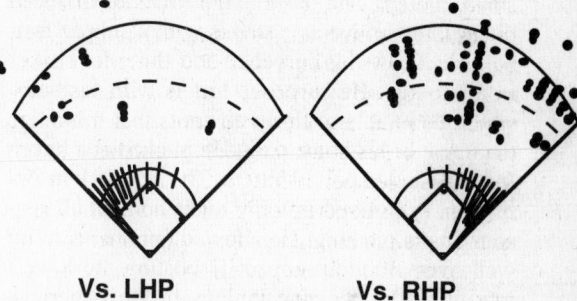

**Vs. LHP**  **Vs. RHP**

### 1995 Situational Stats

|  | AB | H | HR | RBI | Avg |  | AB | H | HR | RBI | Avg |
|---|---|---|---|---|---|---|---|---|---|---|---|
| Home | 228 | 60 | 22 | 54 | .263 | LHP | 142 | 32 | 8 | 21 | .225 |
| Road | 201 | 42 | 10 | 24 | .209 | RHP | 287 | 70 | 24 | 57 | .244 |
| First Half | 224 | 50 | 14 | 37 | .223 | Sc Pos | 104 | 24 | 9 | 49 | .231 |
| Scnd Half | 205 | 52 | 18 | 41 | .254 | Clutch | 52 | 19 | 5 | 12 | .365 |

### 1995 Rankings (American League)

➡ 1st in highest percentage of pitches taken (66.9%)
➡ 2nd in lowest groundball/flyball ratio (0.7)
➡ 3rd in most pitches seen per plate appearance (4.31), lowest batting average on the road (.209) and lowest percentage of swings on the first pitch (7.5%)
➡ 4th in walks and HR frequency (13.4 ABs per HR)
➡ 5th in lowest batting average
➡ 6th in lowest percentage of extra bases taken as a runner (32.7%)
➡ Led the Rangers in home runs, walks, hit by pitch (7) and slugging percentage

# Bob Tewksbury

## 1995 Season

Bob Tewksbury is the kind of player Texas Rangers' president Tom Schieffer loves—he took a drastic pay cut and liked it. Tewksbury has an unusual perspective about the value and responsibilities of athletes. . . not to mention a superb curveball and an allergy to three-ball counts. Tewksbury was a major contributor for the Rangers until he suffered a series of injuries after the All-Star break. He was skilled enough to do what few soft throwers can—succeed while making a jump from the National League to the American.

## Pitching

Tewksbury is a master at the *art* of pitching. He is smart enough, and has enough kinds of offspeed pitches, to survive as a starter with a subpar fastball. He throws his curveball and slider for strikes in all counts. He surprises hitters with fastballs, which he is able to throw to spots that minimize the threat of his home park. He pitched at a haven for left-handed power hitters, The Ballpark in Arlington, yet served up only eight homers all season. That's pitching. He allowed opponents to hit well over .300, but coped by posting the lowest rate of walks per nine innings in the American League.

## Defense

Tewksbury can be easy to run on, as his pitches take their time getting to the plate, but with increased attention to holding runners and Ivan Rodriguez behind the plate, he was much improved in 1995. He's always alert as a fielder. He experienced problems with his legs late last season and might be more vulnerable to bunts this year.

## 1996 Outlook

Tewksbury signed a one-year contract for 1995, making him eligible for free agency again. The Rangers were hoping to sign him again, at about the same $1.5 million salary. His market value was hurt by injuries (stress fracture in a left-side rib, pulled hamstring) that limited him to 21 starts. But there's no reason to believe he won't be a healthy and effective third starter in 1996.

**Position:** SP
**Bats:** R  **Throws:** R
**Ht:** 6' 4"  **Wt:** 208

**Opening Day Age:** 35
**Born:** 11/30/60 in Concord, NH
**ML Seasons:** 10

### Overall Statistics

| | W | L | Pct. | ERA | G | GS | Sv | IP | H | BB | SO | HR | BR/IP |
|---|---|---|---|---|---|---|---|---|---|---|---|---|---|
| 1995 | 8 | 7 | .533 | 4.58 | 21 | 21 | 0 | 129.2 | 169 | 20 | 53 | 8 | 1.46 |
| Career | 85 | 66 | .563 | 3.72 | 214 | 193 | 1 | 1283.1 | 1445 | 198 | 534 | 94 | 1.28 |

### How Often He Throws Strikes

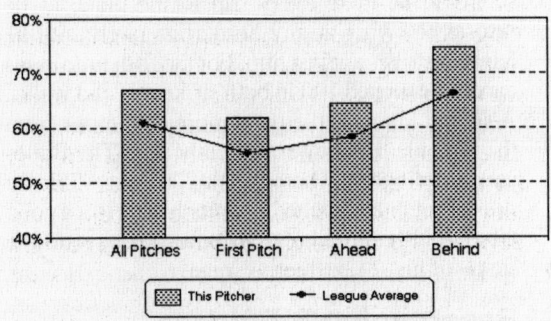

### 1995 Situational Stats

| | W | L | ERA | Sv | IP | | AB | H | HR | RBI | Avg |
|---|---|---|---|---|---|---|---|---|---|---|---|
| Home | 3 | 3 | 3.72 | 0 | 65.1 | LHB | 327 | 98 | 5 | 40 | .300 |
| Road | 5 | 4 | 5.46 | 0 | 64.1 | RHB | 202 | 71 | 3 | 24 | .351 |
| First Half | 7 | 3 | 3.25 | 0 | 91.1 | Sc Pos | 126 | 43 | 3 | 57 | .341 |
| Scnd Half | 1 | 4 | 7.75 | 0 | 38.1 | Clutch | 33 | 9 | 0 | 0 | .273 |

### 1995 Rankings (American League)

➡ 3rd in highest batting average allowed with runners in scoring position (.341)
➡ 8th in complete games (4)
➡ 9th in shutouts (1)
➡ Led the Rangers in complete games (4) and shutouts

# Bobby Witt

## 1995 Season

A lack of run support was all that kept Bobby Witt from having his best season since 1990, when he was 17-10 for Texas. Florida and Texas combined to average 3.8 runs in his 29 starts, leaving him 5-11 despite a decent 4.13 ERA. The Marlins and Rangers were shut out five times in his starts and scored two runs or fewer 12 times. Witt pitched well for Florida, but provided little impact for the Rangers after they dealt two promising minor leaguers to land him in an August 8 trade. His personal highlight came on September 14, when he struck out 12—and walked no one—in eight innings at SkyDome against the Toronto Blue Jays.

## Pitching

Give Oakland pitching coach Dave Duncan credit. Witt hasn't been the same wild man since spending two-plus seasons with the Athletics. The three-time A.L. walk leader walked only 3.6 batters per nine innings last year. He can still hit the 90s with his fastball and has a nasty slider. Duncan helped him get his curveball over the plate and helped him develop a cut fastball that he throws for a change-up. He is a maximum-effort guy who needs his rest between starts; he's not a candidate for a four-man rotation.

## Defense

Witt is slow to the plate, which makes him a target for basestealers. In addition, his pickoff move is telegraphed, not quick. He is an average fielder, rarely hurting himself with the glove.

## 1996 Outlook

For the second year in a row, Witt goes into free agency with marginal credentials. He is unlikely to sign a contract for more than one year, but could be a pleasant surprise for whoever signs him. Texas has some interest in getting him back, but won't slot him into a big salary. There should be a place for an experienced third or fourth starter who has been injury free for four seasons.

**Position:** SP
**Bats:** R  **Throws:** R
**Ht:** 6' 2"  **Wt:** 205

**Opening Day Age:** 31
**Born:** 5/11/64 in Arlington, VA
**ML Seasons:** 10

### Overall Statistics

|  | W | L | Pct. | ERA | G | GS | Sv | IP | H | BB | SO | HR | BR/IP |
|---|---|---|---|---|---|---|---|---|---|---|---|---|---|
| 1995 | 5 | 11 | .313 | 4.13 | 29 | 29 | 0 | 172.0 | 185 | 68 | 141 | 12 | 1.47 |
| Career | 96 | 107 | .473 | 4.52 | 279 | 274 | 0 | 1700.2 | 1586 | 1025 | 1459 | 137 | 1.54 |

### How Often He Throws Strikes

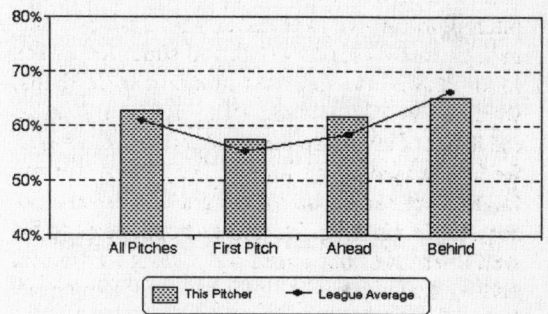

### 1995 Situational Stats

|  | W | L | ERA | Sv | IP |  | AB | H | HR | RBI | Avg |
|---|---|---|---|---|---|---|---|---|---|---|---|
| Home | 4 | 4 | 3.74 | 0 | 86.2 | LHB | 348 | 107 | 8 | 40 | .307 |
| Road | 1 | 7 | 4.54 | 0 | 85.1 | RHB | 317 | 78 | 4 | 35 | .246 |
| First Half | 1 | 6 | 4.74 | 0 | 74.0 | Sc Pos | 179 | 42 | 5 | 61 | .235 |
| Scnd Half | 4 | 5 | 3.67 | 0 | 98.0 | Clutch | 40 | 14 | 0 | 3 | .350 |

### 1995 Rankings (American League)

→ Did not rank near the top or bottom in any category

# Esteban Beltre

**Position**: SS/2B
**Bats**: R **Throws**: R
**Ht**: 5'10" **Wt**: 172

**Opening Day Age**: 28
**Born**: 12/26/67 in
Ingenio Quisfuella, DR
**ML Seasons**: 4
**Pronunciation**:
BELL-tray

## Overall Statistics

| | G | AB | R | H | D | T | HR | RBI | SB | BB | SO | Avg | OBP | Slg |
|---|---|---|---|---|---|---|---|---|---|---|---|---|---|---|
| 1995 | 54 | 92 | 7 | 20 | 8 | 0 | 0 | 7 | 0 | 4 | 15 | .217 | .250 | .304 |
| Career | 159 | 339 | 40 | 79 | 15 | 0 | 1 | 29 | 4 | 24 | 59 | .233 | .282 | .286 |

## 1995 Season

Esteban Beltre was bypassed by Benji Gil for the shortstop vacancy created by Manuel Lee's departure last season. He may never be considered as a major league regular, but he remains a reliable backup with a great attitude. He filled in at both shortstop and second base in 1995, and helped the Rangers win a few games with clutch hits.

## Hitting, Baserunning & Defense

Beltre, a right-handed hitter, had a subpar year at the plate after batting .282 in 1994. He hasn't hit a home run in the majors since 1992, but is strong for his size. He could raise his average with more patience, which might come if he got more of a chance to play. He runs decently, but is not a basestealing threat. His super-strong arm is among the game's best-kept secrets. Beltre resisted attempts by others to convert him to a pitcher in the minors, and still throws as hard as many fastballers.

## 1996 Outlook

Beltre is an insurance policy against both injury and any possible slowing in Gil's development. He is well liked in the organization and could stick around for the next few years if his salary demands remain reasonable. A good 1996 would help ensure his future.

# Danny Darwin

**Position**: SP/RP
**Bats**: R **Throws**: R
**Ht**: 6'3" **Wt**: 202

**Opening Day Age**: 40
**Born**: 10/25/55 in
Bonham, TX
**ML Seasons**: 18

## Overall Statistics

| | W | L | Pct. | ERA | G | GS | Sv | IP | H | BB | SO | HR | BR/IP |
|---|---|---|---|---|---|---|---|---|---|---|---|---|---|
| 1995 | 3 | 10 | .231 | 7.45 | 20 | 15 | 0 | 99.0 | 131 | 31 | 58 | 25 | 1.64 |
| Career | 148 | 150 | .497 | 3.71 | 618 | 297 | 32 | 2546.2 | 2434 | 753 | 1673 | 256 | 1.25 |

## 1995 Season

Toronto looked like the end of the road for Danny Darwin. He was signed as a free agent to fill out the Blue Jays' rotation, but managed only one win in 11 starts before drawing his release. The Texas Rangers were desperate enough to pick him up for an encore. Darwin made four starts while Bob Tewksbury was on the disabled list, then provided some depth as a long reliever. Darwin was happy to be back in Texas, and never complained about his limited role.

## Pitching & Defense

Darwin did more than grow old during the strike— he developed bad mechanical habits while working on his own, and only began to hit his stride after the All-Star break. His fastball has dropped into the mid-80s, making both his forkball and slider less effective. His key is keeping the ball down, where mistakes won't kill him. He is still known as "Dr. Death" for his willingness to knock down hitters. Darwin has a good move to first, but has lost his quick reactions on grounders through the box.

## 1996 Outlook

Darwin turned 40 last October, but still takes his cues from close friend Nolan Ryan. That means he isn't ready to quit. Darwin wants a chance to earn a contract in spring training, preferably with the Rangers. But he'll have to pitch a whole lot better than he did in 1995.

# Lou Frazier

**Position:** LF/CF
**Bats:** B  **Throws:** R
**Ht:** 6' 2"  **Wt:** 180

**Opening Day Age:** 31
**Born:** 1/26/65 in St. Louis, MO
**ML Seasons:** 3

### Overall Statistics

|  | G | AB | R | H | D | T | HR | RBI | SB | BB | SO | Avg | OBP | Slg |
|---|---|---|---|---|---|---|---|---|---|---|---|---|---|---|
| 1995 | 84 | 162 | 25 | 33 | 4 | 0 | 0 | 11 | 13 | 15 | 32 | .204 | .286 | .228 |
| Career | 272 | 491 | 77 | 125 | 14 | 2 | 1 | 41 | 50 | 49 | 79 | .255 | .327 | .297 |

## 1995 Season

The Montreal Expos thought so little of Lou Frazier that they traded him to Texas for "the player to be named later," which turned out to be oft-suspended (and injured) pitcher Hector Fajardo. Frazier salvaged his career with a strong half-season in Texas. Injuries gave him an unexpected opportunity to play, and he contributed—especially as a pinch runner and defensive replacement.

## Hitting, Baserunning & Defense

The switch-hitting Frazier is hard to figure. He hit better right-handed last season, but better left-handed in 1994. Using a short stroke, Frazier hits ground balls from both sides of the plate, allowing him to use his blazing speed. If he was an average runner he'd never escape Triple-A, but his wheels have kept him in the majors. Frazier covers ground in the outfield, playing all three positions. He makes some great catches, but still clunks some, too. His arm is weak. Frazier is an outstanding basestealer who is almost never caught.

## 1996 Outlook

Frazier will compete for an extra outfielder's position with Texas. He has the versatility that Johnny Oates loves, and should remain on the bench. The time has passed when he could be considered for everyday duty, but he understands his limited role.

# Darren Oliver

**Position:** RP/SP
**Bats:** R  **Throws:** L
**Ht:** 6' 2"  **Wt:** 200

**Opening Day Age:** 25
**Born:** 10/6/70 in Kansas City, MO
**ML Seasons:** 3

### Overall Statistics

|  | W | L | Pct. | ERA | G | GS | Sv | IP | H | BB | SO | HR | BR/IP |
|---|---|---|---|---|---|---|---|---|---|---|---|---|---|
| 1995 | 4 | 2 | .667 | 4.22 | 17 | 7 | 0 | 49.0 | 47 | 32 | 39 | 3 | 1.61 |
| Career | 8 | 2 | .800 | 3.78 | 62 | 7 | 2 | 102.1 | 89 | 68 | 93 | 8 | 1.53 |

## 1995 Season

Health has always been the big question with left-hander Darren Oliver. He had arm surgery both during the 1994 strike and the 1995 regular season. Between operations, he was an enigma for Rangers manager Johnny Oates. Oliver excelled as a set-up man in 1994, but pitched horribly early in '95, probably because he was still recovering from surgery. Oates tried him as a starter, and he responded initially. But Oliver's arm broke down after his three longest outings.

## Pitching & Defense

Oliver has great stuff when he's healthy. He throws a sneaky-quick fastball from a smooth delivery, which he complements with a great change-up and a good curve. Control is a key for him. Oliver will beat himself with walks against patient hitters. He owned left-handed hitters in 1994, but struggled to get them out last year. He's got a great pickoff move and is a good athlete, adept at fielding his position.

## 1996 Outlook

The Rangers first need Oliver to get healthy. Then they will decide whether to use him as a starter or a reliever. Despite the most recent setback, Oates and pitching coach Dick Bosman still consider him a candidate for the rotation, believing his personality is too laid-back for the harried pace of bullpen work.

# Luis Ortiz

**Position**: 3B
**Bats**: R  **Throws**: R
**Ht**: 6' 0"  **Wt**: 195

**Opening Day Age**: 25
**Born**: 5/25/70 in Santo Domingo, DR
**ML Seasons**: 3

*Overall Statistics*

|  | G | AB | R | H | D | T | HR | RBI | SB | BB | SO | Avg | OBP | Slg |
|---|---|---|---|---|---|---|---|---|---|---|---|---|---|---|
| 1995 | 41 | 108 | 10 | 25 | 5 | 2 | 1 | 18 | 0 | 6 | 18 | .231 | .270 | .343 |
| Career | 57 | 138 | 13 | 31 | 7 | 2 | 1 | 25 | 0 | 7 | 25 | .225 | .255 | .326 |

## 1995 Season

Acquired from Boston in the Jose Canseco trade, third baseman Luis Ortiz got his first real chance to play at the major league level last year. But Ortiz could not capitalize on Dean Palmer's injury. He was simply too much of a defensive liability to play every day.

## Hitting, Baserunning & Defense

Despite his .231 average last year, Ortiz is capable of hitting the best pitchers in the game. He has a mechanically sound swing, plus a little power. Tough situations don't seem to bother him; he was the Rangers' best hitter with men in scoring position in 1995. But Texas found that he had fallen into bad habits defensively that are very hard to break. In particular, Ortiz has trouble backhanding the ball—and it showed, with eight errors in limited play last season. He runs like a typical third baseman, having never stolen a base in the major leagues.

## 1996 Outlook

The Rangers still like Ortiz. They just don't know what to do with him. Johnny Oates loves versatile players, and is sure to get Ortiz work at positions other than third base. He'll likely see some time in left field and at first base, while continuing to work on his defense at third. With Palmer returning from his injury, Ortiz' value is as a utility man and sometimes designated hitter.

# Mike Pagliarulo

**Position**: 3B/1B
**Bats**: L  **Throws**: R
**Ht**: 6' 2"  **Wt**: 201

**Opening Day Age**: 36
**Born**: 3/15/60 in Medford, MA
**ML Seasons**: 11
**Pronunciation**: pal-yuh-ROO-loh

*Overall Statistics*

|  | G | AB | R | H | D | T | HR | RBI | SB | BB | SO | Avg | OBP | Slg |
|---|---|---|---|---|---|---|---|---|---|---|---|---|---|---|
| 1995 | 86 | 241 | 27 | 56 | 16 | 0 | 4 | 27 | 0 | 15 | 49 | .232 | .277 | .349 |
| Career | 1246 | 3901 | 462 | 942 | 206 | 18 | 134 | 505 | 18 | 343 | 785 | .241 | .306 | .407 |

## 1995 Season

A year after playing in Japan's World Series, Mike Pagliarulo could have been a key to helping the Rangers toward the playoffs. He was signed to a minor league contract in March, then found himself with a huge opportunity when Dean Palmer went out with a season-ending injury June 3. Pagliarulo teased the Rangers by playing well when first put in the lineup, but he quickly wore out. He added toughness to the bench and clubhouse, but left a big hole in the lineup.

## Hitting, Baserunning & Defense

Pagliarulo has lost his bat speed since he was a platoon third baseman with Minnesota in 1991. He is overmatched by anyone with an above-average fastball and seldom pulls any heater. He is a mistake hitter who works the count and looks for hanging curveballs. Pagliarulo is always a threat to hit into a double play, and clogs the bases when he's on. He plays third base like an NHL goalie, taking one-hoppers off the chest and diving to make saves. He has limited range but gets the job done. He can also fill in at first.

## 1996 Outlook

If Pagliarulo wants to, he can probably squeeze in one or two more seasons as a bench player. He did a decent job as a pinch hitter, but there simply aren't any more 200 at-bat seasons in his future.

# Ed Vosberg

**Position**: RP
**Bats**: L **Throws**: L
**Ht**: 6' 1" **Wt**: 190

**Opening Day Age**: 34
**Born**: 9/28/61 in
Tucson, AZ
**ML Seasons**: 4

## Overall Statistics

|  | W | L | Pct. | ERA | G | GS | Sv | IP | H | BB | SO | HR | BR/IP |
|---|---|---|---|---|---|---|---|---|---|---|---|---|---|
| 1995 | 5 | 5 | .500 | 3.00 | 44 | 0 | 4 | 36.0 | 32 | 16 | 36 | 3 | 1.33 |
| Career | 6 | 9 | .400 | 4.41 | 83 | 3 | 4 | 87.2 | 86 | 42 | 68 | 9 | 1.46 |

## 1995 Season

After failing to make the Dodgers' staff in spring training, Ed Vosberg was a major asset in the Texas bullpen, used as the primary lefty against the league's wealth of left-handed sluggers. He didn't back down from that challenge. Nor did he get emotionally destroyed when nailed for the dumbest violation of the season—trying to scalp All-Star tickets at The Ballpark in Arlington.

## Pitching & Defense

Vosberg's best pitch is a sharp-breaking curveball, and it makes him capable of handling the best left-handed hitters if he throws it for a strike. He's always around the plate, but still doesn't get the close-pitch calls when facing a Wade Boggs. Manager Johnny Oates describes him as having "dry hands" in tough situations. He not only has a great pickoff move, but helps his left-handed teammates with their moves. Vosberg remains a fine athlete, competent at fielding his position.

## 1996 Outlook

Vosberg figures to return for a second season with Texas. If he does, it will be the first time he's pitched in the same place two years in a row since he was at Triple-A Las Vegas in 1987-88. He found himself in some save situations late last season and figures to get more this time around. A 15-save season is a possibility.

# Matt Whiteside

**Position**: RP
**Bats**: R **Throws**: R
**Ht**: 6' 0" **Wt**: 205

**Opening Day Age**: 28
**Born**: 8/8/67 in
Charleston, MO
**ML Seasons**: 4

## Overall Statistics

|  | W | L | Pct. | ERA | G | GS | Sv | IP | H | BB | SO | HR | BR/IP |
|---|---|---|---|---|---|---|---|---|---|---|---|---|---|
| 1995 | 5 | 4 | .556 | 4.08 | 40 | 0 | 3 | 53.0 | 48 | 19 | 46 | 5 | 1.26 |
| Career | 10 | 8 | .556 | 4.14 | 167 | 0 | 9 | 215.0 | 220 | 81 | 135 | 19 | 1.40 |

## 1995 Season

With the exception of a stint on the disabled list, righty reliever Matt Whiteside continued last season to show the resilience that makes him valuable. But he also remained inconsistent, having yet to get his big curveball over for strikes. He still hasn't ducked the tendency to give up big-game home runs. Gary Gaetti's blast off Whiteside in early September was a body blow to the Rangers' playoff chances.

## Pitching & Defense

Whiteside improved his change-up while working with pitching coach Dick Bosman, but he basically relies on his curveball, which has a sharp break. He isn't afraid to throw his fastball for strikes, but perhaps he should be. Left-handed hitters tee off on that pitch. On the bright side, he isn't as prone to the dreaded leadoff walk as he was earlier in his career. Whiteside does a fine job of holding runners—he permitted only one steal last year—and he's a fine fielder.

## 1996 Outlook

Whiteside is getting to the point in his career where he needs to either elevate his game or be replaced by someone younger and cheaper. He has yet to fulfill the promise that came with a perfect performance in save situations at three levels in 1992. He figures to get more chances to pitch in the late innings, but his future will depend on how he handles those opportunities.

Texas
Rangers

# Other Texas Rangers

**Jose Alberro** (**Pos**: RHP, **Age**: 27)

A righty reliever, Alberro worked in 12 games with the Rangers last year but struggled with his location. He worked as a starter for the first time in Triple-A, so a swingman role is possible. 1996 Outlook: C

**Steve Buechele** (**Pos**: 3B, **Age**: 34, **Bats**: R)

After being dumped by the Cubs last summer, Buechele went back to the Rangers, his original team. He looked washed up and got dropped again pretty quickly. His career is probably over. 1996 Outlook: D

**Terry Burrows** (**Pos**: LHP, **Age**: 27)

Once considered one of the Rangers' top pitching prospects, Burrows got hit hard in 28 games for the big club last year. Being left-handed and fairly young, he'll probably get more chances. 1996 Outlook: C

**Eric Fox** (**Pos**: OF, **Age**: 32, **Bats**: B)

A fringe player with the A's for several years, Fox got into 10 games for the Rangers last year and went 0-for-15. When you're 32 and a player with marginal skills, that's a problem. 1996 Outlook: D

**Shawn Hare** (**Pos**: RF, **Age**: 29, **Bats**: L)

A line-drive-hitting outfielder with a pretty good minor league record, Hare hasn't shown much in brief trials with the Tigers, Mets and Rangers. He'll need a strong spring to make a major league roster. 1996 Outlook: C.

**Rick Helling** (**Pos**: RHP, **Age**: 25)

A former number-one draft choice, Helling has struggled at both the major league and Triple-A levels over the last two seasons. He's only 25, so there's time to turn it around. 1996 Outlook: C

**Sam Horn** (**Pos**: DH, **Age**: 32, **Bats**: L)

Teams crying for a slugging first baseman or DH could do a lot worse than Horn, who's hit 62 major league homers in a little over 1000 at-bats. He's 32 but can still hit, so there's always a chance. 1996 Outlook: C

**Chris Howard** (**Pos**: LHP, **Age**: 29)

Howard has pitched for three major league teams over the last three years, and his lifetime ERA is 3.13. He's a lefty reliever who can handle left-handed hitters, and a lot of teams could use a guy like that. 1996 Outlook: B

**Candy Maldonado** (**Pos**: OF, **Age**: 35, **Bats**: R)

Maldonado's now 35, but he continued to be a useful player last year, hitting with good power and showing far more patience than in his free-swinging youth. Could help an A.L. team. 1996 Outlook: B

**John Marzano** (**Pos**: C, **Age**: 33, **Bats**: R)

Now 33, Marzano had a big year for the Rangers' Triple-A team last year, hitting .309 with 41 doubles. He might make a roster as a second-string catcher, but his age is against him. 1996 Outlook: C

**Chris Nichting** (**Pos**: RHP, **Age**: 29)

A former Dodger farmhand, Nichting revived his career with some excellent work at the Double- and Triple-A levels the last two years. However, he showed little in 13 games with the Rangers. 1996 Outlook: C

**Scott M. Taylor** (**Pos**: RHP, **Age**: 29)

A well-traveled minor league veteran, Taylor finally got his big chance when the Rangers gave him three starts last year. Unfortunately, he looked awful, giving up six homers and 25 hits in 15.1 innings. 1996 Outlook: C

**Dave Valle** (**Pos**: C, **Age**: 35, **Bats**: R)

The former Mariner catcher get much of a chance to play behind Ivan Rodriguez last year, but he impressed the Rangers with the way he handled the pitching staff. He's signed for '96. 1996 Outlook: B

**Jack Voigt** (**Pos**: RF, **Age**: 29, **Bats**: R)

After struggling with the Rangers in 1995, Voigt was traded to Boston before the trading deadline, but didn't play in September. He showed some promise with Baltimore in 1993, but none since. 1996 Outlook: C

**Craig Worthington** (**Pos**: 3B, **Age**: 30, **Bats**: R)

The Orioles' regular third baseman in 1989-90, Worthington was given a brief opportunity to play with both the Reds and Rangers last year. He's not a bad player and might get another chance this spring. 1996 Outlook: C

# Texas Rangers Minor League Prospects

## Organization Overview:

A few years ago, when the Rangers were in the midst of promoting talent like Juan Gonzalez, Dean Palmer and Ivan Rodriguez, they looked like they might be the class of the A.L. West for years. But the talent pipeline has dried up in recent years, so the Rangers have been forced to patch holes with players obtained via trades, such as Otis Nixon, or through free agency, such as Will Clark. For a while, the Rangers wasted high draft picks by selecting athletes from other sports, such as Donald Harris (football) and Terrell Lowery (basketball), rather than baseball players. The system now looks thin in hitters, especially hitters with power, as well as pitchers with power arms. Many of the Rangers' top prospects competed in the system's lower levels last season and are most likely scheduled to play at Double-A this year. Texas is hopeful that talent can reinvigorate the big league club by the summer of '97.

## Mike Bell

**Position:** 3B      **Opening Day Age:** 21
**Bats:** R **Throws:** R      **Born:** 12/7/74 in
**Ht:** 6' 2" **Wt:** 185      Cincinnati, OH

*Recent Statistics*

|  | G | AB | R | H | D | T | HR | RBI | SB | BB | SO | AVG |
|---|---|---|---|---|---|---|---|---|---|---|---|---|
| 93 R Rangers | 60 | 230 | 48 | 73 | 13 | 6 | 3 | 34 | 9 | 27 | 23 | .317 |
| 94 A Charlstn-SC | 120 | 475 | 58 | 125 | 22 | 6 | 6 | 58 | 16 | 47 | 76 | .263 |
| 95 A Charlotte | 129 | 470 | 49 | 122 | 20 | 1 | 5 | 52 | 9 | 48 | 72 | .260 |

If bloodlines mean anything, Bell should have an excellent shot at a big league career. His grandfather, Gus, and father, Buddy, both enjoyed productive careers, while his brother David made his major league debut last season. Mike was the Rangers' top draft pick in 1993, taken with the supplemental choice awarded after Jose Guzman left as a free agent. Bell is a third baseman like his dad. He hasn't hit with power yet, but that's expected to develop as he matures. Bell will most likely play this season in Double-A.

## Mark Brandenburg

**Position:** P      **Opening Day Age:** 25
**Bats:** R **Throws:** R      **Born:** 7/14/70 in
**Ht:** 6' 0" **Wt:** 170      Houston, TX

*Recent Statistics*

|  | W | L | ERA | G | GS | Sv | IP | H | R | BB | SO | HR |
|---|---|---|---|---|---|---|---|---|---|---|---|---|
| 95 AAA Okla. City | 0 | 5 | 2.02 | 35 | 0 | 2 | 58.0 | 52 | 16 | 15 | 51 | 2 |
| 95 AL Texas | 0 | 1 | 5.93 | 11 | 0 | 0 | 27.1 | 36 | 18 | 7 | 21 | 5 |

Brandenburg a Texas Tech product, wasn't drafted until the 26th round in 1992. He was placed almost immediately in the bullpen by Texas, and doesn't have a fastball that can even be called major league average,

since it rarely leaves the low 80s. Still, in his last four minor league stops Brandenburg has posted successive ERAs of 1.46, 0.87, 1.74 and 2.02. Almost as impressive is the fact that in over 300 minor league innings Brandenburg has surrendered just 10 home runs, including only two at Triple-A Oklahoma City last year. He'll likely never be a stopper in the big leagues, but he can still be an effective set-up man.

## Jim Brower

**Position:** P      **Opening Day Age:** 23
**Bats:** R **Throws:** R      **Born:** 12/29/72 in
**Ht:** 6' 2" **Wt:** 205      Edina, MN

*Recent Statistics*

|  | W | L | ERA | G | GS | Sv | IP | H | R | BB | SO | HR |
|---|---|---|---|---|---|---|---|---|---|---|---|---|
| 94 A Hudson Vall | 2 | 1 | 3.20 | 4 | 4 | 0 | 19.2 | 14 | 10 | 6 | 15 | 0 |
| 94 A Charlstn-SC | 7 | 3 | 1.72 | 12 | 12 | 0 | 78.2 | 52 | 18 | 26 | 84 | 2 |
| 95 A Charlotte | 7 | 10 | 3.89 | 27 | 27 | 0 | 173.2 | 170 | 93 | 62 | 110 | 16 |

The Rangers' system isn't loaded with power pitchers, and Brower is one of the few whose fastball reaches the upper 80s. He also throws a solid breaking ball and change-up. Despite a sparkling professional debut after the Rangers chose him in the seventh round in 1994, Texas resisted the temptation to push him to Double-A last year. Instead, Brower posted a solid though unspectacular season in the Florida State League. Considering the paucity of pitching talent in the Texas organization, Brower now has a chance to move up quickly.

## Kevin Brown

**Position:** C      **Opening Day Age:** 22
**Bats:** R **Throws:** R      **Born:** 4/21/73 in
**Ht:** 6' 2" **Wt:** 200      Valparaiso, IN

*Recent Statistics*

|  | G | AB | R | H | D | T | HR | RBI | SB | BB | SO | AVG |
|---|---|---|---|---|---|---|---|---|---|---|---|---|
| 94 A Hudson Vall | 68 | 232 | 33 | 57 | 19 | 1 | 6 | 32 | 0 | 23 | 86 | .246 |
| 95 A Charlotte | 107 | 355 | 48 | 94 | 25 | 1 | 11 | 57 | 2 | 50 | 96 | .265 |
| 95 AAA Okla. City | 3 | 10 | 1 | 4 | 1 | 0 | 0 | 0 | 0 | 2 | 4 | .400 |

There have been a couple other Kevin Browns to play in the majors in recent years, including the Kevin Brown who pitched briefly for the Mets, Brewers and Mariners, and the Kevin who now pitches for the Orioles but was originally developed by the Rangers. This Kevin Brown is a catcher. He was the Rangers' second-round choice in 1994, but was in fact the first player they selected after losing their number-one pick for the signing of Will Clark. Brown is promising defensively and shows some pop with his bat. He competed in the Florida State League last year, and actually played three games late in the season at Triple-A. With Ivan Rodriguez now catching for Texas, the Rangers are unlikely to rush Brown.

## Edwin Diaz

**Position:** 2B          **Opening Day Age:** 21
**Bats:** R **Throws:** R  **Born:** 1/15/75 in
**Ht:** 5' 11" **Wt:** 170   Bayamon, PR

*Recent Statistics*

|              | G | AB | R | H | D | T | HR | RBI | SB | BB | SO | AVG |
|--------------|---|----|---|---|---|---|----|-----|----|----|----|-----|
| 93 R Rangers | 43 | 154 | 27 | 47 | 10 | 5 | 1 | 23 | 12 | 19 | 21 | .305 |
| 94 A Charlstn-SC | 122 | 413 | 52 | 109 | 22 | 7 | 11 | 60 | 11 | 22 | 107 | .264 |
| 95 A Charlotte | 115 | 450 | 48 | 128 | 26 | 5 | 8 | 56 | 8 | 33 | 94 | .284 |

Most of the Rangers' top prospects played last year in the lower minors, and Diaz is yet another who graduated to fast-A Charlotte from slow-A Charleston. He was a shortstop when drafted in 1993 out of Puerto Rico, but has made the transition to second base. His offensive game shows promise, with some power potential. One area in which Diaz showed improvement while making the jump to a higher level of competition last year was plate discipline, as his walk total rose while his strike-outs dropped.

## Julio Santana

**Position:** P           **Opening Day Age:** 23
**Bats:** R **Throws:** R  **Born:** 1/20/73 in San
**Ht:** 6' 0" **Wt:** 175   Pedro De Macoris, DR

*Recent Statistics*

|              | W | L | ERA | G | GS | Sv | IP | H | R | BB | SO | HR |
|--------------|---|---|-----|---|----|----|----|---|---|----|----|----|
| 94 A Charlstn-SC | 6 | 7 | 2.46 | 16 | 16 | 0 | 91.1 | 65 | 38 | 44 | 103 | 3 |
| 94 AA Tulsa | 7 | 2 | 2.90 | 11 | 11 | 0 | 71.1 | 50 | 26 | 41 | 45 | 1 |
| 95 AAA Okla. City | 0 | 2 | 39.00 | 2 | 2 | 0 | 3.0 | 9 | 14 | 7 | 6 | 3 |
| 95 A Charlotte | 0 | 3 | 3.73 | 5 | 5 | 0 | 31.1 | 32 | 16 | 16 | 27 | 1 |
| 95 AA Tulsa | 6 | 4 | 3.23 | 15 | 15 | 0 | 103.0 | 91 | 40 | 52 | 71 | 8 |

A year ago, Santana was probably the Rangers' hottest prospect. He might still be, but his 1995 campaign was not quite as impressive as 1994, when Santana allowed 115 hits while fanning 148 and compiling a 2.66 ERA in 162.2 innings. He pitched at three levels last year, ascending all the way to Triple-A at age 22. Santana has a fresh arm, since he signed with the Rangers as a shortstop in 1990 and wasn't switched to the mound until three years later. His fastball is his best pitch right now, and he's working on developing a slider that could become another strikeout pitch. Santana may become the Rangers' ace within the next couple years.

## Mike Smith

**Position:** 2B          **Opening Day Age:** 26
**Bats:** R **Throws:** R  **Born:** 12/1/69 in
**Ht:** 6' 0" **Wt:** 180   Piqua, OH

*Recent Statistics*

|              | G | AB | R | H | D | T | HR | RBI | SB | BB | SO | AVG |
|--------------|---|----|---|---|---|---|----|-----|----|----|----|-----|
| 93 A Charlotte | 86 | 327 | 33 | 77 | 16 | 4 | 3 | 43 | 3 | 37 | 55 | .235 |
| 94 A High Desert | 132 | 512 | 96 | 149 | 23 | 6 | 21 | 94 | 28 | 73 | 89 | .291 |
| 95 AA Tulsa | 132 | 499 | 65 | 128 | 22 | 3 | 16 | 64 | 11 | 60 | 72 | .257 |
| 95 MLE | 132 | 491 | 62 | 120 | 20 | 2 | 13 | 61 | 8 | 49 | 77 | .244 |

Smith is 26 now, rather old for a prospect who has yet to play at Triple-A. But you have to notice a second baseman who has hit 16 and 21 homers the past two seasons.

In fact, Smith's 21 homers and 94 RBI in 1994 came while he played at High Desert, an independent team in the California League. Both figures led the club. Smith was originally chosen in the fifth round of 1992 by Texas. He played shortstop while in college at Indiana. Every year is critical for a player of Smith's age who has some obstacles to overcome, but if he continues to produce in Triple-A, he has to be taken seriously as a possible second-base candidate with the Rangers.

## Andy Vessel

**Position:** OF          **Opening Day Age:** 21
**Bats:** R **Throws:** R  **Born:** 3/11/75 in
**Ht:** 6' 3" **Wt:** 205   Richmond, CA

*Recent Statistics*

|              | G | AB | R | H | D | T | HR | RBI | SB | BB | SO | AVG |
|--------------|---|----|---|---|---|---|----|-----|----|----|----|-----|
| 93 R Rangers | 51 | 192 | 23 | 42 | 10 | 2 | 1 | 30 | 6 | 8 | 28 | .219 |
| 94 A Charlstn-SC | 114 | 411 | 40 | 99 | 23 | 2 | 8 | 55 | 7 | 29 | 102 | .241 |
| 95 A Charlotte | 129 | 498 | 67 | 132 | 26 | 2 | 9 | 78 | 3 | 32 | 75 | .265 |

Vessel, the Rangers' third-round pick in 1993, has loads of talent. After hitting just .219 in his first exposure to professional baseball, Vessel's average has actually risen as the level of competition increased, to .241 in the South Atlantic League in 1994, and to .265 in the Florida State League last year. His on-base and slugging percentages have shown similar improvement. Perhaps most encouragingly, Vessel reduced his strikeouts from 102 to 75 despite 87 more at-bats last season. Scouts are impressed with Vessel's speed on the bases as well as the quickness with which he gets his bat through the hitting zone. Even so, he has yet to reach double figures in homers or stolen bases in any season.

## Others to Watch

After pitching out of the bullpen during his first two professional seasons, righthander **Jeff Davis** started 27 games last year with unexpected success (13-7, 2.77 ERA). He even pitched seven shutout innings in his only start following his promotion to Double-A. . . Outfielder **Mark Little** hit 31 doubles and stole 20 bases in the South Atlantic League last season. He also struck out 108 times, too many for a guy with only nine homers. . . Righthander **John Powell** became the NCAA's all-time leading strikeout pitcher while at Auburn. He pitched okay between Single- and Double-A last year (5-5, 3.40 ERA, 74 K in 87.1 IP), but he was no longer exclusively a starter. . . After batting .296 and .293 his first two professional seasons, outfielder **Marc Sagmoen's** production fell dramatically in 1995. He'll need to hit better than the .228 he produced between Double- and Triple-A if he's to keep moving up. . . Third baseman **Fernando Tatis** is one of the few Ranger farmhands with power potential. Tatis hit .303 with 15 taters, 43 doubles and 22 stolen bases at slow-A Charleston, which unfortunately is a long way from the majors.

# Roberto Alomar

## 1995 Season

This 1995 season was both successful and difficult for Roberto Alomar. He was moved to the number-three position in the batting order and concentrated more on power while keeping his average at the .300 mark. He continued to exhibit speed on the basepaths and his defense was as brilliant as ever. However, he also had off-field troubles, including a death threat from a disturbed fan and a season-long contract squabble which may have prevented him from having an even better year. When the year ended Alomar, a free agent, was expected to leave Toronto.

## Hitting

The switch-hitting Alomar has always been a much better hitter from the left side. He generates fine power batting lefty, pulling the ball by shifting all of his weight to his rear leg as he opens up his swing. He's not nearly as good batting righty, as the mechanics of his swing just aren't as smooth. Alomar is an excellent contact hitter who can handle all tough pitches and is very tough to strike out, particularly when he's batting lefty.

## Baserunning & Defense

A perennial Gold Glove winner, Alomar is considered one of the best fielding second baseman in the game. He's very sure-handed, setting an AL record by playing 104 straight errorless games last year, and he often amazes spectators with terrific defensive plays. He is also a legitimate basestealing threat who has twice stolen more than 50 in a season.

## 1996 Outlook

Alomar was coveted by a number of clubs this winter, though his contract demands ($7-8 million per season) narrowed the field. Blue Jays general manager Gord Ash alienated Alomar by dealing David Cone in midyear and by sticking with the club's policy of not negotiating contracts during the season. Alomar figures to have another banner season in 1996. . . but he figures to be doing it in a different uniform.

**Position:** 2B
**Bats:** B **Throws:** R
**Ht:** 6' 0" **Wt:** 185

**Opening Day Age:** 28
**Born:** 2/5/68 in Ponce, PR
**ML Seasons:** 8
**Pronunciation:** AL-a-mar

### Overall Statistics

| | G | AB | R | H | D | T | HR | RBI | SB | BB | SO | Avg | OBP | Slg |
|---|---|---|---|---|---|---|---|---|---|---|---|---|---|---|
| 1995 | 130 | 517 | 71 | 155 | 24 | 7 | 13 | 66 | 30 | 47 | 45 | .300 | .354 | .449 |
| Career | 1151 | 4460 | 697 | 1329 | 230 | 48 | 77 | 499 | 296 | 470 | 522 | .298 | .365 | .423 |

### Where He Hits the Ball

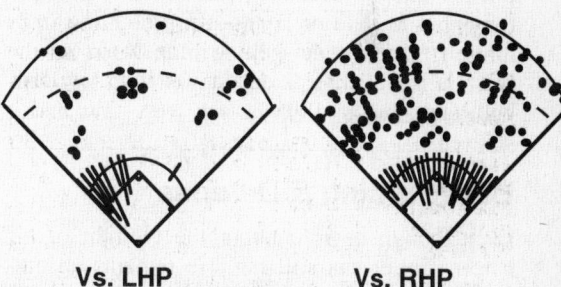

**Vs. LHP**          **Vs. RHP**

### 1995 Situational Stats

| | AB | H | HR | RBI | Avg | | AB | H | HR | RBI | Avg |
|---|---|---|---|---|---|---|---|---|---|---|---|
| Home | 247 | 73 | 7 | 38 | .296 | LHP | 130 | 30 | 2 | 9 | .231 |
| Road | 270 | 82 | 6 | 28 | .304 | RHP | 387 | 125 | 11 | 57 | .323 |
| First Half | 256 | 81 | 10 | 37 | .316 | Sc Pos | 114 | 34 | 1 | 49 | .298 |
| Scnd Half | 261 | 74 | 3 | 29 | .284 | Clutch | 72 | 28 | 2 | 5 | .389 |

### 1995 Rankings (American League)

→ 1st in fielding percentage at second base (.994)
→ 2nd in stolen base percentage (90.9%)
→ 4th in batting average in the clutch (.389)
→ 6th in triples
→ 8th in batting average with the bases loaded (.500) and lowest percentage of swings that missed (10.4%)
→ 9th in stolen bases, lowest on-base percentage vs. left-handed pitchers (.289) and bunts in play (23)
→ Led the Blue Jays in batting average, hits, singles (111), triples, sacrifice flies (7), stolen bases, slugging percentage and stolen base percentage

Toronto Blue Jays

# Joe Carter

## 1995 Season

Joe Carter's reputation as baseball's perennial RBI man took a bit of a hit in 1995, as he failed to reach the 100-RBI plateau for the first time in seven years. Granted it was a short season, but he'd managed 103 RBI in only 111 games the year before. In addition, his homer total dropped to its lowest level since his days in San Diego. But Carter retained his trademark durability while defending multiple outfield positions and first base.

## Hitting

At 36, Carter can still hit the ball with authority, but he seems unable to adjust to the kind of pitching strategies he's seeing these days. Carter is pitched outside constantly, but instead of going to the opposite field or laying off a pitch, he finds himself reaching and getting little wood on the ball. He is still considered a devastating low-fastball hitter, but in 1995 he saw very few, and it showed.

## Baserunning & Defense

Even though he is entering the twilight of his career, Carter can still run. He remains an outstanding percentage basestealer, and has been caught just once in the past two seasons. Carter has always been somewhat inconsistent in the field, and it showed last year in his left-field play. His arm is a little below average for an outfielder, but his versatility remains a strength—he actually manned center field for several games due to injuries to Devon White.

## 1996 Outlook

The Blue Jays are faced with a bit of a puzzle in Carter. He still represents the type of player most teams would want in a cleanup role, but his age and last year's performance should be a concern. It's unlikely he would bring in the type of talent Toronto management is looking for via trade. Carter is in great physical condition, and is a good bet to be reliable. Whether he can regain his 100-RBI form is the big question.

**Position:** LF/CF
**Bats:** R **Throws:** R
**Ht:** 6' 3" **Wt:** 215

**Opening Day Age:** 36
**Born:** 3/7/60 in Oklahoma City, OK
**ML Seasons:** 13

### Overall Statistics

|  | G | AB | R | H | D | T | HR | RBI | SB | BB | SO | Avg | OBP | Slg |
|---|---|---|---|---|---|---|---|---|---|---|---|---|---|---|
| 1995 | 139 | 558 | 70 | 141 | 23 | 0 | 25 | 76 | 12 | 37 | 87 | .253 | .300 | .428 |
| Career | 1749 | 6797 | 959 | 1782 | 345 | 41 | 327 | 1173 | 212 | 419 | 1115 | .262 | .308 | .469 |

### Where He Hits the Ball

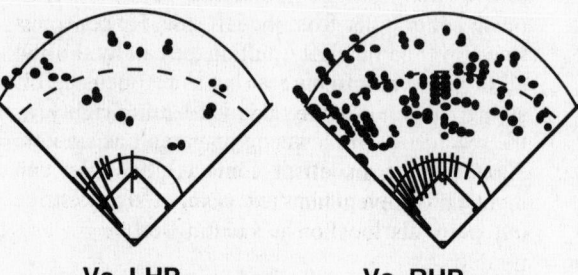

**Vs. LHP**          **Vs. RHP**

### 1995 Situational Stats

|  | AB | H | HR | RBI | Avg |  | AB | H | HR | RBI | Avg |
|---|---|---|---|---|---|---|---|---|---|---|---|
| Home | 275 | 71 | 13 | 34 | .258 | LHP | 136 | 40 | 8 | 20 | .294 |
| Road | 283 | 70 | 12 | 42 | .247 | RHP | 422 | 101 | 17 | 56 | .239 |
| First Half | 256 | 72 | 14 | 42 | .281 | Sc Pos | 157 | 36 | 5 | 50 | .229 |
| Scnd Half | 302 | 69 | 11 | 34 | .228 | Clutch | 88 | 24 | 4 | 11 | .273 |

### 1995 Rankings (American League)

→ 1st in lowest groundball/flyball ratio (0.6), errors in left field (7) and lowest fielding percentage in left field (.971)

→ 2nd in lowest percentage of pitches taken (40.7%)

→ 3rd in lowest on-base percentage and lowest on-base percentage vs. right-handed pitchers (.290)

→ 4th in lowest cleanup slugging percentage (.438)

→ 6th in at-bats, lowest batting average vs. right-handed pitchers (.239) and highest percentage of swings on the first pitch (39.5%)

→ Led the Blue Jays in home runs, at-bats, total bases (239) and RBI

# Tony Castillo

## 1995 Season

Coming off a good season in middle relief in 1994, veteran lefty Tony Castillo became the Blue Jay closer in 1995. Castillo appeared in a career-high 55 games and converted seven saves in a row during July and August, when he was at his best. But he wore down during the latter part of the year, and his lack of a power pitch proved to be a handicap in trying to get those late-inning outs with men on base.

## Pitching

Castillo was forced to change his repertoire as he began to face more righties in the closer role. He still has the big sweeping curve and slider that kept him in baseball as a specialist setting down left-handed batters. But he started going more to his fastball in his new role, throwing it in the 88-89 MPH range and keeping it on the outside edge of the strike zone. By the end of the season, he had actually allowed a lower batting average against righthanders than lefties. However, his age and slight build prevent him from being overpowering, and when his location is not dead-on he is very hittable.

## Defense

Because Castillo is slow to the plate, he can be a target for potential basestealers. But he has a deceptively quick pickoff move and he's done a solid job controlling the running game the past few seasons. He's also proven to be a solid fielding pitcher.

## 1996 Outlook

The Blue Jays will thank Castillo for his moderately successful closer work in '95 but return him to the set-up role this year. He's a good reliever, but the only reason he found himself there in the first place was because no one else could claim the job. Castillo will probably be better off in his old set-up role, to which his stuff is better suited.

**Position:** RP
**Bats:** L  **Throws:** L
**Ht:** 5'10"  **Wt:** 190

**Opening Day Age:** 33
**Born:** 3/1/63 in Lara, VZ
**ML Seasons:** 7
**Pronunciation:** cas-TEE-oh

### Overall Statistics

| | W | L | Pct. | ERA | G | GS | Sv | IP | H | BB | SO | HR | BR/IP |
|---|---|---|---|---|---|---|---|---|---|---|---|---|---|
| 1995 | 1 | 5 | .167 | 3.22 | 55 | 0 | 13 | 72.2 | 64 | 24 | 38 | 7 | 1.21 |
| Career | 18 | 13 | .581 | 3.52 | 259 | 6 | 16 | 342.1 | 348 | 121 | 220 | 29 | 1.37 |

### How Often He Throws Strikes

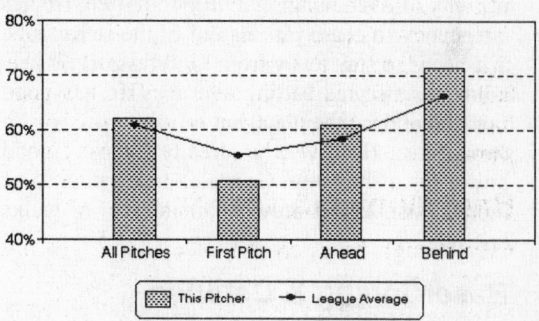

### 1995 Situational Stats

| | W | L | ERA | Sv | IP | | AB | H | HR | RBI | Avg |
|---|---|---|---|---|---|---|---|---|---|---|---|
| Home | 1 | 2 | 1.80 | 4 | 30.0 | LHB | 80 | 21 | 1 | 21 | .263 |
| Road | 0 | 3 | 4.22 | 9 | 42.2 | RHB | 183 | 43 | 6 | 29 | .235 |
| First Half | 0 | 2 | 2.76 | 3 | 42.1 | Sc Pos | 83 | 26 | 1 | 41 | .313 |
| Scnd Half | 1 | 3 | 3.86 | 10 | 30.1 | Clutch | 147 | 36 | 5 | 31 | .245 |

### 1995 Rankings (American League)

- ➡ 1st in lowest save percentage (61.9%)
- ➡ 4th in blown saves (8)
- ➡ 5th in highest percentage of inherited runners scored (47.3%)
- ➡ 6th in relief losses (5) and least strikeouts per 9 innings in relief (4.7)
- ➡ 9th in relief innings (72.2)
- ➡ Led the Blue Jays in games pitched, saves, games finished (31), save opportunities (21), holds (5), save percentage, blown saves, first batter efficiency (.319), relief ERA (3.22), relief losses (5), relief innings and lowest batting average allowed in relief (.243)

Toronto Blue Jays

# Alex Gonzalez

## 1995 Season

Groomed to take over the Toronto shortstop job since the departure of Tony Fernandez, Alex Gonzalez began showing his potential last season. He surprised many with his extra-base power while hitting a respectable .263 during the first half. Youth and overanxious swinging eventually caught up with Gonzalez, inflating his strikeout total after the All-Star break, and his defense also showed some rough edges. But overall Gonzalez had a satisfying season, and it was easy to see why people are so high on him.

## Hitting

As is the case with many young hitters, Gonzalez is guilty of overswinging a little too often. He has a tendency to chase pitches out of the strike zone and needs to stay away from high fastballs if he's going to raise his batting average. He has good fundamentals at the plate, but he often panics with two strikes. However, he already has very good power for a shortstop. Gonzalez is learning to be more selective and drew a fair number of walks last year.

## Baserunning & Defense

Gonzalez had some difficulties at shortstop, recording 17 errors. He has good quickness and a strong arm, but needs to improve his glove work—much of which will come with experience. Strangely, his quickness on the field has not been evident on the bases so far. But his basestealing should improve as he gets to know pitchers' moves better.

## 1996 Outlook

Gonzalez is very young, and his 1995 performance showed enormous promise. He has been deemed the Blue Jays' shortstop of the future, and he figures to be a lot better with a year of experience under his belt. He has both a high level of athleticism and good diamond instincts. It looks like he's going to be a star.

**Position:** SS
**Bats:** R  **Throws:** R
**Ht:** 6' 0"  **Wt:** 182

**Opening Day Age:** 22
**Born:** 4/8/73 in Miami, FL
**ML Seasons:** 2

### Overall Statistics

|  | G | AB | R | H | D | T | HR | RBI | SB | BB | SO | Avg | OBP | Slg |
|---|---|---|---|---|---|---|---|---|---|---|---|---|---|---|
| 1995 | 111 | 367 | 51 | 89 | 19 | 4 | 10 | 42 | 4 | 44 | 114 | .243 | .322 | .398 |
| Career | 126 | 420 | 58 | 97 | 22 | 5 | 10 | 43 | 7 | 48 | 131 | .231 | .310 | .379 |

### Where He Hits the Ball

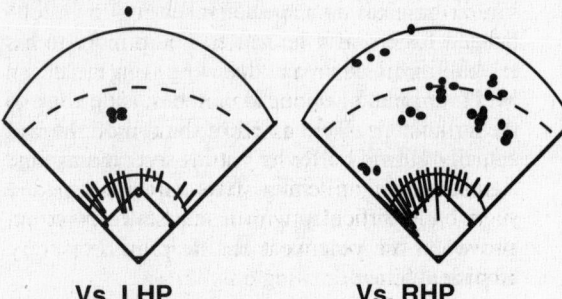

Vs. LHP          Vs. RHP

### 1995 Situational Stats

|  | AB | H | HR | RBI | Avg |  | AB | H | HR | RBI | Avg |
|---|---|---|---|---|---|---|---|---|---|---|---|
| Home | 206 | 54 | 8 | 32 | .262 | LHP | 110 | 30 | 3 | 10 | .273 |
| Road | 161 | 35 | 2 | 10 | .217 | RHP | 257 | 59 | 7 | 32 | .230 |
| First Half | 194 | 51 | 5 | 30 | .263 | Sc Pos | 87 | 24 | 2 | 30 | .276 |
| Scnd Half | 173 | 38 | 5 | 12 | .220 | Clutch | 49 | 12 | 0 | 4 | .245 |

### 1995 Rankings (American League)

→ 1st in lowest fielding percentage at shortstop (.957)
→ 4th in errors at shortstop (17)
→ 7th in highest percentage of swings that missed (28.2%)
→ 8th in strikeouts
→ 9th in sacrifice bunts (9) and lowest percentage of swings put into play (36.8%)
→ Led the Blue Jays in sacrifice bunts, caught stealing (4), strikeouts and on-base percentage vs. left-handed pitchers (.372)

# Shawn Green

**Position:** RF
**Bats:** L  **Throws:** L
**Ht:** 6' 4"  **Wt:** 190

**Opening Day Age:** 23
**Born:** 11/10/72 in Des Plaines, IL
**ML Seasons:** 3

## 1995 Season

The Blue Jays' top draft choice in 1991, Shawn Green reached the majors to stay last year and began to show why he's been considered the club's right fielder of the future. Green bottomed out in June and was hitting just .237 at the All-Star break. But he hit well over .300 from then on, and finished the year with a solid .288 average and 15 homers. Hitting mostly out of the seventh spot, he provided the Jays with strong production from the lower third of their order.

## Hitting

With his lanky frame and smooth swing, Green reminds many scouts of John Olerud. However, Green crouches more at the plate and uncoils with greater force than Olerud did as a rookie. He has excellent plate coverage due to his long reach and will try to pull even outside pitches. He proved to be a quick learner, as his second-half average climbed steadily after he got his second and third looks at enemy pitching staffs. Green seemed to have early difficulty with inside sliders, but improved as the year went on. He proved to be an impatient hitter, drawing only 20 walks.

## Baserunning & Defense

Green has a strong arm and led Toronto outfielders with nine assists, but he also committed six errors and needs to improve his flyball judgment. Green did not show much as a baserunner in his rookie year, but he has good speed and figures to get the go sign more often this year. He has the potential to steal 15-20 bases.

## 1996 Outlook

It's safe to predict that Green's role with Toronto will be bigger this year than it was in 1995. With a successful rookie season under his belt, he'll be expected to provide more power and will likely hit in the middle of the order. Should that occur, look for Green to hit 20-plus homers with better than 80 RBI—goals well within this talented young player's reach.

### Overall Statistics

|  | G | AB | R | H | D | T | HR | RBI | SB | BB | SO | Avg | OBP | Slg |
|---|---|---|---|---|---|---|---|---|---|---|---|---|---|---|
| 1995 | 121 | 379 | 52 | 109 | 31 | 4 | 15 | 54 | 1 | 20 | 68 | .288 | .326 | .509 |
| Career | 138 | 418 | 53 | 112 | 32 | 4 | 15 | 55 | 2 | 21 | 77 | .268 | .306 | .471 |

### Where He Hits the Ball

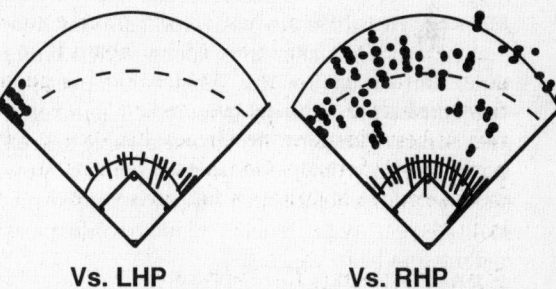

**Vs. LHP**          **Vs. RHP**

### 1995 Situational Stats

|  | AB | H | HR | RBI | Avg |  | AB | H | HR | RBI | Avg |
|---|---|---|---|---|---|---|---|---|---|---|---|
| Home | 182 | 45 | 5 | 26 | .247 | LHP | 45 | 10 | 0 | 4 | .222 |
| Road | 197 | 64 | 10 | 28 | .325 | RHP | 334 | 99 | 15 | 50 | .296 |
| First Half | 156 | 37 | 7 | 22 | .237 | Sc Pos | 110 | 33 | 3 | 38 | .300 |
| Scnd Half | 223 | 72 | 8 | 32 | .323 | Clutch | 56 | 15 | 5 | 7 | .268 |

### 1995 Rankings (American League)

- → 1st in errors in right field (6)
- → 2nd in lowest fielding percentage in right field (.973)
- → 7th in lowest percentage of pitches taken (46.7%)
- → 8th in least GDPs per GDP situation (4.9%)
- → Led the Blue Jays in least GDPs per GDP situation and slugging percentage vs. right-handed pitchers (.533)

**Toronto Blue Jays**

# Juan Guzman

## 1995 Season

Juan Guzman's struggles really began in 1994, when his winning record couldn't hide a 5.68 ERA. Guzman's run support finally dried up last season, and the results weren't very pretty. Injuries played a role in Guzman's poor numbers, as he went on the disabled list twice with a strained right shoulder. But his control remained poor even when he was healthy, and the once-confident Guzman appeared to be a very confused pitcher for much of the year.

## Pitching

There is no question that Guzman's velocity is down from its former 95-MPH level. His fastball topped out at about 92 last year, and then only on occasion. He still has a nasty forkball which he uses in two-strike situations, along with a biting slider. But his control was shakier than ever last year, forcing him to throw an incredible number of pitches each time out. Guzman wasn't able to keep his fastball down and he seemed reluctant to throw his other pitches. His pitch selection caused turmoil all year, with frequent mound conferences and rotating battery mates.

## Defense

Guzman looks at defense and holding runners as afterthoughts. He's not an adept fielder, nor does he have a skillful move to first. Basestealers run on him with great success, stealing 15 against him last year despite his limited workload.

## 1996 Outlook

The best that Toronto management can hope for is that Guzman's health returns, allowing him to pick up better velocity and control. Should his performance continue to deteriorate, the Jays would have to remove him from the rotation and then be saddled with a pitcher who would not be attractive on the trade market. Spring training will be a decisive time for Guzman, and for manager Cito Gaston, who has to make the call.

**Position:** SP
**Bats:** R  **Throws:** R
**Ht:** 5'11"  **Wt:** 195

**Opening Day Age:** 29
**Born:** 10/28/66 in Santo Domingo, DR
**ML Seasons:** 5
**Pronunciation:** GOOZ-man

### Overall Statistics

|        | W  | L  | Pct. | ERA  | G   | GS  | Sv | IP    | H   | BB  | SO  | HR | BR/IP |
|--------|----|----|------|------|-----|-----|----|-------|-----|-----|-----|----|-------|
| 1995   | 4  | 14 | .222 | 6.32 | 24  | 24  | 0  | 135.1 | 151 | 73  | 94  | 13 | 1.66  |
| Career | 56 | 36 | .609 | 4.21 | 133 | 133 | 0  | 823.0 | 760 | 397 | 700 | 62 | 1.41  |

### How Often He Throws Strikes

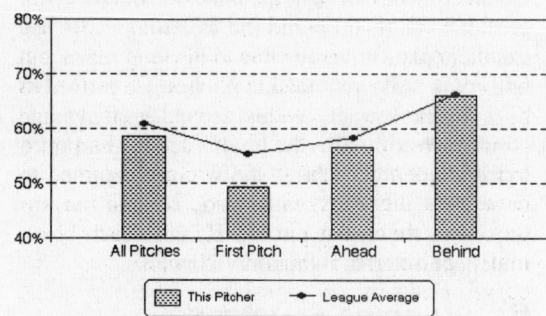

### 1995 Situational Stats

|            | W | L | ERA  | Sv | IP   |       | AB  | H  | HR | RBI | Avg  |
|------------|---|---|------|----|------|-------|-----|----|----|-----|------|
| Home       | 2 | 5 | 5.36 | 0  | 82.1 | LHB   | 298 | 89 | 5  | 48  | .299 |
| Road       | 2 | 9 | 7.81 | 0  | 53.0 | RHB   | 240 | 62 | 8  | 36  | .258 |
| First Half | 2 | 5 | 7.23 | 0  | 61.0 | Sc Pos| 155 | 40 | 2  | 67  | .258 |
| Scnd Half  | 2 | 9 | 5.57 | 0  | 74.1 | Clutch| 35  | 16 | 1  | 9   | .457 |

### 1995 Rankings (American League)

- → 1st in lowest winning percentage (.222)
- → 4th in losses
- → 6th in highest ERA at home (5.36)
- → 10th in pickoff throws (143) and errors at pitcher (2)
- → Led the Blue Jays in losses and pickoff throws

# Pat Hentgen

**Position:** SP
**Bats:** R  **Throws:** R
**Ht:** 6' 2"  **Wt:** 200

**Opening Day Age:** 27
**Born:** 11/13/68 in Detroit, MI
**ML Seasons:** 5
**Pronunciation:** HENT-gen

## 1995 Season

The 1995 season was a difficult one for the Blue Jays as a team, and Pat Hentgen felt a lot of the heat as he endured his first losing season since coming to the majors in 1991. Hentgen posted ERAs above six in both May and June, and never found his groove until September, when he pitched well but won only once because of weak support. Hentgen allowed more hits than innings pitched for the first time in his career, and one outing in Cleveland saw him give up a team-record five homers.

## Pitching

Hentgen presented hitters last year with the same arsenal of pitches which had always worked in the past. His 92-MPH fastball, well-hidden slider and good sloping curveball were all there at times, but he didn't have his usual command of them. His fastball was not as lively in its movement and often flattened out in the hitter's zone. His strike-out-to-walk ratio went in the wrong direction, indicating a slight loss in control. In addition, the lack of a punch-out pitch cost him dearly. Normally poison to right-handed hitters with his curve, Hentgen was constantly forced to pitch from behind in the count and with runners on base, negating his advantage.

## Defense

Generally considered a good-fielding pitcher, Hentgen is mobile after releasing his pitches and comes off the mound quickly. He uses a slide-step to help keep runners in check, and it was effective in '95. Hentgen held the opposition to only nine stolen bases in 16 attempts.

## 1996 Outlook

Considering that Hentgen is only 27 and that his arm appears healthy, he seems a good candidate to bounce back this year. He's under contract for '96, and the Jays will work this spring to make some adjustments to his pitching mechanics. There's a strong chance that he'll again be the ace of the Blue Jay staff.

### Overall Statistics

| | W | L | Pct. | ERA | G | GS | Sv | IP | H | BB | SO | HR | BR/IP |
|---|---|---|---|---|---|---|---|---|---|---|---|---|---|
| 1995 | 10 | 14 | .417 | 5.11 | 30 | 30 | 0 | 200.2 | 236 | 90 | 135 | 24 | 1.62 |
| Career | 47 | 33 | .588 | 4.23 | 119 | 89 | 0 | 649.1 | 663 | 258 | 446 | 80 | 1.42 |

### How Often He Throws Strikes

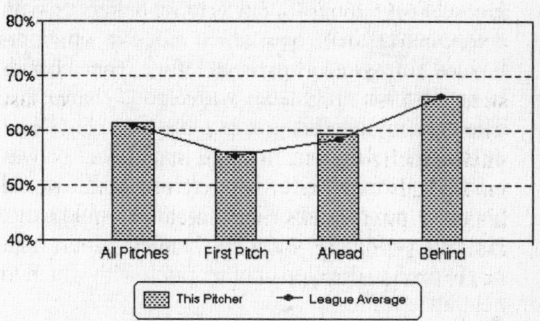

### 1995 Situational Stats

| | W | L | ERA | Sv | IP | | AB | H | HR | RBI | Avg |
|---|---|---|---|---|---|---|---|---|---|---|---|
| Home | 4 | 8 | 5.69 | 0 | 112.1 | LHB | 453 | 135 | 11 | 71 | .298 |
| Road | 6 | 6 | 4.38 | 0 | 88.1 | RHB | 362 | 101 | 13 | 45 | .279 |
| First Half | 6 | 6 | 5.86 | 0 | 90.2 | Sc Pos | 235 | 62 | 5 | 87 | .264 |
| Scnd Half | 4 | 8 | 4.50 | 0 | 110.0 | Clutch | 69 | 14 | 3 | 7 | .203 |

### 1995 Rankings (American League)

- → 1st in hits allowed
- → 2nd in highest batting average allowed (.290), highest on-base percentage allowed (.363) and most baserunners allowed per 9 innings (14.8)
- → 3rd in highest ERA and balks (2)
- → 4th in losses, batters faced (913) and highest ERA at home (5.69)
- → 5th in walks allowed and highest slugging percentage allowed (.444)
- → 7th in pitches thrown (3,396)
- → Led the Blue Jays in losses, games started, innings pitched and hits allowed

# Edwin Hurtado

## 1995 Season

After starting the season at Double-A Knoxville, righthander Edwin Hurtado was called up for good last July to fill a void in Toronto's relief corps. He had several good outings in long relief, and when spot starter Woody Williams was placed on the disabled list, Hurtado joined the starting rotation. He responded exceptionally well, winning four of his first five starts. But his ERA ballooned in August as he became increasingly susceptible to the gopher ball. Hurtado's final numbers weren't great, but he went seven innings or more in six of his 10 starts.

## Pitching

Hurtado's pitching strategy is to set batters up with a 90-plus fastball, one which rides in on right-handed hitters and away from lefties. Then he tries to knock them off balance with a good change-up. The third pitch in his mix is a low-breaking slider designed to complement the fastball. Location was a problem for Hurtado, as often his fastball would get up in the strike zone and his slider would hang. He had problems with left-handed hitters and might need to develop another pitch with which to neutralize lefties.

## Defense

Hurtado fields his position pretty well and is quick to cover first base on right-side grounders. His move to first, featuring a quick body-spin and sharp throw, was very effective as only eight runners attempted to steal against him—a low total considering the number of baserunners he allowed.

## 1996 Outlook

Even though Hurtado had a winning season, his role for 1996 is in question. The Blue Jays intend to go to the market for at least two starters, and Hurtado may find himself back in the bullpen. His league-minimum salary will help his cause, but his ERA will not. He definitely has a future in Toronto but might need more minor league seasoning first.

**Position:** SP
**Bats:** R  **Throws:** R
**Ht:** 6' 3"  **Wt:** 208

**Opening Day Age:** 26
**Born:** 2/1/70 in Barquisimeto, VZ
**ML Seasons:** 1
Pronunciation: her-TAH-doh

### Overall Statistics

|        | W | L | Pct. | ERA  | G  | GS | Sv | IP   | H  | BB | SO | HR | BR/IP |
|--------|---|---|------|------|----|----|----|------|----|----|----|----|-------|
| 1995   | 5 | 2 | .714 | 5.45 | 14 | 10 | 0  | 77.2 | 81 | 40 | 33 | 11 | 1.56  |
| Career | 5 | 2 | .714 | 5.45 | 14 | 10 | 0  | 77.2 | 81 | 40 | 33 | 11 | 1.56  |

### How Often He Throws Strikes

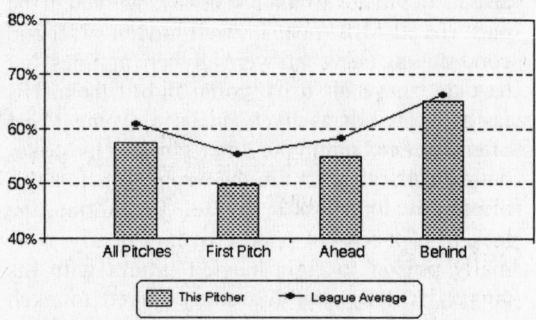

This Pitcher — League Average

### 1995 Situational Stats

|            | W | L | ERA  | Sv | IP   |        | AB  | H  | HR | RBI | Avg  |
|------------|---|---|------|----|------|--------|-----|----|----|-----|------|
| Home       | 2 | 2 | 4.26 | 0  | 38.0 | LHB    | 170 | 50 | 8  | 33  | .294 |
| Road       | 3 | 0 | 6.58 | 0  | 39.2 | RHB    | 125 | 31 | 3  | 14  | .248 |
| First Half | 0 | 0 | 2.25 | 0  | 4.0  | Sc Pos | 70  | 20 | 4  | 35  | .286 |
| Scnd Half  | 5 | 2 | 5.62 | 0  | 73.2 | Clutch | 21  | 10 | 1  | 5   | .476 |

### 1995 Rankings (American League)

➡ 4th in wild pitches (11)

# Al Leiter

## 1995 Season

Rebounding strongly from a rough 1994 campaign, veteran lefty Al Leiter emerged to become Toronto's best overall starter in 1995. Leiter was outstanding in the early going, including one stretch of 23.1 consecutive scoreless innings. He went through a rough stretch in midseason but recovered to finish with 11 wins and a 3.64 ERA, both career bests.

## Pitching

Most scouts feel that Leiter has some of the best stuff of any lefthander in baseball. He has an extremely live fastball that you can hear pop the catcher's mitt from anywhere in the ballpark. It tends to move downward, as do his cutter and hard slider. He also has a big-league curve to keep the hitters honest. What he lacks is consistent control. Even during some of his best performances last year he walked too many batters, and he wound up leading the league in both walks and wild pitches. Fortunately for Leiter, he pitched very well with men on base to help make up for his wildness.

## Defense

Leiter is a good-fielding pitcher who seldom makes an error or wild throw to first. He plays the sacrifice well and gets to first quickly. He has a fine move to first and his low leg-kick allows him to get the ball to the plate in a hurry. Runners had a tough time against Leiter in '95.

## 1996 Outlook

The Blue Jays have indicated that signing Leiter is a priority for next year. He has opted for free agency and may move up significantly in market value from the $795,000 he got in '95. He's 30, but his best days might still be ahead of him if he can improve his control. Being a southpaw enhances his value to any team, and the Jays would certainly like him back.

**Position:** SP
**Bats:** L **Throws:** L
**Ht:** 6' 3" **Wt:** 215

**Opening Day Age:** 30
**Born:** 10/23/65 in Toms River, NJ
**ML Seasons:** 9
**Pronunciation:** LITE-er

### Overall Statistics

|        | W  | L  | Pct. | ERA  | G   | GS | Sv | IP    | H   | BB  | SO  | HR | BR/IP |
|--------|----|----|------|------|-----|----|----|-------|-----|-----|-----|----|-------|
| 1995   | 11 | 11 | .500 | 3.64 | 28  | 28 | 0  | 183.0 | 162 | 108 | 153 | 15 | 1.48  |
| Career | 33 | 32 | .508 | 4.36 | 113 | 83 | 2  | 522.0 | 490 | 309 | 439 | 40 | 1.53  |

### How Often He Throws Strikes

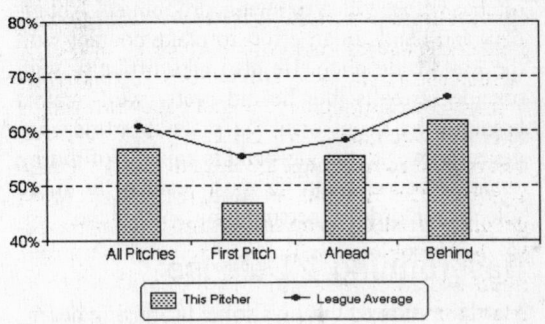

### 1995 Situational Stats

|            | W | L | ERA  | Sv | IP    |        | AB  | H  | HR | RBI | Avg  |
|------------|---|---|------|----|-------|--------|-----|----|----|-----|------|
| Home       | 6 | 4 | 3.05 | 0  | 97.1  | LHB    | 122 | 31 | 4  | 16  | .254 |
| Road       | 5 | 7 | 4.31 | 0  | 85.2  | RHB    | 559 | 131| 11 | 53  | .234 |
| First Half | 5 | 4 | 3.91 | 0  | 76.0  | Sc Pos | 168 | 37 | 2  | 50  | .220 |
| Scnd Half  | 6 | 7 | 3.45 | 0  | 107.0 | Clutch | 36  | 7  | 0  | 2   | .194 |

### 1995 Rankings (American League)

- → 1st in walks allowed, wild pitches (14) and least run support per 9 innings (3.8)
- → 3rd in lowest groundball/flyball ratio allowed (0.9)
- → 4th in lowest slugging percentage allowed (.363) and least GDPs induced per 9 innings (0.5)
- → 5th in runners caught stealing (9), most pitches thrown per batter (3.96) and most strikeouts per 9 innings (7.5)
- → 6th in lowest batting average allowed (.238), least home runs allowed per 9 innings (.74) and lowest batting average allowed with runners in scoring position (.220)

Toronto Blue Jays

# Sandy Martinez

## 1995 Season

It's not often that a Double-A player batting .229 gets called up to the majors to play every other day. But that's exactly what happened to rookie Sandy Martinez when the Blue Jays ran out of patience with catcher Randy Knorr last June. Considering the circumstances, Martinez performed admirably at the plate, hitting .241 overall and .321 with runners in scoring position. But *behind* the plate was a different story, as his lack of experience showed.

## Hitting

Martinez stands in from the left side with a slightly open stance. He showed a tendency to chase low pitches with a golf-type swing, dropping his shoulders and hands in an effort to make contact with the low inside pitch. He also had difficulty with outside fastballs, but he did pretty well against breaking balls out over the plate. Martinez has decent power to the gaps and is capable of hitting some home runs, but he must learn to be more selective in order to see more hittable pitches.

## Baserunning & Defense

Martinez showed the Jays some promising defensive skills behind the plate, but he also displayed a lot of rough edges. He committed five errors and was charged with an ugly 14 passed balls in only 61 games caught. But he displayed a powerful arm and more than held his own controlling the running game. He should become even tougher to steal against as he improves his throwing accuracy. As is the case with most catchers, Martinez is a slow runner and no threat on the bases.

## 1996 Outlook

Martinez will be given every opportunity to make the club this spring, and should have little trouble doing so given the lack of catching depth in the organization. It's possible the club will pursue a free-agent catcher, but in that case Martinez has a strong chance to make the roster as a backup receiver.

**Position:** C
**Bats:** L  **Throws:** R
**Ht:** 6' 2"  **Wt:** 200

**Opening Day Age:** 23
**Born:** 10/3/72 in Villa Mella, DR
**ML Seasons:** 1

### Overall Statistics

|  | G | AB | R | H | D | T | HR | RBI | SB | BB | SO | Avg | OBP | Slg |
|---|---|---|---|---|---|---|---|---|---|---|---|---|---|---|
| 1995 | 62 | 191 | 12 | 46 | 12 | 0 | 2 | 25 | 0 | 7 | 45 | .241 | .270 | .335 |
| Career | 62 | 191 | 12 | 46 | 12 | 0 | 2 | 25 | 0 | 7 | 45 | .241 | .270 | .335 |

### Where He Hits the Ball

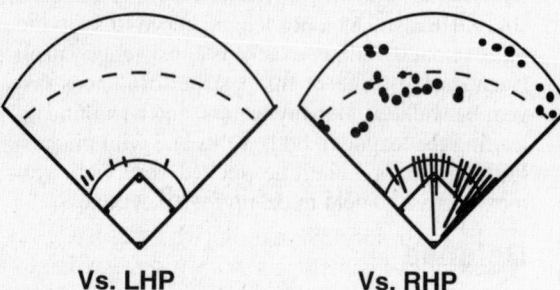

Vs. LHP          Vs. RHP

### 1995 Situational Stats

|  | AB | H | HR | RBI | Avg |  | AB | H | HR | RBI | Avg |
|---|---|---|---|---|---|---|---|---|---|---|---|
| Home | 80 | 18 | 1 | 7 | .225 | LHP | 17 | 2 | 0 | 1 | .118 |
| Road | 111 | 28 | 1 | 18 | .252 | RHP | 174 | 44 | 2 | 24 | .253 |
| First Half | 27 | 7 | 1 | 3 | .259 | Sc Pos | 53 | 17 | 2 | 24 | .321 |
| Scnd Half | 164 | 39 | 1 | 22 | .238 | Clutch | 25 | 7 | 1 | 7 | .280 |

### 1995 Rankings (American League)

➡ 2nd in lowest batting average with two strikes (.108)
➡ 9th in errors at catcher (5)

# Paul Molitor

## 1995 Season

Future Hall of Famer Paul Molitor reached several milestones during 1995. But the season had to be considered a disappointment for Molitor, as his averaged dipped to .270—fortunate, considering that he was struggling at .236 at the All-Star break. Nagging injuries slowed Molitor's bat and affected his confidence. Moved to the number-two spot in the order early in the season, he finally regained his traditional form late in the campaign.

## Hitting

Molitor is a case study in concentration and efficiency. He is a screaming line-drive hitter with occasional home-run power who will hit to both gaps for an abundance of doubles. His level swing has no wasted motion, and he's particularly dangerous with men on base. Molitor is usually a deadly fastball hitter, but minor aches and pains prevented him from turning on the inside stuff early in the season.

## Baserunning & Defense

Molitor is a spry 39 year old who still has good speed. Picking his spots with his usual intelligence, he swiped 12 bases without getting caught last year, making him a perfect 32-for-32 over the last two seasons. He uses that same intelligence when running the bases, where he's still one of the best in the business. Molitor spent all of last year as a designated hitter, but he can do an adequate job at first base in an emergency.

## 1996 Outlook

The Blue Jays didn't pick up their option on Molitor for 1996, and he wound up signing with the Minnesota Twins, where he'll play just across the river from his hometown, St. Paul. His quest for 3,000 hits will likely require two more years of service, and he seems pretty certain to do it. Barring injury, look for Molitor to have a much better season in 1996.

**Position:** DH
**Bats:** R  **Throws:** R
**Ht:** 6' 0"  **Wt:** 190

**Opening Day Age:** 39
**Born:** 8/22/56 in St. Paul, MN
**ML Seasons:** 18
**Pronunciation:** MOLL-uh-ter
**Nickname:** The Igniter

### Overall Statistics

|  | G | AB | R | H | D | T | HR | RBI | SB | BB | SO | Avg | OBP | Slg |
|---|---|---|---|---|---|---|---|---|---|---|---|---|---|---|
| 1995 | 130 | 525 | 63 | 142 | 31 | 2 | 15 | 60 | 12 | 61 | 57 | .270 | .350 | .423 |
| Career | 2261 | 9135 | 1545 | 2789 | 503 | 97 | 211 | 1036 | 466 | 948 | 1058 | .305 | .370 | .451 |

### Where He Hits the Ball

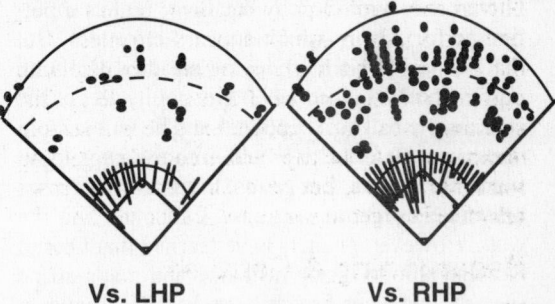

Vs. LHP          Vs. RHP

### 1995 Situational Stats

|  | AB | H | HR | RBI | Avg |  | AB | H | HR | RBI | Avg |
|---|---|---|---|---|---|---|---|---|---|---|---|
| Home | 252 | 68 | 6 | 24 | .270 | LHP | 111 | 31 | 4 | 18 | .279 |
| Road | 273 | 74 | 9 | 36 | .271 | RHP | 414 | 111 | 11 | 42 | .268 |
| First Half | 233 | 55 | 7 | 32 | .236 | Sc Pos | 115 | 35 | 1 | 38 | .304 |
| Scnd Half | 292 | 87 | 8 | 28 | .298 | Clutch | 86 | 19 | 2 | 12 | .221 |

### 1995 Rankings (American League)

→ Led the Blue Jays in highest groundball/flyball ratio (1.4)

# John Olerud

## 1995 Season

John Olerud had a career year by anyone's standards in 1993, when he led the American League with a .363 average and drove in 107 runs. But Olerud hasn't come anywhere close to approaching those numbers over the last two seasons. After hitting .297 in 1994, Olerud reached the All-Star break last year with a lowly .246 average. For the first time since early in his career, he found hiself riding the bench against certain left-handed pitchers. He hit much better during the latter portion of the season, but his power production remained disappointing.

## Hitting

Olerud didn't hit .363 by accident; he has a picture-perfect swing which appears effortless. But that swing has been producing steadily declining power numbers since 1993. His ability to put the stick on the ball is exceptional and he will seldom strike out. He can drive balls into the gaps to all fields. He's also a very patient hitter who increases his value by getting on base frequently via the walk. However, pitchers have learned that Olerud is vulnerable to inside fastballs, and that's all he seems to get when he comes up in RBI situations.

## Baserunning & Defense

Olerud is a vastly underrated first sacker. His 6'5" frame enables him to cover a lot of turf and presents a large target for infielders to throw to. He is also very adept at picking balls up on the short hop. Olerud's baserunning can best be described as "slow and deliberate." He has stolen only one base in his career and did not notch a triple in 1995.

## 1996 Outlook

The Blue Jays are re-tooling their organization and Olerud's name has been circulated in the press as possible trade bait. But given his expensive contract and the team's other priorities, there's a strong chance that he'll be back. While his power production has been disappointing, he'll be an important contributor if he keeps swinging the bat as well as he did late last year.

**Position:** 1B
**Bats:** L  **Throws:** L
**Ht:** 6' 5"   **Wt:** 220

**Opening Day Age:** 27
**Born:** 8/5/68 in Seattle, WA
**ML Seasons:** 7
**Pronunciation:** OHL-uh-rood

### Overall Statistics

|        | G   | AB   | R   | H   | D   | T | HR | RBI | SB | BB  | SO  | Avg  | OBP  | Slg  |
|--------|-----|------|-----|-----|-----|---|----|-----|----|-----|-----|------|------|------|
| 1995   | 135 | 492  | 72  | 143 | 32  | 0 | 8  | 54  | 0  | 84  | 54  | .291 | .398 | .404 |
| Career | 795 | 2705 | 405 | 801 | 188 | 6 | 91 | 410 | 2  | 454 | 393 | .296 | .397 | .471 |

### Where He Hits the Ball

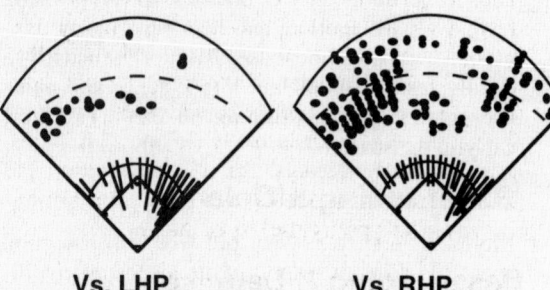

**Vs. LHP**          **Vs. RHP**

### 1995 Situational Stats

|            | AB  | H  | HR | RBI | Avg  |        | AB  | H  | HR | RBI | Avg  |
|------------|-----|----|----|-----|------|--------|-----|----|----|-----|------|
| Home       | 237 | 64 | 1  | 18  | .270 | LHP    | 143 | 37 | 1  | 17  | .259 |
| Road       | 255 | 79 | 7  | 36  | .310 | RHP    | 349 | 106| 7  | 37  | .304 |
| First Half | 248 | 61 | 3  | 21  | .246 | Sc Pos | 142 | 35 | 1  | 45  | .246 |
| Scnd Half  | 244 | 82 | 5  | 33  | .336 | Clutch | 74  | 20 | 0  | 7   | .270 |

### 1995 Rankings (American League)

- ➡ 3rd in lowest percentage of extra bases taken as a runner (29.2%)
- ➡ 4th in fielding percentage at first base (.997)
- ➡ 6th in GDPs (17) and highest percentage of swings put into play (53.4%)
- ➡ 7th in on-base percentage vs. right-handed pitchers (.422)
- ➡ 9th in intentional walks (10)
- ➡ 10th in walks and errors at first base (4)
- ➡ Led the Blue Jays in doubles, walks, intentional walks, times on base (231), on-base percentage, on-base percentage vs. right-handed pitchers and batting average on the road (.310)

# Lance Parrish

## 1995 Season

Veteran catcher Lance Parrish found himself in a Toronto uniform last year after Pat Borders signed with Kansas City and young Carlos Delgado proved unable to handle the position. Brought in to provide experience behind Randy Knorr, the 39-year-old Parrish played a lot more than anticipated, getting 49 starts behind the plate. His throwing arm was as strong as ever, but he struggled with just a .202 batting average. Parrish's main contribution was his behind-the-scenes tutoring of rookie catcher Sandy Martinez.

## Hitting

Parrish has long been a one-dimensional hitter who swings for the seats and hopes for the best. He relies on getting the fastball within his power groove, hoping to use his uppercut swing to hit the ball deep. But last year the home runs came few and far between. At his age he's virtually helpless against any pitch not in his wheelhouse, particularly offspeed offerings. An impatient hitter, he doesn't draw many walks, and if he's not hitting for power he's pretty useless in the lineup.

## Baserunning & Defense

Parrish is very slow and a station-to-station runner on base hits. He didn't commit an error in 1995, but that doesn't take into account the nine passed balls charged against him; he just doesn't have the mobility needed to block pitches any more. Although his reflexes have slowed, Parrish's arm still has plenty of life, and he gunned out baserunners at a 40-percent clip last season.

## 1996 Outlook

Parrish has played for five teams in the last four years, and he might be changing addresses again this season as the Blue Jays probably won't invite him back. He wants to keep playing and his asking price will be low. He can still throw, so despite his woeful offensive performance last year, it's possible that he'll make somebody's roster again this spring.

**Position:** C
**Bats:** R  **Throws:** R
**Ht:** 6' 3"  **Wt:** 225

**Opening Day Age:** 39
**Born:** 6/15/56 in Clairton, PA
**ML Seasons:** 19

### Overall Statistics

|  | G | AB | R | H | D | T | HR | RBI | SB | BB | SO | Avg | OBP | Slg |
|---|---|---|---|---|---|---|---|---|---|---|---|---|---|---|
| 1995 | 70 | 178 | 15 | 36 | 9 | 0 | 4 | 22 | 0 | 15 | 52 | .202 | .265 | .320 |
| Career | 1988 | 7067 | 856 | 1782 | 305 | 27 | 324 | 1070 | 28 | 612 | 1527 | .252 | .313 | .440 |

### Where He Hits the Ball

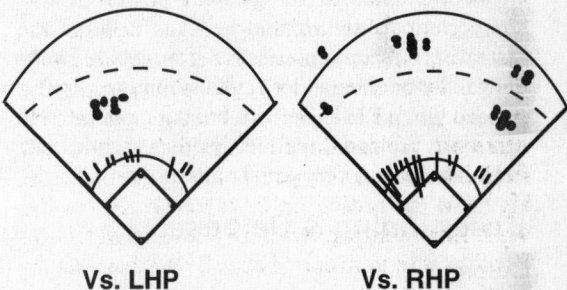

**Vs. LHP**          **Vs. RHP**

### 1995 Situational Stats

|  | AB | H | HR | RBI | Avg |  | AB | H | HR | RBI | Avg |
|---|---|---|---|---|---|---|---|---|---|---|---|
| Home | 100 | 23 | 4 | 16 | .230 | LHP | 58 | 12 | 0 | 7 | .207 |
| Road | 78 | 13 | 0 | 6 | .167 | RHP | 120 | 24 | 4 | 15 | .200 |
| First Half | 118 | 23 | 3 | 9 | .195 | Sc Pos | 58 | 13 | 2 | 19 | .224 |
| Scnd Half | 60 | 13 | 1 | 13 | .217 | Clutch | 33 | 6 | 1 | 6 | .182 |

### 1995 Rankings (American League)

- ➡ 2nd in highest percentage of runners caught stealing as a catcher (39.7%)
- ➡ 6th in lowest batting average on a 3-2 count (.067)

Toronto Blue Jays

# Ed Sprague

## 1995 Season

One of Toronto's most durable players, Ed Sprague played every game of the 1995 season while serving as the only infielder in the lineup who provided consistent power. Sprague smacked a career-high 18 home runs and for a time it looked like he was going to step out of the shadows and become a team leader. But Sprague endured a poor second half at the plate, hitting just .226 after the All-Star break. However, his steady presence at third base remained an asset to the club all year.

## Hitting

Sprague employs a slightly closed batting stance and stands close to the plate, which results in frequent plunkings. He gets his power from a short, compact swing, and he likes to drive the fastball. His main weakness is the curveball. Pitchers will "work the ladder" against Sprague, trying to keep him off balance with breaking pitches. He had more problems with lefties than righties last year, but that's not his usual pattern.

## Baserunning & Defense

Despite committing 16 errors, Sprague had a pretty good year in the field. He has a good arm and will sacrifice his body in front of a hot smash. He's not overly quick on balls hit down the line, but goes to his glove side exceptionally well. He has poor baserunning speed and has attempted just five stolen bases in his career.

## 1996 Outlook

Since it's unlikely that Sprague will ever hit for a high average, he must continue the upward trend in his power numbers to remain an everyday player. But he's a pretty sure bet to open 1996 as Toronto's third baseman. Economics have become a priority with the Blue Jays and Sprague's low salary is one factor in his favor.

**Position:** 3B
**Bats:** R  **Throws:** R
**Ht:** 6' 2"  **Wt:** 210

**Opening Day Age:** 28
**Born:** 7/25/67 in Castro Valley, CA
**ML Seasons:** 5
**Pronunciation:** SPRAYG

### Overall Statistics

|  | G | AB | R | H | D | T | HR | RBI | SB | BB | SO | Avg | OBP | Slg |
|---|---|---|---|---|---|---|---|---|---|---|---|---|---|---|
| 1995 | 144 | 521 | 77 | 127 | 27 | 2 | 18 | 74 | 0 | 58 | 96 | .244 | .333 | .407 |
| Career | 486 | 1679 | 188 | 421 | 86 | 4 | 46 | 218 | 2 | 135 | 326 | .251 | .318 | .389 |

### Where He Hits the Ball

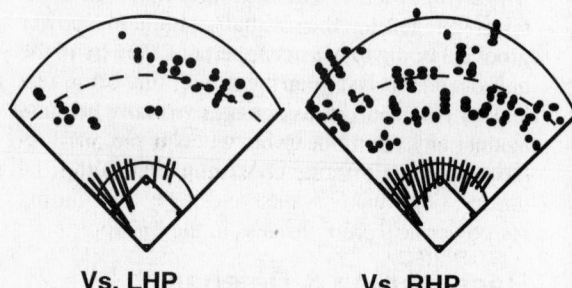

**Vs. LHP**          **Vs. RHP**

### 1995 Situational Stats

|  | AB | H | HR | RBI | Avg |  | AB | H | HR | RBI | Avg |
|---|---|---|---|---|---|---|---|---|---|---|---|
| Home | 252 | 61 | 12 | 39 | .242 | LHP | 135 | 30 | 5 | 14 | .222 |
| Road | 269 | 66 | 6 | 35 | .245 | RHP | 386 | 97 | 13 | 60 | .251 |
| First Half | 238 | 63 | 11 | 35 | .265 | Sc Pos | 153 | 31 | 3 | 53 | .203 |
| Scnd Half | 283 | 64 | 7 | 39 | .226 | Clutch | 80 | 20 | 4 | 11 | .250 |

### 1995 Rankings (American League)

- ➙ 1st in hit by pitch (15)
- ➙ 3rd in GDPs (18), games played, errors at third base (16) and fielding percentage at third base (.958)
- ➙ 4th in lowest batting average with runners in scoring position (.203)
- ➙ 5th in lowest batting average at home (.242)
- ➙ 7th in lowest batting average and lowest on-base percentage vs. left-handed pitchers (.282)
- ➙ 8th in lowest batting average vs. left-handed pitchers (.222)
- ➙ Led the Blue Jays in runs scored, sacrifice flies (7), hit by pitch, GDPs, pitches seen (2,324) and games played

# Mike Timlin

## 1995 Season

Mike Timlin missed considerable time with injuries in 1995, but when he was healthy he was Toronto's most effective reliever. Timlin missed all of July and half of August after arthroscopic surgery to remove bone chips in his right elbow. But he returned from the DL to retire the first 19 batters he faced. Overall, Timlin recorded five saves and posted the lowest ERA of his career.

## Pitching

As with most power relievers, Timlin relies on two basic pitches. He will come directly at the hitter with a ripping 94-MPH fastball and then use his sharp-breaking slider, which he saves especially for right-handed hitters. The slider is less effective against lefthanders, making him somewhat vulnerable to them. The difference in Timlin in '95 compared to other years was that he had greater command of his pitches and got ahead in the count more consistently. He was touched for only one homer all year as he consistently kept the ball down.

## Defense

Timlin is a large man who throws hard, which affects his fielding balance after his delivery. Despite that, he's proven to be very solid in the field. Timlin has a decent move to first, pays close attention to runners and delivers the ball quickly to the plate, making it difficult for runners to steal.

## 1996 Outlook

Injuries have plagued Timlin since 1992, when he had his first elbow operation. The jury is still out as to whether he has the stuff to be a full-time closer rather than a set-up man. The tools are there but he's never really established himself as a closer in his brief opportunities at the job. The Jays will bank on him to at least be their set-up man while they shop for a quality closer; if they don't find one, Timlin could get an extended look.

**Position:** RP
**Bats:** R **Throws:** R
**Ht:** 6' 4" **Wt:** 210

**Opening Day Age:** 30
**Born:** 3/10/66 in Midland, TX
**ML Seasons:** 5

### Overall Statistics

|  | W | L | Pct. | ERA | G | GS | Sv | IP | H | BB | SO | HR | BR/IP |
|---|---|---|---|---|---|---|---|---|---|---|---|---|---|
| 1995 | 4 | 3 | .571 | 2.14 | 31 | 0 | 5 | 42.0 | 38 | 17 | 36 | 1 | 1.31 |
| Career | 19 | 14 | .576 | 3.73 | 208 | 3 | 12 | 289.2 | 281 | 134 | 243 | 19 | 1.43 |

### How Often He Throws Strikes

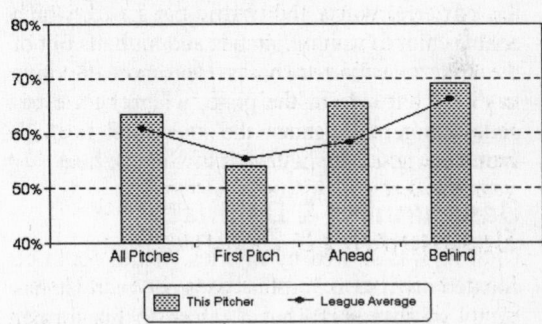

This Pitcher  —— League Average

### 1995 Situational Stats

|  | W | L | ERA | Sv | IP |  | AB | H | HR | RBI | Avg |
|---|---|---|---|---|---|---|---|---|---|---|---|
| Home | 4 | 3 | 2.25 | 1 | 28.0 | LHB | 94 | 28 | 1 | 12 | .298 |
| Road | 0 | 0 | 1.93 | 4 | 14.0 | RHB | 63 | 10 | 0 | 6 | .159 |
| First Half | 3 | 1 | 3.63 | 3 | 22.1 | Sc Pos | 48 | 12 | 1 | 17 | .250 |
| Scnd Half | 1 | 2 | 0.46 | 2 | 19.2 | Clutch | 94 | 24 | 1 | 17 | .255 |

### 1995 Rankings (American League)

→ 10th in highest percentage of inherited runners scored (44.4%)
→ Led the Blue Jays in lowest percentage of inherited runners scored

Toronto
Blue Jays

# Devon White

## 1995 Season

Devon White was enjoying a productive season until the last day of August, when he fractured a bone in his right foot and was sidelined for the remainder of the year. His .283 average was the best of his career, and he earned his fifth consecutive Gold Glove. Aches and pains had also plagued White in 1994 as well, but didn't force him out of the lineup as they did in '95. Through it all, White still represented that rare combination of speed and power from the leadoff position.

## Hitting

White is an impatient switch-hitter who walks infrequently and strikes out too often. But he also has powerful wrists and terrific bat speed, which enables him to wait on pitches and hit balls out of the strike zone for extra bases. He is more effective from the left side of the plate, where he's especially dangerous against the knee-high fastball. From the right side, he favors low inside heat.

## Baserunning & Defense

Until he was slowed by injuries, White could be counted on to steal 30-plus bases per year. He has plenty of speed left, but a return to his former stolen-base level is unlikely. White's outfield abilities remain rank among baseball's best. While he does not have a powerful arm, it is accurate and runners know he's unlikely to throw off line or wild.

## 1996 Outlook

Free agency arrived for White and he took advantage by signing a new three-year contract with the Florida Marlins. The Fish, of course, play their home games in Joe Robbie Stadium, which features natural grass. This might not bode well for White's production as a Marlin. Over the last five seasons, he hit .287 with extra-base power on artificial turf, but just .246 with little power on real grass. And at 33, he's not likely to get better.

**Position:** CF
**Bats:** B  **Throws:** R
**Ht:** 6' 2"  **Wt:** 190

**Opening Day Age:** 33
**Born:** 12/29/62 in Kingston, Jamaica
**ML Seasons:** 11

### Overall Statistics

|  | G | AB | R | H | D | T | HR | RBI | SB | BB | SO | Avg | OBP | Slg |
|---|---|---|---|---|---|---|---|---|---|---|---|---|---|---|
| 1995 | 101 | 427 | 61 | 121 | 23 | 5 | 10 | 53 | 11 | 29 | 97 | .283 | .334 | .431 |
| Career | 1268 | 4942 | 789 | 1284 | 246 | 58 | 131 | 515 | 249 | 353 | 1047 | .260 | .313 | .413 |

### Where He Hits the Ball

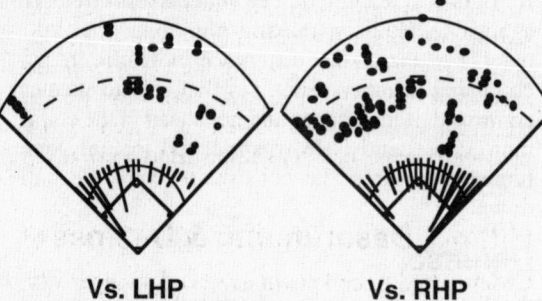

**Vs. LHP**  **Vs. RHP**

### 1995 Situational Stats

|  | AB | H | HR | RBI | Avg |  | AB | H | HR | RBI | Avg |
|---|---|---|---|---|---|---|---|---|---|---|---|
| Home | 210 | 63 | 4 | 24 | .300 | LHP | 100 | 23 | 1 | 13 | .230 |
| Road | 217 | 58 | 6 | 29 | .267 | RHP | 327 | 98 | 9 | 40 | .300 |
| First Half | 233 | 69 | 8 | 33 | .296 | Sc Pos | 82 | 28 | 3 | 42 | .341 |
| Scnd Half | 194 | 52 | 2 | 20 | .268 | Clutch | 56 | 19 | 3 | 13 | .339 |

### 1995 Rankings (American League)

- → 2nd in batting average with the bases loaded (.667)
- → 6th in errors in center field (3)
- → 7th in fielding percentage in center field (.989) and lowest percentage of swings put into play (36.6%)
- → 8th in lowest on-base percentage for a leadoff hitter (.335)
- → 9th in batting average with runners in scoring position (.341)
- → Led the Blue Jays in batting average with runners in scoring position, batting average with the bases loaded, on-base percentage for a leadoff hitter and batting average at home (.300)

# Domingo Cedeno

**Position**: SS/2B
**Bats**: B **Throws**: R
**Ht**: 6' 0" **Wt**: 170

**Opening Day Age**: 27
**Born**: 11/4/68 in La Romana, DR
**ML Seasons**: 3
**Pronunciation**: suh-DAYN-yoh

## Overall Statistics

| | G | AB | R | H | D | T | HR | RBI | SB | BB | SO | Avg | OBP | Slg |
|---|---|---|---|---|---|---|---|---|---|---|---|---|---|---|
| 1995 | 51 | 161 | 18 | 38 | 6 | 1 | 4 | 14 | 0 | 10 | 35 | .236 | .289 | .360 |
| Career | 113 | 304 | 37 | 65 | 8 | 4 | 4 | 31 | 2 | 21 | 76 | .214 | .265 | .306 |

## 1995 Season

After backing up Roberto Alomar for a couple of seasons, Domingo Cedeno moved to the other side of the infield in 1995, playing the majority of his innings at shortstop. His glove work was fine and he displayed occasional power, but Cedeno struggled with his hitting after getting off to a promising start.

## Hitting, Baserunning & Defense

Cedeno used to be known as a wild swinger who would strike out about every third at-bat. But he has cut down on his swing and his strikeouts, and even learned to take a pitch or two. He can surprise pitchers with unexpected power from both sides of the plate but needs to relax more when batting with men on base. Cedeno's glove is what gets him playing time, as he is a very adept fielder at both second and short with a better-than-average arm. Cedeno possesses good speed on the basepaths but does not show the first-step quickness needed for stealing.

## 1996 Outlook

Cedeno's future could be bright in Toronto—Roberto Alomar has gone to free agency, and Alex Gonzalez might be moved to third if the Jays decide to trade Ed Sprague, opening up the shortstop spot as well. At second, Cedeno would be challenged by Tomas Perez, with prospects Tilson Brito and Felipe Crespo also in the wings.

# Danny Cox

**Position**: RP
**Bats**: R **Throws**: R
**Ht**: 6' 4" **Wt**: 250

**Opening Day Age**: 36
**Born**: 9/21/59 in Northhampton, England
**ML Seasons**: 11

## Overall Statistics

| | W | L | Pct. | ERA | G | GS | Sv | IP | H | BB | SO | HR | BR/IP |
|---|---|---|---|---|---|---|---|---|---|---|---|---|---|
| 1995 | 1 | 3 | .250 | 7.40 | 24 | 0 | 0 | 45.0 | 57 | 33 | 38 | 4 | 2.00 |
| Career | 74 | 75 | .497 | 3.64 | 278 | 174 | 8 | 1298.0 | 1292 | 432 | 723 | 102 | 1.33 |

## 1995 Season

An oft-injured pitcher who revived his career after arriving in Toronto and becoming a full-time relief pitcher in 1993, Danny Cox struggled through a horrible, injury-plagued 1995. The big righthander was erratic on the hill, sustained neck and back injuries, went through rehabilitation at Triple-A Syracuse, and saw his ERA soar to the highest level of his career.

## Pitching & Defense

Until last year, Cox had a very live fastball in the 90-plus category, as well as a tough slider. But injuries over the past two seasons have dropped his velocity and cut down the break of his slider. These pitches have become flat for Cox, and the results were ugly last season—he allowed an average of two baserunners per inning. Cox is also slow moving off the mound and prone to making errors. His move to first is average at best, and runners have been very active attempting to steal against him.

## 1996 Outlook

Cox has opted for free agency and the Blue Jays will not be anxious to re-sign him. His age and injury status will certainly hurt him, but he does have World Series experience and may find a club wishing to employ his services.

Toronto Blue Jays

# Tim Crabtree

**Position**: RP
**Bats**: R **Throws**: R
**Ht**: 6' 4"  **Wt**: 195

**Opening Day Age**: 26
**Born**: 10/13/69 in Jackson, MI
**ML Seasons**: 1

### Overall Statistics

|  | W | L | Pct. | ERA | G | GS | Sv | IP | H | BB | SO | HR | BR/IP |
|---|---|---|---|---|---|---|---|---|---|---|---|---|---|
| 1995 | 0 | 2 | .000 | 3.09 | 31 | 0 | 0 | 32.0 | 30 | 13 | 21 | 1 | 1.34 |
| Career | 0 | 2 | .000 | 3.09 | 31 | 0 | 0 | 32.0 | 30 | 13 | 21 | 1 | 1.34 |

## 1995 Season

Recalled last June from Triple-A Syracuse, rookie righthander Tim Crabtree opened some eyes in Toronto. Crabtree didn't allow an earned run in his first eight outings, then survived a shaky August to finish strongly. By season's end he had proven to be one of the few reliable bullpen pitchers the Blue Jays had in 1995. He was particularly tough against right-handed batters, who hit just .167 against him.

## Pitching & Defense

Blessed with a hard slider and a sinking fastball, Crabtree is very effective at keeping the ball down and inducing ground balls. At 26, he needs to gain a bit more control and have better mental preparation when coming in to face the first batter. He also may need to develop another pitch to use against lefties, who gave him some problems last year. Crabtree fields his position well and is agile coming off the mound, but his move to first needs a little work.

## 1996 Outlook

The Blue Jays have plenty of openings in their bullpen this year and Crabtree seems like a good bet to fill one of them. A starting pitcher until fairly recently, he figures to improve as he gets more experience in relief. He might even get an opportunity to close some games.

# Carlos Delgado

Pivotal Season

**Position**: LF
**Bats**: L **Throws**: R
**Ht**: 6' 3"  **Wt**: 206

**Opening Day Age**: 23
**Born**: 6/25/72 in Aguadilla, PR
**ML Seasons**: 3
Pronunciation: del-GAH-doh

### Overall Statistics

|  | G | AB | R | H | D | T | HR | RBI | SB | BB | SO | Avg | OBP | Slg |
|---|---|---|---|---|---|---|---|---|---|---|---|---|---|---|
| 1995 | 37 | 91 | 7 | 15 | 3 | 0 | 3 | 11 | 0 | 6 | 26 | .165 | .212 | .297 |
| Career | 82 | 222 | 24 | 43 | 5 | 0 | 12 | 35 | 1 | 32 | 72 | .194 | .300 | .378 |

## 1995 Season

After a splashy debut early in 1994, much was expected of Carlos Delgado. But that was before people realized that he couldn't hit a major league curve. Delgado was given another chance in '95 in left field but failed to make the grade. He spent most of the year at Triple-A Syracuse, where he flourished once again.

## Hitting, Baserunning & Defense

Delgado can hit fastballs for tape-measure distance. But his problems with major league curveballs have become legendary. While he may take a little time to develop, Delgado's minor league record is so outstanding that he seems certain to become a major league power hitter sooner or later. He does not possess good speed, either on the basepaths or in the outfield. He's adequate defensively in left field, but his arm is average at best. His catching days are almost certainly over.

## 1996 Outlook

Delgado doesn't have anything left to prove at the minor league level, and he figures to make the Jays' roster this spring. But they'll need to find a spot for him. With both Joe Carter and John Olerud under contract, only the DH spot seems available. One way or another, he's got to play.

# Darren Hall

**Position**: RP
**Bats**: R  **Throws**: R
**Ht**: 6' 3"  **Wt**: 205

**Opening Day Age**: 31
**Born**: 7/14/64 in
Marysville, OH
**ML Seasons**: 2

## Overall Statistics

|  | W | L | Pct. | ERA | G | GS | Sv | IP | H | BB | SO | HR | BR/IP |
|---|---|---|---|---|---|---|---|---|---|---|---|---|---|
| 1995 | 0 | 2 | .000 | 4.41 | 17 | 0 | 3 | 16.1 | 21 | 9 | 11 | 2 | 1.84 |
| Career | 2 | 5 | .286 | 3.75 | 47 | 0 | 20 | 48.0 | 47 | 23 | 39 | 5 | 1.46 |

## 1995 Season

Minor league veteran Darren Hall was a pleasant surprise to the Blue Jays in 1994, coming out of nowhere to save 17 games as a 29-year-old rookie. Hall got off to a strong start in 1995, beginning the year with seven scoreless outings. But recurring elbow problems led to surgery in August, putting a damper on any hopes Hall had for a good season. Hall finished the year on the injured list and then signed with the Dodgers after refusing a minor league assignment.

## Pitching & Defense

Hall's pitching arsenal is very similar to that of most top closers. He throws a heavy fastball in the low 90s, and mixes in a "pull the string" curve and a good slider. He keeps his pitches down in the strike zone, resulting in numerous ground balls. Holding runners is an area he'll need to improve, as his move to first is below average. He's considered an average fielder who covers bunts well.

## 1996 Outlook

Hall's hopes of making the Dodger staff depend mostly on the condition of his elbow. While he doesn't figure to be a closer candidate, he's capable of helping his new club in middle relief. . . . if the elbow is healthy. He may need to start the year in the minors and work his way back to the big club.

# Michael Huff

**Position**: CF/RF
**Bats**: R  **Throws**: R
**Ht**: 6' 1"  **Wt**: 190

**Opening Day Age**: 32
**Born**: 8/11/63 in
Honolulu, HI
**ML Seasons**: 6

## Overall Statistics

|  | G | AB | R | H | D | T | HR | RBI | SB | BB | SO | Avg | OBP | Slg |
|---|---|---|---|---|---|---|---|---|---|---|---|---|---|---|
| 1995 | 61 | 138 | 14 | 32 | 9 | 1 | 1 | 9 | 1 | 22 | 21 | .232 | .337 | .333 |
| Career | 358 | 772 | 108 | 193 | 42 | 6 | 9 | 75 | 19 | 108 | 141 | .250 | .349 | .355 |

## 1995 Season

Filling his usual role as a backup outfielder in 1995, veteran Michael Huff was hampered by injuries and a first-half slump. Huff spent two stints on the disabled list with leg injuries, and when he played he was unable to sustain any consistency. As a result, his numbers took a huge tumble from their solid 1994 level. He did hit better during the second half, but he never looked like the .304 hitter he'd been in '94.

## Hitting, Baserunning & Defense

Huff was a tentative hitter for much of 1995, often looking hesitant to swing. It seemed like he was always behind in the count. Huff has limited power and will go the opposite way trying to prevent that third strike. Both his solid baserunning and fine defense in the outfield are the result of intelligence and heads-up play rather than pure speed. Always one to hit the right cutoff man or take the appropriate base on a running play, Huff shows sound baseball instincts.

## 1996 Outlook

Assigned to Triple-A Syracuse after the season, Huff might have trouble making the Toronto roster this spring. However, he's fashioned a career as a useful fourth or fifth outfielder and is likely to return to the majors sometime in 1995.

Toronto
Blue Jays

# Randy Knorr

**Position**: C
**Bats**: R **Throws**: R
**Ht**: 6' 2" **Wt**: 215

**Opening Day Age**: 27
**Born**: 11/12/68 in San Gabriel, CA
**ML Seasons**: 5
**Pronunciation**: NOR

## Overall Statistics

| | G | AB | R | H | D | T | HR | RBI | SB | BB | SO | Avg | OBP | Slg |
|---|---|---|---|---|---|---|---|---|---|---|---|---|---|---|
| 1995 | 45 | 132 | 18 | 28 | 8 | 0 | 3 | 16 | 0 | 11 | 28 | .212 | .273 | .341 |
| Career | 135 | 377 | 50 | 88 | 13 | 2 | 15 | 57 | 0 | 32 | 98 | .233 | .294 | .398 |

## 1995 Season

Expected to replace Pat Borders as Toronto's number-one catcher, Randy Knorr was injured for much of the year and unproductive when available. Knorr fractured his thumb on the last day of June and wasn't reactivated for six weeks. The Jays seemed in no hurry to return a .212 hitter to their lineup. Like Carlos Delgado, Knorr simply was not ready to be Toronto's everyday catcher.

## Hitting, Baserunning & Defense

Knorr likes to extend his arms early in the swing by locking his elbows, similar to a hammer throw. He generates good power from his shoulders but does not make contact often enough to be considered dangerous. His poor knowledge of the strike zone continues, and he's struck out three times for every walk in his major league career. Knorr does not run the bases particularly well, either, and his normally sound defense was missing last year. He couldn't stop opposing baserunners, and he committed eight errors and eight passed balls in only 45 games.

## 1996 Outlook

Since the Blue Jays have decided Delgado is better suited for the outfield and Lance Parrish will not be back, Knorr finds himself competing with only Sandy Martinez for the catching role. . . for now, anyway. The Jays weren't happy with Knorr last year and might bring in yet another receiver to work with Martinez. That would leave Knorr in search of another team.

# Woody Williams

**Position**: RP/SP
**Bats**: R **Throws**: R
**Ht**: 6' 0" **Wt**: 190

**Opening Day Age**: 29
**Born**: 8/19/66 in Houston, TX
**ML Seasons**: 3

## Overall Statistics

| | W | L | Pct. | ERA | G | GS | Sv | IP | H | BB | SO | HR | BR/IP |
|---|---|---|---|---|---|---|---|---|---|---|---|---|---|
| 1995 | 1 | 2 | .333 | 3.69 | 23 | 3 | 0 | 53.2 | 44 | 28 | 41 | 6 | 1.34 |
| Career | 5 | 6 | .455 | 3.84 | 91 | 3 | 0 | 150.0 | 128 | 83 | 121 | 13 | 1.41 |

## 1995 Season

Righthander Woody Williams started the year in the Toronto bullpen, pitched pretty well, and was moved into the rotation in July when the Jays gave up on veteran Danny Darwin. Williams responded with a solid performance in three starts but developed an inflamed right shoulder. He was placed on the 15-day disabled list in mid-July and did not pitch again for the rest of the season.

## Pitching & Defense

Williams throws multiple-speed fastballs and a decent curveball. He attempts to be a location pitcher rather than a fireballer and so far has been pretty successful with that philosophy. He knows how to pitch out of tight situations from his bullpen experience, and can be very tough when he gets ahead in the count. He's downright poor at holding runners, but is a mistake-free fielder.

## 1996 Outlook

Williams will probably return to the role of long reliever and spot starter, depending on what the Jays pick up in the market for their starting rotation. His versatility remains a big strength, as he's proven solid in both roles. His shoulder has had plenty of rest and Williams should be ready for action this spring.

# Other Toronto Blue Jays

### Giovanni Carrara (Pos: RHP, Age: 28)

After a mediocre start at Triple-A, Carrara started seven games for Toronto and was terrible. He moved to the bullpen after that, appearing five more times. At age 28, his role as a starter may be over. 1996 Outlook: C

### Brad Cornett (Pos: RHP, Age: 27)

After pitching at Toronto early in the season, Cornett was placed on the DL in May. He's shown great stuff in the minors, and at 27 he has a chance to bounce back. 1996 Outlook: C

### Ricardo Jordan (Pos: LHP, Age: 25)

Jordan struggled early in Syracuse but was called up in June anyway, and pitched very poorly in 15 games. He has shown flashes of brilliance in the minors, so there is hope. 1996 Outlook: C

### Paul Menhart (Pos: RHP, Age: 27)

After missing most of 1994 on the DL, Menhart split his time as a starter and reliever for the Blue Jays in 1995, pitching poorly in both roles. He has been a good strikeout pitcher, and is far from done. 1996 Outlook: B

### Tomas Perez (Pos: SS, Age: 22, Bats: B)

Perez started most of September for the Blue Jays and struggled at the plate. But he's only 22, so there's plenty of time to develop. Alex Gonzalez is the shortstop of the future, so Perez will have to move if he wants to play. 1996 Outlook: C

### Ken Robinson (Pos: RHP, Age: 26)

Robinson appears to have a great future, allowing just 25 hits in 39 relief innings with Toronto. He's been a very good strikeout pitcher in the minors, which is what you look for in a young hurler. 1996 Outlook: A

### Jimmy Rogers (Pos: RHP, Age: 29)

Given his horrible record of elbow injuries, Rogers will probably get very few opportunities. He pitched very poorly for Toronto in 1995, with serious control problems. 1996 Outlook: C

### Duane Ward (Pos: RHP, Age: 31)

After the season of his life in 1993, Ward has missed most of the past two seasons with shoulder problems. His Toronto and rehab stints were both horrible. If Todd Worrell can come back, maybe Ward can, too. 1996 Outlook: C

### Jeff Ware (Pos: RHP, Age: 25)

Ware was called up in September, starting five games for the Blue Jays and pitching decently in three of them. He has shown poor control and has a history of injuries, so it'll be an uphill fight. 1996 Outlook: C

Toronto
Blue Jays

# Toronto Blue Jays Minor League Prospects

## Organization Overview:

It was a rapid descent for the Blue Jays from World Champions in 1993 to the worst record in baseball two years later. Their vaunted farm system was supposed to prevent such a precipitous slide, but Toronto has had difficulty producing quality pitchers. In addition, megaprospects Carlos Delgado and Alex Gonzalez have yet to make an impact. A trendsetter in global scouting, the Blue Jays have been forced to compete with more teams recently when scouring the world for prospects. All is not doom and gloom for Toronto, however. Shawn Green had a solid rookie season, catcher Sandy Martinez appears to be a force defensively, and Delgado and Gonzalez could yet fulfill their vast potential. In addition, years of solid drafting has filled the system with talented prospects. If a couple of power pitchers come through as the Blue Jays hope, Toronto might return to postseason contention almost as fast as they fell from it.

## Howard Battle

**Position:** 3B     **Opening Day Age:** 24
**Bats:** R **Throws:** R     **Born:** 3/25/72 in Biloxi,
**Ht:** 6' 0" **Wt:** 197     MS

### Recent Statistics

| | G | AB | R | H | D | T | HR | RBI | SB | BB | SO | AVG |
|---|---|---|---|---|---|---|---|---|---|---|---|---|
| 95 AAA Syracuse | 118 | 443 | 43 | 111 | 17 | 4 | 8 | 48 | 10 | 39 | 73 | .251 |
| 95 AL Toronto | 9 | 15 | 3 | 3 | 0 | 0 | 0 | 0 | 1 | 4 | 8 | .200 |
| 95 MLE | 118 | 433 | 35 | 101 | 15 | 3 | 7 | 40 | 7 | 32 | 78 | .233 |

Battle regressed a bit at Syracuse last year. His batting average, homers, RBI and stolen bases all suffered drop-offs, even though it was his second season in Triple-A. Before 1995, Battle had made steady progress through the Toronto system, knocking off one level a year since his selection by the Blue Jays in the fourth round in the 1990 draft. Battle looked like a legitimate power prospect when he belted 20 homers in the South Atlantic League in 1991, and followed with 17 more in the pitcher-friendly Florida State League the following year. He will play this season at age 24, and still has time to rebound.

## Chris Carpenter

**Position:** P     **Opening Day Age:** 20
**Bats:** R **Throws:** R     **Born:** 4/27/75 in
**Ht:** 6' 6" **Wt:** 220     Exeter, NH

### Recent Statistics

| | W | L | ERA | G | GS | Sv | IP | H | R | BB | SO | HR |
|---|---|---|---|---|---|---|---|---|---|---|---|---|
| 94 R Medicne Hat | 6 | 3 | 2.76 | 15 | 15 | 0 | 84.2 | 76 | 40 | 39 | 80 | 3 |
| 95 A Dunedin | 3 | 5 | 2.17 | 15 | 15 | 0 | 99.1 | 83 | 29 | 50 | 56 | 3 |
| 95 AA Knoxville | 3 | 7 | 5.18 | 12 | 12 | 0 | 64.1 | 71 | 47 | 31 | 53 | 3 |

Carpenter was the Blue Jays' top pick in 1993, and is almost certainly the best prospect produced by New Hampshire since Carlton Fisk. Carpenter was Toronto's compensation pick for losing Tom Henke to Texas. He seems to be on the Blue Jays' fast track, as he ascended to Double-A at the age of 20 last year, in just his second professional season. Despite the fine ERA at Dunedin, Carpenter's strikeout-to-walk ratio would tend to indicate that he was less than overpowering. The competition caught up to him at Knoxville, and he would seem to need more time there to gather his bearings.

## Felipe Crespo

**Position:** 2B     **Opening Day Age:** 23
**Bats:** B **Throws:** R     **Born:** 3/5/73 in Rio
**Ht:** 5' 11" **Wt:** 190     Piedras, PR

### Recent Statistics

| | G | AB | R | H | D | T | HR | RBI | SB | BB | SO | AVG |
|---|---|---|---|---|---|---|---|---|---|---|---|---|
| 93 A Dunedin | 96 | 345 | 51 | 103 | 16 | 8 | 6 | 39 | 18 | 47 | 40 | .299 |
| 94 AA Knoxville | 129 | 502 | 74 | 135 | 30 | 4 | 8 | 49 | 20 | 57 | 95 | .269 |
| 95 AAA Syracuse | 88 | 347 | 56 | 102 | 20 | 5 | 13 | 41 | 12 | 41 | 56 | .294 |
| 95 MLE | 88 | 338 | 46 | 93 | 18 | 4 | 12 | 34 | 9 | 34 | 60 | .275 |

Crespo has flipped between second and third base the last couple years. He was back at second in '95 after the Blue Jays traded Chris Stynes to the Royals. Crespo hits well enough to play either position. He draws his share of walks, doesn't appear to be a wild swinger, has the speed to steal a few bases, and boosted his homers to a career-high 13 last season. He's relatively young and could be the heir to Roberto Alomar should the free-agent second sacker depart.

## Tom Evans

**Position:** 3B     **Opening Day Age:** 21
**Bats:** R **Throws:** R     **Born:** 7/9/74 in
**Ht:** 6' 1" **Wt:** 180     Kirkland, WA

### Recent Statistics

| | G | AB | R | H | D | T | HR | RBI | SB | BB | SO | AVG |
|---|---|---|---|---|---|---|---|---|---|---|---|---|
| 93 A Hagerstown | 119 | 389 | 47 | 100 | 25 | 1 | 7 | 54 | 9 | 53 | 61 | .257 |
| 94 A Hagerstown | 95 | 322 | 52 | 88 | 16 | 2 | 13 | 48 | 2 | 51 | 80 | .273 |
| 95 A Dunedin | 130 | 444 | 63 | 124 | 29 | 3 | 9 | 66 | 7 | 51 | 80 | .279 |

Evans has posted the exact same number of walks and strikeouts the past two seasons, which isn't a bad development, considering that he moved to a tougher A league in 1995. At Dunedin he sacrificed a few home runs for more doubles, which may have resulted from the bigger ballparks of the Florida State League. Evans was a pitcher/third baseman coming out of high school, so he definitely has the arm to play the hot corner, if not the quick feet necessary.

## Robert Perez

**Position:** OF　　　　**Opening Day Age:** 26
**Bats:** R **Throws:** R　　**Born:** 6/4/69 in Edo
**Ht:** 6' 3"　**Wt:** 195　　Bolivar, Venezuela

### Recent Statistics

|  | G | AB | R | H | D | T | HR | RBI | SB | BB | SO | AVG |
|---|---|---|---|---|---|---|---|---|---|---|---|---|
| 95 AAA Syracuse | 122 | 502 | 70 | 172 | 38 | 6 | 9 | 67 | 7 | 13 | 60 | .343 |
| 95 AL Toronto | 17 | 48 | 2 | 9 | 2 | 0 | 1 | 3 | 0 | 0 | 5 | .188 |
| 95 MLE | 122 | 486 | 58 | 156 | 35 | 4 | 8 | 55 | 5 | 10 | 64 | .321 |

Perez has proven all he really has to in the minors. The guy can hit, as evidenced by his .343 average in Triple-A last year. Perez has now played in 731 minor league games since beginning his pro career in 1990, and is a .296 lifetime hitter with lots of doubles and occasional home-run power. You have to be skeptical, though, about the long-term prospects for a hitter who drew just 13 walks in over 500 at-bats last year. Still, at age 26, he could be an effective right-handed bat off the Toronto bench.

## Jose Pett

**Position:** P　　　　**Opening Day Age:** 20
**Bats:** R **Throws:** R　　**Born:** 1/8/76 in Sao
**Ht:** 6' 6"　**Wt:** 210　　Paulo, Brazil

### Recent Statistics

|  | W | L | ERA | G | GS | Sv | IP | H | R | BB | SO | HR |
|---|---|---|---|---|---|---|---|---|---|---|---|---|
| 93 R Blue Jays | 1 | 1 | 3.60 | 4 | 4 | 0 | 10.0 | 10 | 4 | 3 | 7 | 0 |
| 94 A Dunedin | 4 | 8 | 3.77 | 15 | 15 | 0 | 90.2 | 103 | 47 | 20 | 49 | 1 |
| 95 AA Knoxville | 8 | 9 | 4.26 | 26 | 25 | 0 | 141.2 | 132 | 87 | 48 | 89 | 16 |

Pett is the much-celebrated Brazilian that the Blue Jays signed at the age of 16, outbidding a half-dozen other organizations with a $700,000 bonus. When he signed, Pett was already 6'6" but weighed just 190 pounds. He has since added about 20 pounds to his frame and could add even more velocity to his good fastball as he fills out further. Despite pitching just 100.2 professional innings before 1995, Pett pitched at Double-A Knoxville all season, and he wasn't overwhelmed. And he didn't leave his teens until this January. He could become a Brazilian phenomenon if he reaches the majors.

## Jose Silva

**Position:** P　　　　**Opening Day Age:** 22
**Bats:** R **Throws:** R　　**Born:** 12/19/73 in
**Ht:** 6' 5"　**Wt:** 210　　Tijuana, Mexico

### Recent Statistics

|  | W | L | ERA | G | GS | Sv | IP | H | R | BB | SO | HR |
|---|---|---|---|---|---|---|---|---|---|---|---|---|
| 93 A Hagerstown | 12 | 5 | 2.52 | 24 | 24 | 0 | 142.2 | 103 | 50 | 62 | 161 | 6 |
| 94 A Dunedin | 0 | 2 | 3.77 | 8 | 7 | 0 | 43.0 | 41 | 32 | 24 | 41 | 4 |
| 94 AA Knoxville | 4 | 8 | 4.14 | 16 | 16 | 0 | 91.1 | 89 | 47 | 31 | 71 | 9 |
| 95 AA Knoxville | 0 | 0 | 9.00 | 3 | 0 | 0 | 2.0 | 3 | 2 | 6 | 2 | 0 |

Silva was probably the Blue Jays top pitching prospect a year ago, but his 1995 season was ruined by a serious offseason car accident in which he suffered major facial damage. When he returned to the mound, he sustained elbow problems when his throwing arm repeatedly hit the brace on his left knee during his follow-through. The elbow was scoped, and he should be able to regain the mid-90s fastball he possessed before all the difficulties. His state of recovery, mentally as well as physically, will determine where he begins 1996. The Blue Jays would like him to play in Triple-A.

## Shannon Stewart

**Position:** OF　　　　**Opening Day Age:** 22
**Bats:** R **Throws:** R　　**Born:** 2/25/74 in
**Ht:** 6' 1"　**Wt:** 185　　Cincinnati, OH

### Recent Statistics

|  | G | AB | R | H | D | T | HR | RBI | SB | BB | SO | AVG |
|---|---|---|---|---|---|---|---|---|---|---|---|---|
| 95 AA Knoxville | 138 | 498 | 89 | 143 | 24 | 6 | 5 | 55 | 42 | 89 | 61 | .287 |
| 95 AL Toronto | 12 | 38 | 2 | 8 | 0 | 0 | 0 | 1 | 2 | 5 | 5 | .211 |
| 95 MLE | 138 | 487 | 78 | 132 | 22 | 5 | 5 | 48 | 31 | 66 | 66 | .271 |

The Blue Jays pushed Stewart from slow-A Hagerstown to Double-A Knoxville last season, and he handled the jump well. Most impressively, his walk total exploded, increasing roughly 75 percent to 89 bases on balls in 498 at-bats. He continued to use his speed to his advantage as well, swiping a career-high 42 bases. The Blue Jays selected Stewart in the first round in 1992 and talked him out of a football scholarship to Florida State. He had been hampered with injuries since signing, playing no more than 75 games in any season before 1995. With Devon White leaving for Florida, Stewart may get a crack at the center-field job in Toronto this spring.

## Others to Watch

The Blue Jays received righthander **Marty Janzen** in the package from the Yankees for David Cone. Janzen finished 16-6 overall last season, with a 2.87 ERA. . . First baseman **Ryan Jones**, a second-round pick in 1993, hit .249 with 18 homers and 78 RBI at Dunedin last year. It virtually duplicated his previous season, although he did reduce his strikeout rate sharply. . . Righthander **Mark Sievert** is a long way from the majors, but he was 12-6 with a 2.91 ERA at Class-A Hagerstown last season. He also allowed just 126 hits in 160.2 innings. . . Reliever **Brian Smith** also pitched in the South Atlantic League and posted gaudy stats (9-1, 21 saves, 0.87 ERA). He was only a 27th-round draft pick in 1994, but a pitcher with a strikeout-to-walk ratio of 101-16 has to be considered a prospect. . . **Paul Spoljaric** was back in Triple-A last year, pitching mostly in relief. He continued to struggle with his control (54 walks in 87.2 IP), but he's a lefthander who throws hard, so he will likely be back in the majors before long. . . **Kevin Witt**, Toronto's top pick in 1994, showed great power for a shortstop in slow-A ball last year (14 HR, 35 doubles in 479 AB). However, he hit just .232 with few walks and one stolen base.

**Toronto Blue Jays**

357

# National League Players

# Steve Avery

## 1995 Season

Steve Avery got off to a solid start in 1995, and by the end of May it looked as if he had put his 1994 troubles behind him. However, as the summer months rolled around Avery began to struggle. Things got so bad for Avery that many Braves fans were calling for him to be traded. However, after a mid-September consultation with Don Sutton, Avery responded with five solid outings to end the season on a positive note. His finest moment came in Game 4 of the World Series, when he held the Indians to one run in six innings.

## Pitching

Avery throws a low-90s fastball, an overhand curve and a change-up. Although he favors the fastball, Avery is most effective when he is throwing his other two pitches for strikes—something he did a lot of in 1995. Despite his difficulties last season, Avery has apparently mastered the control problems he experienced early in his career. He established a career-high strikeout total and kept his walk total at the same low level as 1994. Avery has averaged over 180-plus innings in his six major league seasons and can usually be counted on to last at least six innings.

## Defense & Hitting

Annually among the league leaders in pickoffs, Avery continued this trend with a major league-leading 13 pickoffs in 1995. However, despite his good pickoff move, Avery still has trouble controlling the running game. His slow delivery to the plate allows the baserunner to get a great jump and makes it nearly impossible for his catcher to throw out potential basestealers. Avery is a good hitter and an excellent bunter.

## 1996 Outlook

Although he has been healthy in his first six seasons, Avery has already logged nearly 1,000 innings, which would normally be worrisome for a pitcher not yet 26 years old. However, the Braves are very careful with their starters, who rarely miss a start. His season-ending resurgence and his youth suggest that he'll rebound with a solid 1996.

**Position:** SP
**Bats:** L **Throws:** L
**Ht:** 6' 4" **Wt:** 205

**Opening Day Age:** 25
**Born:** 4/14/70 in Trenton, MI
**ML Seasons:** 6

### Overall Statistics

| | W | L | Pct. | ERA | G | GS | Sv | IP | H | BB | SO | HR | BR/IP |
|---|---|---|---|---|---|---|---|---|---|---|---|---|---|
| 1995 | 7 | 13 | .350 | 4.67 | 29 | 29 | 0 | 173.1 | 165 | 52 | 141 | 22 | 1.25 |
| Career | 65 | 52 | .556 | 3.75 | 179 | 178 | 0 | 1091.1 | 1034 | 331 | 729 | 93 | 1.25 |

### How Often He Throws Strikes

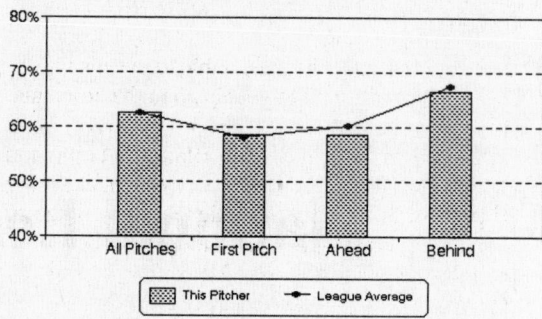

### 1995 Situational Stats

| | W | L | ERA | Sv | IP | | AB | H | HR | RBI | Avg |
|---|---|---|---|---|---|---|---|---|---|---|---|
| Home | 4 | 5 | 4.35 | 0 | 82.2 | LHB | 93 | 18 | 0 | 7 | .194 |
| Road | 3 | 8 | 4.96 | 0 | 90.2 | RHB | 563 | 147 | 22 | 77 | .261 |
| First Half | 4 | 5 | 4.19 | 0 | 86.0 | Sc Pos | 139 | 39 | 6 | 58 | .281 |
| Scnd Half | 3 | 8 | 5.15 | 0 | 87.1 | Clutch | 23 | 5 | 0 | 2 | .217 |

### 1995 Rankings (National League)

- → 1st in stolen bases allowed (30)
- → 2nd in least GDPs induced per 9 innings (0.3)
- → 4th in pickoff throws (191)
- → 5th in losses and highest ERA on the road (4.96)
- → 6th in highest ERA and home runs allowed
- → 7th in runners caught stealing (11), lowest winning percentage and most home runs allowed per 9 innings (1.14)
- → 9th in complete games (3), highest strikeout/walk ratio (2.7), least run support per 9 innings (4.4) and most strikeouts per 9 innings (7.3)
- → Led the Braves in sacrifice bunts (8), losses, games started and home runs allowed

# Jeff Blauser

## 1995 Season

As bad as things were for Jeff Blauser in 1994, he probably never imagined what would become of his offensive abilities in 1995. Batting second in the order for most of the season, Blauser struggled offensively and was eventually dropped to eighth. He recorded career lows in batting average, on-base percentage and slugging percentage. To top it all off, Blauser's season came to a disappointing end when he bruised his thigh and was dropped from the World Series roster. As one of the few players left who suffered through Atlanta's last-place seasons of the late '80s, it was obviously tough for Blauser to watch the Braves win their championship without him.

## Hitting

In the past, Blauser has been able to use his superb strike-zone judgment to get ahead in the count and force pitchers to throw what he loves best: fastballs. Last year, however, Blauser's command of the zone slipped, and he struck out an alarming 25 percent of the time, the highest percentage of his career. One thing that did not escape him, though, was his power—he hit double-digit home runs for the fifth time in his career, which is excellent for a shortstop.

## Baserunning & Defense

Much maligned for his defense early in his career, Blauser has become a consistent fielder. How consistent? He's fielded at a .970 clip—the Atlanta record—in each of the last three seasons. The key to Blauser's defensive success is his positioning, but he also has good range, a strong arm and soft hands. Though not exceptionally fast, Blauser is a smart and aggressive baserunner. His eight stolen bases in 1995 represent the second-highest total of his career.

## 1996 Outlook

Blauser needs to hit to keep his job as a major league shortstop. If he continues at his present level for much longer, the Braves will have to explore other options. Despite his struggles over the last two seasons, the Braves are still fond of Blauser, and he'll have a chance to redeem himself in 1996.

**Position:** SS
**Bats:** R **Throws:** R
**Ht:** 6' 1" **Wt:** 180

**Opening Day Age:** 30
**Born:** 11/8/65 in Los Gatos, CA
**ML Seasons:** 9
**Pronunciation:** BLAU-zer

### Overall Statistics

|  | G | AB | R | H | D | T | HR | RBI | SB | BB | SO | Avg | OBP | Slg |
|---|---|---|---|---|---|---|---|---|---|---|---|---|---|---|
| 1995 | 115 | 431 | 60 | 91 | 16 | 2 | 12 | 31 | 8 | 57 | 107 | .211 | .319 | .341 |
| Career | 950 | 3177 | 463 | 835 | 156 | 23 | 82 | 356 | 50 | 373 | 637 | .263 | .347 | .404 |

### Where He Hits the Ball

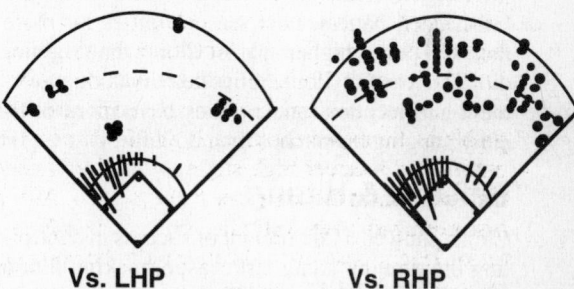

**Vs. LHP**            **Vs. RHP**

### 1995 Situational Stats

|  | AB | H | HR | RBI | Avg |  | AB | H | HR | RBI | Avg |
|---|---|---|---|---|---|---|---|---|---|---|---|
| Home | 203 | 44 | 7 | 19 | .217 | LHP | 84 | 19 | 1 | 5 | .226 |
| Road | 228 | 47 | 5 | 12 | .206 | RHP | 347 | 72 | 11 | 26 | .207 |
| First Half | 261 | 59 | 8 | 20 | .226 | Sc Pos | 83 | 14 | 2 | 19 | .169 |
| Scnd Half | 170 | 32 | 4 | 11 | .188 | Clutch | 58 | 14 | 3 | 8 | .241 |

### 1995 Rankings (National League)

→ 1st in lowest batting average, lowest batting average with runners in scoring position (.169) and lowest batting average vs. right-handed pitchers (.207)

→ 2nd in lowest batting average on the road (.206)

→ 4th in hit by pitch (12), lowest on-base percentage vs. right-handed pitchers (.301) and lowest batting average at home (.217)

→ 5th in lowest slugging percentage and lowest groundball/flyball ratio (0.9)

→ Led the Braves in hit by pitch (12), strikeouts and highest percentage of pitches taken (59.3%)

# Brad Clontz

## 1995 Season

The minor league saves leader in 1994, Brad Clontz was the logical choice to be named Braves closer in 1995. Once he received that distinction, though, Clontz was unable to hold it for long. Hit hard in the first two months, Clontz converted only four of six save opportunities. However, after losing the closer duties Clontz recorded an 18-inning scoreless streak from mid-June to early-August, establishing himself as a dependable right-handed set-up man.

## Pitching

Clontz throws a high-80s fastball, a hard-breaking slider, and a sinker. Like most pitchers with submarine deliveries, Clontz has a lot of trouble with left-handed batters. Last season, lefties hit more than 100 points higher against Clontz than righties did. The reason? Clontz relies heavily upon movement and location, and righties have more difficulty gauging his pitches than do lefties.

## Defense & Hitting

Clontz showed a fair amount of success in controlling the running game last season, making him a bit of an anomaly on the Braves staff. The main reasons for Clontz' success against basestealers are his unique delivery and the fact that he always pitches from the stretch. Clontz stands to the first-base side of the rubber and steps toward third base on his delivery to home plate, making it difficult for runners to gauge where he is throwing the ball. With two eventless plate appearances, Clontz has had little opportunity to show how well he can handle the bat. He has, however, proven to be a competent fielder—he made no errors in 69 innings last season.

## 1996 Outlook

Quality submarine pitchers always seem to have a place on major league clubs because they can be used to get right-handed hitters out and give the opposition a different look. Clontz appears to be a perfect example of this species. Look for the Braves to continue to use him as a right-handed set-up man for Mark Wohlers in 1996.

**Position:** RP
**Bats:** R  **Throws:** R
**Ht:** 6' 1"  **Wt:** 180

**Opening Day Age:** 24
**Born:** 4/25/71 in Stuart, VA
**ML Seasons:** 1

### Overall Statistics

|        | W | L | Pct. | ERA  | G  | GS | Sv | IP   | H  | BB | SO | HR | BR/IP |
|--------|---|---|------|------|----|----|----|------|----|----|----|----|-------|
| 1995   | 8 | 1 | .889 | 3.65 | 59 | 0  | 4  | 69.0 | 71 | 22 | 55 | 5  | 1.35  |
| Career | 8 | 1 | .889 | 3.65 | 59 | 0  | 4  | 69.0 | 71 | 22 | 55 | 5  | 1.35  |

### How Often He Throws Strikes

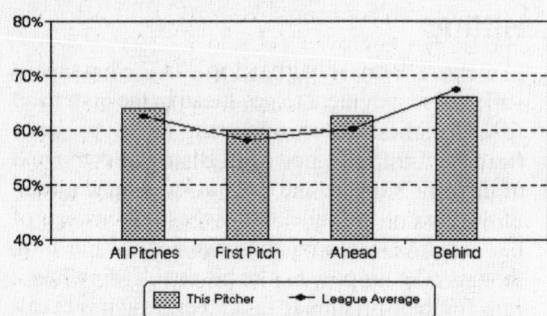

### 1995 Situational Stats

|            | W | L | ERA  | Sv | IP   |        | AB  | H  | HR | RBI | Avg  |
|------------|---|---|------|----|------|--------|-----|----|----|-----|------|
| Home       | 3 | 1 | 2.93 | 1  | 40.0 | LHB    | 93  | 32 | 1  | 19  | .344 |
| Road       | 5 | 0 | 4.66 | 3  | 29.0 | RHB    | 171 | 39 | 4  | 14  | .228 |
| First Half | 2 | 1 | 4.44 | 4  | 26.1 | Sc Pos | 73  | 19 | 0  | 25  | .260 |
| Scnd Half  | 6 | 0 | 3.16 | 0  | 42.2 | Clutch | 93  | 22 | 4  | 14  | .237 |

### 1995 Rankings (National League)

➡ 1st in relief wins (8)
➡ Led the Braves in relief wins (8)

# Tom Glavine

**Position:** SP
**Bats:** L **Throws:** L
**Ht:** 6' 1"  **Wt:** 185

**Opening Day Age:** 30
**Born:** 3/25/66 in Concord, MA
**ML Seasons:** 9
Pronunciation: GLA-vin

## 1995 Season

Once the ace of the Braves pitching staff, Tom Glavine has been overshadowed by teammate Greg Maddux the last three seasons. However, Glavine re-established himself as a superstar with his MVP performance in the World Series. In fact, Glavine's entire 1995 season can be seen as a re-establishment. After seeing his ERA rise steadily over the past four seasons, peaking at 3.97 in 1994, Glavine rebounded with a 3.08 ERA, the third-best mark of his career.

## Pitching

Glavine's arsenal of pitches includes a sinking fastball, a four-seam fastball, and a curveball. By throwing every day and strengthening his arm, Glavine has improved the velocity of his fastball from the mid 80s to the low 90s over the last two seasons. He also possesses one of the league's best change-ups, a variation on the circle change. Throughout his career, Glavine has had difficulty with left-handed batters because he stands to the third-base side of the pitching rubber. He does this to get a better angle on his outside pitches to right-handed batters, but as a result, his curve to lefties isn't as effective.

## Defense & Hitting

Like most Brave starters, Glavine has tremendous difficulty controlling the running game. Potential basestealers achieved a 75-percent success rate against Glavine in 1995. What Glavine lacks in holding runners, he makes up for in other areas. Glavine is a top-notch fielder and is also one of baseball's best-hitting pitchers. He hit .222 and tied Steve Avery for the team lead with eight sacrifices in 1995.

## 1996 Outlook

Glavine is one of the few pitchers who might break Greg Maddux' Cy Young streak in 1996. He is a proven winner and should continue to thrive in the Braves' system. If he can continue to keep his walks down and learn to keep left-handed batters at bay, Glavine should return to his 20-win seasons of the early '90s.

### Overall Statistics

|  | W | L | Pct. | ERA | G | GS | Sv | IP | H | BB | SO | HR | BR/IP |
|---|---|---|---|---|---|---|---|---|---|---|---|---|---|
| 1995 | 16 | 7 | .696 | 3.08 | 29 | 29 | 0 | 198.2 | 182 | 66 | 127 | 9 | 1.25 |
| Career | 124 | 82 | .602 | 3.52 | 262 | 262 | 0 | 1721.0 | 1649 | 579 | 1031 | 113 | 1.29 |

### How Often He Throws Strikes

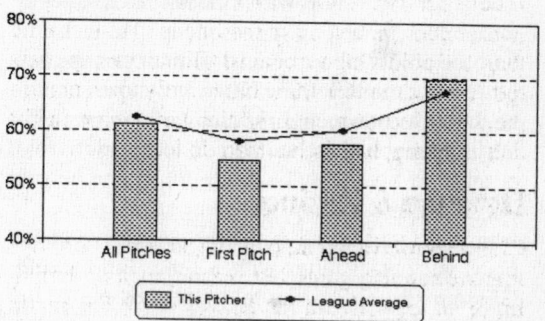

### 1995 Situational Stats

|  | W | L | ERA | Sv | IP |  | AB | H | HR | RBI | Avg |
|---|---|---|---|---|---|---|---|---|---|---|---|
| Home | 6 | 4 | 3.63 | 0 | 91.2 | LHB | 134 | 42 | 2 | 17 | .313 |
| Road | 10 | 3 | 2.61 | 0 | 107.0 | RHB | 605 | 140 | 7 | 51 | .231 |
| First Half | 8 | 4 | 3.49 | 0 | 95.1 | Sc Pos | 163 | 41 | 0 | 52 | .252 |
| Scnd Half | 8 | 3 | 2.70 | 0 | 103.1 | Clutch | 81 | 19 | 1 | 7 | .235 |

### 1995 Rankings (National League)

- → 1st in GDPs induced (26)
- → 2nd in least home runs allowed per 9 innings (.41), most GDPs induced per 9 innings (1.2) and ERA on the road (2.61)
- → 3rd in lowest slugging percentage allowed (.334)
- → 4th in wins
- → 5th in ERA
- → 6th in innings pitched
- → 7th in batters faced (822) and winning percentage
- → Led the Braves in sacrifice bunts (8), games started, hits allowed, batters faced (822) and pitches thrown (3,005)

# Marquis Grissom

## 1995 Season

Acquired from the Montreal Expos on April 6 in a trade for Roberto Kelly and Tony Tarasco, Marquis Grissom was expected to be the final piece in the Braves' 1995 puzzle. Early in the year, it looked as if the Braves might have made a mistake. Grissom was hitting only .239 on June 1 and the club was struggling. Meanwhile, Tarasco and Kelly were tearing the cover off the ball for the surprising Expos. Grissom caught fire in June and again in September, but he never hit as expected. One possible cause: a bruised left heel that bothered him throughout the season.

## Hitting

The biggest question with Grissom as a hitter is, where does he belong in the lineup? He lacks the on-base ability of a true leadoff man and the raw power of a number-three hitter, but those seem to be the spots in which most clubs want to bat him. He is probably best suited for the leadoff role, because of his ability to create runs once he gets on. Grissom's on-base problem stems primarily from the fact that he is overly aggressive at the plate. A contact hitter with a long, fluid swing, Grissom still chases too many pitches out of the strike zone.

## Baserunning & Defense

After leading the league in stolen bases in 1991 and 1992, Grissom's numbers have decreased dramatically over the last two seasons. He remains one of the most aggressive baserunners around, and he led the majors last season by advancing an extra base 76 percent of the time. Another area in which Grissom has always excelled is defense. A Gold Glove center fielder once again, Grissom is known for making difficult plays look easy. He has a strong, accurate arm, and registered nine outfield assists in 1995.

## 1996 Outlook

Grissom capped 1995 with a blistering postseason performance, helping the Braves clinch their first championship. He was rewarded with a new long-term contract with Atlanta, and the club hopes he can get his batting stats to their typical levels.

**Position:** CF
**Bats:** R  **Throws:** R
**Ht:** 5'11"  **Wt:** 190

**Opening Day Age:** 28
**Born:** 4/17/67 in Atlanta, GA
**ML Seasons:** 7

### Overall Statistics

|        | G   | AB   | R   | H   | D   | T  | HR | RBI | SB  | BB  | SO  | Avg  | OBP  | Slg  |
|--------|-----|------|-----|-----|-----|----|----|-----|-----|-----|-----|------|------|------|
| 1995   | 139 | 551  | 80  | 142 | 23  | 3  | 12 | 42  | 29  | 47  | 61  | .258 | .317 | .376 |
| Career | 837 | 3229 | 510 | 889 | 153 | 26 | 66 | 318 | 295 | 255 | 434 | .275 | .329 | .400 |

### Where He Hits the Ball

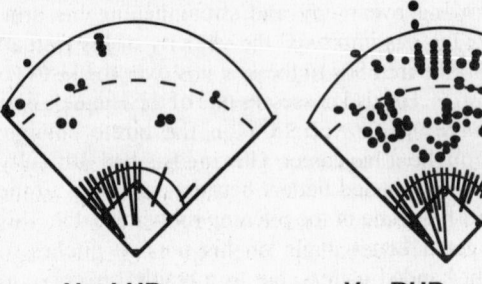

**Vs. LHP**   **Vs. RHP**

### 1995 Situational Stats

|            | AB  | H  | HR | RBI | Avg  |        | AB  | H   | HR | RBI | Avg  |
|------------|-----|----|----|-----|------|--------|-----|-----|----|-----|------|
| Home       | 257 | 59 | 5  | 14  | .230 | LHP    | 132 | 36  | 4  | 8   | .273 |
| Road       | 294 | 83 | 7  | 28  | .282 | RHP    | 419 | 106 | 8  | 34  | .253 |
| First Half | 280 | 80 | 7  | 25  | .286 | Sc Pos | 93  | 27  | 4  | 33  | .290 |
| Scnd Half  | 271 | 62 | 5  | 17  | .229 | Clutch | 81  | 18  | 3  | 10  | .222 |

### 1995 Rankings (National League)

➡ 1st in lowest on-base percentage for a leadoff hitter (.299) and highest percentage of extra bases taken as a runner (76.2%)

➡ 2nd in lowest batting average on a 3-1 count (0.000) and fielding percentage in center field (.994)

➡ 7th in lowest batting average at home (.230)

➡ 8th in at-bats and lowest on-base percentage vs. right-handed pitchers (.311)

➡ 9th in plate appearances (606) and lowest batting average vs. right-handed pitchers (.253)

➡ Led the Braves in at-bats, singles (104), stolen bases, caught stealing (9), plate appearances (606) and stolen base percentage (76.3%)

# Chipper Jones

## 1995 Season

You can call him Mr. Clutch. Throughout the 1995 season, rookie Chipper Jones was one of the Braves' best clutch performers: he hit three ninth-inning, game-winning home runs during the regular season, then another in the Divisional Championship Series, and finished second on the Braves in RBI. In fact, Jones was probably the most feared hitter in the Braves lineup during the postseason, hitting .364 with three homers and eight RBI in 14 games.

## Hitting

Jones lived up to all the hype. With the poise of a 10-year veteran at the plate, Jones seemed to make the jump from the minors to the majors with very little difficulty—despite the fact that he missed all of 1994 after undergoing anterior cruciate ligament surgery. Perhaps taking his new position to heart offensively, Jones became a typical power-hitting third baseman last season, hitting eight more home runs than he had hit in any minor league season. A switch-hitter with a good eye, Jones likes the ball up. He hit for a higher average as a right-handed batter in 1995, but had more power as a lefty—20 of his 23 home runs came against righties.

## Baserunning & Defense

Jones made 25 errors at third base last season, but he was adjusting to both a new position and the brutal Fulton County Stadium infield. He appeared nervous early on, but as the season progressed his hands got softer and he made some excellent plays. He has a strong but erratic throwing arm and above-average range. Despite being slowed somewhat by the knee injury which cost him all of 1994, Jones is still one of the Braves' fastest and most aggressive baserunners.

## 1996 Outlook

It would seem that only another serious injury can stop Jones from becoming a superstar. Still only 23, he should develop into one of baseball's best players over the next few seasons. Though there is still talk about moving him to the outfield, expect Jones to be the Braves' everyday third baseman for quite a while.

**Position:** 3B/LF
**Bats:** B **Throws:** R
**Ht:** 6' 3"  **Wt:** 195

**Opening Day Age:** 23
**Born:** 4/24/72 in DeLand, FL
**ML Seasons:** 2

### Overall Statistics

|  | G | AB | R | H | D | T | HR | RBI | SB | BB | SO | Avg | OBP | Slg |
|---|---|---|---|---|---|---|---|---|---|---|---|---|---|---|
| 1995 | 140 | 524 | 87 | 139 | 22 | 3 | 23 | 86 | 8 | 73 | 99 | .265 | .353 | .450 |
| Career | 148 | 527 | 89 | 141 | 23 | 3 | 23 | 86 | 8 | 74 | 100 | .268 | .355 | .454 |

### Where He Hits the Ball

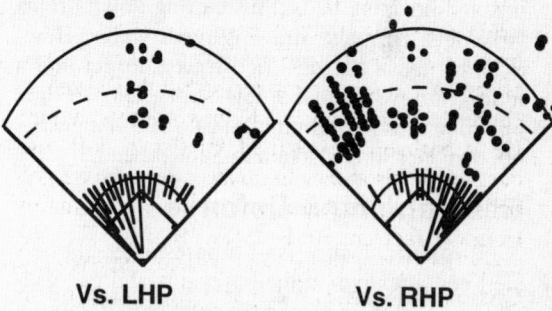

**Vs. LHP**　　　　**Vs. RHP**

### 1995 Situational Stats

|  | AB | H | HR | RBI | Avg |  | AB | H | HR | RBI | Avg |
|---|---|---|---|---|---|---|---|---|---|---|---|
| Home | 268 | 73 | 15 | 46 | .272 | LHP | 127 | 36 | 3 | 13 | .283 |
| Road | 256 | 66 | 8 | 40 | .258 | RHP | 397 | 103 | 20 | 73 | .259 |
| First Half | 258 | 64 | 13 | 47 | .248 | Sc Pos | 121 | 36 | 4 | 57 | .298 |
| Scnd Half | 266 | 75 | 10 | 39 | .282 | Clutch | 87 | 20 | 5 | 9 | .230 |

### 1995 Rankings (National League)

➝ 2nd in errors at third base (25) and lowest fielding percentage at third base (.931)
➝ 7th in walks
➝ 10th in games played and highest percentage of extra bases taken as a runner (63.8%)
➝ Led the Braves in runs scored, walks, pitches seen (2,222), batting average vs. left-handed pitchers (.283) and on-base percentage vs. left-handed pitchers (.393)

# David Justice

## 1995 Season

After some negative comments about Braves fans following Game 5 of the World Series, David Justice was in the Atlanta doghouse. With one swing of the bat, though, he became a hero. Justice's sixth-inning home run in Game 6 proved to be all the offense the Braves would need, as they defeated the Indians 1-0 to win the World Series. It was a satisfying finish for Justice, who struggled for much of the year.

## Hitting

Due to a number of injuries, Justice has been forced to change his swing. His new, more compact swing allows him to wait longer on change-ups and breaking balls, thus cutting down on his strikeouts. He's also drawing more walks. However, he doesn't always find it easy to get into a hitting groove with the new stroke. Justice had only one really solid month last year—August—but then he slumped again in September.

## Baserunning & Defense

A fast runner, Justice isn't a basestealer but he's alert and attentive on the basepaths and can usually be counted on to take the extra base. Learning to use his speed effectively on defense, Justice has become very proficient at chasing down balls in foul territory and has generally improved his range. Once known for a strong throwing arm, Justice has lost some zip in recent years, primarily due to a nagging shoulder injury.

## 1996 Outlook

Although his average took a dip in 1995, Justice was able to increase his walk total while cutting down on his strikeouts. This discipline, combined with his awesome power, makes Justice one of the more feared hitters in the game. If he can find more consistency in his stroke, he could have a big season in 1996.

**Position:** RF
**Bats:** L **Throws:** L
**Ht:** 6' 3" **Wt:** 200

**Opening Day Age:** 29
**Born:** 4/14/66 in Cincinnati, OH
**ML Seasons:** 7

### Overall Statistics

|  | G | AB | R | H | D | T | HR | RBI | SB | BB | SO | Avg | OBP | Slg |
|---|---|---|---|---|---|---|---|---|---|---|---|---|---|---|
| 1995 | 120 | 411 | 73 | 104 | 17 | 2 | 24 | 78 | 4 | 73 | 68 | .253 | .365 | .479 |
| Career | 777 | 2718 | 452 | 741 | 118 | 16 | 154 | 497 | 32 | 431 | 470 | .273 | .372 | .498 |

### Where He Hits the Ball

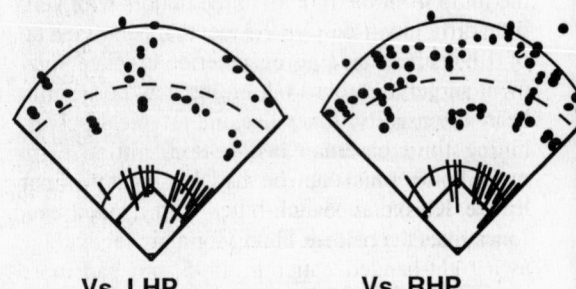

**Vs. LHP**            **Vs. RHP**

### 1995 Situational Stats

|  | AB | H | HR | RBI | Avg |  | AB | H | HR | RBI | Avg |
|---|---|---|---|---|---|---|---|---|---|---|---|
| Home | 189 | 57 | 15 | 39 | .302 | LHP | 141 | 34 | 7 | 23 | .241 |
| Road | 222 | 47 | 9 | 39 | .212 | RHP | 270 | 70 | 17 | 55 | .259 |
| First Half | 159 | 44 | 10 | 38 | .277 | Sc Pos | 111 | 29 | 5 | 51 | .261 |
| Scnd Half | 252 | 60 | 14 | 40 | .238 | Clutch | 65 | 21 | 4 | 12 | .323 |

### 1995 Rankings (National League)

- ⇒ 1st in most pitches seen per plate appearance (4.21)
- ⇒ 3rd in lowest batting average on the road (.212)
- ⇒ 4th in lowest groundball/flyball ratio (0.8) and highest percentage of extra bases taken as a runner (67.4%)
- ⇒ 5th in lowest fielding percentage in right field (.984)
- ⇒ 6th in batting average with the bases loaded (.500)
- ⇒ 7th in lowest batting average, walks and least GDPs per GDP situation (4.5%)
- ⇒ Led the Braves in walks, on-base percentage and HR frequency (17.1 ABs per HR)

# Ryan Klesko

## 1995 Season

Coming off a successful rookie campaign, Ryan Klesko was hoping to play every day in 1995. But despite an incredible spring-training performance by Klesko, Bobby Cox decided to platoon him with Mike Kelly in left field. The news visibly upset Klesko, who responded with a shaky 1-for-11 slump to start the season. After an early-May stint on the disabled list with a torn ligament in his left thumb, though, Klesko was given more playing time (it helped that Kelly was struggling to hit his weight). Klesko finished the year as one of the Braves' leading hitters, establishing career highs in nearly every offensive category.

## Hitting

Klesko is a left-handed power hitter who looks for fastballs that he can drive. After rarely batting against lefties in 1994, Klesko posted respectable numbers against southpaws when given a chance against them in '95. Also as opposed to his rookie season, in which he often looked anxious at the plate, Klesko appeared to be maturing into a very composed, confident hitter in 1995.

## Baserunning & Defense

In the field, Klesko looks like exactly what he is, which is a first baseman playing left field. He has limited range, a poor throwing arm, and he makes a lot of errors. For the second straight season Klesko had the worst fielding percentage among regular left fielders. Although he had some success as a basestealer in the minor leagues, Klesko is not fast or aggressive on the bases.

## 1996 Outlook

If Fred McGriff departs via free agency, Klesko may finally be given the first-base job in 1996. If not, he'll be the regular in left. Given the chance to play every day, Klesko should top 30 home runs and might well lead the National League with 40 or more.

**Position:** LF
**Bats:** L **Throws:** L
**Ht:** 6' 3"  **Wt:** 220

**Opening Day Age:** 24
**Born:** 6/12/71 in Westminster, CA
**ML Seasons:** 4

### Overall Statistics

|        | G   | AB  | R  | H   | D  | T | HR | RBI | SB | BB | SO  | Avg  | OBP  | Slg  |
|--------|-----|-----|----|-----|----|---|----|-----|----|----|-----|------|------|------|
| 1995   | 107 | 329 | 48 | 102 | 25 | 2 | 23 | 70  | 5  | 47 | 72  | .310 | .396 | .608 |
| Career | 234 | 605 | 93 | 176 | 39 | 5 | 42 | 123 | 6  | 76 | 129 | .291 | .370 | .580 |

### Where He Hits the Ball

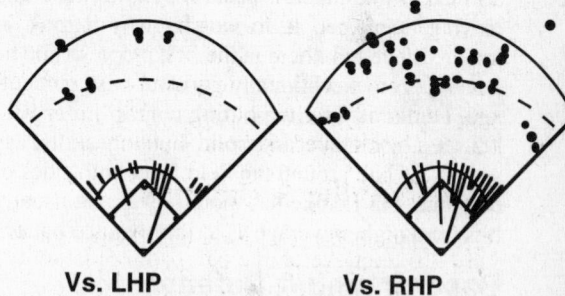

Vs. LHP          Vs. RHP

### 1995 Situational Stats

|            | AB  | H  | HR | RBI | Avg  |        | AB  | H  | HR | RBI | Avg  |
|------------|-----|----|----|-----|------|--------|-----|----|----|-----|------|
| Home       | 172 | 52 | 15 | 41  | .302 | LHP    | 78  | 19 | 3  | 12  | .244 |
| Road       | 157 | 50 | 8  | 29  | .318 | RHP    | 251 | 83 | 20 | 58  | .331 |
| First Half | 128 | 45 | 8  | 25  | .352 | Sc Pos | 82  | 26 | 5  | 42  | .317 |
| Scnd Half  | 201 | 57 | 15 | 45  | .284 | Clutch | 54  | 14 | 2  | 8   | .259 |

### 1995 Rankings (National League)

→ 1st in errors in left field (7) and lowest fielding percentage in left field (.942)
→ 7th in intentional walks (10)
→ 9th in batting average with the bases loaded (.444)
→ Led the Braves in intentional walks (10) and batting average with runners in scoring position (.317)

# Mark Lemke

## 1995 Season

Although his averages were not quite up to his 1994 level, Mark Lemke had another fine season in 1995. Off to a slow start, Lemke was plagued by a strained left hamstring for most of the summer. However, he had an uncharacteristically strong finish, hitting .290 with a season-high 15-game hitting streak during the season's final two months.

## Hitting

After being used as the number-eight hitter in the Brave lineup throughout his career, Lemke was switched to the number-two slot when Jeff Blauser failed to produce early in the season. Lemke seemed to like his new position, batting .301 and leaving many people to wonder why it took so long to move him there in the first place. While he never has an exceptionally good on-base percentage, Lemke is a switch-hitting contact hitter who boasts a good eye and solid bunting skills. He sprays the ball around the field from both sides of the plate, but Lemke has more power and usually hits for a higher average as a right-handed batter.

## Baserunning & Defense

With only four successful stolen bases in 20 career attempts, Lemke would be wise to stay put when he reaches base. Though not particularly fast, Lemke is a smart, aggressive baserunner who is willing to take the extra base when necessary. It is Lemke's ability as a fielder that has made him a successful major leaguer, and he is widely regarded as one of the top defensive second basemen around. Lemke has excellent range, sure hands and is one of the best in all of baseball at turning the double play.

## 1996 Outlook

Like the Energizer bunny, Lemke keeps going and going and going. He has steadily become a respected second baseman and a vital ingredient in the Braves' success. Despite rumors that the Braves will pursue one of the many free-agent second basemen during the offseason, expect Lemke to return in 1996.

**Position:** 2B
**Bats:** B **Throws:** R
**Ht:** 5' 9"  **Wt:** 167

**Opening Day Age:** 30
**Born:** 8/13/65 in Utica, NY
**ML Seasons:** 8

### Overall Statistics

|  | G | AB | R | H | D | T | HR | RBI | SB | BB | SO | Avg | OBP | Slg |
|---|---|---|---|---|---|---|---|---|---|---|---|---|---|---|
| 1995 | 116 | 399 | 42 | 101 | 16 | 5 | 5 | 38 | 2 | 44 | 40 | .253 | .325 | .356 |
| Career | 794 | 2290 | 242 | 565 | 87 | 14 | 25 | 200 | 4 | 256 | 227 | .247 | .320 | .330 |

### Where He Hits the Ball

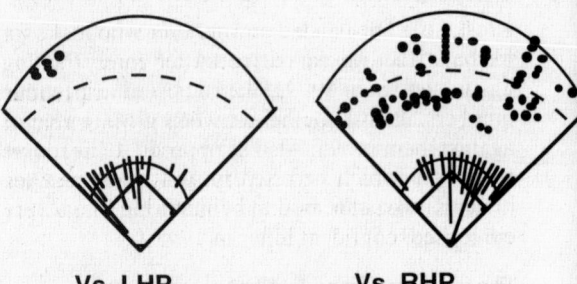

**Vs. LHP**          **Vs. RHP**

### 1995 Situational Stats

|  | AB | H | HR | RBI | Avg |  | AB | H | HR | RBI | Avg |
|---|---|---|---|---|---|---|---|---|---|---|---|
| Home | 191 | 48 | 3 | 17 | .251 | LHP | 93 | 27 | 2 | 12 | .290 |
| Road | 208 | 53 | 2 | 21 | .255 | RHP | 306 | 74 | 3 | 26 | .242 |
| First Half | 166 | 40 | 2 | 16 | .241 | Sc Pos | 84 | 23 | 1 | 29 | .274 |
| Scnd Half | 233 | 61 | 3 | 22 | .262 | Clutch | 55 | 12 | 1 | 9 | .218 |

### 1995 Rankings (National League)

- → 4th in lowest batting average vs. right-handed pitchers (.242) and highest percentage of swings put into play (56.9%)
- → 5th in GDPs (17) and fielding percentage at second base (.990)
- → 6th in least pitches seen per plate appearance (3.26) and lowest slugging percentage vs. right-handed pitchers (.330)
- → 7th in lowest slugging percentage
- → 8th in lowest batting average, most GDPs per GDP situation (18.3%) and lowest batting average with the bases loaded (.125)
- → 9th in highest groundball/flyball ratio (1.9)
- → Led the Braves in triples and highest groundball/flyball ratio (1.9)

# Javy Lopez

## 1995 Season

When Javy Lopez posted an unspectacular rookie season in 1994, many Braves fans questioned whether Lopez had what it takes to be a star in the major leagues. He silenced most of his critics, though, hitting a team-high .315 and maintaining a remarkable level of consistency throughout the season. Unlike '94, when Lopez suffered through a horrendous summer slump, 1995 saw Lopez hit no lower then .261 in any month. The highlight of his season, though, came in Game 2 of the World Series when he hit the game-winning home run and picked a runner off first base.

## Hitting

A free swinger, Lopez generally runs into problems when he becomes impatient and chases pitches that are out of the strike zone. For the second year in a row, Lopez struck out nearly four times as often as he walked. When he is able to control his wild tendencies, however, Lopez is an excellent hitter. Lopez is very strong, and he likes to wait for outside fastballs that he can blast over the fence.

## Baserunning & Defense

Once considered reasonably fast for a catcher, Lopez has shown little speed in his major league career. He has been among the league leaders in grounding into double plays in each of the last two seasons and he has yet to steal a base in the majors. However, the primary area of concern for Lopez is his defense. Although he improved his caught-stealing percentage and decreased his passed balls, the Braves are still not sure that Lopez can handle the everyday catching duties. In fact, Charlie O'Brien caught Greg Maddux and Steve Avery almost exclusively last season.

## 1996 Outlook

Until the Braves are confident in Lopez' ability to handle *all* the Brave starters, he will probably sit at least two times each week. In fact, don't be surprised if Lopez is shifted to another position someday, a move that has become common with good-hitting catchers in recent years. It would be nice to have that big bat in the lineup every day.

**Position:** C
**Bats:** R **Throws:** R
**Ht:** 6' 3"  **Wt:** 200

**Opening Day Age:** 25
**Born:** 11/5/70 in Ponce, PR
**ML Seasons:** 4

**Atlanta Braves**

### Overall Statistics

|  | G | AB | R | H | D | T | HR | RBI | SB | BB | SO | Avg | OBP | Slg |
|---|---|---|---|---|---|---|---|---|---|---|---|---|---|---|
| 1995 | 100 | 333 | 37 | 105 | 11 | 4 | 14 | 51 | 0 | 14 | 57 | .315 | .344 | .498 |
| Career | 197 | 642 | 68 | 185 | 23 | 5 | 28 | 90 | 0 | 31 | 121 | .288 | .327 | .470 |

### Where He Hits the Ball

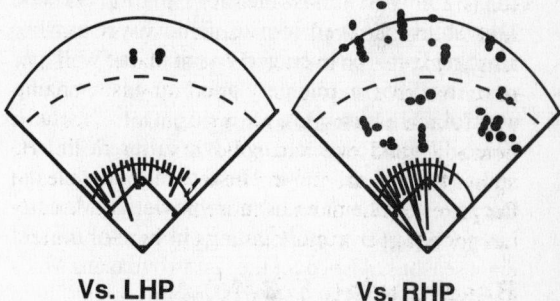

**Vs. LHP**          **Vs. RHP**

### 1995 Situational Stats

|  | AB | H | HR | RBI | Avg |  | AB | H | HR | RBI | Avg |
|---|---|---|---|---|---|---|---|---|---|---|---|
| Home | 178 | 58 | 8 | 23 | .326 | LHP | 86 | 25 | 2 | 8 | .291 |
| Road | 155 | 47 | 6 | 28 | .303 | RHP | 247 | 80 | 12 | 43 | .324 |
| First Half | 175 | 48 | 7 | 25 | .274 | Sc Pos | 78 | 28 | 3 | 37 | .359 |
| Scnd Half | 158 | 57 | 7 | 26 | .361 | Clutch | 60 | 20 | 3 | 15 | .333 |

### 1995 Rankings (National League)

→ 3rd in most GDPs per GDP situation (20.6%) and lowest fielding percentage at catcher (.988)

→ 4th in errors at catcher (8)

→ Led the Braves in batting average in the clutch (.333), batting average on an 0-2 count (.172) and batting average on a 3-2 count (.333)

## 1995 Season

For the fourth straight season, Greg Maddux was baseball's best pitcher. He led the National League in almost every positive pitching category and collected his fourth straight Cy Young Award; no other pitcher has won more than two straight. In an era of explosive hitting, Maddux has posted sub-2.00 ERAs each of the last two seasons. In fact, Maddux' only two losses of the 1995 season came in the only two starts in which he gave up more than three earned runs: May 17 against the Rockies and August 9 against the Reds.

## Pitching

Rarely making a bad pitch, Maddux has the uncanny ability to almost literally paint the corners. This ability allowed him to achieve yet another amazing feat—he averaged less than one walk per start in 1995, a true testament to his amazing control. Maddux throws a high-80s fastball, baseball's best circle change, two different sliders, and an occasional curve. Despite the fact that the last two seasons have been abbreviated, Maddux has pitched 200 or more innings in each of the last eight seasons. Also, over the last two seasons Maddux has an amazing 23-2 road record, including a current 18-game winning streak.

## Defense & Hitting

Never content with just one or two amazing streaks, Maddux has now won six Gold Glove Awards as the league's top defensive pitcher. An excellent athlete, Maddux is a fine-hitting pitcher and a top-notch bunter. The only possible flaw in Maddux' game is that he often has trouble with the running game: basestealers were successful in 26 of 32 attempts against Maddux last season.

## 1996 Outlook

Maddux is arguably the most effective pitcher *ever* over a four-season stretch. And with his current Cy Young streak at four, the question on most people's minds is not whether Maddux will win yet another next year. Rather, most people want to know if Cy Young could have won a Greg Maddux Award. Probably not.

**Position:** SP
**Bats:** R  **Throws:** R
**Ht:** 6' 0"  **Wt:** 175

**Opening Day Age:** 29
**Born:** 4/14/66 in San Angelo, TX
**ML Seasons:** 10

### Overall Statistics

|  | W | L | Pct. | ERA | G | GS | Sv | IP | H | BB | SO | HR | BR/IP |
|---|---|---|---|---|---|---|---|---|---|---|---|---|---|
| 1995 | 19 | 2 | .905 | 1.63 | 28 | 28 | 0 | 209.2 | 147 | 23 | 181 | 8 | 0.81 |
| Career | 150 | 93 | .617 | 2.88 | 301 | 297 | 0 | 2120.2 | 1877 | 561 | 1471 | 108 | 1.15 |

### How Often He Throws Strikes

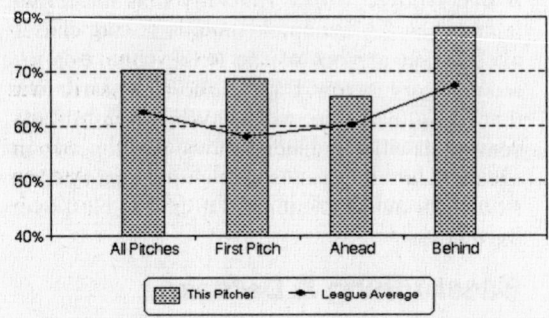

### 1995 Situational Stats

|  | W | L | ERA | Sv | IP |  | AB | H | HR | RBI | Avg |
|---|---|---|---|---|---|---|---|---|---|---|---|
| Home | 6 | 2 | 2.23 | 0 | 97.0 | LHB | 355 | 69 | 2 | 14 | .194 |
| Road | 13 | 0 | 1.12 | 0 | 112.2 | RHB | 393 | 78 | 6 | 21 | .198 |
| First Half | 8 | 1 | 1.64 | 0 | 104.1 | Sc Pos | 127 | 20 | 2 | 26 | .157 |
| Scnd Half | 11 | 1 | 1.62 | 0 | 105.1 | Clutch | 107 | 20 | 2 | 8 | .187 |

### 1995 Rankings (National League)

→ 1st in ERA, wins, complete games (10), shutouts (3), innings pitched, winning percentage, highest strikeout/walk ratio (7.9), lowest slugging percentage allowed (.258), lowest on-base percentage allowed (.224), highest groundball/flyball ratio allowed (3.0), least baserunners allowed per 9 innings (7.5), least home runs allowed per 9 innings (.34) and ERA on the road (1.12)

→ Led the Braves in lowest batting average allowed (.197), lowest slugging percentage allowed (.258), lowest on-base percentage allowed (.224) and least pitches thrown per batter (3.34)

# Fred McGriff

## 1995 Season

Fred McGriff's 30-plus home-run streak has finally come to an end. Partially due to the strike-shortened season and partially due to his first relatively off year since he became a regular, McGriff failed to hit 30 or more home runs for the first time in eight seasons. As if the end of his streak wasn't bad enough, McGriff posted career lows in both on on-base percentage and slugging percentage. McGriff was able to rebound in the postseason, however, batting 19-for-57 and helping lead his team to the World Championship.

## Hitting

McGriff is a power hitter who looks for down-and-in fastballs that he can hit. Although he has shown a tendency to be fooled by good breaking balls in the past, McGriff attempted to solve that problem in 1995. By decreasing his stride, McGriff was able to stay back and adjust to the breaking balls. Since he has been able to successfully handle lefties in previous seasons, McGriff's subpar performance against southpaws in 1995 can probably be dismissed.

## Baserunning & Defense

While he is not a particularly flashy defender, McGriff does a solid job at first base. He has cut down on his errors, is smooth around the bag, and has above-average range. On the basepaths, it's a different story. Though he has only average speed, McGriff had achieved some success as a basestealer prior to 1995. However, last season he stole only three bases in nine attempts, a poor performance by anyone's standards.

## 1996 Outlook

Although it might hurt most players to have the worst season of their career in the last year of a contract, it doesn't really matter in McGriff's case. He remains one of the most feared hitters in baseball and was among the most sought-after free agents this offseason. There was speculation that the Braves might let McGriff depart, but instead he signed a new four-year deal which could have him in Atlanta through the 1999 season.

**Position:** 1B
**Bats:** L  **Throws:** L
**Ht:** 6' 3"  **Wt:** 215

**Opening Day Age:** 32
**Born:** 10/31/63 in Tampa, FL
**ML Seasons:** 10
**Nickname:** Crime Dog

### Overall Statistics

|  | G | AB | R | H | D | T | HR | RBI | SB | BB | SO | Avg | OBP | Slg |
|---|---|---|---|---|---|---|---|---|---|---|---|---|---|---|
| 1995 | 144 | 528 | 85 | 148 | 27 | 1 | 27 | 93 | 3 | 65 | 99 | .280 | .361 | .489 |
| Career | 1291 | 4512 | 788 | 1284 | 229 | 17 | 289 | 803 | 48 | 744 | 1019 | .285 | .386 | .535 |

### Where He Hits the Ball

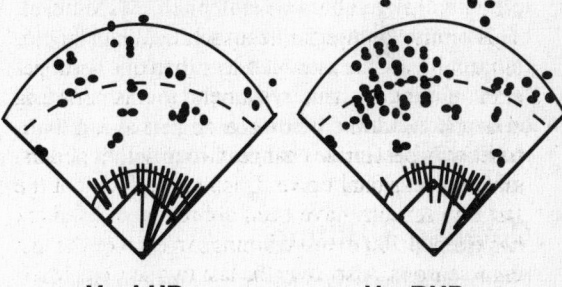

**Vs. LHP**          **Vs. RHP**

### 1995 Situational Stats

|  | AB | H | HR | RBI | Avg |  | AB | H | HR | RBI | Avg |
|---|---|---|---|---|---|---|---|---|---|---|---|
| Home | 261 | 76 | 15 | 45 | .291 | LHP | 188 | 48 | 6 | 28 | .255 |
| Road | 267 | 72 | 12 | 48 | .270 | RHP | 340 | 100 | 21 | 65 | .294 |
| First Half | 252 | 71 | 11 | 45 | .282 | Sc Pos | 134 | 39 | 9 | 68 | .291 |
| Scnd Half | 276 | 77 | 16 | 48 | .279 | Clutch | 81 | 22 | 2 | 8 | .272 |

### 1995 Rankings (National League)

- ➡ 1st in games played
- ➡ 2nd in GDPs (20)
- ➡ 3rd in fielding percentage at first base (.996)
- ➡ 8th in sacrifice flies (6)
- ➡ 9th in errors at first base (5)
- ➡ 10th in RBI, plate appearances (604) and slugging percentage vs. right-handed pitchers (.532)
- ➡ Led the Braves in batting average, home runs, hits, doubles, total bases (258), RBI, sacrifice flies (6), times on base (218), GDPs (20), games played, slugging percentage, batting average vs. right-handed pitchers (.294) and batting average on a 3-1 count (.500)

# Greg McMichael

## 1995 Season

Not really suited for the late-inning role he held for two years, Greg McMichael finally found his niche as a set-up man in 1995. McMichael tied for the National League lead with 20 holds, establishing himself as one of the league's premier set-up men. But although he ended up posting solid numbers, McMichael had a number of prolonged streaks in which he got hit hard.

## Pitching

Utilizing a sidearm delivery which resembles that of former Brave Gene Garber, McMichael throws an average fastball, a slider and a change-up. Although he is a finesse pitcher in the sense that he uses his change-up as an out pitch, McMichael consistently has high strikeout totals. When he got into trouble last season, it was primarily because he was aiming the ball, trying to hit the corners and be too perfect. He's best when he gets ahead with the heater and finishes off the hitter with a nearly unhittable change of pace.

## Defense & Hitting

McMichael has only an average move to first and therefore has difficulty controlling the running game, which means he fits in well with the rest of the Atlanta staff. While he is a decent fielder, McMichael appears to lose his concentration at times, leading him to make three errors in the past two seasons. Although he has had 11 major league at-bats—a lot for a relief pitcher— McMichael has yet to collect a base hit.

## 1996 Outlook

McMichael seems to have found a cozy niche as a set-up man. The Atlanta relief corps has been in flux for nearly as long as anyone can remember. But if Mark Wohlers solidifies his hold on the closer job, McMichael should be racking up the holds all season long.

**Position:** RP
**Bats:** R **Throws:** R
**Ht:** 6' 3" **Wt:** 215

**Opening Day Age:** 29
**Born:** 12/1/66 in Knoxville, TN
**ML Seasons:** 3

### Overall Statistics

|        | W  | L  | Pct. | ERA  | G   | GS | Sv | IP    | H   | BB | SO  | HR | BR/IP |
|--------|----|----|------|------|-----|----|----|-------|-----|----|-----|----|-------|
| 1995   | 7  | 2  | .778 | 2.79 | 67  | 0  | 2  | 80.2  | 64  | 32 | 74  | 8  | 1.19  |
| Career | 13 | 11 | .542 | 2.77 | 192 | 0  | 42 | 231.0 | 198 | 80 | 210 | 12 | 1.20  |

### How Often He Throws Strikes

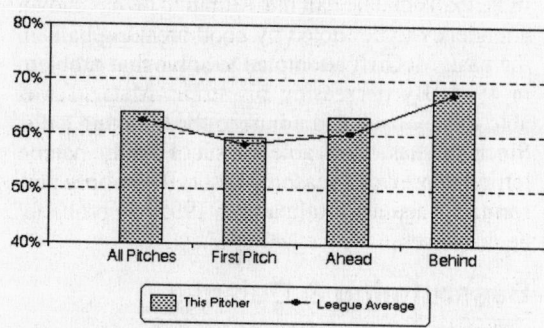

### 1995 Situational Stats

|            | W | L | ERA  | Sv | IP   |        | AB  | H  | HR | RBI | Avg  |
|------------|---|---|------|----|------|--------|-----|----|----|-----|------|
| Home       | 4 | 2 | 3.86 | 0  | 39.2 | LHB    | 130 | 26 | 3  | 10  | .200 |
| Road       | 3 | 0 | 1.76 | 2  | 41.0 | RHB    | 170 | 38 | 5  | 10  | .224 |
| First Half | 5 | 0 | 3.24 | 1  | 41.2 | Sc Pos | 68  | 9  | 0  | 10  | .132 |
| Scnd Half  | 2 | 2 | 2.31 | 1  | 39.0 | Clutch | 156 | 37 | 5  | 11  | .237 |

### 1995 Rankings (National League)

- → 1st in holds (20)
- → 4th in lowest batting average allowed in relief with runners in scoring position (.132) and relief wins (7)
- → 5th in lowest batting average allowed in relief with runners on base (.180)
- → 8th in games pitched and first batter efficiency (.159)
- → 9th in relief innings (80.2) and lowest batting average allowed in relief (.213)
- → 10th in relief ERA (2.79)
- → Led the Braves in games pitched, holds (20) and lowest batting average allowed in relief with runners on base (.180)

# Kent Mercker

**Position:** SP
**Bats:** L **Throws:** L
**Ht:** 6' 2"  **Wt:** 195

**Opening Day Age:** 28
**Born:** 2/1/68 in Dublin, OH
**ML Seasons:** 7

## 1995 Season

Coming off a breakthrough 1994 season that included a no-hitter, Kent Mercker looked like he had finally solidified his position in Atlanta's starting rotation. He started 1995 well, pitching five shutout innings in his first outing, but then alternated good months with bad from there on. The worst part for Mercker was that the bad months were worse than the good months were good, resulting in a career-high 4.15 ERA.

## Pitching

Mercker's biggest weapon is his mid-90s fastball. Although he has yet to find a completely reliable pitch to complement his fastball, Mercker also throws a curveball, a hard slider and a straight change. One of Mercker's biggest problems last year was that he was letting his change float over the heart of the plate. When he experienced trouble throwing his other pitches for strikes, hitters were able to key on the fastball and hit him hard. Mercker continues to have difficulty maintaining the stamina necessary to be a solid major league starter. Last season, he averaged slightly over five innings per start.

## Defense & Hitting

Like most power pitchers, Mercker has a very slow delivery to the plate. That, combined with his lack of a good pickoff, make Mercker extremely easy to run on, especially for a lefty. In fact, would-be basestealers were successful an alarming 90 percent of the time in 1995. However, he fields his position well and rarely makes an error. Although he is not a great hitter or bunter, Mercker showed substantial improvement in the hitting department last season—he achieved a career-high .104 average, including three doubles and six sacrifices.

## 1996 Outlook

With a host of pitching talent emerging from the Braves' minor league system, Mercker will need to improve upon his 1995 performance if he wants to maintain his position in the starting rotation. Although he will not be as hot a commodity as he was last offseason, expect a few clubs to make a bid for Mercker for 1996.

### Overall Statistics

|        | W  | L  | Pct. | ERA  | G   | GS | Sv | IP    | H   | BB  | SO  | HR | BR/IP |
|--------|----|----|------|------|-----|----|----|-------|-----|-----|-----|----|-------|
| 1995   | 7  | 8  | .467 | 4.15 | 29  | 26 | 0  | 143.0 | 140 | 61  | 102 | 16 | 1.41  |
| Career | 31 | 25 | .554 | 3.49 | 233 | 54 | 19 | 515.2 | 440 | 242 | 426 | 49 | 1.32  |

### How Often He Throws Strikes

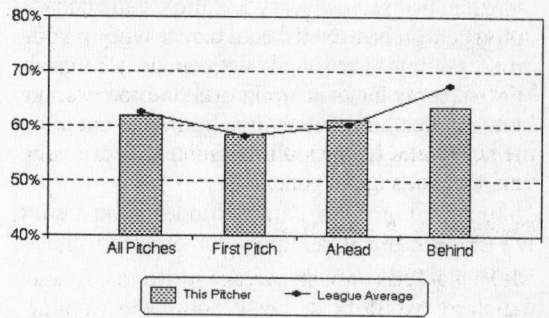

### 1995 Situational Stats

|            | W | L | ERA  | Sv | IP   |        | AB  | H   | HR | RBI | Avg  |
|------------|---|---|------|----|------|--------|-----|-----|----|-----|------|
| Home       | 3 | 4 | 5.01 | 0  | 79.0 | LHB    | 75  | 16  | 2  | 5   | .213 |
| Road       | 4 | 4 | 3.09 | 0  | 64.0 | RHB    | 468 | 124 | 14 | 58  | .265 |
| First Half | 4 | 4 | 4.15 | 0  | 80.1 | Sc Pos | 136 | 31  | 4  | 46  | .228 |
| Scnd Half  | 3 | 4 | 4.16 | 0  | 62.2 | Clutch | 24  | 7   | 1  | 4   | .292 |

### 1995 Rankings (National League)

- ➡ 5th in highest ERA at home (5.01)
- ➡ 8th in balks (2)
- ➡ Led the Braves in balks (2) and bunts in play (13)

# Charlie O'Brien

## 1995 Season

Despite the fact that Javy Lopez finally lived up to his offensive expectations, Charlie O'Brien remained a defensive presence among the Braves' pitching staff in 1995. Catching almost exclusively for Steve Avery and Greg Maddux—apparently at the request of both—O'Brien finished with the second-highest at-bat total of his career. For the second straight season, O'Brien started solidly with the bat, only to falter in the season's latter months.

## Hitting

Though he is a career .219 hitter, O'Brien has shown signs of becoming more of an offensive threat in the last few years. For the second consecutive season he established a career high in home runs, belting nine round-trippers. He also established career highs in walks and on-base average, proving that he is becoming a more patient hitter. However, with his pronounced uppercut swing, O'Brien still looks for pitches to jerk out of the ballpark. Once he gets behind in the count, O'Brien is often easy prey for offspeed pitches outside the strike zone.

## Baserunning & Defense

O'Brien has made a career out of being one of the most solid defensive catchers around. He is one of the best in the business at blocking pitches in the dirt, fielding bunts and handling pop-ups around the plate. Pitchers love the way he calls a game and frames the strike zone. Although he has a strong arm, O'Brien was only able to throw out 10 percent of opposing basestealers last season. However, the difficulties with the running game were more a result of the pitchers he caught than anything else. Not what you'd call fast, O'Brien has stolen one base in his career.

## 1996 Outlook

At 34, O'Brien can't have many years as a major leaguer left. On the other hand, when your biggest booster happens to be the world's best pitcher, you've got security. As long as O'Brien can hit .220 and pop a home run from time to time, he'll have a job with the Braves.

**Position:** C
**Bats:** R **Throws:** R
**Ht:** 6' 2" **Wt:** 205

**Opening Day Age:** 34
**Born:** 5/1/61 in Tulsa, OK
**ML Seasons:** 10

### Overall Statistics

|  | G | AB | R | H | D | T | HR | RBI | SB | BB | SO | Avg | OBP | Slg |
|---|---|---|---|---|---|---|---|---|---|---|---|---|---|---|
| 1995 | 67 | 198 | 18 | 45 | 7 | 0 | 9 | 23 | 0 | 29 | 40 | .227 | .343 | .399 |
| Career | 524 | 1427 | 144 | 312 | 77 | 3 | 33 | 166 | 1 | 145 | 189 | .219 | .302 | .346 |

### Where He Hits the Ball

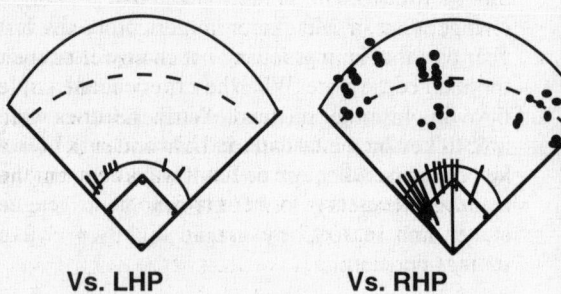

**Vs. LHP**          **Vs. RHP**

### 1995 Situational Stats

|  | AB | H | HR | RBI | Avg |  | AB | H | HR | RBI | Avg |
|---|---|---|---|---|---|---|---|---|---|---|---|
| Home | 83 | 19 | 4 | 10 | .229 | LHP | 35 | 6 | 1 | 3 | .171 |
| Road | 115 | 26 | 5 | 13 | .226 | RHP | 163 | 39 | 8 | 20 | .239 |
| First Half | 80 | 22 | 5 | 13 | .275 | Sc Pos | 64 | 9 | 2 | 14 | .141 |
| Scnd Half | 118 | 23 | 4 | 10 | .195 | Clutch | 32 | 9 | 1 | 3 | .281 |

### 1995 Rankings (National League)

→ 1st in lowest percentage of runners caught stealing as a catcher (10.1%)

→ 7th in lowest batting average with the bases loaded (.125)

→ 9th in lowest batting average with two strikes (.122)

# John Smoltz

## 1995 Season

Coming off a miserable 1994 season and offseason elbow surgery, there were many questions surrounding John Smoltz in 1995. Would he be able to regain his 1993 form? Would the Braves turn to him in their never-ending quest to find a closer? Smoltz remained in the rotation, and broke from the gate strongly with a 2.48 ERA through May. Although he had a number of rocky outings late in the year, including a forgettable performance in Game 3 of the World Series, Smoltz' season was a good indication that he has returned to his All-Star form.

## Pitching

Smoltz throws five pitches: a mid-90s fastball, a circle change, a split-fingered fastball, a curveball and a tight-spinning slider. A pure power pitcher, Smoltz needs to keep his slider down in the strike zone in order to succeed. When he does that, Smoltz can bust his heater in tight and strike out a lot of batters. Although he has always been among the league leaders in strikeouts, Smoltz achieved a career first in 1995 by averaging better than a strikeout per inning. Like most of the Atlanta starters, Smoltz is a workhorse. He's averaged over 190 innings per season.

## Defense & Hitting

As has been the case throughout his career, Smoltz was one of the toughest righties to run on last season. Not one to make many errors, Smoltz has always been a fine defensive player, though he did commit two errors last year. A career .142 hitter, he's also a competent hitter and an excellent bunter—he has 57 sacrifices and three home runs in eight major league seasons.

## 1996 Outlook

A three-time All-Star, Smoltz has shown the ability to dominate hitters. His strong 1995 season solidified his position as the number-three starter on the staff, a position he should occupy again in 1996. However, Smoltz is entering the final season of his contract and he will need to build on last season's performance if he wants to remain a Brave.

**Position:** SP
**Bats:** R  **Throws:** R
**Ht:** 6' 3"  **Wt:** 185

**Opening Day Age:** 28
**Born:** 5/15/67 in Warren, MI
**ML Seasons:** 8

### Overall Statistics

|  | W | L | Pct. | ERA | G | GS | Sv | IP | H | BB | SO | HR | BR/IP |
|---|---|---|---|---|---|---|---|---|---|---|---|---|---|
| 1995 | 12 | 7 | .632 | 3.18 | 29 | 29 | 0 | 192.2 | 166 | 72 | 193 | 15 | 1.24 |
| Career | 90 | 82 | .523 | 3.53 | 231 | 231 | 0 | 1550.2 | 1346 | 572 | 1252 | 131 | 1.24 |

### How Often He Throws Strikes

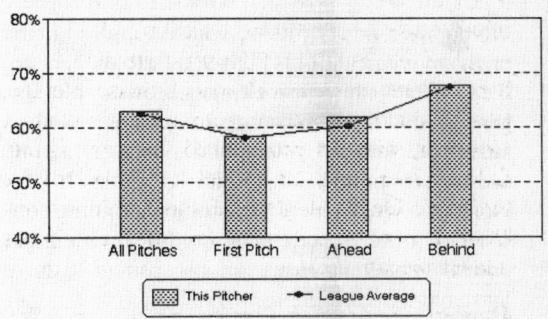

### 1995 Situational Stats

|  | W | L | ERA | Sv | IP |  | AB | H | HR | RBI | Avg |
|---|---|---|---|---|---|---|---|---|---|---|---|
| Home | 6 | 4 | 3.59 | 0 | 102.2 | LHB | 345 | 90 | 7 | 35 | .261 |
| Road | 6 | 3 | 2.70 | 0 | 90.0 | RHB | 369 | 76 | 8 | 33 | .206 |
| First Half | 7 | 4 | 2.84 | 0 | 92.0 | Sc Pos | 174 | 36 | 5 | 51 | .207 |
| Scnd Half | 5 | 3 | 3.49 | 0 | 100.2 | Clutch | 69 | 21 | 2 | 12 | .304 |

### 1995 Rankings (National League)

- ➡ 2nd in strikeouts and most strikeouts per 9 innings (9.0)
- ➡ 3rd in wild pitches (13)
- ➡ 4th in ERA on the road (2.70) and lowest batting average allowed vs. right-handed batters (.206)
- ➡ 5th in lowest slugging percentage allowed (.346)
- ➡ 6th in least home runs allowed per 9 innings (.70) and lowest batting average allowed with runners in scoring position (.207)
- ➡ 7th in ERA and lowest batting average allowed (.232)
- ➡ Led the Braves in games started, walks allowed, strikeouts and wild pitches

# Mark Wohlers

## 1995 Season

Once thought of as the Braves' closer of the future, Mark Wohlers appeared no closer to filling that role at the beginning of the 1995 season then he had in the last four. However, after some shaky outings by Brad Clontz, Wohlers was given the chance to take over the closer duties in June. He responded with one of the outstanding pitching performances of the 1995 season, establishing career bests in ERA, saves, strikeouts and innings pitched. His proudest moment came when he set down the Cleveland Indians in the ninth inning of Game 6 of the World Series to nail down Atlanta's first World Championship.

## Pitching

Wohlers is a power pitcher whose success hinges on the movement of his high-90s fastball, perhaps the swiftest in the game. He also throws a split-fingered fastball, which he uses to set up his fastball against left-handed hitters, and a slider which he uses to set up the fastball against righties. In previous seasons, Wohlers had problems finding consistency, often experiencing control problems in critical situations. However, he seemed to have mastered those problems in 1995.

## Defense & Hitting

Although he has only one career error, Wohlers often appears to have difficulty moving his big body around on the field. Wohlers also has tremendous difficulty controlling the running game. As has been the case throughout his career, Wohlers was unable to stop potential basestealers last year. All five stolen-base attempts against him were successful. Wohlers has a decent swing, but he struck out in all three of his 1995 plate appearances.

## 1996 Outlook

In Wohlers' first five major league seasons, 13 other pitchers recorded a save for the Braves. However, if he truly has mastered his control problems and can again perform as he did in 1995, Wohlers may finally live up to expectations and be *the* Braves closer for the next few years—and potentially one of the best in the game.

**Position:** RP
**Bats:** R **Throws:** R
**Ht:** 6' 4" **Wt:** 207

**Opening Day Age:** 26
**Born:** 1/23/70 in Holyoke, MA
**ML Seasons:** 5
**Pronunciation:** WOHL-ers

### Overall Statistics

|        | W  | L  | Pct. | ERA  | G   | GS | Sv | IP    | H   | BB  | SO  | HR | BR/IP |
|--------|----|----|------|------|-----|----|----|-------|-----|-----|-----|----|-------|
| 1995   | 7  | 3  | .700 | 2.09 | 65  | 0  | 25 | 64.2  | 51  | 24  | 90  | 2  | 1.16  |
| Career | 24 | 10 | .706 | 3.38 | 211 | 0  | 32 | 218.2 | 184 | 106 | 223 | 6  | 1.33  |

### How Often He Throws Strikes

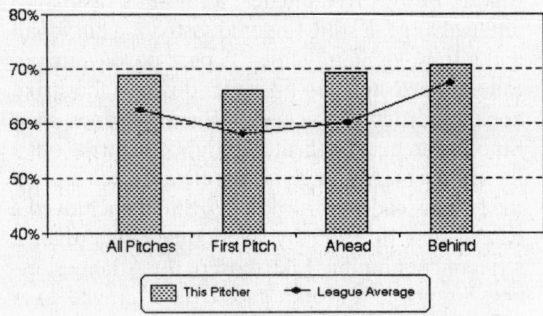

### 1995 Situational Stats

|            | W | L | ERA  | Sv | IP   |        | AB  | H  | HR | RBI | Avg  |
|------------|---|---|------|----|------|--------|-----|----|----|-----|------|
| Home       | 7 | 2 | 0.97 | 14 | 37.0 | LHB    | 111 | 26 | 1  | 9   | .234 |
| Road       | 0 | 1 | 3.58 | 11 | 27.2 | RHB    | 131 | 25 | 1  | 10  | .191 |
| First Half | 3 | 2 | 2.76 | 7  | 29.1 | Sc Pos | 63  | 16 | 2  | 19  | .254 |
| Scnd Half  | 4 | 1 | 1.53 | 18 | 35.1 | Clutch | 159 | 36 | 1  | 14  | .226 |

### 1995 Rankings (National League)

- ➡ 1st in first batter efficiency (.097) and most strikeouts per 9 innings in relief (12.5)
- ➡ 3rd in relief ERA (2.09)
- ➡ 4th in relief wins (7)
- ➡ 5th in save percentage (86.2%)
- ➡ 7th in games finished (49)
- ➡ 8th in lowest batting average allowed in relief (.211) and least baserunners allowed per 9 innings in relief (10.6)
- ➡ 9th in games pitched
- ➡ 10th in saves and save opportunities (29)
- ➡ Led the Braves in saves, games finished (49), save opportunities (29), save percentage (86.2%), blown saves (4), first batter efficiency (.097) and relief ERA (2.09)

# Rafael Belliard

**Position**: SS/2B
**Bats**: R  **Throws**: R
**Ht**: 5' 6"  **Wt**: 160

**Opening Day Age**: 34
**Born**: 10/24/61 in
Pueblo Nuevo, DR
**ML Seasons**: 14

*Overall Statistics*

|  | G | AB | R | H | D | T | HR | RBI | SB | BB | SO | Avg | OBP | Slg |
|---|---|---|---|---|---|---|---|---|---|---|---|---|---|---|
| 1995 | 75 | 180 | 12 | 40 | 2 | 1 | 0 | 7 | 2 | 6 | 28 | .222 | .255 | .244 |
| Career | 989 | 2068 | 198 | 464 | 45 | 14 | 1 | 135 | 40 | 133 | 344 | .224 | .278 | .261 |

## 1995 Season

For the second year in a row, Rafael Belliard started the season hot, hitting .364—albeit in very limited action—during the season's first three weeks. However, Belliard was unable to capitalize when given the chance to play in place of an injured teammate. That was especially evident in the World Series when Belliard, subbing for the injured Jeff Blauser, failed to get on base in his 18 plate appearances and made two uncharacteristic errors. It was, however, another consistent season for the reliable Belliard.

## Hitting, Baserunning & Defense

Belliard is a free-swinging groundball hitter who has a tendency to chase high fastballs. He strikes out a lot, doesn't walk much and has as little power as anyone in the majors. He is, however, an excellent bunter with reasonably good speed. What Belliard lacks on offense, he makes up for on defense. Regarded as one of the finest defensive shortstops in baseball, Belliard has committed just one error in each of the last three seasons. He has good range and an accurate arm whether playing shortstop or second base.

## 1996 Outlook

Although he remains a liability on offense, Belliard is still among the best defensive players around. As a member of a division-winning team in six of the last seven seasons, there is little doubt that Belliard will remain a valuable commodity for the Braves in 1996.

# Pedro Borbon

**Position**: RP
**Bats**: L  **Throws**: L
**Ht**: 6' 1"  **Wt**: 205

**Opening Day Age**: 28
**Born**: 11/15/67 in Mao,
DR
**ML Seasons**: 3
Pronunciation:
bore-BONE

*Overall Statistics*

|  | W | L | Pct. | ERA | G | GS | Sv | IP | H | BB | SO | HR | BR/IP |
|---|---|---|---|---|---|---|---|---|---|---|---|---|---|
| 1995 | 2 | 2 | .500 | 3.09 | 41 | 0 | 2 | 32.0 | 29 | 17 | 33 | 2 | 1.44 |
| Career | 2 | 3 | .400 | 4.11 | 46 | 0 | 2 | 35.0 | 34 | 21 | 36 | 2 | 1.57 |

## 1995 Season

After six strong minor league seasons, Pedro Borbon was finally given the chance to be a full-time major leaguer in 1995. Borbon got off to a rough start, giving up three earned runs in his first outing, but then pitched scoreless ball in his next 13 appearances. The biggest outing of Borbon's season, though, came in Game 4 of the World Series. Borbon replaced a tired Mark Wohlers and shut down the potent Indians lineup, saving the pivotal game for the eventual Series champs.

## Pitching, Defense & Hitting

Borbon is a hard thrower who holds nothing back. He throws a mid-90s fastball, a hard slider, and is working on a change-up as well. The Braves used him primarily as a set-up man against left-handed batters for good reason—he held lefties to a remarkable .167 average and allowed only five of 29 inherited baserunners to score. With only one major league at-bat, Borbon has yet to show whether he has any ability as a hitter or a bunter. However, he is an excellent fielder and has a decent move to first.

## 1996 Outlook

With a solid season as a set-up man under his belt, look for Borbon to remain as a key contributor in the Braves bullpen in 1996. And if Mark Wohlers should continue the trend of past Braves closers and falter next year, look for the club to give Borbon a chance in that role.

# Mike Devereaux

**Position:** RF/LF/CF
**Bats:** R **Throws:** R
**Ht:** 6' 0"  **Wt:** 195

**Opening Day Age:** 32
**Born:** 4/10/63 in
Casper, WY
**ML Seasons:** 9
**Pronunciation:**
DEH-ver-oh

*Overall Statistics*

|  | G | AB | R | H | D | T | HR | RBI | SB | BB | SO | Avg | OBP | Slg |
|---|---|---|---|---|---|---|---|---|---|---|---|---|---|---|
| 1995 | 121 | 388 | 55 | 116 | 24 | 1 | 11 | 63 | 8 | 27 | 62 | .299 | .342 | .451 |
| Career | 921 | 3332 | 434 | 856 | 155 | 31 | 97 | 438 | 76 | 252 | 570 | .257 | .308 | .409 |

## 1995 Season

After signing with the Chicago White Sox on April 8, it looked like Mike Devereaux would finally taste postseason play. However, as the Sox started to come apart at the seams, it appeared that Devereaux would again miss out. But as luck would have it, the Braves came calling in late August, and Devereaux played in October after all. He took advantage of his good fortune with a stellar performance against Cincinnati in the League Championship Series.

## Hitting, Baserunning & Defense

Devereaux is a high-ball hitter who prefers left-handed pitching. He is very impatient and often appears to be swinging for the fences. Devereaux is strong, but not strong enough to justify taking a mighty cut at every pitch. Although he is blessed with above-average speed, Devereaux has always been a cautious baserunner. He is also very cautious in the field. Once known for spectacular catches in the outfield, Devereaux has lost some of the flash that he previously had. He has an average throwing arm and will gun down the occasional overzealous baserunner.

## 1996 Outlook

Although Devereaux will never again be the player who finished seventh in the A.L. MVP vote of 1992, he still has the skills to be a quality major league player. His offensive resurgence in 1995 as well as the natural tools he possesses will make him a sought-after free agent this offseason.

# Mike Kelly

**Position:** LF/RF
**Bats:** R **Throws:** R
**Ht:** 6' 4"  **Wt:** 195

**Opening Day Age:** 25
**Born:** 6/2/70 in Los Angeles, CA
**ML Seasons:** 2

*Overall Statistics*

|  | G | AB | R | H | D | T | HR | RBI | SB | BB | SO | Avg | OBP | Slg |
|---|---|---|---|---|---|---|---|---|---|---|---|---|---|---|
| 1995 | 97 | 137 | 26 | 26 | 6 | 1 | 3 | 17 | 7 | 11 | 49 | .190 | .258 | .314 |
| Career | 127 | 214 | 40 | 47 | 16 | 2 | 5 | 26 | 7 | 13 | 66 | .220 | .273 | .383 |

## 1995 Season

Despite a poor spring-training performance, Mike Kelly was designated as Ryan Klesko's left-field platoon partner to open the 1995 season. However, following a barely acceptable start, Kelly totally fell apart after the All-Star break; he hit .120 over the season's final three months. Kelly's performance was so bad, in fact, that he was demoted to the minors in mid-August and was left off the postseason roster.

## Hitting, Baserunning & Defense

Once thought of as a power hitter, Kelly had trouble reaching the warning track in 1995. His main problem as a hitter is that he is not very selective at the plate. In fact, he struck out once in every three plate appearances last season. One positive note, though, was that he was finally able to achieve success on the basepaths, stealing seven of 10. Relegated to the bench in mid-July, Kelly was used primarily as a late-inning defensive sub for the remainder of the season. Although the Braves stuck with him in that role, Kelly experienced trouble there as well. His arm is not strong and he made four errors, too many for a part-time outfielder.

## 1996 Outlook

The second overall pick in the 1991 draft, Kelly once appeared to be destined for stardom. After a disastrous 1995 season, though, Kelly will be lucky to remain as a backup for the Braves in 1996.

# Mike Mordecai

**Position:** 2B
**Bats:** R **Throws:** R
**Ht:** 5'11" **Wt:** 175

**Opening Day Age:** 28
**Born:** 12/13/67 in
Birmingham, AL
**ML Seasons:** 2
Pronunciation:
mohr-duh-KUY

## Overall Statistics

|  | G | AB | R | H | D | T | HR | RBI | SB | BB | SO | Avg | OBP | Slg |
|---|---|---|---|---|---|---|---|---|---|---|---|---|---|---|
| 1995 | 69 | 75 | 10 | 21 | 6 | 0 | 3 | 11 | 0 | 9 | 16 | .280 | .480 | .353 |
| Career | 73 | 79 | 11 | 22 | 6 | 0 | 4 | 14 | 0 | 10 | 16 | .278 | .506 | .356 |

When Rafeal Belliard was re-signed for the 1995 season, it looked as if infielder Mike Mordecai might have to spend another season at Richmond waiting for his chance to play in the majors. However, with a team-leading .389 average in spring training, Mordecai served notice that he belonged with the big club in 1995. The Braves decided to let Mordecai share the utility duties, and he responded with a solid season.

## Hitting, Baserunning & Defense

Though he is a switch-hitter, Mordecai is much more effective batting right-handed. Unlike the typical utility middle infielder, Mordecai hits a high percentage of fly balls and has a decent amount of power, indicated by his three home runs in only 75 at-bats and his .480 slugging average. Mordecai is also a very solid defensive player. He has superb range, a good arm and is solid at turning the double play. He adjusted well to each of his five positions—all four infield spots and center field—making no errors in 1995. He is not particularly fast and was smart enough not to attempt a stolen base in 1995.

## 1996 Outlook

With a solid rookie season under his belt, look for Mordecai to remain as the Braves' super sub in 1996. In addition, look for Mordecai to enjoy the Braves' Olympics-necessitated road trip next July; he hit an astounding 241 points higher on the road last year.

# Alejandro Pena

**Position:** RP
**Bats:** R **Throws:** R
**Ht:** 6' 1" **Wt:** 228

**Opening Day Age:** 36
**Born:** 6/25/59 in
Cambiaso, DR
**ML Seasons:** 14
**Pronunciation:**
PAIN-yuh

## Overall Statistics

|  | W | L | Pct. | ERA | G | GS | Sv | IP | H | BB | SO | HR | BR/IP |
|---|---|---|---|---|---|---|---|---|---|---|---|---|---|
| 1995 | 3 | 1 | .750 | 4.72 | 44 | 0 | 0 | 55.1 | 55 | 19 | 64 | 8 | 1.34 |
| Career | 56 | 51 | .523 | 3.10 | 499 | 72 | 74 | 1053.1 | 955 | 330 | 834 | 73 | 1.22 |

## 1995 Season

Acquired on August 31 in a trade with the Florida Marlins, Alejandro Pena did a solid job in his second stint with the Braves. After a few rough September outings, Pena did exactly what the Braves wanted once the playoffs rolled around. A shaky performance in a Game 3 World Series loss notwithstanding, Pena had an outstanding postseason run. He gave up only one earned run in his seven innings of work, lowering his career postseason ERA to 2.03.

## Pitching, Defense & Hitting

At 36, Pena can still bring it. His fastball consistently reaches the low 90s and he cleverly mixes in a slider, a change-up and a forkball. Although he has always been good against both right-handed and left-handed batters, Pena is usually more effective against lefties. That was the case again in 1995 as Pena held lefties to a .205 average, while righties hit him to the tune of .282. With only nine hits and 20 sacrifices in 181 career at-bats, it is safe to say that anything Pena does with the bat is unexpected. He also has some problems holding runners. He is, however, a solid defender—he has made only 18 errors in 499 career games.

## 1996 Outlook

Pena still has the tools to pitch in the major leagues. However, with the wealth of pitching talent that the Braves have at Triple-A Richmond, expect Pena to be somewhere else this season.

# Luis Polonia

**Position:** LF
**Bats:** L  **Throws:** L
**Ht:** 5' 8"  **Wt:** 160

**Opening Day Age:** 31
**Born:** 12/10/64 in
Santiago City, DR
**ML Seasons:** 9
Pronunciation:
puh-LONE-yuh

## Overall Statistics

| | G | AB | R | H | D | T | HR | RBI | SB | BB | SO | Avg | OBP | Slg |
|---|---|---|---|---|---|---|---|---|---|---|---|---|---|---|
| 1995 | 95 | 291 | 43 | 76 | 16 | 3 | 2 | 17 | 13 | 28 | 38 | .261 | .322 | .357 |
| Career | 1095 | 3957 | 606 | 1159 | 150 | 56 | 17 | 327 | 283 | 313 | 456 | .293 | .344 | .372 |

## 1995 Season

When the Yankees called up Darryl Strawberry last August, someone in the Yankee outfield had to go, and Luis Polonia was the someone. Looking to improve their bench for the postseason, and with Mike Kelly in a funk, the Braves were only too happy to take the speedy Polonia off the Yankees' hands. Polonia responded with a steady performance over the last two months and was a valuable contributor for the World Champions.

## Hitting, Baserunning & Defense

Polonia is a smart hitter who uses what tools he has effectively. For instance, he hits a lot of ground balls, which allows him to utilize his excellent speed. He also uses his speed effectively on the basepaths. He is an aggressive baserunner and has become an increasingly effective basestealer. Although he has a weak throwing arm, Polonia's defense is pretty solid too. He didn't make an error and had five outfield assists, not bad for a part-time player.

## 1996 Outlook

Although his days of 400-plus at-bats are probably over, the 31-year-old Polonia should be a solid backup outfielder for someone in 1996. Keep in mind, however, that the Braves were very happy with Polonia's performance, and he might get a shot in left field if Klesko moves to first base.

# Dwight Smith

**Position:** RF/LF
**Bats:** L  **Throws:** R
**Ht:** 5'11"  **Wt:** 195

**Opening Day Age:** 32
**Born:** 11/8/63 in
Tallahassee, FL
**ML Seasons:** 7

## Overall Statistics

| | G | AB | R | H | D | T | HR | RBI | SB | BB | SO | Avg | OBP | Slg |
|---|---|---|---|---|---|---|---|---|---|---|---|---|---|---|
| 1995 | 103 | 131 | 16 | 33 | 8 | 2 | 3 | 21 | 0 | 13 | 35 | .252 | .327 | .412 |
| Career | 712 | 1654 | 228 | 466 | 83 | 20 | 43 | 210 | 41 | 133 | 292 | .282 | .338 | .434 |

## 1995 Season

Signed as a free agent by the Braves on April 12, Dwight Smith was a valuable backup outfielder and pinch hitter for the Braves in 1995. Smith ranked among the league' best pinch batters with 16 pinch hits, two pinch homers and 18 pinch-hit RBI.

## Hitting, Baserunning & Defense

Primarily a fastball hitter, Smith uses the entire field and prefers the ball down and in. Throughout his career he has had tremendous difficulty with left-handed pitching and, as a result, he doesn't face them much. Though he is blessed with fairly good speed, Smith is a terrible baserunner. Notorious in his early years for committing ugly baserunning blunders, Smith has curbed that habit in recent years. However, he still remains a liability on the bases—his career stolen-base success rate is just slightly over 50 percent. His fielding is another area where much improvement is needed. Smith often misjudges fly balls and liners, and committed two errors last season in only 25 outfield appearances.

## 1996 Outlook

After spending his first five seasons with the Chicago Cubs, Smith has bounced around over the past two seasons, playing with three different clubs during that time. However, with a .282 career average and his recent success as a pinch hitter, Smith should be able to continue for many seasons as a role player.

# Other Atlanta Braves

**Steve Bedrosian** (**Pos**: RHP, **Age**: 38)

After a brilliant 1993 and a solid 1994, Bedrosian could never get it together in 1995. Carrying a 6.11 ERA on August 11, "Bedrock" retired. 1996 Outlook: D

**Ed Giovanola** (**Pos**: 2B, **Age**: 27, **Bats**: L)

Nobody had heard of Giovanola before 1995. But he got noticed by hitting nearly .400 the first half of the season with Richmond. Giovanola ended up at .321, and he'll have to beat out Mordecai for a job. 1996 Outlook: C

**Brian Kowitz** (**Pos**: RF, **Age**: 26, **Bats**: L)

Kowitz was taken by the Twins in the Rule 5 draft last winter, but they sent him back to the Braves before the season. Good athlete, power lacking for an outfielder, he'll have a tough time breaking in. 1996 Outlook: C

**Rod Nichols** (**Pos**: RHP, **Age**: 31)

In 57 innings with Richmond last year, Nichols struck out 57 batters *while walking only six*. He hasn't fared so well in the majors lately, and will need a break somewhere along the line. 1996 Outlook: C

**Eddie Perez** (**Pos**: C, **Age**: 27, **Bats**: R)

A nine-year Brave farmhand, Perez finally got the call last September. He's not much of a hitter but is okay defensively. Obviously won't play in Atlanta unless somebody gets hurt. 1996 Outlook: D

**Mike Sharperson** (**Pos**: 3B, **Age**: 34, **Bats**: R)

The Braves signed Sharperson as insurance, but he ended up spending most of the season with Richmond, where he hit .319. Still a good enough hitter to help somebody as a utility infielder. 1996 Outlook: B

**Tom Thobe** (**Pos**: LHP, **Age**: 26)

Lefty reliever Thobe has moved up one level in each of his three pro seasons, and has a 2.31 minor league ERA and a 21-11 record. Pedro Borbon is an obstacle, but Thobe should stick. 1996 Outlook: B

**Brad Woodall** (**Pos**: LHP, **Age**: 26)

After a fine 1994 season at Richmond (15-6, 2.42) Woodall was considered an excellent prospect. But he hurt his arm last year and pitched poorly in Triple-A (4-4, 5.10). He still has plenty of time to find himself. 1996 Outlook: C

# Atlanta Braves Minor League Prospects

## Organization Overview:

The Braves are the majors' winningest team in the 1990s. Now that they've finally won a championship, they can be regarded as a *great* team as well. And thanks to a minor league system that's as deep and productive as any in baseball, their level of excellence is unlikely to suffer any dips in the near future. As one of the game's more profitable franchises, the Braves have enjoyed the luxury of seeking talented high-school athletes and being active participants in international player development. The result is a farm system brimming with prospects. Those prospects afford the Braves the option of replacing established players when they become old, unproductive or too expensive, with the likes of Ryan Klesko, Chipper Jones and Javy Lopez. The next wave of exceptional talent may be a year or two away, but when they finally arrive Atlanta should just keep on winning.

### Jermaine Dye

**Position:** OF     **Opening Day Age:** 22
**Bats:** R **Throws:** R     **Born:** 1/28/74 in
**Ht:** 6' 0" **Wt:** 195     Oakland, CA

*Recent Statistics*

|  | G | AB | R | H | D | T | HR | RBI | SB | BB | SO | AVG |
|---|---|---|---|---|---|---|---|---|---|---|---|---|
| 93 R Braves | 31 | 124 | 17 | 43 | 14 | 0 | 0 | 27 | 5 | 5 | 13 | .347 |
| 93 R Danville | 25 | 94 | 6 | 26 | 6 | 1 | 2 | 12 | 4 | 8 | 10 | .277 |
| 94 A Macon | 135 | 506 | 73 | 151 | 41 | 1 | 15 | 98 | 19 | 33 | 82 | .298 |
| 95 AA Greenville | 104 | 403 | 50 | 115 | 26 | 4 | 15 | 71 | 4 | 27 | 74 | .285 |
| 95 MLE | 104 | 386 | 38 | 98 | 22 | 2 | 12 | 54 | 2 | 17 | 77 | .254 |

Dye made the difficult jump from slow-A to Double-A in impressive fashion in 1995. He already has gap power, as evidenced by his doubles totals the last two seasons. His 41 doubles in '94 were a Sally League record. Dye's home-run power is expected to continue to develop, but better plate discipline would help. As a former juco pitcher, Dye has a right fielder's arm, one of the strongest in the minors. He still faces lots of competition for major league playing time in the future, though his great work ethic should be beneficial.

### Damon Hollins

**Position:** OF     **Opening Day Age:** 21
**Bats:** R **Throws:** L     **Born:** 6/12/74 in
**Ht:** 5' 11" **Wt:** 180     Fairfield, CA

*Recent Statistics*

|  | G | AB | R | H | D | T | HR | RBI | SB | BB | SO | AVG |
|---|---|---|---|---|---|---|---|---|---|---|---|---|
| 93 R Danville | 62 | 240 | 37 | 77 | 15 | 2 | 7 | 51 | 10 | 19 | 30 | .321 |
| 94 A Durham | 131 | 485 | 76 | 131 | 28 | 0 | 23 | 88 | 12 | 45 | 115 | .270 |
| 95 AA Greenville | 129 | 466 | 64 | 115 | 26 | 2 | 18 | 77 | 6 | 44 | 120 | .247 |
| 95 MLE | 129 | 450 | 49 | 99 | 22 | 1 | 14 | 59 | 3 | 28 | 125 | .220 |

Hollins is a "tools" player with the kind of power, speed and throwing arm which appeal to scouts. Although his extra-base totals have been good the past few years, his free-swinging tendency is making it easier for pitchers to get him out as he moves up the Braves' chain. His average has dipped the last couple years from .321 in rookie ball to .270 in fast-A, to the .247 he hit at Double-A last season. He's been young for each of those levels, however, and he didn't turn 21 until June of last year. He's played center field in the minors, though he may ultimately end up in right with Atlanta.

### Andruw Jones

**Position:** OF     **Opening Day Age:** 18
**Bats:** R **Throws:** R     **Born:** 4/23/77 in
**Ht:** 6' 1" **Wt:** 170     Curacao, Australia

*Recent Statistics*

|  | G | AB | R | H | D | T | HR | RBI | SB | BB | SO | AVG |
|---|---|---|---|---|---|---|---|---|---|---|---|---|
| 94 R Braves | 27 | 95 | 22 | 21 | 5 | 1 | 2 | 10 | 5 | 16 | 19 | .221 |
| 94 R Danville | 36 | 143 | 20 | 48 | 9 | 2 | 1 | 16 | 16 | 9 | 25 | .336 |
| 95 A Macon | 139 | 537 | 104 | 149 | 41 | 5 | 25 | 100 | 56 | 70 | 122 | .277 |

Jones is one of the most exciting talents in baseball. He's a legitimate five-tool performer who evokes expectations of 30 homers and 60 stolen bases. He came close to posting those gaudy numbers at slow-A Macon in 1995, but here's the kicker: he was only 18 years old, with lots of room for growth. Signed as a 16-year-old free agent from the Netherlands Antilles in 1993, Jones has impressed with not only his power and speed, but also his fielding, throwing arm and plate discipline. If he cuts his strikeouts some, he'll be downright scary. Although the South Atlantic League is a long way from the majors, talents as immense as Jones can advance quickly. He could be one of those rare players who reaches the majors before he turns 20.

### Darrell May

**Position:** P     **Opening Day Age:** 23
**Bats:** L **Throws:** L     **Born:** 6/13/72 in San
**Ht:** 6' 2" **Wt:** 170     Bernardino, CA

*Recent Statistics*

|  | W | L | ERA | G | GS | Sv | IP | H | R | BB | SO | HR |
|---|---|---|---|---|---|---|---|---|---|---|---|---|
| 95 AA Greenville | 2 | 8 | 3.55 | 15 | 15 | 0 | 91.1 | 81 | 44 | 20 | 79 | 18 |
| 95 AAA Richmond | 4 | 2 | 3.71 | 9 | 9 | 0 | 51.0 | 53 | 21 | 16 | 42 | 1 |
| 95 NL Atlanta | 0 | 0 | 11.25 | 2 | 0 | 0 | 4.0 | 10 | 5 | 0 | 1 | 0 |

May wasn't highly regarded when the Braves selected him in the 46th round of 1992, most likely because he doesn't light up the radar gun. Though he doesn't throw hard, he still has had enough stuff to post more strikeouts than hits allowed through 494 professional innings. His career ERA is still under 3.00, and he reached Triple-A by the time he was 23. His numbers have been less impressive with each step up the ladder, though, and Atlanta boasts more imposing throwers in its system. But a lefthander with his record of success will likely get a shot somewhere, sometime.

## Jason Schmidt

**Position:** P
**Bats:** R **Throws:** R
**Ht:** 6' 5" **Wt:** 185

**Opening Day Age:** 23
**Born:** 1/29/73 in
Kelso, WA

*Recent Statistics*

|  | W | L | ERA | G | GS | Sv | IP | H | R | BB | SO | HR |
|---|---|---|---|---|---|---|---|---|---|---|---|---|
| 95 AAA Richmond | 8 | 6 | 2.25 | 19 | 19 | 0 | 116.0 | 97 | 40 | 48 | 95 | 2 |
| 95 NL Atlanta | 2 | 2 | 5.76 | 9 | 2 | 0 | 25.0 | 27 | 17 | 18 | 19 | 2 |

Here's a case where Atlanta's deep pockets allowed them to gamble and win. The Braves' $170,000 bonus offer convinced Schmidt, an eighth-round selection in 1991, to decline an Arizona scholarship. Atlanta then corrected Schmidt's mechanical flaws, and his pitching lines have improved as he's moved up the last couple years. He's a power pitcher whose heater already reaches the mid 90s. And at a lean 6'5" he could gain even more velocity as he matures. Schmidt may be the next in line for Atlanta's rotation should the Braves let Kent Mercker or Steve Avery depart.

## Bobby Smith

**Position:** 3B
**Bats:** R **Throws:** R
**Ht:** 6' 3" **Wt:** 190

**Opening Day Age:** 21
**Born:** 4/10/74 in
Oakland, CA

*Recent Statistics*

|  | G | AB | R | H | D | T | HR | RBI | SB | BB | SO | AVG |
|---|---|---|---|---|---|---|---|---|---|---|---|---|
| 93 A Macon | 108 | 384 | 53 | 94 | 16 | 7 | 4 | 38 | 12 | 23 | 81 | .245 |
| 94 A Durham | 127 | 478 | 49 | 127 | 27 | 2 | 12 | 71 | 18 | 41 | 112 | .266 |
| 95 AA Greenville | 127 | 444 | 75 | 116 | 27 | 3 | 14 | 58 | 12 | 40 | 109 | .261 |
| 95 MLE | 127 | 427 | 57 | 99 | 23 | 1 | 11 | 44 | 7 | 25 | 114 | .232 |

Since the end of the 1994 season, the Braves have chosen to let Terry Pendleton leave as a free agent and then traded third-base prospect Jose Oliva to the Cardinals. Since Chipper Jones is expected to eventually move off third as well, Smith may be the third baseman of the future. His offensive numbers have been solid yet never awe-inspiring, though he's always been relatively young for the levels he's played. It's Smith's defense which draws the highest marks. He has a plus arm and good quickness, and was one of the best defensive third basemen in the Southern League.

## Terrell Wade

**Position:** P
**Bats:** L **Throws:** L
**Ht:** 6' 3" **Wt:** 204

**Opening Day Age:** 23
**Born:** 1/25/73 in
Rembert, SC

*Recent Statistics*

|  | W | L | ERA | G | GS | Sv | IP | H | R | BB | SO | HR |
|---|---|---|---|---|---|---|---|---|---|---|---|---|
| 95 AAA Richmond | 10 | 9 | 4.56 | 24 | 23 | 0 | 142.0 | 137 | 76 | 63 | 124 | 10 |
| 95 NL Atlanta | 0 | 1 | 4.50 | 3 | 0 | 0 | 4.0 | 3 | 2 | 4 | 3 | 1 |

Power-pitching lefthanders are uncommon commodities, and it's hard to believe a lefty with Wade's stuff could go undrafted. Since signing with the Braves as a free agent in 1991, Wade has registered strikeouts at a rate of better than one per inning using two power pitches: an impressive fastball and hard slider. The prob-

lem had been control, but in 1995 Wade reduced his walk rate by more than one per inning, down to four per nine innings. Had Wade been in an organization which didn't already boast three solid lefthanders in its major league rotation, he likely would have received his big-league baptism more than a year ago. He should finally arrive on the scene in 1996.

## Ron Wright

**Position:** 1B
**Bats:** R **Throws:** R
**Ht:** 6' 0" **Wt:** 215

**Opening Day Age:** 20
**Born:** 1/21/76 in Delta,
UT

*Recent Statistics*

|  | G | AB | R | H | D | T | HR | RBI | SB | BB | SO | AVG |
|---|---|---|---|---|---|---|---|---|---|---|---|---|
| 94 R Braves | 45 | 169 | 10 | 29 | 9 | 0 | 1 | 16 | 1 | 10 | 21 | .172 |
| 95 A Macon | 135 | 527 | 93 | 143 | 23 | 1 | 32 | 104 | 2 | 62 | 118 | .271 |

Wright is an example of just how misleading a player's first-season statistics can be. In Wright's case, he batted .172 with little power in his pro debut after being chosen in the seventh round of '94. Last year, despite moving up a level, he increased his batting average by almost .100 points and actually doubled his slugging percentage to .501, tying for the South Atlantic League lead in home runs. To top it off, Wright didn't turn 20 until after the season. Wright has a quick bat and hits well to all fields. He also plays an adequate first base.

## Others to Watch

**Kevin Grijak** hasn't hit with the kind of power you'd like from a first baseman, but he did hit .324 between Double- and Triple-A in 1995. . . Outfielder **Gus Kennedy** was overshadowed by teammates Jones and Wright at Macon last season, but Kennedy posted eye-catching numbers as well (24 HR, 29 doubles, 95 walks, 20 SB in 439 AB). He needs to reduce his 151 strikeouts, though. . . Australian lefthander **Damian Moss** pitched in the Sally League at 18 last year and was dominating at times, with 177 strikeouts in 149.1 innings. He has three good pitches and just needs experience. . . **Aldo Pecorilli** was acquired in a minor league trade with the Cardinals for Ramon Caraballo before last season. Pecorilli then hit .344 between Double- and Triple-A. . . Hard-throwing reliever **Carl Schutz** saved 26 games at Greenville in 1995. More important, he reduced his walk rate to 5.6 per nine innings, a cut of more than two. . . The Braves aren't afraid to draft high-school pitchers, and righthander **Chris Seelbach**, their fourth-round pick in 1991, is another who might pay off. Seelbach was 10-6 with 130 K's in 133.2 innings at the two highest levels last year. . . Outfielder **Juan Williams** clubbed 20 homers and slugged .551 between Greenville and Richmond.

# Jim Bullinger

## 1995 Season

It was hard to believe, but one-time minor league shortstop Jim Bullinger opened 1995 as the Cubs' number-one starter. He justified that perch on Opening Day by throwing six shutout innings to earn the victory. That was no fluke, either. On May 21, Bullinger topped the National League with a 1.95 ERA. Unfortunately, he went on the disabled list that same day with elbow tendinitis. Bullinger returned to the rotation in late June and picked up right where he left off. On July 30 he tossed a three-hit shutout against the Phillies, and those nine innings were the centerpiece of a 24-inning scoreless streak. Before the wheels fell off in September (7.56 ERA), Bullinger was sitting on a fine 3.16 ERA.

## Pitching

For a guy who's only been pitching for seven seasons, Bullinger is a fairly polished hurler. Armed with one of the better curves in the National League, Bullinger has recently developed a cut fastball which he likes to run in on left-handed batters. And the natural sinking action on his regular fastball is a big help at Wrigley Field. Bullinger's problems come when his fastball stays up in the zone, where it's a very hittable pitch.

## Defense & Hitting

How reliable a fielder is Bullinger? In more than 350 major league innings, he has yet to commit an error. On the other hand, his offspeed deliveries and a general lack of interest leave Bullinger quite vulnerable to the running game, and last year basestealers were successful on 27 of 31 attempts, a pretty awful ratio. Bullinger is a decent hitter, .156 lifetime, if not quite what you'd expect from an ex-shortstop. He hasn't homered since his first major league at-bat.

## 1996 Outlook

Though Bullinger finished with just the third-best ERA among Cub hurlers, he did establish himself as a major league starter. As long as his arm holds up—and he hasn't pitched more than 150 innings in a season since 1991—Bullinger will be pitching for the Cubs every fifth day this summer.

**Position:** SP
**Bats:** R **Throws:** R
**Ht:** 6' 2"  **Wt:** 185

**Opening Day Age:** 30
**Born:** 8/21/65 in New Orleans, LA
**ML Seasons:** 4

### Overall Statistics

|        | W  | L  | Pct. | ERA  | G   | GS | Sv | IP    | H   | BB  | SO  | HR | BR/IP |
|--------|----|----|------|------|-----|----|----|-------|-----|-----|-----|----|-------|
| 1995   | 12 | 8  | .600 | 4.14 | 24  | 24 | 0  | 150.0 | 152 | 65  | 93  | 14 | 1.45  |
| Career | 21 | 18 | .538 | 4.12 | 111 | 43 | 10 | 351.2 | 329 | 162 | 211 | 30 | 1.40  |

### How Often He Throws Strikes

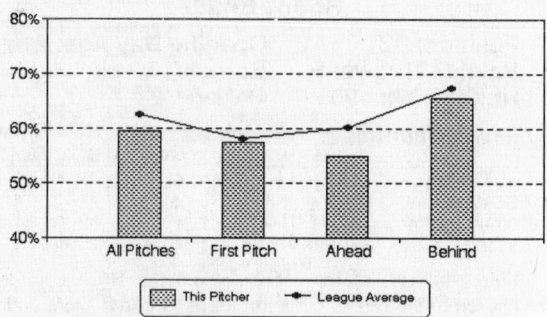

### 1995 Situational Stats

|            | W | L | ERA  | Sv | IP   |        | AB  | H  | HR | RBI | Avg  |
|------------|---|---|------|----|------|--------|-----|----|----|-----|------|
| Home       | 4 | 5 | 5.54 | 0  | 76.1 | LHB    | 264 | 72 | 5  | 36  | .273 |
| Road       | 8 | 3 | 2.69 | 0  | 73.2 | RHB    | 310 | 80 | 9  | 36  | .258 |
| First Half | 6 | 1 | 2.89 | 0  | 56.0 | Sc Pos | 142 | 40 | 3  | 55  | .282 |
| Scnd Half  | 6 | 7 | 4.88 | 0  | 94.0 | Clutch | 23  | 8  | 2  | 5   | .348 |

### 1995 Rankings (National League)

- ➡ 1st in fielding percentage at pitcher (1.000)
- ➡ 2nd in lowest strikeout/walk ratio (1.4) and highest ERA at home (5.54)
- ➡ 3rd in stolen bases allowed (27), highest stolen base percentage allowed (87.1%), most run support per 9 innings (5.9) and ERA on the road (2.69)
- ➡ 5th in most baserunners allowed per 9 innings (13.6)
- ➡ 6th in highest on-base percentage allowed (.346)
- ➡ 7th in hit batsmen (9) and least strikeouts per 9 innings (5.6)
- ➡ Led the Cubs in sacrifice bunts (8), hit batsmen and stolen bases allowed

# Frank Castillo

## 1995 Season

Ever since he struck out 112 batters in 111.1 innings as a minor leaguer in 1990, a lot has been expected of Frank Castillo. In 1995, Castillo finally justified that early promise. Thanks to little support from his teammates, Castillo finished a ho-hum 11-10, a record which belied his staff-low 3.21 ERA. What took so long? According to Cubs broadcaster Steve Stone, the problem was more mental than physical. Castillo himself agreed, saying last year, "I was thinking too much, walking around a lot. I was trying to make every pitch a perfect pitch. Now, it doesn't matter if they score 10 runs off me or one, I'll keep pitching the same." On September 25, Castillo was one out away from a no-hitter before it was spoiled by Bernard Gilkey's triple.

## Pitching

Castillo throws a solid fastball, and he can drop his curve over on occasion. But the pitch that makes the others work, the pitch that drove National League hitters nuts last year, is Castillo's change-up. As Cubs skipper Jim Riggleman observed of Castillo's change, "He'll use it in the hitter's count: 2-and-0 or 3-and-1. He reminds me of Bob Tewksbury that way." Still, Castillo did his best work after getting ahead in the count. When he threw a first-pitch strike, batters averaged just .203; once those unlucky hitters had two strikes, they batted just .141.

## Defense & Hitting

Castillo isn't exactly a wizard with the glove; he's erred four times in the last two seasons. He does hold runners well enough for a righthander. Castillo isn't much of a hitter, either—.114 lifetime—but he can get the sacrifice bunt down when necessary.

## 1996 Outlook

It would be unreasonable to expect Castillo to duplicate that fine ERA of last season. However, one of these years the Cubs are going to average five or six runs in the games Castillo starts, and he's going to post 16 or 17 victories. Or as Harry might say, "Wait 'til next year."

**Position:** SP
**Bats:** R **Throws:** R
**Ht:** 6' 1" **Wt:** 190

**Opening Day Age:** 26
**Born:** 4/1/69 in El Paso, TX
**ML Seasons:** 5
**Pronunciation:** cas-TEE-yoh

### Overall Statistics

|  | W | L | Pct. | ERA | G | GS | Sv | IP | H | BB | SO | HR | BR/IP |
|---|---|---|---|---|---|---|---|---|---|---|---|---|---|
| 1995 | 11 | 10 | .524 | 3.21 | 29 | 29 | 0 | 188.0 | 179 | 52 | 135 | 22 | 1.23 |
| Career | 34 | 37 | .479 | 3.86 | 113 | 109 | 0 | 669.1 | 652 | 192 | 446 | 69 | 1.26 |

### How Often He Throws Strikes

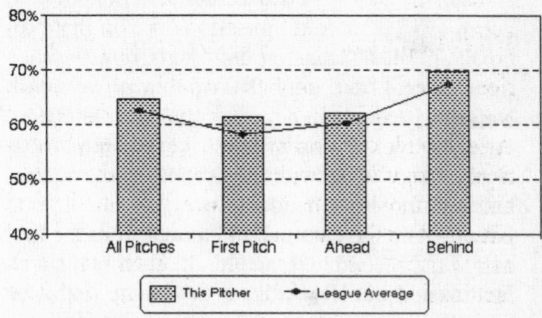

### 1995 Situational Stats

|  | W | L | ERA | Sv | IP |  | AB | H | HR | RBI | Avg |
|---|---|---|---|---|---|---|---|---|---|---|---|
| Home | 5 | 6 | 2.78 | 0 | 90.2 | LHB | 309 | 79 | 6 | 23 | .256 |
| Road | 6 | 4 | 3.61 | 0 | 97.1 | RHB | 414 | 100 | 16 | 46 | .242 |
| First Half | 6 | 4 | 2.88 | 0 | 84.1 | Sc Pos | 146 | 33 | 1 | 45 | .226 |
| Scnd Half | 5 | 6 | 3.47 | 0 | 103.2 | Clutch | 79 | 22 | 3 | 8 | .278 |

### 1995 Rankings (National League)

- 3rd in shutouts (2)
- 6th in home runs allowed, lowest on-base percentage allowed (.302) and least run support per 9 innings (4.2)
- 8th in ERA, pickoff throws (155) and ERA at home (2.78)
- 9th in most home runs allowed per 9 innings (1.05) and least GDPs induced per 9 innings (0.5)
- 10th in least baserunners allowed per 9 innings (11.3) and lowest batting average allowed with runners in scoring position (.226)
- Led the Cubs in ERA, games started, complete games (2), shutouts (2) and highest strikeout/walk ratio (2.6)

# Shawon Dunston

## 1995 Season

It was quite a story. Shawon Dunston—who missed the better part of 1992 and 1993 with a serious back problem, and who the Cubs at one time considered moving to the outfield—was back at shortstop last year, and hitting like he'd never hit before. At the All-Star break, the Wrigley Field "Shawon-O-Meter" listed Dunston's average at .335, the highest among major league shortstops. It couldn't last and it didn't, as Dunston hit just .260 after the break. He went into the season finale with a shot at .300, but went 0-for-4 and finished at .296, the highest full-season mark of his career.

## Hitting

Dunston has always been a champion non-walker, but in 1995 he outdid himself. While on that pre-break .335 tear, Dunston drew only *three*—that's right, three—bases on balls. As they always will, National League pitchers eventually remembered not to throw Dunston many strikes, which probably had a lot to do with his dropoff in the second half. On the other hand, Dunston's strikeout and power totals were virtually identical from the first half to the second half, and it's likely that his luck just evened out. Regardless, any team would be happy with a .296-hitting shortstop with 50 extra-base hits.

## Baserunning & Defense

Though the back woes, not to mention age, have robbed Dunston of some of his speed, he remains very fast for a shortstop and stole 10 bases last year. Just as the injuries have cost Dunston speed, they've also cost him range afield. He still has sure hands, and one of the strongest infield arms in the game.

## 1996 Outlook

Dunston has expressed a desire to break the Cub record for games at shortstop, held by Don Kessinger with 1,618. Dunston's got 1,120 and he might stop right there; with Ryne Sandberg returning, the Cubs were considering moving Rey Sanchez to short and letting Dunston depart via free agency. Whichever club gets him will hope that his back—and his bat—remain healthy, and that he regains some range at shortstop, too.

**Position:** SS
**Bats:** R  **Throws:** R
**Ht:** 6' 1"  **Wt:** 180

**Opening Day Age:** 33
**Born:** 3/21/63 in Brooklyn, NY
**ML Seasons:** 11

### Overall Statistics

|  | G | AB | R | H | D | T | HR | RBI | SB | BB | SO | Avg | OBP | Slg |
|---|---|---|---|---|---|---|---|---|---|---|---|---|---|---|
| 1995 | 127 | 477 | 58 | 141 | 30 | 6 | 14 | 69 | 10 | 10 | 75 | .296 | .317 | .472 |
| Career | 1140 | 4151 | 506 | 1100 | 208 | 44 | 98 | 448 | 146 | 163 | 706 | .265 | .294 | .407 |

### Where He Hits the Ball

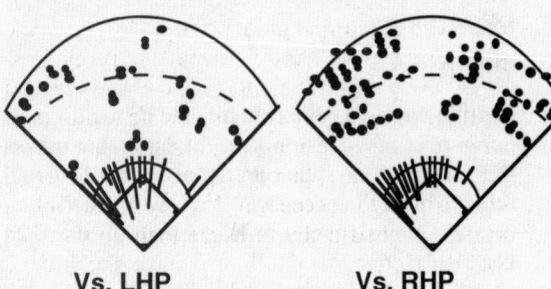

**Vs. LHP**          **Vs. RHP**

### 1995 Situational Stats

|  | AB | H | HR | RBI | Avg |  | AB | H | HR | RBI | Avg |
|---|---|---|---|---|---|---|---|---|---|---|---|
| Home | 232 | 71 | 8 | 37 | .306 | LHP | 138 | 48 | 5 | 24 | .348 |
| Road | 245 | 70 | 6 | 32 | .286 | RHP | 339 | 93 | 9 | 45 | .274 |
| First Half | 227 | 76 | 7 | 36 | .335 | Sc Pos | 121 | 41 | 4 | 55 | .339 |
| Scnd Half | 250 | 65 | 7 | 33 | .260 | Clutch | 84 | 28 | 3 | 10 | .333 |

### 1995 Rankings (National League)

- ➡ 1st in lowest percentage of pitches taken (39.4%)
- ➡ 2nd in lowest on-base percentage vs. right-handed pitchers (.293)
- ➡ 4th in errors at shortstop (17)
- ➡ 5th in least pitches seen per plate appearance (3.25)
- ➡ 7th in lowest fielding percentage at shortstop (.969)
- ➡ 8th in batting average vs. left-handed pitchers (.348)
- ➡ 9th in batting average on an 0-2 count (.292)
- ➡ 10th in lowest on-base percentage
- ➡ Led the Cubs in batting average vs. left-handed pitchers (.348)

# Kevin Foster

## 1995 Season

Kevin Foster's second major league season brought mixed results. He finished with a 12-11 record, a big improvement over his 3-4 mark in 1994. On the other hand, Foster's 4.51 earned-run average was a major comedown from his 2.89 of '94. Back to positives: Foster was healthy all season, he continued to register plenty of strikeouts, and he seems to have solved the control problems he suffered as a minor leaguer.

## Pitching

Foster's stock in trade is a four-seam fastball. He throws it hard and he throws it high. The results are strikeouts and fly balls. . . especially fly balls. Among qualifiers last season, Foster easily finished with the lowest grounder/flyball ratio in the majors, 0.64. That's Sid Fernandez territory. Foster got away with it as a rookie, but last year too many of those high fastballs got blasted; his 32 home runs allowed topped the National League. The standard line is that Foster has to keep the ball down if he's to succeed in Wrigley Field, but he actually pitched better at home than on the road last year.

## Defense & Hitting

Foster's high leg kick would presumably make him an easy mark for basestealers. But all those high fastballs give the catcher good pitches to work with, and opposing runners were just 11-for-21 on stolen-base attempts last year. After batting .074 in 1994, Foster rebounded with a .250 average last season, and he bashed a homer and knocked in nine runs for good measure.

## 1996 Outlook

All those home runs are troublesome, and the Cubs would like Foster to work on the less-home-run-prone two-seam fastball. But either way, Foster showed plenty of good signs last season, and his ERA after July was a satisfactory 3.82. A spot in the Cub rotation is Foster's to lose, and he should be fine in '96. Just don't bet on him when the wind is blowing out.

**Position:** SP
**Bats:** R **Throws:** R
**Ht:** 6' 1" **Wt:** 170

**Opening Day Age:** 27
**Born:** 1/13/69 in Evanston, IL
**ML Seasons:** 3

Chicago Cubs

### Overall Statistics

|        | W  | L  | Pct. | ERA  | G  | GS | Sv | IP    | H   | BB  | SO  | HR | BR/IP |
|--------|----|----|------|------|----|----|----|-------|-----|-----|-----|----|-------|
| 1995   | 12 | 11 | .522 | 4.51 | 30 | 28 | 0  | 167.2 | 149 | 65  | 146 | 32 | 1.28  |
| Career | 15 | 16 | .484 | 4.27 | 45 | 42 | 0  | 255.1 | 232 | 107 | 227 | 42 | 1.33  |

### How Often He Throws Strikes

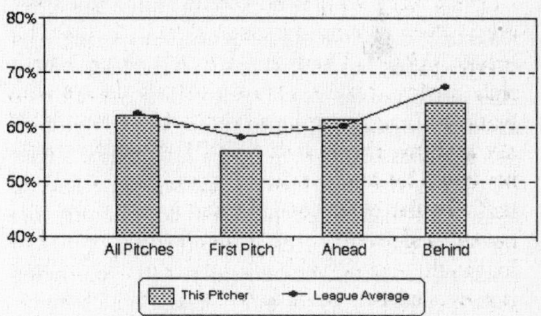

This Pitcher — League Average

### 1995 Situational Stats

|            | W | L | ERA  | Sv | IP   |        | AB  | H  | HR | RBI | Avg  |
|------------|---|---|------|----|------|--------|-----|----|----|-----|------|
| Home       | 7 | 4 | 4.15 | 0  | 78.0 | LHB    | 288 | 75 | 12 | 28  | .260 |
| Road       | 5 | 7 | 4.82 | 0  | 89.2 | RHB    | 334 | 74 | 20 | 51  | .222 |
| First Half | 6 | 5 | 4.57 | 0  | 80.2 | Sc Pos | 114 | 28 | 5  | 47  | .246 |
| Scnd Half  | 6 | 6 | 4.45 | 0  | 87.0 | Clutch | 37  | 10 | 4  | 10  | .270 |

### 1995 Rankings (National League)

- 1st in home runs allowed, lowest groundball/flyball ratio allowed (0.6) and most home runs allowed per 9 innings (1.72)
- 4th in most run support per 9 innings (5.7)
- 5th in most strikeouts per 9 innings (7.8)
- 6th in most pitches thrown per batter (3.86) and least GDPs induced per 9 innings (0.5)
- 7th in highest slugging percentage allowed (.442)
- Led the Cubs in home runs allowed, strikeouts, balks (2), runners caught stealing (10), lowest batting average allowed (.240), lowest stolen base percentage allowed (52.4%) and most strikeouts per 9 innings (7.8)

# Luis Gonzalez

## 1995 Season

When the Cubs went looking for a left fielder with some pop, they turned their covetous eyes toward Houston, and Luis Gonzalez. And why not? At the time (late June), Gonzalez sported a hefty .390 career batting average in Wrigley Field. So on June 28, the Cubs sent Rick Wilkins to Houston in exchange for Gonzalez and Scott Servais. Gonzalez might not have hit .390 as a Cub, but he did bat .291 and reached base with regularity.

## Hitting

Gonzalez' left-handed swing, long and smooth, is regarded as one of the prettier in the National League. He actually struggled upon first arriving in Chicago; he hit just .229 in July. But after making some minor adjustments to his swing—he shortened his leg kick slightly—Gonzalez batted .321 the rest of the way. Described by Steve Stone as "a *great* low-ball hitter," Gonzalez' only obvious weakness is the high fastball, which he sometimes has trouble laying off. Gonzalez shortens up against left-handed pitchers, and he generally hits for about the same average against both types of pitchers. However, he generally—last year being the exception—hits for more power against righties.

## Baserunning & Defense

Gonzalez is built like a tall greyhound, and he swiped 20 bases in 1993 and 15 more in '94. That number dropped to six last year, however, and Gonzalez was gunned down eight times in the process. Once a first baseman as an Astro minor leaguer, Gonzalez has taken amazingly well to the outfield. He gets a good jump on fly balls, and seems to glide effortlessly to the proper spot before sqeezing the baseball. Gonzalez throws well for a left fielder.

## 1996 Outlook

He's not a great hitter, but Gonzalez is certainly better than the Derrick Mays and Scott Bulletts who have patrolled left field for the Cubs in recent years. If he can continue the form he showed the last two months of 1995, Gonzalez might well become a Bleacher Bums favorite.

**Position:** LF
**Bats:** L **Throws:** R
**Ht:** 6' 2"   **Wt:** 180

**Opening Day Age:** 28
**Born:** 9/3/67 in Tampa, FL
**ML Seasons:** 6

### Overall Statistics

| | G | AB | R | H | D | T | HR | RBI | SB | BB | SO | Avg | OBP | Slg |
|---|---|---|---|---|---|---|---|---|---|---|---|---|---|---|
| 1995 | 133 | 471 | 69 | 130 | 29 | 8 | 13 | 69 | 6 | 57 | 63 | .276 | .357 | .454 |
| Career | 670 | 2284 | 300 | 617 | 141 | 27 | 59 | 332 | 58 | 219 | 361 | .270 | .338 | .433 |

### Where He Hits the Ball

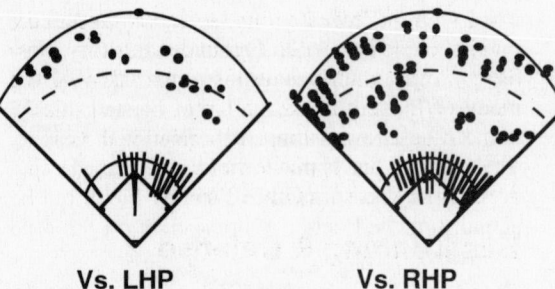

**Vs. LHP**        **Vs. RHP**

### 1995 Situational Stats

| | AB | H | HR | RBI | Avg | | AB | H | HR | RBI | Avg |
|---|---|---|---|---|---|---|---|---|---|---|---|
| Home | 230 | 63 | 6 | 33 | .274 | LHP | 112 | 30 | 4 | 19 | .268 |
| Road | 241 | 67 | 7 | 36 | .278 | RHP | 359 | 100 | 9 | 50 | .279 |
| First Half | 245 | 61 | 6 | 37 | .249 | Sc Pos | 134 | 38 | 2 | 51 | .284 |
| Scnd Half | 226 | 69 | 7 | 32 | .305 | Clutch | 75 | 18 | 3 | 8 | .240 |

### 1995 Rankings (National League)

➡ 2nd in errors in left field (6)
➡ 3rd in triples
➡ 4th in lowest fielding percentage in left field (.977)
➡ 7th in GDPs (16) and batting average with the bases loaded (.444)
➡ 8th in sacrifice flies (6)

# Mark Grace

**Position:** 1B
**Bats:** L **Throws:** L
**Ht:** 6' 2"  **Wt:** 190

**Opening Day Age:** 31
**Born:** 6/28/64 in Winston-Salem, NC
**ML Seasons:** 8

**Chicago Cubs**

## 1995 Season

All things considered, Mark Grace's 1995 campaign has to be considered a triumph. After weighing a number of offers—including one from the crosstown White Sox—the free agent re-signed with the Cubs for one season, and proceeded to post the best all-around numbers of his career. Particularly noteworthy were Grace's power numbers, as his .516 slugging percentage ranked 10th in the National League and tops on the Cubs.

## Hitting

How good was Grace last year? In a shortened season, the lefty swinger set career highs in doubles *and* home runs. With 33 doubles at the All-Star break, Grace was on pace to shatter the single-season record before tailing off in the second half. And he does it without striking out—only 46 last season. How does Grace do it? Well, the most obvious answer is that Grace happily hits the ball wherever it's pitched; a number of those doubles were to the opposite field, and there simply aren't many holes in Grace's swing.

## Baserunning & Defense

Grace is by no means fast, but he just might be the best baserunner in the National League. On July 23, for example, Grace tagged up at first and headed for second on a foul pop to the second baseman. He cruised in standing up, with no throw. Grace is an excellent first baseman—he goes to his left and right equally well, and throws accurately—and last season he garnered his third Gold Glove in four years.

## 1996 Outlook

At this writing, Grace is in exactly the same position he was a year ago: he's a free agent, he wants to play for the Cubs, and the Cubs want him back. That combination, and the lack of a suitable replacement, suggest that he'll be a Cub again. At 31, it's unlikely Grace will duplicate his fine 1995 numbers. But he has to be regarded as one of the top first basemen in the league.

### Overall Statistics

|  | G | AB | R | H | D | T | HR | RBI | SB | BB | SO | Avg | OBP | Slg |
|---|---|---|---|---|---|---|---|---|---|---|---|---|---|---|
| 1995 | 143 | 552 | 97 | 180 | 51 | 3 | 16 | 92 | 6 | 65 | 46 | .326 | .395 | .516 |
| Career | 1155 | 4356 | 608 | 1333 | 261 | 28 | 82 | 589 | 55 | 525 | 347 | .306 | .379 | .435 |

### Where He Hits the Ball

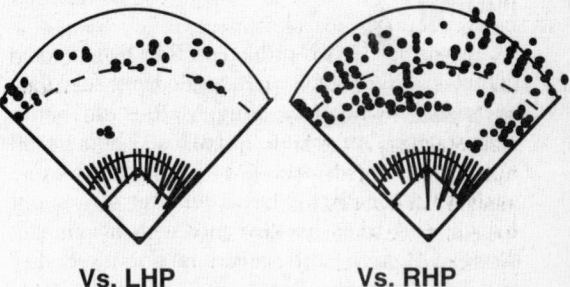

**Vs. LHP**     **Vs. RHP**

### 1995 Situational Stats

|  | AB | H | HR | RBI | Avg |  | AB | H | HR | RBI | Avg |
|---|---|---|---|---|---|---|---|---|---|---|---|
| Home | 280 | 105 | 4 | 41 | .375 | LHP | 186 | 54 | 3 | 30 | .290 |
| Road | 272 | 75 | 12 | 51 | .276 | RHP | 366 | 126 | 13 | 62 | .344 |
| First Half | 262 | 89 | 10 | 49 | .340 | Sc Pos | 129 | 40 | 1 | 66 | .310 |
| Scnd Half | 290 | 91 | 6 | 43 | .314 | Clutch | 89 | 31 | 2 | 7 | .348 |

### 1995 Rankings (National League)

→ 1st in doubles

→ 2nd in cleanup slugging percentage (.664)

→ 3rd in hits, sacrifice flies (7), times on base (247), batting average vs. right-handed pitchers (.344), on-base percentage vs. right-handed pitchers (.425) and errors at first base (7)

→ 4th in games played, batting average at home (.375) and lowest fielding percentage at first base (.995)

→ 5th in batting average, batting average on an 0-2 count (.313) and slugging percentage vs. right-handed pitchers (.560)

→ Led the Cubs in batting average, runs scored, hits (180), singles (110) and doubles

# Brian McRae

## 1995 Season

With the Kansas City Royals facing a huge budget shortfall, they wanted to get *something* for center fielder Brian McRae, who would become a free agent following the 1995 season. So last April, the Royals traded McRae to the Cubs for whatever they could get, which was a pair of mid-level prospects. McRae gave the Cubs exactly what they were looking for: solid, sometimes spectacular defense, and consistency at the top of the order. When McRae was traded to the Cubs, he said, "Leadoff is not my strong suit, but I could do it if there's no one else." There *was* no one else, McRae did it, and he did it as well as anyone could have expected.

## Hitting

As usual, the switch-hitting McRae batted for a higher average against left-handed pitchers. But average was the only thing McRae did better against lefties last season. Ten of his 12 homers, all seven of his triples, and 42 of his 47 walks came against righthanders. McRae hits out of a slight crouch, and takes healthy cuts with a compact swing. Offspeed stuff generally doesn't bother him, but he can be overpowered by good heat.

## Baserunning & Defense

One of the most aggressive baserunners in baseball, McRae runs into the occasional out but generally shows good judgment. He's become a fine basestealer, swiping 55 sacks the last two seasons. McRae has looked like a natural center fielder ever since shifting to the position in his fifth pro season. He takes off after fly balls and liners with the crack of the bat, and anything he gets a glove on, he catches. McRae's one defensive weakness is his throwing arm, not much of a problem in cozy Wrigley Field.

## 1996 Outlook

"The most impressive thing about Brian is the attitude he brings to the clubhouse every day," Jim Riggleman said last season. That shouldn't be a surprise, given that McRae's father Hal was a perennial clubhouse leader. Throw in Brian's not inconsiderable defense and hitting, and the Cubs desperately need him back in 1996.

**Position:** CF
**Bats:** B  **Throws:** R
**Ht:** 6' 0"  **Wt:** 195

**Opening Day Age:** 28
**Born:** 8/27/67 in Bradenton, FL
**ML Seasons:** 6

### Overall Statistics

| | G | AB | R | H | D | T | HR | RBI | SB | BB | SO | Avg | OBP | Slg |
|---|---|---|---|---|---|---|---|---|---|---|---|---|---|---|
| 1995 | 137 | 580 | 92 | 167 | 38 | 7 | 12 | 48 | 27 | 47 | 92 | .288 | .348 | .440 |
| Career | 751 | 2973 | 411 | 794 | 147 | 39 | 42 | 296 | 120 | 213 | 480 | .267 | .320 | .385 |

### Where He Hits the Ball

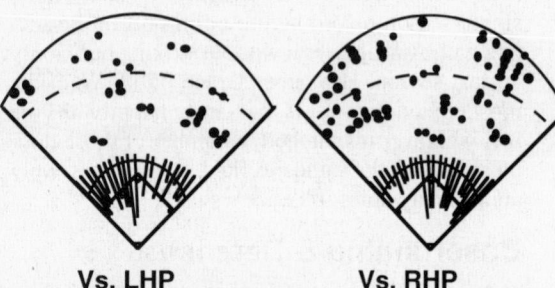

Vs. LHP            Vs. RHP

### 1995 Situational Stats

| | AB | H | HR | RBI | Avg | | AB | H | HR | RBI | Avg |
|---|---|---|---|---|---|---|---|---|---|---|---|
| Home | 283 | 81 | 6 | 30 | .286 | LHP | 163 | 51 | 2 | 12 | .313 |
| Road | 297 | 86 | 6 | 18 | .290 | RHP | 417 | 116 | 10 | 36 | .278 |
| First Half | 282 | 81 | 7 | 26 | .287 | Sc Pos | 108 | 31 | 1 | 37 | .287 |
| Scnd Half | 298 | 86 | 5 | 22 | .289 | Clutch | 92 | 24 | 2 | 8 | .261 |

### 1995 Rankings (National League)

→ 1st in at-bats
→ 2nd in doubles and plate appearances (638)
→ 3rd in highest groundball/flyball ratio (2.2)
→ 4th in hits and fielding percentage in center field (.991)
→ 5th in pitches seen (2,440)
→ 6th in triples
→ 7th in errors in center field (3) and bunts in play (25)
→ 8th in runs scored and singles (110)
→ 10th in lowest on-base percentage for a leadoff hitter (.349)
→ Led the Cubs in at-bats, singles (110), triples, caught stealing (8), hit by pitch (7), GDPs (12) and plate appearances (638)

# Randy Myers

## 1995 Season

After a subpar 1994 campaign which saw him blow five saves and lose five games—and remember, that was a 114-game season—Randy Myers reclaimed his place among the National League's top closers last season. His 38 saves topped the National League, and he only lost twice. Myers pitched well in every month but July (7.15 ERA), and even that month he converted eight of nine save opportunities.

## Pitching

There's nothing fancy about Myers' pitching style. He throws 90-plus fastballs and hard sliders. Neither pitch is overpowering, but Myers knows where and when to throw each of them. Against right-handed batters, Myers likes to get ahead with the heat, then come in with what Cubs general manager Ed Lynch calls "a shoe-eating slider." He'll also throw a curve now and then, but rarely near the strike zone. When he gets behind a right-handed hitter, Myers often goes ahead and issues a semi-intentional walk rather than give in. His slider is *really* rough on left-handed hitters, and Myers held lefties to a lowly .130 average last season.

## Defense & Hitting

Myers' fly-off-the-mound follow-through leaves him in terrible fielding position. But he's not a bad fielder when he has the ball, and he's very tough to run on. Myers has allowed only two stolen bases in the last three seasons, and two runners were nabbed trying last year. Myers almost never bats anymore, but he is a decent .186 lifetime hitter.

## 1996 Outlook

Myers' numbers were more than adequate last season, especially considering that he pitched 28 times in Wrigley Field. He's 33 now, but many closers have pitched well into their late thirties, and it wouldn't be much of a surprise if Myers lasted another five or so years. He should remain a closer until he decisively proves that he's no longer up to the task.

**Position:** RP
**Bats:** L **Throws:** L
**Ht:** 6' 1" **Wt:** 230

**Opening Day Age:** 33
**Born:** 9/19/62 in Vancouver, WA
**ML Seasons:** 11

Chicago Cubs

### Overall Statistics

|        | W  | L  | Pct. | ERA  | G   | GS | Sv  | IP    | H   | BB  | SO  | HR | BR/IP |
|--------|----|----|------|------|-----|----|-----|-------|-----|-----|-----|----|-------|
| 1995   | 1  | 2  | .333 | 3.88 | 57  | 0  | 38  | 55.2  | 49  | 28  | 59  | 7  | 1.38  |
| Career | 34 | 49 | .410 | 3.17 | 543 | 12 | 243 | 709.2 | 592 | 319 | 713 | 54 | 1.28  |

### How Often He Throws Strikes

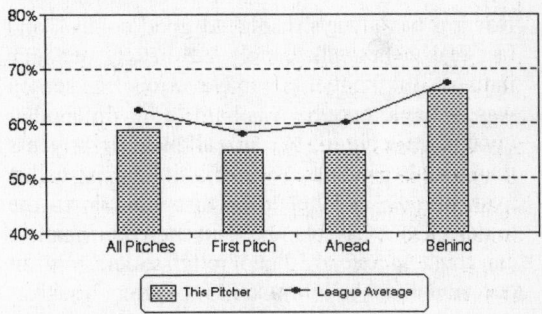

### 1995 Situational Stats

|            | W | L | ERA  | Sv | IP   |        | AB  | H  | HR | RBI | Avg  |
|------------|---|---|------|----|------|--------|-----|----|----|-----|------|
| Home       | 0 | 0 | 4.50 | 17 | 26.0 | LHB    | 46  | 6  | 0  | 6   | .130 |
| Road       | 1 | 2 | 3.34 | 21 | 29.2 | RHB    | 161 | 43 | 7  | 27  | .267 |
| First Half | 0 | 1 | 2.40 | 21 | 30.0 | Sc Pos | 58  | 17 | 3  | 27  | .293 |
| Scnd Half  | 1 | 1 | 5.61 | 17 | 25.2 | Clutch | 168 | 43 | 6  | 32  | .256 |

### 1995 Rankings (National League)

→ 1st in saves and save opportunities (44)
→ 4th in save percentage (86.4%) and most strikeouts per 9 innings in relief (9.5)
→ 6th in blown saves (6)
→ 10th in games finished (47)
→ Led the Cubs in saves, games finished, save opportunities, save percentage, blown saves, lowest batting average allowed in relief (.237), least baserunners allowed per 9 innings in relief (12.4) and most strikeouts per 9 innings in relief

# Jaime Navarro

## 1995 Season

In 1991 and '92, Jaime Navarro went 32-23 with the Milwaukee Brewers and established himself as one of the American League's top young pitchers. But in both '93 and '94, Navarro reported to spring training in poor condition. Perhaps as a result, he posted awful numbers in each of those seasons. Not the way you want to pitch on the eve of free agency. Nevertheless, the Cubs took a flyer on Navarro. He reported to camp 15 pounds lighter, and wound up posting the best numbers of his career. Frank Castillo pitched well, too, but Navarro was the most consistent Cub starter, the centerpiece of a resurgent rotation.

## Pitching

Navarro has always displayed good control, and last season he walked only 2.5 batters per nine innings. But the real key to Navarro's fine season was a simple one; he was hard to hit. In another good year for hitters, Navarro allowed slightly less than a hit per inning. Navarro's sinking fastball is average-plus, and he rarely throws it down the middle. Once he gets ahead in the count, batters can count on a steady diet of tough sliders, with an occasional forkball thrown in for variety's sake.

## Defense & Hitting

Nothing special defensively, Navarro doesn't embarrass himself. Runners generally don't have much trouble, because Navarro rarely varies his stretch motion. He allowed 16 stolen bases last season, with six caught. Navarro batted .185 last season, excellent for any hurler, let alone one batting for the first time in his major league career.

## 1996 Outlook

Navarro's 14-6 record last year virtually guarantees him the number-one spot in the rotation. Assuming his arm is healthy and he reports to camp in good shape, there's no reason to think Navarro won't give the Cubs 200 or so quality innings.

**Position:** SP
**Bats:** R  **Throws:** R
**Ht:** 6' 4"  **Wt:** 225

**Opening Day Age:** 28
**Born:** 3/27/68 in Bayamon, PR
**ML Seasons:** 7
**Pronunciation:** JAY-mee nuh-VAR-roh

### Overall Statistics

|        | W  | L  | Pct. | ERA  | G   | GS  | Sv | IP     | H    | BB  | SO  | HR | BR/IP |
|--------|----|----|------|------|-----|-----|----|--------|------|-----|-----|----|-------|
| 1995   | 14 | 6  | .700 | 3.28 | 29  | 29  | 0  | 200.1  | 194  | 56  | 128 | 19 | 1.25  |
| Career | 76 | 65 | .539 | 4.13 | 212 | 180 | 1  | 1243.1 | 1319 | 374 | 652 | 99 | 1.36  |

### How Often He Throws Strikes

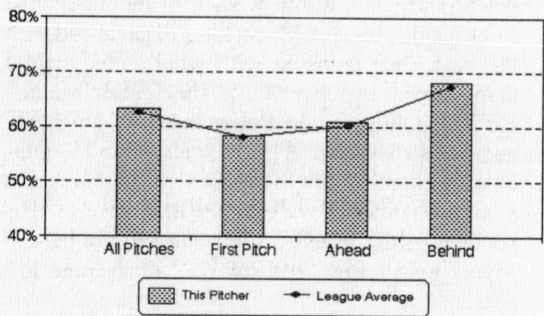

### 1995 Situational Stats

|            | W | L | ERA  | Sv | IP    |        | AB  | H   | HR | RBI | Avg  |
|------------|---|---|------|----|-------|--------|-----|-----|----|-----|------|
| Home       | 5 | 4 | 3.24 | 0  | 97.1  | LHB    | 336 | 84  | 7  | 29  | .250 |
| Road       | 9 | 2 | 3.32 | 0  | 103.0 | RHB    | 437 | 110 | 12 | 40  | .252 |
| First Half | 7 | 2 | 2.82 | 0  | 92.2  | Sc Pos | 167 | 41  | 2  | 45  | .246 |
| Scnd Half  | 7 | 4 | 3.68 | 0  | 107.2 | Clutch | 68  | 14  | 0  | 3   | .206 |

### 1995 Rankings (National League)

➤ 5th in wins, innings pitched, batters faced (837), pitches thrown (3,060) and winning percentage

➤ 8th in lowest on-base percentage allowed (.303) and ERA on the road (3.32)

➤ 9th in hits allowed and least strikeouts per 9 innings (5.8)

➤ 10th in ERA, lowest slugging percentage allowed (.362) and least GDPs induced per 9 innings (0.5)

➤ Led the Cubs in sacrifice bunts (8), wins, games started, innings pitched, hits allowed, batters faced (837), pitches thrown (3,060), GDPs induced (12) and winning percentage

# Mike Perez

**Chicago Cubs**

## 1995 Season

After an impressive 1993 season (7-2, 2.48) with the St. Louis Cardinals, Mike Perez earned the closer job for 1994. He pitched great that April, but a strained shoulder in May sent his season into a headlong spiral ending with an 8.71 ERA. Exit St. Louis, enter the north side of Chicago, as the righthander signed a free-agent deal with the Cubs. Perez might not have regained the form he'd once shown in St. Louis. But he was healthy and he provided a lot of quality innings, as his 68 games pitched ranked fifth in the National League.

## Pitching

At his peak, Perez could blow away hitters with his plus fastball. He can still do that on occasion, as he did last August 18, striking out Larry Walker on a series of 90-plus heaters. But the velocity wasn't always there last season, forcing Perez to nibble with his hard, late-breaking curve and the occasional slider. Every once in a while, Perez unleashes a bat-shattering fastball that bores in on a right-handed batter. Perez' fastball used to afford him the luxury of getting behind in the count, but these days he generally needs to get ahead to be effective.

## Defense & Hitting

Perez is a competent fielder, but his deliberate motion leaves him somewhat vulnerable to the stolen base. Perez doesn't hit much, and after 10 major league at-bats he's still looking for his first hit. On the other hand, he has somehow drawn three walks.

## 1996 Outlook

It looks like Perez' 1994 numbers were an aberration, caused by the shoulder injury. If he can recover fully, there's no reason he can't pitch as well as he did a few years ago. Though he might never be asked to fill the closer role again, a role which he prefers to avoid, Perez should enjoy a productive career as a middle reliever.

**Position:** RP
**Bats:** R  **Throws:** R
**Ht:** 6' 0"  **Wt:** 200

**Opening Day Age:** 31
**Born:** 10/19/64 in Yauco, PR
**ML Seasons:** 6

### Overall Statistics

|        | W  | L  | Pct. | ERA  | G   | GS | Sv | IP    | H   | BB | SO  | HR | BR/IP |
|--------|----|----|------|------|-----|----|----|-------|-----|----|-----|----|-------|
| 1995   | 2  | 6  | .250 | 3.66 | 68  | 0  | 2  | 71.1  | 72  | 27 | 49  | 8  | 1.39  |
| Career | 21 | 16 | .568 | 3.47 | 273 | 0  | 22 | 298.2 | 290 | 99 | 185 | 22 | 1.30  |

### How Often He Throws Strikes

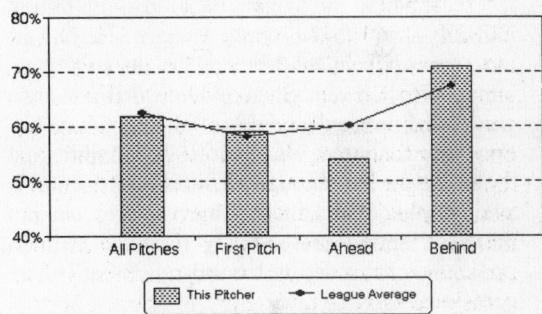

### 1995 Situational Stats

|            | W | L | ERA  | Sv | IP   |        | AB  | H  | HR | RBI | Avg  |
|------------|---|---|------|----|------|--------|-----|----|----|-----|------|
| Home       | 2 | 5 | 3.72 | 0  | 36.1 | LHB    | 93  | 27 | 2  | 9   | .290 |
| Road       | 0 | 1 | 3.60 | 2  | 35.0 | RHB    | 176 | 45 | 6  | 28  | .256 |
| First Half | 1 | 4 | 3.28 | 2  | 35.2 | Sc Pos | 85  | 19 | 2  | 31  | .224 |
| Scnd Half  | 1 | 2 | 4.04 | 0  | 35.2 | Clutch | 139 | 38 | 3  | 23  | .273 |

### 1995 Rankings (National League)

→ 5th in games pitched and relief losses (6)
→ 6th in least strikeouts per 9 innings in relief (6.2)
→ 7th in holds (16)
→ Led the Cubs in games pitched, holds, relief ERA (3.66), relief losses and relief innings (71.1)

# Rey Sanchez

## 1995 Season

Succeeding a legend ain't easy, but Rey Sanchez did it about as well as anyone could expect. There were probably only two or three dozen times last season when Harry Caray said, "You know, Steve, I think Sandberg would've made that play." Sanchez missed late July and early August with tendinitis in his left wrist, and was later hindered by a broken hamate bone in his left hand. But he grittily completed the season. . . only to discover when it ended that the legend was coming back to reclaim his old position.

## Hitting

Sanchez hits for a decent average—he was at .299 last season until the hamate began paining him in mid-July—but it's an empty average. He has almost zero pop in his bat, and he doesn't walk, either. In fact, he and Shawon Dunston made up a great All-Impatient middle infield. Sanchez' hitting style is simple: wait as long as possible, and try to slap the ball through the infield. The result is a fair amount of hits, most of them singles, and not many strikeouts. His ability to make contact makes Sanchez a decent hit-and-run threat.

## Baserunning & Defense

Though he once stole 29 bases in one minor league season, Sanchez doesn't run much anymore. Defensively, Sanchez would have never equalled Ryno's nine Gold Gloves at second, but he *is* a fine second sacker in his own right—perhaps a tad soft on the double play, but with fine range in both directions and very sure hands. Sanchez was also a top shortstop in the minors, and with Sandberg coming out of retirement, he might well get a chance to play his old position again.

## 1996 Outlook

Even though Sandberg is returning, Sanchez might still be a regular this year. There's an excellent chance the Cubs will let Dunston depart via free agency and move Sanchez over to shortstop. Sanchez can certainly handle the position, but he'll probably be waiting for the first time Harry says, "You know, Steve, I think Dunston would've made that play. . ."

**Position:** 2B
**Bats:** R **Throws:** R
**Ht:** 5' 9" **Wt:** 170

**Opening Day Age:** 28
**Born:** 10/5/67 in Rio Piedras, PR
**ML Seasons:** 5

### Overall Statistics

|  | G | AB | R | H | D | T | HR | RBI | SB | BB | SO | Avg | OBP | Slg |
|---|---|---|---|---|---|---|---|---|---|---|---|---|---|---|
| 1995 | 114 | 428 | 57 | 119 | 22 | 2 | 3 | 27 | 6 | 14 | 48 | .278 | .301 | .360 |
| Career | 402 | 1341 | 143 | 369 | 60 | 8 | 4 | 100 | 11 | 63 | 119 | .275 | .313 | .341 |

### Where He Hits the Ball

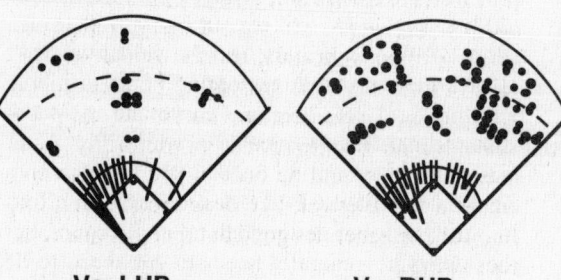

Vs. LHP          Vs. RHP

### 1995 Situational Stats

|  | AB | H | HR | RBI | Avg |  | AB | H | HR | RBI | Avg |
|---|---|---|---|---|---|---|---|---|---|---|---|
| Home | 197 | 58 | 0 | 9 | .294 | LHP | 114 | 30 | 1 | 7 | .263 |
| Road | 231 | 61 | 3 | 18 | .264 | RHP | 314 | 89 | 2 | 20 | .283 |
| First Half | 276 | 83 | 2 | 19 | .301 | Sc Pos | 86 | 22 | 1 | 21 | .256 |
| Scnd Half | 152 | 36 | 1 | 8 | .237 | Clutch | 60 | 17 | 2 | 10 | .283 |

### 1995 Rankings (National League)

→ 3rd in lowest on-base percentage and least pitches seen per plate appearance (3.19)

→ 4th in bunts in play (29) and highest percentage of extra bases taken as a runner (67.4%)

→ 6th in lowest HR frequency (142.7 ABs per HR)

→ 8th in lowest on-base percentage vs. left-handed pitchers (.276)

→ 9th in lowest slugging percentage

→ Led the Cubs in sacrifice bunts (8), bunts in play (29) and highest percentage of extra bases taken as a runner (67.4%)

# Scott Servais

## 1995 Season

It was late June, and N.L. Central rivals Houston and Chicago were both displeased with their starting catchers. Scott Servais was hitting .225 for the Astros, Rick Wilkins was batting .191 for the Cubs, and neither was hitting with any power. The solution? A trade, of course. Wilkins struggled as an Astro, but Servais was reborn in Wrigley Field. He batted .286 as a Cub to finish at a career-high .265, he got on base, he hit home runs, and he played solid defense. The only hitch came in July, when Servais suffered a sprained left knee and spent three weeks on the disabled list.

## Hitting

Servais has shown good power since 1993, when he hit 11 homers in 258 at-bats. He continued that trend in 1995, especially in August. In one 18-game stretch, Servais blasted eight homers and knocked in 15 runs. But Servais did two things in 1995 that he'd *never* done before: he hit for a decent average, and he drew walks. Servais hits out of a Jeff Bagwell-like deep crouch, and like Bagwell, he generates good bat speed with a compact swing.

## Baserunning & Defense

Baserunning? Base*plodding* is more like it. Servais did collect the first two stolen bases of his career last season, but he was also *caught* twice. For a guy with Servais' defensive reputation, he is quite weak against the running game. Over the last two seasons, he's only gunned down 21 percent of opposing basestealers. But Servais blocks the plate well, gets squarely in front of balls in the dirt, and he calls a good game.

## 1996 Outlook

Major leaguers rarely learn to hit when they're 28, so it's likely that Servais' offensive numbers last season were something of a fluke, the product of a career year. However, those numbers guarantee him the starting job this season, and as long as he plays solid defense and hits the occasional homer he'll be in the lineup.

**Position:** C
**Bats:** R  **Throws:** R
**Ht:** 6' 2"  **Wt:** 195

**Opening Day Age:** 28
**Born:** 6/4/67 in LaCrosse, WI
**ML Seasons:** 5
**Pronunciation:** SER-vus

### Overall Statistics

|  | G | AB | R | H | D | T | HR | RBI | SB | BB | SO | Avg | OBP | Slg |
|---|---|---|---|---|---|---|---|---|---|---|---|---|---|---|
| 1995 | 80 | 264 | 38 | 70 | 22 | 0 | 13 | 47 | 2 | 32 | 52 | .265 | .348 | .496 |
| Career | 336 | 1015 | 101 | 237 | 60 | 1 | 33 | 141 | 2 | 79 | 174 | .233 | .297 | .392 |

### Where He Hits the Ball

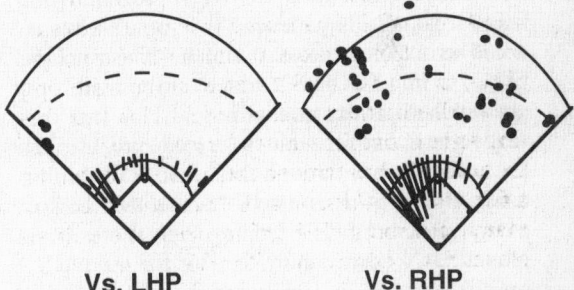

**Vs. LHP**          **Vs. RHP**

### 1995 Situational Stats

|  | AB | H | HR | RBI | Avg |  | AB | H | HR | RBI | Avg |
|---|---|---|---|---|---|---|---|---|---|---|---|
| Home | 129 | 32 | 8 | 25 | .248 | LHP | 69 | 24 | 2 | 18 | .348 |
| Road | 135 | 38 | 5 | 22 | .281 | RHP | 195 | 46 | 11 | 29 | .236 |
| First Half | 120 | 26 | 3 | 16 | .217 | Sc Pos | 70 | 17 | 1 | 31 | .243 |
| Scnd Half | 144 | 44 | 10 | 31 | .306 | Clutch | 45 | 14 | 2 | 7 | .311 |

### 1995 Rankings (National League)

➡ 1st in errors at catcher (12)
➡ Led the Cubs in batting average on a 3-2 count (.389)

# Sammy Sosa

## 1995 Season

Sammy Sosa has always had his critics, and he probably still does. It's just getting harder and harder to find them. Through last July, Sosa was already enjoying a pretty good season. Then came August: 12 home runs, and 33 runs batted in. He ended his amazing run with two homers and a double on September 2. Sosa finished his finest season with career highs in homers, RBI and, tellingly, walks.

## Hitting

Quite possibly the best low-ball hitter in the majors, Sosa regularly turns ankle-high fastballs into extra-base hits. Of course, Sosa has posted good numbers before, but has always suffered one major weakness: impatience. As Jerome Holtzman noted in a column last summer, "The pitching book on him is, 'Don't throw strikes. He's so anxious he'll swing at anything.'" That was certainly true at one time, but Sosa made great strides last year toward rewriting the book. Cubs hitting coach Billy Williams noted, "Sometimes he still overswings, but he's become much more disciplined. He's learned how to wait for his pitch." Sosa's 58 walks in 1995 were 20 more than his previous career high.

## Baserunning & Defense

Once on the bases, Sosa occasionally errs on the side of daring, and he sometimes seems to forget the game situation. He succeeded on 34 of 41 steal attempts last year, fine numbers for anyone. About the only thing Sosa detractors can point to these days is defense. He's got fine range in right field, but he makes too many errors—a whopping 13 last season—and he still misses the cutoff man too often while trying to show off his very strong arm.

## 1996 Outlook

It's hard to imagine that Sosa could get better. . . but don't bet against him. Most people think of him as a "natural," but Sosa is a workaholic. He takes two daily rounds of batting practice, one in the morning and the usual pre-game session. A 40/40 season isn't beyond him, and it's no mystery why Sosa's talents were being sought by a number of clubs over the winter.

**Position:** RF
**Bats:** R  **Throws:** R
**Ht:** 6' 0"  **Wt:** 185

**Opening Day Age:** 27
**Born:** 11/12/68 in San Pedro de Macoris, DR
**ML Seasons:** 7

### Overall Statistics

| | G | AB | R | H | D | T | HR | RBI | SB | BB | SO | Avg | OBP | Slg |
|---|---|---|---|---|---|---|---|---|---|---|---|---|---|---|
| 1995 | 144 | 564 | 89 | 151 | 17 | 3 | 36 | 119 | 34 | 58 | 134 | .268 | .340 | .500 |
| Career | 802 | 2881 | 419 | 738 | 110 | 27 | 131 | 423 | 159 | 198 | 719 | .256 | .308 | .449 |

### Where He Hits the Ball

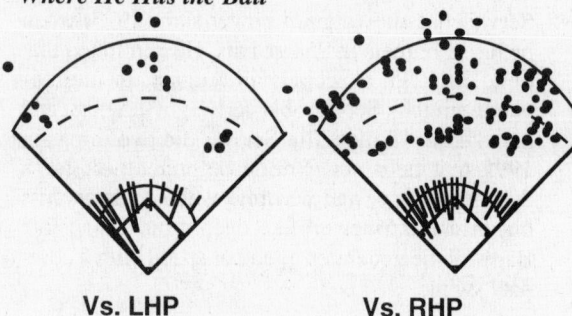

Vs. LHP          Vs. RHP

### 1995 Situational Stats

| | AB | H | HR | RBI | Avg | | AB | H | HR | RBI | Avg |
|---|---|---|---|---|---|---|---|---|---|---|---|
| Home | 276 | 75 | 19 | 62 | .272 | LHP | 148 | 38 | 9 | 27 | .257 |
| Road | 288 | 76 | 17 | 57 | .264 | RHP | 416 | 113 | 27 | 92 | .272 |
| First Half | 278 | 76 | 15 | 54 | .273 | Sc Pos | 164 | 56 | 14 | 84 | .341 |
| Scnd Half | 286 | 75 | 21 | 65 | .262 | Clutch | 84 | 19 | 3 | 11 | .226 |

### 1995 Rankings (National League)

→ 1st in games played and errors in right field (13)
→ 2nd in home runs, RBI, strikeouts, lowest fielding percentage in right field (.962), highest percentage of swings that missed (30.0%) and lowest percentage of swings put into play (34.3%)
→ 3rd in at-bats
→ 4th in pitches seen (2,443)
→ 5th in plate appearances (629)
→ 6th in intentional walks (11) and HR frequency (15.7 ABs per HR)
→ 7th in stolen bases
→ Led the Cubs in home runs, RBI, stolen bases, intentional walks and strikeouts

# Ozzie Timmons

## 1995 Season

After a few years as the Cubs' top minor-league power prospect, Ozzie Timmons finally arrived in 1995. . . sort of. He opened the season in a left-field platoon with Scott Bullett, but saw his playing time shrink considerably after the club traded for Luis Gonzalez in late June. Still, Timmons' season has to be considered a success. Aside from a miserable July (4-for-29), Timmons batted .289 with good power. And he closed the campaign with three homers in September.

## Hitting

Had Timmons shown any ability at all to hit right-handed pitching, the Cubs might not have acquired Gonzalez. But Timmons managed just a .203 average versus righties, which relegated him to part-time duty. His other big weakness as a hitter, at least for now, is a lack of plate patience, which has deteriorated as Timmons moved first to Triple-A and then the majors. If he can conquer that strike-zone foe, his power will make him a productive major league hitter.

## Baserunning & Defense

Timmons runs hard, if not particularly fast, and stole three bases last year without being caught. He's not a great outfielder and doesn't throw well, but he's a good enough athlete that the Cubs worked him out at third and first base in case Todd Zeile or Mark Grace got hurt.

## 1996 Outlook

Like his early-season platoon mate Scott Bullett, Timmons showed enough in limited duty to be a part of the Cubs' plans in 1996. To reach the next level, however, he'll have to do a little better against right-handed pitchers, and draw a few more walks. Chances are he'll again serve as the club's extra righty outfielder, with occasional starts against southpaws.

**Position:** LF
**Bats:** R  **Throws:** R
**Ht:** 6' 2"  **Wt:** 210

**Opening Day Age:** 25
**Born:** 9/18/70 in Tampa, FL
**ML Seasons:** 1

Chicago Cubs

### Overall Statistics

|        | G  | AB  | R  | H  | D  | T | HR | RBI | SB | BB | SO | Avg  | OBP  | Slg  |
|--------|----|-----|----|----|----|---|----|-----|----|----|----|------|------|------|
| 1995   | 77 | 171 | 30 | 45 | 10 | 1 | 8  | 28  | 3  | 13 | 32 | .263 | .314 | .474 |
| Career | 77 | 171 | 30 | 45 | 10 | 1 | 8  | 28  | 3  | 13 | 32 | .263 | .314 | .474 |

### Where He Hits the Ball

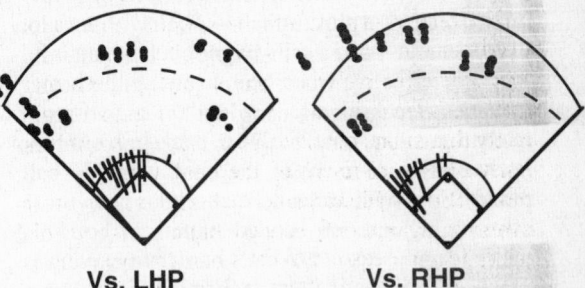

**Vs. LHP**          **Vs. RHP**

### 1995 Situational Stats

|            | AB | H  | HR | RBI | Avg  |        | AB | H  | HR | RBI | Avg  |
|------------|----|----|----|-----|------|--------|----|----|----|-----|------|
| Home       | 90 | 23 | 5  | 10  | .256 | LHP    | 92 | 29 | 3  | 14  | .315 |
| Road       | 81 | 22 | 3  | 18  | .272 | RHP    | 79 | 16 | 5  | 14  | .203 |
| First Half | 96 | 26 | 4  | 17  | .271 | Sc Pos | 44 | 14 | 0  | 16  | .318 |
| Scnd Half  | 75 | 19 | 4  | 11  | .253 | Clutch | 40 | 5  | 0  | 5   | .125 |

### 1995 Rankings (National League)

➡ Did not rank near the top or bottom in any category

# Steve Trachsel

## 1995 Season

How do you go from staff ace to low man on the totem pole, all in one season? Just ask Steve Trachsel. In 1994, the rookie's 3.21 ERA was the best among Cub starters. In 1995, his 5.15 mark was the club's worst. Trachsel's fourth start last season was a three-hit victory over the Giants, but that was as good as it got.

## Pitching

Many observers were quick to notice that Trachsel allowed 25 homers, tied for second most in the league. But 18 of those came with the bases empty. No, the problem last season was simple: Trachsel allowed more hits and he walked more batters than he did in '94. At his best, Trachsel need only rely on two pitches: a plus fastball—albeit without a lot of movement—and a split-finger pitch which is all the more effective when he's throwing the heater to spots. Trachsel also worked on a two-seam fastball, a sinker that he threw back in his minor league days. As is often the case with forkball pitchers, the right-handed Trachsel has been more effective against left-handed batters in both his major league seasons. What's harder to explain is Trachsel's ineffectiveness at Wrigley Field. In his career, he's 3-16 with a 4.75 ERA at home, but 13-6 and 3.76 on the road. At this point, Trachsel may have a mental block about pitching at Wrigley.

## Defense & Hitting

Like most of the Cub starters, Trachsel didn't slow down the opposition running game much. Twenty-six runners tried to steal, and 20 were successful. He's a decent enough fielder. Trachsel batted .265 last season, and he's probably the best-hitting Cub pitcher.

## 1996 Outlook

After Trachsel got roughed up in a late-August start, Cubs manager Bill Riggleman said, "Steve's got a nice arm and a nice repertoire. We're just going to keep putting him out there." That's exactly what they figure to do in 1996, at least for a while. But given his awful numbers at Wrigley Field, a trade might be the best thing for the young righthander.

**Position:** SP
**Bats:** R  **Throws:** R
**Ht:** 6' 4"   **Wt:** 205

**Opening Day Age:** 25
**Born:** 10/31/70 in Oxnard, CA
**ML Seasons:** 3
**Pronunciation:** TRACK-sil

### Overall Statistics

|        | W  | L  | Pct. | ERA  | G  | GS | Sv | IP    | H   | BB  | SO  | HR | BR/IP |
|--------|----|----|------|------|----|----|----|-------|-----|-----|-----|----|-------|
| 1995   | 7  | 13 | .350 | 5.15 | 30 | 29 | 0  | 160.2 | 174 | 76  | 117 | 25 | 1.56  |
| Career | 16 | 22 | .421 | 4.25 | 55 | 54 | 0  | 326.1 | 323 | 133 | 239 | 48 | 1.40  |

### How Often He Throws Strikes

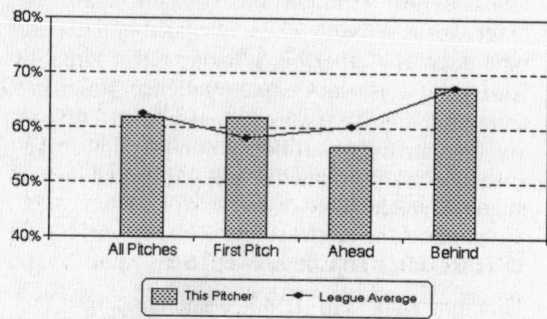

### 1995 Situational Stats

|            | W | L | ERA  | Sv | IP   |        | AB  | H  | HR | RBI | Avg  |
|------------|---|---|------|----|------|--------|-----|----|----|-----|------|
| Home       | 2 | 8 | 6.19 | 0  | 75.2 | LHB    | 295 | 75 | 13 | 38  | .254 |
| Road       | 5 | 5 | 4.24 | 0  | 85.0 | RHB    | 334 | 99 | 12 | 46  | .296 |
| First Half | 3 | 6 | 4.00 | 0  | 83.1 | Sc Pos | 142 | 40 | 4  | 55  | .282 |
| Scnd Half  | 4 | 7 | 6.40 | 0  | 77.1 | Clutch | 29  | 5  | 0  | 1   | .172 |

### 1995 Rankings (National League)

- ➞ 1st in highest ERA at home (6.18)
- ➞ 2nd in home runs allowed and most baserunners allowed per 9 innings (14.0)
- ➞ 3rd in highest ERA, walks allowed, pickoff throws (208), lowest strikeout/walk ratio (1.5) and most home runs allowed per 9 innings (1.40)
- ➞ 4th in highest on-base percentage allowed (.352) and most pitches thrown per batter (3.91)
- ➞ 5th in losses
- ➞ 6th in highest slugging percentage allowed (.453)
- ➞ Led the Cubs in losses, games started, complete games (2) and walks allowed

# Anthony Young

## 1995 Season

If nothing else, the 1995 season was a testament to Anthony Young's strength of will. On August 15, 1994, Young underwent Tommy John tendon-transplant surgery. The normal recovery time is about a year, yet Young vowed to pitch again before the All-Star Game. He beat that goal by a few weeks, returning to the mound on June 13. The season wasn't an unqualified success—Young's 3.70 ERA masks some otherwise unimpressive numbers—but the simple fact that he was pitching on a major league mound made 1995 a positive season.

## Pitching

More so than most pitchers, Young can get away with giving up some hits, because he's an extreme groundball pitcher and induces plenty of double plays. Why all those grounders? Young's best pitch is his hard sinker, and that's backed up by a slider which also breaks downward. He'll also throw a curveball and even an occasional change of pace, but neither of those is a money pitch. Coming off the elbow surgery, Young was forced to make some adjustments upon his return to the mound. His arm strength wasn't quite up to par at first, but Young felt that his velocity was nearly back to normal over the last month or so of the season.

## Defense & Hitting

Young is a good athlete and quick off the mound, but he had his problems on defense last season, committing two errors. He's fairly tough to run on, especially for a righthander. Young doesn't get to wield the bat very often, but he was 2-for-3 last season and sports a decent .163 lifetime average.

## 1996 Outlook

The Cubs never found an entirely reliable set-up man for Randy Myers last year, and Young will likely battle Mike Perez and perhaps Turk Wendell for that job. Even should he lose that fight, Young should stick around as a middle reliever. Remember, Young's career ERA is now 3.84, not bad for a pitcher whose career record is 12-45. With all he's gone through, every day in the majors probably feels like a bonus.

**Position:** RP
**Bats:** R **Throws:** R
**Ht:** 6' 2" **Wt:** 215

**Opening Day Age:** 30
**Born:** 1/19/66 in Houston, TX
**ML Seasons:** 5

Chicago Cubs

### Overall Statistics

|        | W  | L  | Pct. | ERA  | G   | GS | Sv | IP    | H   | BB  | SO  | HR | BR/IP |
|--------|----|----|------|------|-----|----|----|-------|-----|-----|-----|----|-------|
| 1995   | 3  | 4  | .429 | 3.70 | 32  | 1  | 2  | 41.1  | 47  | 14  | 15  | 5  | 1.48  |
| Career | 12 | 45 | .211 | 3.84 | 153 | 51 | 20 | 426.2 | 435 | 145 | 226 | 37 | 1.36  |

### How Often He Throws Strikes

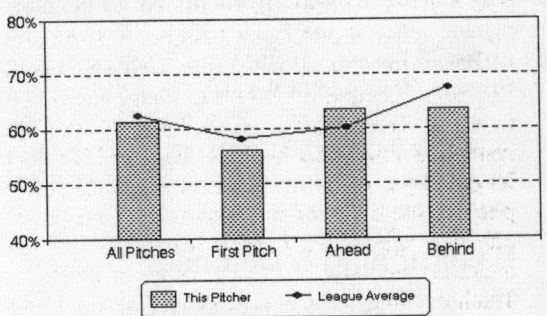

### 1995 Situational Stats

|            | W | L | ERA  | Sv | IP   |        | AB  | H  | HR | RBI | Avg  |
|------------|---|---|------|----|------|--------|-----|----|----|-----|------|
| Home       | 2 | 2 | 4.15 | 1  | 21.2 | LHB    | 59  | 16 | 0  | 2   | .271 |
| Road       | 1 | 2 | 3.20 | 1  | 19.2 | RHB    | 104 | 31 | 5  | 18  | .298 |
| First Half | 0 | 2 | 6.48 | 1  | 8.1  | Sc Pos | 54  | 13 | 0  | 11  | .241 |
| Scnd Half  | 3 | 2 | 3.00 | 1  | 33.0 | Clutch | 37  | 10 | 1  | 6   | .270 |

### 1995 Rankings (National League)

→ Led the Cubs in wild pitches (6)

# Todd Zeile

## 1995 Season

Third base was a mess for the Cubs in 1995. Steve Buechele opened the campaign as the starting third sacker after a couple of decent seasons, but he didn't hit and had apparently retired by season's end. Howard Johnson filled in occasionally, struggling to hit .200. And on June 16, the Cubs traded for Todd Zeile—Mike Morgan going to the Cardinals—but the normally hard-hitting Zeile batted just .227 after donning Cub blue.

## Hitting

Zeile has never hit for a great average, and he *did* hit nine homers as a Cub. In terms of plate discipline, however, Zeile was a totally different hitter after leaving St. Louis. Normally one of the most patient hitters in the league, Zeile drew only 16 walks in 79 games with the Cubs. Upon arriving in Chicago, Zeile said of Wrigley Field, "It's a great park, especially for me." With Waveland Avenue just a long fly ball away, Zeile seemed to lengthen his swing, and the result was too many wild cuts and not enough walks.

## Baserunning & Defense

Though he swiped 17 bases as recently as 1991, Zeile is no longer any kind of threat to steal; he's stolen one sack in each of the last two seasons. A converted catcher, Zeile's defense at third base could charitably be described as erratic. After posting a horrible .923 fielding average in 1993, Zeile upped that figure to .960 in 1994. The Cardinals had him playing first base, but after the trade Zeile moved back to third, where he didn't make anyone forget Ron Santo. Zeile doesn't have much range, and he is often handcuffed by hard grounders just to his left and right.

## 1996 Outlook

Assuming Zeile can get his swing back where it was before the trade, the Cubs just might enjoy their best-hitting third baseman since Ron Cey. If he doesn't, Cub fans might be wishing for the return of Luis Salazar. We're betting that Zeile does bounce back in 1996.

**Position:** 3B/1B
**Bats:** R  **Throws:** R
**Ht:** 6' 1"  **Wt:** 190

**Opening Day Age:** 30
**Born:** 9/9/65 in Van Nuys, CA
**ML Seasons:** 7
**Pronunciation:** ZEAL

### Overall Statistics

|  | G | AB | R | H | D | T | HR | RBI | SB | BB | SO | Avg | OBP | Slg |
|---|---|---|---|---|---|---|---|---|---|---|---|---|---|---|
| 1995 | 113 | 426 | 50 | 105 | 22 | 0 | 14 | 52 | 1 | 34 | 76 | .246 | .305 | .397 |
| Career | 836 | 2993 | 390 | 787 | 165 | 13 | 84 | 424 | 33 | 362 | 463 | .263 | .341 | .411 |

### Where He Hits the Ball

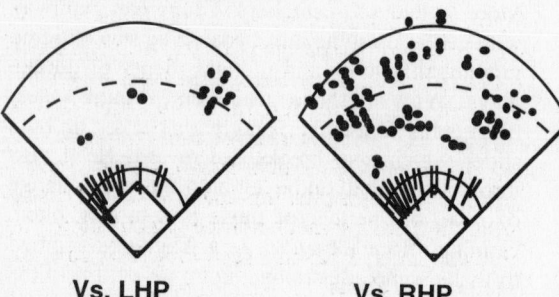

**Vs. LHP**          **Vs. RHP**

### 1995 Situational Stats

|  | AB | H | HR | RBI | Avg |  | AB | H | HR | RBI | Avg |
|---|---|---|---|---|---|---|---|---|---|---|---|
| Home | 180 | 43 | 8 | 24 | .239 | LHP | 106 | 18 | 3 | 10 | .170 |
| Road | 246 | 62 | 6 | 28 | .252 | RHP | 320 | 87 | 11 | 42 | .272 |
| First Half | 223 | 63 | 8 | 31 | .283 | Sc Pos | 92 | 25 | 2 | 33 | .272 |
| Scnd Half | 203 | 42 | 6 | 21 | .207 | Clutch | 62 | 14 | 1 | 8 | .226 |

### 1995 Rankings (National League)

- 1st in lowest batting average vs. left-handed pitchers (.170) and lowest on-base percentage vs. left-handed pitchers (.226)
- 3rd in errors at first base (7) and lowest percentage of swings on the first pitch (16.8%)
- 4th in lowest batting average
- 5th in lowest on-base percentage
- 7th in batting average with the bases loaded (.444), lowest cleanup slugging percentage (.442) and lowest slugging percentage vs. left-handed pitchers (.321)
- 8th in most pitches seen per plate appearance (4.05)
- 9th in highest percentage of pitches taken (60.8%)

# Terry Adams

**Position:** RP
**Bats:** R **Throws:** R
**Ht:** 6' 3" **Wt:** 205

**Opening Day Age:** 23
**Born:** 3/6/73 in Mobile, AL
**ML Seasons:** 1

## Overall Statistics

| | W | L | Pct. | ERA | G | GS | Sv | IP | H | BB | SO | HR | BR/IP |
|---|---|---|---|---|---|---|---|---|---|---|---|---|---|
| 1995 | 1 | 1 | .500 | 6.50 | 18 | 0 | 1 | 18.0 | 22 | 10 | 15 | 0 | 1.78 |
| Career | 1 | 1 | .500 | 6.50 | 18 | 0 | 1 | 18.0 | 22 | 10 | 15 | 0 | 1.78 |

## 1995 Season

Terry Adams was an ineffective starter until 1994, but a switch to the bullpen that season changed his career path in a hurry. He opened 1995 at Double-A Orlando, dominated the hitters there, then stopped briefly in Iowa before a major league call-up in August. His quick Triple-A stint made a believer of Iowa pitching coach Bill Early, who said, "If there's someone in the organization who throws harder, I haven't seen him. The guy was born to be a closer."

## Pitching, Defense & Hitting

Adams has something of a baby face, but don't let that fool you: he can bring the heat. What's more, Adams' fastball has nice bite to it, as he can make it break slightly down and away from right-handed hitters. That fastball hits 90-91 MPH on the slow gun, and Adams' slider tops out around 86. Given his lack of experience—he didn't pitch above Class A until 1995—Adams' 6.50 ERA is no cause for concern. In his brief 18-inning trial, two runners tried to steal, both successfully. Adams hasn't batted in the majors yet, and the Cubs hope he never has to.

## 1996 Outlook

Adams' big-league struggles suggest that he might need a bit more seasoning. But Randy Myers won't be a Cub forever, and Adams just might be closing out games for the club at the turn of the century.

# Scott Bullett

**Position:** LF/CF
**Bats:** L **Throws:** L
**Ht:** 6' 2" **Wt:** 215

**Opening Day Age:** 27
**Born:** 12/25/68 in Martinsburg, WV
**ML Seasons:** 3

## Overall Statistics

| | G | AB | R | H | D | T | HR | RBI | SB | BB | SO | Avg | OBP | Slg |
|---|---|---|---|---|---|---|---|---|---|---|---|---|---|---|
| 1995 | 104 | 150 | 19 | 41 | 5 | 7 | 3 | 22 | 8 | 12 | 30 | .273 | .331 | .460 |
| Career | 138 | 209 | 23 | 52 | 5 | 9 | 3 | 26 | 12 | 15 | 48 | .249 | .304 | .402 |

## 1995 Season

After an impressive 1994 campaign with the Cubs' Triple-A Iowa affiliate, Scott Bullett opened the 1995 season in a left-field platoon with rookie Ozzie Timmons. On June 7, Bullett's average stood at .231, and he'd scored only four runs. The next day, with a right-handed starter on the mound for Colorado, Bullett found himself on the bench. And when the Cubs traded for Luis Gonzalez three weeks later, Bullett's fate was sealed. He didn't pout, and a .367 average after the All-Star break— albeit in limited duty—left Bullett with respectable numbers at season's end.

## Hitting, Baserunning & Defense

Take a look at Bullett's batting line, and one number jumps out at you: *seven* triples in only 150 at-bats. By contrast, it took Brian McRae 580 at-bats to also collect seven three-baggers. Bullett was regarded as a fine minor league center fielder, but McRae's arrival pushed Bullett to left. Despite the presence of the speedy McRae and Sammy Sosa, Bullett probably ranks as the fastest Cub.

## 1996 Outlook

Bullett's speed and defensive skills are useful, and his fine second-half performance will almost certainly guarantee him a job as a spare outfielder somewhere. And if he gets traded, a more regular role isn't out of the question.

# Larry Casian

**Position:** RP
**Bats:** R  **Throws:** L
**Ht:** 6' 0"  **Wt:** 173

**Opening Day Age:** 30
**Born:** 10/28/65 in
Lynwood, CA
**ML Seasons:** 6
**Pronunciation:**
CASS-ee-un

## Overall Statistics

|  | W | L | Pct. | ERA | G | GS | Sv | IP | H | BB | SO | HR | BR/IP |
|---|---|---|---|---|---|---|---|---|---|---|---|---|---|
| 1995 | 1 | 0 | 1.000 | 1.93 | 42 | 0 | 0 | 23.1 | 23 | 15 | 11 | 1 | 1.63 |
| Career | 10 | 9 | .526 | 4.54 | 162 | 3 | 2 | 176.1 | 216 | 57 | 81 | 20 | 1.55 |

## 1995 Season

With the Indians and Twins in 1994, Larry Casian sported an ugly 7.35 earned-run average. Moving to the Cubs in 1995, Casian finished with a sparkling 1.93 ERA. Yet aside from the home-run column, he really didn't pitch all that differently. Still, Casian pitched well enough to see action in 42 games, and that number would have been higher if he hadn't missed seven weeks with shoulder tendinitis.

## Pitching, Defense & Hitting

Casian pitches like your typical situational left-hander: nibble against the right-handed hitters, throw breaking stuff to the lefties. But to his credit, Casian is not afraid to challenge even tough righties from time to time. In one August game, for example, he struck out Mike Piazza with a fastball, the second straight down-the-middle heater in the sequence. But that points up an interesting stat: Casian held right-handed hitters to a .189 average last year. That's great, but lefties—the guys Casian is paid to retire—batted a hefty .308. He's a decent fielder, holds runners extremely well, and rarely gets to hit.

## 1996 Outlook

You have to wonder about Casian. First of all, he's a tad young to be playing the Rick Honeycutt/Tony Fossas role. And second, he hasn't been retiring the left-handed batters anyway. If Casian doesn't start doing just that, his major league days might be numbered.

# Jose Hernandez

**Position:** SS/2B/3B
**Bats:** R  **Throws:** R
**Ht:** 6' 1"  **Wt:** 180

**Opening Day Age:** 26
**Born:** 7/14/69 in Vega
Alta, PR
**ML Seasons:** 4

## Overall Statistics

|  | G | AB | R | H | D | T | HR | RBI | SB | BB | SO | Avg | OBP | Slg |
|---|---|---|---|---|---|---|---|---|---|---|---|---|---|---|
| 1995 | 93 | 245 | 37 | 60 | 11 | 4 | 13 | 40 | 1 | 13 | 69 | .245 | .281 | .482 |
| Career | 197 | 479 | 63 | 110 | 15 | 8 | 14 | 53 | 3 | 24 | 131 | .230 | .267 | .382 |

## 1995 Season

Thanks to the retirement of Ryne Sandberg, Jose Hernandez saw plenty of action in 1994 as the Cubs' top utility infielder. He didn't hit much, but who cared? As we wrote a year ago in these page, "Hernandez is never going to help a club with his bat." It's time to officially eat those words. Hernandez tripled four times and blasted 13 homers last season, mighty impressive numbers for a utility infielder. This from a guy who entered the season with a .278 career slugging percentage.

## Hitting, Baserunning & Defense

Hernandez studied at the Dante Bichette School of Hitting: "Swing hard at everything. You never know, something good might happen." Practiced by Hernandez, this method results in few walks and not much of an average. But good things do happen sometimes, and those are a bonus for the Cubs, because Hernandez does a fine job with the glove. Defensively, he's good enough to play shortstop, second, or third base regularly. Hernandez is an average baserunner.

## 1996 Outlook

Utility infielders with power are a scarce commodity, and Hernandez will be in the majors as long as he can keep it up. Even if he *doesn't* hit double-figure homers every year—and he might never do it again—Hernandez' defensive versatility should ensure him a job for the foreseeable future.

# Howard Johnson

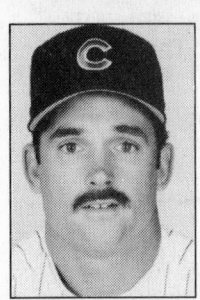

**Position:** 3B/LF
**Bats:** B  **Throws:** R
**Ht:** 5'10"  **Wt:** 195

**Opening Day Age:** 35
**Born:** 11/29/60 in
Clearwater, FL
**ML Seasons:** 14
**Nickname:** HoJo

*Overall Statistics*

|  | G | AB | R | H | D | T | HR | RBI | SB | BB | SO | Avg | OBP | Slg |
|---|---|---|---|---|---|---|---|---|---|---|---|---|---|---|
| 1995 | 87 | 169 | 26 | 33 | 4 | 1 | 7 | 22 | 1 | 34 | 46 | .195 | .330 | .355 |
| Career | 1531 | 4940 | 760 | 1229 | 247 | 22 | 228 | 760 | 231 | 692 | 1053 | .249 | .340 | .446 |

## 1995 Season

You gotta hand it to Howard Johnson; he must be a great guy in the clubhouse. How else to explain the fact that despite hitting .131 at the All-Star break, HoJo did *not* draw his release from the Cubs? Instead, he stuck around as Todd Zeile's backup, and played decently in the second half of the campaign. The highlights of Johnson's campaign were probably his two pinch-hit home runs.

## Hitting, Baserunning & Defense

Technically a switch-hitter, Johnson is nearly impotent against lefthanders, against whom he sees little action anymore. These days, the only pitch Johnson handles with authority is the medium fastball from righties. When he does get his pitch, Johnson can still turn on it, as evidenced by seven homers last season. In fact, Johnson's combination of power and patience probably made him one of the more productive .195 hitters ever. Johnson was once a dangerous runner, but injuries have robbed him of much of his speed. He's not much of a third baseman anymore, and is a liability in the outfield.

## 1996 Outlook

Backup third basemen who struggle to break the Mendoza line generally don't last long in the big leagues. Johnson will certainly be invited to training camp with somebody, but if he doesn't hit his weight in the spring, he might be vacationing in the summer.

# Mark Parent

**Position:** C
**Bats:** R  **Throws:** R
**Ht:** 6'5"  **Wt:** 240

**Opening Day Age:** 34
**Born:** 9/16/61 in
Ashland, OR
**ML Seasons:** 10

*Overall Statistics*

|  | G | AB | R | H | D | T | HR | RBI | SB | BB | SO | Avg | OBP | Slg |
|---|---|---|---|---|---|---|---|---|---|---|---|---|---|---|
| 1995 | 81 | 265 | 30 | 62 | 11 | 0 | 18 | 38 | 0 | 26 | 69 | .234 | .302 | .479 |
| Career | 345 | 940 | 84 | 206 | 36 | 0 | 43 | 124 | 2 | 76 | 213 | .219 | .277 | .395 |

## 1995 Season

Was 1995 Mark Parent's career season? Consider this: In a major league career spanning parts of nine seasons, Parent had *totaled* 25 home runs. In 1995, he walloped 18 homers. What happened? Simply put, he played. Parent opened the season as the Pirates' starting catcher, thanks to a Don Slaught injury. And hours before the September 1 deadline, Parent was traded to the Cubs, with whom he played in 1994, for a player to be named later.

## Hitting, Baserunning & Defense

Power hasn't been a problem for Parent lately; over the last four seasons, his slugging percentage is a hefty .462. So perhaps it shouldn't have been a surprise that he hit those 18 homers when given a chance to play. One of the bigger players in the game, Parent also takes one of the bigger cuts. He runs like a big, slow catcher, not surprising seeing how he's a big, slow catcher. Defensively, Parent is tough to run on, but aside from that he's not a great receiver. He's not quick behind the plate and isn't known for his game-calling skills.

## 1996 Outlook

A standard item on any manager's wish list is "backup catcher with power," so Parent shouldn't have any problems finding work this spring. But his defense will, in all likelihood, limit him to spot duty.

# Ryne Sandberg

**Position:** 2B
**Bats:** R **Throws:** R
**Ht:** 6' 2" **Wt:** 190

**Opening Day Age:** 36
**Born:** 9/18/59 in
Spokane, WA
**ML Seasons:** 14
**Nickname:** Ryno

## Overall Statistics

| | G | AB | R | H | D | T | HR | RBI | SB | BB | SO | Avg | OBP | Slg |
|---|---|---|---|---|---|---|---|---|---|---|---|---|---|---|
| 1995 | | Did Not Play | | | | | | | | | | | | |
| Career | 1879 | 7384 | 1179 | 2133 | 349 | 72 | 245 | 905 | 325 | 679 | 1050 | .289 | .348 | .455 |

## 1995 Season

First Michael Jordan, now Ryne Sandberg. . . can Dick Butkus be far behind? After nearly 17 months away from the game—unless you count sunny afternoons in a Wrigley Field luxury box—Sandberg signed a new contract with the Cubs last Halloween. With hated Larry Himes exiled from Wrigley and the Cubs challenging for a playoff spot, Ryno got the notion that baseball just might be fun again.

## Hitting, Baserunning & Defense

Presumably, the wrist injury which limited Sandberg's power in 1993 and '94 is now healed. If so, he's sure to pound some fastballs onto Waveland Avenue. Sandberg is a fairly patient hitter, but he will wave at the occasional curve in the dirt. As you would expect, Sandberg is no longer the basestealing threat he once was, though he'll still be one of the smarter runners in the game. Sandberg's range at second isn't what it once was, but his knowledge and strong throwing arm make him a better-than-average fielder.

## 1996 Outlook

Can Sandberg come back at age 36? Ted Williams—thanks to the Korean War—missed nearly all of 1952 and 1953, but returned in '54 to hit .345 at the age of 35. More recently, Dave Winfield missed the entire 1989 season with back woes, yet returned in 1990 to hit 21 homers at 38. Ryno might not be an All-Star or win a Gold Glove, but he won't embarrass himself.

# Turk Wendell

**Position:** RP
**Bats:** L **Throws:** R
**Ht:** 6' 2" **Wt:** 190

**Opening Day Age:** 28
**Born:** 5/19/67 in
Pittsfield, MA
**ML Seasons:** 3

## Overall Statistics

| | W | L | Pct. | ERA | G | GS | Sv | IP | H | BB | SO | HR | BR/IP |
|---|---|---|---|---|---|---|---|---|---|---|---|---|---|
| 1995 | 3 | 1 | .750 | 4.92 | 43 | 0 | 0 | 60.1 | 71 | 24 | 50 | 11 | 1.57 |
| Career | 4 | 4 | .500 | 5.83 | 56 | 6 | 0 | 97.1 | 117 | 42 | 74 | 14 | 1.63 |

## 1995 Season

Will Turk Wendell's pitching feats ever equal his flaky fame? At this point, it doesn't look too likely. Wendell opened last season in the minors, battling a minor shoulder problem, but was called up in late May. He spent the rest of the year with the Cubs, and registered three victories while pitching mostly long relief.

## Pitching, Defense & Hitting

Wendell's pitch repertoire is nothing special: average fastball complemented by a slider with pretty good bite. Like most hurlers, Wendell is better off when he keeps the ball down, and when he's pitching well he will get a lot of ground balls. Wendell is fairly athletic on the mound and capable of slick fielding plays. He's collected one base hit in 16 major league at-bats, and has yet to get down a sacrifice.

## 1996 Outlook

Remember when Wendell was one of the top Cub pitching prospects? That was only a few years ago. Hard as it might seem to believe, Wendell turns 29 this May. He just might be one of those so-called "Four-A" pitchers, capable of dominating Triple-A hitters but not quite good enough in the majors. As a right-handed reliever who has yet to define a role for himself, Wendell is still pitching on the fringe.

# Other Chicago Cubs

**Tom Edens (Pos**: RHP, **Age**: 34)

A journeyman? Edens has pitched for six teams, he's 34, and his major league record is a whopping 19-12. Edens doesn't really have major league stuff any more, and pitched only three innings for the Cubs in 1995. 1996 Outlook: C

**Matt Franco (Pos**: 2B, **Age**: 26, **Bats**: L)

A Cub farmhand since 1987, Franco finally made it to Wrigley last year. A first baseman in 1994 and a third baseman in '95, his only start with the Cubs came at second. Might stick as utility man. 1996 Outlook: C

**Todd Haney (Pos**: 2B, **Age**: 30, **Bats**: R)

Someday Haney will tell his kids about 1995, the season he hit .411. Of course, it was only 73 at-bats. His best chance to play in 1996 evaporated when Ryne Sandberg announced his comeback. Haney's a scrapper, though, the type managers like. 1996 Outlook: B

**Felix Jose (Pos**: RF, **Age**: 30, **Bats**: B)

Rarely has a career collapsed so quickly. A year after hitting .303 with the Royals, Jose was released by both Kansas City and the Cubs. He played only 19 games, 10 of them for Triple-A Iowa. 1996 Outlook: C

**Joe Kmak (Pos**: C, **Age**: 32, **Bats**: R)

The backup catcher with the onomatopoetic name gave the Cubs solid defense until a late-August knee injury ended his season. If the club doesn't re-sign Mark Parent, Kmak has a shot at a job. 1996 Outlook: B

**Chris Nabholz (Pos**: LHP, **Age**: 29)

A respectable starter in the early '90s with Montreal, Nabholz has hit a rough patch. He spent part of 1995 on the DL and part in Iowa. As a Cub, he was blasted by right-handed hitters. In November, Nabholz signed with the Mets. 1996 Outlook: B

**Todd Pratt (Pos**: C, **Age**: 29, **Bats**: R)

A few years ago, Pratt carried a good-hit/no-field reputation, but lately he hasn't even been hitting. Sent down after hitting .133 in 60 at-bats, Pratt did better at Iowa. The Cubs aren't turning cartwheels. 1996 Outlook: C

**Roberto Rivera (Pos**: LHP, **Age**: 27)

A solid reliever in the minors, Rivera's pluses are fine control and an excellent change-up. But he doesn't have great velocity, and will need a break to win a roster spot. 1996 Outlook: C

**Kevin Roberson (Pos**: LF, **Age**: 28, **Bats**: B)

Roberson's shown excellent power in three trials with the Cubs, but his tendency to swint at everything has kept his average around the .200 mark. After being dumped by the Cubs last summer, Roberson played for Seattle's Triple-A club, then signed with the Mets after the season. 1996 Outlook: C

**Tanyon Sturtze (Pos**: RHP, **Age**: 25)

A Rule 5 pick from the Athletics, Sturtze spent most of the season at Triple-A Iowa, where he compiled a 6.80 ERA in 23 games. Not the stuff of legends, though Sturtze still has a good arm. 1996 Outlook: C

**Dave Swartzbaugh (Pos**: RHP, **Age**: 28)

Swartzbaugh has a plus fastball, and he looks a little like Goose Gossage on the mound. Not a great pitcher but probably as good as Turk Wendell, and the two will probably fight for a roster spot. 1996 Outlook: B

**Mike Walker (Pos**: RHP, **Age**: 29)

Once a pretty decent prospect in the Cleveland chain, Walker was out of the majors for three years before making it back—briefly—with the Cubs last year. As a middle-aged righthander with mediocre stuff, he'll only pitch in the majors if two or three guys get hurt. 1996 Outlook: C

# Chicago Cubs Minor League Prospects

## Organization Overview:

When the Cubs used their first draft pick to select Ty Griffin in 1988, they began a long string of failed first rounders. Included in that group: Earl Cunningham, Lance Dickson, Doug Glanville and Derek Wallace. Cunningham and Wallace are now with other organizations, while neither Dickson nor Glanville have to worry about autograph hounds. The Cubs seem to have broken their streak with Brooks Kieschnick, a 1993 first rounder who might be the first legitimate power hitter developed by the organization since Rafael Palmeiro, whom the club traded before he developed his power! In the two drafts since Kieschnick, the Cubs have used their top picks on high-school pitchers, Jay Peterson and Kerry Wood. Neither has shown much yet.

### Pat Cline

**Position:** C          **Opening Day Age:** 21
**Bats:** R **Throws:** R     **Born:** 10/9/74 in
**Ht:** 6' 3" **Wt:** 220      Manatee, FL

*Recent Statistics*

|              | G   | AB  | R  | H   | D  | T | HR | RBI | SB | BB | SO | AVG  |
|--------------|-----|-----|----|-----|----|---|----|-----|----|----|----|------|
| 93 R Huntington | 33  | 96  | 17 | 18  | 5  | 0 | 2  | 13  | 0  | 17 | 28 | .188 |
| 94 R Cubs    | 3   | 0   | 0  | 0   | 0  | 0 | 0  | 0   | 0  | 0  | 0  | -    |
| 95 A Rockford | 112 | 390 | 65 | 106 | 27 | 0 | 13 | 77  | 6  | 58 | 93 | .272 |

There's always talk of a catcher shortage, so the Cubs must be thrilled to have two catching prospects in the organization: Pat Cline and Mike Hubbard (below). Cline was named the number-six prospect in the Midwest League by *Baseball America*, on the strength of his strong throwing arm and power potential. Strength aside, Cline only threw out 24 percent of the runners trying to steal, due mostly to poor footwork. Cline topped the Cubbies with 13 homers and 77 RBI, and Rockford manager Steve Roadcap said, "I think Pat can be a Lance Parrish-type catcher. Pat's got a very strong arm and power to all fields."

### Mike Hubbard

**Position:** C          **Opening Day Age:** 25
**Bats:** R **Throws:** R     **Born:** 2/16/71 in
**Ht:** 6' 1" **Wt:** 180      Lynchburg, VA

*Recent Statistics*

|              | G  | AB  | R  | H  | D | T | HR | RBI | SB | BB | SO | AVG  |
|--------------|----|-----|----|----|---|---|----|-----|----|----|----|------|
| 95 AAA Iowa  | 75 | 254 | 28 | 66 | 6 | 3 | 5  | 23  | 6  | 26 | 60 | .260 |
| 95 NL Chicago | 15 | 23  | 2  | 4  | 0 | 0 | 0  | 1   | 0  | 2  | 2  | .174 |
| 95 MLE       | 75 | 248 | 23 | 60 | 5 | 2 | 4  | 19  | 4  | 22 | 62 | .242 |

Regarded as the organization's top catching prospect, Hubbard was summoned to Wrigley in mid-July after hitting .301 in his previous 32 games for Iowa. He was sent back down before long, but returned in September. Though he stole only six bases last season, Hubbard is often compared to a young Craig Biggio, and some have suggested that he too be switched to a less demanding position. However, the Cubs have given no indication that a move is in the offing. That's probably best, because Hubbard really hasn't shown enough with the bat to suggest he could play anywhere else.

### Robin Jennings

**Position:** OF          **Opening Day Age:** 23
**Bats:** L **Throws:** L     **Born:** 4/11/72 in
**Ht:** 6' 2" **Wt:** 200      Singapore

*Recent Statistics*

|              | G   | AB  | R  | H   | D  | T | HR | RBI | SB | BB | SO | AVG  |
|--------------|-----|-----|----|-----|----|---|----|-----|----|----|----|------|
| 93 A Peoria  | 132 | 474 | 65 | 146 | 29 | 5 | 3  | 65  | 11 | 46 | 73 | .308 |
| 94 A Daytona | 128 | 476 | 54 | 133 | 24 | 5 | 8  | 60  | 2  | 45 | 54 | .279 |
| 95 AA Orlando | 132 | 490 | 71 | 145 | 27 | 7 | 17 | 79  | 7  | 44 | 61 | .296 |
| 95 MLE       | 132 | 485 | 67 | 140 | 26 | 5 | 16 | 75  | 5  | 36 | 65 | .289 |

After two-and-a-half seasons in A-ball, Jennings made the big jump to Double-A last spring, and ended up with a breakthrough season. Told that he needed to hit more homers, Jennings worked on his strength and more than doubled his output from 1994. Though he played center last season, the Cubs project him as a left or right fielder. Jennings does have a strong and accurate arm. A 33rd-round pick, Jennings was selected as a draft-and-follow in 1992. He was born in Singapore, where his father was in the foreign service. Late note: Jennings got off to a great start in the Arizona Fall League, which will only enhance his reputation in the organization.

### Brooks Kieschnick

**Position:** OF          **Opening Day Age:** 23
**Bats:** L **Throws:** R     **Born:** 6/6/72 in
**Ht:** 6' 4" **Wt:** 228      Robstown, TX

*Recent Statistics*

|              | G   | AB  | R  | H   | D  | T | HR | RBI | SB | BB | SO | AVG  |
|--------------|-----|-----|----|-----|----|---|----|-----|----|----|----|------|
| 94 AA Orlando | 126 | 468 | 57 | 132 | 25 | 3 | 14 | 55  | 3  | 33 | 78 | .282 |
| 95 AAA Iowa  | 138 | 505 | 61 | 149 | 30 | 1 | 23 | 73  | 2  | 58 | 91 | .295 |
| 95 MLE       | 138 | 492 | 52 | 136 | 27 | 0 | 19 | 62  | 1  | 50 | 95 | .276 |

The Cubs' first-round pick in 1993, Kieschnick posted solid numbers at Triple-A last summer, in just his second full professional season. Those 23 home runs were especially inspiring for an organization which desperately needs power hitters. Kieschnick did show a glaring weakness against left-handed pitchers last year, batting only .224 as opposed to .323 against righties. Kieschnick might end up as a corner infielder, but for now he's an outfielder. As befits a star college pitcher, Kieschnick showed one of the best throwing arms in the American Association last season. He could end up in left field if the Cubs don't re-sign Luis Gonzalez, or first base if Grace doesn't return. No matter what happens, Kieschnick has earned the chance at a major league roster spot.

## Bobby Morris

**Position:** 2B    **Opening Day Age:** 23
**Bats:** L **Throws:** R    **Born:** 11/22/72 in
**Ht:** 6' 0" **Wt:** 180    Hammond, IN

*Recent Statistics*

| | G | AB | R | H | D | T | HR | RBI | SB | BB | SO | AVG |
|---|---|---|---|---|---|---|---|---|---|---|---|---|
| 93 R Huntington | 50 | 170 | 29 | 49 | 8 | 3 | 1 | 24 | 6 | 24 | 29 | .288 |
| 94 A Peoria | 101 | 362 | 61 | 128 | 33 | 1 | 7 | 64 | 7 | 53 | 63 | .354 |
| 95 A Daytona | 95 | 344 | 44 | 106 | 18 | 2 | 2 | 55 | 22 | 38 | 46 | .308 |

There's little question that Bobby, the younger brother of major leaguer Hal Morris, can hit. In 1994, he finished runner-up in the Midwest League batting race with a .354. Morris' problem is defense. He was a third baseman at the University of Iowa, but his lack of power convinced the Cubs to shift him to second. However, last season Morris made 24 errors in his first 64 games at second base, prompting speculation that the Cubs might move the fast-enough Morris to the outfield. His season ended early last year because of a knee injury, not believed to be serious.

## Steve Rain

**Position:** P    **Opening Day Age:** 20
**Bats:** R **Throws:** R    **Born:** 6/2/75 in Los
**Ht:** 6' 6" **Wt:** 225    Angeles, CA

*Recent Statistics*

| | W | L | ERA | G | GS | Sv | IP | H | R | BB | SO | HR |
|---|---|---|---|---|---|---|---|---|---|---|---|---|
| 93 R Cubs | 1 | 3 | 3.89 | 10 | 6 | 0 | 37.0 | 37 | 20 | 17 | 29 | 0 |
| 94 R Huntington | 3 | 3 | 2.65 | 14 | 10 | 0 | 68.0 | 55 | 26 | 19 | 55 | 2 |
| 95 A Rockford | 5 | 2 | 1.21 | 53 | 0 | 23 | 59.1 | 38 | 12 | 23 | 66 | 0 |

Some minor league closers rack up big save totals by throwing a lot of offspeed stuff. Not Steve Rain. Converted to relief last season, Rain dominated Midwest League hitters with a tight slider—which he throws 70-80 percent of the time—and a plus fastball. He has a bulldog mentality on the mound, and can't *wait* to get the ball back from the catcher so he can throw another strike. Perhaps most impressive of all, Rain has only allowed two home runs in 164-plus innings. Not bad for an 11th-round draft pick.

## Amaury Telemaco

**Position:** P    **Opening Day Age:** 22
**Bats:** R **Throws:** R    **Born:** 1/19/74 in
**Ht:** 6' 3" **Wt:** 200    Higuey, DR

*Recent Statistics*

| | W | L | ERA | G | GS | Sv | IP | H | R | BB | SO | HR |
|---|---|---|---|---|---|---|---|---|---|---|---|---|
| 93 A Peoria | 8 | 11 | 3.45 | 23 | 23 | 0 | 143.2 | 129 | 69 | 54 | 133 | 9 |
| 94 A Daytona | 7 | 3 | 3.40 | 11 | 11 | 0 | 76.2 | 62 | 35 | 23 | 59 | 4 |
| 94 AA Orlando | 3 | 5 | 3.45 | 12 | 12 | 0 | 62.2 | 56 | 29 | 20 | 49 | 6 |
| 95 AA Orlando | 8 | 8 | 3.29 | 22 | 22 | 0 | 147.2 | 112 | 60 | 42 | 151 | 13 |

Telemaco's 1994 season ended early, and his 1995 campaign started late due to a sore shoulder. But after his return, Telemaco pitched better than ever. The Cubs' top pitching prospect for two years now, he struck out better than a hitter per inning last season, and again exhibited fine control. Since signing out of the Dominican Republic back in 1991 as a skinny 17-year-old, Telemaco has filled out to 200- plus pounds, and with that extra weight has come extra velocity. His fastball hits the upper 80s, and he also throws a slider and a change-up. Telemaco hasn't gotten much respect yet, but he'll have a great chance to impress at Triple-A Iowa this summer.

## Others to Watch

Outfielder **Pedro Valdes** was regarded by many observers as a better prospect than teammate Robin Jennings. Valdes doesn't have Jennings' power—yet—but he's a year younger and Southern League managers were impressed by his smooth swing. . . The Cubs boast a number of second-line pitching prospects, all righthanders. **Jon Ratliff** was the club's second first-round pick in 1993. He was 8-19 with a high ERA his first two pro seasons, but turned things around last year with a 10-5, 3.47 campaign with Double-A Orlando. Ratliff's fastball is nothing special, but he throws three other pitches and seems to finally be learning what to do with them. . . **Jason Ryan** doesn't have a great arm, but he's the savviest pitcher the Cubs have developed since Greg Maddux. Ryan's fastball tops out in the mid 80s, but he throws two curveballs and a good change-up. . . **Brian Stephenson**, like Jay Peterson and Ryan a 1994 draftee, has only been a full-time pitcher since 1993, so he's still raw. Stephenson spent last season at Daytona in the Florida State League, and struck out 109 batters in 150 innings.

# Bret Boone

## 1995 Season

Building on his breakthrough season of 1994, Bret Boone posted another fine campaign in '95. Boone struggled a bit the last two months of the season, going 194 at-bats between home runs, and he didn't come close to matching his .320 average of 1994. But he improved greatly in the field, and with his combination of power hitting and excellent defense, moved into the National League elite at second base.

## Hitting

Boone swings the bat about as hard as anyone in the game, and that's one reason why his batting average dropped 53 points last year. But Boone prefers to hit for power rather than average, and he was probably never really a .320 hitter anyway. He likes to dig in right on top of the plate, and he doesn't give any ground against right-handed pitching. Over the last two years he has batted nearly .300 against righthanders, with most of his power coming against them. Boone wants to be a big RBI man, and will probably get the chance as he moves up in the Reds' batting order.

## Baserunning & Defense

Boone is an average baserunner, but picks his spots well and should be able to steal 10 bases a year. Perhaps the greatest improvement in Boone's game came in the field in 1995. He showed good range, often making spectacular plays, and didn't make his first error until July. Boone likes to play a deep second base, using his accurate arm and an assortment of deliveries to get the runner at first. He teamed with Barry Larkin to lead National League keystone combos in double plays.

## 1996 Outlook

In 1995, Boone had what probably will become an average season for him. At 26 he is entering his prime and, with more maturity and experience, he will take his place among the best second basemen in the game.

**Position:** 2B
**Bats:** R  **Throws:** R
**Ht:** 5'10"  **Wt:** 180

**Opening Day Age:** 26
**Born:** 4/6/69 in El Cajon, CA
**ML Seasons:** 4

### Overall Statistics

| | G | AB | R | H | D | T | HR | RBI | SB | BB | SO | Avg | OBP | Slg |
|---|---|---|---|---|---|---|---|---|---|---|---|---|---|---|
| 1995 | 138 | 513 | 63 | 137 | 34 | 2 | 15 | 68 | 5 | 41 | 84 | .267 | .326 | .429 |
| Career | 355 | 1294 | 168 | 352 | 75 | 6 | 43 | 189 | 11 | 86 | 244 | .272 | .323 | .439 |

### Where He Hits the Ball

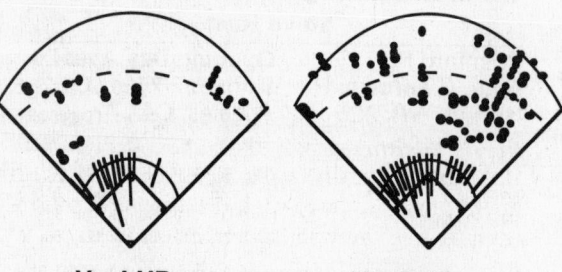

**Vs. LHP**      **Vs. RHP**

### 1995 Situational Stats

| | AB | H | HR | RBI | Avg | | AB | H | HR | RBI | Avg |
|---|---|---|---|---|---|---|---|---|---|---|---|
| Home | 244 | 55 | 6 | 35 | .225 | LHP | 123 | 31 | 4 | 22 | .252 |
| Road | 269 | 82 | 9 | 33 | .305 | RHP | 390 | 106 | 11 | 46 | .272 |
| First Half | 251 | 69 | 5 | 29 | .275 | Sc Pos | 145 | 33 | 3 | 50 | .228 |
| Scnd Half | 262 | 68 | 10 | 39 | .260 | Clutch | 71 | 18 | 3 | 9 | .254 |

### 1995 Rankings (National League)

- ➡ 1st in fielding percentage at second base (.994)
- ➡ 2nd in lowest percentage of extra bases taken as a runner (29.8%)
- ➡ 5th in lowest batting average at home (.225)
- ➡ 7th in doubles
- ➡ 8th in lowest percentage of swings on the first pitch (19.2%)
- ➡ 10th in batting average on the road (.305)
- ➡ Led the Reds in at-bats, GDPs (14), plate appearances (571), games played and highest percentage of swings put into play (47.5%)

# Jeff Branson

## 1995 Season

The Reds' insurance policy, Jeff Branson was there to pick up the pieces last season when Willie Greene failed to hold the starting job at third base. Starting most of the time against right-handed pitchers, Branson played 98 games at third for the Reds, but was versatile enough to see action at all of the infield positions during the year. He wound up playing in 122 contests while continuing to show the surprising power he demonstrated in 1994.

## Hitting

Branson goes to the plate looking for the fastball and can be fooled by offspeed pitches. Pitchers work him with high heat and soft stuff away. Primarily a singles hitter when he first came up, Branson developed more of a power swing the last two years. Looking to pull the ball more often, he reached career highs in extra-base hits and homers in '95, while doubling his home-run output of 1994. Batting in the eight-hole, he was walked intentionally a team-high 14 times. Branson doesn't hit lefties well, which limits him to a platoon role for the foreseeable future.

## Baserunning & Defense

Drafted as a shortstop by the Reds, Branson easily made the transition to third base. He showed good range and ranked second among National League third basemen in fielding percentage. Branson can make the throw from behind the bag and has the accuracy to start the double play. Reconstructive knee surgery has robbed Branson of his speed, but he still does a decent job on the bases. He's never been a basestealer.

## 1996 Outlook

Willie Greene remains the third baseman of the future for Cincinnati and will be given another shot at the starting job in 1996. As usual, though, Branson will be around in case Greene falters. He'll also see action filling in around the Reds infield and as a left-handed bat off the bench.

**Position:** 3B/SS
**Bats:** L  **Throws:** R
**Ht:** 6' 0"  **Wt:** 180

**Opening Day Age:** 29
**Born:** 1/26/67 in Waynesboro, MS
**ML Seasons:** 4

### Cincinnati Reds

### Overall Statistics

|        | G   | AB  | R   | H   | D  | T | HR | RBI | SB | BB | SO  | Avg  | OBP  | Slg  |
|--------|-----|-----|-----|-----|----|---|----|-----|----|----|-----|------|------|------|
| 1995   | 122 | 331 | 43  | 86  | 18 | 2 | 12 | 45  | 2  | 44 | 69  | .260 | .345 | .435 |
| Career | 377 | 936 | 113 | 243 | 44 | 5 | 21 | 98  | 6  | 73 | 174 | .260 | .311 | .385 |

### Where He Hits the Ball

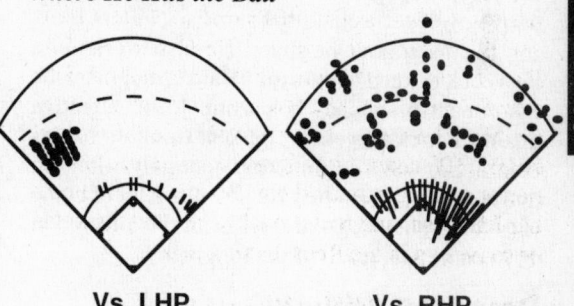

**Vs. LHP**          **Vs. RHP**

### 1995 Situational Stats

|            | AB  | H  | HR | RBI | Avg  |        | AB  | H  | HR | RBI | Avg  |
|------------|-----|----|----|-----|------|--------|-----|----|----|-----|------|
| Home       | 149 | 40 | 9  | 24  | .268 | LHP    | 38  | 6  | 0  | 4   | .158 |
| Road       | 182 | 46 | 3  | 21  | .253 | RHP    | 293 | 80 | 12 | 41  | .273 |
| First Half | 144 | 42 | 5  | 19  | .292 | Sc Pos | 86  | 20 | 2  | 32  | .233 |
| Scnd Half  | 187 | 44 | 7  | 26  | .235 | Clutch | 46  | 9  | 1  | 3   | .196 |

### 1995 Rankings (National League)

- → 1st in lowest batting average with the bases loaded (0.000)
- → 2nd in intentional walks (14) and fielding percentage at third base (.970)
- → 4th in lowest percentage of swings put into play (36.7%)
- → 8th in sacrifice flies (6)
- → Led the Reds in sacrifice flies and intentional walks

# Jeff Brantley

## 1995 Season

Jeff Brantley shared closer duties with other Cincinnati pitchers in 1994, but last year he was the man Davey Johnson called on to finish the game. Brantley responded by going 28-for-32 in save opportunities and Cincinnati won 49 of the 56 games in which he appeared. The 28 saves were a career high for Brantley, who'd never saved more than 19 in any previous season.

## Pitching

Brantley's best pitch is a split-fingered fastball that moves in on right-handed hitters. Mix in a hard-breaking slider and you can see why righthanders hit just .188 against him. Brantley also has an above-average fastball that surprises hitters looking for the splitter or slider. He also works in a curveball to keep batters off balance, and the wide assortment of pitches helps him to be effective against lefties as well as righties. Brantley battles control problems at times, but generally comes in and challenges the hitter. He gives up a lot of home runs for a reliever: 14 of the 22 runs he allowed in 1995 came as a result of the longball.

## Defense & Hitting

Brantley is ready to field after he delivers the pitch. He gets off the mound well and is very good at covering first base. Brantley is used to pitching with runners on. Consequently, he pays them a lot of attention and is not an easy steal. He seldom comes to the plate as a hitter, and didn't pick up a hit or sacrifice last year.

## 1996 Outlook

Brantley did a more than capable job as closer for the Reds. Hector Carrasco, the closer heir apparent, doesn't appear to be ready to challenge him for the role, and Brantley will enter 1996 as the club's sole closer. He can expect plenty of action under new manager Ray Knight.

**Position:** RP
**Bats:** R  **Throws:** R
**Ht:** 5'10"  **Wt:** 190

**Opening Day Age:** 32
**Born:** 9/5/63 in Florence, AL
**ML Seasons:** 8

### Overall Statistics

|        | W  | L  | Pct. | ERA  | G   | GS | Sv | IP    | H   | BB  | SO  | HR | BR/IP |
|--------|----|----|------|------|-----|----|----|-------|-----|-----|-----|----|-------|
| 1995   | 3  | 2  | .600 | 2.82 | 56  | 0  | 28 | 70.1  | 53  | 20  | 62  | 11 | 1.04  |
| Career | 38 | 28 | .576 | 3.12 | 405 | 18 | 85 | 641.0 | 556 | 267 | 509 | 67 | 1.28  |

### How Often He Throws Strikes

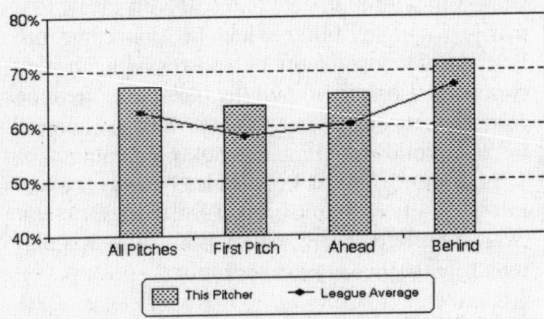

This Pitcher  —— League Average

### 1995 Situational Stats

|           | W | L | ERA  | Sv |  IP  |        | AB  | H  | HR | RBI | Avg  |
|-----------|---|---|------|----|------|--------|-----|----|----|-----|------|
| Home      | 1 | 2 | 3.86 | 12 | 37.1 | LHB    | 119 | 27 | 7  | 15  | .227 |
| Road      | 2 | 0 | 1.64 | 16 | 33.0 | RHB    | 138 | 26 | 4  | 12  | .188 |
| First Half| 3 | 1 | 2.88 | 14 | 40.2 | Sc Pos | 54  | 8  | 1  | 15  | .148 |
| Scnd Half | 0 | 1 | 2.73 | 14 | 29.2 | Clutch | 154 | 29 | 7  | 19  | .188 |

### 1995 Rankings (National League)

- → 2nd in least baserunners allowed per 9 innings in relief (9.5)
- → 3rd in save percentage (87.5%)
- → 4th in lowest batting average allowed in relief with runners on base (.179)
- → 5th in lowest batting average allowed in relief with runners in scoring position (.148)
- → 6th in lowest batting average allowed in relief (.206)
- → 7th in games finished (49)
- → 8th in balks (2)
- → 9th in saves, save opportunities (32) and least GDPs induced per GDP situation (4.2%)
- → Led the Reds in saves, games finished, balks and save opportunities

# Dave Burba

**Position:** RP/SP
**Bats:** R  **Throws:** R
**Ht:** 6' 4"  **Wt:** 240

**Opening Day Age:** 29
**Born:** 7/7/66 in Dayton, OH
**ML Seasons:** 6

Cincinnati Reds

## 1995 Season

When the Reds traded Deion Sanders to the Giants last July, righty starter Mark Portugal was considered the key man from Cincinnati's viewpoint. But Reds general manager Jim Bowden also insisted that Dave Burba be included in the deal, and the big righthander proved that Bowden knew his pitchers. When Portugal got off to a shaky start with his new club, Burba stepped in and provided immediate help to Cincinnati's injury-plagued starting staff. In his first eight appearances for the Reds, including four starts, Brantley went 4-0 with a sparkling 1.02 ERA. Burba loved pitching at Riverfront Stadium, where he had a 37.2-innings scoreless streak that was finally snapped in September.

## Pitching

Burba relies mainly on two pitches: a moving fastball that tops out in the mid-90s, and a hard slider which provides a good complement to the fastball. Burba is a strikeout pitcher who is especially tough against right-handed hitters. Sometimes he struggles with the location of his fastball, which has a tendency to veer out of the strike zone. His walk totals rise when he loses command of the heat, and he can get hit hard when he's behind in the count and has to come in with a little less.

## Defense & Hitting

A power pitcher who falls off the mound toward first, Burba often is out of position to field a ball hit to his right. His pickoff move is decent enough, but he has a high leg kick that gives basestealers extra time on steal attempts. Working as a starter for the Reds, Burba came to the plate more often than usual. He picked up just one hit and laid down four sacrifice bunts.

## 1996 Outlook

Burba has bounced back and forth from starting rotation to bullpen for most of his career. He will probably end up back in the bullpen for the Reds, serving as a right-handed set-up man for Jeff Brantley. But he'll be available to start when needed.

### Overall Statistics

|  | W | L | Pct. | ERA | G | GS | Sv | IP | H | BB | SO | HR | BR/IP |
|---|---|---|---|---|---|---|---|---|---|---|---|---|---|
| 1995 | 10 | 4 | .714 | 3.97 | 52 | 9 | 0 | 106.2 | 90 | 51 | 96 | 9 | 1.32 |
| Career | 27 | 22 | .551 | 4.28 | 214 | 27 | 1 | 391.1 | 366 | 180 | 335 | 38 | 1.40 |

### How Often He Throws Strikes

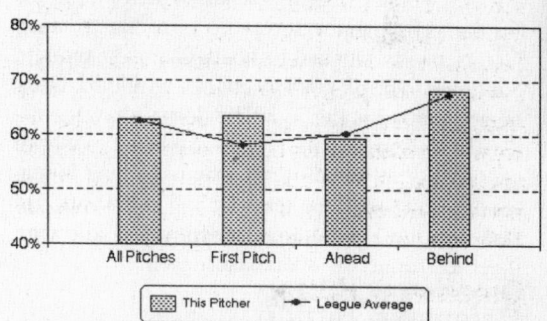

### 1995 Situational Stats

|  | W | L | ERA | Sv | IP |  | AB | H | HR | RBI | Avg |
|---|---|---|---|---|---|---|---|---|---|---|---|
| Home | 4 | 1 | 2.41 | 0 | 59.2 | LHB | 158 | 43 | 5 | 29 | .272 |
| Road | 6 | 3 | 5.94 | 0 | 47.0 | RHB | 237 | 47 | 4 | 19 | .198 |
| First Half | 4 | 2 | 4.50 | 0 | 38.0 | Sc Pos | 108 | 26 | 3 | 38 | .241 |
| Scnd Half | 6 | 2 | 3.67 | 0 | 68.2 | Clutch | 91 | 17 | 2 | 12 | .187 |

### 1995 Rankings (National League)

- ➡ 2nd in lowest batting average allowed vs. right-handed batters (.198)
- ➡ 3rd in winning percentage and most strikeouts per 9 innings in relief (9.7)
- ➡ 8th in relief wins (6)
- ➡ Led the Reds in shutouts (1)

# Hector Carrasco

## 1995 Season

A great middle reliever and set-up man as a rookie in 1994, Hector Carrasco was expected to develop into the club's closer in another year or so. But in 1995, Carrasco's development took several steps backward. His ERA was almost double the 2.24 mark he posted in 1994, and control problems forced manager Davey Johnson to stop using him as a set-up man. Carrasco's concentration seemed to drift when the game wasn't on the line, causing Cincinnati leads to disappear. Team doctors could find nothing wrong when Carrasco complained about numbness in his fingers late in the season.

## Pitching

Blessed with a live arm, Carrasco rifles a high-90s fastball. His mentor Jose Rijo is trying to teach Carrasco his slider and forkball. Carrasco, though, continues to be plagued by control problems. Once he gets behind in the count, he doesn't have confidence in his secondary pitches. So he takes a little off the fastball to get it over the plate, and hitters tee off. Carrasco does keep the ball in the park. He also was the Reds' stingiest reliever at allowing inherited runners to score last season.

## Defense & Hitting

Carrasco's delivery consists of rearing back and firing, which leaves him in poor fielding position. He would rather strike out the batter than pay attention to baserunners, so would-be stealers often get good jumps. It's a good thing Carrasco makes his money pitching, because he hasn't recorded a hit or a sacrifice in two big-league seasons.

## 1996 Outlook

Carrasco played winter ball after the season ended, with Reds bullpen coach Grant Jackson serving as his pitching coach. Cincinnati hopes this special attention will return Carrasco to his 1994 form. He'll have plenty of right-handed competition in the Reds' bullpen, so Carrasco will have to take his pitching to the next level if he expects to be in any game-saving situations come 1996.

**Position:** RP
**Bats:** R **Throws:** R
**Ht:** 6' 2" **Wt:** 180

**Opening Day Age:** 26
**Born:** 10/22/69 in San Pedro de Macoris, DR
**ML Seasons:** 2
**Pronunciation:** kuh-RASS-koh

### Overall Statistics

|  | W | L | Pct. | ERA | G | GS | Sv | IP | H | BB | SO | HR | BR/IP |
|---|---|---|---|---|---|---|---|---|---|---|---|---|---|
| 1995 | 2 | 7 | .222 | 4.12 | 64 | 0 | 5 | 87.1 | 86 | 46 | 64 | 1 | 1.51 |
| Career | 7 | 13 | .350 | 3.38 | 109 | 0 | 11 | 143.2 | 128 | 76 | 105 | 4 | 1.42 |

### How Often He Throws Strikes

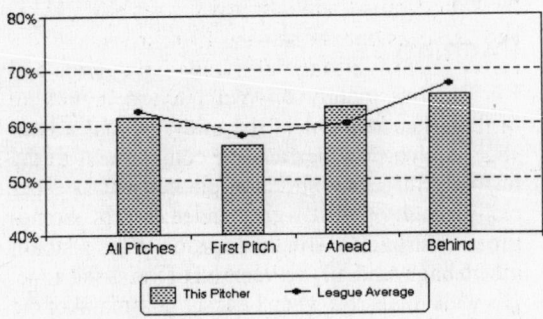

### 1995 Situational Stats

|  | W | L | ERA | Sv | IP |  | AB | H | HR | RBI | Avg |
|---|---|---|---|---|---|---|---|---|---|---|---|
| Home | 1 | 1 | 3.20 | 2 | 39.1 | LHB | 146 | 42 | 0 | 18 | .288 |
| Road | 1 | 6 | 4.88 | 3 | 48.0 | RHB | 189 | 44 | 1 | 18 | .233 |
| First Half | 2 | 3 | 3.30 | 5 | 46.1 | Sc Pos | 92 | 22 | 0 | 33 | .239 |
| Scnd Half | 0 | 4 | 5.05 | 0 | 41.0 | Clutch | 165 | 42 | 0 | 16 | .255 |

### 1995 Rankings (National League)

→ 2nd in wild pitches (15) and relief losses (7)
→ 6th in relief innings (87.1)
→ 10th in games pitched
→ Led the Reds in losses, games pitched, walks allowed, wild pitches, holds (11), blown saves (4) and relief losses

# Mariano Duncan

## 1995 Season

Mariano Duncan came to the Reds by accident in 1995. Jim Bowden simply was trying to block Philadelphia from trading Duncan to Atlanta when he claimed him off waivers. The Reds ended up working out a deal for Duncan, sending 26-year-old minor league shortstop Brian Koelling to the Phillies in the exchange. Though returning to Cincinnati was an accident (Duncan was a Red from 1989 through 1991), he played well. His acquisition added an extra infielder and good right-handed bat to an already deep bench.

## Hitting

Duncan hits for average by going to all fields. He likes the fastball and can drive it for extra bases and an occasional home run. Duncan has made a career out of killing left-handed pitching, and 1995 was no exception. He can hit coming off the bench, as well, batting .389 as a pinch hitter last year. Aggressive at the plate, Duncan is nearly impossible to walk. He picked up just five free passes in '95. Chasing way too many bad pitches is one of Duncan's weaknesses. Another is laying off the high fastball, a pitch he is unable to hit.

## Baserunning & Defense

Duncan has average range and an adequate arm at second. He is versatile enough to play every infield position and in the outfield. The Reds gave him a look at first base and he handled himself well. The once-speedy Duncan is no longer a stolen-base threat. He was successful on just one of his four stolen-base attempts during the season.

## 1996 Outlook

With Bret Boone and Barry Larkin fixed in the Reds lineup, Duncan would get little chance to play in Cincinnati. His skills are still major league caliber and he is just a year removed from starting at second base in the All-Star game. Look for Duncan, a free agent, to try to find a starting job somewhere this winter.

**Position:** 2B/1B/SS
**Bats:** R **Throws:** R
**Ht:** 6' 0" **Wt:** 185

**Opening Day Age:** 33
**Born:** 3/13/63 in San Pedro de Macoris, DR
**ML Seasons:** 10

### Overall Statistics

|  | G | AB | R | H | D | T | HR | RBI | SB | BB | SO | Avg | OBP | Slg |
|---|---|---|---|---|---|---|---|---|---|---|---|---|---|---|
| 1995 | 81 | 265 | 36 | 76 | 14 | 2 | 6 | 36 | 1 | 5 | 62 | .287 | .297 | .423 |
| Career | 1081 | 3938 | 521 | 1031 | 185 | 34 | 78 | 410 | 164 | 180 | 758 | .262 | .298 | .385 |

### Where He Hits the Ball

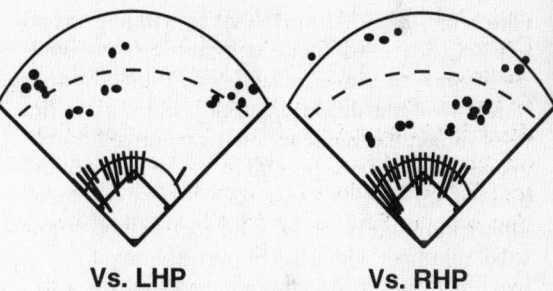

**Vs. LHP**          **Vs. RHP**

### 1995 Situational Stats

|  | AB | H | HR | RBI | Avg |  | AB | H | HR | RBI | Avg |
|---|---|---|---|---|---|---|---|---|---|---|---|
| Home | 118 | 37 | 3 | 18 | .314 | LHP | 114 | 34 | 2 | 17 | .298 |
| Road | 147 | 39 | 3 | 18 | .265 | RHP | 151 | 42 | 4 | 19 | .278 |
| First Half | 155 | 43 | 2 | 13 | .277 | Sc Pos | 65 | 20 | 1 | 26 | .308 |
| Scnd Half | 110 | 33 | 4 | 23 | .300 | Clutch | 46 | 15 | 1 | 7 | .326 |

### 1995 Rankings (National League)

➡ 9th in errors at second base (6)
➡ 10th in batting average on a 3-2 count (.381)

Cincinnati Reds

# Ron Gant

## 1995 Season

Ron Gant didn't miss a beat after sitting out the entire 1994 season while recovering from a broken right leg suffered in a dirt bike accident. Signing Gant paid huge dividends for general manager Jim Bowden and the Reds. Cincinnati, with Gant delivering power and run production in the middle of the lineup, won the National League Central Division. Gant demonstrated the array of hitting and defensive skills that made him a $5 million man in Atlanta, and he garnered Comeback Player of the Year honors for the second time in his career.

## Hitting

Gant's right-handed power was a good fit for Riverfront Stadium. He also performed well in the clutch, batting .368 from the seventh inning on and cracking a record four extra-inning, game-winning home runs in '95. Gant's open stance allows him to cover the inside and middle of the plate, but he is vulnerable to pitches on the outer half. Pitchers who try to work him up in the strike zone are looking for trouble, because his great bat speed allows him to drive those pitches. As if the power wasn't enough, Gant has apparently developed a better batting eye, drawing a career-high 74 walks last season. He still tends to be a streaky hitter who's susceptible to prolonged slumps.

## Baserunning & Defense

Perhaps the biggest question mark was the effect Gant's injury would have on his speed. Although he started the season with an awkward-looking running style, his 23 stolen bases almost matched the 26 he stole in 1993. Gant's speed and aggressiveness allow him to make a lot of plays in left field, but his arm is average at best.

## 1996 Outlook

Gant turned out to be everything the Reds were looking for, but never quite found, in Kevin Mitchell. Will 1995, though, be Gant's only season in a Reds uniform? Cincinnati, overextended with big contracts for 1996, will have trouble meeting the contract demands of this highly sought-after free agent.

**Position:** LF
**Bats:** R **Throws:** R
**Ht:** 6' 0"  **Wt:** 200

**Opening Day Age:** 31
**Born:** 3/2/65 in Victoria, TX
**ML Seasons:** 8

### Overall Statistics

|  | G | AB | R | H | D | T | HR | RBI | SB | BB | SO | Avg | OBP | Slg |
|---|---|---|---|---|---|---|---|---|---|---|---|---|---|---|
| 1995 | 119 | 410 | 79 | 113 | 19 | 4 | 29 | 88 | 23 | 74 | 108 | .276 | .386 | .554 |
| Career | 977 | 3602 | 594 | 949 | 177 | 31 | 176 | 568 | 180 | 374 | 708 | .263 | .334 | .476 |

### Where He Hits the Ball

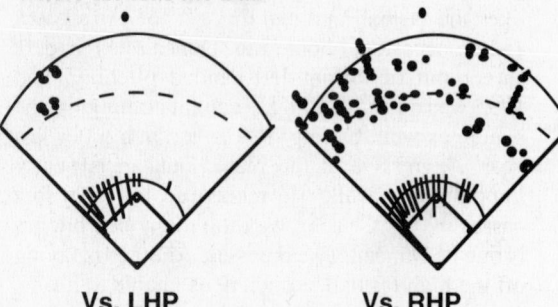

Vs. LHP          Vs. RHP

### 1995 Situational Stats

|  | AB | H | HR | RBI | Avg |  | AB | H | HR | RBI | Avg |
|---|---|---|---|---|---|---|---|---|---|---|---|
| Home | 189 | 52 | 12 | 42 | .275 | LHP | 84 | 21 | 7 | 17 | .250 |
| Road | 221 | 61 | 17 | 46 | .276 | RHP | 326 | 92 | 22 | 71 | .282 |
| First Half | 230 | 67 | 20 | 54 | .291 | Sc Pos | 114 | 34 | 9 | 61 | .298 |
| Scnd Half | 180 | 46 | 9 | 34 | .256 | Clutch | 55 | 23 | 7 | 18 | .418 |

### 1995 Rankings (National League)

- ➡ 1st in batting average in the clutch (.418) and cleanup slugging percentage (.717)
- ➡ 2nd in batting average on an 0-2 count (.333) and fielding percentage in left field (.985)
- ➡ 3rd in HR frequency (14.1 ABs per HR) and lowest groundball/flyball ratio (0.8)
- ➡ 5th in most pitches seen per plate appearance (4.09) and highest percentage of swings that missed (28.5%)
- ➡ 6th in walks and slugging percentage vs. right-handed pitchers (.558)
- ➡ 7th in slugging percentage
- ➡ Led the Reds in home runs, walks and HR frequency

# Xavier Hernandez

**Position:** RP
**Bats:** L  **Throws:** R
**Ht:** 6' 2"  **Wt:** 195

**Opening Day Age:** 30
**Born:** 8/16/65 in Port Arthur, TX
**ML Seasons:** 7

## 1995 Season

The Reds gave veteran reliever Xavier Hernandez a shot when he was let go after a rough 1994 season with the Yankees. Working mainly as a middle reliever, Hernandez wasn't particularly effective, but he was a good luck charm for the Reds, picking up seven wins. Hernandez has a history of throwing at batters, and he was suspended for eight games after precipitating a brawl with Houston in September. He finished the year on a down note, getting lit up for a 12.60 ERA in his last eight appearances.

## Pitching

Hernandez' best pitch is his split-fingered fastball. He also throws a fastball and a slider, but over his career Hernandez has mostly depended on hitters chasing the splitter even when it's out of the strike zone. They don't chase the pitch as much these days, so Hernandez needs to throw it for strikes more frequently. If he can get ahead in the count he can use the splitter very effectively. The problem is that he hasn't had good control the last two years. Lefties were especially tough on him last year.

## Defense & Hitting

Throwing the split-fingered pitch requires Hernandez to be a good fielder—and he is. Hernandez prefers to work on the batter, though, and doesn't keep close tabs on baserunners. They oblige him by stealing whenever possible. As a hitter, Hernandez is in a five-year slump. His one and only major league hit came in 1990. With the way he throws at people, you can't blame him for not digging in at the plate.

## 1996 Outlook

Hernandez has decent stuff and can get the job done in the bullpen when his control keeps him ahead of hitters. The Reds hope he'll be able to return to his '92 and '93 form, when he was an outstanding middle reliever with Houston, but he'll need better command of the splitter in order to do that. He's only 30 and young enough to bounce back.

### Overall Statistics

|  | W | L | Pct. | ERA | G | GS | Sv | IP | H | BB | SO | HR | BR/IP |
|---|---|---|---|---|---|---|---|---|---|---|---|---|---|
| 1995 | 7 | 2 | .778 | 4.60 | 59 | 0 | 3 | 90.0 | 95 | 31 | 84 | 8 | 1.40 |
| Career | 29 | 20 | .592 | 3.76 | 312 | 7 | 28 | 485.2 | 450 | 186 | 404 | 42 | 1.31 |

### How Often He Throws Strikes

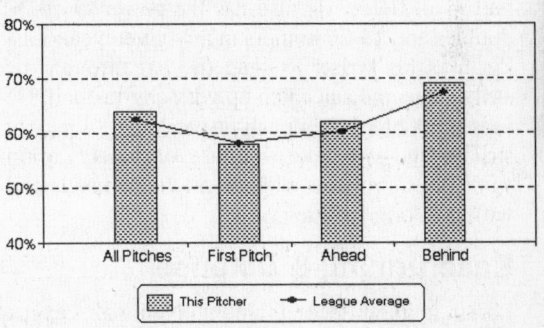

### 1995 Situational Stats

|  | W | L | ERA | Sv | IP |  | AB | H | HR | RBI | Avg |
|---|---|---|---|---|---|---|---|---|---|---|---|
| Home | 5 | 1 | 4.61 | 0 | 41.0 | LHB | 129 | 40 | 5 | 23 | .310 |
| Road | 2 | 1 | 4.59 | 3 | 49.0 | RHB | 219 | 55 | 3 | 18 | .251 |
| First Half | 5 | 1 | 4.18 | 3 | 47.1 | Sc Pos | 98 | 27 | 1 | 29 | .276 |
| Scnd Half | 2 | 1 | 5.06 | 0 | 42.2 | Clutch | 85 | 19 | 3 | 9 | .224 |

### 1995 Rankings (National League)

- ➡ 4th in relief wins and relief innings
- ➡ 9th in highest relief ERA (4.60)
- ➡ 10th in highest batting average allowed in relief (.273)
- ➡ Led the Reds in relief wins (7), relief innings (90.0) and most strikeouts per 9 innings in relief (8.4)

Cincinnati Reds

# Barry Larkin

**Position:** SS
**Bats:** R  **Throws:** R
**Ht:** 6' 0"  **Wt:** 195

**Opening Day Age:** 31
**Born:** 4/28/64 in
Cincinnati, OH
**ML Seasons:** 10

## 1995 Season

Barry Larkin did it all for the Reds in 1995. He hit for average and power, drove in and scored runs, stole bases and played a spectacular shortstop. For the second straight year, Larkin avoided injury and put up the numbers Cincy fans have come to expect. In the clubhouse, Larkin has evolved from leader by example to vocal team leader. His teammates will tell you he was their MVP, and the official voters agreed by naming Larkin the National League's Most Valuable Player.

## Hitting

Larkin is as close to a complete hitter as they come. He has good plate coverage and can line the ball to all fields. He also has the power to hit 30 doubles and 15-20 homers in any given year. Larkin uses his wrists to snap the bat through the strike zone and can catch up with any fastball. He sees a lot of pitches each at-bat, only swings at strikes, and will take the base on balls. Larkin sometimes struggles with the pitch just inside and with breaking balls away.

## Baserunning & Defense

Larkin ranked second among National League shortstops in fielding percentage, but that's only half the story. Now a two-time Gold Glove winner, Larkin executes the spectacular play on a regular basis. He likes making the play up the middle, cutting across the second-base bag and throwing the runner out. Larkin also has the arm to make the throw from deep in the hole. He used his good speed and baserunning instincts to succeed on 51 of his 56 steal attempts, the best success rate in the league. Pitchers must pay attention to Larkin when he's on second because he has a penchant for stealing third.

## 1996 Outlook

At 31, Larkin holds the title of baseball's best shortstop. He should be able to sustain his level of play for the next few years. As usual, the key for Larkin is healthy; if he can play every day he'll once again be an MVP candidate.

### Overall Statistics

|  | G | AB | R | H | D | T | HR | RBI | SB | BB | SO | Avg | OBP | Slg |
|---|---|---|---|---|---|---|---|---|---|---|---|---|---|---|
| 1995 | 131 | 496 | 98 | 158 | 29 | 6 | 15 | 66 | 51 | 61 | 49 | .319 | .394 | .492 |
| Career | 1176 | 4429 | 711 | 1322 | 222 | 44 | 102 | 537 | 239 | 449 | 431 | .298 | .364 | .438 |

### Where He Hits the Ball

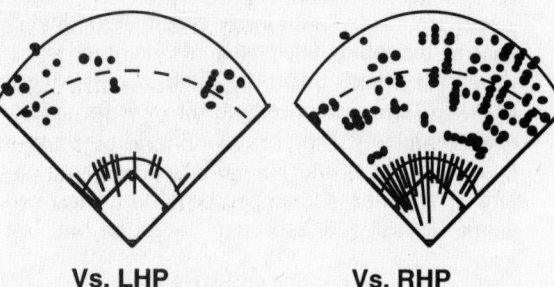

**Vs. LHP**  **Vs. RHP**

### 1995 Situational Stats

|  | AB | H | HR | RBI | Avg |  | AB | H | HR | RBI | Avg |
|---|---|---|---|---|---|---|---|---|---|---|---|
| Home | 253 | 83 | 8 | 34 | .328 | LHP | 111 | 32 | 8 | 20 | .288 |
| Road | 243 | 75 | 7 | 32 | .309 | RHP | 385 | 126 | 7 | 46 | .327 |
| First Half | 225 | 65 | 6 | 29 | .289 | Sc Pos | 109 | 38 | 6 | 54 | .349 |
| Scnd Half | 271 | 93 | 9 | 37 | .343 | Clutch | 68 | 27 | 2 | 11 | .397 |

### 1995 Rankings (National League)

→ 1st in stolen base percentage (91.1%), steals of third (15) and lowest percentage of swings on the first pitch (12.3%)

→ 2nd in stolen bases and fielding percentage at shortstop (.980)

→ 3rd in most pitches seen per plate appearance (4.16) and batting average in the clutch (.397)

→ 5th in runs scored

→ 6th in batting average, batting average vs. right-handed pitchers (.327) and batting average with two strikes (.277)

→ Led the Reds in batting average, runs scored, hits, singles (108), triples, stolen bases and pitches seen (2,356)

# Darren Lewis

## 1995 Season

Center fielder Darren Lewis came to the Reds in the Deion Sanders trade last July 21. While Cincinnati's shortage of starting pitching motivated the trade, the Reds were pleased to acquire the 1994 Gold Glove center fielder in the deal. However, Lewis didn't hit as the Reds had hoped and soon found himself serving as a late-inning defensive replacement. When he was in center, Cincinnati's defense up the middle was one of the best in baseball.

## Hitting

Lewis has the short, slashing-type swing managers like to see from leadoff men with speed. He's a groundball hitter and a good bunter, two more qualities which should help maximize his speed. And he usually makes contact. Unfortunately for Lewis, his hitting style has never translated into a high batting average. Factor in that he doesn't walk a lot, and you have an on-base percentage unworthy of a leadoff hitter. He doesn't hit for power; many of his extra-base hits can be attributed to his speed.

## Baserunning & Defense

Combine speed, great instincts, sure-handedness and the ability to get a great jump on the ball, and you have the makings of a great center fielder. If Lewis gets to the ball, he'll make the play; he holds the major league record for consecutive errorless games by an outfielder, and he committed only two miscues last year. Lewis has a capable arm, but his forte is catching the ball, not throwing it. On the basepaths he needs to read pitchers better. With Cincinnati, he was thrown out on half of his 22 basestealing attempts.

## 1996 Outlook

Darren Lewis, Jerome Walton and Thomas Howard make for a crowded center field in Cincinnati. If Ron Gant doesn't return to the Reds, Walton and Howard would likely move to left and Lewis could regain his starting job. But to keep it, he'll need to hit a lot better than he did in 1995.

**Position:** CF
**Bats:** R **Throws:** R
**Ht:** 6' 0" **Wt:** 189

**Opening Day Age:** 28
**Born:** 8/28/67 in Berkeley, CA
**ML Seasons:** 6

Cincinnati Reds

### Overall Statistics

|  | G | AB | R | H | D | T | HR | RBI | SB | BB | SO | Avg | OBP | Slg |
|---|---|---|---|---|---|---|---|---|---|---|---|---|---|---|
| 1995 | 132 | 472 | 66 | 118 | 13 | 3 | 1 | 24 | 32 | 34 | 57 | .250 | .311 | .297 |
| Career | 579 | 2022 | 303 | 503 | 58 | 23 | 9 | 135 | 151 | 189 | 227 | .249 | .319 | .314 |

### Where He Hits the Ball

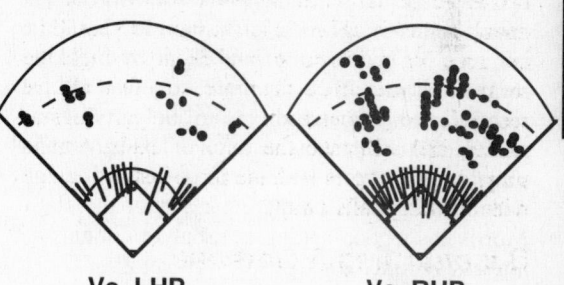

**Vs. LHP**          **Vs. RHP**

### 1995 Situational Stats

|  | AB | H | HR | RBI | Avg |  | AB | H | HR | RBI | Avg |
|---|---|---|---|---|---|---|---|---|---|---|---|
| Home | 220 | 52 | 1 | 14 | .236 | LHP | 104 | 24 | 0 | 3 | .231 |
| Road | 252 | 66 | 0 | 10 | .262 | RHP | 368 | 94 | 1 | 21 | .255 |
| First Half | 284 | 72 | 0 | 15 | .254 | Sc Pos | 86 | 23 | 0 | 22 | .267 |
| Scnd Half | 188 | 46 | 1 | 9 | .245 | Clutch | 64 | 22 | 0 | 5 | .344 |

### 1995 Rankings (National League)

➡ 1st in fielding percentage in center field (.994)
➡ 2nd in caught stealing (18), lowest slugging percentage, lowest HR frequency (472.0 ABs per HR), lowest on-base percentage for a leadoff hitter (.305) and lowest slugging percentage vs. right-handed pitchers (.299)
➡ 3rd in lowest stolen base percentage (64.0%), lowest slugging percentage vs. left-handed pitchers (.288) and bunts in play (33)
➡ 5th in sacrifice bunts (12), lowest on-base percentage vs. left-handed pitchers (.270) and lowest percentage of swings that missed (7.5%)
➡ 6th in lowest batting average (.250) and highest percentage of swings put into play (55.2%)

# Hal Morris

## 1995 Season

Hal Morris, who finally enjoyed an injury-free season in 1994, wasn't as fortunate in 1995. Morris was hampered by hamstring injuries for the first half of the season and was hitting just .209 at the All-Star break. He got things going after the break, raising his average to .279 by season's end. Morris provided a regular left-handed bat in a Reds lineup dominated by right-handed hitters.

## Hitting

Morris has an unusual batting stance. He starts deep in the box and creeps in toward the plate while the pitch is coming. This movement makes him vulnerable to good inside fastballs. Lefthanders are especially troublesome for Morris. He hasn't homered against a lefty since 1992, and he is prone to chasing the outside pitch breaking away from him. He's far more effective against righties, shooting line drives to all parts of the park. He'll take the outside pitch to left-center and pull the inside pitch. He has gap power and can go deep if the pitch is on the inner part of the plate. Morris has a good batting eye, but he remains an aggressive hitter who doesn't walk a lot.

## Baserunning & Defense

While never much of a stealing threat, Morris is usually an average baserunner. However, hamstring problems made him a liability on the basepaths in 1995. For most of the season he went station-to station, and couldn't score from second on a single. Although Morris is just an average fielder, he does a good job pulling throws out of the dirt.

## 1996 Outlook

The Reds, committed to several big-dollar contracts in 1996, don't feel their first baseman's production matched his $3 million salary. Morris, a career .300 hitter who is a free agent, risks pricing himself out of Cincinnati. He's not the prototypical power-hitting first baseman, so it will be interesting to see what his value is in the open market. The Reds would like him back if the price is right.

**Position:** 1B
**Bats:** L **Throws:** L
**Ht:** 6' 4"  **Wt:** 210

**Opening Day Age:** 30
**Born:** 4/9/65 in Fort Rucker, AL
**ML Seasons:** 8

### Overall Statistics

|  | G | AB | R | H | D | T | HR | RBI | SB | BB | SO | Avg | OBP | Slg |
|---|---|---|---|---|---|---|---|---|---|---|---|---|---|---|
| 1995 | 101 | 359 | 53 | 100 | 25 | 2 | 11 | 51 | 1 | 29 | 58 | .279 | .333 | .451 |
| Career | 702 | 2394 | 327 | 737 | 149 | 13 | 55 | 330 | 34 | 210 | 330 | .308 | .363 | .450 |

### Where He Hits the Ball

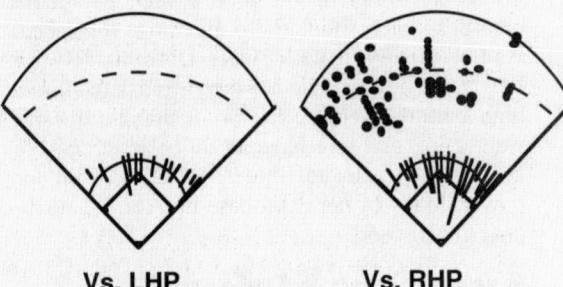

Vs. LHP          Vs. RHP

### 1995 Situational Stats

|  | AB | H | HR | RBI | Avg |  | AB | H | HR | RBI | Avg |
|---|---|---|---|---|---|---|---|---|---|---|---|
| Home | 161 | 54 | 6 | 26 | .335 | LHP | 68 | 15 | 0 | 7 | .221 |
| Road | 198 | 46 | 5 | 25 | .232 | RHP | 291 | 85 | 11 | 44 | .292 |
| First Half | 110 | 23 | 3 | 17 | .209 | Sc Pos | 111 | 24 | 1 | 33 | .216 |
| Scnd Half | 249 | 77 | 8 | 34 | .309 | Clutch | 54 | 13 | 3 | 11 | .241 |

### 1995 Rankings (National League)

→ 3rd in lowest fielding percentage at first base (.994)
→ 9th in lowest batting average with runners in scoring position (.216) and errors at first base (5)

# Mark Portugal

## 1995 Season

After the Reds lost Jose Rijo for the season, general manager Jim Bowden executed a blockbuster deal with San Francisco for several players, with the key man being right-handed starter Mark Portugal. Portugal responded by getting bombed in three of his first four starts. But then he settled down, going 6-2 with a 2.57 ERA in his last 10 starts to help the Reds to a division title.

## Pitching

Portugal is not overpowering. He uses an assortment of pitches to keep hitters off balance. His best offering is his change-up. He also mixes in an above-average curveball and slider, and a lukewarm fastball that he throws to keep hitters honest. Changing speeds effectively is crucial to his success. His control isn't particularly good. Portugal will walk a lot of batters and uncork a wild one from time to time. His stuff makes him more effective against lefthanders.

## Defense & Hitting

Portugal has a nice, easy delivery that leaves him ready to field. He may not look nimble, but he can cover some ground coming off the mound. His slow delivery and offspeed pitches, however, make him an inviting target for basestealers. Portugal's batting average was down considerably from the sizzling .354 he hit in 1994. Still, he can handle the bat. He also picks up an occasional walk and is proficient at getting the bunt down.

## 1996 Outlook

Portugal is signed through 1996 and carries a $4 million price tag. Cincinnati would like to trim it from their payroll, but will be hard-pressed to get anyone to take over the payments. Wherever he pitches, Portugal, who's averaged 11 victories a year for the last six years, won't be the ace, but he'll throw a lot of innings and keep you in games.

**Position:** SP
**Bats:** R  **Throws:** R
**Ht:** 6' 0"  **Wt:** 190

**Opening Day Age:** 33
**Born:** 10/30/62 in Los Angeles, CA
**ML Seasons:** 11

*Cincinnati Reds*

### Overall Statistics

|  | W | L | Pct. | ERA | G | GS | Sv | IP | H | BB | SO | HR | BR/IP |
|---|---|---|---|---|---|---|---|---|---|---|---|---|---|
| 1995 | 11 | 10 | .524 | 4.01 | 31 | 31 | 0 | 181.2 | 185 | 56 | 96 | 17 | 1.33 |
| Career | 84 | 67 | .556 | 3.81 | 259 | 201 | 5 | 1340.0 | 1285 | 487 | 856 | 135 | 1.32 |

### How Often He Throws Strikes

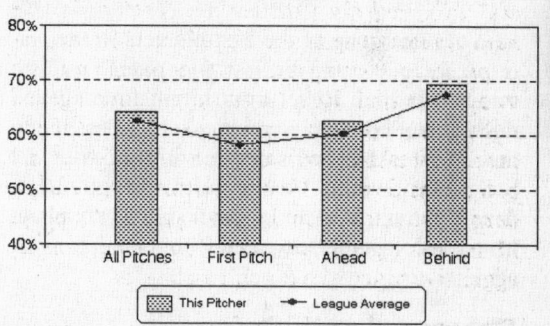

Legend: This Pitcher / League Average

### 1995 Situational Stats

|  | W | L | ERA | Sv | IP |  | AB | H | HR | RBI | Avg |
|---|---|---|---|---|---|---|---|---|---|---|---|
| Home | 4 | 6 | 3.52 | 0 | 99.2 | LHB | 345 | 88 | 5 | 32 | .255 |
| Road | 7 | 4 | 4.61 | 0 | 82.0 | RHB | 360 | 97 | 12 | 47 | .269 |
| First Half | 5 | 3 | 4.32 | 0 | 91.2 | Sc Pos | 172 | 45 | 5 | 58 | .262 |
| Scnd Half | 6 | 7 | 3.70 | 0 | 90.0 | Clutch | 47 | 11 | 0 | 2 | .234 |

### 1995 Rankings (National League)

- → 1st in games started and most run support per 9 innings (6.2)
- → 2nd in highest stolen base percentage allowed (88.2%)
- → 3rd in least strikeouts per 9 innings (4.8)
- → 4th in least pitches thrown per batter (3.43)
- → 8th in lowest strikeout/walk ratio (1.7)
- → 10th in lowest groundball/flyball ratio allowed (1.2) and highest ERA on the road (4.61)

# Jose Rijo

## 1995 Season

The elbow problems that have plagued Jose Rijo for most of his career reached a critical juncture in 1995. Rijo tried to pitch, but the elbow pain rendered him ineffective. He posted his highest ERA since 1987, when he was a struggling young pitcher with Oakland. General Manager Jim Bowden asked Rijo to rest his arm for a possible return during the pennant run. The rest didn't help, forcing Cincinnati's ace to undergo Tommy John ligament-transplant surgery in late August. Rijo's five victories were his fewest since coming to the Reds in 1988, but he still posted a winning record for the eighth straight year.

## Pitching

Rijo has been one of the best pitchers in the National League over the last five years, using a mid-90s fastball to set up a biting forkball and nasty slider. His sore elbow made it impossible to throw his forkball and slider, leaving him with just the heater, which wasn't quite enough. Left-handed hitters, who no longer had to worry about his back-door slider, pounded Rijo for a .328 average.

## Defense & Hitting

Rijo used to enjoy the cat-and-mouse games of battling baserunners, but the ailing pitcher didn't pay much attention to them in 1995. All eight basestealing attempts against him were successful. He is a good athlete who fields his position well. At the plate, Rijo's wild cuts are entertaining but do little damage.

## 1996 Outlook

Just 30 years old, Rijo has a chance to come back from serious elbow surgery. However, for someone who was a power pitcher and relied heavily on the slider, it could be a tough road back. Rijo, a conditioning nut, believes he can return in nine months. Doctors, though, feel a more reasonable recovery period would be 12 to 18 months, making it doubtful that he'll be back on the mound in 1996.

**Position:** SP
**Bats:** R **Throws:** R
**Ht:** 6' 3" **Wt:** 215

**Opening Day Age:** 30
**Born:** 5/13/65 in San Cristobal, DR
**ML Seasons:** 12
**Pronunciation:** REE-ho

### Overall Statistics

|  | W | L | Pct. | ERA | G | GS | Sv | IP | H | BB | SO | HR | BR/IP |
|---|---|---|---|---|---|---|---|---|---|---|---|---|---|
| 1995 | 5 | 4 | .556 | 4.17 | 14 | 14 | 0 | 69.0 | 76 | 22 | 62 | 6 | 1.42 |
| Career | 111 | 87 | .561 | 3.16 | 332 | 260 | 3 | 1786.0 | 1602 | 634 | 1556 | 132 | 1.25 |

### How Often He Throws Strikes

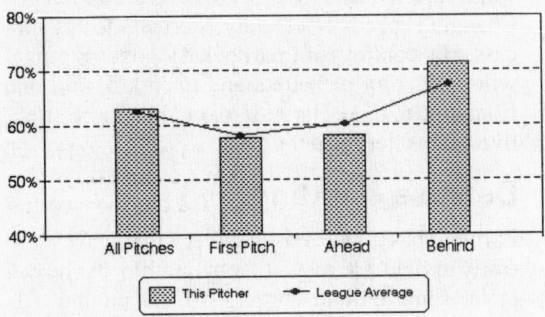

### 1995 Situational Stats

|  | W | L | ERA | Sv | IP |  | AB | H | HR | RBI | Avg |
|---|---|---|---|---|---|---|---|---|---|---|---|
| Home | 2 | 3 | 5.06 | 0 | 32.0 | LHB | 128 | 42 | 4 | 14 | .328 |
| Road | 3 | 1 | 3.41 | 0 | 37.0 | RHB | 139 | 34 | 2 | 14 | .245 |
| First Half | 4 | 4 | 4.21 | 0 | 62.0 | Sc Pos | 61 | 17 | 1 | 21 | .279 |
| Scnd Half | 1 | 0 | 3.86 | 0 | 7.0 | Clutch | 7 | 2 | 1 | 1 | .286 |

### 1995 Rankings (National League)

➜ Did not rank near the top or bottom in any category

# Reggie Sanders

## 1995 Season

Reggie Sanders has begun to live up to the expectations generated by glowing scouting reports and a brilliant minor league career. In 1995, he demonstrated improvement in every area of his game. Sanders established career highs in a number of categories, including batting average, homers, runs batted in and stolen bases. And he finished just two dingers shy of joining the elite 30-30 club. Sanders was a National League All-Star for the first time in his career, and his final numbers were worthy of MVP consideration.

## Hitting

Sanders has a powerful swing, and his strong hands and wrists whip his bat through the hitting zone. He likes the low fastball and offspeed pitches that hang around the middle of the plate. Sanders didn't chase as many bad pitches in '95, and as a result his batting average improved. So did his walk total. He still has problems making contact, however, striking out once every four at-bats last year. Sanders is also a bit slow starting his hands and can be vulnerable to high hard stuff, as the Braves showed in a nightmarish (for Sanders) League Championship Series.

## Baserunning & Defense

Sanders flies around the bases. He can turn a double into a triple, and he circled the sacks for an inside-the-park-homer last year. While his stolen-base totals are impressive, he still needs to work on reading pitchers better to improve his success rate. In the field, Sanders has developed into an outstanding right fielder. He covers a lot of ground, and he gets a better jump on the ball in right than he did when he was playing center. He has a strong, accurate throwing arm that recorded double-digit assists in 1995.

## 1996 Outlook

Only 28, Sanders is at the peak of his talents. There's no reason he can't continue to put up numbers similar to last year's stellar campaign. With continued improvement, Sanders could reach MVP status and possibly the 30-30 club. But first, he'll need to put his LCS problems behind him.

**Position:** RF/CF
**Bats:** R  **Throws:** R
**Ht:** 6' 1"  **Wt:** 185

**Opening Day Age:** 28
**Born:** 12/1/67 in Florence, SC
**ML Seasons:** 5

### Overall Statistics

| | G | AB | R | H | D | T | HR | RBI | SB | BB | SO | Avg | OBP | Slg |
|---|---|---|---|---|---|---|---|---|---|---|---|---|---|---|
| 1995 | 133 | 484 | 91 | 148 | 36 | 6 | 28 | 99 | 36 | 69 | 122 | .306 | .397 | .579 |
| Career | 503 | 1805 | 315 | 501 | 98 | 24 | 78 | 283 | 101 | 209 | 461 | .278 | .355 | .488 |

### Where He Hits the Ball

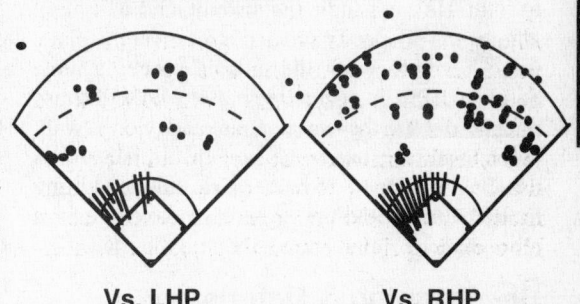

**Vs. LHP**          **Vs. RHP**

### 1995 Situational Stats

| | AB | H | HR | RBI | Avg | | AB | H | HR | RBI | Avg |
|---|---|---|---|---|---|---|---|---|---|---|---|
| Home | 240 | 71 | 9 | 45 | .296 | LHP | 104 | 38 | 8 | 24 | .365 |
| Road | 244 | 77 | 19 | 54 | .316 | RHP | 380 | 110 | 20 | 75 | .289 |
| First Half | 251 | 78 | 15 | 56 | .311 | Sc Pos | 147 | 44 | 7 | 68 | .299 |
| Scnd Half | 233 | 70 | 13 | 43 | .300 | Clutch | 70 | 14 | 1 | 10 | .200 |

### 1995 Rankings (National League)

- ➡ 1st in highest percentage of swings that missed (30.1%)
- ➡ 2nd in slugging percentage vs. left-handed pitchers (.692)
- ➡ 3rd in strikeouts and on-base percentage vs. left-handed pitchers (.447)
- ➡ 4th in doubles, stolen bases, caught stealing (12) and slugging percentage
- ➡ 5th in batting average vs. left-handed pitchers (.365) and fielding percentage in right field (.984)
- ➡ 6th in cleanup slugging percentage (.583)
- ➡ Led the Reds in doubles, triples, total bases (280), RBI and sacrifice flies (6)

# Benito Santiago

## 1995 Season

Reds general manager Jim Bowden rescued Benito Santiago from Camp Homestead last spring for the bargain-basement price of $550,000. Santiago had trouble throwing early in the season, and ended up having arthroscopic surgery to remove debris from his right elbow. He returned on the Fourth of July, then provided the fireworks by hitting .347 during the month. After sharing duties with Eddie Taubensee in the early going, Santiago soon took over as the regular catcher and had one of the better years of his career.

## Hitting

Santiago is a pull hitter who will rarely take a pitch to right. He can handle the fastball, and will jump all over the offspeed pitch that is left over the plate. Pitchers try to work the outside corner against Santiago. He's an aggressive batter who will chase pitches out of the strike zone and won't walk much. Santiago has some pop in his bat and is usually good for 10-15 homers. He enjoyed hitting in Riverfront Stadium, where his average was more than 100 points better than on the road.

## Baserunning & Defense

When Santiago came into the league, he was a stolen-base threat. Now he runs just a little bit better than your average catcher. Elbow problems have hampered his throwing arm; he threw out just 23 percent of potential basestealers in 1995. He still takes his shot at picking off baserunners, though not as frequently as he once did. Pitchers are comfortable working with Santiago, whose defensive skills are decent but a bit overrated. He gets lazy at times, trying to scoop the 58-foot curveball instead of blocking it.

## 1996 Outlook

Though he's not the all-around catcher he once was, Santiago is still a quality major league receiver. It's likely he'll find a better offer in the free agent market than the one he accepted from the Reds last spring, but if the price is right Cincinnati wouldn't mind having him back.

**Position:** C
**Bats:** R  **Throws:** R
**Ht:** 6' 1"  **Wt:** 185

**Opening Day Age:** 31
**Born:** 3/9/65 in Ponce, PR
**ML Seasons:** 10
**Pronunciation:** sahn-tee-AH-go

### Overall Statistics

| | G | AB | R | H | D | T | HR | RBI | SB | BB | SO | Avg | OBP | Slg |
|---|---|---|---|---|---|---|---|---|---|---|---|---|---|---|
| 1995 | 81 | 266 | 40 | 76 | 20 | 0 | 11 | 44 | 2 | 24 | 48 | .286 | .351 | .485 |
| Career | 1110 | 3944 | 436 | 1034 | 177 | 23 | 120 | 510 | 75 | 225 | 709 | .262 | .303 | .410 |

### Where He Hits the Ball

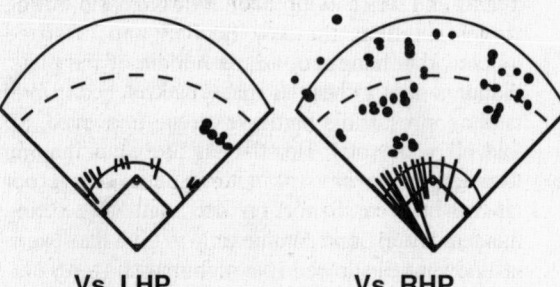

Vs. LHP            Vs. RHP

### 1995 Situational Stats

| | AB | H | HR | RBI | Avg | | AB | H | HR | RBI | Avg |
|---|---|---|---|---|---|---|---|---|---|---|---|
| Home | 144 | 48 | 7 | 23 | .333 | LHP | 62 | 22 | 3 | 14 | .355 |
| Road | 122 | 28 | 4 | 21 | .230 | RHP | 204 | 54 | 8 | 30 | .265 |
| First Half | 54 | 19 | 3 | 7 | .352 | Sc Pos | 68 | 23 | 3 | 34 | .338 |
| Scnd Half | 212 | 57 | 8 | 37 | .269 | Clutch | 34 | 8 | 0 | 2 | .235 |

### 1995 Rankings (National League)

➡ 4th in batting average on a 3-1 count (.750)

# Pete Schourek

## 1995 Season

When Reds general manager Jim Bowden claimed lefthander Pete Schourek off waivers from the New York Mets early in 1994, he may have executed the best acquisition of his tenure. After going 7-2 for the Reds in 1994, Schourek blossomed into the ace of a staff that had lost its number-one starter, Jose Rijo, to career-threatening elbow surgery. Schourek finished second in the league in wins, and eventually the Cy Young vote, behind Greg Maddux. He got stronger as the season wore on, winning 14 of his last 19 starts with a 3.02 ERA.

## Pitching

Schourek gives a lot of credit for his improvement to Reds pitching coach Don Gullett. Gullett worked on shortening the arm swing during his delivery, and Schourek believes that gave him better control and added five miles per hour to his fastball, which now tops out at 92 MPH. Schourek uses that same arm speed to throw a very good change-up. His slow curve can neutralize right-handed hitters, and Schourek was actually more effective against righties than lefties last year.

## Defense & Hitting

Despite a 6-foot-5 frame, Schourek keeps good balance during his delivery and is agile around the mound. He has a deceptive move to first and was, by far, the hardest Reds pitcher to run on. Only 37 percent of potential basestealers succeeded against him. Schourek can do some damage with a bat in his hands. He batted .220 and had three hits in one of his 1995 starts. He also led the team in sacrifices.

## 1996 Outlook

Schourek was arguably the best left-handed starter in the National League last year. Now he will be out to prove that 1995 was no fluke. The young lefty appears to have the kind of stuff that will make him successful for years to come. He will be counted on as a key player in Cincinnati's rotation.

**Position:** SP
**Bats:** L  **Throws:** L
**Ht:** 6' 5"  **Wt:** 205

**Opening Day Age:** 26
**Born:** 5/10/69 in Austin, TX
**ML Seasons:** 5
**Pronunciation:** SHUR-ek

Cincinnati Reds

### Overall Statistics

|  | W | L | Pct. | ERA | G | GS | Sv | IP | H | BB | SO | HR | BR/IP |
|---|---|---|---|---|---|---|---|---|---|---|---|---|---|
| 1995 | 18 | 7 | .720 | 3.22 | 29 | 29 | 0 | 190.1 | 158 | 45 | 160 | 17 | 1.07 |
| Career | 41 | 33 | .554 | 4.14 | 149 | 86 | 2 | 622.1 | 635 | 206 | 428 | 57 | 1.35 |

### How Often He Throws Strikes

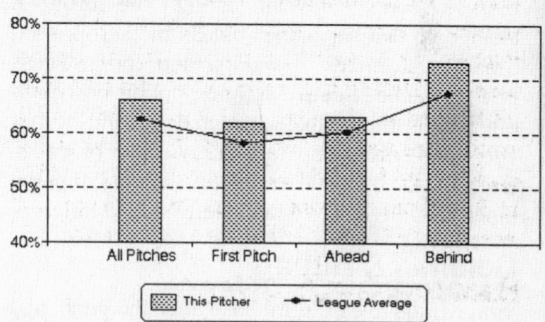

### 1995 Situational Stats

|  | W | L | ERA | Sv | IP |  | AB | H | HR | RBI | Avg |
|---|---|---|---|---|---|---|---|---|---|---|---|
| Home | 13 | 2 | 1.86 | 0 | 106.2 | LHB | 91 | 24 | 4 | 12 | .264 |
| Road | 5 | 5 | 4.95 | 0 | 83.2 | RHB | 602 | 134 | 13 | 55 | .223 |
| First Half | 8 | 4 | 3.49 | 0 | 87.2 | Sc Pos | 115 | 35 | 2 | 45 | .304 |
| Scnd Half | 10 | 3 | 2.98 | 0 | 102.2 | Clutch | 47 | 9 | 0 | 0 | .191 |

### 1995 Rankings (National League)

→ 2nd in wins, winning percentage and ERA at home (1.86)

→ 3rd in highest strikeout/walk ratio (3.6) and least baserunners allowed per 9 innings (10.0)

→ 4th in runners caught stealing (12), lowest on-base percentage allowed (.281) and lowest stolen base percentage allowed (36.8%)

→ 5th in sacrifice bunts (12), lowest batting average allowed (.228) and lowest groundball/flyball ratio allowed (1.0)

→ 6th in highest ERA on the road (4.95)

→ 7th in strikeouts

→ Led the Reds in sacrifice bunts, ERA, wins, losses, games started, innings pitched, batters faced (754) and home runs allowed

# John Smiley

## 1995 Season

John Smiley's third season with the Reds was his best by far. He began the year 5-0, didn't pick up his first loss until June 16 and earned an appearance in the All-Star game. He continued to cruise along until late in the year, when a groin injury put him on the disabled list, limiting his effectiveness in September. Smiley, a competitor who usually gives his team a chance to win, allowed more than four runs just three times, and Cincinnati won 19 of his 27 starts.

## Pitching

Smiley relies mainly on a low-90s fastball that he successfully moves around to hitters. After they've seen the fastball enough, he throws a change-up that has batters out on their front foot. Smiley also mixes in a slider and curve. These pitches can be effective at times, but his best combination is the fastball and change. Smiley has very good control and doesn't issue a lot of walks. He hides the ball well during his delivery, making him especially tough against left-handed hitters.

## Defense & Hitting

Smiley falls toward third base after the pitch, and doesn't move around the infield that well. He will field what's hit to him. He doesn't have a move to keep runners honest, and his leg kick doesn't give catchers a chance to throw anyone out. Smiley broke out the power bat last season, cracking two homers during the year. He also can sacrifice when necessary.

## 1996 Outlook

Smiley is entering the final year of his contract and would like to have a year similar to '95. With good health and command of his pitches, he could finish in the 15-20 win neighborhood. Smiley will team with Pete Schourek and David Wells to make life miserable for left-handed hitters in the National League.

**Position:** SP
**Bats:** L  **Throws:** L
**Ht:** 6' 4"  **Wt:** 210

**Opening Day Age:** 31
**Born:** 3/17/65 in Phoenixville, PA
**ML Seasons:** 10

### Overall Statistics

|  | W | L | Pct. | ERA | G | GS | Sv | IP | H | BB | SO | HR | BR/IP |
|---|---|---|---|---|---|---|---|---|---|---|---|---|---|
| 1995 | 12 | 5 | .706 | 3.46 | 28 | 27 | 0 | 176.2 | 173 | 39 | 124 | 11 | 1.20 |
| Career | 102 | 75 | .576 | 3.67 | 300 | 220 | 4 | 1536.0 | 1451 | 401 | 993 | 139 | 1.21 |

### How Often He Throws Strikes

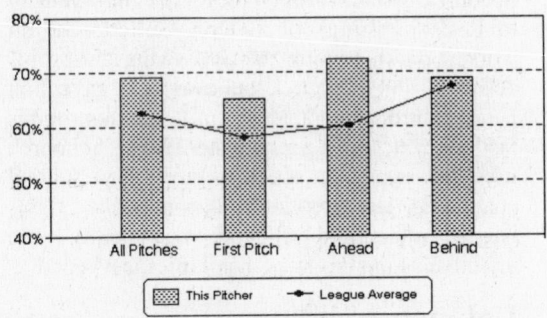

### 1995 Situational Stats

|  | W | L | ERA | Sv | IP |  | AB | H | HR | RBI | Avg |
|---|---|---|---|---|---|---|---|---|---|---|---|
| Home | 4 | 4 | 4.00 | 0 | 72.0 | LHB | 102 | 23 | 4 | 14 | .225 |
| Road | 8 | 1 | 3.10 | 0 | 104.2 | RHB | 557 | 150 | 7 | 51 | .269 |
| First Half | 9 | 1 | 3.06 | 0 | 94.0 | Sc Pos | 151 | 39 | 3 | 50 | .258 |
| Scnd Half | 3 | 4 | 3.92 | 0 | 82.2 | Clutch | 50 | 9 | 1 | 4 | .180 |

### 1995 Rankings (National League)

- → 1st in fielding percentage at pitcher
- → 4th in least home runs allowed per 9 innings (.56) and most GDPs induced per 9 innings (1.1)
- → 5th in GDPs induced (21), highest strikeout/walk ratio (3.2), least pitches thrown per batter (3.46) and ERA on the road (3.10)
- → 6th in winning percentage and least baserunners allowed per 9 innings (11.0)
- → 9th in lowest groundball/flyball ratio allowed (1.2)
- → Led the Reds in hits allowed, GDPs induced, highest groundball/flyball ratio allowed and least pitches thrown per batter

# David Wells

## 1995 Season

Cincinnati gave up top prospect C.J. Nitkowski and others to acquire lefthander David Wells from Detroit. Wells, in the midst of a spectacular season, was 10-3 with a 3.04 ERA despite pitching in hitter-friendly Tiger Stadium. He was 9-2 in his last 15 starts prior to the trade. Wells was just 6-5 with the Reds, but his three complete games took pressure off the bullpen.

## Pitching

Wells throws a low-90s fastball that he keeps down in the strike zone. Wells likes to keep bringing the heat, but will drop in a big curve or change-up when necessary. He has a high leg kick and varying release points that make it tough to pick up his pitches. Wells doesn't walk a lot of batters, but he is prone to giving up the longball when one of his pitches finds too much of the plate.

## Defense & Hitting

Wells falls toward third after the pitch, leaving him in an awkward fielding position that reduces his chances of covering first base successfully. He does have good reactions and can snare the come-backer. Wells has an average move to first, but baserunners gain the advantage when he starts his high leg kick. He didn't embarrass himself in his first action as a hitter, picking up four hits in his brief time in the National League.

## 1996 Outlook

Combining his numbers from both leagues, Wells won 16 games despite playing half the season with the lowly Tigers. Give him a chance to get comfortable in Cincinnati and he might be capable of bigger things in 1996. The Reds should be able to provide run support for Wells and a bullpen that can hang on to his leads.

**Position:** SP
**Bats:** L **Throws:** L
**Ht:** 6' 4"  **Wt:** 225

**Opening Day Age:** 32
**Born:** 5/20/63 in Torrance, CA
**ML Seasons:** 9

*Cincinnati Reds*

### Overall Statistics

| | W | L | Pct. | ERA | G | GS | Sv | IP | H | BB | SO | HR | BR/IP |
|---|---|---|---|---|---|---|---|---|---|---|---|---|---|
| 1995 | 16 | 8 | .667 | 3.24 | 29 | 29 | 0 | 203.0 | 194 | 53 | 133 | 23 | 1.22 |
| Career | 79 | 61 | .564 | 3.77 | 314 | 144 | 13 | 1188.2 | 1149 | 320 | 792 | 133 | 1.24 |

### How Often He Throws Strikes

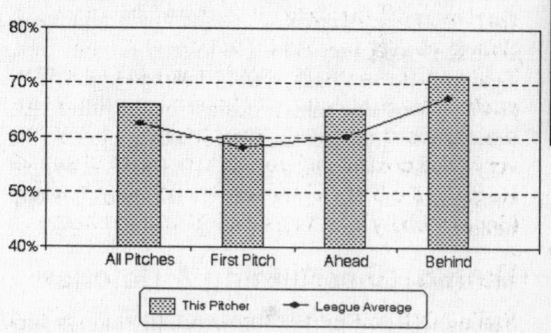

### 1995 Situational Stats

| | W | L | ERA | Sv | IP | | AB | H | HR | RBI | Avg |
|---|---|---|---|---|---|---|---|---|---|---|---|
| Home | 12 | 2 | 2.98 | 0 | 114.2 | LHB | 147 | 36 | 4 | 16 | .245 |
| Road | 4 | 6 | 3.57 | 0 | 88.1 | RHB | 627 | 158 | 19 | 60 | .252 |
| First Half | 8 | 3 | 3.00 | 0 | 108.0 | Sc Pos | 153 | 42 | 3 | 48 | .275 |
| Scnd Half | 8 | 5 | 3.51 | 0 | 95.0 | Clutch | 69 | 17 | 1 | 3 | .246 |

### 1995 Rankings (National League)

➡ 9th in complete games (3)
➡ Led the Reds in complete games (3)

# Lenny Harris

**Position**: 3B/1B
**Bats**: L  **Throws**: R
**Ht**: 5'10"  **Wt**: 210

**Opening Day Age**: 31
**Born**: 10/28/64 in Miami, FL
**ML Seasons**: 8

## Overall Statistics

| | G | AB | R | H | D | T | HR | RBI | SB | BB | SO | Avg | OBP | Slg |
|---|---|---|---|---|---|---|---|---|---|---|---|---|---|---|
| 1995 | 101 | 197 | 32 | 41 | 8 | 3 | 2 | 16 | 10 | 14 | 20 | .208 | .259 | .310 |
| Career | 822 | 2042 | 256 | 553 | 71 | 11 | 12 | 172 | 84 | 149 | 172 | .271 | .322 | .334 |

## 1995 Season

In 1995, Lenny Harris was once again a jack-of-all-trades for Cincinnati. He logged time at first, second and third base, and in left and right field. He also was the team's busiest pinch hitter. Although he wasn't as successful at the plate as he was in 1994, when he batted .310, Harris provided versatility to Manager Davey Johnson's deep bench.

## Hitting, Baserunning & Defense

The left-handed-hitting Harris usually enjoys success against righthanders but struggled last season. He looked like he was trying to pull everything, which could account for his drop in batting average. Harris does have the attributes of a pinch hitter in that he's aggressive and generally puts the ball in play. He also offers speed off the bench; he was caught stealing just once in 11 attempts in '95. Defensively, Harris is best suited for second base. He has the range to play other positions, but not the arm.

## 1996 Outlook

Given the quality of the Reds' starting infield, playing time figures to be limited for Harris in 1996. Most likely he will fill the same role he did last season. The Reds have a lot of middle-infield prospects who may push Harris for a job, and he'll need to hit better to keep his job.

# Thomas Howard

**Position**: CF/LF/RF
**Bats**: B  **Throws**: R
**Ht**: 6' 2"  **Wt**: 205

**Opening Day Age**: 31
**Born**: 12/11/64 in Middletown, OH
**ML Seasons**: 6

## Overall Statistics

| | G | AB | R | H | D | T | HR | RBI | SB | BB | SO | Avg | OBP | Slg |
|---|---|---|---|---|---|---|---|---|---|---|---|---|---|---|
| 1995 | 113 | 281 | 42 | 85 | 15 | 2 | 3 | 26 | 17 | 20 | 37 | .302 | .350 | .402 |
| Career | 556 | 1464 | 185 | 395 | 70 | 10 | 21 | 140 | 56 | 95 | 258 | .270 | .313 | .374 |

## 1995 Season

Veteran outfielder Thomas Howard played two roles for the Reds in 1995. Early in the season he was the team's best pinch hitter, and teamed with Jerome Walton to fill in for the oft-injured Deion Sanders. After Sanders was traded, Howard was the left-handed hitter in a center-field platoon with Walton and Darren Lewis. He did a fine job, batting over .300 in the leadoff spot.

## Hitting, Baserunning & Defense

Though he's a switch-hitter, Howard's troubles hitting lefties relegate him to a platoon role. He is a line-drive hitter who looks to pull inside pitches and takes everything else up the middle. He hits especially well on artificial turf, where his hard-hit ground balls find more holes. The speedy outfielder had a career-high 17 stolen bases last season, but his success rate wasn't spectacular. Howard covers a lot of ground in center field and has a good arm. Still, Manager Davey Johnson liked to replace him with Gold Glover Darren Lewis late in games.

## 1996 Outlook

His fine 1995 performance has probably earned Howard a platoon role in center field next season. If free agent Ron Gant does not return, he could see additional time in left. Either way, he seems a good bet to get 250-300 at-bats.

# Mike Jackson

**Position**: RP
**Bats:** R **Throws:** R
**Ht:** 6' 2" **Wt:** 225

**Opening Day Age:** 31
**Born:** 12/22/64 in
Houston, TX
**ML Seasons:** 10

## Overall Statistics

|  | W | L | Pct. | ERA | G | GS | Sv | IP | H | BB | SO | HR | BR/IP |
|---|---|---|---|---|---|---|---|---|---|---|---|---|---|
| 1995 | 6 | 1 | .857 | 2.39 | 40 | 0 | 2 | 49.0 | 38 | 19 | 41 | 5 | 1.16 |
| Career | 46 | 50 | .479 | 3.30 | 550 | 7 | 38 | 738.0 | 578 | 322 | 651 | 72 | 1.22 |

## 1995 Season

Early in spring training, general manager Jim Bowden asked Jeff Brantley to recruit Mike Jackson for the Reds. Brantley's appeal paid off: Jackson signed and the Reds got a solid set-up man for the bullpen. The big righthander missed the first month-and-a-half of the season, due to tendinitis in his right shoulder. When he returned, he gave the bullpen a much needed boost.

## Pitching, Defense & Hitting

Jackson's primary pitch is a 90-plus fastball with good movement. His strikeout pitch is a hard-breaking slider that starts at the batter's knees and dives down and out of the strike zone. Jackson also has developed a change-up, but will throw it only when ahead in the count. He is aggressive in the field and gets off the mound very well. He has a compact delivery and is quick to home plate, which stymies would-be basestealers.

## 1996 Outlook

Jackson, who may have been victimized by overuse in San Francisco, is now healthy again. He liked the way the Reds handled him out of the bullpen, so he may return to Cincy as a set-up man for Brantley. If not, he could pursue a closer role with another team.

# Mark Lewis

**Position**: 3B
**Bats:** R **Throws:** R
**Ht:** 6' 1" **Wt:** 190

**Opening Day Age:** 26
**Born:** 11/30/69 in
Hamilton, OH
**ML Seasons:** 5

## Overall Statistics

|  | G | AB | R | H | D | T | HR | RBI | SB | BB | SO | Avg | OBP | Slg |
|---|---|---|---|---|---|---|---|---|---|---|---|---|---|---|
| 1995 | 81 | 171 | 25 | 58 | 13 | 1 | 3 | 30 | 0 | 21 | 33 | .339 | .407 | .480 |
| Career | 321 | 1023 | 110 | 278 | 56 | 2 | 10 | 103 | 10 | 63 | 167 | .272 | .313 | .360 |

## 1995 Season

Out of minor league options and frustrated with his lack of development, the Cleveland Indians sent infielder Mark Lewis to Cincinnati in an offseason trade in December of 1994. The trade may have been just what Lewis needed, because he finally began to realize the potential that made him the second overall pick in the 1988 draft. Hitting over .300 for the first time in his major league career, Lewis came off the bench effectively and did stellar work as the right-handed bat in a third-base platoon with Jeff Branson.

## Hitting, Baserunning & Defense

Known primarily as a pull hitter, Lewis started to go to right field last season, a tactic that made him more effective against breaking balls. Driving the ball the opposite way also improved his average. Lewis has gap power but still needs to cut down on his strikeouts. Defensively, the former shortstop has the quick reactions and strong arm needed to play a solid third base. Lewis, who has average speed, didn't steal a base in '95.

## 1996 Outlook

The Reds would like to have kept Lewis, but after the season he became the player to be named later in the David Wells trade. While his .339 batting average was likely an aberration, Lewis is just 26 and should benefit from playing in hitter-friendly Tiger Stadium.

# Chuck McElroy

**Position**: RP
**Bats**: L **Throws**: L
**Ht**: 6' 0" **Wt**: 195

**Opening Day Age**: 28
**Born**: 10/1/67 in Port Arthur, TX
**ML Seasons**: 7
**Pronunciation**: MAK-ull-roy

## Overall Statistics

|  | W | L | Pct. | ERA | G | GS | Sv | IP | H | BB | SO | HR | BR/IP |
|---|---|---|---|---|---|---|---|---|---|---|---|---|---|
| 1995 | 3 | 4 | .429 | 6.02 | 44 | 0 | 0 | 40.1 | 46 | 15 | 27 | 5 | 1.51 |
| Career | 16 | 18 | .471 | 3.43 | 315 | 0 | 14 | 354.2 | 331 | 177 | 295 | 25 | 1.43 |

## 1995 Season

To put it mildly, Chuck McElroy did not get the job done as the left-handed set-up man for the Reds last year. McElroy's 6.02 ERA far exceeded the impressive 2.34 he posted in 1994, his first year with the club, and he wasn't able to handle the left-handed hitters he's paid to retire. Reds manager Davey Johnson eventually lost all confidence in McElroy and by season's end was using him only in mop-up situations.

## Pitching, Defense & Hitting

McElroy throws a fastball and sharp-breaking curve to set up his forkball. His masterful control of 1994 deserted him for much of the 1995 season, which meant he had to scrap the forkball and come over the plate with fastballs. Unfortunately, left-handers could deal with the fastball and hit him hard. McElroy is an adequate fielder. He has a deceptive pickoff move that makes it difficult for baserunners to get a good jump on him. He didn't pick up a hit in '95, but he can handle the bat.

## 1996 Outlook

The Reds were not happy with McElroy's performance and traded for lefthanders Mike Remlinger and Brad Pennington during the season. Cincinnati will search for a lefty reliever during the winter, so it's doubtful that McElroy will return next year. Only 28, he's bound to get another chance with somebody.

# Tim Pugh

**Position**: RP/SP
**Bats**: R **Throws**: R
**Ht**: 6' 6" **Wt**: 225

**Opening Day Age**: 29
**Born**: 1/26/67 in Lake Tahoe, NV
**ML Seasons**: 4
**Pronunciation**: PYOO

## Overall Statistics

|  | W | L | Pct. | ERA | G | GS | Sv | IP | H | BB | SO | HR | BR/IP |
|---|---|---|---|---|---|---|---|---|---|---|---|---|---|
| 1995 | 6 | 5 | .545 | 3.84 | 28 | 12 | 0 | 98.1 | 100 | 32 | 38 | 13 | 1.34 |
| Career | 23 | 25 | .479 | 4.63 | 76 | 55 | 0 | 355.2 | 407 | 130 | 174 | 39 | 1.51 |

## 1995 Season

Righthander Tim Pugh began the 1995 season pitching effectively out of the Cincinnati bullpen. He joined the Reds' starting rotation in May and went 3-0 in his first four starts. But by the end of July he was being hit hard, and eventually was demoted to Triple-A Indianapolis. He completed the cycle by returning in September, pitching good ball once more as a member of the Reds' bullpen.

## Pitching, Defense & Hitting

Pugh throws a sinking fastball, slider and change-up. Only his sinker is outstanding, and when it's working Pugh is a very effective pitcher. However, he has to be careful not to overthrow the pitch, which causes it to straighten out. Pugh induces a lot of ground balls and he does a good job fielding his position. He improved at holding runners in 1995, allowing his catchers to throw out three of 10 potential basestealers. A good hitter for a pitcher, Pugh is a lifetime .202 hitter and can put down the sacrifice when asked.

## 1996 Outlook

The Reds have been waiting for Pugh to show the consistency that would make him a fixture in their rotation. But he proved last year that he can be effective in relief. If he can't earn a spot as a starter, last year's success in relief should help ensure a slot in the club's bullpen.

# Eddie Taubensee

**Position**: C
**Bats**: L **Throws**: R
**Ht**: 6' 4"  **Wt**: 205

**Opening Day Age**: 27
**Born**: 10/31/68 in Beeville, TX
**ML Seasons**: 5
**Pronunciation**: TAW-ben-see

## Overall Statistics

|        | G   | AB   | R   | H   | D  | T | HR | RBI | SB | BB | SO  | Avg  | OBP  | Slg  |
|--------|-----|------|-----|-----|----|---|----|-----|----|----|-----|------|------|------|
| 1995   | 80  | 218  | 32  | 62  | 14 | 2 | 9  | 44  | 2  | 22 | 52  | .284 | .354 | .491 |
| Career | 370 | 1056 | 115 | 269 | 50 | 6 | 31 | 143 | 7  | 94 | 221 | .255 | .316 | .402 |

## 1995 Season

Eddie Taubensee entered the 1995 season expecting to be the Reds' everyday catcher, but the free-agent signing of Benito Santiago changed all that. Taubensee platooned with Santiago for much of the season, but by the end of the year Santiago was starting on a regular basis.

## Hitting, Baserunning & Defense

Taubensee likes the low fastball and pitches on the inner half of the plate. He is vulnerable to pitches away and will chase the high heat. He has some pop in his bat, and could hit 20 homers in a season if he got enough playing time. He doesn't walk much, and lefthanders still give him problems. Taubensee still has plenty of room for improvement behind the plate. He's slow getting the ball to second base, and opposing runners were successful on 86 percent of their stolen-base attempts against him in 1995. He also has some rough edges as a receiver. He has decent speed for a catcher and swiped two bases last year.

## 1996 Outlook

If the Reds don't re-sign Benito Santiago, Taubensee may finally get a shot at a full season behind the plate. While he hit well against right-handed pitching in 1995, the question will be how he'd fare against lefties. But until Taubensee improves his work behind the plate, it's unlikely that he'll play regularly anywhere.

# Jerome Walton

**Position**: CF/LF
**Bats**: R  **Throws**: R
**Ht**: 6' 1"  **Wt**: 185

**Opening Day Age**: 30
**Born**: 7/8/65 in Newnan, GA
**ML Seasons**: 7

## Overall Statistics

|        | G   | AB   | R   | H   | D  | T | HR | RBI | SB | BB  | SO  | Avg  | OBP  | Slg  |
|--------|-----|------|-----|-----|----|---|----|-----|----|-----|-----|------|------|------|
| 1995   | 102 | 162  | 32  | 47  | 12 | 1 | 8  | 22  | 10 | 17  | 25  | .290 | .368 | .525 |
| Career | 523 | 1424 | 220 | 376 | 68 | 8 | 21 | 116 | 58 | 127 | 254 | .264 | .330 | .367 |

## 1995 Season

1989 National League Rookie of the Year Jerome Walton has revived his career in Cincinnati, finding new life as a utility outfielder. After starting center fielder Deion Sanders was traded last July, Walton became a frequent starter against left-handed pitchers. He was especially sharp in the leadoff spot, batting .448 with four homers when starting the first inning.

## Hitting, Baserunning & Defense

Walton has a quick swing and likes to pull the ball, especially the fastball. He's very aggressive at the plate, but he struggles with offspeed pitches. Walton showed surprising power in '95, smacking eight homers in just 162 at-bats. When he didn't start, Walton saw a lot of action as a late-inning defensive replacement for Ron Gant. His good speed allows him to cover a lot of ground in the outfield, but his arm is below average and runners can take the extra base against him. Walton steals bases, but needs to read pitchers' moves better to increase his success rate.

## 1996 Outlook

Walton, who's batted .296 in his two seasons with the Reds, looks like he fits nicely into the niche of reserve outfielder. He gives a team speed, solid defense, and a quality pinch hitter off the bench. Look for him to play the same role for the Reds in 1996.

# Other Cincinnati Reds

**Eric Anthony** (**Pos**: RF/1B, **Age**: 28, **Bats**: L)

Anthony fought the disabled list for most of '95, getting started in June and seeing time at both first base and right field. He had a poor second half, but should keep contributing if healthy. 1996 Outlook: A

**Damon Berryhill** (**Pos**: C, **Age**: 32, **Bats**: B)

Berryhill's '95 was a disaster. He hit just .183 with the Reds before spending a month and a half on the disabled list with bone chips in his elbow. If healthy, he still has value. 1996 Outlook: A

**Matt Grott** (**Pos**: LHP, **Age**: 28)

After a fine '94 at Triple-A, Grott slipped a bit in '95, seeing only two games with the Reds. His control is decent, but he'll have to work to stand out among several young arms for the Reds. 1996 Outlook: C

**Brian Hunter** (**Pos**: 1B, **Age**: 28, **Bats**: R)

Hunter was placed on the disabled list twice in '95, both times after injuring his right hamstring. His batting average continues to dive, and he might have to prove himself in the spring. 1996 Outlook: B

**Kevin Jarvis** (**Pos**: RHP, **Age**: 26)

Jarvis began '95 in the rotation for the Reds, starting 11 games. He threw a two-hit shutout against Florida but struggled otherwise. He eventually moved to the bullpen, and didn't fare much better. 1996 Outlook: A

**Kevin Mitchell** (**Pos**: LF, **Age**: 34, **Bats**: R)

After absolutely blasting the ball for the Reds in 1993 and '94, Mitchell left for Japan. He barely played because of injuries, and desperately wants to return to the National League in 1996. He'll find a job somewhere, and will hit when he can play. 1996 Outlook: B

**Brad Pennington** (**Pos**: LHP, **Age**: 26)

Pennington was traded from Baltimore to Cincinnati in June, and pitched poorly both places. He now has a career ERA over seven in 56 major league games. He needs to prove himself in a hurry. 1996 Outlook: C

**Rick Reed** (**Pos**: RHP, **Age**: 31)

Reed was called up in July, starting three games for the Reds. His debut was excellent, but he struggled after that. The Reds were his fourth team in five seasons, and in November he signed with another: the Mets. 1996 Outlook: C

**Mike Remlinger** (**Pos**: LHP, **Age**: 30)

Remlinger was traded from the Mets to the Reds in May, pitching just twice for Cincinnati after coming over. He's never pitched well when given the chance in the majors. 1996 Outlook: C

**Johnny Ruffin** (**Pos**: RHP, **Age**: 24)

If Ruffin's right knee heals, the future looks great for him. He still needs to work on his control, but he's established himself in the majors before age 24. Batters hit just .093 against him in '95. 1996 Outlook: A

**Pete Smith** (**Pos**: RHP, **Age**: 30)

Smith was a free-agent bust for the Reds, starting twice in May and throwing batting practice both outings. He continues to be victimized by the home-run ball. It's been downhill since '92. 1996 Outlook: C

**Frank Viola** (**Pos**: LHP, **Age**: 35)

Viola, the 1988 A.L. Cy Young Award winner, signed a minor league contract with Cincinnati after starting the season in Toronto. He was shelled in all three of his starts, and his career appears over. 1996 Outlook: D

**Nigel Wilson** (**Pos**: LF, **Age**: 26, **Bats**: L)

Wilson will have to cut down on his strikeouts to have any chance at a major league career. He played in just five games for the Reds in '95. At Triple-A last season, he hit .313 overall, and an amazing .455 when not striking out. Still needs work. 1996 Outlook: B

# Cincinnati Reds Minor League Prospects

## Organization Overview:

Despite the presence of an owner who has never seemed to understand the importance of a productive farm system, the Reds have survived and even thrived. In fact, Cincinnati's minor league teams generated the best overall record of any organization in 1995. In addition, the Reds have developed enough talent over the years to allow the big-league club to finish first or second in their division eight times in the last 11 years. Astute trading has also helped, but you need talent to acquire talent, and the Reds have had enough to get the Boones, Portugals and Lewises recently. Once again in '96, Cincinnati has a number of players knocking on the door, although two of their top prospects, shortstop Pokey Reese and second baseman Eric Owens, play positions where the Reds appear set.

## Aaron Boone

**Position:** 3B    **Opening Day Age:** 23
**Bats:** R **Throws:** R    **Born:** 3/9/73 in La
**Ht:** 6' 2" **Wt:** 190    Mesa, CA

### Recent Statistics

| | G | AB | R | H | D | T | HR | RBI | SB | BB | SO | AVG |
|---|---|---|---|---|---|---|---|---|---|---|---|---|
| 94 R Billings | 67 | 256 | 48 | 70 | 15 | 5 | 7 | 55 | 6 | 36 | 35 | .273 |
| 95 AA Chattanooga | 23 | 66 | 6 | 15 | 3 | 0 | 0 | 3 | 2 | 5 | 12 | .227 |
| 95 A Winston-Sal | 108 | 395 | 61 | 103 | 19 | 1 | 14 | 50 | 11 | 43 | 77 | .261 |

Boone was chosen in the third round of '94 after matriculating at USC, the same college his brother Bret attended. Even though he competed at only the rookie level in his pro debut, the Reds last year tried to skip Class A completely by boosting him to Double-A. He struggled there, but bounced back with a strong performance in high-A. Boone's skills are solid across the board, although his 14 homers may be somewhat of a mirage, since Winston-Salem is a great home-run park. Cincinnati is looking for a third baseman, which may explain his big promotion last year, and having two Boones in the same infield would be quite a story.

## Steve Gibralter

**Position:** OF    **Opening Day Age:** 23
**Bats:** R **Throws:** R    **Born:** 10/9/72 in
**Ht:** 6' 0" **Wt:** 170    Dallas, TX

### Recent Statistics

| | G | AB | R | H | D | T | HR | RBI | SB | BB | SO | AVG |
|---|---|---|---|---|---|---|---|---|---|---|---|---|
| 95 AAA Indianapols | 79 | 263 | 49 | 83 | 19 | 3 | 18 | 63 | 0 | 25 | 70 | .316 |
| 95 NL Cincinnati | 4 | 3 | 0 | 1 | 0 | 0 | 0 | 0 | 0 | 0 | 1 | .333 |
| 95 MLE | 79 | 253 | 40 | 73 | 17 | 1 | 14 | 51 | 0 | 21 | 71 | .289 |

After coming within 11 batting-average points of winning the Midwest League triple crown in 1992, Gibralter's next two seasons were rather disappointing. He rebounded in 1995, slugging a career-high .616 at Triple-A. Drafted in the sixth round of 1990, Gibralter

has enough speed and instincts to be a terrific defensive centerfielder. He missed much of last year due to injury, and at 23 may still need more time in Indianapolis to prove his performance last season wasn't a fluke.

## Willie Greene

**Position:** 3B    **Opening Day Age:** 24
**Bats:** L **Throws:** R    **Born:** 9/23/71 in
**Ht:** 5' 11" **Wt:** 184    Milledgeville, GA

### Recent Statistics

| | G | AB | R | H | D | T | HR | RBI | SB | BB | SO | AVG |
|---|---|---|---|---|---|---|---|---|---|---|---|---|
| 95 AAA Indianapols | 91 | 325 | 57 | 79 | 12 | 2 | 19 | 45 | 3 | 38 | 67 | .243 |
| 95 NL Cincinnati | 8 | 19 | 1 | 2 | 0 | 0 | 0 | 0 | 0 | 3 | 7 | .105 |
| 95 MLE | 91 | 317 | 46 | 71 | 11 | 1 | 17 | 37 | 2 | 32 | 68 | .224 |

It seems as though Greene has been trying, and failing, to land a big-league job forever, and he may in fact turn out to be just a perpetual prospect. He's now spent most of the last three years in Triple-A, never getting settled in four separate major league auditions. He continues to show a quick bat and real home-run power in the minors, but lefthanders and good breaking pitches have seemingly always troubled him with the Reds. Sooner or later, he's gotta run out of chances, and new Reds manager Ray Knight had a run-in with him last year.

## Chad Mottola

**Position:** OF    **Opening Day Age:** 24
**Bats:** R **Throws:** R    **Born:** 10/15/71 in
**Ht:** 6' 3" **Wt:** 215    Augusta, GA

### Recent Statistics

| | G | AB | R | H | D | T | HR | RBI | SB | BB | SO | AVG |
|---|---|---|---|---|---|---|---|---|---|---|---|---|
| 93 A Winston-Sal | 137 | 493 | 76 | 138 | 25 | 3 | 21 | 91 | 13 | 62 | 109 | .280 |
| 94 AA Chattanooga | 118 | 402 | 44 | 97 | 19 | 1 | 7 | 41 | 9 | 30 | 68 | .241 |
| 95 AA Chattanooga | 51 | 181 | 32 | 53 | 13 | 1 | 10 | 39 | 1 | 13 | 32 | .293 |
| 95 AAA Indianapols | 69 | 239 | 40 | 62 | 11 | 1 | 8 | 37 | 8 | 20 | 50 | .259 |
| 95 MLE | 120 | 406 | 59 | 101 | 22 | 0 | 14 | 63 | 6 | 26 | 83 | .249 |

The Reds selected Mottola in the first round of 1992 with the fifth overall pick. Considering his size, power and surprising speed, it's easy to see why he appealed to scouts. He had a couple of very good seasons to begin his pro career, then struggled in making the jump to Double-A in 1994. He performed better last season, mastering the Southern League before moving up to Triple-A. The Reds credit improved bat speed for his improved play. Despite his speed, Mottola is not a basestealer, and he lacks plate discipline.

## Eric Owens

**Position:** 2B    **Opening Day Age:** 25
**Bats:** R **Throws:** R    **Born:** 2/3/71 in
**Ht:** 6' 1" **Wt:** 184    Danville, VA

*Recent Statistics*

| | G | AB | R | H | D | T | HR | RBI | SB | BB | SO | AVG |
|---|---|---|---|---|---|---|---|---|---|---|---|---|
| 95 AAA Indianapols | 108 | 427 | 86 | 134 | 24 | 8 | 12 | 63 | 33 | 52 | 61 | .314 |
| 95 NL Cincinnati | 2 | 2 | 0 | 2 | 0 | 0 | 0 | 1 | 0 | 0 | 0 | 1.000 |
| 95 MLE | 108 | 410 | 70 | 117 | 22 | 5 | 9 | 51 | 25 | 44 | 62 | .285 |

Owens was named the American Association's MVP following a season in which he played a demanding defensive position, hit for average, hit for power, drew his share of walks and led the league in stolen bases. Sounds a bit like a Joe Morgan. He's quite a ways from that level, and he also must try to come back from a torn anterior cruciate ligament which ended his 1995 season in August. There's been talk that Owens may eventually move from second base to the outfield, if only so his path isn't blocked by Bret Boone.

## Pokey Reese

**Position:** SS    **Opening Day Age:** 22
**Bats:** R **Throws:** R    **Born:** 6/10/73 in
**Ht:** 6' 0" **Wt:** 160    Columbia, SC

*Recent Statistics*

| | G | AB | R | H | D | T | HR | RBI | SB | BB | SO | AVG |
|---|---|---|---|---|---|---|---|---|---|---|---|---|
| 93 AA Chattanooga | 102 | 345 | 35 | 73 | 17 | 4 | 3 | 37 | 8 | 23 | 77 | .212 |
| 94 AA Chattanooga | 134 | 484 | 77 | 130 | 23 | 4 | 12 | 49 | 21 | 43 | 75 | .269 |
| 95 AAA Indianapols | 89 | 343 | 51 | 82 | 21 | 1 | 10 | 46 | 8 | 36 | 81 | .239 |
| 95 MLE | 89 | 333 | 42 | 72 | 19 | 0 | 8 | 37 | 6 | 30 | 82 | .216 |

Indianapolis breezed to the best record in the American Association, and Reese was one of the reasons why. He missed time with a broken ankle but showed no lingering effects upon his return. Drafted in the first round of 1991, Reese has been compared defensively to Ozzie Smith almost from day one. He has great range, is acrobatic, and possesses the arm strength to make the play in the hole. Offensively, Reese has shown surprising power, though the Reds might prefer better contact. Reese's timetable for the major leagues depends on the status of Barry Larkin.

## Scott Sullivan

**Position:** P    **Opening Day Age:** 25
**Bats:** R **Throws:** R    **Born:** 3/13/71 in
**Ht:** 6' 3" **Wt:** 210    Tuscaloosa, AL

*Recent Statistics*

| | W | L | ERA | G | GS | Sv | IP | H | R | BB | SO | HR |
|---|---|---|---|---|---|---|---|---|---|---|---|---|
| 95 AAA Indianapls | 4 | 3 | 3.53 | 44 | 0 | 1 | 58.2 | 51 | 31 | 24 | 54 | 2 |
| 95 NL Cincinnati | 0 | 0 | 4.91 | 3 | 0 | 0 | 3.2 | 4 | 2 | 2 | 2 | 0 |

Sullivan was used exclusively in relief last season, the role he performed in college at Auburn. Drafted in the second round of 1993, Sullivan's two power pitches, a hard fastball and slider, may be enough by themselves to let him survive coming out of the bullpen. He's also worked on developing his change-up. His minor league career numbers are strong, with 244 strikeouts and 185 hits allowed in 234 innings. Sullivan was not Indianapolis' closer last season, and he'll probably be used as a set-up man when he arrives for good in Cincinnati.

## Pat Watkins

**Position:** OF    **Opening Day Age:** 23
**Bats:** R **Throws:** R    **Born:** 9/2/72 in
**Ht:** 6' 2" **Wt:** 185    Raleigh, NC

*Recent Statistics*

| | G | AB | R | H | D | T | HR | RBI | SB | BB | SO | AVG |
|---|---|---|---|---|---|---|---|---|---|---|---|---|
| 93 R Billings | 66 | 235 | 46 | 63 | 10 | 3 | 6 | 30 | 15 | 22 | 44 | .268 |
| 94 A Winston-Sal | 132 | 524 | 107 | 152 | 24 | 5 | 27 | 83 | 31 | 62 | 84 | .290 |
| 95 A Winston-Sal | 27 | 107 | 14 | 22 | 3 | 1 | 4 | 13 | 1 | 10 | 24 | .206 |
| 95 AA Chattanooga | 105 | 358 | 57 | 104 | 26 | 2 | 12 | 57 | 5 | 33 | 53 | .291 |
| 95 MLE | 105 | 347 | 49 | 93 | 24 | 1 | 10 | 49 | 3 | 25 | 55 | .268 |

Watkins was taken with the Reds' compensation pick for losing Greg Swindell to free agency in '93. He then came within three home runs of being a 30-30 man at fast-A Wintston-Salem in 1994. After moving up to Chattanooga and struggling with a .232 average early last season, it was discovered that Watkins needed corrective eyewear. He moved back to A-ball while getting adjusted to the new lenses before coming back strong in Double-A. Watkins can play any of the three outfield positions. His arm rates as one of the best in the Reds' system.

## Others to Watch

After slugging .606 in rookie ball in '94, first baseman **Ray Brown**, the Reds' 28th-round selection that year, followed with 19 homers in A-ball last season. . . Outfielder **Adam Hyzdu** was the Giants' top pick in 1990. He's a graduate of famed Moeller High in Cincinnati, the same school that produced Ken Griffey, Jr., among others. He's hit 31 homers since being traded to the Reds organization in '94. . . Righthander **Curt Lyons**, the Reds' sixth-round pick in 1992, went 9-9 with a 2.98 ERA in fast-A last season. . . **Ricky Magdaleno** has some power and the defensive skills to play shortstop, but he hit just .216 in 1995. However, he was just 21, and actually played a few games in Triple-A. . . Despite hitting 25 homers in '94, outfielder **Mike Meggers** was asked to repeat a season at Winston-Salem, where he hit 20 more in '95. The problem is that Meggers doesn't make consistent contact. . . After going 11-1 in rookie ball, righthander **Jason Robbins** remained effective in fast-A last year, with a 9-6 record and 3.06 ERA. . . Shortstop **Brandon Wilson** spent his first five pro seasons in the White Sox chain. He enjoyed his best campaign in '95, hitting .316 with 10 homers and 60 RBI, mostly in Double-A. He was 26, however.

# Jason Bates

## 1995 Season

The 1995 season was a roller-coaster ride for Rockies infielder Jason Bates. He started the year as a backup infielder. By mid-May Bates had won the job at second base by hitting at a .333 clip with a .441 on-base percentage. He lost the job after the All-Star break and then settled in as a utility infielder. However, he showed enough overall to indicate that he can play regularly in the majors if he works on his weaknesses.

## Hitting

Bates is a switch-hitting spray hitter. He hits the fastball very well, but pitchers with good breaking balls and offspeed stuff gave him fits last year. He also hit much better from the left side, and had such problems batting righty that the Rockies wound up platooning him. He'll hit an occasional homer, and he helps his club by drawing a good number of walks. Like most Rockies hitters, he was far more of an offensive threat at Coors Field than on the road last year.

## Baserunning & Defense

Bates has good speed and can go from second to home well, but the first 180 feet give him problems. He gets a poor break out of the batter's box—even from the left side—and his basestealing work showed a lot of rough edges last year. As a fielder, he is sure-handed and turns a good double play but has only average range. His best position is second base, though he doesn't hurt the team at third or short when he plays there as a result of late- inning double switches.

## 1996 Outlook

A hard-nosed kid, Bates showed signs last year that he could develop into a middle infielder who can hit, draw walks, cover his position and turn the double play. If he learns to hit better from the right side, he could win the Rockies' second-base job on an everyday basis.

**Position:** 2B/3B/SS
**Bats:** B **Throws:** R
**Ht:** 5'11" **Wt:** 170

**Opening Day Age:** 25
**Born:** 1/5/71 in Downey, CA
**ML Seasons:** 1

*Overall Statistics*

|  | G | AB | R | H | D | T | HR | RBI | SB | BB | SO | Avg | OBP | Slg |
|---|---|---|---|---|---|---|---|---|---|---|---|---|---|---|
| 1995 | 116 | 322 | 42 | 86 | 17 | 4 | 8 | 46 | 3 | 42 | 70 | .267 | .355 | .419 |
| Career | 116 | 322 | 42 | 86 | 17 | 4 | 8 | 46 | 3 | 42 | 70 | .267 | .355 | .419 |

*Where He Hits the Ball*

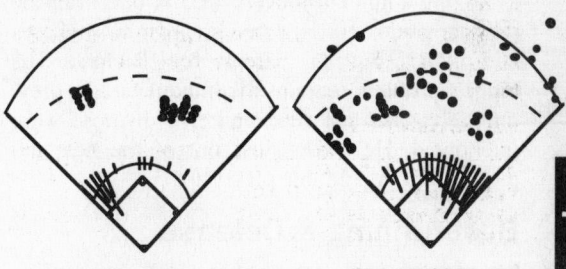

**Vs. LHP**  **Vs. RHP**

*1995 Situational Stats*

|  | AB | H | HR | RBI | Avg |  | AB | H | HR | RBI | Avg |
|---|---|---|---|---|---|---|---|---|---|---|---|
| Home | 157 | 51 | 4 | 28 | .325 | LHP | 71 | 13 | 2 | 10 | .183 |
| Road | 165 | 35 | 4 | 18 | .212 | RHP | 251 | 73 | 6 | 36 | .291 |
| First Half | 194 | 52 | 6 | 26 | .268 | Sc Pos | 73 | 27 | 1 | 36 | .370 |
| Scnd Half | 128 | 34 | 2 | 20 | .266 | Clutch | 48 | 7 | 1 | 3 | .146 |

*1995 Rankings (National League)*

➡ 2nd in batting average with runners in scoring position (.370) and lowest batting average in the clutch (.146)
➡ Led the Rockies in least GDPs per GDP situation (5.8%), batting average with runners in scoring position (.370), batting average with the bases loaded (.429) and batting average on a 3-1 count (.500)

# Dante Bichette

## 1995 Season

Who deserved to win the National League MVP award may be open to debate, but there was no doubt who was the Rockies' MVP in 1995. Dante Bichette had a career year, reaching personal highs in batting average, slugging average, on-base percentage, home runs, RBI, runs scored, hits and total bases. Bichette carried the team in August and September, batting .364 with 20 homers during the heat of the pennant race.

## Hitting

Even granting the fact that Coors Field boosted his numbers considerably, Bichette had a tremendous year. He did his best hitting down the stretch, averaging a home run every 11.3 at-bats after the All-Star break. He is a free swinger who chases bad pitches, but it is hard to fool Bichette. His biggest problem remains his impatience; he drew only 22 walks last year, and five of those were intentional. He's also slow out of the box and prone to hit into double plays.

## Baserunning & Defense

The switch from right field to left field, necessitated by the acquisition of Larry Walker, was not a difficult one for Bichette. He has an above-average arm, which keeps baserunners from taking extra bases on him. His range is limited but he catches everything he gets to. On the basepaths Bichette has lost a step. He posted his lowest steal total of the last five years and his 59-percent success rate was his worst ever. Bichette doesn't take many chances running the sacks.

## 1996 Outlook

Coming off a career year, it wouldn't be much of a disappointment if Bichette drops to .300 with 30 homers next season. A free agent at season's end, Bichette re-signed with the Rockies pretty quickly. He carried the team into their first postseason in the franchise's third year, and he would like to stay and see the first World Series in Coors Field.

**Position:** LF/RF
**Bats:** R  **Throws:** R
**Ht:** 6' 3"  **Wt:** 235

**Opening Day Age:** 32
**Born:** 11/18/63 in West Palm Beach, FL
**ML Seasons:** 8
**Pronunciation:** DON-tay buh-SHET

### Overall Statistics

|  | G | AB | R | H | D | T | HR | RBI | SB | BB | SO | Avg | OBP | Slg |
|---|---|---|---|---|---|---|---|---|---|---|---|---|---|---|
| 1995 | 139 | 579 | 102 | 197 | 38 | 2 | 40 | 128 | 13 | 22 | 96 | .340 | .364 | .620 |
| Career | 820 | 2966 | 413 | 858 | 183 | 15 | 126 | 488 | 88 | 129 | 556 | .289 | .320 | .489 |

### Where He Hits the Ball

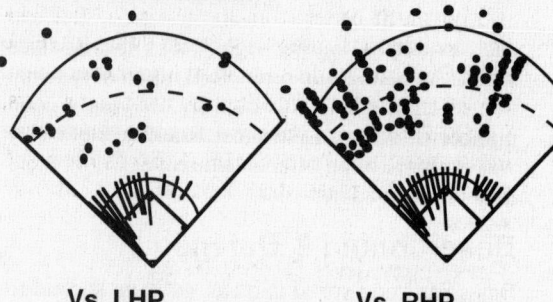

**Vs. LHP**          **Vs. RHP**

### 1995 Situational Stats

|  | AB | H | HR | RBI | Avg |  | AB | H | HR | RBI | Avg |
|---|---|---|---|---|---|---|---|---|---|---|---|
| Home | 302 | 114 | 31 | 83 | .377 | LHP | 149 | 50 | 14 | 40 | .336 |
| Road | 277 | 83 | 9 | 45 | .300 | RHP | 430 | 147 | 26 | 88 | .342 |
| First Half | 274 | 92 | 13 | 48 | .336 | Sc Pos | 158 | 58 | 16 | 93 | .367 |
| Scnd Half | 305 | 105 | 27 | 80 | .344 | Clutch | 76 | 23 | 4 | 20 | .303 |

### 1995 Rankings (National League)

→ 1st in home runs, hits, total bases (359), RBI and slugging percentage

→ 2nd in at-bats, doubles, lowest stolen base percentage (59.1%) and lowest percentage of pitches taken (40.3%)

→ 3rd in batting average, sacrifice flies (7), batting average with runners in scoring position (.367), slugging percentage vs. left-handed pitchers (.691), batting average at home (.377) and fielding percentage in left field (.984)

→ 4th in runs scored, HR frequency (14.5 ABs per HR) and batting average vs. right-handed pitchers (.342)

→ Led the Rockies in batting average, home runs, at-bats, runs scored and hits

# Ellis Burks

## 1995 Season

Veteran outfielder Ellis Burks lost considerable time to wrist problems in 1995 and never really got untracked. When he was healthy, he platooned with Mike Kingery in center field and alternated between the number-two and number-six slots in the lineup. Burks did an adequate job, providing good power and run production for his limited number of at-bats.

## Hitting

Burks has a reputation as a great fastball hitter who also can handle the breaking ball pretty well. He demonstrated good power when he was healthy last year, but the wrist problem, first suffered in 1994, took its toll. Unable to get into a rhythm at the plate and less able to stop his swing once he started it, Burks struck out more often than usual. He had particular trouble against righthanders, who had him at their mercy if they could get ahead in the count. On the other hand, Burks remained patient at the plate, drawing a good number of walks.

## Baserunning & Defense

While various injuries—including a back problem—have slowed him down, Burks has gotten smarter on the bases as he has gotten older. Defensively, he is an above-average outfielder who still gets a good jump on the ball. His range, though, isn't what it used to be. His strong throwing arm remains an asset, particularly for a center fielder who has lost a step.

## 1996 Outlook

Burks seldom is healthy for a whole season. When he stays off the disabled list, he is a capable contributor who can hit 20-25 home runs in a season. As a part-time player fighting off injuries, he yields limited benefits. He doesn't hit righthanders, he strikes out more frequently, and his declining speed is further compromised.

**Position:** CF/LF
**Bats:** R  **Throws:** R
**Ht:** 6' 2"  **Wt:** 205

**Opening Day Age:** 31
**Born:** 9/11/64 in Vicksburg, MS
**ML Seasons:** 9

*Overall Statistics*

| | G | AB | R | H | D | T | HR | RBI | SB | BB | SO | Avg | OBP | Slg |
|---|---|---|---|---|---|---|---|---|---|---|---|---|---|---|
| 1995 | 103 | 278 | 41 | 74 | 10 | 6 | 14 | 49 | 7 | 39 | 72 | .266 | .359 | .496 |
| Career | 1013 | 3720 | 589 | 1044 | 202 | 40 | 137 | 534 | 109 | 366 | 658 | .281 | .347 | .467 |

*Where He Hits the Ball*

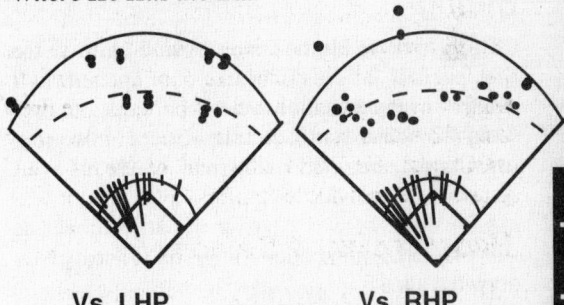

**Vs. LHP**          **Vs. RHP**

*1995 Situational Stats*

| | AB | H | HR | RBI | Avg | | AB | H | HR | RBI | Avg |
|---|---|---|---|---|---|---|---|---|---|---|---|
| Home | 141 | 41 | 8 | 32 | .291 | LHP | 104 | 34 | 5 | 18 | .327 |
| Road | 137 | 33 | 6 | 17 | .241 | RHP | 174 | 40 | 9 | 31 | .230 |
| First Half | 135 | 33 | 6 | 19 | .244 | Sc Pos | 91 | 23 | 3 | 35 | .253 |
| Scnd Half | 143 | 41 | 8 | 30 | .287 | Clutch | 49 | 11 | 1 | 12 | .224 |

*1995 Rankings (National League)*
- ➡ 7th in errors in center field (3)
- ➡ 9th in slugging percentage vs. left-handed pitchers (.567)

Colorado Rockies

# Vinny Castilla

## 1995 Season

Who would replace Charlie Hayes, the everyday third basemen who left via free agency, was one of the biggest questions facing the Rockies entering the 1995 season. Manager Don Baylor found the answer in Vinny Castilla, a 27-year-old who hit both for power and average. Castilla opened the season at third and after getting only three hits in his first 19 at-bats, proceeded to hit .324 from May through August with 30 home runs and 73 RBI. He tailed off a bit in September, but Castilla, who had never before hit more than nine homers in a season, was by far the Rockies' most pleasant surprise.

## Hitting

Castilla loves to hit the fastball. He'll jump on the first pitch if he sees a heater coming, and he's deadly in any situation where he can count on seeing some hard stuff. Another Coors Field prodigy, Castilla struggled on the road, where his average was a whopping 154 points lower than it was at Coors, but he was a power threat wherever he was playing. An impatient hitter, he'll hardly ever draw a walk.

## Baserunning & Defense

The Rockies were boosting Castilla for a Gold Glove, but he still has a ways to go as a third baseman. He has good hands and can turn the 5-4-3 double play, but his range is very limited and his throwing arm is average at best. He makes all the basic plays but few spectacular ones. Castilla is a slow runner and a very poor basestealer, a hideous 6-for-20 in his career.

## 1996 Outlook

Castilla had a wonderful season in 1995, but he will probably find his numbers tough to duplicate. He's never been a very good hitter away from Colorado, and he's going to have difficulty hitting .383 and slugging .730 at home again. More likely he'll develop into a solid everyday third baseman who hits 20-25 homers and bats .280-.300.

**Position:** 3B
**Bats:** R  **Throws:** R
**Ht:** 6' 1"  **Wt:** 180

**Opening Day Age:** 28
**Born:** 7/4/67 in Oaxaca, MX
**ML Seasons:** 5
**Pronunciation:** kas-TEE-yah

### Overall Statistics

|  | G | AB | R | H | D | T | HR | RBI | SB | BB | SO | Avg | OBP | Slg |
|---|---|---|---|---|---|---|---|---|---|---|---|---|---|---|
| 1995 | 139 | 527 | 82 | 163 | 34 | 2 | 32 | 90 | 2 | 30 | 87 | .309 | .347 | .564 |
| Career | 317 | 1015 | 136 | 297 | 55 | 10 | 44 | 139 | 6 | 51 | 161 | .293 | .327 | .497 |

### Where He Hits the Ball

**Vs. LHP**     **Vs. RHP**

### 1995 Situational Stats

|  | AB | H | HR | RBI | Avg |  | AB | H | HR | RBI | Avg |
|---|---|---|---|---|---|---|---|---|---|---|---|
| Home | 274 | 105 | 23 | 58 | .383 | LHP | 134 | 52 | 12 | 35 | .388 |
| Road | 253 | 58 | 9 | 32 | .229 | RHP | 393 | 111 | 20 | 55 | .282 |
| First Half | 262 | 83 | 17 | 48 | .317 | Sc Pos | 129 | 37 | 3 | 52 | .287 |
| Scnd Half | 265 | 80 | 15 | 42 | .302 | Clutch | 72 | 17 | 3 | 8 | .236 |

### 1995 Rankings (National League)

- ➡ 1st in slugging percentage vs. left-handed pitchers (.769)
- ➡ 2nd in batting average vs. left-handed pitchers (.388) and batting average at home (.383)
- ➡ 3rd in total bases (297)
- ➡ 4th in fielding percentage at third base (.958)
- ➡ 5th in home runs and on-base percentage vs. left-handed pitchers (.417)
- ➡ 6th in slugging percentage, batting average on an 0-2 count (.308), lowest batting average on the road (.229) and errors at third base (15)
- ➡ Led the Rockies in batting average on an 0-2 count, slugging percentage vs. left-handed pitchers and batting average at home

# Andres Galarraga

## 1995 Season

Following a couple of excellent but injury-marred years, the 1995 season was one of consistency for Andres Galarraga. He wasn't dogged by a prolonged slump, nor did he ride a lengthy hot streak. Galarraga also avoided hamstring injuries that have plagued him in the past. He credits his healthy year to an offseason strength and conditioning program, which reduced his playing weight to a career-low 225 pounds.

## Hitting

Manager Don Baylor, who resurrected Galarraga's hitting skills a few years ago, was the beneficiary of this free swinger's consistency. Galarraga reached career highs in home runs and RBI. His open stance allows him to be aggressive with pitches anywhere in the strike zone. Why pitchers throw him strikes is sometimes a mystery. Galarraga, who seldom walks, still chases too many bad pitches, but when you hit 30 homers a year nobody's going to complain too much.

## Baserunning & Defense

"El Gato Grande," as he is known in his native Caracas, is called the Big Cat because of his quick reflexes on defense. He moves well in both directions, turning down-the-line doubles into quick outs. Galarraga also is adept at digging out short-hop throws from the infielders. His weight loss has made it easier for him to score from second on base hits. At the age of 34, Galarraga stole more bases last season than he had in any year since 1988.

## 1996 Outlook

A hometown favorite since signing as a free agent before Colorado's inaugural season, Galarraga is cheered regardless of what he does. He's now nearly 35 and his career may be winding down, but in Coors Field another batting title might not be out of reach. More likely, Galarraga will continue to hit between .280 and .320 with 25 homers and 90 RBI. Put a good leadoff hitter in the lineup and those RBI numbers could go up.

**Position:** 1B
**Bats:** R **Throws:** R
**Ht:** 6' 3"  **Wt:** 225

**Opening Day Age:** 34
**Born:** 6/18/61 in Caracas, VZ
**ML Seasons:** 11
**Pronunciation:** gala-RAH-guh
**Nickname:** Big Cat

### Overall Statistics

|  | G | AB | R | H | D | T | HR | RBI | SB | BB | SO | Avg | OBP | Slg |
|---|---|---|---|---|---|---|---|---|---|---|---|---|---|---|
| 1995 | 143 | 554 | 89 | 155 | 29 | 3 | 31 | 106 | 12 | 32 | 146 | .280 | .331 | .511 |
| Career | 1308 | 4848 | 669 | 1371 | 267 | 23 | 200 | 761 | 81 | 310 | 1171 | .283 | .334 | .471 |

### Where He Hits the Ball

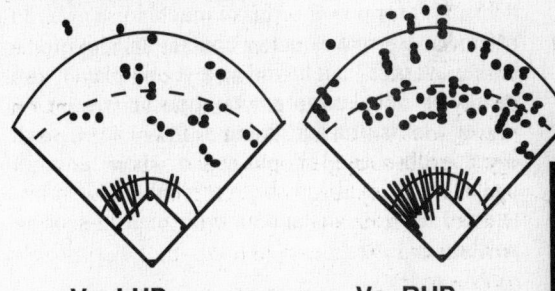

**Vs. LHP**  **Vs. RHP**

### 1995 Situational Stats

|  | AB | H | HR | RBI | Avg |  | AB | H | HR | RBI | Avg |
|---|---|---|---|---|---|---|---|---|---|---|---|
| Home | 273 | 81 | 18 | 55 | .297 | LHP | 137 | 37 | 10 | 33 | .270 |
| Road | 281 | 74 | 13 | 51 | .263 | RHP | 417 | 118 | 21 | 73 | .283 |
| First Half | 258 | 75 | 18 | 55 | .291 | Sc Pos | 157 | 46 | 9 | 72 | .293 |
| Scnd Half | 296 | 80 | 13 | 51 | .270 | Clutch | 82 | 23 | 5 | 12 | .280 |

### 1995 Rankings (National League)

→ 1st in strikeouts, errors at first base (13), lowest fielding percentage at first base (.991) and lowest percentage of swings put into play (33.6%)
→ 3rd in RBI and hit by pitch (13)
→ 4th in games played and highest percentage of swings that missed (29.4%)
→ 5th in at-bats
→ 6th in lowest cleanup slugging percentage (.440)
→ 7th in total bases (283)
→ 8th in home runs
→ Led the Rockies in strikeouts, pitches seen (2,235) and games played

# Joe Girardi

## 1995 Season

In 1995, Joe Girardi once again proved to be a reliable if unspectacular performer. Calling a game was a difficult challenge for Girardi, as the Rockies experiemented with a host of young pitchers who struggled in one of the best hitters' parks in major league history. Still, Girardi provided leadership and solid skills behind the plate. He started quickly at bat, then slumped a bit over the last two months but still finished with career highs in homers and RBI.

## Hitting

Even at Coors Field, Girardi's hitting isn't overly impressive. Primarily a groundball hitter, he doesn't hit for power or make much noise as a run producer. He makes better contact and hits for a higher average than he did as a young player, and he can be called on to go the opposite way. For a player who isn't a sure thing at the plate, Girardi doesn't take enough pitches or draw enough walks. But he's always been a reliable clutch hitter, and he was outstanding with men in scoring position in 1995.

## Baserunning & Defense

Girardi runs better than many big-league catchers, but don't look for double-digit steals. Defensively, he's a big asset. Behind the plate he was a calming influence for a staff that often got lit up in Coors Field. His throwing arm isn't the strongest, but it's accurate and he's quick to get rid of the ball.

## 1996 Outlook

The Rockies surprised a few people by trading Girardi to the Yankees after the season. He's a better defensive catcher than Mike Stanley, who's been the top Yankee receiver the last two years, and Girardi should see plenty of playing time as the Yanks try to field a stronger defensive unit.

**Position:** C
**Bats:** R **Throws:** R
**Ht:** 5'11" **Wt:** 195

**Opening Day Age:** 31
**Born:** 10/14/64 in Peoria, IL
**ML Seasons:** 7

### Overall Statistics

|  | G | AB | R | H | D | T | HR | RBI | SB | BB | SO | Avg | OBP | Slg |
|---|---|---|---|---|---|---|---|---|---|---|---|---|---|---|
| 1995 | 125 | 462 | 63 | 121 | 17 | 2 | 8 | 55 | 3 | 29 | 76 | .262 | .308 | .359 |
| Career | 608 | 1995 | 218 | 536 | 79 | 14 | 18 | 190 | 22 | 127 | 285 | .269 | .315 | .349 |

### Where He Hits the Ball

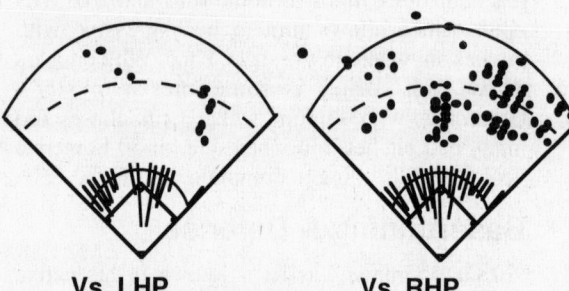

Vs. LHP    Vs. RHP

### 1995 Situational Stats

|  | AB | H | HR | RBI | Avg |  | AB | H | HR | RBI | Avg |
|---|---|---|---|---|---|---|---|---|---|---|---|
| Home | 247 | 72 | 6 | 41 | .291 | LHP | 116 | 29 | 1 | 10 | .250 |
| Road | 215 | 49 | 2 | 14 | .228 | RHP | 346 | 92 | 7 | 45 | .266 |
| First Half | 226 | 67 | 2 | 30 | .296 | Sc Pos | 125 | 42 | 2 | 46 | .336 |
| Scnd Half | 236 | 54 | 6 | 25 | .229 | Clutch | 72 | 22 | 0 | 9 | .306 |

### 1995 Rankings (National League)

- ➡ 2nd in errors at catcher (10) and lowest fielding percentage at catcher (.988)
- ➡ 4th in least pitches seen per plate appearance (3.25)
- ➡ 5th in sacrifice bunts (12), lowest slugging percentage vs. left-handed pitchers (.302), lowest batting average on the road (.228), lowest percentage of pitches taken (45.3%) and highest percentage of swings on the first pitch (44.5%)
- ➡ 6th in lowest on-base percentage (.308) and highest groundball/flyball ratio (2.0)
- ➡ Led the Rockies in sacrifice bunts (12) and bunts in play (19)

# Darren Holmes

## 1995 Season

After two years of struggling to regain his 1992 form, Darren Holmes finally became the pitcher the Rockies thought they were getting when they selected him in the 1992 expansion draft. Manager Don Baylor never really settled on a closer, but Holmes converted 14 of his 18 save opportunities and recorded 13 holds when used in a set-up role. He had an excellent strikeout-to-walk ratio, gave up fewer hits than innings pitched and was excellent in the late innings of close games. He might not have had a full-time closer's role, but he turned in numbers better than many major league closers.

## Pitching

When it is working, Holmes' curveball starts out letter high and crosses the plate below the knees. It can be unhittable. His 90-MPH fastball and late-breaking slider round out an impressive arsenal. When he's got it going, he's even tougher against lefties than he is against righties. He's durable when used several days in a row. All he needs to succeed is good location, and his location was excellent in 1995.

## Defense & Hitting

Holmes' slingshot motion leaves him almost completely out of position for fielding. He finishes up on the right side of the mound, and his fielding is more an exercise in self-defense. He also has problems holding runners. Holmes came to the plate four times last year and successfully sacrificed on three of those occasions.

## 1996 Outlook

With five different pitchers playing key roles in the Rockies bullpen, Holmes had to share the closer role with several other pitchers. But he handled that role in style when given it, and when he wasn't closing he was helping the club in middle relief. However Don Baylor uses him this year, he figures to remain an effective pitcher.

**Position:** RP
**Bats:** R **Throws:** R
**Ht:** 6' 0"  **Wt:** 200

**Opening Day Age:** 29
**Born:** 4/25/66 in Asheville, NC
**ML Seasons:** 6

### Overall Statistics

|        | W | L | Pct. | ERA | G | GS | Sv | IP | H | BB | SO | HR | BR/IP |
|--------|---|---|------|-----|---|----|----|-----|-----|-----|-----|----|-------|
| 1995   | 6 | 1 | .857 | 3.24 | 68 | 0 | 14 | 66.2 | 59 | 28 | 61 | 3 | 1.31 |
| Career | 14 | 16 | .467 | 4.11 | 254 | 0 | 51 | 297.2 | 290 | 121 | 263 | 22 | 1.38 |

### How Often He Throws Strikes

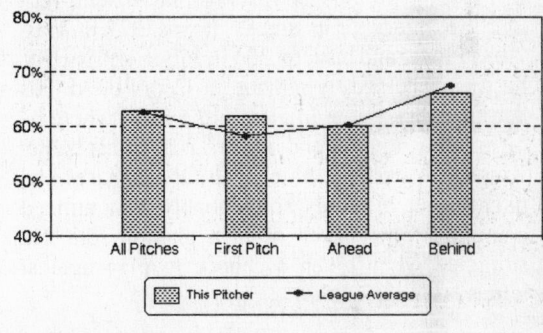

### 1995 Situational Stats

|           | W | L | ERA | Sv | IP |       | AB | H | HR | RBI | Avg |
|-----------|---|---|-----|----|------|-------|-----|----|----|----|------|
| Home      | 3 | 0 | 2.95 | 9 | 39.2 | LHB | 106 | 19 | 2 | 16 | .179 |
| Road      | 3 | 1 | 3.67 | 5 | 27.0 | RHB | 143 | 40 | 1 | 10 | .280 |
| First Half | 5 | 0 | 2.65 | 6 | 34.0 | Sc Pos | 79 | 18 | 1 | 22 | .228 |
| Scnd Half | 1 | 1 | 3.86 | 8 | 32.2 | Clutch | 138 | 31 | 1 | 14 | .225 |

### 1995 Rankings (National League)

- ➠ 5th in games pitched and lowest save percentage (77.8%)
- ➠ 8th in relief wins (6)
- ➠ 10th in holds (13)
- ➠ Led the Rockies in saves, games finished (33), wild pitches (7), save opportunities (18), save percentage (77.8%) and relief wins (6)

Colorado Rockies

# Mike Kingery

## 1995 Season

Coming off a season in which he batted an astonishing .349, Mike Kingery started quickly in 1995. By the end of May he was among the Rockies' leaders in batting, runs scored and stolen bases. Just as he was settling into the leadoff spot, however, came a June swoon. From June through August, Kingery platooned in center field. But in September he lost his job to Ellis Burks, and by year's end his average was down to .269. Kingery's attitude and demeanor never changed. He is a model team player, giving his all, all of the time.

## Hitting

In 1995, one of the few years he played semi-regularly, Kingery hit in streaks. It was .377 in May, .208 in June, and back to .304 in July. Surprisingly, he wasn't helped by playing in Coors Field. His batting average was higher on the road, where he hit as many doubles and homers as he did at home. Kingery is a patient hitter who rarely chases bad pitches, but his tools are probably best utilized coming off the bench or in a platoon role. He struggled when given a chance to play against lefties last year.

## Baserunning & Defense

Kingery is the best center fielder on the Rockies. Although his range is limited, he gets a good jump on the ball and catches everything he gets to. However, his arm is only average. On the bases Kingery has better than average speed. He gets a good lead, which helped him steal 13 bases last year. You can expect him to score from second on base hits.

## 1996 Outlook

Kingery brings more to Coors Field than his numbers show. He works hard, never gives up, and is as solid a team player as there is in the game. The time is coming, however, when that won't be enough. At 35 the end may be near, but Kingery still is capable of contributing. He figures to be a very useful role player again in 1996.

**Position:** CF
**Bats:** L  **Throws:** L
**Ht:** 6' 0"  **Wt:** 185

**Opening Day Age:** 35
**Born:** 3/29/61 in St. James, MN
**ML Seasons:** 9

### Overall Statistics

|        | G   | AB   | R   | H   | D  | T  | HR | RBI | SB | BB  | SO  | Avg  | OBP  | Slg  |
|--------|-----|------|-----|-----|----|----|----|-----|----|-----|-----|------|------|------|
| 1995   | 119 | 350  | 66  | 94  | 18 | 4  | 8  | 37  | 13 | 45  | 40  | .269 | .351 | .411 |
| Career | 702 | 1758 | 260 | 478 | 96 | 24 | 27 | 192 | 43 | 168 | 219 | .272 | .334 | .400 |

### Where He Hits the Ball

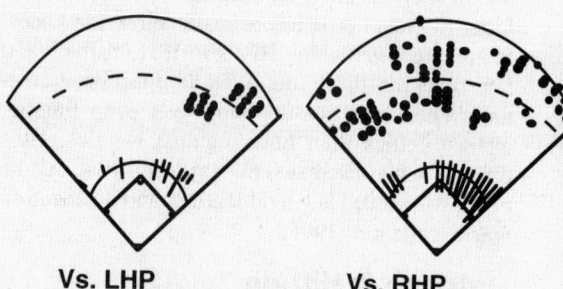

**Vs. LHP**          **Vs. RHP**

### 1995 Situational Stats

|            | AB  | H  | HR | RBI | Avg  |        | AB  | H  | HR | RBI | Avg  |
|------------|-----|----|----|-----|------|--------|-----|----|----|-----|------|
| Home       | 166 | 44 | 4  | 19  | .265 | LHP    | 44  | 10 | 0  | 4   | .227 |
| Road       | 184 | 50 | 4  | 18  | .272 | RHP    | 306 | 84 | 8  | 33  | .275 |
| First Half | 186 | 53 | 5  | 19  | .285 | Sc Pos | 84  | 19 | 1  | 28  | .226 |
| Scnd Half  | 164 | 41 | 3  | 18  | .250 | Clutch | 55  | 14 | 3  | 5   | .255 |

### 1995 Rankings (National League)

➡ 3rd in lowest fielding percentage in center field (.979)
➡ 5th in errors in center field (4)

# Curtis Leskanic

## 1995 Season

His future may be as a starter, but Curt Leskanic had a fabulous season out of the Rockies' bullpen in 1995. After getting off to a slow start, Leskanic found his groove last June. By the end of the season, he was as likely as anyone in the bullpen to be called on in a tough situation. He blew four of his last 10 save opportunities, but that probably was due more to overuse than a lack of ability. Leskanic led the major leagues with 76 mound appearances last year.

## Pitching

Known for his excellent control, Leskanic throws a hard slider and a moving fastball. Both pitches have excellent velocity, and his fastball has been clocked regularly in the 90s. He works down in the strike zone more than most power pitchers, and that gives him two advantages: he gets a good number of groundball outs, and he's less susceptible to the gopher ball at homer-heaven Coors Field. He takes pressure situations in stride, which is perhaps why he's adapted to relief pitching so well.

## Defense & Hitting

Leskanic is an adequate fielder who handles bunts adroitly. He comes off the mound quickly and makes good throws to the bases. He's also shown an ability to help himself with the bat, both hitting and bunting. Like many power pitchers, he's somewhat vulnerable to the running game.

## 1996 Outlook

Leskanic was one of four Colorado pitchers who appeared in 60 or more games in relief last year, and he handled late-inning pressure about as well as any of them. However, he was a starter throughout much of his minor league career, and the Rockies are thinking of returning him to a starting role again. Whatever his role, he has the stuff to be an effective major league pitcher.

**Position:** RP
**Bats:** R  **Throws:** R
**Ht:** 6' 0"  **Wt:** 180

**Opening Day Age:** 27
**Born:** 4/2/68 in Homestead, PA
**ML Seasons:** 3
**Pronunciation:** less-KAN-ick

### Overall Statistics

|  | W | L | Pct. | ERA | G | GS | Sv | IP | H | BB | SO | HR | BR/IP |
|---|---|---|---|---|---|---|---|---|---|---|---|---|---|
| 1995 | 6 | 3 | .667 | 3.40 | 76 | 0 | 10 | 98.0 | 83 | 33 | 107 | 7 | 1.18 |
| Career | 8 | 9 | .471 | 4.31 | 102 | 11 | 10 | 177.1 | 169 | 70 | 154 | 16 | 1.35 |

### How Often He Throws Strikes

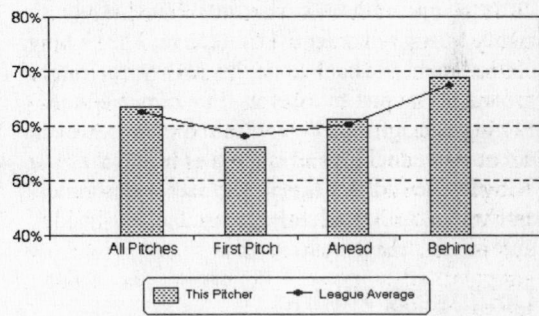

### 1995 Situational Stats

|  | W | L | ERA | Sv | IP |  | AB | H | HR | RBI | Avg |
|---|---|---|---|---|---|---|---|---|---|---|---|
| Home | 4 | 1 | 3.33 | 7 | 51.1 | LHB | 157 | 38 | 4 | 19 | .242 |
| Road | 2 | 2 | 3.47 | 3 | 46.2 | RHB | 211 | 45 | 3 | 17 | .213 |
| First Half | 2 | 1 | 3.27 | 4 | 52.1 | Sc Pos | 101 | 19 | 1 | 24 | .188 |
| Scnd Half | 4 | 2 | 3.55 | 6 | 45.2 | Clutch | 187 | 40 | 3 | 18 | .214 |

### 1995 Rankings (National League)

- ➡ 1st in games pitched
- ➡ 2nd in most strikeouts per 9 innings in relief (9.8)
- ➡ 3rd in holds (19) and relief innings (98.0)
- ➡ 4th in lowest percentage of inherited runners scored (17.4%)
- ➡ 6th in blown saves (6) and first batter efficiency (.147)
- ➡ 8th in relief wins (6)
- ➡ 9th in lowest batting average allowed vs. left-handed batters (.242) and least baserunners allowed per 9 innings in relief (10.7)
- ➡ Led the Rockies in games pitched, holds, blown saves and lowest batting average allowed vs. left-handed batters

# Mike Munoz

## 1995 Season

Like many of his teammates, Mike Munoz suffered from pitching at Coors Field last year, but there is nothing misleading about his 7.42 ERA. On the road, Munoz' ERA was still more than 5.00. In fact, his ERA was more than 5.00 against 10 of the league's 13 other teams, in both halves of the season, and in both day and night games. Manager Don Baylor kept giving him the ball because he was desperate for left-handed relief, but the best thing about Munoz' season was that it ended.

## Pitching

Munoz is not overpowering. He must pinpoint and move around his four pitches—fastball, slider, change-up, and a screwball he throws to righthanders—in order to be effective. The sinking action on his fastball, and its ability to induce ground balls, was an asset in 1994, when Munoz' ERA was a nifty 3.74. The lefthander, however, did not have the same command of his pitches last year that he did in '94. He yielded more homers and wasn't as successful against the left-handed hitters he's paid to get out.

## Defense & Hitting

Munoz came to the plate four times in 1995, and he walked twice and doubled. Still, his future isn't as a hitter. Munoz is a solid fielder. And he allows few stolen-base attempts because of his quick delivery. That's an asset for a pitcher who permitted so many baserunners last year.

## 1996 Outlook

After a successful 1994 against left-handed hitters, Munoz failed miserably in '95 when Manager Don Baylor called on him to perform the same role in '95. Being a left-handed reliever is an asset that has extended many a career, but Munoz will find his Rockies career on the line if he can't recapture his 1994 success. A 30-year-old pitcher without an overpowering fastball, he will need pinpoint control to keep his lefty specialist job.

**Position:** RP
**Bats:** L **Throws:** L
**Ht:** 6' 2"  **Wt:** 200

**Opening Day Age:** 30
**Born:** 7/12/65 in Baldwin Park, CA
**ML Seasons:** 7
**Pronunciation:** moon-YOHS

### Overall Statistics

|        | W | L | Pct. | ERA | G | GS | Sv | IP | H | BB | SO | HR | BR/IP |
|--------|---|---|------|-----|---|----|----|------|-----|-----|-----|----|-------|
| 1995   | 2 | 4 | .333 | 7.42 | 64 | 0 | 2 | 43.2 | 54 | 27 | 37 | 9 | 1.85 |
| Career | 9 | 11 | .450 | 5.06 | 232 | 0 | 5 | 176.0 | 185 | 108 | 117 | 18 | 1.66 |

### How Often He Throws Strikes

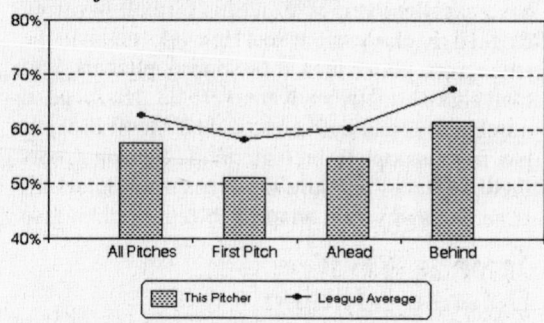

### 1995 Situational Stats

|            | W | L | ERA | Sv | IP |        | AB | H | HR | RBI | Avg |
|------------|---|---|------|----|------|--------|----|----|----|-----|------|
| Home       | 2 | 0 | 9.00 | 0 | 25.0 | LHB    | 84 | 24 | 5 | 19 | .286 |
| Road       | 0 | 4 | 5.30 | 2 | 18.2 | RHB    | 92 | 30 | 4 | 19 | .326 |
| First Half | 1 | 2 | 5.40 | 2 | 23.1 | Sc Pos | 57 | 20 | 3 | 30 | .351 |
| Scnd Half  | 1 | 2 | 9.74 | 0 | 20.1 | Clutch | 70 | 20 | 2 | 10 | .286 |

### 1995 Rankings (National League)

➡ 8th in lowest percentage of inherited runners scored (23.3%)
➡ 10th in games pitched

# Steve Reed

**Position:** RP
**Bats:** R  **Throws:** R
**Ht:** 6' 2"  **Wt:** 205

**Opening Day Age:** 30
**Born:** 3/11/66 in Los Angeles, CA
**ML Seasons:** 4

## 1995 Season

Submariner Steve Reed has improved in each of his three seasons with the Rockies. One of the "Four Horsemen" in the Rockies bullpen who each appeared in over 60 games, Reed was a consistent performer from start to finish in 1995. In fact, his 2.14 ERA was nothing short of miraculous given his home ballpark.

## Pitching

Reed throws a sidearm fastball with pretty good movement and velocity, as well as an effective slider. He's very durable and able to pitch several days in a row if needed. In the past he's had major problems against left-handed hitters, and he also had major problems at the Rockies' former home, Mile High Stadium, where the groundballs he gave up always seemed to scoot through the rough infield surface. The switch to Coors Field seemed to help a lot, and so did working a little bit more over the top against lefties. With his new style Reed was less of a groundballer than before, but he was a lot more effective pitcher.

## Defense & Hitting

Reed had a base hit in only three at-bats last season but he isn't likely to be called upon more often than that. Defensively Reed is solid, even with his sidearm delivery pulling him off the mound. Though he's a little slow to the plate, he does a fine job of controlling the running game.

## 1996 Outlook

With his new-found ability to handle left-handed hitters, Reed has become one of the better middle relievers in the game. In the past he hasn't done well when asked to close games, but the Rockies might be tempted to give him a chance to finish this year. Even if he fails there, he can always return to the set-up role he's handled so well. Many submariners have enjoyed careers, and at 30 Reed could be heading into the best period of his career.

### Overall Statistics

|        | W  | L | Pct. | ERA  | G   | GS | Sv | IP    | H   | BB | SO  | HR | BR/IP |
|--------|----|---|------|------|-----|----|----|-------|-----|----|-----|----|-------|
| 1995   | 5  | 2 | .714 | 2.14 | 71  | 0  | 3  | 84.0  | 61  | 21 | 79  | 8  | 0.98  |
| Career | 18 | 9 | .667 | 3.41 | 214 | 0  | 9  | 248.0 | 233 | 80 | 192 | 32 | 1.26  |

### How Often He Throws Strikes

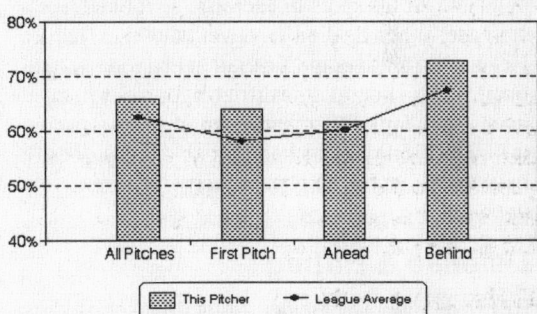

### 1995 Situational Stats

|            | W | L | ERA  | Sv | IP   |        | AB  | H  | HR | RBI | Avg  |
|------------|---|---|------|----|------|--------|-----|----|----|-----|------|
| Home       | 5 | 1 | 3.07 | 2  | 41.0 | LHB    | 102 | 22 | 1  | 8   | .216 |
| Road       | 0 | 1 | 1.26 | 1  | 43.0 | RHB    | 199 | 39 | 7  | 23  | .196 |
| First Half | 1 | 1 | 2.31 | 3  | 35.0 | Sc Pos | 71  | 17 | 2  | 23  | .239 |
| Scnd Half  | 4 | 1 | 2.02 | 0  | 49.0 | Clutch | 107 | 19 | 4  | 9   | .178 |

### 1995 Rankings (National League)

- → 1st in least baserunners allowed per 9 innings in relief (8.9)
- → 3rd in games pitched
- → 4th in relief ERA (2.14)
- → 5th in lowest batting average allowed in relief (.203)
- → 7th in relief innings (84.0)
- → 8th in balks (2) and lowest batting average allowed in relief with runners on base (.189)
- → Led the Rockies in balks, lowest batting average allowed in relief with runners on base, relief ERA, lowest batting average allowed in relief, and fewest baserunners allowed in relief

**Colorado Rockies**

# Kevin Ritz

## 1995 Summary

At the age of 30, Kevin Ritz had the best year of his major league career. He opened the season in the Colorado rotation, and in May ran off a string of six straight starts in which he pitched into the sixth inning or later. He was perhaps the staff ace until an August slump forced him into the bullpen. In the heat of the September pennant race, Ritz made consecutive four-inning relief appearances, shutting down Atlanta and Cincinnati. He earned saves in both games, thereby earning a last shot as a starter. He won twice in his last three starts.

## Pitching

Ritz' success depends on locating his pitches. When he hit his spots last season, he looked like a staff ace. When he didn't, he went down in flames. He throws an average fastball with good movement, and a slider that is difficult for right-handed batters to handle. His change-up must be working or hitters sit on his fastball, which simply doesn't have enough movement or velocity for Ritz to rely upon.

## Defense & Hitting

Ritz is an adequate fielder. Sometimes he is slow getting off the mound, but he has improved his follow-through so that he lands in good position to field the ball. At the plate, Ritz helps the Rockies as much as anyone on the staff. He led all Colorado pitchers in base hits and on-base percentage.

## 1996 Outlook

A pitcher who entered the year with a career ERA well over 5.00, Ritz was one of 1995's biggest surprises. A godsend to a club which was desperate for reliable starters last year, he gave the Rockies quality innings, wasn't overly intimidated by Coors Field, and even helped in relief at a crucial point in the season. He'll enter the year as a member of the Rockies' rotation, and they'll be counting on him to win in double figures again.

**Position:** SP
**Bats:** R **Throws:** R
**Ht:** 6' 4"  **Wt:** 220

**Opening Day Age:** 30
**Born:** 6/8/65 in Eatonstown, NJ
**ML Seasons:** 6

### Overall Statistics

|  | W | L | Pct. | ERA | G | GS | Sv | IP | H | BB | SO | HR | BR/IP |
|---|---|---|---|---|---|---|---|---|---|---|---|---|---|
| 1995 | 11 | 11 | .500 | 4.21 | 31 | 28 | 2 | 173.1 | 171 | 65 | 120 | 16 | 1.36 |
| Career | 22 | 35 | .386 | 5.14 | 96 | 75 | 2 | 424.0 | 453 | 224 | 298 | 28 | 1.60 |

### How Often He Throws Strikes

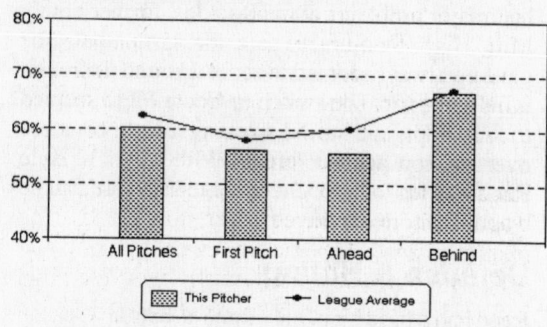

### 1995 Situational Stats

|  | W | L | ERA | Sv | IP |  | AB | H | HR | RBI | Avg |
|---|---|---|---|---|---|---|---|---|---|---|---|
| Home | 5 | 4 | 5.42 | 2 | 76.1 | LHB | 299 | 87 | 3 | 34 | .291 |
| Road | 6 | 7 | 3.25 | 0 | 97.0 | RHB | 360 | 84 | 13 | 55 | .233 |
| First Half | 7 | 3 | 3.50 | 0 | 82.1 | Sc Pos | 160 | 52 | 6 | 73 | .325 |
| Scnd Half | 4 | 8 | 4.85 | 2 | 91.0 | Clutch | 13 | 3 | 0 | 3 | .231 |

### 1995 Rankings (National League)

- → 1st in fielding percentage at pitcher (1.000)
- → 3rd in highest ERA at home (5.42)
- → 6th in ERA on the road (3.25) and highest batting average allowed with runners in scoring position (.325)
- → 8th in highest stolen base percentage allowed (81.8%)
- → 9th in sacrifice bunts (11), lowest strikeout/walk ratio (1.8), highest groundball/flyball ratio allowed (1.7) and most pitches thrown per batter (3.77)
- → 10th in most GDPs induced per 9 innings (0.8)
- → Led the Rockies in ERA, wins, losses, games started, innings pitched, hits allowed, batters faced (743) and home runs allowed

# Bret Saberhagen

## 1995 Season

One start after being rocked by the Rockies, Bret Saberhagen became one. What a strange new world in Denver! Saberhagen found that he could give up 13 hits in a game and receive a standing ovation when he departed. He found that he could give up seven first-inning runs and not be booed leaving the mound. Denver baseball fans, unlike those in New York, love everybody who wears the home uniform. Although Saberhagen and his sore shoulder didn't give Rockies fans much to cheer about, he certainly found a home.

## Pitching

When his shoulder is right, Saberhagen's sinking fastball is a powerful weapon. He mixes it well with an outstanding change-up, and throws a biting curve and slider that are equally impressive. It is his command of his pitches that makes him such a force on the mound. Shoulder problems compromised his pinpoint control in 1995; his 33 walks surpassed his total for the two previous years combined. Still, he averaged less than two per nine innings pitched. Saberhagen learned quickly that walks are especially dangerous in the Mile High City. He had a couple of the worst outings of his career at Coors Field.

## Defense & Hitting

Saberhagen wins games with his arm and not his bat. He does put the ball into play regularly, but he could use some work on his bunting. Defensively Saberhagen is very good. He handles batted balls well and executes the necessary plays consistently. His pickoff move is another asset. If he has a weakness on defense, it is that he is sometimes slow in covering first base.

## 1996 Outlook

Still not yet 32, Saberhagen has already won two Cy Young Awards. If shoulder surgery in the offseason puts him back on track, he is the Rockies' ace. But if the shoulder doesn't improve—or if he doesn't adjust to Coors Field—it could be a long season both for Saberhagen and the Rockies.

**Position:** SP
**Bats:** R  **Throws:** R
**Ht:** 6' 1"  **Wt:** 200

**Opening Day Age:** 31
**Born:** 4/11/64 in Chicago Heights, IL
**ML Seasons:** 12

### Overall Statistics

|        | W   | L   | Pct. | ERA  | G   | GS  | Sv | IP     | H    | BB  | SO   | HR  | BR/IP |
|--------|-----|-----|------|------|-----|-----|----|--------|------|-----|------|-----|-------|
| 1995   | 7   | 6   | .538 | 4.18 | 25  | 25  | 0  | 153.0  | 165  | 33  | 100  | 21  | 1.29  |
| Career | 141 | 100 | .585 | 3.26 | 337 | 309 | 1  | 2227.2 | 2100 | 421 | 1510 | 177 | 1.13  |

### How Often He Throws Strikes

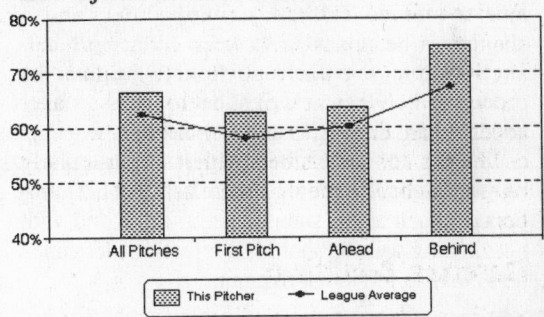

### 1995 Situational Stats

|            | W | L | ERA  | Sv | IP    |        | AB  | H  | HR | RBI | Avg  |
|------------|---|---|------|----|-------|--------|-----|----|----|-----|------|
| Home       | 4 | 3 | 4.84 | 0  | 83.2  | LHB    | 286 | 66 | 8  | 26  | .231 |
| Road       | 3 | 3 | 3.38 | 0  | 69.1  | RHB    | 319 | 99 | 13 | 41  | .310 |
| First Half | 5 | 4 | 3.33 | 0  | 100.0 | Sc Pos | 125 | 32 | 5  | 45  | .256 |
| Scnd Half  | 2 | 2 | 5.77 | 0  | 53.0  | Clutch | 27  | 4  | 0  | 2   | .148 |

### 1995 Rankings (National League)

- → 5th in most home runs allowed per 9 innings (1.24) and highest batting average allowed vs. right-handed batters (.310)
- → 6th in hit batsmen (10), highest strikeout/walk ratio (3.0) and lowest batting average allowed vs. left-handed batters (.231)
- → 7th in lowest groundball/flyball ratio allowed (1.1) and highest ERA at home (4.84)
- → 8th in highest slugging percentage allowed (.441)
- → 9th in complete games (3) and home runs allowed
- → 10th in highest stolen base percentage allowed (80.0%)

**Colorado Rockies**

# Bill Swift

## 1995 Season

As he has done several times in the past, Bill Swift spent the 1995 season battling shoulder injuries. He missed the entire month of August, but came back on September 9 to make his final five starts of the year. In pain, he gave the Rockies five-plus innings in each of those starts and didn't surrender more than two earned runs in any of them. Though he won only nine games and couldn't become the staff anchor the Rockies hoped he would be, the club knew he was giving them everything he had.

## Pitching

Swift is a veteran pitcher who relies on his experience and great movement on his pitches. His arsenal—a sinking fastball, a hard slider, and a change-up he mixes in to keep hitters off balance—induces a disproportionate number of ground balls. When he's right he throws the sinker about as hard as any groundball hurler in the game, and he can dominate hitters with it. . . particularly righties. Coors Field didn't seem to affect his numbers as much as his shoulder injury did, and with his pitching style he should be effective there once he's close to full strength again.

## Defense & Hitting

Swift is good around the mound, and possibly the best fielder on the Colorado staff. He also has a quick move to first and is one of the best righties around when it comes to holding runners. At the plate, Swift is not an easy out, and he's got good power for a pitcher.

## 1996 Outlook

With successful shoulder surgery, Swift is expected to share the staff ace job with Bret Saberhagen. He's 48-22 in four National League seasons, and he has both the experience and the knowledge to be a big winner again. All he needs is a healthy shoulder.

**Position:** SP
**Bats:** R **Throws:** R
**Ht:** 6' 0" **Wt:** 191

**Opening Day Age:** 34
**Born:** 10/27/61 in South Portland, ME
**ML Seasons:** 10

### Overall Statistics

|  | W | L | Pct. | ERA | G | GS | Sv | IP | H | BB | SO | HR | BR/IP |
|---|---|---|---|---|---|---|---|---|---|---|---|---|---|
| 1995 | 9 | 3 | .750 | 4.94 | 19 | 19 | 0 | 105.2 | 122 | 43 | 68 | 12 | 1.56 |
| Career | 78 | 62 | .557 | 3.62 | 353 | 178 | 25 | 1371.1 | 1397 | 425 | 656 | 83 | 1.33 |

### How Often He Throws Strikes

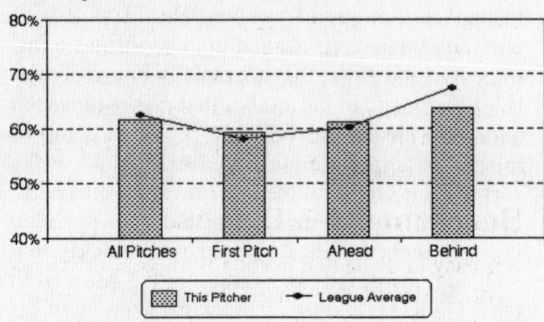

### 1995 Situational Stats

|  | W | L | ERA | Sv | IP |  | AB | H | HR | RBI | Avg |
|---|---|---|---|---|---|---|---|---|---|---|---|
| Home | 4 | 1 | 5.01 | 0 | 55.2 | LHB | 218 | 68 | 6 | 31 | .312 |
| Road | 5 | 2 | 4.86 | 0 | 50.0 | RHB | 194 | 54 | 6 | 27 | .278 |
| First Half | 4 | 2 | 5.90 | 0 | 61.0 | Sc Pos | 93 | 36 | 4 | 46 | .387 |
| Scnd Half | 5 | 1 | 3.63 | 0 | 44.2 | Clutch | 10 | 2 | 0 | 1 | .200 |

### 1995 Rankings (National League)

→ 4th in highest batting average allowed vs. left-handed batters (.312)
→ Led the Rockies in runners caught stealing (5)

# Larry Walker

## 1995 Season

Larry Walker turned out to be everything general manager Bob Gebhard wanted when he signed Walker to the Rockies as a free agent. Strong for most of the season, Walker slumped in August but rebounded for the September pennant race. He is an emotional ballplayer who throws helmets, argues with umpires and glares at pitchers, but he also provides power, speed and solid defense to a young team.

## Hitting

Like most of the Colorado sluggers, Walker hit for both average and power at Coors Field. His numbers weren't nearly as impressive away from Coors, but he continued to provide the longball. In any park, Walker is a line-drive hitter with power to both alleys. He knows the strike zone and smartly shortens his powerful swing late in the count. He crowds the plate and get hits by a good number of pitches.

## Baserunning & Defense

It is easy to argue that Walker is the best defensive right fielder in the National League. He gets a great jump on the ball, runs into walls, dives and, most importantly, catches the ball. His arm rates among the best, and Walker will even attempt to throw runners out at first if they don't run hard on hits to right field. On the bases Walker is fast and smart. He stole 16 bases on the season, nine of them during the September pennant chase, and his success rate is consistently excellent.

## 1996 Outlook

With Coors Field as his home, Walker could have an MVP season in his future. He is expected to bat cleanup and patrol right field for years to come in Denver. With a consistent leadoff hitter in the lineup and Dante Bichette in front of him, Walker will pile up the RBI. If he plays a full 162-game schedule in 1996, he should post even bigger numbers than his impressive '95 stats.

**Position:** RF
**Bats:** L  **Throws:** R
**Ht:** 6' 3"  **Wt:** 215

**Opening Day Age:** 29
**Born:** 12/1/66 in Maple Ridge, BC, Canada
**ML Seasons:** 7

### Overall Statistics

|  | G | AB | R | H | D | T | HR | RBI | SB | BB | SO | Avg | OBP | Slg |
|---|---|---|---|---|---|---|---|---|---|---|---|---|---|---|
| 1995 | 131 | 494 | 96 | 151 | 31 | 5 | 36 | 101 | 16 | 49 | 72 | .306 | .381 | .607 |
| Career | 805 | 2860 | 464 | 817 | 178 | 21 | 135 | 485 | 114 | 313 | 546 | .286 | .361 | .504 |

### Where He Hits the Ball

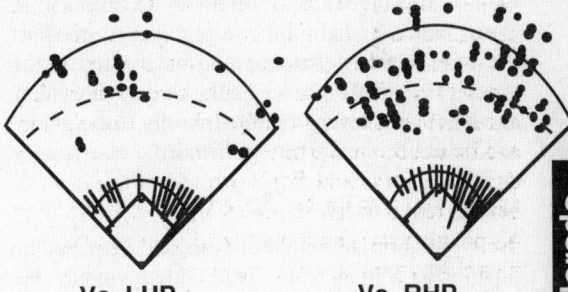

Vs. LHP          Vs. RHP

### 1995 Situational Stats

|  | AB | H | HR | RBI | Avg |  | AB | H | HR | RBI | Avg |
|---|---|---|---|---|---|---|---|---|---|---|---|
| Home | 248 | 85 | 24 | 59 | .343 | LHP | 141 | 45 | 7 | 30 | .319 |
| Road | 246 | 66 | 12 | 42 | .268 | RHP | 353 | 106 | 29 | 71 | .300 |
| First Half | 235 | 75 | 20 | 50 | .319 | Sc Pos | 130 | 36 | 6 | 59 | .277 |
| Scnd Half | 259 | 76 | 16 | 51 | .293 | Clutch | 68 | 19 | 5 | 15 | .279 |

### 1995 Rankings (National League)

➡ 1st in slugging percentage vs. right-handed pitchers (.637)
➡ 2nd in home runs, total bases (300), hit by pitch (14), slugging percentage, HR frequency (13.7 ABs per HR), least pitches seen per plate appearance (3.18) and highest percentage of swings on the first pitch (49.8%)
➡ 3rd in intentional walks (13) and fielding percentage in right field (.988)
➡ 4th in cleanup slugging percentage (.623)
➡ 6th in stolen base percentage (84.2%) and batting average at home (.343)
➡ Led the Rockies in intentional walks (13) and hit by pitch (14)

# Walt Weiss

## 1995 Season

Walt Weiss was the glue that held the Rockies together in 1995. Regardless of how he was hitting, the Colorado pitching staff always felt better knowing he was stationed in the middle of the infield. Though he's not on the team for his hitting ability, Weiss also had a solid year offensively and never went into an extended slump. He also gave the clubhouse an experienced hand in the playoffs.

## Hitting

With the Colorado lineup full of power hitters, the club only needed Weiss to get on base, and that's just what he did. His 98 walks and .403 on-base percentage in 1995 were career highs, and he walked nearly twice as often as he struck out. Weiss batted in the number-eight spot for most of the year, but was also effective when used as the Rockies' leadoff hitter. Still, he provides few extra-base hits, even in hitter-friendly Coors Field. Weiss hit his one homer on the road.

## Baserunning & Defense

Weiss was born to play shortstop, and he plays the position as well as many Gold Glove winners. He goes deep into the hole and up the middle to catch grounders, always making it look easy. He is no speed demon on the bases, but he is a minor threat to steal and avoids hitting into double plays by getting up the line quickly. He stole a career-high 15 bases in 1995.

## 1996 Outlook

The Rockies needed to re-sign Weiss, and they did, so look for Weiss to patrol the middle of the infield in Colorado next season. He'll almost certainly never win a Gold Glove, not with Barry Larkin in the league, but Weiss should continue to play sterling defense while reaching base with regularity.

**Position:** SS
**Bats:** B  **Throws:** R
**Ht:** 6' 0"  **Wt:** 175

**Opening Day Age:** 32
**Born:** 11/28/63 in Tuxedo, NY
**ML Seasons:** 9

### Overall Statistics

|  | G | AB | R | H | D | T | HR | RBI | SB | BB | SO | Avg | OBP | Slg |
|---|---|---|---|---|---|---|---|---|---|---|---|---|---|---|
| 1995 | 137 | 427 | 65 | 111 | 17 | 3 | 1 | 25 | 15 | 98 | 57 | .260 | .403 | .321 |
| Career | 933 | 2958 | 351 | 745 | 102 | 16 | 11 | 226 | 66 | 392 | 391 | .252 | .341 | .308 |

### Where He Hits the Ball

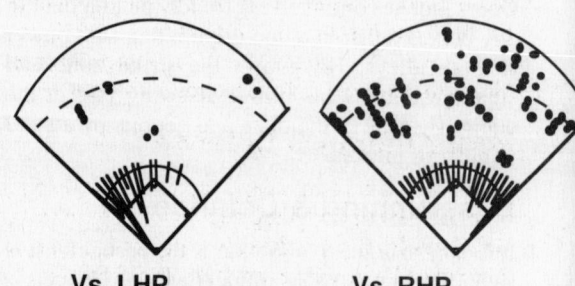

Vs. LHP          Vs. RHP

### 1995 Situational Stats

|  | AB | H | HR | RBI | Avg |  | AB | H | HR | RBI | Avg |
|---|---|---|---|---|---|---|---|---|---|---|---|
| Home | 217 | 61 | 0 | 20 | .281 | LHP | 114 | 30 | 0 | 2 | .263 |
| Road | 210 | 50 | 1 | 5 | .238 | RHP | 313 | 81 | 1 | 23 | .259 |
| First Half | 224 | 54 | 0 | 13 | .241 | Sc Pos | 101 | 18 | 0 | 23 | .178 |
| Scnd Half | 203 | 57 | 1 | 12 | .281 | Clutch | 61 | 15 | 0 | 5 | .246 |

### 1995 Rankings (National League)

- 1st in highest percentage of pitches taken (65.4%)
- 2nd in walks
- 3rd in lowest slugging percentage (.321), lowest HR frequency (427.0 ABs per HR) and lowest batting average with runners in scoring position (.178)
- 4th in on-base percentage, lowest slugging percentage vs. left-handed pitchers (.298) and fielding percentage at shortstop (.974)
- 5th in highest groundball/flyball ratio (2.0) and lowest slugging percentage vs. right-handed pitchers (.329)
- Led the Rockies in walks, on-base percentage and highest groundball/flyball ratio (2.0)

# Eric Young

**Position:** 2B/LF
**Bats:** R **Throws:** R
**Ht:** 5' 9"  **Wt:** 180

**Opening Day Age:** 28
**Born:** 5/18/67 in New
Brunswick, NJ
**ML Seasons:** 4

## 1995 Season

At the end of June, Eric Young was hitting .149 and struggling to stay in the majors. But then Young suddenly found his hitting stroke, batting .355 and stealing 29 bases the rest of the way. Young became an excellent leadoff hitter and the everyday second baseman on a team that needed both.

## Hitting

Young may have turned into the leadoff hitter the Rockies need, because he has all the necessary skills: he has always been a patient hitter, he manipulates the bat very well, and he's fast and a good bunter. Long an excellent fastball hitter, he has become a better hitter by learning to handle offspeed and breaking stuff. He's not just a "Coors hitter," either. . . he was one of only three Rockies hitters to bat over .300 on the road last year.

## Baserunning & Defense

Young is a threat to steal every time he reaches base. He gets a good jump and accelerates quickly. He scores from second easily on most base hits to the outfield and will even try going from first to third on some balls hit to left. Defensively, Young could stand some work. He has limited range at second and only a fair arm. He seems to lose his concentration on easy defensive plays. While he stays in on double plays, he doesn't always pivot quickly enough to complete the play.

## 1996 Outlook

If the second half of 1995 was the real Eric Young, then he could be on his way to a very good career. A fan favorite for hitting the first-ever home run in Denver, Young needs to work on his defense and keep his head in the game in order to become a top-notch player. He's already a pretty good one.

### Overall Statistics

| | G | AB | R | H | D | T | HR | RBI | SB | BB | SO | Avg | OBP | Slg |
|---|---|---|---|---|---|---|---|---|---|---|---|---|---|---|
| 1995 | 120 | 366 | 68 | 116 | 21 | 9 | 6 | 36 | 35 | 49 | 29 | .317 | .404 | .473 |
| Career | 403 | 1216 | 196 | 344 | 51 | 18 | 17 | 119 | 101 | 158 | 96 | .283 | .369 | .396 |

### Where He Hits the Ball

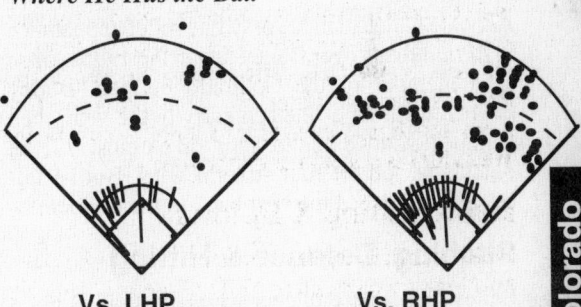

**Vs. LHP**          **Vs. RHP**

### 1995 Situational Stats

| | AB | H | HR | RBI | Avg | | AB | H | HR | RBI | Avg |
|---|---|---|---|---|---|---|---|---|---|---|---|
| Home | 169 | 56 | 5 | 22 | .331 | LHP | 125 | 50 | 4 | 21 | .400 |
| Road | 197 | 60 | 1 | 14 | .305 | RHP | 241 | 66 | 2 | 15 | .274 |
| First Half | 107 | 27 | 2 | 13 | .252 | Sc Pos | 84 | 22 | 1 | 27 | .262 |
| Scnd Half | 259 | 89 | 4 | 23 | .344 | Clutch | 52 | 21 | 0 | 2 | .404 |

### 1995 Rankings (National League)

- → 1st in triples, batting average vs. left-handed pitchers (.400) and errors at second base (11)
- → 2nd in batting average in the clutch (.404) and on-base percentage vs. left-handed pitchers (.449)
- → 3rd in on-base percentage for a leadoff hitter (.402) and steals of third (12)
- → 4th in caught stealing (12) and slugging percentage vs. left-handed pitchers (.648)
- → 5th in lowest batting average with the bases loaded (.100)
- → 6th in stolen bases and lowest percentage of swings that missed (10.1%)
- → Led the Rockies in triples, stolen bases and caught stealing (12)

Colorado Rockies

# Roger Bailey

**Position:** RP/SP
**Bats:** R **Throws:** R
**Ht:** 6' 1"  **Wt:** 180

**Opening Day Age:** 25
**Born:** 10/3/70 in
Chattahoochee, FL
**ML Seasons:** 1

*Overall Statistics*

|  | W | L | Pct. | ERA | G | GS | Sv | IP | H | BB | SO | HR | BR/IP |
|---|---|---|---|---|---|---|---|---|---|---|---|---|---|
| 1995 | 7 | 6 | .538 | 4.98 | 39 | 6 | 0 | 81.1 | 88 | 39 | 33 | 9 | 1.56 |
| Career | 7 | 6 | .538 | 4.98 | 39 | 6 | 0 | 81.1 | 88 | 39 | 33 | 9 | 1.56 |

## 1995 Season

A rookie who had made only one relief appearance in the minors, Roger Bailey began the 1995 season as a member of the Colorado bullpen. Bailey pitched well out of the pen early in the year, then slumped. Called on to start on August 17, he quickly reeled off four straight wins. But he faltered and finished the year back in the bullpen.

## Pitching, Defense & Hitting

Bailey is a finesse pitcher whose fastball is not a strikeout pitch, and his curveball and slider need to be spotted in order for him to be effective. Though he gave it his all in relief, his stuff seems best suited for a starting role, and so does his arm, as he had problems working on short rest last year. His defense was just fair, and he had some problems with opposing baserunners. Though not a great hitter, Bailey looks like he can help himself with the bat on occasion.

## 1996 Outlook

Bailey is still relatively inexperienced, and with a healthy staff this year the Rockies might be better served allowing him to get a full season of experience at the Triple-A level. . . something he hasn't had yet. Judged by his 1995 work, he seems more likely to help the club as a starter than as a reliever.

# Marvin Freeman

**Position:** SP
**Bats:** R **Throws:** R
**Ht:** 6' 7"  **Wt:** 222

**Opening Day Age:** 32
**Born:** 4/10/63 in
Chicago, IL
**ML Seasons:** 9

*Overall Statistics*

|  | W | L | Pct. | ERA | G | GS | Sv | IP | H | BB | SO | HR | BR/9 |
|---|---|---|---|---|---|---|---|---|---|---|---|---|---|
| 1995 | 3 | 7 | .300 | 5.89 | 22 | 18 | 0 | 94.2 | 122 | 41 | 61 | 15 | 1.72 |
| Career | 28 | 19 | .596 | 4.21 | 194 | 54 | 5 | 462.0 | 461 | 191 | 311 | 42 | 1.41 |

## 1995 Season

An assortment of injuries kept Marvin Freeman from pitching as effectively as he did in 1994. In his first three starts, the tall, lanky righthander walked more batters than he struck out, and his control would elude him all season long. By the end of July Freeman was out of the starting rotation, but he struggled in relief as well. He blew his only save opportunity and surrendered runs in three of his four relief appearances.

## Pitching, Defense & Hitting

Freeman throws the basic fastball, curveball and change-up. When he is healthy, his fastball reaches the low 90s on the radar gun, but its movement isn't enough to make it a strikeout pitch. He needs his control to be effective, and he didn't have it last season. Freeman hit a homer in both 1994 and '95, but otherwise he isn't much of a threat at the plate. He also has trouble when called on to sacrifice. His defense is below average because his follow-through on the mound leaves him in poor fielding position.

## 1996 Outlook

Competition will be fierce for starting spots in the Colorado rotation. If Freeman is healthy and regains his form, he can win one of them. If there are a lot of healthy arms in the Rockies camp this spring, Freeman might find himself modeling another uniform.

# Joe Grahe

**Position**: SP/RP
**Bats**: R  **Throws**: R
**Ht**: 6' 0"  **Wt**: 200

**Opening Day Age**: 28
**Born**: 8/14/67 in West
Palm Beach, FL
**ML Seasons**: 6
**Pronunciation**: GRAY

## Overall Statistics

|  | W | L | Pct. | ERA | G | GS | Sv | IP | H | BB | SO | HR | BR/IP |
|---|---|---|---|---|---|---|---|---|---|---|---|---|---|
| 1995 | 4 | 3 | .571 | 5.08 | 17 | 9 | 0 | 56.2 | 69 | 27 | 27 | 6 | 1.69 |
| Career | 21 | 26 | .447 | 4.46 | 174 | 34 | 45 | 367.2 | 411 | 165 | 188 | 26 | 1.57 |

## 1995 Season

The Rockies picked up ailing reliever Joe Grahe last year and tried to return him to his original major league role as a starter. After four relief outings, Grahe made three good starts in June before reality set in. Four of his next five starts were complete disasters and Grahe ended up on the disabled list with arm problems. He returned in mid-September to give his ERA one final boost before being released after the playoffs.

## Pitching, Defense & Hitting

Even during his best seasons, Grahe has never been a control pitcher. Add to the mix that he is not overpowering, then put him in Coors Field, and you have a recipe for disaster. Grahe throws his pitches—fastball, slider, curveball and change-up—with average velocity, but he can be effective when he has good movement on them. He fields his position adequately and can handle the bat better than most. He has problems holding baserunners, however.

## 1996 Outlook

Grahe was released by the Rockies immediately after the playoffs. He is still young enough to be picked up by another team if his arm is healthy. Grahe needs to work on his control and maximize the movement on his pitches to stick in the big leagues.

# Lance Painter

**Position**: RP
**Bats**: L  **Throws**: L
**Ht**: 6' 1"  **Wt**: 195

**Opening Day Age**: 28
**Born**: 7/21/67 in
Bedford, England
**ML Seasons**: 3

## Overall Statistics

|  | W | L | Pct. | ERA | G | GS | Sv | IP | H | BB | SO | HR | BR/IP |
|---|---|---|---|---|---|---|---|---|---|---|---|---|---|
| 1995 | 3 | 0 | 1.000 | 4.37 | 33 | 1 | 1 | 45.1 | 55 | 10 | 36 | 9 | 1.43 |
| Career | 9 | 8 | .529 | 5.58 | 58 | 21 | 1 | 158.0 | 198 | 45 | 93 | 23 | 1.54 |

## 1995 Season

Lefthander Lance Painter had the best season of his three-year career in 1995. Like most Rockies pitchers, Painter was hurt by the thin air in Coors Field, but his overall work was excellent. Used primarily as a starter in 1993 and '94, he adapted very well to life as a relief pitcher.

## Pitching, Defense & Hitting

"Painter" is the perfect name for the young left-hander, who can paint the corners with pinpoint precision. He sports a good slider and has excellent movement on his fastball. As a lefty reliever his one major drawback is that he's had some problems with left-handed hitters, though lefties seldom take him out of the yard. He fields his position well, leaving himself in good position when he comes off the mound, and he has a quick move to first. Painter's offensive abilities were impressive enough to warrant pinch-hitting duties during the playoffs.

## 1996 Outlook

Spots will be tough to find if the Rockies staff is healthy this year, but Painter is a good insurance policy if injuries occur. He has the ability to pitch at the major league level and should find a role somewhere in 1996.

# Bryan Rekar

**Position**: SP
**Bats**: R **Throws**: R
**Ht**: 6' 3" **Wt**: 208

**Opening Day Age**: 23
**Born**: 6/3/72 in Oak Lawn, Illinois
**ML Seasons**: 1

## Overall Statistics

| | W | L | Pct. | ERA | G | GS | Sv | IP | H | BB | SO | HR | BR/IP |
|---|---|---|---|---|---|---|---|---|---|---|---|---|---|
| 1995 | 4 | 6 | .400 | 4.98 | 15 | 14 | 0 | 85.0 | 95 | 24 | 60 | 11 | 1.40 |
| Career | 4 | 6 | .400 | 4.98 | 15 | 14 | 0 | 85.0 | 95 | 24 | 60 | 11 | 1.40 |

## 1995 Season

In April the Rockies believed Bryan Rekar might be two years away from the big leagues. By July, they thought Rekar was ready for the major leagues, and it looks like they were right. He immediately gave the Rockies three consecutive strong outings, claiming a spot in the rotation for the rest of the year. Rekar wore down as the season wore on, but he gained invaluable experience and confidence in his abilities. His season was one of the most successful on the Rockies staff.

## Pitching, Defense & Hitting

A four-pitch pitcher with decent command, Rekar throws a fastball with good movement and velocity. His slider, curveball and change are above-average pitches, as well. He aggressively challenges each hitter. Rekar needs to improve at setting up hitters with his pitch selection, but his control will carry him a long way. Rekar hustles in the field and is effective at knocking down balls hit back up the middle. He also does a fine job of holding runners. As a hitter, Rekar comes from the Hank Aguirre school of hitting, where foul balls are cause for celebration.

## 1996 Outlook

If Rekar isn't overwhelmed by his meteoric rise, he can establish himself as a solid part of the starting rotation. If all arms are healthy, spring training will be a battleground for a number of starter candidates. Rekar has the stuff to win a spot.

# Armando Reynoso

**Position**: SP
**Bats**: R **Throws**: R
**Ht**: 6' 0" **Wt**: 196

**Opening Day Age**: 29
**Born**: 5/1/66 in San Luis Potosi, MX
**ML Seasons**: 5
**Pronunciation**: ray-NOH-so

## Overall Statistics

| | W | L | Pct. | ERA | G | GS | Sv | IP | H | BB | SO | HR | BR/IP |
|---|---|---|---|---|---|---|---|---|---|---|---|---|---|
| 1995 | 7 | 7 | .500 | 5.32 | 20 | 18 | 0 | 93.0 | 116 | 36 | 40 | 12 | 1.63 |
| Career | 25 | 23 | .521 | 4.61 | 68 | 63 | 1 | 365.1 | 413 | 133 | 194 | 45 | 1.49 |

## 1995 Season

Armando Reynoso spent most of 1995 building up his stamina from the elbow transplant surgery he underwent the previous year. While Reynoso showed signs of attaining his previous arm strength, he was seldom able to put together back-to-back strong outings. His control was good, but he didn't have the movement he needed to be effective.

## Pitching, Defense & Hitting

Reynoso is a control pitcher who throws a variety of pitches. His fastball is a cutter with good movement, and he'll also use a screwball, forkball and curve. He changes speeds on his pitches to keep hitters off balance, and he'll use all manner of deliveries from overhand to sidearm. Reynoso moves well on the mound and fields his position adequately. His pickoff move is among the best in the majors and he nabbed seven runners last year despite his limited workload. Reynoso is not a threat at the plate.

## 1996 Outlook

Reynoso will work in the offseason at rebuilding the strength in his arm. In the spring he will have every opportunity to regain his spot in the starting rotation. If he can get back to where he was before the surgery, he'll make a good number-four or five starter.

# Bruce Ruffin

**Position**: RP
**Bats**: B **Throws**: L
**Ht**: 6' 2"  **Wt**: 213

**Opening Day Age**: 32
**Born**: 10/4/63 in
Lubbock, TX
**ML Seasons**: 10

## Overall Statistics

| | W | L | Pct. | ERA | G | GS | Sv | IP | H | BB | SO | HR | BR/IP |
|---|---|---|---|---|---|---|---|---|---|---|---|---|---|
| 1995 | 0 | 1 | .000 | 2.12 | 37 | 0 | 11 | 34.0 | 26 | 19 | 23 | 1 | 1.32 |
| Career | 53 | 75 | .414 | 4.19 | 375 | 152 | 32 | 1176.1 | 1272 | 518 | 738 | 84 | 1.52 |

## 1995 Season

Ruffin saved 11 games in 12 opportunities last year, and seemed to develop the closer mentality he needed to be effective. But injuries sidelined Ruffin for all of July and most of August. When he came back, he wasn't the closer anymore. His new role was to come in to face a left-handed batter. Though Ruffin wasn't as effective in that role, he had a quality season, posting the lowest ERA of his 10-year career.

## Pitching, Defense & Hitting

Ruffin's slider is a mean pitch for both left- and right-handed hitters. It not only moves downward, but also sweeps in on right-handed batters. When hitters lay off the slider, they draw walks. Ruffin's fastball has average velocity but good movement. Ruffin is an adequate fielder who is quick to cover the bag at first. As a hitter, his career is over. He is only fair at holding runners.

## 1996 Season

Despite their postseason appearance, Colorado's pitching was a weakness and changes will come. If Ruffin is healthy, he has the stuff to develop into a big-league closer. Or he may serve as a set-up man. However, lefties have hit him better than righthanders the last two years, which may not bode well for a set-up role in '96.

# John Vander Wal

**Position**: 1B
**Bats**: L **Throws**: L
**Ht**: 6' 2"  **Wt**: 190

**Opening Day Age**: 29
**Born**: 4/29/66 in Grand
Rapids, MI
**ML Seasons**: 5

## Overall Statistics

| | G | AB | R | H | D | T | HR | RBI | SB | BB | SO | Avg | OBP | Slg |
|---|---|---|---|---|---|---|---|---|---|---|---|---|---|---|
| 1995 | 105 | 101 | 15 | 35 | 8 | 1 | 5 | 21 | 1 | 16 | 23 | .347 | .432 | .594 |
| Career | 428 | 700 | 86 | 176 | 30 | 9 | 20 | 94 | 12 | 84 | 138 | .251 | .331 | .406 |

## 1995 Season

Deadly off the bench, John Vander Wal had one the greatest seasons any pinch hitter ever had in 1995. He finished the year with 28 pinch hits, surpassing Jose Morales' major league record by three. Vander Wal's totals included a dozen extra-base hits. After never hitting above .245 in a major league season, he batted .347.

## Hitting, Baserunning & Defense

Vander Wal is a good enough hitter to play first base when necessary. Of course, no one is going to move a healthy Andres Galarraga from there. Manager Don Baylor accused Vander Wal of being too picky when his pinch hitter slumped in mid-season, but Vander Wal does his best hitting when he is selective. When he works a count in his favor, he will look for the fastballs he is so adept at driving. Vander Wal has enough speed that he can steal a base or play the outfield. His arm limits him to left field or first base.

## 1996 Outlook

Vander Wal has turned himself into one of the most valuable bench players in baseball. He will continue to be the man off the bench late in the game. He may not duplicate his '95 season in 1996, but he will continue to be a valuable role player.

# Other Colorado Rockies

**Jorge Brito** (**Pos**: C, **Age**: 29, **Bats**: R)

After bouncing around the minors for a decade, Brito finally got his chance with the Rockies in '95 but hit poorly in 51 at-bats. He showed a decent arm, nailing four of 11 runners, but little else. 1996 Outlook: B

**Pedro Castellano** (**Pos**: 3B, **Age**: 26, **Bats**: R)

Castellano started the season with Colorado, but was sent down quickly after Ellis Burks got healthy. After two solid seasons at Triple-A, he struggled in '95. He's young, so another shot will come. 1996 Outlook: B

**Craig Counsell** (**Pos**: SS, **Age**: 25, **Bats**: L)

Counsell saw just three games with the Rockies in '95, but he should get the chance to supplant Walt Weiss sooner or later. He's shown a decent eye in the minors, with a little speed. 1996 Outlook: C

**Bryan Hickerson** (**Pos**: RP, **Age**: 32, **Throws**: L)

Hickerson was traded from the Cubs to Colorado in late July, and was simply terrible for the Rockies, who eventually released him in October. His career is in jeopardy. 1996 Outlook: C

**Trent Hubbard** (**Pos**: CF, **Age**: 29, **Bats**: R)

After a monster season at Triple-A, Hubbard was called up in August and made the most of his opportunity, hitting .310 in 24 games. He stayed with the team into the playoffs, and should hang around. 1996 Outlook: A

**Roberto Mejia** (**Pos**: 2B, **Age**: 23, **Throws**: R)

After stints with the Rockies the previous two seasons, Mejia's star took a dive in '95. His batting average tumbled, and he failed to draw a walk all season before being sent down to Triple-A in June. 1996 Outlook: B.

**Dave Nied** (**Pos**: RP, **Age**: 27, **Throws**: R)

It's hard to believe how far he's fallen in three seasons. Nied spent most of '95 fighting injuries to his pitching elbow. He was awful with the Rockies and not much better during rehabilitation. 1996 Outlook: B

**Matt Nokes** (**Pos**: C, **Age**: 32, **Bats**: L)

Nokes no longer has a bat to offer, and was released by both Baltimore and Colorado in '95. His injuries certainly didn't help. He's 32, but might be able to find a spot somewhere. 1996 Outlook: C

**Jayhawk Owens** (**Pos**: C, **Age**: 27, **Bats**: R)

Owens was called up in early August and stayed with the Rockies through the playoffs, throwing out five of eight runners along the way. He needs to prove he can handle a pitching staff. 1996 Outlook: A

**Harvey Pulliam** (**Pos**: LF, **Age**: 28, **Bats**: R)

Pulliam will probably do no better than backing up Dante Bichette in Colorado, but it's a role he might fit well. He had a solid season at Triple-A in '95, and has a lot to offer. 1996 Outlook: B

**A.J. Sager** (**Pos**: RP, **Age**: 31, **Throws**: R)

After a promising Triple-A season in '94, Sager showed nothing with the Rockies in '95 during 10 relief appearances. He's always had excellent control in the minors, but it left him with Colorado. 1996 Outlook: C

**Jimmy Tatum** (**Pos**: LF, **Age**: 28, **Throws**: R)

An expansion-draft selection by the Rockies, Tatum split his time between Colorado and Triple-A in '95, used almost exclusively as a pinch-hitter in the majors. It'll be tough to find him a spot. 1996 Outlook: B.

# Colorado Rockies Minor League Prospects

## Organization Overview:

The Rockies have done things unconventionally, but you can't argue with their success, having reached baseball's playoffs in just their third year of existence. Of course, no other expansion team had drawn roughly 4.5 million fans in its first year, allowing Colorado to pay huge contracts to stars like Larry Walker, Bill Swift and Bret Saberhagen. The organization has placed an emphasis on using its highest draft picks on quality arms, and the results are beginning to show. Last year, homegrown pitching products Bryan Rekar, Mark Thompson and Juan Acevedo all pitched at times for Colorado, and Acevedo was the bait the Rockies used to close the Saberhagen deal with the Mets. On the other hand, no position player the Rockies drafted has yet made an impact.

### John Burke

**Position:** P          **Opening Day Age:** 26
**Bats:** B **Throws:** R          **Born:** 2/9/70 in
**Ht:** 6' 4"  **Wt:** 220          Durango, CO

#### Recent Statistics

|  | W | L | ERA | G | GS | Sv | IP | H | R | BB | SO | HR |
|---|---|---|---|---|---|---|---|---|---|---|---|---|
| 93 A Central Val | 7 | 8 | 3.18 | 20 | 20 | 0 | 119.0 | 104 | 62 | 64 | 114 | 5 |
| 93 AAA Col Sprng | 3 | 2 | 3.14 | 8 | 8 | 0 | 48.2 | 44 | 22 | 23 | 38 | 0 |
| 94 AAA Col Sprng | 0 | 0 | 19.64 | 8 | 0 | 0 | 11.0 | 16 | 25 | 22 | 6 | 0 |
| 94 A Asheville | 0 | 1 | 1.06 | 4 | 4 | 0 | 17.0 | 5 | 3 | 5 | 16 | 1 |
| 95 AAA Col Sprng | 7 | 1 | 4.55 | 19 | 17 | 1 | 87.0 | 79 | 46 | 48 | 65 | 7 |

Burke has already had an eventful baseball career, having been drafted three separate times, including twice in the first round. He refused to sign with Houston after the Astros chose him in the opening round of '91, before becoming the Rockies' first draft pick ever the following year. Since then, Burke has avoided the arm injuries which plagued him in college, but suffered a mysterious loss of control in 1994 (6 K, 22 BB in 11 IP). As his 7-1 record in high-altitude Colorado Springs would indicate, he pitched better in '95, though he still had trouble locating the plate at times.

### Derrick Gibson

**Position:** OF          **Opening Day Age:** 21
**Bats:** R **Throws:** R          **Born:** 2/5/75 in Winter
**Ht:** 6' 2"  **Wt:** 227          Haven, FL

#### Recent Statistics

|  | G | AB | R | H | D | T | HR | RBI | SB | BB | SO | AVG |
|---|---|---|---|---|---|---|---|---|---|---|---|---|
| 93 R Rockies | 34 | 119 | 13 | 18 | 2 | 2 | 0 | 10 | 3 | 5 | 55 | .151 |
| 94 A Bend | 73 | 284 | 47 | 75 | 19 | 5 | 12 | 57 | 14 | 29 | 102 | .264 |
| 95 A Asheville | 135 | 506 | 91 | 148 | 16 | 10 | 32 | 115 | 31 | 29 | 136 | .292 |

Gibson would have played football at Auburn if inadequate test scores hadn't stopped him. His interest in football may be the reason he wasn't selected until the 13th round in '93 by the Rockies. His future in baseball looks bright, however. Gibson is a terrific package of speed and power, turning in a 30-30 performance in the South Atlantic League last year. His 32 homers tied for the league lead, and no one had more RBI. He may need to shorten his swing as he moves up the minor league chain, however.

### Quinton McCracken

**Position:** OF          **Opening Day Age:** 26
**Bats:** B **Throws:** R          **Born:** 3/16/70 in
**Ht:** 5' 8"  **Wt:** 170          Wilmington, NC

#### Recent Statistics

|  | G | AB | R | H | D | T | HR | RBI | SB | BB | SO | AVG |
|---|---|---|---|---|---|---|---|---|---|---|---|---|
| 95 AA New Haven | 55 | 221 | 33 | 79 | 11 | 4 | 1 | 26 | 26 | 21 | 32 | .357 |
| 95 AAA Col Sprng | 61 | 244 | 55 | 88 | 14 | 6 | 3 | 28 | 17 | 23 | 30 | .361 |
| 95 NL Colorado | 3 | 1 | 0 | 0 | 0 | 0 | 0 | 0 | 0 | 0 | 1 | .000 |
| 95 MLE | 116 | 467 | 73 | 169 | 26 | 11 | 4 | 45 | 30 | 34 | 61 | .362 |

McCracken has persevered through long odds and is now knocking on the door for a major league job. Drafted in the 25th round in 1992 as a second baseman, the 5'8" McCracken has moved to the outfield and been a very effective top-of-the-order hitter, scoring 94, 94 and 88 runs the past three seasons. McCracken has shown patience at the plate and stolen as many as 60 bases in a season, but his .359 batting average last year was 76 points above his previous career mark. At 26, McCracken can at least be an effective bench player, even if last year's average was a fluke.

### Doug Million

**Position:** P          **Opening Day Age:** 20
**Bats:** L **Throws:** L          **Born:** 10/13/75 in Fort
**Ht:** 6' 4"  **Wt:** 175          Thomas, KY

#### Recent Statistics

|  | W | L | ERA | G | GS | Sv | IP | H | R | BB | SO | HR |
|---|---|---|---|---|---|---|---|---|---|---|---|---|
| 94 R Rockies | 1 | 0 | 1.50 | 3 | 3 | 0 | 12.0 | 8 | 3 | 3 | 19 | 0 |
| 94 A Bend | 5 | 3 | 2.34 | 10 | 10 | 0 | 57.2 | 50 | 23 | 21 | 75 | 4 |
| 95 A Salem | 5 | 7 | 4.62 | 24 | 23 | 0 | 111.0 | 111 | 71 | 79 | 85 | 6 |

Million was very impressive in his 1994 pro debut following his selection by the Rockies as the seventh player taken overall that year. He was quite advanced after coming from a solid baseball program at Sarasota High, and struck out over 12 batters per nine innings in his first pro exposure. On the slight side when drafted, Million went on a conditioning program which added more weight than the Rockies expected. His 1995 season was a disappointment, but Million has three solid pitches and could progress quickly.

## Neifi Perez

**Position:** SS          **Opening Day Age:** 20
**Bats:** B **Throws:** R          **Born:** 6/2/75 in Villa
**Ht:** 6' 0"  **Wt:** 164          Mella, DR

*Recent Statistics*

|                | G | AB | R | H | D | T | HR | RBI | SB | BB | SO | AVG |
|----------------|-----|-----|----|-----|----|---|----|-----|----|----|----|------|
| 94 A Central Val | 134 | 506 | 64 | 121 | 16 | 7 | 1 | 35 | 9 | 32 | 79 | .239 |
| 95 AAA Col Sprng | 11 | 36 | 4 | 10 | 4 | 0 | 0 | 2 | 1 | 0 | 5 | .278 |
| 95 AA New Haven | 116 | 427 | 59 | 108 | 28 | 3 | 5 | 43 | 5 | 24 | 52 | .253 |
| 95 MLE | 127 | 471 | 59 | 126 | 36 | 4 | 7 | 42 | 3 | 19 | 56 | .268 |

Perez was signed as a free agent from the Dominican Republic in 1992. He's a hard worker and intelligent player who learned to switch-hit and speak English on his own. Defensively, he's an instinctive shortstop with a better-than-average throwing arm. His offensive game improved last season despite moving up a level to AA, as he started to hit with a bit more power. Only 20 years of age, Perez is the Rockies' most likely heir apparent to Walt Weiss and could be ready by the end of 1996.

## Mark Thompson

**Position:** P          **Opening Day Age:** 24
**Bats:** R **Throws:** R          **Born:** 4/7/71 in
**Ht:** 6' 2"  **Wt:** 205          Russellville, KY

*Recent Statistics*

|                | W | L | ERA | G | GS | Sv | IP | H | R | BB | SO | HR |
|----------------|---|---|------|----|----|----|------|----|----|----|----|----|
| 95 AAA Col Sprng | 5 | 3 | 6.10 | 11 | 10 | 0 | 62.0 | 73 | 43 | 25 | 38 | 2 |
| 95 NL Colorado | 2 | 3 | 6.53 | 21 | 5 | 0 | 51.0 | 73 | 42 | 22 | 30 | 7 |

Thompson was the Rockies' second pick in their first draft back in '92. His recent minor league record has not been scintillating, but it's important to keep in mind that Colorado Springs is a pitcher's nightmare just as Coors Field is. Thompson throws a fastball, change-up and hard slider, which is probably his best pitch. He could be in Colorado's rotation at the start of the '96 season.

## John Thomson

**Position:** P          **Opening Day Age:** 22
**Bats:** R **Throws:** R          **Born:** 10/1/73 in
**Ht:** 6' 3"  **Wt:** 170          Vicksburg, MS

*Recent Statistics*

|                | W | L | ERA | G | GS | Sv | IP | H | R | BB | SO | HR |
|----------------|---|---|------|----|----|----|-------|-----|----|----|----|----|
| 93 R Rockies | 3 | 5 | 4.62 | 11 | 11 | 0 | 50.2 | 43 | 40 | 31 | 36 | 0 |
| 94 A Asheville | 6 | 6 | 2.85 | 19 | 15 | 0 | 88.1 | 70 | 34 | 33 | 79 | 3 |
| 94 A Central Val | 3 | 1 | 3.28 | 9 | 8 | 0 | 49.1 | 43 | 20 | 18 | 41 | 0 |
| 95 AA New Haven | 7 | 8 | 4.18 | 26 | 24 | 0 | 131.1 | 132 | 69 | 56 | 82 | 8 |

The Rockies have demonstrated a tendency to select pitchers with their premium picks in the amateur draft, figuring few free agent hurlers would elect to toil in an environment as hostile to their species as Colorado. Thomson was the last of six pitchers drafted by Colorado in the first seven rounds of 1993. He throws the basic three pitches—fastball, curve and change—and delivers them with solid mechanics. He'll likely pitch this season in Triple-A at the age of 22.

## Andy Velazquez

**Position:** OF          **Opening Day Age:** 20
**Bats:** R **Throws:** R          **Born:** 12/15/75 in
**Ht:** 6' 0"  **Wt:** 170          Santurce, PR

*Recent Statistics*

|                | G | AB | R | H | D | T | HR | RBI | SB | BB | SO | AVG |
|----------------|-----|-----|----|-----|----|---|----|-----|----|----|-----|------|
| 93 R Rockies | 39 | 147 | 20 | 36 | 4 | 2 | 2 | 20 | 7 | 16 | 35 | .245 |
| 94 A Asheville | 119 | 447 | 50 | 106 | 22 | 3 | 11 | 39 | 9 | 23 | 120 | .237 |
| 95 A Salem | 131 | 497 | 74 | 149 | 25 | 6 | 13 | 69 | 7 | 40 | 102 | .300 |

Velazquez, the nephew of Roberto Clemente, has many of the same skills as his Hall-of-Fame uncle. Velazquez finished third in batting in the Carolina League last season and was voted the circuit's top defensive outfielder. His throwing arm also ranked as the league's strongest, although it's unfair to compare that to Clemente's legendary bazooka. Velazquez showed great improvement in just his second full professional season, and didn't turn 20 until December.

## Others to Watch

Righthander **Garvin Alston** pitched exclusively in relief for the first time in 1995, with solid results (2.84 ERA, 73 K's in 66.2 IP at Double-A). . . Outfielder **Angel Echevarria** was chosen in the 17th round of the '92 draft out of Rutgers. The 24 year old enjoyed his best pro season in '95, hitting .300 with 21 homers and 100 RBI at Double-A New Haven. . . After belting 28 homers in low A-ball in 1994, first baseman **Nate Holdren** followed with 15 homers in fast-A. He has yet to post a batting average above last year's .245, however. . . Outfielder **Terry Jones** has little power, but he can steal bases and score runs (51 SB, 78 runs in 124 games at Double-A). . . Lefthander **Mike Kusiewicz** was drafted in '94 but didn't make his pro debut until last year, when he was sensational in 22 Class-A starts (8-4, 2.03 ERA, 110 K, 34 BB, 99 hits in 128.1 IP). . . **Lloyd Peever**, a righthander, has more strikeouts than hits allowed and a strikeout to walk ratio of better than three to one in 283.1 minor league innings. A heavy college workload at LSU may have caught up to him, however, as he started just eight games in 1995. . . **Chris Sexton** plays shortstop and shows some valuable offensive traits. He's walked better than 90 times and scored over 80 runs each of the past two seasons in single-A. . . Reliever **Jake Viano** pitched in Double-A last season at the age of 21. He saved 19 games and struck out 85 batters while allowing just 51 hits in 72 innings.

# Kurt Abbott

## 1995 Season

After showing some power potential with nine home runs in 1994, Kurt Abbott had a firm grip on the Marlins' shortstop job despite his sometimes shaky defense. He took advantage of the opportunity. After an early slump which saw him benched for a brief stretch, Abbott came alive in the summer months, blasting 12 homers and driving home 44 runs. He finished the season with 17 home runs, tops among National League shortstops. His defense, though, was still shaky.

## Hitting

Just as Holmes had his Moriarty, Ahab had his whale, and Nixon had the press, Kurt Abbott has a mortal enemy of his own: the slider. Abbott's May benching came because of his struggles against a steady diet of the slider-ball, and he never really solved the pitch. Abbott's troubles with breaking balls leaves him nearly helpless after he gets behind in the count. Amazingly, Abbott didn't draw a single walk in those situations, and he hit just .154 with two strikes. On the other hand, nine of Abbott's 17 homers came with two strikes: *let 'er rip!*

## Baserunning & Defense

Abbott has pretty good speed for a shortstop, as suggested by his 10 triples over the last two seasons, but he's never going to steal more than four or five bases per season. Like a lot of power-hitting middle infielders, Abbott sports a strong throwing arm. But despite the solid arm and decent hands, Abbott is not a good shortstop; he simply lacks the range—in both directions—necessary for the position. In fact, Abbott might be the worst defensive shortstop in the National League.

## 1996 Outlook

Most managers will trade a little defense for offense, but championship teams need quality shortstop play. If Abbott continues to hit for power, he'll eventually be shifted to third base. For now, he'll open 1996 as the Marlins' starting shortstop.

**Position:** SS
**Bats:** R  **Throws:** R
**Ht:** 6' 0"  **Wt:** 185

**Opening Day Age:** 26
**Born:** 6/2/69 in Zanesville, OH
**ML Seasons:** 3

### Overall Statistics

| | G | AB | R | H | D | T | HR | RBI | SB | BB | SO | Avg | OBP | Slg |
|---|---|---|---|---|---|---|---|---|---|---|---|---|---|---|
| 1995 | 120 | 420 | 60 | 107 | 18 | 7 | 17 | 60 | 4 | 36 | 110 | .255 | .318 | .452 |
| Career | 241 | 826 | 112 | 208 | 36 | 10 | 29 | 102 | 9 | 55 | 228 | .252 | .304 | .425 |

### Where He Hits the Ball

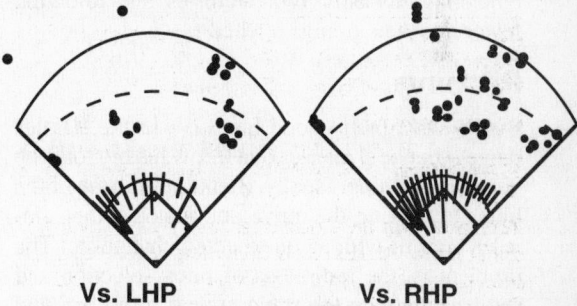

Vs. LHP                Vs. RHP

### 1995 Situational Stats

| | AB | H | HR | RBI | Avg | | AB | H | HR | RBI | Avg |
|---|---|---|---|---|---|---|---|---|---|---|---|
| Home | 207 | 61 | 12 | 34 | .295 | LHP | 119 | 29 | 3 | 13 | .244 |
| Road | 213 | 46 | 5 | 26 | .216 | RHP | 301 | 78 | 14 | 47 | .259 |
| First Half | 181 | 47 | 8 | 26 | .260 | Sc Pos | 89 | 22 | 3 | 41 | .247 |
| Scnd Half | 239 | 60 | 9 | 34 | .251 | Clutch | 68 | 13 | 2 | 9 | .191 |

### 1995 Rankings (National League)

- ➡ 2nd in lowest fielding percentage at shortstop (.959)
- ➡ 3rd in errors at shortstop (19)
- ➡ 4th in lowest batting average on the road (.216)
- ➡ 5th in lowest percentage of swings put into play (37.1%)
- ➡ 6th in triples and strikeouts
- ➡ 9th in lowest batting average (.255) and highest percentage of swings that missed (27.4%)
- ➡ Led the Marlins in triples and strikeouts

**Florida Marlins**

# Willie Banks

## 1995 Season

Not many pitchers can say they pitched for three different major league teams in one season; then again, not many would want to. After a disastrous second half in 1994, Willie Banks opened last season in the Cub bullpen. Ten outings and a 15.43 ERA—no, that isn't a typo—later, Banks was designated for assignment and shortly thereafter traded to Los Angeles, where he became a starter again. Banks started six games for the Dodgers, pitched well in a couple of them, and posted a respectable 4.03 ERA. Nevertheless, Banks was the odd man out when the Dodgers needed roster space, and the Marlins acquired him on waivers on August 10. He started nine games with Florida, collecting his only two victories and allowing fewer hits than innings pitched.

## Pitching

Banks has a pretty good fastball—in the 90-plus range—but he'd just as soon throw his big lollipop curve as anything. Ideally, Banks gets ahead of the hitter by mixing the curve and fastball, then finishes him off with an unexpected change-up. The problem is, the rudiments of pitch selection and setting hitters up too often appear forgotten, and Banks ends up grooving a fastball or walking a banjo hitter. Banks pitches with a lazy motion, at least until the arm starts moving forward.

## Defense & Hitting

A good athlete, Banks is quick off the mound to pounce on grounders and usually throws well to the bases. He was vulnerable to the running game, presumably because his various pitching coaches suggested that he focus on the hitters—not bad advice. Banks likes to hit and his career average is now .179, with two doubles.

## 1996 Outlook

Despite Banks' relatively good showing with the Marlins, he once again was dumped. This time the Phillies picked him up, and he'll be vying for a rotation spot this spring. The arm is still there, and perhaps Phillies pitching coach Johnny Podres can do something about the rest of the package.

**Position:** SP/RP
**Bats:** R  **Throws:** R
**Ht:** 6' 1"  **Wt:** 200

**Opening Day Age:** 27
**Born:** 2/27/69 in Jersey City, NJ
**ML Seasons:** 5

### Overall Statistics

| | W | L | Pct. | ERA | G | GS | Sv | IP | H | BB | SO | HR | BR/IP |
|---|---|---|---|---|---|---|---|---|---|---|---|---|---|
| 1995 | 2 | 6 | .250 | 5.66 | 25 | 15 | 0 | 90.2 | 106 | 58 | 62 | 14 | 1.81 |
| Career | 26 | 35 | .426 | 5.03 | 100 | 83 | 0 | 488.2 | 532 | 241 | 344 | 54 | 1.58 |

### How Often He Throws Strikes

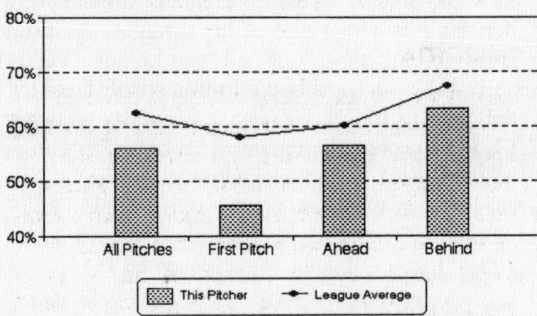

### 1995 Situational Stats

| | W | L | ERA | Sv | IP | | AB | H | HR | RBI | Avg |
|---|---|---|---|---|---|---|---|---|---|---|---|
| Home | 2 | 2 | 5.14 | 0 | 49.0 | LHB | 166 | 48 | 8 | 33 | .289 |
| Road | 0 | 4 | 6.26 | 0 | 41.2 | RHB | 195 | 58 | 6 | 28 | .297 |
| First Half | 0 | 2 | 9.47 | 0 | 25.2 | Sc Pos | 107 | 32 | 6 | 51 | .299 |
| Scnd Half | 2 | 4 | 4.15 | 0 | 65.0 | Clutch | 28 | 10 | 1 | 7 | .357 |

### 1995 Rankings (National League)

➡ Did not rank near the top or bottom in any category

# John Burkett

## 1995 Season

It was something of a strange season for John Burkett. In December of 1994, he was traded from San Francisco to Texas for a pair of minor league prospects. But with the "resolution" of the labor situation, the Rangers decided they couldn't afford Burkett, who became a free agent on April 7. The next day, he signed a two-year contract with Florida. The Marlins were looking for a workhorse, and that's just what they got with Burkett, who didn't miss a turn and wound up tied for sixth in the National League with 30 starts. Durability, of course, is nothing new for Burkett, who has never hit the disabled list in his seven-year career. The only negative of Burkett's season was his 4.30 ERA, the highest full-season mark of his career.

## Pitching

Burkett was better against left-handed hitters last year, and there's a good reason: a running fastball, the pitch that made Burkett a winner in the National League. Thrown inside to lefty hitters, it heads toward them when it's working, before veering back to catch a piece of the plate. The effect is almost that of a very hard screwball, and it's practically unhittable. Burkett also throws a tough slider, a decent curve, and the occasional Roger Craig-taught split-fingered fastball. He keeps the ball down nearly all of the time, and the result is plenty of ground balls and double plays.

## Defense & Hitting

Burkett's motion leaves him off-balance to the left side of the rubber after releasing the ball, which in turn leaves him in terrible position to field bunts and nubbers between the mound and third base. Burkett's move to first is average. Famously awful as a hitter, Burkett went 7-for-66 last season yet *raised* his career average. . . to .076.

## 1996 Outlook

He's signed through 1996, so Burkett will spend another season in the Marlin rotation. Joined by Patt Rapp and Chris Hammond—assuming those two remain—Burkett anchors a rotation that should be the foundation of a Florida club which could surprise in 1996.

**Position:** SP
**Bats:** R  **Throws:** R
**Ht:** 6' 3"  **Wt:** 211

**Opening Day Age:** 31
**Born:** 11/28/64 in New Brighton, PA
**ML Seasons:** 7
**Pronunciation:** BURR-ket

### Overall Statistics

|  | W | L | Pct. | ERA | G | GS | Sv | IP | H | BB | SO | HR | BR/IP |
|---|---|---|---|---|---|---|---|---|---|---|---|---|---|
| 1995 | 14 | 14 | .500 | 4.30 | 30 | 30 | 0 | 188.1 | 208 | 57 | 126 | 22 | 1.41 |
| Career | 81 | 56 | .591 | 3.90 | 193 | 187 | 1 | 1185.2 | 1233 | 302 | 717 | 106 | 1.29 |

### How Often He Throws Strikes

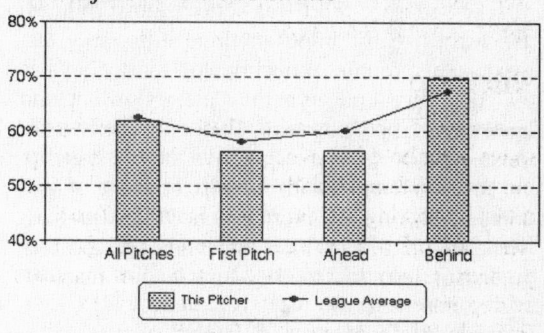

### 1995 Situational Stats

|  | W | L | ERA | Sv | IP |  | AB | H | HR | RBI | Avg |
|---|---|---|---|---|---|---|---|---|---|---|---|
| Home | 7 | 7 | 4.42 | 0 | 95.2 | LHB | 361 | 99 | 6 | 39 | .274 |
| Road | 7 | 7 | 4.18 | 0 | 92.2 | RHB | 376 | 109 | 16 | 47 | .290 |
| First Half | 6 | 8 | 4.96 | 0 | 85.1 | Sc Pos | 172 | 42 | 5 | 58 | .244 |
| Scnd Half | 8 | 6 | 3.76 | 0 | 103.0 | Clutch | 71 | 23 | 1 | 7 | .324 |

### 1995 Rankings (National League)

➡ 1st in GDPs induced (26), most GDPs induced per 9 innings (1.2) and fielding percentage at pitcher (1.000)
➡ 2nd in losses
➡ 4th in hits allowed
➡ 5th in wins, complete games (4) and highest slugging percentage allowed (.455)
➡ 6th in games started, home runs allowed, pickoff throws (157) and highest batting average allowed (.282)
➡ 8th in highest on-base percentage allowed (.339)
➡ Led the Marlins in wins, losses, games started, complete games, innings pitched, hits allowed and batters faced (810)

# Chuck Carr

## 1995 Season

Chuck Carr is living proof of the old adage, "You can't steal first base." After leading the National League with 58 stolen bases in 1993, Carr hasn't come close to matching that total. In 1995, Carr missed a month with tendinitis in his left leg, missed some time with cramps in his left hamstring, and finally was benched against right-handed pitchers in favor of Jesus Tavarez. At the time of the benching, Carr was hitting .212 overall and just .188 vs. righthanders.

## Hitting

The strangest thing about Carr's season was his utter inability to hit right-handed pitchers. In his first two seasons, Carr was better against righties. He wasn't really doing anything differently last year, so his troubles probably won't last. Carr has two major weaknesses at the plate: a slow bat, and poor strike-zone judgment. Of course, the two are related. Because he doesn't have the bat speed to make adjustments, Carr swings at a lot of bad pitches. He did show more patience than usual last year, and his .330 on-base percentage was a career high. But that's still too low for a leadoff man.

## Baserunning & Defense

Carr is built like a small greyhound, and that's just what he runs like. Though he has the speed to be a great basestealer, Carr's occasional inability to read pitchers' moves drops him from the "excellent" to the "very good" category. Though he doesn't always get the best jump in center field, Carr's wheels allow him to outrun many of his mistakes. He plays deep, which results in plenty of nice warning-track grabs while costing him outs in shallow center.

## 1996 Outlook

To Carr's credit, he took his benching better than most expected. However, the Marlins signed free-agent Devon White in late November, leaving Carr expendable, and before long he was traded to Milwaukee. Given the infatuation with speed which most recent Brewer managers seem to share, Carr should see plenty of playing time.

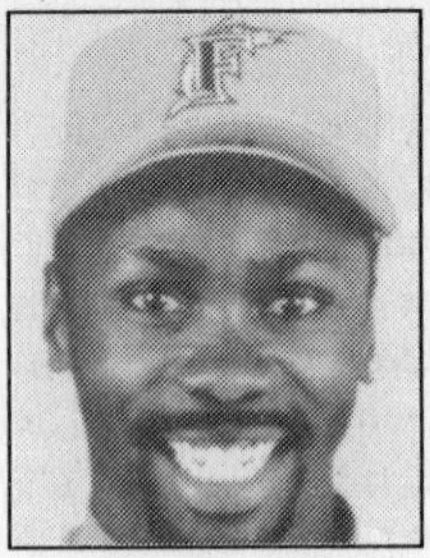

**Position:** CF
**Bats:** R **Throws:** R
**Ht:** 5'10" **Wt:** 165

**Opening Day Age:** 27
**Born:** 8/10/68 in San Bernardino, CA
**ML Seasons:** 6

### *Overall Statistics*

| | G | AB | R | H | D | T | HR | RBI | SB | BB | SO | Avg | OBP | Slg |
|---|---|---|---|---|---|---|---|---|---|---|---|---|---|---|
| 1995 | 105 | 308 | 54 | 70 | 20 | 0 | 2 | 20 | 25 | 46 | 49 | .227 | .330 | .312 |
| Career | 391 | 1369 | 199 | 347 | 61 | 4 | 8 | 95 | 127 | 126 | 204 | .253 | .319 | .321 |

### *Where He Hits the Ball*

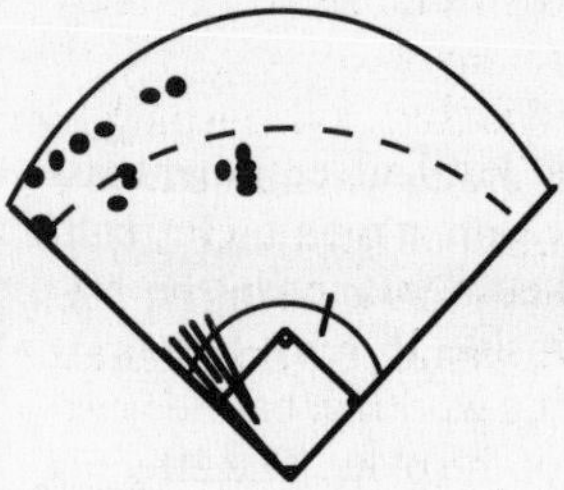

Vs. LHP

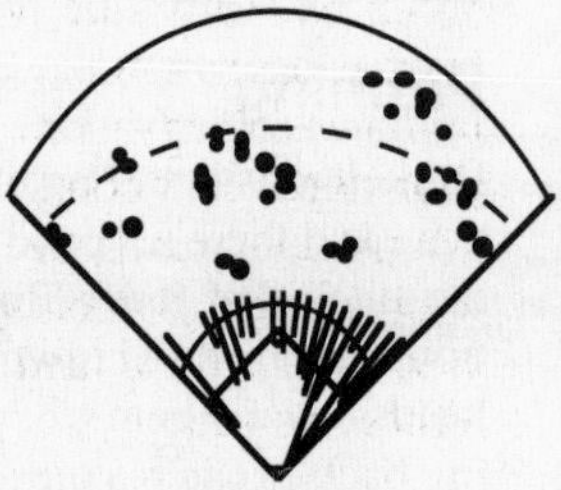

Vs. RHP

### *1995 Situational Stats*

| | AB | H | HR | RBI | Avg | | AB | H | HR | RBI | Avg |
|---|---|---|---|---|---|---|---|---|---|---|---|
| Home | 151 | 40 | 1 | 9 | .265 | LHP | 116 | 36 | 2 | 8 | .310 |
| Road | 157 | 30 | 1 | 11 | .191 | RHP | 192 | 34 | 0 | 12 | .177 |
| First Half | 143 | 32 | 0 | 10 | .224 | Sc Pos | 66 | 15 | 0 | 16 | .227 |
| Scnd Half | 165 | 38 | 2 | 10 | .230 | Clutch | 45 | 11 | 0 | 4 | .244 |

### *1995 Rankings (National League)*

- ➡ 2nd in least GDPs per GDP situation (3.2%)
- ➡ 5th in lowest fielding percentage in center field (.987)
- ➡ 6th in bunts in play (26)
- ➡ 7th in errors in center field (3)
- ➡ 8th in caught stealing (11)
- ➡ 9th in lowest stolen base percentage (69.4%) and on-base percentage vs. left-handed pitchers (.403)
- ➡ Led the Marlins in least GDPs per GDP situation (3.2%)

# Greg Colbrunn

## 1995 Season

Finally, Greg Colbrunn didn't hurt himself. Last season was the first of Colbrunn's professional career in which he played more than 125 games, and the first since 1992 that he topped 100. Given a full season at first base, Colbrunn gave the Marlins the consistent production they'd hoped for, finishing second on the club to Jeff Conine in both home runs and RBI.

## Hitting

Colbrunn's reputation outweighs his performance. A lot of that reputation is due to Colbrunn's pretty swing. He's got decent power, obviously, but it's nothing special for a first baseman. Worse, Colbrunn has very little plate discipline so he rarely reaches base via walk. All things considered, Colbrunn wasn't any more productive last season than shortstop Kurt Abbott. Colbrunn was also pathetic against southpaws. Seeing as how he had a relatively normal platoon split in 1994, it's likely that 1995 was a fluke, and he should do fine against lefties this year.

## Baserunning & Defense

Colbrunn runs well for a first baseman, and he swiped 11 bases last season while being caught only three times. Though Colbrunn has only been a first baseman for a few years—he was a catcher in the Montreal system—he's become a fairly solid defender.

## 1996 Outlook

Early last season, there was talk in Florida of signing free agent Fred McGriff for 1996. But then Colbrunn came on and hit 23 home runs, and given that he comes about $3 million cheaper than McGriff, there will certainly be some sentiment in the Marlin front office to keep Colbrunn. If the Marlins do sign McGriff, Colbrunn and his 89 RBI shouldn't have much trouble finding work. But he'll need to move his game to another level if he's to find long-term security. Still only 26, Colbrunn has plenty of room left for improvement.

**Position:** 1B
**Bats:** R **Throws:** R
**Ht:** 6' 0"  **Wt:** 200

**Opening Day Age:** 26
**Born:** 7/26/69 in Fontana, CA
**ML Seasons:** 4

### Overall Statistics

| | G | AB | R | H | D | T | HR | RBI | SB | BB | SO | Avg | OBP | Slg |
|---|---|---|---|---|---|---|---|---|---|---|---|---|---|---|
| 1995 | 138 | 528 | 70 | 146 | 22 | 1 | 23 | 89 | 11 | 22 | 69 | .277 | .311 | .453 |
| Career | 307 | 1004 | 114 | 277 | 49 | 1 | 35 | 161 | 19 | 43 | 163 | .276 | .309 | .431 |

### Where He Hits the Ball

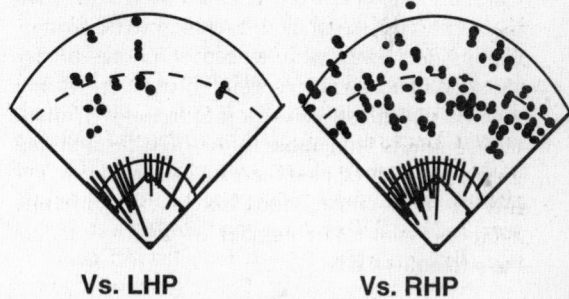

**Vs. LHP**          **Vs. RHP**

### 1995 Situational Stats

| | AB | H | HR | RBI | Avg | | AB | H | HR | RBI | Avg |
|---|---|---|---|---|---|---|---|---|---|---|---|
| Home | 260 | 73 | 12 | 41 | .281 | LHP | 144 | 31 | 3 | 14 | .215 |
| Road | 268 | 73 | 11 | 48 | .272 | RHP | 384 | 115 | 20 | 75 | .299 |
| First Half | 242 | 66 | 8 | 37 | .273 | Sc Pos | 147 | 49 | 8 | 70 | .333 |
| Scnd Half | 286 | 80 | 15 | 52 | .280 | Clutch | 84 | 19 | 4 | 14 | .226 |

### 1995 Rankings (National League)

➡ 1st in batting average on an 0-2 count (.345)
➡ 3rd in lowest on-base percentage vs. left-handed pitchers (.257)
➡ 4th in lowest batting average vs. left-handed pitchers (.215) and fielding percentage at first base (.996)
➡ 8th in lowest on-base percentage and lowest slugging percentage vs. left-handed pitchers (.326)
➡ 9th in GDPs (15) and errors at first base (5)
➡ Led the Marlins in at-bats, GDPs, games played, batting average with runners in scoring position (.333), batting average vs. right-handed pitchers (.299) and batting average on an 0-2 count (.345)

# Jeff Conine

## 1995 Season

It was another solid season for Jeff Conine, who posted numbers very similar to his 1994 breakthrough campaign. Not that the season was without its negatives. On May 29, Conine's N.L.-high consecutive-games streak was napped at 307 because of a strained hamstring, and he later missed 10 days with shoulder soreness after a collision. But those downers were balanced by Conine's eighth-inning, pinch-hit home run that gave the National League a 3-2 victory in the All-Star Game. For that swing, Conine was named MVP of the Mid-Summer Classic.

## Hitting

Conine starts with his hands a bit forward, which means he's got to get them back before he swings. Conine gets away with it because he has a very short, compact swing, especially for such a strong guy. He doesn't strike out a lot for a power hitter, but Conine is vulnerable to the high fastball and goes through stretches where he has problems laying off other pitches, too. But his .300 lifetime average—with a fair number of walks—renders the strikeouts trivial.

## Baserunning & Defense

No one can accuse Conine of not running the bases *hard*. But he does know his limitations, and rarely moves around more than one base at a time. That lack of speed—not to mention experience—makes Conine a liability in left field. He'll generally catch what he gets to, and has a decent arm. Conine's best position is first base—the one he played in the minors—but so far the Marlins have been reluctant to move him back.

## 1996 Outlook

Based on the last two seasons, Conine probably should be considered one of the top 10 hitters in the National League. The club appreciates Conine, and last June they signed him to a three-year contract extension that should have him in Marlin teal through the 1998 season, at least.

**Position:** LF/1B
**Bats:** R  **Throws:** R
**Ht:** 6' 1"  **Wt:** 220

**Opening Day Age:** 29
**Born:** 6/27/66 in Tacoma, WA
**ML Seasons:** 5
**Pronunciation:** COH-nine

### Overall Statistics

| | G | AB | R | H | D | T | HR | RBI | SB | BB | SO | Avg | OBP | Slg |
|---|---|---|---|---|---|---|---|---|---|---|---|---|---|---|
| 1995 | 133 | 483 | 72 | 146 | 26 | 2 | 25 | 105 | 2 | 66 | 94 | .302 | .379 | .520 |
| Career | 447 | 1640 | 220 | 492 | 84 | 13 | 55 | 277 | 5 | 168 | 349 | .300 | .363 | .468 |

### Where He Hits the Ball

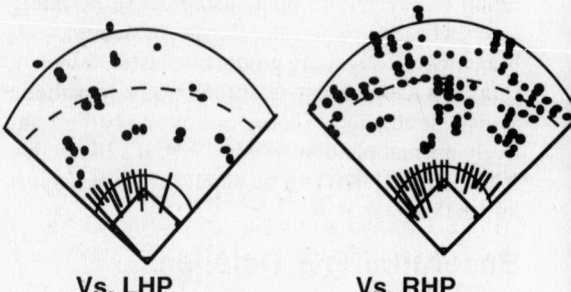

**Vs. LHP**          **Vs. RHP**

### 1995 Situational Stats

| | AB | H | HR | RBI | Avg | | AB | H | HR | RBI | Avg |
|---|---|---|---|---|---|---|---|---|---|---|---|
| Home | 243 | 85 | 13 | 52 | .350 | LHP | 120 | 38 | 9 | 24 | .317 |
| Road | 240 | 61 | 12 | 53 | .254 | RHP | 363 | 108 | 16 | 81 | .298 |
| First Half | 227 | 73 | 14 | 48 | .322 | Sc Pos | 149 | 48 | 7 | 80 | .322 |
| Scnd Half | 256 | 73 | 11 | 57 | .285 | Clutch | 74 | 17 | 2 | 19 | .230 |

### 1995 Rankings (National League)

- ➤ 1st in sacrifice flies (12)
- ➤ 2nd in lowest groundball/flyball ratio (0.7)
- ➤ 3rd in lowest fielding percentage in left field (.976)
- ➤ 4th in RBI and errors in left field (5)
- ➤ 5th in batting average at home (.350)
- ➤ 6th in slugging percentage vs. left-handed pitchers (.592)
- ➤ 7th in on-base percentage vs. left-handed pitchers (.407)
- ➤ 9th in slugging percentage
- ➤ Led the Marlins in batting average, home runs, total bases (251), RBI, sacrifice flies, times on base (213), plate appearances (562) and slugging percentage

# Andre Dawson

## 1995 Season

The plan was for Andre Dawson to close his career living the life of ease: start occasionally, pinch hit frequently, and provide that "veteran leadership" which every team thinks it needs. A good plan, perhaps, but it didn't work out that way, not with an injury to Gary Sheffield in June. Dawson wound up starting 46 games in right field, and 11 more in left for good measure.

## Hitting

Dawson's bat isn't as quick as it once was, but it's still hard to get a fastball by him. Unfortunately, National League pitchers are well aware of that fact, and they also know that Dawson is—as he has always been—vulnerable to the breaking ball, especially when delivered from righthanders low and away. On the other hand, Dawson brutalized southpaws last season for 11 extra-base hits in 80 at-bats.

## Baserunning & Defense

Andre Dawson owns two of the more famous knees in sports history; they'd been operated on 10 times entering 1995. So even if he weren't 41, Dawson wouldn't exactly be burning up the basepaths. He does make good decisions, which most of the time means stopping where he is. Dawson's slowness afoot limits his range in the outfield, of course. He committed eight errors as well, so the defensive package at this point is not a pretty one.

## 1996 Outlook

Believe it or not, Dawson underwent yet *another* knee surgery after the season. Nevertheless, he expressed a desire to play again, but only in Florida. Though Dawson appears to have very little left, Rene Lachemann appreciated Dawson's contributions and might want him back. Used in a limited role—specifically, as a pinch hitter against lefties—Dawson wouldn't be a bad guy to have on the club. Let's hope for a dignified end to Dawson's Hall of Fame career.

**Position:** RF/LF
**Bats:** R **Throws:** R
**Ht:** 6' 3" **Wt:** 197

**Opening Day Age:** 41
**Born:** 7/10/54 in Miami, FL
**ML Seasons:** 20
**Nickname:** Hawk

### Overall Statistics

|  | G | AB | R | H | D | T | HR | RBI | SB | BB | SO | Avg | OBP | Slg |
|---|---|---|---|---|---|---|---|---|---|---|---|---|---|---|
| 1995 | 79 | 226 | 30 | 58 | 10 | 3 | 8 | 37 | 0 | 9 | 45 | .257 | .305 | .434 |
| Career | 2585 | 9869 | 1367 | 2758 | 501 | 98 | 436 | 1577 | 314 | 587 | 1496 | .279 | .323 | .483 |

### Where He Hits the Ball

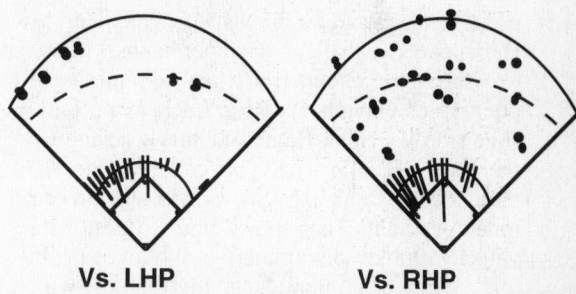

**Vs. LHP**　　　　**Vs. RHP**

### 1995 Situational Stats

|  | AB | H | HR | RBI | Avg |  | AB | H | HR | RBI | Avg |
|---|---|---|---|---|---|---|---|---|---|---|---|
| Home | 110 | 24 | 1 | 13 | .218 | LHP | 80 | 25 | 4 | 18 | .313 |
| Road | 116 | 34 | 7 | 24 | .293 | RHP | 146 | 33 | 4 | 19 | .226 |
| First Half | 104 | 24 | 4 | 15 | .231 | Sc Pos | 68 | 17 | 4 | 27 | .250 |
| Scnd Half | 122 | 34 | 4 | 22 | .279 | Clutch | 44 | 7 | 0 | 0 | .159 |

### 1995 Rankings (National League)

➡ 4th in errors in right field (6)
➡ 5th in lowest batting average in the clutch (.159)
➡ 9th in lowest batting average on a 3-2 count (.091)

**Florida Marlins**

# Chris Hammond

## 1995 Season

At the All-Star break, Chris Hammond's 2.55 ERA ranked third in the National League. And he opened the second half of the season with a three-hit shutout of the Dodgers, dropping the ERA to 2.28. But hard times hit in August, as they seem to every year for Hammond. First he spent 18 days on the disabled list with biceps tendinitis. And when he returned to the rotation Hammond was pounded, posting a 6.19 ERA over the season's final two months. Overall, though, it was a successful campaign, Hammond's second in as many years.

## Pitching

Hammond's change-up is feared around the National League, and he throws a decent slider, too. Hammond's fastball, on the other hand, is nothing to write home about. But when he's mixing his pitches, it's enough. As Rene Lachemann said in June after watching Hammond throw a shutout at the Mets, "That's what you call pitching right there. I don't think his velocity was over 86 or 87 miles per hour. That shows you it doesn't take velocity. It takes disrupting the rhythm of the hitter." When Hammond gets in trouble—which doesn't happen much anymore—it's often when he loses confidence in his fastball.

## Defense & Hitting

Hammond helps himself defensively and at the plate. He is perhaps the toughest pitcher in the majors to steal against. All seven runners trying to steal last season were caught, and Hammond picked another two runners off base himself. He is agile around the mound but will make an occasional error. One of the best-hitting pitchers around, Hammond batted .271 last season with a home run, the fourth of his career.

## 1996 Outlook

Thanks to an injury in 1994, Hammond's record over the last two seasons is just 13-10. But his ERA over that same span is 3.57, a fine mark in this hitter-happy era. If he can somehow avoid the second-half woes which have troubled him in recent years, *and* stay healthy, Hammond is a great bet for 14 or more wins.

**Position:** SP
**Bats:** L **Throws:** L
**Ht:** 6' 1" **Wt:** 195

**Opening Day Age:** 30
**Born:** 1/21/66 in Atlanta, GA
**ML Seasons:** 6

### Overall Statistics

| | W | L | Pct. | ERA | G | GS | Sv | IP | H | BB | SO | HR | BR/IP |
|---|---|---|---|---|---|---|---|---|---|---|---|---|---|
| 1995 | 9 | 6 | .600 | 3.80 | 25 | 24 | 0 | 161.0 | 157 | 47 | 126 | 17 | 1.27 |
| Career | 38 | 41 | .481 | 4.13 | 121 | 116 | 0 | 683.2 | 697 | 251 | 407 | 59 | 1.39 |

### How Often He Throws Strikes

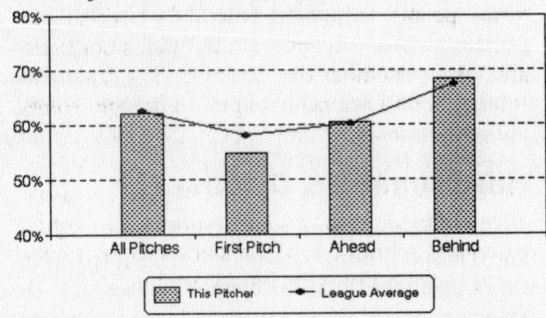

### 1995 Situational Stats

| | W | L | ERA | Sv | IP | | AB | H | HR | RBI | Avg |
|---|---|---|---|---|---|---|---|---|---|---|---|
| Home | 5 | 3 | 3.15 | 0 | 80.0 | LHB | 106 | 23 | 2 | 12 | .217 |
| Road | 4 | 3 | 4.44 | 0 | 81.0 | RHB | 507 | 134 | 15 | 53 | .264 |
| First Half | 5 | 2 | 2.55 | 0 | 74.0 | Sc Pos | 141 | 26 | 1 | 36 | .184 |
| Scnd Half | 4 | 4 | 4.86 | 0 | 87.0 | Clutch | 44 | 17 | 2 | 10 | .386 |

### 1995 Rankings (National League)

→ 1st in lowest stolen base percentage allowed (0.0%)
→ 2nd in lowest batting average allowed with runners in scoring position (.184)
→ 3rd in shutouts (2)
→ 5th in most run support per 9 innings (5.7)
→ 7th in hit batsmen (9)
→ 9th in complete games (3)
→ 10th in highest strikeout/walk ratio (2.7) and most strikeouts per 9 innings (7.0)
→ Led the Marlins in shutouts, hit batsmen, strikeouts, highest strikeout/walk ratio and lowest on-base percentage allowed (.315)

# Charles Johnson

## 1995 Season

On June 22, rookie catcher Charles Johnson, playing nearly every day, was hitting just .142. The Marlins must have been tempted to send him to Triple-A—Johnson skipped that level on his way to the majors—but they resisted because the young backstop was playing so well defensively. That was a good move, because he soon went on a tear with the bat. By the time his season ended on September 18—thanks to a minor knee injury, on the heels of a hand injury which cost him three weeks in August—Johnson had lifted his average from that lowly .142 to .251.

## Hitting

When people talk about Johnson's hitting, they usually focus on his power. And that's considerable. But remember this number: .351. That was Johnson's on-base percentage last season, something most people didn't notice, and it was better than that of teammates Kurt Abbott, Terry Pendleton and even Greg Colbrunn. In fact, on a per at-bat basis Johnson was just as productive as first baseman Colbrunn. Johnson's ability to work the count bodes well for his future as a hitter.

## Baserunning & Defense

For a young player, even a catcher, Johnson is slow. Now on to the good stuff. . . Even when Johnson was below the Mendoza Line, his defense was so impressive that Marlins GM Dave Dombrowski touted him as the best catcher in the league, and Terry Pendleton suggested that Johnson was worthy of All-Star consideration. Johnson backed those opinions up with his throwing arm. He tossed out 41 percent of the runners trying to steal, the best figure in the National League. How impressed were N.L. managers and coaches? Johnson captured a Gold Glove despite his injuries and inexperience.

## 1996 Outlook

How good can Charles Johnson be? Only time will tell. In the short term, he has already been recognized as the top defensive catcher in the National League. His second-half hitting surge suggests that he might soon be one of the better *hitting* catchers in the league, too.

**Position:** C
**Bats:** R **Throws:** R
**Ht:** 6' 2"  **Wt:** 215

**Opening Day Age:** 24
**Born:** 7/20/71 in Fort Pierce, Florida
**ML Seasons:** 2

### Overall Statistics

|  | G | AB | R | H | D | T | HR | RBI | SB | BB | SO | Avg | OBP | Slg |
|---|---|---|---|---|---|---|---|---|---|---|---|---|---|---|
| 1995 | 97 | 315 | 40 | 79 | 15 | 1 | 11 | 39 | 0 | 46 | 71 | .251 | .351 | .410 |
| Career | 101 | 326 | 45 | 84 | 16 | 1 | 12 | 43 | 0 | 47 | 75 | .258 | .355 | .423 |

### Where He Hits the Ball

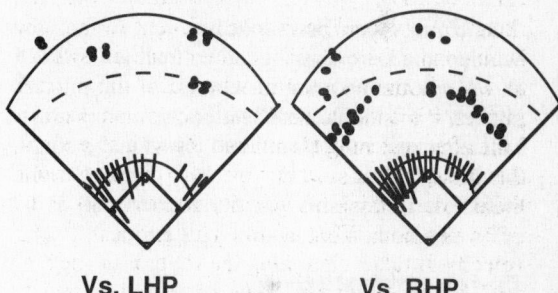

**Vs. LHP**          **Vs. RHP**

### 1995 Situational Stats

|  | AB | H | HR | RBI | Avg |  | AB | H | HR | RBI | Avg |
|---|---|---|---|---|---|---|---|---|---|---|---|
| Home | 157 | 36 | 3 | 12 | .229 | LHP | 83 | 24 | 3 | 12 | .289 |
| Road | 158 | 43 | 8 | 27 | .272 | RHP | 232 | 55 | 8 | 27 | .237 |
| First Half | 189 | 39 | 6 | 22 | .206 | Sc Pos | 79 | 20 | 1 | 25 | .253 |
| Scnd Half | 126 | 40 | 5 | 17 | .317 | Clutch | 47 | 11 | 2 | 6 | .234 |

### 1995 Rankings (National League)

- ➡ 1st in highest percentage of runners caught stealing as a catcher (41.4%)
- ➡ 10th in errors at catcher (6) and highest percentage of swings that missed (27.3%)

**Florida Marlins**

# Terry Mathews

## 1995 Season

A fifth-round draft pick of the Texas Rangers in 1987, Terry Mathews established himself as a prospect by going 13-6 a year later in the Florida State League. After two partial seasons with the major league Rangers, Mathews spent a year in the Houston organization before signing with Florida for 1994. After splitting that season between Triple-A and the majors, Mathews enjoyed his first full big-league season in 1995. Perhaps the most versatile member of the Marlin bullpen, Mathews had outings ranging from one batter to four innings, and generally pitched well no matter how he was used.

## Pitching

The chunky Mathews pitches out of a slow windup, but generates a good fastball which he'll throw repeatedly when his control of the pitch is sharp. Against left-handed hitters, he cuts the fastball to make it run away. When ahead in the count, Mathews will throw a big-breaking curve. His one weakness last season was the gopher ball, as he allowed nine homers in only 82.2 innings.

## Defense & Hitting

Mathews is a competent fielder, though he doesn't exactly roam around the infield looking for extra plays to make. Carrying on the tradition of portly pitchers like Terry Forster and Don Robinson, Mathews is—so far at least—a pretty good hitter. In college, Mathews played first base and even designated hitter when he wasn't pitching, and he is now 9-for-19 at the plate in the majors.

## 1996 Outlook

In two seasons, Mathews' National League ERA stands at a respectable 3.37. His fine overall performance last season marks him as the number-one candidate to serve as Robb Nen's primary set-up man in 1996. Barring that, Mathews won't have any trouble finding work, and well-paid work at that.

**Position:** RP
**Bats:** L **Throws:** R
**Ht:** 6' 2"  **Wt:** 225

**Opening Day Age:** 31
**Born:** 10/5/64 in Alexandria, LA
**ML Seasons:** 4

### Overall Statistics

|  | W | L | Pct. | ERA | G | GS | Sv | IP | H | BB | SO | HR | BR/IP |
|---|---|---|---|---|---|---|---|---|---|---|---|---|---|
| 1995 | 4 | 4 | .500 | 3.38 | 57 | 0 | 3 | 82.2 | 70 | 27 | 72 | 9 | 1.17 |
| Career | 12 | 9 | .571 | 3.91 | 155 | 4 | 4 | 225.1 | 217 | 85 | 170 | 22 | 1.34 |

### How Often He Throws Strikes

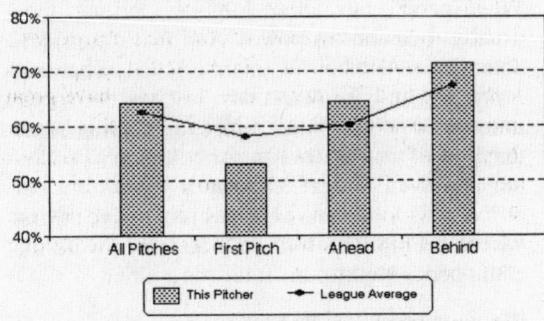

### 1995 Situational Stats

|  | W | L | ERA | Sv | IP |  | AB | H | HR | RBI | Avg |
|---|---|---|---|---|---|---|---|---|---|---|---|
| Home | 2 | 2 | 2.74 | 1 | 46.0 | LHB | 119 | 27 | 4 | 16 | .227 |
| Road | 2 | 2 | 4.17 | 2 | 36.2 | RHB | 179 | 43 | 5 | 24 | .240 |
| First Half | 2 | 1 | 2.79 | 2 | 48.1 | Sc Pos | 72 | 20 | 2 | 31 | .278 |
| Scnd Half | 2 | 3 | 4.19 | 1 | 34.1 | Clutch | 99 | 27 | 3 | 17 | .273 |

### 1995 Rankings (National League)

→ 8th in highest percentage of inherited runners scored (37.1%) and relief innings (82.2)
→ Led the Marlins in relief innings, lowest batting average allowed in relief (.235) and least baserunners allowed per 9 innings in relief (10.7)

# Robb Nen

## 1995 Season

Robb Nen was brilliant in 1994, converting all 15 of his save opportunities and striking out a batter per inning. So with Bryan Harvey still not healthy, Nen opened 1995 as the Marlins' closer. But after he gave up a game-ending home run June 5 against the Astros for his fourth loss, manager Rene Lachemann soon demoted him from closer to set-up man. Nen pitched well in that role for a month, and no one could establish themself as the club's closer. So Nen was returned to his old job in mid-July, and from then on he compiled a 2.45 ERA, struck out 40 batters in 33 innings, and most importantly, he converted 19 of 22 save chances.

## Pitching

In May, Lachemann told Nen that he simply had to throw his curveball more. True, Nen's fastball tops out in the mid-90s range, but it doesn't have great movement and even a 95-MPH fastball isn't un-hittable when it's straight. After a brief period of adjustment, Nen was better able to mix his fast-ball, curve, and tight slider, and as a result was one of the game's dominant pitchers over the second half of the season.

## Defense & Hitting

Nen doesn't have a particularly wild motion; in fact, he has a fairly compact delivery for such a hard thrower. However, basestealers had an easy time of it last season, succeeding on all 12 of their attempts. Nen doesn't look very graceful—not surprising given his size—but he's a decent fielder. Despite his brief foray into the wonderful world of middle relief, Nen didn't get to bat last year. He is hitless in seven major league at-bats.

## 1996 Outlook

Last year's struggles were a normal roadblock for a young pitcher in just his first full season as a closer. With top N.L. closers like Randy Myers and Tom Henke approaching baseball old age, Nen appears poised to take his place among the league's premier relievers, and it could happen as soon as this summer.

**Position:** RP
**Bats:** R **Throws:** R
**Ht:** 6' 4" **Wt:** 190

**Opening Day Age:** 26
**Born:** 11/28/69 in San Pedro, CA
**ML Seasons:** 3

### Overall Statistics

|        | W | L  | Pct. | ERA  | G   | GS | Sv | IP    | H   | BB | SO  | HR | BR/IP |
|--------|---|----|------|------|-----|----|----|-------|-----|----|-----|----|-------|
| 1995   | 0 | 7  | .000 | 3.29 | 62  | 0  | 23 | 65.2  | 62  | 23 | 68  | 6  | 1.29  |
| Career | 7 | 13 | .350 | 4.26 | 130 | 4  | 38 | 179.2 | 171 | 86 | 167 | 18 | 1.43  |

### How Often He Throws Strikes

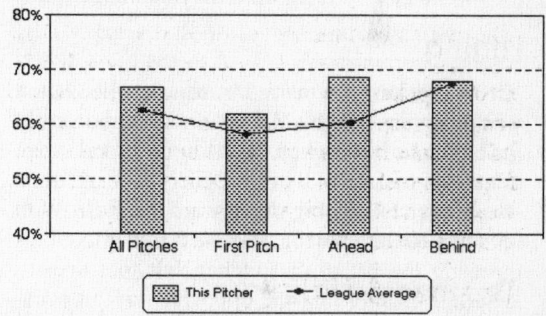

### 1995 Situational Stats

|            | W | L | ERA  | Sv | IP   |        | AB  | H  | HR | RBI | Avg  |
|------------|---|---|------|----|------|--------|-----|----|----|-----|------|
| Home       | 0 | 5 | 4.30 | 11 | 37.2 | LHB    | 121 | 33 | 3  | 16  | .273 |
| Road       | 0 | 2 | 1.93 | 12 | 28.0 | RHB    | 133 | 29 | 3  | 12  | .218 |
| First Half | 0 | 5 | 4.26 | 4  | 31.2 | Sc Pos | 84  | 17 | 2  | 21  | .202 |
| Scnd Half  | 0 | 2 | 2.38 | 19 | 34.0 | Clutch | 154 | 37 | 5  | 23  | .240 |

### 1995 Rankings (National League)

- → 1st in games finished (54)
- → 2nd in relief losses (7)
- → 5th in most strikeouts per 9 innings in relief (9.3)
- → 6th in lowest save percentage (79.3%) and blown saves (6)
- → 10th in save opportunities (29)
- → Led the Marlins in saves, games finished, stolen bases allowed (12), save opportunities, save percentage, blown saves, lowest batting average allowed in relief with runners on base (.212), relief ERA (3.29), relief losses and most strikeouts per 9 innings in relief

**Florida Marlins**

# Terry Pendleton

## 1995 Season

With Chipper Jones healthy, the Braves made no attempt to re-sign free-agent Terry Pendleton for 1995. So the Marlins came calling, with the hopes that Pendleton could do for them exactly what he'd done for Atlanta in 1991: collect some key hits and stabilize the infield defense. Convinced that the strike would last until June or July, Pendleton gave up his offseason conditioning program in February, and as a result he reported to training camp 10 pounds overweight, which might explain his .239 May average. In the summer months, however, Pendleton batted a sizzling .337 with 47 RBI. Unfortunately, he slumped in September to drop his average below .300. Throughout, he gave the Marlins the solid defense they had hoped for.

## Hitting

After a 1994 season marred by injuries, Pendleton was relatively healthy last year, and it showed in his hitting as he cranked out 14 homers and drove home 78 runs. Pendleton begins with an open stance, then takes a big step toward the plate. With his long, looping swing, it almost looks like he's throwing the bat at the pitcher, but that doesn't keep him from going the opposite way on occasion. The switch-hitter prefers low pitches when he's batting lefty, high pitches when batting righty. As usual, Pendleton hit for better power as a right-handed hitter.

## Baserunning & Defense

Once fairly fast despite his pudgy build, Pendleton's age and injuries have cost him most of that speed. He's a decent baserunner but doesn't steal anymore. Pendleton's defensive skills have also deteriorated. Though he's still capable of making the lightning stab to snare hard grounders, Pendleton's Gold Glove range is just a memory. He leads the universe in visits to the mound.

## 1996 Season

Pendleton is a free agent at this writing, and it's unclear as to whether or not the Fish want him back. The Marlins currently don't have any other candidates for third base, so Pendleton might be back in 1996. Either way, he'll play somewhere.

**Position:** 3B
**Bats:** B **Throws:** R
**Ht:** 5' 9" **Wt:** 195

**Opening Day Age:** 35
**Born:** 7/16/60 in Los Angeles, CA
**ML Seasons:** 12

### Overall Statistics

|  | G | AB | R | H | D | T | HR | RBI | SB | BB | SO | Avg | OBP | Slg |
|---|---|---|---|---|---|---|---|---|---|---|---|---|---|---|
| 1995 | 133 | 513 | 70 | 149 | 32 | 1 | 14 | 78 | 1 | 38 | 84 | .290 | .339 | .439 |
| Career | 1611 | 6114 | 772 | 1673 | 311 | 38 | 125 | 825 | 122 | 418 | 805 | .274 | .318 | .398 |

### Where He Hits the Ball

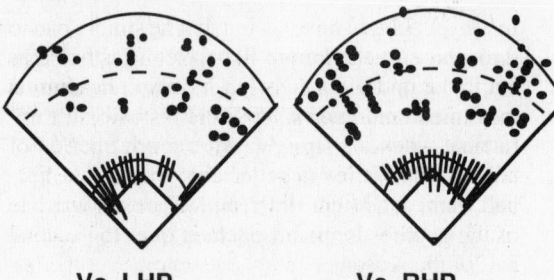

**Vs. LHP**          **Vs. RHP**

### 1995 Situational Stats

|  | AB | H | HR | RBI | Avg |  | AB | H | HR | RBI | Avg |
|---|---|---|---|---|---|---|---|---|---|---|---|
| Home | 267 | 85 | 8 | 43 | .318 | LHP | 149 | 50 | 3 | 23 | .336 |
| Road | 246 | 64 | 6 | 35 | .260 | RHP | 364 | 99 | 11 | 55 | .272 |
| First Half | 239 | 71 | 6 | 39 | .297 | Sc Pos | 134 | 43 | 4 | 59 | .321 |
| Scnd Half | 274 | 78 | 8 | 39 | .285 | Clutch | 85 | 25 | 1 | 12 | .294 |

### 1995 Rankings (National League)

- ➡ 1st in batting average on a 3-1 count (.750)
- ➡ 3rd in errors at third base (18)
- ➡ 4th in lowest cleanup slugging percentage (.432)
- ➡ 5th in fielding percentage at third base (.951) and lowest percentage of extra bases taken as a runner (37.7%)
- ➡ 9th in batting average at home (.318)
- ➡ 10th in batting average on an 0-2 count (.286)
- ➡ Led the Marlins in hits, singles (102), doubles, batting average vs. left-handed pitchers (.336) , batting average on a 3-1 count and batting average with two strikes (.241)

# Yorkis Perez

## 1995 Season

How many pitchers have gone to Japan, then made a successful return to the major leagues? Let's see, there's Goose Gossage, Bill Gullickson. . . and Yorkis Perez. After nine years in the minors—not including three games with the Cubs in 1991—Perez pitched briefly for the Yomiuri Giants in 1992. Following one season as an Expo farmhand, Perez signed with the Marlins as a free agent, and he's been their situational lefty ever since. And don't let that 5.21 ERA fool you; Perez did exactly what he's paid to do last year, which is retire left-handed hitters every game or two. His 69 mound appearances ranked fourth in the National League.

## Pitching

As opposed to someone like Tony Fossas, Perez isn't your prototypical lefty junkballer. In addition to his fine curve and slider, Perez throws a decent fastball as well. Against left-handed hitters, of course, Perez tries to get ahead with the fastball and then fool them with the offspeed stuff. He usually succeeds; he held lefties to a .157 batting average last season, and a .173 mark over the last two campaigns. Perez' fastball gives him a decent chance against righties, too. Against them, he mostly nibbles on the outside with all three of his pitches, resulting in too many walks. His other weakness is a penchant for giving up home runs.

## Defense & Hitting

Though he's been a pro for 13 seasons now, some of the finer points of the game—like fielding and holding runners—continue to elude Perez. He's not real quick off the mound, and a mediocre move to first allowed basestealers to succeed last season on seven of eight attempts. Perez is 0-for-4, with three strikeouts, as a hitter in his career.

## 1996 Outlook

If Perez can continue doing what he's done so far—shut down left-handed hitters along with a fair share of righties—he'll be a major leaguer for another decade. As the only reliable lefty in the Marlin bullpen last season, Perez is wanted back in Flordida.

**Position:** RP
**Bats:** L  **Throws:** L
**Ht:** 6' 0"  **Wt:** 180

**Opening Day Age:** 28
**Born:** 9/30/67 in Bajos de Haina, DR
**ML Seasons:** 3

### Overall Statistics

|        | W | L | Pct. | ERA  | G   | GS | Sv | IP   | H  | BB | SO | HR | BR/IP |
|--------|---|---|------|------|-----|----|----|------|----|----|----|----|-------|
| 1995   | 2 | 6 | .250 | 5.21 | 69  | 0  | 1  | 46.2 | 35 | 28 | 47 | 6  | 1.35  |
| Career | 6 | 6 | .500 | 4.32 | 116 | 0  | 1  | 91.2 | 70 | 44 | 91 | 10 | 1.24  |

### How Often He Throws Strikes

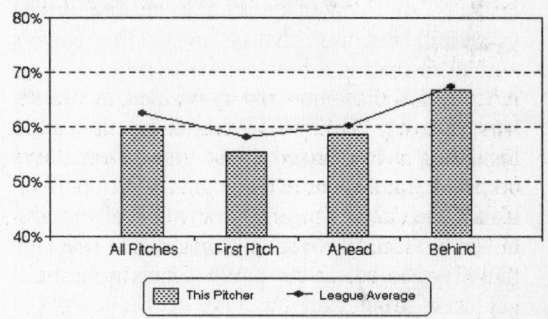

### 1995 Situational Stats

|            | W | L | ERA   | Sv | IP   |        | AB | H  | HR | RBI | Avg  |
|------------|---|---|-------|----|------|--------|----|----|----|-----|------|
| Home       | 1 | 2 | 1.67  | 1  | 32.1 | LHB    | 83 | 13 | 3  | 10  | .157 |
| Road       | 1 | 4 | 13.19 | 0  | 14.1 | RHB    | 89 | 22 | 3  | 13  | .247 |
| First Half | 0 | 3 | 6.41  | 1  | 26.2 | Sc Pos | 50 | 9  | 1  | 12  | .180 |
| Scnd Half  | 2 | 3 | 3.60  | 0  | 20.0 | Clutch | 89 | 22 | 4  | 13  | .247 |

### 1995 Rankings (National League)

- ➡ 2nd in first batter efficiency (.105) and lowest percentage of inherited runners scored (14.3%)
- ➡ 4th in games pitched
- ➡ 5th in relief losses (6)
- ➡ 7th in holds (16)
- ➡ Led the Marlins in games pitched, holds, first batter efficiency, lowest batting average allowed in relief with runners in scoring position (.180) and lowest percentage of inherited runners scored

# Pat Rapp

## Pitching

After leading Marlin starters with a 3.85 ERA in 1994, Pat Rapp got off to a slow start in 1995. By the end of July he was muddling along at 4-6 with a 4.64 ERA. But Rapp was simply brilliant from then on. In 12 August/September starts, Rapp went 10-1 with a 2.14 ERA, and assumed the mantle of staff ace. The highlight of Rapp's season was probably September 7, when he no-hit the Braves for 6.1 innings before settling for a four-hit victory. Rapp finished with a fine 3.44 ERA, breaking the team mark he set in 1994.

## Pitching

Rapp has a very good curveball, throws two fastballs, and worked on a circle change-up last year. Neither of his fastballs is outstanding. Rapp's normal fastball is a four-seamer that behaves almost like a slider, moving down and in to left-handed hitters. His two-seamer comes in a little faster and a lot straighter. At times Rapp loses confidence in his curve and wants to rely only on his fastballs, which rarely works to his advantage. Given his lack of velocity, Rapp has to keep the ball down to be effective. When he's right, he'll get lots of groundball outs.

## Defense & Hitting

Rapp is perhaps the toughest righthander in the majors to run on, due to his extreme quickness to the plate. Of the 20 runners who attempted to steal last season, 15 were gunned down! Otherwise, Rapp is adequate defensively. He's a .131 lifetime hitter—about average—and a pretty good bunter.

## 1996 Outlook

Not only has Rapp been the most effective starter in the Marlins' (admittedly) brief history, he's also been the healthiest, and hasn't missed a start since 1993. Though he doesn't strike out enough batters to be regarded as a dominant starter, Rapp is a solid major league pitcher and deserves an Opening Day assignment.

**Position:** SP
**Bats:** R **Throws:** R
**Ht:** 6' 3" **Wt:** 215

**Opening Day Age:** 28
**Born:** 7/13/67 in Jennings, LA
**ML Seasons:** 4

### Overall Statistics

|  | W | L | Pct. | ERA | G | GS | Sv | IP | H | BB | SO | HR | BR/IP |
|---|---|---|---|---|---|---|---|---|---|---|---|---|---|
| 1995 | 14 | 7 | .667 | 3.44 | 28 | 28 | 0 | 167.1 | 158 | 76 | 102 | 10 | 1.40 |
| Career | 25 | 23 | .521 | 3.80 | 71 | 69 | 0 | 404.2 | 399 | 190 | 237 | 30 | 1.46 |

### How Often He Throws Strikes

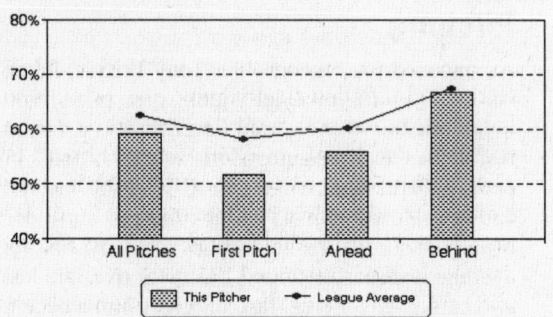

### 1995 Situational Stats

|  | W | L | ERA | Sv | IP |  | AB | H | HR | RBI | Avg |
|---|---|---|---|---|---|---|---|---|---|---|---|
| Home | 6 | 4 | 3.55 | 0 | 78.2 | LHB | 293 | 71 | 4 | 25 | .242 |
| Road | 8 | 3 | 3.35 | 0 | 88.2 | RHB | 332 | 87 | 6 | 35 | .262 |
| First Half | 3 | 5 | 4.95 | 0 | 72.2 | Sc Pos | 163 | 34 | 2 | 41 | .209 |
| Scnd Half | 11 | 2 | 2.28 | 0 | 94.2 | Clutch | 10 | 4 | 1 | 2 | .400 |

### 1995 Rankings (National League)

- ➙ 1st in runners caught stealing (15), lowest strikeout/walk ratio (1.3) and most pitches thrown per batter (3.95)
- ➙ 2nd in most run support per 9 innings (6.2)
- ➙ 3rd in shutouts (2), walks allowed, lowest stolen base percentage allowed (25.0%) and least home runs allowed per 9 innings (.54)
- ➙ 5th in wins
- ➙ 6th in lowest slugging percentage allowed (.350) and least strikeouts per 9 innings (5.5)
- ➙ 7th in highest on-base percentage allowed (.340) and most GDPs induced per 9 innings (0.9)
- ➙ Led the Marlins in sacrifice bunts (9), ERA, wins, shutouts and walks allowed

# Gary Sheffield

## 1995 Season

On June 10, Gary Sheffield suffered a torn ligament in his left thumb, and the initial prognosis was that he'd be lost for the season. The injury was especially crushing because at the time, Sheffield was third in the National League in on-base average, second in walks and third in stolen bases. His power and RBI were down, but that was largely because National League pitchers refused to throw him strikes in critical situations. Anyway, Sheffield stumped the doctors by returning to the lineup in September; what's more, he showed no ill effects from the injury, walloping four homers in his first five games back.

## Hitting

In a sense, Sheffield defies the laws of baseball. How can a man who swings so hard strike out so rarely? Perhaps that's the answer: His swing is *so* quick that he can wait until the very last instant to trigger it, and the result is that he's very hard to fool. Pitchers don't dare throw him fastballs in the strike zone, which leaves them reduced to throwing offspeed stuff. Sheffield is rarely fooled by those offerings, either, and the result in 1995 was all those walks. Give him credit, too. Instead of getting frustrated and expanding his strike zone, Sheffield took the free base.

## Baserunning & Defense

After becoming less aggressive on the basepaths a few years ago to avoid injuries, Sheffield broke loose last season, and would have swiped 40 or more bases if he hadn't been sidelined. He is still learning to play the outfield, and his range remains poor. Given his speed and decent arm strength, one would think there is potential. But if Sheffield doesn't start getting better, the Marlins should probably consider the ultimate shift: first base.

## 1996 Outlook

If Sheffield can stay healthy for the entire season, he will almost certainly rank among the top four or five hitters in the National League. Remember, back in 1992 he came just a few homers and RBI short of a Triple Crown. And you know the scary thing? Sheffield is still only 27.

**Position:** RF
**Bats:** R  **Throws:** R
**Ht:** 5'11"  **Wt:** 190

**Opening Day Age:** 27
**Born:** 11/18/68 in Tampa, FL
**ML Seasons:** 8

### Overall Statistics

| | G | AB | R | H | D | T | HR | RBI | SB | BB | SO | Avg | OBP | Slg |
|---|---|---|---|---|---|---|---|---|---|---|---|---|---|---|
| 1995 | 63 | 213 | 46 | 69 | 8 | 0 | 16 | 46 | 19 | 55 | 45 | .324 | .467 | .587 |
| Career | 730 | 2696 | 399 | 774 | 139 | 12 | 117 | 430 | 96 | 298 | 295 | .287 | .361 | .478 |

### Where He Hits the Ball

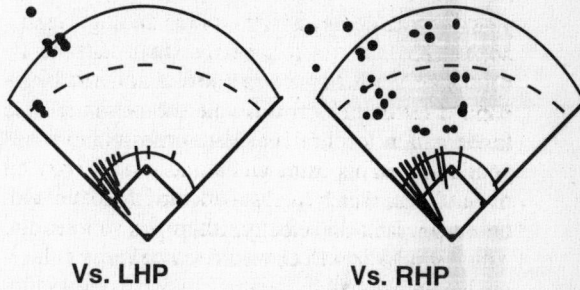

**Vs. LHP**          **Vs. RHP**

### 1995 Situational Stats

| | AB | H | HR | RBI | Avg | | AB | H | HR | RBI | Avg |
|---|---|---|---|---|---|---|---|---|---|---|---|
| Home | 102 | 34 | 4 | 17 | .333 | LHP | 61 | 20 | 3 | 8 | .328 |
| Road | 111 | 35 | 12 | 29 | .315 | RHP | 152 | 49 | 13 | 38 | .322 |
| First Half | 143 | 45 | 6 | 19 | .315 | Sc Pos | 51 | 15 | 6 | 34 | .294 |
| Scnd Half | 70 | 24 | 10 | 27 | .343 | Clutch | 33 | 10 | 2 | 8 | .303 |

### 1995 Rankings (National League)

- → 5th in errors in right field (5)
- → 10th in least GDPs per GDP situation (5.5%) and batting average with the bases loaded (.429)
- → Led the Marlins in intentional walks (8), stolen base percentage (82.6%), batting average in the clutch (.303) and batting average with the bases loaded

**Florida Marlins**

# Quilvio Veras

## 1995 Season

You have to give the Marlins a lot of credit. Quilvio Veras posted .400-plus on-base percentages at every stop in the Mets' minor league system, until 1994 when he suffered the effects of a partial shoulder tear. That November, Florida acquired Veras in exchange for Carl Everett. Veras was a revelation. He carried a poor batting average for most of the season but he walked a ton, and Marcel Lachemann put him in the leadoff slot and left him there. Sometimes Veras' inexperience showed, as when he was benched for one game in May after missing yet another sign. Overall, though, 1995 was marred only by a pulled hamstring that cost Veras the last eight games of the campaign.

## Hitting

The 5'9" Veras has a small strike zone to begin with. Throw in a crouch and the patience of a kindergarten teacher, and Veras can make things very tough on opposing pitchers. He starts from an open stance, then steps back toward the plate with an exaggerated kick before taking a vicious cut. You'd think that swing would leave Veras vulnerable to breaking balls, but his quick bat allows him to wait that extra split second when necessary. Even though he swings hard, Veras doesn't have much pop. His five homers last year were his most ever as a pro.

## Baserunning & Defense

Obviously one of the fastest men in the league, Veras wound up leading the majors with 56 steals. Of course, he also topped the majors with 21 times *caught* stealing, so there is some work to be done there. Veras' defense was a question mark entering the season, but he showed good range and was very strong on the double-play pivot.

## 1996 Outlook

Despite his rookie status, Veras generally looked like he knew what he was doing last season, both at the plate and in the field. Given another year of experience, who knows? As a premier leadoff man and a fine fielder, Veras might already be considered among the league's elite.

**Position:** 2B
**Bats:** B  **Throws:** R
**Ht:** 5' 9"  **Wt:** 166

**Opening Day Age:** 24
**Born:** 4/3/71 in Santo Domingo, DR
**ML Seasons:** 1

### Overall Statistics

|  | G | AB | R | H | D | T | HR | RBI | SB | BB | SO | Avg | OBP | Slg |
|---|---|---|---|---|---|---|---|---|---|---|---|---|---|---|
| 1995 | 124 | 440 | 86 | 115 | 20 | 7 | 5 | 32 | 56 | 80 | 68 | .261 | .384 | .373 |
| Career | 124 | 440 | 86 | 115 | 20 | 7 | 5 | 32 | 56 | 80 | 68 | .261 | .384 | .373 |

### Where He Hits the Ball

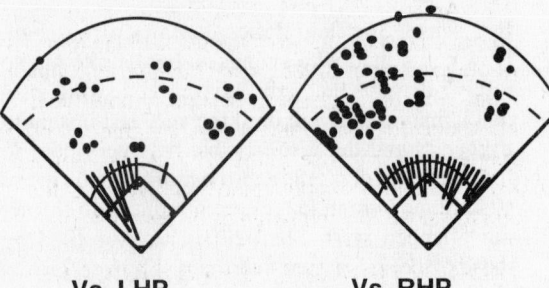

Vs. LHP        Vs. RHP

### 1995 Situational Stats

|  | AB | H | HR | RBI | Avg |  | AB | H | HR | RBI | Avg |
|---|---|---|---|---|---|---|---|---|---|---|---|
| Home | 195 | 52 | 2 | 19 | .267 | LHP | 119 | 29 | 3 | 10 | .244 |
| Road | 245 | 63 | 3 | 13 | .257 | RHP | 321 | 86 | 2 | 22 | .268 |
| First Half | 218 | 51 | 3 | 13 | .234 | Sc Pos | 86 | 18 | 2 | 24 | .209 |
| Scnd Half | 222 | 64 | 2 | 19 | .288 | Clutch | 68 | 19 | 0 | 4 | .279 |

### 1995 Rankings (National League)

→ 1st in stolen bases and caught stealing (21)
→ 2nd in most pitches seen per plate appearance (4.16), highest percentage of pitches taken (64.7%) and steals of third (14)
→ 3rd in walks
→ 4th in on-base percentage for a leadoff hitter (.387), lowest fielding percentage at second base (.986) and bunts in play (29)
→ 5th in lowest batting average with runners in scoring position (.209), errors at second base (9) and lowest percentage of swings on the first pitch (18.0%)
→ 6th in triples
→ Led the Marlins in runs scored, triples, stolen bases, caught stealing and walks

# Alex Arias

**Position:** SS/3B
**Bats:** R **Throws:** R
**Ht:** 6' 3" **Wt:** 185

**Opening Day Age:** 28
**Born:** 11/20/67 in New York, NY
**ML Seasons:** 4
**Pronunciation:** AIR-ee-us

## Overall Statistics

|  | G | AB | R | H | D | T | HR | RBI | SB | BB | SO | Avg | OBP | Slg |
|---|---|---|---|---|---|---|---|---|---|---|---|---|---|---|
| 1995 | 94 | 216 | 22 | 58 | 9 | 2 | 3 | 26 | 1 | 22 | 20 | .269 | .337 | .370 |
| Career | 281 | 677 | 67 | 181 | 25 | 3 | 5 | 68 | 2 | 69 | 70 | .267 | .339 | .335 |

## 1995 Season

Alex Arias began 1995 in the same role that he'd played since coming from the Cubs to the Marlins in the expansion draft: utility infielder and pinch hitter. He did start seven straight games in late May, and hit two homers and a game-winning single against those Cubs. But Arias' defense keeps him from staying in the lineup for very long, and he ended the campaign as he began it.

## Hitting, Baserunning & Defense

Arias is a contact hitter, and usually just tries to lay the bat on the ball. He draws a fair number of walks and doesn't strike out much. A basestealing threat in the minors, Arias rarely runs anymore despite pretty good speed. The reason the Cubs didn't protect Arias in the expansion draft, and the reason he's never been a regular, is his defense. He simply doesn't have the range to play shortstop regularly in the majors. Arias plays reasonably well at third base and second.

## 1996 Outlook

Arias doesn't hit enough to be a valuable bat, and his defense is shaky to the point that he's not a suitable late-inning replacement. But he does have two things going for him: he can play three positions, and he's had a job for four seasons. Arias should fill the same role in 1996 as he has before.

# Jerry Browne

**Position:** 2B/LF/CF/RF
**Bats:** B **Throws:** R
**Ht:** 5'10" **Wt:** 170

**Opening Day Age:** 30
**Born:** 2/3/66 in St. Croix, Virgin Islands
**ML Seasons:** 10

## Overall Statistics

|  | G | AB | R | H | D | T | HR | RBI | SB | BB | SO | Avg | OBP | Slg |
|---|---|---|---|---|---|---|---|---|---|---|---|---|---|---|
| 1995 | 77 | 184 | 21 | 47 | 4 | 0 | 1 | 17 | 1 | 25 | 20 | .255 | .346 | .293 |
| Career | 982 | 3190 | 431 | 866 | 135 | 25 | 23 | 288 | 73 | 393 | 325 | .271 | .351 | .351 |

## 1995 Season

Jerry Browne hit .295 as a spare part in 1994, but he was under no illusions as to his job in 1995: play a part-time role, just as he'd done for years. In 1995, Browne played second when Quilvio Veras got hurt, plus the outfield and a little third. Throw in the periodic pinch-hitting appearance, and "The Governor" was a very busy (utility) man.

## Hitting, Baserunning & Defense

Browne has never been what you'd call a power hitter, but he took that to ridiculous extremes last season with just five extra-base hits in 184 at-bats. Browne hits from an open stance, and will pull inside pitches through the hole, or happily line outside offerings the opposite way. As always, Browne was very patient. He doesn't run much these days, but is still fast enough to play the outfield, and he even started eight games in center last season. Browne is a decent left fielder, not so hot at the other spots. His primary position has always been second base, where he has decent range but is awful on the double-play pivot.

## 1996 Outlook

Browne gets on base, he plays many positions, and he doesn't whine when he's not in the lineup. That all adds up to a good utility player, and Browne will certainly be filling that role in 1996, whether for the Marlins or some other club.

**Florida Marlins**

# Mark Gardner

**Position:** RP/SP
**Bats:** R **Throws:** R
**Ht:** 6' 1"  **Wt:** 205

**Opening Day Age:** 34
**Born:** 3/1/62 in Los Angeles, CA
**ML Seasons:** 7

*Overall Statistics*

| | W | L | Pct. | ERA | G | GS | Sv | IP | H | BB | SO | HR | BR/IP |
|---|---|---|---|---|---|---|---|---|---|---|---|---|---|
| 1995 | 5 | 5 | .500 | 4.49 | 39 | 11 | 1 | 102.1 | 109 | 43 | 87 | 14 | 1.49 |
| Career | 41 | 48 | .461 | 4.38 | 170 | 128 | 1 | 813.1 | 771 | 316 | 593 | 92 | 1.34 |

## 1995 Season

Mark Gardner opened last season in the Florida rotation. But an 8.68 ERA in four starts put a stop to that, and Gardner headed for the bullpen, where he spent a good part of the rest of the season. Gardner did start seven more times, and one of those was a seven-hit shutout over the Cardinals on July 9, his first whitewash since 1990.

## Pitching, Defense & Hitting

Gardner's best pitch has always been his sharp curve, and it's still a good one. But he's lost some arm strength over the last few years, and the curve doesn't have the same bite it once had. That loss of arm strength, of course, has also cost Gardner velocity on his fastball. He made a couple of errors last year, but finishes his pitching motion in good fielding position. Gardner has a decent move for a righthander. On the other hand, he hasn't learned to hit over the years and is just a .114 lifetime hitter.

## 1996 Outlook

Gardner's ERA over the last three seasons is 5.15. With the Marlin pitching staff improving as it has, it's unlikely that management will be burning up the phone lines negotiating with Gardner's agent. The experienced righthander will have to impress someone in spring training or risk opening the season in Triple-A.

# Buddy Groom

**Position:** RP/SP
**Bats:** L **Throws:** L
**Ht:** 6' 2"  **Wt:** 200

**Opening Day Age:** 30
**Born:** 7/10/65 in Dallas, TX
**ML Seasons:** 4

*Overall Statistics*

| | W | L | Pct. | ERA | G | GS | Sv | IP | H | BB | SO | HR | BR/IP |
|---|---|---|---|---|---|---|---|---|---|---|---|---|---|
| 1995 | 2 | 5 | .286 | 7.44 | 37 | 4 | 1 | 55.2 | 81 | 32 | 35 | 8 | 2.03 |
| Career | 2 | 13 | .133 | 6.07 | 108 | 14 | 3 | 163.0 | 208 | 80 | 92 | 20 | 1.77 |

## 1995 Season

After a decent 1994 campaign with the Tigers, Buddy Groom was counted on by Sparky Anderson as his lefty set-up man. But on August 7, saddled with a 7.52 ERA, Groom was traded to the Marlins. He fared just as poorly in Florida, posting a 7.20 ERA with the Fish. Groom's 1995 lowlight came on August 18, when he became the first pitcher to lose both ends of a doubleheader since Don Aase accomplished the feat for Baltimore in 1986.

## Pitching, Defense & Hitting

Though 33 of Groom's 37 appearances last year came in relief, he still has a starter's mentality on the mound and will throw his fastball, slider and curve at any point in the count. However, Groom knows the limitations of his fastball—normally a sinker—and rarely throws it near the middle of the plate. Occasionally, though, he will muscle up and throw high heat past a hitter looking for the slider. Groom's motion can be tricky for baserunners, but his follow-through leaves him in poor fielding position. He's yet to bat in the majors.

## 1996 Outlook

It would be easy to write off a pitcher with a 6.07 lifetime ERA. But Groom has two factors working in his favor. He's left-handed, and he pitched fairly well in 1994. That combination will get him invited to spring training somewhere; it'll be up to Groom to retire some hitters.

# Richie Lewis

**Position:** RP
**Bats:** R **Throws:** R
**Ht:** 5'10" **Wt:** 175

**Opening Day Age:** 30
**Born:** 1/25/66 in Muncie, IN
**ML Seasons:** 4

### Overall Statistics

| | W | L | Pct. | ERA | G | GS | Sv | IP | H | BB | SO | HR | BR/IP |
|---|---|---|---|---|---|---|---|---|---|---|---|---|---|
| 1995 | 0 | 1 | .000 | 3.75 | 21 | 1 | 0 | 36.0 | 30 | 15 | 32 | 9 | 1.25 |
| Career | 8 | 9 | .471 | 4.40 | 125 | 3 | 0 | 174.0 | 173 | 103 | 146 | 24 | 1.59 |

## 1995 Season

What can one make of Richie Lewis' 1995 season? After a particularly rough stretch that saw him allow home runs in four consecutive relief appearances, Lewis was sent to the minors. Recalled on July 23, he had one bad relief outing and one good one. Then came his only start of the season, and Lewis responded with 6.2 strong innings. But he was demoted three days later, and remained in the minors until September.

## Pitching, Defense & Hitting

Lewis has always featured a knee-buckling curve that rates among the better yakkers in baseball. His fastball isn't bad, either, average-minus at the very worst. But Lewis has never had any kind of offspeed pitch he could count on, which is why he's been a reliever in the majors. Lewis pitches with a compact motion, and his follow-through leaves him in good fielding position. He's not real attentive with runners on base. Lewis is 1-for-8 as a hitter in his three N.L. seasons.

## 1996 Outlook

He's always been able to get people out. Unfortunately, Lewis suffers chronic arm problems. As one National League scout put it, "You never know when his elbow's going to blow out." As a result, the Marlins released Lewis in October and at this writing he's a free agent. If healthy this spring, Lewis should have little problem finding work, and might be a reliable set-up man.

# Jesus Tavarez

**Position:** CF/RF
**Bats:** B **Throws:** R
**Ht:** 6' 0" **Wt:** 170

**Opening Day Age:** 25
**Born:** 3/26/71 in Santo Domingo, DR
**ML Seasons:** 2

### Overall Statistics

| | G | AB | R | H | D | T | HR | RBI | SB | BB | SO | Avg | OBP | Slg |
|---|---|---|---|---|---|---|---|---|---|---|---|---|---|---|
| 1995 | 63 | 190 | 31 | 55 | 6 | 2 | 2 | 13 | 7 | 16 | 27 | .289 | .346 | .374 |
| Career | 80 | 229 | 35 | 62 | 6 | 2 | 2 | 17 | 8 | 17 | 32 | .271 | .323 | .341 |

## 1995 Season

After posting decent numbers at Double-A in 1994, speedy outfielder Jesus Tavarez opened last season in Triple-A Charlotte. With Chuck Carr on the DL with a pulled hamstring, Tavarez was recalled in late May. . . only to suffer a hamstring injury himself. Tavarez arrived in the majors for good in late July, and eventually replaced the struggling Carr in the lineup against right-handed pitchers. Tavarez was a pleasant surprise, hitting .289 and performing adequately in center field.

## Hitting, Baserunning & Defense

Tavarez employs a quick, slashing swing that is best matched against fastballs between the knee and the belt. He can be overpowered by high heat. A slap hitter, Tavarez would be lucky to hit three or four homers in a full season, barring a big change in his hitting style. A prolific basestealer in the minors, he hasn't displayed that same derring-do lately. He's a shade slower than Carr, but that's still pretty fast. Tavarez has the skills to play center field in the majors, and his arm is strong enough that he was often shifted to right field in late innings.

## 1996 Outlook

All things being equal, Tavarez' performance last season would have earned him a shot at the regular center-field job. But the Marlins signed free-agent Devon White last November, so Tavarez will once again open the season as a part-time player.

**Florida Marlins**

# Randy Veres

**Position:** RP
**Bats:** R  **Throws:** R
**Ht:** 6' 3"  **Wt:** 210

**Opening Day Age:** 30
**Born:** 11/25/65 in
Sacramento, CA
**ML Seasons:** 4
**Pronunciation:**
VAIR-ez

*Overall Statistics*

|  | W | L | Pct. | ERA | G | GS | Sv | IP | H | BB | SO | HR | BR/IP |
|---|---|---|---|---|---|---|---|---|---|---|---|---|---|
| 1995 | 4 | 4 | .500 | 3.88 | 47 | 0 | 1 | 48.2 | 46 | 22 | 31 | 6 | 1.40 |
| Career | 5 | 9 | .357 | 3.99 | 86 | 1 | 2 | 108.1 | 105 | 44 | 60 | 14 | 1.38 |

## 1995 Season

By Randy Veres standards, 1995 has to be considered a major breakthrough. At 29, Veres quadrupled his career victory total with four, and he set a career high with 48.2 innings pitched.

## Pitching, Defense & Hitting

Veres made it to the majors back in 1990 because he had a good arm, and he still throws a decent fastball and slider. What's held him back over the years is the lack of a dependable offspeed offering. Once a starter, Veres' limited repertoire will probably limit him to the bullpen from now on. Veres' numbers last season were actually a little better than they look. Of the 22 walks he issued, seven were intentional, so his "true" strikeout-to-walk ratio was a decent 31/15. Veres looks like a competent fielder, and his move to first is average at best. Veres has batted four times as a major leaguer, and he's still looking for that elusive first hit.

## 1996 Outlook

Middle-aged right-handed relievers with questionable track records don't buy houses in major league cities, because they're unlikely to stay there long. Veres is certainly no exception. If he pitches well in spring training, he'll make somebody's roster. If not, it's back to Triple-A and waiting for a phone call.

# David Weathers

**Position:** SP/RP
**Bats:** R  **Throws:** R
**Ht:** 6' 3"  **Wt:** 220

**Opening Day Age:** 26
**Born:** 9/25/69 in
Lawrenceburg, TN
**ML Seasons:** 5

*Overall Statistics*

|  | W | L | Pct. | ERA | G | GS | Sv | IP | H | BB | SO | HR | BR/IP |
|---|---|---|---|---|---|---|---|---|---|---|---|---|---|
| 1995 | 4 | 5 | .444 | 5.98 | 28 | 15 | 0 | 90.1 | 104 | 52 | 60 | 8 | 1.73 |
| Career | 15 | 20 | .429 | 5.48 | 83 | 45 | 0 | 289.0 | 347 | 143 | 182 | 26 | 1.70 |

## 1995 Season

Fate didn't smile on David Weathers last year, but he's probably used to that by now. After two straight poor seasons in Florida, Weathers was off to another rough start in 1995. But on June 25 in Cincinnati, Weathers had a no-hitter through five innings. In the top of the sixth, he came to the plate to bunt. One Tim Pugh fastball later, Weathers had a shattered little finger on his pitching hand, requiring stitches, and his season went downhill from there. The end result was his third five-plus ERA in as many seasons.

## Pitching, Defense & Hitting

Weathers has always had a good arm, and that's why the Marlins grabbed him from Toronto in the expansion draft. He throws an average-plus fastball with good sinking movement, and a tight slider. What Weathers lacks is a reliable third pitch. He rarely changes speeds, so hitters can generally sit on the hard stuff. Weathers' compact delivery leaves him in decent fielding position, and his move to first is average for a righthander. Lifetime, Weathers is a .100 hitter.

## 1996 Outlook

It's probably too early to give up on Weathers. Though he didn't pitch well as a reliever last season, his two-pitch repertoire might be better suited to the bullpen. The Marlins have probably seen enough, however, and Weathers will likely be pitching elsewhere in 1996.

# Other Florida Marlins

**Ryan Bowen** (**Pos**: RHP, **Age**: 28)

Bowen missed nearly all of last season with a knee injury. But his arm is fine, and he closed the season with a pair of solid starts. Not much star potential, but a decent fourth starter who might be a big surprise. 1996 Outlook: A

**Steve Decker** (**Pos**: C, **Age**: 30, **Bats**: R)

Considered one of baseball's hottest prospects back in 1990, Decker is now reduced to fighting for a job as a backup catcher. With a .211 lifetime batting average, it won't be handed to him. 1996 Outlook: B

**Mario Diaz** (**Pos**: 2B, **Age**: 34, **Bats**: R)

After hitting .325 in 1994—albeit in just 77 at-bats—Diaz slumped to .230 last season. Almost certainly nearing the end of the line. 1996 Outlook: C

**Rich Garces** (**Pos**: RHP, **Age**: 24)

Once considered the Twins' closer of the future, Garces ate himself out of that opportunity. He pitched for both the Cubs and Marlins last season, and the velocity on his fastball and slider weren't great. 1996 Outlook: C

**Tommy Gregg** (**Pos**: RF, **Age**: 32, **Bats**: L)

After spending all of 1994 in the minors, Gregg opened last season in Triple-A Charlotte, where he absolutely killed the ball. Summoned to Miami, Gregg played some right field and didn't hit. 1996 Outlook: C

**Bryan Harvey** (**Pos**: RHP, **Age**: 32)

After suffering serious elbow problems each of the last two seasons, it might be time to give up on Harvey. He'll undoubtedly be in camp with somebody, but has only pitched 10 innings since 1993. 1996 Outlook: C

**Wilson Heredia** (**Pos**: RHP, **Age**: 24)

Once considered a decent relief prospect with the Rangers, Heredia was sent to Florida in the Bobby Witt deal last August. He's got a decent arm, but lacks the repertoire to start and the stuff to close. 1996 Outlook: C

**Jeremy Hernandez** (**Pos**: RHP, **Age**: 29)

He's missed most of the last two seasons after undergoing two surgeries on a disk in his neck, so it's hard to be optimistic. Hernandez did pitch twice in September, though not particularly well. 1996 Outlook: B

**John Johnstone** (**Pos**: RHP, **Age**: 27)

After posting 5.91 ERAs in both 1993 and 1994, Johnstone missed nearly all of 1995 with a serious elbow injury. 'Nuff said. 1996 Outlook: D

**Matt Mantei** (**Pos**: RHP, **Age**: 22)

The Marlins snatched Mantei from Seattle in the Rule 5 draft, and he was excellent in two minor league stops. After 12 games with the Fish, Mantei went on the DL with a herniated disk in his back. 1996 Outlook: B

**Russ Morman** (**Pos**: RF, **Age**: 33, **Bats**: R)

A righty-hitting version of Tommy Gregg, Morman also was called up after killing the ball (.314) at Triple-A Charlotte. He'll have to prove himself again in the minors, and he's 33. 1996 Outlook: C

**Rob Murphy** (**Pos**: LHP, **Age**: 35)

Murphy was released by both the Dodgers and the Marlins last summer. That might not be particularly worrisome, but the fact that no one else picked him up probably should be. Remember, he's a lefty. 1996 Outlook: C

**Bob Natal** (**Pos**: C, **Age**: 30, **Bats**: R)

It's fun to watch Natal's distinctive batting stance, but don't stare too long at his batting *stats*, which haven't matched his minor league numbers yet. Could easily find work as a backup, and might surprise. 1996 Outlook: B

**Rich Scheid** (**Pos**: LHP, **Age**: 31)

Scheid has no fastball to speak of, but one of these years he's going to be given the role of one-out lefty, and there's a 50 percent chance he'll keep it. On the other hand, he could be out of baseball soon. 1996 Outlook: C

**Aaron Small** (**Pos**: RHP, **Age**: 24)

A longtime Toronto farmhand, Small came to the Marlins early last season. With Triple-A Charlotte, he posted decent numbers including 10 saves. Looks like a candidate for right-handed set-up man. 1996 Outlook: B

**Darrell Whitmore** (**Pos**: CF, **Age**: 27, **Bats**: L)

Whitmore's got a .203 average in 330 major league at-bats, and missed most of last season with a sore shoulder. Now at his peak baseball age, he is running out of chances. 1996 Outlook: C

**Eddie Zosky** (**Pos**: SS, **Age**: 28, **Bats**: R)

Zosky was once regarded as Toronto's future shortstop, but that was five years ago. Now he's trying to hang on as a utility man, and so far it's not going too well. Only five at-bats last season. 1996 Outlook: C

# Florida Marlins Minor League Prospects

## Organization Overview:

The Marlins haven't enjoyed the success of their expansion brethren Colorado Rockies, but Florida's future could be just as bright. The Marlins have made a committment to building through the farm system, and they already boast more prospects than a number of more-established organizations. Since many in the Marlins' player development department, including General Manager Dave Dombrowski, were responsible for constructing Montreal's impressive talent base, Florida's minor league success is no surprise. The fact that the Marlins market themselves to the Latin American fan base and are the team of choice for many prospects in the Caribbean could have important future ramifications. The Marlins play in a division with other good young teams, not the least of which is World Champion Atlanta, but Florida could be a team to contend with for years to come.

### Luis Castillo

**Position:** 2B
**Bats:** R **Throws:** R
**Ht:** 5' 11" **Wt:** 146
**Opening Day Age:** 20
**Born:** 9/12/75 in San Pedro de Marcoris, DR

*Recent Statistics*

| | G | AB | R | H | D | T | HR | RBI | SB | BB | SO | AVG |
|---|---|---|---|---|---|---|---|---|---|---|---|---|
| 94 R Marlins | 57 | 216 | 49 | 57 | 8 | 0 | 0 | 16 | 31 | 37 | 36 | .264 |
| 95 A Kane County | 89 | 340 | 71 | 111 | 4 | 4 | 0 | 23 | 41 | 55 | 50 | .326 |

Castillo may never hit for power. At 5'11" and 146 pounds, his career isolated power (slugging average minus batting average) is a pathetic .036. But that doesn't mean he isn't an effective offensive player. His .326 batting average, combined with lots of walks, produced an on-base percentage well over .400 and 71 runs in 89 games. In addition, he has disruptive speed on the bases. A second baseman from the renowned San Pedro de Macoris in the Dominican Republic, Castillo is expected to make a complete recovery from the separated shoulder which sidelined him last season.

### Will Cunnane

**Position:** P
**Bats:** R **Throws:** R
**Ht:** 6' 2" **Wt:** 165
**Opening Day Age:** 21
**Born:** 4/24/74 in Suffern, NY

*Recent Statistics*

| | W | L | ERA | G | GS | Sv | IP | H | R | BB | SO | HR |
|---|---|---|---|---|---|---|---|---|---|---|---|---|
| 93 R Marlins | 3 | 3 | 2.70 | 16 | 9 | 2 | 66.2 | 75 | 32 | 8 | 64 | 1 |
| 94 A Kane County | 11 | 3 | 1.43 | 32 | 16 | 1 | 138.2 | 110 | 27 | 23 | 106 | 2 |
| 95 AA Portland | 9 | 2 | 3.67 | 21 | 21 | 0 | 117.2 | 120 | 48 | 34 | 83 | 10 |

Cunnane produced the minors' lowest ERA of 1994, and has compiled a sterling 20-5 record over the last two seasons. All that from a guy who wasn't even drafted in 1993 and didn't become a starter until midway through his first campaign. Cunnane throws a fastball in the 90s and delivers it with great control. His career strikeout-to-walk ratio is nearly four to one. Last year was the first time minor league batters had any success hitting the long ball against Cunnane, as he had allowed just three homers in his first 205 professional innings.

### Billy McMillon

**Position:** OF
**Bats:** L **Throws:** L
**Ht:** 5' 11" **Wt:** 172
**Opening Day Age:** 24
**Born:** 11/17/71 in Otero, NM

*Recent Statistics*

| | G | AB | R | H | D | T | HR | RBI | SB | BB | SO | AVG |
|---|---|---|---|---|---|---|---|---|---|---|---|---|
| 93 A Elmira | 57 | 227 | 38 | 69 | 14 | 2 | 6 | 35 | 5 | 30 | 44 | .304 |
| 94 A Kane County | 137 | 496 | 88 | 125 | 25 | 3 | 17 | 101 | 7 | 84 | 99 | .252 |
| 95 AA Portland | 141 | 518 | 92 | 162 | 29 | 3 | 14 | 93 | 15 | 96 | 90 | .313 |
| 95 MLE | 141 | 498 | 73 | 142 | 25 | 2 | 10 | 74 | 10 | 65 | 96 | .285 |

The Marlins have a number of prospects who already display the remarkable strike-zone judgment evidenced by McMillon. A player who hits .313 and draws as many walks as McMillon is going to score bunches of runs, and he's scored 180 over the last two years. An eighth-round draft pick from Clemson in 1993, McMillon has now delivered three straight solid seasons. His power is not overwhelming, but McMillon will drive the ball to the gaps, knock in runs, and steal a few bases. The left-handed swinger will be 24 when he plays in 1996, most likely in Triple-A.

### Kevin Millar

**Position:** 1B
**Bats:** R **Throws:** R
**Ht:** 6' 1" **Wt:** 195
**Opening Day Age:** 24
**Born:** 9/24/71 in Los Angeles, CA

*Recent Statistics*

| | G | AB | R | H | D | T | HR | RBI | SB | BB | SO | AVG |
|---|---|---|---|---|---|---|---|---|---|---|---|---|
| 94 A Kane County | 135 | 477 | 75 | 144 | 35 | 2 | 19 | 93 | 3 | 74 | 88 | .302 |
| 95 A Brevard Cty | 129 | 459 | 53 | 132 | 32 | 2 | 13 | 68 | 4 | 70 | 66 | .288 |

Millar turned 24 last September and has yet to play above Class A, but his production the last two seasons is hard to ignore. The Marlins signed Millar after he played in the independent Northern League during 1993. Since then, he's averaged .295 with 17 homers, 86 RBI, 36 doubles, 77 walks and 68 runs scored per 500 at-bats. The right-handed-hitting Millar may be limited to first base defensively, but it'll be interesting to see how he handles any future increase in classification level.

## Ralph Milliard

**Position:** 2B    **Opening Day Age:** 22
**Bats:** R **Throws:** R    **Born:** 12/30/73 in
**Ht:** 5' 10" **Wt:** 160    Wilhelmstad, Curacao

*Recent Statistics*

| | G | AB | R | H | D | T | HR | RBI | SB | BB | SO | AVG |
|---|---|---|---|---|---|---|---|---|---|---|---|---|
| 93 R Marlins | 53 | 192 | 35 | 45 | 15 | 0 | 0 | 25 | 11 | 30 | 17 | .234 |
| 94 A Kane County | 133 | 515 | 97 | 153 | 34 | 2 | 8 | 67 | 10 | 68 | 63 | .297 |
| 95 AA Portland | 128 | 464 | 104 | 124 | 22 | 3 | 11 | 40 | 22 | 85 | 83 | .267 |
| 95 MLE | 128 | 449 | 83 | 109 | 19 | 2 | 8 | 31 | 14 | 57 | 88 | .243 |

The Marlins are an organization blessed with exciting middle-infield prospects, and Milliard is a case in point. At just 21 years of age, Milliard handled the jump to Double-A in fine fashion last season, as he continued to develop his home-run power and basestealing prowess. His most impressive skill may be his patience at the plate, which allowed him to draw 85 walks and led to over 100 runs scored. Defensively, Milliard displays exceptional range at second base and has little difficulty turning the double play.

## Jay Powell

**Position:** P    **Opening Day Age:** 24
**Bats:** R **Throws:** R    **Born:** 1/19/72 in
**Ht:** 6' 4" **Wt:** 220    Meridian, MS

*Recent Statistics*

| | W | L | ERA | G | GS | Sv | IP | H | R | BB | SO | HR |
|---|---|---|---|---|---|---|---|---|---|---|---|---|
| 95 AA Portland | 5 | 4 | 1.87 | 50 | 0 | 24 | 53.0 | 42 | 12 | 15 | 53 | 2 |
| 95 NL Florida | 0 | 0 | 1.08 | 9 | 0 | 0 | 8.1 | 7 | 2 | 6 | 4 | 0 |

Powell had been a disappointment to the Baltimore organization following his first-round selection by the Orioles in 1993. He couldn't keep his ERA under 4.50 in either of his first two pro seasons and was subsequently sent to Florida in exchange for Bret Barberie. But Powell seemed to turn the corner in '95 and actually made nine September appearances with the Marlins. He was used exclusively in relief by Florida, his role in college at Mississippi State, something Baltimore had gotten away from in '94. He could be an effective set-up man with the capability to move into the closer role for Florida.

## Edgar Renteria

**Position:** SS    **Opening Day Age:** 20
**Bats:** R **Throws:** R    **Born:** 8/7/75 in
**Ht:** 6' 1" **Wt:** 172    Barranquilla, Colombia

*Recent Statistics*

| | G | AB | R | H | D | T | HR | RBI | SB | BB | SO | AVG |
|---|---|---|---|---|---|---|---|---|---|---|---|---|
| 93 A Kane County | 116 | 384 | 40 | 78 | 8 | 0 | 1 | 35 | 7 | 35 | 94 | .203 |
| 94 A Brevard Cty | 128 | 439 | 46 | 111 | 15 | 1 | 0 | 36 | 6 | 35 | 56 | .253 |
| 95 AA Portland | 135 | 508 | 70 | 147 | 15 | 7 | 7 | 68 | 30 | 32 | 85 | .289 |
| 95 MLE | 135 | 491 | 55 | 130 | 13 | 5 | 5 | 54 | 21 | 21 | 91 | .265 |

Renteria improved by leaps and bounds last season, increasing his batting over the previous year from .253 to .289, his steals from six to 30, and home runs from zero to seven. Considering that Renteria was making the sometimes tricky jump from Class A to Double-A, and that he was the Eastern League's youngest player at 19 (he turned 20 in August), it was quite an accomplishment. There's no concern that Renteria has the defensive skills to play shortstop. The native of Colombia will almost certainly be the Marlin shortstop as they enter the 21st century.

## Marc Valdes

**Position:** P    **Opening Day Age:** 24
**Bats:** R **Throws:** R    **Born:** 12/20/71 in
**Ht:** 6' 0" **Wt:** 170    Dayton, OH

*Recent Statistics*

| | W | L | ERA | G | GS | Sv | IP | H | R | BB | SO | HR |
|---|---|---|---|---|---|---|---|---|---|---|---|---|
| 95 AAA Charlotte | 9 | 13 | 4.86 | 27 | 27 | 0 | 170.1 | 189 | 98 | 59 | 104 | 19 |
| 95 NL Florida | 0 | 0 | 14.14 | 3 | 3 | 0 | 7.0 | 17 | 13 | 9 | 2 | 1 |

Valdes is a product of Jesuit High in Tampa and the University of Florida, where he was the Gators' all-time leader in victories. The Marlins drafted Valdes in the first round in 1993, and he's made a rapid rise through the system since, actually reaching Miami last season. Valdes throws a fastball with sinking action, and mixes in a hard slider and change-up. He wasn't as impressive in 1995 as he was the year before, and appeared overmatched in his three starts with the Marlins. The 24 year old could spend his second season in Triple-A this year.

## Others to Watch

Lefthander **Joel Adamson** was involved in the Danny Jackson trade with Philadelphia the day of the expansion draft. He was 8-4 with 80 K's, 20 walks and a 3.29 ERA in Triple-A last year. . . Third baseman **Josh Booty** looked like a $1.6 million bust when he was hitting .101 through 109 Midwest League at-bats last year. The fifth player taken overall in 1994, Booty then hit .220 with 6 homers and 37 RBI when demoted to a short-season A league. . . Righthander **Andy Larkin** missed much of last season due to back problems. He had looked like the Marlins' top pitching prospect after going 9-7 with a 2.83 ERA at Kane County in '94. . . Like other Marlin prospects, third baseman **Lou Lucca** draws lots of walks. He's also been a consistent .280 hitter with doubles power in four minor league seasons. . . At one time righthander **Kurt Miller** was considered among the best pitching prospects in all of baseball. However, he's now posted three straight mediocre to poor seasons, and was 8-11 with a 4.62 ERA in '95. . . **Clemente Nunez** was 12-6 with a 2.48 ERA in his second season in the California League. The righthander was only 20 last year. . . 21-year-old **Tony Saunders** has spent the last two years with Class-A Brevard County. Saunders compiled a 3.09 ERA with 100 strikeouts and 24 walks in 131 innings during that span. . . Hard-throwing lefthander **Matt Whisenant** finally reached Double-A in his sixth pro season, going 10-6 with a 3.50 ERA at Portland.

**Florida Marlins**

# Jeff Bagwell

## 1995 Season

A slow start plagued Jeff Bagwell for the first six weeks of the 1995 season. Just about the time he hit a consistent groove and started displaying the form that made him a unanimous National League MVP the year before, Bagwell was sidelined with a broken left hand for the third year in a row. He nevertheless finished with a club-high 87 RBI, and would almost certainly have topped 100 RBI for the second straight year had he not been injured.

## Hitting

Bagwell's trademark wide-open stance, which culminates with a powerful uppercut, leaves his left hand exposed to inside pitches. His .290 batting average represented a 78-point drop from his team-record .368 in '94, largely as a result of that six-week slump, and some wondered if Bagwell was pulling off the ball because of a subconscious fear of being hit in the same hand again. However, he came back to set a club record with 31 RBI in July. Still, some people think he should experiment with a slightly different stance, one which won't leave his hand so vulnerable.

## Baserunning & Defense

Bagwell is an aggressive baserunner for a power hitter, but he's not the type to stretch a gap hit into a triple. He's among the best at breaking up potential double plays with hard slides into second base. Bagwell excels at scooping low throws to first out of the dirt, a trait which was vital since the Astros went through several shortstops and third basemen last season.

## 1996 Outlook

If he can avoid another lengthy stay on the disabled list, Bagwell could threaten his own club records for batting average, home runs and RBI. Already regarded as the best overall player in franchise history, Bagwell will be just 27 years old on Opening Day and is just entering his prime. He is a legitimate Triple Crown threat—if the Astros provide him with protection in the order so opposing pitchers can't pitch around him.

**Position:** 1B
**Bats:** R  **Throws:** R
**Ht:** 6' 0"  **Wt:** 195

**Opening Day Age:** 27
**Born:** 5/27/68 in Boston, MA
**ML Seasons:** 5

### Overall Statistics

|  | G | AB | R | H | D | T | HR | RBI | SB | BB | SO | Avg | OBP | Slg |
|---|---|---|---|---|---|---|---|---|---|---|---|---|---|---|
| 1995 | 114 | 448 | 88 | 130 | 29 | 0 | 21 | 87 | 12 | 79 | 102 | .290 | .399 | .496 |
| Career | 684 | 2523 | 434 | 771 | 158 | 16 | 113 | 469 | 57 | 365 | 453 | .306 | .395 | .515 |

### Where He Hits the Ball

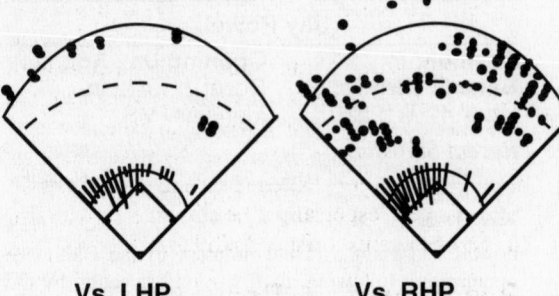

Vs. LHP          Vs. RHP

### 1995 Situational Stats

|  | AB | H | HR | RBI | Avg |  | AB | H | HR | RBI | Avg |
|---|---|---|---|---|---|---|---|---|---|---|---|
| Home | 221 | 63 | 10 | 41 | .285 | LHP | 84 | 25 | 2 | 15 | .298 |
| Road | 227 | 67 | 11 | 46 | .295 | RHP | 364 | 105 | 19 | 72 | .288 |
| First Half | 265 | 69 | 10 | 45 | .260 | Sc Pos | 137 | 37 | 5 | 62 | .270 |
| Scnd Half | 183 | 61 | 11 | 42 | .333 | Clutch | 76 | 21 | 4 | 15 | .276 |

### 1995 Rankings (National League)

- → 2nd in lowest fielding percentage at first base (.994)
- → 3rd in errors at first base (7)
- → 4th in intentional walks (12)
- → 5th in walks
- → 6th in on-base percentage
- → 7th in lowest groundball/flyball ratio (1.0)
- → 8th in sacrifice flies (6)
- → 9th in on-base percentage vs. right-handed pitchers (.390)
- → 10th in lowest stolen base percentage (70.6%)
- → Led the Astros in RBI, intentional walks, strikeouts, slugging percentage, HR frequency (21.3 ABs per HR) and most pitches seen per plate appearance (3.93)

# Derek Bell

## 1995 Season

Had it not been for Derek Bell's tremendous offensive production in 1995, the Astros would have had little to show for their blockbuster trade with San Diego the year before. Bell was perhaps the most productive offensive player left off the N.L. All-Star team, after hitting .337 with 56 RBI during the first half of the season. He was a legitimate MVP candidate until sidelined for the season's final five weeks with a muscle tear in his thigh.

## Hitting

Bell has developed into one of the league's best hitters by consistently punishing left-handed pitchers. He has become a more mature hitter since joining the Astros, and is less of a wild swinger than he was in the past. Bell still doesn't walk much for a cleanup hitter, but he's good at making contact and possesses outstanding bat speed. He has above-average gap power, is an excellent fastball hitter, and has improved against breaking pitches. He might challenge for the league batting title this year, especially if he continues to exercise discipline against offspeed pitchers.

## Baserunning & Defense

Bell is an active basestealer, but could become a much more complete player if he worked on reading an opposing pitcher's moves, which would enable him to get a bigger jump. In the outfield, he'll often make a superb catch that robs an opposing player of an extra-base hit, then have problems with a routine fly ball. His biggest fielding asset is a strong arm that was much more accurate in '95 than in previous seasons.

## 1996 Outlook

Bell is a player whose stock is on the rise, and he's entrenched himself as the Astros' starting right fielder. He has proven he can consistently hit .300 and thrive in clutch situations. But he must improve his baserunning and fielding if he is to earn All-Star recognition.

**Position:** RF/CF
**Bats:** R  **Throws:** R
**Ht:** 6' 2"   **Wt:** 215

**Opening Day Age:** 27
**Born:** 12/11/68 in Tampa, FL
**ML Seasons:** 5

### Overall Statistics

|  | G | AB | R | H | D | T | HR | RBI | SB | BB | SO | Avg | OBP | Slg |
|---|---|----|---|---|---|---|----|-----|----|----|----|-----|-----|-----|
| 1995 | 112 | 452 | 63 | 151 | 21 | 2 | 8 | 86 | 27 | 33 | 71 | .334 | .385 | .442 |
| Career | 449 | 1617 | 218 | 471 | 66 | 6 | 45 | 228 | 87 | 106 | 320 | .291 | .342 | .423 |

### Where He Hits the Ball

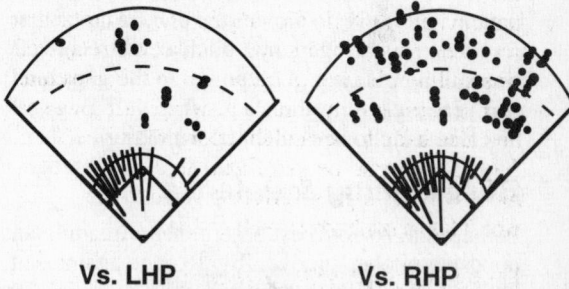

**Vs. LHP**          **Vs. RHP**

### 1995 Situational Stats

|  | AB | H | HR | RBI | Avg |  | AB | H | HR | RBI | Avg |
|---|----|---|----|-----|-----|---|----|---|----|-----|-----|
| Home | 219 | 67 | 3 | 33 | .306 | LHP | 100 | 41 | 2 | 28 | .410 |
| Road | 233 | 84 | 5 | 53 | .361 | RHP | 352 | 110 | 6 | 58 | .313 |
| First Half | 276 | 93 | 5 | 56 | .337 | Sc Pos | 152 | 47 | 2 | 78 | .309 |
| Scnd Half | 176 | 58 | 3 | 30 | .330 | Clutch | 74 | 22 | 1 | 12 | .297 |

### 1995 Rankings (National League)

→ 2nd in batting average on the road (.361)
→ 3rd in errors in right field (8)
→ 4th in batting average, singles (120) and highest groundball/flyball ratio (2.1)
→ 8th in sacrifice flies (6), batting average vs. right-handed pitchers (.313) and lowest cleanup slugging percentage (.448)
→ 9th in steals of third (6)
→ Led the Astros in batting average, singles, caught stealing (9), highest groundball/flyball ratio (2.1), cleanup slugging percentage (.448), batting average at home (.306), batting average on the road (.361) and batting average with two strikes (.262)

**Houston Astros**

# Craig Biggio

## 1995 Season

Craig Biggio was the glue that held the injury-plagued Astros together in 1995. He led the club in at-bats, hits, runs scored, doubles, home runs, walks and stolen bases. In fact, his 22 home runs were a career high, despite the strike-shortened season. Biggio was the first Houston player voted by fans to start in the All-Star game since 1972, ending the longest such drought of any major league team.

## Hitting

Biggio uses quick hands to turn on the ball, and sprays hits to all fields—an extremely valuable asset for a player who has blossomed into perhaps the best number-two hitter in baseball. A very patient hitter, Biggio crowds the plate, a tactic that resulted in his being hit by a pitch a club-record 22 times in '95. He has good power to the gaps, and last year picked up the slack when Jeff Bagwell and Derek Bell were sidelined with injuries.

## Baserunning & Defense

Perhaps the Astros' best baserunner at reading an opposing pitcher's move, Biggio once again used a long lead and quick stride to steal a club-high 33 bases last season. He is among the best in the league at going from first to third on singles to right field, and seldom hits into double plays. Biggio, who won his second straight Gold Glove in '95, continues to show above-average fielding range at second base, and is extremely adept at turning the double play.

## 1996 Outlook

Biggio provides a big headache for equipment managers—getting his uniform dirty in the early innings of ballgames. A constant factor because of his hustle, Biggio is in the midst of his peak of baseball productivity. His excellent fielding and deft baserunning are overshadowed by his ability to hit for average and power. A free agent who figures to cash in big, Biggio should continue to be one of the game's best table-setters and biggest run-scorers in '96.

**Position:** 2B
**Bats:** R  **Throws:** R
**Ht:** 5'11"  **Wt:** 180

**Opening Day Age:** 30
**Born:** 12/14/65 in Smithtown, NY
**ML Seasons:** 8
**Pronunciation:** BIDG-jee-oh

### Overall Statistics

|  | G | AB | R | H | D | T | HR | RBI | SB | BB | SO | Avg | OBP | Slg |
|---|---|---|---|---|---|---|---|---|---|---|---|---|---|---|
| 1995 | 141 | 553 | 123 | 167 | 30 | 2 | 22 | 77 | 33 | 80 | 85 | .302 | .406 | .483 |
| Career | 1055 | 3880 | 615 | 1105 | 221 | 24 | 79 | 389 | 196 | 475 | 574 | .285 | .369 | .415 |

### Where He Hits the Ball

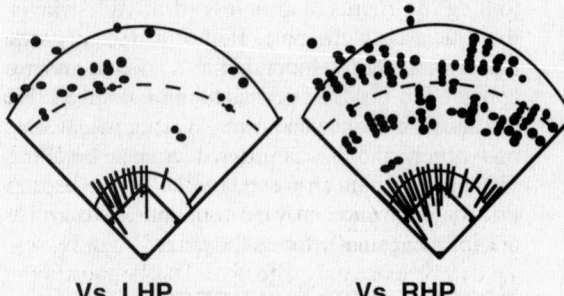

**Vs. LHP**            **Vs. RHP**

### 1995 Situational Stats

|  | AB | H | HR | RBI | Avg |  | AB | H | HR | RBI | Avg |
|---|---|---|---|---|---|---|---|---|---|---|---|
| Home | 265 | 73 | 6 | 31 | .275 | LHP | 107 | 41 | 7 | 18 | .383 |
| Road | 288 | 94 | 16 | 46 | .326 | RHP | 446 | 126 | 15 | 59 | .283 |
| First Half | 264 | 74 | 10 | 41 | .280 | Sc Pos | 145 | 38 | 4 | 51 | .262 |
| Scnd Half | 289 | 93 | 12 | 36 | .322 | Clutch | 109 | 31 | 2 | 13 | .284 |

### 1995 Rankings (National League)

- ➞ 1st in runs scored, hit by pitch (22), pitches seen (2,488), plate appearances (673) and on-base percentage vs. left-handed pitchers (.493)
- ➞ 2nd in times on base (269) and on-base percentage
- ➞ 3rd in sacrifice flies (7), walks (80), batting average vs. left-handed pitchers (.383) and errors at second base (10)
- ➞ 4th in hits, batting average on the road (.326) and steals of third (10)
- ➞ Led the Astros in home runs, at-bats, runs scored, hits, doubles, total bases (267), sacrifice bunts (11), sacrifice flies, stolen bases, walks and hit by pitch

# Jim Dougherty

## 1995 Season

After progressing through the Astros' minor league system for four years, righty reliever Jim Dougherty made his major league debut in '95. All 56 of his appearances came in short relief, usually in situations in which he could face right-handed hitters. His 8-4 record was largely a result of being the beneficiary of Houston comebacks. Dougherty started strongly, putting together seven straight scoreless appearances in late May and early June, but was less effective late in the season as opposing hitters became more familiar with his unusual pitching motion. He had particular problems with left-handed hitters.

## Pitching

Dougherty is a classic example of a pitcher who uses a combination sidearm/submarine delivery to get the most out of his sinkers and sliders. He befuddled right-handed hitters during most of his rookie season, but was battered by lefties, who hit .420 against him. Dougherty often struggled with his control, which enabled some hitters to tee off when he eventually found the plate. When he's on, he can be extremely effective. But he must work on keeping the ball down and pitching more inside.

## Defense & Hitting

Dougherty doesn't have the quickest delivery to the plate, which gives baserunners the chance to be aggressive. He's an average fielder, with only moderate agility off the mound while fielding bunts. Dougherty had only one hit in eight at-bats as a rookie but made good contact, striking out just twice.

## 1996 Outlook

If Dougherty is to remain a fixture in the Astro bullpen, he must improve his effectiveness against left-handed hitters. He also must learn to adjust to his role as a middle reliever after being primarily as a closer in the minors. Adding another pitch to his repertoire would help his future as well.

**Position:** RP
**Bats:** R  **Throws:** R
**Ht:** 6' 0"  **Wt:** 210

**Opening Day Age:** 28
**Born:** 3/8/68 in Brentwood, NY
**ML Seasons:** 1

### Overall Statistics

|        | W | L | Pct. | ERA | G | GS | Sv | IP | H | BB | SO | HR | BR/IP |
|--------|---|---|------|-----|---|----|----|-----|----|----|----|----|-------|
| 1995   | 8 | 4 | .667 | 4.92 | 56 | 0 | 0 | 67.2 | 76 | 25 | 49 | 7 | 1.49 |
| Career | 8 | 4 | .667 | 4.92 | 56 | 0 | 0 | 67.2 | 76 | 25 | 49 | 7 | 1.49 |

### How Often He Throws Strikes

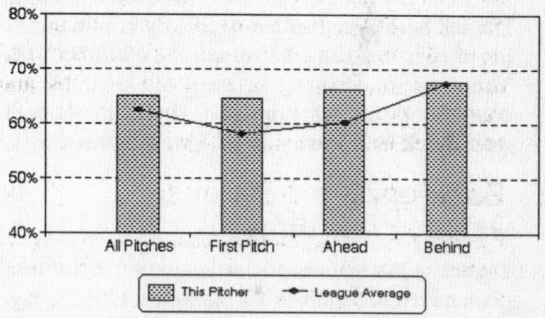

### 1995 Situational Stats

|            | W | L | ERA | Sv | IP   |        | AB  | H  | HR | RBI | Avg  |
|------------|---|---|-----|----|------|--------|-----|----|----|-----|------|
| Home       | 3 | 1 | 4.50 | 0 | 32.0 | LHB    | 88  | 37 | 5  | 23  | .420 |
| Road       | 5 | 3 | 5.30 | 0 | 35.2 | RHB    | 172 | 39 | 2  | 19  | .227 |
| First Half | 4 | 1 | 4.75 | 0 | 41.2 | Sc Pos | 81  | 26 | 3  | 37  | .321 |
| Scnd Half  | 4 | 3 | 5.19 | 0 | 26.0 | Clutch | 77  | 25 | 2  | 12  | .325 |

### 1995 Rankings (National League)

- → 1st in relief wins (8)
- → 6th in highest relief ERA (4.92) and highest batting average allowed in relief (.292)
- → 10th in highest batting average allowed in relief with runners on base (.325), most baserunners allowed per 9 innings in relief (13.8) and least strikeouts per 9 innings in relief (6.5)
- → Led the Astros in most GDPs induced per GDP situation (16.7%) and relief wins

# Doug Drabek

## 1995 Season

Although he came through with an occasional gem, Doug Drabek struggled during most of the '95 season. He finished with only two complete games—his lowest total since 1987—and a career-high 4.77 ERA. Right- and left-handed hitters were equally effective against Drabek, whose biggest drawback was inconsistency. He yielded more than a hit per inning, and had uncharacteristic problems finding the strike zone.

## Pitching

Drabek's fastball is still above average by major league standards, but he continues to rely primarily on a variety of curves and a sinker. Long noted for his ability to throw strikes on a consistent basis, Drabek no longer has the necessary command of his pitches that helped him win the 1990 N.L. Cy Young Award. Drabek frequently fell behind in the count in '95, allowing opposing hitters to be more selective. His knowledge of hitters, however, is among the best in the league.

## Defense & Hitting

Drabek remains one of the league's best-hitting pitchers. He's collected 14 hits in each of the last two seasons, and drove in eight runs in '95 while laying down eight successful sacrifices. He does an adequate job of holding runners. Drabek's quickness, utilized occasionally as a pinch runner, enables him to field his position better than most pitchers.

## 1996 Outlook

Drabek tends to excel in even-numbered years, and there is plenty of room for improvement in 1996. He has reached the stage in his career where he may be relying more on knowledge then sheer athletic ability. Although he is no longer in a position to be considered the workhorse of the staff, he's been able to avoid injuries, and once again could be a 12- to 14-game winner if he regains consistent command of his pitches.

**Position:** SP
**Bats:** R **Throws:** R
**Ht:** 6' 1" **Wt:** 185

**Opening Day Age:** 33
**Born:** 7/25/62 in Victoria, TX
**ML Seasons:** 10
**Pronunciation:** DRAY-bek

### Overall Statistics

|        | W   | L   | Pct. | ERA  | G   | GS  | Sv | IP     | H    | BB  | SO   | HR  | BR/IP |
|--------|-----|-----|------|------|-----|-----|----|--------|------|-----|------|-----|-------|
| 1995   | 10  | 9   | .526 | 4.77 | 31  | 31  | 0  | 185.0  | 205  | 54  | 143  | 18  | 1.40  |
| Career | 130 | 103 | .558 | 3.32 | 314 | 305 | 0  | 2081.2 | 1932 | 546 | 1317 | 175 | 1.19  |

### How Often He Throws Strikes

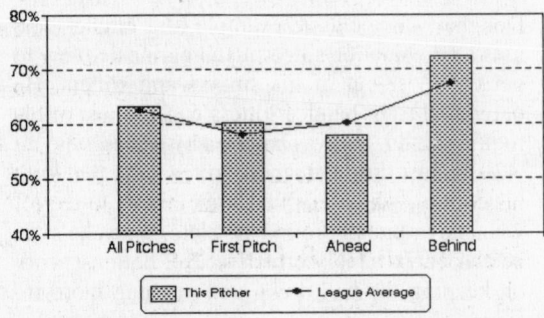

### 1995 Situational Stats

|            | W | L | ERA  | Sv | IP    |       | AB  | H   | HR | RBI | Avg  |
|------------|---|---|------|----|-------|-------|-----|-----|----|-----|------|
| Home       | 4 | 6 | 3.95 | 0  | 100.1 | LHB   | 381 | 110 | 10 | 44  | .289 |
| Road       | 6 | 3 | 5.74 | 0  | 84.2  | RHB   | 347 | 95  | 8  | 52  | .274 |
| First Half | 4 | 5 | 4.83 | 0  | 87.2  | Sc Pos| 179 | 61  | 4  | 72  | .341 |
| Scnd Half  | 6 | 4 | 4.72 | 0  | 97.1  | Clutch| 30  | 4   | 1  | 1   | .133 |

### 1995 Rankings (National League)

- ➡ 1st in games started
- ➡ 2nd in highest ERA on the road (5.74)
- ➡ 3rd in highest batting average allowed with runners in scoring position (.341)
- ➡ 4th in least GDPs induced per 9 innings (0.4)
- ➡ 5th in highest ERA
- ➡ 6th in hits allowed
- ➡ 7th in highest batting average allowed (.282)
- ➡ 9th in most baserunners allowed per 9 innings (13.0)
- ➡ 10th in hit batsmen (8), stolen bases allowed (21), runners caught stealing (10) and highest slugging percentage allowed (.427)
- ➡ Led the Astros in wins, games started, hits allowed, batters faced (797) and balks (1)

# Tony Eusebio

**Position:** C
**Bats:** R **Throws:** R
**Ht:** 6' 2" **Wt:** 180

**Opening Day Age:** 28
**Born:** 4/27/67 in San Jose De Los Llamos, DR
**ML Seasons:** 3
**Pronunciation:** you-SAY-bee-oh

## 1995 Season

The most unheralded player on the Astros in '95—and perhaps the most underrated catcher in club history—Tony Eusebio did everything the team asked in his first full season in the majors. After a tremendous summer stretch, only a September slump kept him from a .300 season. Used primarily against right-handed pitchers, Eusebio also excelled against lefties when pressed into duty following a harrowing succession of injuries that afflicted the other Houston catchers.

## Hitting

Primarily an opposite-field hitter, Eusebio became more selective at the plate last season. He didn't turn into Frank Thomas or anything, but his on-base percentage was among the highest on the club. . . pretty astonishing for a guy who had a reputation for swinging at everything. Eusebio also proved he could hit in the clutch, excelling with runners in scoring position and in late-inning pressure situations. He loves the fastball, but when he's in a groove he can handle just about any pitch.

## Baserunning & Defense

As can be expected from a catcher, Eusebio grounded into his share of double plays, and was unsuccessful on his only two stolen base attempts last season. But he improved greatly on his ability to handle the Astros' young pitchers, allowing Houston to trade Scott Servais at midseason. Eusebio has a quick release, and makes strong, accurate throws.

## 1996 Season

The biggest question for Eusebio in '96 is what he will do for an encore. Matching his .299 average might be a challenge if he's platooned with left-handed-hitting Rick Wilkins. But Eusebio's success against righthanders and improved skills behind the plate make him a solid and productive major league player at baseball's most demanding position.

### Overall Statistics

| | G | AB | R | H | D | T | HR | RBI | SB | BB | SO | Avg | OBP | Slg |
|---|---|---|---|---|---|---|---|---|---|---|---|---|---|---|
| 1995 | 113 | 368 | 46 | 110 | 21 | 1 | 6 | 58 | 0 | 31 | 59 | .299 | .354 | .410 |
| Career | 178 | 546 | 68 | 159 | 31 | 2 | 11 | 88 | 0 | 45 | 100 | .291 | .343 | .416 |

### Where He Hits the Ball

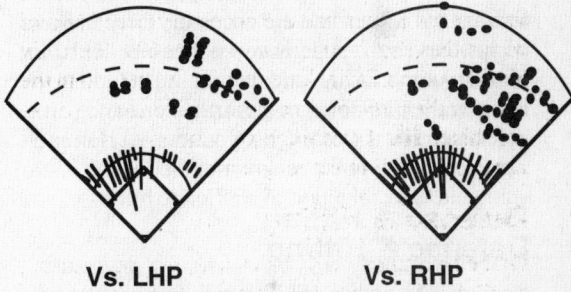

**Vs. LHP**          **Vs. RHP**

### 1995 Situational Stats

| | AB | H | HR | RBI | Avg | | AB | H | HR | RBI | Avg |
|---|---|---|---|---|---|---|---|---|---|---|---|
| Home | 182 | 52 | 5 | 28 | .286 | LHP | 88 | 24 | 1 | 13 | .273 |
| Road | 186 | 58 | 1 | 30 | .312 | RHP | 280 | 86 | 5 | 45 | .307 |
| First Half | 159 | 50 | 2 | 29 | .314 | Sc Pos | 115 | 36 | 2 | 51 | .313 |
| Scnd Half | 209 | 60 | 4 | 29 | .287 | Clutch | 78 | 25 | 2 | 15 | .321 |

### 1995 Rankings (National League)

➡ 3rd in fielding percentage at catcher (.993)

**Houston Astros**

# Mike Hampton

## 1995 Season

Although just a kid who turned 23 late in the season, Mike Hampton wound up as the ace of Houston's starting rotation . His effectiveness in a starting role was a major surprise, considering that he'd been used exclusively in short relief in 44 appearances the year before. Hampton overcame occasional groin and elbow injuries to help keep the Astros in the wild-card race with a streak of quality starts in September—allowing the Cubs just three hits in 8.1 innings in his final outing.

## Pitching

Hampton possesses an excellent assortment of pitches for a young lefthander. His cut fastball, which has a nice sinking action, tails away from left-handed hitters and enhances the effectiveness of his curveball, slider and change-up. He's not afraid to pitch inside, and does an outstanding job keeping the ball down in the strike zone and painting the corners. Despite his young age, Hampton shows as much poise as any member of the Astro staff, and isn't reluctant to challenge hitters.

## Defense & Hitting

Regarded as perhaps the Astros' best natural athlete, Hampton fields his position exceptionally well because of his overall quickness. He has an above-average pickoff move, but he's a little slow to the plate and runners who can read his move steal fairly easily against him. Hampton hit only .146 with only four sacrifices last season, statistics that could easily improve.

## 1996 Outlook

No player on the Houston roster has a more promising future in the majors than Hampton. If he can add a little speed to his fastball and avoid the occasional injuries that bothered him in '95, he could become a consistent 15-game winner who averages 200 innings per year.

**Position:** SP
**Bats:** R  **Throws:** L
**Ht:** 5'10"  **Wt:** 180

**Opening Day Age:** 23
**Born:** 9/9/72 in Brooksville, FL
**ML Seasons:** 3

### Overall Statistics

| | W | L | Pct. | ERA | G | GS | Sv | IP | H | BB | SO | HR | BR/IP |
|---|---|---|---|---|---|---|---|---|---|---|---|---|---|
| 1995 | 9 | 8 | .529 | 3.35 | 24 | 24 | 0 | 150.2 | 141 | 49 | 115 | 13 | 1.26 |
| Career | 12 | 12 | .500 | 3.92 | 81 | 27 | 1 | 209.0 | 215 | 82 | 147 | 20 | 1.42 |

### How Often He Throws Strikes

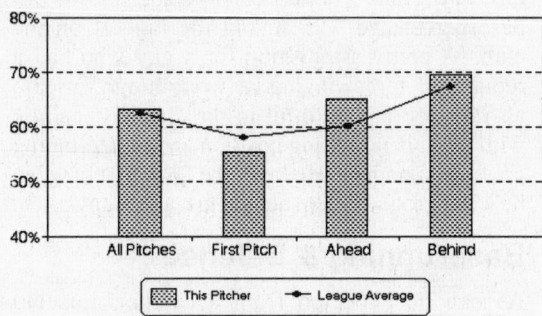

### 1995 Situational Stats

| | W | L | ERA | Sv | IP | | AB | H | HR | RBI | Avg |
|---|---|---|---|---|---|---|---|---|---|---|---|
| Home | 4 | 4 | 2.48 | 0 | 80.0 | LHB | 114 | 31 | 3 | 14 | .272 |
| Road | 5 | 4 | 4.33 | 0 | 70.2 | RHB | 458 | 110 | 10 | 46 | .240 |
| First Half | 4 | 3 | 2.78 | 0 | 55.0 | Sc Pos | 139 | 32 | 5 | 47 | .230 |
| Scnd Half | 5 | 5 | 3.67 | 0 | 95.2 | Clutch | 30 | 7 | 0 | 1 | .233 |

### 1995 Rankings (National League)

➡ 5th in errors at pitcher (3)
➡ 6th in highest groundball/flyball ratio allowed (2.0), ERA at home (2.47) and lowest fielding percentage at pitcher (.919)
➡ 7th in most run support per 9 innings (5.6)
➡ 10th in pickoff throws (141)
➡ Led the Astros in ERA, balks (1), GDPs induced (12), lowest batting average allowed (.247), lowest slugging percentage allowed (.364), most run support per 9 innings, most GDPs induced per 9 innings (0.7) and ERA at home

# Mike Henneman

## 1995 Season

When the Astros needed a proven closer in August, they acquired veteran Tiger reliever Mike Henneman to replace the injured John Hudek. Henneman appeared to regain the form he had lost in Detroit by compiling a 1.65 ERA in his first 15 N.L. appearances. He slumped a bit down the stretch, but overall appeared to still have what it takes to be a closer. He was especially tough against right-handed hitters, and he permitted only one home run all season.

## Pitching

Although some teams with AstroTurf parks might have been reluctant to use a groundball pitcher like Henneman as a closer, Detroit's all-time save leader thrived early in his new surroundings. From the outset, the effectiveness of Henneman's slider and sinker reminded longtime Astro fans of Houston's all-time save leader, Dave Smith. Henneman's pitches still had their big breaking motion, forcing Houston's infielders to be on their toes in order to field the many ground balls that ensued. Henneman isn't afraid to pitch inside, and can challenge hitters with an average fastball when necessary.

## Defense & Hitting

Tough to run on, Henneman relies upon a quick delivery to the plate that discourages all but the speediest runners from trying to steal. He fields his position well and isn't reluctant to make a quick throw trying to force the lead runner on sacrifice attempts. Henneman did not make a plate appearance for the Astros in '95 and has batted just once in his major league career.

## 1996 Outlook

The Astros must be wondering whether the real Henneman was the one they saw over his first 15 appearances, or the one they saw down the stretch. Regardless, Henneman has hinted that the upcoming season might be his last. He has reached the point of his career where his experience is as valuable as his ability.

**Position:** RP
**Bats:** R **Throws:** R
**Ht:** 6' 3" **Wt:** 212

**Opening Day Age:** 34
**Born:** 12/11/61 in St. Charles, MO
**ML Seasons:** 9
**Pronunciation:** HENN-uh-min

### Overall Statistics

|  | W | L | Pct. | ERA | G | GS | Sv | IP | H | BB | SO | HR | BR/IP |
|---|---|---|---|---|---|---|---|---|---|---|---|---|---|
| 1995 | 0 | 2 | .000 | 2.15 | 50 | 0 | 26 | 50.1 | 45 | 13 | 43 | 1 | 1.15 |
| Career | 57 | 35 | .620 | 3.05 | 512 | 0 | 162 | 690.2 | 645 | 254 | 499 | 41 | 1.30 |

### How Often He Throws Strikes

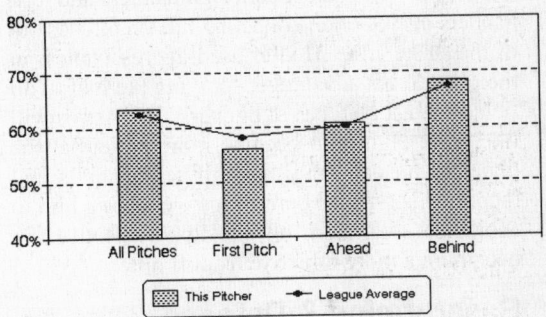

### 1995 Situational Stats

|  | W | L | ERA | Sv | IP |  | AB | H | HR | RBI | Avg |
|---|---|---|---|---|---|---|---|---|---|---|---|
| Home | 0 | 0 | 1.13 | 15 | 24.0 | LHB | 99 | 28 | 1 | 13 | .283 |
| Road | 0 | 2 | 3.08 | 11 | 26.1 | RHB | 88 | 17 | 0 | 13 | .193 |
| First Half | 0 | 1 | 1.85 | 17 | 24.1 | Sc Pos | 52 | 15 | 0 | 23 | .288 |
| Scnd Half | 0 | 1 | 2.42 | 9 | 26.0 | Clutch | 130 | 29 | 1 | 20 | .223 |

### 1995 Rankings (National League)

➡ Did not rank near the top or bottom in any category

Houston Astros

# Brian Hunter

## 1995 Season

Easily one of the Astros' most impressive young players to reach the majors in recent years, Brian Hunter returned from a stint at Triple-A Tuscon to earn the starting center-field job by midseason. Hunter became an impact player shortly after he was called up from the minors on June 13, and used his outstanding speed to steal 24 bases and run down numerous fly balls in the gaps. The Astros won 15 of the first 21 games in which he played. After a spell on the disabled list with a broken right hand, Hunter returned and played well the remainder of the season.

## Hitting

Hunter hit well against both righthanders and left-handers in '95, often collecting hits on pitches out of the strike zone. Hunter used aggressiveness at the plate to his advantage, spraying the ball to all fields against all types of pitchers. The Astros will likely ask Hunter to become more patient at the plate, so he can draw more bases on balls and increase his on-base percentage—enabling him to capitalize even more on his superb speed while becoming a more effective leadoff hitter.

## Baserunning & Defense

Perhaps the quickest player to ever wear an Astros uniform, Hunter makes third basemen and short-stops hurry their throws on routine grounders. If anything, he's penalized by the quick AstroTurf bounces which might be infield singles on grass fields. Once he sharpens his baserunning skills, he could average 50 thefts a year. Hunter also covers a tremendous amount of ground in center field, turning potential gap hits into outs. He did commit nine errors, many resulting from erratic throws.

## 1996 Outlook

If Hunter becomes more selective at the plate and learns to read opposing pitchers' pickoff moves, he could quickly develop into one of the Astros' best-ever leadoff hitters and one of the top table-setters in the majors. Hunter's overall aggressive style of play makes him an exciting commodity, and a valuable defensive anchor in the spacious Astro-dome outfield.

**Position:** CF
**Bats:** R  **Throws:** R
**Ht:** 6' 4"  **Wt:** 180

**Opening Day Age:** 25
**Born:** 3/5/71 in Portland, OR
**ML Seasons:** 2

### Overall Statistics

| | G | AB | R | H | D | T | HR | RBI | SB | BB | SO | Avg | OBP | Slg |
|---|---|---|---|---|---|---|---|---|---|---|---|---|---|---|
| 1995 | 78 | 321 | 52 | 97 | 14 | 5 | 2 | 28 | 24 | 21 | 52 | .302 | .346 | .396 |
| Career | 84 | 345 | 54 | 103 | 15 | 5 | 2 | 28 | 26 | 22 | 58 | .299 | .341 | .388 |

### Where He Hits the Ball

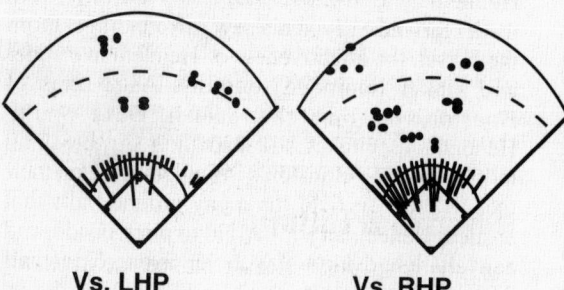

**Vs. LHP**          **Vs. RHP**

### 1995 Situational Stats

| | AB | H | HR | RBI | Avg | | AB | H | HR | RBI | Avg |
|---|---|---|---|---|---|---|---|---|---|---|---|
| Home | 153 | 42 | 0 | 10 | .275 | LHP | 80 | 23 | 0 | 9 | .288 |
| Road | 168 | 55 | 2 | 18 | .327 | RHP | 241 | 74 | 2 | 19 | .307 |
| First Half | 99 | 37 | 1 | 12 | .374 | Sc Pos | 74 | 22 | 0 | 26 | .297 |
| Scnd Half | 222 | 60 | 1 | 16 | .270 | Clutch | 54 | 19 | 1 | 5 | .352 |

### 1995 Rankings (National League)

- ➡ 1st in errors in center field (9)
- ➡ 9th in batting average in the clutch (.352) and lowest on-base percentage for a leadoff hitter (.345)
- ➡ Led the Astros in triples and batting average in the clutch

# Todd Jones

## 1995 Season

After a strong first half in which he continued to display his solid 1994 form, reliever Todd Jones fizzled during the second half of the 1995 season. He had problems finding the plate, and was the losing pitcher in two critical extra-inning games during the season's final week—games that ultimately cost the club a wild-card berth. Opponents only hit .237 against Jones, but they learned to be more selective and wait for the righthander to unravel.

## Pitching

Jones isn't a finesse pitcher. He tries to overpower hitters with a big overhand curveball, an above-average fastball that approaches the mid-90s, and a strong change-up. But he sometimes struggles with wildness, leaving pitches high in the zone and allowing hitters to tee off. That became a frequent problem for Jones in '95 as the innings piled up. He made 20 more appearances than in 1994, with much of that duty coming late in the season.

## Defense & Hitting

Jones is an average fielder but he has a major problem holding runners, who swiped nine bases in 10 attempts against him last year. He doesn't react quickly to grounders up the middle. As a closer, Jones rarely gets to hit. He finished with one double in just five plate appearances last season.

## 1996 Outlook

Jones almost certainly will play a key role in the Astro bullpen, but whether he will be used primarily as a set-up man or a closer remains to be seen. With Mike Henneman nearing the end of the line, Jones just might get a chance to replace him. He could develop into one of the league's premier relievers if he can improve the command of his pitches, especially his curve and change-up.

**Position:** RP
**Bats:** L  **Throws:** R
**Ht:** 6' 3"  **Wt:** 200

**Opening Day Age:** 27
**Born:** 4/24/68 in Marietta, GA
**ML Seasons:** 3

### Overall Statistics

| | W | L | Pct. | ERA | G | GS | Sv | IP | H | BB | SO | HR | BR/IP |
|---|---|---|---|---|---|---|---|---|---|---|---|---|---|
| 1995 | 6 | 5 | .545 | 3.07 | 68 | 0 | 15 | 99.2 | 89 | 52 | 96 | 8 | 1.41 |
| Career | 12 | 9 | .571 | 2.96 | 143 | 0 | 22 | 209.2 | 169 | 93 | 184 | 15 | 1.25 |

### How Often He Throws Strikes

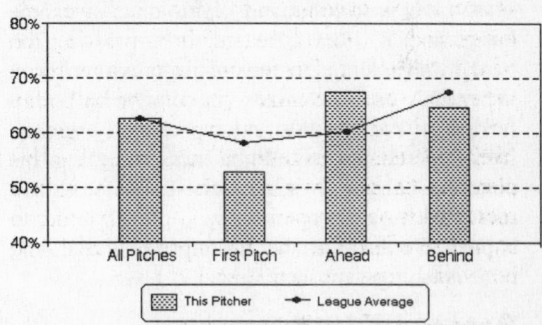

This Pitcher  •— League Average

### 1995 Situational Stats

| | W | L | ERA | Sv | IP | | AB | H | HR | RBI | Avg |
|---|---|---|---|---|---|---|---|---|---|---|---|
| Home | 3 | 4 | 2.86 | 5 | 50.1 | LHB | 166 | 44 | 3 | 16 | .265 |
| Road | 3 | 1 | 3.28 | 10 | 49.1 | RHB | 209 | 45 | 5 | 27 | .215 |
| First Half | 5 | 1 | 1.83 | 6 | 54.0 | Sc Pos | 119 | 25 | 2 | 35 | .210 |
| Scnd Half | 1 | 4 | 4.53 | 9 | 45.2 | Clutch | 219 | 49 | 3 | 25 | .224 |

### 1995 Rankings (National League)

→ 1st in lowest save percentage (75.0%)
→ 2nd in relief innings (99.2)
→ 5th in games pitched
→ 8th in relief wins (6)
→ 9th in lowest batting average allowed with runners in scoring position (.210)
→ Led the Astros in saves, games finished (40), save opportunities (20), save percentage (75.0%), blown saves (5), lowest batting average allowed with runners in scoring position (.210), lowest batting average allowed in relief with runners on base (.224), relief losses (5), lowest batting average allowed in relief (.237) and most strikeouts per 9 innings in relief (8.7)

**Houston Astros**

# Darryl Kile

## 1995 Season

Of all the disappointments the Astros experienced in '95, one of the biggest was the performance of Darryl Kile. Blessed with a curveball rated the league's best in a poll of N.L. managers, Kile struggled with his mechanics, his control, and his confidence before being sent to Triple-A Tucson shortly after midseason. The end result was a puzzling 4-12 record with Houston, in which he walked 73 batters in just 127 innings and finished with an ERA approaching five.

## Pitching

A 15-game winner only two years ago, Kile admitted his mechanics were on the brink of disaster last season. He lost command of his once-awesome curve, and at times appeared to be pressing too hard in an attempt to regain his previous form. When he's on, Kile mixes his curve with both a fastball in the low 90s and a potentially wicked split-fingered fastball. When he's struggling, his control is abysmal—and every delivery with a runner on base is a potential wild pitch waiting to happen. No Astro pitcher has more potential, and none is a bigger mystery.

## Defense & Hitting

Kile has problems holding runners on base, in part because of his wildness; his catchers often have trouble just blocking his errant pitches, let alone catching them and throwing out a runner. His 6-foot-5 frame gives him decent range on grounders hit toward the mound. Learning to help himself at the plate, or at least make contact a majority of the time, would be a big plus. He's a liability when batting, collecting just four hits in 36 at-bats while striking out 20 times last year.

## 1996 Outlook

Kile's career is at a crossroads. He has displayed the natural ability to become one of the majors' biggest winners, yet has been unable to harness that talent or develop the mental toughness that separates the best from the rest. Two sharp relief appearances in the Astros' final four games of the season may have provided a much-needed boost of confidence.

**Position:** SP
**Bats:** R **Throws:** R
**Ht:** 6' 5" **Wt:** 185

**Opening Day Age:** 27
**Born:** 12/2/68 in Garden Grove, CA
**ML Seasons:** 5

### Overall Statistics

|  | W | L | Pct. | ERA | G | GS | Sv | IP | H | BB | SO | HR | BR/IP |
|---|---|---|---|---|---|---|---|---|---|---|---|---|---|
| 1995 | 4 | 12 | .250 | 4.96 | 25 | 21 | 0 | 127.0 | 114 | 73 | 113 | 5 | 1.47 |
| Career | 40 | 47 | .460 | 4.09 | 140 | 115 | 0 | 725.1 | 687 | 371 | 549 | 54 | 1.46 |

### How Often He Throws Strikes

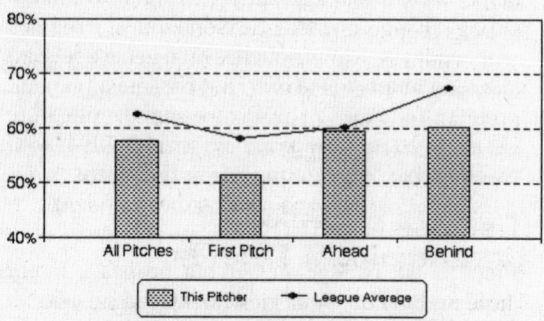

### 1995 Situational Stats

|  | W | L | ERA | Sv | IP |  | AB | H | HR | RBI | Avg |
|---|---|---|---|---|---|---|---|---|---|---|---|
| Home | 1 | 8 | 5.82 | 0 | 60.1 | LHB | 216 | 54 | 3 | 32 | .250 |
| Road | 3 | 4 | 4.19 | 0 | 66.2 | RHB | 259 | 60 | 2 | 25 | .232 |
| First Half | 3 | 9 | 5.02 | 0 | 84.1 | Sc Pos | 148 | 37 | 1 | 49 | .250 |
| Scnd Half | 1 | 3 | 4.85 | 0 | 42.2 | Clutch | 24 | 7 | 1 | 2 | .292 |

### 1995 Rankings (National League)

→ 2nd in hit batsmen (12)
→ 4th in lowest winning percentage
→ 5th in wild pitches (11) and errors at pitcher (3)
→ 7th in walks allowed and lowest fielding percentage at pitcher (.923)
→ 8th in losses
→ Led the Astros in losses, walks allowed, hit batsmen, wild pitches, balks (1), lowest batting average allowed vs. left-handed batters (.250) and lowest batting average allowed vs. right-handed batters (.232)

# Dave Magadan

## 1995 Season

Signed as a free agent just before the start of the season, veteran infielder Dave Magadan provided the Astros with what they were looking for in 1995—a left-handed hitting third baseman who could platoon with Craig Shipley. He was particularly effective down the stretch, as his on-base percentage of .488 in September topped the National League. He was also able to avoid the injuries that plagued him the previous season with the Florida Marlins.

## Hitting

Without question, Magadan's biggest value as a hitter is his selectivity at the plate. He is one of the league's best players at putting the ball in play, but he lacks the necessary power to earn himself a spot as a regular. Opposing fielders generally shade Magadan to the opposite field because of his knack of keeping his hands back and spraying the ball to left and left-center field. He also is an above-average hitter in the clutch, but he has trouble with lefthanders and needs to be platooned.

## Baserunning & Defense

These are two big liabilities for Magadan, who is a roadblock on the bases, averaging fewer than one stolen base per season during his major league career. His lack of speed and quickness also saddles him with limited range at third, a drawback that led to 18 fielding errors last season. Magadan's best position is first base, but the Astros used him sparingly there last year, even when Jeff Bagwell was sidelined for a month.

## 1996 Outlook

The fact that Magadan was able to raise his batting average 38 points from the previous season will keep him in the majors for at least another year or two. He's the type of player who would make a capable designated hitter if he could generate more power. If the Astros come up with a regular third baseman, Magadan could be used as a left-handed hitter off the bench.

**Position:** 3B/1B
**Bats:** L  **Throws:** R
**Ht:** 6' 3"  **Wt:** 205

**Opening Day Age:** 33
**Born:** 9/30/62 in Tampa, FL
**ML Seasons:** 10

### Overall Statistics

|  | G | AB | R | H | D | T | HR | RBI | SB | BB | SO | Avg | OBP | Slg |
|---|---|---|---|---|---|---|---|---|---|---|---|---|---|---|
| 1995 | 127 | 348 | 44 | 109 | 24 | 0 | 2 | 51 | 2 | 71 | 56 | .313 | .428 | .399 |
| Career | 1039 | 3102 | 398 | 901 | 164 | 11 | 29 | 372 | 9 | 537 | 392 | .290 | .393 | .378 |

### Where He Hits the Ball

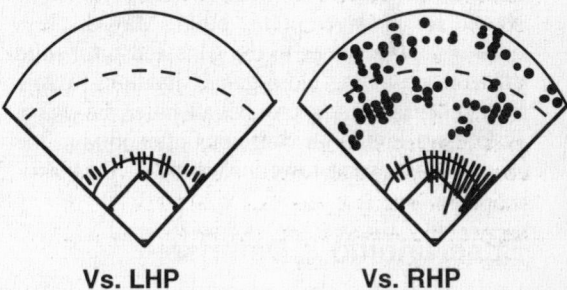

| Vs. LHP | Vs. RHP |
|---|---|

### 1995 Situational Stats

|  | AB | H | HR | RBI | Avg |  | AB | H | HR | RBI | Avg |
|---|---|---|---|---|---|---|---|---|---|---|---|
| Home | 157 | 54 | 0 | 24 | .344 | LHP | 35 | 6 | 0 | 4 | .171 |
| Road | 191 | 55 | 2 | 27 | .288 | RHP | 313 | 103 | 2 | 47 | .329 |
| First Half | 125 | 36 | 1 | 19 | .288 | Sc Pos | 100 | 33 | 0 | 49 | .330 |
| Scnd Half | 223 | 73 | 1 | 32 | .327 | Clutch | 74 | 16 | 0 | 10 | .216 |

### 1995 Rankings (National League)

→ 1st in lowest fielding percentage at third base (.923) and lowest percentage of extra bases taken as a runner (25.6%)

→ 2nd in on-base percentage vs. right-handed pitchers (.446)

→ 3rd in errors at third base (18) and highest percentage of pitches taken (64.7%)

→ 4th in batting average with the bases loaded (.500)

→ 5th in batting average vs. right-handed pitchers (.329)

→ 8th in batting average on a 3-1 count (.571)

→ 9th in walks

→ Led the Astros in batting average with runners in scoring position (.330)

**Houston Astros**

# Derrick May

## 1995 Season

Acquired from the Brewers in midseason as the Astros tinkered with their starting outfield, Derrick May blossomed into a pleasant surprise. He played a big role, frequently hitting in the cleanup spot against righthanders when right fielder Derek Bell missed the final month with a thigh injury. After a slow start with the Brewers, May sizzled when it counted most, hitting over .300 after moving on to Houston while providing occasional power. He came up huge in the crucial season-ending series with the Cubs, collecting 10 hits (two home runs) in four games.

## Hitting

Although he doesn't reach the fences as often as he should for a player of his build, May displays above-average power to the gaps and hit a solid .321 in late-inning close-game situations. While he's still primarily a groundball hitter, he was a little more home-run conscious after joining the Astros and hit some towering, rainbow-like blasts.

## Baserunning & Defense

May is heavy-legged and isn't a big threat to steal, although he was successful in all five of his attempts after the Astros acquired him from Milwaukee. He overcame a reputation as an outfielder with limited range and a suspect throwing arm by serving the Astros well in right field during the season's final month. But he still needs to improve his ability to read line drives.

## 1996 Outlook

May made a good impression after joining the Astros last year and could stick around this year as a reserve outfielder and a left-handed hitter off the bench. However, he's still only 27 and could yet establish himself as a major league regular. The tools are certainly there.

**Position:** LF/RF
**Bats:** L  **Throws:** R
**Ht:** 6' 4"   **Wt:** 225

**Opening Day Age:** 27
**Born:** 7/14/68 in Rochester, NY
**ML Seasons:** 6

### Overall Statistics

|        | G   | AB   | R   | H   | D  | T | HR | RBI | SB | BB  | SO  | Avg  | OBP  | Slg  |
|--------|-----|------|-----|-----|----|---|----|-----|----|-----|-----|------|------|------|
| 1995   | 110 | 319  | 44  | 90  | 18 | 2 | 9  | 50  | 5  | 24  | 42  | .282 | .333 | .436 |
| Career | 494 | 1563 | 194 | 441 | 78 | 6 | 37 | 237 | 24 | 103 | 165 | .282 | .326 | .411 |

### Where He Hits the Ball

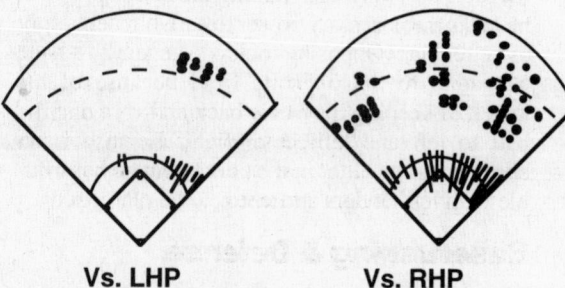

**Vs. LHP**          **Vs. RHP**

### 1995 Situational Stats

|           | AB  | H  | HR | RBI | Avg  |        | AB  | H  | HR | RBI | Avg  |
|-----------|-----|----|----|-----|------|--------|-----|----|----|-----|------|
| Home      | 168 | 44 | 4  | 30  | .262 | LHP    | 39  | 10 | 0  | 5   | .256 |
| Road      | 151 | 46 | 5  | 20  | .305 | RHP    | 280 | 80 | 9  | 45  | .286 |
| First Half| 132 | 34 | 1  | 11  | .258 | Sc Pos | 99  | 26 | 5  | 43  | .263 |
| Scnd Half | 187 | 56 | 8  | 39  | .299 | Clutch | 56  | 18 | 2  | 13  | .321 |

### 1995 Rankings (National League)

➡ 7th in batting average on a 3-1 count (.600)
➡ Led the Astros in batting average on a 3-1 count

# Orlando Miller

## 1995 Season

Orlando Miller became the Astros' regular short-stop when Andujar Cedeno was traded to San Diego at the end of the '94 season. He provided ample production at the plate and displayed above-average range at shortstop during his rookie season. But Miller missed the final month with what originally was diagnosed as a knee sprain, casting a shadow over what otherwise would have been considered a hopeful debut.

## Hitting

Miller likes to take his cuts at the plate. . . maybe a little too much. He's extremely aggressive with the bat, and takes huge rips—two qualities the Astros probably would rather see from a cleanup hitter than a shortstop usually batting eighth in the order. Miller hasn't yet learned how to take advantage of lefties, and he needs to become much more selective at the plate if he is to improve on his .244 average with runners in scoring position. He also needs to work on drawing more walks, and quit chasing low breaking pitches.

## Baserunning & Defense

Miller was successful on only three of seven stolen-base attempts as a rookie, but he does have the ability to go from first to third and challenge outfielders on singles to right field. In the field, Miller didn't make anyone forget about Cedeno at short. Although he possesses a strong arm, he has problems making accurate throws from deep short and lacks the necessary range to be considered among the league's best talents at that position.

## 1996 Outlook

Miller is the Astros' shortstop of the present, but the future is still up for grabs. He has the natural ability to make a name for himself, and apparently has overcome the occasional temper tantrums that slowed his path to the majors. Just how good he can become depends on how much more selective he can be at the plate, and whether he improves his range at short.

**Position:** SS
**Bats:** R **Throws:** R
**Ht:** 6' 1" **Wt:** 180

**Opening Day Age:** 27
**Born:** 1/13/69 in Changuinola, Panama
**ML Seasons:** 2

### Overall Statistics

|  | G | AB | R | H | D | T | HR | RBI | SB | BB | SO | Avg | OBP | Slg |
|---|---|---|---|---|---|---|---|---|---|---|---|---|---|---|
| 1995 | 92 | 324 | 36 | 85 | 20 | 1 | 5 | 36 | 3 | 22 | 71 | .262 | .319 | .377 |
| Career | 108 | 364 | 39 | 98 | 20 | 2 | 7 | 45 | 4 | 24 | 83 | .269 | .327 | .393 |

### Where He Hits the Ball

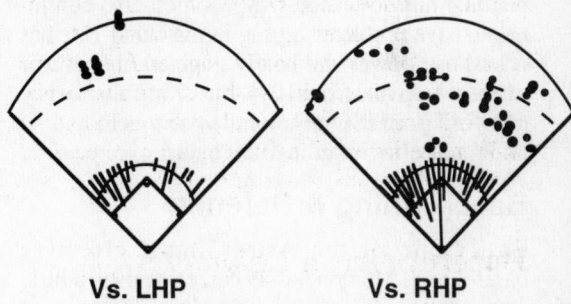

Vs. LHP          Vs. RHP

### 1995 Situational Stats

|  | AB | H | HR | RBI | Avg |  | AB | H | HR | RBI | Avg |
|---|---|---|---|---|---|---|---|---|---|---|---|
| Home | 158 | 37 | 1 | 18 | .234 | LHP | 72 | 18 | 0 | 7 | .250 |
| Road | 166 | 48 | 4 | 18 | .289 | RHP | 252 | 67 | 5 | 29 | .266 |
| First Half | 226 | 63 | 3 | 27 | .279 | Sc Pos | 82 | 20 | 1 | 28 | .244 |
| Scnd Half | 98 | 22 | 2 | 9 | .224 | Clutch | 63 | 17 | 0 | 5 | .270 |

### 1995 Rankings (National League)

➡ 5th in lowest fielding percentage at shortstop (.964)
➡ 7th in batting average on a 3-2 count (.400)
➡ 10th in errors at shortstop (15)
➡ Led the Astros in batting average on an 0-2 count (.250) and batting average on a 3-2 count

Houston Astros

# James Mouton

## 1995 Season

A bench player during the early months of the season, James Mouton regained a starting role in the Astros' outfield when Luis Gonzalez was traded to the Chicago Cubs in midyear. Mouton responded by playing better defense than any of the club's other outfielders, but he struggled against right-handed pitchers to the point where he became a part-time starter during the season's final stages.

## Hitting

Mouton can pound lefties and sprays hits to all fields against them, but righthanders have been able to defuse his aggressiveness at the plate by pitching him low and away. Mouton also continues to have problems hitting in the clutch. He has occasional power and nearly doubled his number of extra-base hits from 1994, but he has a tendency to swing from the heels a little too much, and he might be better off going for contact over power.

## Baserunning & Defense

Easily one of the Astros' most effective baserunners, Mouton has 49 career steals in a little over 200 major league games—many of them contests in which he only played a few innings. He is as aggressive on the bases as he is at the plate, a trait which also extends to his play in the outfield. Mouton did not commit an error in 94 games and made a series of spectacular running catches. But his throwing arm is only average, at best, and runners aren't afraid to take the extra base against him.

## 1996 Outlook

Mouton's speed and his effectiveness against left-handers should ensure him a spot on the Astros' roster, if not a starting outfield role. He appears best suited for left field. Mouton is typical of a young player who is still learning, and he can contribute to a club which historically has stressed speed more than power in the spacious Astrodome.

**Position:** LF/CF/RF
**Bats:** R  **Throws:** R
**Ht:** 5' 9"  **Wt:** 175

**Opening Day Age:** 27
**Born:** 12/29/68 in Denver, Colorado
**ML Seasons:** 2
**Pronunciation:** MOO-tawn

### Overall Statistics

|  | G | AB | R | H | D | T | HR | RBI | SB | BB | SO | Avg | OBP | Slg |
|---|---|---|---|---|---|---|---|---|---|---|---|---|---|---|
| 1995 | 104 | 298 | 42 | 78 | 18 | 2 | 4 | 27 | 25 | 25 | 59 | .262 | .326 | .376 |
| Career | 203 | 608 | 85 | 154 | 29 | 2 | 6 | 43 | 49 | 52 | 128 | .253 | .320 | .337 |

### Where He Hits the Ball

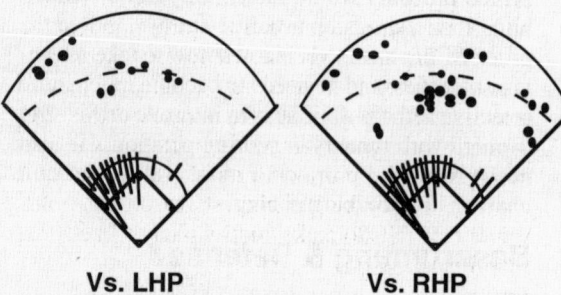

Vs. LHP          Vs. RHP

### 1995 Situational Stats

|  | AB | H | HR | RBI | Avg |  | AB | H | HR | RBI | Avg |
|---|---|---|---|---|---|---|---|---|---|---|---|
| Home | 155 | 41 | 2 | 10 | .265 | LHP | 116 | 38 | 3 | 10 | .328 |
| Road | 143 | 37 | 2 | 17 | .259 | RHP | 182 | 40 | 1 | 17 | .220 |
| First Half | 130 | 35 | 3 | 13 | .269 | Sc Pos | 77 | 18 | 1 | 22 | .234 |
| Scnd Half | 168 | 43 | 1 | 14 | .256 | Clutch | 57 | 11 | 2 | 8 | .193 |

### 1995 Rankings (National League)

➡ Did not rank near the top or bottom in any category

# Shane Reynolds

## 1995 Season

Easily one of Houston's biggest surprises in '95, Shane Reynolds more than doubled his career victory total while becoming the club's most consistent right-handed starter. Used primarily as a reliever by the Astros during his first three seasons, Reynolds thrived in the rotation—leading the club in innings pitched, strikeouts, complete games, and shutouts. He was especially tough in the Astrodome, where he posted a nifty 2.82 ERA.

## Pitching

Reynolds kept hitters guessing in '95 with a nasty split-fingered fastball that tails away from left-handed hitters. The pitch actually made him *more* effective against lefties than against righties, which is fairly common for splitter-dependant pitchers. The underlying key to Reynolds' success was his ability to mix his trademark pitch with both a fastball that consistently reached the low-90s and a sharp-breaking curveball that was second-best on the club to Darryl Kile's. A lack of experience may be the biggest reason Reynolds sometimes fails to make quality pitches in critical situations.

## Hitting & Defense

When Reynolds makes contact at the plate, it's usually because he's in a sacrifice situation. He laid down 10 sacrifices in '95, but also struck out in nearly 50 percent of his plate appearances, finishing with just one RBI. An average fielding pitcher, Reynolds occasionally provides baserunners an edge with his methodical delivery, and it showed as 16 of 22 runners attempting to steal against him were successful.

## 1996 Outlook

In two short years, Reynolds has gone from relative obscurity to being regarded as the top right-handed starter on the Astros' staff. If he challenges hitters a bit more and receives adequate run support, Reynolds has the potential to become a 15-game winner.

**Position:** SP
**Bats:** R  **Throws:** R
**Ht:** 6' 3"  **Wt:** 210

**Opening Day Age:** 28
**Born:** 3/26/68 in Bastrop, LA
**ML Seasons:** 4

### Overall Statistics

| | W | L | Pct. | ERA | G | GS | Sv | IP | H | BB | SO | HR | BR/IP |
|---|---|---|---|---|---|---|---|---|---|---|---|---|---|
| 1995 | 10 | 11 | .476 | 3.47 | 30 | 30 | 0 | 189.1 | 196 | 37 | 175 | 15 | 1.23 |
| Career | 19 | 19 | .500 | 3.50 | 76 | 50 | 0 | 349.2 | 377 | 70 | 305 | 27 | 1.28 |

### How Often He Throws Strikes

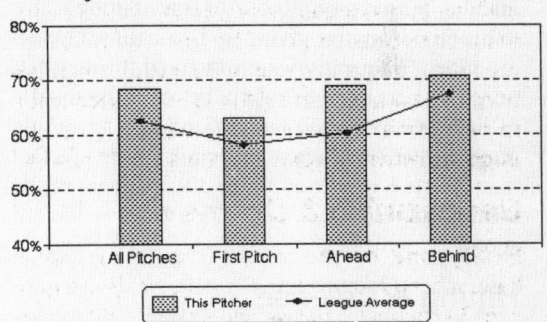

### 1995 Situational Stats

| | W | L | ERA | Sv | IP | | AB | H | HR | RBI | Avg |
|---|---|---|---|---|---|---|---|---|---|---|---|
| Home | 4 | 4 | 2.82 | 0 | 83.0 | LHB | 354 | 92 | 6 | 34 | .260 |
| Road | 6 | 7 | 3.98 | 0 | 106.1 | RHB | 391 | 104 | 9 | 40 | .266 |
| First Half | 5 | 5 | 2.60 | 0 | 86.2 | Sc Pos | 191 | 47 | 3 | 58 | .246 |
| Scnd Half | 5 | 6 | 4.21 | 0 | 102.2 | Clutch | 63 | 18 | 1 | 5 | .286 |

### 1995 Rankings (National League)

→ 2nd in highest strikeout/walk ratio (4.7) and highest groundball/flyball ratio allowed (2.7)
→ 3rd in shutouts (2) and most strikeouts per 9 innings (8.3)
→ 4th in strikeouts
→ 5th in lowest on-base percentage allowed (.300)
→ 6th in games started
→ 7th in least pitches thrown per batter (3.49), least baserunners allowed per 9 innings (11.2) and least home runs allowed per 9 innings (.71)
→ Led the Astros in wins, complete games (3), shutouts, innings pitched, strikeouts, balks (1) and highest strikeout/walk ratio

**Houston Astros**

# Greg Swindell

## 1995 Season

Greg Swindell probably pitched more out of the stretch in 1995 than at any other time in his major league career for two reasons. First, he allowed a whopping 180 hits in only 153 innings. And second, he made seven relief appearances after continued inconsistency as a starter. Although he retained his above-average control, Swindell also gave up a team-high 21 homers in what may have been his last season in a Houston uniform.

## Pitching

Swindell's fastball now peaks in the mid-80s and his curve has become inconsistent, prompting him to rely on his slider as his most effective pitch. His inability to find the corners is a contributing factor to his propensity for giving up home runs. Opposing hitters frequently were rewarded for their patience by being served fat pitches over the middle of the plate. Swindell has learned to pitch inside more effectively against left-handed hitters, a fact that resulted in his move to the bullpen in the waning stages of the Astros' run at the wild-card spot.

## Hitting & Defense

Despite his lack of quickness, Swindell remains an above-average fielder who does a fine job holding runners on first base—runners enjoyed just a 54-percent success rate attempting to steal against him in '95. He also has become one of the Astros' best pitchers at making contact while at bat, finishing with a .240 average and laying down six sacrifices in '95.

## 1996 Outlook

Although his weight is officially listed at 225, that's probably very low, and Swindell may have lost an edge off some of his pitches over the years because of his hefty build. Now 31, his career is at a crossroads. A major disappointment during his three seasons in Houston, Swindell will be gone if the Astros can find someone willing to assume his big contract. 1996 could be Swindell's make-or-break season in the major leagues.

**Position:** SP/RP
**Bats:** R **Throws:** L
**Ht:** 6' 3" **Wt:** 225

**Opening Day Age:** 31
**Born:** 1/2/65 in Fort Worth, TX
**ML Seasons:** 10
**Pronunciation:** Swin-DELL

### Overall Statistics

|        | W   | L  | Pct. | ERA  | G   | GS  | Sv | IP     | H    | BB  | SO   | HR  | BR/IP |
|--------|-----|----|------|------|-----|-----|----|--------|------|-----|------|-----|-------|
| 1995   | 10  | 9  | .526 | 4.47 | 33  | 26  | 0  | 153.0  | 180  | 39  | 96   | 21  | 1.43  |
| Career | 102 | 94 | .520 | 3.80 | 272 | 262 | 0  | 1748.1 | 1839 | 372 | 1188 | 188 | 1.26  |

### How Often He Throws Strikes

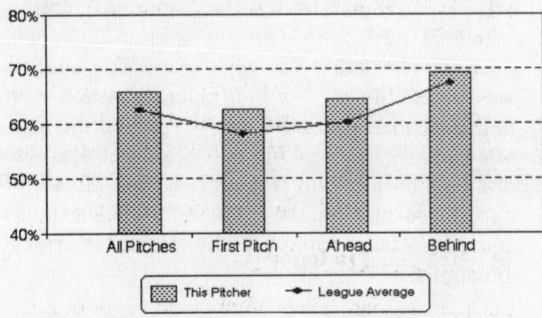

### 1995 Situational Stats

|            | W | L | ERA  | Sv | IP   |        | AB  | H   | HR | RBI | Avg  |
|------------|---|---|------|----|------|--------|-----|-----|----|-----|------|
| Home       | 5 | 5 | 3.78 | 0  | 85.2 | LHB    | 106 | 26  | 1  | 9   | .245 |
| Road       | 5 | 4 | 5.35 | 0  | 67.1 | RHB    | 500 | 154 | 20 | 72  | .308 |
| First Half | 6 | 3 | 4.17 | 0  | 77.2 | Sc Pos | 127 | 38  | 6  | 60  | .299 |
| Scnd Half  | 4 | 6 | 4.78 | 0  | 75.1 | Clutch | 33  | 9   | 0  | 2   | .273 |

### 1995 Rankings (National League)

➡ 2nd in highest slugging percentage allowed (.474)

➡ 3rd in highest batting average allowed (.297)

➡ 4th in pickoff throws (191) and runners caught stealing (12)

➡ 5th in most home runs allowed per 9 innings (1.24)

➡ 6th in highest batting average allowed vs. right-handed batters (.308)

➡ 8th in most baserunners allowed per 9 innings (13.0), most run support per 9 innings (5.5) and least strikeouts per 9 innings (5.6)

➡ Led the Astros in wins, home runs allowed and pickoff throws (191)

# Dave Veres

## 1995 Season

Righthander Dave Veres unquestionably was the Astros' most consistent reliever in 1995. Used almost exclusively as a set-up man, he led all National League relievers with 103.1 innings. Veres was the man the Astros called upon to pass leads along to closers John Hudek, Todd Jones and Mike Henneman. He responded to that challenge by averaging almost a strikeout per inning in only his second season in the majors.

## Pitching

Veres excels at the primary responsibility of any relief pitcher—he throws strikes. He issued only 30 walks and consistently came up with big strikeouts in key situations. Batters his just .196 against him with runners in scoring position. Veres doesn't have a wide variety of pitches, relying mainly on a fastball, a split-fingered fastball, and a slider. But he can paint the corners and isn't reluctant to challenge hitters by coming inside. The most compelling statistic describing Veres' control might be that he allowed only five homers all season.

## Hitting & Defense

As a set-up man, Veres often is removed for pinch hitters and seldom makes a plate appearance. He went hitless in five at-bats, striking out four times. He fielded his position adequately, especially when it came to charging off the mound on sacrifice attempts. He has a pretty good move to first.

## 1996 Outlook

The big question is what Veres will do for an encore. Although used primarily as a starter much of his nine-year career in the minors, he has displayed the necessary command of his pitches to remain a standout major league reliever. His 1995 season proved that his 1994 campaign was no fluke. After two seasons as a member of the Houston bullpen, he has become the team's best set-up man since Larry Andersen.

**Position:** RP
**Bats:** R  **Throws:** R
**Ht:** 6' 2"  **Wt:** 195

**Opening Day Age:** 29
**Born:** 10/19/66 in Montgomery, AL
**ML Seasons:** 2
**Pronunciation:** VEERZ

### Overall Statistics

|        | W | L | Pct. | ERA | G | GS | Sv | IP | H | BB | SO | HR | BR/IP |
|--------|---|---|------|-----|---|----|----|----|---|----|----|----|-------|
| 1995   | 5 | 1 | .833 | 2.26 | 72 | 0 | 1 | 103.1 | 89 | 30 | 94 | 5 | 1.15 |
| Career | 8 | 4 | .667 | 2.31 | 104 | 0 | 2 | 144.1 | 128 | 37 | 122 | 9 | 1.14 |

### How Often He Throws Strikes

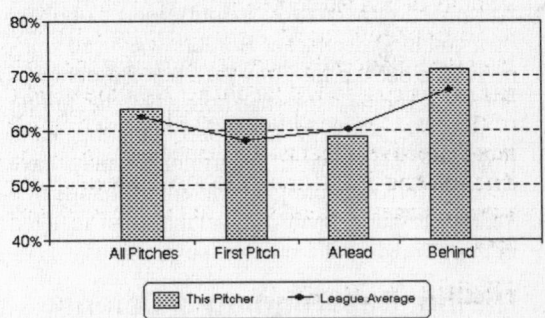

### 1995 Situational Stats

|            | W | L | ERA | Sv | IP |  |        | AB | H | HR | RBI | Avg |
|------------|---|---|-----|----|-----|--|--------|-----|----|----|-----|------|
| Home       | 2 | 0 | 2.52 | 0 | 50.0 |  | LHB    | 140 | 34 | 3 | 6 | .243 |
| Road       | 3 | 1 | 2.03 | 1 | 53.1 |  | RHB    | 230 | 55 | 2 | 25 | .239 |
| First Half | 3 | 1 | 1.74 | 0 | 51.2 |  | Sc Pos | 97 | 19 | 0 | 25 | .196 |
| Scnd Half  | 2 | 0 | 2.79 | 1 | 51.2 |  | Clutch | 162 | 37 | 3 | 16 | .228 |

### 1995 Rankings (National League)

- ➜ 1st in relief innings (103.1)
- ➜ 2nd in games pitched
- ➜ 3rd in holds (19)
- ➜ 5th in relief ERA (2.26)
- ➜ Led the Astros in games pitched, holds, first batter efficiency (.177), relief ERA, relief innings and least baserunners allowed per 9 innings in relief (10.7)

**Houston Astros**

# Pat Borders

**Position:** C
**Bats:** R **Throws:** R
**Ht:** 6' 2" **Wt:** 195

**Opening Day Age:** 32
**Born:** 5/14/63 in
Columbus, OH
**ML Seasons:** 8

## Overall Statistics

| | G | AB | R | H | D | T | HR | RBI | SB | BB | SO | Avg | OBP | Slg |
|---|---|---|---|---|---|---|---|---|---|---|---|---|---|---|
| 1995 | 63 | 178 | 15 | 37 | 8 | 1 | 4 | 13 | 0 | 9 | 29 | .208 | .246 | .331 |
| Career | 804 | 2473 | 219 | 624 | 135 | 10 | 57 | 282 | 6 | 120 | 391 | .252 | .287 | .384 |

## 1995 Season

Acquired by the Astros at midseason to bolster their catching depth, Pat Borders was used sparingly as a backup for Tony Eusebio. Borders was not the factor the Astros had hoped he'd be, failing to drive in a run in 35 at-bats with the team. Ironically, his biggest "contribution" may have been his role in inciting a beanball exchange in a September game against Cincinnati that resulted in three brawls and a series of suspensions.

## Hitting, Baserunning & Defense

Borders' overall skills have eroded to the point where opposing pitchers can get him out with a steady diet of breaking pitches and fastballs on the corners. Until he joined the Astros last season, Borders had spent his entire career in the A.L., so his hitting might improve once he learns his new league. He does a good job blocking the plate, but seemed to have trouble in '95 stopping pitches in the dirt. His throwing arm is mediocre, at best, and he indeed runs like a 32-year-old catcher.

## 1996 Outlook

The Astros are committed to platooning Eusebio and Rick Wilkins in '96, so Borders is expendable. But major league teams are always looking for catchers with experience, and Borders might extend his career if he regains his batting stroke.

# Doug Brocail

**Position:** RP/SP
**Bats:** L **Throws:** R
**Ht:** 6' 5" **Wt:** 235

**Opening Day Age:** 28
**Born:** 5/16/67 in
Clearfield, PA
**ML Seasons:** 4
**Pronunciation:**
Broh-KAIL

## Overall Statistics

| | W | L | Pct. | ERA | G | GS | Sv | IP | H | BB | SO | HR | BR/IP |
|---|---|---|---|---|---|---|---|---|---|---|---|---|---|
| 1995 | 6 | 4 | .600 | 4.19 | 36 | 7 | 1 | 77.1 | 87 | 22 | 39 | 10 | 1.41 |
| Career | 10 | 17 | .370 | 4.64 | 75 | 34 | 1 | 236.2 | 268 | 74 | 135 | 29 | 1.45 |

## 1995 Season

After being obtained by the Astros in the blockbuster trade with San Diego, righthander Doug Brocail provided the Astros with some flashes of brilliance during his first season with the club. A series of injuries to Houston's pitching staff prompted the team to use him as both a spot starter and in long relief. He seemed to adapt better to pitching out of the bullpen, posting an ERA as a reliever more than two runs below his figure as a starter.

## Pitching, Defense & Hitting

Brocail throws a fastball, slider and change-up. He isn't going to overpower many hitters, but he works the corners well. When he does make a fat pitch, he pays for it—he allowed 10 home runs in just 77.1 innings last season. In addition, lefties continue to be a problem for him. Brocail fields his position well, and is no slouch at the plate; he batted .250 last season with four sacrifices in a limited number of plate appearances. He's slow to the plate and very easy to run on.

## 1996 Outlook

Brocail needs to work on improving the overall consistency of his pitches, but he did some fine work last year and he's versatile enough to fit into the Astros' plans. He may be used as a combination fifth starter/long reliever once again—the type of pitcher who can provide several innings when needed.

# John Cangelosi  Surprise

**Position:** CF/LF
**Bats:** B **Throws:** L
**Ht:** 5' 8" **Wt:** 160

**Opening Day Age:** 33
**Born:** 3/10/63 in
Brooklyn, NY
**ML Seasons:** 9

*Overall Statistics*

| | G | AB | R | H | D | T | HR | RBI | SB | BB | SO | Avg | OBP | Slg |
|---|---|---|---|---|---|---|---|---|---|---|---|---|---|---|
| 1995 | 90 | 201 | 46 | 64 | 5 | 2 | 2 | 18 | 21 | 48 | 42 | .318 | .457 | .393 |
| Career | 716 | 1373 | 232 | 341 | 45 | 11 | 9 | 96 | 130 | 265 | 221 | .248 | .377 | .317 |

## 1995 Season

Probably the Astros' best find in '95, John Cangelosi turned in a superb season as a part-time outfielder and effective pinch hitter for a club decimated by injuries. By the time the season ended, Cangelosi had been penciled into the Astros' leadoff position because of his .318 batting average, his high on-base percentage, and his quickness on the bases.

## Hitting, Baserunning & Defense

Cangelosi is very selective at the plate. His small strike zone forces pitches to bear down and pitch too fine, which enables him to draw walks and wait on pitches he can hit to the opposite field. As a bonus in '95, he actually hit lefthanders well. He was outstanding as a basestealer last season (21-for-26), and is adept at stretching singles into extra-base hits. Cangelosi covers ample ground for a player his size. His throwing arm isn't strong, but it is accurate.

## 1996 Outlook

Cangelosi proved to be a bargain in '95 and should play an integral role as a reserve outfielder and valuable bat off the bench. He brings plenty of hustle and experience, two vital commodities for any club. Cangelosi might not match his '95 level of production, but he is the type of player who can come in and be productive when a regular is injured.

# John Hudek

**Position:** RP
**Bats:** B **Throws:** R
**Ht:** 6' 1" **Wt:** 200

**Opening Day Age:** 29
**Born:** 8/8/66 in Tampa, FL
**ML Seasons:** 2
**Pronunciation:** HOO-dek

*Overall Statistics*

| | W | L | Pct. | ERA | G | GS | Sv | IP | H | BB | SO | HR | BR/IP |
|---|---|---|---|---|---|---|---|---|---|---|---|---|---|
| 1995 | 2 | 2 | .500 | 5.40 | 19 | 0 | 7 | 20.0 | 19 | 5 | 29 | 3 | 1.20 |
| Career | 2 | 4 | .333 | 3.79 | 61 | 0 | 23 | 59.1 | 43 | 23 | 68 | 8 | 1.11 |

## 1995 Season

Coming off a year in which he finished second in the N.L. Rookie of the Year balloting and made the All-Star team, John Hudek took a big tumble in 1995. He appeared in only 19 games before being sidelined with a career-threatening circulation problem that reduced the velocity of his fastball and nearly doubled his ERA. Hudek had averaged well over a strikeout per inning while used as the Astros' closer before hitting the disabled list in June.

## Pitching, Defense & Hitting

Hudek relies on the motion of a live fastball that was clocked in the mid-90s before he began to experience arm problems early last season. He also throws an occasional slider. Hudek has still not allowed a home run to a right-handed hitter in the majors, and is especially tough when ahead in the count. He's adept at fielding his position, and his quick delivery makes it easier for catchers to thwart potential basestealers. Hudek doesn't bat often, but managed to drive in two runs in his lone at-bat last season.

## 1996 Outlook

If healthy, Hudek has the potential to be one of the league's standout closers. But that's a huge if, and the Astros right now would consider a return to his previous form strictly a bonus. For now they'll be happy just to have him on the mound, working toward recovery.

Houston Astros

# Craig Shipley

**Position:** 3B/SS
**Bats:** R **Throws:** R
**Ht:** 6' 1" **Wt:** 190

**Opening Day Age:** 33
**Born:** 1/7/63 in Sydney, Australia
**ML Seasons:** 8

*Overall Statistics*

| | G | AB | R | H | D | T | HR | RBI | SB | BB | SO | Avg | OBP | Slg |
|---|---|---|---|---|---|---|---|---|---|---|---|---|---|---|
| 1995 | 92 | 232 | 23 | 61 | 8 | 1 | 3 | 24 | 6 | 8 | 28 | .263 | .291 | .345 |
| Career | 409 | 967 | 102 | 259 | 42 | 5 | 12 | 95 | 25 | 33 | 134 | .268 | .298 | .359 |

## 1995 Season

Craig Shipley had big shoes to fill from the start of the '95 season after he was acquired by the Astros from San Diego in a blockbuster deal that sent third baseman Ken Caminiti to the Padres. Shipley was used in a platoon role at third with Dave Magadan, and certainly didn't make Astros fans forget Caminiti in the field or at the plate, as his batting average dropped 70 points from the previous season.

## Hitting, Baserunning & Defense

Shipley is an average hitter against breaking-ball pitchers, preferring to wait for a fastball he can drive. He grounded into a team-high 13 double plays last season, and is something of a liability on the bases. He did have a good year basestealing (6 for 7) in 1995. By using him almost exclusively at third base, the Astros learned what the Padres knew all along—limited range and a below-average throwing arm put Shipley in a position to be best used as a utility player.

## 1996 Outlook

Ideally, the Astros would like to use Shipley as a part-timer who can make contact as a right-handed stick off the bench. His limitations in the field make him an unlikely candidate to become a regular, although he might secure his roster status if he becomes more productive at the plate in clutch situations.

# Mike Simms

**Position:** 1B/RF
**Bats:** R **Throws:** R
**Ht:** 6' 4" **Wt:** 185

**Opening Day Age:** 29
**Born:** 1/12/67 in Orange, CA
**ML Seasons:** 5

*Overall Statistics*

| | G | AB | R | H | D | T | HR | RBI | SB | BB | SO | Avg | OBP | Slg |
|---|---|---|---|---|---|---|---|---|---|---|---|---|---|---|
| 1995 | 50 | 121 | 14 | 31 | 4 | 0 | 9 | 24 | 1 | 13 | 28 | .256 | .341 | .512 |
| Career | 132 | 293 | 37 | 67 | 12 | 0 | 14 | 45 | 3 | 33 | 84 | .229 | .312 | .413 |

## 1995 Season

Mike Simms made the most of his limited tour of duty with the Astros in 1995. Recalled from the minors when Jeff Bagwell went down with a broken left hand for the third year in a row, Simms stepped in and provided occasional punch at the plate when the club needed it. He cranked nine home runs in August and September as the Astros fought a losing battle for the N.L. wild-card spot.

## Hitting, Baserunning & Defense

Simms gets full extension with his long arms and can quickly transform a pitcher's mistake into a home run. However, he's always struck out a lot, and he's pretty easy to handle once he gets behind in the count. He also has problems with right-handed pitching. Simms compensates for his lack of speed on the bases by knowing his limitations— he doesn't try to stretch a single into a double unless it's a sure thing. He's an above-average fielder at first, and possesses an adequate arm and decent range in the outfield.

## 1996 Outlook

The fact that Simms can hit for power and play both first base and the outfield makes him a valuable commodity. He's a bona fide power threat as a right-handed hitter off the bench—a role he'll likely have to accept, since Jeff Bagwell is firmly entrenched as the Astros' starting first baseman. After five seasons of call-ups from the minors, it might be time for Simms to finally stick around.

# Milt Thompson

**Position:** RF/LF
**Bats:** L **Throws:** R
**Ht:** 5'11" **Wt:** 190

**Opening Day Age:** 37
**Born:** 1/5/59 in
Washington, DC
**ML Seasons:** 12

*Overall Statistics*

| | G | AB | R | H | D | T | HR | RBI | SB | BB | SO | Avg | OBP | Slg |
|---|---|---|---|---|---|---|---|---|---|---|---|---|---|---|
| 1995 | 92 | 132 | 14 | 29 | 9 | 0 | 2 | 19 | 4 | 14 | 37 | .220 | .297 | .333 |
| Career | 1297 | 3695 | 488 | 1022 | 154 | 37 | 47 | 354 | 213 | 329 | 622 | .277 | .338 | .376 |

## 1995 Season

In his first full season with Houston, veteran outfielder Milt Thompson provided the Astros with a quality left-handed hitter off the bench. He hit only .220, but frequently came through in the clutch while helping guide the team's younger players. Thompson was a major reason Houston's pinch hitters finished second in the league with a .297 average.

## Hitting, Baserunning & Defense

Thompson is an aggressive contact hitter who likes to hit to the opposite field. He's especially tough with runners in scoring position, hitting .324 last season. His major weakness is that he frequently chases high fastballs out of the strike zone. At 37, he no longer has his threatening speed but is a very intelligent baserunner who isn't afraid to challenge outfielders' throws to the plate. Thompson played only sparingly in the outfield for the Astros in '95 and didn't embarrass himself. His arm is about average.

## 1996 Outlook

In the twilight of his career, Thompson is the type of role player who can still help most clubs with his leadership skills and postseason experience. Few active players can match Thompson's ability to come off the bench and ignite a late rally against right-handed relievers, which is what the Astros will expect him to do again.

# Rick Wilkins

**Position:** C
**Bats:** L **Throws:** R
**Ht:** 6' 2" **Wt:** 215

**Opening Day Age:** 28
**Born:** 6/4/67 in
Jacksonville, FL
**ML Seasons:** 5

*Overall Statistics*

| | G | AB | R | H | D | T | HR | RBI | SB | BB | SO | Avg | OBP | Slg |
|---|---|---|---|---|---|---|---|---|---|---|---|---|---|---|
| 1995 | 65 | 202 | 30 | 41 | 3 | 0 | 7 | 19 | 0 | 46 | 61 | .203 | .351 | .322 |
| Career | 470 | 1408 | 193 | 358 | 69 | 4 | 58 | 175 | 9 | 183 | 355 | .254 | .344 | .433 |

## 1995 Season

Acquired from the Chicago Cubs at midseason to serve as the Astros' starting catcher against right-handed pitchers, Rick Wilkins was placed on the disabled list because of a neck injury shortly after his arrival. Wilkins underwent surgery, missed almost two months, and wound up playing only 15 games for his new club. The Astros—who unsuccessfully tried to get the deal voided because they felt the Cubs had given them damaged goods—were never able to gauge his full ability.

## Hitting, Baserunning & Defense

Wilkins is a classic example of a fastball hitter who has trouble with breaking pitches. The Astros hope he can regain his hitting ability in night games, where his .304 career average compensates for an eye condition that makes it more difficult for him to see the ball in daylight. Wilkins is exceptional throwing out baserunners—stopping them at above the league rate last season—but is certainly no speedster on the bases himself.

## 1996 Outlook

Wilkins is still living off 1993, when he batted .303 with 30 homers for the Cubs. Since then he's hit .217 with 14 homers in 515 at-bats, and while injuries have been a factor, it's possible that his big '93 numbers were just a fluke. Wilkins likely will be platooned with Tony Eusebio at the start of 1996, but unless he's healthy and hitting he won't be able to stay in the lineup.

# Other Houston Astros

**Erik Bennett** (**Pos**: RHP, **Age**: 27)

After pitching in just one game for the Angels, Bennett was acquired off waivers by Houston in July, finishing his season in Triple-A. After a solid '94 in the minors, he struggled last season. 1996 Outlook: C

**Mike Brumley** (**Pos**: SS, **Age**: 32, **Bats**: B)

Used almost exclusively as a pinch hitter, Brumley did nothing to help his case in '95 with the Astros. A .206 career major league hitter, he doesn't have much to offer. 1996 Outlook: D

**Jerry Goff** (**Pos**: C, **Age**: 31, **Bats**: L)

Goff got the call to Houston in July, after Rick Wilkins went on the DL. He hit poorly with the Astros, but did an adequate job defensively behind the plate. He'll be lucky to have the same role in '96. 1996 Outlook: C

**Ricky Gutierrez** (**Pos**: SS, **Age**: 25, **Bats**: R)

After coming over in the mega-trade with San Diego, Gutierrez got his chance to start at shortstop after Orlando Miller got hurt. He hit .313 in September and probably earned another season. 1996 Outlook: A

**Dave Hajek** (**Pos**: SS, **Age**: 28, **Bats**: R)

After a second solid season at Triple-A, Hajek was called up in September but saw very little action. He'll have to fight hard for an infield spot in Houston. 1996 Outlook: C

**Dean Hartgraves** (**Pos**: LHP, **Age**: 29)

If Hartgraves pitched only in the Astrodome, he'd win the Cy Young Award. He posted a 0.45 ERA at home last season, but a 6.61 mark on the road. He should nevertheless continue his role as a lefty set-up man. 1996 Outlook: A

**Pedro Martinez** (**Pos**: LHP, **Age**: 27)

After coming from San Diego in the mega-trade, the Astros sent him back to the Padres after a disappointing '95. After two solid seasons in San Diego, his control was horrible for Houston. 1996 outlook: A

**Craig McMurtry** (**Pos**: RHP, **Age**: 36)

After being banished from the majors for four seasons, McMurtry struggled in 11 relief appearances with the Astros after an outstanding year as a Triple-A starter. He'll be lucky to get another chance, and the fact that he was a replacement player won't make things easier. 1996 Outlook: C

**Andy Stankiewicz** (**Pos**: SS, **Age**: 31, **Bats**: R)

Stankiewicz might have had his last chance in '95, hitting very poorly for Houston and fighting a knee injury. At 31 he'll have to show somebody a lot of defense to find a spot. 1996 Outlook: C

**Jeff Tabaka** (**Pos**: LHP, **Age**: 32)

After being traded from San Diego in July, Tabaka pitched fairly well for the Astros, posting a 2.22 ERA in 24 relief appearances. He'll have to improve his control to keep his relief role. 1996 Outlook: A

**Donne Wall** (**Pos**: RHP, **Age**: 28)

After finishing a fine year as a Triple-A starter, Wall got five starts for the Astros in September, pitching pretty well in three of them. His control remains outstanding, and will keep him around. 1996 Outlook: B

# Houston Astros Minor League Prospects

## Organization Overview:

The days when Astro ownership would spend millions of dollars to acquire a high-priced free agent like Doug Drabek or Greg Swindell seem to be long-gone. That became abundantly clear when the Astros dumped millions of dollars worth of salary in their blockbuster deal with San Diego last December. So for the near term, at least, the Astros are adopting a small-market strategy of downsizing the payroll and promoting from within. For that tactic to work, however, the Astros must be able to replace the veterans they deem too expensive with competent newcomers. The Astros had high hopes for three rookies entering last season. Two of them, Brian Hunter and Orlando Miller, came through with solid results. The third, Phil Nevin, ultimately wore out his welcome and was traded to Detroit. Two out of three may not be bad, but the Astros could have difficulty producing those three prospects every year. Although Houston still has a couple of grade-A talents making their way up the organization, the depth behind them appears a bit thin right now.

### Bob Abreu

**Position:** OF
**Bats:** L **Throws:** R
**Ht:** 6' 0" **Wt:** 160

**Opening Day Age:** 22
**Born:** 3/11/74 in
Maracay, Venez

*Recent Statistics*

| | G | AB | R | H | D | T | HR | RBI | SB | BB | SO | AVG |
|---|---|---|---|---|---|---|---|---|---|---|---|---|
| 93 A Osceola | 129 | 474 | 62 | 134 | 21 | 17 | 5 | 55 | 10 | 51 | 90 | .283 |
| 94 AA Jackson | 118 | 400 | 61 | 121 | 25 | 9 | 16 | 73 | 12 | 42 | 81 | .303 |
| 95 AAA Tucson | 114 | 415 | 72 | 126 | 24 | 17 | 10 | 75 | 16 | 67 | 120 | .304 |
| 95 MLE | 114 | 392 | 53 | 103 | 20 | 10 | 6 | 55 | 10 | 49 | 133 | .263 |

Abreu, a native of Venezuela, was signed at the age of 16 and has been one of the youngest players at every level he's competed at ever since. He reached Triple-A at the age of 21 last year and ranked among the PCL's best talents, hitting .304, leading the league in triples, and playing a solid right field. Although he struck out 120 times, his strike-zone judgement actually improved, as he drew a career-high 67 walks. Abreu's ultimate position with the Astros may be left field.

### Ramon Castro

**Position:** C
**Bats:** R **Throws:** R
**Ht:** 6' 3" **Wt:** 195

**Opening Day Age:** 20
**Born:** 3/1/76 in Vega
Baja, PR

*Recent Statistics*

| | G | AB | R | H | D | T | HR | RBI | SB | BB | SO | AVG |
|---|---|---|---|---|---|---|---|---|---|---|---|---|
| 94 R Astros | 37 | 123 | 17 | 34 | 7 | 0 | 3 | 14 | 5 | 17 | 14 | .276 |
| 95 A Kissimmee | 36 | 120 | 6 | 25 | 5 | 0 | 0 | 8 | 0 | 6 | 21 | .208 |
| 95 A Auburn | 63 | 224 | 40 | 67 | 17 | 0 | 9 | 49 | 0 | 24 | 27 | .299 |

Castro is probably a few years away from the Astrodome, or wherever else the Astros eventually call home.

He was the first Puerto Rican ever drafted in the first round, when Houston chose him 17th overall in 1994. Castro excites scouts because he's a catcher with power potential. He outclassed the short-season New York-Penn league last year, but appeared overwhelmed in his 36-game stint in the fast-A Florida State League. Since he was still a teenager, he obviously has plenty of time to make the necessary adjustments.

### Tim Forkner

**Position:** 3B
**Bats:** L **Throws:** R
**Ht:** 5' 11" **Wt:** 180

**Opening Day Age:** 23
**Born:** 3/28/73 in
Montrose, CO

*Recent Statistics*

| | G | AB | R | H | D | T | HR | RBI | SB | BB | SO | AVG |
|---|---|---|---|---|---|---|---|---|---|---|---|---|
| 93 A Auburn | 72 | 267 | 32 | 76 | 14 | 9 | 0 | 39 | 3 | 38 | 29 | .285 |
| 94 A Quad City | 124 | 429 | 57 | 128 | 23 | 4 | 6 | 57 | 6 | 57 | 72 | .298 |
| 95 A Kissimmee | 89 | 296 | 42 | 84 | 20 | 4 | 1 | 34 | 4 | 60 | 40 | .284 |
| 95 AA Jackson | 35 | 119 | 19 | 32 | 11 | 0 | 3 | 23 | 1 | 19 | 14 | .269 |

Forkner will probably need to learn to drive the ball if he is to be anything more than a major league backup. His position, third base, virtually demands more than six home runs a year, his single-season high. Even without much power, however, Forkner is not an offensive liability. He coaxes walks, hits some doubles, and is a career .288 hitter. The Astros' 14th-round pick in 1993, Forkner will probably return to Double-A this season at the age of 23.

### Richard Hidalgo

**Position:** OF
**Bats:** R **Throws:** R
**Ht:** 6' 2" **Wt:** 175

**Opening Day Age:** 20
**Born:** 7/2/75 in
Caracas, Venez

*Recent Statistics*

| | G | AB | R | H | D | T | HR | RBI | SB | BB | SO | AVG |
|---|---|---|---|---|---|---|---|---|---|---|---|---|
| 93 A Asheville | 111 | 403 | 49 | 109 | 23 | 3 | 10 | 55 | 21 | 30 | 76 | .270 |
| 94 A Quad City | 124 | 476 | 68 | 139 | 47 | 6 | 12 | 76 | 12 | 23 | 80 | .292 |
| 95 AA Jackson | 133 | 489 | 59 | 130 | 28 | 6 | 14 | 59 | 8 | 32 | 76 | .266 |
| 95 MLE | 133 | 478 | 56 | 119 | 26 | 4 | 12 | 56 | 6 | 25 | 86 | .249 |

The Astros have enjoyed recent success signing and developing players from Venezuela such as Hidalgo, Abreu and Roberto Petagine, who was involved in the trade with San Diego. It's possible that Hidalgo, who started last year in Double-A as a teenager, will ultimately be better than any of them. After leading the Midwest League with 47 doubles in 1994, Hidalgo's batting average and extra-base total both fell last year. He did show slightly better plate discipline, although he can definitely improve that area of his game. In right field, Hidalgo's arm has already gained a great reputation.

## Chris Holt

| | | |
|---|---|---|
| **Position:** P | **Opening Day Age:** 24 |
| **Bats:** R **Throws:** R | **Born:** 9/18/71 in |
| **Ht:** 6' 4" **Wt:** 205 | Dallas, TX |

*Recent Statistics*

| | W | L | ERA | G | GS | Sv | IP | H | R | BB | SO | HR |
|---|---|---|---|---|---|---|---|---|---|---|---|---|
| 93 A Quad City | 11 | 10 | 2.27 | 26 | 26 | 0 | 186.1 | 162 | 70 | 54 | 176 | 10 |
| 94 AA Jackson | 10 | 9 | 3.45 | 26 | 25 | 0 | 167.0 | 169 | 78 | 22 | 111 | 11 |
| 95 AA Jackson | 2 | 2 | 1.67 | 5 | 5 | 0 | 32.1 | 27 | 8 | 5 | 24 | 2 |
| 95 AAA Tucson | 5 | 8 | 4.10 | 20 | 19 | 0 | 118.2 | 155 | 65 | 32 | 69 | 5 |

Holt was the Astros' third-round draft pick in 1992 out of Navarro Junior College in Texas. After leading the Midwest League in complete games with 10 in 1993, he then walked just 1.19 batters per nine innings in '94, the lowest rate of any minor leaguer. He started out well at Jackson again last year, which earned him a promotion to Tucson, where Triple-A batters hit over .300 against him. Holt's fastball is no better than major league average, so even though his control is pinpoint, his future depends on how well he develops his other pitches.

## Doug Mlicki

| | | |
|---|---|---|
| **Position:** P | **Opening Day Age:** 24 |
| **Bats:** R **Throws:** R | **Born:** 4/23/71 in |
| **Ht:** 6' 3" **Wt:** 175 | Cleveland, OH |

*Recent Statistics*

| | W | L | ERA | G | GS | Sv | IP | H | R | BB | SO | HR |
|---|---|---|---|---|---|---|---|---|---|---|---|---|
| 93 A Osceola | 11 | 10 | 3.91 | 26 | 23 | 0 | 158.2 | 158 | 81 | 65 | 111 | 16 |
| 94 AA Jackson | 13 | 7 | 3.38 | 23 | 23 | 0 | 138.2 | 107 | 62 | 54 | 130 | 20 |
| 95 AA Jackson | 8 | 3 | 2.79 | 16 | 16 | 0 | 96.2 | 73 | 41 | 33 | 72 | 6 |
| 95 AAA Tucson | 1 | 2 | 5.56 | 6 | 6 | 0 | 34.0 | 44 | 27 | 6 | 22 | 3 |

Mlicki is the younger brother of Dave, who pitched with the Mets last season after coming up through Cleveland's system. Doug was the Astros' 12th-round selection in 1992 and made it to Triple-A last year. He isn't a hard thrower but has a decent curveball and change-up. For some reason the Astros forced Mlicki to spend almost two full seasons at Double-A Jackson, even though his 21-10 record and 3.14 ERA there would indicate he was overqualified for the level. Mlicki will turn 25 in April and will probably spend most of 1996 in Tucson.

## Bryant Nelson

| | | |
|---|---|---|
| **Position:** SS | **Opening Day Age:** 22 |
| **Bats:** B **Throws:** R | **Born:** 1/27/74 in |
| **Ht:** 5' 10" **Wt:** 170 | Crossett, AR |

*Recent Statistics*

| | G | AB | R | H | D | T | HR | RBI | SB | BB | SO | AVG |
|---|---|---|---|---|---|---|---|---|---|---|---|---|
| 94 A Quad City | 45 | 156 | 20 | 38 | 6 | 0 | 1 | 6 | 3 | 11 | 15 | .244 |
| 94 A Auburn | 65 | 261 | 53 | 84 | 16 | 7 | 6 | 35 | 2 | 11 | 13 | .322 |
| 95 A Kissimmee | 105 | 395 | 47 | 129 | 34 | 5 | 3 | 52 | 14 | 20 | 37 | .327 |
| 95 A Quad City | 6 | 26 | 1 | 1 | 1 | 0 | 0 | 2 | 0 | 0 | 3 | .038 |

Nelson was drafted in the 44th-round out of a Texas junior college back in 1993. His .327 average and 34 doubles in the Florida State League show he has offensive potential, but Nelson's ticket to the majors may be his versatility. He can play virtually any position in the infield or in the outfield, and he's currently doing an adequate job playing shortstop. He's also a switch-hitter, so he can used in either platoon situation. He'll be 22 this season and will probably be bumped to Double-A.

## Billy Wagner

| | | |
|---|---|---|
| **Position:** P | **Opening Day Age:** 24 |
| **Bats:** L **Throws:** L | **Born:** 7/25/71 in |
| **Ht:** 5' 10" **Wt:** 180 | Tannersville, VA |

*Recent Statistics*

| | W | L | ERA | G | GS | Sv | IP | H | R | BB | SO | HR |
|---|---|---|---|---|---|---|---|---|---|---|---|---|
| 95 AA Jackson | 2 | 2 | 2.57 | 12 | 12 | 0 | 70.0 | 49 | 25 | 36 | 77 | 7 |
| 95 AAA Tucson | 5 | 3 | 3.18 | 13 | 13 | 0 | 76.1 | 70 | 28 | 32 | 80 | 3 |
| 95 NL Houston | 0 | 0 | 0.00 | 1 | 0 | 0 | 0.1 | 0 | 0 | 0 | 0 | 0 |

Although he's listed at just 5'10" and might be a tad shorter than that, Wagner is an extreme power pitcher, averaging better than a strikeout per inning at every one of his four minor league stops. Wagner's fastball nears triple figures on occasion, but usually resides in the low to mid 90s. He actually averaged over 16 strikeouts per nine innings during his three seasons at Ferrum College in Virginia, convincing Houston to draft him with the 12th overall selection of 1993. When he arrives in the Astrodome for good, Wagner will revive memories of Nolan Ryan and J.R. Richard.

## Others to Watch

The Astros are fairly thin in catching prospects, but **Raul Chavez** may be the closest to the majors. He hit .278 with 4 homers and 35 RBI between Double- and Triple-A last year, though he faces a future challenge from Ramon Castro... Houston's $750,000 bonus convinced righthander **Scott Elarton** to forego a scholarship to Stanford. Elarton is 6'7", throws over 90 MPH, is very bright, and was 21-8 in the low minors as a teenager... Righthander **Tim Kester** reversed his 1994 5-12 record with a 12-5 ledger at Quad Cities last year. He reduced his ERA by almost two points, to 2.97, and boasted a strikeout-to-walk ratio of 5.6 to one... Lefthander **Tony Mounce** was another pitcher enjoying a nice year in the Midwest League. Mounce, Houston's seventh-round pick in 1994, was 16-8 with a 2.43 ERA and allowed just 118 hits in 159 innings. At 21 he was also three years younger than Kester... Shortstop **Jhonny Perez** played in the Florida State League at the age of 18 and more than held his own, which by itself is quite an accomplishment. He hit .271 and stole 23 bases in just 65 games.

# Billy Ashley

## 1995 Season

Billy Ashley and his parents petitioned the National League office for special consideration before the 1995 season because he had accumulated a few too many at-bats to be eligible for Rookie of the Year. They should have saved themselves the postage. Ashley began the year as the Dodgers' starting left fielder, but after striking out in 36 percent of his plate appearances and misplaying many fly balls, the big, strong kid landed squarely on the bench. He totaled just 33 at-bats after the All-Star break.

## Hitting

It is a lot of fun to watch Ashley hit. . . in batting practice, at least. He smacks long, towering shots to deep left field, showing as much power as anyone in baseball. When the pitcher is actually trying to get him out, however, it is a different story. There are big holes in his swing, and he exacerbates his troubles by swinging at bad balls. Breaking stuff away gets him every time. He has shown the ability to hit the ball up the middle and to right-center, and needs to develop that stroke more.

## Baserunning & Defense

Ashley is very slow and cautious on the basepaths, strictly a station-to-station guy. He is absolutely atrocious in the outfield, an embarassment at times. He gets no jump, will almost always let a ball bounce in front of him and has no clue on balls over his head. When he finally gets to the ball, Ashley has a pretty good arm. Still, his future is either at first base or as a designated hitter.

## 1996 Outlook

He has awesome, Dave Kingman-like power, but Ashley must make contact more often. He held his own against left-handed pitching, so a left-field platoon of he and Todd Hollandsworth is a possibility. But it was Ashley's lack of defensive skills that put him in Tommy Lasorda's doghouse, and he is a manager who likes to use the same lineup every day. Ashley's days on the club could be numbered.

**Position:** LF
**Bats:** R  **Throws:** R
**Ht:** 6' 7"  **Wt:** 235

**Opening Day Age:** 25
**Born:** 7/11/70 in Taylor, MI
**ML Seasons:** 4

### Overall Statistics

|        | G   | AB  | R  | H  | D  | T | HR | RBI | SB | BB | SO  | Avg  | OBP  | Slg  |
|--------|-----|-----|----|----|----|---|----|-----|----|----|-----|------|------|------|
| 1995   | 81  | 215 | 17 | 51 | 5  | 0 | 8  | 27  | 0  | 25 | 88  | .237 | .320 | .372 |
| Career | 126 | 353 | 23 | 83 | 11 | 0 | 10 | 33  | 0  | 32 | 135 | .235 | .301 | .351 |

### Where He Hits the Ball

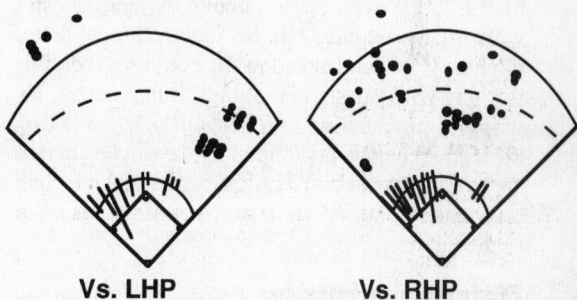

Vs. LHP          Vs. RHP

### 1995 Situational Stats

|            | AB  | H  | HR | RBI | Avg  |        | AB  | H  | HR | RBI | Avg  |
|------------|-----|----|----|-----|------|--------|-----|----|----|-----|------|
| Home       | 117 | 35 | 6  | 22  | .299 | LHP    | 68  | 19 | 2  | 5   | .279 |
| Road       | 98  | 16 | 2  | 5   | .163 | RHP    | 147 | 32 | 6  | 22  | .218 |
| First Half | 182 | 46 | 8  | 27  | .253 | Sc Pos | 51  | 11 | 3  | 22  | .216 |
| Scnd Half  | 33  | 5  | 0  | 0   | .152 | Clutch | 26  | 4  | 0  | 1   | .154 |

### 1995 Rankings (National League)

➡ 3rd in lowest batting average on an 0-2 count (.037)
➡ 9th in errors in left field (3)

# Pedro Astacio

## 1995 Season

Pedro Astacio began the year as a solid member of the rotation, but was moved to the bullpen in June after a series of ineffective starts. The change served him well, as his ERA was almost a run-and-a-half lower in relief than as a starter. Perhaps more important on the image-conscious Dodgers, the young Dominican did not complain or sulk. He performed like a true professional.

## Pitching

Everything hinges on Astacio's hard sinking fastball. He must keep it down, yet in the strike zone, to be effective. The 90-plus MPH heater is complemented by a good change-up, and if he can get his curveball over, that's a bonus. Astacio doesn't walk many people, but he makes much better pitches when he is ahead in the count. In fact, this is a guy who rides an emotional rollercoaster. He wriggles his pitching arm nervously when taking the sign. When he is pumped up, he pitches better, and like a less showy Carlos Perez, Astacio will punctuate an inning-ending strikeout by sprinting to the dugout.

## Defense & Hitting

Astacio has developed a good move to first and delivers the ball quickly to the plate as well. Opposing basestealers were just 7-for-13 in 1995. He has quick hands and feet and is just as fast off the mound during an inning as he is after the third out. He is game but awkward at the plate.

## 1996 Outlook

A smaller-market team would have probably stuck with Astacio a bit longer. The Dodgers went with Willie Banks, then brought out their fat wallet to rent Kevin Tapani. Neither was very good, and Astacio's lifetime ERA in August through October is 2.23. They may be paying the price now for rushing him to the majors in 1992, but Astacio has a live arm and is just 26 years old. He could prove to be a valuable member of their staff, regardless of his role.

**Position:** RP/SP
**Bats:** R  **Throws:** R
**Ht:** 6' 2"  **Wt:** 195

**Opening Day Age:** 26
**Born:** 11/28/69 in Hato Mayor, DR
**ML Seasons:** 4
**Pronunciation:** a-STA-see-oh

### Overall Statistics

|        | W  | L  | Pct. | ERA  | G   | GS | Sv | IP    | H   | BB  | SO  | HR | BR/IP |
|--------|----|----|------|------|-----|----|----|-------|-----|-----|-----|----|-------|
| 1995   | 7  | 8  | .467 | 4.24 | 48  | 11 | 0  | 104.0 | 103 | 29  | 80  | 12 | 1.27  |
| Career | 32 | 30 | .516 | 3.66 | 113 | 76 | 0  | 521.1 | 490 | 164 | 353 | 45 | 1.25  |

### How Often He Throws Strikes

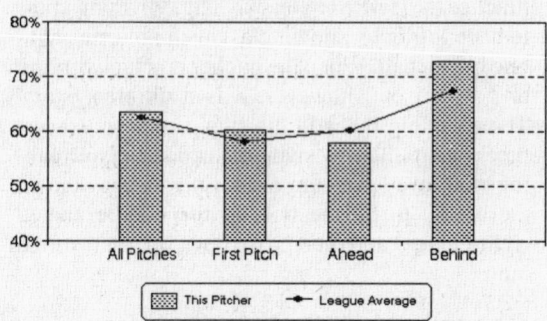

### 1995 Situational Stats

|            | W | L | ERA  | Sv | IP   |       | AB  | H  | HR | RBI | Avg  |
|------------|---|---|------|----|------|-------|-----|----|----|-----|------|
| Home       | 4 | 3 | 4.04 | 0  | 49.0 | LHB   | 194 | 50 | 8  | 24  | .258 |
| Road       | 3 | 5 | 4.42 | 0  | 55.0 | RHB   | 201 | 53 | 4  | 25  | .264 |
| First Half | 1 | 7 | 4.50 | 0  | 72.0 | Sc Pos| 91  | 22 | 1  | 33  | .242 |
| Scnd Half  | 6 | 1 | 3.66 | 0  | 32.0 | Clutch| 82  | 22 | 2  | 10  | .268 |

### 1995 Rankings (National League)

- ➡ 6th in worst first batter efficiency (.324)
- ➡ 8th in relief wins (6)
- ➡ Led the Dodgers in relief wins

# Brett Butler

## 1995 Season

1995 had to be the strangest of Brett Butler's 15-year career. Cast adrift by the Dodgers for his pro-union stance and/or high salary demands, he finally accepted a modest offer from the Mets. Hitting just .255 at the All-Star break and with his mother battling cancer, Butler considered retirement before rekindling his spirit with a scorching July. He was then re-acquired by the Dodgers, fought off an ugly replacement player tiff and helped lead them to the playoffs. . . only to see the club get swept by the Reds. Strange days indeed.

## Hitting

Nothing new here. Butler spanked the ball enough times to hit .300 on the nose. He led the league with 43 infield hits and walked more times than he struck out, something he has failed to accomplish only three times in his career. Though he will occasionally try to yank the first pitch down the right-field line just to keep 'em honest, Butler is a classic good pitch spoiler. He usually likes to wait until he can hit one hard to the left side. Then he runs like hell.

## Baserunning & Defense

If the 38 year old has lost a step, he makes it up with moxie. Butler stole 32 bases and his 80-percent success rate was the highest full-season mark of his career. Just like at the plate, he is a pitcher's pest on the basepaths and seldom makes a mistake. Butler is not quite as flawless defensively as he once was and his arm isn't as strong, but he remains one of the steadier center fielders in the game.

## 1996 Outlook

Though he must be tiring of the uncertainty, once Butler is between the lines his game remains remarkably consistent. Roger Cedeno is still considered the Dodgers' center fielder of the future, but he's also still green, and Butler signed a one-year deal with the Dodgers for 1996.

**Position:** CF
**Bats:** L **Throws:** L
**Ht:** 5'10" **Wt:** 161

**Opening Day Age:** 38
**Born:** 6/15/57 in Los Angeles, CA
**ML Seasons:** 15

### Overall Statistics

|  | G | AB | R | H | D | T | HR | RBI | SB | BB | SO | Avg | OBP | Slg |
|---|---|---|---|---|---|---|---|---|---|---|---|---|---|---|
| 1995 | 129 | 513 | 78 | 154 | 18 | 9 | 1 | 38 | 32 | 67 | 51 | .300 | .377 | .376 |
| Career | 2074 | 7706 | 1285 | 2243 | 268 | 127 | 54 | 552 | 535 | 1078 | 845 | .291 | .379 | .380 |

### Where He Hits the Ball

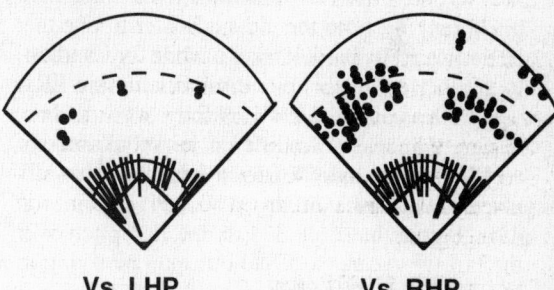

**Vs. LHP**      **Vs. RHP**

### 1995 Situational Stats

|  | AB | H | HR | RBI | Avg |  | AB | H | HR | RBI | Avg |
|---|---|---|---|---|---|---|---|---|---|---|---|
| Home | 253 | 75 | 0 | 19 | .296 | LHP | 130 | 36 | 1 | 11 | .277 |
| Road | 260 | 79 | 1 | 19 | .304 | RHP | 383 | 118 | 0 | 27 | .308 |
| First Half | 255 | 65 | 0 | 22 | .255 | Sc Pos | 106 | 29 | 0 | 36 | .274 |
| Scnd Half | 258 | 89 | 1 | 16 | .345 | Clutch | 98 | 29 | 0 | 8 | .296 |

### 1995 Rankings (National League)

- → 1st in triples, lowest HR frequency (513.0 ABs per HR), highest groundball/flyball ratio (2.6) and bunts in play (46)
- → 2nd in singles (126) and lowest percentage of swings that missed (5.5%)
- → 3rd in fielding percentage in center field (.993)
- → 5th in on-base percentage for a leadoff hitter (.375)
- → 7th in pitches seen (2,376)
- → 8th in sacrifice flies (6)
- → 9th in stolen bases
- → Led the Dodgers in batting average on a 3-1 count (.667) and on-base percentage for a leadoff hitter (.368)

# Tom Candiotti

## 1995 Season

With his calm demeanor and tantalizing knuckle-ball, Tom Candiotti has the unique ability of putting two offenses to sleep: his own as well as that of the opposition. The Dodgers were shut out 12 times in 1995, half of them with Candiotti on the mound, and he did not allow an earned run in three of those. In fact, they averaged 3.0 runs per game over his last 25 starts, and that includes one contest in which the offense scored 10 runs. It was just another frustrating year for the veteran, who kept his club in almost every game he started.

## Pitching

It all starts with the knuckler. Candiotti actually has several different versions of his trademark pitch, ranging from the classic floater to one that he throws pretty hard. It takes a while for Candiotti to get the feel of this pitch; his first inning ERA was 7.80, as opposed to a 2.69 the rest of the time. Candiotti mixes in two different curveballs, one of which drops straight downward. He will also mix in a cut fastball that might tip 80 MPH on his good days. Batters have hit .374 on the first pitch over the last two years, so Candiotti may be trying to slip that one in for a strike too often.

## Defense & Hitting

Candiotti has developed a fine move to first and it paid dividends in '95. Basestealers were just 10-for-23 against him. His pickoff throws seem harder than any of his pitches and they are very accurate as well. In the field, Candiotti is cautious rather than quick. He is not an automatic out at the plate and can get the bunt down when asked.

## 1996 Outlook

Candiotti went 33-46 in his four years with the Dodgers, but pitched much better than that. His ERA over that span was 3.39. He will probably not be back with the club, but appears to have at least a couple of decent years left. An experienced innings-eater who never gets rattled, Candiotti should have no trouble finding a rotation spot somewhere.

**Position:** SP
**Bats:** R **Throws:** R
**Ht:** 6' 2"  **Wt:** 221

**Opening Day Age:** 38
**Born:** 8/31/57 in Walnut Creek, CA
**ML Seasons:** 12
**Pronunciation:** kan-dee-AH-tee

### Overall Statistics

|        | W   | L   | Pct. | ERA  | G   | GS  | Sv | IP     | H    | BB  | SO   | HR  | BR/IP |
|--------|-----|-----|------|------|-----|-----|----|--------|------|-----|------|-----|-------|
| 1995   | 7   | 14  | .333 | 3.50 | 30  | 30  | 0  | 190.1  | 187  | 58  | 141  | 18  | 1.29  |
| Career | 117 | 124 | .485 | 3.47 | 331 | 319 | 0  | 2165.1 | 2054 | 707 | 1428 | 167 | 1.28  |

### How Often He Throws Strikes

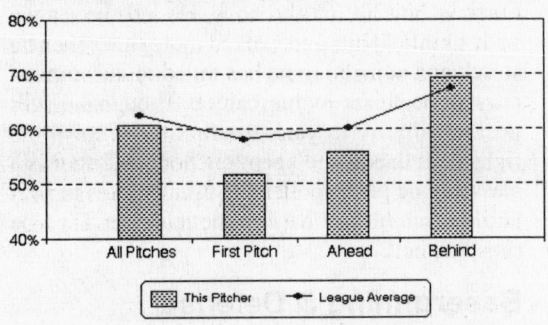

### 1995 Situational Stats

|            | W | L | ERA  | Sv | IP    |        | AB  | H  | HR | RBI | Avg  |
|------------|---|---|------|----|-------|--------|-----|----|----|-----|------|
| Home       | 3 | 9 | 3.35 | 0  | 102.0 | LHB    | 330 | 88 | 7  | 27  | .267 |
| Road       | 4 | 5 | 3.67 | 0  | 88.1  | RHB    | 402 | 99 | 11 | 56  | .246 |
| First Half | 4 | 6 | 2.82 | 0  | 95.2  | Sc Pos | 187 | 39 | 6  | 62  | .209 |
| Scnd Half  | 3 | 8 | 4.18 | 0  | 94.2  | Clutch | 72  | 17 | 3  | 7   | .236 |

### 1995 Rankings (National League)

- ➡ 1st in least run support per 9 innings (3.5)
- ➡ 2nd in losses and runners caught stealing (13)
- ➡ 6th in games started, pitches thrown (3,052), lowest winning percentage and lowest stolen base percentage allowed (43.5%)
- ➡ 7th in hit batsmen (9) and lowest batting average allowed with runners in scoring position (.209)
- ➡ 9th in batters faced (812)
- ➡ 10th in most pitches thrown per batter (3.76)
- ➡ Led the Dodgers in losses, games started, hits allowed, hit batsmen, pickoff throws (91), runners caught stealing, highest ground-ball/flyball ratio allowed (1.5) and lowest stolen base percentage allowed

# Delino DeShields

## 1995 Season

Delino DeShields followed up a disappointing 1994 campaign—his first as a member of the Dodgers—with a carbon copy in 1995. He suffered through the first half with mysterious ailments to his back and legs. After losing his job for a month to rookie sparkplug Chad Fonville, DeShields returned to the starting lineup on August 20th with a vengeance. Using lighter bats left behind by Willie Banks, he hit .305 through the end of the season with 18 stolen bases. He thus revived hopes that his career is back on track.

## Hitting

DeShields swings a quick bat, though there are plenty of holes in it. He is quite selective, too much so at times. He often gets behind in the count and is not able to make contact on a tough third strike pitch. After cutting down on his strikeouts every year since leading the league with 151 in 1991, DeShields regressed and went down 83 times in '95. Though he has surprising power, he is at his best when he uses the whole field and lets his legs do the work.

## Baserunning & Defense

When healthy, the thin Delaware native can really motor. He has a 74-percent stolen-base success rate over his six-year career. DeShields does not dazzle in the field. He has great range to his left, but is shaky to his right. His arm is a bit on the weak side and he is just fair at turning the double play. He plays too deep for a natural-grass infield, a leftover from his days on turf, so he has to hurry on anything hit slowly.

## 1996 Outlook

DeShields is a thoughtful, brooding guy who has never seemed at home in Los Angeles and he does not buy Tommy Lasorda's schtick at all. With Chad Fonville the heir apparent at second base, the free agent will probably head back east. He should look for a team that plays on turf; it enhances every part of his game.

**Position:** 2B
**Bats:** L  **Throws:** R
**Ht:** 6' 1"  **Wt:** 175

**Opening Day Age:** 27
**Born:** 1/15/69 in Seaford, DE
**ML Seasons:** 6

### Overall Statistics

|        | G   | AB   | R   | H   | D   | T  | HR | RBI | SB  | BB  | SO  | Avg  | OBP  | Slg  |
|--------|-----|------|-----|-----|-----|----|----|-----|-----|-----|-----|------|------|------|
| 1995   | 127 | 425  | 66  | 109 | 18  | 3  | 8  | 37  | 39  | 63  | 83  | .256 | .353 | .369 |
| Career | 754 | 2818 | 426 | 764 | 108 | 31 | 33 | 251 | 253 | 404 | 555 | .271 | .363 | .367 |

### Where He Hits the Ball

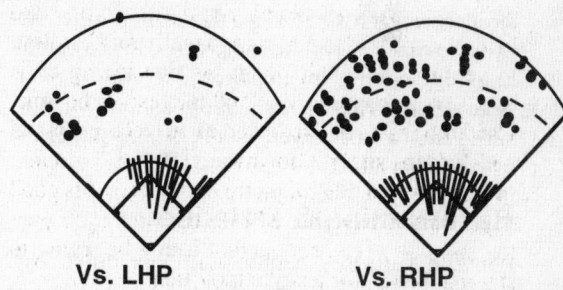

**Vs. LHP**          **Vs. RHP**

### 1995 Situational Stats

|            | AB  | H  | HR | RBI | Avg  |        | AB  | H  | HR | RBI | Avg  |
|------------|-----|----|----|-----|------|--------|-----|----|----|-----|------|
| Home       | 205 | 43 | 2  | 15  | .210 | LHP    | 121 | 25 | 2  | 11  | .207 |
| Road       | 220 | 66 | 6  | 22  | .300 | RHP    | 304 | 84 | 6  | 26  | .276 |
| First Half | 253 | 62 | 4  | 16  | .245 | Sc Pos | 75  | 27 | 1  | 29  | .360 |
| Scnd Half  | 172 | 47 | 4  | 21  | .273 | Clutch | 80  | 18 | 1  | 8   | .225 |

### 1995 Rankings (National League)

- → 1st in errors at second base (11) and lowest fielding percentage at second base (.980)
- → 2nd in lowest batting average at home (.210)
- → 3rd in stolen bases, caught stealing (14) and lowest batting average vs. left-handed pitchers (.207)
- → 4th in batting average with runners in scoring position (.360), lowest on-base percentage for a leadoff hitter (.320) and highest percentage of pitches taken (63.9%)
- → 6th in most pitches seen per plate appearance (4.07) and lowest slugging percentage vs. left-handed pitchers (.314)
- → Led the Dodgers in stolen bases and caught stealing

**Los Angeles Dodgers**

# Chad Fonville

## 1995 Season

There was no bigger surprise on the Dodgers—and maybe in all of baseball—in 1995 than the performance of Chad Fonville. Plucked from Montreal (who had just plucked him from San Francisco) via the Rule 5 draft, the scrappy little guy flat out hustled his way into the starting lineup. He played second base, then moved to left field before finally settling in at shortstop for the last month. Bottom line: the club was 40-27 with Fonville in the starting lineup.

## Hitting

Fonville is a spray hitter with no power. Almost half (40 of 89) of his hits stayed in the infield, and 19 of those were bunts. Though he looks a bit stronger on the right side, the switch-hitter approaches each at-bat the same way. He is a battler, hanging in there even when seemingly overmatched. Fonville could be more patient; with his speed and lack of power, a walk is almost literally as good as a hit.

## Baserunning & Defense

Fonville surprises people with his quickness. From the left side, he gets down the line as fast as anyone this side of Deion Sanders before the ankle surgery. He stole 20 bases in his last 24 attempts. In the field, he attacks the ball and shows great range no matter the position. In fact, Fonville adapted wonderfully to the outfield. He showed good natural instincts and a decent arm, though it is probably not strong enough to play shortstop every day.

## 1996 Outlook

Even with all the praise, this is a 25 year old who had never played above A-ball before the 1995 season. The Dodgers sent him to the Arizona Fall League to play every day at second base, where he is expected to start next year. He brought a lot of energy to a team that had gotten too comfortable, but when all was said and done, his on-base percentage was 61 points lower than displaced Jose Offerman. Fonville could disappoint when the league catches up with him.

**Position:** 2B/SS
**Bats:** B **Throws:** R
**Ht:** 5' 6" **Wt:** 155

**Opening Day Age:** 25
**Born:** 3/5/71 in Jacksonville, NC
**ML Seasons:** 1

### Overall Statistics

|  | G | AB | R | H | D | T | HR | RBI | SB | BB | SO | Avg | OBP | Slg |
|---|---|---|---|---|---|---|---|---|---|---|---|---|---|---|
| 1995 | 102 | 320 | 43 | 89 | 6 | 1 | 0 | 16 | 20 | 23 | 42 | .278 | .328 | .303 |
| Career | 102 | 320 | 43 | 89 | 6 | 1 | 0 | 16 | 20 | 23 | 42 | .278 | .328 | .303 |

### Where He Hits the Ball

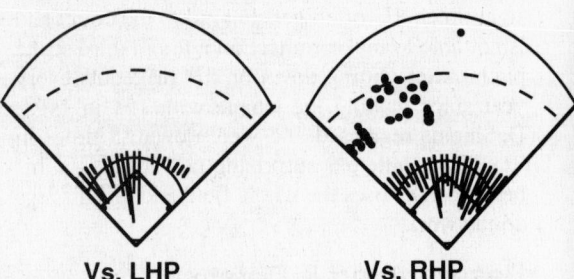

**Vs. LHP**          **Vs. RHP**

### 1995 Situational Stats

|  | AB | H | HR | RBI | Avg |  | AB | H | HR | RBI | Avg |
|---|---|---|---|---|---|---|---|---|---|---|---|
| Home | 147 | 39 | 0 | 4 | .265 | LHP | 87 | 21 | 0 | 4 | .241 |
| Road | 173 | 50 | 0 | 12 | .289 | RHP | 233 | 68 | 0 | 12 | .292 |
| First Half | 47 | 13 | 0 | 1 | .277 | Sc Pos | 64 | 18 | 0 | 16 | .281 |
| Scnd Half | 273 | 76 | 0 | 15 | .278 | Clutch | 43 | 6 | 0 | 1 | .140 |

### 1995 Rankings (National League)

→ 1st in lowest batting average in the clutch (.140)
→ 2nd in bunts in play (38)
→ 9th in errors at second base (6)
→ Led the Dodgers in bunts in play

# Eric Karros

## 1995 Season

No one has benefited more from hitting coach Reggie Smith's patient tutelage than Eric Karros. He came out of the blocks hot last year, was still hitting .359 at the end of May, and went on to establish new career highs in almost every offensive category. Karros was the most dangerous clutch hitter on the club all year long. In the final two months of the season, with the division up for grabs, he hit 15 homers with 46 RBI.

## Hitting

Karros has a short, powerful stroke with a lot of power to left. The secret to his increased success, however, is using the whole field. He has always been difficult to jam, so when he takes the outside pitch the opposite way, the burly first sacker is a very tough out. He has also become more patient, collecting more walks than ever before. Karros can still be fooled with breaking stuff away, but the increased strikeout total (another career high) is tolerable when combined with the production.

## Baserunning & Defense

Cursed with a bad back, Karros has worked hard at maintaining flexibility and it has worked wonders. Far from speedy, he stole four bases in 1995 and runs aggressively when appropriate. He looks much more limber in the field as well. In fact, Karros showed as much improvement on defense as he did at the plate. He still has little range, but has become quite adept at scooping low throws.

## 1996 Outlook

Karros hit over .300 at every minor league stop, so the talent has always been there. Now he is evolving into a team leader, patiently learning the ropes from veterans like Brett Butler and Tim Wallach. The only place he could possibly go in the immediate future would be across the diamond to third if the team decides to try Mike Piazza at first. After the improvements Karros showed last year, anything is possible.

**Position:** 1B
**Bats:** R  **Throws:** R
**Ht:** 6' 4"  **Wt:** 222

**Opening Day Age:** 28
**Born:** 11/4/67 in Hackensack, NJ
**ML Seasons:** 5
**Pronunciation:** CARE-ose

### Overall Statistics

|        | G   | AB   | R   | H   | D   | T | HR | RBI | SB | BB  | SO  | Avg  | OBP  | Slg  |
|--------|-----|------|-----|-----|-----|---|----|-----|----|-----|-----|------|------|------|
| 1995   | 143 | 551  | 83  | 164 | 29  | 3 | 32 | 105 | 4  | 61  | 115 | .298 | .369 | .535 |
| Career | 575 | 2135 | 271 | 566 | 108 | 7 | 89 | 320 | 8  | 162 | 359 | .265 | .317 | .447 |

### Where He Hits the Ball

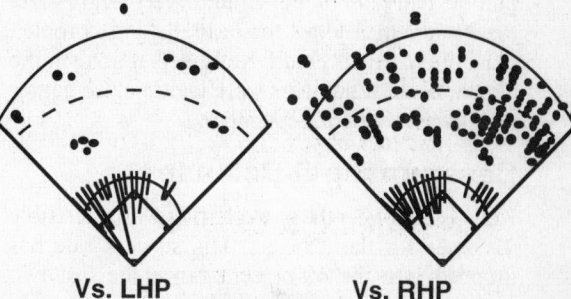

**Vs. LHP**          **Vs. RHP**

### 1995 Situational Stats

|            | AB  | H  | HR | RBI | Avg  |        | AB  | H   | HR | RBI | Avg  |
|------------|-----|----|----|-----|------|--------|-----|-----|----|-----|------|
| Home       | 263 | 77 | 19 | 51  | .293 | LHP    | 124 | 39  | 4  | 17  | .315 |
| Road       | 288 | 87 | 13 | 54  | .302 | RHP    | 427 | 125 | 28 | 88  | .293 |
| First Half | 267 | 82 | 14 | 48  | .307 | Sc Pos | 145 | 50  | 8  | 72  | .345 |
| Scnd Half  | 284 | 82 | 18 | 57  | .289 | Clutch | 74  | 25  | 7  | 19  | .338 |

### 1995 Rankings (National League)

- ➥ 2nd in pitches seen (2,485)
- ➥ 3rd in errors at first base (7)
- ➥ 4th in total bases (295), RBI, strikeouts and games played
- ➥ 5th in home runs, times on base (229) and fielding percentage at first base (.995)
- ➥ 6th in lowest batting average with the bases loaded (.111)
- ➥ 7th in hits (164), plate appearances (620) and slugging percentage vs. right-handed pitchers (.550)
- ➥ Led the Dodgers in home runs, at-bats, hits, doubles, total bases, RBI, hit by pitch (4), times on base, strikeouts, GDPs (14) and pitches seen

**Los Angeles Dodgers**

# Roberto Kelly

## 1995 Season

One of the last of a dying breed, expensive mercenary Roberto Kelly has played on four teams in the last two years. He is a consistent veteran whose oversized contract made him expendable several times. After playing just 24 games for the Expos, he was acquired by the Dodgers to fill Brett Butler's departed shoes. In due time, Kelly was benched, moved to left, then reinstated to the lineup, albeit in the number-eight spot in the order.

## Hitting

Kelly is a streaky free swinger. He went one stretch of 27 games without drawing a walk. There is a little pop in his bat, though he is more likely to pull the ball hard on the ground. Very aggressive, the Panamanian looks for fastballs and is fooled quite often. To his credit, Kelly gets it done in the clutch; his best numbers were late in close games and in the month of September.

## Baserunning & Defense

Kelly is no longer the speed burner who once stole 42 bases for the Yankees. His success rate has dropped into the 60-percent range the last two years. Though he appears to have above-average speed, it is difficult to tell as Kelly rarely runs hard. His defensive skills are alarmingly mediocre. He gets a terrible jump and often misjudges balls. Acquired to anchor the outfield, he was routinely replaced by rookie Roger Cedeno late in ballgames for defensive purposes.

## 1996 Outlook

With his athletic physique and all that gold around his neck, Kelly looks like a better ballplayer than he really is. It takes a while before each new club realizes how many of the little things he does poorly. Overthrown cutoffs, outs dropping for singles, collisions with fellow outfielders, it all gets old quickly and even the forgiving Dodger Stadium crowd often booed him. Kelly will play somewhere this year, but it will not be Los Angeles.

**Position:** CF/LF
**Bats:** R **Throws:** R
**Ht:** 6' 2"  **Wt:** 202

**Opening Day Age:** 31
**Born:** 10/1/64 in Panama City, Panama
**ML Seasons:** 9
**Nickname:** Gray

### Overall Statistics

| | G | AB | R | H | D | T | HR | RBI | SB | BB | SO | Avg | OBP | Slg |
|---|---|---|---|---|---|---|---|---|---|---|---|---|---|---|
| 1995 | 136 | 504 | 58 | 140 | 23 | 2 | 7 | 57 | 19 | 22 | 79 | .278 | .312 | .373 |
| Career | 962 | 3535 | 495 | 1006 | 173 | 20 | 81 | 395 | 210 | 242 | 633 | .285 | .333 | .414 |

### Where He Hits the Ball

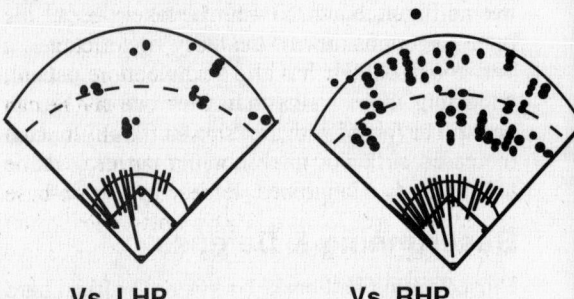

Vs. LHP          Vs. RHP

### 1995 Situational Stats

| | AB | H | HR | RBI | Avg | | AB | H | HR | RBI | Avg |
|---|---|---|---|---|---|---|---|---|---|---|---|
| Home | 236 | 66 | 2 | 21 | .280 | LHP | 117 | 35 | 2 | 14 | .299 |
| Road | 268 | 74 | 5 | 36 | .276 | RHP | 387 | 105 | 5 | 43 | .271 |
| First Half | 269 | 76 | 2 | 25 | .283 | Sc Pos | 125 | 39 | 0 | 46 | .312 |
| Scnd Half | 235 | 64 | 5 | 32 | .272 | Clutch | 76 | 25 | 3 | 16 | .329 |

### 1995 Rankings (National League)

- ➡ 3rd in sacrifice flies (7)
- ➡ 5th in batting average with the bases loaded (.500) and lowest on-base percentage vs. right-handed pitchers (.306)
- ➡ 6th in lowest stolen base percentage (65.5%)
- ➡ 7th in lowest slugging percentage vs. right-handed pitchers (.354) and errors in center field (3)
- ➡ 9th in lowest on-base percentage, errors in left field (3) and lowest percentage of pitches taken (45.7%)
- ➡ 10th in singles (108) and caught stealing (10)
- ➡ Led the Dodgers in sacrifice flies nd hit by pitch (4)

# Ramon Martinez

## 1995 Season

Ramon Martinez firmly established himself as the stopper of the Dodger staff in 1995. He got off to an uncharacteristic slow start, but his confidence was buoyed by his first no-hitter on July 14 vs. Florida. From that point on, the long, lean Dominican was consistently dominant. He won his last six decisions during the stretch drive in September, fashioning a 2.74 ERA in the process.

## Pitching

Martinez seems to have fully recovered from his early '90s arm problems, and it shows in his fastball. It now registers 93-94 MPH on his best days, and he used no other pitch after the third inning in the no-hitter. Now that the heater is back, his three-finger change-up becomes more effective. It is one of the best in the league when he doesn't telegraph it. Martinez also has a slurve that he can occasionally drop in for strikes. Right-handed hitters have a lot of trouble with Martinez, but he still tends to nibble with lefties, whose on-base percentage was almost 100 points higher than righties last year. Martinez has learned to cruise along until he needs to bear down and he's at his best in the late innings of a game.

## Defense & Hitting

Martinez continues to improve in every area of his game. Surprisingly agile, he has always been methodically solid as a fielder. He has really improved his move to first and has held opposing basestealers under .500 over the last two years. Now a full-fledged switch-hitter after years of experimentation, he swatted 11 base hits, including four doubles, and led the club with 13 sacrifices.

## 1996 Outlook

Martinez declared free agency after last season, but his marriage to the Dodger organization is a happy one and he quickly signed a new three-year deal. He should be a solid starter for years to come.

**Position:** SP
**Bats:** B  **Throws:** R
**Ht:** 6' 4"  **Wt:** 186

**Opening Day Age:** 28
**Born:** 3/22/68 in Santo Domingo, DR
**ML Seasons:** 8

### Overall Statistics

|  | W | L | Pct. | ERA | G | GS | Sv | IP | H | BB | SO | HR | BR/IP |
|---|---|---|---|---|---|---|---|---|---|---|---|---|---|
| 1995 | 17 | 7 | .708 | 3.66 | 30 | 30 | 0 | 206.1 | 176 | 81 | 138 | 19 | 1.25 |
| Career | 91 | 63 | .591 | 3.48 | 201 | 198 | 0 | 1327.2 | 1166 | 509 | 970 | 114 | 1.26 |

### How Often He Throws Strikes

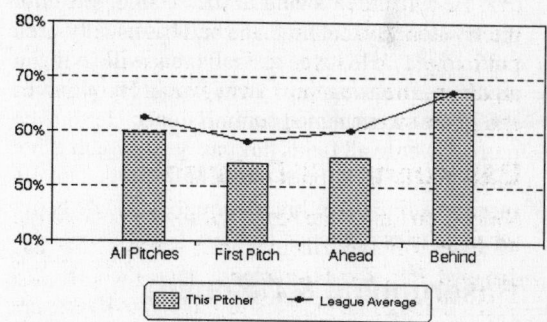

### 1995 Situational Stats

|  | W | L | ERA | Sv | IP |  | AB | H | HR | RBI | Avg |
|---|---|---|---|---|---|---|---|---|---|---|---|
| Home | 8 | 5 | 3.57 | 0 | 118.1 | LHB | 320 | 81 | 8 | 34 | .253 |
| Road | 9 | 2 | 3.78 | 0 | 88.0 | RHB | 441 | 95 | 11 | 48 | .215 |
| First Half | 8 | 6 | 4.85 | 0 | 94.2 | Sc Pos | 156 | 41 | 5 | 62 | .263 |
| Scnd Half | 9 | 1 | 2.66 | 0 | 111.2 | Clutch | 48 | 11 | 2 | 6 | .229 |

### 1995 Rankings (National League)

- ➡ 1st in walks allowed and pitches thrown (3,349)
- ➡ 2nd in batters faced (859)
- ➡ 3rd in sacrifice bunts (13), wins, shutouts (2) and innings pitched
- ➡ 4th in winning percentage
- ➡ 5th in complete games (4), most pitches thrown per batter (3.90) and errors at pitcher (3)
- ➡ 6th in games started (30), GDPs induced (19), lowest strikeout/walk ratio (1.7) and lowest batting average allowed (.231)
- ➡ Led the Dodgers in sacrifice bunts, wins, games started, innings pitched, batters faced and home runs allowed

**Los Angeles Dodgers**

# Raul Mondesi

## 1995 Season

Had the 1995 season ended at the All-Star break, Raul Mondesi might have been the National League MVP. There are two halves to every season, however, even a strike-shortened one, and the dynamic Dominican's performance suffered in the last three months. Nevertheless, Mondesi is gifted enough to contribute even when he is slumping and showed his courage by playing every day down the stretch despite needing surgery on his right knee.

## Hitting

Mondesi is very impatient at the plate and took a cut at the first pitch in 49 percent of his at-bats in '95. He will often swing at the second and third pitches, too. By that time, the ball has usually been put into play. He loves fastballs, but will swing at anything. Breaking stuff away would be outlawed if Mondesi were named commissioner. He showed more power to all fields this past year, which is not surprising as he is built like a bull. He is actually more of a line-drive hitter, though, and hits better when he tries to do just that.

## Baserunning & Defense

Mondesi had a breakthrough year in the stolen-base department, getting caught just four times in 31 tries, vastly improving on his 63-percent rate before '95. He has blazing speed; a Mondesi triple is one of baseball's most exciting plays. That is, until one sees him in the outfield. Mondesi gets to the ball and releases it with such force and accuracy that it is quite simply hard to believe. There cannot be a better right fielder in the game today, and Mondesi was rewarded with his first Gold Glove.

## 1996 Outlook

There are areas in which Mondesi has room to improve, which is scary. If he can learn to be more patient at the plate like he learned to steal bases, there are no limits for him. He has all the skills; now it is simply a matter of endurance and concentration. The club would like to keep him in right field where he seems most comfortable, and he should be patrolling that area for a long time to come.

**Position:** RF/CF
**Bats:** R  **Throws:** R
**Ht:** 5'11"  **Wt:** 212

**Opening Day Age:** 25
**Born:** 3/12/71 in San Cristobal, DR
**ML Seasons:** 3
**Pronunciation:** MON-de-see

### Overall Statistics

|  | G | AB | R | H | D | T | HR | RBI | SB | BB | SO | Avg | Slg | OBA |
|---|---|---|---|---|---|---|---|---|---|---|---|---|---|---|
| 1995 | 139 | 536 | 91 | 153 | 23 | 6 | 26 | 88 | 27 | 33 | 96 | .285 | .328 | .496 |
| Career | 293 | 1056 | 167 | 311 | 53 | 15 | 46 | 154 | 42 | 53 | 190 | .295 | .329 | .504 |

### Where He Hits the Ball

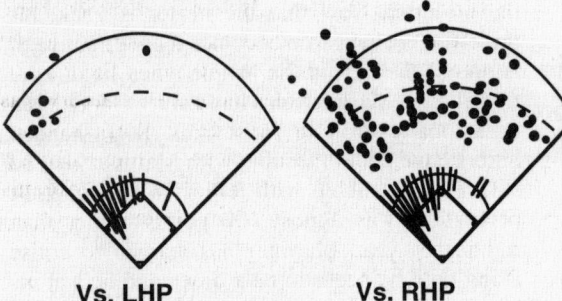

Vs. LHP        Vs. RHP

### 1995 Situational Stats

|  | AB | H | HR | RBI | Avg |  | AB | H | HR | RBI | Avg |
|---|---|---|---|---|---|---|---|---|---|---|---|
| Home | 257 | 74 | 13 | 45 | .288 | LHP | 112 | 28 | 5 | 16 | .250 |
| Road | 279 | 79 | 13 | 43 | .283 | RHP | 424 | 125 | 21 | 72 | .295 |
| First Half | 270 | 85 | 13 | 40 | .315 | Sc Pos | 127 | 36 | 10 | 61 | .283 |
| Scnd Half | 266 | 68 | 13 | 48 | .256 | Clutch | 77 | 21 | 1 | 8 | .273 |

### 1995 Rankings (National League)

- → 3rd in sacrifice flies (7), lowest percentage of pitches taken (44.3%) and highest percentage of swings on the first pitch (48.5%)
- → 4th in stolen base percentage (87.1%) and lowest fielding percentage in right field (.984)
- → 6th in highest percentage of extra bases taken as a runner (66.0%)
- → 7th in errors in right field (4)
- → 8th in highest percentage of swings that missed (27.6%)
- → 9th in runs scored
- → 10th in at-bats
- → Led the Dodgers in runs scored, triples, sacrifice flies, hit by pitch (4) and stolen base percentage

**Position:** SP
**Bats:** R **Throws:** R
**Ht:** 6' 2"  **Wt:** 210

**Opening Day Age:** 27
**Born:** 8/31/68 in Kobe, Japan
**ML Seasons:** 1
**Pronunciation:**
Hid-AY-oh NOH-moh

## 1995 Season

Wow. Not even the Dodgers' braintrust could have envisioned the level of success that Hideo Nomo reached in his rookie year. The Japanese import was virtually unhittable in the first half of the season and started the All-Star Game after going 6-0 in June with a 0.89 ERA. Though he faded down the stretch, Nomo showed he could win even without his best stuff. He went 3-1 in September despite topping off at 84 MPH on the gun.

## Pitching

Whirling out of the most twisted delivery since Luis Tiant, Nomo shows his numbers to the hitter. When healthy, his fastball will reach 90 MPH. He will occasionally flip a little curveball up there, just to keep the hitters honest, but they all know what's coming. The Tornado actually throws two different forkballs: a slow tailing one that serves as a nasty change-up and the devastating knee-rattler—Nomo's strikeout pitch—which drops a foot-and-a-half. Nomo has control problems sometimes, especially early in the game.

## Defense & Hitting

Nomo has problems holding runners. Though the twisted delivery is less pronounced from the stretch position, he is easy prey for basestealers. A poor move is not enough to keep them honest. The unique windup leaves him in surprisingly good fielding position, and Nomo holds his own in that department. Despite his willingness, Nomo is pretty hapless at the plate. He struck out in exactly half his at-bats, but did collect four RBI and five sacrifice bunts.

## 1996 Outlook

Nomo has pitched himself into a mighty enviable bargaining position. Not only was he successful on the hill, but at the box office as well. The Dodgers will be competing with the other rich clubs for his services, but there are rumors that he could earn much more in his native land now that he is an international superstar. How much can a team afford to pay a two-pitch hurler with a history of elbow, shoulder and fingernail problems?

### Overall Statistics

|        | W  | L | Pct. | ERA  | G  | GS | Sv | IP    | H   | BB | SO  | HR | BR/IP |
|--------|----|---|------|------|----|----|----|-------|-----|----|-----|----|-------|
| 1995   | 13 | 6 | .684 | 2.54 | 28 | 28 | 0  | 191.1 | 124 | 78 | 236 | 14 | 1.06  |
| Career | 13 | 6 | .684 | 2.54 | 28 | 28 | 0  | 191.1 | 124 | 78 | 236 | 14 | 1.06  |

### How Often He Throws Strikes

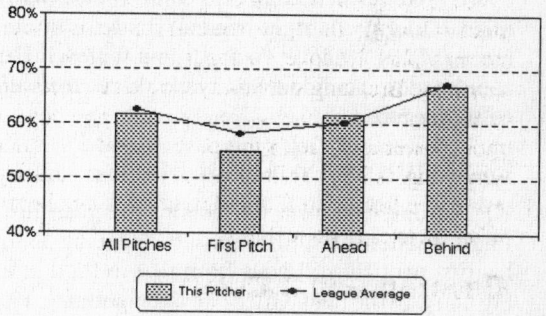

### 1995 Situational Stats

|            | W | L | ERA  | Sv | IP    |        | AB  | H  | HR | RBI | Avg  |
|------------|---|---|------|----|-------|--------|-----|----|----|-----|------|
| Home       | 8 | 2 | 1.73 | 0  | 99.0  | LHB    | 317 | 63 | 8  | 28  | .199 |
| Road       | 5 | 4 | 3.41 | 0  | 92.1  | RHB    | 364 | 61 | 6  | 25  | .168 |
| First Half | 6 | 1 | 1.99 | 0  | 90.1  | Sc Pos | 156 | 30 | 3  | 42  | .192 |
| Scnd Half  | 7 | 5 | 3.03 | 0  | 101.0 | Clutch | 53  | 6  | 1  | 2   | .113 |

### 1995 Rankings (National League)

→ 1st in shutouts (3), strikeouts, wild pitches (19), balks (5), lowest batting average allowed (.182), least GDPs induced per 9 innings (0.2), most strikeouts per 9 innings (11.1), ERA at home (1.73) and lowest batting average allowed vs. right-handed batters (.168)

→ 2nd in ERA, walks allowed, stolen bases allowed (29), lowest slugging percentage allowed (.286) and lowest on-base percentage allowed (.270)

→ Led the Dodgers in highest strikeout/walk ratio (3.0), lowest batting average allowed and lowest slugging percentage allowed

**Los Angeles Dodgers**

# Jose Offerman

## 1995 Season

It was the best of times, it was the worst of times for Jose Offerman in 1995. Batting .303 at the time, he was named to the All-Star team by Felipe Alou, only to have the announcement booed by the Dodger Stadium crowd. Then he lost his job to Rule 5 draftee Chad Fonville and sat on the bench during the entire month of September as his team won the division.

## Hitting

Offerman is a patient hitter with an excellent eye. The switch-hitter looks like two different batters on either side of the plate. As a lefty, he hits from a crouch and his swing has a loop to it. He can be overpowered by hard throwers and is fooled more often. Offerman's right-handed stance is more erect and his swing is compact and forceful. He appears more confident and really drives the ball batting righty.

## Baserunning & Defense

For reasons unknown, Offerman has stolen just four bases in the last two years after swiping 53 in his first two. He still goes from first to third in a big hurry. In the field, Offerman is a nightmare. He does not attack the ball so he gets to a lot of grounders between hops. When he has time to think, his arm is erratic as well. He is at his best when he simply reacts and makes the play.

## 1996 Outlook

Offerman has probably played his last game as a Dodger, especially with the Dodgers signing Greg Gagne last November. It should be noted that opposing shortstops also have major problems on the notoriously bad Chavez Ravine infield surface, so perhaps Offerman is not all to blame. The guy is in his prime and his OBP was just five ticks below that of Barry Larkin. He will be in someone's starting lineup, and a fresh start might do wonders for his career.

**Position:** SS
**Bats:** B **Throws:** R
**Ht:** 6' 0" **Wt:** 188

**Opening Day Age:** 27
**Born:** 11/8/68 in San Pedro de Macoris, DR
**ML Seasons:** 6

### Overall Statistics

|  | G | AB | R | H | D | T | HR | RBI | SB | BB | SO | Avg | OBP | Slg |
|---|---|---|---|---|---|---|---|---|---|---|---|---|---|---|
| 1995 | 119 | 429 | 69 | 123 | 14 | 6 | 4 | 33 | 2 | 69 | 67 | .287 | .389 | .375 |
| Career | 579 | 1967 | 257 | 503 | 65 | 24 | 8 | 160 | 61 | 264 | 324 | .256 | .344 | .325 |

### Where He Hits the Ball

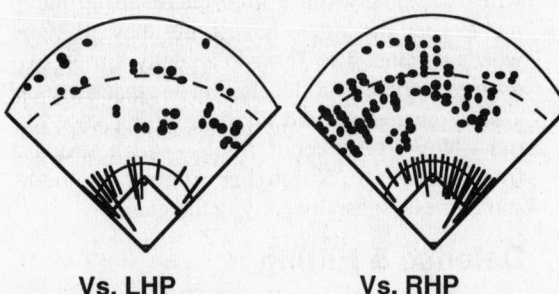

**Vs. LHP**        **Vs. RHP**

### 1995 Situational Stats

|  | AB | H | HR | RBI | Avg |  | AB | H | HR | RBI | Avg |
|---|---|---|---|---|---|---|---|---|---|---|---|
| Home | 207 | 58 | 2 | 18 | .280 | LHP | 123 | 37 | 1 | 7 | .301 |
| Road | 222 | 65 | 2 | 15 | .293 | RHP | 306 | 86 | 3 | 26 | .281 |
| First Half | 251 | 76 | 1 | 16 | .303 | Sc Pos | 89 | 23 | 0 | 26 | .258 |
| Scnd Half | 178 | 47 | 3 | 17 | .264 | Clutch | 60 | 17 | 0 | 7 | .283 |

### 1995 Rankings (National League)

→ 1st in errors at shortstop (35) and lowest fielding percentage at shortstop (.932)

→ 7th in highest percentage of pitches taken (61.4%)

→ 8th in lowest HR frequency (107.3 ABs per HR), bunts in play (24) and highest percentage of extra bases taken as a runner (64.0%)

→ 10th in walks, on-base percentage, batting average on a 3-1 count (.563) and on-base percentage vs. left-handed pitchers (.403)

→ Led the Dodgers in triples, walks, on-base percentage vs. left-handed pitchers, lowest percentage of swings that missed (14.8%) and highest percentage of swings put into play (48.3%)

# Antonio Osuna

Rookie righthander Antonio Osuna looked like an overmatched 22 year old at the beginning of the 1995 campaign. But after a short stint on the disabled list with a groin pull and subsequent demotion to Triple-A Albuquerque, he came back looking like a future closer. Best of all, the young Mexican was around the plate; he walked just nine while striking out 37 after the All-Star break.

## Pitching

Osuna throws very hard, consistently in the low- to mid-90s. Day in and day out, no one on the staff has a better fastball. The heater has little movement, however, so location is crucial. Osuna's curveball and change-up are just mediocre at this point in his career, but if he can occasionally get them over it raises enough doubt to add a couple of ticks to the fastball. Like any pitcher, control is the key to Osuna's success. Though he always pitches from the stretch position, opponents hit over 70 points better with men on base. He has not yet perfected the ability to make better pitches in the clutch.

## Defense & Hitting

Osuna ends his pitching motion in good fielding position and appears to have good instincts. Like most Dodger farmhands, the fundamentals have been ingrained into him. He has a compact delivery, and opposing baserunners must be cautious as he has a fine move. Osuna looks to be a future closer even at the plate, making just two token plate appearances.

## 1996 Outlook

Osuna appeared ready to close games late in the year, but that horrible first half raises some questions. . . as does the opponents' .351 average with runners in scoring position. However, Osuna took very well to the set-up role, and one more year as caddie to Todd Worrell (or another veteran) should give the youngster the experience and confidence to close in the years to come. He certainly has the stuff.

**Position:** RP
**Bats:** R **Throws:** R
**Ht:** 5'11" **Wt:** 160

**Opening Day Age:** 22
**Born:** 4/12/73 in Sinaloa, MX
**ML Seasons:** 1
**Pronunciation:** oh-SOO-nuh

### Overall Statistics

|  | W | L | Pct. | ERA | G | GS | Sv | IP | H | BB | SO | HR | BR/IP |
|---|---|---|---|---|---|---|---|---|---|---|---|---|---|
| 1995 | 2 | 4 | .333 | 4.43 | 39 | 0 | 0 | 44.2 | 39 | 20 | 46 | 5 | 1.32 |
| Career | 2 | 4 | .333 | 4.43 | 39 | 0 | 0 | 44.2 | 39 | 20 | 46 | 5 | 1.32 |

### How Often He Throws Strikes

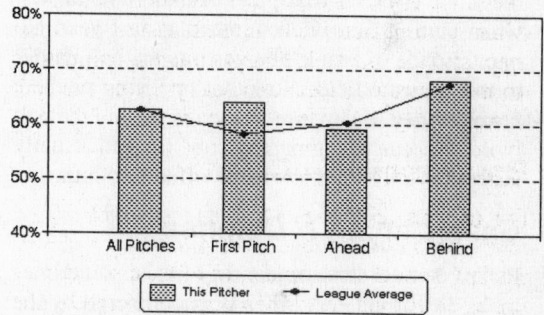

### 1995 Situational Stats

|  | W | L | ERA | Sv | IP |  | AB | H | HR | RBI | Avg |
|---|---|---|---|---|---|---|---|---|---|---|---|
| Home | 0 | 1 | 2.11 | 0 | 21.1 | LHB | 58 | 16 | 1 | 4 | .276 |
| Road | 2 | 3 | 6.56 | 0 | 23.1 | RHB | 104 | 23 | 4 | 15 | .221 |
| First Half | 1 | 2 | 8.16 | 0 | 14.1 | Sc Pos | 37 | 13 | 0 | 13 | .351 |
| Scnd Half | 1 | 2 | 2.67 | 0 | 30.1 | Clutch | 105 | 26 | 1 | 14 | .248 |

### 1995 Rankings (National League)
➡ Led the Dodgers in holds (11) and most GDPs induced per GDP situation (13.8%)

# Mike Piazza

## 1995 Season

Mike Piazza just keeps getting better. Despite spending most of May on the disabled list with a torn ligament in his left thumb, Piazza hit his way onto the All-Star team as teammate Hideo Nomo's battery mate. After getting hit on the left wrist with a Mark Leiter fastball in late September, Piazza refused to leave the lineup. Playing just 112 games, he finished in the top 10 in all three Triple Crown categories.

## Hitting

Very few ballplayers combine power and average like Piazza. He is a great situational hitter, adjusting his stroke for the pitcher, the count, the inning, the score. He loves first-pitch fastballs and hit .474 when putting first pitches into play last year. No one this side of Frank Thomas hits the ball harder to the opposite field. Now that opposing pitchers have decided to jam him, Piazza is pulling the ball more. He can be impatient, but he will usually accept a walk if that is what is offered to him.

## Baserunning & Defense

Piazza is not a slow runner. In fact, he sometimes looks downright spry when unencumbered by the tools of ignorance. He takes great pride in his defensive game, so the recent whispers about his poor pitch selection, inability to block pitches and erratic throwing arm have raised his hackles. He will admit, however, that catching every day wears him down. It shows in all areas of his game.

## 1996 Outlook

One thing is for sure: Piazza will be in the middle of the order for the Dodgers. The only question is whether he will remain behind the plate. Though he likes the control of calling every pitch, the time is near when he must listen to reason. Third base is probably up for grabs. So is left field. One intriguing idea has Eric Karros moving to third and Piazza taking over at first from his former roommate. Perhaps with a full spring training. . .

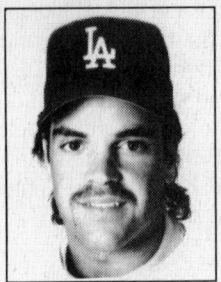

**Position:** C
**Bats:** R **Throws:** R
**Ht:** 6' 3" **Wt:** 215

**Opening Day Age:** 27
**Born:** 9/4/68 in Norristown, PA
**ML Seasons:** 4
**Pronunciation:** pee-AH-zuh

### Overall Statistics

|        | G   | AB   | R   | H   | D  | T | HR | RBI | SB | BB  | SO  | Avg  | OBP  | Slg  |
|--------|-----|------|-----|-----|----|---|----|-----|----|-----|-----|------|------|------|
| 1995   | 112 | 434  | 82  | 150 | 17 | 0 | 32 | 93  | 1  | 39  | 80  | .346 | .400 | .606 |
| Career | 389 | 1455 | 232 | 469 | 62 | 2 | 92 | 304 | 5  | 122 | 243 | .322 | .375 | .557 |

### Where He Hits the Ball

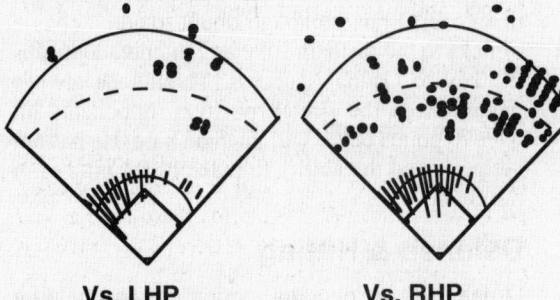

**Vs. LHP**          **Vs. RHP**

### 1995 Situational Stats

|            | AB  | H  | HR | RBI | Avg  |        | AB  | H   | HR | RBI | Avg  |
|------------|-----|----|----|-----|------|--------|-----|-----|----|-----|------|
| Home       | 205 | 62 | 9  | 36  | .302 | LHP    | 89  | 29  | 8  | 15  | .326 |
| Road       | 229 | 88 | 23 | 57  | .384 | RHP    | 345 | 121 | 24 | 78  | .351 |
| First Half | 162 | 61 | 13 | 37  | .377 | Sc Pos | 112 | 40  | 9  | 60  | .357 |
| Scnd Half  | 272 | 89 | 19 | 56  | .327 | Clutch | 61  | 22  | 4  | 10  | .361 |

### 1995 Rankings (National League)

→ 1st in HR frequency (13.6 ABs per HR) and batting average on the road (.384)
→ 2nd in batting average and batting average vs. right-handed pitchers (.351)
→ 3rd in slugging percentage , slugging percentage vs. right-handed pitchers (.606) and errors at catcher (9)
→ 4th in lowest percentage of extra bases taken as a runner (33.3%)
→ 5th in home runs, on-base percentage and batting average with runners in scoring position (.357)
→ Led the Dodgers in batting average, home runs, singles (101), intentional walks (10) and slugging percentage

# Kevin Tapani

## 1995 Season

The Dodgers acquired Kevin Tapani from Minnesota on July 31, the last day before he would have had to clear waivers. Carrying a $3.6 million contract, the veteran righthander is just the type of player that a rich team can afford in its run for the pennant. Though his numbers in the National League were downright ugly, the club went 8-3 in his starts. The fifth spot in the rotation had gone 3-8 before Tapani came over.

## Pitching

Tapani has mediocre stuff. He hits corners with a tailing fastball in the mid- to upper-80s. He throws two different curveballs, a little dinker and a huge looper, and a very good change-up that drops off the table. Everything comes out of a nice compact delivery. He survives via sheer guile and great control. The veteran has walked less than two batters per nine innings over his career. Tapani makes the hitters put the ball into play, but they've been increasingly successful as his ERA has risen every year since 1991. For some reason he has had trouble with right-handed hitters, who have hit over .300 against him in each of the last two years.

## Defense & Hitting

Tapani's compact delivery does not help him in holding baserunners, who were 21-for-25 in 1995. It does leave him, however, in good position to field the ball. He moves well and gets off the mound quickly. For a guy coming over from the American League, he held his own at the plate. He usually makes contact and even drove in a couple of runs.

## 1996 Outlook

Tapani is one of those guys who may or may not be a free agent, depending on strike-related service time. No matter what the economic ground rules will be next year, he will earn a lot less money. The Dodgers have so many question marks that Tapani is down the list a bit. Though his numbers are less than gaudy, he has not missed a start due to injury since August of 1990. He will fill a rotation spot somewhere.

**Position:** SP
**Bats:** R  **Throws:** R
**Ht:** 6' 0"  **Wt:** 189

**Opening Day Age:** 32
**Born:** 2/18/64 in Des Moines, IA
**ML Seasons:** 7
**Pronunciation:** TAP-uh-nee

### Overall Statistics

| | W | L | Pct. | ERA | G | GS | Sv | IP | H | BB | SO | HR | BR/IP |
|---|---|---|---|---|---|---|---|---|---|---|---|---|---|
| 1995 | 10 | 13 | .435 | 4.96 | 33 | 31 | 0 | 190.2 | 227 | 48 | 131 | 29 | 1.44 |
| Career | 79 | 65 | .549 | 4.10 | 197 | 191 | 0 | 1235.2 | 1305 | 273 | 769 | 118 | 1.28 |

### How Often He Throws Strikes

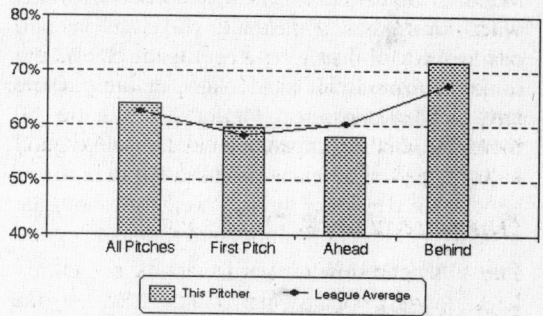

### 1995 Situational Stats

| | W | L | ERA | Sv | IP | | AB | H | HR | RBI | Avg |
|---|---|---|---|---|---|---|---|---|---|---|---|
| Home | 5 | 6 | 5.68 | 0 | 95.0 | LHB | 419 | 119 | 15 | 56 | .284 |
| Road | 5 | 7 | 4.23 | 0 | 95.2 | RHB | 351 | 108 | 14 | 48 | .308 |
| First Half | 4 | 9 | 4.84 | 0 | 106.0 | Sc Pos | 198 | 57 | 7 | 72 | .288 |
| Scnd Half | 6 | 4 | 5.10 | 0 | 84.2 | Clutch | 38 | 10 | 0 | 2 | .263 |

### 1995 Rankings (National League)

➡ Did not rank near the top or bottom in any category

# Ismael Valdes

## 1995 Season

Ismael Valdes began the 1995 season as a spot starter and/or long relief man. He had proven to be quite valuable in the latter role the previous year, so the Dodgers were reluctant to move him. By June, he had pitched his way into the rotation to stay. Despite a tendency to win and lose in streaks, Valdes was actually very steady and quite durable. He led the club with six complete games and held opponents to a .171 average after the 90-pitch mark.

## Pitching

Watch him pitch and one sees why Valdes reminds Bobby Cox of the seemingly incomparable Greg Maddux. He has command way beyond his years of all four pitches: fastball, slider, curve and change-up. Furthermore, every pitch looks the same as it leaves his hand. Same delivery, same arm speed, same release point. Though the 90 MPH fastball has just average velocity, it has good tailing action and Valdes can usually put it where he wants it. He hides the ball well from both the windup and stretch position, and retains his good stuff from the latter.

## Defense & Hitting

Valdes comes out of his pitching delivery in great shape, facing square to the hitter. He has very quick hands and made several spectacular snags of hard-hit liners back through the box. The young Mexican also gets off the hill quickly and runs pretty well. He holds his own at the plate and was third on the club with seven sacrifices.

## 1996 Outlook

Valdes has pitched himself into the third spot in the rotation behind Ramon Martinez and Hideo Nomo. Quite a feat for a 22 year old who had never pitched in Triple-A until the strike in 1994. To show the command and poise that he does at so young an age, and with the fine results. . . He has to be considered the most treasured member of the Dodgers' pitching staff.

**Position:** SP/RP
**Bats:** R  **Throws:** R
**Ht:** 6' 3"  **Wt:** 207

**Opening Day Age:** 22
**Born:** 8/21/73 in Victoria, MX
**ML Seasons:** 2
**Pronunciation:** ISH-mail Val-DEZZ

### *Overall Statistics*

|  | W | L | Pct. | ERA | G | GS | Sv | IP | H | BB | SO | HR | BR/IP |
|---|---|---|---|---|---|---|---|---|---|---|---|---|---|
| 1995 | 13 | 11 | .542 | 3.05 | 33 | 27 | 1 | 197.2 | 168 | 51 | 150 | 17 | 1.11 |
| Career | 16 | 12 | .571 | 3.07 | 54 | 28 | 1 | 226.0 | 189 | 61 | 178 | 19 | 1.11 |

### *How Often He Throws Strikes*

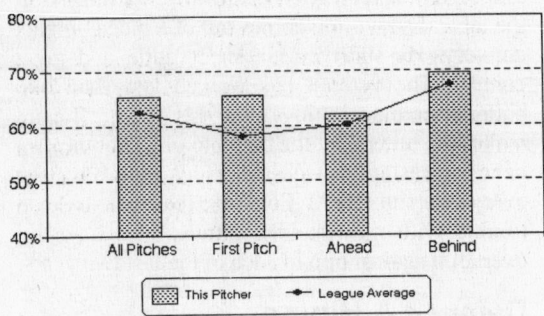

### *1995 Situational Stats*

|  | W | L | ERA | Sv | IP |  | AB | H | HR | RBI | Avg |
|---|---|---|---|---|---|---|---|---|---|---|---|
| Home | 6 | 5 | 2.30 | 0 | 98.0 | LHB | 359 | 82 | 13 | 38 | .228 |
| Road | 7 | 6 | 3.79 | 1 | 99.2 | RHB | 378 | 86 | 4 | 30 | .228 |
| First Half | 5 | 5 | 3.30 | 1 | 92.2 | Sc Pos | 155 | 37 | 6 | 53 | .239 |
| Scnd Half | 8 | 6 | 2.83 | 0 | 105.0 | Clutch | 94 | 22 | 3 | 9 | .234 |

### *1995 Rankings (National League)*

➡ 3rd in complete games (6), shutouts (2) and lowest on-base percentage allowed (.277)

➡ 4th in ERA, balks (3), lowest batting average allowed (.228), lowest slugging percentage allowed (.343), least baserunners allowed per 9 innings (10.0) and lowest batting average allowed vs. left-handed batters (.228)

➡ 5th in least run support per 9 innings (4.0) and ERA at home (2.30)

➡ 6th in lowest batting average on an 0-2 count (.045)

➡ 7th in innings pitched and least GDPs induced per 9 innings (0.5) thrown per batter (3.51)

# Todd Worrell

## 1995 Season

After entering the season with a total of 19 saves in the 1990s, Todd Worrell came out of nowhere to save 32. Worrell started the year competing with Rudy Seanez as the Dodger closer, but quickly regained Tommy Lasorda's confidence and went to the All-Star Game having allowed only one earned run. Though he faded a bit in July and August, Worrell closed the season just as he started. His ERA in September: 0.00.

## Pitching

Finally healthy again, Worrell threw harder in 1995 than he had in years, registering 95 MPH on the gun on his good days. That radar reading changes considerably when he pitches two days in a row, so perhaps most impressive was his performance on the days when he did not have his best fastball. He junked his trademark slider in spring training and started throwing a curveball. It gave the batters a much different look from the Worrell of years past. He will even mix in a sloppy change-up once in a while. So even though he remains a power pitcher at heart, the offspeed stuff makes Worrell that much tougher.

## Defense & Hitting

Worrell is absolutely hopeless at holding runners. He has never developed a decent move, has a big leg kick, and baserunners often take second without even drawing a throw. The big man is a bit awkward getting off the mound and has not collected a hit since 1987.

## 1996 Outlook

Facing the end of his career, Worrell got healthy and focused. He returned to the level of effectiveness he'd shown with the Cardinals in the late 1980s, when he reeled off three straight 30-save seasons. A free agent, he figures to cash in. The Dodgers need him in 1996, but anyone who signs this guy for more than one season is asking for trouble.

**Position:** RP
**Bats:** R  **Throws:** R
**Ht:** 6' 5"  **Wt:** 227

**Opening Day Age:** 36
**Born:** 9/28/59 in Arcadia, CA
**ML Seasons:** 9
**Pronunciation:** Wohr-RELL

### Overall Statistics

|  | W | L | Pct. | ERA | G | GS | Sv | IP | H | BB | SO | HR | BR/IP |
|---|---|---|---|---|---|---|---|---|---|---|---|---|---|
| 1995 | 4 | 1 | .800 | 2.02 | 59 | 0 | 32 | 62.1 | 50 | 19 | 61 | 4 | 1.11 |
| Career | 44 | 40 | .524 | 2.86 | 480 | 0 | 177 | 568.2 | 478 | 209 | 501 | 48 | 1.21 |

### How Often He Throws Strikes

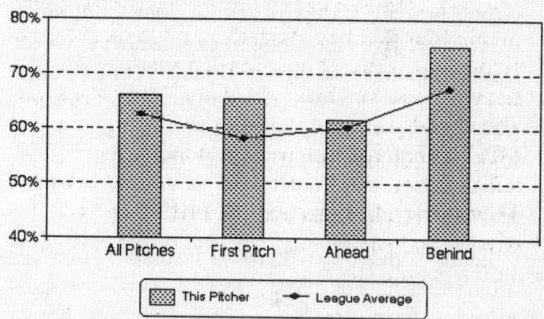

### 1995 Situational Stats

|  | W | L | ERA | Sv | IP |  | AB | H | HR | RBI | Avg |
|---|---|---|---|---|---|---|---|---|---|---|---|
| Home | 3 | 1 | 3.21 | 18 | 33.2 | LHB | 115 | 22 | 1 | 10 | .191 |
| Road | 1 | 0 | 0.63 | 14 | 28.2 | RHB | 111 | 28 | 3 | 14 | .252 |
| First Half | 2 | 0 | 0.32 | 12 | 28.1 | Sc Pos | 59 | 14 | 1 | 19 | .237 |
| Scnd Half | 2 | 1 | 3.44 | 20 | 34.0 | Clutch | 168 | 37 | 4 | 24 | .220 |

### 1995 Rankings (National League)

→ 2nd in save percentage (88.9%) and relief ERA (2.02)
→ 3rd in games finished (53) and first batter efficiency (.109)
→ 4th in saves
→ 6th in least baserunners allowed per 9 innings in relief (10.1)
→ 7th in save opportunities (36)
→ 8th in most strikeouts per 9 innings in relief (8.8)
→ Led the Dodgers in games pitched, saves, games finished, save opportunities, save percentage, blown saves (4), first batter efficiency, relief ERA and relief innings (62.1)

Los Angeles Dodgers

# John Cummings

**Position:** RP
**Bats:** L  **Throws:** L
**Ht:** 6' 3"  **Wt:** 200

**Opening Day Age:** 26
**Born:** 5/10/69 in
Torrance, CA
**ML Seasons:** 3

## Overall Statistics

|  | W | L | Pct. | ERA | G | GS | Sv | IP | H | BB | SO | HR | BR/IP |
|---|---|---|---|---|---|---|---|---|---|---|---|---|---|
| 1995 | 3 | 1 | .750 | 4.06 | 39 | 0 | 0 | 44.1 | 46 | 17 | 25 | 3 | 1.42 |
| Career | 5 | 11 | .313 | 5.30 | 66 | 16 | 0 | 154.2 | 171 | 70 | 77 | 16 | 1.56 |

## 1995 Season

After a horrible start with Seattle, John Cummings was picked up by the Dodgers in a late May waiver deal. He spent some time in Double-A before joining the Dodgers' annual parade of bullpen lefties. Surprisingly, Cummings held his own and stuck with the club through the end of the season.

## Pitching, Defense & Hitting

Cummings throws an 85 MPH fastball that moves a bit and a decent curve. He will also sometimes mix in a change-up. None of his pitches are above average, so he must get ahead in the count in order to be effective; batters hit .178 off him after a first-pitch strike, .345 when starting with ball one. Much of his success in the National League was due to cutting down on his walks. His move to first, like everything else, is just average, but Cummings is able to keep runners close by getting rid of the ball quickly. He appears to be an average fielder as well. At the plate, he needs a designated hitter.

## 1996 Outlook

Cummings survived the late-season acquisition of Mark Guthrie, a much more experienced and higher-paid southpaw, and was often used in critical situations down the stretch. Despite allowing left-handed hitters to hit .306, Cummings faces little competition in the Dodger bullpen. If he continues to challenge hitters, he should be with the club next year and there is even some half-hearted talk of using him as a starter.

# Omar Daal

**Position:** RP
**Bats:** L  **Throws:** L
**Ht:** 6' 3"  **Wt:** 185

**Opening Day Age:** 24
**Born:** 3/1/72 in
Maracaibo, VZ
**ML Seasons:** 3
**Pronunciation:** DOLL

## Overall Statistics

|  | W | L | Pct. | ERA | G | GS | Sv | IP | H | BB | SO | HR | BR/IP |
|---|---|---|---|---|---|---|---|---|---|---|---|---|---|
| 1995 | 4 | 0 | 1.000 | 7.20 | 28 | 0 | 0 | 20.0 | 29 | 15 | 11 | 1 | 2.20 |
| Career | 6 | 3 | .667 | 5.35 | 99 | 0 | 0 | 69.0 | 77 | 41 | 39 | 7 | 1.71 |

## 1995 Season

After a sterling winter season as a starting pitcher in his home country of Venezuela, lefthander Omar Daal came to spring training as a candidate for the Dodger rotation. He made the Opening Day staff, but back in his familiar role as the bullpen lefty. It turned out to be a setback year for the 23-year-old Daal, however, as he was ineffective and spent most of the year in Triple-A.

## Pitching, Defense & Hitting

Daal has an excellent curveball with a big, looping break. He is tough when he can get it over. His sinking fastball has just average velocity, so the change-up, while quite good, is only mildly effective. He nibbles too much, walking more guys than he struck out, but since opponents hit .354 against him (righthanders hit .459!), perhaps nibbling is not such a bad idea. Daal is a decent fielder with a good pickoff move. He has yet to make a big-league plate appearance.

## 1996 Outlook

Were he not left-handed, Daal's career would be in deep trouble. John Cummings beat him out as the main southpaw out of the pen, and should be back. Daal is young enough to turn things around, but it had better happen soon. Winter league success means nothing unless it translates to the States.

# Mark Guthrie

**Position:** RP
**Bats:** R  **Throws:** L
**Ht:** 6' 4"  **Wt:** 207

**Opening Day Age:** 30
**Born:** 9/22/65 in Buffalo, NY
**ML Seasons:** 7

## Overall Statistics

| | W | L | Pct. | ERA | G | GS | Sv | IP | H | BB | SO | HR | BR/IP |
|---|---|---|---|---|---|---|---|---|---|---|---|---|---|
| 1995 | 5 | 5 | .500 | 4.21 | 60 | 0 | 0 | 62.0 | 66 | 25 | 67 | 6 | 1.47 |
| Career | 29 | 29 | .500 | 4.17 | 264 | 43 | 8 | 509.1 | 546 | 183 | 407 | 49 | 1.43 |

## 1995 Season

Veteran lefty Mark Guthrie came over to the Dodgers as a relatively expensive throw-in to the Kevin Tapani deal. His presence doubled Tommy Lasorda's options for bullpen southpaws and Guthrie did an adequate job. Guthrie, traditionally a second-half pitcher, compiled a scoreless September. That may be deceiving, as he was often used for just one left-handed batter, and first batters touched him for a .333 average.

## Pitching, Defense & Hitting

Guthrie has a peek-a-boo wind-up, hiding the ball behind his right knee. He throws pretty hard, though the fastball runs a bit straight for a southpaw. He also throws a curveball and a little change-up, but his out pitch is a forkball that does not seem to have the bite that it had before Guthrie developed a blood clot in his shoulder a few years back. He uses a slide-step from the stretch position and has a good enough move to hold guys close. He is an average fielder and made contact in his only National League plate appearance.

## 1996 Outlook

Guthrie did a decent job for the Dodgers, but younger, cheaper John Cummings was often used in hold situations. With experienced lefthanders such a valuable commodity, someone else will probably offer him a better deal. He may make less money in today's market, but he will definitely have a job.

# Chris Gwynn

**Position:** LF
**Bats:** L  **Throws:** L
**Ht:** 6' 0"  **Wt:** 220

**Opening Day Age:** 31
**Born:** 10/13/64 in Los Angeles, CA
**ML Seasons:** 9

## Overall Statistics

| | G | AB | R | H | D | T | HR | RBI | SB | BB | SO | Avg | OBP | Slg |
|---|---|---|---|---|---|---|---|---|---|---|---|---|---|---|
| 1995 | 67 | 84 | 8 | 18 | 3 | 2 | 1 | 10 | 0 | 6 | 23 | .214 | .272 | .333 |
| Career | 518 | 917 | 111 | 247 | 32 | 11 | 16 | 108 | 2 | 61 | 143 | .269 | .313 | .381 |

## 1995 Season

Chris Gwynn settled back into his usual place on Tommy Lasorda's bench last season, getting a start every couple of months. He has totaled 155 at-bats in the last two years combined, so there is little chance to get into a rhythm. His 1995 highlight was a late-season, game-winning home run that older brother Tony watched sail over his head into the Dodger Stadium bullpen.

## Hitting, Baserunning & Defense

Gwynn is more of a pull hitter than his brother, only occasionally slapping hits left of second base. Like most lefties, he likes the ball down and in. Gwynn has decent power when the situation calls for it. Though pear-shaped, he has deceptive speed and legs out a fair number of triples. Gwynn is not, however, a basestealing threat. He is a decent outfielder despite seldom getting any game time to hone those skills. His throwing arm is just average.

## 1996 Outlook

Gwynn has refused a minor league assignment and is again a free agent. That does not necessarily mean he is leaving the club. One of the most personable people around, he is very popular with his teammates. Lasorda likes to use the same lineup card day after day, so he needs guys like Gwynn to keep him company on the bench until it is time to take a few hacks late in the game.

Los Angeles Dodgers

# Dave Hansen

**Position**: 3B
**Bats**: L **Throws**: R
**Ht**: 6' 0"  **Wt**: 195

**Opening Day Age**: 27
**Born**: 11/24/68 in Long Beach, CA
**ML Seasons**: 6

## Overall Statistics

|  | G | AB | R | H | D | T | HR | RBI | SB | BB | SO | Avg | OBP | Slg |
|---|---|---|---|---|---|---|---|---|---|---|---|---|---|---|
| 1995 | 100 | 181 | 19 | 52 | 10 | 0 | 1 | 14 | 0 | 28 | 28 | .287 | .384 | .359 |
| Career | 414 | 734 | 68 | 194 | 31 | 0 | 12 | 77 | 1 | 90 | 110 | .264 | .345 | .359 |

## 1995 Season

Dave Hansen was promised more at-bats in 1995 and he got to the plate 211 times, more than in the previous two years combined. It took a couple of injuries to Tim Wallach to achieve that, but Hansen is not one to complain and he performs well when asked. In fact, his ability to produce off the bench (he hit .314 as a pinch hitter) may be part of the reason he spends so much time there.

## Hitting, Baserunning & Defense

Hansen approaches each at-bat aggressively, yet he has a very good eye. Though he can yank one over the right-field fence, a line drive up the middle is more his style. He makes contact and usually hits the ball hard somewhere. Hansen is an intelligent, alert and earnest ballplayer, which partially makes up for a basic lack of skills. Hands, feet, speed, quickness: all are average at best. So he is barely adequate in the field and a very cautious baserunner.

## 1996 Outlook

Look at Hansen's last three years as one full season and you have Tim Wallach with slightly less power. Will he finally get his chance now that Wallach is considering retirement? Doubtful. With the Dodgers trading for Mike Blowers, Hansen will probably continue to be an important bench player and key pinch hitter. When is that next expansion anyway?

# Todd Hollandsworth

**Position**: CF
**Bats**: L **Throws**: L
**Ht**: 6' 2"  **Wt**: 193

**Opening Day Age**: 22
**Born**: 4/20/73 in Dayton, OH
**ML Seasons**: 1

## Overall Statistics

|  | G | AB | R | H | D | T | HR | RBI | SB | BB | SO | Avg | OBP | Slg |
|---|---|---|---|---|---|---|---|---|---|---|---|---|---|---|
| 1995 | 41 | 103 | 16 | 24 | 2 | 0 | 5 | 13 | 2 | 10 | 29 | .233 | .304 | .398 |
| Career | 41 | 103 | 16 | 24 | 2 | 0 | 5 | 13 | 2 | 10 | 29 | .233 | .304 | .398 |

## 1995 Season

Heralded prospect Todd Hollandsworth hit a few speed bumps on the road to stardom in 1995. Two injuries to his right hand, a broken hamate bone in May and a fractured thumb in August derailed what was looking like a promising rookie season. In fact, Hollandsworth had won the starting center field job from rent-a-player Roberto Kelly when his season was virtually terminated by his second stint on the disabled list.

## Hitting, Baserunning & Defense

Hollandsworth has a nice compact swing that produces surprising pop from the left side of the plate. He should develop into a decent contact hitter with a lot of doubles power to both gaps. Opposing lefties give him some trouble, however, and a platoon situation might be in order at this stage of his career. Hollandsworth has good speed and is delightfully reckless, both on the bases and especially in the outfield. He looks to be a natural center fielder as he gets a great jump and has great instincts. His arm, though not Mondesi's, is strong and accurate.

## 1996 Outlook

If he can stay healthy, Hollandsworth will play a lot next year in either left or center. He turns 23 right after Opening Day and looks to have a very bright future. Just don't expect him to repeat his gaudy numbers from Albuquerque in pitcher-friendly Chavez Ravine.

# Rudy Seanez

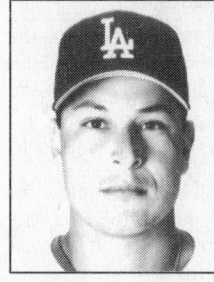

**Position:** RP
**Bats:** R **Throws:** R
**Ht:** 5'10" **Wt:** 190

**Opening Day Age:** 27
**Born:** 10/20/68 in
Brawley, CA
**ML Seasons:** 6
**Pronunciation:**
see-AHN-ez

## Overall Statistics

| | W | L | Pct. | ERA | G | GS | Sv | IP | H | BB | SO | HR | BR/IP |
|---|---|---|---|---|---|---|---|---|---|---|---|---|---|
| 1995 | 1 | 3 | .250 | 6.75 | 37 | 0 | 3 | 34.2 | 39 | 18 | 29 | 5 | 1.64 |
| Career | 4 | 5 | .444 | 6.00 | 91 | 0 | 3 | 99.0 | 104 | 65 | 86 | 12 | 1.71 |

## 1995 Season

Rudy Seanez opened the 1995 season with two saves in the very first series. It all went downhill rather quickly. Seanez pulled a groin in late May and was never the same upon his return. Though he appeared to be fine physically, his confidence wavered and finally broke. Seanez was sent to the minors in late August and was not recalled in September.

## Pitching, Defense & Hitting

The Seanez fastball is still there, consistently popping the mitt at 90-plus MPH. He also throws a good hard slider and mixes in a decent curve. He could use an offspeed pitch, but his biggest problem is his inability to make good pitches at crucial times. He gets rattled, loses his edge, gets behind in the count, then either walks the hitter or leaves a pitch up. Seanez fields his position fairly well. He doesn't hold runners well, as it takes him a while to deliver the ball to the plate. A career reliever, he has made just two lifetime plate appearances.

## 1996 Outlook

The Dodgers thought enough of his arm to sign Seanez to a two-year deal before the 1995 season. In the past, physical problems had held the young fireballer back. Now it is his emotional makeup that's in question. No longer a closer candidate, Seanez will simply strive to make the big-league staff in a set-up role.

# Tim Wallach

**Position:** 3B
**Bats:** R **Throws:** R
**Ht:** 6'3" **Wt:** 207

**Opening Day Age:** 38
**Born:** 9/14/57 in
Huntington Park, CA
**ML Seasons:** 16

## Overall Statistics

| | G | AB | R | H | D | T | HR | RBI | SB | BB | SO | Avg | OBP | Slg |
|---|---|---|---|---|---|---|---|---|---|---|---|---|---|---|
| 1995 | 97 | 327 | 24 | 87 | 22 | 2 | 9 | 38 | 0 | 27 | 69 | .266 | .326 | .428 |
| Career | 2110 | 7747 | 871 | 2003 | 422 | 35 | 248 | 1083 | 50 | 619 | 1228 | .259 | .317 | .418 |

## 1995 Seaon

Tim Wallach missed the first 22 games of the 1995 season with a bulging disc in his lower back and ended the year playing with a torn posterior cruciate ligament in his left knee. While his courage provided inspiration for the Dodgers in their pennant drive, his career would appear to literally be on its last legs. At 38, Wallach can no longer be considered an everyday player, and his at-bats have decreased every year since 1990.

## Hitting, Baserunning & Defense

Though the bad back has reduced his power somewhat, Wallach can still drive the ball to all fields. He preys on fastballs, so getting ahead in the count is crucial. Sliders just off the outside corner seduce him every time. Wallach is a steady third sacker with limited range. If he can reach it, he will make the play. He makes up for a short arm with a quick release. On the basepaths, Wallach often appears to be setting picks as he moves gingerly from station to station.

## 1996 Outlook

Wallach's contributions in the clubhouse far outweigh those on the field at this point in his career. Given the Dodgers' trade for Mike Blowers, any contributions Wallach makes will almost certainly be with another club.

# Other Los Angeles Dodgers

**Jim Bruske** (**Pos**: RP, **Age**:31, **Throws**: R)

A 31-year-old starter/reliever who previously pitched for the Indian and Astro organizations, Bruske got into nine games with the Dodgers last year, all in relief. His work was just fair. 1996 Outlook: C

**Mike Busch** (**Pos**: 3B, **Age**:27, **Bats**: R)

A replacement player, Busch created a rift on the Dodgers when they brought him up late last year. Brett Butler, for one, was outraged. Busch made peace and went on to hit three homers, but he's no prospect. 1996 Outlook: C

**Juan Castro** (**Pos**: 3B, **Age**:23, **Bats**: R)

An infielder with a decent glove but no power, Castro got into a few games last year as a late-inning sub, and even started a game at short. He won't hit enough to make it. 1996 Outlook: C

**Joey Eischen** (**Pos**: RP, **Age**:25, **Throws**: L)

A lefty who was considered a pretty good prospect by the Expos, Eischen came to the Dodgers in a deal last year and pitched pretty well in 17 relief games. Tough on lefties. 1996 Outlook: A

**Carlos Hernandez** (**Pos**: C, **Age**:28, **Bats**: R)

Hernandez has been Mike Piazza's backup for three years now, and obviously hasn't had much chance to play. He's very sound defensively and a fine defensive catcher. A Piazza position switch would help. 1996 Outlook: A

**Garey Ingram** (**Pos**: 3B, **Age**:25, **Bats**: R)

Ingram got into 44 games with the Dodgers, mostly as an infield fill-in. He can run, draw some walks and field a little, but he's at best a good utility player. He just can't hit enough. 1996 Outlook: C

**Derek Lilliquist** (**Pos**: RP, **Age**:30, **Throws**: L)

The well-traveled Lilliquist has pitched for several teams, and had a couple of fine seasons with the Indians. He got cuffed around with the Red Sox last year, but he's only 30 and better than that. 1996 Outlook: B

**Noe Munoz** (**Pos**: C, **Age**:25, **Bats**: R)

A Mexican catcher, Munoz got one at-bat with the Dodgers last year. He's supposed to be good in the field, but he didn't hit in the minors and won't hit in the majors. 1996 Outlook: D

**Rick Parker** (**Pos**: LF, **Age**:33, **Bats**: R)

Now 33 years old, Parker has been a sub outfielder for the Giants, Astros and Mets, and he played the same role with the Dodgers last year. If he hits like he did last year (.276), he could be back. 1996 Outlook: C

**Tom Prince** (**Pos**: C, **Age**:31, **Bats**: R)

Your basic third-string catcher, Prince can field and throw, but his lifetime major league average is .181. On the other hand, Prince seems to have developed good power over the last few seasons. He'll probably be back in the minors this year, waiting for some catcher to get hurt. 1996 Outlook: C.

**Eddie Pye** (**Pos**: 3B, **Age**:29, **Bats**: R)

Pye has now had four-plus seasons with the Dodgers' Triple-A team at Albuquerque, and he's hit as high as .335. But he lacks power and his other skills aren't quite good enough. 1996 Outlook: C.

**Felix Rodriguez** (**Pos**: RP, **Age**:23, **Throws**: R)

Rodriguez broke in as a catcher but was switched to the mound in 1993. Still only 23, he has a good arm but is still working on his control. Could stick this spring, but a Triple-A stint seems likely. 1996 Outlook: B.

**Mitch Webster** (**Pos**: LF/RF, **Age**:36, **Bats**: B)

Webster has spent the last four years with the Dodgers as a reserve outfielder/pinch hitter, but he batted only .179 last year and at 36 the end is near. Will need a big spring to make a team. 1996 Outlook: C.

**Reggie Williams** (**Pos**: LF, **Age**:29, **Bats**: B)

A former Angel prospect, Williams has great speed in the outfield, and he's had two straight good years in Triple-A. He's nearly 30 and his age is against him, but some team might give him a chance. 1996 Outlook: C.

# Los Angeles Dodgers Minor League Prospects

## Organization Overview:

The Dodgers probably boast more good young prospects than any team in baseball. And by young we mean *really* young. . . players who are quite advanced for their age and experience. Just last season, Los Angeles received contributions from a couple of 22 year olds, Todd Hollandsworth and Antonio Osuna, both of whom might be considered old when compared to other diaper dandies who will soon arrive in Dodger Stadium. 21-year-old Roger Cedeno has a good shot at cracking the Dodger outfield this season, with 20-year-old Karim Garcia soon to follow. The Dodger organization simply isn't afraid to push prospects through their system at a rapid pace. In addition, Los Angeles is a very active participant in international scouting, grabbing the best talent it can find between the Pacific rim and Latin America. In part because of its aggressive approach to player development, Los Angeles is now in the enviable position of possessing excess talent at multiple positions. How many clubs can say the same?

### Roger Cedeno

**Position:** OF
**Bats:** B **Throws:** R
**Ht:** 6' 1" **Wt:** 165

**Opening Day Age:** 21
**Born:** 8/16/74 in
Valencia, Venez

*Recent Statistics*

|  | G | AB | R | H | D | T | HR | RBI | SB | BB | SO | AVG |
|---|---|---|---|---|---|---|---|---|---|---|---|---|
| 95 AAA Albuquerq | 99 | 367 | 67 | 112 | 19 | 9 | 2 | 44 | 23 | 53 | 56 | .305 |
| 95 NL Los Angeles | 40 | 42 | 4 | 10 | 2 | 0 | 0 | 3 | 1 | 3 | 10 | .238 |
| 95 MLE | 99 | 341 | 44 | 86 | 12 | 3 | 1 | 29 | 15 | 34 | 58 | .252 |

Cedeno marked himself as a potentially special talent when he held his own in Double-A at the age of 18. He's now 21 and has played parts of the past three seasons in Triple-A, hitting .311 at that level. Cedeno is a switch-hitting center fielder with exceptional speed and impressive plate discipline for someone so young. The one skill Cedeno has yet to display is home-run power. The power could still develop, but he's already an acceptable top-of-the-order hitter.

### Karim Garcia

**Position:** OF
**Bats:** L **Throws:** L
**Ht:** 6' 0" **Wt:** 200

**Opening Day Age:** 20
**Born:** 10/29/75 in Cd.
Obregon, Sonora,
Mexico

*Recent Statistics*

|  | G | AB | R | H | D | T | HR | RBI | SB | BB | SO | AVG |
|---|---|---|---|---|---|---|---|---|---|---|---|---|
| 95 AAA Albuquerq | 124 | 474 | 88 | 151 | 26 | 10 | 20 | 91 | 12 | 38 | 102 | .319 |
| 95 NL Los Angeles | 13 | 20 | 1 | 4 | 0 | 0 | 0 | 0 | 0 | 0 | 4 | .200 |
| 95 MLE | 124 | 438 | 58 | 115 | 18 | 4 | 12 | 60 | 8 | 24 | 107 | .263 |

If Garcia was really 19 last year, then his production in Triple-A was truly exceptional. He signed as a free agent out of Mexico in 1992 and has posted three very consistent seasons as a pro, with the exception of a batting average which has increased from .241 to .265 to .319 as he's faced better pitching. After leading the Florida State League with 21 homers in '94, the Dodgers decided to skip Garcia past Double-A entirely. The results last year indicate he was not only ready for that move, but may very well be prepared for the next logical step.

### Wilton Guerrero

**Position:** SS
**Bats:** R **Throws:** R
**Ht:** 5' 11" **Wt:** 145

**Opening Day Age:** 21
**Born:** 10/24/74 in
Nizao, Bani, DR

*Recent Statistics*

|  | G | AB | R | H | D | T | HR | RBI | SB | BB | SO | AVG |
|---|---|---|---|---|---|---|---|---|---|---|---|---|
| 93 R Great Falls | 66 | 256 | 44 | 76 | 5 | 1 | 0 | 21 | 20 | 24 | 33 | .297 |
| 94 A Vero Beach | 110 | 402 | 55 | 118 | 11 | 4 | 1 | 32 | 23 | 29 | 71 | .294 |
| 95 AA San Antonio | 95 | 382 | 53 | 133 | 13 | 6 | 0 | 26 | 21 | 26 | 63 | .348 |
| 95 AAA Albuquerq | 14 | 49 | 10 | 16 | 1 | 1 | 0 | 2 | 2 | 1 | 7 | .327 |
| 95 MLE | 109 | 411 | 51 | 129 | 10 | 3 | 0 | 23 | 17 | 18 | 74 | .314 |

Guerrero is yet another prospect whom the Dodgers haven't hesitated to promote despite his relative youth. He won the Texas League batting title last season at the age of 20 before playing the final half-month in Triple-A. Guerrero's strike-zone judgment is poor for someone with so little power, but he has yet to steal fewer than 20 bases in any season and is a .315 lifetime hitter in the minor leagues. Defensively, Guerrero figures to be an improvement over Jose Offerman once he reaches Los Angeles.

### Paul Konerko

**Position:** C
**Bats:** R **Throws:** R
**Ht:** 6' 2" **Wt:** 205

**Opening Day Age:** 20
**Born:** 3/5/76 in
Providence, RI

*Recent Statistics*

|  | G | AB | R | H | D | T | HR | RBI | SB | BB | SO | AVG |
|---|---|---|---|---|---|---|---|---|---|---|---|---|
| 94 A Yakima | 67 | 257 | 25 | 74 | 15 | 2 | 6 | 58 | 1 | 36 | 52 | .288 |
| 95 A San Bernrdo | 118 | 448 | 77 | 124 | 21 | 1 | 19 | 77 | 3 | 59 | 88 | .277 |

Konerko was the Dodgers' top pick in 1994 and the first catcher taken by anybody in that draft. His first full pro season last year was very encouraging, as Konerko flashed tremendous offensive potential. He obviously has the power to hit for extra bases and the eye to draw walks. He also led the Northwest League in RBI in his '94 pro debut. His defensive game lags behind his offense, but he won't turn 20 until spring training. With Mike Piazza entrenched in L.A., Konerko should have plenty of time to develop.

Los Angeles Dodgers

## Chris Latham

**Position:** OF  
**Bats:** B **Throws:** R  
**Ht:** 5' 11" **Wt:** 174  
**Opening Day Age:** 22  
**Born:** 5/26/73 in Coeur D'Alene, ID

*Recent Statistics*

| | G | AB | R | H | D | T | HR | RBI | SB | BB | SO | AVG |
|---|---|---|---|---|---|---|---|---|---|---|---|---|
| 93 A Yakima | 54 | 192 | 46 | 50 | 2 | 6 | 4 | 17 | 24 | 39 | 53 | .260 |
| 93 A Bakersfield | 6 | 27 | 1 | 5 | 1 | 0 | 0 | 3 | 2 | 4 | 5 | .185 |
| 94 A Bakersfield | 52 | 191 | 29 | 41 | 5 | 2 | 5 | 15 | 28 | 28 | 49 | .215 |
| 94 A Yakima | 71 | 288 | 69 | 98 | 19 | 8 | 5 | 32 | 33 | 55 | 66 | .340 |
| 95 A Vero Beach | 71 | 259 | 53 | 74 | 13 | 4 | 6 | 39 | 42 | 56 | 54 | .286 |
| 95 AA San Antonio | 58 | 214 | 38 | 64 | 14 | 5 | 9 | 37 | 11 | 33 | 59 | .299 |
| 95 AAA Albuquerq | 5 | 18 | 2 | 3 | 0 | 1 | 0 | 3 | 1 | 1 | 4 | .167 |
| 95 MLE | 63 | 222 | 33 | 57 | 10 | 2 | 7 | 32 | 8 | 23 | 67 | .257 |

Latham was one of the fastest-rising players in the Dodger system in '95, ascending from fast-A to Triple-A in the space of a couple months. Latham was drafted as a shortstop in 1991 and hit like one through most of his first three years a pro. He now plays center field and started to hit with more power last year, totaling 52 extra-base hits between the three levels at which he played. His basestealing speed is unquestioned, as he's swiped at least 50 bases each of the last two years.

## Chan Ho Park

**Position:** P  
**Bats:** R **Throws:** R  
**Ht:** 6' 2" **Wt:** 185  
**Opening Day Age:** 22  
**Born:** 6/30/73 in Kong Ju City, Korea

*Recent Statistics*

| | W | L | ERA | G | GS | Sv | IP | H | R | BB | SO | HR |
|---|---|---|---|---|---|---|---|---|---|---|---|---|
| 95 AAA Albuquerq | 6 | 7 | 4.91 | 23 | 22 | 0 | 110.0 | 93 | 64 | 76 | 101 | 10 |
| 95 NL Los Ang. | 0 | 0 | 4.50 | 2 | 1 | 0 | 4.0 | 2 | 2 | 2 | 7 | 1 |

Park has been sort of an enigma for the Dodgers since they signed him a couple of years ago for a $1.2 million bonus. He actually started the '94 season with Los Angeles before being demoted to Double-A, where he later suffered elbow problems. When healthy, Park throws a mid-90s fastball and good breaking pitch. His strikeout rates have been good, but he walks too many hitters. A 4.91 ERA in the PCL is actually respectable, and it isn't out of the question that Park could begin the '96 season in the Dodger rotation.

## Gary Rath

**Position:** P  
**Bats:** L **Throws:** L  
**Ht:** 6' 2" **Wt:** 185  
**Opening Day Age:** 23  
**Born:** 1/10/73 in Gulfport, MS

*Recent Statistics*

| | W | L | ERA | G | GS | Sv | IP | H | R | BB | SO | HR |
|---|---|---|---|---|---|---|---|---|---|---|---|---|
| 94 A Vero Beach | 5 | 6 | 2.73 | 13 | 11 | 0 | 62.2 | 55 | 26 | 23 | 50 | 3 |
| 95 AA San Antonio | 13 | 3 | 2.77 | 18 | 18 | 0 | 117.0 | 96 | 42 | 48 | 81 | 6 |
| 95 AAA Albuquerq | 3 | 5 | 5.08 | 8 | 8 | 0 | 39.0 | 46 | 31 | 20 | 23 | 4 |

By the end of Rath's first full pro season he had already reached Triple-A. He was the Dodgers' second-round selection in 1994 and last year pitched enough at Double-A San Antonio to qualify for the ERA title and share the Texas League lead in victories. His fastball isn't exceptionally quick but it does have good left-handed movement. He also gets high marks for his pitching smarts. Rath found the going tougher in Albuquerque, and will likely spend the summer of '96 there once again.

## Adam Riggs

**Position:** 2B  
**Bats:** R **Throws:** R  
**Ht:** 6' 0" **Wt:** 190  
**Opening Day Age:** 23  
**Born:** 10/4/72 in Steubenville, OH

*Recent Statistics*

| | G | AB | R | H | D | T | HR | RBI | SB | BB | SO | AVG |
|---|---|---|---|---|---|---|---|---|---|---|---|---|
| 94 R Great Falls | 62 | 234 | 55 | 73 | 20 | 3 | 5 | 44 | 19 | 31 | 38 | .312 |
| 94 A Yakima | 4 | 7 | 1 | 2 | 1 | 0 | 0 | 0 | 0 | 0 | 1 | .286 |
| 95 A San Bernrdo | 134 | 542 | 111 | 196 | 39 | 5 | 24 | 106 | 31 | 54 | 93 | .362 |

Riggs generated one of the best offensive seasons of anyone in the minors last year, leading the California League in batting average and being named its Most Valuable Player. Though he was only 22, there are some observers who question just how high Riggs' ceiling is. He wasn't drafted until the 22nd round in 1994, and the Dodgers then shifted him from the outfield to second base, where he faces a lot of work to become adequate. But the range of offensive skills Riggs has displayed can compensate for a lot of defensive problems.

## Others to Watch

The Dodger rotation already enlists pitchers from Mexico, Japan and the Dominican Republic, and may soon use one from Korea. Eventually, **Kym Ashworth** could be Australia's representative on the League of Nations staff. Ashworth, a 19-year-old lefthander, was 7-4 with a 3.53 ERA at Vero Beach last year. . . Lefthander **Will Brunson** got off to a 10-0 start in the California League in '95 before earning a mid-season promotion to Double-A. He finished 4-5 with San Antonio. . . Catcher **Ken Huckaby** hit .324 at Albuquerque but has never hit with power and doesn't draw walks. . . Outfielder **Scott Hunter** was the Dodgers' fifth-round pick in 1993. He hit .285 with fair power and 27 stolen bases for San Bernadino. . . Reliever **Joe Jacobsen** saved 34 games last year, all in Class A. He's allowed only seven home runs in 243.2 professional innings. . . Lefty **Mark Mimbs**, the brother of Phillie Mike, compiled a 2.97 ERA to go along with 96 strikeouts and 22 walks in Triple-A. . . **Righthander Hugo Pivaral** was only 18 years old last year when he went 6-4 with a 4.63 ERA in the fast-A California League. He's a big guy at 6'5" and 220 pounds, and he throws a mean fastball.

# Moises Alou

## 1995 Season

Coming off a 1994 campaign in which he finished third in the National League MVP balloting, Moises Alou was a major disappointment last year. Despite missing 50 games with shoulder injuries and a death in his family, Alou still tied for the club lead in home runs with 14 and ranked second on the Expos with 58 RBI. However, those were the worst numbers for Alou since he became an every-day player in 1993. His average fell 24 points in the second half of the season after he first damaged his left shoulder, then re-aggravated an old injury to his *right* shoulder.

## Hitting

Bothered by the weakened shoulders, Alou had trouble turning on pitches consistently last year. When healthy he sports one of the quicker bats in the league and can catch up to nearly any fastball. He will get impatient and chase breaking pitches when behind in the count, and he also has some trouble with low offspeed stuff. However, he is maturing as a hitter with gap power to the opposite field. Alou is also capable of bunting his way on base in the right situation.

## Baserunning & Defense

The gruesome leg and ankle injuries Alou suffered late in 1993 have taken some of his speed. Now that he's set in the third spot of the batting order, he is rarely asked to steal bases anyway. Alou is an outstanding outfielder, and seems to have settled into left field where he has excellent range and a strong and accurate arm.

## 1996 Outlook

Alou had offseason rotator-cuff surgery on both shoulders, but the Expos expect him ready to open the season. Assuming he has no physical complications, Montreal would like to sign him to a multi-year deal and make him the centerpiece of their always-evolving club. Wherever he plays, Alou can be counted on to return to his star heights this season.

**Position:** LF/RF
**Bats:** R  **Throws:** R
**Ht:** 6' 3"  **Wt:** 195

**Opening Day Age:** 29
**Born:** 7/3/66 in Atlanta, GA
**ML Seasons:** 5
**Pronunciation:** MOY-sezz ah-LOO

### Overall Statistics

|  | G | AB | R | H | D | T | HR | RBI | SB | BB | SO | Avg | OBP | Slg |
|---|---|---|---|---|---|---|---|---|---|---|---|---|---|---|
| 1995 | 93 | 344 | 48 | 94 | 22 | 0 | 14 | 58 | 4 | 29 | 56 | .273 | .342 | .459 |
| Career | 467 | 1609 | 256 | 475 | 110 | 14 | 63 | 277 | 44 | 134 | 221 | .295 | .351 | .498 |

### Where He Hits the Ball

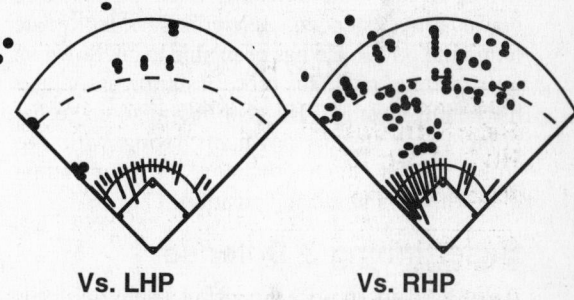

**Vs. LHP**          **Vs. RHP**

### 1995 Situational Stats

|  | AB | H | HR | RBI | Avg |  | AB | H | HR | RBI | Avg |
|---|---|---|---|---|---|---|---|---|---|---|---|
| Home | 151 | 37 | 4 | 25 | .245 | LHP | 82 | 28 | 5 | 19 | .341 |
| Road | 193 | 57 | 10 | 33 | .295 | RHP | 262 | 66 | 9 | 39 | .252 |
| First Half | 239 | 71 | 8 | 39 | .297 | Sc Pos | 98 | 35 | 2 | 42 | .357 |
| Scnd Half | 105 | 23 | 6 | 19 | .219 | Clutch | 50 | 14 | 1 | 8 | .280 |

### 1995 Rankings (National League)

→ 1st in lowest batting average on a 3-1 count (.000)
→ 5th in lowest cleanup slugging percentage (.437)
→ 6th in batting average with runners in scoring position (.357)
→ 8th in hit by pitch (9)
→ Led the Expos in home runs, hit by pitch, batting average with runners in scoring position and cleanup slugging percentage (.437)

# Sean Berry

## 1995 Season

Sean Berry earned the Expos' Opening Day third-base job last year, but wound up sharing the position, mostly with rookie Shane Andrews. For the third straight season, the consistent Berry batted around 300 times. His on-base percentages in those seasons were .348, .347 and .367, and he has hit 14, 11, and 14 homers. The big news was his career-high .318 batting average, a 40-point improvement over 1994. Berry also established career highs in RBI, hits and doubles.

## Hitting

The key for Berry is to avoid getting jammed. He does not have exceptional bat speed and can get tied up inside with hard stuff. When he is able to get his arms extended, Berry displays legitimate home-run power. He has been able to cut down on his strikeouts and in the process significantly raise his batting average. He also has matured to the point where he cuts down his swing with two strikes and in clutch situations, last year batting .333 with men in scoring position.

## Baserunning & Defense

Berry used to surprise opposing teams with his speed, succeeding on 26 of 28 steal attempts in 1993 and '94. But last year, pitchers seemed to catch on, as Berry was nailed on eight of his 11 attempts. At third base, Berry is a defensive liability with his limited range and very erratic arm. He is also tentative charging balls, and often gun-shy when he has to cut loose with a throw. The Expos took a brief look at him at first base, but they felt he lacked the good hands necessary for the position.

## 1996 Outlook

Berry has become a solid hitter. However, his fielding woes make him suspect as a regular player. With service time making him more expensive, Berry is a likely candidate for the Expos to shop in trade talks, especially with Shane Andrews and Wil Cordero around.

**Position:** 3B
**Bats:** R  **Throws:** R
**Ht:** 5'11"  **Wt:** 200

**Opening Day Age:** 30
**Born:** 3/22/66 in Santa Monica, CA
**ML Seasons:** 6

### Overall Statistics

|  | G | AB | R | H | D | T | HR | RBI | SB | BB | SO | Avg | OBP | Slg |
|---|---|---|---|---|---|---|---|---|---|---|---|---|---|---|
| 1995 | 103 | 314 | 38 | 100 | 22 | 1 | 14 | 55 | 3 | 25 | 53 | .318 | .367 | .529 |
| Career | 391 | 1073 | 143 | 299 | 61 | 6 | 40 | 154 | 31 | 106 | 212 | .279 | .344 | .459 |

### Where He Hits the Ball

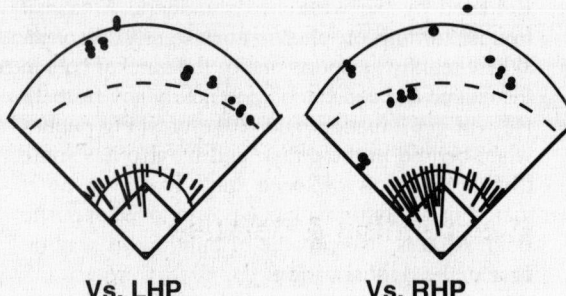

**Vs. LHP**          **Vs. RHP**

### 1995 Situational Stats

|  | AB | H | HR | RBI | Avg |  |  | AB | H | HR | RBI | Avg |
|---|---|---|---|---|---|---|---|---|---|---|---|---|
| Home | 157 | 42 | 5 | 26 | .268 | LHP |  | 74 | 21 | 1 | 13 | .284 |
| Road | 157 | 58 | 9 | 29 | .369 | RHP |  | 240 | 79 | 13 | 42 | .329 |
| First Half | 134 | 40 | 5 | 24 | .299 | Sc Pos |  | 81 | 27 | 4 | 42 | .333 |
| Scnd Half | 180 | 60 | 9 | 31 | .333 | Clutch |  | 52 | 14 | 2 | 3 | .269 |

### 1995 Rankings (National League)

➡ 10th in errors at third base (12)
➡ Led the Expos in home runs, sacrifice flies (5) and caught stealing (8)

# Wil Cordero

## 1995 Season

After a spectacular 1994 campaign in which he was arguably the National League's top-hitting shortstop, Wil Cordero hoped to build on that success in 1995. But by the end of a strange and disappointing season, Cordero was a left fielder. His move from shortstop triggered a 6-for-46 slump in an otherwise-solid offensive season, one in which he set career highs with 35 doubles and 147 hits.

## Hitting

Cordero has one of the quickest bats around and is practically impossible to jam. However, he is too anxious early in the count, and he also struggled last season after falling behind. He began fishing for breaking balls out of the strike zone and also got into a bad habit of pulling off pitches, resulting in too many strikeouts and routine fly balls. At his best, Cordero slashes the ball to all fields, because he has the bat speed and strength to reach the gap anywhere.

## Baserunning & Defense

In addition to slumping at the plate, Cordero suddenly became a tentative runner, going 9-for-14 on steal attempts. He has the speed and quickness to easily steal 15 or 20 bases per season. Cordero's days at shortstop could be over, despite his impressive physical tools. The Expos have grown weary of his erratic throwing arm and lack of range. However, Cordero's stint in left field was not a success, as he made five errors in his 26 outfield starts. Some feel that Cordero's best position might be third base.

## 1996 Outlook

The sky's still the limit for Cordero, who slugged .489 at the age of 22 in 1994. Still only 24, Cordero has the tools to be a star but has allowed his game to drift, especially in the field. The Expos are beginning to lose patience, but Cordero remains a big-time talent waiting to happen. It'll take a little more maturity and a lot more defense.

**Position:** SS/LF
**Bats:** R  **Throws:** R
**Ht:** 6' 2"  **Wt:** 195

**Opening Day Age:** 24
**Born:** 10/3/71 in Mayaguez, PR
**ML Seasons:** 4
**Pronunciation:** cor-DAIR-oh

### Overall Statistics

|  | G | AB | R | H | D | T | HR | RBI | SB | BB | SO | Avg | OBP | Slg |
|---|---|---|---|---|---|---|---|---|---|---|---|---|---|---|
| 1995 | 131 | 514 | 64 | 147 | 35 | 2 | 10 | 49 | 9 | 36 | 88 | .286 | .341 | .420 |
| Career | 424 | 1530 | 202 | 425 | 101 | 8 | 37 | 178 | 37 | 120 | 241 | .278 | .338 | .427 |

### Where He Hits the Ball

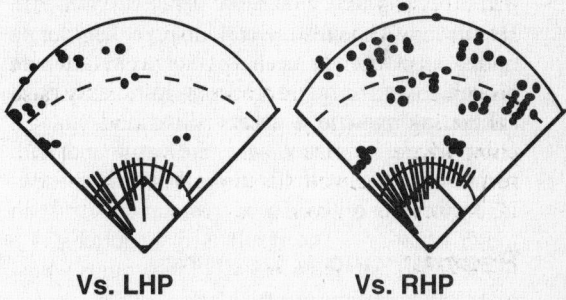

**Vs. LHP**          **Vs. RHP**

### 1995 Situational Stats

|  | AB | H | HR | RBI | Avg |  | AB | H | HR | RBI | Avg |
|---|---|---|---|---|---|---|---|---|---|---|---|
| Home | 247 | 72 | 2 | 23 | .291 | LHP | 124 | 38 | 3 | 19 | .306 |
| Road | 267 | 75 | 8 | 26 | .281 | RHP | 390 | 109 | 7 | 30 | .279 |
| First Half | 273 | 82 | 5 | 28 | .300 | Sc Pos | 109 | 29 | 2 | 36 | .266 |
| Scnd Half | 241 | 65 | 5 | 21 | .270 | Clutch | 66 | 16 | 0 | 6 | .242 |

### 1995 Rankings (National League)

→ 3rd in lowest fielding percentage at shortstop (.960)

→ 4th in errors at shortstop (17) and errors in left field (5)

→ 5th in doubles

→ 7th in lowest percentage of extra bases taken as a runner (40.8%)

→ 8th in hit by pitch (9)

→ Led the Expos in at-bats, hits, singles (100), doubles, hit by pitch, times on base (192), strikeouts (88), pitches seen (1,985), plate appearances (564), games played and batting average on an 0-2 count (.261)

# Jose DeLeon

## 1995 Season

Acquired from the White Sox in late August, veteran righthander Jose DeLeon was ineffective in his seven appearances for Montreal. He was scored upon in four of the seven outings, going 0-1 with a 7.56 ERA. That performance came after DeLeon struggled in Chicago, going 5-3 but with an ugly 5.19 ERA.

## Pitching

Since he was a kid, DeLeon has confounded baseball people with his inability to translate excellent stuff and a good attitude into better results. Now he's at an age where he's just trying to hang on as an innings-eater. DeLeon still throws a fastball that is occasionally clocked in the low to mid 90s. However, he can only maintain that velocity for an inning or two, which means his days as a starter are probably over for good. DeLeon also has a good splitter, along with a decent slider and change. However, he does not have the command with them that he has with his fastball, which unfortunately he has always been reluctant to trust in tough situations. The result is that DeLeon is a nibbler who runs unnecessarily long counts which often end up as hits or walks.

## Defense & Hitting

DeLeon employs an average-plus move to first, though its effectiveness is somewhat negated by his slow delivery to the plate. He is an adequate fielder. He hasn't hit for a few years but he can at least handle the bat and make occasional contact.

## 1996 Outlook

There is very little certain about the Expos these days, so it shouldn't be a surprise that Montreal has little idea what will happen with this 35-year-old journeyman. Veteran right-handed middle relievers are a dime a dozen, and where—or if—DeLeon winds up will all come down to price.

**Position:** RP
**Bats:** R  **Throws:** R
**Ht:** 6' 3"  **Wt:** 226

**Opening Day Age:** 35
**Born:** 12/20/60 in Rancho Viejo, La Vega, DR
**ML Seasons:** 13
**Pronunciation:** DAY-lee-own

*Overall Statistics*

|  | W | L | Pct. | ERA | G | GS | Sv | IP | H | BB | SO | HR | BR/IP |
|---|---|---|---|---|---|---|---|---|---|---|---|---|---|
| 1995 | 5 | 4 | .556 | 5.45 | 45 | 0 | 0 | 76.0 | 67 | 35 | 65 | 12 | 1.34 |
| Career | 86 | 119 | .420 | 3.76 | 415 | 264 | 6 | 1897.1 | 1556 | 841 | 1594 | 153 | 1.26 |

*How Often He Throws Strikes*

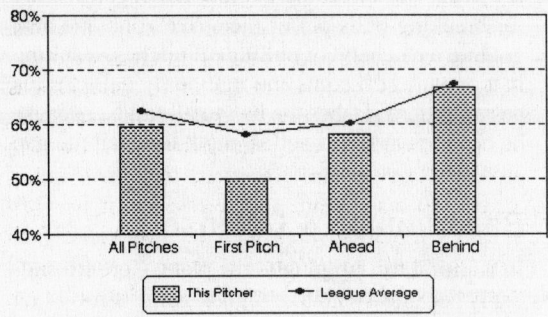

*1995 Situational Stats*

|  | W | L | ERA | Sv | IP |  | AB | H | HR | RBI | Avg |
|---|---|---|---|---|---|---|---|---|---|---|---|
| Home | 3 | 0 | 4.73 | 0 | 40.0 | LHB | 123 | 34 | 2 | 19 | .276 |
| Road | 2 | 4 | 6.25 | 0 | 36.0 | RHB | 159 | 33 | 10 | 25 | .208 |
| First Half | 3 | 3 | 5.44 | 0 | 41.1 | Sc Pos | 78 | 18 | 2 | 30 | .231 |
| Scnd Half | 2 | 1 | 5.45 | 0 | 34.2 | Clutch | 97 | 24 | 2 | 11 | .247 |

*1995 Rankings (National League)*

➡ Did not rank near the top or bottom in any category

# Jeff Fassero

Tough on Lefties

**Position:** SP
**Bats:** L **Throws:** L
**Ht:** 6' 1" **Wt:** 195

**Opening Day Age:** 33
**Born:** 1/5/63 in Springfield, IL
**ML Seasons:** 5
**Pronunciation:** fuh-SAIR-oh

## 1995 Season

Shifted to the rotation in the middle of 1993, left-hander Jeff Fassero quickly established himself as one of the game's top lefty starters, and entered 1995 with a 2.64 career ERA. With the departure of Ken Hill, Fassero was expected to become the Expos' number-one starter. At first he thrived in the role; on June 2 he was 7-1 and seemingly on the way to his best season. But he came down with a groin problem and pitched well in only six of his last 22 starts, with a 4.97 earned- run average over that span.

## Pitching

Few lefthanders in the National League have better stuff than Fassero. He has a heavy, sinking fastball that is thrown consistently in the low 90s, plus a hard slider and a good split-fingered pitch. When Fassero is down in the strike zone, he's as unhittable as any pitcher in the league, especially for left-handed hitters, who managed just a .175 average last season. However, the groin injury hampered his rhythm and release point. He lost much of the downward movement on his fastball *and* much of his control. Fassero's walk total soared, as did the number of hits he allowed.

## Defense & Hitting

Fassero has a very average pickoff move and is also rather slow delivering to the plate, so holding runners is one flaw in his game. He is a solid fielder who makes all the routine plays. Fassero is a weak hitter, and he collected four hits and 29 strikeouts in his 57 at-bats last season. He did handle the bat well enough to execute eight sacrifice bunts.

## 1996 Outlook

In his two-and-a-half seasons as a starter, Fassero has emerged as one of the league's best lefthanders, good for 12 to 15 wins every year. He might become too expensive for the Expos, but he can pitch for anyone.

### Overall Statistics

|        | W  | L  | Pct. | ERA  | G   | GS | Sv | IP    | H   | BB  | SO  | HR | BR/IP |
|--------|----|----|------|------|-----|----|----|-------|-----|-----|-----|----|-------|
| 1995   | 13 | 14 | .481 | 4.33 | 30  | 30 | 0  | 189.0 | 207 | 74  | 164 | 15 | 1.49  |
| Career | 43 | 37 | .538 | 3.16 | 228 | 66 | 10 | 618.1 | 565 | 219 | 528 | 37 | 1.27  |

### How Often He Throws Strikes

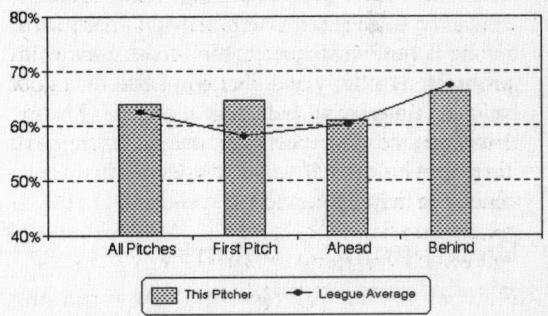

This Pitcher — League Average

### 1995 Situational Stats

|           | W | L  | ERA  | Sv | IP    |        | AB  | H   | HR | RBI | Avg  |
|-----------|---|----|------|----|-------|--------|-----|-----|----|-----|------|
| Home      | 6 | 10 | 4.65 | 0  | 110.1 | LHB    | 103 | 18  | 0  | 10  | .175 |
| Road      | 7 | 4  | 3.89 | 0  | 78.2  | RHB    | 628 | 189 | 15 | 79  | .301 |
| First Half| 8 | 6  | 3.90 | 0  | 87.2  | Sc Pos | 181 | 50  | 3  | 68  | .276 |
| Scnd Half | 5 | 8  | 4.71 | 0  | 101.1 | Clutch | 42  | 10  | 2  | 4   | .238 |

### 1995 Rankings (National League)

- ➡ 2nd in losses and pickoff throws (209)
- ➡ 3rd in errors at pitcher (4)
- ➡ 4th in stolen bases allowed (26) and runners caught stealing (12)
- ➡ 5th in hits allowed, highest batting average allowed (.283), highest on-base percentage allowed (.348), highest groundball/flyball ratio allowed (2.0) and lowest fielding percentage at pitcher (.913)
- ➡ 6th in games started, batters faced (833), walks allowed, strikeouts, most baserunners allowed per 9 innings (13.5) and most strikeouts per 9 innings (7.8)
- ➡ Led the Expos in sacrifice bunts (8), losses, games started and hits allowed

# Darrin Fletcher

## 1995 Season

For the fourth straight season, Darrin Fletcher saw significant action as the Expos' not-quite regular catcher. Playing almost entirely against right-handed pitching, Fletcher set personal highs in a number of offensive categories. He was especially effective in the second half, hitting .294 after the All-Star break. As usual, Fletcher was a durable backstop. Since arriving in the majors for good in June, 1992, Fletcher has had just one DL stint.

## Hitting

Fletcher was generally platooned with Tim Laker, and 10 of his 11 homers came against right-handed pitchers. He does not have great bat speed, and his sometimes-slow bat produces many lazy fly balls. He can be tied up with high-and-tight hard stuff, but he'll pull mistakes in the strike zone with power. He is a fairly good breaking-ball hitter and has good bat control, which accounts for his low strikeout totals. Fletcher has worked to improve his hitting from year to year, opening his stance slightly to help add some bat speed.

## Baserunning & Defense

Fletcher is the quintessential slow-running catcher; he's never stolen a base in the majors and is not a threat to end that streak anytime soon. The Expo coaches have great confidence in his handling of pitchers and allow him latitude in calling his own game. Fletcher is also a good receiver and has made strides to improve his throwing. He has quickened his release and last year had the best success rate of his career, throwing out nearly a third of the runners who tried to steal against him.

## 1996 Outlook

Fletcher is being pressed by the improving Tim Laker, but he remains a very solid professional. With his salary getting up and the Expos' limited resources placing their priorities elsewhere, Fletcher himself could end up elsewhere. But he'll be a plus no matter where he plays.

**Position:** C
**Bats:** L  **Throws:** R
**Ht:** 6' 1"  **Wt:** 205

**Opening Day Age:** 29
**Born:** 10/3/66 in Elmhurst, IL
**ML Seasons:** 7

### Overall Statistics

|  | G | AB | R | H | D | T | HR | RBI | SB | BB | SO | Avg | OBP | Slg |
|---|---|---|---|---|---|---|---|---|---|---|---|---|---|---|
| 1995 | 110 | 350 | 42 | 100 | 21 | 1 | 11 | 45 | 0 | 32 | 23 | .286 | .351 | .446 |
| Career | 482 | 1420 | 125 | 367 | 78 | 5 | 34 | 203 | 0 | 112 | 135 | .258 | .315 | .392 |

### Where He Hits the Ball

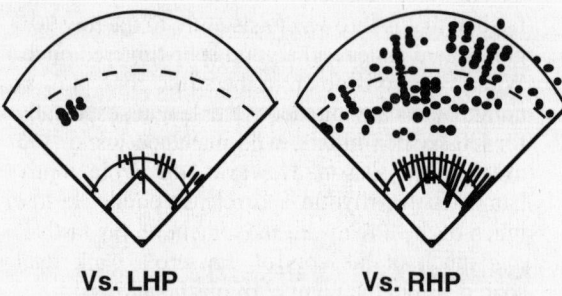

**Vs. LHP**              **Vs. RHP**

### 1995 Situational Stats

|  | AB | H | HR | RBI | Avg |  | AB | H | HR | RBI | Avg |
|---|---|---|---|---|---|---|---|---|---|---|---|
| Home | 163 | 46 | 3 | 23 | .282 | LHP | 44 | 10 | 1 | 8 | .227 |
| Road | 187 | 54 | 8 | 22 | .289 | RHP | 306 | 90 | 10 | 37 | .294 |
| First Half | 156 | 43 | 6 | 22 | .276 | Sc Pos | 103 | 22 | 3 | 36 | .214 |
| Scnd Half | 194 | 57 | 5 | 23 | .294 | Clutch | 52 | 14 | 1 | 7 | .269 |

### 1995 Rankings (National League)

- → 2nd in fielding percentage at catcher (.994)
- → 4th in most GDPs per GDP situation (20.3%)
- → 5th in highest percentage of swings put into play (55.9%)
- → 7th in batting average with two strikes (.276)
- → 8th in lowest batting average with runners in scoring position (.214)
- → 9th in GDPs (15)
- → 10th in lowest percentage of swings that missed (10.9%)
- → Led the Expos in GDPs, batting average vs. right-handed pitchers (.294), slugging percentage vs. right-handed pitchers (.461) and on-base percentage vs. right-handed pitchers (.353)

# Mark Grudzielanek

## 1995 Season

In two separate tours of duty last season, rookie Mark Grudzielanek demonstrated that he has a promising future with the Expos. He held his own offensively, especially when given the chance to play every day at shortstop over the season's final month. He provided glimpses of both extra-base power and basestealing speed.

## Hitting

At this early point in his career, Grudzielanek is something of a one-dimensional hitter. He hit .343 against left-handed pitching and only .211 vs. righthanders. He also hit over 200 points better on artificial turf. However, the Expos think Grudzielanek has excellent offensive potential. He has good bat speed, and hitting out of a slightly open stance he can turn on inside pitches or drive outside offerings to the opposite field. He tends to overswing at times, which accounts for his high strikeout rate. And he will chase offspeed stuff out of the strike zone. However, Grudzielanek is a battler who the Expos think can eventually reach .280 with double-figure homers.

## Baserunning & Defense

Grudzielanek does not have blinding speed, but a very quick first step and good acceleration make him a solid basestealing threat. He is very aggressive running the bases. Grudzielanek played second and third base in addition to shortstop, and all that moving around accounted for him making 10 errors. He's best at shortstop, where he has adequate range and good hands.

## 1996 Outlook

He doesn't have the stand-out tools of Wil Cordero, but Grudzielanek could end up being the Expos' shortstop this year. The club loves his work ethic and thinks he can be a dependable player in the field with decent offensive skills. At the very least, Grudzielanek should be a very useful utility man. It would be wise to learn how to spell, not to mention pronounce, his name.

**Position:** SS/2B/3B
**Bats:** R **Throws:** R
**Ht:** 6' 1"  **Wt:** 180

**Opening Day Age:** 25
**Born:** 6/30/70 in Milwaukee, WI
**ML Seasons:** 1
**Pronunciation:** gruz-ELL-uh-neck

### Overall Statistics

| | G | AB | R | H | D | T | HR | RBI | SB | BB | SO | Avg | OBP | Slg |
|---|---|---|---|---|---|---|---|---|---|---|---|---|---|---|
| 1995 | 78 | 269 | 27 | 66 | 12 | 2 | 1 | 20 | 8 | 14 | 47 | .245 | .300 | .316 |
| Career | 78 | 269 | 27 | 66 | 12 | 2 | 1 | 20 | 8 | 14 | 47 | .245 | .300 | .316 |

### Where He Hits the Ball

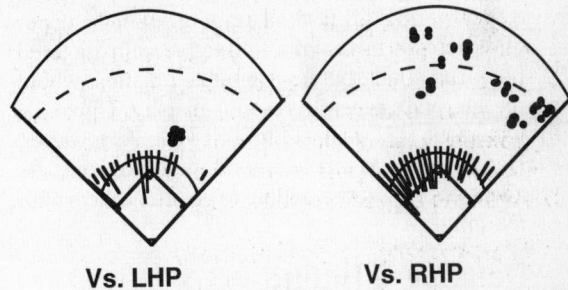

**Vs. LHP**      **Vs. RHP**

### 1995 Situational Stats

| | AB | H | HR | RBI | Avg | | AB | H | HR | RBI | Avg |
|---|---|---|---|---|---|---|---|---|---|---|---|
| Home | 112 | 37 | 1 | 11 | .330 | LHP | 70 | 24 | 0 | 9 | .343 |
| Road | 157 | 29 | 0 | 9 | .185 | RHP | 199 | 42 | 1 | 11 | .211 |
| First Half | 153 | 38 | 1 | 11 | .248 | Sc Pos | 69 | 15 | 0 | 18 | .217 |
| Scnd Half | 116 | 28 | 0 | 9 | .241 | Clutch | 43 | 9 | 0 | 4 | .209 |

### 1995 Rankings (National League)

➡ Led the Expos in batting average with the bases loaded (.400)

# Gil Heredia

## 1995 Season

Coming off his most productive season ever, righthander Gil Heredia opened 1995 in the Montreal rotation. He struggled, and after a July 7 start in which he failed to retire a single batter, Heredia was sent to the bullpen. He returned to start five games in August and pitched pretty well, but went back to the pen anyway. Overall, Heredia was just 4-6 with a 5.20 ERA as a starter, but he posted a sparkling 1.32 ERA in relief.

## Pitching

Few pitchers in baseball have better control than Heredia, who has walked only 48 batters in 252 innings over the last three seasons. He needs such command because his stuff is not what you'd call overpowering, his fastball topping out in the upper 80s. Heredia mixes in an effective split-fingered pitch and slider, but he is a pitcher against whom the ball will generally be put in play. Opposing batters hit .291 against him last year. As a starter, Heredia tends to nibble around the strike zone. As a reliever, he is more willing to go after hitters with the splitter.

## Defense & Hitting

Heredia pays close attention to baserunners and can surprise with his quick pickoff move. He is a good athlete who does not get rattled in the field and makes the routine plays. Heredia has always been a good-hitting pitcher, and he was 6-for-33 (.182) last season.

## 1996 Outlook

In Heredia, the Expos have a versatile pitcher who can do a competent job as a starter but is probably better suited to the bullpen. If they can fill out their rotation in satisfactory fashion, look for Montreal to use Heredia in the set-up role in which he flourished last season.

**Position:** RP/SP
**Bats:** R  **Throws:** R
**Ht:** 6' 1"  **Wt:** 205

**Opening Day Age:** 30
**Born:** 10/26/65 in Nogales, AZ
**ML Seasons:** 5
**Pronunciation:** herr-AY-dee-uh

### Overall Statistics

|        | W  | L  | Pct. | ERA  | G   | GS | Sv | IP    | H   | BB | SO  | HR | BR/IP |
|--------|----|----|------|------|-----|----|----|-------|-----|----|-----|----|-------|
| 1995   | 5  | 6  | .455 | 4.31 | 40  | 18 | 1  | 119.0 | 137 | 21 | 74  | 7  | 1.33  |
| Career | 17 | 16 | .515 | 3.99 | 126 | 39 | 3  | 329.1 | 359 | 75 | 211 | 26 | 1.32  |

### How Often He Throws Strikes

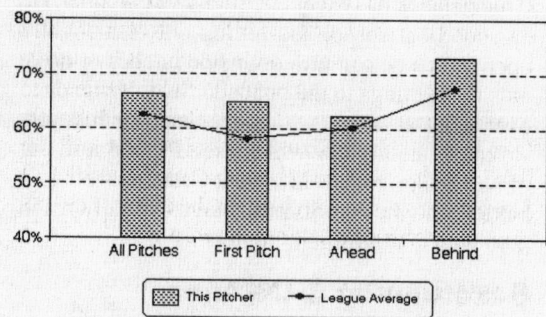

### 1995 Situational Stats

|            | W | L | ERA  | Sv | IP   |        | AB  | H  | HR | RBI | Avg  |
|------------|---|---|------|----|------|--------|-----|----|----|-----|------|
| Home       | 3 | 2 | 4.85 | 0  | 42.2 | LHB    | 207 | 62 | 4  | 21  | .300 |
| Road       | 2 | 4 | 4.01 | 1  | 76.1 | RHB    | 263 | 75 | 3  | 29  | .285 |
| First Half | 3 | 5 | 6.04 | 0  | 67.0 | Sc Pos | 110 | 39 | 2  | 42  | .355 |
| Scnd Half  | 2 | 1 | 2.08 | 1  | 52.0 | Clutch | 21  | 8  | 0  | 2   | .381 |

### 1995 Rankings (National League)

➡ 1st in fielding percentage at pitcher (1.000)

# Mike Lansing

## 1995 Season

Without much fanfare, Mike Lansing has emerged as one of the most productive second basemen in the National League. He led the Expos with 62 RBI last year, fourth best among N.L. second basemen. He added 10 homers, 27 steals and 30 doubles despite missing the first half of June with a hamstring injury. Lansing endured a horrendous 6-for-63 slump after coming off the DL, leaving us to wonder what he'd have done with a healthy hammy.

## Hitting

Lansing has added strength through lifting weights, and he is not a hitter to be taken lightly. He can drive the ball to the gaps against both left- and right-handed pitching, and he's an excellent fastball hitter. Lansing occasionally has trouble with breaking balls and change-ups, but he has learned to wait on the offspeed stuff much better. During his slump, Lansing was pulling off too many pitches, but he rebounded over the last 70 games. He is also a tough out in the clutch. His one weakness is that he seldom draws a walk.

## Baserunning & Defense

With excellent speed, a quick first step and excellent knowledge of opposing pitchers, Lansing has developed into an outstanding basestealer who was caught only four times in 31 attempts last season, despite laboring for a month with that bad hamstring. Originally a shortstop, Lansing has become one of baseball's best second baseman. He has outstanding range, soft hands, a strong arm with a quick release, and he hangs in on the double play as well as anyone.

## 1996 Outlook

There are few questions left unanswered about Lansing. He has established himself as a legitimate run producer and an outstanding defensive player. The Expos also liked the way he battled his way out of a serious slump last season to finish with a flourish. He has become one of Montreal's mainstays.

**Position:** 2B
**Bats:** R **Throws:** R
**Ht:** 6' 0"  **Wt:** 180

**Opening Day Age:** 27
**Born:** 4/3/68 in Rawlins, WY
**ML Seasons:** 3

### Overall Statistics

|        | G   | AB   | R   | H   | D  | T | HR | RBI | SB | BB  | SO  | Avg  | OBP  | Slg  |
|--------|-----|------|-----|-----|----|---|----|-----|----|-----|-----|------|------|------|
| 1995   | 127 | 467  | 47  | 119 | 30 | 2 | 10 | 62  | 27 | 28  | 65  | .255 | .299 | .392 |
| Career | 374 | 1352 | 155 | 365 | 80 | 5 | 18 | 142 | 62 | 104 | 158 | .270 | .327 | .376 |

### Where He Hits the Ball

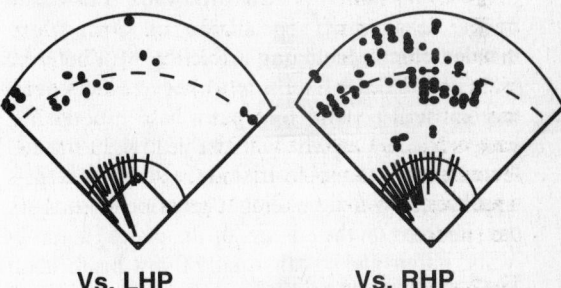

**Vs. LHP**      **Vs. RHP**

### 1995 Situational Stats

|            | AB  | H  | HR | RBI | Avg  |        | AB  | H  | HR | RBI | Avg  |
|------------|-----|----|----|-----|------|--------|-----|----|----|-----|------|
| Home       | 243 | 63 | 4  | 27  | .259 | LHP    | 107 | 29 | 4  | 19  | .271 |
| Road       | 224 | 56 | 6  | 35  | .250 | RHP    | 360 | 90 | 6  | 43  | .250 |
| First Half | 193 | 42 | 5  | 24  | .218 | Sc Pos | 124 | 40 | 6  | 54  | .323 |
| Scnd Half  | 274 | 77 | 5  | 38  | .281 | Clutch | 70  | 20 | 1  | 10  | .286 |

### 1995 Rankings (National League)

- ➡ 1st in lowest on-base percentage vs. right-handed pitchers (.292)
- ➡ 2nd in lowest on-base percentage
- ➡ 4th in stolen base percentage (87.1%) and fielding percentage at second base (.991)
- ➡ 6th in batting average on a 3-1 count (.600) and steals of third (8)
- ➡ 8th in lowest batting average vs. right-handed pitchers (.250)
- ➡ 9th in least pitches seen per plate appearance (3.36) and errors at second base (6)
- ➡ 10th in lowest batting average
- ➡ Led the Expos in RBI, stolen bases, batting average in the clutch (.286), batting average on a 3-1 count and steals of third

# Dave Leiper

## 1995 Season

Lefthander Dave Leiper began last season in Oakland, continuing his second stint as an Athletic. Despite pitching decently, Leiper was first demoted to Triple-A, then traded to the Expos on July 25. After two outings in Ottawa, Leiper was summoned to Montreal where he did a solid job, posting a 2.86 ERA in 26 appearances. Felipe Alou was so impressed that he allowed Leiper to record a pair of saves in August. In general, though, Leiper was used in his accustomed role as a situational lefty.

## Pitching

With outstanding control and an excellent split-fingered fastball, Leiper has revived his career in recent seasons by specializing in retiring left-handed hitters. Including his action with both the Athletics and the Expos, left-handed hitters averaged just .197 with four extra-base hits against Leiper. He is somewhat vulnerable to right-handed bats, but not to a worrisome extent. Leiper is sneaky fast, with a sinker that occasionally hits 90, and he lives on the corners of the plate. He rarely walks hitters and he can usually throw his forkball for strikes, even when behind in the count.

## Defense & Hitting

Leiper has a fairly slow delivery to the plate, which can make him vulnerable to impatient baserunners. However, he does a fair job of holding runners, and he's a dependable fielder. Leiper rarely stays in a game long enough to bat, and is 1-for-4 lifetime.

## 1996 Outlook

One of the more uplifting stories of the last few years, Leiper has come back from a heart problem to establish himself as one of the more effective specialty lefthanders. Leiper is now 33, but he's got three things going for him: a 3.66 career ERA, a left arm, and a manager who likes him.

**Position:** RP
**Bats:** L  **Throws:** L
**Ht:** 6' 1"  **Wt:** 175

**Opening Day Age:** 33
**Born:** 6/18/62 in Whittier, CA
**ML Seasons:** 7
**Pronunciation:** LEE-per

### Overall Statistics

| | W | L | Pct. | ERA | G | GS | Sv | IP | H | BB | SO | HR | BR/IP |
|---|---|---|---|---|---|---|---|---|---|---|---|---|---|
| 1995 | 1 | 3 | .250 | 3.22 | 50 | 0 | 2 | 44.2 | 39 | 19 | 22 | 5 | 1.30 |
| Career | 10 | 7 | .588 | 3.66 | 231 | 0 | 7 | 253.0 | 242 | 105 | 137 | 21 | 1.37 |

### How Often He Throws Strikes

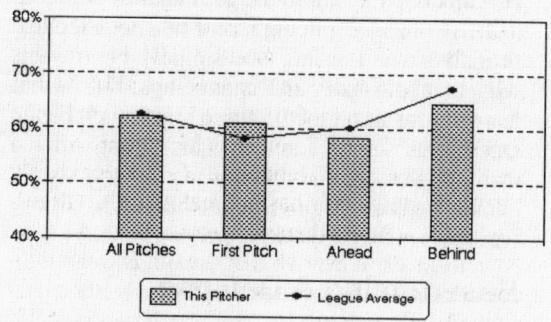

### 1995 Situational Stats

| | W | L | ERA | Sv | IP | | AB | H | HR | RBI | Avg |
|---|---|---|---|---|---|---|---|---|---|---|---|
| Home | 1 | 2 | 2.45 | 0 | 29.1 | LHB | 76 | 15 | 2 | 8 | .197 |
| Road | 0 | 1 | 4.70 | 2 | 15.1 | RHB | 93 | 24 | 3 | 15 | .258 |
| First Half | 1 | 1 | 3.57 | 0 | 22.2 | Sc Pos | 39 | 10 | 1 | 16 | .256 |
| Scnd Half | 0 | 2 | 2.86 | 2 | 22.0 | Clutch | 56 | 15 | 2 | 8 | .268 |

### 1995 Rankings (National League)

➡ Did not rank near the top or bottom in any category

# Pedro Martinez

**Montreal Expos**

## 1995 Season

Pedro Martinez had another excellent season in 1995, intimidating hitters and winning games. He plunked 11 batters—tied for third most in the league—but won 14 while pacing the Expo staff in victories, innings, starts and strikeouts. Martinez was consistent from start to finish, with the highlight coming June 3 against the Padres when he threw nine perfect innings only to see his no-hit bid end in the 10th.

## Pitching

Long silenced are the skeptics who predicted that Martinez was not physically strong enough to survive as a top starting pitcher. He instead has established himself as a durable pitcher who holds his stuff late into ballgames. Martinez has a world of stuff, beginning with a running fastball which is consistently clocked in the low to mid 90s. He mixes in an outstanding circle change which he sinks to both corners of the plate, along with a sharp-breaking overhand curve. Everybody knows that Martinez has no qualms about throwing inside, and the threat of getting beaned has to be in the back of every hitter's mind. However, he doesn't really deserve the headhunter label. His fastball runs so hard and late that it can start off just inside but wind up a foot off the plate.

## Defense & Hitting

Martinez' agility and quickness allow him to field his position very well. He pays close attention to baserunners, but he's easy to steal against anyway because it's obvious when he's coming home. Martinez swings from the heels but rarely connects, managing seven singles and 30 strikeouts last season.

## 1996 Outlook

If he can avoid getting hurt by someone charging the mound, Martinez should continue his rise as one of the game's best young pitchers. He is a knowledgeable, enthusiastic worker who loves to win, and there's no reason why he won't do just that for years to come.

**Position:** SP
**Bats:** R  **Throws:** R
**Ht:** 5'11"  **Wt:** 170

**Opening Day Age:** 24
**Born:** 10/25/71 in Manoguyabo, DR
**ML Seasons:** 4

### Overall Statistics

|  | W | L | Pct. | ERA | G | GS | Sv | IP | H | BB | SO | HR | BR/IP |
|---|---|---|---|---|---|---|---|---|---|---|---|---|---|
| 1995 | 14 | 10 | .583 | 3.51 | 30 | 30 | 0 | 194.2 | 158 | 66 | 174 | 21 | 1.15 |
| Career | 35 | 21 | .625 | 3.25 | 121 | 56 | 3 | 454.1 | 355 | 169 | 443 | 37 | 1.15 |

### How Often He Throws Strikes

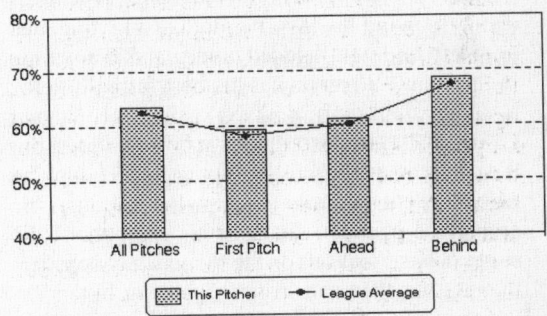

### 1995 Situational Stats

|  | W | L | ERA | Sv | IP |  | AB | H | HR | RBI | Avg |
|---|---|---|---|---|---|---|---|---|---|---|---|
| Home | 6 | 7 | 3.59 | 0 | 105.1 | LHB | 366 | 80 | 8 | 33 | .219 |
| Road | 8 | 3 | 3.43 | 0 | 89.1 | RHB | 331 | 78 | 13 | 36 | .236 |
| First Half | 6 | 5 | 3.00 | 0 | 96.0 | Sc Pos | 117 | 29 | 2 | 44 | .248 |
| Scnd Half | 8 | 5 | 4.01 | 0 | 98.2 | Clutch | 50 | 14 | 1 | 5 | .280 |

### 1995 Rankings (National League)

→ 2nd in runners caught stealing (13)
→ 3rd in shutouts (2), hit batsmen (11), lowest batting average allowed (.227), most pitches thrown per batter (3.92) and lowest batting average allowed vs. left-handed batters (.219)
→ 4th in pitches thrown (3,074), lowest ground-ball/flyball ratio allowed (1.0) and most strikeouts per 9 innings (8.0)
→ 5th in wins, strikeouts, lowest stolen base percentage allowed (40.9%), least baserunners allowed per 9 innings (10.9) and least GDPs induced per 9 innings (0.5)
→ Led the Expos in ERA, wins, games started, complete games (2) and shutouts

# Carlos Perez

## 1995 Season

For half a season, Carlos Perez was one of baseball's most refreshing stories. The eccentric rookie lefthander won seven of his first eight decisions on the way to being named to the National League All-Star team. But Perez went 3-6 after the break, then was arrested for a sexual assault in late September, ending his season.

## Pitching

Perez' fastball usually does not exceed the 88-90 MPH range, but it looks much better than that because of his great change-up. Perez has excellent arm motion that disguises the change beautifully. He can also turn the change over, giving it even more sinking action. And Perez is fearless about throwing his favorite pitch, using it against both left- and right-handed hitters, and at any time in the count. When he has his best fastball, Perez is dominating, retiring hitters with strikeouts and ground balls. He also throws a decent slider, but it's not a consistently reliable pitch yet. Though he has excellent control, Perez will sometimes be around the plate too much, as his 18 gopher balls suggest. His gyrations on the mound may be entertaining, but they can irritate opposing hitters. . . which just might play right into Perez' plans.

## Defense & Hitting

Perez can occasionally surprise opponents with his pickoff move, but he has a high leg kick and is slow to the plate, leaving him vulnerable to stolen bases. He is also prone to balks. His delivery often takes him out of prime fielding position. He hit a home run and knocked in five runs, and is something of a threat if only because he swings from the heels.

## 1996 Outlook

Perez' legal problems could seriously impact his career. He could be a solid part of the Expo rotation for years to come. But he might also be indefinitely unavailable pending resolution of the charges against him.

**Position:** SP/RP
**Bats:** L  **Throws:** L
**Ht:** 6' 3"  **Wt:** 195

**Opening Day Age:** 25
**Born:** 1/14/71 in Nigua, DR
**ML Seasons:** 1

### Overall Statistics

|  | W | L | Pct. | ERA | G | GS | Sv | IP | H | BB | SO | HR | BR/IP |
|---|---|---|------|-----|---|----|----|-----|-----|----|-----|----|-------|
| 1995 | 10 | 8 | .556 | 3.69 | 28 | 23 | 0 | 141.1 | 142 | 28 | 106 | 18 | 1.20 |
| Career | 10 | 8 | .556 | 3.69 | 28 | 23 | 0 | 141.1 | 142 | 28 | 106 | 18 | 1.20 |

### How Often He Throws Strikes

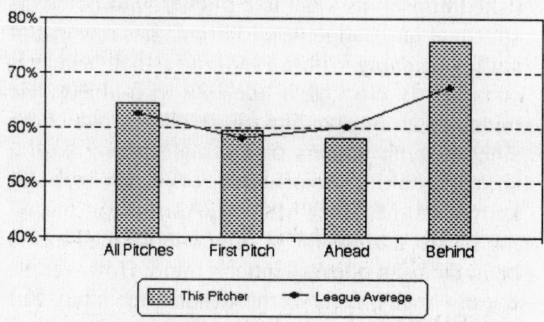

### 1995 Situational Stats

|  | W | L | ERA | Sv | IP |  | AB | H | HR | RBI | Avg |
|---|---|---|------|----|------|--------|-----|-----|----|-----|------|
| Home | 9 | 3 | 2.86 | 0 | 88.0 | LHB | 101 | 18 | 1 | 5 | .178 |
| Road | 1 | 5 | 5.06 | 0 | 53.1 | RHB | 451 | 124 | 17 | 51 | .275 |
| First Half | 7 | 2 | 3.26 | 0 | 69.0 | Sc Pos | 135 | 26 | 5 | 37 | .193 |
| Scnd Half | 3 | 6 | 4.11 | 0 | 72.1 | Clutch | 23 | 3 | 0 | 0 | .130 |

### 1995 Rankings (National League)
- 2nd in balks (4)
- 4th in lowest batting average allowed with runners in scoring position (.193)
- 9th in lowest fielding percentage at pitcher (.935)
- Led the Expos in complete games (2), wild pitches (8), balks, ERA at home (2.86) and lowest batting average allowed with runners in scoring position

# Mel Rojas

## 1995 Season

When John Wetteland was dealt to the Yankees last season, set-up man Mel Rojas became the Expo closer. Rojas had an up-and-down season in his new role. He managed 30 saves but also blew nine opportunities, four of the blown saves coming against San Francisco. Rojas' 4.12 ERA was very high for a closer.

## Pitching

With a 90-plus fastball and a sharp split-fingered pitch, Rojas can be dominant. However, he wore down physically over the season's last month. At times he lost his aggressiveness and became a nibbler instead of a power pitcher, which greatly irritated the Expo brass. Rojas used to throw a slider fairly often, but he has largely junked that pitch in favor of his splitter, which occasional stays up and gets hammered. Rojas' control was also shaky. He walked 29, hit seven batters, and fell behind in too many counts. With his stuff, the Expos found it hard to believe that Rojas could allow more than a hit per inning, and they were just as disappointed that right-handed batters hit him as well as lefties did.

## Defense & Hitting

Rojas flies open with his delivery, which leaves him in poor fielding position. He pays little attention to baserunners and has virtually no pickoff move, making things extremely easy for opposing baserunners. Over the last two seasons, basestealers are 21-for-22 against Rojas. He is helpless at the plate, going 4-for-50 lifetime.

## 1996 Outlook

Given his first chance to be a full-time closer, Rojas saved 30 games despite the other disappointing numbers. However, the Expos want to see more. They are losing patience with Rojas' concentration lapses and his habit of making excuses when he blows saves. With his stuff, Rojas can be a premier closer. The Expos are ready for that to happen.

**Position:** RP
**Bats:** R  **Throws:** R
**Ht:** 5'11"  **Wt:** 195

**Opening Day Age:** 29
**Born:** 12/10/66 in Haina, DR
**ML Seasons:** 6
**Pronunciation:** ROH-hoss

### Overall Statistics

|        | W  | L  | Pct. | ERA  | G   | GS | Sv | IP    | H   | BB  | SO  | HR | BR/IP |
|--------|----|----|------|------|-----|----|----|-------|-----|-----|-----|----|-------|
| 1995   | 1  | 4  | .200 | 4.12 | 59  | 0  | 30 | 67.2  | 69  | 29  | 61  | 2  | 1.45  |
| Career | 22 | 19 | .537 | 3.00 | 311 | 0  | 73 | 428.2 | 367 | 151 | 326 | 30 | 1.21  |

### How Often He Throws Strikes

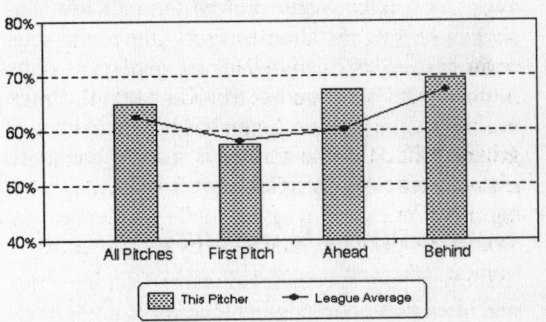

### 1995 Situational Stats

|            | W | L | ERA  | Sv | IP   |        | AB  | H  | HR | RBI | Avg  |
|------------|---|---|------|----|------|--------|-----|----|----|-----|------|
| Home       | 1 | 1 | 4.19 | 13 | 34.1 | LHB    | 130 | 34 | 1  | 17  | .262 |
| Road       | 0 | 3 | 4.05 | 17 | 33.1 | RHB    | 133 | 35 | 1  | 17  | .263 |
| First Half | 1 | 3 | 3.93 | 14 | 34.1 | Sc Pos | 89  | 22 | 0  | 29  | .247 |
| Scnd Half  | 0 | 1 | 4.32 | 16 | 33.1 | Clutch | 186 | 49 | 2  | 31  | .263 |

### 1995 Rankings (National League)

- → 2nd in blown saves (9)
- → 3rd in save opportunities (39) and lowest save percentage (76.9%)
- → 7th in saves
- → 9th in games finished (48) and most baserunners allowed per 9 innings in relief (14.0)
- → Led the Expos in saves, games finished, save opportunities, save percentage, blown saves and relief innings (67.2)

# David Segui

## 1995 Season

Injuries to Cliff Floyd and Henry Rodriguez forced the Expos to deal for a first baseman last June. But their bad fortune turned to good when they acquired switch-hitting David Segui from the Mets for pitching prospect Reid Cornelius. Segui flourished when given a chance to play every day, ending up among the league's top hitters with a .309 average.

## Hitting

For most of his career, Segui has not been considered a power threat. However, he has added strength over the last few seasons and now has the ability to pull a dozen or so balls a year for home runs. As a lefty, Segui prefers the ball low, but overall he hits for almost exactly the same stats from both sides of the plate. He generally waits well with his short quick stroke and can slash the ball where it's pitched. Segui has excellent knowledge of the strike zone and is among the more difficult hitters in the league to strike out.

## Baserunning & Defense

With very poor speed, Segui is a risk on the bases and often uses poor judgment; he was caught stealing seven times in nine attempts last season. He also grounds into a lot of double plays. Segui's range is limited at first base. Otherwise he's an excellent first baseman with soft hands and an accurate arm. He can play the outfield and has a good arm there, but doesn't have the range for anything but routine plays.

## 1996 Outlook

Segui opened a lot of eyes in Montreal with his outstanding season. Though he is not the classic power-hitting first baseman most teams prefer, Segui made a big believer of Felipe Alou. As a result, unless something very strange happens, Segui will open the season with a lock on the regular first-base job.

**Position:** 1B/LF
**Bats:** B  **Throws:** L
**Ht:** 6' 1"  **Wt:** 202

**Opening Day Age:** 29
**Born:** 7/19/66 in Kansas City, KS
**ML Seasons:** 6
**Pronunciation:** suh-GEE

### Overall Statistics

|  | G | AB | R | H | D | T | HR | RBI | SB | BB | SO | Avg | OBP | Slg |
|---|---|---|---|---|---|---|---|---|---|---|---|---|---|---|
| 1995 | 130 | 456 | 68 | 141 | 25 | 4 | 12 | 68 | 2 | 40 | 47 | .309 | .367 | .461 |
| Career | 609 | 1766 | 218 | 478 | 92 | 5 | 37 | 225 | 6 | 174 | 200 | .271 | .335 | .391 |

### Where He Hits the Ball

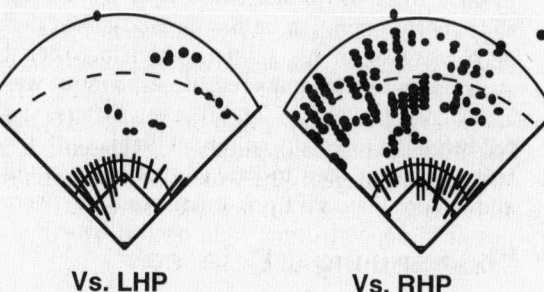

Vs. LHP          Vs. RHP

### 1995 Situational Stats

|  | AB | H | HR | RBI | Avg |  | AB | H | HR | RBI | Avg |
|---|---|---|---|---|---|---|---|---|---|---|---|
| Home | 234 | 69 | 6 | 36 | .295 | LHP | 112 | 37 | 2 | 17 | .330 |
| Road | 222 | 72 | 6 | 32 | .324 | RHP | 344 | 104 | 10 | 51 | .302 |
| First Half | 178 | 61 | 3 | 23 | .343 | Sc Pos | 119 | 36 | 4 | 55 | .303 |
| Scnd Half | 278 | 80 | 9 | 45 | .288 | Clutch | 61 | 11 | 2 | 7 | .180 |

### 1995 Rankings (National League)

- ➡ 2nd in fielding percentage at first base (.997)
- ➡ 5th in batting average on the road (.324)
- ➡ 8th in batting average (.309) and on-base percentage vs. left-handed pitchers (.403)
- ➡ 10th in lowest batting average in the clutch (.180)

# Tony Tarasco

## 1995 Season

One of three players the Expos received from Atlanta last April for Marquis Grissom, Tony Tarasco was asked to take over the right-field spot vacated by Larry Walker. In his first season as an everyday player, Tarasco largely held his own, showing encouraging power with 14 homers. Through June, Tarasco was hitting .287 with good power, but a second-half slump—especially a 3-for-43 slump in August—left him with subpar totals for a right fielder.

## Hitting

Tarasco has a quick bat and can produce big-time power when he turns around fastballs over the plate. On the other hand, he often gets overly aggressive, chasing breaking pitches and offspeed stuff. Unlike many young left-handed hitters, Tarasco has shown the ability to hang in against left-handed pitching when given the chance. Though he suffers his share of strikeouts, Tarasco has a decent knowledge of the strike zone for a young hitter, and led the Expos in walks last year.

## Baserunning & Defense

With a quick first step and outstanding speed, Tarasco is an excellent baserunner. He stole 24 bases in 27 attempts, and with more experience and more times on base, he might eventually reach 40 steals in a season. Tarasco is also as quick as anyone getting out of the batter's box and was the toughest player in the National League to double up last season. He can play any of the three outfield positions, though most of his action last year came in right field, where he settled in nicely. He has excellent range and a strong, accurate arm.

## 1996 Outlook

Tarasco had some rough periods while adjusting to everyday action last season. However, on balance he held his own, and the Expos think he can be a solid all-around outfielder for the next several years. He has the potential to blossom into a 25-homer, 40-steal talent.

**Position:** RF/LF
**Bats:** L **Throws:** R
**Ht:** 6' 1"  **Wt:** 205

**Opening Day Age:** 25
**Born:** 12/9/70 in New York, NY
**ML Seasons:** 3

### Overall Statistics

|        | G   | AB  | R  | H   | D  | T | HR | RBI | SB | BB | SO  | Avg  | OBP  | Slg  |
|--------|-----|-----|----|-----|----|---|----|-----|----|----|-----|------|------|------|
| 1995   | 126 | 438 | 64 | 109 | 18 | 4 | 14 | 40  | 24 | 51 | 78  | .249 | .329 | .404 |
| Career | 237 | 605 | 86 | 153 | 26 | 4 | 19 | 61  | 29 | 60 | 100 | .253 | .321 | .403 |

### Where He Hits the Ball

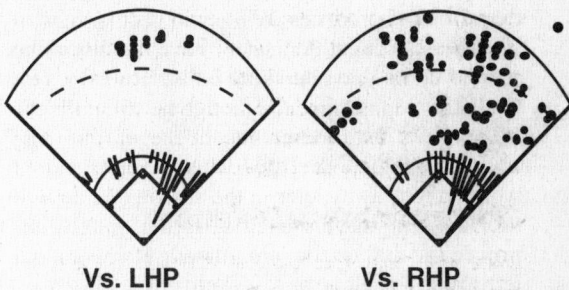

**Vs. LHP**          **Vs. RHP**

### 1995 Situational Stats

|            | AB  | H  | HR | RBI | Avg  |        | AB  | H  | HR | RBI | Avg  |
|------------|-----|----|----|-----|------|--------|-----|----|----|-----|------|
| Home       | 230 | 58 | 7  | 19  | .252 | LHP    | 89  | 22 | 1  | 7   | .247 |
| Road       | 208 | 51 | 7  | 21  | .245 | RHP    | 349 | 87 | 13 | 33  | .249 |
| First Half | 251 | 68 | 8  | 25  | .271 | Sc Pos | 93  | 26 | 3  | 26  | .280 |
| Scnd Half  | 187 | 41 | 6  | 15  | .219 | Clutch | 63  | 11 | 0  | 3   | .175 |

### 1995 Rankings (National League)

- ➡ 1st in least GDPs per GDP situation (2.2%)
- ➡ 3rd in stolen base percentage (88.9%)
- ➡ 4th in intentional walks (12) and fielding percentage in right field (.987)
- ➡ 5th in lowest batting average
- ➡ 7th in lowest batting average vs. right-handed pitchers (.249) and lowest on-base percentage for a leadoff hitter (.333)
- ➡ 9th in lowest batting average in the clutch (.175)
- ➡ 10th in lowest batting average at home (.252)
- ➡ Led the Expos in home runs, triples, walks, intentional walks, HR frequency (31.3 ABs per HR), stolen base percentage and least GDPs per GDP situation

# Rondell White

## 1995 Season

With a blistering last two months, Rondell White ended his first full season poised for stardom. White hit .345 in August and September, finishing off a strong year in which he was second on the Expos with 140 hits and 25 steals, while scoring 87 runs to pace the club. With the trade of Roberto Kelly in late May, White took over center field full time, and except for a missed week due to a hamstring pull, he was the regular from that point on.

## Hitting

Comparisons start with ex-Montreal outfielders Marquis Grissom and Andre Dawson. Like those former Expo stars, White generates exceptional bat speed that will likely translate into more power than Grissom produces. White will get his share of strikeouts, because he doesn't have the discipline to hold up on good breaking balls. However, few fastballs get past him, and though he still pulls the majority of extra-base hits, he began showing power to the opposite field when pitchers started working him away later in the season. White will take a walk, and his pitch selection greatly improved as the season progressed. He wore out left-handed pitching at a .377 clip.

## Baserunning & Defense

Lessons from Expo baserunning coach Tommy Harper and White's own thrilling speed are a potent combination, as opposing pitchers and catchers found out. White should become a 40-steal man before his career is over, especially if he continues batting leadoff. He wasn't exceptionally aggressive on the basepaths last year, but that should improve with experience. Not many center fielders are in Marquis Grissom's class, but Montreal suffered little if any dropoff after White took over the position. He has excellent range and judgment, and compensates for an average arm with an aggressive charge and quick release.

## 1996 Outlook

The sky's the limit for White, who is poised to ascend into the league's group of top outfielders. With a full season under his belt, White could break through and become one of the loop's dominant players.

**Position:** CF
**Bats:** R **Throws:** R
**Ht:** 6' 1" **Wt:** 205

**Opening Day Age:** 24
**Born:** 2/23/72 in Milledgeville, GA
**ML Seasons:** 3

*Overall Statistics*

|  | G | AB | R | H | D | T | HR | RBI | SB | BB | SO | Avg | OBP | Slg |
|---|---|---|---|---|---|---|---|---|---|---|---|---|---|---|
| 1995 | 130 | 474 | 87 | 140 | 33 | 4 | 13 | 57 | 25 | 41 | 87 | .295 | .356 | .464 |
| Career | 193 | 644 | 112 | 186 | 46 | 6 | 17 | 85 | 27 | 57 | 121 | .289 | .352 | .458 |

*Where He Hits the Ball*

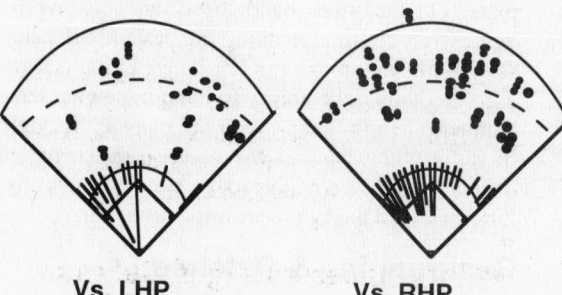

**Vs. LHP**   **Vs. RHP**

*1995 Situational Stats*

|  | AB | H | HR | RBI | Avg |  | AB | H | HR | RBI | Avg |
|---|---|---|---|---|---|---|---|---|---|---|---|
| Home | 232 | 71 | 6 | 29 | .306 | LHP | 122 | 46 | 2 | 18 | .377 |
| Road | 242 | 69 | 7 | 28 | .285 | RHP | 352 | 94 | 11 | 39 | .267 |
| First Half | 168 | 46 | 7 | 26 | .274 | Sc Pos | 111 | 26 | 2 | 45 | .234 |
| Scnd Half | 306 | 94 | 6 | 31 | .307 | Clutch | 69 | 16 | 3 | 11 | .232 |

*1995 Rankings (National League)*

→ 4th in batting average vs. left-handed pitchers (.377), on-base percentage vs. left-handed pitchers (.437) and lowest fielding percentage in center field (.984)
→ 5th in errors in center field (4)
→ 6th in on-base percentage for a leadoff hitter (.375)
→ 7th in highest groundball/flyball ratio (2.0) and stolen base percentage (83.3%)
→ 10th in doubles and lowest percentage of extra bases taken as a runner (42.1%)
→ Led the Expos in batting average, runs scored, triples, total bases (220), slugging percentage, on-base percentage and highest groundball/flyball ratio

# Shane Andrews

**Position**: 3B/1B
**Bats**: R **Throws**: R
**Ht**: 6' 1"  **Wt**: 215

**Opening Day Age**: 24
**Born**: 8/28/71 in
Dallas, TX
**ML Seasons**: 1

## Overall Statistics

| | G | AB | R | H | D | T | HR | RBI | SB | BB | SO | Avg | OBP | Slg |
|---|---|---|---|---|---|---|---|---|---|---|---|---|---|---|
| 1995 | 84 | 220 | 27 | 47 | 10 | 1 | 8 | 31 | 1 | 17 | 68 | .214 | .271 | .377 |
| Career | 84 | 220 | 27 | 47 | 10 | 1 | 8 | 31 | 1 | 17 | 68 | .214 | .271 | .377 |

## 1995 Season

The 11th overall pick in the 1990 amateur draft, Shane Andrews reached the majors last season despite a career .239 batting average in the minor leagues. Playing both third base and first, Andrews showed flashes of what could be big-time power. He bombed eight home runs and 10 doubles in 220 at-bats, with six of his homers coming against right-handed pitching.

## Hitting, Baserunning & Defense

Andrews has a big swing that has its share of holes, resulting in the expected strikeout problems. He can be tied up with hard stuff up in the strike zone, and he has problems waiting on offspeed pitches. However, Andrews has the strength to drive the ball out of any part of a ballpark, and he should raise his batting average as he learns better plate discipline. Andrews can steal a base on occasion but is a below-average runner. Losing weight has made him a much more agile infielder. His footwork improved at third and he has become more consistent with his throws. He also plays a serviceable first base.

## 1996 Outlook

Andrews has legitimate 20-homer potential, and if he continues to stay in shape and show improvement in the field, the Expos' third-base job is likely his to lose this spring.

# Cliff Floyd

**Position**: 1B
**Bats**: L **Throws**: R
**Ht**: 6' 4"  **Wt**: 230

**Opening Day Age**: 23
**Born**: 12/5/72 in
Chicago, IL
**ML Seasons**: 3

## Overall Statistics

| | G | AB | R | H | D | T | HR | RBI | SB | BB | SO | Avg | OBP | Slg |
|---|---|---|---|---|---|---|---|---|---|---|---|---|---|---|
| 1995 | 29 | 69 | 6 | 9 | 1 | 0 | 1 | 8 | 3 | 7 | 22 | .130 | .221 | .188 |
| Career | 139 | 434 | 52 | 110 | 20 | 4 | 6 | 51 | 13 | 31 | 94 | .253 | .307 | .359 |

## 1995 Season

In one of the scariest plays of the season, Montreal youngster Cliff Floyd nearly saw his career end in a freak accident at first base which resulted in six broken bones in his left wrist and hand. After three operations, he returned—much earlier than expected—for the season's final three weeks.

## Hitting, Baserunning & Defense

Before his injury in mid-May, Floyd was off to a slow start. He was having trouble laying off breaking balls in the dirt, and he seemed unable to consistently adjust to high fastballs. He has shown excellent power potential in the minors but has been a tentative swinger since coming to the majors. Montreal would like to see him become more aggressive, even if it means more strikeouts. For a big man, Floyd has outstanding speed and can be a dangerous basestealer. Last year's injury may relegate him to the outfield for good. As an outfielder, Floyd has decent range and an average left-field arm.

## 1996 Outlook

The Expos want to see Floyd slim down and become more aggressive with the bat, and he could also use more outfield practice. All of which might leave Floyd in the minors this spring. As Felipe Alou said, "He's got to play every day. . . whether it's in the majors or the minors, not sit on the bench. That's the main thing."

# Greg Harris

**Position**: RP
**Bats**: B **Throws**: R
**Ht**: 6' 0"  **Wt**: 175

**Opening Day Age**: 40
**Born**: 11/2/55 in
Lynwood, CA
**ML Seasons**: 15

### Overall Statistics

| | W | L | Pct. | ERA | G | GS | Sv | IP | H | BB | SO | HR | BR/IP |
|---|---|---|------|-----|---|----|----|-----|-----|-----|------|-----|-------|
| 1995 | 2 | 3 | .400 | 2.61 | 45 | 0 | 0 | 48.1 | 45 | 16 | 47 | 6 | 1.26 |
| Career | 74 | 90 | .451 | 3.69 | 703 | 98 | 54 | 1467.1 | 1329 | 652 | 1141 | 129 | 1.35 |

## 1995 Season

During the course of another workmanlike season for the veteran righthander, Greg Harris made major league history by pitching both left-handed and right-handed in the same inning. That head-line-making episode aside, Harris was solid in middle and long relief.

## Pitching, Defense & Hitting

Harris has been able to fashion a long career through a combination of pitching savvy and an overhand curve that when right can be effective against either left- or right-handed hitters. The curve gives Harris a proven strikeout pitch, and in fact he has averaged nearly a strikeout per inning over the last three seasons. When he isn't throwing the curve for strikes, he has trouble because his fastball is a rather straight, low-to-mid-80s offering, and his splitter is just average. He is much more effective against right-handed hitters, who batted .202 against him last season, compared to the .294 hit by lefties. Harris is an excellent fielder, capable of making outstanding plays, and a life-time .221 hitter.

## 1996 Outlook

Throughout his long career, Harris has rarely had any guarantees heading into a new season, and this one is no exception. He will likely need to battle for a job in Montreal but could help almost any club in a middle-inning role. And watch for that famous ambidextrous glove.

# Butch Henry

**Position:** SP
**Bats:** L  **Throws:** L
**Ht:** 6' 1"  **Wt:** 205

**Opening Day Age:** 27
**Born:** 10/7/68 in El
Paso, TX
**ML Seasons:** 4

### Overall Statistics

| | W | L | Pct. | ERA | G | GS | Sv | IP | H | BB | SO | HR | BR/IP |
|---|---|---|------|-----|---|----|----|-----|-----|-----|-----|-----|-------|
| 1995 | 7 | 9 | .438 | 2.84 | 21 | 21 | 0 | 126.2 | 133 | 28 | 60 | 11 | 1.27 |
| Career | 24 | 30 | .444 | 3.81 | 103 | 80 | 1 | 502.2 | 550 | 117 | 273 | 52 | 1.33 |

## 1995 Season

It was a hard-luck season for lefthander Butch Henry. He started the year 0-4 and had four no-decisions in which he allowed only four runs in 28.2 innings. He ended the season with a 2.84 ERA, which would have been third best in the league had he pitched enough innings to qualify. Why didn't he pitch enough innings? Henry ripped an elbow ligament on August 15, requiring Tommy John transplant surgery.

## Pitching, Defense & Hitting

Henry will give up his share of hits. However, he is tough to score on because he does not issue many walks, and he has increased the velocity of his sinking fastball to the point where it's a fine complement to his outstanding change-up. He has a better-than-average pickoff move and does a good job of holding runners. He is also a very competent fielder. Henry was only 2-for-42 as a hitter last season, but handles the bat better than that mark suggests.

## 1996 Outlook

Red Sox general manager Dan Duquette scooped up Henry when the Expos tried to sneak him through postseason waivers. Henry won't be able to throw until midseason at the very earliest, but Duquette is gambling that if Henry is able to overcome his elbow injury, the Red Sox will have a very underrated lefthander who has not yet seen his 30th birthday.

# Tim Laker

**Position**: C
**Bats**: R  **Throws**: R
**Ht**: 6' 3"  **Wt**: 200

**Opening Day Age**: 26
**Born**: 11/27/69 in Encino, CA
**ML Seasons**: 3

## Overall Statistics

|  | G | AB | R | H | D | T | HR | RBI | SB | BB | SO | Avg | OBP | Slg |
|---|---|---|---|---|---|---|---|---|---|---|---|---|---|---|
| 1995 | 64 | 141 | 17 | 33 | 8 | 1 | 3 | 20 | 0 | 14 | 38 | .234 | .306 | .369 |
| Career | 135 | 273 | 28 | 60 | 13 | 2 | 3 | 31 | 3 | 18 | 68 | .220 | .271 | .315 |

## 1995 Season

Serving as Darrin Fletcher's backup, young catcher Tim Laker managed 20 RBI in 42 starts last season. In the process he gave the Expos hope that all the glowing scouting reports they've been reading over the years might come true.

## Hitting, Baserunning & Defense

Laker moved up through Montreal's minor league chain because of his defense; his hitting was anemic at nearly every stop. But in 1994 he batted .309 with 12 homers for Triple-A Ottawa, and last season he showed further signs of becoming a decent major league hitter. He is a good fastball hitter and is beginning to get the hang of breaking balls, too. He still has difficulty waiting on offspeed pitches, and has worked on cutting down his swing to better protect the plate when behind in the count. Laker runs fairly well for a catcher. He has one of the stronger throwing arms around, but his throw-out rates have never been good—25 percent last year—because of poor footwork. He is an improving receiver and handler of pitchers.

## 1996 Outlook

Montreal has mulled dealing away the more expensive Darrin Fletcher. They probably wouldn't consider such a move if they didn't think Laker was ready for an expanded role. If Fletcher *is* dealt, Laker will take over the regular catching chores and finish '96 with 350-odd at-bats.

# Henry Rodriguez

**Position**: RF/1B
**Bats**: L  **Throws**: L
**Ht**: 6' 1"  **Wt**: 209

**Opening Day Age**: 28
**Born**: 11/8/67 in Santo Domingo, DR
**ML Seasons**: 4

## Overall Statistics

|  | G | AB | R | H | D | T | HR | RBI | SB | BB | SO | Avg | OBP | Slg |
|---|---|---|---|---|---|---|---|---|---|---|---|---|---|---|
| 1995 | 45 | 138 | 13 | 33 | 4 | 1 | 2 | 15 | 0 | 11 | 28 | .239 | .293 | .326 |
| Career | 278 | 766 | 77 | 186 | 35 | 3 | 21 | 101 | 1 | 47 | 155 | .243 | .286 | .379 |

## 1995 Season

Henry Rodriguez made headlines last spring by hitting four homers in one preseason game for the Dodgers. But there was no position for him in Los Angeles, and on May 23 Rodriguez was traded to Montreal, where the Expos hoped he'd fill the hole at first base left by Cliff Floyd's injury. Unfortunately, he had little chance to nail down the job. Nine games after becoming an Expo, Rodriguez broke his right leg and would not return until September, when he played sparingly.

## Hitting, Baserunning & Defense

Rodriguez has excellent power, especially to the opposite field. However, he still has the bad habit of trying to pull too many pitches and sometimes becomes a wild swinger, chasing pitches way out of the strike zone. A good low-ball hitter, Rodriguez would be a more consistent hitter were he willing to cut down his swing in some situations. He is largely a station-to-station baserunner with little basestealing potential. Rodriguez is an outstanding first baseman with soft hands and good range. He is an adequate outfielder, prone to misjudging balls. His arm, for the outfield, is subpar.

## 1996 Outlook

Rodriguez never got a chance to be the Expos' first baseman because of his injury and the excellence of David Segui. If he re-signs with Montreal, Rodriguez will start the year as an outfielder/utility man.

# Kirk Rueter

**Position:** SP
**Bats:** L **Throws:** L
**Ht:** 6' 3" **Wt:** 195

**Opening Day Age:** 25
**Born:** 12/1/70 in Centralia, IL
**ML Seasons:** 3
**Pronunciation:** REE-ter

## Overall Statistics

| | W | L | Pct. | ERA | G | GS | Sv | IP | H | BB | SO | HR | BR/IP |
|---|---|---|---|---|---|---|---|---|---|---|---|---|---|
| 1995 | 5 | 3 | .625 | 3.23 | 9 | 9 | 0 | 47.1 | 38 | 9 | 28 | 3 | 0.99 |
| Career | 20 | 6 | .769 | 3.83 | 43 | 43 | 0 | 225.1 | 229 | 50 | 109 | 19 | 1.24 |

## 1995 Season

It's been a strange last three years for lefthander Kirk Rueter. In 1993 Rueter was a sensation, posting eight victories without a loss after a midseason call-up. The next year he struggled, going 7-3 but with a 5.17 ERA. In 1995, Rueter was sent to the minors after two poor early starts and did not return until late August. However, he returned to his 1993 form, winning five of his last seven starts with a 1.82 ERA in those seven games.

## Pitching, Defense & Hitting

Rueter won't overpower anyone, so when his control wavered early in the season, he got hit hard. With a good tailwind behind it, Rueter's fastball reaches the mid 80s. However, he has an outstanding change-up which he turns over. That's probably his most effective pitch against left-handed hitters, who batted only .143 against him last year. Rueter also has a good curve and the willingness to pitch inside. He fields his position with agility and has one of the better pickoff moves on the staff. Rueter was hitless last year but can help himself with the bat.

## 1996 Outlook

Rueter's margin for error is slim, but when he has his good control and change-up, he can beat anyone. Montreal will likely give him every chance at their rotation, and he *might* look like Tom Glavine if things break right.

# Tim Scott

**Position:** RP
**Bats:** R **Throws:** R
**Ht:** 6' 2" **Wt:** 205

**Opening Day Age:** 29
**Born:** 11/16/66 in Hanford, CA
**ML Seasons:** 5

## Overall Statistics

| | W | L | Pct. | ERA | G | GS | Sv | IP | H | BB | SO | HR | BR/IP |
|---|---|---|---|---|---|---|---|---|---|---|---|---|---|
| 1995 | 2 | 0 | 1.000 | 3.98 | 62 | 0 | 2 | 63.1 | 52 | 23 | 57 | 6 | 1.18 |
| Career | 18 | 5 | .783 | 3.61 | 194 | 0 | 4 | 227.0 | 213 | 96 | 190 | 14 | 1.36 |

## 1995 Season

The workhorse of the Montreal bullpen, Tim Scott was the main set-up man for closer Mel Rojas last year. Among his club-leading 62 appearances, Scott tied for third in the league with 19 holds while converting two save chances.

## Pitching, Defense & Hitting

Scott is one of the better-kept secrets in the National League, because he's been stuck behind John Wetteland and Mel Rojas for the last three years. But make no mistake about it: Scott has stuff worthy of a closer. He can throw his fastball consistently in the low 90s, and when he keeps it down in the strike zone, running away from lefties and into righties, that fastball is an extremely tough pitch. Always tough against left-handed hitters, Scott has improved against righties with the addition of a solid split-fingered pitch. He is an adequate fielder but does not hold runners well. Scott has no pickoff move and is slow coming to the plate. He rarely hits but can handle the bat fairly well.

## 1996 Outlook

The Expo staff has largely changed around him, but Scott continues to provide solid set-up work and will likely once again be an unsung workhorse out of their bullpen. He might also get more chances for saves due to Mel Rojas' inconsistency.

# Other Montreal Expos

**Tavo Alvarez** (**Pos**: RHP, **Age**: 24)

After missing all of 1994 with a torn rotator cuff, Alvarez got eight starts for the Expos, pitching very poorly and struggling with his control. But his fine Triple-A season should yield another chance. 1996 Outlook: B

**Bryan Eversgerd** (**Pos**: LHP, **Age**: 27)

Eversgerd came to Montreal from St. Louis in April, sandwiching two poor major league stints around an outstanding year at Triple-A. His struggles were very similar to his '94 season with the Cardinals. 1996 Outlook: B

**Tom Foley** (**Pos**: INF, **Age**: 36, **Bats**: L)

A veteran utility infielder, Foley fought both the disabled list and a poor bat in 1995, seeing just 11 games with the Expos after signing as a free agent. If healthy, he'll once again find a team. 1996 Outlook: B

**Willie Fraser** (**Pos**: RHP, **Age**: 31)

Once heavily used by the Angels, Fraser appears to be nearing the end of the line, pitching poorly in relief for the Expos and declaring himself a free agent. He hasn't pitched well since 1990. 1996 Outlook: C

**Curtis Pride** (**Pos**: LF, **Age**: 27, **Bats**: L)

Pride, who is 95% deaf, was called up twice by the Expos in 1995, managing just one extra-base hit in 63 at-bats. A six-year free agent, a number of teams were bidding for his services this winter. 1996 Outlook: C

**F.P. Santangelo** (**Pos**: LF, **Age**: 28, **Bats**: B)

After six seasons in the minors, Santangelo put together a solid major league debut after his August call-up, hitting for a better average than in the minors, and walking more than he struck out. 1996 Outlook: B

**Curt Schmidt** (**Pos**: RHP, **Age**: 26)

Drafted by the Expos in 1992, Schmidt and his sidearm delivery put together a stellar relief season at Triple-A, but showed none of that promise during 11 games with Montreal. His control needs a lot of work. 1996 Outlook: B

**Joe Siddall** (**Pos**: C, **Age**: 28, **Bats**: L)

After hitting just .214 at Triple-A in 1995, Siddall was called up in September, and didn't show much. Runners were 7-for-7 stealing against him. He has no power or ability to draw walks. 1996 Outlook: C

**Dave Silvestri** (**Pos**: 2B, **Age**: 28, **Bats**: R)

A slow start and broken left hand sent Silvestri from the Yankees to the Expos in July. He hit better in Montreal, and managed to start at all four infield positions over the course of the season. 1996 Outlook: B

**Tim Spehr** (**Pos**: C, **Age**: 29, **Bats**: R)

The perennial backup catcher in Montreal, Spehr's solid play came to an abrupt halt in August when he was diagnosed with testicular cancer. He's excellent defensively and will play, health permitting: 1996 Outlook: A

**J.J. Thobe** (**Pos**: RHP, **Age**: 25)

A starter previously in the minors, Thobe was used heavily in relief at Triple-A, seeing only four games with the Expos. He was acquired off waivers by the Red Sox after the season. 1996 Outlook: D

**Jeff Treadway** (**Pos**: 2B, **Age**: 33, **Bats**: L)

A member of Atlanta's pennant winners in 1991 and '92, Treadway went downhill in a hurry in '95. After being traded from the Dodgers to the Expos, he hit poorly, went to the DL, and retired. 1996 Outlook: D

**Gabe White** (**Pos**: LHP, **Age**: 24)

A top Expo prospect since 1990, White was awful in 1995 for the Expos, but still showed some promising strikeout ability. He has plenty of time to develop into a quality pitcher. 1996 Outlook: B

# Montreal Expos Minor League Prospects

## Organization Overview:

Despite the problems inherent with playing in a city that's the very epitome of small market, in a province that will likely never be called baseball-mad, the Expos have remained competitive in recent years through judicious use of the draft and solid player development. The problem for the Expos, though, is that their lifeline is threatening to dry up. Oh, they still have a few prospects. It's just that they're not as plentiful, and may not measure up to the caliber of the Grissoms, Walkers, Corderos or Whites of recent vintage. And for a team strapped for cash like Montreal, whose turnover will tend to be high as long as it can't pay players what they can get elsewhere on the open market, losing its edge in the one area in which it can excel will make it especially difficult to compete.

### Israel Alcantara

**Position:** 3B     **Opening Day Age:** 22
**Bats:** R **Throws:** R     **Born:** 5/6/73 in Santo
**Ht:** 6' 2" **Wt:** 165     Domingo, DR

#### Recent Statistics

| | G | AB | R | H | D | T | HR | RBI | SB | BB | SO | AVG |
|---|---|---|---|---|---|---|---|---|---|---|---|---|
| 93 A Burlington | 126 | 470 | 65 | 115 | 26 | 3 | 18 | 73 | 6 | 20 | 125 | .245 |
| 94 A W. Palm Bch | 125 | 471 | 65 | 134 | 26 | 4 | 15 | 69 | 9 | 26 | 130 | .285 |
| 95 AA Harrisburg | 71 | 237 | 25 | 50 | 12 | 2 | 10 | 29 | 1 | 21 | 81 | .211 |
| 95 A W. Palm Bch | 39 | 134 | 16 | 37 | 7 | 2 | 3 | 22 | 3 | 9 | 35 | .276 |
| 95 MLE | 71 | 230 | 19 | 43 | 11 | 1 | 6 | 22 | 0 | 14 | 86 | .187 |

Alcantara showed promise in 1994 when he hit .285 with 15 homers in the Florida State League. However, he found the jump to Double-A a little too difficult last season and was eventually dispatched back to West Palm Beach, where his hitting returned to its previous level. Alcantara's biggest offensive deficiency had been his poor plate discipline, but that was one area of his game which actually showed slight improvement last season. He'll turn 23 in May, and he'll probably be back at Harrisburg.

### Yamil Benitez

**Position:** OF     **Opening Day Age:** 23
**Bats:** R **Throws:** R     **Born:** 10/5/72 in San
**Ht:** 6' 2" **Wt:** 180     Juan, PR

#### Recent Statistics

| | G | AB | R | H | D | T | HR | RBI | SB | BB | SO | AVG |
|---|---|---|---|---|---|---|---|---|---|---|---|---|
| 95 AAA Ottawa | 127 | 474 | 66 | 123 | 24 | 6 | 18 | 69 | 14 | 44 | 128 | .259 |
| 95 NL Montreal | 14 | 39 | 8 | 15 | 2 | 1 | 2 | 7 | 0 | 1 | 7 | .385 |
| 95 MLE | 127 | 458 | 52 | 107 | 23 | 4 | 12 | 55 | 10 | 36 | 134 | .234 |

Benitez possesses offensive skills similiar to Alcantara's. Like Alcantara, Benitez has been a .260-.270 hitter with medium-range power and poor plate discipline. He also strikes out frequently, but will steal a few more bases than Alcantara. Benitez finished second in the Eastern League in 1994 with 91 RBI. The jump to Triple-A Ottawa generally didn't affect his overall numbers last year, and he was very impressive in his brief trial with Montreal. Given the rapid turnover in the Expo outfield recently, Benitez could soon be getting a big-league shot.

### Hiram Bocachica

**Position:** SS     **Opening Day Age:** 20
**Bats:** R **Throws:** R     **Born:** 3/4/76 in Ponce,
**Ht:** 5' 11" **Wt:** 165     PR

#### Recent Statistics

| | G | AB | R | H | D | T | HR | RBI | SB | BB | SO | AVG |
|---|---|---|---|---|---|---|---|---|---|---|---|---|
| 94 R Expos | 43 | 168 | 31 | 47 | 9 | 0 | 5 | 16 | 11 | 15 | 42 | .280 |
| 95 A Albany | 96 | 380 | 65 | 108 | 20 | 10 | 2 | 30 | 47 | 52 | 78 | .284 |

The Expos have concerns that Wil Cordero is a legitimate major league shortstop, as last year's trial in left field would indicate. Bocachica, the second Puerto Rican ever drafted in the first round, could be the eventual long-term solution. In addition to his defensive skills, he should rate as an above-average offensive shortstop with some extra-base power. Unlike many Latin players, Bocachica has not shown an aversion to drawing walks. Add in over 40 steals a year, plus the fact that he was just 19 last season, and you can see why Bocachica is such a valuable property.

### Steve Falteisek

**Position:** P     **Opening Day Age:** 24
**Bats:** R **Throws:** R     **Born:** 1/28/72 in
**Ht:** 6' 2" **Wt:** 200     Mineola, NY

#### Recent Statistics

| | W | L | ERA | G | GS | Sv | IP | H | R | BB | SO | HR |
|---|---|---|---|---|---|---|---|---|---|---|---|---|
| 93 A Burlington | 3 | 5 | 5.90 | 14 | 14 | 0 | 76.1 | 86 | 59 | 35 | 63 | 4 |
| 94 A W. Palm Bch | 9 | 4 | 2.54 | 27 | 24 | 0 | 159.2 | 144 | 72 | 49 | 91 | 3 |
| 95 AA Harrisburg | 9 | 6 | 2.95 | 25 | 25 | 0 | 168.0 | 152 | 74 | 64 | 112 | 3 |
| 95 AAA Ottawa | 2 | 0 | 1.17 | 3 | 3 | 0 | 23.0 | 17 | 4 | 5 | 18 | 0 |

Falteisek took a couple years to really get going after the Expos chose him in the 10th round of 1992. But in 1994 his 2.54 ERA was the Florida State League's third-best mark, and last year he went a combined 11-6 with a 2.73 ERA between Double- and Triple-A. Falteisek's strikeout rate has never been particulary high, although he's never struggled with his control, either. The relative ease with which Falteisek handled the two jumps in level last year is a positive indicator.

## Scott Gentile

**Position:** P  
**Bats:** R **Throws:** R  
**Ht:** 5' 11" **Wt:** 210  

**Opening Day Age:** 25  
**Born:** 12/21/70 in New Britain, CT  

### Recent Statistics

|  | W | L | ERA | G | GS | Sv | IP | H | R | BB | SO | HR |
|---|---|---|---|---|---|---|---|---|---|---|---|---|
| 93 A W. Palm Bch | 8 | 9 | 4.03 | 25 | 25 | 0 | 138.1 | 132 | 72 | 54 | 108 | 8 |
| 94 AA Harrisburg | 0 | 1 | 17.42 | 6 | 2 | 0 | 10.1 | 16 | 21 | 25 | 14 | 1 |
| 94 A W. Palm Bch | 5 | 2 | 1.93 | 53 | 1 | 26 | 65.1 | 44 | 16 | 19 | 90 | 0 |
| 95 AA Harrisburg | 2 | 2 | 3.44 | 37 | 0 | 11 | 49.2 | 36 | 19 | 15 | 48 | 3 |

The Expos used Gentile as a starter for two years before allowing him to finally succeed in the closer role he was destined to fill. He was untouchable the last three months of 1994, not allowing a run in his last 40 appearances covering 43 innings. Gentile was not as dominant upon reaching Double-A, but his mid-90s fastball and hard slider were still highly effective. Felipe Alou uses his bullpen a lot in Montreal, and Gentile has a chance to soon be a valuable contributor in some capacity.

## Vladimir Guerrero

**Position:** OF  
**Bats:** R **Throws:** R  
**Ht:** 6' 2" **Wt:** 158  

**Opening Day Age:** 20  
**Born:** 2/9/76 in Nizao Bani, DR  

### Recent Statistics

|  | G | AB | R | H | D | T | HR | RBI | SB | BB | SO | AVG |
|---|---|---|---|---|---|---|---|---|---|---|---|---|
| 94 R Expos | 37 | 137 | 24 | 43 | 13 | 3 | 5 | 25 | 0 | 11 | 18 | .314 |
| 95 A Albany | 110 | 421 | 77 | 140 | 21 | 10 | 16 | 63 | 12 | 30 | 45 | .333 |

Most of the Expos' best position prospects are young, and many of them, such as Bocachica, Brad Fullmer and Guerrero, played at low Class-A Albany last year. Like Bocachica, Guerrero excelled there at just 19 years, leading the Sally League in batting average. He already has plus power, which should only get better as he matures. As his triple and stolen-base totals would indicate, Guerrero has good speed, and he has the arm to play right field in the majors.

## Everett Stull

**Position:** P  
**Bats:** R **Throws:** R  
**Ht:** 6' 3" **Wt:** 195  

**Opening Day Age:** 24  
**Born:** 8/24/71 in Fort Riley, GA  

### Recent Statistics

|  | W | L | ERA | G | GS | Sv | IP | H | R | BB | SO | HR |
|---|---|---|---|---|---|---|---|---|---|---|---|---|
| 93 A Burlington | 4 | 9 | 3.83 | 15 | 15 | 0 | 82.1 | 68 | 44 | 59 | 85 | 8 |
| 94 A W. Palm Bch | 10 | 10 | 3.31 | 27 | 26 | 0 | 147.0 | 116 | 60 | 78 | 165 | 3 |
| 95 AA Harrisburg | 3 | 12 | 5.54 | 24 | 24 | 0 | 126.2 | 114 | 88 | 79 | 132 | 12 |

Stull's walk rate, which had decreased his previous two years, rose in 1995, with the results reflected in his won-lost record. Stull has a "fresh" arm, meaning he didn't pitch much before the Expos selected him in the third round of 1992. His stuff can be overpowering, with a fastball that flirts with the high 90s and a knee-buckling curve that at times breaks so much it's difficult to keep in the strike zone. If he can harness his control,

Stull is probably closer to the big leagues than his record last year might indicate.

## Ugueth Urbina

**Position:** P  
**Bats:** R **Throws:** R  
**Ht:** 6' 2" **Wt:** 170  

**Opening Day Age:** 22  
**Born:** 2/15/74 in Caracas, VZ  

### Recent Statistics

|  | W | L | ERA | G | GS | Sv | IP | H | R | BB | SO | HR |
|---|---|---|---|---|---|---|---|---|---|---|---|---|
| 95 A W. Palm Bch | 1 | 0 | 0.00 | 2 | 2 | 0 | 9.0 | 4 | 0 | 1 | 11 | 0 |
| 95 AAA Ottawa | 6 | 2 | 3.04 | 13 | 11 | 0 | 68.0 | 46 | 26 | 26 | 55 | 1 |
| 95 NL Montreal | 2 | 2 | 6.17 | 7 | 4 | 0 | 23.1 | 26 | 17 | 14 | 15 | 6 |

Urbina rebounded nicely from a traumatic 1994 in which he missed a month of the season to mourn following the murder of his father. He also battled arm problems that year. 1995 was better for him, and at 21 he tasted a couple cups of coffee in the big leagues. As his hits-to-innings ratio indicates, Triple-A batters had a tough time hitting Urbina. His strikeout totals have never been eye-catching, although they will likely improve as he develops a better breaking ball to complement his mid-90s fastball and effective change-up.

## Others to Watch

Shortstop **Jolbert Cabrera** hit .286 at West Palm Beach and played a handful of games in Double-A at the age of 22. He has some speed but little power. . . Third baseman **Brad Fullmer**, 21, is almost without question the Expos' best hitting prospect. He was a second-round draft pick in 1993 who signed late and then missed all of '94 due to injury. But he hit .323 with 38 doubles in his first pro exposure last season at Albany. . . Righthander **Rod Henderson** struggled in 1994 and was 3-6 in just 12 starts last year. When Henderson's right, he's a power pitcher with command of four pitches. . . Catcher **Bob Henley** enjoyed a spectacular season in the Midwest League in '94, hitting .301 with 20 homers. Last year's numbers weren't as eye-popping, though he still hit .281 with 83 walks for a .436 on-base percentage. Again, that's a catcher producing those numbers. . . Second baseman **Jose Vidro** hit .325 at West Palm Beach before getting promoted to Double-A last year. He was a sixth-round pick out of Puerto Rico in 1993, and will play this year at the age of 21.

# Edgardo Alfonzo

## 1995 Season

Mets manager Dallas Green saw Edgardo Alfonzo playing winter ball in Venezuela after the 1994 season, and immediately decided he could skip Triple-A and help the Mets in '95. Green said the rookie's offensive production was about what he expected from Alfonzo. He was a shortstop, then a second baseman in the minors, but played mostly third in the majors. He was playing fairly regularly before a herniated disk in his lower back put him on the disabled list late in the year.

## Hitting

Because he has played year-round, Alfonzo has more experience than most players his age. Said Mets batting coach Tom McCraw, "He's a very good learner, very attentive, and doesn't ever panic. He really knows what to do with the ball. By the time he's 25 or 26, all hell should break loose." Alfonzo already has shown he can hit both righthanders and lefthanders, and that he has some power. He needs to work only on developing patience at the plate.

## Baserunning & Defense

Alfonzo stole only once last season, and wasn't a big basestealer in the minors. His speed shows more in taking extra bases and in getting out of the batter's box quickly, as evidenced by his five triples. Defensively, he showed he can play all three infield skill positions. Like most former shortstops, he is adept at fielding grounders and throwing from either second or third. Again, his year-round experience has made him a more mature player.

## 1996 Outlook

Alfonzo avoided surgery, instead spending the offseason resting his back. The only question is whether he'll be the Mets' regular third baseman or second baseman (with Jeff Kent the other half of this question). Alfonzo shouldn't have any defensive worries at either position, which would allow him to develop even faster as a hitter. Depending on where he bats in the lineup, he could drive in plenty of runs.

**Position:** 3B/2B
**Bats:** R **Throws:** R
**Ht:** 5'11" **Wt:** 187

**Opening Day Age:** 22
**Born:** 8/11/73 in St. Teresa, VZ
**ML Seasons:** 1

### Overall Statistics

|  | G | AB | R | H | D | T | HR | RBI | SB | BB | SO | Avg | OBP | Slg |
|---|---|---|---|---|---|---|---|---|---|---|---|---|---|---|
| 1995 | 101 | 335 | 26 | 93 | 13 | 5 | 4 | 41 | 1 | 12 | 37 | .278 | .301 | .382 |
| Career | 101 | 335 | 26 | 93 | 13 | 5 | 4 | 41 | 1 | 12 | 37 | .278 | .301 | .382 |

### Where He Hits the Ball

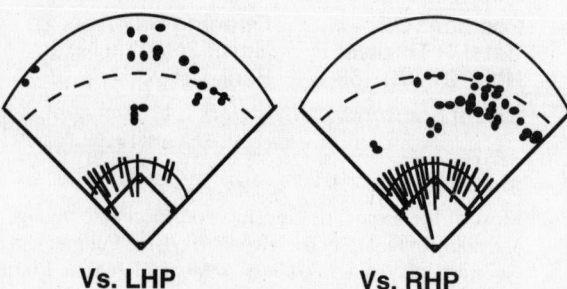

**Vs. LHP**          **Vs. RHP**

### 1995 Situational Stats

|  | AB | H | HR | RBI | Avg |  | AB | H | HR | RBI | Avg |
|---|---|---|---|---|---|---|---|---|---|---|---|
| Home | 167 | 47 | 0 | 16 | .281 | LHP | 98 | 28 | 2 | 15 | .286 |
| Road | 168 | 46 | 4 | 25 | .274 | RHP | 237 | 65 | 2 | 26 | .274 |
| First Half | 193 | 49 | 3 | 22 | .254 | Sc Pos | 81 | 26 | 2 | 36 | .321 |
| Scnd Half | 142 | 44 | 1 | 19 | .310 | Clutch | 61 | 18 | 0 | 4 | .295 |

### 1995 Rankings (National League)

➡ 4th in lowest batting average on a 3-2 count (.056)
➡ Led the Mets in batting average with runners in scoring position (.321)

# Rico Brogna

## 1995 Season

Rico Brogna followed up a breakthrough 1994 season with a solid year as the Mets' main power source after Bobby Bonilla was traded. Brogna hit most of his home runs during the second half of the year, after a hip injury slowed him during May. Season highlights included driving in the winning run in a 10-inning game against the Rockies, and beating Houston with a two-run homer September 14.

## Hitting

Unlike the Tigers, who wanted Brogna to pull the ball, the Mets have encouraged the big slugger to drive the ball to all fields. They want him to knock in runs, not draw walks, so he hasn't taken many free passes despite seeing a lot of pitches. He held up well following his monstrous half-season in 1994. Brogna's smooth swing marks him as an accomplished hitter. His biggest problem is picking up breaking pitches from lefthanders.

## Baserunning & Defense

Typical of the Mets, Brogna is not a good baserunner. He has stolen one base in his year-and-a-half in New York. Once aboard, he goes station to station. The team's slickest-fielding first baseman since Keith Hernandez, Brogna can turn 3-6-3 double plays because he gets rid of the ball quickly, and is fast enough to get back to the base for the return throw.

## 1996 Outlook

If Brogna learns to hit lefthanders better, Dallas Green can use him every day. Brogna's defense is good enough that he can move down in the lineup against lefties and stay in the game. There is a Gold Glove in his future. He is young enough that he can continue to develop as a hitter, with a .300 average and 30 home runs also possible down the road. Better hitters surrounding him in the lineup would help him see better pitches, too. The future looks bright.

**Position:** 1B
**Bats:** L  **Throws:** L
**Ht:** 6' 2"  **Wt:** 205

**Opening Day Age:** 25
**Born:** 4/18/70 in Turner Falls, MA
**ML Seasons:** 3
**Pronunciation:** BROHN-yuh

### Overall Statistics

| | G | AB | R | H | D | T | HR | RBI | SB | BB | SO | Avg | OBP | Slg |
|---|---|---|---|---|---|---|---|---|---|---|---|---|---|---|
| 1995 | 134 | 495 | 72 | 143 | 27 | 2 | 22 | 76 | 0 | 39 | 111 | .289 | .342 | .485 |
| Career | 182 | 652 | 91 | 194 | 39 | 4 | 30 | 99 | 1 | 48 | 145 | .298 | .347 | .508 |

### Where He Hits the Ball

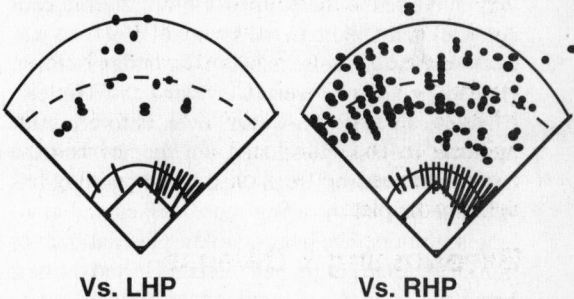

Vs. LHP          Vs. RHP

### 1995 Situational Stats

| | AB | H | HR | RBI | Avg | | AB | H | HR | RBI | Avg |
|---|---|---|---|---|---|---|---|---|---|---|---|
| Home | 243 | 71 | 13 | 43 | .292 | LHP | 118 | 27 | 2 | 14 | .229 |
| Road | 252 | 72 | 9 | 33 | .286 | RHP | 377 | 116 | 20 | 62 | .308 |
| First Half | 229 | 63 | 9 | 31 | .275 | Sc Pos | 135 | 36 | 4 | 52 | .267 |
| Scnd Half | 266 | 80 | 13 | 45 | .301 | Clutch | 88 | 30 | 6 | 18 | .341 |

### 1995 Rankings (National League)

- ➡ 1st in fielding percentage at first base (.998)
- ➡ 5th in strikeouts
- ➡ 6th in lowest on-base percentage vs. left-handed pitchers (.272) and batting average on a 3-2 count (.400)
- ➡ 8th in lowest batting average vs. left-handed pitchers (.229)
- ➡ 9th in lowest slugging percentage vs. left-handed pitchers (.339)
- ➡ Led the Mets in batting average, home runs, runs scored, doubles, total bases (240), RBI, times on base (184), strikeouts, pitches seen (1,956), slugging percentage, on-base percentage and HR frequency (22.5 ABs per HR)

# Jerry DiPoto

## 1995 Season

The Mets acquired righty reliever Jerry DiPoto in a trade from Cleveland before last season, and installed him as a middle reliever. He stumbled coming out of the gate, losing his first three decisions and blowing four save opportunities. In his first 25 games, the Mets won just three. Then in 10 games on either side of the All-Star Game, he picked up three victories. The Mets then showed more confidence in DiPoto, who became the workhorse of their bullpen.

## Pitching

A starter until 1992, DiPoto had a limited repertoire (fastball/slider and occasional splitter) and was converted to the bullpen. Before thyroid cancer sidelined DiPoto in the spring of 1994, he was as close as anyone else to being the Indians' closer. He had 23 saves between Cleveland and Triple-A Charlotte in 1993. However, even before his illness the Indians questioned whether he had the makeup of a closer. He pitched better for the Mets when he started throwing more strikes and challenging hitters. His heavy, sinking fastball makes him an extreme groundball pitcher. He had the best home-run ratio of any regular Mets pitcher.

## Defense & Hitting

DiPoto is a passable fielder who was erratic at times during 1995. Few Mets pitchers hold baserunners as well as he does; four of nine stolen-base attempts against DiPoto were cut down last year. DiPoto never batted before 1995, and he went 0-for-5 with the Mets.

## 1996 Outlook

Late last season, DiPoto became a more reliable pitcher, but he was never indispensable. He's not a star, in other words. Unless the Mets acquire a better right-handed reliever, or move a starter such as Dave Mlicki to the pen, DiPoto should be able to keep his set-up job. If not, he would still be a long-relief candidate. He can throw virtually every day, and has no history of arm injuries.

**Position:** RP
**Bats:** R  **Throws:** R
**Ht:** 6' 2"  **Wt:** 200

**Opening Day Age:** 27
**Born:** 5/24/68 in Jersey City, NJ
**ML Seasons:** 3
**Pronunciation:** duh-POE-toe

### Overall Statistics

|        | W | L | Pct. | ERA | G | GS | Sv | IP | H | BB | SO | HR | BR/IP |
|--------|---|---|------|-----|---|----|----|------|-----|----|----|----|-------|
| 1995   | 4 | 6 | .400 | 3.78 | 58 | 0 | 2 | 78.2 | 77 | 29 | 49 | 2 | 1.35 |
| Career | 8 | 10 | .444 | 3.70 | 111 | 0 | 13 | 150.2 | 160 | 69 | 99 | 3 | 1.52 |

### How Often He Throws Strikes

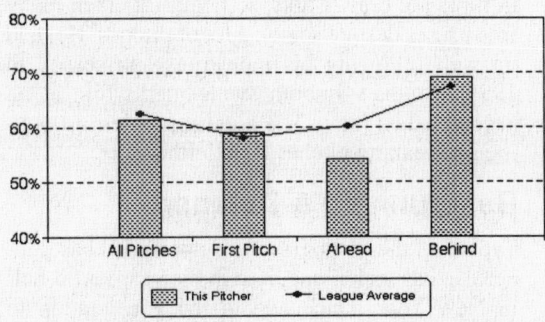

### 1995 Situational Stats

|            | W | L | ERA | Sv | IP |       | AB | H | HR | RBI | Avg |
|------------|---|---|------|----|------|-------|-----|----|----|-----|------|
| Home       | 0 | 1 | 3.43 | 1 | 39.1 | LHB   | 123 | 33 | 0 | 14 | .268 |
| Road       | 4 | 5 | 4.12 | 1 | 39.1 | RHB   | 165 | 44 | 2 | 24 | .267 |
| First Half | 1 | 3 | 5.86 | 0 | 35.1 | Sc Pos | 85 | 26 | 1 | 36 | .306 |
| Scnd Half  | 3 | 3 | 2.08 | 2 | 43.1 | Clutch | 117 | 36 | 0 | 18 | .308 |

### 1995 Rankings (National League)

→ 4th in least strikeouts per 9 innings in relief (5.6)
→ 5th in errors at pitcher (3) and relief losses (6)
→ Led the Mets in games pitched, holds (8), lowest percentage of inherited runners scored (24.1%), relief losses and relief innings (78.2)

# Carl Everett

## 1995 Season

At first, Florida seemed to get the best of the Carl Everett-for-Quilvio Veras trade. Everett made the Mets in the spring but slumped to .193 with a .233 on-base percentage and was demoted to Norfolk. He returned a different player, and was one of the best in the National League in September—hitting with power, drawing walks and playing great defense.

## Hitting

Playing under Toby Harrah at Norfolk, Everett developed his batting eye. After walking in just six percent of his at-bats in 1994, he soared to a 13-percent rate with the Mets. He doesn't describe his new style as being patient, but says his aggressiveness is now channeled more into actively looking for the right pitch. He has also developed more power, with a career-high 18 homers in Triple-A and the majors combined. Lefthanders still give him some trouble.

## Baserunning & Defense

Said Mets outfield coach Frank Howard, "His arm is what you notice first. It's a 6.5 on a scale of 7, and we don't use 7 much." Everett used that arm, considered the Mets' best since Ellis Valentine two decades ago, for nine assists in 68 games in right field. He has enough speed to play center field, and is improving day to day. Everett hasn't yet unleashed his speed as a basestealer. He was just 2-for-7 last year.

## 1996 Outlook

The Mets should like the answers to the only questions surrounding Everett. Will he play center field or right? Will he bat first or third? He has the talent to succeed in either position in the field and either slot in the batting order. Last year he realized the potential the Yankees recognized when they drafted him in the first round in 1990. Now the Everett-Veras trade is considered one that helped both teams.

**Position:** RF
**Bats:** B  **Throws:** R
**Ht:** 6' 0"  **Wt:** 190

**Opening Day Age:** 24
**Born:** 6/3/71 in Tampa, FL
**ML Seasons:** 3

### Overall Statistics

|  | G | AB | R | H | D | T | HR | RBI | SB | BB | SO | Avg | OBP | Slg |
|---|---|---|---|---|---|---|---|---|---|---|---|---|---|---|
| 1995 | 79 | 289 | 48 | 75 | 13 | 1 | 12 | 54 | 2 | 39 | 67 | .260 | .352 | .436 |
| Career | 106 | 359 | 55 | 88 | 14 | 1 | 14 | 60 | 7 | 43 | 91 | .245 | .329 | .407 |

### Where He Hits the Ball

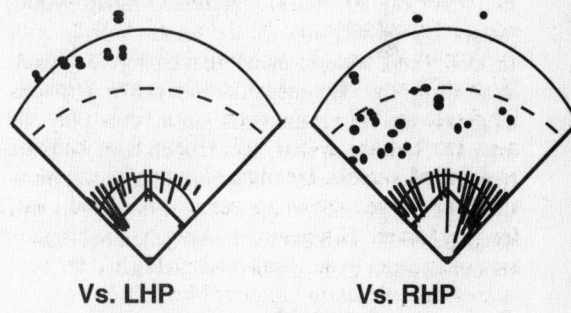

**Vs. LHP**          **Vs. RHP**

### 1995 Situational Stats

|  | AB | H | HR | RBI | Avg |  | AB | H | HR | RBI | Avg |
|---|---|---|---|---|---|---|---|---|---|---|---|
| Home | 138 | 43 | 9 | 24 | .312 | LHP | 100 | 21 | 4 | 14 | .210 |
| Road | 151 | 32 | 3 | 30 | .212 | RHP | 189 | 54 | 8 | 40 | .286 |
| First Half | 57 | 11 | 3 | 6 | .193 | Sc Pos | 95 | 29 | 4 | 46 | .305 |
| Scnd Half | 232 | 64 | 9 | 48 | .276 | Clutch | 48 | 10 | 1 | 3 | .208 |

### 1995 Rankings (National League)

→ 3rd in batting average with the bases loaded (.556)

→ Led the Mets in batting average with the bases loaded

# John Franco

## 1995 Season

The reigning N.L. saves champ a year ago, John Franco turned down a bigger offer from the Orioles to re-sign with his hometown Mets for $5 million for 1995-1996. Then he contributed to their slow start by blowing four of his first 10 save opportunities. For the second consecutive year, he got hot later in the year, posting 22 saves and three wins in his final 30 appearances. Seven of those saves came in the Mets' 13-5 finish, including three in consecutive games September 14-16.

## Pitching

Because Franco's best pitch is a fadeaway change-up, righthanders have more trouble hitting against him than do left-handed batters. Franco works hitters on either side of the plate, inside with fastballs and sliders, using the change-up away against righties. He keeps the ball down, and gets as many outs on groundballs and double plays as anyone. Because of that, he relies on help from his infielders, and doesn't hesitate to suggest how they should position themselves. Franco can still reach back and strike out a batter when necessary, though ground balls are his basic style.

## Defense & Hitting

Franco holds runners well, thanks to a good pick-off move. During the last two seasons, they're just 2-for-4 in steal attempts against him. That's just part of his solid overall fielding ability; he is alert and quick off the mound. He is not a good hitter, but in his closer role, he rarely needs that skill.

## 1996 Outlook

Franco is a leader in the clubhouse, and The Man in the Mets' bullpen. With an increased emphasis on defense in the New York organization, the groundball-inducing Franco can look forward to continued success. He just missed recording 30-plus saves for the seventh time last year. He clearly ranks among the game's most valuable relievers.

**Position:** RP
**Bats:** L **Throws:** L
**Ht:** 5'10" **Wt:** 185

**Opening Day Age:** 35
**Born:** 9/17/60 in Brooklyn, NY
**ML Seasons:** 12

### Overall Statistics

|        | W  | L  | Pct. | ERA  | G   | GS | Sv  | IP    | H   | BB  | SO  | HR | BR/IP |
|--------|----|----|------|------|-----|----|-----|-------|-----|-----|-----|----|-------|
| 1995   | 5  | 3  | .625 | 2.44 | 48  | 0  | 29  | 51.2  | 48  | 17  | 41  | 4  | 1.26  |
| Career | 68 | 54 | .557 | 2.62 | 661 | 0  | 295 | 822.0 | 752 | 315 | 600 | 46 | 1.30  |

### How Often He Throws Strikes

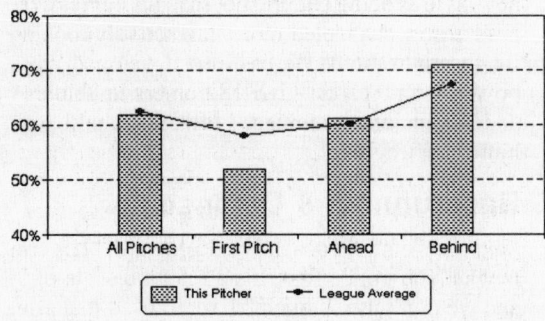

### 1995 Situational Stats

|            | W | L | ERA  | Sv | IP   |        | AB  | H  | HR | RBI | Avg  |
|------------|---|---|------|----|------|--------|-----|----|----|-----|------|
| Home       | 4 | 1 | 2.51 | 18 | 32.1 | LHB    | 32  | 9  | 0  | 3   | .281 |
| Road       | 1 | 2 | 2.33 | 11 | 19.1 | RHB    | 159 | 39 | 4  | 17  | .245 |
| First Half | 3 | 1 | 3.00 | 9  | 24.0 | Sc Pos | 51  | 10 | 1  | 15  | .196 |
| Scnd Half  | 2 | 2 | 1.95 | 20 | 27.2 | Clutch | 156 | 37 | 3  | 18  | .237 |

### 1995 Rankings (National League)

➡ 3rd in blown saves (7)
➡ 7th in save opportunities (36), lowest save percentage (80.6%) and relief ERA (2.44)
➡ 8th in saves
➡ Led the Mets in saves, games finished (41), save opportunities, save percentage (80.6%), blown saves and relief ERA

# Pete Harnisch

## 1995 Season

The Mets traded with Houston to get local hero Pete Harnisch (a Fordham alumnus from Commack, N.Y.), knowing he was damaged goods. A damaged tendon in his shoulder hampered Harnisch in 1994. The Mets nonetheless gave him a three-year, $9-million contract. His best early starts were no-decisions, so he was just 1-7, despite pitching fairly well, when he left his July 6th start because of shoulder pain. He came back 10 days later, but made just four more starts before the shoulder shut him down.

## Pitching

One benefit of Harnisch's ongoing shoulder trouble was that it forced him to become a pitcher rather than a thrower with a 92 MPH fastball. He has learned to spot the fastball and use a hard slider that makes him tough against right-handed hitters. He also has worked on a cut fastball to help him against lefthanders. His breaking pitches have been less effective when arm soreness limits his velocity. Harnisch is a tough-minded competitor. Being a flyball pitcher works almost as well at Shea Stadium as it did at the Astrodome.

## Defense & Hitting

Because of his competitiveness, Harnisch does everything pretty well. He's a decent hitter with occasional gap power. He's a sure-handed fielder. Harnisch has developed a good pickoff move, but basestealers were 12-for-17 against him last year.

## 1996 Outlook

The Mets could use Harnisch's veteran savvy in a rotation that could have as many as three starters who were in the minors a year ago. However, he underwent shoulder surgery during the offseason. A recovery would make him far more valuable than the injury-plagued pitcher with 10 wins over the last two seasons. More arm trouble could put his career in jeopardy. Key to watch: early-season radar-gun readings.

**Position:** SP
**Bats:** R **Throws:** R
**Ht:** 6' 0" **Wt:** 207

**Opening Day Age:** 29
**Born:** 9/23/66 in Commack, NY
**ML Seasons:** 8

### Overall Statistics

|  | W | L | Pct. | ERA | G | GS | Sv | IP | H | BB | SO | HR | BR/IP |
|---|---|---|---|---|---|---|---|---|---|---|---|---|---|
| 1995 | 2 | 8 | .200 | 3.68 | 18 | 18 | 0 | 110.0 | 111 | 24 | 82 | 13 | 1.23 |
| Career | 63 | 63 | .500 | 3.72 | 186 | 185 | 0 | 1151.0 | 1032 | 448 | 867 | 106 | 1.29 |

### How Often He Throws Strikes

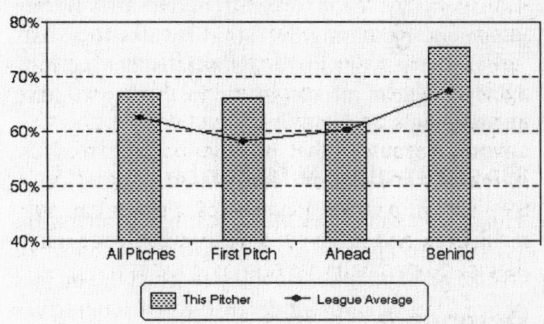

### 1995 Situational Stats

|  | W | L | ERA | Sv | IP |  | AB | H | HR | RBI | Avg |
|---|---|---|---|---|---|---|---|---|---|---|---|
| Home | 1 | 4 | 2.73 | 0 | 66.0 | LHB | 199 | 60 | 6 | 26 | .302 |
| Road | 1 | 4 | 5.11 | 0 | 44.0 | RHB | 226 | 51 | 7 | 24 | .226 |
| First Half | 1 | 7 | 4.23 | 0 | 83.0 | Sc Pos | 102 | 28 | 2 | 37 | .275 |
| Scnd Half | 1 | 1 | 2.00 | 0 | 27.0 | Clutch | 22 | 8 | 0 | 2 | .364 |

### 1995 Rankings (National League)

➡ 8th in highest batting average allowed vs. left-handed batters (.302)
➡ Led the Mets in runners caught stealing (5)

# Todd Hundley

## 1995 Season

After offseason surgery to remove a bone spur from his left wrist, Todd Hundley had a career year, even though he missed a week in May with a sore foot and six weeks after a home-plate collision July 22. Hundley became the ninth player in major league history to hit grand slams from both sides of the plate in the same season.

## Hitting

Three major developments propelled Hundley to his big year. First, he started to hit lefthanders well enough that he no longer was in a strict platoon with Kelly Stinnett. Second, Hundley had an exceptional year hitting with runners in scoring position. Finally, he exercised better strike-zone judgment, increasing his ratio of walks to at-bats from nine percent to 15. Especially batting left-handed, he can turn on inside fastballs and drive them with power.

## Baserunning & Defense

Hundley is one of the Mets' best baserunners. He is extremely aggressive, and knows how and when to take an extra base. Hundley reached the majors at age 21 because of his defensive skills, but never has thrown out basestealers as well as predicted by scouts (26 percent last year). He controlled the running game better than Stinnett, but they were equally effective in handling the Mets' staff.

## 1996 Outlook

For the Mets, re-signing Hundley was a major priority. He is the only major league catcher with power from both sides of the plate. He is a leader in the clubhouse and sets an example with the hard-nosed style learned from his father, Randy Hundley. Todd won't have to catch every day, as his father did, because the Mets have other alternatives in Stinnett and Alberto Castillo. Hundley doesn't have to be platooned; New York was 10-6 in games he started against lefthanders.

**Position:** C
**Bats:** B **Throws:** R
**Ht:** 5'11" **Wt:** 185

**Opening Day Age:** 26
**Born:** 5/27/69 in Martinsville, VA
**ML Seasons:** 6

### Overall Statistics

|        | G   | AB   | R   | H   | D  | T | HR | RBI | SB | BB  | SO  | Avg  | OBP  | Slg  |
|--------|-----|------|-----|-----|----|---|----|-----|----|-----|-----|------|------|------|
| 1995   | 90  | 275  | 39  | 77  | 11 | 0 | 15 | 51  | 1  | 42  | 64  | .280 | .382 | .484 |
| Career | 491 | 1468 | 169 | 338 | 61 | 4 | 50 | 187 | 7  | 121 | 307 | .230 | .293 | .379 |

### Where He Hits the Ball

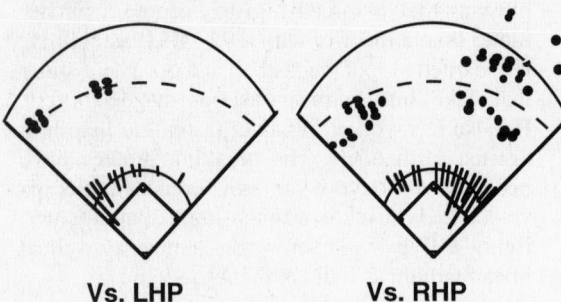

**Vs. LHP**          **Vs. RHP**

### 1995 Situational Stats

|            | AB  | H  | HR | RBI | Avg  |        | AB  | H  | HR | RBI | Avg  |
|------------|-----|----|----|-----|------|--------|-----|----|----|-----|------|
| Home       | 125 | 34 | 6  | 20  | .272 | LHP    | 60  | 18 | 3  | 12  | .300 |
| Road       | 150 | 43 | 9  | 31  | .287 | RHP    | 215 | 59 | 12 | 39  | .274 |
| First Half | 173 | 45 | 12 | 36  | .260 | Sc Pos | 66  | 22 | 4  | 36  | .333 |
| Scnd Half  | 102 | 32 | 3  | 15  | .314 | Clutch | 49  | 12 | 2  | 12  | .245 |

### 1995 Rankings (National League)

→ 1st in lowest fielding percentage at catcher (.987)
→ 5th in errors at catcher (7)

# Jason Isringhausen

## 1995 Season

After a fast start at Double-A Binghamton, including a 14-strikeout game, highly regarded pitching project Jason Isringhausen was promoted to Triple-A Norfolk. He was there only long enough to post a 9-1 record and 1.55 ERA that made him the International League Pitcher of the Year and Rookie of the Year. After pitching in the Triple-A All-Star Game, he joined the Mets, allowing two hits in seven innings in his debut. He quickly became the club's most effective starter as the Mets put together a 40-30 finish.

## Pitching

Montreal's David Segui hit a home run against Isringhausen, then called him "The best pitcher I have seen in the National League for being tough to hit. He can throw his curveball anywhere, and has the change-up and fastball to go with it." It's a tailing fastball, giving Isringhausen pitches that break away from both left-handed and right-handed batters. He conservatively estimated his velocity at 88 MPH, and said the key to his success is establishing his curve early in a game. For a young pitcher, he's economical; he needed just 4.95 pitches per out in the majors. He still has room for improvement against lefthanders.

## Defense & Hitting

Isringhausen so dominated his competition coming up that he didn't need to develop skills that will help him more in the majors. National Leaguers ran wild against him, with 22 steals in 26 attempts. He'll need to work on holding runners, fielding and hitting.

## 1996 Outlook

When the Mets asked San Francisco about Matt Williams, the first name the Giants brought up was Isringhausen's. No deal. He can't be expected to maintain his .818 winning percentage, but he should be plenty good enough to keep a place high in the Mets' rotation. He and the other young pitchers are the key to their future. After last year's success, that future looks extremely bright.

**Position:** SP
**Bats:** R  **Throws:** R
**Ht:** 6' 3"  **Wt:** 196

**Opening Day Age:** 23
**Born:** 9/7/72 in Brighton, IL
**ML Seasons:** 1
**Pronunciation:** IZ-ring-how-zen

### Overall Statistics

|  | W | L | Pct. | ERA | G | GS | Sv | IP | H | BB | SO | HR | BR/IP |
|---|---|---|---|---|---|---|---|---|---|---|---|---|---|
| 1995 | 9 | 2 | .818 | 2.81 | 14 | 14 | 0 | 93.0 | 88 | 31 | 55 | 6 | 1.28 |
| Career | 9 | 2 | .818 | 2.81 | 14 | 14 | 0 | 93.0 | 88 | 31 | 55 | 6 | 1.28 |

### How Often He Throws Strikes

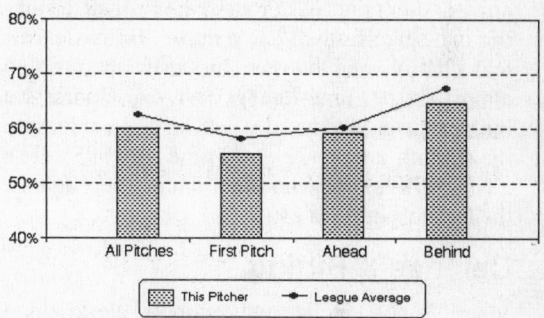

### 1995 Situational Stats

|  | W | L | ERA | Sv | IP |  | AB | H | HR | RBI | Avg |
|---|---|---|---|---|---|---|---|---|---|---|---|
| Home | 5 | 2 | 2.92 | 0 | 52.1 | LHB | 183 | 55 | 3 | 15 | .301 |
| Road | 4 | 0 | 2.66 | 0 | 40.2 | RHB | 163 | 33 | 3 | 11 | .202 |
| First Half | 0 | 0 | - | 0 | 0.0 | Sc Pos | 87 | 15 | 1 | 20 | .172 |
| Scnd Half | 9 | 2 | 2.81 | 0 | 93.0 | Clutch | 23 | 5 | 0 | 0 | .217 |

### 1995 Rankings (National League)

➡ 7th in most GDPs induced per GDP situation (19.6%)
➡ 8th in stolen bases allowed (22)
➡ Led the Mets in most GDPs induced per GDP situation (19.6%)

# Bobby Jones

## 1995 Season

Bobby Jones was the Mets' Opening Day starter. From that point on, he was the one constant in their rotation, missing just one start. After winning four of his first six decisions, he lost four in a row, then went 6-4 down the stretch to finish as the team's biggest winner. Jones' best start came on September 8, when he tossed a complete-game three-hitter to beat the Expos, 5-0.

## Pitching

Jones is one of those pitchers whose head is even better than his arm. He's a finesse pitcher who throws a straight change as deceptive as any in the majors. He can use it effectively because he has an array of other pitches: a four-seam fastball, a sinking two-seam fastball and a curve. He has excellent control, and boosted his strikeout ratio to almost six per nine innings last year. Jones is a bullpen-saver who usually gets his team at least to the seventh inning (22 of 30 times in 1995). He's a competitive type who often pitches best against the league's best teams.

## Defense & Hitting

Jones is a good athlete and a smooth, alert fielder. His game has two holes. He can't hit—though he is a good bunter—and he has done a poor job holding baserunners. Last year he gave up 24 stolen bases in 27 attempts.

## 1996 Outlook

One of the greatest signs of the Mets' improvement is Jones' status. He started last season number two in the rotation, behind Bret Saberhagen. This year, he could be as low as fourth on the pitching totem pole behind youngsters Jason Isringhausen, Bill Pulsipher and Paul Wilson. As an offspeed pitcher behind flamethrowers such as those, Jones could become even more effective in keeping hitters off balance. He also would be one of the younger rotation "veterans" in baseball.

**Position:** SP
**Bats:** R  **Throws:** R
**Ht:** 6' 4"  **Wt:** 225

**Opening Day Age:** 26
**Born:** 2/10/70 in Fresno, California
**ML Seasons:** 3

### Overall Statistics

|  | W | L | Pct. | ERA | G | GS | Sv | IP | H | BB | SO | HR | BR/IP |
|---|---|---|---|---|---|---|---|---|---|---|---|---|---|
| 1995 | 10 | 10 | .500 | 4.19 | 30 | 30 | 0 | 195.2 | 209 | 53 | 127 | 20 | 1.34 |
| Career | 24 | 21 | .533 | 3.71 | 63 | 63 | 0 | 417.1 | 427 | 131 | 242 | 36 | 1.34 |

### How Often He Throws Strikes

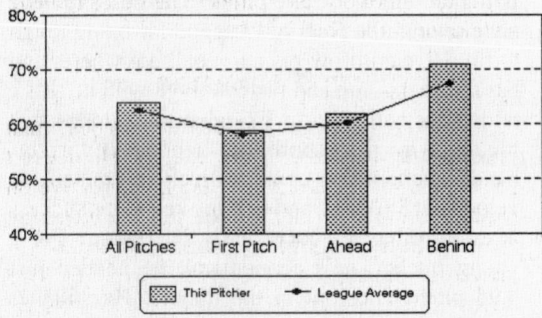

### 1995 Situational Stats

|  | W | L | ERA | Sv | IP |  | AB | H | HR | RBI | Avg |
|---|---|---|---|---|---|---|---|---|---|---|---|
| Home | 5 | 3 | 3.28 | 0 | 96.0 | LHB | 347 | 86 | 9 | 34 | .248 |
| Road | 5 | 7 | 5.06 | 0 | 99.2 | RHB | 415 | 123 | 11 | 60 | .296 |
| First Half | 4 | 6 | 3.08 | 0 | 105.1 | Sc Pos | 184 | 44 | 2 | 64 | .239 |
| Scnd Half | 6 | 4 | 5.48 | 0 | 90.1 | Clutch | 69 | 15 | 1 | 7 | .217 |

### 1995 Rankings (National League)

- ➡ 1st in sacrifice bunts (18), highest stolen base percentage allowed (88.9%), lowest batting average on an 0-2 count (0.000) and errors at pitcher (6)
- ➡ 2nd in lowest fielding percentage at pitcher (.872)
- ➡ 3rd in hits allowed
- ➡ 4th in batters faced (839) and highest ERA on the road (5.06)
- ➡ 6th in games started and least pitches thrown per batter (3.47)
- ➡ 7th in stolen bases allowed (24)
- ➡ 8th in innings pitched
- ➡ Led the Mets in sacrifice bunts, ERA, wins, losses and games started

# Jeff Kent

**Position:** 2B
**Bats:** R **Throws:** R
**Ht:** 6' 1"  **Wt:** 185

**Opening Day Age:** 28
**Born:** 3/7/68 in
Bellflower, CA
**ML Seasons:** 4

## 1995 Season

Jeff Kent continued to be one of the majors' leading power hitters at second base. In his fourth major league season, he reached 20 home runs for the second time and equaled his career high in extra-base hits even though he spent some time on the disabled list. He showed more season-long consistency than in the other years when he had extreme hot streaks and slumps.

## Hitting

Kent tends to be an all-or-nothing hitter. He hits many fly balls, which can be a problem in the National League's largest parks. He also strikes out frequently without drawing many walks. His bat is too quick for any pitcher, righty or lefty, to try blowing a fastball by him.

## Baserunning & Defense

Kent has some speed, but has been a less-than break-even basestealer in the majors. He doesn't get a good jump on pitchers. He is aggressive on the bases, and will challenge outfielders by taking an extra base. A former shortstop, Kent has improved at second base, dropping his error total down to 10 from 14 in 1994 and 18 in 1993. He has slightly better-than-average range, but last year did not turn double plays as frequently as in 1994.

## 1996 Outlook

Either Kent or Edgardo Alfonzo could spend 1996 at third base, which both can handle defensively. Kent has above-average power, even for a third baseman. At times he has stepped forward as a clubhouse leader, offering the experience of having gone through the Mets' lean years, and the appreciation for any improvement they can now show. Conversely, with many talented young infielders arriving in 1996, there has been chatter in the Shea press box about Kent being dispensable. He was eligible for arbitration and looking forward to a big '96 salary.

### Overall Statistics

| | G | AB | R | H | D | T | HR | RBI | SB | BB | SO | Avg | OBP | Slg |
|---|---|---|---|---|---|---|---|---|---|---|---|---|---|---|
| 1995 | 125 | 472 | 65 | 131 | 22 | 3 | 20 | 65 | 3 | 29 | 89 | .278 | .327 | .464 |
| Career | 474 | 1688 | 235 | 459 | 91 | 10 | 66 | 263 | 10 | 109 | 337 | .272 | .326 | .455 |

### Where He Hits the Ball

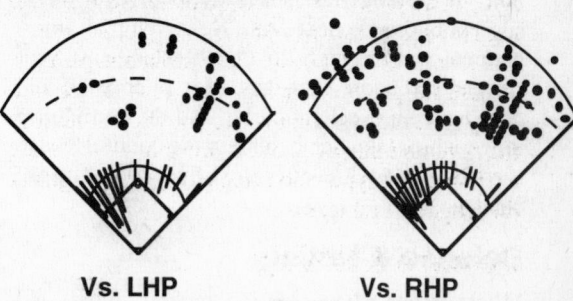

**Vs. LHP**          **Vs. RHP**

### 1995 Situational Stats

| | AB | H | HR | RBI | Avg | | AB | H | HR | RBI | Avg |
|---|---|---|---|---|---|---|---|---|---|---|---|
| Home | 243 | 69 | 11 | 33 | .284 | LHP | 133 | 33 | 3 | 10 | .248 |
| Road | 229 | 62 | 9 | 32 | .271 | RHP | 339 | 98 | 17 | 55 | .289 |
| First Half | 223 | 60 | 10 | 25 | .269 | Sc Pos | 137 | 27 | 4 | 45 | .197 |
| Scnd Half | 249 | 71 | 10 | 40 | .285 | Clutch | 85 | 23 | 5 | 7 | .271 |

### 1995 Rankings (National League)

- ➡ 3rd in errors at second base (10) and lowest fielding percentage at second base (.984)
- ➡ 4th in lowest batting average with runners in scoring position (.197)
- ➡ 6th in lowest percentage of pitches taken (45.5%)
- ➡ 8th in highest percentage of swings on the first pitch (41.9%)
- ➡ 9th in lowest cleanup slugging percentage (.451)
- ➡ 10th in lowest groundball/flyball ratio (1.0)
- ➡ Led the Mets in hit by pitch (8)

# Dave Mlicki

## 1995 Season

Dave Mlicki was the best of three pitchers the Mets obtained in a preseason trade with Cleveland. After earning a win from the bullpen in his National League debut, Mlicki took over the fifth starter's role. He went back to the pen briefly in August when Jason Isringhausen and Reid Cornelius arrived, then returned to the rotation when Pete Harnisch was lost. From that point on, Mlicki went 5-2.

## Pitching

Mlicki overcame offseason surgery to remove "loose bodies" from his elbow. Then he learned not to give in with predictable fastballs when behind in the count. When he does give in, he is susceptible to the home run. He gave up an International League-high 26 in 1994, and last year surrendered more than any Met pitcher. Mlicki does have an excellent curve, and the confidence now to throw it when behind in the count. He also throws a knuckle-curve, slider and straight change.

## Defense & Hitting

Mlicki doesn't have a good pickoff move, and because he's a breaking-ball pitcher and a bit slow to the plate, he's easy to run against. His fielding is adequate. Last year he got just two hits in his first year in the N.L., but he did show a good eye with eight walks.

## 1996 Outlook

With young pitchers coming up to New York, Mlicki is a prime candidate to be dropped from the rotation. He could keep his job if Pete Harnisch doesn't recover from surgery or the Mets decide Paul Wilson isn't ready. But unlike a year ago, the Mets and Mlicki both know he is capable of starting in the majors. At worst, he's an insurance policy as a swing man. At best, he goes every five days for the Mets or another team.

**Position:** SP
**Bats:** R  **Throws:** R
**Ht:** 6' 4"  **Wt:** 190

**Opening Day Age:** 27
**Born:** 6/8/68 in Cleveland, OH
**ML Seasons:** 3
**Pronunciation:** ma-LICK-ee

### Overall Statistics

|  | W | L | Pct. | ERA | G | GS | Sv | IP | H | BB | SO | HR | BR/IP |
|---|---|---|---|---|---|---|---|---|---|---|---|---|---|
| 1995 | 9 | 7 | .563 | 4.26 | 29 | 25 | 0 | 160.2 | 160 | 54 | 123 | 23 | 1.33 |
| Career | 9 | 9 | .500 | 4.28 | 36 | 32 | 0 | 195.2 | 194 | 76 | 146 | 28 | 1.38 |

### How Often He Throws Strikes

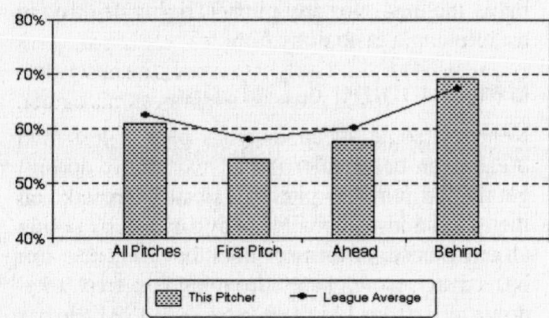

### 1995 Situational Stats

|  | W | L | ERA | Sv | IP |  | AB | H | HR | RBI | Avg |
|---|---|---|---|---|---|---|---|---|---|---|---|
| Home | 4 | 3 | 3.66 | 0 | 83.2 | LHB | 278 | 86 | 12 | 34 | .309 |
| Road | 5 | 4 | 4.91 | 0 | 77.0 | RHB | 347 | 74 | 11 | 40 | .213 |
| First Half | 4 | 4 | 4.09 | 0 | 77.0 | Sc Pos | 141 | 35 | 5 | 51 | .248 |
| Scnd Half | 5 | 3 | 4.41 | 0 | 83.2 | Clutch | 42 | 9 | 2 | 6 | .214 |

### 1995 Rankings (National League)

→ 2nd in most pitches thrown per batter (3.93)
→ 3rd in least GDPs induced per 9 innings (0.3)
→ 4th in most home runs allowed per 9 innings (1.29)
→ 5th in sacrifice bunts (12), home runs allowed, highest stolen base percentage allowed (85.0%) and highest batting average allowed vs. left-handed batters (.309)
→ 6th in lowest groundball/flyball ratio allowed (1.1), most run support per 9 innings (5.6) and lowest batting average allowed vs. right-handed batters (.213)
→ 7th in highest ERA on the road (4.91)
→ Led the Mets in home runs allowed, walks allowed and pickoff throws (86)

# Joe Orsulak

## 1995 Season

The Mets haven't built any big plans around outfielder Joe Orsulak during any of his three seasons in New York, but he always plays his way into an important role. Orsulak can pinch hit and play solidly in left field, right field, or at first base. Orsulak had as many big hits in '95 as any Met, including a game-winning 10th-inning single June 15, a sacrifice fly to beat Pittsburgh July 30 and a three-run pinch-hit homer in a 5-2 win August 7.

## Hitting

Orsulak is strictly a platoon player now. He never hit more than 11 home runs in a season, and showed even less power in 1995. Orsulak still can drive the ball into the outfield gaps. He makes good contact and uses all fields, hitting the ball where it's pitched. The last two years he has shown less patience at the plate than earlier in his career.

## Baserunning & Defense

Never a high-percentage basestealer, Orsulak was just 1-for-4 last year. He'll stay put unless he sees an obvious opportunity to steal. He is a good, alert baserunner. Defensively, he makes up for his reduced speed by studying hitters and positioning himself well. He no longer is quick enough to play center field. Even playing mostly in left field, he showed some decline in '95, registering just three assists with four errors.

## 1996 Outlook

Orsulak was eligible for free agency. He can still be valuable as a pinch hitter and double-switch defensive replacement. Having slowed slightly but noticeably, he may not play often with a defense-oriented team like the Mets. His most marketable skill is that he makes the most of his talent and intelligence, and has that long track record of always playing himself into a larger-than-expected supporting role.

**Position:** LF/RF
**Bats:** L  **Throws:** L
**Ht:** 6' 1"  **Wt:** 205

**Opening Day Age:** 33
**Born:** 5/31/62 in Glen Ridge, NJ
**ML Seasons:** 12
**Pronunciation:** ORR-suh-lack

### Overall Statistics

| | G | AB | R | H | D | T | HR | RBI | SB | BB | SO | Avg | OBP | Slg |
|---|---|---|---|---|---|---|---|---|---|---|---|---|---|---|
| 1995 | 108 | 290 | 41 | 82 | 19 | 2 | 1 | 37 | 1 | 19 | 35 | .283 | .323 | .372 |
| Career | 1268 | 3926 | 523 | 1091 | 168 | 35 | 54 | 379 | 92 | 284 | 347 | .278 | .328 | .380 |

### Where He Hits the Ball

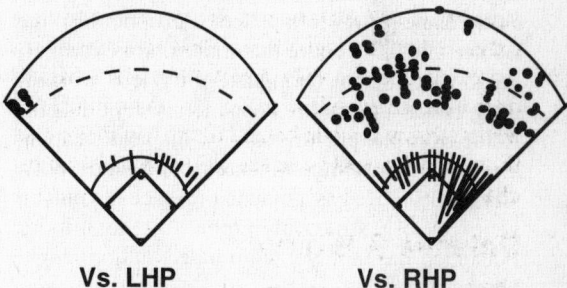

**Vs. LHP**          **Vs. RHP**

### 1995 Situational Stats

| | AB | H | HR | RBI | Avg | | AB | H | HR | RBI | Avg |
|---|---|---|---|---|---|---|---|---|---|---|---|
| Home | 126 | 41 | 1 | 22 | .325 | LHP | 25 | 4 | 0 | 6 | .160 |
| Road | 164 | 41 | 0 | 15 | .250 | RHP | 265 | 78 | 1 | 31 | .294 |
| First Half | 151 | 43 | 0 | 15 | .285 | Sc Pos | 66 | 23 | 1 | 34 | .348 |
| Scnd Half | 139 | 39 | 1 | 22 | .281 | Clutch | 79 | 21 | 1 | 16 | .266 |

### 1995 Rankings (National League)

→ 6th in errors in left field (4)
→ 8th in sacrifice flies (6) and least GDPs per GDP situation (4.7%)
→ Led the Mets in sacrifice flies and batting average with two strikes (.255)

# Bill Pulsipher

## 1995 Season

When the 1995 season began, Bill Pulsipher was the Mets' top pitching prospect. After a 6-4, 3.14 start at Triple-A Norfolk, he joined the major league rotation in New York on June 17. He was hit hard in his first two starts, then gave up just three hits in 7.1 innings in a 2-0 win over the Marlins. The rookie went at least six innings in every start before September 11, when pitching 200-plus innings two years in a row sidelined him with a sprained elbow ligament.

## Pitching

Pulsipher throws a low-90s fastball with good movement, including a cutter that bears in on right-handed batters. He gets them out about as easily as he retires lefthanders. Pulsipher also has a sharp-breaking curve that makes him extremely tough when he has command of it. He is working on a change-up that has been inconsistent thus far. Aside from his pitching ability, his best weapons are his bulldog competitiveness, confidence, poise and maturity. He has a mound presence beyond his years. A big strikeout pitcher in the minors, Pulsipher has not yet dominated major league hitters.

## Defense & Hitting

Very much a modern-day player in dress and appearance, Pulsipher also is a throwback. He's as good an athlete as there is among today's pitchers. He's an aggressive fielder, and he holds runners well enough that only 9 of 14 steal attempts were successful against him. He is confident, if not accomplished, in his hitting ability.

## 1996 Outlook

The only question about Pulsipher's progress is the elbow injury that shut him down last September. He didn't undergo surgery, but couldn't throw at all for eight weeks before beginning his rehabilitation. Control of his offspeed pitches could restore his strikeout level to nearly one per inning. If his elbow is sound, he has the stuff to become the Mets' ace as early as this season.

**Position:** SP
**Bats:** L  **Throws:** L
**Ht:** 6' 3"  **Wt:** 208

**Opening Day Age:** 22
**Born:** 10/9/73 in Fort Benning, GA
**ML Seasons:** 1
**Pronunciation:** PUL-suh-fer

### Overall Statistics

|  | W | L | Pct. | ERA | G | GS | Sv | IP | H | BB | SO | HR | BR/IP |
|---|---|---|---|---|---|---|---|---|---|---|---|---|---|
| 1995 | 5 | 7 | .417 | 3.98 | 17 | 17 | 0 | 126.2 | 122 | 45 | 81 | 11 | 1.32 |
| Career | 5 | 7 | .417 | 3.98 | 17 | 17 | 0 | 126.2 | 122 | 45 | 81 | 11 | 1.32 |

### How Often He Throws Strikes

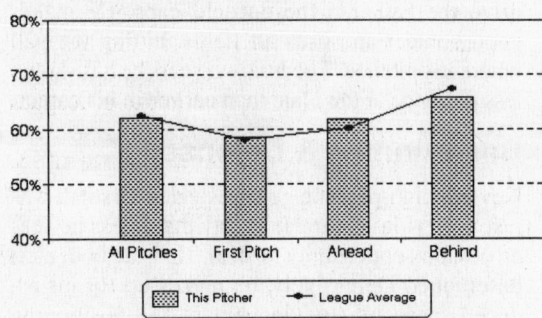

### 1995 Situational Stats

|  | W | L | ERA | Sv | IP |  | AB | H | HR | RBI | Avg |
|---|---|---|---|---|---|---|---|---|---|---|---|
| Home | 4 | 4 | 3.76 | 0 | 69.1 | LHB | 71 | 18 | 1 | 6 | .254 |
| Road | 1 | 3 | 4.24 | 0 | 57.1 | RHB | 407 | 104 | 10 | 45 | .256 |
| First Half | 1 | 4 | 4.50 | 0 | 36.0 | Sc Pos | 132 | 37 | 4 | 43 | .280 |
| Scnd Half | 4 | 3 | 3.77 | 0 | 90.2 | Clutch | 58 | 18 | 4 | 9 | .310 |

### 1995 Rankings (National League)

➨ Led the Mets in runners caught stealing (5) and GDPs induced (16)

# Kelly Stinnett

## 1995 Season

When the 1995 season began, Mets catcher Kelly Stinnett figured to spend another season platooning with Todd Hundley. Injuries to Hundley increased Stinnett's playing time, but he missed an opportunity to play even more because he sprained his right knee in May—during the same time Hundley was injured. A weak second half left Stinnett with a reduced role as the season drew to a close.

## Hitting

Stinnett has proven himself as a mistake-punisher at the plate, but the National League's pitchers have learned to stay away from his power stroke. Stinnett continues to have trouble hitting lefthanders, and his average against righties slid from his surprising .284 in 1994. He's a patient hitter who can draw walks, but his time in the major leagues thus far has worked in favor of opposing pitchers, who nearly doubled Stinnett's strikeout rate in '95.

## Baserunning & Defense

Opponents can't take Stinnett for granted on the bases just because he's a catcher. He has enough speed and has picked his spots well enough that he is 4-for-4 in his career as a basestealer. Stinnett received his major league opportunity because of his defensive ability, but last year he threw out only 14 percent of those who tried to steal against him. Stinnett and Hundley's winning rates were in a dead heat; the Mets were 37-39 in Hundley's starts, 28-30 in Stinnett's.

## 1996 Outlook

The Mets have a more than adequate supply of major league catchers. With Stinnett, Hundley and defensive whiz Alberto Castillo available, New York has trade bait. If the switch-hitting Hundley stays in New York, he isn't likely to be platooned, and Stinnett's role will be more limited than it was in 1994-1995. Stinnett is still good enough to be a backup on anybody's roster.

**Position:** C
**Bats:** R  **Throws:** R
**Ht:** 5'11"  **Wt:** 195

**Opening Day Age:** 26
**Born:** 2/14/70 in Lawton, OK
**ML Seasons:** 2

New York Mets

### Overall Statistics

|  | G | AB | R | H | D | T | HR | RBI | SB | BB | SO | Avg | OBP | Slg |
|---|---|---|---|---|---|---|---|---|---|---|---|---|---|---|
| 1995 | 77 | 196 | 23 | 43 | 8 | 1 | 4 | 18 | 2 | 29 | 65 | .219 | .338 | .332 |
| Career | 124 | 346 | 43 | 81 | 14 | 3 | 6 | 32 | 4 | 40 | 93 | .234 | .332 | .344 |

### Where He Hits the Ball

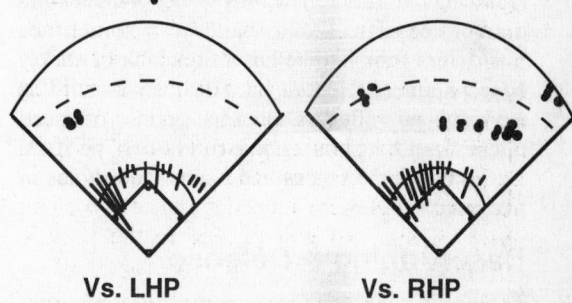

**Vs. LHP**          **Vs. RHP**

### 1995 Situational Stats

|  | AB | H | HR | RBI | Avg |  | AB | H | HR | RBI | Avg |
|---|---|---|---|---|---|---|---|---|---|---|---|
| Home | 95 | 17 | 1 | 5 | .179 | LHP | 76 | 17 | 3 | 10 | .224 |
| Road | 101 | 26 | 3 | 13 | .257 | RHP | 120 | 26 | 1 | 8 | .217 |
| First Half | 57 | 16 | 2 | 6 | .281 | Sc Pos | 50 | 11 | 1 | 14 | .220 |
| Scnd Half | 139 | 27 | 2 | 12 | .194 | Clutch | 34 | 7 | 0 | 5 | .206 |

### 1995 Rankings (National League)

➡ 1st in lowest batting average on a 3-1 count (.000)
➡ 2nd in lowest percentage of runners caught stealing as a catcher (14.3%)
➡ 5th in errors at catcher (7)

# Ryan Thompson

## 1995 Season

Dallas Green said the 1995 season would be a make-or-break year for Ryan Thompson. He didn't make it. Thompson began the year on the disabled list with a torn elbow ligament. His arm never seemed to be the same. In the second half of the season, he suffered from hamstring pulls. Thompson batted .340 in a Triple-A rehab assignment, but at the big-league level he mostly sat and watched Brett Butler, then Damon Buford and Carl Everett, playing center field. Thompson backed up at all three outfield positions.

## Hitting

The biggest problem with Thompson's game is a recurring inability to keep his swing compact and disciplined. His innate eagerness sometimes makes him look like he has a total lack of strike-zone judgment. He can hit a fastball as hard as anybody, but often is clueless against offspeed pitches. After he hits a home run or two, he starts swinging for the fences and opens more holes in his swing.

## Baserunning & Defense

Thompson has shown improvement as a baserunner. He has good speed, and for the first time in his career used it effectively as a basestealer (3-for-4). He can take an extra base. In the outfield, Thompson has good range and a strong arm, but because of last year's injury he had just four assists in '95. He usually plays hard in the field and on the bases.

## 1996 Outlook

Thompson and Jeff Kent were obtained from Toronto for David Cone, and Thompson never has risen to the task of trying to justify that deal. With young, talented outfielders coming up, his days as a Met could be numbered; if he stays, his role is in question. Thompson is talented enough to have value to other teams, but he really needs to find someone who can teach him, permanently, how to take a pitch. At 28, that might be a tall order.

**Position:** CF/LF/RF
**Bats:** R **Throws:** R
**Ht:** 6' 3" **Wt:** 215

**Opening Day Age:** 28
**Born:** 11/4/67 in Chestertown, MD
**ML Seasons:** 4

### Overall Statistics

|        | G   | AB  | R   | H   | D  | T | HR | RBI | SB | BB | SO  | Avg  | OBP  | Slg  |
|--------|-----|-----|-----|-----|----|---|----|-----|----|----|-----|------|------|------|
| 1995   | 75  | 267 | 39  | 67  | 13 | 0 | 7  | 31  | 3  | 19 | 77  | .251 | .306 | .378 |
| Career | 283 | 997 | 127 | 238 | 53 | 4 | 39 | 126 | 8  | 74 | 276 | .239 | .300 | .417 |

### Where He Hits the Ball

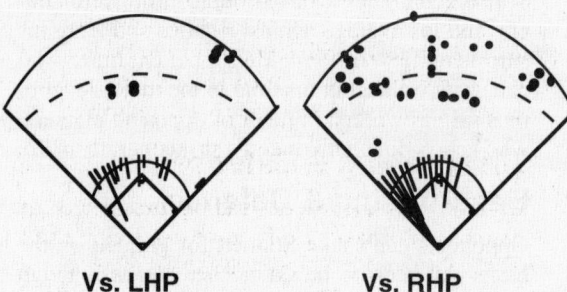

**Vs. LHP**        **Vs. RHP**

### 1995 Situational Stats

|            | AB  | H  | HR | RBI | Avg  |        | AB  | H  | HR | RBI | Avg  |
|------------|-----|----|----|-----|------|--------|-----|----|----|-----|------|
| Home       | 150 | 36 | 3  | 17  | .240 | LHP    | 73  | 21 | 2  | 7   | .288 |
| Road       | 117 | 31 | 4  | 14  | .265 | RHP    | 194 | 46 | 5  | 24  | .237 |
| First Half | 114 | 35 | 5  | 16  | .307 | Sc Pos | 69  | 16 | 1  | 22  | .232 |
| Scnd Half  | 153 | 32 | 2  | 15  | .209 | Clutch | 38  | 9  | 0  | 3   | .237 |

### 1995 Rankings (National League)

➡ 10th in lowest batting average on a 3-2 count (.100)

# Jose Vizcaino

## 1995 Season

"All I do is try to do my job and don't make much noise," says Mets shortstop Jose Vizcaino. Last year Vizcaino quietly played more than any other Met, established a career high in RBI and was named the team's best player in the second half by *USA Today Baseball Weekly*. He was at his noisiest August 21, when he drove in the winning run against the Giants in the 11th inning. That capped a five-game winning streak that propelled New York to a 28-15 finish.

## Hitting

The biggest improvement in Vizcaino's offense last year came from making sharper contact and hitting more line drives. He drilled a career-high 29 extra-base hits. Vizcaino uses the whole field and is aggressive with any pitch in or around the strike zone. He is best suited to the bottom of the batting order because he does not draw walks.

## Baserunning & Defense

Vizcaino was the Mets' leading basestealer at season's end. That in itself was no big deal. He had only eight, but his 73-percent success rate was a gigantic improvement after going 1-for-12 in 1994. For someone with decent raw speed, he has been somewhat shy about taking extra bases. Vizcaino has the arm and sure hands needed to play shortstop, and he has improved his range to the point that it's probably as good as any National Leaguer's.

## 1996 Outlook

The Mets wanted to re-sign Vizcaino as insurance in case heralded prospect Rey Ordonez isn't ready this year. The career year in 1995 gave him some bargaining leverage to stay up near the $1.355-million, one-year deal he negotiated for last season. Vizcaino has value even if he isn't the regular shortstop because he can play second or third base. He is in some demand; the Angels wanted him when Gary DiSarcina was injured last season.

**Position:** SS
**Bats:** B  **Throws:** R
**Ht:** 6' 1"  **Wt:** 180

**Opening Day Age:** 28
**Born:** 3/26/68 in Palenque de San Cristobal, DR
**ML Seasons:** 7
**Pronunciation:** vis-KAH-ee-no

New York Mets

### Overall Statistics

| | G | AB | R | H | D | T | HR | RBI | SB | BB | SO | Avg | OBP | Slg |
|---|---|---|---|---|---|---|---|---|---|---|---|---|---|---|
| 1995 | 135 | 509 | 66 | 146 | 21 | 5 | 3 | 56 | 8 | 35 | 76 | .287 | .332 | .365 |
| Career | 612 | 1961 | 224 | 527 | 69 | 17 | 11 | 172 | 27 | 137 | 271 | .269 | .315 | .338 |

### Where He Hits the Ball

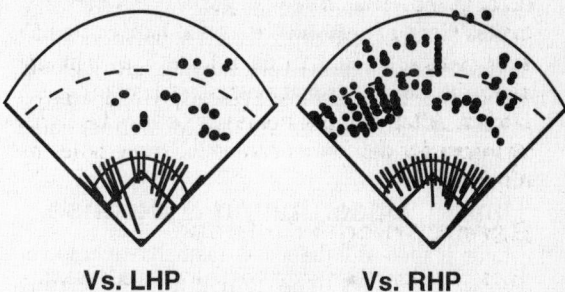

**Vs. LHP**          **Vs. RHP**

### 1995 Situational Stats

| | AB | H | HR | RBI | Avg | | AB | H | HR | RBI | Avg |
|---|---|---|---|---|---|---|---|---|---|---|---|
| Home | 263 | 76 | 2 | 31 | .289 | LHP | 130 | 45 | 0 | 9 | .346 |
| Road | 246 | 70 | 1 | 25 | .285 | RHP | 379 | 101 | 3 | 47 | .266 |
| First Half | 233 | 62 | 1 | 24 | .266 | Sc Pos | 126 | 40 | 1 | 50 | .317 |
| Scnd Half | 276 | 84 | 2 | 32 | .304 | Clutch | 97 | 24 | 0 | 13 | .247 |

### 1995 Rankings (National League)

- → 1st in fielding percentage at shortstop (.984)
- → 3rd in sacrifice bunts (13)
- → 5th in singles (117) and lowest HR frequency (169.7 ABs per HR)
- → 7th in batting average on an 0-2 count (.297) and highest percentage of swings on the first pitch (42.3%)
- → 8th in highest groundball/flyball ratio (1.9)
- → 9th in batting average vs. left-handed pitchers (.346), lowest on-base percentage vs. right-handed pitchers (.313), bunts in play (22) and steals of third (6)
- → Led the Mets in at-bats, hits, singles, GDPs (14) and plate appearances (561)

# Tim Bogar

**Position**: SS/3B
**Bats**: R  **Throws**: R
**Ht**: 6' 2"  **Wt**: 198

**Opening Day Age**: 29
**Born**: 10/28/66 in
Indianapolis, IN
**ML Seasons**: 3

## Overall Statistics

| | G | AB | R | H | D | T | HR | RBI | SB | BB | SO | Avg | OBP | Slg |
|---|---|---|---|---|---|---|---|---|---|---|---|---|---|---|
| 1995 | 78 | 145 | 17 | 42 | 7 | 0 | 1 | 21 | 1 | 9 | 25 | .290 | .329 | .359 |
| Career | 206 | 402 | 41 | 100 | 20 | 0 | 6 | 51 | 2 | 27 | 65 | .249 | .299 | .343 |

## 1995 Season

Tim Bogar is a less-talented role player in sharp contrast to the underachieving "superstars" who inhabited Shea Stadium a decade ago. He accepted and thrived in a utility role, playing left field and all four infield positions. Typically, Bogar coaxed a bases-loaded walk to win the Mets' final game in the 11th inning.

## Hitting, Baserunning & Defense

Major league righthanders' fastballs overpower Bogar, so he isn't likely to return to the starting shortstop role that he had in 1993. His value is off the bench, because he can fill in capably at so many positions. He can pinch hit because he handles left-handed pitching well and has some power. He also can pinch run—not because he's fast, but because he's alert. He's a steady fielder, but below average in range. Bogar realizes his talent is limited, and works hard and keeps himself in the game to compensate. He's a coach or manager in the making.

## 1996 Outlook

As long as he can hit lefthanders, Bogar can be valuable as a right-handed pinch hitter and defensive replacement. He is a positive influence in the clubhouse who could help the Mets develop young infielders such as Rey Ordonez and Edgardo Alfonzo. Other players have made longer careers out of less.

# Damon Buford

**Position**: CF/LF
**Bats**: R  **Throws**: R
**Ht**: 5'10"  **Wt**: 170

**Opening Day Age**: 25
**Born**: 6/12/70 in
Baltimore, MD
**ML Seasons**: 3

## Overall Statistics

| | G | AB | R | H | D | T | HR | RBI | SB | BB | SO | Avg | OBP | Slg |
|---|---|---|---|---|---|---|---|---|---|---|---|---|---|---|
| 1995 | 68 | 168 | 30 | 34 | 5 | 0 | 4 | 14 | 10 | 25 | 35 | .202 | .318 | .304 |
| Career | 125 | 249 | 50 | 53 | 10 | 0 | 6 | 23 | 12 | 34 | 55 | .213 | .318 | .325 |

## 1995 Season

Damon Buford struggled early last season with Baltimore (2-for-32), but put his game back together at Triple-A Rochester (.309 in 188 at-bats, with 17 steals). The Mets obtained Buford in the Bobby Bonilla trade and gave him his first extended major league chance. He didn't do much to impress, at least as a hitter.

## Hitting, Baserunning & Defense

Buford's skills—speed and a good batting eye, but not much power—make him a candidate to be a leadoff hitter if he can learn to handle major league pitching. And that's the big question. He did reasonably well against left-handed pitching last year, but righthanders simply overpowered him. Buford was only a .500 basestealer in '95, but he runs with the instinct of a second-generation major leaguer whose father (Don) has managed in the minors. He is a good center fielder with excellent range. He can play shallow, and has to because his arm comes up a bit short. He played mostly left field for the Mets.

## 1996 Outlook

Buford has only a long-shot chance for the everyday center-field job. There are better prospects—Carl Everett and Alex Ochoa—coming up. However, in Dallas Green's ever-shifting lineup, Buford could find playing time in left field or platooning with Everett in center.

# Paul Byrd

**Position**: RP
**Bats**: R  **Throws**: R
**Ht**: 6' 1"  **Wt**: 185

**Opening Day Age**: 25
**Born**: 12/3/70 in
Louisville, KY
**ML Seasons**: 1

*Overall Statistics*

|  | W | L | Pct. | ERA | G | GS | Sv | IP | H | BB | SO | HR | BR/IP |
|---|---|---|---|---|---|---|---|---|---|---|---|---|---|
| 1995 | 2 | 0 | 1.000 | 2.05 | 17 | 0 | 0 | 22.0 | 18 | 7 | 26 | 1 | 1.14 |
| Career | 2 | 0 | 1.000 | 2.05 | 17 | 0 | 0 | 22.0 | 18 | 7 | 26 | 1 | 1.14 |

## 1995 Season

Righthander Paul Byrd was a minor leaguer added to a trade between the Mets and Indians before last season. After pitching well as a starter and closer at Triple-A Norfolk (3-5, 2.79 ERA, 6 saves), he made his major league debut on July 28. In his short time with the Mets, Byrd quickly graduated from mop-up work to critical situations.

## Pitching, Defense & Hitting

Two adjustments helped Byrd make the final step to the majors. Mets coach Al Jackson and Norfolk pitching coach Bob Apodaca had Byrd abandon his overhead windup, keeping his hands in front of him so he could maintain focus on his target. He also started using his cut fastball more. Byrd also throws a sinking fastball, overhand curve. slurve and change-up. He throws only 86-87 MPH, so he relies on control of his curve to hit spots. He needs to work on holding runners and defense, and is no threat at bat.

## 1996 Outlook

Byrd was a pleasant surprise last season. Beginning in 1996, he's in a role almost interchangeable with Doug Henry and Jerry DiPoto. So Byrd is vulnerable to a shrinking role if he doesn't keep the pinpoint control that made him so good in 1995.

# Doug Henry

**Position**: RP
**Bats**: R  **Throws**: R
**Ht**: 6' 4"  **Wt**: 205

**Opening Day Age**: 32
**Born**: 12/10/63 in
Sacramento, CA
**ML Seasons**: 5

*Overall Statistics*

|  | W | L | Pct. | ERA | G | GS | Sv | IP | H | BB | SO | HR | BR/IP |
|---|---|---|---|---|---|---|---|---|---|---|---|---|---|
| 1995 | 3 | 6 | .333 | 2.96 | 51 | 0 | 4 | 67.0 | 48 | 25 | 62 | 7 | 1.09 |
| Career | 12 | 18 | .400 | 3.72 | 230 | 0 | 65 | 254.1 | 227 | 111 | 200 | 28 | 1.33 |

## 1995 Season

A one-pitch pitcher who had lost his closer role with Milwaukee, Doug Henry came up with a slider and a forkball in Puerto Rico the winter before the '95 season. After signing with the Mets he struggled early, but eventually rose to be the Mets' top righty reliever. Although he remained in the shadow of John Franco, Henry got some saves for the first time since mid-1993.

## Pitching, Defense & Hitting

With the Brewers, Henry threw only heat, and not always over the plate. Batters, especially lefthanders, learned to time his fastball. Last season, in addition to adding the breaking pitches and a change-up, he improved control of his four-seam fastball. Now he's a new pitcher who believes he can throw all four pitches for strikes at any time. Henry is improving at holding runners. He rarely bats.

## 1996 Outlook

In September, ex-closer Henry said that being number two in the Mets pen is fine with him. "I feel like I'm all the way back. I'm having fun setting up Franco." Henry can't be expected to displace John Franco, but he could increase his saves total with a team likely to win more often in '96.

# Butch Huskey

**Position:** 3B
**Bats:** R **Throws:** R
**Ht:** 6' 3"  **Wt:** 244

**Opening Day Age:** 24
**Born:** 11/10/71 in
Anadarko, OK
**ML Seasons:** 2

*Overall Statistics*

|  | G | AB | R | H | D | T | HR | RBI | SB | BB | SO | Avg | OBP | Slg |
|---|---|---|---|---|---|---|---|---|---|---|---|---|---|---|
| 1995 | 28 | 90 | 8 | 17 | 1 | 0 | 3 | 11 | 1 | 10 | 16 | .189 | .267 | .300 |
| Career | 41 | 131 | 10 | 23 | 2 | 0 | 3 | 14 | 1 | 11 | 29 | .176 | .234 | .260 |

## 1995 Season

Butch Huskey grew up last year. He learned to lay off the outside breaking pitches that he couldn't hit anyway, and waited for pitchers to throw him his pitch. The result was 28 home runs, 87 RBI and an International League MVP award, then an encouraging power run with the Mets before a wrist injury ended his season.

## Hitting, Baserunning & Defense

Power is Huskey's greatest strength. Spreading his feet out at the plate helped him see the ball better. Working with Norfolk manager Toby Harrah, who was an expert at drawing walks, also helped Huskey's patience. He enjoyed playing with young, hungry prospects, rather than over-the-hill Triple-A veterans. He willingly plays all three outfield positions as well as first and third base, and holds his own. His sure hands are his biggest asset at third. Especially for a big man, Huskey runs swiftly.

## 1996 Outlook

Huskey was perhaps the most improved player in the minors last season. He's out of options, but the Mets were not inclined to let him get away. They're not sure whether to use him at third or in left field, the position he was set to play in the Dominican Republic winter league. Versatility could get him 400 at-bats.

# Chris Jones

**Position:** RF/LF
**Bats:** R **Throws:** R
**Ht:** 6' 2"  **Wt:** 205

**Opening Day Age:** 30
**Born:** 12/16/65 in
Utica, NY
**ML Seasons:** 5

*Overall Statistics*

|  | G | AB | R | H | D | T | HR | RBI | SB | BB | SO | Avg | OBP | Slg |
|---|---|---|---|---|---|---|---|---|---|---|---|---|---|---|
| 1995 | 79 | 182 | 33 | 51 | 6 | 2 | 8 | 31 | 2 | 13 | 45 | .280 | .327 | .467 |
| Career | 292 | 583 | 89 | 158 | 22 | 10 | 17 | 74 | 16 | 34 | 159 | .271 | .310 | .431 |

## 1995 Season

Chris Jones was among the Mets' biggest success stories of 1995. Signed as a minor league free agent, he tore up the International League (.333 in 114 at-bats) and earned a promotion to his fourth major league club. He added to the Mets' bench strength with three game-winning pinch hits, including homers May 31 and July 29.

## Hitting, Baserunning & Defense

Jones, the Reds' first-round draft choice out of high school in 1984, is a line-drive hitter with pretty good power. He has adapted well to coming off the bench. He can hit righthanders or lefthanders, but he swings and misses too often. He also lacks patience at the plate. He has some speed, which he uses intelligently. Defensively, he has good range in left or right field. He has a strong arm, but it isn't accurate enough to discourage runners from trying for extra bases.

## 1996 Outlook

A Dallas Green favorite, Jones can continue in a similar role, as a potent right-handed bat off the bench and occasional platoon partner at first base for Rico Brogna or for an outfielder. He's the kind of role player who can make the difference for a team in contention.

# Blas Minor

**Position**: RP
**Bats**: R **Throws**: R
**Ht**: 6' 3" **Wt**: 203

**Opening Day Age**: 30
**Born**: 3/20/66 in
Merced, CA
**ML Seasons**: 4

## Overall Statistics

| | W | L | Pct. | ERA | G | GS | Sv | IP | H | BB | SO | HR | BR/IP |
|---|---|---|---|---|---|---|---|---|---|---|---|---|---|
| 1995 | 4 | 2 | .667 | 3.66 | 35 | 0 | 1 | 46.2 | 44 | 13 | 43 | 6 | 1.22 |
| Career | 12 | 9 | .571 | 4.44 | 118 | 0 | 4 | 162.0 | 168 | 48 | 144 | 18 | 1.33 |

## 1995 Season

Former Pirate Blas Minor worked in his usual middle-relief role for the Mets. He was a work-horse early in the season, then went out for a month. He returned August 25 and pitched three innings to earn his only save. By that time, Doug Henry, Jerry DiPoto and Paul Byrd had established themselves, so Blas played a truly minor role.

## Pitching, Defense & Hitting

Minor has an adequate fastball which he mixes with a curve and splitter. His repertoire was big enough to be a starter before he reached the major leagues. He needs a better change-up to retire left-handed batters. He is a good athlete who fields well, and he can hit the ball hard if he makes contact. He has a good pickoff move and holds runners very well. Only three of six basestealers last year succeeded against him.

## 1996 Outlook

Minor looked like the odd man out of the Mets bullpen in late '95. He could beat Paul Byrd out of a job, or he could resurface elsewhere. Minor has obvious talent, but hasn't really found a role in the majors, where there isn't much of a market for righty-righty match-up specialists.

# Bill Spiers

**Position**: 3B
**Bats**: L **Throws**: R
**Ht**: 6' 2" **Wt**: 190

**Opening Day Age**: 29
**Born**: 6/5/66 in
Orangeburg, SC
**ML Seasons**: 7
**Pronunciation**:
SPY-ers

## Overall Statistics

| | G | AB | R | H | D | T | HR | RBI | SB | BB | SO | Avg | OBP | Slg |
|---|---|---|---|---|---|---|---|---|---|---|---|---|---|---|
| 1995 | 63 | 72 | 5 | 15 | 2 | 1 | 0 | 11 | 0 | 12 | 15 | .208 | .314 | .264 |
| Career | 620 | 1764 | 236 | 448 | 59 | 18 | 16 | 189 | 52 | 132 | 275 | .254 | .307 | .335 |

## 1995 Season

The Mets signed veteran infielder Bill Spiers from Milwaukee, where he had his last big season before back surgery in 1991. Spiers played hurt last year, and spent some time on the disabled list because of a strained rotator cuff. A shortstop with the Brewers, he played only at second and third last year. He batted a career-low .208, with only three extra-base hits.

## Hitting, Baserunning & Defense

Spiers' development as a hitter was slowed by an inability to hit lefthanders. He's a fastball hitter who can be overmatched by sharp breaking stuff. He realizes his limited power, and compensates by keeping the ball on the ground. Spiers has developed better patience at the plate. He's not a basestealing threat, but he is an intelligent runner. Spiers used to be considered a decent infielder, but he's now a shadow of his former defensive self. He positions himself well, but primarily because of his sore arm last year he made seven errors in 11 games at third base.

## 1996 Outlook

Spiers was eligible for free agency. At this point, he must be viewed as an injury risk. Given his troubles afield in '95, he will have to show an improved arm to spark much interest. As a pinch hitter he is useful only against righties.

# Other New York Mets

### Jeff Barry (Pos: LF, Age: 27, Bats: B)

Barry is a 27-year-old outfielder who's had an erratic minor league hitting record. He has some speed and a little power, but the Mets' outfield situation is crowded, and they have better prospects. 1996 Outlook: C

### Mike Birkbeck (Pos: RHP, Age: 35)

A 10-game winner with the Brewers in 1988, Birkbeck made an improbable return to the majors last year and looked great in four starts. A lot of clubs need pitching, but at 35 his chances are slim. 1996 Outlook: C

### Alberto Castillo (Pos: C, Age: 26, Bats: R)

Still only 26, Castillo broke in at age 17 and has spent nine seasons in the minors. He's considered an excellent catcher, but probably won't hit enough to be more than a backup. 1996 Outlook: B

### Reid Cornelius (Pos: RHP, Age: 25)

Once considered a top prospect by the Expos, Cornelius came to the Mets in midseason last year and showed some promise in 10 starts. But they have better young pitchers, and his only hope is a trade. 1996 Outlook: C

### Don Florence (Pos: LHP, Age: 29)

A former Red Sox prospect, Florence came to the Mets in a minor league deal last year and had sub-2.00 ERAs in both Triple-A and the majors last year. He's not that good. . . doesn't throw hard enough. 1996 Outlook: C

### Brook Fordyce (Pos: C, Age: 25, Bats: R)

Considered the Mets' catcher of the future a few years ago, Fordyce hasn't developed as a hitter and now ranks well behind Todd Hundley and Kelly Stinnett. A trade would help. 1996 Outlook: C

### Aaron Ledesma (Pos: 3B, Age: 24, Bats: R)

Ledesma hit .297 at Triple-A Norfolk last year, but didn't hit homer. He has good speed, but his lack of power makes him a long shot. 1996 Outlook: C

### Kevin Lomon (Pos: RHP, Age: 24)

A former Braves prospect, Lomon came to the Mets in a deal last year and got hit hard in a six-game trial. Only 24, he will probably be in Triple-A this season, and could be back if he's effective there. 1996 Outlook: C

### Ricky Otero (Pos: LF, Age: 23, Bats: B)

One of the Mets' better prospects, Otero has speed and surprising power for a little man. He attempted to jump from Double-A to the majors last year, but failed to hit. A full year in Triple-A is likely. 1996 Outlook: C

### Dave Telgheder (Pos: RHP, Age: 29)

Telgheder has pitched for the Mets in each of the last three seasons without doing much to impress. He's running out of chances, and a move to another team would help. 1996 Outlook: C

### Pete Walker (Pos: RHP, Age: 26)

A righty reliever, Walker got into 13 games with the Mets last year and didn't do a lot to impress. His minor league record isn't that great, and he'll probably be back in Triple-A this year. 1996 Outlook: C

# New York Mets Minor League Prospects

## Organization Overview:

With New York's next generation of young pitching prodigies ready, the Mets appear poised to challenge the Braves' supremacy in the National League East. It's a familiar formula for the Mets, who in previous incarnations developed two dominant pitching staffs in winning two World Championships. Whether the current contigent measures up remains to be seen. But as if Bill Pulsipher and Jason Isringhausen's arrivals in the Big Apple last season weren't enough, along comes Paul Wilson. For more on him, see below. In addition, New York was possibly the only team in baseball to acquire quality prospects during last July's firesale of high-priced veterans. Alex Ochoa and Juan Acevedo could turn out to be equitable compensation for the departed Bobby Bonilla and Bret Saberhagen. Both will vie for playing time in 1996, and could be major components when the Mets expect to contend for a title in 1997.

### Juan Acevedo

**Position:** P
**Opening Day Age:** 25
**Bats:** R **Throws:** R
**Born:** 5/5/70 in Juarez,
**Ht:** 6' 2"  **Wt:** 195
Mexico

*Recent Statistics*

|  | W | L | ERA | G | GS | Sv | IP | H | R | BB | SO | HR |
|---|---|---|---|---|---|---|---|---|---|---|---|---|
| 95 AAA Col Spmg | 1 | 1 | 6.14 | 3 | 3 | 0 | 14.2 | 18 | 11 | 7 | 7 | 0 |
| 95 AAA Norfolk | 0 | 0 | 0.00 | 2 | 2 | 0 | 3.0 | 0 | 0 | 1 | 2 | 0 |
| 95 NL Colorado | 4 | 6 | 6.44 | 17 | 11 | 0 | 65.2 | 82 | 53 | 20 | 40 | 15 |

Acevedo is the pitcher the Mets held out for when they traded Bret Saberhagen to the Rockies last July. There are some people who believe Acevedo was the best pitcher in the Eastern League in 1994. That's quite a statement when you consider Bill Pulsipher and Jason Isringhausen were in the same league. Acevedo was hit hard during his tenure with Colorado last year. But if he's completely healthy and back to his previous form, Acevedo will give the Mets yet another young gun.

### Jason Hardtke

**Position:** 2B
**Opening Day Age:** 24
**Bats:** B **Throws:** R
**Born:** 9/15/71 in
**Ht:** 5' 10"  **Wt:** 175
Milwaukee, WI

*Recent Statistics*

|  | G | AB | R | H | D | T | HR | RBI | SB | BB | SO | AVG |
|---|---|---|---|---|---|---|---|---|---|---|---|---|
| 94 AA Wichita | 75 | 255 | 26 | 60 | 15 | 1 | 5 | 29 | 1 | 21 | 44 | .235 |
| 94 A Rancho Cuca | 4 | 13 | 2 | 4 | 0 | 0 | 0 | 0 | 0 | 3 | 2 | .308 |
| 95 AAA Norfolk | 4 | 7 | 1 | 2 | 1 | 0 | 0 | 0 | 1 | 2 | 0 | .286 |
| 95 AA Binghamton | 121 | 455 | 65 | 130 | 42 | 4 | 4 | 52 | 6 | 66 | 58 | .286 |
| 95 MLE | 125 | 444 | 52 | 114 | 35 | 2 | 3 | 41 | 4 | 44 | 62 | .257 |

Hardtke is a pretty good defensive second baseman with the offensive skills to bat high in the order. Because he's been a .290 career hitter in the minors with the ability to draw walks, Hardtke has scored as many as 104 and 98 runs in a single season. He also has gap power, as last year's doubles total (42) suggests. Drafted as a shortstop by Cleveland in 1990, Hardtke has also played some third base, and could eventually be a valuable utility player.

### Alex Ochoa

**Position:** OF
**Opening Day Age:** 24
**Bats:** R **Throws:** R
**Born:** 3/29/72 in Miami
**Ht:** 6' 0"  **Wt:** 185
Lakes, FL

*Recent Statistics*

|  | G | AB | R | H | D | T | HR | RBI | SB | BB | SO | AVG |
|---|---|---|---|---|---|---|---|---|---|---|---|---|
| 95 AAA Rochester | 91 | 336 | 41 | 92 | 18 | 2 | 8 | 46 | 17 | 26 | 50 | .274 |
| 95 AAA Norfolk | 34 | 123 | 17 | 38 | 6 | 2 | 2 | 15 | 7 | 14 | 12 | .309 |
| 95 NL New York | 11 | 37 | 7 | 11 | 1 | 0 | 0 | 1 | 2 | 10 | .297 |
| 95 MLE | 125 | 441 | 46 | 112 | 20 | 2 | 6 | 48 | 17 | 31 | 64 | .254 |

Ochoa was the guy the Mets insisted on when they dealt Bobby Bonilla to the Orioles. Ochoa is the prototypical "tools" player with the ability to hit for average and power, steal bases, and make plays in the field. His throwing arm in right field may have been the best in the minors last year. He's a .290 career hitter in professional baseball, though he hasn't yet demonstrated the home-run stroke that many observers project. He could open the '96 season with the Mets.

### Rey Ordonez

**Position:** SS
**Opening Day Age:** 24
**Bats:** B **Throws:** R
**Born:** 1/11/72 in
**Ht:** 5' 9"  **Wt:** 159
Havana, Cuba

*Recent Statistics*

|  | G | AB | R | H | D | T | HR | RBI | SB | BB | SO | AVG |
|---|---|---|---|---|---|---|---|---|---|---|---|---|
| 94 A St. Lucie | 79 | 314 | 47 | 97 | 21 | 2 | 2 | 40 | 11 | 14 | 28 | .309 |
| 94 AA Binghamton | 48 | 191 | 22 | 50 | 10 | 2 | 1 | 20 | 4 | 4 | 18 | .262 |
| 95 AAA Norfolk | 125 | 439 | 49 | 94 | 21 | 4 | 2 | 50 | 11 | 27 | 50 | .214 |
| 95 MLE | 125 | 431 | 43 | 86 | 18 | 3 | 1 | 44 | 8 | 23 | 52 | .200 |

There's no doubt that Ordonez possesses the requisite range, instincts and body control to be a terrific major league defensive shortstop. He draws raves for his fielding excellence, and his wizardry with the glove has been favorably compared to Ozzie Smith. But put a bat in his hands, and unfortunately Ordonez compares to Jose Lind. Ordonez hit .214 at Triple-A Norfolk in 1995, and it was an empty .214: few walks, stolen bases, or extra-base hits. Because Ordonez is so dazzling afield, the Mets may tolerate his weak stick. But on-base and slugging percentages in the mid-to-high .200s could sorely test their patience.

## Jay Payton

**Position:** OF
**Bats:** R **Throws:** R
**Ht:** 5' 10" **Wt:** 190

**Opening Day Age:** 23
**Born:** 11/22/72 in
Zanesville, OH

### Recent Statistics

| | G | AB | R | H | D | T | HR | RBI | SB | BB | SO | AVG |
|---|---|---|---|---|---|---|---|---|---|---|---|---|
| 94 A Pittsfield | 58 | 219 | 47 | 80 | 16 | 2 | 3 | 37 | 10 | 23 | 18 | .365 |
| 94 AA Binghamton | 8 | 25 | 3 | 7 | 1 | 0 | 0 | 1 | 1 | 2 | 3 | .280 |
| 95 AA Binghamton | 85 | 357 | 59 | 123 | 20 | 3 | 14 | 54 | 16 | 29 | 32 | .345 |
| 95 AAA Norfolk | 50 | 196 | 33 | 47 | 11 | 4 | 4 | 30 | 11 | 11 | 22 | .240 |
| 95 MLE | 135 | 533 | 76 | 150 | 26 | 5 | 13 | 69 | 19 | 28 | 57 | .281 |

Payton is a line-drive hitter who in 1994 led the NCAA Division I in RBI and the New York-Penn League in batting. He was arguably the Eastern League's best hitter before earning a midseason promotion to Triple-A in 1995. Although he continued to be a .300 hitter, Payton surpised some people in the organization by generating 18 home runs. Though he lacks a strong arm, Payton displays enough speed to cover center field and steal 30 bases a year. He could be ready for the majors sometime in '96.

## Robert Person

**Position:** P
**Bats:** R **Throws:** R
**Ht:** 5' 11" **Wt:** 180

**Opening Day Age:** 26
**Born:** 10/6/69 in St.
Louis, MO

### Recent Statistics

| | W | L | ERA | G | GS | Sv | IP | H | R | BB | SO | HR |
|---|---|---|---|---|---|---|---|---|---|---|---|---|
| 95 AA Binghamton | 5 | 4 | 3.11 | 26 | 7 | 7 | 66.2 | 46 | 27 | 25 | 65 | 4 |
| 95 AAA Norfolk | 2 | 1 | 4.50 | 5 | 4 | 0 | 32.0 | 30 | 17 | 13 | 33 | 2 |
| 95 NL New York | 1 | 0 | 0.75 | 3 | 1 | 0 | 12.0 | 5 | 1 | 2 | 10 | 1 |

Person now has seven minor league seasons under his belt, but he appears to have finally found his niche. Originally selected by Cleveland in the 25th round of the 1989 draft as a shortstop/outfielder, Person's live arm convinced the Indians to convert him to the mound. He worked mostly as a starter until 1994, when he began to work some games in relief. Last year he struck out roughly one man per inning in both Double- and Triple-A. His good velocity makes him a future closer candidate.

## Paul Wilson

**Position:** P
**Bats:** R **Throws:** R
**Ht:** 6' 5" **Wt:** 235

**Opening Day Age:** 23
**Born:** 3/28/73 in
Orlando, FL

### Recent Statistics

| | W | L | ERA | G | GS | Sv | IP | H | R | BB | SO | HR |
|---|---|---|---|---|---|---|---|---|---|---|---|---|
| 94 R Mets | 0 | 2 | 3.00 | 3 | 3 | 0 | 12.0 | 8 | 4 | 4 | 13 | 0 |
| 94 A St. Lucie | 0 | 5 | 5.06 | 8 | 8 | 0 | 37.1 | 32 | 23 | 17 | 37 | 3 |
| 95 AA Binghamton | 6 | 3 | 2.17 | 16 | 16 | 0 | 120.1 | 89 | 34 | 24 | 127 | 5 |
| 95 AAA Norfolk | 5 | 3 | 2.85 | 10 | 10 | 0 | 66.1 | 59 | 25 | 20 | 67 | 3 |

Bill Pulsipher and Jason Isringhausen generated a lot of excitement last summer with their impressive major league debuts, but in the long run Wilson could have the greatest impact for the Mets. Wilson was the first pick of the entire 1994 draft, and despite decent peripheral stats was winless in seven decisions his first season. The Mets weren't concerned, though, and bumped him up to Double-A, where Wilson dominated the first half of '95 before moving to the next level. Wilson is a classic power pitcher with a good fastball, slider and disruptive change.

## Preston Wilson

**Position:** OF
**Bats:** R **Throws:** R
**Ht:** 6' 3" **Wt:** 190

**Opening Day Age:** 21
**Born:** 7/19/74 in
Bamberg, SC

### Recent Statistics

| | G | AB | R | H | D | T | HR | RBI | SB | BB | SO | AVG |
|---|---|---|---|---|---|---|---|---|---|---|---|---|
| 93 R Kingsport | 66 | 259 | 44 | 60 | 9 | 0 | 16 | 48 | 6 | 24 | 75 | .232 |
| 93 A Pittsfield | 8 | 29 | 6 | 16 | 5 | 1 | 1 | 12 | 1 | 2 | 7 | .552 |
| 94 A Columbia | 131 | 474 | 55 | 108 | 17 | 4 | 14 | 58 | 13 | 20 | 135 | .228 |
| 95 A Columbia | 111 | 442 | 70 | 119 | 26 | 5 | 20 | 61 | 20 | 19 | 114 | .269 |

Yes, Preston is the stepson of Mookie, but he doesn't have the same hitting style as the Mets' former leadoff hitter. Preston probably possesses the greatest power potential of any Met farmhand. He was New York's top draft pick in 1992 out of high school, but it took more than a year for him to adjust to the pitching in the South Atlantic League. Wilson continues to be a free-swinger with little plate discipline. Drafted as a shortstop, it appears his home will be the outfield.

## Others to Watch

Second baseman **Jesus Azuaje** played at three levels last season, ulimately reaching Triple-A at age 22. He didn't hit as well as he did in 1994, when he batted .282 with 21 stolen bases in slow-A. . . First baseman **Omar Garcia** has spent seven seasons in the Mets' system since being drafted in the 18th round in 1989. Garcia hits for average but not much power, especially for a corner position. . . Righthander **Erik Hiljus** got to Double-A last year after going 8-4 with an ERA under three at Port St. Lucie. Maintaining his control will be key to Hiljus' future advancement. . . After slugging 12 home runs in his 1994 pro debut, the Mets were comparing outfielder **Terrance Long** favorably to Ben Grieve, the second player taken overall that season. Long struggled in A-ball last year, and will have to make some adjustments. . . Righthander **Eric Ludwick** was 13-6 with a 3.69 ERA last season. The Mets' second-round pick in '93 made it to Triple-A late last season. . . After going 7-13 with a 5.52 ERA at Triple-A in 1995, it appears **Chris Roberts** has been passed by the other good young Met pitchers. Roberts was a first-round pick in 1992, but the left-hander just isn't a strikeout pitcher. . . Which is what lefthander **Jesus Sanchez** could be. Sanchez struck out 177 Sally League batters in 169.2 innings last year.

# Toby Borland

## 1995 Season

On a Phillies pitching staff that saw more casualties than an inner-city emergency ward, Toby Borland was a much-needed durable bullpen arm. In his first full major league season, Borland was employed primarily as a middle reliever and setup man; he did see nine save opportunities, converting six of them. He had 74 relief innings—second most on the Philadelphia staff.

## Pitching

Borland uses a sidearm delivery that can be tough on right-handed hitters. However, to be successful he must keep his sinking fastball and developing split-finger fastball down in the strike zone because of their only average velocity. At his best, Borland will induce ground balls, and he can ride his fastball in on righties for the strikeout. When he gets the ball up against lefties, he gets hit, as evidenced by the .295 batting average which opposing left-handed batters compiled against him. His control is also inconsistent, and he is vulnerable when pitching behind in the count. But Borland does get decent movement with most of his pitches, which usually helps him keep the ball in the park.

## Defense & Hitting

The 6-foot-6 Borland is rather slow to the plate with his delivery, and it showed in '95, as opposing baserunners were 7-for-7 stealing against him. He's a good athlete with solid defensive instincts, but still committed two errors last season. As a reliever, Borland rarely gets to bat. He went just 1-for-5 in '95, and has just eight at-bats in his major league career.

## 1996 Outlook

Still inexpensive in terms of salary and still young enough to improve, Borland will likely be counted on to fill the same middle-inning role he held competently last season. He will probably never have a closer's stuff. But Borland is a solid, uncomplaining competitor of the type every bullpen needs.

**Position:** RP
**Bats:** R  **Throws:** R
**Ht:** 6' 6"  **Wt:** 190

**Opening Day Age:** 26
**Born:** 5/29/69 in Quitman, LA
**ML Seasons:** 2

*Philadelphia Phillies*

### Overall Statistics

|        | W | L | Pct. | ERA  | G  | GS | Sv | IP    | H   | BB | SO | HR | BR/IP |
|--------|---|---|------|------|----|----|----|-------|-----|----|----|----|-------|
| 1995   | 1 | 3 | .250 | 3.77 | 50 | 0  | 6  | 74.0  | 81  | 37 | 59 | 3  | 1.59  |
| Career | 2 | 3 | .400 | 3.32 | 74 | 0  | 7  | 108.1 | 112 | 51 | 85 | 4  | 1.50  |

### How Often He Throws Strikes

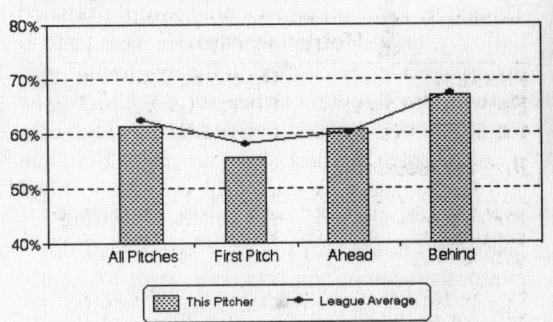

This Pitcher | League Average

### 1995 Situational Stats

|            | W | L | ERA  | Sv | IP   |        | AB  | H  | HR | RBI | Avg  |
|------------|---|---|------|----|------|--------|-----|----|----|-----|------|
| Home       | 1 | 2 | 5.56 | 3  | 34.0 | LHB    | 122 | 36 | 1  | 16  | .295 |
| Road       | 0 | 1 | 2.25 | 3  | 40.0 | RHB    | 170 | 45 | 2  | 19  | .265 |
| First Half | 0 | 0 | 6.45 | 1  | 22.1 | Sc Pos | 91  | 25 | 1  | 29  | .275 |
| Scnd Half  | 1 | 3 | 2.61 | 5  | 51.2 | Clutch | 113 | 29 | 1  | 10  | .257 |

### 1995 Rankings (National League)

→ 4th in wild pitches (12) and most baserunners allowed per 9 innings in relief (15.0)

→ 8th in highest batting average allowed in relief (.277)

→ Led the Phillies in wild pitches and most GDPs induced per GDP situation (17.9%)

# Ricky Bottalico

## 1995 Season

Rookie reliever Ricky Bottalico proved himself to be a rare jewel from the Phillies' otherwise undistinguished farm system last year. Establishing himself as one of the tougher right-handed relievers in the National League, Bottalico led the club in appearances and relief innings, while holding opposing hitters to a .167 batting average. Used almost exclusively as a set-up man, Bottalico gave up most of his hits and runs in clusters, with *two* stretches of at least 10 consecutive appearances in which he was unscored upon. He also averaged nearly a strikeout per inning pitched.

## Pitching

Though he has worked on a change-up, Bottalico basically throws everything hard. He has a fastball that is consistently clocked in the low to mid-90s. He will also throw a cut fastball. In addition, he features a late-breaking slider in the high-80s, which is often his best strikeout pitch. Bottalico still has some lapses of control and was touched for seven home runs—the result of getting his fastball up in the strike zone. He did wear down late in the season, and was shut down for nearly two weeks to rest his tired shoulder.

## Defense & Hitting

Like many power pitchers, Bottalico has plenty of room to improve his fielding. He is also vulnerable to the stolen base, though he has worked on developing at least an adequate move to first, holding runners to 6-for-9 basestealing in '95. He's no threat with the bat.

## 1996 Outlook

With the likelihood that Philadelphia will shop veteran Heathcliff Slocumb in order to drop his salary, Bottalico could enter spring training with the closer's job his to lose. The Phillies love his makeup and believe he's definitely a closer of the future. In order to make that a reality, Bottalico will need to develop better consistency with his location and pitching mechanics.

**Position:** RP
**Bats:** L  **Throws:** R
**Ht:** 6' 1"  **Wt:** 209

**Opening Day Age:** 26
**Born:** 8/26/69 in New Britain, CT
**ML Seasons:** 2
**Pronunciation:** Buh-TAL-ico

### Overall Statistics

|  | W | L | Pct. | ERA | G | GS | Sv | IP | H | BB | SO | HR | BR/IP |
|---|---|---|---|---|---|---|---|---|---|---|---|---|---|
| 1995 | 5 | 3 | .625 | 2.46 | 62 | 0 | 1 | 87.2 | 50 | 42 | 87 | 7 | 1.05 |
| Career | 5 | 3 | .625 | 2.38 | 65 | 0 | 1 | 90.2 | 53 | 43 | 90 | 7 | 1.06 |

### How Often He Throws Strikes

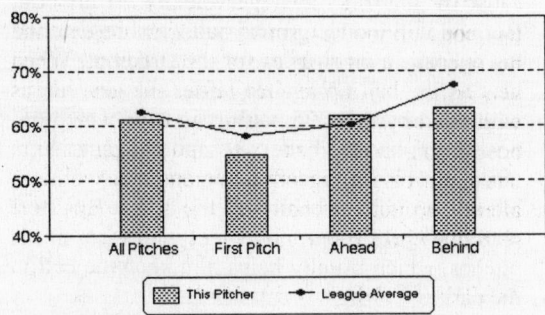

### 1995 Situational Stats

|  | W | L | ERA | Sv | IP |  | AB | H | HR | RBI | Avg |
|---|---|---|---|---|---|---|---|---|---|---|---|
| Home | 3 | 2 | 1.88 | 0 | 48.0 | LHB | 113 | 21 | 3 | 15 | .186 |
| Road | 2 | 1 | 3.18 | 1 | 39.2 | RHB | 187 | 29 | 4 | 22 | .155 |
| First Half | 3 | 1 | 1.96 | 1 | 36.2 | Sc Pos | 73 | 18 | 4 | 32 | .247 |
| Scnd Half | 2 | 2 | 2.82 | 0 | 51.0 | Clutch | 204 | 33 | 4 | 23 | .162 |

### 1995 Rankings (National League)

→ 1st in holds (20) and lowest batting average allowed in relief (.167)
→ 3rd in least baserunners allowed per 9 innings in relief (9.9)
→ 5th in relief innings (87.2)
→ 6th in most strikeouts per 9 innings in relief (8.9)
→ 8th in relief ERA (2.46)
→ 9th in highest percentage of inherited runners scored (36.1%)
→ 10th in first batter efficiency (.176)
→ Led the Phillies in games pitched, holds first batter efficiency, relief ERA, relief innings and lowest batting average allowed in relief

# Darren Daulton

## 1995 Season

The wear and tear of catching finally caught up to Darren Daulton in 1995. Daulton struggled at the plate for much of the season before seeing it end in August with torn ligaments in his right knee. Daulton previously had trouble with his shredded left knee, as well as with his shoulder. Through it all, he still managed 55 RBI—third best on what was one of baseball's lightest-hitting clubs. However, Daulton spent much of the season mired in various offensive slumps.

## Hitting

Usually a fanatical offseason conditioning advocate, Daulton cut back on his routine because of the strike and personal issues. He simply wasn't in top condition when spring training began, and never really caught up. As a result, his bat speed was noticeably slower. He pulled far fewer balls with power and lost much of his usual effectiveness hitting to left-center. He also fell back into a bad habit of jerking off too many pitches in an attempt to pull the ball. But Daulton remains a selective hitter, capable of taking a walk.

## Baserunning & Defense

All his physical difficulties have not lessened Daulton's aggressiveness on the bases, and he will still surprise with an occasional stolen base. Meanwhile, his recent shoulder difficulties have caused Daulton to develop a hitch in his throwing motion. But his quick release helps compensate for his shoulder, and he still has one of the more feared arms in the game. As a handler of pitchers, Daulton has few peers. It was a skill sorely tested last year as the Phillies employed 26 different hurlers.

## 1996 Outlook

No catcher has ever come back from reconstructive surgery on both knees, but don't bet against Daulton, who is confident about his chances of being ready for spring training. But at age 34, he simply can't be expected to catch six out of every seven games. His days as one of the game's best catchers may be behind him.

**Position:** C
**Bats:** L **Throws:** R
**Ht:** 6' 2" **Wt:** 200

**Opening Day Age:** 34
**Born:** 1/3/62 in Arkansas City, KS
**ML Seasons:** 12

### Overall Statistics

|  | G | AB | R | H | D | T | HR | RBI | SB | BB | SO | Avg | OBP | Slg |
|---|---|---|---|---|---|---|---|---|---|---|---|---|---|---|
| 1995 | 98 | 342 | 44 | 85 | 19 | 3 | 9 | 55 | 3 | 55 | 52 | .249 | .359 | .401 |
| Career | 1020 | 3223 | 440 | 785 | 176 | 17 | 123 | 525 | 44 | 546 | 647 | .244 | .354 | .423 |

### Where He Hits the Ball

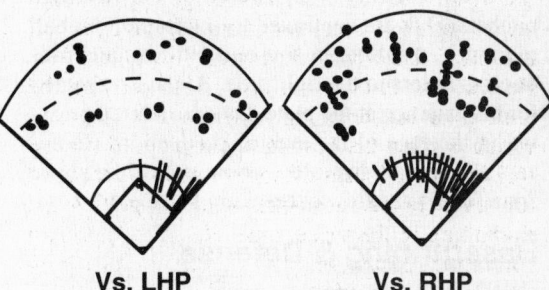

Vs. LHP       Vs. RHP

### 1995 Situational Stats

|  | AB | H | HR | RBI | Avg |  | AB | H | HR | RBI | Avg |
|---|---|---|---|---|---|---|---|---|---|---|---|
| Home | 176 | 45 | 7 | 29 | .256 | LHP | 111 | 27 | 2 | 23 | .243 |
| Road | 166 | 40 | 2 | 26 | .241 | RHP | 231 | 58 | 7 | 32 | .251 |
| First Half | 213 | 47 | 6 | 31 | .221 | Sc Pos | 111 | 28 | 2 | 41 | .252 |
| Scnd Half | 129 | 38 | 3 | 24 | .295 | Clutch | 57 | 13 | 1 | 7 | .228 |

### 1995 Rankings (National League)

→ 1st in lowest cleanup slugging percentage (.364) and fielding percentage at catcher (.994)

→ 3rd in least GDPs per GDP situation (3.9%)

→ Led the Phillies in walks and least GDPs per GDP situation

# Lenny Dykstra

## 1995 Season

For the fourth time in five years, Lenny Dykstra missed a large portion of the season due to injuries. This time it was a back problem—believed caused by excessive weightlifting—that sidelined Dykstra intermittently and kept him from developing any momentum. Then came the knee injury that required season-ending surgery. In all, Dykstra was barely a factor in '95, managing only 18 extra-base hits and 37 runs scored while leaving a huge hole atop the Philadelphia lineup.

## Hitting

Whether it was his back or lack of conditioning, Dykstra's bat speed noticeably decreased last season. He was easily overpowered by only average pitchers. Dykstra continued trying to pull the ball too much, resulting in soft outfield flies and routine grounders to the right side. Always respected for his patience at the plate, Dykstra started pressing in the face of his lack of production. He became more anxious, often going out of the strike zone for low-and-away breaking balls.

## Baserunning & Defense

Injuries and advancing age have robbed Dykstra of much of his quickness. As a result, he has become only a fair percentage basestealer. In '95 he was noticeably slower on the bases, and was rarely able to take an extra base. His defense has suffered significant slippage as well. Dykstra's range has decreased to the point where the Phillies sent him to left field prior to his season-ending knee injury. His arm remains one of the weakest in the National League.

## 1996 Outlook

With nearly $10 million committed to Dykstra over the next two years, the Phillies are resigned to hoping he can get himself in shape and return to something close to the 1993 form that nearly made him N.L. MVP. After years of suspect conditioning habits, the Phillies were encouraged by Dykstra's offseason regimen, but he enters this season a very big question mark.

**Position:** CF
**Bats:** L **Throws:** L
**Ht:** 5'10" **Wt:** 190

**Opening Day Age:** 33
**Born:** 2/10/63 in Santa Ana, CA
**ML Seasons:** 11
**Pronunciation:** DIKE-struh
**Nickname:** Nails

### Overall Statistics

|  | G | AB | R | H | D | T | HR | RBI | SB | BB | SO | Avg | OBP | Slg |
|---|---|---|---|---|---|---|---|---|---|---|---|---|---|---|
| 1995 | 62 | 254 | 37 | 67 | 15 | 1 | 2 | 18 | 10 | 33 | 28 | .264 | .353 | .354 |
| Career | 1238 | 4425 | 781 | 1263 | 275 | 40 | 78 | 391 | 282 | 614 | 478 | .285 | .374 | .419 |

### Where He Hits the Ball

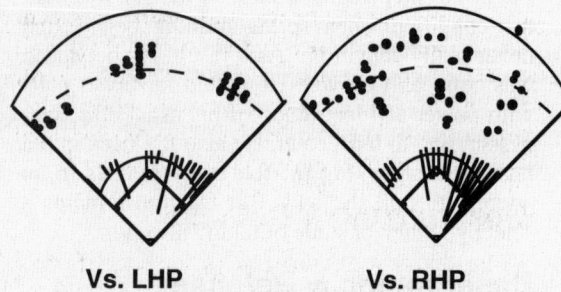

Vs. LHP          Vs. RHP

### 1995 Situational Stats

|  | AB | H | HR | RBI | Avg |  | AB | H | HR | RBI | Avg |
|---|---|---|---|---|---|---|---|---|---|---|---|
| Home | 131 | 31 | 2 | 10 | .237 | LHP | 88 | 27 | 1 | 9 | .307 |
| Road | 123 | 36 | 0 | 8 | .293 | RHP | 166 | 40 | 1 | 9 | .241 |
| First Half | 191 | 50 | 0 | 15 | .262 | Sc Pos | 53 | 16 | 0 | 15 | .302 |
| Scnd Half | 63 | 17 | 2 | 3 | .270 | Clutch | 44 | 9 | 0 | 3 | .205 |

### 1995 Rankings (National League)

→ 9th in on-base percentage for a leadoff hitter (.354)
→ Led the Phillies in stolen bases and on-base percentage for a leadoff hitter

# Jim Eisenreich

## 1995 Season

In an ideal world, Jim Eisenreich would be a platoon-type player who could be spotted to conserve his energy. However, the Phillies were anything but an ideal team in '95, and Eisenreich was forced to play virtually every day. Out of the gate quickly and among the league's leading hitters through the season's first three months, Eisenreich cooled off after the All-Star break, though he still led the Philadelphia regulars with a solid .316 average.

## Hitting

Eisenreich wears out right-handed pitching, batting .341 against righties last year. He hit 128 points lower against lefties, whom he had to see far too often last season. His hitting approach is a paradigm of simplicity, with little spare movement and a short, quick stroke that can catch up with most fastballs. He also stays back on pitches well, making him tough against breaking pitches and offspeed offerings. He usually makes contact, and is difficult to strike out except when fatigued.

## Baserunning & Defense

There are few baserunners in the league more intelligent than Eisenreich, who, despite average speed, stole 10 bases last year without being caught. He is also a model of good judgment when trying to take the extra base. A dependable outfielder, Eisenreich rarely if ever misjudges a ball, and is sure-handed on everything he reaches. His arm is average, but accurate. He makes up for his lack of arm strength by charging balls well and throwing with a quick delivery.

## 1996 Outlook

Because of the medication he must take to control his Tourette's Syndrome, Eisenreich is vulnerable to becoming fatigued. To get the maximum out of his ability, the Phillies cannot overplay him. However, given the proper rest Eisenreich should remain a quality player.

**Position:** RF/LF
**Bats:** L **Throws:** L
**Ht:** 5'11" **Wt:** 195

**Opening Day Age:** 36
**Born:** 4/18/59 in St. Cloud, MN
**ML Seasons:** 12
**Pronunciation:** EYE-zen-rike

*Philadelphia Phillies*

### Overall Statistics

|  | G | AB | R | H | D | T | HR | RBI | SB | BB | SO | Avg | OBP | Slg |
|---|---|---|---|---|---|---|---|---|---|---|---|---|---|---|
| 1995 | 129 | 377 | 46 | 119 | 22 | 2 | 10 | 55 | 10 | 38 | 44 | .316 | .375 | .464 |
| Career | 1084 | 3173 | 390 | 915 | 175 | 33 | 46 | 389 | 88 | 247 | 339 | .288 | .337 | .408 |

### Where He Hits the Ball

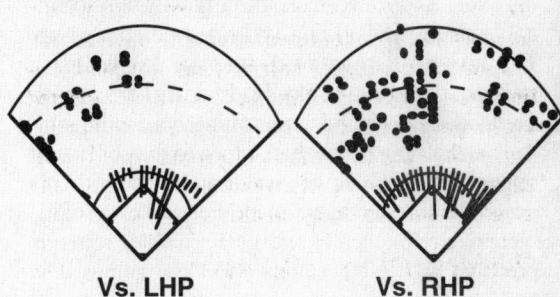

**Vs. LHP**    **Vs. RHP**

### 1995 Situational Stats

|  | AB | H | HR | RBI | Avg |  | AB | H | HR | RBI | Avg |
|---|---|---|---|---|---|---|---|---|---|---|---|
| Home | 183 | 61 | 5 | 29 | .333 | LHP | 75 | 16 | 0 | 9 | .213 |
| Road | 194 | 58 | 5 | 26 | .299 | RHP | 302 | 103 | 10 | 46 | .341 |
| First Half | 184 | 61 | 4 | 27 | .332 | Sc Pos | 110 | 33 | 1 | 43 | .300 |
| Scnd Half | 193 | 58 | 6 | 28 | .301 | Clutch | 73 | 18 | 1 | 7 | .247 |

### 1995 Rankings (National League)

→ 4th in batting average on an 0-2 count (.318) and batting average with two strikes (.304)
→ 9th in batting average on a 3-1 count (.571), batting average on a 3-2 count (.387) and highest percentage of swings put into play (53.0%)
→ Led the Phillies in stolen bases, batting average with the bases loaded (.294), batting average on a 3-1 count, batting average on an 0-2 count and highest percentage of pitches taken (59.0%)

# Sid Fernandez

## 1995 Season

Picked up after being released by Baltimore, Sid Fernandez enjoyed a surprising, albeit brief, renaissance with the Phillies. He made 11 starts for Philadelphia, six of them quality outings. With the Phillies, Fernandez was as tough to hit as he was during his glory years with the Mets, fanning 79 in 64.2 innings while holding opposing batters to a .200 average. The bad news was that Fernandez spent the last month on the sidelines with shoulder problems.

## Pitching

Taking quickly to the teachings of Phillies pitching coach Johnny Podres, Fernandez largely junked his slider and relied instead on his always-formidable rising fastball and an improved change-up. The added offspeed offering gave Fernandez a needed different look. Podres tinkered with Fernandez' mechanics, improving his erratic control and helping his fastball return to the consistent upper-80s MPH range that, combined with his deceptive motion, again made Fernandez a legitimate power pitcher. However, Fernandez remains prone to high pitch counts and slow games. His best stuff usually lasts no more than six or seven innings.

## Defense & Hitting

Despite his lumbering appearance, Fernandez is not a bad athlete. He has quick reactions and good instincts in the field; however, his slowness makes his fielding range almost nonexistent. Fernandez has a decent pickoff move to first, but his deliberate delivery home makes him very easy for basestealers to measure. Fernandez can do occasional damage as a hitter, and is a career .185 hitter.

## 1996 Outlook

The prognosis for El Sid is basically the same as for every Phillies starting pitcher. He had flashes of excellence last season that provide the promise of future rewards. However, Fernandez ended the season injured and a question mark, primarily because he has had a long history of poor conditioning. He'll arrive in spring training with something to prove.

**Position:** SP
**Bats:** L  **Throws:** L
**Ht:** 6' 1"  **Wt:** 225

**Opening Day Age:** 33
**Born:** 10/12/62 in Honolulu, HI
**ML Seasons:** 13

### Overall Statistics

|        | W   | L  | Pct. | ERA  | G   | GS  | Sv | IP     | H    | BB  | SO   | HR  | BR/IP |
|--------|-----|----|------|------|-----|-----|----|--------|------|-----|------|-----|-------|
| 1995   | 6   | 5  | .545 | 4.56 | 19  | 18  | 0  | 92.2   | 84   | 38  | 110  | 20  | 1.32  |
| Career | 110 | 90 | .550 | 3.35 | 295 | 288 | 1  | 1798.2 | 1367 | 687 | 1663 | 185 | 1.14  |

### How Often He Throws Strikes

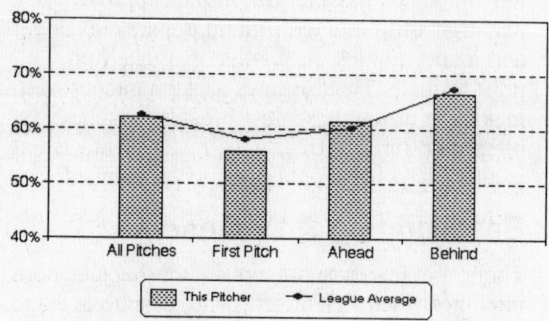

This Pitcher  —●— League Average

### 1995 Situational Stats

|            | W | L | ERA  | Sv | IP   |        | AB  | H  | HR | RBI | Avg  |
|------------|---|---|------|----|------|--------|-----|----|----|-----|------|
| Home       | 4 | 1 | 3.88 | 0  | 46.1 | LHB    | 52  | 7  | 1  | 2   | .135 |
| Road       | 2 | 4 | 5.24 | 0  | 46.1 | RHB    | 306 | 77 | 19 | 45  | .252 |
| First Half | 0 | 4 | 7.39 | 0  | 28.0 | Sc Pos | 72  | 19 | 4  | 25  | .264 |
| Scnd Half  | 6 | 1 | 3.34 | 0  | 64.2 | Clutch | 17  | 4  | 0  | 0   | .235 |

### 1995 Rankings (National League)

➡ 4th in least GDPs induced per GDP situation (2.4%)

# Tyler Green

## 1995 Season

There were two Tyler Greens pitching for Philadelphia in 1995. One of them was a member of the National League All-Star team, who rolled up eight wins and four complete games prior to the break, and seemed on his way to establishing himself as one of the league's big-time righthanders. The other Tyler Green was the second-half version, an increasingly tentative and ineffective pitcher who did not win a game after June and was ultimately yanked from the starting rotation by exasperated manager Jim Fregosi.

## Pitching

Ever since being selected as the Phillies' top draft pick in 1991, Green has been known for his tantalizing knuckle-curve. But during his excellent stretch of pitching last year, Green used the knuckle-curve as a complementary pitch to a hard, sinking fastball. He would throw the knuckle-curve and an improved change-up after being aggressive with his good fastball. But once Green suffered a few losses, he lost his aggressiveness, got away from this effective pattern, and became a nibbler—all while trying to throw a perfect pitch with his curve. The result was more walks, many more hits, and 15 home runs.

## Defense & Hitting

Green has only a fair move to first and is slow coming home, making him a target for potential basestealers. He is also just an average fielder and often finds himself in a less-than-favorable fielding position. Green has worked to become a good-hitting pitcher, and last year produced eight hits (including five doubles), a home run and five RBI, as well as eight sacrifice bunts.

## 1996 Outlook

Unlike many of his teammates, Green at least ended the 1995 season healthy. However, he had become buried in Fregosi's doghouse, and was sent to the Instructional League to work on his straying mechanics and shattered confidence. Green has shown the stuff to win in the majors. If he can learn to relax and regain his aggressiveness, he can be an important part of the Phillies' rotation.

**Position:** SP
**Bats:** R **Throws:** R
**Ht:** 6' 5" **Wt:** 204

**Opening Day Age:** 26
**Born:** 2/18/70 in Springfield, OH
**ML Seasons:** 2

Philadelphia Phillies

### Overall Statistics

|  | W | L | Pct. | ERA | G | GS | Sv | IP | H | BB | SO | HR | BR/IP |
|---|---|---|---|---|---|---|---|---|---|---|---|---|---|
| 1995 | 8 | 9 | .471 | 5.31 | 26 | 25 | 0 | 140.2 | 157 | 66 | 85 | 15 | 1.59 |
| Career | 8 | 9 | .471 | 5.41 | 29 | 27 | 0 | 148.0 | 173 | 71 | 92 | 16 | 1.65 |

### How Often He Throws Strikes

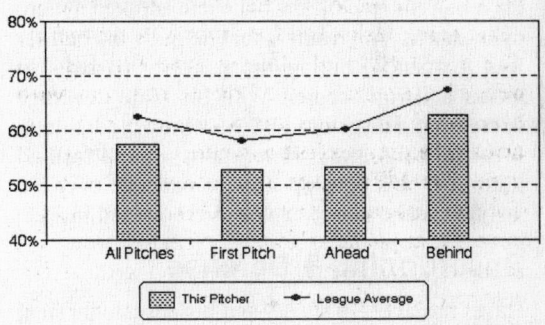

### 1995 Situational Stats

|  | W | L | ERA | Sv | IP |  | AB | H | HR | RBI | Avg |
|---|---|---|---|---|---|---|---|---|---|---|---|
| Home | 4 | 5 | 5.85 | 0 | 64.2 | LHB | 224 | 68 | 7 | 40 | .304 |
| Road | 4 | 4 | 4.86 | 0 | 76.0 | RHB | 318 | 89 | 8 | 35 | .280 |
| First Half | 8 | 4 | 2.81 | 0 | 96.0 | Sc Pos | 142 | 42 | 4 | 60 | .296 |
| Scnd Half | 0 | 5 | 10.68 | 0 | 44.2 | Clutch | 32 | 12 | 0 | 3 | .375 |

### 1995 Rankings (National League)

- ➡ 3rd in shutouts (2)
- ➡ 5th in complete games (4)
- ➡ 7th in wild pitches (9) and highest batting average allowed vs. left-handed batters (.304)
- ➡ 8th in balks (2) and highest ERA on the road (4.86)
- ➡ 10th in walks allowed
- ➡ Led the Phillies in complete games, shutouts , pickoff throws (112), runners caught stealing (7) and GDPs induced (15)

# Charlie Hayes

## 1995 Season

Philadelphia could not have asked for much more out of Charlie Hayes. He appeared in all but three games and was the Phillies' most dependable hitter. His 85 RBI led the club and were 29 more than any other Philadelphia batter. But Hayes wore down toward the end of the season, both at the plate and in the field, with his RBI production falling off considerably after the All-Star break. Although the Phillies did not expect big home-run numbers from Hayes, the fact that he managed only 11 came as a bit of a disappointment.

## Hitting

Ever since getting hit in the face by a pitch in 1994, Hayes has moved off the plate and adopted a more open stance. The result is that he pulls the ball far less frequently, hitting the majority of balls to center and right-center. With his plate coverage decreasing, Hayes has also become vulnerable to breaking balls away. He remains a good fastball hitter and he's developed more patience over the last few years, but he can be overpowered inside.

## Baserunning & Defense

Hayes has average speed, and his occasional steal attempts succeeded at a good percentage in '95. However, he is not aggressive on the bases, occasionally taking balls for granted by going less than all-out, while also being prone to hitting into double plays. His hands are as good as any third baseman's in the league, and his range is average. But Hayes continues to be plagued by an erratic throwing arm. Errors on routine plays directly led to three crucial losses during a midseason period when the Phillies were trying to keep their season together.

## 1996 Outlook

For the second time in his career, Hayes has soured the Phillies with his sometimes lackadaisical style. So despite Hayes' solid production, the Phillies will probably not re-sign him, meaning he will land on the free-agent market. At just 30 years of age, he's likely to become a solid acquisition for someone.

**Position:** 3B
**Bats:** R  **Throws:** R
**Ht:** 6' 0"  **Wt:** 224

**Opening Day Age:** 30
**Born:** 5/29/65 in Hattiesburg, MS
**ML Seasons:** 8

### Overall Statistics

|        | G   | AB   | R   | H   | D   | T  | HR | RBI | SB | BB  | SO  | Avg  | OBP  | Slg  |
|--------|-----|------|-----|-----|-----|----|----|-----|----|-----|-----|------|------|------|
| 1995   | 141 | 529  | 58  | 146 | 30  | 3  | 11 | 85  | 5  | 50  | 88  | .276 | .340 | .406 |
| Career | 941 | 3370 | 361 | 904 | 175 | 13 | 94 | 452 | 32 | 212 | 560 | .268 | .312 | .412 |

### Where He Hits the Ball

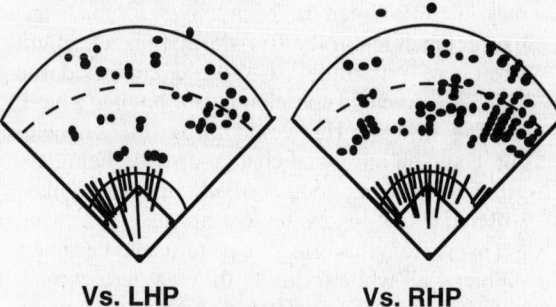

Vs. LHP          Vs. RHP

### 1995 Situational Stats

|            | AB  | H  | HR | RBI | Avg  |        | AB  | H   | HR | RBI | Avg  |
|------------|-----|----|----|-----|------|--------|-----|-----|----|-----|------|
| Home       | 257 | 74 | 6  | 45  | .288 | LHP    | 147 | 46  | 3  | 25  | .313 |
| Road       | 272 | 72 | 5  | 40  | .265 | RHP    | 382 | 100 | 8  | 60  | .262 |
| First Half | 243 | 74 | 6  | 51  | .305 | Sc Pos | 180 | 51  | 4  | 77  | .283 |
| Scnd Half  | 286 | 72 | 5  | 34  | .252 | Clutch | 88  | 23  | 2  | 14  | .261 |

### 1995 Rankings (National League)

- ➔ 1st in GDPs (23)
- ➔ 3rd in fielding percentage at third base (.963)
- ➔ 7th in errors at third base (14)
- ➔ 8th in sacrifice flies (6) and games played
- ➔ Led the Phillies in home runs, at-bats, total bases (215), RBI, sacrifice flies (6), times on base (200), strikeouts, GDPs, pitches seen (2,147), plate appearances (589) and games played

# Gregg Jefferies

## 1995 Season

Although Gregg Jefferies' statistics suggest a solid 1995 season, the numbers don't reveal just how little impact Jefferies had on the Phillies' season. During Philadelphia's early-season run of excellence, Jefferies was slumping badly. Then as the Phillies plummeted, Jefferies was often sidelined with injuries to his hamstring and thumb. And when Jefferies finally got hot over the last three months of the season, it was when the Phillies were all but out of the National League playoff hunt.

## Hitting

Jefferies' basic switch-hitting skills are as good as anyone's. His short swing allows him to wait on pitches well, and he knows the strike zone. Although he batted 65 points higher from the right side in '95, Jefferies has historically been consistent with his hitting from both sides of the plate However, he walks too infrequently for someone with his hitting ability. And with runners in scoring position, he becomes a below-average hitter, so anxious to performthat he goes after pitches off the plate.

## Baserunning & Defense

Jefferies' stolen-base totals over the last three years have gone from 46 to 12 to only nine last season. One reason for that can be traced to his hitting third in the lineup, but it is also a reflection of his leg problems and his declining degree of aggressiveness. The Phillies had hoped he could adapt to playing left field, but he was barely adequate in the outfield. He was eventually moved back to first, where he is an average fielder at best. His arm is weak.

## 1996 Outlook

With three years left on a $16 million contract, Jefferies won't be going anywhere. However, by midseason few in the Phillies' clubhouse would have been unhappy to see him leave. His cockiness turned off teammates and his refusal to take advice turned off coaches, all of which is nothing new in Jefferies' career. But he remains a top-notch hitter. If healthy, he will likely rebound with solid numbers in '96.

**Position:** 1B/LF
**Bats:** B **Throws:** R
**Ht:** 5'10" **Wt:** 185

**Opening Day Age:** 28
**Born:** 8/1/67 in Burlingame, CA
**ML Seasons:** 9
**Nickname:** Puggsly

Philadelphia Phillies

### Overall Statistics

| | G | AB | R | H | D | T | HR | RBI | SB | BB | SO | Avg | OBP | Slg |
|---|---|---|---|---|---|---|---|---|---|---|---|---|---|---|
| 1995 | 114 | 480 | 69 | 147 | 31 | 2 | 11 | 56 | 9 | 35 | 26 | .306 | .349 | .448 |
| Career | 976 | 3738 | 522 | 1106 | 214 | 18 | 91 | 474 | 149 | 325 | 247 | .296 | .352 | .436 |

### Where He Hits the Ball

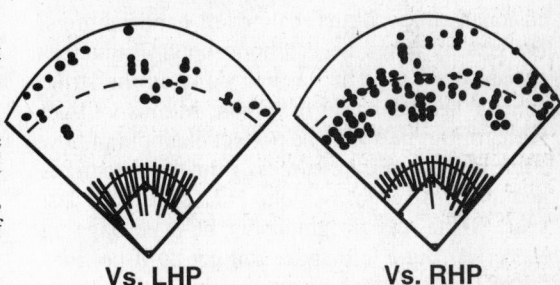

Vs. LHP          Vs. RHP

### 1995 Situational Stats

| | AB | H | HR | RBI | Avg | | AB | H | HR | RBI | Avg |
|---|---|---|---|---|---|---|---|---|---|---|---|
| Home | 211 | 69 | 4 | 31 | .327 | LHP | 151 | 53 | 4 | 15 | .351 |
| Road | 269 | 78 | 7 | 25 | .290 | RHP | 329 | 94 | 7 | 41 | .286 |
| First Half | 202 | 52 | 5 | 19 | .257 | Sc Pos | 114 | 29 | 2 | 41 | .254 |
| Scnd Half | 278 | 95 | 6 | 37 | .342 | Clutch | 90 | 29 | 2 | 12 | .322 |

### 1995 Rankings (National League)

→ 1st in lowest percentage of swings that missed (5.1%)
→ 2nd in batting average with two strikes (.315), highest percentage of swings put into play (59.0%) and lowest percentage of swings on the first pitch (14.4%)
→ 3rd in lowest percentage of extra bases taken as a runner (32.7%)
→ 7th in batting average vs. left-handed pitchers (.351)
→ Led the Phillies in batting average, home runs, runs scored, hits and singles (103)

# Michael Mimbs

## 1995 Season

Plucked from the baseball bargain basement, Michael Mimbs surprised one and all by earning a spot in the Phillies' starting rotation last spring. He proceeded to win six of his first seven decisions—including two complete games and a shutout. However, the league eventually caught up with Mimbs and he wound up in the bullpen, where he had some success in set-up and long relief roles. In all, it was a valuable season for someone who had never pitched in the major leagues.

## Pitching

No one will ever compare Mimbs to Sandy Koufax, as his sinking fastball rarely exceeds the mid-80s. He has a decent change-up and will occasionally throw a curveball to left-handed hitters. He gets by when he has good control, changes speeds, and keeps his fastball down in the strike zone. When behind in the count, Mimbs will get hit hard. But he's still the perfect example of how a lefthander can have success if he throws strikes and changes speeds. As one N.L. scout said last year, "If he was a righthander he'd be bagging groceries. But a lefthander can get by if he finds the plate, no matter how average his stuff."

## Defense & Hitting

Mimbs does not have a great pickoff move, but he'll occasionally use a slide-step to quicken his delivery home, and he allowed just four steals in 11 attempts last season. Mimbs is a decent athlete who fields his position fairly well. He's not much of a factor as a hitter, but he had eight successful sacrifices.

## 1996 Outlook

The Phillies acknowledge that Mimbs' early success was largely a mirage. But for a spot starter and long-relieving lefthander in the bullpen, the Phillies could do a lot worse on a staff riddled by injuries and question marks. Mimbs has a solid chance of sticking with the team in some kind of role.

**Position:** SP/RP
**Bats:** L **Throws:** L
**Ht:** 6' 2"  **Wt:** 180

**Opening Day Age:** 27
**Born:** 2/13/69 in Macon, GA
**ML Seasons:** 1

### Overall Statistics

|  | W | L | Pct. | ERA | G | GS | Sv | IP | H | BB | SO | HR | BR/IP |
|---|---|---|---|---|---|---|---|---|---|---|---|---|---|
| 1995 | 9 | 7 | .563 | 4.15 | 35 | 19 | 1 | 136.2 | 127 | 75 | 93 | 10 | 1.48 |
| Career | 9 | 7 | .563 | 4.15 | 35 | 19 | 1 | 136.2 | 127 | 75 | 93 | 10 | 1.48 |

### How Often He Throws Strikes

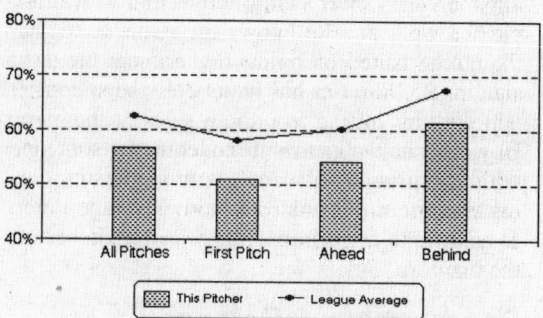

### 1995 Situational Stats

|  | W | L | ERA | Sv | IP |  | AB | H | HR | RBI | Avg |
|---|---|---|---|---|---|---|---|---|---|---|---|
| Home | 6 | 6 | 4.52 | 1 | 85.2 | LHB | 98 | 21 | 1 | 11 | .214 |
| Road | 3 | 1 | 3.53 | 0 | 51.0 | RHB | 410 | 106 | 9 | 52 | .259 |
| First Half | 6 | 4 | 3.86 | 0 | 79.1 | Sc Pos | 123 | 30 | 4 | 52 | .244 |
| Scnd Half | 3 | 3 | 4.55 | 1 | 57.1 | Clutch | 44 | 9 | 0 | 4 | .205 |

### 1995 Rankings (National League)

- ➡ 5th in walks allowed
- ➡ 7th in wild pitches (9)
- ➡ 10th in highest ERA at home (4.52)
- ➡ Led the Phillies in walks allowed, hit batsmen (6), runners caught stealing (7), winning percentage, ERA at home (4.52) and lowest batting average allowed with runners in scoring position (.244)

# Mickey Morandini

## 1995 Season

In a career that continues to show what hard work can produce, Mickey Morandini took another step by earning his first All-Star berth in 1995. Morandini achieved career highs in several offensive categories while leading the Phillies in doubles and triples. He added 49 RBI despite hitting in the number-one or -two spots for most of the season. Morandini also solidified himself as a leader on a team that went through a dizzying array of personnel changes.

## Hitting

Morandini has built up his strength to the point where he can drive the ball with authority to either right or left center, and also pull an occasional pitch for a home run. He struck out too often last year, sometimes falling into the habit of trying to pull the ball too much. Lefthanders can still make Morandini look bad, especially with fastballs. But he has become one of the better clutch hitters in the league, leading all Philadelphia regulars in hitting with men in scoring position. During Lenny Dykstra's absence, Morandini was pressed into a leadoff role. That's not his best spot, considering his strikeouts and infrequent walks.

## Baserunning & Defense

Morandini has always had solid baserunning instincts, but his speed is only average at best. He is fearless in breaking up double plays and uses excellent judgment in taking the extra base. Morandini has above-average range in the field, and hangs in as well as any second baseman while turning the double play. He's very sure-handed (only seven errors last season) and his accurate arm rounds out a complete defensive package.

## 1996 Outlook

On a team loaded with injuries, questions, and changes, Morandini has become one of the Phillies' few islands of stability. He has improved with each season, and with so many other problems on the team, Philadelphia at least knows it has a dependable second baseman. His health remains excellent, and there's no reason to believe he won't continue to produce.

**Position:** 2B
**Bats:** L **Throws:** R
**Ht:** 5'11" **Wt:** 176

**Opening Day Age:** 29
**Born:** 4/22/66 in Leechburg, PA
**ML Seasons:** 6
**Pronunciation:** Mor-an-DEE-nee

Philadelphia Phillies

### Overall Statistics

|  | G | AB | R | H | D | T | HR | RBI | SB | BB | SO | Avg | OBP | Slg |
|---|---|---|---|---|---|---|---|---|---|---|---|---|---|---|
| 1995 | 127 | 494 | 65 | 140 | 34 | 7 | 6 | 49 | 9 | 42 | 80 | .283 | .350 | .417 |
| Career | 584 | 2019 | 256 | 537 | 92 | 33 | 16 | 161 | 56 | 170 | 314 | .266 | .328 | .368 |

### Where He Hits the Ball

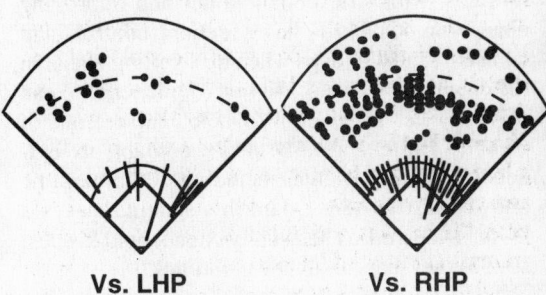

**Vs. LHP**          **Vs. RHP**

### 1995 Situational Stats

|  | AB | H | HR | RBI | Avg |  | AB | H | HR | RBI | Avg |
|---|---|---|---|---|---|---|---|---|---|---|---|
| Home | 242 | 73 | 3 | 25 | .302 | LHP | 105 | 24 | 1 | 14 | .229 |
| Road | 252 | 67 | 3 | 24 | .266 | RHP | 389 | 116 | 5 | 35 | .298 |
| First Half | 227 | 64 | 4 | 27 | .282 | Sc Pos | 107 | 37 | 2 | 44 | .346 |
| Scnd Half | 267 | 76 | 2 | 22 | .285 | Clutch | 89 | 20 | 2 | 8 | .225 |

### 1995 Rankings (National League)

- ➡ 6th in triples (7) and fielding percentage at second base (.989)
- ➡ 7th in doubles, lowest batting average vs. left-handed pitchers (.229) and errors at second base (7)
- ➡ 8th in hit by pitch (9) and batting average with runners in scoring position (.346)
- ➡ 9th in lowest on-base percentage vs. left-handed pitchers (.287)
- ➡ 10th in on-base percentage for a leadoff hitter (.353) and lowest slugging percentage vs. left-handed pitchers (.343)
- ➡ Led the Phillies in doubles, triples, caught stealing (6), hit by pitch and on-base percentage

# Paul Quantrill

## 1995 Season

No one expected Paul Quantrill to end the season as Philadelphia's most dependable starting pitcher. Then again, no one expected five different Phillies starters to land on the disabled list. But nothing should be taken away from the gritty Quantrill. He was the only Philadelphia pitcher to reach double figures in victories, and he led the staff in innings pitched—missing only one start due to injury. His durability was very valuable on a pitching staff full of scar tissue.

## Pitching

No particular pitch sets Quantrill apart. Rather, he mixes in a decent sinking fastball, usually in the mid-80s, with an excellent slider and improving change-up. Quantrill has excellent control, and can battle most lineups when he's getting ahead in the count. But he's not the sort of pitcher who can regularly get a strikeout to help him get out of trouble. Batters usually make contact, as evidenced by the 212 hits (including 20 homers) he allowed last season. Quantrill's stamina leaves a lot to be desired, as he usually cannot hold his best stuff longer than six or seven innings.

## Defense & Hitting

A former hockey player and an excellent athlete, Quantrill has outstanding instincts and fields his position very well. But his pickoff move is only average, and his quick delivery to the plate didn't do much to control the running game in '95. Runners were 20-for-24 stealing against him. Quantrill is largely overmatched as a hitter, managing six singles and seven sacrifices in '95.

## 1996 Outlook

Quantrill hardly has the stuff worthy of a number-one starter. But his continuing health and ability to eat up innings made him a fairly valuable commodity last winter, and the Toronto Blue Jays scored something of a public-relations coup by trading for Quantrill, an Ontario native. He should get a great shot at a rotation spot.

**Position:** SP
**Bats:** L **Throws:** R
**Ht:** 6' 1" **Wt:** 185

**Opening Day Age:** 27
**Born:** 11/3/68 in London, Ontario, Canada
**ML Seasons:** 4
**Pronunciation:** KWAN-trill

### Overall Statistics

|        | W  | L  | Pct. | ERA  | G   | GS | Sv | IP    | H   | BB  | SO  | HR | BR/IP |
|--------|----|----|------|------|-----|----|----|-------|-----|-----|-----|----|-------|
| 1995   | 11 | 12 | .478 | 4.67 | 33  | 29 | 0  | 179.1 | 212 | 44  | 103 | 20 | 1.43  |
| Career | 22 | 30 | .423 | 4.16 | 144 | 44 | 3  | 419.2 | 482 | 118 | 221 | 41 | 1.43  |

### How Often He Throws Strikes

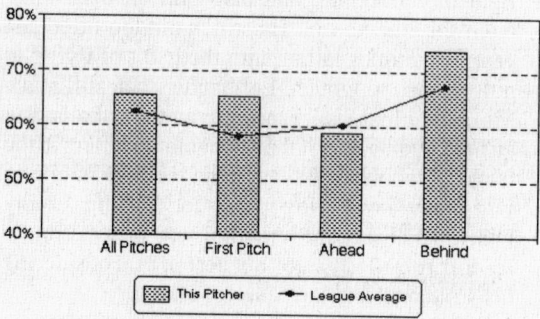

### 1995 Situational Stats

|            | W | L | ERA  | Sv | IP   |        | AB  | H   | HR | RBI | Avg  |
|------------|---|---|------|----|------|--------|-----|-----|----|-----|------|
| Home       | 5 | 6 | 4.82 | 0  | 97.0 | LHB    | 308 | 108 | 10 | 44  | .351 |
| Road       | 6 | 6 | 4.48 | 0  | 82.1 | RHB    | 411 | 104 | 10 | 49  | .253 |
| First Half | 7 | 4 | 4.31 | 0  | 87.2 | Sc Pos | 192 | 53  | 8  | 77  | .276 |
| Scnd Half  | 4 | 8 | 5.01 | 0  | 91.2 | Clutch | 45  | 13  | 3  | 8   | .289 |

### 1995 Rankings (National League)

→ 1st in highest batting average allowed vs. left-handed batters (.351)
→ 2nd in hits allowed
→ 4th in balks (3), highest batting average allowed (.295), highest slugging percentage allowed (.459) and least strikeouts per 9 innings (5.2)
→ 6th in highest stolen base percentage allowed (83.3%)
→ 7th in highest ERA and most baserunners allowed per 9 innings (13.1)
→ Led the Phillies in ERA, wins, losses, games started, innings pitched, hits allowed, batters faced (784) and home runs allowed

# Curt Schilling

## 1995 Season

Bad luck and an arm injury spoiled what looked like a return to baseball's top echelon for Phillies righty Curt Schilling. The MVP of the 1993 National League Championship Series came out of the gate pitching well, landing among the league leaders in strikeouts after three months of the season. But then Schilling developed arm problems that resulted in season-ending surgery after only 17 starts.

## Pitching

At full health early in the season, Schilling was again throwing both of his fastballs—a cutter that rides away from lefthanders, and a sinker that breaks in to lefties—consistently in the low 90s. Schilling was also able to throw strikes almost at will, not only with the fastballs, but with his excellent change-up and an occasional slider. Schilling also regained his aggressiveness. He throws inside when required, and will go after the strikeout when ahead in the count. He's prone to giving up home runs because he's around the plate so much, but his small number of walks limit that damage.

## Defense & Hitting

Schilling has worked hard to be a complete pitcher, which includes holding runners on base. He has an above-average pickoff move and a fairly quick delivery to the plate. But he's slipped a bit at controlling the running game since 1993, and baserunners did well against him last season. He rarely hurts himself in the field and is far from an automatic out at the plate. He had seven hits last year and handles the bat fairly well in bunt situations.

## 1996 Outlook

Though they'll hold their breath all spring, the Phillies seem confident that Schilling will bounce back from his latest injuries. If he's healthy and confident of his arm strength, Schilling can be one of the league's toughest righthanders—and someone capable of being Philadelphia's needed staff ace.

**Position:** SP
**Bats:** R **Throws:** R
**Ht:** 6' 4" **Wt:** 225

**Opening Day Age:** 29
**Born:** 11/14/66 in Anchorage, AK
**ML Seasons:** 8
**Pronunciation:** SHILL-ing

### Overall Statistics

| | W | L | Pct. | ERA | G | GS | Sv | IP | H | BB | SO | HR | BR/IP |
|---|---|---|---|---|---|---|---|---|---|---|---|---|---|
| 1995 | 7 | 5 | .583 | 3.57 | 17 | 17 | 0 | 116.0 | 96 | 26 | 114 | 12 | 1.05 |
| Career | 43 | 42 | .506 | 3.56 | 206 | 95 | 13 | 805.0 | 731 | 241 | 618 | 64 | 1.21 |

### How Often He Throws Strikes

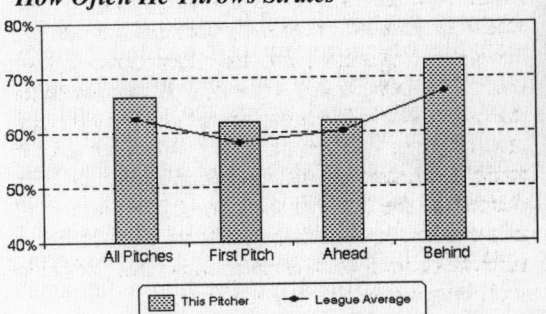

### 1995 Situational Stats

| | W | L | ERA | Sv | IP | | AB | H | HR | RBI | Avg |
|---|---|---|---|---|---|---|---|---|---|---|---|
| Home | 1 | 4 | 3.94 | 0 | 48.0 | LHB | 176 | 41 | 8 | 23 | .233 |
| Road | 6 | 1 | 3.31 | 0 | 68.0 | RHB | 261 | 55 | 4 | 20 | .211 |
| First Half | 5 | 5 | 3.41 | 0 | 103.0 | Sc Pos | 85 | 18 | 2 | 27 | .212 |
| Scnd Half | 2 | 0 | 4.85 | 0 | 13.0 | Clutch | 40 | 14 | 5 | 10 | .350 |

### 1995 Rankings (National League)

→ 5th in lowest batting average allowed vs. right-handed batters (.211)
→ 7th in lowest batting average allowed vs. left-handed batters (.233)
→ Led the Phillies in strikeouts, lowest batting average allowed vs. left-handed batters and lowest batting average allowed vs. right-handed batters

Philadelphia Phillies

# Heathcliff Slocumb

## 1995 Season

Although he cooled off in the second half, Heathcliff Slocumb had a breakthrough campaign in 1995. Given the opportunity to close games for the first time in his career, Slocumb made the N.L. All-Star team and ranked among the league leaders with 32 saves. He started off sensationally and had 20 saves and a 0.91 ERA by the end of June. Slocumb then went into a slump, once losing four times in a span of five appearances. But he rebounded, converting seven of his final eight opportunities.

## Pitching

Slocumb throws a riding fastball that is consistently in the low to mid 90s, and a hard slider capable of eating up left-handed hitters. Slocumb's control can cause him problems, however. He still hangs sliders too often, and has stretches in which he labors to get ahead in the count—forcing him to rely on fastballs that yield too many hits for someone in a closer's role. In fact, some scouts believe that despite last season's success, Slocumb's stuff is not overpowering enough to consistently make him a top-notch closer.

## Defense & Hitting

Slocumb's delivery does not leave him in good fielding position, but he has decent athletic skills. He is only average at holding runners. Opponents didn't run often against Slocumb in '95, but were usually successful when they tried. As either a set-up man or a closer, Slocumb rarely will be required to hit, which is just as well, considering he's struck out in half of his career at-bats.

## 1996 Outlook

Slocumb probably had a career season last year, which is one reason why the Phillies were shopping him late in the year in an effort to both extract prospects and dump his salary. But although he might not again have a 30-save season, Slocumb could still be of the league's better relievers. In a perfect situation he would be a set-up man, only occasionally asked to close a game.

**Position:** RP
**Bats:** R **Throws:** R
**Ht:** 6' 3"  **Wt:** 215

**Opening Day Age:** 29
**Born:** 6/7/66 in Jamaica, NY
**ML Seasons:** 5

### Overall Statistics

|  | W | L | Pct. | ERA | G | GS | Sv | IP | H | BB | SO | HR | BR/IP |
|---|---|---|---|---|---|---|---|---|---|---|---|---|---|
| 1995 | 5 | 6 | .455 | 2.89 | 61 | 0 | 32 | 65.1 | 64 | 35 | 63 | 2 | 1.52 |
| Career | 16 | 12 | .571 | 3.64 | 225 | 0 | 34 | 274.1 | 279 | 134 | 204 | 11 | 1.51 |

### How Often He Throws Strikes

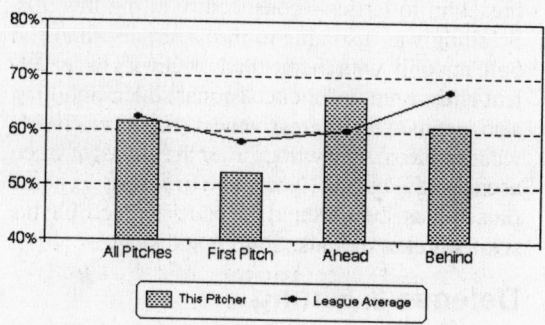

### 1995 Situational Stats

|  | W | L | ERA | Sv | IP |  |  | AB | H | HR | RBI | Avg |
|---|---|---|---|---|---|---|---|---|---|---|---|---|
| Home | 4 | 1 | 3.19 | 13 | 31.0 | LHB | | 107 | 24 | 0 | 5 | .224 |
| Road | 1 | 5 | 2.62 | 19 | 34.1 | RHB | | 142 | 40 | 2 | 25 | .282 |
| First Half | 1 | 0 | 2.14 | 20 | 33.2 | Sc Pos | | 75 | 23 | 2 | 28 | .307 |
| Scnd Half | 4 | 6 | 3.69 | 12 | 31.2 | Clutch | | 198 | 49 | 2 | 27 | .247 |

### 1995 Rankings (National League)

→ 1st in games finished (54)
→ 4th in saves and save opportunities (38)
→ 5th in relief losses (6)
→ 6th in save percentage (84.2%) and blown saves (6)
→ Led the Phillies in saves, games finished (54), save opportunities, save percentage , blown saves and relief losses

# Kevin Stocker

## 1995 Season

At a point where he should have been solidifying his career, Kevin Stocker took a major step backward in 1995. Stocker turned in a poor season both offensively and defensively, and even Phillies coach Larry Bowa, who has been Stocker's biggest supporter, was moved to say late in the season, "He's been one of our biggest disappointments this year because he let himself get beaten by a slump." Indeed, Stocker did not get his average above .200 for good until right before the All-Star break. He got very little production from his .218 batting average, and was erratic in the field to the point where he was often benched during the last two months.

## Hitting

Stocker was overpowered by both righthanders and lefthanders last year. He started chasing hard stuff out of the strike zone and often got overpowered inside. As a result, his strikeouts increased noticeably, and he lost the contact-hitting approach that had been so successful for him the previous two seasons. Stocker also started pressing as his bad year continued, and batted just .174 with men in scoring position.

## Baserunning & Defense

Stocker has only average speed but he is a good percentage basestealer. In the field, the Phillies were greatly disappointed by Stocker's performance, as he took his hitting woes to shortstop. He continued his ongoing problems with an erratic throwing arm, and last season committed several errors on routine plays. His play was a disappointment considering his solid range, good knowledge of hitters, and normally steady hands.

## 1996 Outlook

Without any realistic alternative, the Phillies are not likely to give up on Stocker. However, they'll need to see more mental toughness from him. In addition, Stocker must show he can make the adjustments necessary to return to the level that made him a solid young prospect. At age 26, he still has time to prove he can return to that level.

**Position:** SS
**Bats:** B **Throws:** R
**Ht:** 6' 1" **Wt:** 175

**Opening Day Age:** 26
**Born:** 2/13/70 in Spokane, WA
**ML Seasons:** 3

Philadelphia Phillies

### Overall Statistics

|        | G   | AB  | R   | H   | D  | T | HR | RBI | SB | BB  | SO  | Avg  | OBP  | Slg  |
|--------|-----|-----|-----|-----|----|---|----|-----|----|-----|-----|------|------|------|
| 1995   | 125 | 412 | 42  | 90  | 14 | 3 | 1  | 32  | 6  | 43  | 75  | .218 | .304 | .274 |
| Career | 277 | 942 | 126 | 248 | 37 | 8 | 5  | 91  | 13 | 117 | 159 | .263 | .357 | .335 |

### Where He Hits the Ball

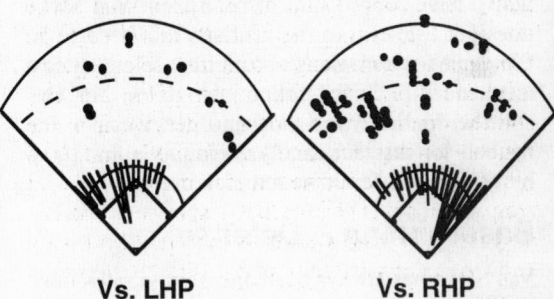

**Vs. LHP**          **Vs. RHP**

### 1995 Situational Stats

|            | AB  | H  | HR | RBI | Avg  |        | AB  | H  | HR | RBI | Avg  |
|------------|-----|----|----|-----|------|--------|-----|----|----|-----|------|
| Home       | 209 | 41 | 1  | 23  | .196 | LHP    | 115 | 25 | 0  | 9   | .217 |
| Road       | 203 | 49 | 0  | 9   | .241 | RHP    | 297 | 65 | 1  | 23  | .219 |
| First Half | 194 | 40 | 0  | 21  | .206 | Sc Pos | 109 | 19 | 0  | 31  | .174 |
| Scnd Half  | 218 | 50 | 1  | 11  | .229 | Clutch | 71  | 17 | 1  | 5   | .239 |

### 1995 Rankings (National League)

→ 1st in lowest slugging percentage, lowest slugging percentage vs. left-handed pitchers (.252), lowest slugging percentage vs. right-handed pitchers (.283) and lowest batting average at home (.196)

→ 2nd in lowest batting average, lowest batting average with runners in scoring position (.174) and lowest batting average vs. right-handed pitchers (.219)

→ 4th in lowest on-base percentage , lowest HR frequency (412.0 ABs per HR), lowest on-base percentage vs. left-handed pitchers (.268) and errors at shortstop (17)

→ Led the Phillies in sacrifice bunts (10), intentional walks (9) and hit by pitch (9)

# Andy Van Slyke

## 1995 Season

Picked up by Philadelphia in a trade after a brief, ill-fated stay in Baltimore, Andy Van Slyke showed flashes of his former All-Star form, but was otherwise hampered by assorted injuries—in particular, a badly bruised side that lingered for several weeks. Van Slyke had his moments, including a homer in his first game for Philadelphia, but overall he was unable to find any kind of groove. He finished the season with the lowest batting average of his career.

## Hitting

Many scouts believe Van Slyke's days as a premier player are behind him because of back problems, which have robbed him of bat speed. Van Slyke does not catch up to the fastballs that used to be fair game for him. He is also all but useless against left-handed pitching, hitting just .169 in '95. Despite his demise, Van Slyke can still drive an inside fastball for distance, and he remains a good gap hitter who can be difficult to defense.

## Baserunning & Defense

Van Slyke has always been one of baseball's most intelligent baserunners, but the years and the injuries have taken their toll on what used to be 30-steal speed. Although he's now only an occasional threat to run, he remains an outstanding percentage basestealer, going 7-for-7 in each of the last two seasons. No longer at his Gold Glove level, Van Slyke still performs creditibly in center field, but his range and throwing arm are perhaps more suited to left field at this point.

## 1996 Outlook

Van Slyke's future, both in Philadelphia and in major league baseball, appears to be up in the air. No team is likely to guarantee Van Slyke significant money after his two straight off-seasons. It would not be a surprise if he elected to retire and pursue a broadcasting career, which would seem perfect for his well-known wit.

**Position:** CF
**Bats:** L  **Throws:** R
**Ht:** 6' 2"  **Wt:** 198

**Opening Day Age:** 35
**Born:** 12/21/60 in Utica, NY
**ML Seasons:** 13

### Overall Statistics

|  | G | AB | R | H | D | T | HR | RBI | SB | BB | SO | Avg | OBP | Slg |
|---|---|---|---|---|---|---|---|---|---|---|---|---|---|---|
| 1995 | 80 | 277 | 32 | 62 | 11 | 2 | 6 | 24 | 7 | 33 | 56 | .224 | .309 | .343 |
| Career | 1658 | 5711 | 835 | 1562 | 293 | 91 | 164 | 792 | 245 | 667 | 1063 | .274 | .349 | .443 |

### Where He Hits the Ball

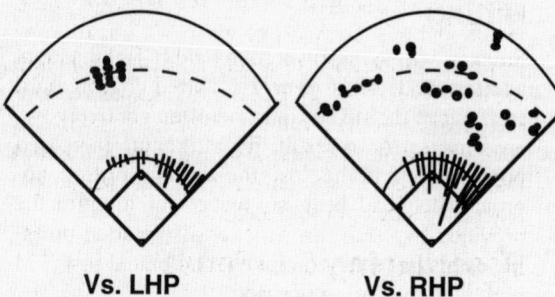

**Vs. LHP**          **Vs. RHP**

### 1995 Situational Stats

|  | AB | H | HR | RBI | Avg |  | AB | H | HR | RBI | Avg |
|---|---|---|---|---|---|---|---|---|---|---|---|
| Home | 143 | 29 | 1 | 9 | .203 | LHP | 59 | 10 | 0 | 5 | .169 |
| Road | 134 | 33 | 5 | 15 | .246 | RHP | 218 | 52 | 6 | 19 | .239 |
| First Half | 69 | 12 | 4 | 10 | .174 | Sc Pos | 68 | 11 | 0 | 13 | .162 |
| Scnd Half | 208 | 50 | 2 | 14 | .240 | Clutch | 60 | 12 | 1 | 2 | .200 |

### 1995 Rankings (National League)

➡ 1st in lowest batting average on a 3-2 count
➡ 2nd in lowest batting average with two strikes (.082)

# Mark Whiten

**Position:** RF
**Bats:** B **Throws:** R
**Ht:** 6' 3"  **Wt:** 235

**Opening Day Age:** 29
**Born:** 11/25/66 in Pensacola, FL
**ML Seasons:** 6
**Pronunciation:** WIT-en

## 1995 Season

Such a bust in Boston that he was banished to the minors, Mark Whiten resurfaced in Philadelphia last season and showed signs of reviving his career. Although he was with the Phillies for only 60 games, Whiten's 11 homers tied for the club lead. He also had several key RBI for the run-starved Phillies, supplying them with a reasonable cleanup bat after Darren Daulton was lost for the season.

## Hitting

Whiten is a notorious first-ball fastball hitter, and his impatience often gets him quickly behind in the count. It's then that he becomes highly vulnerable to strikeouts, whiffing more than once per game last season as a Phillie. He will also chase breaking balls away from him. Whiten has the power to hit the ball out to any field, and can chop the ball to get it in play. But overall, he has become too predictable as a hitter and needs to work on seeing more pitches instead of swinging at the first fastball he sees. A switch-hitter, Whiten has power from both sides of the plate.

## Baserunning & Defense

Whiten has had assorted pulled-muscle problems with his legs and groin the past couple of seasons, and as a result he's not the basestealer he once promised to be. But he remains an excellent percentage stealer, and will take the extra base if available. It's no secret that Whiten has one of baseball's best outfield throwing arms, which he too often shows off for no good reason. And though he has good range, he will occasionally get a sluggish jump on the ball.

## 1996 Outlook

Whiten's laid-back, unenthusiastic style did not sit well with many of his teammates. But his excellent athletic talent remains a tease for the Phillies—as it's been for four other major league teams. With little power within their organization and the lowest home-run total in the majors, Philadelphia seems likely to bring Whiten back, hoping he returns to the big numbers he had in St. Louis.

### Overall Statistics

| | G | AB | R | H | D | T | HR | RBI | SB | BB | SO | Avg | OBP | Slg |
|---|---|---|---|---|---|---|---|---|---|---|---|---|---|---|
| 1995 | 92 | 320 | 51 | 77 | 13 | 1 | 12 | 47 | 8 | 39 | 86 | .241 | .324 | .400 |
| Career | 633 | 2219 | 320 | 569 | 82 | 19 | 71 | 294 | 55 | 243 | 472 | .256 | .330 | .406 |

### Where He Hits the Ball

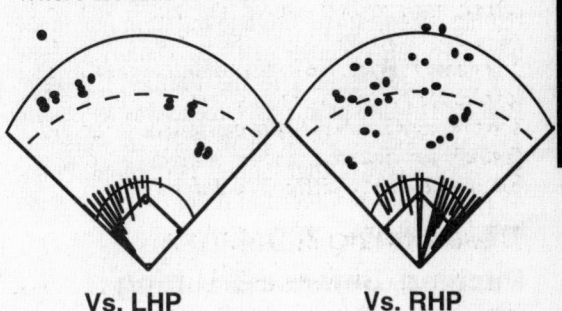

**Vs. LHP**          **Vs. RHP**

### 1995 Situational Stats

| | AB | H | HR | RBI | Avg | | AB | H | HR | RBI | Avg |
|---|---|---|---|---|---|---|---|---|---|---|---|
| Home | 177 | 43 | 5 | 26 | .243 | LHP | 110 | 23 | 6 | 15 | .209 |
| Road | 143 | 34 | 7 | 21 | .238 | RHP | 210 | 54 | 6 | 32 | .257 |
| First Half | 92 | 17 | 1 | 8 | .185 | Sc Pos | 106 | 27 | 2 | 31 | .255 |
| Scnd Half | 228 | 60 | 11 | 39 | .263 | Clutch | 62 | 14 | 4 | 12 | .226 |

### 1995 Rankings (National League)

→ 7th in errors in right field (4)
→ Led the Phillies in home runs (11) and cleanup slugging percentage (.489)

# Tommy Greene

**Position**: SP/RP
**Bats**: R **Throws**: R
**Ht**: 6' 5"  **Wt**: 222

**Opening Day Age**: 28
**Born**: 4/6/67 in
Lumberton, NC
**ML Seasons**: 7

## Overall Statistics

|  | W | L | Pct. | ERA | G | GS | Sv | IP | H | BB | SO | HR | BR/IP |
|---|---|---|---|---|---|---|---|---|---|---|---|---|---|
| 1995 | 0 | 5 | .000 | 8.29 | 11 | 6 | 0 | 33.2 | 45 | 20 | 24 | 6 | 1.93 |
| Career | 38 | 24 | .613 | 4.10 | 117 | 95 | 0 | 619.0 | 581 | 236 | 450 | 60 | 1.32 |

## 1995 Season

Failing once again to return to the form that made him a 16-game winner in 1993, Tommy Greene was a disappointment to the Phillies last year. Bothered by arm problems, Greene was winless in 11 appearances—six of them starts in which he averaged just over four innings per outing. Philadelphia looked at Greene in relief, but he was no better in that role.

## Pitching, Defense & Hitting

Even when Greene could pump his fastball in the 90s, the Phillies had to climb all over him to cut loose and stay aggressive with his hard stuff. There was also much organizational suspicion that Greene would not pitch with even a small amount of soreness in his arm. He now rarely throws harder than the mid 80s, and in addition, his control has become erratic. Greene is a solid fielder, with at best an average move to first. But considering how hard he was hit in '95, there was little reason for runners to try stealing. Though hitless last year, Greene has always been an excellent hitting pitcher.

## 1996 Outlook

Though their many pitching injuries could force the Phillies to bring Greene back for another look, there seems to be too much frustration with Greene to give him much chance to return to Philadelphia. A move to another organization is more likely.

# Jeff Juden

**Position**: SP
**Bats**: B **Throws**: R
**Ht**: 6' 8"  **Wt**: 265

**Opening Day Age**: 25
**Born**: 1/19/71 in
Salem, MA
**ML Seasons**: 4
**Pronunciation**:
JEW-den

## Overall Statistics

|  | W | L | Pct. | ERA | G | GS | Sv | IP | H | BB | SO | HR | BR/IP |
|---|---|---|---|---|---|---|---|---|---|---|---|---|---|
| 1995 | 2 | 4 | .333 | 4.02 | 13 | 10 | 0 | 62.2 | 53 | 31 | 47 | 6 | 1.34 |
| Career | 3 | 11 | .214 | 4.92 | 25 | 18 | 0 | 113.1 | 105 | 54 | 87 | 14 | 1.40 |

## 1995 Season

For eternal prospect Jeff Juden, 1995 turned into another year of teasing a team with his potential. Juden had a handful of strong outings for the Phillies, including his first complete game. But he eventually bounced between the majors and minors because of his inconsistency, pitching poorly in three of his final four starts of what was a 10-start trial in Philadelphia. They traded him to the Giants almost as soon as the season ended.

## Pitching, Defense & Hitting

The 6-foot-8 Juden can throw in the low 90s, but his habit of gaining weight and his inconsistent mechanics cause his velocity to often drop into the mid 80s. Juden also struggles to get consistent movement on his fastball, and his offspeed and breaking stuff are still not imposing. He's a ponderous fielder, and like many large pitchers has trouble keeping runners close. They ran at will against him in '95. Juden's only hit last year was a grand-slam home run, one of those aberrations akin to the arrival of Halley's Comet.

## 1996 Outlook

Like Houston before them, Philadelphia tired of dealing with Juden's unappetizing combination of a cocky attitude, lazy work habits and infrequent results. He was dumped to the pitching-needy Giants, who will take their turn at trying to light a fire under this former first-round draft pick who has never approached his potential.

# Tony Longmire

**Position**: LF
**Bats**: L **Throws**: R
**Ht**: 6' 1"  **Wt**: 202

**Opening Day Age:** 27
**Born:** 8/12/68 in
Vallejo, CA
**ML Seasons:** 3

*Overall Statistics*

|  | G | AB | R | H | D | T | HR | RBI | SB | BB | SO | Avg | OBP | Slg |
|---|---|---|---|---|---|---|---|---|---|---|---|---|---|---|
| 1995 | 59 | 104 | 21 | 37 | 7 | 0 | 3 | 19 | 1 | 11 | 19 | .356 | .419 | .510 |
| Career | 139 | 256 | 32 | 73 | 18 | 0 | 3 | 37 | 3 | 21 | 47 | .285 | .340 | .391 |

## 1995 Season

Tony Longmire was on the verge of establishing himself as a legitimate everyday major leaguer last year when a wrist injury sidelined him for the season. He had homered three times as a pinch-hitter—a role he filled well—and was hitting as a platoon regular in left field before his injury. Longmire batted .438 with men in scoring position, and demonstrated the ability to hit left-handed pitching for the first time, thus enhancing his value.

## Hitting, Baserunning & Defense

Longmire lowered his hands and shortened his stroke last year, and the results were significant. His bat speed was much improved and he was able to wait longer on breaking balls, while hanging in better against lefthanders. Longmire has used his injury time over the last two years to build himself up, and he now has legitimate power to right field. Longmire is no more than an average baserunner and has much work to do as an outfielder, where he has below-average arm strength and average range.

## 1996 Outlook

Assuming he's healthy, Longmire will likely be given a long look in the Philadelphia outfield. The Phillies need all the offense they can get, and the brief glimpses of promise shown last year by Longmire did not go unnoticed. He might make a big splash if given a full season in '96.

# Tom Marsh

**Position**: LF
**Bats**: R **Throws**: R
**Ht**: 6' 2"  **Wt**: 190

**Opening Day Age:** 30
**Born:** 12/27/65 in
Toledo, OH
**ML Seasons:** 3

*Overall Statistics*

|  | G | AB | R | H | D | T | HR | RBI | SB | BB | SO | Avg | OBP | Slg |
|---|---|---|---|---|---|---|---|---|---|---|---|---|---|---|
| 1995 | 43 | 109 | 13 | 32 | 3 | 1 | 3 | 15 | 0 | 4 | 25 | .294 | .316 | .422 |
| Career | 93 | 252 | 23 | 62 | 7 | 4 | 5 | 34 | 0 | 7 | 49 | .246 | .266 | .365 |

## 1995 Season

If effort counted for everything, then Tom Marsh would be a major league superstar. As it is, the overachieving Marsh proved his worth last year as a hard-nosed reserve outfielder and pinch hitter with occasional power. His aggressiveness was at times costly, contributing to two long spells on the injured list—one after he ran into a fence, and another following a frightening collision while trying to break up a double play.

## Hitting, Baserunning & Defense

Marsh is a free swinger who always takes his cuts early in the count. However, he has not learned to cut down his swing or protect the plate when behind in the count. Consequently, he's prone to strikeouts, especially on breaking balls. Marsh hangs in well against right-handed pitching, and can occasionally drive an inside pitch for power. He's a fearless baserunner, though his speed is just average. And he struggled last season in left field, a victim of poor range and a mediocre throwing arm.

## 1996 Outlook

The Phillies like Marsh's hard-nosed approach and his persistence through several seasons in the minors. He is not a front-line talent, but Marsh still has some value as a willing and able role player off the bench.

*Philadelphia Phillies*

# Gene Schall

**Position**: 1B
**Bats**: R **Throws**: R
**Ht**: 6' 3" **Wt**: 201

**Opening Day Age**: 25
**Born**: 6/5/70 in
Abington, PA
**ML Seasons**: 1
**Pronunciation**: Shawl

## Overall Statistics

| | G | AB | R | H | D | T | HR | RBI | SB | BB | SO | Avg | OBP | Slg |
|---|---|---|---|---|---|---|---|---|---|---|---|---|---|---|
| 1995 | 24 | 65 | 2 | 15 | 2 | 0 | 0 | 5 | 0 | 6 | 16 | .231 | .306 | .262 |
| Career | 24 | 65 | 2 | 15 | 2 | 0 | 0 | 5 | 0 | 6 | 16 | .231 | .306 | .262 |

## 1995 Season

A Philadelphia native and a graduate of Villanova, Gene Schall became a rare local product to play for the Phillies in 1995. Schall showed some flashes of promise shortly after his June call-up, but he soon began to struggle with offspeed pitches and never displayed the power he had shown in the minors. He struggled through September, striking out 15 times in just 51 at-bats.

## Hitting, Baserunning & Defense

Schall is a good fastball hitter with power to left and right-center, but he needs to quicken his long swing to adapt to major league pitching. He also lacks the discipline to lay off breaking pitches, especially when behind in the count. Schall is a below-average runner, but he does show good judgment on the bases. A first baseman with limited range and fair agility throughout his young career, the Phillies had Schall go to the Instructional League to play left field.

## 1996 Outlook

If Schall shows some power in the Instructional League and in spring training, the Phillies will likely try to make room for him. He's had two solid seasons at Triple-A and it's time for him to prove his value at the major league level. Considering the lack of power in the Philadelphia lineup last season, he's likely to get a very close look.

# Gary Varsho

**Position**: RF
**Bats**: L **Throws**: R
**Ht**: 5'11" **Wt**: 185

**Opening Day Age**: 34
**Born**: 6/20/61 in
Marshfield, WI
**ML Seasons**: 8

## Overall Statistics

| | G | AB | R | H | D | T | HR | RBI | SB | BB | SO | Avg | OBP | Slg |
|---|---|---|---|---|---|---|---|---|---|---|---|---|---|---|
| 1995 | 72 | 103 | 7 | 26 | 1 | 1 | 0 | 11 | 2 | 7 | 17 | .252 | .310 | .282 |
| Career | 571 | 837 | 101 | 204 | 41 | 11 | 10 | 84 | 27 | 55 | 146 | .244 | .294 | .355 |

## 1995 Season

In between various stints on the disabled list, which were more for the convenience of the Phillies than for any serious injury, Gary Varsho demonstrated that he remains a decent bit player off a major league bench. Spotted almost exclusively against right-handed pitching, Varsho managed 11 RBI in his limited playing time, but faded badly after the All-Star break.

## Hitting, Baserunning & Defense

Varsho has long been resigned to part-time duty. He's never been able to hit lefthanders, making him a weapon to be used only against righties. He does not have the strength to turn on hard stuff, but in the past has been capable of spraying the ball with occasional gap power. However, that power was almost completely lacking in 1995. He has decent speed, and has usually been successful in his career picking spots to steal. Varsho was able to fill in at both left and right field last season, without hurting his team defensively.

## 1996 Outlook

As he's done in virtually every season of his career, Varsho will come to spring training without a job guaranteed. However, his savvy and experience off the bench should be of value to some club, if not Philadelphia. Approaching age 35, Varsho's experience is clearly his biggest asset.

# Lenny Webster

**Position**: C
**Bats**: R  **Throws**: R
**Ht**: 5' 9"  **Wt**: 195

**Opening Day Age**: 31
**Born**: 2/10/65 in New Orleans, LA
**ML Seasons**: 7

## Overall Statistics

|  | G | AB | R | H | D | T | HR | RBI | SB | BB | SO | Avg | OBP | Slg |
|---|---|---|---|---|---|---|---|---|---|---|---|---|---|---|
| 1995 | 49 | 150 | 18 | 40 | 9 | 0 | 4 | 14 | 0 | 16 | 27 | .267 | .337 | .407 |
| Career | 242 | 577 | 66 | 151 | 35 | 1 | 14 | 67 | 1 | 62 | 83 | .262 | .339 | .399 |

## 1995 Season

Signed as a backup catcher to Darren Daulton, Lenny Webster ended up playing more than anticipated when Daulton was lost for the season with a knee injury. After struggling during his time as an occasional fill-in when Daulton was healthy, Webster played better when he got more time. His .343 batting average in August was the highest on the Phillies, and he finished the season having started 39 games behind the plate.

## Hitting, Baserunning & Defense

Webster is a good fastball hitter who won't miss mistake pitches up and over the plate. He also will hold his own on breaking pitches, and will battle for a walk in key situations. Like most catchers, he has no speed, making him a prime double-play candidate. While a competent receiver who handles pitchers well, Webster has a very poor arm and slow release, making him susceptible to basestealers. He threw out just five of 53 runners attempting to steal in '95.

## 1996 Outlook

Philadelphia may view Webster as too expensive to keep as their backup, especially if Daulton is healthy enough to catch regularly. However, solid backup catchers with power are rare commodities, and Webster would fit on the roster of several major league clubs.

# David West

**Position**: SP
**Bats**: L  **Throws**: L
**Ht**: 6' 6"  **Wt**: 247

**Opening Day Age**: 31
**Born**: 9/1/64 in Memphis, TN
**ML Seasons**: 8

## Overall Statistics

|  | W | L | Pct. | ERA | G | GS | Sv | IP | H | BB | SO | HR | BR/IP |
|---|---|---|---|---|---|---|---|---|---|---|---|---|---|
| 1995 | 3 | 2 | .600 | 3.79 | 8 | 8 | 0 | 38.0 | 34 | 19 | 25 | 5 | 1.39 |
| Career | 29 | 36 | .446 | 4.58 | 191 | 72 | 3 | 539.0 | 487 | 293 | 411 | 64 | 1.45 |

## 1995 Season

Though he managed eight starts during the first half of the season, David West was never healthy in 1995 and ended up being lost in July with a season-ending shoulder injury. It was evident that West did not have his usual velocity, as his strikeout rate dropped from the encouraging level he had established the previous two seasons.

## Pitching, Defense & Hitting

West has developed a good curveball and effective change-up. But without his 90 plus fastball to help set them up, his other pitches are not nearly as effective. Although his ailing shoulder cut down his velocity by a significant amount, West remained very tough against left-handed hitters last season. In fact, teams continue to sit down most of their lefties against him. With a slow delivery home and no pickoff move to speak of, West remains vulnerable to the stolen base. His size contributes to his below-average fielding ability and lack of agility. But he can surprise occasionally with his bat, hitting a three-run homer last season.

## 1996 Outlook

Conditioning has always been a problem for West. Now he must overcome a major arm injury which makes his future very uncertain. If he can overcome the physical hurdles, he still has the stuff to be a winner. But that is a big "if" at this stage of his career.

Philadelphia Phillies

# Other Philadelphia Phillies

**Kyle Abbott (Pos**: LHP, **Age**: 28)

After spending 1994 in Japan, Abbott was reacquired by the Phillies for '95, but shoulder injuries continued to burden him. His performance was hopeful, but his health remains a big problem. 1996 Outlook: A

**Gary Bennett (Pos**: PH, **Age**: 23, **Bats**: R)

A catcher drafted by the Phillies in 1990, Bennett struggled for the second straight season in the minors, seeing just one game with the Phillies. 1996 Outlook: C

**Andy Carter (Pos**: LHP, **Age**: 27)

Carter was banished to the minors after four early appearances with the Phillies. He struggled at Triple-A as well, and his future is fading. 1996 Outlook: B

**Jim Deshaies (Pos**: LHP, **Age**: 35)

Hammered in Minnesota in 1994, Deshaies was a free-agent bust for the Phillies. He was released, and things look bleak at age 35. 1996 Outlook: D

**Kevin Elster (Pos**: SS, **Age**: 31, **Bats**: R)

Elster fought to keep his head above water in 1995, working his way through three organizations (Yankees, Royals, Phillies) and hit very poorly playing mostly shortstop. He has little to offer. 1996 Outlook: D

**Paul Fletcher (Pos**: RHP, **Age**: 29)

Drafted as a starting pitcher by the Phillies in 1988, Fletcher saw some heavy work at Triple-A before pitching poorly in 10 relief appearances in the majors. His age is creeping up on him. 1996 Outlook: C

**Kevin Flora (Pos**: CF, **Age**: 26, **Bats**: R)

Struggling in the minors since 1987, Flora started 1995 with California before coming over to the Phillies in August trade. He hit very poorly in Philadelphia, and declared himself a free agent. 1996 Outlook: C

**Steve Frey (Pos**: LHP, **Age**: 32)

After a rough 1994, Frey managed to play for three clubs in 1995—San Francisco, Seattle, and Philadelphia. Despite a stint on the disabled list, he put together a respectable season in relief. 1996 Outlook: A

**Mike Grace (Pos**: RHP, **Age**: 25)

Drafted by the Phillies in 1991, Grace worked his way up the ladder in 1995, spending most of the season in Double-A, but finishing with an excellent starting effort in September for Philadelphia. 1996 Outlook: B

**Pete Incaviglia (Pos**: LF, **Age**: 31)

After a year in Japan, Inky is reportedly headed back to Philadelphia, where he'd play against lefthanders and hit the ball very hard. 1996 Outlook: A

**Ryan Karp (Pos**: LHP, **Age**: 25)

A career minor leaguer, Karp pitched in just one game for the Phils. He split time between Double- and Triple-A, and his control remains sharp. 1996 Outlook: C

**Mike Lieberthal (Pos**: C, **Age**: 24, **Bats**: R)

Philadelphia's first pick in the 1990 draft, Lieberthal played a bunch last September. He hit okay, but struggled with his throwing. 1996 Outlook: B

**Bobby Munoz (Pos**: RHP, **Age**: 28)

Munoz had a disastrous 1995, spending two stints on the disabled list with elbow problems—the second one ending his season. He was rocky when he could pitch, after a brilliant 1994 for the Phillies. 1996 Outlook: A

**Omar Olivares (Pos**: RHP, **Age**: 28)

Colorado sent Olivares to the bullpen after six mostly horrible starts, and the Phillies eventually picked him up off waivers in July. He didn't pitch much better there. It's been downhill for him since 1991. 1996 Outlook: B

**Randy Ready (Pos**: 1B, **Age**: 36, **Bats**: R)

Ready came back to earth after a solid 1994, hitting very poorly for the Phillies as a pinch hitter. He's been versatile, but his career is about over. 1996 Outlook: C

**Chuck Ricci (Pos**: RHP, **Age**: 27)

Ricci made the most of his opportunity in 1995, performing well in seven relief stints while striking out nearly a batter per inning. His Triple-A season was also outstanding. 1996 Outlook: B

**Kevin Sefcik (Pos**: 3B, **Age**: 25, **Bats**: R)

Drafted by the Phils in '93, Sefcik was a September call-up who saw little action. He loves to run the bases, but hasn't drawn walks in the minors. 1996 Outlook: C

**Dennis Springer (Pos**: RHP, **Age**: 31)

Originally drafted by the Dodgers, Springer and his knuckleball were handed four starts by the Phillies in September, getting shelled in three of them. His major league chances are dwindling, but you should never count a knuckleballer out. 1996 Outook: C

**Russ Springer (Pos**: RHP, **Age**: 27)

After a poor start in California, Springer was traded to the Phillies in August, and pitched considerably better. His control has gotten better the last two seasons, and maybe his new league will help. 1996 Outlook: A

**Mike Williams (Pos**: RHP, **Age**: 27)

Williams ended 1995 on a roll, pitching extremely well in four of his last five starts during September. Batters hit just .239 against him, and his control was much better. He has a lot of promise. 1996 Outlook: A

# Philadelphia Phillies Minor League Prospects

## Organization Overview:

The Phillies made it to the World Series in 1993 with virtually no contributions from players they signed and developed themselves. Much of the credit for the Phillies' success that season was due General Manager Lee Thomas, who built the club with sharp trades and other creative roster management, knowing help from within was limited to a Kevin Stocker here or a Mike Williams there. Although the Phillies still aren't bursting at the seams with high-level talent, they do appear headed in the right direction. The last few drafts have been better, and the farm system has been injected with some quality pitching prospects. The 1994 draft, when Philadelphia selected nine pitchers in the first 11 rounds, appears especially productive. The Phillies could receive contributions from a couple of second-line talents like Gene Schall and Mike Lieberthal this season, but the impact players are probably a year or two away.

### Dave Doster

**Position:** 2B          **Opening Day Age:** 25
**Bats:** R **Throws:** R  **Born:** 10/8/70 in New
**Ht:** 5' 10" **Wt:** 185   Haven, IN

*Recent Statistics*

|  | G | AB | R | H | D | T | HR | RBI | SB | BB | SO | AVG |
|---|---|---|---|---|---|---|---|---|---|---|---|---|
| 93 A Spartanburg | 60 | 223 | 34 | 61 | 15 | 0 | 3 | 20 | 1 | 25 | 36 | .274 |
| 93 A Clearwater | 9 | 28 | 4 | 10 | 3 | 1 | 0 | 2 | 0 | 2 | 2 | .357 |
| 94 A Clearwater | 131 | 480 | 76 | 135 | 42 | 4 | 13 | 74 | 12 | 54 | 71 | .281 |
| 95 AA Reading | 139 | 551 | 84 | 146 | 39 | 3 | 21 | 79 | 11 | 51 | 61 | .265 |
| 95 MLE | 139 | 532 | 64 | 127 | 36 | 1 | 16 | 60 | 7 | 33 | 66 | .239 |

Doster wasn't drafted until the 27th round in 1993, and he played at Double-A at the age of 24 last season. But his production the last couple years has to catch somebody's attention. Doster's offensive performance has been terrific, especially for a middle infielder. In addition to last year's 21 homers at Reading, Doster has cracked more than 80 doubles since '94. His defensive numbers have also been strong, and there doesn't appear to be any reason why he can't have a major league career.

### Wayne Gomes

**Position:** P          **Opening Day Age:** 23
**Bats:** R **Throws:** R  **Born:** 1/15/73 in
**Ht:** 6' 0" **Wt:** 215   Hampton, VA

*Recent Statistics*

|  | W | L | ERA | G | GS | Sv | IP | H | R | BB | SO | HR |
|---|---|---|---|---|---|---|---|---|---|---|---|---|
| 93 A Batavia | 1 | 0 | 1.23 | 5 | 0 | 0 | 7.1 | 1 | 1 | 8 | 11 | 0 |
| 93 A Clearwater | 0 | 0 | 1.17 | 9 | 0 | 4 | 7.2 | 4 | 1 | 9 | 13 | 0 |
| 94 A Clearwater | 6 | 8 | 4.74 | 23 | 21 | 0 | 104.1 | 85 | 63 | 82 | 102 | 5 |
| 95 AA Reading | 7 | 4 | 3.96 | 22 | 22 | 0 | 104.2 | 89 | 54 | 70 | 102 | 8 |

Gomes is probably the hardest thrower in the Phillies' organization, with a fastball which stays in the mid 90s. Minor league batters have had a tough time making contact against Gomes, as his strikeout rate has hovered at roughly one per inning throughout his career. However, Gomes has struggled finding his control since being taken by Philadelphia in the first round of 1993. The Phillies have been starting Gomes so he can get more experience, but they still feel that his ultimate destination is the bullpen.

### Rich Hunter

**Position:** P          **Opening Day Age:** 21
**Bats:** R **Throws:** R  **Born:** 9/25/74 in
**Ht:** 6' 1" **Wt:** 180   Pasadena, CA

*Recent Statistics*

|  | W | L | ERA | G | GS | Sv | IP | H | R | BB | SO | HR |
|---|---|---|---|---|---|---|---|---|---|---|---|---|
| 93 R Martinsvlle | 0 | 6 | 9.55 | 13 | 9 | 0 | 49.0 | 82 | 61 | 27 | 36 | 9 |
| 94 R Martinsvlle | 3 | 2 | 4.50 | 18 | 0 | 5 | 38.0 | 31 | 19 | 9 | 39 | 3 |
| 95 A Piedmont | 10 | 2 | 2.77 | 15 | 15 | 0 | 104.0 | 79 | 37 | 19 | 80 | 3 |
| 95 A Clearwater | 6 | 0 | 2.93 | 9 | 9 | 0 | 58.1 | 62 | 23 | 7 | 46 | 3 |
| 95 AA Reading | 3 | 0 | 2.05 | 3 | 3 | 0 | 22.0 | 14 | 6 | 6 | 17 | 1 |

Hunter's numbers in his pro debut, following his selection by the Phillies in the 14th round of 1993, were downright ugly (0-6, 9.55 ERA, 82 hits allowed in 49 innings). It's hard to believe how much progress he's made in the two years since then. He was one of the minors' most successful pitchers last season, going 19-2 with a 2.73 ERA between three stops which ended in Double-A. Another positive indicator was Hunter's strikeout-to-walk ratio of 143-32, accomplished at the tender age of 20.

### Kevin Jordan

**Position:** 2B          **Opening Day Age:** 26
**Bats:** R **Throws:** R  **Born:** 10/9/69 in San
**Ht:** 6' 1" **Wt:** 185   Francisco, CA

*Recent Statistics*

|  | G | AB | R | H | D | T | HR | RBI | SB | BB | SO | AVG |
|---|---|---|---|---|---|---|---|---|---|---|---|---|
| 93 Albany-Colonie | 135 | 513 | 87 | 145 | 33 | 4 | 16 | 87 | 8 | 41 | 53 | .283 |
| 94 AAA Scrntn-WB | 81 | 314 | 44 | 91 | 22 | 1 | 12 | 57 | 0 | 29 | 28 | .290 |
| 95 AAA Scrntn-WB | 106 | 410 | 61 | 127 | 29 | 4 | 5 | 60 | 3 | 28 | 36 | .310 |
| 95 NL Philadelphia | 24 | 54 | 6 | 10 | 1 | 0 | 2 | 6 | 0 | 2 | 9 | .185 |
| 95 MLE | 106 | 394 | 48 | 111 | 27 | 2 | 3 | 47 | 2 | 22 | 38 | .282 |

Jordan finally saw some major league action with the Phillies last season. His minor league hitting record, which includes a Carolina League batting title in 1992, has always been impressive. Jordan is a .297 career hitter and has shown occasional power. He isn't flashy as a second baseman, but he gets the job done. Since he's a righthanded hitter, Jordan would seem to be a natural platoon partner for Mickey Morandini, although the Phillies may have other ideas.

## Carlton Loewer

**Position:** P | **Opening Day Age:** 22
**Bats:** B **Throws:** R | **Born:** 9/24/73 in
**Ht:** 6' 6" **Wt:** 220 | Lafayette, LA

*Recent Statistics*

|  | W | L | ERA | G | GS | Sv | IP | H | R | BB | SO | HR |
|---|---|---|---|---|---|---|---|---|---|---|---|---|
| 95 A Clearwater | 7 | 5 | 3.30 | 20 | 20 | 0 | 114.2 | 124 | 59 | 36 | 83 | 6 |
| 95 AA Reading | 4 | 1 | 2.16 | 8 | 8 | 0 | 50.0 | 42 | 17 | 31 | 35 | 3 |

The Phillies chose Loewer with the 23rd pick of the first round in 1994. He signed late and didn't make his debut until last season, when he showed little difficulty making the transition to pro ball. He never quite lived up to his potential in college, but he's a big guy with a 90 MPH fastball and a decent curve. While his record and ERA were solid last season, Loewer was not overpowering. Still, in an organization not blessed with high-level pitching talent, he could be pushed quickly.

## Ryan Nye

**Position:** P | **Opening Day Age:** 22
**Bats:** R **Throws:** R | **Born:** 6/24/73 in Biloxi,
**Ht:** 6' 2" **Wt:** 195 | MS

*Recent Statistics*

|  | W | L | ERA | G | GS | Sv | IP | H | R | BB | SO | HR |
|---|---|---|---|---|---|---|---|---|---|---|---|---|
| 94 A Batavia | 7 | 2 | 2.64 | 13 | 12 | 0 | 71.2 | 64 | 27 | 15 | 71 | 3 |
| 95 A Clearwater | 12 | 7 | 3.40 | 27 | 27 | 0 | 167.0 | 164 | 71 | 33 | 116 | 8 |

Nye was the Phillies' second round pick in 1994 out of Texas Tech. He's been successful in his two minor league seasons, posting an overall record of 19-9 to go along with an ERA of 3.17. The velocity on Nye's fastball is not more than ordinary, but it's effective because of its good sinking movement. Through 238.2 professional innings, he's yielded only 11 home runs. Nye also has command of a nice slider and rarely walks anyone.

## Scott Rolen

**Position:** 3B | **Opening Day Age:** 20
**Bats:** R **Throws:** R | **Born:** 4/4/75 in
**Ht:** 6' 4" **Wt:** 210 | Evansville, IN

*Recent Statistics*

|  | G | AB | R | H | D | T | HR | RBI | SB | BB | SO | AVG |
|---|---|---|---|---|---|---|---|---|---|---|---|---|
| 93 R Martinsvlle | 25 | 80 | 8 | 25 | 5 | 0 | 0 | 12 | 3 | 10 | 15 | .313 |
| 94 A Spartanburg | 138 | 513 | 83 | 151 | 34 | 5 | 14 | 72 | 6 | 55 | 90 | .294 |
| 95 A Clearwater | 66 | 238 | 45 | 69 | 13 | 2 | 10 | 39 | 4 | 37 | 46 | .290 |
| 95 AA Reading | 20 | 76 | 16 | 22 | 3 | 0 | 3 | 15 | 1 | 7 | 14 | .289 |

Rolen is probably the Phillies' top position prospect, though he could still be a couple years away. Drafted in the second round of 1993 out of high school, Rolen shows a nice range of skills, including power, plate discipline and the ability to hit for average. He's also a fine defensive third baseman who reached Double-A at the age of 20 last season. At 6'4" and 210 pounds, Rolen will probably get even stronger. He's very much in the Phillies' plans as their third baseman of the future.

## Larry Wimberly

**Position:** P | **Opening Day Age:** 20
**Bats:** L **Throws:** L | **Born:** 8/22/75 in
**Ht:** 6' 2" **Wt:** 185 | Winter Garden, FL

*Recent Statistics*

|  | W | L | ERA | G | GS | Sv | IP | H | R | BB | SO | HR |
|---|---|---|---|---|---|---|---|---|---|---|---|---|
| 94 R Martinsvlle | 3 | 2 | 2.58 | 13 | 13 | 0 | 69.2 | 55 | 24 | 25 | 67 | 6 |
| 95 A Piedmont | 10 | 3 | 2.67 | 24 | 24 | 0 | 135.0 | 99 | 48 | 44 | 139 | 9 |

The 1994 draft could eventually produce three starters for the Phillies' rotation. Loewer and Nye were chosen in the first two rounds that year, and were followed in round three by Wimberly. Although you wouldn't know it by glancing at Wimberly's strikeout and hits allowed totals last year, he is far from overpowering. His fastball rarely leaves the low 80s, but he throws it and a good curveball and changeup for strikes. Wimberly is roughly two years younger than Loewer and Nye, and is furthest from the majors.

## Others to Watch

Lefthander **Matt Beech** is yet another pitching prospect selected in the 1994 draft, in round seven. Beech was 11-8 with with 155 strikeouts last year, and made it to Double-A . . .Catcher **Bobby Estalella** cracked 15 homers in the Florida State League, before adding two more in AA last year. He also showed good patience at the plate, and is only 21. . .First baseman **Dan Held** was 24 last year, a tad old for high-A, but he's hit 18 and 22 homers the past two seasons. . .Outfielder **Jeremy Kendall** stole 62 bases and scored 98 runs at Spartanburg in 1994. He was limited to 36 games last year, is now 24, and has yet to establish himself in high-A . . .Outfielder **Wendell Magee** hit .353 at Clearwater before posting a .294 mark in the season's final month at Double-A. He was Philadelphia's 12th-round selection in '94. . . Reliever **Brian Stumpf** saved 28 games in low-A last year. He struck out 66 batters in 61.2 innings, but at age 23 was a little old for the classification.

# Jay Bell

**Position:** SS
**Bats:** R **Throws:** R
**Ht:** 6' 0" **Wt:** 185

**Opening Day Age:** 30
**Born:** 12/11/65 in Eglin AFB, FL
**ML Seasons:** 10

## 1995 Season

The National League player representative to the Major League Baseball Players Association, Jay Bell seemed distracted when he returned to work after the strike. Bell was hitting just .198 on June 24, but rebounded to bat .297 in his last 88 games. His inconsistency at the plate didn't carry over onto the field. He played his usual steady game and finished third among N.L. shortstops with a .978 fielding percentage.

## Hitting

As a hitter, Bell does many things well. He has decent power, especially to the gaps, and he hits the ball to all fields. Bell has a Dr. Jekyll and Mr. Hyde persona about hitting with runners on base. With no one on, he is a free swinger and prone to strike out. With men on, however, he is much more patient and makes better contact. Despite his propensity for striking out, Bell is a good number-two hitter. He is very good on the hit-and-run and an exceptional bunter.

## Baserunning & Defense

Bell has average speed and no longer steals bases. Still, he moves well enough that he doesn't clog the bases. Outfielders can't get lazy or he will take the extra base. Despite lacking great range, Bell is a solid shortstop. He is very good at going up the middle and compensates for his lack of range with good positioning and instincts. Bell has developed a softer touch over the years and his arm is above average, which could make for an easy conversion to third base later in his career.

## 1996 Outlook

After serving on the union's negotiating team during the strike, Bell showed signs of mental fatigue early last season. He is still one of the better shortstops in the game, though, and has more good years ahead. How much longer he stays in Pittsburgh is questionable. He has two years remaining on a contract paying him $9.3 million, and the budget-minded Pirates would move him in the right trade.

### Overall Statistics

| | G | AB | R | H | D | T | HR | RBI | SB | BB | SO | Avg | OBP | Slg |
|---|---|---|---|---|---|---|---|---|---|---|---|---|---|---|
| 1995 | 138 | 530 | 79 | 139 | 28 | 4 | 13 | 55 | 2 | 55 | 110 | .262 | .336 | .404 |
| Career | 1071 | 4002 | 598 | 1070 | 220 | 43 | 70 | 390 | 58 | 403 | 759 | .267 | .337 | .396 |

### Where He Hits the Ball

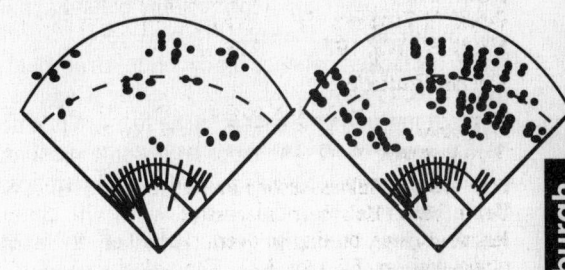

**Vs. LHP**          **Vs. RHP**

### 1995 Situational Stats

| | AB | H | HR | RBI | Avg | | AB | H | HR | RBI | Avg |
|---|---|---|---|---|---|---|---|---|---|---|---|
| Home | 260 | 59 | 8 | 25 | .227 | LHP | 144 | 44 | 7 | 17 | .306 |
| Road | 270 | 80 | 5 | 30 | .296 | RHP | 386 | 95 | 6 | 38 | .246 |
| First Half | 239 | 54 | 5 | 18 | .226 | Sc Pos | 135 | 31 | 3 | 40 | .230 |
| Scnd Half | 291 | 85 | 8 | 37 | .292 | Clutch | 91 | 24 | 0 | 9 | .264 |

### 1995 Rankings (National League)

- → 2nd in highest percentage of extra bases taken as a runner (70.5%)
- → 3rd in fielding percentage at shortstop (.978)
- → 4th in most pitches seen per plate appearance (4.09) and lowest batting average on an 0-2 count (.038)
- → 6th in strikeouts, pitches seen (2,428), lowest batting average vs. right-handed pitchers (.246) and lowest batting average at home (.227)
- → 9th in lowest slugging percentage vs. right-handed pitchers (.355)
- → Led the Pirates in at-bats, runs scored, triples, walks, strikeouts, GDPs (13), pitches seen and plate appearances (593)

# Jacob Brumfield

## 1995 Season

After coming to the Pirates last year in an offseason deal with Cincinnati, Jacob Brumfield became an everyday player for the first time in his major league career. Brumfield started slowly—a quadriceps strain that disabled him for two weeks in May was a contributing factor—but he rebounded to set career highs in nearly every offensive category. Despite suffering facial lacerations and a deep thigh bruise in an outfield collision with Dave Clark on July 25, Brumfield batted .313 and scored 27 runs in August.

## Hitting

The speedy Brumfield is mostly a singles hitter, but he has enough pop to drive some balls into the gap. While he has the speed to be a good leadoff hitter, his lack of patience hinders him. Brumfield, though, is a much better hitter when he is aggressive and jumps on the first pitch he likes. When he tries to work counts, he tends to become passive, producing strings of weak grounders and pop-ups. Brumfield is a high-ball hitter who will chase low-and-away breaking stuff. He needs to learn the strike zone and hit more balls on the ground.

## Baserunning & Defense

Brumfield has exceptional speed, but not playing regularly in the majors has compromised his ability to take full advantage of it. He doesn't get good reads on pitchers' moves and too often runs the bases with his head down. He is a very aggressive runner who has stolen home on straight steals twice in his career. Brumfield is fast enough to cover more than one outfield position, and his strong throwing arm is equally impressive.

## 1996 Outlook

Brumfield's strong finish and the Pirates' lack of a true leadoff hitter offer another chance to play on a regular basis in 1996. At 30, it's hard to imagine that he will suddenly blossom into a star. Though better suited as a fourth outfielder, he should produce another decent season as a regular.

**Position:** CF
**Bats:** R **Throws:** R
**Ht:** 6' 0" **Wt:** 185

**Opening Day Age:** 30
**Born:** 5/27/65 in Bogalusa, LA
**ML Seasons:** 4

### Overall Statistics

|  | G | AB | R | H | D | T | HR | RBI | SB | BB | SO | Avg | OBP | Slg |
|---|---|---|---|---|---|---|---|---|---|---|---|---|---|---|
| 1995 | 116 | 402 | 64 | 109 | 23 | 2 | 4 | 26 | 22 | 37 | 71 | .271 | .339 | .368 |
| Career | 311 | 826 | 146 | 224 | 50 | 7 | 14 | 62 | 54 | 75 | 140 | .271 | .335 | .400 |

### Where He Hits the Ball

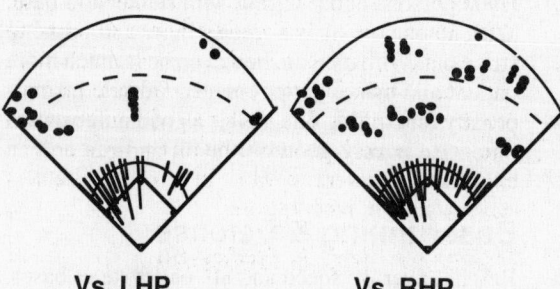

**Vs. LHP**          **Vs. RHP**

### 1995 Situational Stats

|  | AB | H | HR | RBI | Avg |  |  | AB | H | HR | RBI | Avg |
|---|---|---|---|---|---|---|---|---|---|---|---|---|
| Home | 208 | 58 | 4 | 17 | .279 | | LHP | 124 | 37 | 1 | 6 | .298 |
| Road | 194 | 51 | 0 | 9 | .263 | | RHP | 278 | 72 | 3 | 20 | .259 |
| First Half | 163 | 44 | 1 | 12 | .270 | | Sc Pos | 82 | 21 | 1 | 22 | .256 |
| Scnd Half | 239 | 65 | 3 | 14 | .272 | | Clutch | 68 | 21 | 2 | 7 | .309 |

### 1995 Rankings (National League)

➡ 1st in lowest fielding percentage in center field (.969)
➡ 2nd in errors in center field (8)
➡ 4th in caught stealing (12)
➡ 5th in lowest stolen base percentage (64.7%) and lowest on-base percentage for a leadoff hitter (.333)
➡ 10th in least GDPs per GDP situation (5.5%)
➡ Led the Pirates in stolen bases, caught stealing, hit by pitch (5), stolen base percentage (64.7%) and batting average in the clutch (.309)

# Dave Clark

## 1995 Season

Dave Clark was enjoying another productive season as a role player when he suffered a broken left collarbone in a horrific outfield collision with Jacob Brumfield on July 25. Clark was hitting .314 at the time of the injury, but batted just .150 in 18 games after returning from the disabled list in mid-September. He started 24 games in left field and another 20 in right for manager Jim Leyland.

## Hitting

The veteran outfielder is one of the few Pirates capable of hitting the ball out of the park on a regular basis. Clark, who is extremely strong with impressive bat speed, is strictly a fastball hitter. His forte is driving low pitches to all corners of the park. Pitchers succeed against him by changing speeds and going up the ladder. While Clark usually draws a decent number of walks, he also is prone to strikeouts. His struggles with left-handed pitching forced him into a platoon role, but he's handled lefties very well in limited chances against them in recent years.

## Baserunning & Defense

Clark is no threat as a basestealer, but he is very aggressive on the bases. He looks to take the extra base, always goes in hard at second to break up double plays, and doesn't hesitate to run over a catcher. Clark is a poor fielder with no range, limiting him to playing the corners. He also has major problems with balls hit over his head. Clark has a strong arm, but it is inaccurate and runners will take chances on him.

## 1996 Outlook

At the close of last season, Clark was one of just three Pirates signed for 1996 so his return is all but assured. Clark has become a terrific role player in Pittsburgh because manager Jim Leyland spots him in the right situations. He gives the Pirates some much-needed power, and he is a veteran influence in the clubhouse, something that cannot be discounted with a young Pittsburgh team.

**Position:** LF/RF
**Bats:** L  **Throws:** R
**Ht:** 6' 2"  **Wt:** 209

**Opening Day Age:** 33
**Born:** 9/3/62 in Tupelo, MS
**ML Seasons:** 10

### Overall Statistics

| | G | AB | R | H | D | T | HR | RBI | SB | BB | SO | Avg | OBP | Slg |
|---|---|---|---|---|---|---|---|---|---|---|---|---|---|---|
| 1995 | 77 | 196 | 30 | 55 | 6 | 0 | 4 | 24 | 3 | 24 | 38 | .281 | .359 | .372 |
| Career | 603 | 1464 | 189 | 387 | 54 | 6 | 49 | 212 | 15 | 155 | 319 | .264 | .333 | .410 |

### Where He Hits the Ball

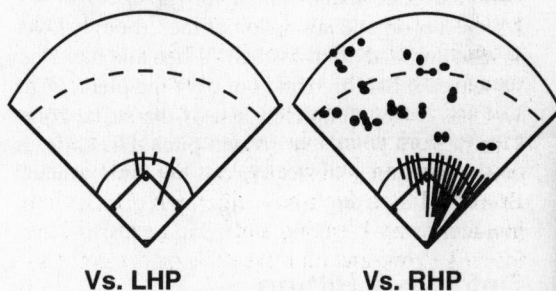

**Vs. LHP**          **Vs. RHP**

### 1995 Situational Stats

| | AB | H | HR | RBI | Avg | | AB | H | HR | RBI | Avg |
|---|---|---|---|---|---|---|---|---|---|---|---|
| Home | 88 | 25 | 2 | 13 | .284 | LHP | 23 | 8 | 1 | 4 | .348 |
| Road | 108 | 30 | 2 | 11 | .278 | RHP | 173 | 47 | 3 | 20 | .272 |
| First Half | 131 | 44 | 4 | 22 | .336 | Sc Pos | 57 | 15 | 2 | 21 | .263 |
| Scnd Half | 65 | 11 | 0 | 2 | .169 | Clutch | 31 | 9 | 1 | 7 | .290 |

### 1995 Rankings (National League)

→ 9th in errors in left field (3)

# Mike Dyer

## 1995 Season

Mike Dyer's first full season in the majors since 1989 was an up-and-down affair. He started poorly, yielding eight earned runs in his first 14 innings. And he struggled at the end of the year, giving up 12 earned runs in his final 13 appearances. In between, his ERA was a respectable 3.30. Dyer was durable, capable of taking over when Pittsburgh starters departed early. His 74.2 innings was tops among Pirate relievers.

## Pitching

Dyer's arm is now fully recovered from surgery that removed a blood clot from his shoulder in 1991. Once again Dyer showed the 94-MPH fastball that once made him a top prospect in the Minnesota organization. Sometimes, though, Dyer loses command of his fastball. When that happens, he leaves it belt-high and out over the plate, or he watches it run completely out of the strike zone. Dyer lacks a consistent second pitch. His slider is effective when it breaks sharply, but his command of it often fails him. His change-up is primarily for show.

## Defense & Hitting

Dyer is a solid fielder, quick off the mound with good reflexes. Holding runners is more of a problem. His delivery to the plate is slow and he doesn't have much of a pickoff move. Dyer proved to be a tough out last year, going 4-for-7. He also is a pretty good bunter.

## 1996 Season

Pirates manager Jim Leyland abhors walks, so winning a job in 1996 will be a challenge for Dyer. His days as a starter are over and he lacks the consistency to be a closer. When he has command of his pitches, he is a competent and versatile reliever. If he becomes a consistent performer, he can find a niche in the majors. If he doesn't, he's gone.

**Position:** RP
**Bats:** R  **Throws:** R
**Ht:** 6' 3"  **Wt:** 200

**Opening Day Age:** 29
**Born:** 9/8/66 in Upland, CA
**ML Seasons:** 3

### Overall Statistics

|  | W | L | Pct. | ERA | G | GS | Sv | IP | H | BB | SO | HR | BR/IP |
|---|---|---|---|---|---|---|---|---|---|---|---|---|---|
| 1995 | 4 | 5 | .444 | 4.34 | 55 | 0 | 0 | 74.2 | 81 | 30 | 53 | 9 | 1.49 |
| Career | 9 | 13 | .409 | 4.70 | 85 | 12 | 4 | 161.0 | 170 | 79 | 103 | 12 | 1.55 |

### How Often He Throws Strikes

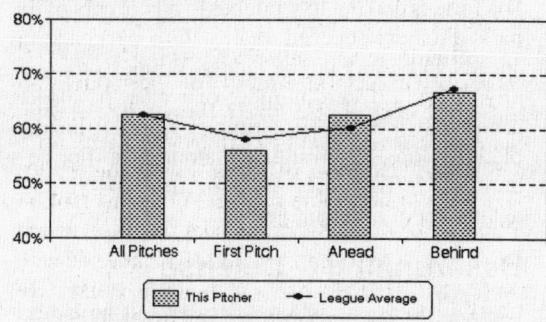

### 1995 Situational Stats

|  | W | L | ERA | Sv | IP |  | AB | H | HR | RBI | Avg |
|---|---|---|---|---|---|---|---|---|---|---|---|
| Home | 2 | 2 | 3.46 | 0 | 41.2 | LHB | 95 | 34 | 4 | 19 | .358 |
| Road | 2 | 3 | 5.45 | 0 | 33.0 | RHB | 193 | 47 | 5 | 21 | .244 |
| First Half | 1 | 1 | 4.46 | 0 | 34.1 | Sc Pos | 93 | 23 | 1 | 31 | .247 |
| Scnd Half | 3 | 4 | 4.24 | 0 | 40.1 | Clutch | 66 | 18 | 2 | 9 | .273 |

### 1995 Rankings (National League)

→ 4th in worst first batter efficiency (.354)
→ 6th in most GDPs induced per GDP situation (20.8%)
→ 7th in lowest percentage of inherited runners scored (23.1%), highest batting average allowed in relief (.281) and least strikeouts per 9 innings in relief (6.4)
→ 8th in most baserunners allowed per 9 innings in relief (14.0)
→ Led the Pirates in balks (1), most GDPs induced per GDP situation, lowest percentage of inherited runners scored and relief innings (74.2)

# John Ericks

## 1995 Season

Selected in the first round of the 1988 draft by St. Louis, righthander John Ericks was released by the Cardinals four years later after undergoing reconstructive shoulder surgery. After sitting out the 1993 season, Ericks pitched for the Pittsburgh organization in 1994 and finally reached the big leagues when he was promoted last June. Like most of Pittsburgh's young pitchers, Ericks had his good and bad outings. He had a respectable 2-3 record entering August, but lost his final five decisions.

## Pitching

The big righthander rears back and fires a 90-plus fastball. He also throws a big-breaking curveball that equally confounds right- and left-handed hitters. Ericks lacks an effective offspeed pitch and consistent control. He rarely throws his straight change for strikes and tips off the pitch with poor arm action. Because of his size, his mechanics have been troublesome at times. When his motion is out of whack, his pitches take off all over the place. For a pitcher with limited major league experience, Ericks has outstanding poise. He didn't rattle last season, even in games where he was hit hard. Durability is still a concern because of the nature of his shoulder operation, and the Pirates pitched him sparingly last September.

## Defense & Hitting

While his move to first is just ordinary, Ericks does a decent job of stopping the running game. He pays close attention to runners and frequently steps off the rubber to disrupt their timing. A lumbering kind of guy, Ericks is particularly slow off the mound to field bunts and cover first base. Ericks isn't much of a hitter, either, though he is a good bunter.

## 1996 Outlook

Ericks exhibited a live arm and some promise in his rookie season. Look for him to stick in the Pirates rotation, because manager Jim Leyland loves hard throwers with poise. It's hard to project Ericks as a big winner, but he's a battler.

**Position:** SP
**Bats:** R **Throws:** R
**Ht:** 6' 7" **Wt:** 225

**Opening Day Age:** 28
**Born:** 9/16/67 in Oak Lawn, IL
**ML Seasons:** 1

### Overall Statistics

| | W | L | Pct. | ERA | G | GS | Sv | IP | H | BB | SO | HR | BR/IP |
|---|---|---|---|---|---|---|---|---|---|---|---|---|---|
| 1995 | 3 | 9 | .250 | 4.58 | 19 | 18 | 0 | 106.0 | 108 | 50 | 80 | 7 | 1.49 |
| Career | 3 | 9 | .250 | 4.58 | 19 | 18 | 0 | 106.0 | 108 | 50 | 80 | 7 | 1.49 |

### How Often He Throws Strikes

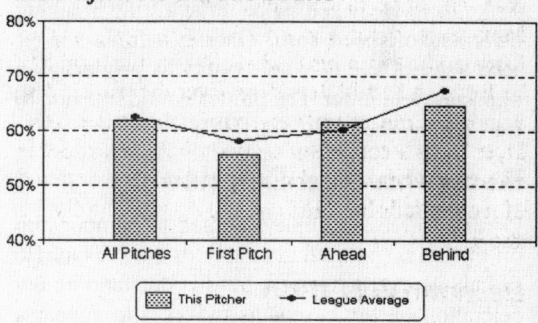

### 1995 Situational Stats

| | W | L | ERA | Sv | IP | | AB | H | HR | RBI | Avg |
|---|---|---|---|---|---|---|---|---|---|---|---|
| Home | 3 | 4 | 4.30 | 0 | 67.0 | LHB | 207 | 59 | 4 | 23 | .285 |
| Road | 0 | 5 | 5.08 | 0 | 39.0 | RHB | 203 | 49 | 3 | 29 | .241 |
| First Half | 2 | 1 | 2.45 | 0 | 22.0 | Sc Pos | 105 | 35 | 1 | 42 | .333 |
| Scnd Half | 1 | 8 | 5.14 | 0 | 84.0 | Clutch | 33 | 12 | 0 | 5 | .364 |

### 1995 Rankings (National League)

➡ 5th in wild pitches (11), least GDPs induced per GDP situation (2.5%), highest batting average allowed with runners in scoring position (.333) and errors at pitcher (3)

➡ Led the Pirates in wild pitches (11)

# Carlos Garcia

## 1995 Season

Carlos Garcia started the 1995 season slowly after straining knee ligaments while playing winter ball in his native Venezuela. Once he was fully healed, Garcia turned it on and set career highs in batting average and runs batted in. He also had hitting streaks of 21, 15 and 14 games. He started 12 games at shortstop, the first time he'd played that position in the majors since 1992.

## Hitting

For a middle infielder, Garcia's power potential is outstanding. Eventually he may average 12-15 homers per season. Garcia is primarily a fastball hitter who will jump all over mistakes up in the strike zone. He is getting better at hitting breaking balls and offspeed stuff. Garcia, a free swinger who doesn't like to work counts, is primarily an opposite-field hitter. The Pirates would like him to start pulling the ball more.

## Baserunning & Defense

Garcia's offseason injury seemed to hamper him on the bases, particularly early in the season. He has above-average speed, but his outstanding acceleration on the basepaths makes him appear a little faster than he really is. He is not a high percentage basestealer, and must improve on reading pitchers' moves and getting better jumps. A shortstop throughout his minor-league career, Garcia continues to improve at second base. He has sure hands, a very strong arm, and goes to his right extremely well. Garcia isn't as sound going to his left or turning double plays. If ever given the chance, he could be a Gold Glove-caliber shortstop.

## 1996 Outlook

Assuming the Pirates don't use Garcia in the leadoff spot, as they did for much of 1994, he should blossom into a solid RBI man this season. He is an impressive young player who works extremely hard. Garcia's biggest problem is that he is his own toughest critic. He needs to relax. He has enough natural ability to become one of the game's better second basemen.

**Position:** 2B/SS
**Bats:** R  **Throws:** R
**Ht:** 6' 1"  **Wt:** 193

**Opening Day Age:** 28
**Born:** 10/15/67 in Tachira, VZ
**ML Seasons:** 6

*Overall Statistics*

| | G | AB | R | H | D | T | HR | RBI | SB | BB | SO | Avg | OBP | Slg |
|---|---|---|---|---|---|---|---|---|---|---|---|---|---|---|
| 1995 | 104 | 367 | 41 | 108 | 24 | 2 | 6 | 50 | 8 | 25 | 55 | .294 | .340 | .420 |
| Career | 381 | 1392 | 174 | 385 | 65 | 11 | 24 | 130 | 44 | 73 | 208 | .277 | .317 | .391 |

*Where He Hits the Ball*

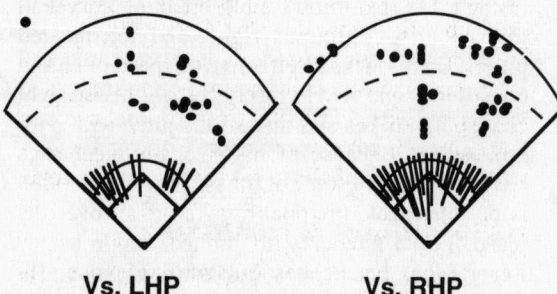

**Vs. LHP**          **Vs. RHP**

*1995 Situational Stats*

| | AB | H | HR | RBI | Avg | | AB | H | HR | RBI | Avg |
|---|---|---|---|---|---|---|---|---|---|---|---|
| Home | 200 | 63 | 4 | 31 | .315 | LHP | 105 | 31 | 1 | 12 | .295 |
| Road | 167 | 45 | 2 | 19 | .269 | RHP | 262 | 77 | 5 | 38 | .294 |
| First Half | 199 | 56 | 3 | 26 | .281 | Sc Pos | 93 | 27 | 1 | 40 | .290 |
| Scnd Half | 168 | 52 | 3 | 24 | .310 | Clutch | 43 | 8 | 0 | 5 | .186 |

*1995 Rankings (National League)*

➡ 2nd in lowest fielding percentage at second base (.982)
➡ 5th in errors at second base (9)
➡ 9th in least GDPs per GDP situation (4.9%) and batting average with two strikes (.271)
➡ Led the Pirates in least GDPs per GDP situation, batting average with two strikes (.271), lowest percentage of swings that missed (13.7%) and highest percentage of swings put into play (48.8%)

# Mark Johnson

## 1995 Season

After winning Southern League MVP honors in 1994, his third season at Double-A Carolina, Mark Johnson made the Pirates out of spring training last year. He got off to a decent start, hitting .242 with nine homers through the end of June, but departed for Triple-A Calgary in August after hitting just .125 in a 27-game stretch. He broke his left thumb 10 days later and underwent season-ending surgery.

## Hitting

Johnson is the classic all-or-nothing hitter. He takes a huge swing and either drives the ball a mile or flails at air. Johnson also has a big leg kick. With all the motion in his swing, Johnson isn't able to catch up with good inside heat. He has trouble with breaking balls and offspeed pitches as well. For Johnson to have any kind of long-term success in the majors, he needs to develop outstanding plate discipline. He must force pitchers into situations where he sees fastballs in his limited hitting zone.

## Baserunning & Defense

Johnson has adequate speed for a big guy. He seldom will steal a base, but he is very aggressive and will take the extra base. Johnson has worked hard on his fielding, but is still a below-average first baseman. His range is limited and his hands are stiff. He does have a strong arm, which is only natural since he threw for more than 4,000 yards while playing quarterback at Dartmouth.

## 1996 Outlook

The Pirates are in desperate need of power and will give Johnson another look this spring. His success hangs on how well he can make adjustments at the plate. He's a bright guy with a psychology degree from an Ivy League school, so he can't be counted out. Still, it took him three seasons to escape Double-A, which certainly suggests that his upside potential is limited.

**Position:** 1B
**Bats:** L  **Throws:** L
**Ht:** 6' 4"  **Wt:** 230

**Opening Day Age:** 28
**Born:** 10/17/67 in Worcester, MA
**ML Seasons:** 1

### Overall Statistics

|  | G | AB | R | H | D | T | HR | RBI | SB | BB | SO | Avg | OBP | Slg |
|---|---|---|---|---|---|---|---|---|---|---|---|---|---|---|
| 1995 | 79 | 221 | 32 | 46 | 6 | 1 | 13 | 28 | 5 | 37 | 66 | .208 | .326 | .421 |
| Career | 79 | 221 | 32 | 46 | 6 | 1 | 13 | 28 | 5 | 37 | 66 | .208 | .326 | .421 |

### Where He Hits the Ball

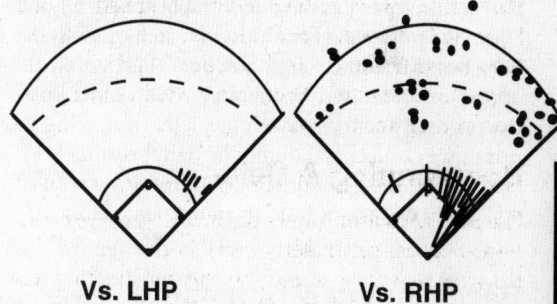

**Vs. LHP**            **Vs. RHP**

### 1995 Situational Stats

|  | AB | H | HR | RBI | Avg |  | AB | H | HR | RBI | Avg |
|---|---|---|---|---|---|---|---|---|---|---|---|
| Home | 100 | 21 | 7 | 14 | .210 | LHP | 22 | 4 | 1 | 4 | .182 |
| Road | 121 | 25 | 6 | 14 | .207 | RHP | 199 | 42 | 12 | 24 | .211 |
| First Half | 141 | 36 | 9 | 21 | .255 | Sc Pos | 62 | 7 | 2 | 13 | .113 |
| Scnd Half | 80 | 10 | 4 | 7 | .125 | Clutch | 34 | 6 | 1 | 1 | .176 |

### 1995 Rankings (National League)

➡ 2nd in errors at first base (8)
➡ 5th in lowest batting average with two strikes (.099)

# Jeff King

## 1995 Season

Pirate infielder Jeff King got off to a hot start in 1995, batting .310 with six homers and 34 RBI in his first 32 games. Then a sprained left wrist put him on the disabled list in mid-June, and King cooled off considerably when he returned. He eventually rebounded to lead the Pirates in homers (a career-high 18) and runs batted in. He also became just the second player in club history, and the first since 1894, to hit two homers in one inning when he hit two out at San Francisco on August 8.

## Hitting

A quick glance at King's skills suggests a premier power hitter. He has outstanding bat speed, a good eye at the plate, and the ability to catch up with the very best fastballs. King, however, has never put up the expected power numbers. He seems hesitant to really cut loose at the plate, preferring to just make contact and dump the ball the other way. He rarely pulls a pitch. King doesn't draw a lot of walks but he doesn't strike out much, either. He has a good knowledge of the strike zone.

## Baserunning & Defense

King has just average speed at best. Still, he is a very sound baserunner; he has good instincts and knows when to take the extra base. Traditionally one of the National League's most underrated defensive players, King struggled in the field in 1995, particularly with his throwing. He goes to his left extremely well and is good at charging balls. His arm is barely average. Normally a third baseman, he also saw some action at first base last season. He played well, exhibiting outstanding range and good hands.

## 1996 Outlook

King is a hard guy to figure. He alternates between strong seasons and poor ones. The Pirates have miscast King as a cleanup hitter the past three years. He'd be a fine complementary player in a good lineup, but can't be expected to carry the power load by himself.

**Position:** 3B/1B
**Bats:** R  **Throws:** R
**Ht:** 6' 1"  **Wt:** 185

**Opening Day Age:** 31
**Born:** 12/26/64 in Marion, IN
**ML Seasons:** 7

### Overall Statistics

| | G | AB | R | H | D | T | HR | RBI | SB | BB | SO | Avg | OBP | Slg |
|---|---|---|---|---|---|---|---|---|---|---|---|---|---|---|
| 1995 | 122 | 445 | 61 | 118 | 27 | 2 | 18 | 87 | 7 | 55 | 63 | .265 | .342 | .456 |
| Career | 739 | 2570 | 328 | 657 | 137 | 12 | 69 | 382 | 32 | 226 | 310 | .256 | .314 | .399 |

### Where He Hits the Ball

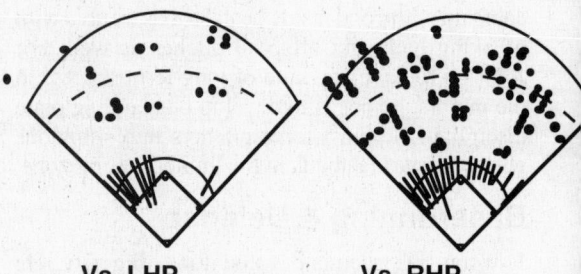

Vs. LHP          Vs. RHP

### 1995 Situational Stats

| | AB | H | HR | RBI | Avg | | AB | H | HR | RBI | Avg |
|---|---|---|---|---|---|---|---|---|---|---|---|
| Home | 222 | 53 | 7 | 41 | .239 | LHP | 112 | 27 | 7 | 19 | .241 |
| Road | 223 | 65 | 11 | 46 | .291 | RHP | 333 | 91 | 11 | 68 | .273 |
| First Half | 183 | 50 | 6 | 40 | .273 | Sc Pos | 137 | 36 | 3 | 60 | .263 |
| Scnd Half | 262 | 68 | 12 | 47 | .260 | Clutch | 77 | 19 | 2 | 13 | .247 |

### 1995 Rankings (National League)

- ➡ 2nd in sacrifice flies (8)
- ➡ 6th in lowest groundball/flyball ratio (0.9)
- ➡ 7th in most pitches seen per plate appearance (4.06)
- ➡ 8th in errors at third base (13)
- ➡ 9th in lowest batting average at home (.239) and lowest percentage of swings on the first pitch (19.3%)
- ➡ 10th in lowest batting average vs. left-handed pitchers (.241) and lowest cleanup slugging percentage (.486)
- ➡ Led the Pirates in home runs, RBI, sacrifice flies, walks, HR frequency (24.7 ABs per HR), cleanup slugging percentage (.486) and highest percentage of pitches taken (59.7%)

# Esteban Loaiza

## 1995 Season

Expected to start the season at Triple-A Calgary, rookie righthander Esteban Loaiza was thrust into the Pirates' rotation when Rick White suffered a sprained elbow ligament in spring training. Loaiza won his major league debut in Philadelphia on April 29, and was 6-3 with a 5.12 ERA at the All-Star break. The overmatched rookie went 2-6 in the second half. Loaiza tied for the National League lead in starts with 31, but also gave up more runs than any other pitcher in the National League.

## Pitching

Loaiza has the arm to be a star. He throws a 90-plus fastball with outstanding movement. He also has an above-average slider and curveball. His change-up still needs work. Loaiza delivers all his pitches with a textbook motion. His smooth delivery keeps him from tipping his pitches, a problem that plagues many youngsters. Loaiza, though, was maddeningly inconsistent. In some starts he was overpowering, throwing all his pitches for strikes and challenging hitters. At other times he seemed intimidated by major league hitters. He would nibble at the plate and wind up exiting early.

## Defense & Hitting

Loaiza is good defensively with outstanding reflexes. Like many young pitchers, he needs work on his pickoff move and keeping runners close. His mind wanders at times, and occasionally he forgets to cover first or back up a base. Loaiza was a catcher in high school and likes to hit. He is far from an automatic out and also is a good bunter.

## 1996 Outlook

Pittsburgh has a wealth of young, unproven pitching prospects, but Loaiza has the best arm of the bunch. He has a good assortment of pitches and the look of a staff ace. To become a star, though, Loaiza will have to improve his concentration, stay aggressive, and learn how to work the league's hitters. In fairness to Loaiza, he was rushed from Double-A to the majors last season. He has a bright future.

**Position:** SP
**Bats:** R  **Throws:** R
**Ht:** 6' 4"  **Wt:** 190

**Opening Day Age:** 24
**Born:** 12/31/71 in Tijuana, MX
**ML Seasons:** 1
**Pronunciation:** low-WAY-zah

### Overall Statistics

|  | W | L | Pct. | ERA | G | GS | Sv | IP | H | BB | SO | HR | BR/IP |
|---|---|---|---|---|---|---|---|---|---|---|---|---|---|
| 1995 | 8 | 9 | .471 | 5.16 | 32 | 31 | 0 | 172.2 | 205 | 55 | 85 | 21 | 1.51 |
| Career | 8 | 9 | .471 | 5.16 | 32 | 31 | 0 | 172.2 | 205 | 55 | 85 | 21 | 1.51 |

### How Often He Throws Strikes

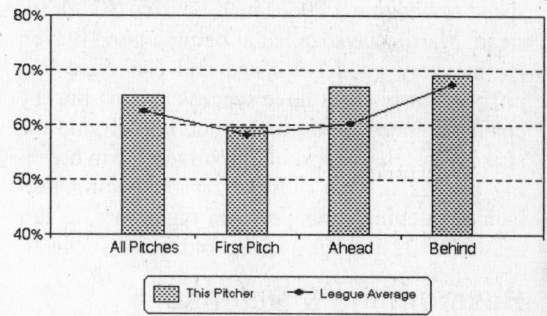

This Pitcher — League Average

### 1995 Situational Stats

|  | W | L | ERA | Sv | IP |  | AB | H | HR | RBI | Avg |
|---|---|---|---|---|---|---|---|---|---|---|---|
| Home | 3 | 6 | 5.01 | 0 | 88.0 | LHB | 304 | 84 | 6 | 46 | .276 |
| Road | 5 | 3 | 5.31 | 0 | 84.2 | RHB | 379 | 121 | 15 | 57 | .319 |
| First Half | 6 | 3 | 5.12 | 0 | 84.1 | Sc Pos | 178 | 62 | 2 | 76 | .348 |
| Scnd Half | 2 | 6 | 5.20 | 0 | 88.1 | Clutch | 23 | 4 | 0 | 0 | .174 |

### 1995 Rankings (National League)

→ 1st in games started and least pitches thrown per batter (3.28)
→ 2nd in highest ERA, highest batting average allowed (.300), highest on-base percentage allowed (.352), least strikeouts per 9 innings (4.4) and highest batting average allowed with runners in scoring position (.348)
→ 3rd in highest slugging percentage allowed (.464), most baserunners allowed per 9 innings (13.8), highest ERA on the road (5.32) and highest batting average allowed vs. right-handed batters (.319)
→ Led the Pirates in sacrifice bunts (7), games started and home runs allowed

Pittsburgh Pirates

# Al Martin

## 1995 Season

After a slow start, Al Martin turned his season around with a big second half, hitting .329 in 66 games following the All-Star break. His batting average bottomed out at .215 in late June, but Martin countered with .368 in July, .326 in August, and .318 from September 1 on. Manager Jim Leyland plugged Martin into the leadoff spot for much of the season. He's not ideally suited for the role, but Martin handled it adequately and he led off four games with home runs.

## Hitting

Martin seemingly has the tools to become an offensive force. He certainly has enough power and speed to become a 20/20 man or even 30/30. Instead, Martin stays stalled at being a good player. He has very good bat speed and can drive low pitches, but pitchers have success against him by changing speeds and moving the ball around the strike zone. He is particularly vulnerable to breaking pitches off the outside corner. Facing left-handed pitching is his personal nightmare, as last season's .132 average against southpaws suggests.

## Baserunning & Defense

Martin is extremely fast. Often he steals bases on sheer speed, because he doesn't always read pitchers' moves well. At the plate he is always a threat for an extra-base hit because of his exceptional acceleration as he rounds first base. Though a very aggressive runner, he rarely runs into outs. He is best suited to left field because his arm is below average. He has outstanding range, though, and runs into the gap or to the foul line to take away extra-base hits. Martin seems more comfortable and confident in center field, where he can put that range to better use.

## 1996 Outlook

Time is running out fast on Martin's chances of becoming an impact player. That's not to say that he isn't a good player who does numerous things to help his team win. He also plays the game with great intensity and fire, something the Pirates have lacked in recent years.

**Position:** LF/CF
**Bats:** L **Throws:** L
**Ht:** 6' 2"  **Wt:** 210

**Opening Day Age:** 28
**Born:** 11/24/67 in West Covina, CA
**ML Seasons:** 4

### Overall Statistics

| | G | AB | R | H | D | T | HR | RBI | SB | BB | SO | Avg | OBP | Slg |
|---|---|---|---|---|---|---|---|---|---|---|---|---|---|---|
| 1995 | 124 | 439 | 70 | 124 | 25 | 3 | 13 | 41 | 20 | 44 | 92 | .282 | .351 | .442 |
| Career | 361 | 1207 | 204 | 340 | 63 | 16 | 40 | 140 | 51 | 120 | 275 | .282 | .348 | .460 |

### Where He Hits the Ball

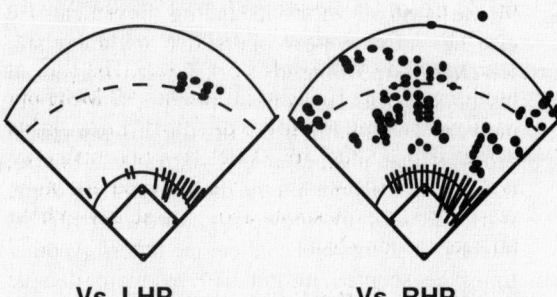

Vs. LHP          Vs. RHP

### 1995 Situational Stats

| | AB | H | HR | RBI | Avg | | AB | H | HR | RBI | Avg |
|---|---|---|---|---|---|---|---|---|---|---|---|
| Home | 224 | 69 | 8 | 24 | .308 | LHP | 68 | 9 | 1 | 7 | .132 |
| Road | 215 | 55 | 5 | 17 | .256 | RHP | 371 | 115 | 12 | 34 | .310 |
| First Half | 208 | 48 | 7 | 17 | .231 | Sc Pos | 96 | 21 | 2 | 24 | .219 |
| Scnd Half | 231 | 76 | 6 | 24 | .329 | Clutch | 76 | 18 | 2 | 6 | .237 |

### 1995 Rankings (National League)

- → 2nd in lowest fielding percentage in left field (.970)
- → 4th in lowest stolen base percentage (64.5%)
- → 6th in errors in left field (4) and highest percentage of swings that missed (28.3%)
- → 8th in caught stealing (11)
- → 9th in batting average vs. right-handed pitchers (.310)
- → 10th in lowest batting average with runners in scoring position (.219)
- → Led the Pirates in highest groundball/flyball ratio (1.3)

# Jeff McCurry

## 1995 Season

Pittsburgh's last cut in spring training a year ago, rookie righty Jeff McCurry quickly made it to the majors for the first time in his career. Promoted in May from Triple-A Calgary, McCurry pitched effectively out of the bullpen for more than a month. His ERA was a season-low 2.65 on June 13. That was the high point of his season; he was inconsistent the rest of the summer. He did have a decent September and recorded his first major league save in his final appearance, September 27, at Houston.

## Pitching

McCurry established himself as a prospect by saving 43 minor league games from 1992-94. After a good start last season, it became clear he was overmatched by major league hitters. His stuff is ordinary at best. His fastball reaches 90 MPH but has little movement. He has difficulty throwing his curveball and slider for strikes, and his change-up is strictly for show. McCurry's arm tired late in the season, raising questions about his ability to hold up over the long haul.

## Defense & Hitting

A good athlete, McCurry fields his position well, snaring comebackers through the box and charging bunts. He also is very good at holding runners. He has a good move to first, pays close attention to runners, and keeps them off balance by varying his delivery. McCurry rarely bats, so it's hard to say if he's capable of making contact against big-league pitching.

## 1996 Outlook

On the whole, McCurry had a horrible rookie season in 1995. That he spent almost the entire year with the Pirates is more an indictment of their pitching talent than McCurry's promise. Though McCurry pitched well in the minors, he was overmatched in the majors. If he doesn't pitch better this season, he won't be around much longer.

**Position:** RP
**Bats:** R  **Throws:** R
**Ht:** 6' 7"  **Wt:** 210

**Opening Day Age:** 26
**Born:** 1/21/70 in Tokyo, Japan
**ML Seasons:** 1

### Overall Statistics

|        | W | L | Pct. | ERA  | G  | GS | Sv | IP   | H  | BB | SO | HR | BR/IP |
|--------|---|---|------|------|----|----|----|------|----|----|----|----|-------|
| 1995   | 1 | 4 | .200 | 5.02 | 55 | 0  | 1  | 61.0 | 82 | 30 | 27 | 9  | 1.84  |
| Career | 1 | 4 | .200 | 5.02 | 55 | 0  | 1  | 61.0 | 82 | 30 | 27 | 9  | 1.84  |

### How Often He Throws Strikes

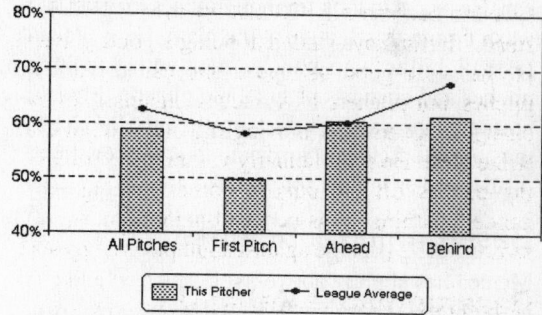

### 1995 Situational Stats

|            | W | L | ERA  | Sv | IP   |        | AB  | H  | HR | RBI | Avg  |
|------------|---|---|------|----|------|--------|-----|----|----|-----|------|
| Home       | 1 | 1 | 7.08 | 0  | 34.1 | LHB    | 86  | 33 | 3  | 13  | .384 |
| Road       | 0 | 3 | 2.36 | 1  | 26.2 | RHB    | 157 | 49 | 6  | 27  | .312 |
| First Half | 0 | 2 | 5.08 | 0  | 28.1 | Sc Pos | 78  | 22 | 3  | 30  | .282 |
| Scnd Half  | 1 | 2 | 4.96 | 1  | 32.2 | Clutch | 55  | 17 | 1  | 8   | .309 |

### 1995 Rankings (National League)

➡ 1st in highest batting average allowed in relief (.337) and least strikeouts per 9 innings in relief (4.0)
➡ 2nd in most baserunners allowed per 9 innings in relief (17.3)
➡ 4th in highest relief ERA (5.02)
➡ 9th in most GDPs induced per GDP situation (19.2%)

Pittsburgh Pirates

# Orlando Merced

## 1995 Season

Playing primarily in right field, Orlando Merced had the best year of his career in 1995. He posted career highs in at-bats, hits, doubles, home runs and runs batted in. He also hit .300 for the second time in his career. He was a consistent performer at the plate, slumping only briefly in June before finishing strong. On June 1 against Cincinnati, Merced hit two homers in a game for the first time in his career.

## Hitting

Merced is a solid major league hitter who makes good contact. With the Pirates lacking power, Merced changed his approach somewhat last season. He began to look for more pitches to drive and wasn't quite as selective at the plate. He is a dead fastball hitter who can be had with breaking pitches and change-ups high and outside. Merced normally sprays line drives up the middle and to the opposite field, but he began to pull a few more inside pitches last season.

## Baserunning & Defense

Merced has slightly above-average speed and can motor pretty well when he keeps his weight down, which has been a problem at times. Though he doesn't steal many bases, he is very aggressive on the basepaths. Merced has spent his career shuttling between first base and right field. He is shaky in the outfield, unsure on most fly balls, and his arm is not strong or accurate. He is better at first base, where he displays above-average range and decent hands.

## 1996 Outlook

Merced can become a free agent at the end of the '96 season, and the Pirates would like to lock him up with a long-term deal. While not a star, he is a good offensive player who is capable of hitting .280-.300 with some homers and RBI. He also seemed to mature last season, losing weight and becoming more of a veteran leader on a very young club.

**Position:** RF/1B
**Bats:** L  **Throws:** R
**Ht:** 5'11"  **Wt:** 185

**Opening Day Age:** 29
**Born:** 11/2/66 in San Juan, PR
**ML Seasons:** 6
**Pronunciation:** mer-SED

### Overall Statistics

|  | G | AB | R | H | D | T | HR | RBI | SB | BB | SO | Avg | OBP | Slg |
|---|---|---|---|---|---|---|---|---|---|---|---|---|---|---|
| 1995 | 132 | 487 | 75 | 146 | 29 | 4 | 15 | 83 | 7 | 52 | 74 | .300 | .365 | .468 |
| Career | 656 | 2160 | 327 | 609 | 122 | 18 | 48 | 314 | 27 | 288 | 349 | .282 | .366 | .422 |

### Where He Hits the Ball

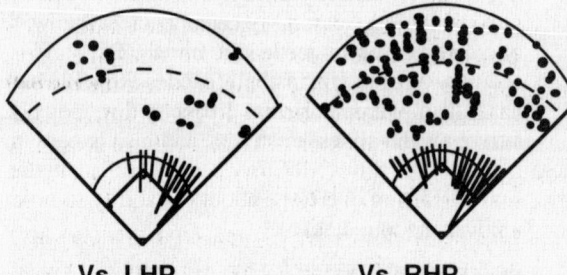

Vs. LHP          Vs. RHP

### 1995 Situational Stats

|  | AB | H | HR | RBI | Avg |  | AB | H | HR | RBI | Avg |
|---|---|---|---|---|---|---|---|---|---|---|---|
| Home | 242 | 74 | 8 | 47 | .306 | LHP | 120 | 27 | 5 | 17 | .225 |
| Road | 245 | 72 | 7 | 36 | .294 | RHP | 367 | 119 | 10 | 66 | .324 |
| First Half | 206 | 62 | 6 | 31 | .301 | Sc Pos | 140 | 47 | 6 | 70 | .336 |
| Scnd Half | 281 | 84 | 9 | 52 | .299 | Clutch | 83 | 21 | 3 | 14 | .253 |

### 1995 Rankings (National League)

- 3rd in lowest fielding percentage in right field (.976)
- 5th in errors in right field (5)
- 6th in lowest batting average vs. left-handed pitchers (.225)
- 7th in batting average vs. right-handed pitchers (.324)
- 10th in on-base percentage vs. right-handed pitchers (.386)
- Led the Pirates in batting average, hits, singles (98), doubles, triples, total bases (228), intentional walks (9), times on base (199), slugging percentage and on-base percentage

# Dan Miceli

## 1995 Season

Danny Miceli had a club-high 21 saves in his first full major-league season, the most by a Pirate since Bill Landrum saved 26 in 1989. Miceli also blew six save opportunities and allowed 11 of 24 inherited runners to score. Most of Miceli's troubles came in the season's final weeks. He allowed runs in seven of his last nine outings, a total of 11 runs in 9.1 innings.

## Pitching

Miceli is the classic closer who throws hard. His fastball routinely reaches the mid-90s and has good movement. Occasionally the heat rises too high out of the strike zone or stays flat at belt level. Walks and gopher balls are the result. Basically a one-pitch pitcher when he joined the Pirates' bullpen, Miceli is developing a slider. When it's working, the slider is a nice complement to the fastball that keeps hitters guessing. Miceli is smaller than most closers and seemed to tire late last season.

## Defense & Hitting

Like many closers, Miceli doesn't do a good job of controlling the running game. He is hurt by a weak pickoff move and a slow delivery to the plate. He is a decent fielder, adequate on balls hit back through the box, and he's always alert to covering first and backing up bases. As far as hitting, Miceli rarely bats. That's just as well, as he looks uncomfortable with a bat in his hands.

## 1996 Outlook

Despite his poor finish in 1995, Miceli will begin 1996 as the Pirates' closer. He has the arm for the job. He simply needs to gain some consistency. The Pirates are confident he will continue to grow into the job. Miceli also has the ideal closer's mentality. He is a quiet and intense guy, who has shown the ability to shake off bad outings and not let them carry over into his next save opportunity. He could develop into one of the game's better closers.

**Position:** RP
**Bats:** R  **Throws:** R
**Ht:** 6' 0"  **Wt:** 207

**Opening Day Age:** 25
**Born:** 9/9/70 in Newark, NJ
**ML Seasons:** 3
**Pronunciation:** muh-SELL-ee

### Overall Statistics

|  | W | L | Pct. | ERA | G | GS | Sv | IP | H | BB | SO | HR | BR/IP |
|---|---|---|---|---|---|---|---|---|---|---|---|---|---|
| 1995 | 4 | 4 | .500 | 4.66 | 58 | 0 | 21 | 58.0 | 61 | 28 | 56 | 7 | 1.53 |
| Career | 6 | 5 | .545 | 5.06 | 95 | 0 | 23 | 90.2 | 95 | 42 | 87 | 12 | 1.51 |

### How Often He Throws Strikes

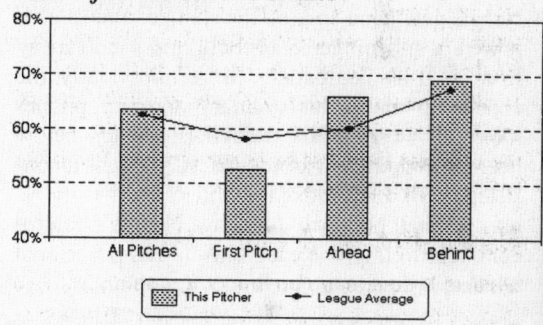

### 1995 Situational Stats

|  | W | L | ERA | Sv | IP |  | AB | H | HR | RBI | Avg |
|---|---|---|---|---|---|---|---|---|---|---|---|
| Home | 2 | 1 | 4.06 | 12 | 31.0 | LHB | 92 | 33 | 5 | 21 | .359 |
| Road | 2 | 3 | 5.33 | 9 | 27.0 | RHB | 134 | 28 | 2 | 18 | .209 |
| First Half | 1 | 3 | 4.15 | 10 | 26.0 | Sc Pos | 80 | 21 | 4 | 35 | .263 |
| Scnd Half | 3 | 1 | 5.06 | 11 | 32.0 | Clutch | 140 | 38 | 5 | 25 | .271 |

### 1995 Rankings (National League)

→ 2nd in least GDPs induced per GDP situation (1.8%)
→ 4th in lowest save percentage (77.8%)
→ 5th in games finished (51)
→ 6th in blown saves (6) and most baserunners allowed per 9 innings in relief (14.4)
→ 7th in highest relief ERA (4.66)
→ Led the Pirates in saves, games finished, save opportunities (27), save percentage (77.8%), blown saves, lowest batting average allowed in relief with runners on base (.248) and most strikeouts per 9 innings in relief (8.7)

# Denny Neagle

## 1995 Season

Denny Neagle blossomed into a top-flight left-hander in 1995, anchoring a young Pittsburgh staff in desperate need of consistent and successful starters. The highlight of his season may have been his first All-Star appearance. Coming in with no outs and a man on third, he induced Edgar Martinez to fly out, struck out Mo Vaughn, and retired Albert Belle on a grounder. Neagle finished the year with career highs in most pitching categories, including 13 wins, a team-high 150 strikeouts, and five complete games.

## Pitching

The key to Neagle's success is his change-up. Neagle gets good sink on his change, almost as if it were a split-fingered fastball, and it tails away from right-handed batters. More importantly, the change-up makes his ordinary array of pitches look much better. His fastball is a notch below average, topping out around 85 MPH. He is inconsistent with a late-breaking slider, and he throws his curveball primarily for show. Neagle's control continues to improve each season. His occasional bouts of wildness are no longer a problem.

## Defense & Hitting

Although he is getting better at holding runners, Neagle's move still needs work. He is quick off the mound and has improved at fielding balls hit back through the box. Despite starting his career with 40 hitless at-bats, Neagle takes a healthy cut and has homered in each of the past two seasons. He is a solid bunter who can be counted on to sacrifice.

## 1996 Outlook

Still only 27, Neagle had a breakthrough season in 1995 and seems poised to become a consistent 15-game winner. A pitcher whose out pitch is a change-up normally isn't the staff ace, but Neagle has assumed that role for now. Neagle is an extremely bright guy who follows the game closer than many of his fellow players. He knows the hitters and he understands the art of pitching.

**Position:** SP
**Bats:** L  **Throws:** L
**Ht:** 6' 2"  **Wt:** 216

**Opening Day Age:** 27
**Born:** 9/13/68 in Gambrills, MD
**ML Seasons:** 5
**Pronunciation:** NAY-gull

### Overall Statistics

|  | W | L | Pct. | ERA | G | GS | Sv | IP | H | BB | SO | HR | BR/IP |
|---|---|---|------|-----|---|----|----|-----|---|----|----|----|-------|
| 1995 | 13 | 8 | .619 | 3.43 | 31 | 31 | 0 | 209.2 | 221 | 45 | 150 | 20 | 1.27 |
| Career | 29 | 30 | .492 | 4.35 | 167 | 71 | 3 | 534.1 | 547 | 181 | 436 | 60 | 1.36 |

### How Often He Throws Strikes

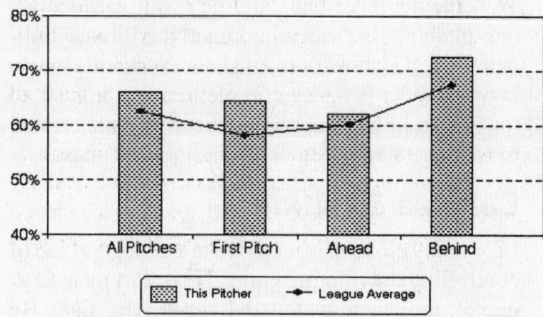

This Pitcher ▨    League Average ●

### 1995 Situational Stats

|  | W | L | ERA | Sv | IP |  | AB | H | HR | RBI | Avg |
|---|---|---|-----|----|----|---|----|---|----|-----|-----|
| Home | 6 | 0 | 3.56 | 0 | 81.0 | LHB | 125 | 34 | 5 | 14 | .272 |
| Road | 7 | 8 | 3.36 | 0 | 128.2 | RHB | 684 | 187 | 15 | 66 | .273 |
| First Half | 9 | 4 | 3.34 | 0 | 107.2 | Sc Pos | 162 | 43 | 1 | 56 | .265 |
| Scnd Half | 4 | 4 | 3.53 | 0 | 102.0 | Clutch | 51 | 8 | 1 | 4 | .157 |

### 1995 Rankings (National League)

- ➡ 1st in games started, innings pitched, hits allowed and batters faced (876)
- ➡ 2nd in pitches thrown (3,165)
- ➡ 4th in complete games (5) and highest strikeout/walk ratio (3.3)
- ➡ 7th in runners caught stealing (11)
- ➡ 8th in strikeouts and lowest groundball/flyball ratio allowed (1.1)
- ➡ 9th in wins and GDPs induced (18)
- ➡ 10th in highest batting average allowed (.273) and lowest stolen base percentage allowed (54.2%)
- ➡ Led the Pirates in ERA, wins, games started, complete games and shutouts (1)

# Steve Parris

**Position:** SP
**Bats:** R  **Throws:** R
**Ht:** 6' 0"  **Wt:** 190

**Opening Day Age:** 28
**Born:** 12/17/67 in Joliet, IL
**ML Seasons:** 1

## 1995 Season

After being released by Philadelphia, Los Angeles and Seattle, then undergoing reconstructive shoulder surgery in 1993, righthander Steve Parris managed to reach the major leagues last June. He started the year at Double-A Carolina and was 9-1 with a 2.51 ERA when the Pirates came calling. Parris continued to pitch pretty well after being called up, going 6-4 with a 4.10 ERA in his first 13 starts. But he wore out late in the summer, allowing 15 earned runs in his final two appearances before Pittsburgh shut him down with a tired arm.

## Pitching

Parris' best pitch is a curveball that bores in hard on lefthanders and goes down and away from righthanders. Controlling the curveball is the key to Parris' success. If he's throwing it for strikes, he's tough to beat. Though he doesn't appear to throw hard, Parris' fastball deceptively reaches 90 MPH and sinks. Parris also has a decent slider and change-up to complement the curve and fastball. Durability is a concern. Even a strike-shortened 1995 campaign severely tested Parris' rebuilt shoulder.

## Defense & Hitting

Parris does a good job of holding runners. He has a quick move and steps off often to disrupt runners' timing. He also is a good fielder. He reacts quickly to batted balls and covers first well. He was dangerous at the plate last season, going 7-for-28 with four RBI. He also knows how to lay down a bunt.

## 1996 Outlook

Parris' stuff is good enough to keep him in a major league rotation, but is his shoulder? Missing most of September in 1995 is not a good sign, but Parris insists it was arm fatigue rather than injury. Parris may not develop into a big winner, but he should be a competent fourth or fifth starter if his shoulder holds up.

### Overall Statistics

|        | W | L | Pct. | ERA  | G  | GS | Sv | IP   | H  | BB | SO | HR | BR/IP |
|--------|---|---|------|------|----|----|----|------|----|----|----|----|-------|
| 1995   | 6 | 6 | .500 | 5.38 | 15 | 15 | 0  | 82.0 | 89 | 33 | 61 | 12 | 1.49  |
| Career | 6 | 6 | .500 | 5.38 | 15 | 15 | 0  | 82.0 | 89 | 33 | 61 | 12 | 1.49  |

### How Often He Throws Strikes

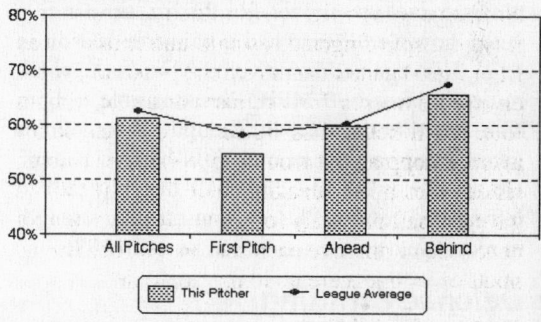

### 1995 Situational Stats

|            | W | L | ERA  | Sv | IP   |         | AB  | H  | HR | RBI | Avg  |
|------------|---|---|------|----|------|---------|-----|----|----|-----|------|
| Home       | 4 | 3 | 4.70 | 0  | 46.0 | LHB     | 140 | 34 | 5  | 18  | .243 |
| Road       | 2 | 3 | 6.25 | 0  | 36.0 | RHB     | 175 | 55 | 7  | 26  | .314 |
| First Half | 1 | 2 | 8.15 | 0  | 17.2 | Sc Pos  | 59  | 17 | 5  | 30  | .288 |
| Scnd Half  | 5 | 4 | 4.62 | 0  | 64.1 | Clutch  | 10  | 2  | 0  | 0   | .200 |

### 1995 Rankings (National League)

→ Led the Pirates in shutouts (1) and hit batsmen (7)

# Dan Plesac

## 1995 Season

Signed as a free agent to provide stability to a young Pirate bullpen, Dan Plesac did what was asked. Plesac began the season sensationally, and had a 2-0 mark and an 0.54 ERA at the end of May. He then went through a long rough stretch. He recovered, however, allowing just three earned runs in his final 18 innings.

## Pitching

When he broke in with Milwaukee in the late 1980s, Plesac quickly became one of the game's dominant closers. He threw a fastball that could light up the radar gun, but a chronic case of shoulder tendinitis robbed Plesac of velocity and turned him into a set-up reliever. For the first time in five years, however, Plesac had a pain-free season in 1995. His regained some velocity on his fastball, routinely hitting 90 MPH. Plesac is able to both sink and ride the fastball, though he sometimes gets burned on high heat to right-handed batters. He also throws a big curveball that is death to left-handed batters. Plesac's command, a strength in recent years, deserted him at times in 1995.

## Defense & Hitting

As a lefthander pitching in the late innings, Plesac rarely has runners try to steal against him. If they pick their spots, they can succeed because his move is nothing special. Plesac is big and somewhat slow, but fairly agile at making all the plays in the field. He isn't much of a threat at the plate, although he did record his first major league hit last season.

## 1996 Outlook

Healthy for the first time in years, Plesac was coveted by many clubs for the pennant stretch in 1995, but the Pirates couldn't get him through waivers to make a trade. His days of closing are over, but he can nail down an occasional game and pitch effectively against lefthanders. His leadership and professionalism are assets that should rub off on any staff.

**Position:** RP
**Bats:** L  **Throws:** L
**Ht:** 6' 5"  **Wt:** 215

**Opening Day Age:** 34
**Born:** 2/4/62 in Gary, IN
**ML Seasons:** 10
**Pronunciation:**
PLEE-sack

### Overall Statistics

|        | W  | L  | Pct. | ERA  | G   | GS | Sv  | IP    | H   | BB  | SO  | HR | BR/IP |
|--------|----|----|------|------|-----|----|-----|-------|-----|-----|-----|----|-------|
| 1995   | 4  | 4  | .500 | 3.58 | 58  | 0  | 3   | 60.1  | 53  | 27  | 57  | 3  | 1.33  |
| Career | 37 | 45 | .451 | 3.49 | 534 | 14 | 137 | 702.0 | 648 | 247 | 605 | 65 | 1.27  |

### How Often He Throws Strikes

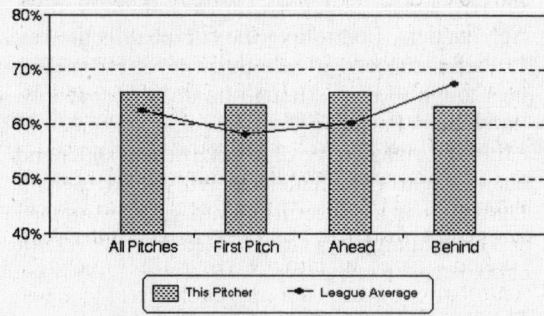

### 1995 Situational Stats

|            | W | L | ERA  | Sv | IP   |        | AB  | H  | HR | RBI | Avg  |
|------------|---|---|------|----|------|--------|-----|----|----|-----|------|
| Home       | 2 | 2 | 3.77 | 1  | 28.2 | LHB    | 81  | 18 | 2  | 16  | .222 |
| Road       | 2 | 2 | 3.41 | 2  | 31.2 | RHB    | 143 | 35 | 1  | 9   | .245 |
| First Half | 3 | 0 | 2.08 | 2  | 30.1 | Sc Pos | 62  | 17 | 0  | 20  | .274 |
| Scnd Half  | 1 | 4 | 5.10 | 1  | 30.0 | Clutch | 104 | 28 | 2  | 14  | .269 |

### 1995 Rankings (National League)

➡ Led the Pirates in relief ERA (3.58) and least baserunners allowed per 9 innings in relief (12.1)

# Paul Wagner

## 1995 Season

Although he was twice removed from the Pirates' starting rotation, Paul Wagner still managed to lose a major league-high 16 games in 1995. Wagner dropped his first five decisions and was 1-10 on June 18. In his defense, he was receiving very poor support—the Pirates were held to one run or less in nine of his 25 starts. He came within one out of a no-hitter against Colorado on August 29, instead settling for a one-hitter after Andres Galarraga's infield single.

## Pitching

Wagner's moving fastball routinely tops 90 miles per hour. He also throws an excellent slider that is hard to distinguish from his fastball because of its sudden, late break. Wagner, however, has never mastered the change of pace that could make him a star pitcher. He's failed to effectively incorporate his straight change and split-fingered pitch, but had some success with a palmball late last summer. Until he uses it regularly, hitters will time his hard stuff and tee off on him. Wagner is strong and can go the distance, but rarely keeps hitters off balance enough to throw a complete game. His control also is spotty at times, particularly with his fastball, and he falls behind too many hitters.

## Defense & Hitting

Wagner puts a lot of runners on base and struggles with the running game. His move is below average, his delivery to the plate is slow, and he sometimes forgets about baserunners. As a hitter, Wagner delivers an occasional single, but as a bunter he doesn't always help himself with a sacrifice.

## 1996 Outlook

Despite his struggles, Wagner deserves another crack at the starting rotation. He has a terrific arm and could be a big winner if he adds an offspeed pitch. His above-average hard stuff makes him a strong candidate for short relief, but the Pirates, perhaps stubbornly, keep believing he can become a top-notch starter.

**Position:** SP/RP
**Bats:** R **Throws:** R
**Ht:** 6' 1" **Wt:** 202

**Opening Day Age:** 28
**Born:** 11/14/67 in Milwaukee, WI
**ML Seasons:** 4

### Overall Statistics

|  | W | L | Pct. | ERA | G | GS | Sv | IP | H | BB | SO | HR | BR/IP |
|---|---|---|---|---|---|---|---|---|---|---|---|---|---|
| 1995 | 5 | 16 | .238 | 4.80 | 33 | 25 | 1 | 165.0 | 174 | 72 | 120 | 18 | 1.49 |
| Career | 22 | 32 | .407 | 4.45 | 112 | 60 | 3 | 439.0 | 462 | 169 | 325 | 40 | 1.44 |

### How Often He Throws Strikes

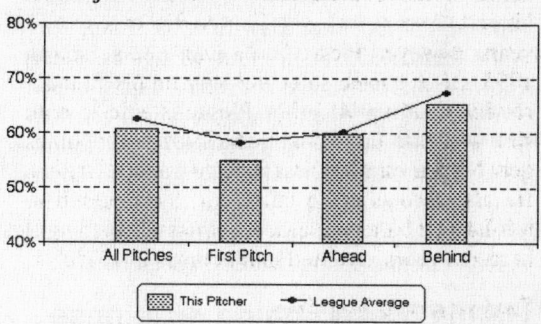

### 1995 Situational Stats

|  | W | L | ERA | Sv | IP |  | AB | H | HR | RBI | Avg |
|---|---|---|---|---|---|---|---|---|---|---|---|
| Home | 4 | 9 | 5.10 | 1 | 83.0 | LHB | 285 | 79 | 5 | 33 | .277 |
| Road | 1 | 7 | 4.50 | 0 | 82.0 | RHB | 352 | 95 | 13 | 54 | .270 |
| First Half | 1 | 10 | 5.60 | 0 | 70.2 | Sc Pos | 180 | 48 | 6 | 69 | .267 |
| Scnd Half | 4 | 6 | 4.20 | 1 | 94.1 | Clutch | 34 | 10 | 1 | 3 | .294 |

### 1995 Rankings (National League)

→ 1st in losses and fielding percentage at pitcher (1.000)
→ 2nd in lowest winning percentage
→ 3rd in highest on-base percentage allowed (.352)
→ 4th in highest ERA, most baserunners allowed per 9 innings (13.8), least run support per 9 innings (3.9) and highest ERA at home (5.10)
→ 5th in lowest strikeout/walk ratio (1.7) and most GDPs induced per 9 innings (1.0)
→ 6th in stolen bases allowed (25), GDPs induced (19)
→ Led the Pirates in losses, shutouts (1), walks allowed and hit batsmen (7)

# Rich Aude

**Position:** 1B
**Bats:** R **Throws:** R
**Ht:** 6' 5" **Wt:** 209

**Opening Day Age:** 24
**Born:** 7/13/71 in Van Nuys, CA
**ML Seasons:** 2
**Pronunciation:** AW-day

*Overall Statistics*

|  | G | AB | R | H | D | T | HR | RBI | SB | BB | SO | Avg | OBP | Slg |
|---|---|---|---|---|---|---|---|---|---|---|---|---|---|---|
| 1995 | 42 | 109 | 10 | 27 | 8 | 0 | 2 | 19 | 1 | 6 | 20 | .248 | .287 | .376 |
| Career | 55 | 135 | 11 | 30 | 9 | 0 | 2 | 23 | 1 | 7 | 27 | .222 | .261 | .333 |

## 1995 Season

Pittsburgh's Opening Day first baseman, Rich Aude batted .333 in his first 18 games. Never known to hit for average, the rookie then slumped, dropping his average into more realistic territory. The right-handed hitter platooned with fellow-rookie Mark Johnson until his demotion to Triple-A Calgary on July 1. Aude hit .333 with nine homers and 42 RBI in 50 games with Calgary before returning to the Pirates on September 5.

## Hitting, Baserunning & Defense

Aude certainly looks the part of a power hitter, resembling Dave Kingman or Dick Stuart. While he has developed good gap power, he has yet to hit the ball over the fence consistently. One reason may be his effort to make better contact and shed the label of all-or-nothing hitter. Though a big guy, Aude isn't a plodder on the bases. Once a brutal defensive first baseman, Aude has worked hard on that aspect of the game. He is still below average, though, with limited range, stiff hands and an erratic arm.

## 1996 Outlook

The Pirates need power hitters, but there are indications they don't think Aude is the answer. They didn't give him many at-bats last season and rarely mention his name when talking of their rebuilding efforts. He is still young enough to blossom into a good player.

# Jason Christiansen

**Position:** RP
**Bats:** R **Throws:** L
**Ht:** 6' 5" **Wt:** 230

**Opening Day Age:** 26
**Born:** 9/21/69 in Omaha, NE
**ML Seasons:** 1

*Overall Statistics*

|  | W | L | Pct. | ERA | G | GS | Sv | IP | H | BB | SO | HR | BR/IP |
|---|---|---|---|---|---|---|---|---|---|---|---|---|---|
| 1995 | 1 | 3 | .250 | 4.15 | 63 | 0 | 0 | 56.1 | 49 | 34 | 53 | 5 | 1.47 |
| Career | 1 | 3 | .250 | 4.15 | 63 | 0 | 0 | 56.1 | 49 | 34 | 53 | 5 | 1.47 |

## 1995 Season

At the start of the season Jason Christiansen had never appeared in a big league game, but he wound up making a team-high 63 appearances in 1995. Christiansen started strongly and had a 0.98 ERA through his first 23 outings. But his effectiveness evaporated, and his ERA was 5.68 the rest of the way. He was tough on left-handed hitters, limiting them to a .207 batting average.

## Pitching, Defense & Hitting

The big lefthander has an excellent fastball, and he complements the heat with a sweeping curveball that is all but impossible for lefthanders to hit. But he was inconsistent with the curve during the second half. And his control, outstanding throughout his minor league career, deserted him as the season wore on. Christiansen is not a good fielder; he moves awkwardly around the mound and needs work on covering bunts. He's about average at holding runners. He struck out in his one at-bat last season.

## 1996 Outlook

Highly regarded by the Pirates, Christiansen showed more promise than his 1995 numbers indicated. With an up-and-down rookie year out of the way, look for better results in 1996. Once again he will be a left-handed specialist out of the Pirates' bullpen. He has the ability to develop into a solid set-up man who could even close a game if needed.

# Midre Cummings

**Position:** CF/RF
**Bats:** L **Throws:** R
**Ht:** 6' 0" **Wt:** 196

**Opening Day Age:** 24
**Born:** 10/14/71 in St. Croix, Virgin Islands
**ML Seasons:** 3
**Pronunciation:** MEE-dray CUMM-ings

*Overall Statistics*

|  | G | AB | R | H | D | T | HR | RBI | SB | BB | SO | Avg | OBP | Slg |
|---|---|---|---|---|---|---|---|---|---|---|---|---|---|---|
| 1995 | 59 | 152 | 13 | 37 | 7 | 1 | 2 | 15 | 1 | 13 | 30 | .243 | .303 | .342 |
| Career | 96 | 274 | 29 | 62 | 12 | 1 | 3 | 30 | 1 | 21 | 57 | .226 | .282 | .310 |

## 1995 Season

Highly touted Midre Cummings was given the Pirates' right-field job when spring training started. However, he played his way out of the role before the shortened camp ended, and spent most of the first half at Triple-A Calgary. When Pittsburgh gave him an extended look after the All-Star break, Cummings' overall game and work habits were uninspiring.

## Hitting, Baserunning & Defense

Coming up through the minors, Cummings was supposed to be a guy who could hit .300 in his sleep. That hasn't happened. He occasionally shows flashes of ability, pulling a ball 430 feet or smoking a line drive the other way. Most of the time, though, he goes to the plate without a plan and simply flails away. Cummings has good speed but rarely uses it on the basepaths. He showed decent range in center and right field last season, but a weak throwing arm might eventually limit him to left.

## 1996 Outlook

In 1992 the Pirates traded 20-game winner John Smiley to Minnesota for Cummings and left-hander Denny Neagle. Cummings was supposed to be the key, a player the Pirates might eventually rebuild around. Instead, it's Neagle's emergence that has salvaged the trade. The Pirates have given up on Cummings and his lackadaisical attitude. Unless he quickly undergoes a serious attitude adjustment, his chances of becoming a regular, let alone a star, are slim.

# Jon Lieber

**Position:** SP/RP
**Bats:** L **Throws:** R
**Ht:** 6' 3" **Wt:** 220

**Opening Day Age:** 25
**Born:** 4/2/70 in Council Bluffs, IA
**ML Seasons:** 2
**Pronunciation:** LEE-burr

*Overall Statistics*

|  | W | L | Pct. | ERA | G | GS | Sv | IP | H | BB | SO | HR | BR/IP |
|---|---|---|---|---|---|---|---|---|---|---|---|---|---|
| 1995 | 4 | 7 | .364 | 6.32 | 21 | 12 | 0 | 72.2 | 103 | 14 | 45 | 7 | 1.61 |
| Career | 10 | 14 | .417 | 4.76 | 38 | 29 | 0 | 181.1 | 219 | 39 | 116 | 19 | 1.42 |

## 1995 Season

After a promising debut in 1994, Jon Lieber was Pittsburgh's Opening Day starter in 1995. But he wound up at Triple-A Calgary after going 2-7 with a 7.48 ERA in 11 starts. Lieber fared no better at Calgary, but returned to pitch well out of the Pirates' bullpen in September, registering a 1.50 ERA in nine relief appearances.

## Pitching, Defense & Hitting

After showing great command of his pitches in 1994, Lieber looked lost last season. When he's on, he throws a heavy 90 MPH fastball with good sinking action, and an outstanding, late-breaking slider. Too many of his sinkers didn't sink last year, and he was inconsistent with his slider. Lieber must also develop a decent change-up to offset his hard stuff. Chunky and not in the best of shape, Lieber also presents durability concerns. He is slow and not a good-fielding pitcher, and also below average at holding runners. He may be built like the Babe, but he doesn't hit like him.

## 1996 Outlook

Lieber is not a lock to even make the Pirates' Opening Day roster in 1996. He has to prove himself all over again after being out of shape, both mentally and physically, last year. He still has a chance to become a solid starter, but this certainly is a crossroads season in his career.

# Nelson Liriano

**Position**: 2B
**Bats**: B **Throws**: R
**Ht**: 5'10" **Wt**: 178

**Opening Day Age**: 31
**Born**: 6/3/64 in Puerto Plata, DR
**ML Seasons**: 8

## Overall Statistics

| | G | AB | R | H | D | T | HR | RBI | SB | BB | SO | Avg | OBP | Slg |
|---|---|---|---|---|---|---|---|---|---|---|---|---|---|---|
| 1995 | 107 | 259 | 29 | 74 | 12 | 1 | 5 | 38 | 2 | 24 | 34 | .286 | .347 | .398 |
| Career | 623 | 1894 | 263 | 498 | 85 | 25 | 21 | 199 | 57 | 192 | 259 | .263 | .331 | .367 |

## 1995 Season

Veteran infielder Nelson Liriano performed brilliantly as a part-time player after joining the Pirates last season. He made 51 of his 55 starts at second base, filling in admirably when Carlos Garcia went on the disabled list in late July. He batted over .300 in July and August, and over the season hit a team-high .365 with runners in scoring position.

## Hitting, Baserunning & Defense

Liriano is a good-hitting backup infielder. He hits for average and occasionally drives the ball into the gap. Although a switch hitter, he is usually ineffective from the right side and rarely bats against lefties at this stage of his career. He has slowed a little over the years and no longer steals many bases. Second base is still, by far, his best position. Liriano shows good range and can turn a double play. He isn't as good at other infield positions. He lacks the necessary range of a shortstop and the strong arm of a third baseman.

## 1996 Outlook

It's been years since Liriano was touted as Toronto's second baseman of the future. He has bounced around the majors since those days. Though not a great player, he has a wonderful attitude and does enough things well to make him an effective bench player.

# Steve Pegues

**Position**: LF/RF
**Bats**: R **Throws**: R
**Ht**: 6' 2" **Wt**: 190

**Opening Day Age**: 27
**Born**: 5/21/68 in Pontotoc, MS
**ML Seasons**: 2
**Pronunciation**: puh-GHEEZ

## Overall Statistics

| | G | AB | R | H | D | T | HR | RBI | SB | BB | SO | Avg | OBP | Slg |
|---|---|---|---|---|---|---|---|---|---|---|---|---|---|---|
| 1995 | 82 | 171 | 17 | 42 | 8 | 0 | 6 | 16 | 1 | 4 | 36 | .246 | .263 | .398 |
| Career | 100 | 207 | 19 | 55 | 10 | 0 | 6 | 18 | 2 | 6 | 41 | .266 | .286 | .401 |

## 1995 Season

Steve Pegues spent his first full season in the majors in 1995, starting 36 games in the Pirates' outfield. On June 19 he enjoyed the first two-homer game of his career against San Francisco. Overall, though, he left a lot to be desired. He went 8-for-34 as a pinch hitter and batted just .081 with runners in scoring position.

## Hitting, Baserunning & Defense

A good hitter in the minor leagues, Pegues had his ups and downs in 1995. Though not noted for his power, he turned on some inside fastballs and sent them soaring. More notable was Pegues' complete lack of patience at the plate. He swung at everything, avoiding walks like they were IRS auditors. Pegues has some offensive skills, but they are negated by his free swinging. Pegues has good speed and can steal a base on occasion. He is an adequate defensive outfielder who is capable of playing all three spots. He has good range and an average arm.

## 1996 Outlook

The Pirates outrighted Pegues off the 40-man roster at the end of last season. He refused assignment to Triple-A Calgary and became a free agent. If Pegues couldn't stick with the worst team in the National League, what are his chances of making it somewhere else?

# Don Slaught

**Position**: C
**Bats**: R  **Throws**: R
**Ht**: 6' 1"  **Wt**: 185

**Opening Day Age**: 37
**Born**: 9/11/58 in Long Beach, CA
**ML Seasons**: 14
**Nickname**: Sluggo

### Overall Statistics

|  | G | AB | R | H | D | T | HR | RBI | SB | BB | SO | Avg | OBP | Slg |
|---|---|---|---|---|---|---|---|---|---|---|---|---|---|---|
| 1995 | 35 | 112 | 13 | 34 | 6 | 0 | 0 | 13 | 0 | 9 | 8 | .304 | .361 | .357 |
| Career | 1231 | 3800 | 388 | 1075 | 225 | 28 | 71 | 440 | 18 | 291 | 533 | .283 | .337 | .413 |

## 1995 Season

Another typical year for Don Slaught: a .300 average and a lot of time on the disabled list. Slaught missed the first five games of the season with a bruised right shoulder, then went on the disabled list twice with hamstring problems. But when Slaught played he produced, topping .300 for the fourth time with the Pirates.

## Hitting, Baserunning & Defense

Slaught is a line-drive hitter who uses the entire field and successfully executes the hit-and-run. He is primarily a fastball hitter, but has good enough bat control to foul off breaking balls until he gets his pitch. Numerous injuries over the years have robbed him of his speed. Never a great defensive catcher, Slaught threw out just five of 37 baserunners attempting to steal last season. He also doesn't move well behind the plate anymore, and has a hard time blocking balls in the dirt.

## 1996 Outlook

Slaught's days as a starting catcher may be over. He is just too fragile and cannot be counted on to catch 80-100 games. Because Slaught works hard at conditioning, he may hang on as a backup for a year or two. The Pirates would consider bringing him back to serve as a mentor to a young catcher, either Jason Kendall or Angelo Encarnacion, provided Slaught takes a pay cut from his 1995 salary.

# Kevin Young

**Position**: 3B
**Bats**: R  **Throws**: R
**Ht**: 6' 2"  **Wt**: 219

**Opening Day Age**: 26
**Born**: 6/16/69 in Alpena, MI
**ML Seasons**: 4

### Overall Statistics

|  | G | AB | R | H | D | T | HR | RBI | SB | BB | SO | Avg | OBP | Slg |
|---|---|---|---|---|---|---|---|---|---|---|---|---|---|---|
| 1995 | 56 | 181 | 13 | 42 | 9 | 0 | 6 | 22 | 1 | 8 | 53 | .232 | .268 | .381 |
| Career | 266 | 759 | 68 | 177 | 40 | 5 | 13 | 84 | 4 | 54 | 169 | .233 | .290 | .350 |

## 1995 Season

Kevin Young began the season at Triple-A Calgary, but returned to Pittsburgh in June after hitting .356 with eight homers and 34 RBI in 45 games there. Young spent the remainder of the season with the Pirates, spending time at both first base and third. He hit better than during any previous stint with the team. . .which is not to say he hit very well.

## Hitting, Baserunning & Defense

The Pirates thought Young would blossom into a major league hitter after a strong 1992 season at Triple-A Buffalo, but he hasn't developed into the .300 hitter with 15-20 homers that they anticipated. Young has a long swing and slow hands, making him susceptible to hard stuff inside. Pitchers pounds him inside, then go away with breaking balls in the dirt. He has tried dozen of adjustments with little success. Young has good speed but he doesn't steal many bases. He has decent range at both first and third base, but his arm is erratic at times.

## 1996 Outlook

Young showed signs of improvement last season, earning another chance with the Pirates. If free agent Jeff King isn't re-signed, Young becomes the front-runner to start at third base. Despite Young's impressive work habits, time is running out on him. He must prove he belongs in the majors.

# Other Pittsburgh Pirates

**Angelo Encarnacion** (**Pos**: C, **Age**: 22, **Bats**: R)

Encarnacion showed flashes of his cannon arm, throwing out a respectable 21 of 59 runners in '95. Both his defense and hitting have a lot of room to improve, but at his age there's plenty of time. 1996 Outlook: A

**Freddy Garcia** (**Pos**: LF, **Age**: 23, **Bats**: R)

Garcia needs a lot of work, both in the field and at the plate. His defense has never been great, and he had just two extra-base hits in 57 at-bats last season. Still young enough to improve. 1996 Outlook: B

**Jim Gott** (**Pos**: RHP, **Age**: 36)

Gott's career appears to be winding down. He pitched poorly after returning to the Pirates from Los Angeles. His three trips to the disabled list last season might have finally finished him. 1996 Outlook: C

**Lee Hancock** (**Pos**: LHP, **Age**: 28)

After struggling at Triple-A, Hancock made the most of his opportunity as a September call-up, pitching well in 11 relief appearances. He needs to do something special, and in a hurry. 1996 Outlook: B

**John Hope** (**Pos**: RHP, **Age**: 25)

Hope got another brief stint with the Pirates in '95, allowing eight earned runs in two-plus innings. He was outstanding at Triple-A as a starter, with a strikeout-to-walk ratio nearing four. He's just 25. 1996 Outlook: B

**Dennis Konuszewski** (**Pos**: RHP, **Age**: 25)

Konuszewksi didn't gain a lot in '95, pitching in just one game for the Pirates after a brief call-up in August. He's spent the rest of the last two seasons in Double-A pitching long relief, which doesn't say a lot for his future. 1996 Outloook: C

**Ravelo Manzanillo** (**Pos**: LHP, **Age**: 32)

The Pirates had a quick trigger with Manzanillo, sending him to the minors after he struggled in five relief appearances. He didn't help his cause at Triple-A, and his career is on the line. 1996 Outlook: C

**Ross Powell** (**Pos**: LHP, **Age**: 28)

After pitching poorly with Houston to start the season, Powell was traded to Pittsburgh in July, and didn't pitch much better. He was pummeled in his three starts for the Astros, finishing in the bullpen. 1996 Outlook: B

**Mackey Sasser** (**Pos**: C, **Age**: 33, **Bats**: L)

Sasser's '95 was very similar to his '94. Fighting both injuries and a slow start, he was released in May, and didn't resurface the rest of the season. He has little to offer at this point. 1996 Outlook: D

**John Wehner** (**Pos**: 3B/LF, **Age**: 28, **Bats**: R)

Wehner saw time with the Pirates for the fifth consecutive year, playing six positions along the way. He hit a nifty .308 in 52 games, spending most of his time in left field or at third base. 1996 Outlook: A

**Rick White** (**Pos**: RHP, **Age**: 27)

The Pirates gave White a chance to prove himself with nine starts last season. The results were mixed, with batters hitting .299 against him. Given that he started the year on the disabled list, it wasn't bad. 1996 Outlook: A

**Gary Wilson** (**Pos**: RHP, **Age**: 26)

Wilson had a tough '95, pitching poorly at Triple-A and during two stints with Pittsburgh in a relief role.. He was very solid as a minor league starter in '94, so maybe Pittsburgh will change his role. 1996 Outlook: B

# Pittsburgh Pirates Minor League Prospects

## Organization Overview:

Only three seasons removed from a heartbreaking seven-game loss in the 1992 National League Championship Series, the Pirates last year fell to the worst record in the N.L. It was a reminder of just how quickly the fortunes of a small-market team can drop in today's economic conditions. Pittsburgh simply couldn't afford to retain the services of its star players. The Pirates have given ample opportunity to their farmhands in recent years, virtually turning over their entire roster since the end of '92. So far, the newcomers haven't been up to the challenge, but that won't stop the Pirates from continuing the policy. There are a couple of prospects with star potential who could make the jump this season. Trey Beamon and Jason Kendall give Pirate fans at least some reason for optimism, but many of the youngsters already in Pittsburgh will have to show improvement for the Pirates to have any real chance in the near future.

### Jermaine Allensworth

**Position:** OF          **Opening Day Age:** 24
**Bats:** R **Throws:** R     **Born:** 1/11/72 in
**Ht:** 5' 11" **Wt:** 180     Anderson, IN

*Recent Statistics*

|  | G | AB | R | H | D | T | HR | RBI | SB | BB | SO | AVG |
|---|---|---|---|---|---|---|---|---|---|---|---|---|
| 93 A Welland | 67 | 263 | 44 | 81 | 16 | 4 | 1 | 32 | 18 | 24 | 38 | .308 |
| 94 AA Carolina | 118 | 452 | 63 | 109 | 26 | 8 | 1 | 34 | 16 | 39 | 79 | .241 |
| 95 AA Carolina | 56 | 219 | 37 | 59 | 14 | 2 | 1 | 14 | 13 | 25 | 34 | .269 |
| 95 AAA Calgary | 51 | 190 | 46 | 60 | 13 | 4 | 3 | 11 | 13 | 13 | 30 | .316 |
| 95 MLE | 107 | 388 | 59 | 98 | 23 | 3 | 1 | 17 | 17 | 25 | 67 | .253 |

Allensworth was the second of three first-round choices for the Pirates in 1993. He was in fact selected with one of the picks awarded Pittsburgh for losing Doug Drabek to free agency. Allensworth actually hit the best of his career following his promotion to Triple-A last season. His three home runs for Calgary matched his previous career total in over 900 at-bats. He's projected as a leadoff hitter, though his walk rate hasn't been high. He's an excellent defensive center fielder.

### Jimmy Anderson

**Position:** P          **Opening Day Age:** 20
**Bats:** L **Throws:** L     **Born:** 1/22/76 in
**Ht:** 6' 1" **Wt:** 180     Portsmouth, VA

*Recent Statistics*

|  | W | L | ERA | G | GS | Sv | IP | H | R | BB | SO | HR |
|---|---|---|---|---|---|---|---|---|---|---|---|---|
| 94 R Pirates | 5 | 1 | 1.60 | 10 | 10 | 0 | 56.1 | 35 | 21 | 27 | 66 | 1 |
| 95 A Augusta | 4 | 2 | 1.53 | 14 | 14 | 0 | 76.2 | 51 | 15 | 31 | 75 | 1 |
| 95 A Lynchburg | 1 | 5 | 4.13 | 10 | 9 | 0 | 52.1 | 56 | 29 | 21 | 32 | 1 |

Anderson breezed through the first half of 1995 in slow-A ball. His performance at Augusta earned Anderson a midseason promotion to the Carolina League, where he

produced his first ERA over 1.60 as a pro. He was the Pirates' ninth-round draft choice in 1994, and was pitching last season at the age of 19. The lefthander has the makings to be a power pitcher. His fastball already reaches the 90s, and he also throws a hard slider.

### Trey Beamon

**Position:** OF          **Opening Day Age:** 22
**Bats:** L **Throws:** R     **Born:** 2/11/74 in
**Ht:** 6' 3" **Wt:** 195     Dallas, TX

*Recent Statistics*

|  | G | AB | R | H | D | T | HR | RBI | SB | BB | SO | AVG |
|---|---|---|---|---|---|---|---|---|---|---|---|---|
| 93 A Augusta | 104 | 373 | 64 | 101 | 18 | 6 | 0 | 45 | 19 | 48 | 60 | .271 |
| 94 AA Carolina | 112 | 434 | 69 | 140 | 18 | 9 | 5 | 47 | 24 | 33 | 53 | .323 |
| 95 AAA Calgary | 118 | 452 | 74 | 151 | 29 | 5 | 5 | 62 | 18 | 39 | 55 | .334 |
| 95 MLE | 118 | 417 | 46 | 116 | 23 | 2 | 3 | 38 | 11 | 24 | 57 | .278 |

Beamon won the Southern League batting championship with a .323 average in 1994, and followed that with a .334 average in Triple-A last season. Last year's performance was especially impressive since Beamon was not only moving up a level, but was also just 21 years of age. The Pirates expect Beamon to hit with more power as he matures, and his fine speed should be good for 20 stolen bases a year. The majors are the next logical step for 1996.

### Lou Collier

**Position:** SS          **Opening Day Age:** 22
**Bats:** R **Throws:** R     **Born:** 8/21/73 in
**Ht:** 5' 10" **Wt:** 170     Chicago, IL

*Recent Statistics*

|  | G | AB | R | H | D | T | HR | RBI | SB | BB | SO | AVG |
|---|---|---|---|---|---|---|---|---|---|---|---|---|
| 93 A Welland | 50 | 201 | 35 | 61 | 6 | 2 | 1 | 19 | 8 | 12 | 31 | .303 |
| 94 A Augusta | 85 | 318 | 48 | 89 | 17 | 4 | 7 | 40 | 32 | 25 | 53 | .280 |
| 94 A Salem | 43 | 158 | 25 | 42 | 4 | 1 | 6 | 16 | 5 | 15 | 29 | .266 |
| 95 A Lynchburg | 114 | 399 | 68 | 110 | 19 | 3 | 4 | 38 | 31 | 51 | 60 | .276 |

Collier was drafted by the Pirates in 1992, but chose to remain at Triton (Illinois) Junior College, where he was named the National Junior College Player of the Year for 1993. Signed that spring, Collier has continued to show offensive ability as a shortstop. His walk rate rose sharply last season, and he again stole over 30 bases. His range may not be wide enough to remain at the position, though, so a move to third base could be forthcoming.

## Micah Franklin

**Position:** OF     **Opening Day Age:** 23
**Bats:** B **Throws:** R     **Born:** 4/25/72 in San
**Ht:** 6' 0" **Wt:** 195     Francisco, CA

*Recent Statistics*

| | G | AB | R | H | D | T | HR | RBI | SB | BB | SO | AVG |
|---|---|---|---|---|---|---|---|---|---|---|---|---|
| 93 A Winston-Sal | 20 | 69 | 10 | 16 | 1 | 1 | 3 | 6 | 0 | 10 | 19 | .232 |
| 93 A Charlstn-WV | 102 | 343 | 56 | 90 | 14 | 4 | 17 | 68 | 6 | 47 | 109 | .262 |
| 94 A Winston-Sal | 42 | 150 | 44 | 45 | 7 | 0 | 21 | 44 | 7 | 27 | 48 | .300 |
| 94 AA Chattanooga | 79 | 279 | 46 | 77 | 17 | 0 | 10 | 40 | 2 | 33 | 79 | .276 |
| 95 AAA Calgary | 110 | 358 | 64 | 105 | 28 | 0 | 21 | 71 | 3 | 47 | 95 | .293 |
| 95 MLE | 110 | 334 | 40 | 81 | 23 | 0 | 12 | 44 | 1 | 29 | 99 | .243 |

The Pirates are Franklin's third organization. He was originally signed by the Mets in the third round of 1990, before New York released him due to supposed attitude problems. Cincinnati gave Franklin a chance, but despite 31 homers between A and Double-A in 1994, the Reds still traded him to the Pirates. Franklin's power is certainly legitimate, though Calgary is a good hitter's park. The Pirates are not set at first base, and Franklin, who'll turn 24 in April, figures to compete for the position.

## Jason Kendall

**Position:** C     **Opening Day Age:** 21
**Bats:** R **Throws:** R     **Born:** 6/26/74 in San
**Ht:** 6' 0" **Wt:** 170     Diego, CA

*Recent Statistics*

| | G | AB | R | H | D | T | HR | RBI | SB | BB | SO | AVG |
|---|---|---|---|---|---|---|---|---|---|---|---|---|
| 93 A Augusta | 102 | 366 | 43 | 101 | 17 | 4 | 1 | 40 | 8 | 22 | 30 | .276 |
| 94 A Salem | 101 | 371 | 68 | 118 | 19 | 2 | 7 | 66 | 14 | 47 | 21 | .318 |
| 94 AA Carolina | 13 | 47 | 6 | 11 | 2 | 0 | 0 | 6 | 0 | 2 | 3 | .234 |
| 95 AA Carolina | 117 | 429 | 87 | 140 | 26 | 1 | 8 | 71 | 10 | 56 | 22 | .326 |
| 95 MLE | 117 | 413 | 73 | 124 | 24 | 0 | 6 | 59 | 7 | 39 | 23 | .300 |

Kendall's .326 batting average was the Southern League's second-highest mark in 1995. He complemented the average with walks and a few extra-base hits. Kendall was the Pirates' first-round draft pick in 1992 out of high school, and is only 21. He's the son of Fred Kendall, the catcher who played parts of 12 seasons in the big leagues, and he knows how to call a game from behind the plate. His throwing arm is strong and he handles pitchers well. He may get a shot to stick with the Pirates as early as this season.

## Ramon Morel

**Position:** P     **Opening Day Age:** 21
**Bats:** R **Throws:** R     **Born:** 8/15/74 in Villa
**Ht:** 6' 2" **Wt:** 170     Gonzalez, DR

*Recent Statistics*

| | W | L | ERA | G | GS | Sv | IP | H | R | BB | SO | HR |
|---|---|---|---|---|---|---|---|---|---|---|---|---|
| 95 A Lynchburg | 3 | 7 | 3.47 | 12 | 12 | 0 | 72.2 | 80 | 35 | 13 | 44 | 2 |
| 95 AA Carolina | 3 | 3 | 3.52 | 10 | 10 | 0 | 69.0 | 71 | 31 | 10 | 34 | 4 |
| 95 NL Pittsburgh | 0 | 1 | 2.84 | 5 | 0 | 0 | 6.1 | 6 | 2 | 2 | 3 | 0 |

Morel's performance in 1994 was outstanding, particularly his strikeout-to-walk ratio of more than six to one. He was a bit more hittable in moving up a couple levels last season, and his strikeout rate decreased. But he continued to demonstrate remarkable control, and made it to Double-A before he turned 21. Morel throws four pitches, including a 90-MPH fastball. Signed as a free agent from the Dominican Republic in 1992, he receives high marks for his competitiveness and pitching smarts.

## Charles Peterson

**Position:** OF     **Opening Day Age:** 21
**Bats:** R **Throws:** R     **Born:** 5/8/74 in
**Ht:** 6' 3" **Wt:** 200     Laurens, SC

*Recent Statistics*

| | G | AB | R | H | D | T | HR | RBI | SB | BB | SO | AVG |
|---|---|---|---|---|---|---|---|---|---|---|---|---|
| 93 R Pirates | 49 | 188 | 28 | 57 | 11 | 3 | 1 | 23 | 8 | 22 | 22 | .303 |
| 94 A Augusta | 108 | 415 | 55 | 106 | 14 | 6 | 4 | 40 | 27 | 35 | 78 | .255 |
| 95 A Lynchburg | 107 | 391 | 61 | 107 | 9 | 4 | 7 | 51 | 31 | 43 | 73 | .274 |
| 95 AA Carolina | 20 | 70 | 13 | 23 | 3 | 1 | 0 | 7 | 2 | 9 | 15 | .329 |

Peterson chose baseball over football after a terrific high school career in which he was named all-state and helped lead his school to state titles on the gridiron. Peterson's physical skills are obvious. He has great speed, which he's used to steal 27 and 33 bases the past two seasons. He's also very strong, which has yet to translate into much extra-base power though it eventually should. The Pirates' top pick in 1993, Peterson may return to Double-A this season.

## Others to Watch

Righthander **Elmer Dessens** finished 15-8 with a 2.49 ERA in the Southern League last season. His control was phenomenal, as he walked just 1.24 batters per nine innings. . . **John Dillinger** was Pittsburgh's 20th-round selection in 1992 out of a Florida junior college. He was 6-6 with a 4.02 ERA at fast-A Lynchburg last year. . . Righthander **Joe Maskivish**, a 37th-round pick in 1994, made 26 appearances last year and saved 20 games. He did turn 24 in August and was still in single-A. . . Catcher **Keith Osik** turned 27 in October of last year. He enjoyed a fine season in Triple-A, hitting .336 with 10 homers and 59 RBI. . . Lefthander **Chris Peters** became a starter in 1995, and the results were encouraging. He was 13-5 with a 2.33 ERA between A and Double-A, and his strikeout-to-walk ratio was 139-37. . . Another lefthander, **Matt Ruebel**, also went 13-5, exclusively at Double-A. Ruebel produced a 2.76 ERA, 136 strikeouts and 45 walks at age 25. . . **Tony Womack** doesn't draw walks and has no power, but he can play both middle-infield positions and could stick with the Pirates as a utilityman.

# Rene Arocha

## 1995 Season

Cuban righthander Rene Arocha signed with the Cardinals back in 1992, and joined the major league rotation the following season. Despite pitching fairly well in that role, Arocha was shifted to the bullpen in 1994 and collected 11 saves. But he wasn't great as a closer, and last year was used exclusively as a set-up reliever. Arocha had a so-so year that was interrupted by his second elbow operation in two years. Opposing batters ended up hitting .297 against him and he was touched for six home runs. What's worse, three of those gopher balls blew late-inning leads. By the time injuries ended his season, Arocha had gradually slipped in terms of importance within the St. Louis bullpen.

## Pitching

St. Louis had hoped that Arocha would be a power-pitching complement to Tom Henke in their bullpen. However, Arocha's velocity slipped back into the mid 80s for most of last year and his fastball thus became less useful. He has a serviceable slider and forkball, and also throws a change-up, but his location is too inconsistent for any of them to be dependable out pitches. Arocha does not have especially high walk numbers but he too often is wild within the strike zone, resulting in too many pitches down the middle. And with his fastball not good enough to overpower anyone, Arocha can be a very hittable pitcher in a role where every hit often is costly.

## Defense & Hitting

Arocha has a quick delivery home and works hard to keep runners close, so he is very solid in defensing the running game. He also has decent reactions in the field and can handle routine responsibilities. Not much of a hitter, Arocha only batted once last season and is 7-for-68 (.103) lifetime.

## 1996 Outlook

Once considered a front-line starter, Arocha has slipped back into a middle-relief role and was unremarkable even there. His arm problems and dropping velocity have raised questions in St. Louis. Arocha will have to prove himself to new manager Tony La Russa.

**Position:** RP
**Bats:** R **Throws:** R
**Ht:** 6' 0" **Wt:** 205

**Opening Day Age:** 30
**Born:** 2/24/66 in Havana, Cuba
**ML Seasons:** 3
**Pronunciation:** uh-ROACH-uh

### Overall Statistics

|        | W  | L  | Pct. | ERA  | G   | GS | Sv | IP    | H   | BB | SO  | HR | BR/IP |
|--------|----|----|------|------|-----|----|----|-------|-----|----|-----|----|-------|
| 1995   | 3  | 5  | .375 | 3.99 | 41  | 0  | 0  | 49.2  | 55  | 18 | 25  | 6  | 1.47  |
| Career | 18 | 17 | .514 | 3.87 | 118 | 36 | 11 | 320.2 | 346 | 70 | 183 | 35 | 1.30  |

### How Often He Throws Strikes

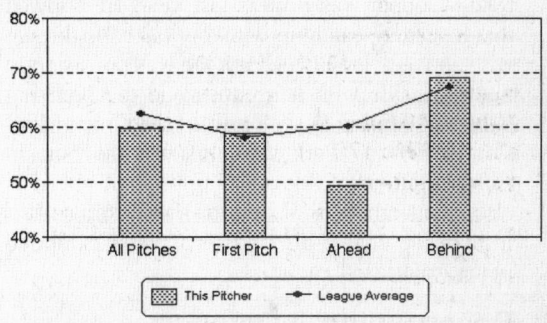

### 1995 Situational Stats

|           | W | L | ERA  | Sv | IP   |        | AB  | H  | HR | RBI | Avg  |
|-----------|---|---|------|----|------|--------|-----|----|----|-----|------|
| Home      | 1 | 1 | 3.47 | 0  | 23.1 | LHB    | 97  | 27 | 3  | 14  | .278 |
| Road      | 2 | 4 | 4.44 | 0  | 26.1 | RHB    | 88  | 28 | 3  | 13  | .318 |
| First Half | 3 | 4 | 3.57 | 0  | 40.1 | Sc Pos | 58  | 15 | 1  | 22  | .259 |
| Scnd Half | 0 | 1 | 5.79 | 0  | 9.1  | Clutch | 129 | 40 | 3  | 23  | .310 |

### 1995 Rankings (National League)

→ 2nd in worst first batter efficiency (.378) and least strikeouts per 9 innings in relief (4.5)
→ 3rd in blown saves (7)
→ 5th in highest batting average allowed in relief (.297)
→ 9th in holds (14)
→ Led the Cardinals in blown saves

St. Louis Cardinals

# Scott Cooper

## 1995 Season

The Cardinals weren't expecting Scott Cooper to be the second coming of Ken Boyer at third base, but neither did they expect Cooper—a two-time American League All-Star—to be such a huge disappointment. He was overmatched from the start by National League pitching, and never mounted any momentum on his way to an eventual late-season benching. Even worse, Cooper was eaten alive defensively by the Busch Stadium artificial turf.

## Hitting

In every conceivable category—vs. righties and lefties, in clutch situations, at home and on the road—Cooper was a mess last year. He showed that he cannot catch up with any fastballs thrown with above-average velocity. He was consistently tied up inside with hard stuff, and the breaking balls that he used to send toward the Green Monster in Fenway Park were just routine outs in Busch Stadium. Cooper's sluggish bat speed is also a concern for St. Louis, as the Cardinals saw little of the double-digit power Cooper exhibited in the American League.

## Baserunning & Defense

Cooper is an exceptionally slow runner, so slow that he is too much of a risk to use on hit-and-run plays. His best asset as a fielder is a strong throwing arm, but that doesn't make up for his poor range, which is especially exposed on the artificial turf which St. Louis will replace in 1996 with real grass. Cooper's fielding mechanics are poor, which contributes to his being out of position on too many balls.

## 1996 Outlook

By season's end, the Cardinals were scrambling for alternatives at third base. As one exasperated club executive put it, "No one had any idea how weak a player Cooper was when we got him from Boston." There was talk St. Louis would not even tender Cooper a 1996 contract. If he does return, he'll have to show much more than he did last season to warrant an everyday role.

**Position:** 3B
**Bats:** L  **Throws:** R
**Ht:** 6' 3"  **Wt:** 215

**Opening Day Age:** 28
**Born:** 10/13/67 in St. Louis, MO
**ML Seasons:** 6

### Overall Statistics

| | G | AB | R | H | D | T | HR | RBI | SB | BB | SO | Avg | OBP | Slg |
|---|---|---|---|---|---|---|---|---|---|---|---|---|---|---|
| 1995 | 118 | 374 | 29 | 86 | 18 | 2 | 3 | 40 | 0 | 49 | 85 | .230 | .321 | .313 |
| Career | 517 | 1642 | 185 | 446 | 88 | 11 | 30 | 196 | 6 | 176 | 267 | .272 | .343 | .393 |

### Where He Hits the Ball

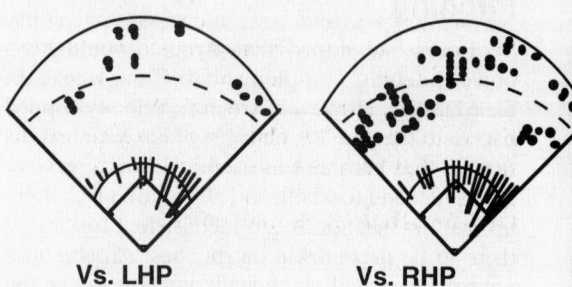

**Vs. LHP**          **Vs. RHP**

### 1995 Situational Stats

| | AB | H | HR | RBI | Avg | | AB | H | HR | RBI | Avg |
|---|---|---|---|---|---|---|---|---|---|---|---|
| Home | 189 | 43 | 1 | 20 | .228 | LHP | 97 | 20 | 0 | 18 | .206 |
| Road | 185 | 43 | 2 | 20 | .232 | RHP | 277 | 66 | 3 | 22 | .238 |
| First Half | 231 | 59 | 2 | 31 | .255 | Sc Pos | 100 | 21 | 0 | 35 | .210 |
| Scnd Half | 143 | 27 | 1 | 9 | .189 | Clutch | 60 | 11 | 0 | 10 | .183 |

### 1995 Rankings (National League)

➡ 2nd in lowest batting average vs. left-handed pitchers (.206) and lowest slugging percentage vs. left-handed pitchers (.268)

➡ 3rd in errors at third base (18)

➡ 4th in lowest fielding percentage at third base (.945)

➡ 7th in lowest batting average with runners in scoring position (.210)

➡ Led the Cardinals in batting average on a 3-2 count (.326), highest percentage of pitches taken (56.4%) and lowest percentage of swings that missed (18.8%)

# Tripp Cromer

## 1995 Season

The Cardinals saw the post-Ozzie Smith era at shortstop last season, and they weren't thrilled with what they saw in Tripp Cromer. Given the job after Smith went down with a shoulder injury, Cromer raised little hope that he would be the heir apparent. Though displaying occasional power, Cromer was largely overmatched at the plate. He also did little to make Cards fans forget Ozzie in the field.

## Hitting

Cromer surprises people with his gap power and occasional home-run strength, but he has such a big swing that he can be tied up with even average fastballs. He is easily fooled by decent breaking balls and often chases balls out of the strike zone, resulting in too many strikeouts and not enough walks. Cromer is far too anxious at the plate and has not yet learned to wait on offspeed pitches. He also visibly pressed in clutch situations, batting an anemic .133 with men in scoring position.

## Baserunning & Defense

Cromer hardly fits the mold of the classic Cardinals infielder. He has below-average speed and did not even attempt a stolen base while grounding into the second-most double plays on the club. Cromer is sure-handed in the field, but his range is only average and his throwing arm is more erratic than you'd like from your shortstop. He is also less than slick when turning the double play.

## 1996 Outlook

The decline of Ozzie Smith leaves the Cardinals—and their new manager—in search of a shortstop. Cromer enters the season as a decided long shot, and will have to show significant improvement this spring if he's to win a regular job. Cromer's minor league record suggests that he's a bit better than he showed last season, but if he does stick with the new Cardinal regime, it almost certainly will be as a reserve.

**Position:** SS/2B
**Bats:** R  **Throws:** R
**Ht:** 6' 2"  **Wt:** 170

**Opening Day Age:** 28
**Born:** 11/21/67 in Lake City, SC
**ML Seasons:** 3
**Pronunciation:** CROW-mer

### Overall Statistics

|        | G   | AB  | R  | H  | D  | T | HR | RBI | SB | BB | SO | Avg  | OBP  | Slg  |
|--------|-----|-----|----|----|----|---|----|-----|----|----|----|------|------|------|
| 1995   | 105 | 345 | 36 | 78 | 19 | 0 | 5  | 18  | 0  | 14 | 66 | .226 | .261 | .325 |
| Career | 117 | 368 | 38 | 80 | 19 | 0 | 5  | 18  | 0  | 15 | 72 | .217 | .253 | .310 |

### Where He Hits the Ball

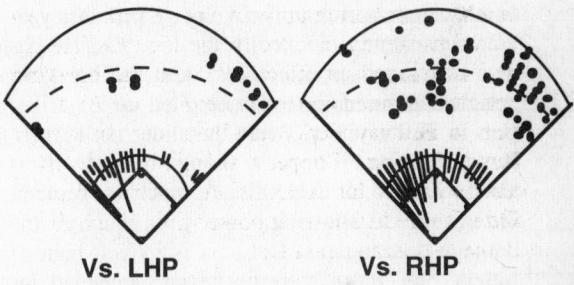

Vs. LHP          Vs. RHP

### 1995 Situational Stats

|            | AB  | H  | HR | RBI | Avg  |        | AB  | H  | HR | RBI | Avg  |
|------------|-----|----|----|-----|------|--------|-----|----|----|-----|------|
| Home       | 164 | 41 | 2  | 8   | .250 | LHP    | 84  | 16 | 2  | 6   | .190 |
| Road       | 181 | 37 | 3  | 10  | .204 | RHP    | 261 | 62 | 3  | 12  | .238 |
| First Half | 207 | 50 | 5  | 12  | .242 | Sc Pos | 60  | 8  | 0  | 11  | .133 |
| Scnd Half  | 138 | 28 | 0  | 6   | .203 | Clutch | 47  | 11 | 0  | 3   | .234 |

### 1995 Rankings (National League)

→ 4th in lowest fielding percentage at shortstop (.960)
→ 6th in most GDPs per GDP situation (18.4%)
→ 7th in errors at shortstop (16)
→ Led the Cardinals in sacrifice flies (5)

# Rich DeLucia

## 1995 Season

Once a 12-game winner as a starter with Seattle, Rich DeLucia was plucked off the baseball scrap heap by St. Louis and given a career revival as a middle and long reliever. He made 55 relief outings, second-most on the club, with opponents hitting only .213 against him for the season. He was valuable in several innings-eating, long-relief stints, especially during an early-season stretch in which Cardinal starters were struggling. DeLucia actually led the Cardinals with eight victories, which is obviously more a testament to the rotation's problems than anything else.

## Pitching

DeLucia has overcome arm problems from earlier in his career and regained velocity that last year was consistently clocked in the low 90s. He has also developed an effective, late-breaking slider which was the main reason he piled up 76 strikeouts in 82.1 innings. When the slider isn't working, he can be hit because though his velocity is good, his fastball doesn't have much movement. He is prone to allowing home runs. Much of the damage done against DeLucia is by left-handed hitters, one reason why he never succeeded for long as a starter. When spotted against right-handed hitters, who batted under .200 against him last year, DeLucia is much more effective.

## Hitting & Defense

DeLucia is a good athlete who fields his position well. He has a fairly quick delivery home, though no pickoff move to speak of. He handles the bat reasonably well and usually puts the ball in play when needed as a hitter, striking out only three times last season in 10 at-bats, his first as a major leaguer.

## 1996 Outlook

St. Louis was pleasantly surprised by DeLucia's emergence and he could be a key source of bullpen innings for Tony La Russa, a proven master at extracting the maximum from his relief corps.

**Position:** RP
**Bats:** R  **Throws:** R
**Ht:** 6' 0"  **Wt:** 185

**Opening Day Age:** 31
**Born:** 10/7/64 in Wyomissing, PA
**ML Seasons:** 6
duh-LOOSH-shuh

### Overall Statistics

|        | W  | L  | Pct. | ERA  | G   | GS | Sv | IP    | H   | BB  | SO  | HR | BR/IP |
|--------|----|----|------|------|-----|----|----|-------|-----|-----|-----|----|-------|
| 1995   | 8  | 7  | .533 | 3.39 | 56  | 1  | 0  | 82.1  | 63  | 36  | 76  | 9  | 1.20  |
| Career | 27 | 34 | .443 | 4.53 | 161 | 49 | 1  | 437.1 | 424 | 186 | 323 | 64 | 1.39  |

### How Often He Throws Strikes

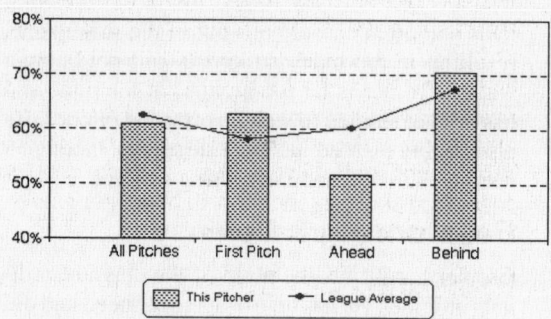

This Pitcher    — League Average

### 1995 Situational Stats

|            | W | L | ERA  | Sv | IP   |        | AB  | H  | HR | RBI | Avg  |
|------------|---|---|------|----|------|--------|-----|----|----|-----|------|
| Home       | 4 | 3 | 4.02 | 0  | 40.1 | LHB    | 114 | 27 | 5  | 15  | .237 |
| Road       | 4 | 4 | 2.79 | 0  | 42.0 | RHB    | 182 | 36 | 4  | 21  | .198 |
| First Half | 3 | 3 | 3.54 | 0  | 48.1 | Sc Pos | 79  | 19 | 2  | 27  | .241 |
| Scnd Half  | 5 | 4 | 3.18 | 0  | 34.0 | Clutch | 95  | 19 | 5  | 12  | .200 |

### 1995 Rankings (National League)

- ➡ 1st in relief wins (8)
- ➡ 3rd in lowest batting average allowed in relief (.201)
- ➡ 5th in relief losses (6)
- ➡ 6th in highest percentage of inherited runners scored (39.3%)
- ➡ 10th in relief innings (79.0)
- ➡ Led the Cardinals in wins, winning percentage, relief wins, relief innings and lowest batting average allowed in relief

# Bernard Gilkey

## 1995 Season

After a 1994 campaign that saw his numbers drop alarmingly, Bernard Gilkey revived his career with his most solid overall season. Being forced to bat leadoff most of the campaign hurt Gilkey's RBI total, but he still knocked in 69 runs, just one fewer than his career high. Gilkey was also among club leaders in total bases and runs scored as he solidified his position as St. Louis' everyday left fielder.

## Hitting

Gilkey abandoned what had become an exaggerated crouch, moved off the plate slightly and began catching up to the fastballs which were thrown past him in his disappointing 1994 season. He regained power and showed his extra-base ability to both right- and left-center fields. Though he will never be a walking machine, Gilkey has improved his patience, cut down his swing and limited his strikeouts. He is annually one of the best hitters in the league with men in scoring position, a skill that ideally will have him batting lower in the order in the future.

## Baserunning & Defense

An above-average runner, Gilkey has never developed into more than an average basestealer. However, he is aggressive in taking the extra base and breaking up double plays. Gilkey's range is just fair, but along with Ray Lankford and Brian Jordan he is part of one of baseball's fastest outfields. Gilkey's arm is above average for a left fielder, and his quick release makes things dangerous for baserunners.

## 1996 Outlook

If needed, Gilkey will again be the Cardinals' leadoff hitter. However, St. Louis hopes to find a more prototypical leadoff man, allowing them to bat Gilkey lower in the order, where his burgeoning power will be better utilized. Whatever happens, Gilkey will wind up somewhere in the St. Louis lineup, looking to build on his excellent 1995.

**Position:** LF
**Bats:** R  **Throws:** R
**Ht:** 6' 0"  **Wt:** 200

**Opening Day Age:** 29
**Born:** 9/24/66 in St. Louis, MO
**ML Seasons:** 6

### Overall Statistics

|        | G   | AB   | R   | H   | D   | T  | HR | RBI | SB | BB  | SO  | Avg  | OBP  | Slg  |
|--------|-----|------|-----|-----|-----|----|----|-----|----|-----|-----|------|------|------|
| 1995   | 121 | 480  | 73  | 143 | 33  | 4  | 17 | 69  | 12 | 42  | 70  | .298 | .358 | .490 |
| Career | 593 | 2133 | 319 | 602 | 126 | 18 | 52 | 250 | 80 | 223 | 291 | .282 | .354 | .431 |

### Where He Hits the Ball

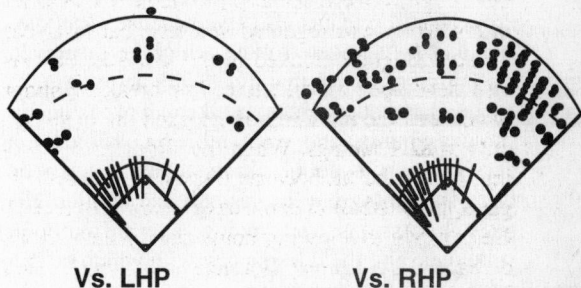

**Vs. LHP**                    **Vs. RHP**

### 1995 Situational Stats

|            | AB  | H  | HR | RBI | Avg  |        | AB  | H   | HR | RBI | Avg  |
|------------|-----|----|----|-----|------|--------|-----|-----|----|-----|------|
| Home       | 238 | 66 | 5  | 36  | .277 | LHP    | 106 | 33  | 2  | 15  | .311 |
| Road       | 242 | 77 | 12 | 33  | .318 | RHP    | 374 | 110 | 15 | 54  | .294 |
| First Half | 222 | 69 | 8  | 36  | .311 | Sc Pos | 95  | 31  | 0  | 43  | .326 |
| Scnd Half  | 258 | 74 | 9  | 33  | .287 | Clutch | 83  | 23  | 3  | 16  | .277 |

### 1995 Rankings (National League)

➡ 1st in fielding percentage in left field (.986)
➡ 5th in GDPs (17) and most GDPs per GDP situation (20.0%)
➡ 6th in batting average on the road (.318)
➡ 7th in lowest stolen base percentage (66.7%)
➡ 8th in lowest on-base percentage for a leadoff hitter (.344)
➡ 9th in errors in left field (3)
➡ 10th in doubles
➡ Led the Cardinals in batting average, triples, GDPs, highest groundball/flyball ratio (1.3), batting average with runners in scoring position (.326) and batting average vs. left-handed pitchers (.311)

**St. Louis Cardinals**

# Tom Henke

## 1995 Season

After a 1994 season which saw him throw three or four bad pitches which ruined his ERA, Tom Henke re-asserted himself as one of the game's premier closers. An All-Star selection in his first season in the National League, Henke blew only two save opportunities and was unscored upon for nearly the entire first half of the season. It was a dynamic performance, especially considering how infrequently he was given chances to save games by the otherwise woeful St. Louis pitching staff.

## Pitching

Little has been lost from the great Henke fastball, which he still runs up there consistently in the 92- to 95-MPH range. And when his velocity does drop, he still remains effective because of an outstanding split-fingered pitch which he throws in the mid-80s, a pitch that dives with an exceptionally hard and quick break. Henke will occasionally show a change and even more occasionally a curve, but he's doing hitters a favor when he throws anything but the fastball and splitter. His main concessions to advancing years are a drop in strikeouts, and the infrequency with which he can pitch more than one inning.

## Defense & Hitting

Like most closers, Henke is largely oblivious to the other parts of a pitcher's job. He has no move to first and his big delivery rarely leaves him in good fielding position. Henke is not particularly agile, and he batted only once last season, which was one too many times.

## 1996 Outlook

No manager in baseball knows better how to nurse the maximum from his closer than Tony La Russa. Late last season, Henke made some noises about retiring. But the presence of La Russa is certain to be attractive for Henke. That, plus the fact that he lives year-round in Missouri, makes St. Louis a perfect spot for Henke, and the Cardinals expect him to return for another big year.

**Position:** RP
**Bats:** R **Throws:** R
**Ht:** 6' 5" **Wt:** 230

**Opening Day Age:** 38
**Born:** 12/21/57 in Kansas City, MO
**ML Seasons:** 14
**Nickname:** The Terminator
**Pronunciation:** HEN-kee

### Overall Statistics

|        | W  | L  | Pct. | ERA  | G   | GS | Sv  | IP    | H   | BB  | SO  | HR | BR/IP |
|--------|----|----|------|------|-----|----|-----|-------|-----|-----|-----|----|-------|
| 1995   | 1  | 1  | .500 | 1.82 | 52  | 0  | 36  | 54.1  | 42  | 18  | 48  | 2  | 1.10  |
| Career | 41 | 42 | .494 | 2.67 | 642 | 0  | 311 | 789.2 | 607 | 255 | 861 | 64 | 1.09  |

### How Often He Throws Strikes

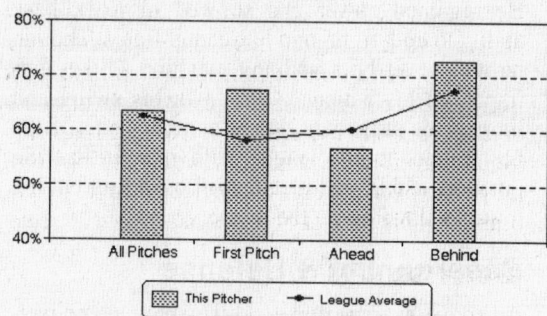

### 1995 Situational Stats

|            | W | L | ERA  | Sv | IP   |        | AB  | H  | HR | RBI | Avg  |
|------------|---|---|------|----|------|--------|-----|----|----|-----|------|
| Home       | 1 | 1 | 1.72 | 20 | 31.1 | LHB    | 99  | 19 | 2  | 5   | .192 |
| Road       | 0 | 0 | 1.96 | 16 | 23.0 | RHB    | 102 | 23 | 0  | 9   | .225 |
| First Half | 0 | 0 | 1.65 | 17 | 27.1 | Sc Pos | 59  | 9  | 0  | 10  | .153 |
| Scnd Half  | 1 | 1 | 2.00 | 19 | 27.0 | Clutch | 152 | 33 | 1  | 11  | .217 |

### 1995 Rankings (National League)

→ 1st in save percentage (94.7%) and relief ERA (1.82)
→ 2nd in saves
→ 4th in save opportunities (38) and least baserunners allowed per 9 innings in relief (9.9)
→ 7th in lowest batting average allowed in relief with runners in scoring position (.153) and lowest batting average allowed in relief (.209)
→ Led the Cardinals in saves, games finished, save opportunities, save percentage, relief ERA and least baserunners allowed per 9 innings in relief

# Danny Jackson

## 1995 Season

There were few more expensive disappointments than Danny Jackson. Weakened by an offseason cancer scare and unable to regain strength because of heavy medication, Jackson lost his first nine decisions with St. Louis. His ERA at that point was over seven. However, after his medication was better regulated and he got over some other aches and pains, Jackson eventually showed some encouraging flashes, winning two of his final five decisions and allowing fewer than four runs per game over his last eight starts.

## Pitching

Without his usual bulldog stamina, Jackson lost at least five miles per hour off his fastball. And with his weakness came mechanical problems in his delivery which resulted in his slider flattening out. However, at full strength Jackson can still be a solid power pitcher with his heavy sinking fastball and an outstanding slider. In addition, Jackson throws an effective change-up which he occasionally turns over against right-handed batters. He has improved his control over the last couple of years.

## Defense & Hitting

Jackson is one of those lefthanders who is fairly easy to run on. He has a relatively high leg kick, so runners can usually gauge when he's going home and thus get excellent jumps. He is a decent fielder who does not get rattled when forced to make decisions. And though he strikes out in roughly half his at-bats, when he does make contact, he can do some damage. Two of his five hits last year were doubles.

## 1996 Outlook

Stuck with two more years of his big contract, the Cardinals might as well be optimistic about Jackson. And they may have good reason. He seemed completely over his medical condition by the end of last season, and he then embarked on a vigorous offseason conditioning program, similar to what he did prior to his big 1994 campaign with Philadelphia. The Cards think Jackson can come back and again be a big winner.

**Position:** SP
**Bats:** R **Throws:** L
**Ht:** 6' 0" **Wt:** 220

**Opening Day Age:** 34
**Born:** 1/5/62 in San Antonio, TX
**ML Seasons:** 13

### Overall Statistics

|  | W | L | Pct. | ERA | G | GS | Sv | IP | H | BB | SO | HR | BR/IP |
|---|---|---|---|---|---|---|---|---|---|---|---|---|---|
| 1995 | 2 | 12 | .143 | 5.90 | 19 | 19 | 0 | 100.2 | 120 | 48 | 52 | 10 | 1.67 |
| Career | 109 | 121 | .474 | 3.88 | 323 | 307 | 1 | 1968.2 | 1979 | 772 | 1166 | 119 | 1.40 |

### How Often He Throws Strikes

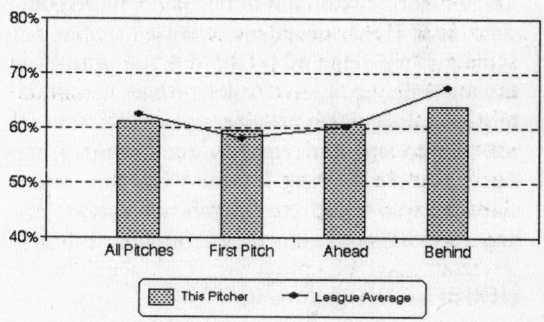

### 1995 Situational Stats

|  | W | L | ERA | Sv | IP |  | AB | H | HR | RBI | Avg |
|---|---|---|---|---|---|---|---|---|---|---|---|
| Home | 1 | 5 | 6.26 | 0 | 46.0 | LHB | 58 | 15 | 1 | 10 | .259 |
| Road | 1 | 7 | 5.60 | 0 | 54.2 | RHB | 338 | 105 | 9 | 62 | .311 |
| First Half | 1 | 9 | 6.71 | 0 | 63.0 | Sc Pos | 115 | 37 | 3 | 57 | .322 |
| Scnd Half | 1 | 3 | 4.54 | 0 | 37.2 | Clutch | 25 | 10 | 1 | 6 | .400 |

### 1995 Rankings (National League)

→ 1st in lowest winning percentage
→ 4th in highest batting average allowed vs. right-handed batters (.311)
→ 5th in errors at pitcher (3)
→ 8th in losses and highest batting average allowed with runners in scoring position (.322)
→ Led the Cardinals in losses, complete games (2), shutouts (1), walks allowed and hit batsmen (6)

St. Louis
Cardinals

# Brian Jordan

## 1995 Season

Who says baseball loses all the great athletes? After flirting with a return to pro football for years, Brian Jordan has finally made the commitment to baseball. And if last season is any indication, Jordan made the right decision. After a blistering start followed by a six-week swoon, Jordan rebounded over the last three months and put together a breakthrough season in which he led the Cards in hits, runs scored and steals, and was second in homers and RBI. Jordan fell just four points short of hitting .300.

## Hitting

Jordan has worked hard with Cards batting instructor Chris Chambliss to become a more complete hitter. He shortened his swing somewhat, but without sacrificing any power, and the result was a swing better equipped to catch up with hard stuff. Jordan is also solid against breaking balls. He will still pile up strikeouts, mainly due to impatience that causes him to chase too many balls and rarely walk. He was solid in the clutch last season, batting over .300 with runners in scoring position.

## Baserunning & Defense

There are few better athletes in baseball than Jordan. He has come on strong as a basestealer and there's no reason why his combination of speed, instincts and aggressiveness won't someday translate into 30 or more steals. He does need better judgment, but that should come as he becomes more schooled regarding N.L. pitchers. Jordan has also improved steadily as an outfielder, becoming reliably sure-handed with a strong and accurate throwing arm.

## 1996 Outlook

The questions about Jordan finally were answered last season, and —barring any physical setbacks— he could be poised for stardom. His blend of power, speed and athleticism make Jordan a candidate to be baseball's next 30-30 man, and it could happen in 1996.

**Position:** RF/CF
**Bats:** R **Throws:** R
**Ht:** 6' 1" **Wt:** 215

**Opening Day Age:** 29
**Born:** 3/29/67 in Baltimore, MD
**ML Seasons:** 4

### Overall Statistics

|  | G | AB | R | H | D | T | HR | RBI | SB | BB | SO | Avg | OBP | Slg |
|---|---|---|---|---|---|---|---|---|---|---|---|---|---|---|
| 1995 | 131 | 490 | 83 | 145 | 20 | 4 | 22 | 81 | 24 | 22 | 79 | .296 | .339 | .488 |
| Career | 306 | 1084 | 147 | 300 | 47 | 16 | 42 | 162 | 41 | 60 | 202 | .277 | .323 | .466 |

### Where He Hits the Ball

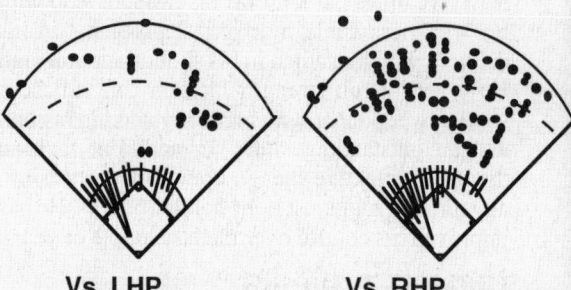

Vs. LHP          Vs. RHP

### 1995 Situational Stats

|  | AB | H | HR | RBI | Avg |  | AB | H | HR | RBI | Avg |
|---|---|---|---|---|---|---|---|---|---|---|---|
| Home | 259 | 81 | 14 | 53 | .313 | LHP | 121 | 33 | 5 | 21 | .273 |
| Road | 231 | 64 | 8 | 28 | .277 | RHP | 369 | 112 | 17 | 60 | .304 |
| First Half | 259 | 76 | 10 | 42 | .293 | Sc Pos | 131 | 42 | 5 | 57 | .321 |
| Scnd Half | 231 | 69 | 12 | 39 | .299 | Clutch | 85 | 20 | 2 | 15 | .235 |

### 1995 Rankings (National League)

→ 1st in fielding percentage in right field (.996)
→ 3rd in highest percentage of extra bases taken as a runner (69.6%)
→ 5th in least GDPs per GDP situation (4.3%)
→ 6th in hit by pitch (11) and highest percentage of swings on the first pitch (42.4%)
→ 8th in cleanup slugging percentage (.534)
→ 10th in least pitches seen per plate appearance (3.39) and batting average at home (.313)
→ Led the Cardinals in at-bats, runs scored, hits, singles (99), triples, stolen bases, caught stealing (9), hit by pitch, least GDPs per GDP situation (4.3%), batting average vs. right-handed pitchers (.304) and cleanup slugging percentage

# Ray Lankford

## 1995 Season

After drifting for a couple of years, Ray Lankford has renewed the promise that once had people labeling him a potential MVP. He hit a career-high 25 home runs, adding 82 RBI and 24 steals in the kind of all-around production St. Louis has been expecting from him. Lankford was especially strong in the second half of the season when he settled into the middle of the St. Louis batting order.

## Hitting

Lankford has been criticized for his high number of strikeouts, but now that he's entrenched as a middle-of-the-order hitter, the strikeouts are much more acceptable. He has a good knowledge of the strike zone and will take more than his share of walks. However, he has a big swing which he will not cut down when behind in the count. As a result, he is especially vulnerable to offspeed pitches. On the other hand, Lankford is rarely overpowered by fastballs. He is also a solid clutch hitter and last year, for the first time, he stayed in against left-handers, against whom he hit .275.

## Baserunning & Defense

Lankford has the pure speed to be a big-time basestealer. However, he has never been a quick starter off first base nor does he get the best of jumps. That, combined with his new place in the batting order, should result in Lankford's steals peaking in the 25 to 30 range. For someone with such outstanding skills, Lankford is an average outfielder. He has the speed to make up for mistakes but is often tentative, especially on balls hit over his head. His arm is better than average.

## 1996 Outlook

Some people wanted to compare a younger Lankford to Barry Bonds, but that was a stretch. However, if the Cardinals can improve their lineup ahead of Lankford, he can continue to grow into one of the league's better players, and is capable of being a consistent 85-100 RBI man.

**Position:** CF
**Bats:** L  **Throws:** L
**Ht:** 5'11"  **Wt:** 200

**Opening Day Age:** 28
**Born:** 6/5/67 in Los Angeles, CA
**ML Seasons:** 6

### Overall Statistics

|  | G | AB | R | H | D | T | HR | RBI | SB | BB | SO | Avg | OBP | Slg |
|---|---|---|---|---|---|---|---|---|---|---|---|---|---|---|
| 1995 | 132 | 483 | 81 | 134 | 35 | 2 | 25 | 82 | 24 | 63 | 110 | .277 | .360 | .513 |
| Career | 711 | 2596 | 416 | 695 | 150 | 32 | 83 | 351 | 143 | 328 | 622 | .268 | .351 | .446 |

### Where He Hits the Ball

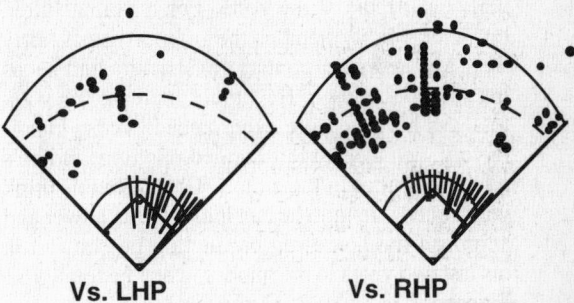

Vs. LHP          Vs. RHP

### 1995 Situational Stats

|  | AB | H | HR | RBI | Avg |  | AB | H | HR | RBI | Avg |
|---|---|---|---|---|---|---|---|---|---|---|---|
| Home | 237 | 73 | 16 | 48 | .308 | LHP | 142 | 39 | 3 | 29 | .275 |
| Road | 246 | 61 | 9 | 34 | .248 | RHP | 341 | 95 | 22 | 53 | .279 |
| First Half | 256 | 69 | 10 | 35 | .270 | Sc Pos | 124 | 38 | 9 | 61 | .306 |
| Scnd Half | 227 | 65 | 15 | 47 | .286 | Clutch | 74 | 23 | 4 | 15 | .311 |

### 1995 Rankings (National League)

→ 5th in doubles and fielding percentage in center field (.990)
→ 6th in strikeouts and lowest percentage of swings on the first pitch (18.1%)
→ 7th in errors in center field (3)
→ 8th in lowest percentage of swings put into play (37.6%)
→ 9th in lowest groundball/flyball ratio (1.0), most pitches seen per plate appearance (4.03) and slugging percentage vs. right-handed pitchers (.543)
→ Led the Cardinals in home runs, doubles, total bases (248), RBI, sacrifice flies (5), stolen bases, walks and intentional walks (6)

St. Louis Cardinals

# John Mabry

## 1995 Season

After Gregg Jefferies left St. Louis via free agency, the Cardinals experimented with various options before deciding to use converted outfielder John Mabry as the everyday first baseman. Mabry, long considered a top hitting prospect, took full advantage of his chance. He hit over .300, showed occasional power and was competent in the field.

## Hitting

With a fluid, short stroke, Mabry has the ability to hit the ball hard to all fields. He is a good fastball hitter and unlike most left-handed hitters, he can handle his share of hard stuff up in the strike zone. Changes of speed can bother him, as can breaking balls out of the strike zone. For a young hitter, however, Mabry handles the offspeed stuff fairly well, and he makes contact consistently and keeps his strikeouts down. He should increase his walk totals as he gets more experienced. Mabry hangs in very well against left-handed pitching, and he's a focused hitter in the clutch. The Cardinals think with added strength, he can increase his power and approach the home-run production he showed in his last two years in the minors, when he totaled 31 homers.

## Baserunning & Defense

Mabry will never earn his living with his running. He is slow and not a threat to steal. However, he does have good judgment on the bases and will take the extra base. He had his rough moments at first base, especially throwing the ball. However, he appears to have decent hands and acceptable range, while still needing work on footwork. He is also an experienced outfielder, though his range and arm are a little suspect.

## 1996 Outlook

Ideally, the Cardinals would like to add power to their lineup, and finding a slugging first baseman might be one way to do that. However, Mabry impressed St. Louis to the point where they might first look at other positions, leaving Mabry in place with the hope that he'll develop more power as he gains experience.

**Position:** 1B/LF/RF
**Bats:** L  **Throws:** R
**Ht:** 6' 4"  **Wt:** 205

**Opening Day Age:** 25
**Born:** 10/17/70 in Wilmington, DE
**ML Seasons:** 2

### Overall Statistics

|        | G   | AB  | R  | H   | D  | T | HR | RBI | SB | BB | SO | Avg  | OBP  | Slg  |
|--------|-----|-----|----|-----|----|---|----|-----|----|----|----|------|------|------|
| 1995   | 129 | 388 | 35 | 119 | 21 | 1 | 5  | 41  | 0  | 24 | 45 | .307 | .347 | .405 |
| Career | 135 | 411 | 37 | 126 | 24 | 1 | 5  | 44  | 0  | 26 | 49 | .307 | .348 | .406 |

### Where He Hits the Ball

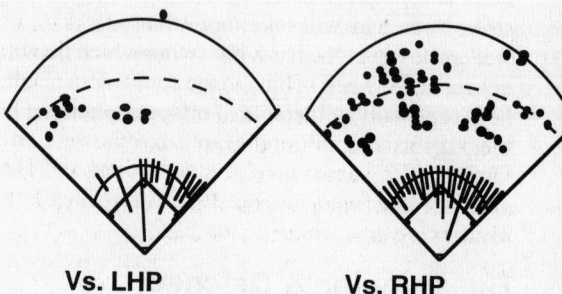

**Vs. LHP**          **Vs. RHP**

### 1995 Situational Stats

|           | AB  | H  | HR | RBI | Avg  |        | AB  | H  | HR | RBI | Avg  |
|-----------|-----|----|----|-----|------|--------|-----|----|----|-----|------|
| Home      | 204 | 66 | 2  | 22  | .324 | LHP    | 100 | 33 | 2  | 14  | .330 |
| Road      | 184 | 53 | 3  | 19  | .288 | RHP    | 288 | 86 | 3  | 27  | .299 |
| First Half| 157 | 48 | 1  | 13  | .306 | Sc Pos | 92  | 27 | 2  | 35  | .293 |
| Scnd Half | 231 | 71 | 4  | 28  | .307 | Clutch | 72  | 27 | 0  | 10  | .375 |

### 1995 Rankings (National League)

➡ 6th in batting average in the clutch (.375)
➡ Led the Cardinals in batting average in the clutch

# Mike Morgan

## 1995 Season

Acquired from the Cubs in a controversial June 16 trade that sent Todd Zeile to Chicago, Mike Morgan immediately joined the Cardinals' starting rotation, but after starting four games he was sidelined with a strained left hamstring. But over the season's second half, Morgan pitched solid ball for St. Louis. His overall earned-run average topped all Cardinal starters, and he tossed one of only four complete games thrown by St. Louis pitchers.

## Pitching

Though he has a lot of mileage on his arm, Morgan remains a hard thrower with a heavy sinking fastball that still consistently arrives at 90 miles per hour. Morgan's secondary pitch is a hard, late-breaking slider. He'll also mix in an occasional change-up and curve, but the key for him now, just as it's been for all his 15 major league seasons, is keeping his hard stuff down in the strike zone. Morgan has always given up his share of home runs, because when he gets the ball up he gets hit hard. Morgan's frequent groin and knee injuries have been a factor in his inconsistent location. When he cannot adequately drive off the rubber, his pitches tend to stay high.

## Defense & Hitting

Morgan does not have any kind of move that should worry a baserunner. He does try to vary his delivery to give his catchers a fighting chance. Morgan does a solid job of fielding his position. He is no threat with the bat, last year fanning in more than half his at-bats. Lifetime, Morgan is a .091 hitter, with only two extra-base hits (both doubles) in 385 at-bats.

## 1996 Outlook

St. Louis is under no illusions about Morgan suddenly becoming a 20-game winner. However, they would like to keep him around because when healthy he is a proven innings-eater who can stabilize what is likely to be a mostly youthful starting rotation. Given decent support, Morgan should win at least a dozen games.

**Position:** SP
**Bats:** R **Throws:** R
**Ht:** 6' 2" **Wt:** 220

**Opening Day Age:** 36
**Born:** 10/8/59 in Tulare, CA
**ML Seasons:** 15

### Overall Statistics

|  | W | L | Pct. | ERA | G | GS | Sv | IP | H | BB | SO | HR | BR/IP |
|---|---|---|---|---|---|---|---|---|---|---|---|---|---|
| 1995 | 7 | 7 | .500 | 3.56 | 21 | 21 | 0 | 131.1 | 133 | 34 | 61 | 12 | 1.27 |
| Career | 102 | 144 | .415 | 3.98 | 366 | 306 | 3 | 2045.0 | 2101 | 689 | 1012 | 176 | 1.36 |

### How Often He Throws Strikes

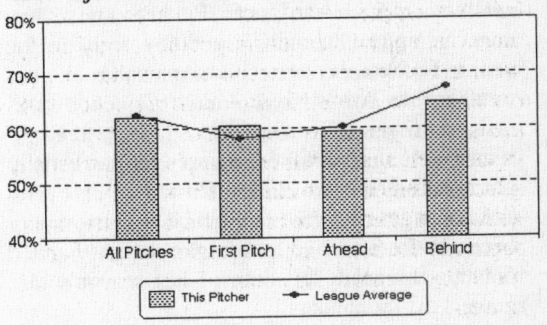

### 1995 Situational Stats

|  | W | L | ERA | Sv | IP |  | AB | H | HR | RBI | Avg |
|---|---|---|---|---|---|---|---|---|---|---|---|
| Home | 4 | 4 | 2.69 | 0 | 73.2 | LHB | 227 | 62 | 5 | 22 | .273 |
| Road | 3 | 3 | 4.68 | 0 | 57.2 | RHB | 264 | 71 | 7 | 28 | .269 |
| First Half | 4 | 3 | 2.58 | 0 | 52.1 | Sc Pos | 123 | 25 | 3 | 38 | .203 |
| Scnd Half | 3 | 4 | 4.22 | 0 | 79.0 | Clutch | 21 | 3 | 1 | 1 | .143 |

### 1995 Rankings (National League)

➡ 4th in most GDPs induced per GDP situation (21.6%)
➡ 5th in lowest batting average allowed with runners in scoring position (.203)
➡ 6th in GDPs induced (19)
➡ 7th in ERA at home (2.69)

St. Louis
Cardinals

# Jose Oquendo

## 1995 Season

For a portion of Ozzie Smith's absence last year, veteran middle infielder Jose Oquendo filled in at shortstop. He also saw significant action at second base. Oquendo provided the Cardinals with his usual versatility and tepid offensive production. He did manage his first two home runs since 1991, but otherwise struggled offensively while batting more often than in any season since '91.

## Hitting

Throughout his career, Oquendo has been known as a patient hitter willing to take his share of walks and work long counts. Nothing has changed, except that Oquendo increasingly has a tough time catching up with hard stuff. Pitchers know they can challenge Oquendo, especially early in the count, because he almost always takes pitches until he has two strikes. And if Oquendo does swing at first-pitch strikes, there is little threat of him driving the ball for extra bases. He can usually put breaking balls into play but has trouble with good changes of speed. Though he has historically been a more effective hitter against right-handed pitching, Oquendo hit both of last season's rare homers off lefthanders.

## Baserunning & Defense

Oquendo hasn't had basestealing speed in a decade, and that certainly won't change at this stage of his career. However, the veteran usually runs the bases intelligently. Oquendo is a more reliable player at second than at short, where both his range and arm have deteriorated of late. He of course has played nearly everywhere at one point in his career, including the outfield and even pitcher, but Oquendo is no longer physically able to exhibit such versatility.

## 1996 Outlook

Tony La Russa has always liked the options attendant with versatile bench players, so Oquendo's experience will be a plus. However, Oquendo has been a physical risk for a few years and his offense has slipped to the point where he does not bring much production to the table. If he's still with St. Louis this spring, he'll face a fight for a job.

**Position:** 2B/SS
**Bats:** B **Throws:** R
**Ht:** 5'10" **Wt:** 171

**Opening Day Age:** 32
**Born:** 7/4/63 in Rio Piedras, PR
**ML Seasons:** 12
**Pronunciation:** oh-KEN-doh

### Overall Statistics

|  | G | AB | R | H | D | T | HR | RBI | SB | BB | SO | Avg | OBP | Slg |
|---|---|---|---|---|---|---|---|---|---|---|---|---|---|---|
| 1995 | 88 | 220 | 31 | 46 | 8 | 3 | 2 | 17 | 1 | 35 | 21 | .209 | .316 | .300 |
| Career | 1190 | 3202 | 339 | 821 | 104 | 24 | 14 | 254 | 35 | 448 | 376 | .256 | .346 | .317 |

### Where He Hits the Ball

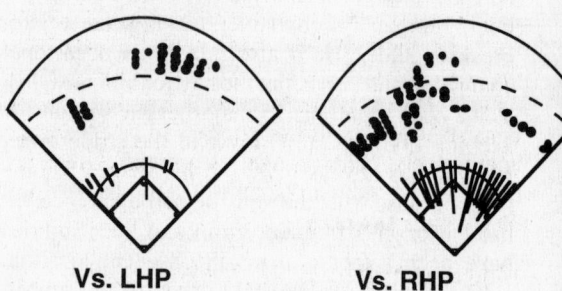

**Vs. LHP**          **Vs. RHP**

### 1995 Situational Stats

|  | AB | H | HR | RBI | Avg |  |  | AB | H | HR | RBI | Avg |
|---|---|---|---|---|---|---|---|---|---|---|---|---|
| Home | 100 | 23 | 0 | 7 | .230 | LHP | | 54 | 11 | 2 | 6 | .204 |
| Road | 120 | 23 | 2 | 10 | .192 | RHP | | 166 | 35 | 0 | 11 | .211 |
| First Half | 129 | 28 | 1 | 11 | .217 | Sc Pos | | 40 | 13 | 1 | 13 | .325 |
| Scnd Half | 91 | 18 | 1 | 6 | .198 | Clutch | | 43 | 8 | 0 | 3 | .186 |

### 1995 Rankings (National League)

→ Did not rank near the top or bottom in any category

# Tom Pagnozzi

## 1995 Season

Injuries continue to be an annual occurrence for Tom Pagnozzi, whose 1995 season was shortened by physical problems for a third straight year. To make matters worse, he produced precious little when he did play. Pagnozzi managed only 15 RBI in 219 at-bats while batting below .200 with men in scoring position. His overall numbers were the worst since he became the Cardinals' number-one catcher back in 1991.

## Hitting

Pagnozzi has never resembled the second coming of Johnny Bench. But after at least achieving a form of respectability as a batter, Pagnozzi nosedived last year. He managed only 17 extra-base hits and was particularly overmatched against even the most average hard stuff. For such an ordinary hitter, Pagnozzi is unfortunately also impatient. He rarely works a walk and his lack of consistent power allows pitchers to go after him aggressively. He is known as a good change-up hitter, so of course pitchers rarely throw him change-ups anymore.

## Baserunning & Defense

Once an above-average runner for a catcher, Pagnozzi is now no factor on the bases. He's attempted only one stolen base the last two years and has become one of the easier batters with whom to turn a double play. He has built his career on his catching skills and they remain excellent. When healthy, he still has a solid throwing arm and perfect mechanics, which allowed him to gun down 35 percent of attempting basestealers last season. Pagnozzi is also considered a good handler of pitchers.

## 1996 Outlook

On a club in need of offense, a catcher of Pagnozzi's infrequent offensive production could be viewed as a luxury. However, his veteran savvy and knowledge of National League hitters are valuable to the St. Louis pitching staff. For those reasons, he will likely remain an asset even if asked to serve just a part-time role.

**Position:** C
**Bats:** R  **Throws:** R
**Ht:** 6' 1"  **Wt:** 195

**Opening Day Age:** 33
**Born:** 7/30/62 in Tucson, AZ
**ML Seasons:** 9
Pronunciation: pag-NAHZ-ee

### Overall Statistics

|  | G | AB | R | H | D | T | HR | RBI | SB | BB | SO | Avg | OBP | Slg |
|---|---|---|---|---|---|---|---|---|---|---|---|---|---|---|
| 1995 | 62 | 219 | 17 | 47 | 14 | 1 | 2 | 15 | 0 | 11 | 31 | .215 | .254 | .315 |
| Career | 732 | 2279 | 188 | 577 | 118 | 11 | 29 | 247 | 14 | 150 | 328 | .253 | .299 | .353 |

### Where He Hits the Ball

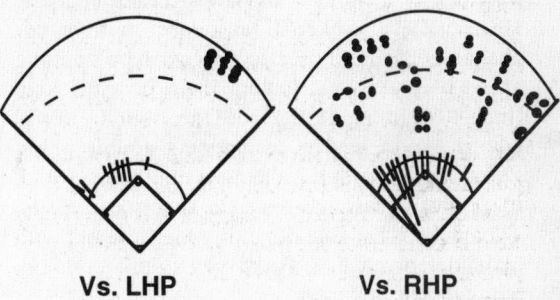

**Vs. LHP**          **Vs. RHP**

### 1995 Situational Stats

|  | AB | H | HR | RBI | Avg |  | AB | H | HR | RBI | Avg |
|---|---|---|---|---|---|---|---|---|---|---|---|
| Home | 115 | 29 | 1 | 8 | .252 | LHP | 33 | 8 | 0 | 1 | .242 |
| Road | 104 | 18 | 1 | 7 | .173 | RHP | 186 | 39 | 2 | 14 | .210 |
| First Half | 185 | 42 | 1 | 11 | .227 | Sc Pos | 44 | 8 | 1 | 12 | .182 |
| Scnd Half | 34 | 5 | 1 | 4 | .147 | Clutch | 38 | 3 | 1 | 3 | .079 |

### 1995 Rankings (National League)

→ 3rd in highest percentage of runners caught stealing as a catcher (35.1%)

→ 10th in lowest batting average on an 0-2 count (.056)

# Mark Petkovsek

## 1995 Season

Righthander Mark Petkovsek bounced through assorted organizations—and pitched briefly for both the Rangers and Pirates—before getting picked up last year by the Cardinals. When injuries decimated the Redbirds' starting rotation, Petkovsek wound up with the longest major league stay of his career. He topped the St. Louis staff with 137.1 innings and 21 starts—including a complete-game shutout—and proved to be a durable, albeit unspectacular, addition to the mound corps.

## Pitching

Pitchers who throw strikes and stay healthy can last a long time in baseball these days, which is one reason why Petkovsek has kept getting chances. He is a basic sinker/slider pitcher with a fair change-up, and is most effective when he's getting ahead of hitters and having them beat his hard (high 80s) sinking fastball into the ground. He was among league leaders in inducing double plays. Petkovsek keeps his walks to a minimum, which makes his occasional mistakes much less costly. Though he is capable of getting the strikeout with his slider or change, Petkovsek's stuff certainly won't dazzle anyone.

## Defense & Hitting

Having played professionally since 1987, Petkovsek has learned the fundamentals of playing his position. He works hard to hold runners close—only 10 of 17 prospective basestealers were successful last season—and he's a decent fielder with good instincts. Petkovsek held his own as a hitter, driving in a pair of runs and showing he can lay down the sacrifice when necessary.

## 1996 Outlook

The Cardinals have plenty of young starting pitchers with better stuff than Petkovsek, but he impressed the organization with his ability to keep his team in most games he started. He will have to earn a spot in the rotation, but barring that he'll stick as a spot starter and long reliever.

**Position:** SP/RP
**Bats:** R  **Throws:** R
**Ht:** 6' 0"  **Wt:** 195

**Opening Day Age:** 30
**Born:** 11/18/65 in Beaumont, TX
**ML Seasons:** 3
**Pronunciation:** pet-KUY-zek

### Overall Statistics

|        | W | L | Pct. | ERA | G | GS | Sv | IP | H | BB | SO | HR | BR/IP |
|--------|---|---|------|-----|---|----|----|------|-----|----|----|----|-------|
| 1995   | 6 | 6 | .500 | 4.00 | 26 | 21 | 0 | 137.1 | 136 | 35 | 71 | 11 | 1.25 |
| Career | 9 | 7 | .563 | 5.08 | 56 | 22 | 0 | 179.0 | 200 | 48 | 91 | 22 | 1.39 |

### How Often He Throws Strikes

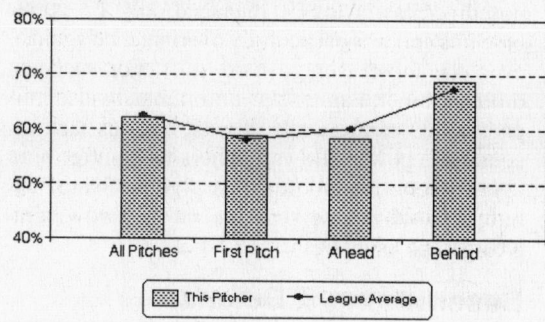

### 1995 Situational Stats

|            | W | L | ERA | Sv | IP |      | AB | H | HR | RBI | Avg |
|------------|---|---|------|----|------|------|-----|----|----|-----|------|
| Home       | 4 | 1 | 2.92 | 0 | 77.0 | LHB  | 235 | 67 | 4 | 33 | .285 |
| Road       | 2 | 5 | 5.37 | 0 | 60.1 | RHB  | 285 | 69 | 7 | 29 | .242 |
| First Half | 3 | 2 | 4.38 | 0 | 51.1 | Sc Pos | 118 | 36 | 4 | 52 | .305 |
| Scnd Half  | 3 | 4 | 3.77 | 0 | 86.0 | Clutch | 32 | 8 | 0 | 3 | .250 |

### 1995 Rankings (National League)

➡ 9th in GDPs induced (18) and highest batting average allowed with runners in scoring position (.305)

➡ Led the Cardinals in games started, shutouts (1), innings pitched, hits allowed, batters faced (569), hit batsmen (6), pitches thrown (2,053), GDPs induced, ERA at home (2.92), lowest batting average allowed vs. left-handed batters (.285) and lowest batting average allowed vs. right-handed batters (.242)

# Ozzie Smith

## 1995 Season

The great career of Ozzie Smith fell into serious decline last season as a serious shoulder injury kept him sidelined for two-thirds of the season. When Smith did play, his skills were severely diminished. He managed one more hit with men in scoring position (eight) and one less extra-base hit (six) than he had errors (seven), ratios not exactly what you're looking for from an everyday short-stop.

## Hitting

For the last decade, Ozzie has been an over-achiever as a hitter, thanks to hard work and great conditioning. But with his sore shoulder preventing him from taking extra work or keeping up his usual training regimen, Smith's bat speed dropped to practically nothing. He could not get around on fastballs, which often became weak grounders. He was also susceptible to chasing breaking balls—especially when batting right-handed, where he managed only a .143 average. Even when struggling, Smith is a patient batter who will work counts and take his share of walks.

## Baserunning & Defense

Smith's days as a big-time basestealer are over, though he remains an above-average runner. Easily the most unsettling development is his slippage in the field. The Wizard will someday enter the Hall of Fame because of his brilliant defensive skills, but he's now just a shadow of his former self. His weak shoulder allows him to throw only soft rainbow tosses across the diamond. His range is ordinary and even his sure hands have started to betray him.

## 1996 Outlook

The Cardinals openly label shortstop as one of their biggest question marks—an indication that their expectations of Ozzie this season are not very high. There were questions all winter about the condition of his shoulder, but the Cards assume he'll be back for what will almost certainly be his final season. If his skills are what they were in '95, Smith may end up finishing his career on the bench.

**Position:** SS
**Bats:** B  **Throws:** R
**Ht:** 5'10"  **Wt:** 170

**Opening Day Age:** 41
**Born:** 12/26/54 in Mobile, AL
**ML Seasons:** 18
**Nickname:** The Wizard of Oz

### Overall Statistics

|  | G | AB | R | H | D | T | HR | RBI | SB | BB | SO | Avg | OBP | Slg |
|---|---|---|---|---|---|---|---|---|---|---|---|---|---|---|
| 1995 | 44 | 156 | 16 | 31 | 5 | 1 | 0 | 11 | 4 | 17 | 12 | .199 | .282 | .244 |
| Career | 2491 | 9169 | 1221 | 2396 | 392 | 67 | 26 | 775 | 573 | 1047 | 580 | .261 | .337 | .327 |

### Where He Hits the Ball

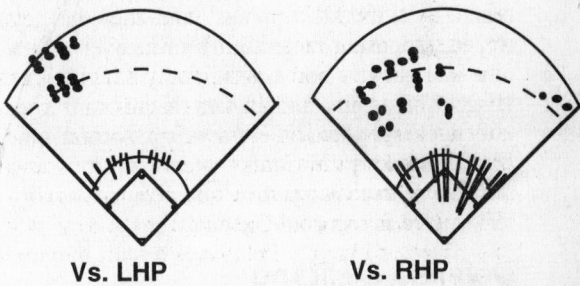

**Vs. LHP**　　　　　**Vs. RHP**

### 1995 Situational Stats

|  | AB | H | HR | RBI | Avg |  | AB | H | HR | RBI | Avg |
|---|---|---|---|---|---|---|---|---|---|---|---|
| Home | 97 | 17 | 0 | 7 | .175 | LHP | 35 | 5 | 0 | 2 | .143 |
| Road | 59 | 14 | 0 | 4 | .237 | RHP | 121 | 26 | 0 | 9 | .215 |
| First Half | 68 | 17 | 0 | 3 | .250 | Sc Pos | 37 | 8 | 0 | 11 | .216 |
| Scnd Half | 88 | 14 | 0 | 8 | .159 | Clutch | 27 | 7 | 0 | 3 | .259 |

### 1995 Rankings (National League)

➡ Led the Cardinals in sacrifice bunts (5) and bunts in play (9)

# Tom Urbani

**Position:** SP/RP
**Bats:** L  **Throws:** L
**Ht:** 6' 1"  **Wt:** 190

**Opening Day Age:** 28
**Born:** 1/21/68 in Santa Cruz, CA
**ML Seasons:** 3
Pronunciation: ur-BANN-ee

## 1995 Season

Shoulder problems sidelined lefthander Tom Urbani early in the 1995 season, but he came back and wound up pitching in 24 games, 13 of them as a starter. Urbani was just 2-5 as a starter, but did some fine work out of the bullpen, striking out 16 batters in 13.1 innings. He ended the season in the bullpen, a logical role given that he's a lefthander who doesn't throw hard and has limited stamina.

## Pitching

Urbani cannot afford to be off in his location, because when he is he gets hammered. His assortment of sinking fastballs thrown in the mid 80s, sliders and change-ups can be effective for a time. However, Urbani tends to get the ball up as he reaches the middle innings, and then he gets ripped. Opposing batters hit him at over a .300 clip, including 11 home runs in only 82.2 innings. His lack of stamina and the fact that his stuff loses effectiveness when hitters see it a second time have convinced the Cards that his future is as a reliever, where his relative effectiveness against left-handed hitters could be an asset.

## Defense & Hitting

A good athlete, Urbani helps himself in many different ways. He is an excellent fielding pitcher with one of the better pickoff moves on the St. Louis pitching staff. Urbani picked one runner off last year, and three others were caught trying to steal. He is also one of the better hitting pitchers in baseball, and one of his six hits last season was a home run.

## 1996 Outlook

Left-handed relievers are one of baseball's most valuable commodities, and no manager likes having loads of bullpen options more than Tony La Russa. So look for Urbani to be used exclusively as a reliever, probably in middle- and long-relief roles. He is likely to get another starting chance only if the Cardinals again suffer an epidemic of injuries to their rotation.

### Overall Statistics

|        | W  | L  | Pct. | ERA  | G  | GS | Sv | IP    | H   | BB | SO  | HR | BR/IP |
|--------|----|----|------|------|----|----|----|-------|-----|----|-----|----|-------|
| 1995   | 3  | 5  | .375 | 3.70 | 24 | 13 | 0  | 82.2  | 99  | 21 | 52  | 11 | 1.45  |
| Career | 7  | 15 | .318 | 4.48 | 62 | 32 | 0  | 225.0 | 270 | 68 | 128 | 27 | 1.50  |

### How Often He Throws Strikes

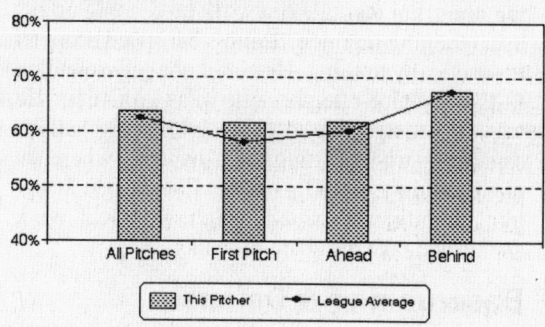

This Pitcher — League Average

### 1995 Situational Stats

|            | W | L | ERA  | Sv | IP   |        | AB  | H  | HR | RBI | Avg  |
|------------|---|---|------|----|------|--------|-----|----|----|-----|------|
| Home       | 1 | 3 | 3.75 | 0  | 36.0 | LHB    | 74  | 18 | 3  | 6   | .243 |
| Road       | 2 | 2 | 3.66 | 0  | 46.2 | RHB    | 251 | 81 | 8  | 29  | .323 |
| First Half | 2 | 3 | 3.53 | 0  | 51.0 | Sc Pos | 73  | 18 | 2  | 21  | .247 |
| Scnd Half  | 1 | 2 | 3.98 | 0  | 31.2 | Clutch | 24  | 9  | 0  | 0   | .375 |

### 1995 Rankings (National League)

→ 1st in highest batting average allowed vs. right-handed batters (.323)
→ 2nd in most GDPs induced per GDP situation (22.2%)
→ Led the Cardinals in most GDPs induced per GDP situation

# Allen Watson

## 1995 Season

Former number-one draft choice Allen Watson still hasn't posted the spectacular numbers of his minor league career, but he did show signs last year of becoming a decent major league starter. Watson did suffer the first physical problems of his pro career, though none of his ailments were serious.

## Pitching

When St. Louis selected Watson in the first round of the 1991 amateur draft, they thought that he would develop into a legitimate power pitcher with a 90-plus fastball. However, Watson's velocity continues to languish in the high 80s, and therefore location is crucial to his success. When Watson is getting his fastball and slider in on hitters, he is effective. However, when he catches too much of the plate, he is very hittable, especially by right-handed hitters. Watson also allows hitters of all kinds to make far too much contact. He fanned only 49 of the nearly 500 batters he faced last year. That number will have to go up—a lot—if he's to become a premier starter.

## Defense & Hitting

Watson was among the league leaders in pickoffs. However, he is easy pickings for any basestealer who can recognize his move to first, because he is exceptionally slow coming to the plate. His delivery also leaves him out of position for many balls hit through the box. Watson has quickly established himself as one of the league's best-hitting pitchers. He was among the league leaders in hits and led St. Louis pitchers in RBI for a second straight year.

## 1996 Outlook

The Cardinals once projected Watson as a possible star. Those expectations have not been realized. That said, the Cards still think Watson can be a productive pitcher and are counting on him to be part of their rotation. While stardom is no longer expected, they think he can win 12 to 15 games per season.

**Position:** SP
**Bats:** L **Throws:** L
**Ht:** 6' 3" **Wt:** 200

**Opening Day Age:** 25
**Born:** 11/18/70 in Jamaica, NY
**ML Seasons:** 3

### Overall Statistics

|        | W  | L  | Pct. | ERA  | G  | GS | Sv | IP    | H   | BB  | SO  | HR | BR/IP |
|--------|----|----|------|------|----|----|----|-------|-----|-----|-----|----|-------|
| 1995   | 7  | 9  | .438 | 4.96 | 21 | 19 | 0  | 114.1 | 126 | 41  | 49  | 17 | 1.46  |
| Career | 19 | 21 | .475 | 5.07 | 59 | 56 | 0  | 316.0 | 346 | 122 | 172 | 43 | 1.48  |

### How Often He Throws Strikes

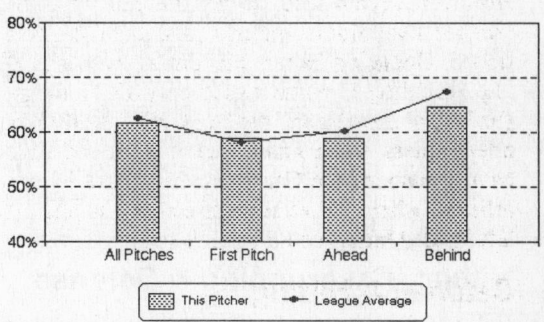

### 1995 Situational Stats

|            | W | L | ERA  | Sv | IP   |        | AB  | H  | HR | RBI | Avg  |
|------------|---|---|------|----|------|--------|-----|----|----|-----|------|
| Home       | 6 | 4 | 4.86 | 0  | 63.0 | LHB    | 75  | 15 | 3  | 11  | .200 |
| Road       | 1 | 5 | 5.08 | 0  | 51.1 | RHB    | 367 | 111| 14 | 43  | .302 |
| First Half | 2 | 2 | 6.75 | 0  | 32.0 | Sc Pos | 100 | 22 | 1  | 33  | .220 |
| Scnd Half  | 5 | 7 | 4.26 | 0  | 82.1 | Clutch | 14  | 2  | 0  | 1   | .143 |

### 1995 Rankings (National League)

➡ 7th in runners caught stealing (11) and highest batting average allowed vs. right-handed batters (.302)
➡ 8th in balks (2)
➡ 10th in lowest winning percentage
➡ Led the Cardinals in home runs allowed, pickoff throws (111) and runners caught stealing

# David Bell

**Position:** 2B
**Bats:** R **Throws:** R
**Ht:** 5'10" **Wt:** 175

**Opening Day Age:** 23
**Born:** 9/14/72 in
Cincinnati, OH
**ML Seasons:** 1

## Overall Statistics

| | G | AB | R | H | D | T | HR | RBI | SB | BB | SO | Avg | OBP | Slg |
|---|---|---|---|---|---|---|---|---|---|---|---|---|---|---|
| 1995 | 41 | 146 | 13 | 36 | 7 | 2 | 2 | 19 | 1 | 4 | 25 | .247 | .275 | .363 |
| Career | 41 | 146 | 13 | 36 | 7 | 2 | 2 | 19 | 1 | 4 | 25 | .247 | .275 | .363 |

## 1995 Season

Acquired in the trade that sent Ken Hill to Cleveland, infielder David Bell showed the Cardinals enough in a six-week audition to become part of the club's future plans. Bell played both third base—his primary position in the minors—and second, and showed potential at both spots. He also showed decent batting pop, with 11 extra-base hits and 19 RBI in only 41 games.

## Hitting, Baserunning & Defense

Bell will need to cut down on his swing a bit to become the .280-type hitter he is capable of being. He can be overpowered up and in, and shows a youngster's inexperience against quality breaking balls and change-ups. However, he has some power potential and can drive the ball to the opposite field. Not surprisingly, the son of Buddy Bell has mostly played third, where he has solid range and a good arm. The Cards would like to see more of him at second, where he was given on-the-job training and made several errors as a result. Also not surprisingly, the son of Buddy Bell—and grandson of Gus—will not threaten anyone with his speed.

## 1996 Outlook

The unprecedented phenomenon of second- and third-generation major leaguers continues. Bell might not end up being the star his father and grandfather were, but the Cardinals love his work ethic and attitude. They think he will fit into Tony La Russa's mix.

# Darnell Coles

**Position:** 3B/1B
**Bats:** R **Throws:** R
**Ht:** 6' 1" **Wt:** 180

**Opening Day Age:** 33
**Born:** 6/2/62 in San
Bernardino, CA
**ML Seasons:** 13

## Overall Statistics

| | G | AB | R | H | D | T | HR | RBI | SB | BB | SO | Avg | OBP | Slg |
|---|---|---|---|---|---|---|---|---|---|---|---|---|---|---|
| 1995 | 63 | 138 | 13 | 31 | 7 | 0 | 3 | 16 | 0 | 16 | 20 | .225 | .316 | .341 |
| Career | 936 | 2869 | 332 | 702 | 141 | 14 | 74 | 366 | 20 | 237 | 439 | .245 | .306 | .381 |

## 1995 Season

Used largely as a pinch hitter and spot starter at third and first, Darnell Coles continued to find a niche as a veteran bench player last year. He managed only a .225 average but provided 16 RBI in 138 at-bats, not a bad ratio for a bit player, especially on a St. Louis bench that provided little power elsewhere.

## Hitting, Baserunning & Defense

Coles still has a quick bat and can occasionally turn around a mistake fastball out and over the plate. However, he has never shown any ability to consistently hit breaking balls and is largely reduced to working the count his way, hoping to make the pitcher throw one of Coles' beloved heaters. Never a patient hitter, Coles won't be challenging for the walks title. He has average speed at best and has never been a basestealer. Originally a third baseman who had horrendous early-career fielding problems, Coles can adequately fill in at first, third, left field and second base. His arm is below average.

## 1996 Outlook

In the baseball scheme of things, the Darnell Coles of the world usually go year to year, wondering where their next job might surface. Tony La Russa covets veteran bench players like Coles, but it will come down to money and who else is available. Coles will likely surface somewhere.

# Tony Fossas

Tough On Lefties

**Position**: RP
**Bats**: L  **Throws**: L
**Ht**: 6' 0"  **Wt**: 198

**Opening Day Age**: 38
**Born**: 9/23/57 in Havana, Cuba
**ML Seasons**: 8

### Overall Statistics

| | W | L | Pct. | ERA | G | GS | Sv | IP | H | BB | SO | HR | BR/IP |
|---|---|---|---|---|---|---|---|---|---|---|---|---|---|
| 1995 | 3 | 0 | 1.000 | 1.47 | 58 | 0 | 0 | 36.2 | 28 | 10 | 40 | 1 | 1.04 |
| Career | 14 | 10 | .583 | 3.84 | 385 | 0 | 5 | 293.1 | 293 | 116 | 224 | 23 | 1.39 |

## 1995 Season

Signed as a minor league free agent just prior to the start of the season, Tony Fossas was everything the Cardinals could have asked for. As a situational left-handed reliever, usually spotted to face one or two hitters only, Fossas had a super year in which he posted a 1.47 ERA, a surprise after consecutive seasons with 5.18 and 4.76 marks. He also posted 40 strikeouts in 36.2 innings and, most important, limited left-handed hitters to zero home runs and a .181 average.

## Pitching, Defense & Hitting

There are no surprises when Fossas arrives on the mound. He eats left-handed hitters alive with his running mid-80s fastball and a sidearm slider which he consistently throws for strikes and almost never hangs. Right-handed hitters can hurt Fossas, but he can battle them when he has his good cut fastball. Besides, he almost never faces quality right-handed hitters in crucial situations anyway. Fossas holds runners fairly well but is an average fielder at best. He did not bat last year and is unlikely to ever hit because he faces only a handful of hitters before leaving for a pinch-hitter.

## 1996 Outlook

At the ripe age of 38 and after a long, up-and-down career, Fossas might have finally found some security. The Cardinals were considering giving him the first multi-year contract of his career. Specialists like Fossas are hard to find, and few are better at what they do.

# Jose Oliva

**Position**: 3B
**Bats**: R  **Throws**: R
**Ht**: 6' 3"  **Wt**: 215

**Opening Day Age**: 25
**Born**: 3/3/71 in San Pedro de Macoris, DR
**ML Seasons**: 2

### Overall Statistics

| | G | AB | R | H | D | T | HR | RBI | SB | BB | SO | Avg | OBP | Slg |
|---|---|---|---|---|---|---|---|---|---|---|---|---|---|---|
| 1995 | 70 | 183 | 15 | 26 | 5 | 0 | 7 | 20 | 0 | 12 | 46 | .142 | .202 | .284 |
| Career | 89 | 242 | 24 | 43 | 10 | 0 | 13 | 31 | 0 | 19 | 56 | .178 | .242 | .380 |

## 1995 Season

When the Atlanta Braves tired of third baseman Jose Oliva's moody presence in their clubhouse, they quickly dumped him on the first taker, namely the Cardinals. St. Louis was willing to gamble on Oliva's considerable power potential, but he was a bust in the short term, batting an astounding .122 as a Cardinal—after hitting .156 with Atlanta—and striking out once every four at-bats. Overall, Oliva's .142 average in 183 at-bats was nothing short of disastrous.

## Hitting, Baserunning & Defense

Oliva's seven home runs in limited play last year underscore his huge power potential, evident since he was a farmhand with Texas. However, Oliva does not take advice well, he's not a hard worker, and thus has not altered a big, uppercut, all-or-nothing swing that is eaten alive by major league breaking stuff and changes of speed. He is a below-average baserunner, no threat to steal. Oliva has a great arm and decent hands, but he is lackadaisical on too many balls and throws erratically, making for a mixed bag defensively.

## 1996 Outlook

If Tony La Russa can light a fire under Oliva, the Cardinals could have a sleeper with 25-homer potential. But so far, no manager or coach has been successful at getting Oliva to realize both his strengths and his limitations. Until someone does, he will be an underachiever.

St. Louis Cardinals

# Donovan Osborne

**Position:** SP
**Bats:** L **Throws:** L
**Ht:** 6' 2"  **Wt:** 195

**Opening Day Age:** 26
**Born:** 6/21/69 in
Roseville, CA
**ML Seasons:** 3

*Overall Statistics*

|  | W | L | Pct. | ERA | G | GS | Sv | IP | H | BB | SO | HR | BR/IP |
|---|---|---|---|---|---|---|---|---|---|---|---|---|---|
| 1995 | 4 | 6 | .400 | 3.81 | 19 | 19 | 0 | 113.1 | 112 | 34 | 82 | 17 | 1.29 |
| Career | 25 | 22 | .532 | 3.78 | 79 | 74 | 0 | 448.0 | 458 | 119 | 269 | 49 | 1.29 |

## 1995 Season

It took over a year for Donovan Osborne to rebound from shoulder trouble—he missed the entire 1994 season and most of the first half of 1995. But Osborne finally settled back into the Cardinal rotation last July and, though rusty, proved he was healthy. He struck out 82 batters in 113.1 innings and pitched fairly well in 15 of his 19 starts.

## Pitching, Defense & Hitting

Osborne has his velocity back to the 90-plus range, and throws an improving change-up and slider. For Osborne, location is the key. When he struggles, it's generally because he leaves too many balls up in the strike zone. He also tends to leave the ball over too much of the plate when he tries to pitch inside, a problem that results in a career-long penchant for allowing home runs. In addition, he makes too many mistakes against left-handed hitters, who are not intimidated by his stuff. Osborne has an improved pickoff move and is an adequate fielder. He can also do some damage as a hitter, and batted .161 with four RBI last year.

## 1996 Outlook

Though a former top draft pick, Osborne is not likely to ever be an ace. However, he is still young enough to improve his pitching savvy. Given good health, there's no reason Osborne can't be a double-digit winner for the Cardinals.

# Jeff Parrett

**Position:** RP
**Bats:** R **Throws:** R
**Ht:** 6' 3"  **Wt:** 205

**Opening Day Age:** 34
**Born:** 8/26/61 in
Indianapolis, IN
**ML Seasons:** 9

*Overall Statistics*

|  | W | L | Pct. | ERA | G | GS | Sv | IP | H | BB | SO | HR | BR/IP |
|---|---|---|---|---|---|---|---|---|---|---|---|---|---|
| 1995 | 4 | 7 | .364 | 3.64 | 59 | 0 | 0 | 76.2 | 71 | 28 | 71 | 8 | 1.29 |
| Career | 53 | 40 | .570 | 3.84 | 440 | 11 | 22 | 658.1 | 608 | 314 | 552 | 59 | 1.40 |

## 1995 Season

Bouncing back from elbow damage, righthander Jeff Parrett did a workingman's job of middle relief for the Cardinals in 1995. He led the club with 59 appearances and averaged close to a strikeout per inning. Heady stuff for a pitcher who stumbled to a 5.38 ERA with pitcher's nightmare Colorado back in 1994.

## Pitching, Defense & Hitting

Parrett still throws around 90, and at times he can unleash an effective split-fingered fastball. However, his splitter is often inconsistent, and when it stays up in the strike zone Parrett can get hit hard. His control will also waver at times and he cannot be successful when he has to pitch from behind in the count because his fastball is not good enough by itself to get him by. Parrett has trouble holding runners, with no pickoff move to speak of. He usually gets in good fielding position. Parrett doesn't scare anyone as a hitter, and is 4-for-36 lifetime.

## 1996 Outlook

Parrett had one of his best seasons three years ago in Oakland, so Tony La Russa is very familiar with what he can do. So are the Cardinals, who were generally pleased with his workhorse performance. As long as he's kept in middle-relief and mop-up roles, Parrett can be a solid part of the St. Louis bullpen.

# Geronimo Pena

**Position:** 2B
**Bats:** B  **Throws:** R
**Ht:** 6' 1"  **Wt:** 195

**Opening Day Age:** 29
**Born:** 3/29/67 in
Distrito Nacional, DR
**ML Seasons:** 6
**Pronunciation:**
PAYN-yuh

*Overall Statistics*

|  | G | AB | R | H | D | T | HR | RBI | SB | BB | SO | Avg | OBP | Slg |
|---|---|---|---|---|---|---|---|---|---|---|---|---|---|---|
| 1995 | 32 | 101 | 20 | 27 | 6 | 1 | 1 | 8 | 3 | 16 | 30 | .267 | .367 | .376 |
| Career | 373 | 1001 | 161 | 264 | 60 | 8 | 29 | 122 | 54 | 111 | 251 | .264 | .346 | .427 |

## 1995 Season

Injuries destroyed another season for Geronimo Pena in 1995, and time might be running out on what was once a promising career. Pena got only 101 at-bats and showed little of the pop which once set him apart from most other middle infielders. Pena went to the disabled list three times in 1995, with three different injuries: a fractured tibia, a strained hamstring, and a sore knee. Ouch.

## Hitting, Baserunning & Defense

The switch-hitting Pena batted over 150 points higher against left-handed pitching last year, continuing a career-long pattern. He is too easily overpowered by good hard stuff and has difficulty protecting the plate and shortening his swing when behind in the count. Pena has good extra-base power from either side of the plate, but he strikes out too much. He has been a decent basestealer during his career, though he runs infrequently. Pena does not have great range at second, but he does have good hands and a strong arm. He also turns the double play very well.

## 1996 Outlook

Pena's baseball tools remain tantalizing, and he still has the offensive potential to be one of the better second baseman. His unreliability and penchant for getting hurt might have worn out the Cardinals' patience, but he still could have that one season in him when he stays healthy, cuts down his strikeouts and emerges as a big-time player. However, time is running out.

# Danny Sheaffer

**Position:** C
**Bats:** R  **Throws:** R
**Ht:** 6' 0"  **Wt:** 195

**Opening Day Age:** 34
**Born:** 8/2/61 in
Jacksonville, FL
**ML Seasons:** 5

*Overall Statistics*

|  | G | AB | R | H | D | T | HR | RBI | SB | BB | SO | Avg | OBP | Slg |
|---|---|---|---|---|---|---|---|---|---|---|---|---|---|---|
| 1995 | 76 | 208 | 24 | 48 | 10 | 1 | 5 | 30 | 0 | 23 | 38 | .231 | .306 | .361 |
| Career | 234 | 616 | 67 | 141 | 24 | 2 | 11 | 79 | 2 | 43 | 80 | .229 | .277 | .328 |

## 1995 Season

After two seasons with the Rockies, reserve catcher Danny Sheaffer joined the Cardinals last season. Given extensive playing time when Tom Pagnozzi was injured, Sheaffer provided the Cards with a workmanlike performance. He managed five home runs and 30 RBI, which by recent St. Louis standards was solid production from their catcher.

## Hitting, Baserunning & Defense

Sheaffer can pull hanging breaking balls and high fastballs for occasional power, so pitchers have to at least approach him with some care. He does not help himself with his over-aggressiveness and can be tempted to chase breaking balls low and outside. He also does not adjust well on good changeups. Sheaffer is no threat to steal but is a good enough runner to take the occasional extra base. He is a solid receiver with a usually accurate and strong arm, though he tossed out only 22 percent of the runners trying to steal. Sheaffer can also fill in at first, third, or even the outfield in an emergency.

## 1996 Outlook

The classic backup catcher, Sheaffer will stick somewhere if not St. Louis. He is perfectly suited to spelling an everyday catcher once or twice a week. Anything more and his lack of overall production becomes a problem. But Sheaffer should help someone's bench in 1996.

# Other St. Louis Cardinals

**Cory Bailey** (**Pos**: RHP, **Age**: 25)

An ex-Red Sox farmhand, Bailey is a career reliever who has recorded some nice minor league save totals, including 25 at Triple-A Louisville in 1995. Control has been a problem for him. 1996 Outlook: B

**Allen Battle** (**Pos**: LF/RF, **Age**: 27, **Bats**: R)

Battle has speed and gap power, and he's had excellent minor league OBPs. He did a good job of getting on base in 61 games with the Cards last year, but showed no power. Should make the club. 1996 Outlook: B

**Ramon Caraballo** (**Pos**: 2B, **Age**: 26, **Bats**: B)

Caraballo is a diminutive second baseman with good speed but a spotty minor league hitting record. He showed fine range in a trial with the Cards last year, but made some errors and didn't hit at all. 1996 Outlook: C

**Doug Creek** (**Pos**: LHP, **Age**: 27)

Creek is a short, stocky left-handed pitcher whose career took off when he was switched to relief in 1995. He looked awesome in six games for the Cards last year; he's not that good, but he can pitch. 1996 Outlook: A

**John Frascatore** (**Pos**: RHP, **Age**: 26)

A righty swingman, Frascatore got into 14 games for the Cards last year and didn't do a lot to distinguish himself. The Cards need pitching, but he's a long shot to make the club this spring. 1996 Outlook: C

**Ray Giannelli** (**Pos**: 1B, **Age**: 30, **Bats**: L)

An ex-Blue Jay farmhand, Gianelli has hit for pretty good power in the minors, and had 16 homers at Louisville last year. He's 30, though, and the odds are against him. 1996 Outlook: C

**Scott Hemond** (**Pos**: C, **Age**: 30, **Bats**: R)

Hemond spent several years with the A's, and he must be happy Tony La Russa is taking over the Cards; Tony will probably overlook Hemond's .144 average last year. He can catch and play other positions, too. 1996 Outlook: B

**Tim Hulett** (**Pos**: 2B, **Age**: 36, **Bats**: R)

Nearing the end of the line, Hulett played for the Rangers' Triple-A affiliate last year and hit .213 with no power. At his best he was a versatile infielder with some pop, but his career is probably over. 1996 outlook: D

**Manuel Lee** (**Pos**: 2B, **Age**: 30, **Bats**: B)

Picked up by the Cardinals to provide infield depth, Lee missed almost the entire season with injuries. At his best he's capable of playing regularly at both shortstop and second base, but he's not at his best. 1996 Outlook: C

**T.J. Mathews** (**Pos**: RHP, **Age**: 26)

With the Cardinals hurting for pitching last year, Mathews came up from Louisville and did a great job in a set-up role. He has a strong chance to be the number-one set-up man this year. 1996 Outlook: A

**Vince Palacios** (**Pos**: RHP, **Age**: 32)

Palacios has a great arm, but he keeps hurting it. He didn't pitch well when available last year, and he may never be healthy enough to realize his potential. He's 32 and the clock is ticking. 1996 Outlook: C

**Gerald Perry** (**Pos**: 1B, **Age**: 35, **Bats**: L)

One of baseball's best pinch hitters in recent years, Perry had a horrible season in 1995. He's 35 but he works cheap, and will probably get another chance to show he's not washed up. 1996 Outlook: C

**Rich Rodriguez** (**Pos**: LHP, **Age**: 33)

A durable reliever for several years, Rodriguez came down with shoulder trouble last year and missed almost the entire season. He will need to prove he's healthy; if so, he can help a team. 1996 Outlook: C

**Chris Sabo** (**Pos**: DH, **Age**: 34, **Bats**: R)

Sabo began the year as the White Sox DH, but didn't hit and got released. He signed with the Cardinals, but couldn't help them, either. A comeback is not impossible, but it's unlikely. 1996 Outlook: C

**Mark Sweeney** (**Pos**: 1B, **Age**: 26, **Bats**: L)

A first baseman with a nice stroke but not much power, Sweeney did a pretty good job as a bench player for the Cards last year. Should have the same role again; a long shot to play regularly. 1996 Outlook: A

# St. Louis Cardinals Minor League Prospects

## Organization Overview:

The Cardinals are something of an enigma, in that their commitment to player development is unquestioned, yet the system has experienced recent difficulties producing players of star quality. In 1990 the Cardinals decided not to re-sign free agents Terry Pendleton, Vince Coleman and Willie McGee. Flush with five of the first 39 picks in the 1991 draft, St. Louis thought it was building a solid foundation for the future. Five years later, none of the players have made an impact, though the Cards still have hopes for Dmitri Young, Allen Watson and Brian Barber. St. Louis has tended to be conservative when drafting, spending most of its premium picks on more-polished college products, especially pitchers. Watson, Barber, and Alan Benes, the jewel of the system, should pitch this season in St. Louis. Others will soon follow. Their success will help determine how quickly the Cardinals can get back into contention under Tony La Russa.

### Brian Barber

**Position:** P          **Opening Day Age:** 23
**Bats:** R **Throws:** R     **Born:** 3/4/73 in
**Ht:** 6' 1" **Wt:** 172     Hamilton, OH

*Recent Statistics*

| | W | L | ERA | G | GS | Sv | IP | H | R | BB | SO | HR |
|---|---|---|---|---|---|---|---|---|---|---|---|---|
| 95 AAA Louisville | 6 | 5 | 4.70 | 20 | 19 | 0 | 107.1 | 105 | 67 | 40 | 94 | 14 |
| 95 NL St. Louis | 2 | 1 | 5.22 | 9 | 4 | 0 | 29.1 | 31 | 17 | 16 | 27 | 4 |

The Cardinals selected Barber just one pick after they chose Allen Watson in the first round of '91. Barber is a product of Dr. Phillips High School in Orlando, Florida, the same school which produced Royals prospect Johnny Damon. Barber throws quite hard for someone who isn't big. He also has a slider and change, and can be overpowering when he has command of them. He's pitched parts of the last three seasons in Triple-A, was not embarrassed in nine appearances with St. Louis last year, and is a candidate for the rotation this spring.

### Alan Benes

**Position:** P          **Opening Day Age:** 24
**Bats:** R **Throws:** R     **Born:** 1/21/72 in
**Ht:** 6' 5" **Wt:** 215     Evansville, IN

*Recent Statistics*

| | W | L | ERA | G | GS | Sv | IP | H | R | BB | SO | HR |
|---|---|---|---|---|---|---|---|---|---|---|---|---|
| 95 AAA Louisville | 4 | 2 | 2.41 | 11 | 11 | 0 | 56.0 | 37 | 16 | 14 | 54 | 5 |
| 95 NL St. Louis | 1 | 2 | 8.44 | 3 | 3 | 0 | 16.0 | 24 | 15 | 4 | 20 | 2 |

Benes was almost untouchable his last two seasons in the minor leagues, going a combined 21-5 with a 2.30 ERA during that span. After being selected by St. Louis in the first round of 1993, Benes has added a few miles per hour to a fastball that now reaches the 90s. His slider is probably his best pitch, and he throws strikes. Unlike his brother Andy, Alan receives high grades for his competitive nature and positive reaction to adversity. It would be a surprise if Benes isn't in the Cardinal rotation in '96.

### Terry Bradshaw

**Position:** OF          **Opening Day Age:** 27
**Bats:** L **Throws:** R      **Born:** 2/3/69 in
**Ht:** 6' 0" **Wt:** 180     Franklin, VA

*Recent Statistics*

| | G | AB | R | H | D | T | HR | RBI | SB | BB | SO | AVG |
|---|---|---|---|---|---|---|---|---|---|---|---|---|
| 95 AAA Louisville | 111 | 389 | 65 | 110 | 24 | 8 | 8 | 42 | 20 | 53 | 60 | .283 |
| 95 NL St. Louis | 19 | 44 | 6 | 10 | 1 | 1 | 0 | 2 | 1 | 2 | 10 | .227 |
| 95 MLE | 111 | 378 | 53 | 99 | 22 | 5 | 6 | 34 | 14 | 43 | 62 | .262 |

Bradshaw is not a youngster, since he'll turn 27 before the 1996 campaign begins. His career was stalled when he missed the entire 1992 season due to knee surgery. It's been a slow climb back, but Bradshaw could be ready to help the Cardinals as a spare outfielder. He won't be stealing 64 bases in one season like he did before the injury, though he still has enough speed to cover the alleys as a center fielder. He has gap power and also draws enough walks to be a decent leadoff hitter.

### Mike Gulan

**Position:** 3B          **Opening Day Age:** 25
**Bats:** R **Throws:** R      **Born:** 12/18/70 in
**Ht:** 6' 1" **Wt:** 190     Stubenville, OH

*Recent Statistics*

| | G | AB | R | H | D | T | HR | RBI | SB | BB | SO | AVG |
|---|---|---|---|---|---|---|---|---|---|---|---|---|
| 93 A Springfield | 132 | 455 | 81 | 118 | 28 | 4 | 23 | 76 | 8 | 34 | 135 | .259 |
| 94 A St. Pete | 120 | 466 | 39 | 113 | 30 | 2 | 8 | 56 | 2 | 26 | 108 | .242 |
| 95 AA Arkansas | 64 | 242 | 47 | 76 | 16 | 3 | 12 | 48 | 4 | 11 | 52 | .314 |
| 95 AAA Louisville | 58 | 195 | 21 | 46 | 10 | 4 | 5 | 27 | 2 | 10 | 53 | .236 |
| 95 MLE | 122 | 426 | 58 | 111 | 24 | 4 | 13 | 64 | 4 | 16 | 110 | .261 |

The Cardinals haven't developed a real power hitter for what seems like eons, but Gulan does have home-run potential. His performance at Arkansas last year has to be tempered somewhat by his .242 average and eight home runs in the Florida State League in '94, as well as his drop in production upon reaching Triple-A. Also disheartening is Gulan's low walk rate. Still, Gulan has hit as many as 23 home runs in a season, and he's a very good defensive third baseman.

## Aaron Holbert

**Position:** SS    **Opening Day Age:** 23
**Bats:** R **Throws:** R    **Born:** 1/9/73 in
**Ht:** 6' 0" **Wt:** 160    Torrance, CA

*Recent Statistics*

| | G | AB | R | H | D | T | HR | RBI | SB | BB | SO | AVG |
|---|---|---|---|---|---|---|---|---|---|---|---|---|
| 93 A St. Pete | 121 | 457 | 60 | 121 | 18 | 3 | 2 | 31 | 45 | 28 | 61 | .265 |
| 94 R Cardinals | 5 | 12 | 3 | 2 | 0 | 0 | 0 | 0 | 2 | 2 | 2 | .167 |
| 94 AA Arkansas | 59 | 233 | 41 | 69 | 10 | 6 | 2 | 19 | 9 | 14 | 25 | .296 |
| 95 AAA Louisville | 112 | 401 | 57 | 103 | 16 | 4 | 9 | 40 | 14 | 20 | 60 | .257 |
| 95 MLE | 112 | 389 | 46 | 91 | 15 | 2 | 7 | 32 | 10 | 16 | 62 | .234 |

Holbert has been considered the heir apparent to Ozzie Smith almost from the day the Cardinals drafted him in the first round back in 1990. He has the requisite range, hands and throwing arm to play shortstop in the bigs, though comparing him to the Wizard is unfair. Holbert muscled up for nine home runs in Triple-A last year, more than his career total of the previous five seasons. His power may not make up for an on-base percentage that fell under .300, however. Sooner or later, Ozzie has got to call it quits. At 23, Holbert is probably first in line to replace him.

## Bret Wagner

**Position:** P    **Opening Day Age:** 22
**Bats:** L **Throws:** L    **Born:** 4/17/73 in New
**Ht:** 6' 0" **Wt:** 190    Cumberland, PA

*Recent Statistics*

| | W | L | ERA | G | GS | Sv | IP | H | R | BB | SO | HR |
|---|---|---|---|---|---|---|---|---|---|---|---|---|
| 94 A New Jersey | 0 | 1 | 5.11 | 3 | 3 | 0 | 12.1 | 10 | 9 | 4 | 10 | 0 |
| 94 A Savannah | 4 | 1 | 1.23 | 7 | 7 | 0 | 44.0 | 27 | 8 | 6 | 43 | 2 |
| 95 A St. Pete | 5 | 4 | 2.12 | 17 | 17 | 0 | 93.1 | 77 | 36 | 28 | 59 | 3 |
| 95 AA Arkansas | 1 | 2 | 3.19 | 6 | 6 | 0 | 36.2 | 34 | 14 | 18 | 31 | 1 |

The Cardinals love to draft college pitchers in the first round, and they've done so in each of the past six drafts. Wagner was St. Louis' top pick in 1994, and he's made a smooth transition to the pro game. He was dominant at Savannah in '94 and St. Petersburg in '95, and his 3.19 ERA at Double-A suggests that he wasn't overmatched at that level in the final month last season. Like other top Cardinal pitching prospects, Wagner throws a good fastball and slider. He could wind up as a left-handed closer.

## Jay Witasick

**Position:** P    **Opening Day Age:** 23
**Bats:** R **Throws:** R    **Born:** 8/28/72 in
**Ht:** 6' 4" **Wt:** 205    Baltimore, MD

*Recent Statistics*

| | W | L | ERA | G | GS | Sv | IP | H | R | BB | SO | HR |
|---|---|---|---|---|---|---|---|---|---|---|---|---|
| 93 R Johnson Cty | 4 | 3 | 4.12 | 12 | 12 | 0 | 67.2 | 65 | 42 | 19 | 74 | 8 |
| 93 A Savannah | 1 | 0 | 4.50 | 1 | 1 | 0 | 6.0 | 7 | 3 | 2 | 8 | 0 |
| 94 A Madison | 10 | 4 | 2.32 | 18 | 18 | 0 | 112.1 | 74 | 36 | 42 | 141 | 5 |
| 95 A St. Pete | 7 | 7 | 2.74 | 18 | 18 | 0 | 105.0 | 80 | 39 | 36 | 109 | 4 |
| 95 AA Arkansas | 2 | 4 | 6.88 | 7 | 7 | 0 | 34.0 | 46 | 29 | 16 | 26 | 4 |

Witasick was a second-round selection in 1993. He hasn't received as much notice as some of the recent first-rounders, but Witasick's record has been very im-

pressive. He's averaged nearly 10 strikeouts and just 7.5 hits allowed per nine innings through 56 pro starts. Witasick's best pitch is a curveball that complements a high-80s fastball. He experienced his first real failure when he moved up to Double-A in the middle of last season, and he could return to that level in 1996.

## Dmitri Young

**Position:** OF    **Opening Day Age:** 22
**Bats:** B **Throws:** R    **Born:** 10/11/73 in
**Ht:** 6' 2" **Wt:** 215    Vicksburg, MS

*Recent Statistics*

| | G | AB | R | H | D | T | HR | RBI | SB | BB | SO | AVG |
|---|---|---|---|---|---|---|---|---|---|---|---|---|
| 93 A St. Pete | 69 | 270 | 31 | 85 | 13 | 3 | 5 | 43 | 3 | 24 | 28 | .315 |
| 93 AA Arkansas | 45 | 166 | 13 | 41 | 11 | 2 | 3 | 21 | 4 | 9 | 29 | .247 |
| 94 AA Arkansas | 125 | 453 | 53 | 123 | 33 | 2 | 8 | 54 | 0 | 36 | 60 | .272 |
| 95 AA Arkansas | 97 | 367 | 54 | 107 | 18 | 6 | 10 | 62 | 2 | 30 | 46 | .292 |
| 95 AAA Louisville | 2 | 7 | 3 | 2 | 0 | 0 | 0 | 0 | 0 | 1 | 1 | .286 |
| 95 MLE | 99 | 365 | 49 | 100 | 18 | 4 | 8 | 55 | 1 | 22 | 49 | .274 |

Young is still a prospect, though he is almost certainly regarded as a disappointment by many Cardinal observers. He was chosen with the fourth overall selection in the 1991 draft, when he was the first high-school hitter selected. Young owns a .289 career average in the minors, but he hasn't developed his power as expected. It could be that St. Louis rushed him to Double-A too quickly at age 19. Young has also had problems finding a defensive position, moving from third base to first, and now the outfield.

## Others to Watch

Righthander **Mike Busby** was 9-8 with a 3.29 ERA between Double- and Triple-A last year. He was a 14th-round pick in 1991. . . **Kris Detmers** was signed as a draft-and-follow in 1994. The lefthander fanned 150 in 146.2 innings at St. Petersburg last year. . . Outfielder **Anthony Lewis** has spent seven seasons in the minors. He hit a career-high 24 homers in Double-A last season at age 24. . . Reliever **Steve Montgomery** led the Texas League with 36 saves in 1995. He's now spent the past two-and-a-half seasons in Double-A, and he's 25. That tells you something about his arm.

# Andy Ashby

**Position:** SP
**Bats:** R  **Throws:** R
**Ht:** 6' 5"  **Wt:** 190

**Opening Day Age:** 28
**Born:** 7/11/67 in Kansas City, MO
**ML Seasons:** 5

## 1995 Season

It now looks like one of the more lopsided trades of the decade. In 1993, the Padres sent Bruce Hurst and Greg Harris to the Rockies, and received Andy Ashby, Brad Ausmus and Doug Bochtler. A 6-11 record notwithstanding, Ashby pitched well in 1994, and last season he continued to pitch well despite a rough start (6.15 ERA in his first seven starts). Few people noticed—probably because of his ho-hum 12-10 record—but Ashby finished behind only Greg Maddux and Hideo Nomo in the National League ERA battle.

## Pitching

Ashby has always had a fine arm, but over the last couple of years he's mastered a cut fastball which tails away from right-handed hitters. Add that to his other four pitches—sinking fastball, curve, slider, change-up—and Ashby features a variety of weapons with which to retire N.L. batters. Aside from the cut fastball, Ashby's success can be credited to his willingness to trust his stuff, rather than always nibbling around the corners. Ashby's outstanding sinker helps him keep the ball down, and last season he was an extreme groundball pitcher. That's a good quality in cozy Jack Murphy Stadium. As you'd expect, Ashby is very tough on right-handed hitters, and he's no picnic for lefties, either.

## Defense & Hitting

Ashby's slow to the plate, so fast runners salivate upon reaching first. He did show an improved move to first last year, and not so many liberties were taken. Ashby is a .146 hitter in his career, right around average for a pitcher. He's a fine bunter, and finished second in the major leagues with 17 sacrifice hits last season.

## 1996 Outlook

Pay no attention to that 23-39 career record; based purely on *how well he pitches*, Andy Ashby is already one of the top starters in the National League. Given another healthy season and some support from his teammates, Ashby is a good bet for 15-18 victories this season.

### Overall Statistics

|        | W  | L  | Pct. | ERA  | G   | GS | Sv | IP    | H   | BB  | SO  | HR | BR/IP |
|--------|----|----|------|------|-----|----|----|-------|-----|-----|-----|----|-------|
| 1995   | 12 | 10 | .545 | 2.94 | 31  | 31 | 0  | 192.2 | 180 | 62  | 150 | 17 | 1.26  |
| Career | 23 | 39 | .371 | 4.46 | 105 | 92 | 1  | 559.0 | 576 | 201 | 398 | 63 | 1.39  |

### How Often He Throws Strikes

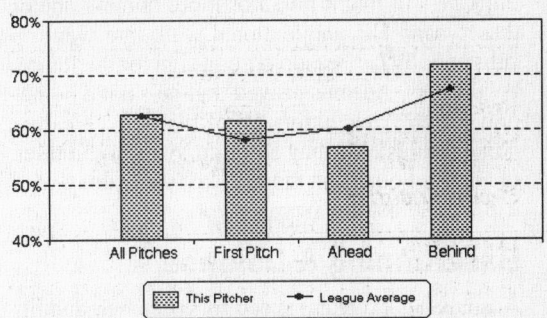

Legend: This Pitcher — League Average

### 1995 Situational Stats

|            | W | L | ERA  | Sv | IP    |        | AB  | H  | HR | RBI | Avg  |
|------------|---|---|------|----|-------|--------|-----|----|----|-----|------|
| Home       | 7 | 3 | 2.21 | 0  | 93.2  | LHB    | 330 | 90 | 5  | 29  | .273 |
| Road       | 5 | 7 | 3.64 | 0  | 99.0  | RHB    | 382 | 90 | 12 | 40  | .236 |
| First Half | 6 | 5 | 3.33 | 0  | 92.0  | Sc Pos | 159 | 38 | 2  | 47  | .239 |
| Scnd Half  | 6 | 5 | 2.59 | 0  | 100.2 | Clutch | 41  | 7  | 1  | 3   | .171 |

### 1995 Rankings (National League)

- ➡ 1st in games started
- ➡ 2nd in sacrifice bunts (17)
- ➡ 3rd in ERA, shutouts (2), hit batsmen (11), GDPs induced (24), most GDPs induced per 9 innings (1.1) and ERA at home (2.21)
- ➡ 4th in highest groundball/flyball ratio allowed (2.1)
- ➡ 8th in strikeouts
- ➡ 10th in pitches thrown (2,995), runners caught stealing (10) and least run support per 9 innings (4.4)
- ➡ Led the Padres in sacrifice bunts, ERA, wins, losses, games started, complete games (2), shutouts and home runs allowed

647

# Brad Ausmus

## 1995 Season

More fruits of a 1993 trade with the Rockies, Brad Ausmus brings a lot of things to the table. He's fast, he's a fine defensive catcher, and he can hit a little, too. Only a couple things marred an otherwise fine season for Ausmus: he wasn't able to start the five games before the All-Star break because of a wrist injury suffered when he punched a water cooler, and he wasn't really the everyday catcher as Brian Johnson got significant playing time.

## Hitting

Ausmus has yet to show much power, but he's strong and he takes a full rip, and some scouts think he still might hit 15 or more homers one of these years. His unintentional walk rate went up substantially last season, a good sign for the future. By the way, Ausmus proved that he's not a home-only hitter. After hitting 10 of his first 12 career homers at Jack Murphy Stadium, Ausmus hit three of his five homers on the road last year, along with a .323 road batting average.

## Baserunning & Defense

Ausmus has excellent speed for a catcher, and his ratio of 16 stolen bases in 103 games last season would be very good for a lot of center fielders. He doesn't have a great arm, but he *does* have great footwork and a quick release. As a result, he threw out 38 percent of prospective basestealers last season, the third-best figure in the major leagues and behind only Gold Glove winners Ivan Rodriguez and Charles Johnson. The San Diego staff last season had a much better ERA with Brian Johnson behind the plate than it did with Ausmus. This was likely a fluke, given that Ausmus had better numbers in 1994.

## 1996 Outlook

On a team with a number of promising young pitchers, Ausmus' defensive skills are particularly valuable. And if he can develop his power and continue to steal an occasional base, he'll have to be considered one of the more valuable catchers in the league.

**Position:** C
**Bats:** R  **Throws:** R
**Ht:** 5'11"  **Wt:** 190

**Opening Day Age:** 26
**Born:** 4/14/69 in New Haven, CT
**ML Seasons:** 3
**Pronunciation:** AHS-mus

### Overall Statistics

| | G | AB | R | H | D | T | HR | RBI | SB | BB | SO | Avg | OBP | Slg |
|---|---|---|---|---|---|---|---|---|---|---|---|---|---|---|
| 1995 | 103 | 328 | 44 | 96 | 16 | 4 | 5 | 34 | 16 | 31 | 56 | .293 | .353 | .412 |
| Career | 253 | 815 | 107 | 219 | 36 | 6 | 17 | 70 | 23 | 67 | 147 | .269 | .324 | .390 |

### Where He Hits the Ball

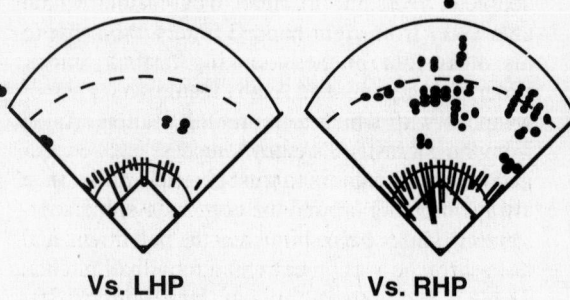

**Vs. LHP**          **Vs. RHP**

### 1995 Situational Stats

| | AB | H | HR | RBI | Avg | | AB | H | HR | RBI | Avg |
|---|---|---|---|---|---|---|---|---|---|---|---|
| Home | 173 | 46 | 2 | 15 | .266 | LHP | 70 | 22 | 3 | 7 | .314 |
| Road | 155 | 50 | 3 | 19 | .323 | RHP | 258 | 74 | 2 | 27 | .287 |
| First Half | 161 | 46 | 1 | 12 | .286 | Sc Pos | 69 | 20 | 1 | 27 | .290 |
| Scnd Half | 167 | 50 | 4 | 22 | .299 | Clutch | 51 | 10 | 1 | 3 | .196 |

### 1995 Rankings (National League)

→ 2nd in highest percentage of runners caught stealing as a catcher (37.9%)
→ 10th in errors at catcher (6)

# Willie Blair

**Position:** RP/SP
**Bats:** R  **Throws:** R
**Ht:** 6' 1"  **Wt:** 185

**Opening Day Age:** 30
**Born:** 12/18/65 in
Paintsville, KY
**ML Seasons:** 6

## 1995 Season

After a rough 1994 season with the Colorado Rockies—and who could blame him?—Willie Blair signed a free-agent contract with the Padres last April. He opened the season in the bullpen, and pitched better than his 5.04 relief ERA would suggest. With Scott Sanders hitting the disabled list in late July, Blair took his place in the rotation on August 3 and responded with six shutout innings in his first start. Overall, Blair went 4-4 in 12 starts, with a 3.89 ERA.

## Pitching

Blair doesn't have a great arm at this point, but he'll throw four different pitches, three of them at least major league average. Blair's favorite pitch is his slider, which sometimes looks almost like a very fast change-up because it breaks almost straight down. Blair's fastball has decent movement, and he also throws an effective change-up. Rounding out Blair's repertoire is a big curve that doesn't often fool the hitters. Probably due to all those pitches, Blair shows very little platoon differential. Over the last five seasons, lefties have hit Blair at a .294 clip, righties .292. His ERA was hurt last season by his lack of success with runners in scoring position.

## Defense & Hitting

Blair does a decent job of holding runners. Of the 14 runners who tried to steal with him on the mound last year, half were caught. He doesn't throw to first base a lot, but Blair employs an effective slide-step which gives his catchers a great chance at nailing the runner. Blair is a poor hitter. After going 0-for-24 last year, he's at .060 lifetime.

## 1996 Outlook

On a pitching staff—and for that matter, a bull-pen—composed of live young arms, Blair provides a veteran presence and versatility. And he's still got pretty good stuff, too, so the Padres would like to bring him back if the price isn't too high.

### Overall Statistics

|      | W  | L  | Pct. | ERA  | G   | GS | Sv | IP    | H   | BB  | SO  | HR | BR/IP |
|------|----|----|------|------|-----|----|----|-------|-----|-----|-----|----|-------|
| 1995 | 7  | 5  | .583 | 4.34 | 40  | 12 | 0  | 114.0 | 112 | 45  | 83  | 11 | 1.38  |
| Career | 23 | 35 | .397 | 4.75 | 200 | 50 | 3  | 521.0 | 592 | 189 | 339 | 56 | 1.50  |

### How Often He Throws Strikes

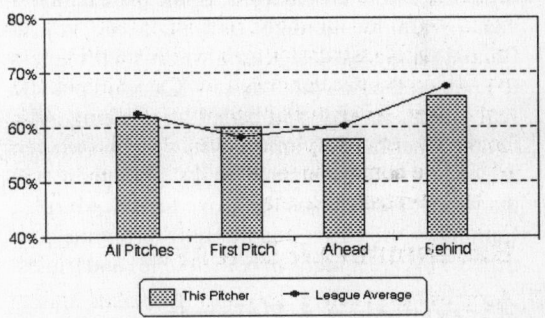

### 1995 Situational Stats

|           | W | L | ERA  | Sv | IP   |       | AB  | H  | HR | RBI | Avg  |
|-----------|---|---|------|----|------|-------|-----|----|----|-----|------|
| Home      | 3 | 1 | 3.20 | 0  | 59.0 | LHB   | 163 | 44 | 5  | 23  | .270 |
| Road      | 4 | 4 | 5.56 | 0  | 55.0 | RHB   | 265 | 68 | 6  | 38  | .257 |
| First Half| 1 | 0 | 5.02 | 0  | 28.2 | Sc Pos| 84  | 32 | 4  | 47  | .381 |
| Scnd Half | 6 | 5 | 4.11 | 0  | 85.1 | Clutch| 54  | 14 | 0  | 6   | .259 |

### 1995 Rankings (National League)

➡ Did not rank near the top or bottom in any category

# Ken Caminiti

## 1995 Season

Of all the players in the 12-player trade between Houston and San Diego back in December of 1994, perhaps the chief beneficiary was third baseman Ken Caminiti. Trapped in the Astrodome for eight years, Caminiti welcomed the move to San Diego and homer-happy Jack Murphy. And he took advantage, setting career highs in nearly every hitting category: doubles, homers, RBI, walks, all three averages, and even stolen bases. In the process, Caminiti helped transform the Padres from an awful offensive club to a good one.

## Hitting

The switch-hitting Caminiti has always been a little better from the right side of the plate, and last year he simply murdered lefties. A big key to Caminiti's success last season was his willingness to jump on the first pitch he saw. Caminiti put 102 first pitches in play, and batted an amazing .441. On the other hand, Caminiti was no wild swinger, as he drew a career-high 69 walks. Then there was the power. As much as the move to Jack Murphy, Caminiti's offseason conditioning program contributed to career highs in both doubles and triples.

## Baserunning & Defense

Caminiti is by no means fast, but he is a heady baserunner and finished with a dozen steals last season, a career high. With Matt Williams out for much of the season, Caminiti finally garnered his first Gold Glove. He excels at snaring scorchers to either side, and owns the strongest third-base arm in the majors. The only negative last year was Caminiti's 27 errors, the most of any third sacker in either league.

## 1996 Outlook

Caminiti's two best seasons have come in the last two years, at age 31 and 32; it'll be interesting to see if he can continue this unlikely trend. Though he became a free agent after last season, Caminiti was eager to return to San Diego, and he signed a new deal which should have him in a Padre uniform through at least the 1997 season.

**Position:** 3B
**Bats:** B **Throws:** R
**Ht:** 6' 0"   **Wt:** 200

**Opening Day Age:** 32
**Born:** 4/21/63 in Hanford, CA
**ML Seasons:** 9
**Pronunciation:** kam-un-NET-ee

### Overall Statistics

|  | G | AB | R | H | D | T | HR | RBI | SB | BB | SO | Avg | OBP | Slg |
|---|---|---|---|---|---|---|---|---|---|---|---|---|---|---|
| 1995 | 143 | 526 | 74 | 159 | 33 | 0 | 26 | 94 | 12 | 69 | 94 | .302 | .380 | .513 |
| Career | 1091 | 3967 | 483 | 1055 | 213 | 13 | 101 | 539 | 51 | 367 | 658 | .266 | .328 | .403 |

### Where He Hits the Ball

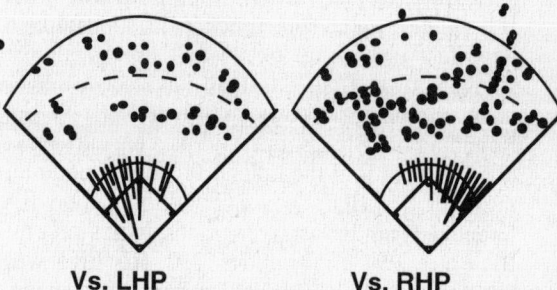

**Vs. LHP**          **Vs. RHP**

### 1995 Situational Stats

|  | AB | H | HR | RBI | Avg |  | AB | H | HR | RBI | Avg |
|---|---|---|---|---|---|---|---|---|---|---|---|
| Home | 261 | 79 | 16 | 51 | .303 | LHP | 169 | 56 | 10 | 32 | .331 |
| Road | 265 | 80 | 10 | 43 | .302 | RHP | 357 | 103 | 16 | 62 | .289 |
| First Half | 251 | 72 | 11 | 45 | .287 | Sc Pos | 146 | 42 | 8 | 68 | .288 |
| Scnd Half | 275 | 87 | 15 | 49 | .316 | Clutch | 71 | 18 | 1 | 4 | .254 |

### 1995 Rankings (National League)

- ➡ 1st in errors at third base (27)
- ➡ 3rd in lowest fielding percentage at third base (.936)
- ➡ 4th in games played
- ➡ 5th in times on base (229)
- ➡ 8th in sacrifice flies (6) and slugging percentage vs. left-handed pitchers (.574)
- ➡ 9th in hits, RBI and cleanup slugging percentage (.516)
- ➡ 10th in doubles, total bases and lowest stolen base percentage (70.6%)
- ➡ Led the Padres in home runs, doubles, total bases (270), RBI, sacrifice flies, walks, strikeouts and games played

# Andujar Cedeno

## 1995 Season

Of the five players traded from Houston to San Diego in the December 1994 mega-deal, Andujar Cedeno perhaps figured to benefit the most. He'd be installed as the starter at shortstop for the Padres, and his power stroke would find a happy home in hitter-friendly Jack Murphy Stadium. Cedeno played okay at shortstop, but his hitting was simply atrocious; in fact, he might have been the worst-hitting regular in the majors.

## Hitting

One well-known baseball writer, whom we shall leave nameless, once compared Cedeno's wrists to those of Henry Aaron. Unfortunately, Cedeno doesn't have Aaron's power, Aaron's batting average, or Aaron's strike-zone judgment. That last weakness is what kept Cedeno hitting for average or power. He simply swung at far too many bad pitches last season, both high fastballs and offspeed stuff outside the zone. Cedeno's troubles were particularly pronounced after the All-Star game, when he produced these eye-popping averages: .173 batting, .266 on-base, .200 slugging!

## Baserunning & Defense

Cedeno has decent speed, and he's an average baserunner. At his best, Cedeno might steal 10 or 12 bases in a season. He was a bit steadier at shortstop than he'd been with Houston, and has a strong arm and average range.

## 1996 Outlook

A look at Cedeno's numbers from last season sounds an alarm, and without a big improvement his career will be a short one. But Cedeno suffered some off-the-field problems last year. The Padres are hopeful that with those behind him, he can return to the production he showed as an Astro. If not, shortstop could be a big hole for the club this season.

**Position:** SS
**Bats:** R  **Throws:** R
**Ht:** 6' 1"  **Wt:** 170

**Opening Day Age:** 26
**Born:** 8/21/69 in La Romana, DR
**ML Seasons:** 6
**Pronunciation:** suh-DAYN-yo

### Overall Statistics

|        | G   | AB   | R   | H   | D  | T  | HR | RBI | SB | BB  | SO  | Avg  | OBP  | Slg  |
|--------|-----|------|-----|-----|----|----|----|-----|----|-----|-----|------|------|------|
| 1995   | 120 | 390  | 42  | 82  | 16 | 2  | 6  | 31  | 5  | 28  | 92  | .210 | .271 | .308 |
| Career | 512 | 1716 | 191 | 414 | 92 | 10 | 37 | 185 | 21 | 128 | 418 | .241 | .300 | .371 |

### Where He Hits the Ball

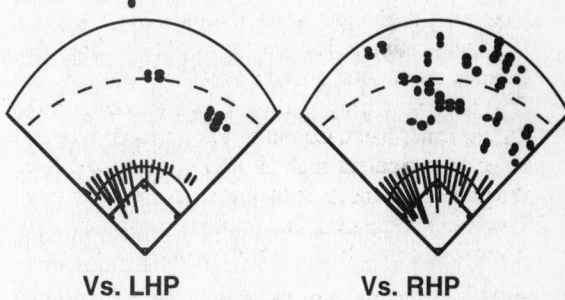

**Vs. LHP**          **Vs. RHP**

### 1995 Situational Stats

|            | AB  | H  | HR | RBI | Avg  |        | AB  | H  | HR | RBI | Avg  |
|------------|-----|----|----|-----|------|--------|-----|----|----|-----|------|
| Home       | 180 | 39 | 3  | 14  | .217 | LHP    | 96  | 26 | 2  | 9   | .271 |
| Road       | 210 | 43 | 3  | 17  | .205 | RHP    | 294 | 56 | 4  | 22  | .190 |
| First Half | 240 | 56 | 6  | 26  | .233 | Sc Pos | 100 | 28 | 3  | 26  | .280 |
| Scnd Half  | 150 | 26 | 0  | 5   | .173 | Clutch | 62  | 14 | 1  | 2   | .226 |

### 1995 Rankings (National League)

- 1st in lowest batting average on the road (.205)
- 3rd in highest percentage of swings that missed (29.6%) and lowest percentage of swings put into play (35.0%)
- 4th in lowest percentage of pitches taken (45.2%)
- 6th in lowest fielding percentage at shortstop (.965)
- 7th in errors at shortstop (16)
- 8th in lowest batting average with the bases loaded (.125)
- Led the Padres in hit by pitch (5)

# Glenn Dishman

## 1995 Season

In one of the more unlikely success stories you'll find, lefthander Glenn Dishman won a spot in the Padre rotation in just his third professional season. Why so unlikely? Because Dishman wasn't even drafted out of college. After signing with San Diego in 1993, he blazed through the minors, pitching with poise at nearly every juncture on his way to the major leagues. After his promotion from Triple-A Las Vegas last June, Dishman pitched well in his first six starts (2.23 ERA) but was generally roughed up later in the season as his fastball seemed to lose some zip.

## Pitching

Once a TCU Horned Frog, Dishman is now a San Diego Crafty Lefty. His fastball is below average, and it's easily the slowest among the Padre starters (not including Fernando, of course). Often compared to Tom Glavine, Dishman will throw his curve and change-up on any count. In a July 22 game, for instance, he struck out Fred McGriff on a 3-2 change of pace. While Dishman averaged around a strikeout per inning in the lower minors, his K rate has dropped drastically since moving to first Triple-A and now the majors. He's very tough against left-handed hitters, but righties have had success against him.

## Defense & Hitting

As befitting a smart southpaw, Dishman is a good fielder and he holds runners well. Of the eight who tried to steal against him last year, four were gunned down. He went 6-for-30 and knocked in four runs as a hitter.

## 1996 Outlook

Despite his impressive strikeout numbers in the minors, Dishman's stuff simply might not be good enough to retire major league hitters for six or seven innings every fifth day. However, Dishman's offspeed pitches make him very tough on left-handed hitters, and he might be perfect as a southpaw specialist. Either way, he's got plenty of time to discover the right role.

**Position:** SP
**Bats:** R **Throws:** L
**Ht:** 6' 1"  **Wt:** 195

**Opening Day Age:** 25
**Born:** 11/5/70 in Baltimore, MD
**ML Seasons:** 1

### Overall Statistics

|        | W | L | Pct. | ERA | G | GS | Sv | IP | H | BB | SO | HR | BR/IP |
|--------|---|---|------|------|----|----|----|------|-----|----|----|----|-------|
| 1995   | 4 | 8 | .333 | 5.01 | 19 | 16 | 0 | 97.0 | 104 | 34 | 43 | 11 | 1.42 |
| Career | 4 | 8 | .333 | 5.01 | 19 | 16 | 0 | 97.0 | 104 | 34 | 43 | 11 | 1.42 |

### How Often He Throws Strikes

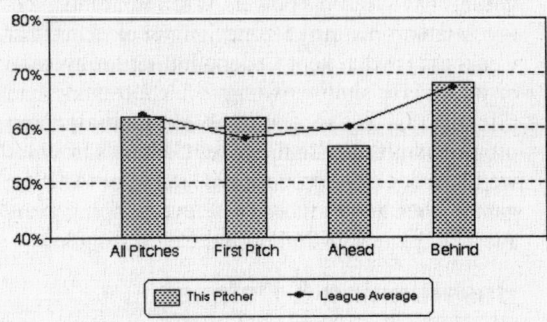

### 1995 Situational Stats

|            | W | L | ERA | Sv | IP |        | AB | H | HR | RBI | Avg |
|------------|---|---|------|----|------|--------|-----|----|----|-----|------|
| Home       | 2 | 3 | 4.57 | 0 | 43.1 | LHB    | 66  | 11 | 1  | 7   | .167 |
| Road       | 2 | 5 | 5.37 | 0 | 53.2 | RHB    | 308 | 93 | 10 | 40  | .302 |
| First Half | 1 | 2 | 2.77 | 0 | 26.0 | Sc Pos | 77  | 23 | 3  | 38  | .299 |
| Scnd Half  | 3 | 6 | 5.83 | 0 | 71.0 | Clutch | 20  | 3  | 0  | 0   | .150 |

### 1995 Rankings (National League)

→ 8th in highest batting average allowed vs. right-handed batters (.302)

# Steve Finley

## 1995 Season

Yet another component of the dozen-player deal involving the Padres and Astros, center fielder Steve Finley rivaled Ken Caminiti as the biggest beneficiary—so far—of the trade. Batting leadoff or number two all season, Finley was a major reason that the Padres jumped from number 12 in the National League in runs scored, in 1994, to number six in 1995. And of course, he performed his usual sterling job in center field.

## Hitting

"To me," Finley said in August, "I'm not doing anything I haven't done in years past." Well, that wasn't precisely true. Finley set career highs in batting average and walks, the latter despite the abbreviated schedule. He entered the season with a .324 career on-base percentage, very low for a leadoff man. But all those hits and walks added up to a .366 OBP and 104 runs, two *more* career highs. Finley actually took slightly fewer pitches per plate appearance than usual. The difference was, he took fewer strikes but more balls. Finley batted .339 in the leadoff spot, but saw his average fall to just .246 in the two slot.

## Baserunning & Defense

One of the faster players in the league, Finley's 36 steals were a welcome surprise given his total of 32 in 1993 and '94 combined. He's a solid, aggressive baserunner. Finley has always drawn raves for his play in center field, and deservedly so. His range remains excellent, and his arm is fine. He had a little trouble with errors last year, making seven, but that's an anomaly. Like fellow Houston expatriate Ken Caminiti, Finley was rewarded for his fielding prowess with his first Gold Glove.

## 1996 Outlook

Finley's 1995 numbers can't be attributed to his move from Houston, because he was much better last year away from San Diego. Most likely, it was just a case of a good player having his career season. Even should his hitting stats fall off, Finley gives the Padres good defense in center field and speed at the top of the order.

**Position:** CF
**Bats:** L  **Throws:** L
**Ht:** 6' 2"  **Wt:** 180

**Opening Day Age:** 31
**Born:** 3/12/65 in Union City, TN
**ML Seasons:** 7

### Overall Statistics

| | G | AB | R | H | D | T | HR | RBI | SB | BB | SO | Avg | OBP | Slg |
|---|---|---|---|---|---|---|---|---|---|---|---|---|---|---|
| 1995 | 139 | 562 | 104 | 167 | 23 | 8 | 10 | 44 | 36 | 59 | 62 | .297 | .366 | .420 |
| Career | 919 | 3364 | 486 | 935 | 132 | 55 | 47 | 292 | 185 | 262 | 390 | .278 | .331 | .392 |

### Where He Hits the Ball

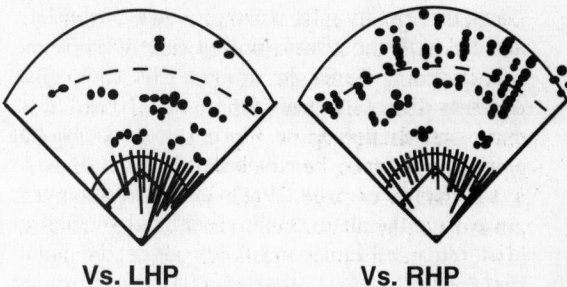

**Vs. LHP**          **Vs. RHP**

### 1995 Situational Stats

| | AB | H | HR | RBI | Avg | | AB | H | HR | RBI | Avg |
|---|---|---|---|---|---|---|---|---|---|---|---|
| Home | 255 | 70 | 4 | 17 | .275 | LHP | 187 | 61 | 3 | 9 | .326 |
| Road | 307 | 97 | 6 | 27 | .316 | RHP | 375 | 106 | 7 | 35 | .283 |
| First Half | 282 | 79 | 5 | 18 | .280 | Sc Pos | 103 | 31 | 2 | 34 | .301 |
| Scnd Half | 280 | 88 | 5 | 26 | .314 | Clutch | 91 | 29 | 2 | 10 | .319 |

### 1995 Rankings (National League)

→ 2nd in singles (126), on-base percentage for a leadoff hitter (.405) and lowest fielding percentage in center field (.977)

→ 3rd in runs scored, triples and errors in center field (7)

→ 4th in at-bats, hits, stolen bases, caught stealing (12), plate appearances (630) and steals of third (10)

→ 5th in times on base (229)

→ 7th in batting average on the road (.316) and highest percentage of extra bases taken as a runner (65.2%)

→ Led the Padres in at-bats, runs scored, triples, stolen bases and caught stealing

**San Diego Padres**

# Bryce Florie

## 1995 Season

After spending his entire pro career as a starter, righthander Bryce Florie became a relief pitcher in 1994 and compiled a 5.15 ERA for the Padres' Triple-A farm team at Las Vegas. Undaunted, the Padres listed Florie on their Opening Day roster last April. He spent the entire season in the majors, and though he struggled with his control at times, Florie proved very tough to hit, holding opposition hitters to a .202 batting average. He spent the entire season in the bullpen and provided reliable service as a middle reliever.

## Pitching

Florie relies on two pitches, but his arm is so live that those two pitches often look like five. Florie's fastball normally tails down and away from left-handed hitters, but sometimes it simply drops and sometimes it comes in straight. His slider also behaves differently from pitch to pitch, and at its best is almost unhittable. Florie suffers occasional control problems, largely because his stuff is so good that pitches which begin as strikes often veer away from the plate. On the other hand, the unpredictability of Florie's pitches gives the small righthander a great weapon against left-handed hitters, who managed just a .202 batting average last season.

## Defense & Hitting

Aside from a moderate leg kick, Florie pitches with a compact motion which leaves him in good fielding position after releasing the ball. He pays little attention to baserunners, who were a perfect 12-for-12 on steal attempts last season. Florie has batted twice in the majors, and he whiffed both times.

## 1996 Outlook

The Padres love Florie's stuff, but with Trevor Hoffman around he'll be relegated to middle relief. If he can harness his stuff just a bit more, he should post some nice numbers as Hoffman's right-handed set-up man.

**Position:** RP
**Bats:** R  **Throws:** R
**Ht:** 5'11"  **Wt:** 190

**Opening Day Age:** 25
**Born:** 5/21/70 in Charleston, SC
**ML Seasons:** 2

### Overall Statistics

|  | W | L | Pct. | ERA | G | GS | Sv | IP | H | BB | SO | HR | BR/IP |
|---|---|---|---|---|---|---|---|---|---|---|---|---|---|
| 1995 | 2 | 2 | .500 | 3.01 | 47 | 0 | 1 | 68.2 | 49 | 38 | 68 | 8 | 1.27 |
| Career | 2 | 2 | .500 | 2.77 | 56 | 0 | 1 | 78.0 | 57 | 41 | 76 | 8 | 1.26 |

### How Often He Throws Strikes

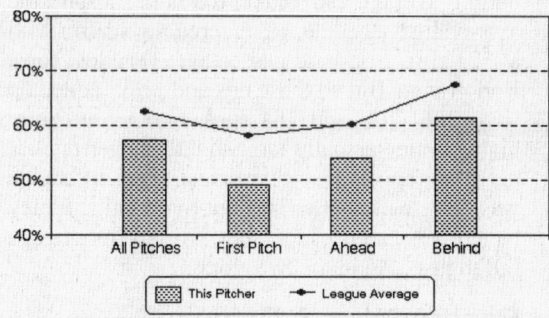

### 1995 Situational Stats

|  | W | L | ERA | Sv | IP |  | AB | H | HR | RBI | Avg |
|---|---|---|---|---|---|---|---|---|---|---|---|
| Home | 0 | 1 | 2.78 | 1 | 32.1 | LHB | 109 | 22 | 2 | 10 | .202 |
| Road | 2 | 1 | 3.22 | 0 | 36.1 | RHB | 133 | 27 | 6 | 24 | .203 |
| First Half | 2 | 0 | 2.39 | 0 | 37.2 | Sc Pos | 84 | 15 | 1 | 25 | .179 |
| Scnd Half | 0 | 2 | 3.77 | 1 | 31.0 | Clutch | 101 | 19 | 5 | 15 | .188 |

### 1995 Rankings (National League)

➡ Did not rank near the top or bottom in any category

# Tony Gwynn

## 1995 Season

What could Tony Gwynn do for an encore? In 1994, he batted .394, leaving us to wonder what he might have accomplished given a full season. Well, he didn't hit .400 last season. But he did bat .368, good for his second straight batting title and the sixth of his Hall of Fame career. Gwynn also knocked in 90 runs, a career high. All this despite the fact that the never-svelte Gwynn reported to training camp at 236 pounds. . . also a career high. Maybe he was right, and it *was* all muscle.

## Hitting

Everything Gwynn does at the plate is designed with two things in mind: avoid strikeouts, and hit for average. How do you avoid strikeouts? By not taking pitches. Gwynn averaged 3.07 pitches per plate appearances last season, fewest in the National League. The first good pitch he sees, he hits. Though some commentators raved about Gwynn's career-high 90 RBI last season, his power numbers were actually down significantly, on a per at-bat basis, from 1994. All those RBI came because (1) Gwynn batted .394 with runners in scoring position, and (2) Bip Roberts, Steve Finley and Jody Reed were getting on base at the top of the order.

## Baserunning & Defense

After swiping only five bases in 1994, Gwynn stole 17 last season. He's not fast anymore, but he's smart enough to pick his spots. While he's no longer a Gold Glove-caliber right fielder, Gwynn remains a solid defender who positions himself well and has good instincts. His arm might be a little short for right field, but it's accurate and Gwynn recorded eight assists last season.

## 1996 Outlook

You'd think Gwynn would slow down one of these years, given that he's now in his mid 30s and seems to get a little fatter, or perhaps more "muscular," each season. But he's hit .379 over the last two seasons, and has to be considered a favorite to win his seventh batting title in 1996.

**Position:** RF
**Bats:** L **Throws:** L
**Ht:** 5'11" **Wt:** 215

**Opening Day Age:** 35
**Born:** 5/9/60 in Los Angeles, CA
**ML Seasons:** 14

### Overall Statistics

|  | G | AB | R | H | D | T | HR | RBI | SB | BB | SO | Avg | OBP | Slg |
|---|---|---|---|---|---|---|---|---|---|---|---|---|---|---|
| 1995 | 135 | 535 | 82 | 197 | 33 | 1 | 9 | 90 | 17 | 35 | 15 | .368 | .404 | .484 |
| Career | 1830 | 7144 | 1073 | 2401 | 384 | 80 | 87 | 804 | 285 | 625 | 344 | .336 | .388 | .449 |

### Where He Hits the Ball

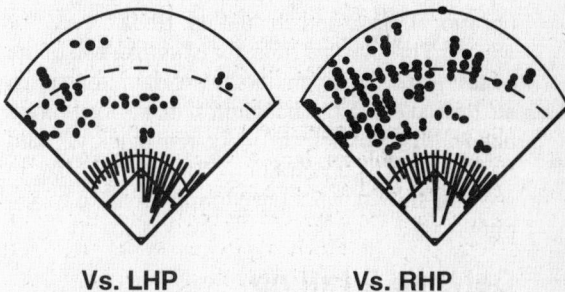

**Vs. LHP**        **Vs. RHP**

### 1995 Situational Stats

|  | AB | H | HR | RBI | Avg |  | AB | H | HR | RBI | Avg |
|---|---|---|---|---|---|---|---|---|---|---|---|
| Home | 266 | 103 | 5 | 45 | .387 | LHP | 188 | 62 | 2 | 27 | .330 |
| Road | 269 | 94 | 4 | 45 | .349 | RHP | 347 | 135 | 7 | 63 | .389 |
| First Half | 269 | 98 | 6 | 52 | .364 | Sc Pos | 137 | 54 | 4 | 82 | .394 |
| Scnd Half | 266 | 99 | 3 | 38 | .372 | Clutch | 80 | 31 | 3 | 18 | .388 |

### 1995 Rankings (National League)

→ 1st in batting average, hits, singles (154), least pitches seen per plate appearance (3.07), batting average with runners in scoring position (.394), batting average vs. right-handed pitchers (.389), batting average at home (.387) and highest percentage of swings put into play (62.8%)

→ 2nd in highest groundball/flyball ratio (2.5), batting average with the bases loaded (.636) and fielding percentage in right field (.992)

→ Led the Padres in doubles, sacrifice flies (6 ), intentional walks (10), times on base (233), on-base percentage, highest groundball/flyball ratio and batting average with runners in scoring position

**San Diego Padres**

# Joey Hamilton

## 1995 Season

Talk about a frustrating season. Second-year man Joey Hamilton started 30 games and finished with a fine 3.08 ERA—numbers almost identical to those posted by Tom Glavine. But where Glavine finished 16-7, Hamilton could manage only a 6-9 mark thanks to poor support from both his hitters and his bullpen. Hamilton opened and closed the season with eight-start winless streaks.

## Pitching

Hamilton's best pitch is his sinking fastball, a 90-plus offering which results in a lot of first-pitch groundball outs. Like teammate Andy Ashby, Hamilton is an extreme groundball pitcher. He also throws an effective slider, along with the occasional curve and change-up. He is a very fast worker. Through late June, for example, two of the fastest games in the majors were Hamilton starts, at 1:59 and 1:55. That didn't make everybody happy. "It's possible to work too quickly," said Padres pitching coach Sonny Siebert. "I'd like to see him slow down, concentrating more on each pitch."

## Defense & Hitting

For a righthander, Hamilton is tough to run on. Of 16 runners trying to steal, eight were nailed, and Hamilton picked three men off base himself. Otherwise, he had a pretty awful defensive season, tying Bobby Jones for the major league lead with six errors. On a happier note, Hamilton doubled off Pete Harnisch on June 9. So what? That two-bagger broke Hamilton's 0-for-57 streak, believed to be the longest hitless streak at the start of any career in major league history. He finished the season 7-for-65 (.108).

## 1996 Outlook

Along with Andy Ashby and Scott Sanders, Hamilton is part of one of the game's more impressive young rotations. Given just average luck, he should easily double last season's victory total.

**Position:** SP
**Bats:** R  **Throws:** R
**Ht:** 6' 4"  **Wt:** 230

**Opening Day Age:** 25
**Born:** 9/9/70 in Statesboro, GA
**ML Seasons:** 2

### Overall Statistics

|  | W | L | Pct. | ERA | G | GS | Sv | IP | H | BB | SO | HR | BR/IP |
|---|---|---|---|---|---|---|---|---|---|---|---|---|---|
| 1995 | 6 | 9 | .400 | 3.08 | 31 | 30 | 0 | 204.1 | 189 | 56 | 123 | 17 | 1.20 |
| Career | 15 | 15 | .500 | 3.05 | 47 | 46 | 0 | 313.0 | 287 | 85 | 184 | 24 | 1.19 |

### How Often He Throws Strikes

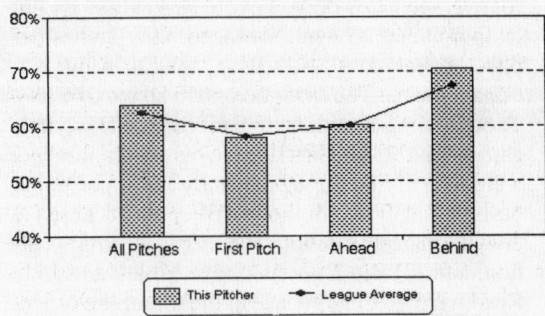

### 1995 Situational Stats

|  | W | L | ERA | Sv | IP |  | AB | H | HR | RBI | Avg |
|---|---|---|---|---|---|---|---|---|---|---|---|
| Home | 3 | 6 | 2.84 | 0 | 107.2 | LHB | 340 | 78 | 9 | 36 | .229 |
| Road | 3 | 3 | 3.35 | 0 | 96.2 | RHB | 427 | 111 | 8 | 42 | .260 |
| First Half | 3 | 2 | 2.87 | 0 | 97.1 | Sc Pos | 161 | 43 | 2 | 58 | .267 |
| Scnd Half | 3 | 7 | 3.28 | 0 | 107.0 | Clutch | 80 | 25 | 1 | 5 | .313 |

### 1995 Rankings (National League)

→ 1st in errors at pitcher (6)
→ 2nd in least run support per 9 innings (3.6)
→ 3rd in shutouts (2), batters faced (850), hit batsmen (11), pitches thrown (3,114), highest groundball/flyball ratio allowed (2.3) and lowest fielding percentage at pitcher (.875)
→ 4th in innings pitched and GDPs induced (22)
→ 5th in least strikeouts per 9 innings (5.4) and lowest batting average allowed vs. left-handed batters (.229)
→ 6th in ERA, games started and most GDPs induced per 9 innings (1.0)
→ Led the Padres in complete games (2), shutouts, innings pitched, hits allowed, batters faced and home runs allowed

# Trevor Hoffman

## 1995 Season

Trevor Hoffman may have allowed 10 homers and slipped to a 3.88 ERA last season, but the Padres were more impressed with him than ever. Why? A couple of reasons. First, Hoffman did save 31 games, sixth most in the National League. And second, he did it while pitching nearly all season with a partially-torn shoulder muscle. Sure, he could pitch. But it hurt, and his velocity was certainly affected. Hoffman's ability to pitch through that pain won him admirers throughout the organization, only enhancing his reputation as a bulldog closer who will do whatever it takes to win.

## Pitching

At his best, Hoffman throws a low-90s fastball with good movement, which is about all he needs. For the sake of variety, he'll mix in a slider and curve, too. Unfortunately, Hoffman's shoulder woes cost him a mile or two off his fastball, which is more important than it sounds. Though his numbers weren't on par with 1994, they were generally excellent across the board except for one thing: home runs allowed, 10. In '94, Hoffman only tossed four gopher balls. He still has good control. Hoffman rarely walks a batter, and he's hit just one in nearly 200 career innings despite his willingness to pitch inside.

## Defense & Hitting

Hoffman, who began his professional career as a shortstop, is a pretty good athlete who fields his position well. Over the last two seasons, only three runners have attempted to steal and each was successful. Hoffman batted only twice last season but came up with a two-run double.

## 1996 Outlook

What can Trevor Hoffman do with a healthy shoulder? The Padres hope to find out this season. If he *is* recovered fully from the shoulder surgery—and the early reports were positive—Hoffman should take his place among the National League's top closers.

**Position:** RP
**Bats:** R  **Throws:** R
**Ht:** 6' 0"  **Wt:** 205

**Opening Day Age:** 28
**Born:** 10/13/67 in Bellflower, CA
**ML Seasons:** 3

### Overall Statistics

|  | W | L | Pct. | ERA | G | GS | Sv | IP | H | BB | SO | HR | BR/IP |
|---|---|---|---|---|---|---|---|---|---|---|---|---|---|
| 1995 | 7 | 4 | .636 | 3.88 | 55 | 0 | 31 | 53.1 | 48 | 14 | 52 | 10 | 1.16 |
| Career | 15 | 14 | .517 | 3.52 | 169 | 0 | 56 | 199.1 | 167 | 73 | 199 | 24 | 1.20 |

### How Often He Throws Strikes

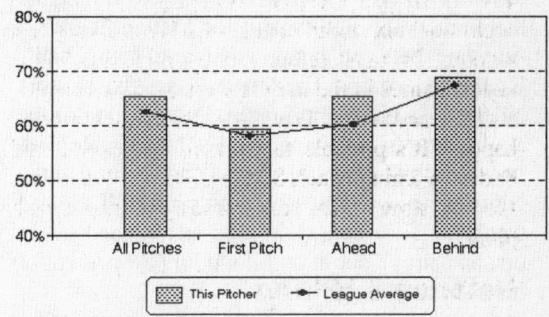

### 1995 Situational Stats

|  | W | L | ERA | Sv | IP |  | AB | H | HR | RBI | Avg |
|---|---|---|---|---|---|---|---|---|---|---|---|
| Home | 6 | 1 | 3.00 | 15 | 27.0 | LHB | 99 | 20 | 3 | 9 | .202 |
| Road | 1 | 3 | 4.78 | 16 | 26.1 | RHB | 105 | 28 | 7 | 17 | .267 |
| First Half | 4 | 2 | 4.21 | 11 | 25.2 | Sc Pos | 44 | 12 | 4 | 18 | .273 |
| Scnd Half | 3 | 2 | 3.58 | 20 | 27.2 | Clutch | 140 | 34 | 5 | 20 | .243 |

### 1995 Rankings (National League)

- ➡ 3rd in blown saves (7)
- ➡ 4th in save opportunities (38) and relief wins (7)
- ➡ 5th in games finished (51)
- ➡ 6th in saves
- ➡ 7th in save percentage (81.6%) and least baserunners allowed per 9 innings in relief (10.5)
- ➡ 9th in most strikeouts per 9 innings in relief (8.8)
- ➡ Led the Padres in games pitched, saves, games finished, save opportunities, save percentage, blown saves, relief wins and least baserunners allowed per 9 innings in relief

San Diego Padres

# Melvin Nieves

## 1995 Season

With the Padres desperate for punch in their out-field, power prospect Melvin Nieves opened the season as the club's starting left fielder. However, he batted just .184 in his first 49 at-bats—with 16 strikeouts—and was relegated to spot duty for the rest of the campaign. Nieves was out of options, and the Padres would have risked losing him if they'd tried to send him to the minors.

## Hitting

Nieves is probably the most powerful hitter in the organization, and don't think the Padres don't know it. Batting coach Merv Rettenmund, who worked overtime with Nieves, observed, "He has a chance to carry this club. He's big and strong and has tremendous ability. But for Melvin, there's a fine line between being good and being bad." Unable to control the strike zone last season, Nieves was bad far too often. Perhaps due to the slight hitch in his swing, Nieves has trouble with inside fastballs and sliders, and once behind in the count he waves helplessly at offspeed stuff. He had trouble against both right- and left-handed pitchers, and struck out in an astounding 38 percent of his at-bats.

## Baserunning & Defense

Nieves is slow, and doesn't show great baserunning judgment. Defensively, he does have a right fielder's arm, but his lack of range makes him a below-average outfielder whether in left or right. If he ends up sticking in the majors—by no means a foregone conclusion—it might well be as a first baseman.

## 1996 Outlook

Back in June, Bruce Bochy said, "Mike Schmidt, Matt Williams, Keith Hernandez—these guys certainly took some time, and that's how we feel about Melvin." Perhaps, but Nieves didn't get much better as last season progressed, and at some point the Padres will lose patience. This past winter, Nieves was being considered as a first-base option, possibly in a platoon with lefty-hitting Roberto Petagine.

**Position:** LF/RF
**Bats:** B **Throws:** R
**Ht:** 6' 2" **Wt:** 210

**Opening Day Age:** 24
**Born:** 12/28/71 in San Juan, PR
**ML Seasons:** 4
**Pronunciation:** nee-EV-uhz

*Overall Statistics*

|  | G | AB | R | H | D | T | HR | RBI | SB | BB | SO | Avg | OBP | Slg |
|---|---|---|---|---|---|---|---|---|---|---|---|---|---|---|
| 1995 | 98 | 234 | 32 | 48 | 6 | 1 | 14 | 38 | 2 | 19 | 88 | .205 | .276 | .419 |
| Career | 139 | 319 | 38 | 66 | 8 | 1 | 17 | 46 | 2 | 27 | 126 | .207 | .279 | .398 |

*Where He Hits the Ball*

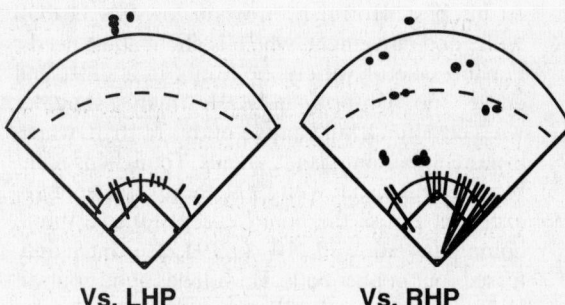

Vs. LHP          Vs. RHP

*1995 Situational Stats*

|  | AB | H | HR | RBI | Avg |  | AB | H | HR | RBI | Avg |
|---|---|---|---|---|---|---|---|---|---|---|---|
| Home | 111 | 17 | 5 | 17 | .153 | LHP | 56 | 10 | 5 | 9 | .179 |
| Road | 123 | 31 | 9 | 21 | .252 | RHP | 178 | 38 | 9 | 29 | .213 |
| First Half | 142 | 29 | 6 | 18 | .204 | Sc Pos | 75 | 14 | 2 | 23 | .187 |
| Scnd Half | 92 | 19 | 8 | 20 | .207 | Clutch | 42 | 9 | 4 | 9 | .214 |

*1995 Rankings (National League)*

- ➡ 3rd in lowest batting average with two strikes (.095)
- ➡ 7th in most GDPs per GDP situation (18.4%)
- ➡ 8th in lowest batting average on an 0-2 count (.053)
- ➡ Led the Padres in hit by pitch (5)

# Phil Plantier

## 1995 Season

What happened to Phil Plantier? As recently as 1993—when he blasted 34 homers in only 462 at-bats with his hometown Padres—Plantier looked like one of the game's top young power hitters. But after an injury-marred 1994 in which he batted just .220, Plantier was one of six players traded to Houston. He played fairly well but missed two months with a broken hand, and on July 19 he was traded *back* to the Padres. Some figured a return home would mean a hitting surge, but Plantier did little with the bat as a second-time Padre.

## Hitting

As anyone who has seen Plantier knows, he hits with one of the more unorthodox stances in the game. Settling into a deep crouch—though not as deep as it once was—Plantier explodes with an uppercut swing somewhat like his ex-teammate in Houston, Jeff Bagwell. The difference is, Plantier's swing isn't nearly as quick, so he is often fooled by breaking balls—especially when they're thrown by lefthanders. Though he actually hit lefties well last season, he is normally helpless against them, with a .199 average since 1991.

## Baserunning & Defense

Listed at 195 pounds, Plantier probably goes 10 or 15 pounds more than that, and he runs about as well as you'd expect. He's got two career triples and 11 stolen bases. Plantier is not a good left fielder, with poor range and a throwing arm getting sorer by the year. First base, if not designated hitter, probably waits in his near future.

## 1996 Outlook

Plantier is only 27, so it's a bit early to give up on him. Remember, this is a player who hit 34 home runs just three seasons ago, and he remains an immensely strong hitter with a good batting eye. But the Padres had seen enough, and they made no effort to re-sign the free-agent slugger. Plantier wound up signing with Detroit, and if he can't revive his career in homer-happy Tiger Stadium, he can't do it anywhere. Watch for reports on Plantier's health; if it's good, expect power.

**Position:** LF/RF
**Bats:** L **Throws:** R
**Ht:** 5'11" **Wt:** 195

**Opening Day Age:** 27
**Born:** 1/27/69 in Manchester, NH
**ML Seasons:** 6
**Pronunciation:** plan-TEER

### Overall Statistics

|  | G | AB | R | H | D | T | HR | RBI | SB | BB | SO | Avg | OBP | Slg |
|---|---|---|---|---|---|---|---|---|---|---|---|---|---|---|
| 1995 | 76 | 216 | 33 | 55 | 6 | 0 | 9 | 34 | 1 | 28 | 48 | .255 | .339 | .407 |
| Career | 485 | 1531 | 218 | 378 | 74 | 2 | 79 | 243 | 11 | 196 | 390 | .247 | .336 | .453 |

### Where He Hits the Ball

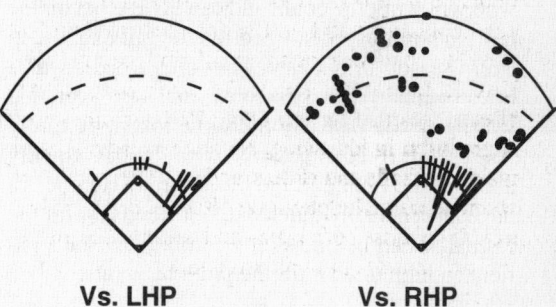

**Vs. LHP**          **Vs. RHP**

### 1995 Situational Stats

|  | AB | H | HR | RBI | Avg |  | AB | H | HR | RBI | Avg |
|---|---|---|---|---|---|---|---|---|---|---|---|
| Home | 93 | 20 | 1 | 5 | .215 | LHP | 45 | 15 | 3 | 8 | .333 |
| Road | 123 | 35 | 8 | 29 | .285 | RHP | 171 | 40 | 6 | 26 | .234 |
| First Half | 56 | 15 | 4 | 11 | .268 | Sc Pos | 71 | 21 | 3 | 27 | .296 |
| Scnd Half | 160 | 40 | 5 | 23 | .250 | Clutch | 34 | 4 | 2 | 2 | .118 |

### 1995 Rankings (National League)
➡ 9th in errors in left field (3)

# Jody Reed

**Position:** 2B
**Bats:** R  **Throws:** R
**Ht:** 5' 9"  **Wt:** 157

**Opening Day Age:** 33
**Born:** 7/26/62 in
Tampa, FL
**ML Seasons:** 9

## 1995 Season

Jody Reed signed so late, he didn't even make it into the Padres' media guide. Reed was one of those homeless Homestead free agents, floating around last April looking for a team. He finally found one on April 19, as the Padres found themselves in need of a durable second baseman. In May, Reed only played about half the time and batted just .173. But as his playing time picked up in June, Reed's bat heated up, and he hit .269 from June 1 on.

## Hitting

When managers fantasize about the ideal number-two hitter, they're usually thinking about a guy who will work the count and can lay the bat on the ball. In both respects, Reed fits the bill exactly. In every season of his career but one, Reed's walks have exceeded his strikeouts, and last year that was again the case. By the same token, he rarely strikes out. Reed is an artist with the bat, equally adept at the bunt and the hit-and-run. He doesn't have an especially quick bat, but Reed *can* hit the fastball when he knows it's coming, and he's patient enough to wait for the pitch he wants.

## Baserunning & Defense

Reed will occasionally surprise with a stolen base, but he's not a fast runner and rarely takes chances. Reed is a major league regular because of his defense. He's not flashy but he *is* one of the most consistent second basemen around. After leading his leagues in fielding percentage in both 1993 and '94, Reed was just edged by Brett Boone last season. He's got great range going both ways, and is always fine on the double-play pivot. . . the complete package.

## 1996 Outlook

Except for a few seasons in Boston when he was hitting 40-plus doubles, Reed has rarely gotten much respect, because the two things he does best—draw walks and play defense—aren't particularly popular skills. Still, major league managers know what Reed can do, and he should remain a regular until his batting average drops below .240 or so.

### Overall Statistics

|  | G | AB | R | H | D | T | HR | RBI | SB | BB | SO | Avg | OBP | Slg |
|---|---|---|---|---|---|---|---|---|---|---|---|---|---|---|
| 1995 | 131 | 445 | 58 | 114 | 18 | 1 | 4 | 40 | 6 | 59 | 38 | .256 | .348 | .328 |
| Career | 1086 | 3947 | 515 | 1088 | 241 | 10 | 25 | 335 | 35 | 473 | 339 | .276 | .355 | .361 |

### *Where He Hits the Ball*

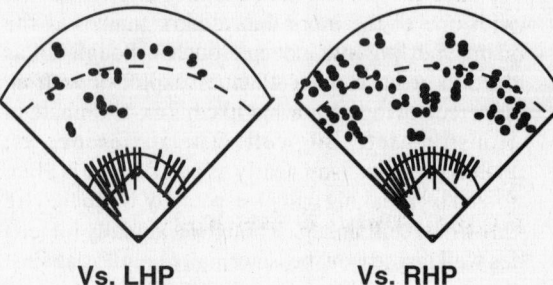

Vs. LHP          Vs. RHP

### *1995 Situational Stats*

|  | AB | H | HR | RBI | Avg |  | AB | H | HR | RBI | Avg |
|---|---|---|---|---|---|---|---|---|---|---|---|
| Home | 212 | 59 | 4 | 23 | .278 | LHP | 131 | 38 | 0 | 9 | .290 |
| Road | 233 | 55 | 0 | 17 | .236 | RHP | 314 | 76 | 4 | 31 | .242 |
| First Half | 178 | 46 | 1 | 14 | .258 | Sc Pos | 103 | 30 | 1 | 36 | .291 |
| Scnd Half | 267 | 68 | 3 | 26 | .255 | Clutch | 71 | 21 | 0 | 5 | .296 |

### *1995 Rankings (National League)*

→ 2nd in fielding percentage at second base (.994)

→ 3rd in lowest slugging percentage vs. right-handed pitchers (.312) and highest percentage of swings put into play (58.5%)

→ 4th in lowest slugging percentage, lowest percentage of swings that missed (6.8%) and lowest percentage of swings on the first pitch (17.1%)

→ 5th in lowest batting average vs. right-handed pitchers (.242) and highest percentage of pitches taken (63.9%)

→ Led the Padres in hit by pitch (5), most pitches seen per plate appearance (3.80) and on-base percentage vs. left-handed pitchers (.400)

# Bip Roberts

## 1995 Season

As usual, Bip Roberts' season was ruined by an injury. This time, it was a strained right quadriceps which, except for one at-bat in July, kept him out of the lineup from late June through late August. When healthy, Roberts played effectively as usual, though he didn't have one of his better years. He batted leadoff and saw action both in left field (35 starts) and second base (23).

## Hitting

Having Tony Gwynn as a teammate has apparently affected Bip Roberts' hitting style. Where once he took lots of pitches and drew a fair number of walks, Roberts' walk rate last season was the lowest since his rookie season. He still hit .304, of course, but his .346 on-base percentage wasn't quite what you'd like from your leadoff man. Roberts has typically hit better from the left side of the plate, and last year was no exception as he batted .323 with nearly all of his power against right-handed pitching.

## Baserunning & Defense

Despite all the injuries Roberts has suffered through the years, he remains one of the faster players in the National League. Last season, in roughly half a season, Roberts stole 20 bases and was caught only twice. He also shows very good judgment when running the bases otherwise. Defensive position has always been a big question with Roberts, and last season he played left field and second base. He doesn't get great jumps on fly balls and has a weak arm, but his speed gives him good range in left. At second base, Roberts has decent range but is weak on the double-play pivot.

## 1996 Outlook

Of Roberts' eight full seasons in the majors, he has played more than 120 games only twice. In those two seasons he scored 104 and 92 runs. The last of those seasons was 1992, and Roberts doesn't seem to be getting any healthier. Granted, when he can play he'll score runs, and he's signed through 1996. He just doesn't play enough.

**Position:** LF/2B
**Bats:** B **Throws:** R
**Ht:** 5' 7"  **Wt:** 165

**Opening Day Age:** 32
**Born:** 10/27/63 in Berkeley, CA
**ML Seasons:** 9

### Overall Statistics

|        | G   | AB   | R   | H   | D   | T  | HR | RBI | SB  | BB  | SO  | Avg  | OBP  | Slg  |
|--------|-----|------|-----|-----|-----|----|----|-----|-----|-----|-----|------|------|------|
| 1995   | 73  | 296  | 40  | 90  | 14  | 0  | 2  | 25  | 20  | 17  | 36  | .304 | .346 | .372 |
| Career | 897 | 3082 | 516 | 915 | 145 | 27 | 25 | 232 | 218 | 312 | 405 | .297 | .363 | .386 |

### Where He Hits the Ball

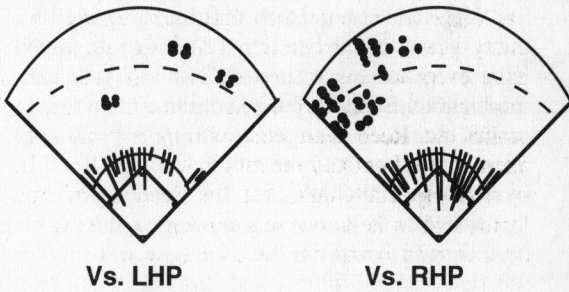

**Vs. LHP**          **Vs. RHP**

### 1995 Situational Stats

|            | AB  | H  | HR | RBI | Avg  |        | AB  | H  | HR | RBI | Avg  |
|------------|-----|----|----|-----|------|--------|-----|----|----|-----|------|
| Home       | 172 | 53 | 2  | 18  | .308 | LHP    | 79  | 20 | 0  | 3   | .253 |
| Road       | 124 | 37 | 0  | 7   | .298 | RHP    | 217 | 70 | 2  | 22  | .323 |
| First Half | 208 | 66 | 1  | 19  | .317 | Sc Pos | 63  | 24 | 1  | 24  | .381 |
| Scnd Half  | 88  | 24 | 1  | 6   | .273 | Clutch | 51  | 17 | 1  | 10  | .333 |

### 1995 Rankings (National League)

- ➡ 2nd in stolen base percentage (90.9%)
- ➡ 6th in lowest on-base percentage for a leadoff hitter (.333)
- ➡ Led the Padres in stolen base percentage and batting average on an 0-2 count (.211)

# Scott Sanders

## 1995 Season

For the second season in a row, injuries marred an otherwise promising season for righthander Scott Sanders. In 1994, a rib-cage injury landed Sanders on the disabled list early, and he was never quite the same after coming back. And last season, elbow tendinitis cost Sanders nearly the entire second half of the season. On a happier note, Sanders averaged nearly a strikeout per inning, also for the second straight year, and he solidified his status as an up-and-coming major league starter.

## Pitching

Sanders has a great arm, demonstrated best by his 90-plus fastball, which he can either sink or run in on right-handed hitters. In addition, his slider is a nice, tight pitch, and he showed a much-improved change-up early last season. Control has been a problem for Sanders, but he continued to improve in that area last season. After issuing 3.9 walks per nine innings—not to mention leading the N.L. with 10 wild pitches—in 1994, Sanders lowered his walk rate to 3.1 last season, while retaining his excellent strikeout rate. As usual, he was murder on right-handed hitters, and has held them to a .196 average in his career.

## Defense & Hitting

Sanders pays attention to baserunners, who calmed down last year after getting nailed frequently in '94. Of the eight who tried in 1995, three were gunned down. He's agile around the mound and a reliable fielder. Sanders is a pretty good hitter, .173 lifetime, and last season he hit .296 (8-for-27).

## 1996 Outlook

His ERAs the last two seasons have been 4.78 and 4.30. Assuming he's healthy to start the season— and the severity of the elbow injury was still a question mark as this book went to press—Sanders should get his ERA even lower and serve as a fine number-three starter behind Andy Ashby and Joey Hamilton.

**Position:** SP
**Bats:** R **Throws:** R
**Ht:** 6' 4"  **Wt:** 220

**Opening Day Age:** 27
**Born:** 3/25/69 in Hannibal, MO
**ML Seasons:** 3

### Overall Statistics

|        | W  | L  | Pct. | ERA  | G  | GS | Sv | IP    | H   | BB  | SO  | HR | BR/IP |
|--------|----|----|------|------|----|----|----|-------|-----|-----|-----|----|-------|
| 1995   | 5  | 5  | .500 | 4.30 | 17 | 15 | 0  | 90.0  | 79  | 31  | 88  | 14 | 1.22  |
| Career | 12 | 16 | .429 | 4.48 | 49 | 44 | 1  | 253.1 | 236 | 102 | 234 | 28 | 1.33  |

### How Often He Throws Strikes

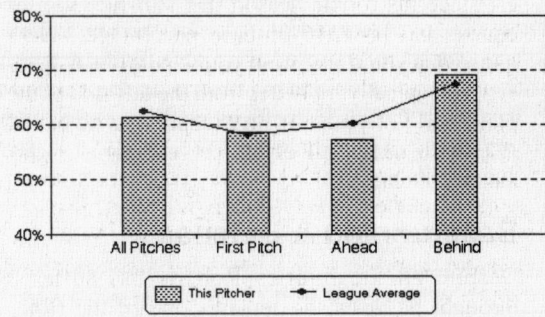

### 1995 Situational Stats

|            | W | L | ERA  | Sv | IP   |        | AB  | H  | HR | RBI | Avg  |
|------------|---|---|------|----|------|--------|-----|----|----|-----|------|
| Home       | 4 | 2 | 5.11 | 0  | 56.1 | LHB    | 134 | 37 | 5  | 19  | .276 |
| Road       | 1 | 3 | 2.94 | 0  | 33.2 | RHB    | 212 | 42 | 9  | 21  | .198 |
| First Half | 5 | 5 | 4.10 | 0  | 85.2 | Sc Pos | 61  | 19 | 3  | 26  | .311 |
| Scnd Half  | 0 | 0 | 8.31 | 0  | 4.1  | Clutch | 14  | 0  | 0  | 0   | .000 |

### 1995 Rankings (National League)

➡ 2nd in least GDPs induced per GDP situation (1.8%)

# Brian Williams

## 1995 Season

Brian Williams is a living, breathing argument for minor league seasoning. A so-called "sandwich pick" by the Astros back in 1990, Williams now has a career ERA of 4.99 in the major leagues, yet he's only pitched in 45 minor league games. After one promising season in Houston followed by two disappointing ones, Williams was traded to San Diego in the mega-trade of two Decembers ago. He opened last season in the bullpen, didn't pitch too well, and pitched even worse in six starts after the All-Star game. Williams closed his season in style, throwing a game-losing gopher ball on the campaign's final day.

## Pitching

Scouts have been drooling over Williams' right arm ever since he starred as a pitcher/outfielder for South Carolina. That right arm is capable of launching 90-plus fastballs inning after inning. As you would expect, however, Williams has yet to find a reliable breaking pitch. His curve is awesome when he throws it just right, but he doesn't throw it just right with any consistency. Williams did rack up plenty of strikeouts last season. Unfortunately, his control was shaky as always, and he simply won't be successful in the major leagues until he throws more strikes.

## Defense & Hitting

After making four errors in 1994, Williams fielded flawlessly last season. He's got a quick move to first, and only four runners tried to steal on him in 1995; two of them were nailed. Though he was just 1-for-14 last season as a hitter, Williams was an outfielder on Team USA seven summers ago, and he remains a fine athlete. Earlier in his career, Williams was even used as a pinch runner on occasion.

## 1996 Outlook

It's highly unlikely that Williams will be a Padre in 1996. However, there's always a place for a guy with a million-dollar arm. Just ask Bobby Witt.

**Position:** RP/SP
**Bats:** R  **Throws:** R
**Ht:** 6' 2"  **Wt:** 225

**Opening Day Age:** 27
**Born:** 2/15/69 in Lancaster, SC
**ML Seasons:** 5

### Overall Statistics

|  | W | L | Pct. | ERA | G | GS | Sv | IP | H | BB | SO | HR | BR/IP |
|---|---|---|---|---|---|---|---|---|---|---|---|---|---|
| 1995 | 3 | 10 | .231 | 6.00 | 44 | 6 | 0 | 72.0 | 79 | 38 | 75 | 3 | 1.63 |
| Career | 20 | 26 | .435 | 4.99 | 124 | 42 | 3 | 340.2 | 370 | 163 | 238 | 31 | 1.56 |

### How Often He Throws Strikes

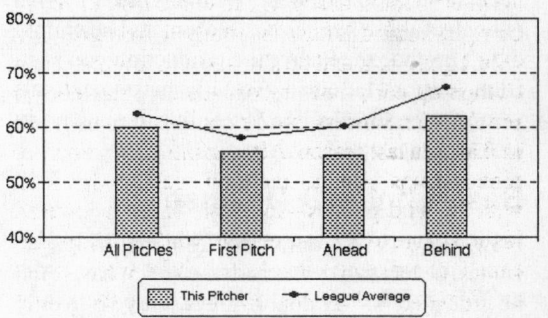

### 1995 Situational Stats

|  | W | L | ERA | Sv | IP |  | AB | H | HR | RBI | Avg |
|---|---|---|---|---|---|---|---|---|---|---|---|
| Home | 1 | 4 | 5.52 | 0 | 29.1 | LHB | 111 | 31 | 0 | 17 | .279 |
| Road | 2 | 6 | 6.33 | 0 | 42.2 | RHB | 172 | 48 | 3 | 23 | .279 |
| First Half | 1 | 7 | 5.81 | 0 | 31.0 | Sc Pos | 84 | 27 | 3 | 39 | .321 |
| Scnd Half | 2 | 3 | 6.15 | 0 | 41.0 | Clutch | 78 | 26 | 2 | 16 | .333 |

### 1995 Rankings (National League)

- ➡ 1st in relief losses (8)
- ➡ 3rd in lowest winning percentage
- ➡ 5th in first batter efficiency (.143)
- ➡ 10th in hit batsmen (8)
- ➡ Led the Padres in losses, wild pitches (7), first batter efficiency and relief losses

# Eddie Williams

## 1995 Season

Was 1994 a fluke? After three seasons away from the majors—including stints in Japan and with a semi-pro team—Eddie Williams completed his comeback by hitting .331 with great power in 49 games with the Padres. That performance assured him a regular job at first base in 1995. But Williams lost that regular job in early August because he wasn't hitting, and spent the rest of the season sharing first base with Scott Livingstone.

## Hitting

Williams settles into his exaggerated closed stance well off the plate, looking for fastballs below the belt that he can drive, to the opposite field if necessary. Problem was, Williams didn't drive enough of those pitches last season, and he simply didn't provide the Padres the production you need from your first baseman. Actually, his power totals were nearly identical to 1994, but they came in 121 more at-bats.

## Baserunning & Defense

How slow is Williams? In 263 major league games, he has two triples and one stolen base. And he grounded into 21 double plays last year in only 296 at-bats, an amazing ratio. In his "first" major league career, Williams was a third baseman, but only by the loosest definition as his fielding percentages were consistently atrocious. Now a first baseman, Williams doesn't make as many errors as he used to but is still a liability in the field. Williams doesn't throw well and he's tentative around the bag.

## 1996 Outlook

Like Phils Clark and Plantier, Williams fell short in the power department last season, and each member of that trio is likely to be elsewhere this season. As far as Williams goes, his swing didn't look bad last year, and he could be useful as a part-time first baseman and pinch hitter.

**Position:** 1B
**Bats:** R **Throws:** R
**Ht:** 6' 0" **Wt:** 210

**Opening Day Age:** 31
**Born:** 11/1/64 in Shreveport, LA
**ML Seasons:** 7

### Overall Statistics

|  | G | AB | R | H | D | T | HR | RBI | SB | BB | SO | Avg | OBP | Slg |
|---|---|----|---|---|---|---|----|-----|----|----|----|-----|-----|-----|
| 1995 | 97 | 296 | 35 | 77 | 11 | 1 | 12 | 47 | 0 | 23 | 47 | .260 | .320 | .426 |
| Career | 263 | 806 | 111 | 218 | 37 | 2 | 30 | 109 | 1 | 70 | 135 | .270 | .336 | .433 |

### Where He Hits the Ball

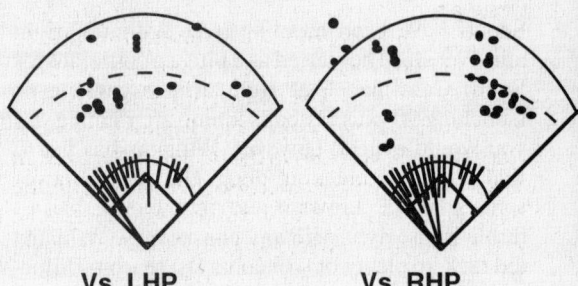

Vs. LHP          Vs. RHP

### 1995 Situational Stats

|  | AB | H | HR | RBI | Avg |  | AB | H | HR | RBI | Avg |
|---|----|---|----|-----|-----|---|----|---|----|-----|-----|
| Home | 138 | 37 | 4 | 19 | .268 | LHP | 118 | 34 | 7 | 19 | .288 |
| Road | 158 | 40 | 8 | 28 | .253 | RHP | 178 | 43 | 5 | 28 | .242 |
| First Half | 181 | 48 | 7 | 32 | .265 | Sc Pos | 92 | 22 | 2 | 33 | .239 |
| Scnd Half | 115 | 29 | 5 | 15 | .252 | Clutch | 53 | 14 | 1 | 7 | .264 |

### 1995 Rankings (National League)

➡ 1st in most GDPs per GDP situation (29.4%)
➡ 2nd in GDPs (21)
➡ 3rd in errors at first base (7)
➡ Led the Padres in GDPs

# Doug Bochtler

**Position**: RP
**Bats**: R **Throws**: R
**Ht**: 6' 3" **Wt**: 200

**Opening Day Age**: 25
**Born**: 7/5/70 in West Palm Beach, FL
**ML Seasons**: 1
**Pronunciation**: BOCK-ler

## Overall Statistics

|  | W | L | Pct. | ERA | G | GS | Sv | IP | H | BB | SO | HR | BR/IP |
|---|---|---|---|---|---|---|---|---|---|---|---|---|---|
| 1995 | 4 | 4 | .500 | 3.57 | 34 | 0 | 1 | 45.1 | 38 | 19 | 45 | 5 | 1.26 |
| Career | 4 | 4 | .500 | 3.57 | 34 | 0 | 1 | 45.1 | 38 | 19 | 45 | 5 | 1.26 |

## 1995 Season

Once a top prospect in the Montreal organization, Doug Bochtler suffered shoulder problems in 1992 but was selected in the expansion draft by Colorado anyway. The following season, Bochtler accompanied Andy Ashby and Brad Ausmus in a trade from the Rockies to the Padres. After a rough 1994 as a Triple-A starter, Bochtler moved to the bullpen last season, and it was as a reliever that he made it to the majors. He posted solid numbers, including four victories and eight holds.

## Pitching, Defense & Hitting

Bochtler's fastball isn't quite what it was before the shoulder injury, but he's still got good stuff, and throws a fastball, slider and change-up. He throws with a herky-jerky delivery that provides some deception. Baserunners went wild with Bochtler on the mound, attempting 11 steals, but they weren't particularly successful. Bochtler nailed three runners, and his catcher got two more. He batted twice, unsuccessfully.

## 1996 Outlook

Bochtler is one of the lesser lights in the San Diego bullpen, but that's only because there are so many nice arms in that bullpen. With a number of clubs, Bochtler would be a top candidate for righty set-up man. But he'll probably have to pitch exceptionally well this spring to assume that role for the Padres.

# Archi Cianfrocco

**Position**: 1B/SS
**Bats**: R **Throws**: R
**Ht**: 6' 5" **Wt**: 215

**Opening Day Age**: 29
**Born**: 10/6/66 in Rome, NY
**ML Seasons**: 4
**Pronunciation**: sin-FROCK-oh

## Overall Statistics

|  | G | AB | R | H | D | T | HR | RBI | SB | BB | SO | Avg | OBP | Slg |
|---|---|---|---|---|---|---|---|---|---|---|---|---|---|---|
| 1995 | 51 | 118 | 22 | 31 | 7 | 0 | 5 | 31 | 0 | 11 | 28 | .263 | .333 | .449 |
| Career | 292 | 792 | 86 | 191 | 31 | 4 | 27 | 122 | 7 | 42 | 202 | .241 | .285 | .393 |

## 1995 Season

After losing the third-base job early in 1994 and spending part of the season in the minors, Archi Cianfrocco was waived by the Padres that November. But they eventually re-signed him to a minor league contract, and after a hot start (.311-10-58) at Triple-A Las Vegas last season, Cianfrocco was recalled to San Diego. He kept hitting, and played all over the field.

## Hitting, Baserunning & Defense

Cianfrocco has never been one to take a walk, and he lives for the first-pitch fastball. But if a pitcher can get ahead Cianfrocco's in trouble, because he's pretty helpless against offspeed stuff. In his first three big-league seasons, Cianfrocco was 7-for-7 stealing bases, but last year he was 0-for-2. Quite frankly, Cianfrocco had no business starting 14 games at shortstop last season; his range was about what you'd expect from a player whose best position is probably first base. Aside from his action at shortstop, Cianfrocco put in time at first, third, second, left field and right field.

## 1996 Outlook

There are certainly utility players out there with more defensive skills than Cianfrocco. But few have his power, his attitude or his ability to play nearly every position on the field. He'll likely be back in San Diego, performing his normal chores.

San Diego Padres

# Brian Johnson

**Position**: C
**Bats**: R  **Throws**: R
**Ht**: 6' 2"  **Wt**: 210

**Opening Day Age:** 28
**Born:** 1/8/68 in
Oakland, CA
**ML Seasons:** 2

*Overall Statistics*

|  | G | AB | R | H | D | T | HR | RBI | SB | BB | SO | Avg | OBP | Slg |
|---|---|---|---|---|---|---|---|---|---|---|---|---|---|---|
| 1995 | 68 | 207 | 20 | 52 | 9 | 0 | 3 | 29 | 0 | 11 | 39 | .251 | .287 | .338 |
| Career | 104 | 300 | 27 | 75 | 13 | 1 | 6 | 45 | 0 | 16 | 60 | .250 | .286 | .360 |

## 1995 Season

The highlight of Brian Johnson's 1995 season came on May 14, when his pinch-hit, grand-slam homer off Randy Myers gave the Padres a 9-7 victory over the Cubs. Despite the presence of Brad Ausmus, Johnson carved a niche for himself and saw more action than your average backup catcher. Beginning in mid-June, Johnson served as Andy Ashby's personal catcher, and he also caught for Andy Benes until Benes was traded.

## Hitting, Baserunning & Defense

Johnson first drew attention in 1993, when he hit .339 with good power at Triple-A Las Vegas. He's not really that good a hitter—not even close—and brings little to the plate. He *is* strong, but swings at too many bad pitches to take good advantage of his power. Johnson runs okay for a catcher. He's just fair defensively, and doesn't throw particularly well. On the other hand, Johnson can fill in at first or third base if necessary, which his manager appreciates.

## 1996 Outlook

It's quickly becoming clear that Johnson's prolific hitting in 1993 was a fluke, but he's established himself as more than just a once-a-week backstop. At the very least, Johnson should retain his role as Andy Ashby's catcher of choice. Otherwise, his playing time will depend on the health and production of Brad Ausmus.

# Scott Livingstone

**Position**: 1B/3B
**Bats**: L  **Throws**: R
**Ht**: 6' 0"  **Wt**: 190

**Opening Day Age:** 30
**Born:** 7/15/65 in
Dallas, TX
**ML Seasons:** 5

*Overall Statistics*

|  | G | AB | R | H | D | T | HR | RBI | SB | BB | SO | Avg | OBP | Slg |
|---|---|---|---|---|---|---|---|---|---|---|---|---|---|---|
| 1995 | 99 | 196 | 26 | 66 | 15 | 0 | 5 | 32 | 2 | 15 | 22 | .337 | .380 | .490 |
| Career | 430 | 1184 | 138 | 346 | 64 | 3 | 15 | 139 | 8 | 72 | 141 | .292 | .329 | .389 |

## 1995 Season

There's not much call in the major leagues for corner infielders with no power, and that's just what Scott Livingstone is. Livingstone played a lot after being traded from Detroit to San Diego in 1994, but he lost his job when the Padres traded for Ken Caminiti. So through the first three months last season, Livingstone was mostly a pinch hitter. He surged in July (.360), and in August began taking playing time away from Eddie Williams. Livingstone never cooled off, ending the season with a .337 batting average and half the first-base job.

## Hitting, Baserunning & Defense

A pure contact hitter, Livingstone sent line drives to all fields last season. He likes the ball low, and rarely gets a chance to face left-handed pitchers despite a .327 career average against southpaws. Livingstone has below-average wheels. A third baseman by trade, Livingstone played a little first base in the minors and with Detroit, and he should get better with experience.

## 1996 Outlook

You can obviously discount last year's batting average as a fluke. But in five major league seasons, Livingstone has only batted below .282 once. An "empty" .282, perhaps, but one that will keep him in the majors for a while. Still, don't look for Livingstone to play regularly unless he goes to another team, Caminiti gets hurt, or the other first-base prospects wash out.

# Marc Newfield

**Position:** LF
**Bats:** R **Throws:** R
**Ht:** 6' 4" **Wt:** 205

**Opening Day Age:** 23
**Born:** 10/19/72 in
Sacramento, CA
**ML Seasons:** 3

## Overall Statistics

|  | G | AB | R | H | D | T | HR | RBI | SB | BB | SO | Avg | OBP | Slg |
|---|---|---|---|---|---|---|---|---|---|---|---|---|---|---|
| 1995 | 45 | 140 | 13 | 33 | 8 | 1 | 4 | 21 | 0 | 5 | 24 | .236 | .267 | .393 |
| Career | 79 | 244 | 21 | 55 | 12 | 1 | 6 | 32 | 0 | 9 | 36 | .225 | .258 | .357 |

## 1995 Season

The sixth overall pick in the 1990 draft, Marc Newfield spent the better part of five seasons hitting the cover off the ball in the Seattle farm system. Unfortunately, he also spent much of that time looking bad in the outfield and alienating his managers. Still, Newfield's star looked bright when he hit .349 and 44 doubles with Triple-A Calgary in 1994. Given a brief trial in left field last June, Newfield didn't hit. He returned to Calgary, and on July 31 was sent to San Diego in the Andy Benes trade.

## Hitting, Baserunning & Defense

Newfield apparently just needed a change of scenery to get his bat going. After struggling in Seattle and Calgary, he hit .328 with power for San Diego and Las Vegas. At 23, Newfield is still developing his power but he's strong enough right now to hit 15-20 homers per season. He should also hit in the .280 range with a fair number of walks. Of course, there's more to baseball than hitting, and it's that "more" which has thus far held Newfield back. At 6-4 and 205 pounds, he lumbers around the bases and is no whippet in left field.

## 1996 Outlook

The Padre lineup is sorely in need of power, and Newfield might be the guy to supply it. If he can't handle left field in the majors, the club will probably try him at first base, possibly in a platoon with fellow prospect Roberto Petagine. Either way, expect to see Newfield in the lineup at some point this season.

# Roberto Petagine

**Position:** 1B
**Bats:** L **Throws:** L
**Ht:** 6' 1" **Wt:** 170

**Opening Day Age:** 24
**Born:** 6/2/71 in Nueva
Esparita, VZ
**ML Seasons:** 2
**Pronunciation:**
pet-uh-JEEN-ee

## Overall Statistics

|  | G | AB | R | H | D | T | HR | RBI | SB | BB | SO | Avg | OBP | Slg |
|---|---|---|---|---|---|---|---|---|---|---|---|---|---|---|
| 1995 | 89 | 124 | 15 | 29 | 8 | 0 | 3 | 17 | 0 | 26 | 41 | .234 | .367 | .371 |
| Career | 97 | 131 | 15 | 29 | 8 | 0 | 3 | 17 | 0 | 27 | 44 | .221 | .354 | .351 |

## 1995 Season

A top prospect in the Houston organization, first baseman Roberto Petagine's path to the majors was blocked by a pretty fair player named Jeff Bagwell. So after the 1994 season, Petagine was part of the 12-player blockbuster trade between the Padres and Astros. He opened the season with the big club, but spent most of the year shuffling between San Diego and Triple-A Las Vegas. All the while, Petagine never really got on track with the bat.

## Hitting, Baserunning & Defense

Petagine is an extremely patient hitter, and he's got a pretty, uncomplicated swing which hitting coach Merv Rettenmund compared to Tony Gwynn's. It's just that Rettenmund wanted to see more of them. Petagine averaged nearly four pitches per plate appearance; a lot of those pitches were called strikes, which helps explain his high strikeout rate. Petagine will have to make it on the strength of his bat, because he's not a good baserunner and is, at best, an average first baseman.

## 1996 Outlook

Though he failed to win a regular job in 1995, Petagine is still a big part of the Padre game plan. Eddie Williams was a big disappointment at first base last season, so that position is wide open in 1996. If Petagine doesn't win the job outright, he might end up platooning with Williams, Melvin Nieves, or even Newfield.

San Diego Padres

# Fernando Valenzuela

**Position:** SP/RP
**Bats:** L **Throws:** L
**Ht:** 5'11" **Wt:** 200

**Opening Day Age:** 35
**Born:** 11/1/60 in
Navajoa, Sonora, MX
**ML Seasons:** 15
Pronunciation:
val-un-ZWAY-luh

### Overall Statistics

| | W | L | Pct. | ERA | G | GS | Sv | IP | H | BB | SO | HR | BR/IP |
|---|---|---|---|---|---|---|---|---|---|---|---|---|---|
| 1995 | 8 | 3 | .727 | 4.98 | 29 | 15 | 0 | 90.1 | 101 | 34 | 57 | 16 | 1.49 |
| Career | 158 | 133 | .543 | 3.49 | 402 | 375 | 2 | 2669.1 | 2435 | 1038 | 1918 | 197 | 1.30 |

## 1995 Season

How many lives does Fernando Valenzuela have? The Padres signed Valenzuela for 1995 largely as a box-office draw, and he spent most of the season struggling. He opened the campaign in the rotation, but was hit hard and sent to the bullpen, making an occasional spot start. But Valenzuela returned to the rotation on August 27, and allowed two or fewer runs in five of his last seven starts, winning all five. Did Valenzuela boost attendance? The club averaged 13,354 fans in his starts, 14,727 overall.

## Pitching, Defense & Hitting

Valenzuela's once-fearsome screwball is now just another pitch, and rarely used. What got Valenzuela back to the majors is his cut fastball, now his primary pitch. He'll also mix in change-ups and sliders, all thrown at varying speeds. Valenzuela is quick off the mound despite his girth. He's got a good move to first, and runners have to be careful not to stray too far from the bag. One of the best-hitting pitchers of the last 20 years, Valenzuela batted .250 last season with a pair of homers, giving him 10 for his career.

## 1996 Outlook

He's not particularly effective against left-handed hitters, so Valenzuela isn't a situational lefty. And there's not really room for him in the Padre rotation. But his relatively strong finish left the door open for 1996, and he should get a chance to pitch somewhere.

# Ron Villone

**Position:** RP
**Bats:** L **Throws:** L
**Ht:** 6'3" **Wt:** 235

**Opening Day Age:** 26
**Born:** 1/16/70 in
Englewood, NJ
**ML Seasons:** 1

### Overall Statistics

| | W | L | Pct. | ERA | G | GS | Sv | IP | H | BB | SO | HR | BR/IP |
|---|---|---|---|---|---|---|---|---|---|---|---|---|---|
| 1995 | 2 | 3 | .400 | 5.80 | 38 | 0 | 1 | 45.0 | 44 | 34 | 63 | 11 | 1.73 |
| Career | 2 | 3 | .400 | 5.80 | 38 | 0 | 1 | 45.0 | 44 | 34 | 63 | 11 | 1.73 |

## 1995 Season

Lefthander Ron Villone was a Mariners first-round draft pick back in 1992. After struggling in the minors as a starter, he shifted to relief work in 1994 and opened last season in the Seattle bullpen. Sent back to Triple-A at the cut-down date, Villone was recalled and demoted once more. While he struggled against A.L. hitters, Villone was dominant in Tacoma. Impressed, the Padres made sure Villone was included in the July 31 trade which sent Andy Benes to Seattle. Immediately promoted to the Padre bullpen, Villone showed plenty in the last two months.

## Pitching, Defense & Hitting

For a relatively inexperienced pitcher with an excellent arm—his fastball tops 90 miles per hour—Villone throws a surprisingly effective change-up, probably his best pitch. With the Mariners, Villone wasn't getting his fastball over often enough to use the change-up. But in San Diego, Villone improved his control, and the result was 37 strikeouts in 25.2 innings. His follow-through leaves him in poor fielding position. But he's got a funky motion that baserunners haven't quite figured out yet. Villone batted just once last season.

## 1996 Outlook

Bruce Bochy said of Villone last summer, "I see him doing more than just getting a left-handed hitter out now and then." Perhaps. But there are other good young arms in the bullpen, and Villone is the only lefty. He should see plenty of situational work in 1996.

# Other San Diego Padres

**Billy Bean** (**Pos**: LF, **Age**: 31, **Bats**: L)

Here's all you need to know about Billy Bean: Though the Padres were desperate for power in the outfield last year, they let Bean waste away in Las Vegas, where he hit .290 with 15 homers. 1996 Outlook: C

**Andres Berumen** (**Pos**: RHP, **Age**: 24)

Berumen has been a pro for seven seasons, but he's still only 24. Scouts rave about his arm, but Berumen walked 36 hitters in 44 innings last year, and he won't have a real role until he finds control. 1996 Outlook: B

**Phil Clark** (**Pos**: RF/LF, **Age**: 27, **Bats**: R)

Since hitting spectacularly as a part-timer in 1993, Clark has struggled just to hit his weight and was a major disappointment last season. He had some value when he could catch, but those days appear to be over. 1996 Outlook: C

**Donnie Elliott** (**Pos**: RHP, **Age**: 27)

Elliott is trying to come back from shoulder woes, and his only mound appearance last year came on September 19, when he pitched two innings of relief. He'll have to fight just for a chance. 1996 Outlook: C

**Ray Holbert** (**Pos**: SS, **Age**: 25, **Bats**: R)

The speedy Holbert missed a month with an ankle injury, and played little even when healthy. In October, he was traded to the Astros for Pedro Martinez. Could compete with Miller for shortstop job. 1996 Outlook: B

**Tim Hyers** (**Pos**: 1B, **Age**: 24, **Bats**: L)

For a spell in 1994, Hyers was San Diego's regular first baseman. His star has fallen considerably since then, and he collected only five major league at-bats last season. He's a singles-hitting first baseman. 1996 Outlook: C

**Luis Lopez** (**Pos**: 2B, **Age**: 25, **Bats**: B)

Lopez would have been the Padres' everyday second baseman last year, but he hurt his knee in the spring and didn't play at all. He should be okay this season, and should have a regular job if the Padres don't sign one of the big-name free agents available. 1996 Outlook: B

**Tim Mauser** (**Pos**: RHP, **Age**: 29)

Mauser saw plenty of action in 1994, but he's been passed up by younger relievers with better arms. He's not awful, but as a mediocre right-handed reliever he'll need a break to make it back. 1996 Outlook: C

**Tim Worrell** (**Pos**: RHP, **Age**: 28)

Worrell is attempting to recover from a torn elbow ligament, and he pitched decently out of the bullpen last September. He's got a ways to go, but might be ready to contribute sometime this summer. 1996 Outlook: B

# San Diego Padres Minor League Prospects

## Organization Overview:

How successful was the Padres' draft last June? We won't *really* know for a few years, of course, but *Baseball America* rated it "baseball's best draft," and then-Director of Scouting Kevin Towers was rewarded with a promotion to general manager after the season. Then there was the Pioneer League, whose top prospects included a monastery's worth of Padres. Heading the list was catcher Ben Davis, the second player selected in the draft. Unfortunately, all those 1995 draftees are a few years away from the majors, and the upper levels of the minor league system are relatively bare. The top Padre prospect who didn't spend most of last season in Class A was probably Marc Kroon, a power-pitching righthander who could use another year of seasoning. Still, the Padres are on the right track, encouraging for a small-market franchise.

## Gabe Alvarez

**Position:** SS       **Opening Day Age:** 22
**Bats:** R **Throws:** R   **Born:** 3/6/74 in
**Ht:** 6' 1"  **Wt:** 185    Novojoa, Sonora,
                             Mexico

*Recent Statistics*

|               | G | AB | R | H | D | T | HR | RBI | SB | BB | SO | AVG |
|---------------|---|----|---|---|---|---|----|-----|----|----|----|-----|
| 95 A Rancho Cuca | 59 | 212 | 41 | 73 | 17 | 2 | 6 | 36 | 1 | 29 | 30 | .344 |
| 95 AA Memphis | 2 | 9 | 0 | 5 | 1 | 0 | 0 | 4 | 0 | 1 | 1 | .556 |

Alvarez, a second-round pick out of USC last summer, wasn't listed among the California League's top prospects by *Baseball America* last fall. However, he's a polished hitter and perhaps the top prospect in the entire San Diego organization. Why wasn't Alvarez more highly regarded by league managers? Well, he played shortstop—his position in college—and didn't look good at all there, making a ton of errors. He may not be a shortstop, but he most certainly *is* a hitter. Alvarez will probably play third base this summer for Double-A Memphis, and if he takes to the position could be pushing Ken Caminiti by 1997.

## Robbie Beckett

**Position:** P        **Opening Day Age:** 23
**Bats:** R **Throws:** L   **Born:** 7/16/72 in
**Ht:** 6' 5"  **Wt:** 235    Austin, TX

*Recent Statistics*

|                 | W | L | ERA | G | GS | Sv | IP | H | R | BB | SO | HR |
|-----------------|---|---|------|----|----|----|------|----|----|----|----|----|
| 93 A Rancho Cuca | 2 | 4 | 6.02 | 37 | 10 | 4 | 83.2 | 75 | 62 | 93 | 88 | 7 |
| 94 A Wichita | 1 | 3 | 5.85 | 33 | 0 | 2 | 40.0 | 30 | 28 | 40 | 59 | 2 |
| 94 AAA Las Vegas | 0 | 1 | 11.79 | 23 | 0 | 0 | 23.2 | 27 | 36 | 39 | 30 | 4 |
| 95 AA Memphis | 3 | 4 | 4.80 | 36 | 8 | 0 | 86.1 | 65 | 57 | 73 | 98 | 3 |

Has Robbie Beckett finally found his control? No, but he's getting warmer. Last season, for the first time since he was a first-year pro in 1990, Beckett actually walked

*fewer* than one batter per inning. Okay, so that's nothing to boast about, but it was a major step forward for the big southpaw who was once a first-round draft pick. As you'd expect, Beckett has the standard repertoire of the power pitcher: low-90s fastball and hard slider. Obviously, he still doesn't throw enough strikes even after six years as a pro, and his makeup has been questioned. But Beckett still has that great arm, and one time in a hundred that great arm will turn out to be Randy Johnson.

## Raul Casanova

**Position:** C        **Opening Day Age:** 23
**Bats:** R **Throws:** R   **Born:** 8/23/72 in
**Ht:** 6' 0"  **Wt:** 192    Humacao, PR

*Recent Statistics*

|                 | G | AB | R | H | D | T | HR | RBI | SB | BB | SO | AVG |
|-----------------|----|-----|----|-----|----|---|----|-----|----|----|----|------|
| 93 A Waterloo | 76 | 227 | 32 | 58 | 12 | 0 | 6 | 30 | 0 | 21 | 46 | .256 |
| 94 A Rancho Cuca | 123 | 471 | 83 | 160 | 27 | 2 | 23 | 120 | 1 | 43 | 97 | .340 |
| 95 AA Memphis | 89 | 306 | 42 | 83 | 18 | 0 | 12 | 44 | 1 | 25 | 51 | .271 |
| 95 MLE | 89 | 296 | 34 | 73 | 15 | 0 | 11 | 35 | 2 | 17 | 54 | .247 |

After four so-so seasons in the Met and Padre systems, Raul Casanova broke through in 1994 with 23 homers and a .340 average for Rancho Cucamonga. Elevated to Double-A Memphis last season, Casanova's power and average fell off, but he still hit 12 homers in 306 at-bats, impressive for a catcher barely into his 20s. Casanova does have some holes in his game: he's slow, and he could draw more walks. But he's got a good arm and has decent skills behind the plate. With those skills, he doesn't need to hit like Yogi Berra. Casanova should open this season with Triple-A Las Vegas, and if one of the major leaguers gets hurt Casanova might be first in line for a call-up.

## Ben Davis

**Position:** C        **Opening Day Age:** 19
**Bats:** B **Throws:** R   **Born:** 3/10/77 in
**Ht:** 6' 3"  **Wt:** 185    Chester, PA

*Recent Statistics*

|               | G | AB | R | H | D | T | HR | RBI | SB | BB | SO | AVG |
|---------------|----|-----|----|----|---|---|----|-----|----|----|----|------|
| 95 R Idaho Falls | 52 | 197 | 36 | 55 | 8 | 3 | 5 | 46 | 0 | 17 | 36 | .279 |

With the second overall pick in the draft last June, the Padres selected Ben Davis, a catcher who was named High School Player of the Year by *Baseball America*. The history of catchers drafted in early rounds isn't particularly encouraging, but the early returns on Davis are optimistic indeed. His batting average wasn't particularly impressive, but Davis knocked in 46 runs in only 197 at-bats, a fine ratio. Pioneer League managers only had praise for Davis' defense and his overall makeup, and they voted him the circuit's top prospect. Though Davis is four years younger than Raul Casanova, it should be an interesting race to the majors between the pair of backstop prospects.

## Dustin Hermanson

**Position:** P
**Bats:** R **Throws:** R
**Ht:** 6' 3" **Wt:** 195

**Opening Day Age:** 23
**Born:** 12/21/72 in Springfield, OH

### Recent Statistics

|  | W | L | ERA | G | GS | Sv | IP | H | R | BB | SO | HR |
|---|---|---|---|---|---|---|---|---|---|---|---|---|
| 95 AAA Las Vegas | 0 | 1 | 3.50 | 31 | 0 | 11 | 36.0 | 35 | 23 | 29 | 42 | 5 |
| 95 NL San Diego | 3 | 1 | 6.82 | 26 | 0 | 0 | 31.2 | 35 | 26 | 22 | 19 | 8 |

Sure, Hermanson was lit up after arriving in San Diego last season. But remember, he was in just his second professional season after being selected with the third pick in the 1994 draft. Hermanson tore through the Texas League that summer, but he's run into trouble since. A classic power pitcher, Hermanson throws a low-90s fastball and a hard slider, but in 1995 his mechanics were all screwed up and the velocity on his fastball dropped to the upper 80s. With a quality bullpen in place at the major league level, the Padres aren't compelled to rush Hermanson, so they'll be patient as he works through his troubles.

## Marc Kroon

**Position:** P
**Bats:** B **Throws:** R
**Ht:** 6' 2" **Wt:** 175

**Opening Day Age:** 22
**Born:** 4/2/73 in Bronx, NY

### Recent Statistics

|  | W | L | ERA | G | GS | Sv | IP | H | R | BB | SO | HR |
|---|---|---|---|---|---|---|---|---|---|---|---|---|
| 95 AA Memphis | 7 | 5 | 3.51 | 22 | 19 | 2 | 115.1 | 90 | 49 | 61 | 123 | 12 |
| 95 NL San Diego | 0 | 1 | 10.80 | 2 | 0 | 0 | 1.2 | 1 | 2 | 2 | 2 | 0 |

Baseball men love great pitching arms, so baseball men love Mark Kroon. Originally a Met farmhand and a second-round draft pick back in 1991, Kroon came to the Padres in a trade two years ago. The other players involved have all faded into obscurity, while Kroon is on the verge of pitching in the majors. He's averaged better than a strikeout per inning over the last four seasons, thanks to a fastball consistently clocked in the mid-90s. One caveat with Kroon: he still hasn't developed an effective offspeed pitch, and he might be destined for the bullpen. That might not be a bad idea, because he certainly has closer stuff.

## Derrek Lee

**Position:** 1B
**Bats:** R **Throws:** R
**Ht:** 6' 5" **Wt:** 205

**Opening Day Age:** 20
**Born:** 9/6/75 in Sacramento, CA

### Recent Statistics

|  | G | AB | R | H | D | T | HR | RBI | SB | BB | SO | AVG |
|---|---|---|---|---|---|---|---|---|---|---|---|---|
| 93 R Padres | 15 | 52 | 11 | 17 | 1 | 1 | 2 | 5 | 4 | 6 | 7 | .327 |
| 93 A Rancho Cuca | 20 | 73 | 13 | 20 | 5 | 1 | 1 | 10 | 0 | 10 | 20 | .274 |
| 94 A Rancho Cuca | 126 | 442 | 66 | 118 | 19 | 2 | 8 | 53 | 18 | 42 | 95 | .267 |
| 95 A Rancho Cuca | 128 | 502 | 82 | 151 | 25 | 2 | 23 | 95 | 14 | 49 | 130 | .301 |
| 95 AA Memphis | 2 | 9 | 0 | 1 | 0 | 0 | 0 | 1 | 0 | 0 | 2 | .111 |

In his second full season in the fast-A California League, Derrek Lee finally posted the numbers expected by the Padres since they made him their first-round draft pick back in 1993. Though he struggled at Rancho Cucamonga in 1994, the Cal League is an awfully tough place for a raw 18 year old. Returned there last year, Lee became one of the more feared hitters in the league. After a rough 1994 at third base, Lee played well at first last season. However, he's got good wheels and might wind up in the outfield. Lee has good bloodlines; his father Leon was a star in Japan, and Derrek's uncle Leron was a major leaguer here. Lee the Younger will open 1996 in Double-A, and will be on a fast track to the majors if he can cut his strikeouts some.

## Ray McDavid

**Position:** OF
**Bats:** L **Throws:** R
**Ht:** 6' 3" **Wt:** 195

**Opening Day Age:** 24
**Born:** 7/20/71 in San Diego, CA

### Recent Statistics

|  | G | AB | R | H | D | T | HR | RBI | SB | BB | SO | AVG |
|---|---|---|---|---|---|---|---|---|---|---|---|---|
| 95 R Padres | 9 | 28 | 13 | 13 | 2 | 1 | 1 | 6 | 3 | 8 | 7 | .464 |
| 95 AAA Las Vegas | 52 | 166 | 28 | 45 | 8 | 1 | 5 | 27 | 7 | 30 | 35 | .271 |
| 95 NL San Diego | 11 | 17 | 2 | 3 | 0 | 0 | 0 | 0 | 1 | 2 | 6 | .176 |

It's taken a while, but Ray McDavid might finally be ready to contribute at the major league level. He's been tabbed as a top prospect ever since 1991, when he drew 106 walks and stole 60 bases in the Sally League. Since then, McDavid has hit about .270 at every minor league stop and continued to draw plenty of walks. McDavid seems to have lost some of his speed, but he remains a decent center fielder with a subpar arm. At this point, McDavid's biggest problem is finding a spot in the crowded Padre outfield. Steve Finley and Tony Gwynn are established regulars, but neither is a power threat so the club would like a big hitter in left. McDavid is no weakling, but unless he puts on a big power show in the spring he'll probably be relegated to spot duty.

## Others to Watch

Shortstop **Juan Melo** hit .282 last year with Clinton, a more than credible season for a 19 year old in the slow-A Midwest League. A switch-hitter with good defensive skills, Melo has few negatives, but he's still two or three years away from the majors. . . First basemen, **Jason Thompson** is still a prospect though his star has fallen somewhat. He did hit 20 homers last season, but a .272 batting average and 131 strikeouts in Double-A give cause for concern. At 24, Thompson will be watched closely this season at Triple-A Las Vegas. He could be in the majors sometime soon if first base remains a problem position for the Padres. . . Among Ben Davis' teammates at Idaho Falls was first baseman **Sean Watkins**, a Bradley product and the club's eighth-round pick last June. Watkins probably should have started his pro career in a higher league, seeing as how he batted Pioneer League pitchers for a .372 average and 13 homers. Managers loved his power and his tough-guy attitude, but at his age (22) he needs to prove himself at higher levels, and fairly soon.

# Jose Bautista

## 1995 Season

Jose Bautista's least productive season characterized the San Francisco bullpen. Picked up to pitch long relief and perhaps start occasionally, Bautista posted the league's worst ERA among pitchers with at least 66 innings. An elbow contusion suffered late in 1994 may have disrupted Bautista's pitching. In only 100.2 innings, Bautista coughed up 24 home runs, fourth-highest total in the league. About all you can say for his season is that he kept taking the ball without complaint. He even started six games, though he won only one of them.

## Pitching

When his arm is right, Bautista throws a good fastball and slider, along with an average change-up and a forkball at two different speeds. Most of the home runs were the result of hanging forkballs. Lefty hitters gave him particular trouble, and he pitched weakly with runners on base. Bautista struggled with his first batter, but improved with more pitches. Highly durable, Bautista showed fine control, allowing only 2.3 walks per nine innings. Outfielders can expect most of the action when Bautista is on the mound.

## Defense & Hitting

Bautista snaps up comebackers but will occasionally throw wildly to first. His deliberate delivery does not preclude a pretty good pickoff move. Bautista is no hitter. In 19 plate appearances, he whiffed nine times and reached base once via walk; his lifetime average is .098.

## 1996 Outlook

Although Bautista proved early on that his arm was lacking something, the Giants allowed him to post his third consecutive year with over 50 appearances, triggering the club's contractual obligation to guarantee Bautista's salary in 1996. As a result, Bautista will be given every opportunity to prove that 1995 was a fluke. If healthy, he should do just that.

**Position:** RP/SP
**Bats:** R **Throws:** R
**Ht:** 6' 2" **Wt:** 205

**Opening Day Age:** 31
**Born:** 7/26/64 in Bani, DR
**ML Seasons:** 7
**Pronunciation:**
baw-TEES-tah

### Overall Statistics

|        | W  | L  | Pct. | ERA  | G   | GS | Sv | IP    | H   | BB  | SO  | HR | BR/IP |
|--------|----|----|------|------|-----|----|----|-------|-----|-----|-----|----|-------|
| 1995   | 3  | 8  | .273 | 6.44 | 52  | 6  | 0  | 100.2 | 120 | 26  | 45  | 24 | 1.45  |
| Career | 27 | 36 | .429 | 4.59 | 243 | 48 | 3  | 563.1 | 596 | 142 | 277 | 88 | 1.31  |

### How Often He Throws Strikes

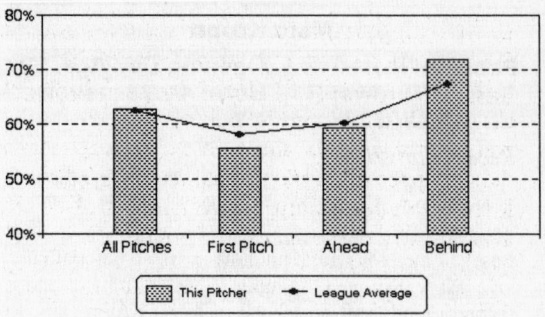

### 1995 Situational Stats

|            | W | L | ERA  | Sv | IP   |        | AB  | H  | HR | RBI | Avg  |
|------------|---|---|------|----|------|--------|-----|----|----|-----|------|
| Home       | 1 | 5 | 5.26 | 0  | 53.0 | LHB    | 161 | 52 | 9  | 35  | .323 |
| Road       | 2 | 3 | 7.74 | 0  | 47.2 | RHB    | 246 | 68 | 15 | 47  | .276 |
| First Half | 2 | 4 | 5.57 | 0  | 63.0 | Sc Pos | 98  | 35 | 5  | 52  | .357 |
| Scnd Half  | 1 | 4 | 7.88 | 0  | 37.2 | Clutch | 62  | 19 | 3  | 10  | .306 |

### 1995 Rankings (National League)

- → 1st in least GDPs induced per GDP situation (1.6%) and worst first batter efficiency (.405)
- → 2nd in highest relief ERA (6.96)
- → 3rd in highest batting average allowed vs. left-handed batters (.323), highest batting average allowed in relief (.317) and least strikeouts per 9 innings in relief (4.6)
- → 4th in home runs allowed
- → 5th in highest percentage of inherited runners scored (40.6%)
- → 7th in most baserunners allowed per 9 innings in relief (14.3)
- → 8th in balks (2)
- → Led the Giants in relief innings (64.2)

# Rod Beck

## 1995 Season

Perfection is not a human quality, as Rod Beck learned last year. From August of 1993 to May of 1995, Beck strung together 41 straight saves. But when he fell, he fell hard. Although he finished third in the league with 33 saves, Beck's 10 blown chances topped the majors. His roughest patch came in July, when he allowed 15 earned runs and blew four saves in one 9.2-inning stretch. But from August 1 on, usually pitching no more than one inning at a time, Beck walked two batters, struck out 13, and compiled a stingy 2.25 ERA. And he finished the season with 127 career saves, tying Gary Lavelle's franchise record.

## Pitching

Beck's biggest problem last season—and in 1994—was probably that the velocity on his fastball was down slightly. Beck can no longer get away with throwing his sinker up in the strike zone. Once he gets ahead in the count—which didn't happen often enough last season—Beck lets loose with a devastating split-fingered fastball. He also throws a curve and slider, both of them hard. Though his ERA didn't show it, Beck's problems began in 1994 when he allowed more than a hit per inning, a trend which continued last season.

## Defense & Hitting

Beck prefers to focus his attention toward the hitter rather than baserunners. That and his delivery make Beck fairly easy to run on, and he's permitted five steals over the last two seasons. Beck is a nimble fielder, at least for a man his size. Beck rarely hits, of course; he's 3-for-14 lifetime with seven strikeouts.

## 1996 Outlook

Beck seems awfully young to be over the hill, but (1) he's been worked hard, and (2) he hasn't kept in good shape. That is not a good combination. On the other hand, Beck pitched well last season if you throw out July. With arbitration looming, the Giants have a tough decision to make this winter.

**Position:** RP
**Bats:** R  **Throws:** R
**Ht:** 6' 1"  **Wt:** 236

**Opening Day Age:** 27
**Born:** 8/3/68 in Burbank, CA
**ML Seasons:** 5

### Overall Statistics

|  | W | L | Pct. | ERA | G | GS | Sv | IP | H | BB | SO | HR | BR/IP |
|---|---|---|---|---|---|---|---|---|---|---|---|---|---|
| 1995 | 5 | 6 | .455 | 4.45 | 60 | 0 | 33 | 58.2 | 60 | 21 | 42 | 7 | 1.38 |
| Career | 14 | 15 | .483 | 2.80 | 280 | 0 | 127 | 331.0 | 281 | 75 | 292 | 36 | 1.08 |

### How Often He Throws Strikes

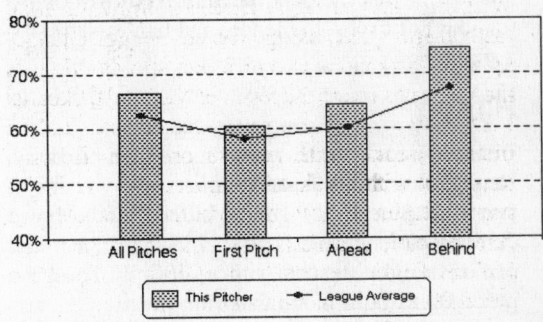

### 1995 Situational Stats

|  | W | L | ERA | Sv | IP |  | AB | H | HR | RBI | Avg |
|---|---|---|---|---|---|---|---|---|---|---|---|
| Home | 5 | 3 | 4.54 | 16 | 35.2 | LHB | 109 | 30 | 3 | 22 | .275 |
| Road | 0 | 3 | 4.30 | 17 | 23.0 | RHB | 116 | 30 | 4 | 13 | .259 |
| First Half | 4 | 3 | 3.34 | 15 | 32.1 | Sc Pos | 59 | 14 | 2 | 26 | .237 |
| Scnd Half | 1 | 3 | 5.81 | 18 | 26.1 | Clutch | 158 | 47 | 7 | 33 | .297 |

### 1995 Rankings (National League)

- ➡ 1st in blown saves (10)
- ➡ 2nd in save opportunities (43) and lowest save percentage (76.7%)
- ➡ 3rd in saves
- ➡ 4th in games finished (52)
- ➡ 5th in relief losses (6)
- ➡ 8th in least strikeouts per 9 innings in relief (6.4)
- ➡ 10th in highest relief ERA (4.45)
- ➡ Led the Giants in games pitched, saves, games finished, save opportunities, save percentage (76.7%), blown saves, relief ERA, relief losses and lowest batting average allowed in relief (.267)

**S. F. Giants**

# Barry Bonds

Immortal

## 1995 Season

Postseason success remains Barry Bonds' only unconquered goal. As usual, he topped the National League in walks and on-base percentage. Bonds ranked second in runs, fourth in home runs, fifth in slugging, sixth in RBI. . . and first in extra-base hits among non-Rockies. Bonds became the first Giant to hit 30 home runs and steal 30 bases since his father reached those marks in 1973. There were a couple of flies in Bonds' 1995 ointment. A bruised hand limited him to a .204 average in August. And a pair of mental mistakes drew deserved negative reviews. In one game, Bonds ignored a ball hit over his head, thinking it was going to be a home run. It wasn't. And in a reversal of that incident, he admired a ball he hit to—but not over—the fence, and had to settle for a single.

## Hitting

Bonds swings with his wrists more than his body. He pummels fastballs, and pitchers throw inside to jam him. A dead-pull flyball hitter, Bonds shows extreme patience and is now working on a streak of six straight seasons with a .400-plus on-base percentage. With men in scoring position, Bonds walks a third of the time and reaches base safely more than half the time. A clutch performer, Bonds won three games in late June and early July with late-inning home runs, and hit .357 after the sixth inning.

## Baserunning & Defense

A daring, occasionally unwise baserunner, Bonds has been known to steal with Matt Williams up, go for third on a double, or try to make an inside-the-park homer out of a triple. Bonds displays excellent range in left field, has the best arm for that position in the majors, and consistently posts double figures in assists.

## 1996 Outlook

Simply put, Bonds is the most productive hitter of his generation. He'll inevitably see a slow dropoff in performance. . . eventually. For now, Bonds is still in his early 30s and should be a fantastic hitter for a number of years.

**Position:** LF
**Bats:** L  **Throws:** L
**Ht:** 6' 1"  **Wt:** 190

**Opening Day Age:** 31
**Born:** 7/24/64 in Riverside, CA
**ML Seasons:** 10
**Nickname:** Sledgehammer

### Overall Statistics

|  | G | AB | R | H | D | T | HR | RBI | SB | BB | SO | Avg | OBP | Slg |
|---|---|---|---|---|---|---|---|---|---|---|---|---|---|---|
| 1995 | 144 | 506 | 109 | 149 | 30 | 7 | 33 | 104 | 31 | 120 | 83 | .294 | .431 | .577 |
| Career | 1425 | 5020 | 999 | 1436 | 306 | 48 | 292 | 864 | 340 | 931 | 795 | .286 | .398 | .541 |

### Where He Hits the Ball

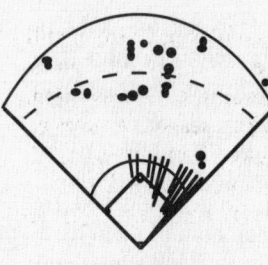

**Vs. LHP**

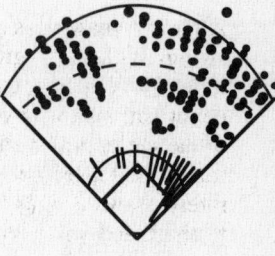

**Vs. RHP**

### 1995 Situational Stats

|  | AB | H | HR | RBI | Avg |  | AB | H | HR | RBI | Avg |
|---|---|---|---|---|---|---|---|---|---|---|---|
| Home | 238 | 73 | 16 | 51 | .307 | LHP | 138 | 37 | 5 | 28 | .268 |
| Road | 268 | 76 | 17 | 53 | .284 | RHP | 368 | 112 | 28 | 76 | .304 |
| First Half | 248 | 76 | 16 | 53 | .306 | Sc Pos | 117 | 38 | 4 | 57 | .325 |
| Scnd Half | 258 | 73 | 17 | 51 | .283 | Clutch | 80 | 28 | 7 | 29 | .350 |

### 1995 Rankings (National League)

- 1st in walks, intentional walks (22), times on base (274), games played, on-base percentage, lowest groundball/flyball ratio (0.7) and on-base percentage vs. right-handed pitchers (.447)
- 2nd in runs scored, slugging percentage vs. right-handed pitchers (.614) and errors in left field (6)
- 3rd in pitches seen (2,452) and plate appearances (635)
- 4th in home runs and fielding percentage in left field (.980)
- Led the Giants in batting average , home runs, runs scored, hits, doubles and triples

# Mark Carreon

## 1995 Season

Mark Carreon can play every day. Given a bad rap because he had his worst batting average (.232) the only year (1992) he played regularly, Carreon smacked .301 last year. He claimed the Giants' first-base job in June, filling the vacuum created by the departure of Will Clark, the weakness of Todd Benzinger, and the utter failure of J. R. Phillips to hit major league pitching. A left-handed thrower with a weak arm and not much speed, Carreon was miscast as an outfielder. But first base. . . that he could do. The emergence of Carreon as an everyday player was one of the bright spots of the Giants' season.

## Hitting

After two seasons as a bench player, Carreon still swings with the aggressive mentality of a pinch hitter. Nonetheless, Carreon struck out less often, per at-bat, than in any previous season. A devotee of the see-ball-hit-ball religion, Carreon has to hit for a good average to get on base, because he rarely draws a walk. Carreon feasts on the high fastball, and will take it to all fields with decent power. His 17 homers were a career best, and he was effective against both left- and righthanders.

## Baserunning & Defense

Carreon is, to put it kindly, not fast, and he hasn't stolen a base since 1993. He does hustle around the bases. Early in the season, Dusty Baker removed Carreon for defense in the late innings. But Carreon took to first base well, and by the end of the season Baker was letting him finish the close games.

## 1996 Outlook

At this writing, there are three candidates for the Giants' first-base job in 1996: Mark Carreon (.301 average in '95), Dave McCarty (.250) and J.R. Phillips (.195). Obviously, Carreon has a big edge, and he'll almost certainly open the season in the lineup.

**Position:** 1B/RF
**Bats:** R **Throws:** L
**Ht:** 6' 0" **Wt:** 195

**Opening Day Age:** 32
**Born:** 7/9/63 in Chicago, IL
**ML Seasons:** 9
**Pronunciation:** CARRY-on

### Overall Statistics

|  | G | AB | R | H | D | T | HR | RBI | SB | BB | SO | Avg | OBP | Slg |
|---|---|---|---|---|---|---|---|---|---|---|---|---|---|---|
| 1995 | 117 | 396 | 53 | 119 | 24 | 0 | 17 | 65 | 0 | 23 | 37 | .301 | .343 | .490 |
| Career | 619 | 1578 | 190 | 435 | 74 | 2 | 58 | 224 | 9 | 107 | 204 | .276 | .324 | .435 |

### Where He Hits the Ball

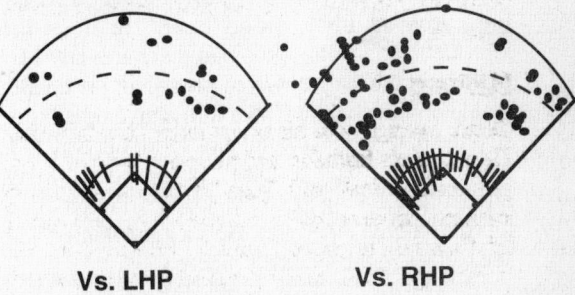

**Vs. LHP**  **Vs. RHP**

### 1995 Situational Stats

|  | AB | H | HR | RBI | Avg |  | AB | H | HR | RBI | Avg |
|---|---|---|---|---|---|---|---|---|---|---|---|
| Home | 191 | 51 | 7 | 29 | .267 | LHP | 97 | 30 | 3 | 11 | .309 |
| Road | 205 | 68 | 10 | 36 | .332 | RHP | 299 | 89 | 14 | 54 | .298 |
| First Half | 137 | 38 | 8 | 18 | .277 | Sc Pos | 111 | 35 | 0 | 40 | .315 |
| Scnd Half | 259 | 81 | 9 | 47 | .313 | Clutch | 66 | 20 | 2 | 11 | .303 |

### 1995 Rankings (National League)

→ 3rd in lowest cleanup slugging percentage (.430)
→ 9th in errors at first base (5)
→ 10th in lowest percentage of extra bases taken as a runner (42.1%)
→ Led the Giants in batting average with the bases loaded (.364), batting average on a 3-1 count (.556), batting average with two strikes (.260), lowest percentage of swings that missed (11.8%) and highest percentage of swings put into play (48.1%)

S. F. Giants

# Royce Clayton

## 1995 Season

Rarely absent from the lineup in 1995, Royce Clayton scored the most runs of his career, hit the most doubles, tied his career high in walks, and set a career high in stolen bases. On the other hand, he hit just .244 and continued to exhibit the plate discipline of Eric Gregg. Defensively, Clayton composed half of what was perhaps baseball's best left-side infield defense, at least when Matt Williams was healthy.

## Hitting

A line-drive hitter, Clayton lacks patience to say the least. Only eight National Leaguers struck out more often than Clayton, who was frequently fooled by the split-fingered fastball and has trouble catching up to good heat. He does hit knuckleballers well. . . too bad there are only two of them in the league. Given his speed, the Giants would obviously like Clayton to choke up a little, slap the ball on the ground and sprint his way to a single, but so far that hasn't happened with any regularity. Lacking great bat speed, Clayton often hits the ball the other way. He's a good bunter, and specializes in the suicide squeeze.

## Baserunning & Defense

Always a slow starter, Clayton failed on four of his first seven steal attempts, then swiped 21 of his last 26. Among the Giants, only Deion Sanders is faster. Clayton displays fine range and a strong arm at shortstop, but he's prone to the occasional lapse and his 20 miscues last season trailed only Jose Offerman among major league shortstops.

## 1996 Outlook

The Giants are tired of waiting for Clayton to meet the expectations which have long been held for him. There was talk last fall that the club would let Clayton go, and award the regular shortstop job to prospect Rich Aurilia. Clayton will no doubt play somewhere, and if he's going to have a big year it will probably be soon.

**Position:** SS
**Bats:** R **Throws:** R
**Ht:** 6' 0" **Wt:** 183

**Opening Day Age:** 26
**Born:** 1/2/70 in Burbank, CA
**ML Seasons:** 5

### Overall Statistics

|  | G | AB | R | H | D | T | HR | RBI | SB | BB | SO | Avg | OBP | Slg |
|---|---|---|---|---|---|---|---|---|---|---|---|---|---|---|
| 1995 | 138 | 509 | 56 | 124 | 29 | 3 | 5 | 58 | 24 | 38 | 109 | .244 | .298 | .342 |
| Career | 506 | 1790 | 179 | 445 | 72 | 18 | 18 | 184 | 66 | 133 | 343 | .249 | .302 | .339 |

### Where He Hits the Ball

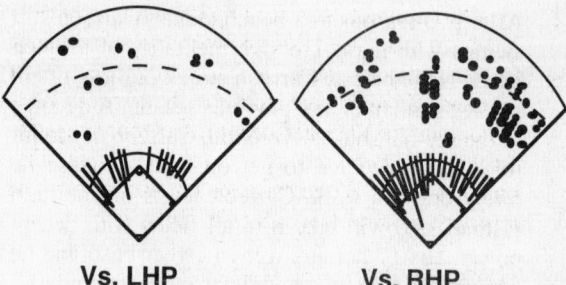

**Vs. LHP**        **Vs. RHP**

### 1995 Situational Stats

|  | AB | H | HR | RBI | Avg |  | AB | H | HR | RBI | Avg |
|---|---|---|---|---|---|---|---|---|---|---|---|
| Home | 251 | 54 | 2 | 23 | .215 | LHP | 104 | 27 | 4 | 11 | .260 |
| Road | 258 | 70 | 3 | 35 | .271 | RHP | 405 | 97 | 1 | 47 | .240 |
| First Half | 245 | 62 | 3 | 38 | .253 | Sc Pos | 142 | 36 | 1 | 52 | .254 |
| Scnd Half | 264 | 62 | 2 | 20 | .235 | Clutch | 90 | 19 | 1 | 9 | .211 |

### 1995 Rankings (National League)

- ➡ 1st in lowest on-base percentage
- ➡ 2nd in errors at shortstop (20)
- ➡ 3rd in lowest batting average, lowest batting average vs. right-handed pitchers (.240), lowest on-base percentage vs. right-handed pitchers (.297) and lowest batting average at home (.215)
- ➡ 4th in lowest slugging percentage vs. right-handed pitchers (.321)
- ➡ 6th in lowest slugging percentage and fielding percentage at shortstop (.969)
- ➡ Led the Giants in at-bats, singles (87), strikeouts and highest groundball/flyball ratio (1.9)

# Glenallen Hill

**Position:** RF
**Bats:** R  **Throws:** R
**Ht:** 6' 2"  **Wt:** 220

**Opening Day Age:** 31
**Born:** 3/22/65 in Santa Cruz, CA
**ML Seasons:** 7

## 1995 Season

Glenallen Hill has been one of baseball's more unlikely success stories over the last two years. Always regarded as a player with great raw tools, Hill's never seemed to live up to the stardom for which he was predicted. But he made great strides in 1994 as a Cub—particularly when it came to drawing walks—and impressed even more after taking over in right field for the Giants last season. Hill opened the campaign with five homers in his first 11 games, and by season's end had knocked in 86 runs in his first full season—at age 30—as a full-time player.

## Hitting

Oddly, Hill was successful last season even as his plate discipline returned to its impatient pre-1994 level. An unabashed free swinger, Hill stands close to the plate and takes a full swing even when jammed. He may have led the club in broken bats. No one in the National League was more eager to hit than Hill, who swung at 50 percent of the first pitches he saw. When he keeps his elbow down, he hits with more power and pulls the ball.

## Baserunning & Defense

Just as Hill has improved at the plate, his baserunning has picked up, too. Given that he played regularly for the first time in his career, Hill's career-high 25 steals weren't a big surprise. But he was only caught five times, and that was a surprise. A one-time center fielder, Hill doesn't always get great jumps on the ball, but his speed helps him outrun a lot of mistakes. He's always had a strong arm, and gunned down 10 too-greedy runners last season.

## 1996 Outlook

Hill's success carries a price tag, and the Giants may not be willing to risk arbitration. Giant fans will be most disappointed if Hill leaves the Bay Area. Hill, on the other hand, should be able to convert his 24 home runs into a hefty contract and a regular job, whether in San Francisco or elsewhere.

### Overall Statistics

|  | G | AB | R | H | D | T | HR | RBI | SB | BB | SO | Avg | OBP | Slg |
|---|---|---|---|---|---|---|---|---|---|---|---|---|---|---|
| 1995 | 132 | 497 | 71 | 131 | 29 | 4 | 24 | 86 | 25 | 39 | 98 | .264 | .317 | .483 |
| Career | 595 | 1929 | 270 | 501 | 90 | 13 | 88 | 284 | 77 | 149 | 427 | .260 | .313 | .457 |

### Where He Hits the Ball

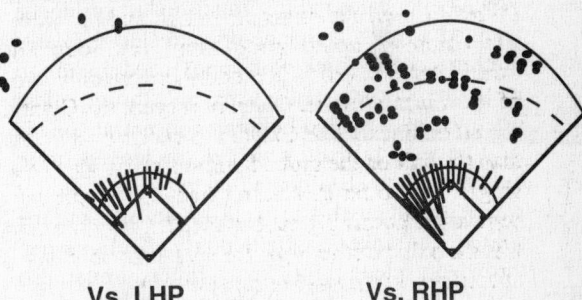

**Vs. LHP**   **Vs. RHP**

### 1995 Situational Stats

|  | AB | H | HR | RBI | Avg |  | AB | H | HR | RBI | Avg |
|---|---|---|---|---|---|---|---|---|---|---|---|
| Home | 234 | 61 | 13 | 49 | .261 | LHP | 91 | 28 | 8 | 22 | .308 |
| Road | 263 | 70 | 11 | 37 | .266 | RHP | 406 | 103 | 16 | 64 | .254 |
| First Half | 252 | 65 | 8 | 43 | .258 | Sc Pos | 159 | 38 | 7 | 60 | .239 |
| Scnd Half | 245 | 66 | 16 | 43 | .269 | Clutch | 99 | 21 | 4 | 20 | .212 |

### 1995 Rankings (National League)

➡ 1st in lowest fielding percentage in right field (.959) and highest percentage of swings on the first pitch (50.0%)

➡ 2nd in errors in right field (10)

➡ 7th in stolen base percentage (83.3%), lowest on-base percentage vs. right-handed pitchers (.308) and highest percentage of swings that missed (27.9%)

➡ 10th in lowest batting average vs. right-handed pitchers (.254)

➡ Led the Giants in stolen base percentage

# Mark Leiter

## 1995 Season

It was an interesting year for the Leiter family. While both Mark (Giants) and Al (Blue Jays) were arguably the ace starters for their respective teams, neither ended up with a winning record. Mark, the elder Leiter, has four shoulder surgeries and chronic groin injuries on his medical chart, and was never a full-time starter before 1995. However, he was pressed into service as an emergency starter for the Giants' home opener, and never left the rotation. He topped the Giants in wins, innings and starts, and his seven complete games trailed only Greg Maddux in the National League.

## Pitching

When Leiter came to San Francisco last spring, he featured a fastball, change-up, and slurve. Giants pitching coach Dick Pole convinced Leiter to make the slurve a real curve, and throw it less often. He also wanted Leiter to concentrate on his split-fingered fastball, which was in his repertoire but rarely used. By the end of the season, Leiter was using mainly his fastball—a sinker—and the splitter. The sinker was particularly effective when thrown outside to right-handed hitters. Leiter also learned that he had to back hitters off the plate, and as a result he topped the majors with 17 hit batters.

## Defense & Hitting

Leiter had a rough year defensively; his four errors yielded an awful .867 fielding percentage. He's got a pretty good move to first, though, and caught four runners napping last season. Leiter's first National League action gave him a chance to hit, and he went 6-for-61 with a staff-leading five RBI.

## 1996 Outlook

Most of the evidence suggests that Leiter posted a career season in 1995. Even if he really did learn how to pitch better, there's no reason to think his body can stand up to another year of starting every fifth day. Leiter will open the season in the rotation, but it will be something of a surprise if he's still there in August.

**Position:** SP
**Bats:** R  **Throws:** R
**Ht:** 6' 3"  **Wt:** 210

**Opening Day Age:** 32
**Born:** 4/13/63 in Joliet, IL
**ML Seasons:** 6
**Pronunciation:** LITE-er

### Overall Statistics

|        | W  | L  | Pct. | ERA  | G   | GS | Sv | IP    | H   | BB  | SO  | HR | BR/IP |
|--------|----|----|------|------|-----|----|----|-------|-----|-----|-----|----|-------|
| 1995   | 10 | 12 | .455 | 3.82 | 30  | 29 | 0  | 195.2 | 185 | 55  | 129 | 19 | 1.23  |
| Career | 38 | 38 | .500 | 4.35 | 178 | 81 | 3  | 670.2 | 669 | 236 | 469 | 79 | 1.35  |

### How Often He Throws Strikes

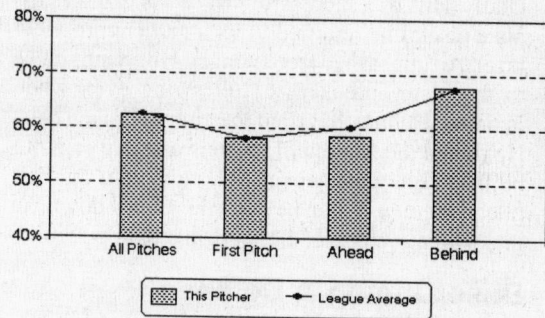

### 1995 Situational Stats

|            | W | L | ERA  | Sv | IP    |        | AB  | H   | HR | RBI | Avg  |
|------------|---|---|------|----|-------|--------|-----|-----|----|-----|------|
| Home       | 5 | 5 | 3.87 | 0  | 100.0 | LHB    | 315 | 76  | 9  | 33  | .241 |
| Road       | 5 | 7 | 3.76 | 0  | 95.2  | RHB    | 414 | 109 | 10 | 48  | .263 |
| First Half | 3 | 6 | 4.08 | 0  | 81.2  | Sc Pos | 154 | 50  | 0  | 59  | .325 |
| Scnd Half  | 7 | 6 | 3.63 | 0  | 114.0 | Clutch | 65  | 12  | 1  | 4   | .185 |

### 1995 Rankings (National League)

- ➞ 1st in hit batsmen (17), pickoff throws (218) and lowest fielding percentage at pitcher (.867)
- ➞ 2nd in complete games (7)
- ➞ 3rd in lowest groundball/flyball ratio allowed (1.0), least run support per 9 innings (3.7) and errors at pitcher (4)
- ➞ 4th in balks (3)
- ➞ 7th in wild pitches (9) and highest batting average allowed with runners in scoring position (.325)
- ➞ Led the Giants in sacrifice bunts (9), ERA, wins, games started and complete games

# Kirt Manwaring

## 1995 Season

With Kirt Manwaring behind the plate, the Giants don't care how well he hits. Good thing, too, because Manwaring is no hitter; what you see in his mediocre batting average is all you get. Manwaring hit .251 with no power or walks in 1995, and he's hit .253 with no power or walks over the last five seasons. Like any weak hitter, Manwaring has his moments: on July 14 he blasted two of his four homers, both of them off Greg Swindell. Four days later, Manwaring cracked five ribs when diving to stop a throw, but he finished the season without complaint.

## Hitting

Pitchers like to jam Manwaring inside, while he prefers to spray the ball around. Manwaring does well when he swings at the first pitch, probably because that keeps him from getting behind in the count. He scored the fewest runs of any season since he took over the catching job in 1992. Manwaring did do one thing well at the plate last season: he was hit by 10 pitches, seventh most in the National League. That hurt his body but helped his needy OBP.

## Baserunning & Defense

Manwaring is slow and cautious on the bases. Probably *too* cautious: he posted the majors' worst ratio of times on base to runs scored last year. He calls pitches well and is famous for stopping the running game. However, he fell to eighth in the league in opponents' steal success rate. Manwaring has good instincts behind the plate, and a knack for sensing when a pitcher needs a few calming words. He makes highlight films annually, taking hard hits at the plate from baserunners but holding on tight to the baseball.

## 1996 Outlook

Manwaring will never amount to much at the plate. But *behind* the plate, he's one of the best. And when you've got Barry Bonds and Matt Williams in your lineup, you can afford to carry a weak hitter or two. Manwaring has a guaranteed contract for 1996, so he'll be providing his usual sterling defense.

**Position:** C
**Bats:** R  **Throws:** R
**Ht:** 5'11"  **Wt:** 203

**Opening Day Age:** 30
**Born:** 7/15/65 in Elmira, NY
**ML Seasons:** 9
**Pronunciation:** man-WAIR-ing

### Overall Statistics

| | G | AB | R | H | D | T | HR | RBI | SB | BB | SO | Avg | OBP | Slg |
|---|---|---|---|---|---|---|---|---|---|---|---|---|---|---|
| 1995 | 118 | 379 | 21 | 95 | 15 | 2 | 4 | 36 | 1 | 27 | 72 | .251 | .314 | .332 |
| Career | 660 | 1990 | 165 | 492 | 77 | 12 | 15 | 193 | 8 | 144 | 315 | .247 | .308 | .321 |

### Where He Hits the Ball

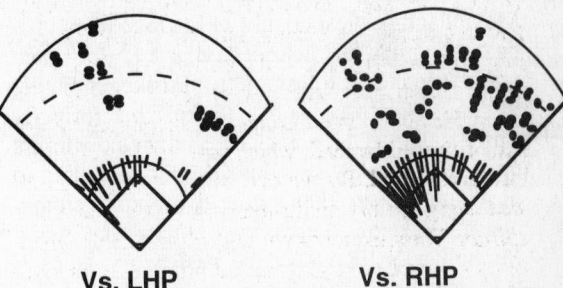

**Vs. LHP**          **Vs. RHP**

### 1995 Situational Stats

| | AB | H | HR | RBI | Avg | | AB | H | HR | RBI | Avg |
|---|---|---|---|---|---|---|---|---|---|---|---|
| Home | 183 | 49 | 4 | 16 | .268 | LHP | 85 | 21 | 3 | 7 | .247 |
| Road | 196 | 46 | 0 | 20 | .235 | RHP | 294 | 74 | 1 | 29 | .252 |
| First Half | 174 | 43 | 1 | 15 | .247 | Sc Pos | 105 | 22 | 0 | 29 | .210 |
| Scnd Half | 205 | 52 | 3 | 21 | .254 | Clutch | 58 | 14 | 0 | 3 | .241 |

### 1995 Rankings (National League)

➡ 4th in lowest batting average with the bases loaded (.077), lowest batting average on an 0-2 count (.038) and lowest fielding percentage at catcher (.990)

➡ 5th in errors at catcher (7)

➡ 6th in lowest batting average with runners in scoring position (.210)

➡ 7th in hit by pitch (10) and lowest batting average on the road (.235)

➡ Led the Giants in sacrifice flies (4)

# Terry Mulholland

## 1995 Season

It's been a rapid fall for Terry Mulholland, who started the 1993 All-Star Game. After a disastrous 1994 season with the Yankees, Mulholland hoped to rejuvenate his career by returning to his first major league club, the San Francisco Giants. But except for a six-start stretch late in the season—in which Mulholland went 3-1 with a 2.44 ERA—it was not a successful comeback. Given 24 starts, Mulholland finished with the National League's worst ERA, and only Kevin Foster allowed more home runs. To make matters worse, Mulholland missed most of June with elbow soreness and surgery to remove bone chips.

## Pitching

Mulholland has lost control of his four-seam fastball—the pitch that he relied on as a Phillie—and failed to make the transition from strikeout pitcher to finesse pitcher. Unable to trust his formerly trusty sinker, slider and change-up, he now offers up long hits in key situations. Mulholland used to bust hitters inside, then nibble away, but he simply doesn't have the necessary velocity any more. Mulholland's ERA over the past two seasons is 6.11, which speaks volumes.

## Defense & Hitting

Mulholland just might be the toughest pitcher to run on in baseball history. He has the majors' best move to first, and has allowed just four stolen bases over the last four seasons. However, his delivery leaves him in poor position to field grounders, and he moves slowly off the mound. Though he's a poor hitter for average, he subscribes to the "Swing hard in case you hit it" school: three of his five hits last season went for extra bases, including a home run.

## 1996 Outlook

Mulholland has experienced shoulder, knee, and hip problems since 1991. He is a free agent, and the Giants are not calling. But the demand for experienced lefthanders remains high, and Mulholland should get at least one more chance to come back.

**Position:** SP/RP
**Bats:** R  **Throws:** L
**Ht:** 6' 3"  **Wt:** 212

**Opening Day Age:** 33
**Born:** 3/9/63 in Uniontown, PA
**ML Seasons:** 9

### Overall Statistics

|        | W  | L  | Pct. | ERA  | G   | GS  | Sv | IP     | H    | BB  | SO  | HR  | BR/IP |
|--------|----|----|------|------|-----|-----|----|--------|------|-----|-----|-----|-------|
| 1995   | 5  | 13 | .278 | 5.80 | 29  | 24  | 0  | 149.0  | 190  | 38  | 65  | 25  | 1.53  |
| Career | 68 | 78 | .466 | 4.24 | 230 | 197 | 0  | 1318.1 | 1385 | 330 | 706 | 127 | 1.30  |

### How Often He Throws Strikes

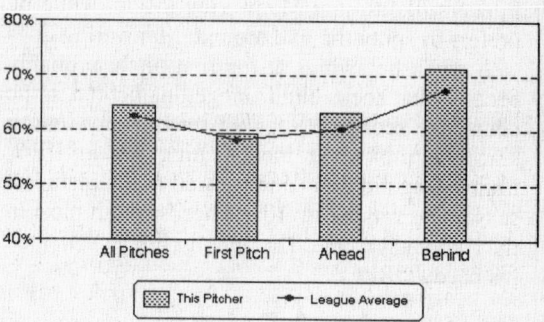

This Pitcher — League Average

### 1995 Situational Stats

|            | W | L | ERA  | Sv | IP   |        | AB  | H   | HR | RBI | Avg  |
|------------|---|---|------|----|------|--------|-----|-----|----|-----|------|
| Home       | 2 | 5 | 4.66 | 0  | 65.2 | LHB    | 107 | 30  | 3  | 17  | .280 |
| Road       | 3 | 8 | 6.70 | 0  | 83.1 | RHB    | 500 | 160 | 22 | 80  | .320 |
| First Half | 2 | 7 | 6.40 | 0  | 57.2 | Sc Pos | 135 | 49  | 3  | 67  | .363 |
| Scnd Half  | 3 | 6 | 5.42 | 0  | 91.1 | Clutch | 29  | 6   | 0  | 1   | .207 |

### 1995 Rankings (National League)

- → 1st in highest ERA, highest batting average allowed (.313), highest slugging percentage allowed (.494), highest on-base percentage allowed (.354), most baserunners allowed per 9 innings (14.0), least strikeouts per 9 innings (3.9), highest ERA on the road (6.70) and highest batting average allowed with runners in scoring position (.363)
- → 2nd in home runs allowed, lowest stolen base percentage allowed (14.3%) and most home runs allowed per 9 innings (1.51)
- → Led the Giants in losses, hits allowed, home runs allowed and runners caught stealing

# Deion Sanders

## 1995 Season

Deion Sanders may be a superstar in the NFL, but he's got a ways to go as a baseball player. One play from last May offers a good example. Despite the fact that the Reds—his club at the time—had a six-run lead, Sanders attempted to steal third. Failing to slide while being tagged, he sprained his left ankle and missed seven weeks. As it turned out, that was pretty much the end of his Cincinnati career. A few days after coming off the DL in July, Sanders went to San Francisco in a four-player deal. Sanders eventually ended his season a few days early to undergo arthroscopic surgery on his ankle. He also missed four games with migraines while negotiating his mega-contract with the Dallas Cowboys.

## Hitting

Sanders obviously has the speed of a leadoff hitter, but he doesn't have the patience of one. Despite average bat speed at best, Sanders takes a full rip on every pitch and is frequently fooled by offspeed offerings. Like a younger Sammy Sosa, Sanders' favorite pitch is the low fastball. Sanders drops his hands as he starts his swing, which costs power. He is a good bunter and adept at dropping them down for base hits.

## Baserunning & Defense

Sanders didn't appear hobbled much by the ankle injury. He stole 24 bases in all, including 16 as a Red, and was fast enough to collect eight triples, third-most in the league. Once on the bases, Sanders occasionally makes bad decisions which he can't outrun. In center field, however, his speed makes up for the occasional misjudged fly ball. A weak arm and poor mechanics leave Sanders ill-equipped to throw out baserunners.

## 1996 Outlook

For all his fame, Sanders is now 28 years old and has never collected more than 375 at-bats in a major league season. He has talent, though, and the Giants would like him back this year. Of course, where Deion will play is always a soap opera, no matter what the sport.

**Position:** CF
**Bats:** L **Throws:** L
**Ht:** 6' 1" **Wt:** 195

**Opening Day Age:** 28
**Born:** 8/9/67 in Ft. Myers, FL
**ML Seasons:** 7
**Nickname:** Neon Deion

### Overall Statistics

|        | G   | AB   | R   | H   | D  | T  | HR | RBI | SB  | BB  | SO  | Avg  | OBP  | Slg  |
|--------|-----|------|-----|-----|----|----|----|-----|-----|-----|-----|------|------|------|
| 1995   | 85  | 343  | 48  | 92  | 11 | 8  | 6  | 28  | 24  | 27  | 60  | .268 | .327 | .399 |
| Career | 494 | 1583 | 249 | 418 | 57 | 36 | 33 | 141 | 127 | 121 | 275 | .264 | .320 | .408 |

### Where He Hits the Ball

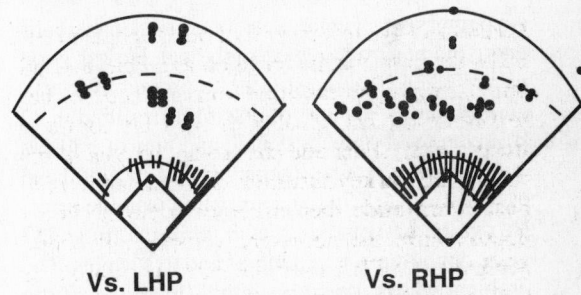

**Vs. LHP**          **Vs. RHP**

### 1995 Situational Stats

|            | AB  | H  | HR | RBI | Avg  |        | AB  | H  | HR | RBI | Avg  |
|------------|-----|----|----|-----|------|--------|-----|----|----|-----|------|
| Home       | 159 | 46 | 3  | 12  | .289 | LHP    | 89  | 19 | 0  | 7   | .213 |
| Road       | 184 | 46 | 3  | 16  | .250 | RHP    | 254 | 73 | 6  | 21  | .287 |
| First Half | 114 | 28 | 1  | 8   | .246 | Sc Pos | 61  | 16 | 0  | 21  | .262 |
| Scnd Half  | 229 | 64 | 5  | 20  | .279 | Clutch | 53  | 12 | 0  | 4   | .226 |

### 1995 Rankings (National League)

- → 3rd in triples and lowest on-base percentage for a leadoff hitter (.320)
- → 4th in errors in center field (5)
- → 7th in steals of third (7)
- → 9th in bunts in play (22)
- → 10th in lowest batting average with the bases loaded (.143)
- → Led the Giants in on-base percentage for a leadoff hitter (.346)

S. F. Giants

# Steve Scarsone

## 1995 Season

The consummate utility player, Steve Scarsone filled in for the injured Robby Thompson and Matt Williams, and played plenty of first base as well, as opportunity blossomed in an infield rife with injuries and disappointment. Scarsone missed a few games himself with an abdominal strain and a bruised finger, but remained basically healthy. Rarely used in the opening weeks, Scarsone was hitting .364 with six homers and a whopping .782 slugging percentage on June 15 . He didn't keep that up, of course, but he did finish with respectable totals while batting nearly as often as in his other three seasons combined.

## Hitting

An aggressive swinger, Scarsone turns on fastballs down but has trouble with high heat. He has good power when he connects, as he proved last year. Unfortunately, his lack of discipline resulted in 82 strikeouts and only 18 walks, and almost half his outs were strikeouts. Pitchers trying to get ahead of Scarsone early in the count often paid the price. He put the first pitch in play 35 times, hitting .457 with four homers, two doubles and two triples. The problem was that he missed that first pitch a little too often.

## Baserunning & Defense

Scarsone managed his first career triple and first career steal last year, finishing with three of each. He hustles on the bases, and once scored from second on a sacrifice bunt when the defense fell asleep. He is deft at sliding into home and avoiding tags. Scarsone made too many fielding errors last season, but he's a pretty good second baseman and doesn't embarrass himself at first or third.

## 1996 Outlook

In 469 career at-bats, Scarsone sports a .424 slugging percentage, excellent for a utility infielder. He quite likely had his career year in 1995, but plenty of managers would love to have him around. With Mike Benjamin gone, Scarsone should again be a busy man in 1996.

**Position:** 3B/1B/2B
**Bats:** R **Throws:** R
**Ht:** 6' 2"  **Wt:** 195

**Opening Day Age:** 29
**Born:** 4/11/66 in Anaheim, CA
**ML Seasons:** 4
**Pronunciation:** scar-SONE-ee

### Overall Statistics

|        | G   | AB  | R  | H   | D  | T | HR | RBI | SB | BB | SO  | Avg  | OBP  | Slg  |
|--------|-----|-----|----|-----|----|---|----|-----|----|----|-----|------|------|------|
| 1995   | 80  | 233 | 33 | 62  | 10 | 3 | 11 | 29  | 3  | 18 | 82  | .266 | .333 | .476 |
| Career | 194 | 469 | 73 | 121 | 27 | 3 | 15 | 57  | 3  | 34 | 146 | .258 | .314 | .424 |

### Where He Hits the Ball

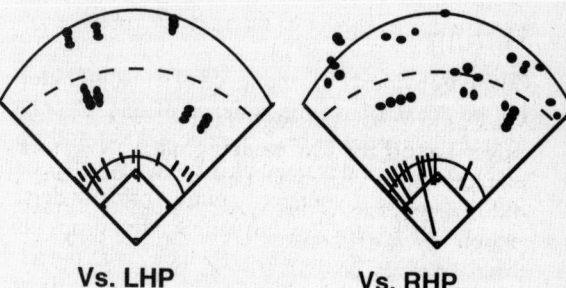

Vs. LHP            Vs. RHP

### 1995 Situational Stats

|            | AB  | H  | HR | RBI | Avg  |      | AB  | H  | HR | RBI | Avg  |
|------------|-----|----|----|-----|------|------|-----|----|----|-----|------|
| Home       | 128 | 29 | 7  | 17  | .227 | LHP  | 71  | 23 | 3  | 7   | .324 |
| Road       | 105 | 33 | 4  | 12  | .314 | RHP  | 162 | 39 | 8  | 22  | .241 |
| First Half | 98  | 31 | 7  | 16  | .316 | Sc Pos | 64 | 13 | 2  | 16  | .203 |
| Scnd Half  | 135 | 31 | 4  | 13  | .230 | Clutch | 40 | 11 | 3  | 7   | .275 |

### 1995 Rankings (National League)

➡ Did not rank near the top or bottom in any category

# Robby Thompson

## 1995 Season

Robby Thompson's fine career has fallen victim to injuries, and his 1995 campaign epitomized that decline. In early May, Thompson hurt his right quadriceps while running out a grounder and missed three games. Later that month, an inflamed left groin sent Thompson to the disabled list. Minor aches kept him out of three games in June, and a similar number in July. On Labor Day, he strained his left rotator cuff and sat for four games. Finally, Thompson's season ended early with surgery to repair cartilage damage caused by diving for a ground ball. In recent seasons, Thompson suffered a torn rotator cuff, a stiff back and a pulled rib cage muscle. We spied a glimpse of the old Thompson in September, when he hit .333, but that was too few at-bats to be taken as a hopeful sign.

## Hitting

Thompson loves the high fastball, but can no longer lay off the low breaking pitch. A serious shoulder injury cursed Thompson in 1994, and a still-apparent loss of bat speed has led to wasted motion and a wild swing. Over the last two seasons, he's hit just .219 with reduced power. Thompson has at least partially offset his batting weakness by taking more pitches, and his walk ratio last season was very good.

## Baserunning & Defense

Once good for 10 or 15 steals a year, Thompson hardly runs at all any more, whether because of injuries or in an effort to avoid more of them. Thompson remains an excellent fielder, who positions himself smartly and shows true savvy on relays from the outfield. He still turns the double play fairly well, but is no longer the standout that he once was.

## 1996 Outlook

With a guaranteed contract, Thompson will try again in 1996, but a full season is unlikely. The Giants need to start thinking about a second baseman of the future, because Thompson's days as a regular appear to be nearly over.

**Position:** 2B
**Bats:** R  **Throws:** R
**Ht:** 5'11"  **Wt:** 173

**Opening Day Age:** 33
**Born:** 5/10/62 in West Palm Beach, FL
**ML Seasons:** 10

### Overall Statistics

| | G | AB | R | H | D | T | HR | RBI | SB | BB | SO | Avg | OBP | Slg |
|---|---|---|---|---|---|---|---|---|---|---|---|---|---|---|
| 1995 | 95 | 336 | 51 | 75 | 15 | 0 | 8 | 23 | 1 | 42 | 76 | .223 | .317 | .339 |
| Career | 1241 | 4385 | 636 | 1139 | 227 | 38 | 114 | 437 | 101 | 415 | 918 | .260 | .331 | .407 |

### Where He Hits the Ball

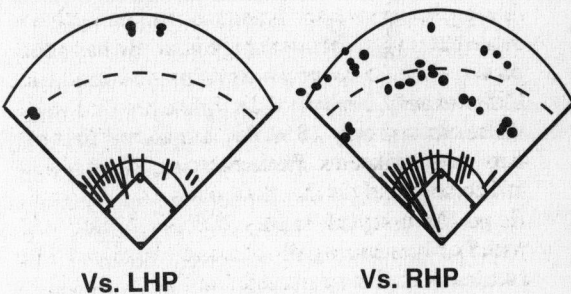

**Vs. LHP**          **Vs. RHP**

### 1995 Situational Stats

| | AB | H | HR | RBI | Avg | | AB | H | HR | RBI | Avg |
|---|---|---|---|---|---|---|---|---|---|---|---|
| Home | 170 | 36 | 4 | 10 | .212 | LHP | 77 | 19 | 1 | 5 | .247 |
| Road | 166 | 39 | 4 | 13 | .235 | RHP | 259 | 56 | 7 | 18 | .216 |
| First Half | 164 | 33 | 2 | 10 | .201 | Sc Pos | 69 | 19 | 3 | 18 | .275 |
| Scnd Half | 172 | 42 | 6 | 13 | .244 | Clutch | 59 | 11 | 3 | 8 | .186 |

### 1995 Rankings (National League)

→ 3rd in fielding percentage at second base (.993)
→ 10th in lowest batting average with two strikes (.126)
→ Led the Giants in sacrifice bunts (9), least GDPs per GDP situation (5.7%) and highest percentage of extra bases taken as a runner (61.1%)

S. F. Giants

# William VanLandingham

## 1995 Season

3Com Park, once known as Candlestick, is a pitcher's park, and right now the pitcher is William VanLandingham, who is 9-0 with a 2.95 ERA at home since jumping to the majors from Double-A in 1994. VanLandingham opened the 1995 season on the disabled list with a sore rib cage, then went just 1-2 in his first 10 starts. But he saved his season with an August/September run of five wins in six decisions and a 2.84 ERA. Unfortunately, VanLandingham was sidelined in mid-September after he strained his left groin trying to beat out a bunt.

## Pitching

VanLandingham's fastball has just average velocity, but it's got great downward movement. He also throws a hard, often wild slider, and is working on a change-up. For the first time in his professional career, VanLandingham had homer problems. In four pro seasons prior to 1995, he allowed one home run every 37 innings. Last summer he allowed a round-tripper every *nine* innings. But there were positive signs too, as VanLandingham's walk rate went down and his strikeout rate was up over '94. It's probably a fluke, but he's a perfect 12-0 in day games. . . most of them, of course, at Candlestick.

## Defense & Hitting

VanLandingham fields his position decently if unspectacularly. He needs work holding runners, surrendering 13 steals last season with only four caught stealing. He has learned how to hit, walloping three extra-base hits, including one of two homers hit by Giant pitchers. His decent footspeed is wasted by poor judgment on the bases.

## 1996 Outlook

VanLandingham has a quality arm *and* he's not yet eligible for arbitration, which makes it easy and cheap for the Giants to plop him into the rotation. Perhaps still a year or two from his prime, VanLandingham just might be the staff ace as soon as this summer.

**Position:** SP
**Bats:** R  **Throws:** R
**Ht:** 6' 2"  **Wt:** 210

**Opening Day Age:** 25
**Born:** 7/16/70 in Columbia, TN
**ML Seasons:** 2

### Overall Statistics

|        | W  | L | Pct. | ERA  | G  | GS | Sv | IP    | H   | BB | SO  | HR | BR/IP |
|--------|----|---|------|------|----|----|----|-------|-----|----|-----|----|-------|
| 1995   | 6  | 3 | .667 | 3.67 | 18 | 18 | 0  | 122.2 | 124 | 40 | 95  | 14 | 1.34  |
| Career | 14 | 5 | .737 | 3.61 | 34 | 32 | 0  | 206.2 | 194 | 83 | 151 | 18 | 1.34  |

### How Often He Throws Strikes

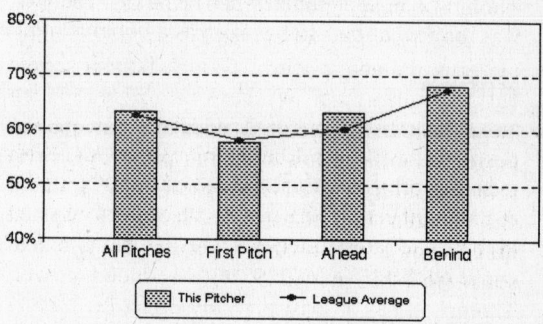

### 1995 Situational Stats

|            | W | L | ERA  | Sv | IP   |        | AB  | H  | HR | RBI | Avg  |
|------------|---|---|------|----|------|--------|-----|----|----|-----|------|
| Home       | 5 | 0 | 3.05 | 0  | 73.2 | LHB    | 216 | 65 | 4  | 22  | .301 |
| Road       | 1 | 3 | 4.59 | 0  | 49.0 | RHB    | 254 | 59 | 10 | 30  | .232 |
| First Half | 1 | 2 | 4.35 | 0  | 41.1 | Sc Pos | 92  | 21 | 5  | 37  | .228 |
| Scnd Half  | 5 | 1 | 3.32 | 0  | 81.1 | Clutch | 60  | 16 | 1  | 5   | .267 |

### 1995 Rankings (National League)

➝ 2nd in balks (4)
➝ 9th in highest batting average allowed vs. left-handed batters (.301)
➝ Led the Giants in balks, stolen bases allowed (13), ERA at home (3.05) and lowest batting average allowed vs. right-handed batters (.232)

# Matt Williams

## 1995 Season

The June 5 issue of *Sports Illustrated* featured Matt Williams. On June 3, Williams broke his right foot with a foul ball. A coincidence, of course. At the time, the one-time one-dimensional slugger was leading the National League not only in home runs (13) and RBI (35), but batting average as well with a .381 mark. Williams cooled off after his mid-August return, but he was certainly no slouch, not with a .295 average and 10 homers in 149 at-bats.

## Hitting

Williams destroys fastballs, as always, and has learned to lay off curveballs and hit deep to all fields. He is especially tough on lefties. Williams has steadily improved his batting average by laying off unhittable pitches. Though he still strikes out more than most, Williams has become much more selective in general, which results in two positives: walks, and better pitches to hit. With men in scoring position, he walked once every 3.9 at-bats. Otherwise, his walk rate sagged to once every 19 at-bats. Either Williams got more patient or the pitchers got more scared.

## Baserunning & Defense

The burly Williams doesn't run particularly well, and he takes few chances as he navigates his way around the diamond. The accolades for Williams' hitting apply equally to his fielding, as he might be the slickest third baseman in the game. He possesses quick feet, soft hands, and a strong arm. Among other things, Williams excels at charging slow rollers and bunts.

## 1996 Outlook

With a guaranteed contract through 1998, Williams will likely be exciting Bay Area fans for at least three more seasons. Assuming he can stay healthy, Williams will again be among the leaders in many offensive categories. What's more, a full season of his outstanding power and defense could help make the Giants one of the National League's surprise teams in 1996.

**Position:** 3B
**Bats:** R  **Throws:** R
**Ht:** 6' 2"  **Wt:** 216

**Opening Day Age:** 30
**Born:** 11/28/65 in Bishop, CA
**ML Seasons:** 9

### Overall Statistics

|  | G | AB | R | H | D | T | HR | RBI | SB | BB | SO | Avg | OBP | Slg |
|---|---|---|---|---|---|---|---|---|---|---|---|---|---|---|
| 1995 | 76 | 283 | 53 | 95 | 17 | 1 | 23 | 65 | 2 | 30 | 58 | .336 | .399 | .647 |
| Career | 1015 | 3735 | 525 | 970 | 163 | 24 | 225 | 647 | 28 | 233 | 781 | .260 | .306 | .497 |

### Where He Hits the Ball

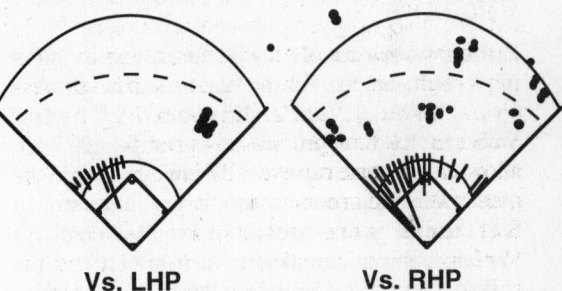

**Vs. LHP**          **Vs. RHP**

### 1995 Situational Stats

|  | AB | H | HR | RBI | Avg |  | AB | H | HR | RBI | Avg |
|---|---|---|---|---|---|---|---|---|---|---|---|
| Home | 120 | 39 | 9 | 22 | .325 | LHP | 53 | 20 | 6 | 16 | .377 |
| Road | 163 | 56 | 14 | 43 | .344 | RHP | 230 | 75 | 17 | 49 | .326 |
| First Half | 134 | 51 | 13 | 35 | .381 | Sc Pos | 75 | 23 | 7 | 40 | .307 |
| Scnd Half | 149 | 44 | 10 | 30 | .295 | Clutch | 43 | 17 | 2 | 10 | .395 |

### 1995 Rankings (National League)

➡ 3rd in cleanup slugging percentage (.643)
➡ 4th in batting average in the clutch (.395)
➡ 8th in batting average on a 3-2 count (.391)
➡ Led the Giants in batting average in the clutch, cleanup slugging percentage and batting average on a 3-2 count

S. F. Giants

# Trevor Wilson

## 1995 Season

Not many pitchers go 19 months between wins, as Trevor Wilson did. After missing the entire 1994 season with a shoulder injury, Wilson returned to the mound last April 29 and his first start was a triumphant one: six innings, two hits, and one victory. Unfortunately, that was the high point of Wilson's season. He retooled his delivery to avoid the tendon problems he experienced earlier, but could not avoid the disabled list. In June, biceps tendinitis sent Wilson to the DL. And in August, a torn labrum ended his season for good. Wilson's final ERA was certainly respectable, but he averaged fewer than five innings per start and walked as many as he struck out.

## Pitching

Wilson tosses an 88-MPH fastball with good movement, along with an adequate curveball, a so-so change-up, and a slider that needs work. Wilson pitches with finesse rather than power, stays ahead in the count, and is always around the plate. He sometimes becomes hyper, and needs to take the time to settle himself down. Wilson didn't appear to have completely recovered from the shoulder injury, as he did his best pitching when working on five or more days of rest (1.88 ERA in four starts).

## Defense & Hitting

A good pickoff move and quickness to the plate make Wilson tough to run on. He shows fine range as a fielder, finishing his delivery in good position to pounce on bunts and dribblers. Wilson batted .233 last season and his lifetime mark is a solid .176, with a couple of homers tossed in for good measure. He strikes out about a third of the time and is a good bunter.

## 1996 Outlook

Giant patience and dollars may have run out for Wilson. As a free agent, Wilson can shop around, and San Francisco may be willing to let the southpaw reside on some other team's DL. He is certainly capable of pitching some quality innings... just not many of them.

**Position:** SP
**Bats:** L **Throws:** L
**Ht:** 6' 0"  **Wt:** 204

**Opening Day Age:** 29
**Born:** 6/7/66 in Torrance, CA
**ML Seasons:** 7

### Overall Statistics

|        | W  | L  | Pct. | ERA  | G   | GS  | Sv | IP    | H   | BB  | SO  | HR | BR/IP |
|--------|----|----|------|------|-----|-----|----|-------|-----|-----|-----|----|-------|
| 1995   | 3  | 4  | .429 | 3.92 | 17  | 17  | 0  | 82.2  | 82  | 38  | 38  | 8  | 1.45  |
| Career | 41 | 46 | .471 | 3.87 | 154 | 115 | 0  | 720.1 | 657 | 300 | 425 | 61 | 1.33  |

### How Often He Throws Strikes

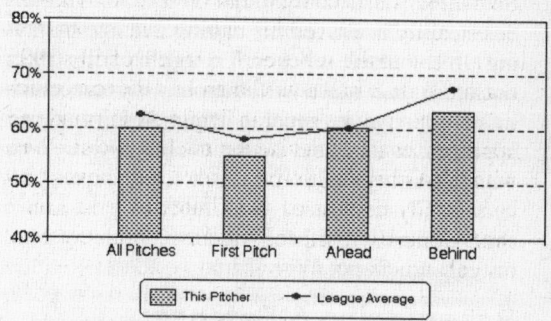

### 1995 Situational Stats

|            | W | L | ERA  | Sv | IP   |        | AB  | H  | HR | RBI | Avg  |
|------------|---|---|------|----|------|--------|-----|----|----|-----|------|
| Home       | 2 | 1 | 3.14 | 0  | 43.0 | LHB    | 47  | 12 | 0  | 3   | .255 |
| Road       | 1 | 3 | 4.76 | 0  | 39.2 | RHB    | 258 | 70 | 8  | 24  | .271 |
| First Half | 3 | 3 | 3.79 | 0  | 54.2 | Sc Pos | 69  | 12 | 3  | 20  | .174 |
| Scnd Half  | 0 | 1 | 4.18 | 0  | 28.0 | Clutch | 16  | 4  | 0  | 1   | .250 |

### 1995 Rankings (National League)

→ 1st in most GDPs induced per GDP situation (23.9%)
→ Led the Giants in GDPs induced (17) and most GDPs induced per GDP situation

# Shawn Barton

**Position:** RP
**Bats:** R  **Throws:** L
**Ht:** 6' 1"  **Wt:** 195

**Opening Day Age:** 32
**Born:** 5/14/63 in Los
Angeles, CA
**ML Seasons:** 2

## Overall Statistics

|  | W | L | Pct. | ERA | G | GS | Sv | IP | H | BB | SO | HR | BR/IP |
|---|---|---|------|-----|---|----|----|------|----|----|----|----|-------|
| 1995 | 4 | 1 | .800 | 4.26 | 52 | 0 | 1 | 44.1 | 37 | 19 | 22 | 3 | 1.26 |
| Career | 4 | 2 | .667 | 3.97 | 66 | 0 | 1 | 56.2 | 47 | 26 | 26 | 4 | 1.29 |

## 1995 Season

Shawn Barton, a 32-year-old career minor leaguer, emerged from nowhere to serve as San Francisco's only left-handed reliever for much of the 1995 season. Barton had bounced around the minors for 11 years, including eight in Triple-A. He made 53 appearances for Phoenix over the last two seasons, with ERAs below 2.00 both years, and those numbers finally convinced the Giants to give him a shot. Generally used for less than an inning after his call-up, Barton allowed no home runs with a 1.74 ERA before the All-Star break, but was hit pretty hard the second half.

## Pitching, Defense & Hitting

His assigned role was left-handed specialist, and Barton did the job last year, as opposing lefties had a .290 slugging average against him. A junkball pitcher with no fastball, Barton requires good control, but he did not always have it last season. Baserunners had a tough time reading Barton's move, and were nailed four times in six steal attempts. He's also an excellent fielder with very quick reactions on the mound. Barton batted once, and laid down a sacrifice.

## 1996 Outlook

The Giants gave up on Kevin Rogers, so they'll again be looking for a lefty specialist this spring. Barton's certainly not the best available, but he has to be considered a decent bet for a roster spot because he had some stretches of success last year.

# Mike Benjamin

**Position:** 3B/SS
**Bats:** R  **Throws:** R
**Ht:** 6' 0"  **Wt:** 169

**Opening Day Age:** 30
**Born:** 11/22/65 in
Euclid, OH
**ML Seasons:** 7

## Overall Statistics

|  | G | AB | R | H | D | T | HR | RBI | SB | BB | SO | Avg | OBP | Slg |
|---|---|----|---|---|---|---|----|-----|----|----|----|-----|-----|-----|
| 1995 | 68 | 186 | 19 | 41 | 6 | 0 | 3 | 12 | 11 | 8 | 51 | .220 | .256 | .301 |
| Career | 299 | 637 | 79 | 125 | 26 | 3 | 13 | 51 | 21 | 36 | 142 | .196 | .250 | .308 |

## 1995 Season

Someday you'll win a bar bet by remembering Mike Benjamin's record 14 hits in three games. Of course, the Giants always had faith in Benjamin. He was protected in the 1993 expansion draft, costing the club Pat Rapp or Steve Reed. And with Benjamin on the roster, the Giants had no spot for Chad Fonville, lost in the Rule 5 draft a year ago. This is the same Benjamin who entered last season with a .186 career batting average. Yet last June, that same Mike Benjamin went 14-for-18 in one three-game stretch. That interlude aside, Benjamin hit a pathetic .161 with a .203 on-base percentage and a pithy .206 slugging average.

## Hitting, Baserunning & Defense

What hitting Benjamin does manage is best done against lefthanders. He tries to pull too much and is overly aggressive for a lightweight. Benjamin is most successful when swinging at the first pitch, and he tends to hit the ball on the ground. His 11 steals last season exceeded his previous career total. Benjamin's excellent defense at second, third and shortstop is obviously what has kept him employed over the years.

## 1996 Outlook

The Giants apparently realized that Benjamin would never be an All-Star, and after the season they traded him to the Phillies for elephantine righthander Jeff Juden. With the Phils, Benjamin will compete for a utility infield job.

S. F. Giants

# Jamie Brewington

**Position:** SP
**Bats:** R **Throws:** R
**Ht:** 6' 4" **Wt:** 190

**Opening Day Age:** 24
**Born:** 9/28/71 in
Greenville, NC
**ML Seasons:** 1

### Overall Statistics

| | W | L | Pct. | ERA | G | GS | Sv | IP | H | BB | SO | HR | BR/IP |
|---|---|---|------|------|----|----|----|------|----|----|----|----|-------|
| 1995 | 6 | 4 | .600 | 4.54 | 13 | 13 | 0 | 75.1 | 68 | 45 | 45 | 8 | 1.50 |
| Career | 6 | 4 | .600 | 4.54 | 13 | 13 | 0 | 75.1 | 68 | 45 | 45 | 8 | 1.50 |

## 1995 Season

Jamie Chancellor Brewington, the lanky son of a one-time Oakland Raiders offensive tackle, arrived at Candlestick (now 3Com) Park in midseason from Shreveport, where he was 8-3 with a 3.06 ERA in 16 starts. Brewington debuted with a quality start and victory. He dominated hitters through August, suffered a two-week slump, then finished strong.

## Pitching, Defense & Hitting

In 1994, Brewington led all Giants minor leaguers with 127 strikeouts in 129 innings, and he kept his strikeout rate fairly high in both Double-A and the majors last season. Most of those K's come courtesy of a 90-plus fastball, which Brewington likes to throw on the corners. He mixes in a good slider and curve, but troubles come when Brewington gets his pitches up, because the fastball is relatively straight. Opponents found him difficult to run on, getting caught half the time, and he fielded his position very well. Brewington can also swing the bat—he collected five hits in 23 at-bats—and lay down the sacrifice.

## 1996 Outlook

Obviously, Brewington won't succeed long in the majors with a 1:1 strikeout/walk ratio, and he was sent to the Arizona Fall League, presumably to work on his control. But given the promise Brewington showed last season, he'll have to pitch himself *out* of a rotation spot this spring.

# Mark Dewey

**Position:** RP
**Bats:** R **Throws:** R
**Ht:** 6' 0" **Wt:** 216

**Opening Day Age:** 31
**Born:** 1/3/65 in Grand
Rapids, MI
**ML Seasons:** 5

### Overall Statistics

| | W | L | Pct. | ERA | G | GS | Sv | IP | H | BB | SO | HR | BR/IP |
|---|---|---|-------|------|-----|----|----|-------|-----|----|-----|----|-------|
| 1995 | 1 | 0 | 1.000 | 3.13 | 27 | 0 | 0 | 31.2 | 30 | 17 | 32 | 2 | 1.48 |
| Career | 6 | 4 | .600 | 3.37 | 127 | 0 | 8 | 165.2 | 164 | 61 | 111 | 9 | 1.36 |

## 1995 Season

When all else fails, go back to where you started. Mark Dewey returned to the Giants, with whom he began his professional career in 1987, after stops in New York and Pittsburgh. Unfortunately, a rib stress fracture left Dewey on the disabled list for almost three months, and he missed most of the second half of the season before returning in September with 7.1 scoreless innings.

## Pitching, Defense & Hitting

Dewey specializes in blowing away right-handed hitters with a three-quarter/sidearm curveball, set up by an 88-MPH sinker. His repertoire also includes a slider and a change-up. Dewey was extremely tough on righties last season, limiting them to a .195 average with no homers, but left-handed hitters returned the favor by pounding him at a .389 clip. Dewey's move to first is excellent for a righthander, and runners rarely bother moving when he's on the mound. In six career plate appearances, Dewey has a single and two walks to his credit.

## 1996 Outlook

Dewey is one of those marginal righthanders who has never quite gotten the breaks, or perhaps just the chance to pitch that he deserved. His lifetime stats suggest that given a full, healthy season in the majors, Dewey could post some nice numbers as Rod Beck's set-up man. But given his career to this point, it's just as likely that he'll once again be toiling in the minors.

# John Patterson

**Position:** 2B
**Bats:** B **Throws:** R
**Ht:** 5' 9" **Wt:** 168

**Opening Day Age:** 29
**Born:** 2/11/67 in Key West, FL
**ML Seasons:** 4

## Overall Statistics

|        | G   | AB  | R  | H   | D  | T | HR | RBI | SB | BB | SO  | Avg  | OBP  | Slg  |
|--------|-----|-----|----|-----|----|---|----|-----|----|----|-----|------|------|------|
| 1995   | 95  | 205 | 27 | 42  | 5  | 3 | 1  | 14  | 4  | 14 | 41  | .205 | .294 | .273 |
| Career | 228 | 564 | 74 | 121 | 16 | 5 | 5  | 52  | 22 | 35 | 113 | .215 | .289 | .287 |

## 1995 Season

Once groomed to play second base for the Giants, John Patterson now occupies the bench. The popular backup infielder saw both his slugging and on-base percentages drop below .300 last year. Injuries have plagued Patterson throughout his career, and his 1995 campaign ended prematurely when he suffered a severe left wrist dislocation while making a tag.

## Hitting, Baserunning & Defense

Strictly a singles hitter, Patterson scatters ground balls and posted the worst slugging percentage in the National League among hitters with at least 200 at-bats. He is much too aggressive, striking out once every five at-bats. Lefthanders mow him down, and Patterson did not perform well as a pinch hitter or in late innings. One thing he did do well was get plunked, as his 12 HBPs ranked fourth in the league. Once fast enough that the Giants briefly shifted him to center field, Patterson has lost much of his speed to injuries. He remains a solid second baseman, and capably fills in for Robby Thompson when the latter is hurt.

## 1996 Outlook

There are hundreds of Triple-A players who can hit better than Patterson. He's eligible for arbitration, but the Giants certainly have no intention of going that route. Patterson needs to play well in spring training, wherever he is, or face a trip back to the minors.

# J.R. Phillips

**Position:** 1B
**Bats:** L **Throws:** L
**Ht:** 6' 1" **Wt:** 185

**Opening Day Age:** 25
**Born:** 4/29/70 in West Covina, CA
**ML Seasons:** 3

## Overall Statistics

|        | G   | AB  | R  | H  | D  | T | HR | RBI | SB | BB | SO | Avg  | OBP  | Slg  |
|--------|-----|-----|----|----|----|---|----|-----|----|----|----|------|------|------|
| 1995   | 92  | 231 | 27 | 45 | 9  | 0 | 9  | 28  | 1  | 19 | 69 | .195 | .256 | .351 |
| Career | 118 | 285 | 29 | 55 | 10 | 1 | 11 | 35  | 2  | 20 | 87 | .193 | .245 | .351 |

## 1995 Season

In 1994, J.R. Phillips hit .300 with 27 homers in just 95 games at Triple-A Phoenix. With Will Clark a vague memory and Todd Benzinger a recent nightmare at first base, Phillips was handed the job for 1995. He couldn't hold it. By the All-Star break, Phillips' batting average was .152 and his days as a regular were over. The Giants would have sent him to the minors, but Phillips was out of options so he could have been claimed by another club. Playing but a part-time role in the second half, Phillips rebounded to hit .288 with good power.

## Hitting, Baserunning & Defense

Late last season, Dusty Baker said of Phillips, "I gave him some books about hitting. We've been trying to get through to him [that] you don't have to pull every ball." And that is Phillips' problem in a nutshell. All the pitchers in the National League knew what Phillips wanted, so instead they threw outside breaking pitches. The results? Look at the stats. Phillips did play well at first base. He runs the bases recklessly for someone with little speed.

## 1996 Outlook

With Mark Carreon now established at first base, the Giants are talking about shifting Phillips to right field, where he played in the low minors. At this point, however, his defensive position seems much less important than his hitting. If he can't top .200, it won't really matter where he plays.

# Jeff Reed

**Position**: C
**Bats**: L  **Throws**: R
**Ht**: 6' 2"  **Wt**: 190

**Opening Day Age**: 33
**Born**: 11/12/62 in
Joliet, IL
**ML Seasons**: 12

## Overall Statistics

| | G | AB | R | H | D | T | HR | RBI | SB | BB | SO | Avg | OBP | Slg |
|---|---|---|---|---|---|---|---|---|---|---|---|---|---|---|
| 1995 | 66 | 113 | 12 | 30 | 2 | 0 | 0 | 9 | 0 | 20 | 17 | .265 | .376 | .283 |
| Career | 722 | 1760 | 136 | 411 | 71 | 6 | 20 | 147 | 2 | 187 | 263 | .234 | .306 | .315 |

## 1995 Season

Most managers would rather kiss an umpire than pinch hit with their second-string catcher. But left-handed-hitting Jeff Reed did just that 30 times last year, batting .179 with five walks. Through the end of May, Reed's on-base percentage stood at .441. Although he slumped after that, Reed still finished with the third-best OBP on the Giants. . . quite a feat for an aging receiver who's lasted 12 seasons in the majors because of his defense. Of course, Reed also finished with the third-worst slugging percentage on the club. You want everything?

## Hitting, Baserunning & Defense

Reed swings stiffly, pushing the ball the opposite way with no power. As his on-base success improved, his power decreased; in 113 at-bats, Reed collected *two* extra-base hits, an unbelievably low ratio. How slow is Reed? His last triple came in 1991, and he last stole a base in 1988! Reed does yeoman work behind the plate, and after a tough year throwing in 1994, Reed tossed out 45 percent of would-be basestealers in 1995. Pitchers enjoy working with Reed, and he moves fairly well behind the plate.

## 1996 Outlook

After the season, the Giants re-signed Tom Lampkin, another lefty-swinging catcher who can't hit. Now a 33-year-old free agent, Reed will almost certainly find a job somewhere if he's willing to work cheap.

# Sergio Valdez

**Position**: SP
**Bats**: R  **Throws**: R
**Ht**: 6' 1"  **Wt**: 190

**Opening Day Age**: 30
**Born**: 9/7/65 in Elias
Pina, DR
**ML Seasons**: 8

## Overall Statistics

| | W | L | Pct. | ERA | G | GS | Sv | IP | H | BB | SO | HR | BR/IP |
|---|---|---|---|---|---|---|---|---|---|---|---|---|---|
| 1995 | 4 | 5 | .444 | 4.75 | 13 | 11 | 0 | 66.1 | 78 | 17 | 29 | 12 | 1.43 |
| Career | 12 | 20 | .375 | 5.06 | 116 | 31 | 0 | 302.2 | 332 | 109 | 190 | 46 | 1.46 |

## 1995 Season

Decimation of the Giants' pitching staff created an opportunity for journeyman Sergio Valdez, pitching for his fifth organization. In half a season at Phoenix, Valdez won six and lost seven with a 4.45 ERA. After a pair of relief stints with the Giants, Valdez made his first start on July 28, and got no decision despite allowing just three hits in eight innings. After a 1-3, 5.58 start, Valdez pitched better the rest of the way, even tossing the first complete game of his career.

## Pitching, Defense & Hitting

Valdez must keep his sinkerball and forkball low to get the ground balls he needs to succeed. If his 88-MPH fastball stays up, Valdez becomes very hittable. He allowed a slim 2.3 walks per nine innings, but batters slugged .511 with a home run every 5.5 innings. Valdez has some problems holding runners, and his defense can be shaky as well. He hit 2-for-18 at the plate with seven strikeouts, and is a serviceable bunter.

## 1996 Outlook

Thirty-year-old Sergio should not be confused with young reliever Carlos Valdez. Carlos has a future with the Giants, while Sergio. . . well, let's just say there's a good chance he'll be pitching for his *sixth* organization in 1996.

# Other San Francisco Giants

**Luis Aquino (Pos**: RHP, **Age**: 30)

After a 1995 season marred by minor injuries, Aquino signed to play in Japan this year. 1996 Outlook: D

**Rich Aurilia (Pos**: SS, **Age**: 24, **Bats**: R)

A virtual on-base machine, Aurilia seems to have recovered nicely from a subpar 1994 campaign. He played well at both Double- and Triple-A last season, and might well take over shortstop this summer. 1996 Outlook: A

**Marvin Benard (Pos**: CF, **Age**: 26, **Bats**: L)

A center fielder with good wheels, Benard hit .304 at Triple-A Phoenix last season, and went 13-for-34 with the big club. He's not good enough to play regularly, but could win a part-time job. 1996 Outlook: B

**Enrique Burgos (Pos**: LHP, **Age**: 30)

Perhaps the top minor league strikeout pitcher of the '90s, Burgos simply doesn't have the control to pitch in the majors. Great fastball, but no reliable offspeed pitch. 1996 Outlook: C

**Shawn Estes (Pos**: LHP, **Age**: 23)

This 1991 first-round draft pick looked like a bust in the Seattle system, but he appeared to turn the corner with the Giants last season. Estes went 7-2 with a 2.13 ERA at Double- and Triple-A, and still has a great arm. 1996 Oulook: B

**Rikkert Faneyte (Pos**: CF/RF, **Age**: 26, **Bats**: R)

Always a decent hitter in the minors, Faneyte has a .173 average in 127 major league at-bats. The Dutch native is regarded as a fine outfielder, and he'll probably get another chance this season. 1996 Outlook: B

**Pat Gomez (Pos**: LHP, **Age**: 28)

He'll be somewhere this spring, looking to earn a spot as a lefty reliever. Gomez' stats suggest that he'd be decent in that role, as he's held lefty hitters to a .221 average in his career. 1996 Outlook: B

**Kenny Greer (Pos**: RHP, **Age**: 28)

This guy is *really* marginal. Now 28, Greer has 13 major league innings to his credit, and the Giants are his third organization. Won't pitch in the majors unless injuries hit, lots of them. 1996 Outlook: C

**Chris Hook (Pos**: RHP, **Age**: 27)

Despite a rough 1994 season in Triple-A, Hook spent nearly all of 1995 in the National League. He didn't pitch too well, 5-1 record notwithstanding. The Giant bullpen is full of question marks. 1996 Outlook: B

**Tom Lampkin (Pos**: C, **Age**: 32, **Bats**: L)

Given a choice at the end of last season, the Giants re-signed Lampkin rather than Jeff Reed as their primary backup catcher. He's no hitter but throws well. 1996 Outlook: B

**Mark Leonard (Pos**: RF, **Age**: 31, **Bats**: L)

In his second tour with the Giants, Leonard once again posted solid numbers for Triple-A Phoenix but failed to hit in San Francisco. No outfielder, Leonard is a pinch hitter waiting to happen. 1996 Outlook: C

**Dave McCarty (Pos**: 1B, **Age**: 26, **Bats**: R)

Perennial Twins prospect McCarty wound up with the Giants. As usual, he pasted Triple-A pitchers but struggled in the majors. You never know, he might come through one of these years. 1996 Outlook: B

**Steve Mintz (Pos**: RHP, **Age**: 27)

Mintz doesn't have a great arm, but he's generally pitched well at every pro stop. In between two call-ups and demotions last season, he went 5-2 with a 2.39 ERA with hitter-friendly Phoenix. 1996 Outlook: B

**John Roper (Pos**: RHP, **Age**: 24)

Once a top minor league prospect, Roper's ERA in 35 major league games—including 32 starts—is 5.35. He came from Cincinnati in a trade last summer, and is still young. 1996 Outlook: B

**Scott Service (Pos**: RHP, **Age**: 29)

He's 29 years old now and missed most of 1994 with an injury, but Service is a quality pitcher. There's even talk of making him the closer if Rod Beck isn't re-signed. 1996 Outlook: A

**Carlos Valdez (Pos**: RHP, **Age**: 24)

Not to be confused with Sergio Valdez, who started 11 games for the Giants last year, Carlos is a young reliever with a nice arm. Pitched great at two minor league stops last year (4-2, 1.74). 1996 Outlook: B

# San Francisco Giants Minor League Prospects

## Organization Overview:

Just two years removed from a 103-win campaign, the Giants last year sank into the National League's West Division basement. A return to title contention will not be easy, although the N.L. West didn't have a dominant team last season. The Giants' farm system appears a bit thin right now in quality prospects. San Francisco strung together a series of poor high draft picks in the late '80s and early '90s. Steve Hosey in '89, Adam Hyzdu and Eric Christopherson in '90, and Calvin Murray in '92 can all be considered first-round disappointments for the Giants. Better success with those premium choices could be making a difference right now. San Francisco needs help on the mound, and there are some pitchers with quality arms who'll be given an opportunity this season. Several position prospects also show promise, but an impact talent is not readily apparent.

## Jason Canizaro

**Position:** 2B     **Opening Day Age:** 22
**Bats:** R **Throws:** R     **Born:** 7/4/73 in
**Ht:** 5' 10" **Wt:** 175     Orange, TX

*Recent Statistics*

|                  | G   | AB  | R   | H   | D  | T | HR | RBI | SB | BB | SO  | AVG  |
|------------------|-----|-----|-----|-----|----|---|----|-----|----|----|-----|------|
| 93 R Giants      | 49  | 180 | 34  | 47  | 10 | 6 | 3  | 41  | 12 | 22 | 40  | .261 |
| 94 A San Jose    | 126 | 464 | 77  | 117 | 16 | 2 | 15 | 69  | 12 | 46 | 98  | .252 |
| 95 AA Shreveport | 126 | 440 | 83  | 129 | 25 | 7 | 12 | 60  | 16 | 58 | 98  | .293 |
| 95 MLE           | 126 | 425 | 72  | 114 | 22 | 4 | 10 | 52  | 11 | 43 | 106 | .268 |

Canizaro has handled two difficult jumps in competition level with aplomb the past two seasons. In fact, he enjoyed his best season as a pro at Double-A Shreveport last year. San Francisco drafted Canizaro in the fourth round of 1993 out of a Texas junior college. He's hit with power and plate discipline since then, although he's fanned 98 times each of the last two seasons. Afield, Canizaro has good range and turns the double play well at second base. He was originally drafted as a shortstop, and could be moved back there.

## Jesse Ibarra

**Position:** DH-1B     **Opening Day Age:** 23
**Bats:** B **Throws:** R     **Born:** 7/12/72 in Los
**Ht:** 6' 3" **Wt:** 195     Angeles, CA

*Recent Statistics*

|                 | G   | AB  | R  | H   | D  | T | HR | RBI | SB | BB | SO | AVG  |
|-----------------|-----|-----|----|-----|----|---|----|-----|----|----|----|------|
| 94 A Everett    | 67  | 252 | 32 | 57  | 15 | 1 | 10 | 37  | 0  | 34 | 82 | .226 |
| 95 A Burlington | 129 | 437 | 72 | 144 | 30 | 1 | 34 | 96  | 1  | 77 | 94 | .330 |
| 95 A San Jose   | 3   | 9   | 1  | 3   | 2  | 0 | 0  | 4   | 0  | 1  | 1  | .333 |

Ibarra's hitting prowess is unquestioned. He drove in an even 100 runs last season while slugging .635. He also complemented his .330 batting average with plenty of walks, which helped produce an on-base percentage well over .400. The concern is finding a defensive posi-

tion for him. Ibarra was a combination DH-third base-man-pitcher in college, and is being tried at first base with the Giants. But with a bat as promising as Ibarra's, San Francisco can live with some defensive deficiencies.

## Marcus Jensen

**Position:** C     **Opening Day Age:** 23
**Bats:** B **Throws:** R     **Born:** 12/14/72 in
**Ht:** 6' 4" **Wt:** 195     Oakland, CA

*Recent Statistics*

|                  | G   | AB  | R  | H   | D  | T | HR | RBI | SB | BB | SO  | AVG  |
|------------------|-----|-----|----|-----|----|---|----|-----|----|----|-----|------|
| 93 A Clinton     | 104 | 324 | 53 | 85  | 24 | 2 | 11 | 56  | 1  | 66 | 98  | .262 |
| 94 A San Jose    | 118 | 418 | 56 | 101 | 18 | 0 | 7  | 47  | 1  | 61 | 100 | .242 |
| 95 AA Shreveport | 95  | 321 | 55 | 91  | 22 | 8 | 4  | 45  | 0  | 41 | 68  | .283 |
| 95 MLE           | 95  | 310 | 48 | 80  | 19 | 4 | 3  | 39  | 0  | 31 | 74  | .258 |

Jensen's tenure with the Giants goes back to 1990, when San Francisco chose him with a pick acquired for losing Craig Lefferts to free agency. Jensen has taken his time moving up the Giants' chain, but he's still just 23 years old and continues to demonstrate valuable offensive skills as a switch-hitting catcher. Jensen's plate discipline is a given, and San Francisco hopes his power will develop. Defensively, Jensen has had success throwing out runners and is a solid receiver.

## Bill Mueller

**Position:** 3B     **Opening Day Age:** 25
**Bats:** B **Throws:** R     **Born:** 3/17/71 in
**Ht:** 5' 11" **Wt:** 173     Maryland Hts, MO

*Recent Statistics*

|                  | G   | AB  | R  | H   | D  | T | HR | RBI | SB | BB  | SO | AVG  |
|------------------|-----|-----|----|-----|----|---|----|-----|----|-----|----|------|
| 93 A Everett     | 58  | 200 | 31 | 60  | 8  | 2 | 1  | 24  | 13 | 42  | 17 | .300 |
| 94 A San Jose    | 120 | 431 | 79 | 130 | 20 | 9 | 5  | 72  | 4  | 103 | 47 | .302 |
| 95 AA Shreveport | 88  | 330 | 56 | 102 | 16 | 2 | 1  | 39  | 6  | 53  | 36 | .309 |
| 95 AAA Phoenix   | 41  | 172 | 23 | 51  | 13 | 6 | 2  | 19  | 0  | 19  | 31 | .297 |
| 95 MLE           | 129 | 480 | 66 | 131 | 24 | 4 | 1  | 48  | 4  | 54  | 72 | .273 |

After reaching Triple-A last season, Mueller's on-base percentage fell below .400 for the first time in his pro career. Drafted in the 15th round out of Southwest Missouri State in 1993, Mueller has been a walk machine, drawing 103 bases on balls in only 431 at-bats in 1994. He has minimal power and little speed, so Mueller's ability to get on base is his one central skill. The switch-hitting third baseman isn't going to push Matt Williams off the position in San Francisco, so Mueller will likely return to Phoenix in '96.

## Dante Powell

**Position:** OF  **Opening Day Age:** 22
**Bats:** R **Throws:** R  **Born:** 8/25/73 in Long
**Ht:** 6' 2"  **Wt:** 185  Beach, CA

*Recent Statistics*

|  | G | AB | R | H | D | T | HR | RBI | SB | BB | SO | AVG |
|---|---|---|---|---|---|---|---|---|---|---|---|---|
| 94 A Everett | 41 | 165 | 31 | 51 | 15 | 1 | 5 | 25 | 27 | 19 | 47 | .309 |
| 94 A San Jose | 1 | 4 | 0 | 2 | 0 | 1 | 0 | 0 | 0 | 0 | 1 | .500 |
| 95 A San Jose | 135 | 505 | 74 | 125 | 23 | 8 | 10 | 70 | 43 | 46 | 131 | .248 |

Powell was the Giants' top selection in 1994. Right now, speed is his best asset. He stole 27 of 28 bases in his pro debut, and followed with 43 more last season. He's also a far-ranging center fielder with an okay throwing arm. It's Powell's hitting game which needs the most work. His batting average in the California League was a disappointment, and he didn't walk enough to be an effective leadoff man. The Giants hope he doesn't turn out to be another Calvin Murray.

## Joe Rosselli

**Position:** P  **Opening Day Age:** 23
**Bats:** R **Throws:** L  **Born:** 5/28/72 in
**Ht:** 6' 1"  **Wt:** 170  Burbank, CA

*Recent Statistics*

|  | W | L | ERA | G | GS | Sv | IP | H | R | BB | SO | HR |
|---|---|---|---|---|---|---|---|---|---|---|---|---|
| 95 AAA Phoenix | 4 | 3 | 4.99 | 13 | 13 | 0 | 79.1 | 94 | 47 | 12 | 34 | 8 |
| 95 NL San Fran | 2 | 1 | 8.70 | 9 | 5 | 0 | 30.0 | 39 | 29 | 20 | 7 | 5 |

Somehow, Rosselli won two of three decisions with San Francisco last year despite an 8.70 ERA and an ugly strikeout-to-walk ratio of 7-20. Rosselli underwent shoulder surgery in 1993, and his strikeout rates, which were never staggering, have dropped since then. Meanwhile, his ERAs have risen in Triple-A, but ERAs under 5.00 in Phoenix are not indecent. Roselli throws the four basic pitches, and throws them for strikes. His control within the strikezone is the key to his success.

## Steve Soderstrom

**Position:** P  **Opening Day Age:** 23
**Bats:** R **Throws:** R  **Born:** 4/3/72 in
**Ht:** 6' 3"  **Wt:** 195  Turlock, CA

*Recent Statistics*

|  | W | L | ERA | G | GS | Sv | IP | H | R | BB | SO | HR |
|---|---|---|---|---|---|---|---|---|---|---|---|---|
| 94 A San Jose | 2 | 3 | 4.20 | 8 | 8 | 0 | 40.2 | 34 | 20 | 26 | 40 | 2 |
| 95 AA Shreveport | 9 | 5 | 3.41 | 22 | 22 | 0 | 116.0 | 106 | 53 | 51 | 91 | 6 |

Soderstrom has struggled with injuries since San Francisco used the sixth selection overall to choose him in 1993. After missing that season with elbow tendinitis, a circulation problem in '94 limited him to eight starts. Finally healthy last year, Soderstrom pitched well at the Double-A level. His repertoire is mostly hard stuff, with a fastball and good slider. Both pitches have good movement. If Soderstrom can avoid injury, he could pitch in the majors at some point in '96.

## Keith Williams

**Position:** OF  **Opening Day Age:** 23
**Bats:** R **Throws:** R  **Born:** 4/21/72 in
**Ht:** 6' 0"  **Wt:** 190  Bedford, PA

*Recent Statistics*

|  | G | AB | R | H | D | T | HR | RBI | SB | BB | SO | AVG |
|---|---|---|---|---|---|---|---|---|---|---|---|---|
| 93 A Everett | 75 | 288 | 57 | 87 | 21 | 5 | 12 | 49 | 21 | 48 | 73 | .302 |
| 94 A San Jose | 128 | 504 | 91 | 151 | 30 | 8 | 21 | 97 | 4 | 60 | 102 | .300 |
| 95 AA Shreveport | 75 | 275 | 39 | 84 | 20 | 1 | 9 | 55 | 5 | 23 | 39 | .305 |
| 95 AAA Phoenix | 24 | 83 | 7 | 25 | 4 | 1 | 2 | 14 | 0 | 5 | 11 | .301 |
| 95 MLE | 99 | 343 | 39 | 94 | 20 | 0 | 9 | 58 | 3 | 20 | 53 | .274 |

Williams was the Giants' seventh-round selection in 1993 and has hit between .300 and .305 at each of four stops since then. His 1994 campaign, when he hit 21 homers and drove in 97 runs at San Jose, a poor hitter's park, was outstanding. He followed with a .304 average, 11 homers and 69 RBI between Double- and Triple-A last year. While his batting average has remained nearly constant, Williams' on-base and slugging percentages have slipped as he's moved up the Giants' system.

## Others to Watch

Righthander **Steve Bourgeois** spent most of 1995 in Double-A, where he was 12-3 with a 2.85 ERA. The Giants feel he could be ready by midseason of '96. . . Outfielder **Jake Cruz** was a supplemental first-round pick in 1994 out of Arizona State. He hit .297 with 13 homers and 77 RBI at Shreveport last year. . . **Keith Foulke**, the Giants' ninth-round pick in '94, was 13-6 at San Jose last year. He fanned 168 batters while walking only 32, a ratio better than 5-1. . . Lefthander **Ricky Pickett** was involved in the Deion Sanders' trade with Cincinnati last season. Overall, Pickett saved 12 games with 92 strikeouts in 67.2 innings. . . **Andy Taulbee** was a second-round pick in 1994. The righthander was 7-7 last year, spending part of the year in Double-A. . . **Chris Wimmer** is a product of Wichita State and played on the 1992 U.S. Olympic team. He's a good defensive second baseman, but not a force offensively.

# About STATS, Inc.

STATS, Inc. is the nation's leading independent sports information and statistical analysis company, providing detailed sports services for a wide array of clients.

One of the fastest-growing sports companies in the country, STATS provides the most up-to-the-minute sports information to professional teams, print and broadcast media, software developers and interactive service providers around the country. Some of our major clients are ESPN, Turner Sports, the Associated Press, *The Sporting News*, Electronic Arts and Motorola. Much of the information we provide is available to the public via STATS On-Line. And keep an eye out for STATS' baseball debut on America Online during spring training, 1996.

STATS Publishing, a division of STATS, Inc., produces 10 annual books, including the *STATS Major League Handbook*, the *Pro Football Handbook*, and the *Pro Basketball Handbook*. You might be particularly interested in the *Minor League Scouting Notebook*, this book's sister publication. All of our books deliver STATS expertise to fans, scouts, general managers and media around the country.

In addition, STATS offers the most innovative—and fun—fantasy sports games around, from *Bill James Fantasy Baseball* and *Bill James Classic Baseball* to *STATS Fantasy Football* and *STATS Fantasy Hoops*.

Information technology has grown by leaps and bounds in the last decade, and STATS will continue to be at the forefront as both a vendor and supplier of the most up-to-date, in-depth sports information available. If you haven't already, you will most certainly be seeing us at an infobahn rest stop in the near future.

For more information on our products, or on joining our reporter network, write us at:

**STATS, Inc.**
**8131 Monticello Ave.**
**Skokie, IL 60076-3300**

...or call us at 1-800-63-STATS (1-800-637-8287). Outside the U.S., dial 1-847-676-3383.

# Index

| | | | |
|---|---|---|---|
| Harvey, Bryan | 477 | Huson, Jeff | 45 |
| Haselman, Bill | 65 | Hyers, Tim | 669 |
| Hatcher, Billy | 187 | | |
| Hatteberg, Scott | 69 | | |
| Hawkins, LaTroy | 234 | | |
| Hayes, Charlie | 582 | **I** | |
| Haynes, Jimmy | 46 | | |
| Helfand, Eric | 282 | Ibanez, Raul | 308 |
| Hemond, Scott | 644 | Ibarra, Jesse | 692 |
| Henderson, Rickey | 269 | Ignasiak, Mike | 211 |
| Henke, Tom | 628 | Incaviglia, Pete | 596 |
| Henneman, Mike | 487 | Ingram, Garey | 526 |
| Henry, Butch | 546 | Ingram, Riccardo | 233 |
| Henry, Doug | 569 | Isringhausen, Jason | 559 |
| Henry, Dwayne | 163 | | |
| Hentgen, Pat | 341 | | |
| Heredia, Gil | 536 | | |
| Heredia, Wilson | 477 | **J** | |
| Hermanson, Dustin | 671 | | |
| Hernandez, Carlos | 526 | Jackson, Damian | 142 |
| Hernandez, Jeremy | 477 | Jackson, Danny | 629 |
| Hernandez, Jose | 402 | Jackson, Mike | 427 |
| Hernandez, Roberto | 102 | Jacome, Jason | 175 |
| Hernandez, Xavier | 415 | Jaha, John | 195 |
| Herrera, Jose | 279 | James, Chris | 69 |
| Hershiser, Orel | 124 | James, Dion | 256 |
| Hiatt, Phil | 163 | James, Mike | 91 |
| Hickerson, Bryan | 454 | Janicki, Pete | 95 |
| Hidalgo, Richard | 503 | Jarvis, Kevin | 430 |
| Higginson, Bob | 154 | Javier, Stan | 270 |
| Hill, Glenallen | 677 | Jefferies, Gregg | 583 |
| Hill, Ken | 125 | Jefferson, Reggie | 66 |
| Hitchcock, Sterling | 239 | Jennings, Robin | 406 |
| Hocking, Denny | 233 | Jensen, Marcus | 692 |
| Hoffman, Trevor | 657 | Jeter, Derek | 261 |
| Hoiles, Chris | 32 | Johns, Doug | 282 |
| Holbert, Aaron | 646 | Johnson, Brian | 666 |
| Holbert, Ray | 669 | Johnson, Charles | 465 |
| Hollandsworth, Todd | 524 | Johnson, Howard | 403 |
| Hollins, Damon | 382 | Johnson, Lance | 103 |
| Hollins, Dave | 66 | Johnson, Mark | 605 |
| Holmes, Darren | 439 | Johnson, Randy | 296 |
| Holt, Chris | 504 | Johnston, Joel | 69 |
| Holzemer, Mark | 93 | Johnstone, John | 477 |
| Honeycutt, Rick | 240 | Jones, Andruw | 382 |
| Hook, Chris | 691 | Jones, Bobby | 560 |
| Hope, John | 620 | Jones, Chipper | 365 |
| Horn, Sam | 332 | Jones, Chris | 570 |
| Horsman, Vince | 233 | Jones, Doug | 33 |
| Hosey, Dwayne | 69 | Jones, Todd | 489 |
| Howard, Chris | 332 | Jordan, Brian | 630 |
| Howard, Davis | 184 | Jordan, Kevin | 597 |
| Howard, Thomas | 426 | Jordan, Ricardo | 355 |
| Howe, Steve | 241 | Jose, Felix | 405 |
| Hubbard, Mike | 406 | Joyner, Wally | 176 |
| Hubbard, Trent | 454 | Juden, Jeff | 592 |
| Hudek, John | 499 | Justice, David | 366 |
| Hudler, Rex | 91 | | |
| Hudson, Joe | 69 | | |
| Huff, Michael | 353 | | |
| Huisman, Rick | 187 | | |
| Hulett, Tim | 644 | **K** | |
| Hulse, David | 208 | | |
| Hundley, Todd | 558 | Kamieniecki, Scott | 256 |
| Hunter, Brian | 488 | Karchner, Matt | 104 |
| Hunter, Rich | 597 | Karkovice, Ron | 105 |
| Hunter, Torii | 234 | Karl, Scott | 208 |
| Hurtado, Edwin | 342 | Karp, Ryan | 596 |
| Huskey, Butch | 570 | Karros, Eric | 511 |

| | | | |
|---|---|---|---|
| Karsay, Steve | 282 | Lloyd, Graeme | 209 |
| Kelly, Mike | 378 | Loaiza, Esteban | 607 |
| Kelly, Pat | 242 | Lockhart, Keith | 177 |
| Kelly, Roberto | 512 | Loewer, Carlton | 598 |
| Kendall, Jason | 622 | Lofton, Kenny | 126 |
| Kent, Jeff | 561 | Lomon, Kevin | 572 |
| Key, Jimmy | 257 | Longmire, Tony | 593 |
| Keyser, Brian | 116 | Looney, Brian | 69 |
| Kiefer, Mark | 211 | Lopez, Albie | 138 |
| Kieschnick, Brooks | 406 | Lopez, Javy | 369 |
| Kile, Darryl | 490 | Lopez, Luis | 669 |
| King, Jeff | 606 | Loretta, Mark | 212 |
| King, Kevin | 307 | Lorraine, Andrew | 118 |
| Kingery, Mike | 440 | Lyons, Barry | 116 |
| Kirby, Wayne | 137 | | |
| Klesko, Ryan | 367 | | |
| Klingenbeck, Scott | 233 | **M** | |
| Kmak, Joe | 405 | | |
| Knoblauch, Chuck | 217 | | |
| Knorr, Randy | 354 | Maas, Kevin | 259 |
| Konerko, Paul | 527 | Mabry, John | 632 |
| Konuszewski, Dennis | 620 | MacDonald, Bob | 259 |
| Kowitz, Brian | 381 | MacFarlane, Mike | 56 |
| Kreuter, Chad | 307 | Maddux, Greg | 370 |
| Krivda, Rick | 43 | Maddux, Mike | 67 |
| Kroon, Marc | 671 | Maduro, Calvin | 47 |
| Krueger, Bill | 307 | Magadan, Dave | 491 |
| Kruk, John | 116 | Magnante, Mike | 184 |
| | | Mahomes, Pat | 219 |
| | | Malave, Jose | 70 |
| | | Maldonado, Candy | 332 |
| **L** | | Mantei, Matt | 477 |
| | | Manto, Jeff | 34 |
| Laker, Tim | 547 | Manwaring, Kirt | 679 |
| Lampkin, Tom | 691 | Manzanillo, Josias | 259 |
| Langston, Mark | 82 | Manzanillo, Ravelo | 620 |
| Lankford, Ray | 631 | Marquez, Isidro | 116 |
| Lansing, Mike | 537 | Marsh, Tom | 593 |
| Larkin, Barry | 416 | Martin, Al | 608 |
| Latham, Chris | 528 | Martin, Norberto | 113 |
| LaValliere, Mike | 112 | Martinez, Carlos | 93 |
| Lawton, Matt | 234 | Martinez, Dave | 106 |
| Ledesma, Aaron | 572 | Martinez, Dennis | 127 |
| Lee, Derrek | 671 | Martinez, Edgar | 297 |
| Lee, Manuel | 644 | Martinez, Felix | 188 |
| Lee, Mark | 45 | Martinez, Pedro | 539 |
| Leiper, Dave | 538 | Martinez, Pedro A. | 502 |
| Leiter, Al | 343 | Martinez, Ramon | 513 |
| Leiter, Mark | 678 | Martinez, Sandy | 344 |
| Leius, Scott | 218 | Martinez, Tino | 298 |
| Lemke, Mark | 368 | Marzano, John | 332 |
| Leonard, Mark | 691 | Masteller, Dan | 231 |
| Lesher, Brian | 284 | Matheny, Mike | 209 |
| Leskanic, Curt | 441 | Mathews, T.J. | 644 |
| Levis, Jesse | 141 | Mathews, Terry | 466 |
| Lewis, Darren | 417 | Mattingly, Don | 244 |
| Lewis, Mark | 427 | Mauser, Tim | 669 |
| Lewis, Richie | 475 | Maxcy, Brian | 161 |
| Leyritz, Jim | 243 | May, Darrell | 382 |
| Lieber, Jon | 617 | May, Derrick | 492 |
| Lieberthal, Mike | 596 | Mayne, Brent | 178 |
| Lilliquist, Derek | 526 | McCarty, Dave | 691 |
| Lima, Jose | 160 | McCaskill, Kirk | 113 |
| Lind, Jose | 93 | McCracken, Quinton | 455 |
| Linton, Doug | 187 | McCurry, Jeff | 609 |
| Lira, Felipe | 155 | McDavid, Ray | 671 |
| Liriano, Nelson | 618 | McDonald, Ben | 35 |
| Listach, Pat | 196 | McDonald, Jason | 284 |
| Livingstone, Scott | 666 | McDowell, Jack | 245 |

| | | | | | | |
|---|---|---|---|---|---|---|
| McDowell, Roger | 317 | Myers, Mike | 163 | | Pride, Curtis | 549 |
| McElroy, Chuck | 428 | Myers, Randy | 391 | | Prieto, Ariel | 282 |
| McGee, Willie | 67 | | | **P** | Prince, Tom | 526 |
| McGinnis, Russ | 187 | | | | Puckett, Kirby | 222 |
| McGriff, Fred | 371 | | | Pagliarulo, Mike | 330 | Pugh, Tim | 428 |
| McGwire, Mark | 271 | **N** | | Pagnozzi, Tom | 635 | Pulliam, Harvey | 454 |
| McLemore, Mark | 318 | | | Painter, Lance | 451 | Pulsipher, Bill | 564 |
| McMichael, Greg | 372 | | | Palacios, Vince | 644 | Pye, Eddie | 526 |
| McMillon, Billy | 478 | Nabholz, Chris | 405 | Palmeiro, Orlando | 93 | | |
| McMurtry, Craig | 502 | Naehring, Tim | 57 | Palmeiro, Rafael | 39 | | |
| McRae, Brian | 390 | Nagy, Charles | 130 | Palmer, Dean | 320 | | |
| Meacham, Rusty | 179 | Natal, Bob | 477 | Paquette, Craig | 273 | **Q** | |
| Meares, Pat | 220 | Navarro, Jaime | 392 | Parent, Mark | 403 | | |
| Mecir, Jim | 307 | Neagle, Denny | 612 | Park, Chan Ho | 528 | | |
| Mejia, Roberto | 454 | Neel, Troy | 282 | Parker, Rick | 526 | Quantrill, Paul | 586 |
| Menhart, Paul | 355 | Nelson, Bryant | 504 | Parra, Jose | 233 | | |
| Merced, Orlando | 610 | Nelson, Jeff | 299 | Parrett, Jeff | 642 | | |
| Mercedes, Henry | 187 | Nen, Robb | 467 | Parris, Steve | 613 | **R** | |
| Mercedes, Jose | 211 | Nevin, Phil | 163 | Parrish, Lance | 347 | | |
| Mercker, Kent | 373 | Newfield, Marc | 667 | Patterson, Bob | 92 | | |
| Merullo, Matt | 231 | Newson, Warren | 304 | Patterson, Jeff | 259 | Raabe, Brian | 233 |
| Mesa, Jose | 128 | Nichols, Rod | 381 | Patterson, John | 689 | Radinsky, Scott | 114 |
| Miceli, Danny | 611 | Nichting, Chris | 332 | Pavlas, Dave | 259 | Radke, Brad | 223 |
| Mieske, Matt | 197 | Nied, Dave | 454 | Pavlik, Roger | 321 | Rain, Steve | 407 |
| Millar, Kevin | 478 | Nieves, Melvin | 658 | Payton, Jay | 574 | Raines, Tim | 108 |
| Miller, Keith | 187 | Nilsson, Dave | 199 | Pegues, Steve | 618 | Ramirez, Manny | 133 |
| Miller, Orlando | 493 | Nitkowski, C.J. | 156 | Pemberton, Rudy | 165 | Randa, Joe | 187 |
| Miller, Travis | 234 | Nixon, Otis | 319 | Pena, Alejandro | 379 | Rapp, Pat | 470 |
| Milliard, Ralph | 479 | Nixon, Trot | 70 | Pena, Geronimo | 643 | Rasmussen, Dennis | 187 |
| Million, Doug | 455 | Nokes, Matt | 454 | Pena, Tony | 138 | Rath, Gary | 528 |
| Mills, Alan | 45 | Nomo, Hideo | 515 | Pendleton, Terry | 468 | Ray, Ken | 189 |
| Mimbs, Michael | 584 | Norman, Les | 187 | Penn, Shannon | 163 | Reboulet, Jeff | 232 |
| Minor, Blas | 571 | Nunnally, Jon | 181 | Pennington, Brad | 430 | Reed, Jeff | 690 |
| Mintz, Steve | 691 | Nye, Ryan | 598 | Percibal, Billy | 47 | Reed, Jody | 660 |
| Miranda, Angel | 198 | | | Percival, Troy | 84 | Reed, Rick | 430 |
| Mitchell, Kevin | 430 | | | Perez, Carlos | 540 | Reed, Steve | 443 |
| Mlicki, Dave | 562 | | | Perez, Eddie | 381 | Reese, Pokey | 432 |
| Mohler, Mike | 279 | **O** | | Perez, Melido | 247 | Rekar, Bryan | 452 |
| Molitor, Paul | 345 | | | Perez, Mike | 393 | Relaford, Desmond | 309 |
| Mondesi, Raul | 514 | O'Brien, Charlie | 374 | Perez, Neifi | 456 | Remlinger, Mike | 430 |
| Monteleone, Rich | 93 | O'Leary, Troy | 58 | Perez, Robert | 357 | Renteria, Edgar | 479 |
| Montgomery, Jeff | 180 | O'Neill, Paul | 246 | Perez, Tomas | 355 | Reyes, Al | 211 |
| Moore, Mike | 163 | Obando, Sherman | 45 | Perez, Yorkis | 469 | Reyes, Carlos | 280 |
| Moore, Trey | 308 | Ochoa, Alex | 573 | Perry, Gerald | 644 | Reynolds, Shane | 495 |
| Morandini, Mickey | 585 | Offerman, Jose | 516 | Perry, Herbert | 139 | Reynoso, Armando | 452 |
| Mordecai, Mike | 379 | Ogea, Chad | 131 | Person, Robert | 574 | Rhodes, Arthur | 43 |
| Morel, Ramon | 622 | Olerud, John | 346 | Petagine, Roberto | 667 | Rhodes, Karl | 69 |
| Morgan, Mike | 633 | Oliva, Jose | 641 | Peterson, Charles | 622 | Ricci, Chuck | 596 |
| Morman, Russ | 477 | Olivares, Omar | 596 | Petkovsek, Mark | 636 | Rigby, Brad | 284 |
| Morris, Bobby | 407 | Oliver, Darren | 329 | Pett, Jose | 357 | Riggs, Adam | 528 |
| Morris, Hal | 418 | Oliver, Joe | 200 | Pettitte, Andy | 248 | Righetti, Dave | 116 |
| Mota, Jose | 187 | Olson, Gregg | 185 | Phillips, J.R. | 689 | Rightnowar, Ron | 211 |
| Mottola, Chad | 431 | Ontiveros, Steve | 272 | Phillips, Tony | 85 | Rijo, Jose | 420 |
| Mouton, James | 494 | Oquendo, Jose | 634 | Phoenix, Steve | 282 | Ripken, Billy | 141 |
| Mouton, Lyle | 107 | Oquist, Mike | 45 | Piazza, Mike | 518 | Ripken, Cal | 40 |
| Moyer, Jamie | 36 | Ordonez, Rey | 573 | Pichardo, Hipolito | 182 | Risley, Bill | 300 |
| Mueller, Bill | 692 | Orellano, Rafael | 71 | Pierce, Jeff | 69 | Ritz, Kevin | 444 |
| Mulholland, Terry | 680 | Orosco, Jesse | 38 | Pirkl, Greg | 307 | Rivera, Mariano | 257 |
| Munoz, Bobby | 596 | Orsulak, Joe | 563 | Pittsley, Jim | 188 | Rivera, Roberto | 405 |
| Munoz, Mike | 442 | Ortiz, Luis | 330 | Plantier, Phil | 659 | Rivera, Ruben | 261 |
| Munoz, Noe | 526 | Osborne, Donovan | 642 | Plesac, Dan | 614 | Roa, Joe | 141 |
| Munoz, Oscar | 233 | Osuna, Antonio | 517 | Plunk, Eric | 132 | Roberson, Kevin | 405 |
| Munoz, Pedro | 221 | Otero, Ricky | 572 | Polonia, Luis | 380 | Roberson, Sid | 210 |
| Murphy, Rob | 477 | Owen, Spike | 92 | Poole, Jim | 139 | Roberts, Bip | 661 |
| Murray, Eddie | 129 | Owens, Eric | 432 | Portugal, Mark | 419 | Robertson, Rich | 232 |
| Murray, Glenn | 70 | Owens, Jayhawk | 454 | Posada, Jorge | 261 | Robinson, Ken | 355 |
| Murray, Matt | 69 | | | Powell, Dante | 693 | Rodriguez, Alex | 305 |
| Musselwhite, Jim | 261 | | | Powell, Jay | 479 | Rodriguez, Carlos | 69 |
| Mussina, Mike | 37 | | | Powell, Ross | 620 | Rodriguez, Felix | 526 |
| Myers, Greg | 83 | | | Pozo, Arquimedez | 309 | Rodriguez, Frankie | 224 |
| | | | | Pratt, Todd | 405 | | |

# Y

# Z

# Perfect For Your Fantasy Draft!

## STATS Presents...

### The 1996 Projections Update

**ONLY $9.95 Available 3/1/96**

*The 1996 Projections Update* is the most up-to-date, amazingly accurate set of projections ever assembled, perfect for your March fantasy draft! The updates for every 1995 major league player take into account all winter and spring trades, free agent signings, and much more! *Projections Update* is a must for those who live to win!

*The 1996 Projections Update* is the perfect complement to your *Major League Handbook 1996*, giving you a second set of accurate projections updated for all hitters and pitchers.

**Includes projections updated for all players based on:**

- ☆ Players in new ballparks
- ☆ Trades
- ☆ Free Agency
- ☆ Releases
- ☆ Injury developments
- ☆ More accurate playing time projections

*"Take our word for it...we really hit the nail on the head."*

—Bill James

## Order from STATS INC. Today!

### Use Order Form in This Book, or Call 1-800-63-STATS or 708-676-3383!

# STATS INC.
# Meet the Winning Lineup...

**Bill James Presents:**
## STATS 1996 Major League Handbook
- Bill James' exclusive 1996 player projections
- Career data for every 1995 Major League Baseball player
- Leader boards, fielding stats and stadium data
- **Price: $17.95, Item #HB96, Available NOW!**

**Bill James Presents:**
## STATS 1996 Minor League Handbook

- Year-by-year career statistical data for AA and AAA players
- Bill James' exclusive Major League Equivalencies
- Complete 1995 Single-A player statistics
- **Price: $17.95, Item #MH96, Available NOW!**

## STATS 1996 Player Profiles
- Exclusive 1995 breakdowns for pitchers and hitters, over 30 in all: lefty/righty, home/road, clutch situations, ahead/behind in the count, month-by-month, etc.
- Complete breakdowns by player for the last five seasons
- **Price: $17.95, Item #PP96, Available NOW!**

## STATS Scouting Notebook: 1996
- Extensive scouting reports on over 700 major league players
- Evaluations of nearly 200 minor league prospects
- **Price: $16.95, Item #SN96, Available 1/1/96**

## STATS 1996 Minor League Scouting Notebook
- Evaluation of each organization's top prospects
- Essays, stat lines and grades for more than 400 prospects
- **Price: $16.95, Item #MN96, Available 1/15/96**

### Bill James Presents:
### STATS 1996 Batter Versus Pitcher Match-Ups!

- Complete stats for pitchers vs. batters (5+ career AB against them)
- Leader boards and stats for all 1995 Major League players
- **Price: $12.95, Item #BP96, Available 1/15/96**

## STATS 1996 Baseball Scoreboard

- Entertaining essays interpreting baseball stats
- Easy-to-understand statistical charts
- Specific coverage of every major team
- Appendices that invite further reader analysis
- **Price: $16.95, Item #SB96, Available 3/1/96**

### STATS 1995-96 Pro Basketball Handbook

- Career stats for every player who logged minutes during 1994-95
- Team game logs with points, rebounds, assists and much more
- Leader boards from points per game to triple doubles
- **Price: $17.95, Item #BH96, Available NOW!**

## STATS 1996 Pro Football Handbook

- A complete season-by-season register for every active 1995 player
- Numerous statistical breakdowns for hundreds of NFL players
- Leader boards in a number of innovative and traditional categories
- **Price: $17.95, Item #FH96, Available 2/1/96**

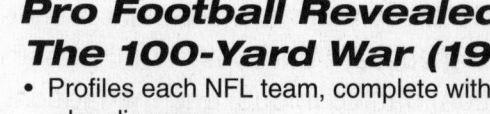

### Pro Football Revealed: The 100-Yard War (1996 Edition)

- Profiles each NFL team, complete with essays, charts and play diagrams
- Detailed statistical breakdowns on players, teams and coaches
- Essays about NFL trends and happenings by leading experts
- **Price: $16.95, Item #PF96 , Available 7/1/96**
- **1995 EDITION AVAILABLE NOW for ONLY $15.95!**

# Order from STATS INC. Today!
## Use Order Form in This Book, or Call 1-800-63-STATS or 708-676-3383!

# Bill James Classic Baseball

### *Joe Jackson, Walter Johnson, and Roberto Clemente are back on the field of your dreams!*

If you're not ready to give up baseball in the fall, or if you're looking to relive its glorious past, then Bill James Classic Baseball is the game for you!

The Classic Game features players from all eras of Major League Baseball at all performance levels - not just the stars. You could see Honus Wagner, Josh Gibson, Carl Yastrzemski, Bob Uecker, Billy Grabarkewitz, and Dick Fowler...on the SAME team!

## As owner, GM and manager all in one, you'll be able to...

- "Buy" your team of up to 25 players from our catalog of over 2,000 historical players (You'll receive $1 million to buy your favorite players)
- Choose the park your team will call home—current or historical, 63 in all!
- Rotate batting lineups for a right- or left-handed starting pitcher
- Change your pitching rotation for each series. Determine your set-up man, closer, and long reliever
- Alter in-game strategies, including stealing frequency, holding runners on base, hit-and-run, and much more!
- Select your best pinch hitter and late-inning defensive replacements (For example, Curt Flood will get to more balls than Hack Wilson!)

## How to Play The Classic Game:

1. Sign up to be a team owner TODAY! Leagues forming year-round
2. STATS, Inc. will supply you with a catalog of eligible players and a rule book
3. You'll receive $1 million to buy your favorite major leaguers
4. Take part in a player and ballpark draft with 11 other owners
5. Set your pitching rotation, batting lineup, and managerial strategies
6. STATS runs the game simulation...a 154-game schedule, 14 weeks!
7. You'll receive customized in-depth weekly reports, featuring game summaries, stats, and boxscores

# Order from STATS INC. Today!

### *Use Order Form in This Book, or Call 1-800-63-STATS or 708-676-3383!*

# Bill James Fantasy Baseball

Bill James Fantasy Baseball enters its eighth season of offering baseball fans the most unique, realistic and exciting game fantasy sports has to offer.

You draft a 25-player roster and can expand to as many as 28. Players aren't ranked like in rotisserie leagues—you'll get credit for everything a player does, like hitting homers, driving in runs, turning double plays, pitching quality outings and more!

Also, the team which scores the most points among all leagues, plus wins the World Series, will receive the John McGraw Award, which includes a one-week trip to the Grapefruit League in spring training, a day at the ballpark with Bill James, and a new fantasy league named in his/her honor!

## Unique Features Include:

- **Live fantasy experts** — available seven days a week

- **The best weekly reports in the business** — detailing who is in the lead, win-loss records, MVPs, and team strengths and weaknesses

- **On-Line computer system** — a world of information, including daily updates of fantasy standings and stats

- **Over twice as many statistics as rotisserie**

- **Transactions that are effective the very next day!**

"My goal was to develop a fantasy league based on the simplest yet most realistic principle possible. A league in which the values are as nearly as possible what they ought to be, without being distorted by artificial category values or rankings...."

— **Bill James**

*All this, all summer long...for less than $5 per week!*

# Order from *STATS* INC. Today!

*Use Order Form in This Book, or Call 1-800-63-STATS or 708-676-3383!*

# STATS Fantasy Hoops

Soar into the 1995-96 season with STATS Fantasy Hoops! SFH puts YOU in charge. Don't just sit back and watch Grant Hill, Shawn Kemp, and Alonzo Mourning - get in the game and coach your team to the top!

### How to Play SFH:
1. Sign up to coach a team.
2. You'll receive a full set of rules and a draft form with SFH point values for all eligible players - anyone who played in the NBA in 1994-95, plus all 1995 NBA draft picks.
3. Complete the draft form and return it to STATS.
4. You will take part in the draft with nine other owners, and we will send you league rosters.
5. You make unlimited weekly transactions including trades, free agent signings, activations, and benchings.
6. Six of the 10 teams in your league advance to postseason play, with two teams ultimately advancing to the Finals.

SFH points values are tested against actual NBA results, mirroring the real thing. Weekly reports will tell you everything you need to know to lead your team to the SFH Championship!

# STATS Fantasy Football

STATS Fantasy Football puts YOU in charge! You draft, trade, cut, bench, activate players and even sign free agents each week. SFF pits you head-to-head against 11 other owners.

STATS' scoring system applies realistic values, tested against actual NFL results. Each week, you'll receive a superb in-depth report telling you all about both team and league performances.

### How to Play SFF:
1. Sign up today!
2. STATS sends you a draft form listing all eligible NFL players.
3. Fill out the draft form and return it to STATS, and you will take part in the draft along with 11 other team owners.
4. Go head-to-head against the other owners in your league. You'll make week-by-week roster moves and transactions through STATS' Fantasy Football experts, via phone, fax, or on-line!

## Order from STATS INC. Today!
### Use Order Form in This Book, or Call 1-800-63-STATS or 708-676-3383!

# STATS On-Line

Now you can have a direct line to a world of sports information just like the pros use with STATS On-Line. If you love to keep up with your favorite teams and players, STATS On-Line is for you. From Shaquille O'Neal's fast-breaking dunks to Ken Griffey's tape-measure blasts — if you want baseball, basketball, football and hockey stats, we put them at your fingertips!

## *STATS On-Line*

- **Player Profiles and Team Profiles** — The #1 resource for scouting your favorite professional teams and players with information you simply can't find anywhere else! The most detailed info you've ever seen, including real-time stats. Follow baseball pitch-by-pitch, foot ball snap-by-snap, and basketball and hockey shot-by-shot, with scores and player stats updated continually!

- **NO monthly or annual fees**

- **Local access numbers** — avoid costly long-distance charges!

- **Unlimited access** — 24 hours a day, seven days a week

- **Downloadable files** — get year-to-date stats in an ASCII format for baseball, football, basketball, and hockey

- **In-progress box scores** — You'll have access to the most up-to-the-second scoring stats for every team and player. When you log into STATS On-Line, you'll get detailed updates, including player stats and scoring plays while the games are in progress!

- **Other exclusive features** — transactions and injury information, team and player profiles and updates, standings, leader and trailer boards, game-by-game logs, fantasy game features, and much more!

*Sign-up fee of $30 (applied towards future use), 24-hour access with usage charges of $.75/min. Mon.-Fri., 8am-6pm CST; $.25/min. all other hours and weekends.*

# Order from STATS INC. Today!
## *Use Order Form in This Book, or Call 1-800-63-STATS or 708-676-3383!*

# STATS INC Order Form

Name_____ Phone_____

Address_____ Fax_____

City_____ State_____ Zip_____

## Method of Payment (U.S. Funds Only):

❏ Check/Money Order ❏ Visa ❏ MasterCard

Cardholder Name_____

Credit Card Number_____ Exp. _____

Signature_____

### BOOKS

| Qty | Product Name | Item # | Price | Total |
|-----|--------------|--------|-------|-------|
| | STATS 1996 Major League Handbook | HB96 | $17.95 | |
| | 1996 Major League Hndbk. (Comb-bnd) | HC96 | $19.95 | |
| | STATS 1996 Projections Update | PJUP | $9.95 | |
| | The Scouting Notebook: 1996 | SN96 | $16.95 | |
| | STATS 1996 Player Profiles | PP96 | $17.95 | |
| | 1996 Player Profiles (Comb-bound) | PC96 | $19.95 | |
| | STATS 1996 Minor Lg. Scouting Ntbk. | MN96 | $16.95 | |
| | STATS 1996 Minor League Handbook | MH96 | $17.95 | |
| | 1996 Minor League Hndbk. (Comb-bnd) | MC96 | $19.95 | |
| | STATS 1996 BVSP Match-Ups! | BP96 | $12.95 | |
| | STATS 1996 Baseball Scoreboard | SB96 | $16.95 | |
| | STATS 1995-96 Pro Basketball Hndbk. | BH96 | $17.95 | |
| | Pro Football Revealed (1996 Edition) | PF96 | $16.95 | |
| | STATS 1996 Pro Football Handbook | FH96 | $17.95 | |
| | For previous editions, circle appropriate years: | | | |
| | Major League Handbook  91  92  93  94  95 | | $9.95 | |
| | Scouting Report/Notebook  92  94  95 | | $9.95 | |
| | Player Profiles  93  94  95 | | $9.95 | |
| | Minor League Handbook  92  93  94  95 | | $9.95 | |
| | Baseball Scoreboard  92  93  94  95 | | $9.95 | |
| | Basketball Scoreboard  94  95 | | $9.95 | |
| | Pro Football Handbook  95 | | $9.95 | |
| | Pro Football Revealed  94  95 | | $9.95 | |

### FANTASY GAMES & STATSfax

| Qty | Product Name | Item # | Price | Total |
|-----|--------------|--------|-------|-------|
| | Bill James Classic Baseball | BJCG | $129.00 | |
| | How to Win The Classic Game (book) | CGBK | $16.95 | |
| | The Classic Game STATSfax | CGX5 | $20.00 | |
| | Bill James Fantasy Baseball | BJFB | $89.00 | |
| | BJFB STATSfax/5-day | SFX5 | $20.00 | |
| | BJFB STATSfax/7-day | SFX7 | $25.00 | |
| | STATS Fantasy Hoops | SFH | $85.00 | |
| | SFH STATSfax/5-day | SFH5 | $20.00 | |
| | SFH STATSfax/7-day | SFH7 | $25.00 | |
| | STATS Fantasy Football | SFF | $69.00 | |
| | SFF STATSfax/3-day | SFF3 | $15.00 | |

### STATS ON-LINE

| Qty | Product Name | Item # | Price | Total |
|-----|--------------|--------|-------|-------|
| | STATS On-Line | ONLE | $30.00 | |

**For faster service, call**
**1-800-63-STATS or 708-676-3383,**
**or fax this form to STATS at**
**708-676-0821**

1st Fantasy Team Name (ex. Colt 45's):_____ _____

What Fantasy Game is this team for?_____

2nd Fantasy Team Name (ex. Colt 45's):_____ _____

What Fantasy Game is this team for?_____

NOTE: $1.00/player is charged for all roster moves and transactions.

**For Bill James Fantasy Baseball**

Would you like to play in a league drafted by Bill James?   ❏ Yes   ❏ No

### TOTALS

| | Price | Total |
|--|-------|-------|
| **Product Total** (excl. Fantasy Games and On-Line) | | |
| For first class mailing in U.S. add: | +$2.50/book | |
| Canada—all orders—add: | +$3.50/book | |
| Order 2 or more books—subtract: | -$1.00/book | |
| IL residents add 8.5% sales tax | | |
| **Subtotal** | | |
| Fantasy Games & On-Line Total | | |
| **GRAND TOTAL** | | |

### FREE Information Kits:

❏ STATS Reporter Networks
❏ Bill James Classic Baseball
❏ Bill James Fantasy Baseball
❏ STATS On-Line
❏ STATS Fantasy Hoops
❏ STATS Fantasy Football
❏ STATS Year-end Reports
❏ STATSfax

BOOK

**Mail to: STATS, Inc., 8131 Monticello Ave., Skokie, IL 60076-3300**